STATISTICS
for
BUSINESS & ECONOMICS
Fourth Edition

PAUL NEWBOLD
University of Illinois,
Urbana-Champaign

Prentice Hall, Upper Saddle River, New Jersey 07458

Library of Congress Cataloging-in-Publication Data

Newbold, Paul.
    Statistics for business and economics / Paul Newbold. — 4th ed.
    880 pp.   cm.
    Includes bibliographical references and index.
    ISBN 0-13-181595-4
    1. Commercial statistics.   2. Economics—Statistical methods.
  3. Statistics. I. Title.
  HF1017.N48   1994
  519.5—dc20   94–33610

To My Parents

Editor-in-Chief: *Rich Wohl*
Acquisitions Editor: *Tom Tucker*
Managing Editor: *Joyce Turner*
Production Editor: *Anne Graydon*
Design Director: *Patricia Wosczyk*
Interior/Cover Designer: *Rosemarie Votta*
Cover Artist: *Phyllis Cement*
Manufacturing Buyer: *Marie McNamara*
Assistant Editor: *Andrea Cuperman*
Production Assistant: *Renee Pelletier*
Marketing Manager: *Sandra Steiner*

 © 1995 by Prentice-Hall, Inc.
A Simon & Schuster Company
Upper Saddle River, New Jersey 07458

Printed in the United States of America
10 9

0-13-181595-4

Prentice-Hall International (UK) Limited, *London*
Prentice-Hall of Australia Pty. Limited, *Sydney*
Prentice-Hall Canada Inc., *Toronto*
Prentice-Hall Hispanoamericana, S.A., *Mexico*
Prentice-Hall of India Private Limited, *New Delhi*
Prentice-Hall of Japan, Inc., *Tokyo*
Simon & Schuster Asia Pte. Ltd., *Singapore*
Editora Prentice-Hall do Brasil, Ltda., *Rio de Janeiro*

BRIEF CONTENTS

CHAPTER 1 ■ What Is Statistics? *1*

CHAPTER 2 ■ Summarizing Numerical Information *6*

CHAPTER 3 ■ Probability *74*

CHAPTER 4 ■ Discrete Random Variables and Probability Distributions *129*

CHAPTER 5 ■ Continuous Random Variables and Probability Distribution *179*

CHAPTER 6 ■ Sampling and Sampling Distributions *223*

CHAPTER 7 ■ Point Estimation *257*

CHAPTER 8 ■ Interval Estimation *271*

CHAPTER 9 ■ Hypothesis Testing *323*

CHAPTER 10 ■ Some Nonparametric Tests *385*

CHAPTER 11 ■ Goodness-of-Fit Tests and Contingency Tables *405*

CHAPTER 12 ■ Linear Correlation and Regression *427*

CHAPTER 13 ■ Multiple Regression *477*

CHAPTER 14 ■ Additional Topics in Regression Analysis *535*

CHAPTER 15 ■ Analysis of Variance *595*

CHAPTER 16 ■ Statistical Quality Control *643*

CHAPTER 17 ■ Time Series Analysis and Forecasting *677*

CHAPTER 18 ■ Survey Sampling Methods *735*

CHAPTER 19 ■ Statistical Decision Theory *781*

APPENDIX ■ Tables *829*

Answers to Selected Exercises *847*

Index *863*

C O N T E N T S

PREFACE   xi

1

WHAT IS STATISTICS?   1

1.1   Making Sense of Numerical Information   1
1.2   Dealing with Uncertainty   2
1.3   Sampling   3
1.4   Analyzing Relationships   4
1.5   Forecasting   4
1.6   Decision Making in an Uncertain Environment   5

2

SUMMARIZING NUMERICAL INFORMATION   6

2.1   Populations and Samples   6
2.2   Numerical Summary: Measures of Central Tendency   8
    (i)   The Mean   8
    (ii)   The Median   12
    (iii)   The Mode   14
2.3   Numerical Summary: Measures of Dispersion   14
    (i)   The Variance and the Standard Deviation   15
    (ii)   The Mean Absolute Deviation   23
    (iii)   The Range   24
    (iv)   The Interquartile Range   25
2.4   Grouped Data and Histograms   29
2.5   Numerical Summary of Grouped Data   37
2.6   Some Other Graphical Methods   53
    (i)   Bar Charts   53
    (ii)   Time Plots   56
    (iii)   Pie Charts   56
    (iv)   Scatter Plots   57
    (v)   Box-and-Whisker Plots   59
2.7   Lying with Statistics   61
    (i)   Emotive and Loaded Statements   61
    (ii)   Inadequate Numerical Summaries   62
    (iii)   Choice of Scale for Time Plots   63
    (iv)   Improper Graphical Size Comparisons   64

      (v) Coincidences That Really Are Just That   66
     (vi) Generalizing from Very Small Samples   67
Review Exercises   70

3

PROBABILITY   74

3.1   Introduction   74
3.2   Random Experiment, Outcomes, Events   75
3.3   What Is Probability?   83
3.4   Probability and Its Postulates   85
3.5   Permutations and Combinations   91
3.6   Probability Rules   96
3.7   Bivariate Probabilities   108
3.8   Bayes' Theorem   113
Review Exercises   122

4

DISCRETE RANDOM VARIABLES AND PROBABILITY DISTRIBUTIONS   129

4.1   Random Variables   129
4.2   Probability Distributions for Discrete Random Variables   131
4.3   Expectations for Discrete Random Variables   135
4.4   Jointly Distributed Discrete Random Variables   144
4.5   The Binomial Distribution   157
4.6   The Hypergeometric Distribution   163
4.7   The Poisson Distribution   166
Review Exercises   174

5

CONTINUOUS RANDOM VARIABLES AND PROBABILITY DISTRIBUTIONS   179

5.1   Continuous Random Variables   179
5.2   Probability Distributions for Continuous Random Variables   180
5.3   Expectations for Continuous Random Variables   186
5.4   Jointly Distributed Continuous Random Variables   190
5.5   The Normal Distribution   194
5.6   The Central Limit Theorem   207
5.7   The Normal Distribution as an Approximation to the Binomial and Poisson Distributions   209

5.8   The Exponential Distribution   216
Review Exercises   218

6

SAMPLING AND SAMPLING DISTRIBUTIONS   223

6.1   Sampling from a Population   223
6.2   Sampling Distribution of the Sample Mean   227
6.3   Sampling Distribution of a Sample Proportion   233
6.4   Sampling Distribution of the Sample Variance   243
Review Exercises   251
Appendix A6.1   255

7

POINT ESTIMATION   257

7.1   Introduction   257
7.2   Unbiased Estimators and Their Efficiency   260
7.3   Choice of Point Estimator   265
Review Exercises   267

8

INTERVAL ESTIMATION   271

8.1   Confidence Intervals   271
8.2   Confidence Intervals for the Mean of a Normal Distribution: Population Variance Known   273
8.3   The Student's t Distribution   282
8.4   Confidence Intervals for the Mean of a Normal Population: Population Variance Unknown   285
8.5   Confidence Intervals for the Population Proportion (Large Samples)   292
8.6   Confidence Intervals for the Variance of a Normal Population   295
8.7   Confidence Intervals for the Difference Between the Means of Two Normal Populations   300
8.8   Confidence Intervals for the Difference Between Two Population Proportions (Large Samples)   309
8.9   Estimating the Sample Size   314
Review Exercises   318

9

HYPOTHESIS TESTING   323

9.1 Concepts of Hypothesis Testing 323
9.2 Tests of the Mean of a Normal Distribution: Population Variance Known 329
9.3 Tests of the Mean of a Normal Distribution: Population Variance Unknown 339
9.4 Tests of the Variance of a Normal Distribution 344
9.5 Tests of the Population Proportion (Large Samples) 347
9.6 Tests for the Difference Between Two Means 352
9.7 Tests for the Difference Between Two Population Proportions (Large Samples) 359
9.8 Testing the Equality of the Variances of Two Normal Populations 365
9.9 Measuring the Power of a Test 368
9.10 Some Comments on Hypothesis Testing 374
Review Exercises 377

10

SOME NONPARAMETRIC TESTS 385

10.1 Introduction 385
10.2 The Sign Test 386
10.3 The Wilcoxin Test 391
10.4 The Mann-Whitney Test 394
10.5 Discussion 399
Review Exercises 402

11

GOODNESS-OF-FIT TESTS AND CONTINGENCY TABLES 405

11.1 Goodness-of-Fit Tests 405
11.2 Goodness-of-Fit Tests: Population Parameters Unknown 410
11.3 Contingency Tables 415
Review Exercises 422

12

LINEAR CORRELATION AND REGRESSION 427

12.1 Correlation 427
12.2 Rank Correlation 436
12.3 The Linear Regression Model 441
12.4 Least Squares Estimation 447
12.5 Standard Assumptions for the Linear Regression Model 450

12.6 The Gauss-Markov Theorem   451

12.7 The Explanatory Power of a Linear Regression Equation   452

12.8 Confidence Intervals and Hypothesis Tests   458

12.9 Prediction   463

Review Exercises   471

Appendix A12.1   476

13

MULTIPLE REGRESSION   477

13.1 The Multiple Regression Model   477

13.2 Least Squares Estimation   485

13.3 Standard Assumptions for the Multiple Regression Model   487

13.4 The Gauss-Markov Theorem   488

13.5 The Explanatory Power of a Multiple Regression Equation   489

13.6 Confidence Intervals and Hypothesis Tests for Individual Regression Parameters   497

13.7 Tests on Sets of Regression Parameters   505

13.8 Prediction   511

13.9 Computer Packages for Regression Calculations   517

Review Exercises   523

Appendix A13.1   531

14

ADDITIONAL TOPICS IN REGRESSION ANALYSIS   535

14.1 Model-Building Methodology   535

     (i) Model Specification   536

     (ii) Coefficient Estimation   536

     (iii) Model Verification   537

     (iv) Interpretation and Inference   537

14.2 Dummy Variables   538

14.3 Lagged Dependent Variables   541

14.4 Nonlinear Models   553

14.5 Specification Bias   556

14.6 Multicollinearity   558

14.7 Heteroscedasticity   567

14.8 Autocorrelated Errors   572

14.9 Summary   585

Review Exercises   587

15

ANALYSIS OF VARIANCE   595

15.1   Comparison of Several Population Means   595
15.2   One-Way Analysis of Variance   598
15.3   The Kruskal-Wallis Test   606
15.4   Two-Way Analysis of Variance: One Observaton Per Cell, Randomized Blocks   613
15.5   Two-Way Analysis of Variance: More Than One Observation Per Cell   624
  (i) Group Means   625
  (ii) Block Means   626
  (iii) Cell Means   626
  (iv) Overall Mean   627
Review Exercises   635

16

STATISTICAL QUALITY CONTROL   643

16.1   The Importance of Quality Control   643
16.2   Control Charts for Means and Standard Deviations   645
16.3   Process Capability   656
16.4   Control Charts for Proportions   659
16.5   Control Charts for Number of Occurrences   663
16.6   Summary   664
Review Exercises   668
Appendix A16.1   671
Appendix A16.2   674

17

TIME SERIES ANALYSIS AND FORECASTING   677

17.1   Time Series Data: Problems and Opportunities   677
17.2   Index Numbers   678
17.3   A Nonparametric Test for Randomness   688
17.4   Components of a Time Series   692
17.5   Moving Averages   696
17.6   Extraction of the Seasonal Component Through Moving Averages   699
17.7   Simple Exponential Smoothing   708
17.8   The Holt-Winters Exponential Smoothing Forecasting Model   712
17.9   Autoregressive Models   723
17.10 Autoregressive Integrated Moving Average Models   729
Review Exercises   731

18

SURVEY SAMPLING METHODS   735
18.1   Introduction   735
18.2   Sampling and Nonsampling Errors   740
18.3   Simple Random Sampling   742
18.4   Stratified Sampling   750
18.5   Determining the Sample Size   762
18.6   Other Sampling Methods   767
Review Exercises   778

19

STATISTICAL DECISION THEORY   781
19.1   Decision Making Under Uncertainty   781
19.2   Solutions Not Involving Specification of Probabilities   785
    (i)   Maximin Criterion   785
    (ii)   Minimax Regret Criterion   787
19.3   Expected Monetary Value   790
19.4   Use of Sample Information: Bayesian Analysis   798
19.5   The Value of Sample Information   803
19.6   Allowing for Risk: Utility Analysis   818
Review Exercises   827

APPENDIX TABLES   829
1   Probability Function of the Binomial Distribution   829
2   Values of $e^{-\lambda}$ 834
3   Cumulative Distribution Function of the Standard Normal Distribution   835
4   Some Uniformly Distributed Random Numbers   837
5   Cutoff Points of the Chi-Square Distribution Function   838
6   Cutoff Points for the Student's t Distribution   839
7   Cutoff Points for the F Distribution   840
8   Cutoff Points for the Distribution of the Wilcoxon Test Statistic   842
9   Cutoff Points for the Distribution of Spearman's Rank Correlation Coefficient   843
10   Cutoff Points for the Distribution of the Durbin-Watson Test Statistic   844
11   Cumulative Distribution Function of the Runs Test Statistic   846

ANSWERS TO SELECTED EVEN-NUMBERED EXERCISES   847

INDEX   863

Statistics courses are offered in virtually all college business programs and are required in the great majority. They are somewhat less popular than influenza shots, but at least as useful. An understanding of statistical ideas and the potential for their application is essential to the modern manager. Statistical methods are widely implemented throughout business, where numerical information has to be collected and sensibly interpreted as an aid to decision making in an uncertain environment.

In preparing the fourth edition of this text, I have kept in mind that not all statistical concepts are easily grasped on initial exposure. I have tried to make clear the rationale behind the various techniques, and to illustrate the practical application of these techniques. It is hoped that the student will discover both how and why particular methods of data analysis are appropriate in specific situations. The student should approach the subject from this perspective. Understanding of the basis of statistical methods is far more important than attempting to memorize their details as if they were recipes in a cookbook. The majority of readers of this book will become consumers rather than producers of statistical information. It is hoped that this book will help them become well-informed consumers, with an understanding of the basis for, and the ability to critically evaluate, statistical claims. As an aid to understanding the methodology, I have included a very large number of numerical examples. These are intended to provide realistic illustrations of circumstances in which particular methods are useful. The text includes a great many exercises. Working through several exercises on each topic should shape the student's understanding of the material and provide valuable hands-on experience.

To persuade students of the practical relevance of the subject, I have included many real and realistic examples and exercises, drawn from a range of business areas. These areas include accounting, economics, finance, marketing, industrial organization, organizational behavior, and business ethics. It is hoped that the accumulation of these illustrations will convince the reader of the importance of statistical methods in the modern business world, and heighten his or her interest in the subject.

This text is suitable for a one- or two-semester course for business or economics majors. There is more than enough material for a two-semester course, and many instructors will not want to cover every chapter in detail, particularly if a large amount of course time is spent on project work. All or parts of Chapters 10, 11, and 14–19 can be omitted without loss of continuity. One of many possibilities for a one-semester course is to cover Chapters 1–9, 12, and perhaps 13. In such a course, instructors may prefer to omit some of the following sections: 2.6, 2.7, 4.6, 4.7, 5.8, 7.3, 9.9, and 12.2.

This book developed from a two-semester course at the University of Illinois, where we covered most of the material in Chapters 1–9, 11–14, and 17. I am deeply indebted to many colleagues, teaching assistants, and most of all students for helpful discussions, suggestions, and criticisms. Many of these prompted revisions, which I hope have improved the clarity of the exposition.

In preparing this new edition, I have incorporated some additional material, particularly on statistical quality control, and have added many examples of particular statistical methods in action. However, I have tried to maintain and enhance two crucial features of previous editions. These were care and clarity in explaining, using no mathematics beyond basic algebra, how and why the various techniques work, and the provision of large numbers of examples and exercises involving real business and economic data.

The numbers of colleagues, teaching assistants, and students who have helped in some way in the preparation of this and previous editions are far too large to permit specific recognition. However, it is important here to acknowledge the following colleagues for their input on this edition:

Y. C. Chang
University of Notre Dame

Janice Lonergan
Augustana College

S. B. Fotopoulos
Washington State University

William I. Notz
Ohio State University

Frank P. Jozsa, Jr.
Allentown College

Donald Richter
NYU School of Business

Stan Taylor
*California State University,
Sacramento*

I would also like to thank my Prentice Hall editors Rich Wohl and Tom Tucker, and Naoko Miki for expert typing. Of course, all remaining imperfections are the author's responsibility.

To that tiny minority of students who actually read prefaces, I wish you success in your studies of business statistics. I hope you will become convinced of the relevance and value of statistics in many fields of business.

—*Paul Newbold*

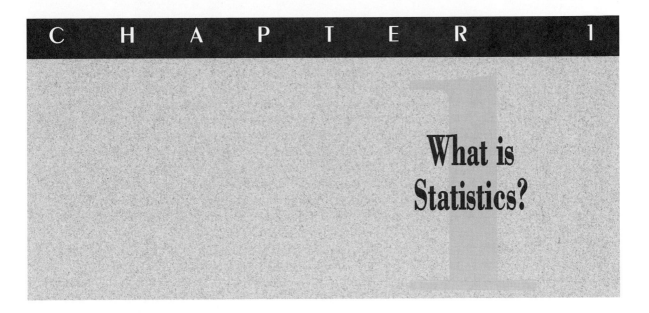

What is Statistics?

Since the majority of readers tend to skip the introductory chapter of a text, it is tempting to answer the question of the title with "Statistics is what statisticians do" and to proceed immediately to the next chapter. Unfortunately, my editor argued forcibly that rather more might be expected. In the end, I decided to compromise with convention and to keep these introductory remarks as brief as possible.

Compulsory statistics courses have received bad press. Indeed, on the typical college campus, enrollment in such a course ranks somewhere in popularity between laws establishing a minimum drinking age and mandatory draft registration. In part, this reputation is deserved. The concepts involved are not always easy to grasp at first, and it is certainly necessary to work hard to keep up with any worthwhile course in the subject. However, one complaint heard occasionally is definitely unjustified. **Statistics is not irrelevant.** The remainder of this chapter is devoted to an expansion of this point, particularly with respect to business and economic problems.

Statistics *is* what statisticians do. What is remarkable is the range of activities in which statisticians are involved. These activities impinge on virtually every aspect of daily business and economic life. We will group these activities under six broad headings.

1.1 MAKING SENSE OF NUMERICAL INFORMATION

Any manager operating in the business environment requires as much information as possible about the characteristics of that environment. In the modern era, thanks in part to the massive information storage capacities of computer systems, much of the

1

available information is **quantitative.** For example, it may be necessary to assimilate movements in interest rates, stock market prices, money supply, or unemployment. Market research surveys are carried out to determine the strength of product demand. An auditor is concerned about the number and size of errors found in accounts receivable. A personnel manager may be able to use aptitude test scores, in addition to subjective judgment of candidates for employment. The list is virtually endless.

The common features of these examples are that the information to be absorbed is *numerical,* and that the sheer amount of that information renders it, in its raw form, virtually impossible to comprehend fully. The statistician's role involves the extraction and synthesis of the important features of a large body of numerical information. One objective is to try to make sense of numerical data by summarizing it in such a way that a readily understood picture emerges while little of importance is lost.

Many issues are involved in a comprehensive analysis and synthesis of numerical data. The most appropriate method will depend on the nature of the numerical information and how it is to be used. In some circumstances, it will be desirable to employ some of the heavy artillery of formal techniques to be discussed in the later chapters of this book. On other occasions, a relatively straightforward numerical or graphical summary may be sufficient and should, in any event, provide a good basis for a deeper analysis. In Chapter 2, we will consider some useful techniques for summarizing numerical information.

1.2 DEALING WITH UNCERTAINTY

A second answer to the question posed at the beginning of this chapter is "Statistics is the science of uncertainty." In statistics, we do not deal with questions of what *is* but of what *could be,* what *might be,* or what *probably is.* Consider the following statements:

> "The price of IBM stock will be higher in six months than it is now."

> "If the federal budget deficit is as high as predicted, interest rates will remain high for the rest of the year."

> "If a bid of this level is submitted, it will be lower than competitors' bids and the contract will be secured."

> "The best opportunities for improvement in market share for this product lie in an advertising campaign aimed at the 18-to-25-year-old age group."

Each of these statements contains language suggesting a spurious amount of certainty. At the time the assertions were made, it would have been impossible to be *sure* of their truth. Although an analyst may believe that anticipated developments over the next few months are such that the price of IBM stock is likely to rise over the period, he or she will not be certain of this. Thus, from a purely semantic point of view, the statements should be modified, as indicated by the following examples:

> "The price of IBM stock *is likely to be* higher in six months than it is now."

> "If a bid of this level is submitted, *it is probable that* it will be lower than competitors' bids and the contract will be secured."

However, our concern about uncertainty is not merely semantical. All we have done so far is to replace unwarrantedly precise statements with unnecessarily vague statements. After all, what is meant by "is likely to be" or "it is probable that"? Perhaps the two modified statements could be interpreted as assertions that the events of interest are more likely than not to occur. But *how much* more likely? The English language is rich in words that describe uncertainty, and, indeed, some of these suggest a gradation from the impossible to the certain. Nevertheless, language alone is inadequate to provide a satisfactory description of the degree of uncertainty attached to the occurrence of a particular event. Rather, we need a more formal structure for this purpose.

In the majority of this book, we will be discussing procedures for attacking problems where the conclusion will necessarily be couched in the formal language of uncertainty. As a prelude, that language—**probability**—is introduced in Chapter 3.

1.3 SAMPLING

Before bringing a new product to market, a manufacturer wants to arrive at some assessment of the likely level of demand, and a market research survey may be undertaken. The manufacturer is, in fact, interested in the **population** of all potential buyers. However, it is prohibitively expensive, if not impossible, for a typical market research survey to contact every member of that population. Rather, a small subset— or **sample**—of population members will be contacted, and any conclusions about the population will be based on information obtained from the sample.

The technique of sampling large populations is commonly used in business. For example, decisions about whether a production process is operating correctly are based on the quality of a sample from its output. Again, an audit of accounts receivable will generally be based on a sample of all accounts.

When we have information on a sample from a population, it is generally straightforward to summarize the numerical sample data. However, taking a sample is merely a means to an end. The objective is not to make statements about the sample but, rather, to draw conclusions about the wider population. Thus, an important problem for the statistician involves the extent to which it is possible to generalize about a population, based on results obtained from a sample.

Of course, if a sample is taken from a population, we will not be able to learn *precisely* the population characteristics. For example, suppose that a sample of accounts receivable is examined, and it is found that 8.2% of these are in error. It does not follow that *exactly* 8.2% of all the accounts receivable in the population are in error. We will have learned something about this population percentage, but we will not know its exact value. Some uncertainty will remain. Hence, in making inferences about a population based on the results of a sample, any conclusions will naturally involve the language of uncertainty, as discussed in the preceding section.

We begin our exploration of procedures for the analysis of sample data in Chapter 6, postponing to Chapter 18 a comprehensive discussion of methods for selecting samples.

An important application of sampling methods is in product quality control; this topic will be discussed in Chapter 16.

1.4 ANALYZING RELATIONSHIPS

Does the rate of growth of the money supply influence the inflation rate?

If General Motors increases the price of mid-size cars by 5%, what will be the effect on the sales of these cars?

Are companies whose dividends are a high percentage of total cash flow viewed as high or low risk?

Are utilities more profitable in areas where they have local monopoly power than where they are subject to competition?

Does minimum wage legislation affect the level of unemployment?

Each of these questions is concerned with the possibility and nature of a relationship between two or more variables of interest. For example, how might we begin to answer the question about the effect on the demand for automobiles of a 5% increase in prices? Simple economic theory tells us that, all other things being equal, an increase in price will lead to a decrease in demand. However, such theory is purely qualitative. It does not tell us *by how much* demand will fall. Subject matter theory is extremely valuable in suggesting the influential factors for such quantities of interest as product demand. To proceed further, we must collect quantitative information in order to assess how demand has responded to price changes in the past. We would then base our assessment on the premise that what happened in the past is likely to be repeated after the proposed current price increase.

In the automobile example, the objective is to use numerical information to learn something about the relationship between the variables of interest. Procedures for analyzing relationships are discussed in Chapters 11–14.

1.5 FORECASTING

The desire to be able to foretell the future is a very human characteristic. However, the need for reliable predictions in business goes far beyond curiosity. Investment decisions must be made well ahead of the time at which a new product can be brought to market, and forecasts of likely market conditions some years into the future would obviously be desirable. For established products, short-term sales forecasts are important in the setting of inventory levels and production schedules. Predictions of future interest rates are important to a company deciding whether to issue new debt. In formulating a coherent economic policy, the government requires forecasts of the likely outcomes for variables such as gross domestic product, unemployment, and inflation under various policy options.

Essentially, forecasts of future values are obtained through the discovery of regularities in past behavior. Thus, data are collected on the past behavior of the variable to be predicted, and on the behavior of other related variables. The analysis of this information may then suggest likely future trends.

Some of the methods of business forecasting are introduced in Chapter 17.

1.6 DECISION MAKING IN AN UNCERTAIN ENVIRONMENT

In any business, decisions are made regularly in an environment where the decision maker cannot be certain of the future behavior of those factors that will eventually affect the outcomes following from the various options under consideration.

In submitting a bid for a contract, a manufacturer will not be completely certain of the total future cost involved in fulfilling it. Moreover, he will not know the levels of the bids to be submitted by his competitors. In spite of this uncertainty, a decision as to where to pitch the bid must be made. An investor, deciding how to balance her portfolio among stocks, bonds, and money market instruments, must make this decision when future market movements are unknown. She may take some view on probable future developments, but she will not be able to predict the future with perfect accuracy.

These examples demonstrate that in order to think about possible options when business decisions are to be made, it is inevitable that techniques for dealing with uncertainty will be relevant. Some useful procedures will be outlined in Chapter 19.

In the remainder of this book we present an array of techniques useful in the analysis of numerical information. Their goal is to help in the understanding of an uncertain environment so that better decisions are likely to be made. It should be emphasized, however, that these techniques are simply useful tools for the manager. They are not intended as substitutes for the familiarity with the business environment that develops through years of study and accumulated experience but, rather, as aids to the sharpening of that familiarity. Thus, even though a careful technical analysis of numerical information will often be of considerable value, that analysis may not be very profitable unless it is allied with the expertise that comes from studying the qualitative characteristics of the relevant environment. It is in alliance with other relevant expertise in the business environment that statistical methods have proved most valuable as management tools.

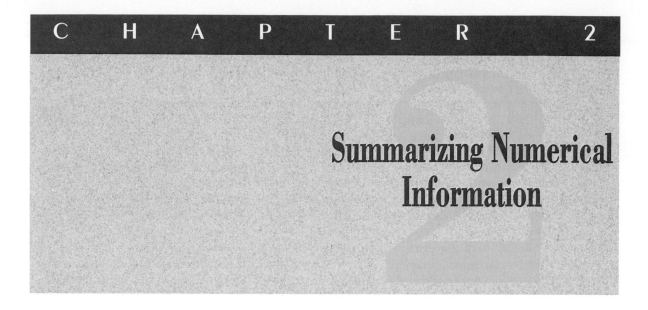

CHAPTER 2

Summarizing Numerical Information

2.1 POPULATIONS AND SAMPLES

It is commonplace to come across the assertion that in today's world we are assaulted on all sides by a veritable barrage of numbers. It is impossible to read a newspaper or listen to a news report without having to digest the impact of such statements as "the Dow-Jones average fell 6 points today," "the Consumer Price Index rose by .8% last month," or "the latest survey indicates that the president's approval rating now stands at 40%." Now, issues such as the state of the stock market, the rate of price inflation, and the electorate's opinion of the performance of the president are likely to be of concern to many of us. It is becoming the case that in order to obtain an intelligent appreciation of current developments in such fields, one must absorb and interpret substantial amounts of numerical information. Certainly, the amount of such information that is collected has grown at a phenomenal rate over the past few years. Government has contributed to this development, both through its own collection efforts and through requirements on corporations to release information. The private sector, too, has played its part. The well-publicized Gallup surveys of voters' attitudes and Nielsen ratings of the week's television shows are merely the tip of a vast iceberg of market research studies. The annual reports of large corporations are rendered somewhat indigestible by the sheer mass of numerical information contained on the many facets of the organization. To a considerable extent, the electronic computer is responsible for this trend. Developments in computing have made relatively straightforward the storage, retrieval, and analysis of information in quantities that would have been completely overwhelming a few years ago. In consequence, it is a fact of life that we are being forced more and more to think about the numerical aspects of any issue of

6

interest. To many people, this development is a source of confusion; to many others, a source of irritation. To statisticians, it is a source of income.

Somebody has to make sense of all the numerical information. Certainly, we are all free to interpret the numbers as we choose, just as we are all free to carry out our own electrical repairs. Nevertheless, the task of making sense of all the numerical information is by no means trivially easy. Faced with a mass of data on, say, the annual incomes of every family in a large city, what can be done? Concentration on the individual incomes will produce nothing more rewarding than a headache. The trick is to extract the essence from the data in as straightforward and simple a form as possible. The statistician's objective is to summarize succinctly, bringing out the important characteristics of the numbers in such a way that a clear and accurate picture emerges. One wants to reduce the mass of information as far as possible, while guarding against the possibility of obscuring important features through too extreme a reduction. As we shall see in later chapters, there is much science involved in the analysis of numerical data, but there is considerably more art.

In this chapter, our aim is to survey some of the methods employed in the summarization of numerical information. Some of the techniques involve the production of numerical summary measures, while others are graphical in nature. All have attractions and can, in particular applications, have drawbacks. Unfortunately, there is no single "right way" to analyze data. Rather, the appropriate line of attack is typically problem-specific, depending on the characteristics of the data and the purposes of the analysis.

Before beginning our discussion on the summarization of numerical data, we pause to distinguish between two types of data sets. In a study of household incomes in a small town of 1,000 households, one might conceivably obtain the income of every household. The data would then constitute the complete set, or **population,** of household incomes of this town. Assuming that the information gained was accurate, we would then have discovered everything that was to be learned about this population. However, as we noted in the previous chapter, it is very often prohibitively expensive to obtain the complete set of data from a population. Far more often, an investigator will be able to gather only a subset, or **sample,** of the population values. Thus, we may collect a sample of, say, fifty household incomes from this town. However, if only a sample has been obtained, the analysis does not end at this point, for the investigator's objective is to learn about the population. In subsequent chapters of this book, we will discuss many techniques for making inferences about a population based on sample information. In this chapter, we will deal only with procedures for the summarization of numerical information, whether it originates from a sample or from the whole population. The techniques are very similar in either case, though we will find it convenient to make some notational distinctions on occasion.

Definitions

The **population** is the complete set of numerical information on a particular quantity in which an investigator is interested.

A **sample** is an observed subset of population values.

In Sections 2.2 and 2.3 we will consider numerical summary measures of data sets, and some graphical procedures will be presented in Sections 2.4–2.6. In many practical applications, the use of both numerical and graphical approaches is likely to be the best strategy.

2.2 NUMERICAL SUMMARY: MEASURES OF CENTRAL TENDENCY

Table 2.1 shows the annual salaries of the seven shop-floor supervisory staff members employed by a small corporation. A casual glance at the numbers in the table reveals one simple fact: They are not all the same; that is to say, there is a spread, or **distribution,** of salaries. This is most easily illustrated by plotting the data along a line, as in Figure 2.1, where each point represents a single observation.

In trying to summarize the numbers in Table 2.1, we may begin by looking for the center of their distribution. Summary measures with such an objective as their goal are called **measures of central tendency.** Several measures of this kind are used in business problems. In this section we will discuss three of them.

(i) THE MEAN

One measure of central location that springs readily to mind is the average. In statistics, an average is referred to as a **mean.**

Definition

The **mean** of a set of numerical observations is the sum of the set divided by the number of observations, that is, their average.

Thus, the mean annual salary for the shop-floor supervisory staff of Table 2.1 is

$$\text{Mean} = \frac{34,500 + 30,700 + 32,900 + 36,000 + 34,100 + 33,800 + 32,500}{7}$$

$$= \$33,500$$

The mean, or average, salary for these staff members is $33,500.

Now, the computations involved in finding a mean are not difficult to describe verbally. However, later on we will encounter arithmetic manipulations that are more conveniently described algebraically. Let us see how to produce a simple algebraic

TABLE 2.1 Annual salaries of shop-floor supervisory staff

$34,500	$30,700	$32,900	$36,000	$34,100	$33,800	$32,500

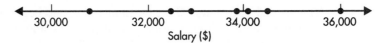

FIGURE 2.1 Annual salaries of shop-floor supervisory staff: data of Table 2.1

formula to describe the operation of finding the mean for any arbitrary set of data. First, if population data are involved, we let N denote the number of observations, so in our example

$$N = 7$$

Next, we let x_1 denote the first observation, x_2 the second, and so on, so x_N denotes the last observation. Thus, for the data of Table 2.1,

$$x_1 = 34,500 \qquad x_2 = 30,700 \qquad x_3 = 32,900 \qquad x_4 = 36,000$$

$$x_5 = 34,100 \qquad x_6 = 33,800 \qquad x_7 = 32,500$$

With sample data, the notation is slightly different, as n is used to denote the number of observations. The notation is summarized in the accompanying box.

Notation

POPULATION N observations, labeled $x_1, x_2, \ldots, x_N$

SAMPLE n observations, labeled $x_1, x_2, \ldots, x_n$

The mean is found by adding up all the observations and dividing the result by the number of observations. Therefore, we can write an algebraic expression for the population mean as

---

$$\text{Population mean} = \frac{x_1 + x_2 + \cdots + x_N}{N} \qquad (2.2.1)$$

Now, the numerator of the right-hand side of Eq. (2.2.1) is, of course, the *sum* of the numbers $x_1, x_2, \ldots, x_N$. In subsequent sections of this book, we will want to refer regularly to the act of **summation.** It is therefore convenient to introduce a notation to represent this act. For this purpose, the symbol Σ (Greek capital "sigma") is employed, and rather than write

$$x_1 + x_2 + \cdots + x_N$$

we will write

$$\sum_{i=1}^{N} x_i$$

This is read as follows: "Take the numbers x_i, and beginning at $i = 1$ (that is, with x_1), form their sum, adding in turn the numbers x_2, x_3, and so on, terminating the process at $i = N$ (that is, when x_N has been added in)."

Summation notation can be put to more general use. Suppose that our interest is not primarily in the numbers x_i but in some function (such as the logarithm or the square) of the individual numbers. In general, we will use $g(x_i)$ to denote a function of the quantity x_i. Then, the sum of these functions for our N numbers is

$$g(x_1) + g(x_2) + \cdots + g(x_N)$$

Using summation notation, this is more compactly written as

$$\sum_{i=1}^{N} g(x_i)$$

Summation Notation

(i) Let $x_1, x_2, \ldots, x_N$ be a set of numbers. Then

$$\sum_{i=1}^{N} x_i = x_1 + x_2 + \cdots + x_N$$

(ii) If $g(x_i)$ is any function of x_i, then

$$\sum_{i=1}^{N} g(x_i) = g(x_1) + g(x_2) + \cdots + g(x_N)$$

To illustrate the second formula in the box, we can write the sum of the squares of the numbers $x_1, x_2, \ldots, x_N$ as

$$\sum_{i=1}^{N} x_i^2 = x_1^2 + x_2^2 + \cdots + x_N^2$$

Expressions for the mean can now be written using summation notation. We use the symbol μ (Greek lowercase "mu") to denote a population mean and $\bar{x}$ (read "x bar") to denote a sample mean.

Algebraic Expressions for Means

(i) Let $x_1, x_2, \ldots, x_N$ be the N population members. Then, the **population mean** is

$$\mu = \frac{\sum_{i=1}^{N} x_i}{N}$$

(ii) Let $x_1, x_2, \ldots, x_n$ be the n sample members. Then, the **sample mean** is

$$\bar{x} = \frac{\sum\limits_{i=1}^{n} x_i}{n}$$

EXAMPLE 2.1

A sample of eight U.S. corporations showed the following percentage changes in earnings per share in the current year compared with the previous year:

13.6%	25.5%	43.6%	−19.8%	−13.8%

12.0%	36.3%	14.3%

Find the sample mean percentage change in earnings per share.
The sample contains $n = 8$ observations, so the mean is

$$\bar{x} = \frac{\sum\limits_{i=1}^{n} x_i}{n}$$

$$= \frac{13.6 + 25.5 + 43.6 + (-19.8) + (-13.8) + 12.0 + 36.3 + 14.3}{8}$$

$$= 13.9625\%$$

Thus, the mean percentage change in earnings per share for this sample is 13.9625%, or approximately 14.0%.

EXAMPLE 2.2

Over a 7-year period, the annual percentage returns on common stocks were

4.0%	14.3%	19.0%	−14.7%	−26.5%	37.2%	23.8%

Find the population mean percentage return over this period.
Regarding the seven observations as the population of interest, we have $N = 7$, so their mean is

$$\mu = \frac{\sum\limits_{i=1}^{N} x_i}{N}$$

$$= \frac{4.0 + 14.3 + 19.0 + (-14.7) + (-26.5) + 37.2 + 23.8}{7}$$

$$= 8.1571\%$$

The mean percentage return from investment in common stocks over this 7-year period was 8.1571%. For purposes of presentation, it is best to round such results—to

8.2% in this case. However, more significant figures are needed if the result is to be carried, as an intermediate step, in the calculation of other quantities, as in Example 2.4 in the next section.

(ii) *THE MEDIAN*

The mean provides an intuitively plausible and easily interpreted measure of central tendency and, indeed, is calculated more often than any other. However, an alternative measure may be preferable for some purposes.

Consider again the seven salaries of Table 2.1. Arranging these in ascending order, we have

$30,700 $32,500 $32,900 $33,800

$34,100 $34,500 $36,000

Now, when the data are arranged in this fashion, the middle value is $33,800. Three members of the staff have higher salaries, and three lower. This middle value is called the **median** of these observations. In this particular instance, the number of observations is odd, and their median is easily located. When there is an even number of values, however, there is not a single middle one. In such situations, the median is conventionally taken as the average of the middle pair when the observations are arranged in ascending order.

Definition

The **median** of a set of observations is the middle one if the number of observations is odd and the average of the middle pair if their number is even when these observations are arranged in increasing order. Thus, if there are N observations arranged in increasing order, the median is the $[(N + 1)/2]$th observation when N is odd and the average of the $(N/2)$th and $[(N + 2)/2]$th observation when N is even.

For the data of Table 2.1, we have seen that the mean is $33,500 and the median is $33,800. These two values are very close, and, as can be seen in Figure 2.2, it makes very little difference which is used in acquiring a feel for the center of these observations. However, such is not invariably the case.

My journey from home to the University of Illinois takes me by three banks, each of which has a device that displays the current temperature. On one particular day, the temperature recorded at the first bank was 19°F, while that at the second was 31°F. This was rather perplexing, but if at that stage I had been forced to estimate the true temperature, perhaps the best that could have been done was to take the average of these two numbers. According to the third bank on my route, the temperature was 20°F. Given the three readings of 19, 31, and 20, the option of estimating the true temperature by their mean (23⅓°F) remained open. However, this seemed rather unattractive. Given two other readings so close together, it was natural to suspect that equip-

FIGURE 2.2 Annual salaries of shop-floor supervisory staff, with mean and median salaries shown

ment registering 31°F was malfunctioning. Thus, the median of the three observations (20°F) provided a more plausible estimate of the true temperature. Since I was due to teach a statistics class on this day and the clamor of my students for real examples could not justifiably be resisted much longer, I detoured to pass a fourth bank. Here the temperature was given as 20°F. At this stage, then, the available data consisted of four observations:

$$19 \quad 20 \quad 20 \quad 31$$

The mean of these values is 22.5°F and the median is 20°F, as shown in Figure 2.3. In this case, the mean and median do differ somewhat, and most of us would probably prefer the median. The observation of 31°F differs so much from the other three that it inevitably arouses suspicion. Thus, in finding a measure of central tendency, one's inclination is to give relatively little weight to this observation.

This simple example serves to illustrate a general point. The mean can be quite markedly affected by extreme observations, whereas the median is not susceptible to such strong influence. For example, the median temperature would remain unchanged if the highest of the four recordings had been 21°F or 41°F, rather than 31°F.

In circumstances where it is deemed inappropriate to give much weight to extreme observations, the median is often preferred to the mean as a measure of central tendency. Distributions of the incomes or wealth of households in a city, state, or country tend to contain a relatively small proportion of very high values. As a result, the mean of such distributions is typically quite a bit higher than the median, and the median would be preferred as the measure of central tendency. It is easily interpreted as that level of income or wealth exceeded by half the households in the population. The mean, which is pushed up by the very wealthy, gives rather too rosy a picture of the economic well-being of the typical household in the community.

In spite of its advantage in discounting extreme observations, the median is used less frequently than the mean. The reason for this is that the theoretical development

FIGURE 2.3 Four temperature recordings, with mean and median recordings shown

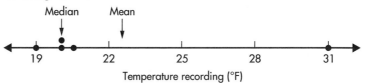

of inferential procedures based on the mean, and measures related to it, is considerably more straightforward than the development of procedures based on the median. Accordingly, most statisticians work with the mean and related measures, incorporating into their analysis special techniques to deal with those situations in which it is suspected that extreme outlying observations could exert undue influence.

(iii) THE MODE

We briefly note another measure of central location, which is defined in the box.

Definition

The **mode** of a set of observations is the value that occurs most frequently.

The concept of a mode is relevant in cases of multiple occurrences of observation values, as the following example illustrates.

EXAMPLE 2.3

A manufacturer of portable radios obtained a sample of fifty radios from a week's output. The radios were thoroughly checked and the number of defects was recorded as follows:

NUMBER OF DEFECTS	0	1	2	3
NUMBER OF RADIOS	12	15	17	6

Find the modal number of defects for this sample.

Since two defects occur more than any other number, the mode of this sample is 2.

The mode is used less than either the mean or the median in business applications. Perhaps its most obvious use is by manufacturers who produce goods, such as clothing, in various sizes. The modal size of items sold is then the one in heaviest demand.

2.3 NUMERICAL SUMMARY: MEASURES OF DISPERSION

Table 2.2 shows the salaries of seven shop-floor workers in a second corporation. The data of Table 2.2 have precisely the same mean ($33,500) as those of Table 2.1. Moreover, both data sets have the same median ($33,800). Thus, if we restrict ourselves to measures of central location, we have no basis for distinguishing between the salary distributions in the two corporations. Yet these distributions do differ in an important way, as is apparent from Figure 2.4. Clearly, the second set of data is more *dispersed* than the first.

TABLE 2.2 Annual salaries of shop-floor supervisory staff in a second corporation

$34,900	$27,500	$31,600	$39,700	$35,300	$33,800	$31,700

A measure of central location is almost never, by itself, sufficient to provide an adequate summary of the characteristics of a set of data. We will usually require, in addition, a measure of the amount of **dispersion** in the data. In this section we consider several such measures.

(i) *THE VARIANCE AND THE STANDARD DEVIATION*

Let $x_1, x_2, \ldots, x_N$ represent a population of numerical values, with mean μ. Since our interest is in the dispersion of these values, it is natural to look at their discrepancies from the mean, that is, the differences

$$x_1 - \mu, x_2 - \mu, \ldots, x_N - \mu$$

Since some population members will be higher than the mean and some lower, some of these differences will be positive and some negative. Indeed, they "balance out" in the sense that their sum is zero.[1] However, in assessing spread, the *sign* of the discrepancy between an observation and the mean is of no interest. We want to treat a negative discrepancy in exactly the same fashion as a positive discrepancy of the same amount. For example, a salary that is $1,000 below the mean should be treated in the same way as a salary that exceeds the mean by $1,000. One way to achieve this is to look not at the discrepancies themselves but at their *squares:*

$$(x_1 - \mu)^2, (x_2 - \mu)^2, \ldots, (x_N - \mu)^2$$

FIGURE 2.4 Annual salaries of shop-floor supervisory staff

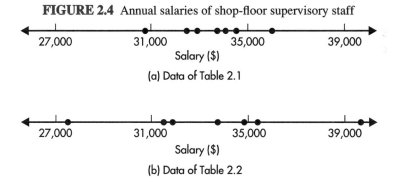

(a) Data of Table 2.1

(b) Data of Table 2.2

---

[1] This follows, since

$$\sum_{i=1}^{N}(x_i - \mu) = (x_1 - \mu) + (x_2 - \mu) + \cdots + (x_N - \mu)$$

$$= (x_1 + x_2 + \cdots + x_N) - N\mu = N\mu - N\mu = 0$$

The average of these squared discrepancies provides a measure of dispersion called the **variance** of the observations. Using summation notation, we may express the variance, denoted by the symbol σ^2 (σ is a Greek lowercase "sigma"), as

$$\sigma^2 = \frac{\sum_{i=1}^{N}(x_i - \mu)^2}{N}$$

The calculations for the variance of the salaries of the staff of Table 2.1 are set out in Table 2.3. We have used the fact that the population mean is $33,500.

From Table 2.3, we see that the sum of squared discrepancies of the observations about their mean is

$$\sum_{i=1}^{N}(x_i - \mu)^2 = 16,900,000$$

Therefore, the variance of this population is

$$\sigma^2 = \frac{\sum_{i=1}^{N}(x_i - \mu)^2}{N} = \frac{16,900,000}{7} = 2,414,286$$

In exactly the same way, we can find the variance of the salaries of Table 2.2, which again have mean $33,500. The calculations are set out in Table 2.4.

The sum of squared discrepancies of the observations about their mean is

$$\sum_{i=1}^{N}(x_i - \mu)^2 = 86,580,000$$

Hence, the variance of this population is

$$\sigma^2 = \frac{\sum_{i=1}^{N}(x_i - \mu)^2}{N} = \frac{86,580,000}{7} = 12,368,571$$

TABLE 2.3 Calculations for the variance of the data of Table 2.1

x_i	$x_i - \mu = x_i - 33{,}500$	$(x_i - \mu)^2$
34,500	1,000	1,000,000
30,700	−2,800	7,840,000
32,900	−600	360,000
36,000	2,500	6,250,000
34,100	600	360,000
33,800	300	90,000
32,500	−1,000	1,000,000
Sums	0	16,900,000

TABLE 2.4 Calculations for the variance of the data of Table 2.2

x_i	$x_i - \mu = x_i - 33,500$	$(x_i - \mu)^2$
34,900	1,400	1,960,000
27,500	−6,000	36,000,000
31,600	−1,900	3,610,000
39,700	6,200	38,440,000
35,300	1,800	3,240,000
33,800	300	90,000
31,700	−1,800	3,240,000
Sums	0	86,580,000

We see, then, that the variance of the salaries in the second corporation is higher than the variance of those in the first corporation. This confirms the visual impression, gained from Figure 2.4, of greater dispersion in the second population.

For purposes of computational convenience, the following alternative but equivalent formula is sometimes used for calculating the population variance:[2]

$$\sigma^2 = \frac{\sum\limits_{i=1}^{N} x_i^2}{N} - \mu^2$$

This formulation is easily remembered as *the mean of the squares, less the square of the mean.*

Now, the variance can be used to compare the dispersions of two or more population distributions. However, since the discrepancies from the mean are squared in computing a variance, it is rather difficult to interpret the variance of a single population. A simple way of returning to the original units of measurement is to take the square root of the variance. The resulting quantity, denoted σ, is called the **standard deviation.** For the shop-floor supervisory staff of the first corporation, the standard deviation of salaries is

$$\sigma = \sqrt{\sigma^2} = \sqrt{2,414,286} = \$1,554$$

Similarly, for the staff of the second corporation, the salaries have standard deviation

$$\sigma = \sqrt{\sigma^2} = \sqrt{12,368,571} = \$3,517$$

---

[2] The equivalence is shown as follows:

$$\sum_{i=1}^{N} (x_i - \mu)^2 = \sum_{i=1}^{N} (x_i^2 - 2\mu x_i + \mu^2)$$

$$= \sum_{i=1}^{N} x_i^2 - 2\mu \sum_{i=1}^{N} x_i + \sum_{i=1}^{N} \mu^2$$

$$= \sum_{i=1}^{N} x_i^2 - 2N\mu^2 + N\mu^2 = \sum_{i=1}^{N} x_i^2 - N\mu^2$$

EXAMPLE 2.4

In Example 2.2, we analyzed the annual percentage returns on common stocks over a 7-year period. Over the same period, the annual percentage returns on U.S. Treasury bills were

6.5%	4.4%	3.8%	6.9%	8.0%	5.8%	5.1%

Compare these two population distributions in terms of means and standard deviations.

For the common stocks, we found in Example 2.2 that the mean percentage return over this 7-year period was

$$\mu = 8.1571\%$$

The sum of squares of these returns is

$$\sum_{i=1}^{7}x_i^2 = (4.0)^2 + (14.3)^2 + (19.0)^2 + (-14.7)^2 + (-26.5)^2 + (37.2)^2$$

$$+(23.8)^2 = 3,450.11$$

Hence, the variance is

$$\sigma^2 = \frac{\sum_{i=1}^{N}x_i^2}{N} - \mu^2 = \frac{3,450.11}{7} - (8.1571)^2 = 426.3346$$

and the standard deviation is

$$\sigma = \sqrt{\sigma^2} = \sqrt{426.3346} = 20.6479\%$$

The mean percentage return on Treasury bills in this period was

$$\mu = \frac{\sum_{i=1}^{N}x_i}{N} = \frac{6.5 + 4.4 + 3.8 + 6.9 + 8.0 + 5.8 + 5.1}{7}$$

$$= 5.7857\%$$

The variance of these percentage returns may be found by first computing the sum of squares

$$\sum_{i=1}^{7} x_i^2 = (6.5)^2 + (4.4)^2 + (3.8)^2 + (6.9)^2 + (8.0)^2 + (5.8)^2 + (5.1)^2$$

$$= 247.31$$

The variance is then

$$\sigma^2 = \frac{\sum_{i=1}^{N} x_i^2}{N} - \mu^2 = \frac{247.31}{7} - (5.7857)^2 = 1.8557$$

Therefore, the standard deviation is

$$\sigma = \sqrt{\sigma^2} = \sqrt{1.8557} = 1.3622\%$$

We summarize the data on percentage returns on these two types of investment over this 7-year period in the following table, where all figures have been rounded to one decimal place.

	COMMON STOCKS	U.S. TREASURY BILLS
Mean	8.2%	5.8%
Standard deviation	20.6%	1.4%

It can be seen that while investment in common stocks yielded the higher average rate of return, the returns on Treasury bills were considerably less variable. In the context of this example, the standard deviation can be viewed as providing a measure of the uncertainty, or risk, associated with investment returns. We see that while average returns were higher for common stocks than for Treasury bills, the associated risk, as measured by the standard deviation of returns, was also higher. (Similar results, which are predicted by finance theory, emerge from the analysis of larger sets of returns data.)

INTERPRETATION OF THE POPULATION STANDARD DEVIATION

So far, we have seen how the variance or the standard deviation can be used to compare the dispersions of two populations. It is also possible to interpret the standard deviation for a single population. Specifically, this quantity can be used to estimate the percentage of population members that lie within a specified distance of the mean. Two rules are commonly used for forming such estimates. The first is true for *any* population.

> Tchebychev's Rule
>
> For *any* population with mean μ and standard deviation σ, *at least* $100(1 - 1/m^2)\%$ of the population members lie within m standard deviations around the mean, for any number $m > 1$.

To see how Tchebychev's rule works in practice, we construct the following table:

m		1.5	2	2.5	3
$100(1 - 1/m^2)\%$		55.6%	75%	84%	88.9%

Hence, according to Tchebychev's rule, at least 55.6% of the population values lie within 1.5 standard deviations around the mean and so on. Tchebychev's rule is shown diagramatically in Figure 2.5. There we show a set of population values, with the range from $(\mu - 1.5\sigma)$ to $(\mu + 1.5\sigma)$ indicated. Tchebychev's rule guarantees that *at least* 55.6% of the population members lie within this range. (In fact, for this particular population, the actual percentage of observations within this range is much higher than 55.6%.)

To provide a numerical illustration, consider the population of Table 2.1, which has mean \$33,500 and standard deviation \$1,554. It follows from Tchebychev's rule that for this population, at least 55.6% of the salaries must fall within $(1.5)(1,554) = $ \$2,331 around the mean—that is, within the range \$31,169 to \$35,831. Similarly, at least 75% of the salaries in this population must fall within \$3,108 around the mean—that is, within the range \$30,392 to \$36,608.

The advantage of Tchebychev's rule is that its applicability extends to *any* population. However, it is within this guarantee that its major drawback lies. For many populations, the percentage of values falling in any specified range is much higher than the minimum assured by Tchebychev's rule. For one "standard" distribution,[3] which describes the shape of many large populations in the real world, it is possible to state a rule of thumb that often provides reliable estimates.

FIGURE 2.5 Illustration of Tchebychev's rule

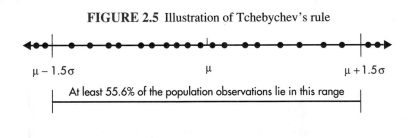

---

[3] The "normal distribution" will be introduced in Section 5.5. It has been found to describe well the distributions of many actual populations.

> **Rule of Thumb**
>
> For many large populations, approximately 68% of the population members lie within one standard deviation of the mean, and approximately 95% lie within two standard deviations of the mean.

Suppose that we have a large population of salaries with mean \$33,500 and standard deviation \$1,554. The rule of thumb would then estimate that roughly 68% of the salaries are between \$31,946 and \$35,054 and that approximately 95% fall within the range \$30,392 to \$36,608.

SAMPLE VARIANCE AND STANDARD DEVIATION

We can define also the variance and standard deviation for a sample of n observations, $x_1, x_2, \ldots, x_n$. Again, we will denote the sample mean by $\bar{x}$. The sample variance is based on the squared discrepancies of the sample values from their mean, that is

$$(x_1 - \bar{x})^2, (x_2 - \bar{x})^2, \ldots, (x_n - \bar{x})^2$$

However, in computing the sample variance, we do not average these squared discrepancies. Instead, their sum is divided by one less than the number of observations. Thus, the **sample variance,** s^2, is defined as

$$s^2 = \frac{\sum_{i=1}^{n}(x_i - \bar{x})^2}{n - 1} \qquad (2.3.1)$$

As we have defined it, the sample variance has desirable properties as an estimate of the corresponding population variance. One way to explain division by $(n - 1)$ rather than n in Eq. (2.3.1) is that we have to use, in that formula, the sample mean rather than the population mean as the measure of central location. If the population mean, μ, were known, a natural quantity to calculate when looking at the dispersion in a sample would be the average of the squared discrepancies

$$(x_1 - \mu)^2, (x_2 - \mu)^2, \ldots, (x_n - \mu)^2$$

However, since μ will not be known in practice, it must be replaced by a suitable proxy—the sample mean, $\bar{x}$. Essentially, it is as compensation for using the sample mean as proxy for the population mean in Eq. (2.3.1) that the divisor is $(n - 1)$ rather than n. We will return to this point in considerably more detail in Chapters 6 and 7. The essential point is that on average, defined this way, s^2 will be neither higher nor lower than the true σ^2 when sampling in the long run.

As in the case of a population, the **standard deviation** for a sample is the square root of the variance.

> **Definitions**
>
> Let $x_1, x_2, \ldots, x_n$ denote the n members of a sample, whose mean is $\bar{x}$. The **sample variance,** s^2, is defined as
>
> $$s^2 = \frac{\sum\limits_{i=1}^{n}(x_i - \bar{x})^2}{n - 1}$$
>
> An equivalent formula for computation is
>
> $$s^2 = \frac{\sum\limits_{i=1}^{n}x_i^2 - n\bar{x}^2}{n - 1}$$
>
> The **sample standard deviation,** s, is the (positive) square root of the variance.

EXAMPLE 2.5

Find the sample standard deviation of percentage increase in earnings for the eight corporations of Example 2.1.

In Example 2.1, we found

$$n = 8 \qquad \bar{x} = 13.9625\%$$

The sum of squares of the sample values is

$$\sum_{i=1}^{n}x_i^2 = (13.6)^2 + (25.2)^2 + (43.6)^2 + (-19.8)^2$$
$$+ (-13.8)^2 + (12.0)^2 + (36.3)^2 + (14.3)^2$$
$$= 4{,}984.83$$

The sample variance is, therefore,

$$s^2 = \frac{\sum\limits_{i=1}^{n}x_i^2 - n\bar{x}^2}{n-1} = \frac{4{,}984.83 - (8)(13.9625)^2}{7} = 489.3170$$

Hence, the sample standard deviation is

$$s = \sqrt{s^2} = \sqrt{489.3170} = 22.1\%$$

The variance and standard deviation are the most commonly used numerical measures of dispersion in a set of data. The reason for their popularity lies in the fact that making inferences about a population, based on a sample, is most conveniently carried out using these measures. However, there are occasions when alternative measures of spread might be preferable. In the remainder of this section, we briefly discuss three alternatives.

(ii) THE MEAN ABSOLUTE DEVIATION

Consider a population of N members, $x_1, x_2, \ldots, x_N$, with population mean μ. In assessing dispersion, we noted earlier that the deviations from the mean

$$x_1 - \mu, x_2 - \mu, \ldots, x_N - \mu$$

might be used to provide relevant information, as long as a negative deviation is treated the same way as a positive deviation of the same amount. In forming the variance, this requirement is met by squaring the discrepancies. Another solution is provided by looking at their absolute values. (The **absolute value** of a positive number is the number itself, while that of a negative number is obtained by multiplying the number by -1.) The **mean absolute deviation** is then the average of the absolute deviations.

Definition

Let $x_1, x_2, \ldots, x_N$ denote the N members of a population whose mean is μ. Their **mean absolute deviation** is the average of the absolute discrepancies from their mean; that is

$$\text{MAD} = \frac{\sum\limits_{i=1}^{N} |x_i - \mu|}{N}$$

The **sample mean absolute deviation** is defined analogously as the average of the absolute deviations of the sample observations from their mean.

EXAMPLE 2.6

Find the mean absolute deviation of the annual salaries of the shop-floor supervisory staff in Table 2.1.

The mean salary for these staff members is

$$\mu = \$33{,}500$$

The calculations for the mean absolute deviation are set out in the table.

x_i	$x_i - \mu = x_i - 33{,}500$	$|x_i - \mu|$
34,500	1,000	1,000
30,700	−2,800	2,800
32,900	−600	600
36,000	2,500	2,500
34,100	600	600
33,800	300	300
32,500	−1,000	1,000
Sums	0	8,800

From this table, we see that

$$\sum_{i=1}^{N} |x_i - \mu| = 8,800$$

Thus, the mean absolute deviation is

$$\text{MAD} = \frac{\sum_{i=1}^{N} |x_i - \mu|}{N} = \frac{8,800}{7} = \$1,257$$

Hence, the average absolute discrepancy of these salaries from their mean is $1,257.

The mean absolute deviation has two advantages over the standard deviation as a descriptive measure of the amount of dispersion in a set of data. First, it is conceptually easier to interpret. It is far simpler to form a mental picture of "the average absolute deviation from the mean" than of "the square root of the average squared deviation from the mean." Second, because the individual deviations are squared in the calculation of the variance and the standard deviation, these two measures are more seriously influenced by odd extremely large or extremely small observations than is the mean absolute deviation. In spite of these points, the mean absolute deviation is employed relatively infrequently in practice because complications can arise from its use in making inferences about a population, based on sample observations.

(iii) THE RANGE

Perhaps the simplest, and most obvious, measure of the dispersion in a set of numerical observations is the difference between the largest and the smallest values. This is know as the **range.**

Definition

The **range** of a set of data is the difference between the largest and smallest observations.

EXAMPLE 2.7

Find the range of the annual salaries of the shop-floor supervisory staff in Table 2.1.

From the table, we see that the highest salary is $36,000, and the lowest is $30,700. The range is, therefore

Range = 36,000 – 30,700 = $5,300

The range is certainly easy to interpret and in some applications may itself be of interest. However, because it takes into account only the largest and smallest observations, it is susceptible to considerable distortion if there is an unusual extreme observation. Moreover, its value is likely to be influenced by the number of observations. In general, we would expect that the range of a large sample would be higher than that of a small sample taken from the same population.

To illustrate the drawback of looking at only the largest and smallest values, suppose that a corporation has seven employees, one with salary $36,000, one with salary $30,700, and each of the other five with salary $33,800. We would all find it easy to agree that there is less dispersion in these salaries than in those of Table 2.1, yet in each case the range is $5,300.

The most common business application of the range is in statistical quality control. Here, sequences of small samples of measurements, as characteristics of the outputs of production processes, are taken over time. These data are analyzed on the shop floor as they are obtained. Because of its computational simplicity, the range of sample values is then often used as a measure of dispersion in place of the standard deviation. In Chapter 16, we will illustrate this application of the range.

(iv) THE INTERQUARTILE RANGE

We have indicated that the range may be an unsatisfactory measure of dispersion because it is too much influenced by a single very high or very low observation. One way around this difficulty is to arrange the observations in ascending order, discard a few of the highest and lowest, and find the range of those remaining. A particular possibility of this sort involves dividing the data into four groups of equal size. The values that serve as the dividing lines between the groups are called **quartiles.** In Figure 2.6, the seven salaries of Table 2.1 are ranked in ascending order; the second observation marks the **first quartile,** the fourth is the **second quartile** (which is the same as the median), and the sixth is the **third quartile.** Quartiles are defined in such a way that the same number of observations occurs before and after each quartile. For these data, then, the first quartile is $32,500, the second quartile is $33,800, and the third quartile is $34,500.

Now, the difference between the third and first quartiles provides a measure of dispersion that is particularly attractive when the median is employed as the measure of central tendency. This difference is called the **interquartile range** of the data. In our example

$$\text{Interquartile range} = 34,500 - 32,500 = \$2,000$$

The general procedure for finding this measure of dispersion is described in the accompanying box.

FIGURE 2.6 The quartiles for the salary data of Table 2.1

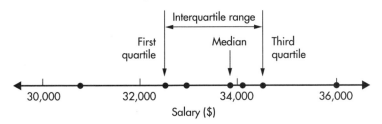

> Quartiles and Interquartile Range
>
> Suppose that N observations are arranged in ascending order. Then, the **first quartile** is the $[(N + 1)/4]$th observation and the **third quartile** is the $[3(N + 1)/4]$th observation. The **second quartile** (the median) is the $[(N + 1)/2]$th observation.
>
> When $(N + 1)$ is not an integer multiple of 4, the quartiles are found by interpolation. For example, suppose that we have $N = 12$ observations, so $(N + 1) = 13$. Then $(N + 1)/4 = 3\frac{1}{4}$, and the first quartile is taken to be the number that is one-quarter of the way from the third observation to the fourth. Similarly, $3(N + 1)/4 = 9\frac{3}{4}$, so the third quartile is taken as the number that is three-quarters of the way from the ninth observation to the tenth.
>
> The difference between the third and first quartiles provides a measure of dispersion called the **interquartile range.**

The interquartile range has an easy and sometimes convenient interpretation. For large data sets, it is the range containing the middle half of all the observations.

EXAMPLE 2.8

Find the interquartile range of the eight sample percentage changes in earnings per share for the corporations of Example 2.1.

Arranged in ascending order, these observations are

$$-19.8\% \quad -13.8\% \quad 12.0\% \quad 13.6\%$$
$$14.3\% \quad 25.5\% \quad 36.3\% \quad 43.6\%$$

For these data, the median is the average of the fourth and fifth observations—that is, 13.95%.

Since there are $n = 8$ observations, we have $(n + 1)/4 = 2\frac{1}{4}$. Hence, the first quartile is one-quarter of the way from the second observation (–13.8) to the third (12.0). Therefore

$$\text{First quartile} = -13.8 + \frac{1}{4}[12.0 - (-13.8)] = -7.35\%$$

Similarly, since $3(n + 1)/4 = 6\frac{3}{4}$, the third quartile is three-quarters of the way from the sixth observation (25.5) to the seventh (36.3). Thus, we have

$$\text{Third quartile} = 25.5 + \frac{3}{4}(36.3 - 25.5) = 33.60\%$$

Finally, the interquartile range is the difference between the third and first quartiles:

$$\text{Interquartile range} = 33.60 - (-7.35) = 40.95\%$$

The interquartile range provides a measure of dispersion that is very little influenced by an occasional extreme observation. On theoretical grounds, however, it is not very convenient as a basis for making inferences about a population from sample data. For this reason, statisticians usually employ the mean and standard deviation as summary numerical measures of central location and dispersion, respectively.

EXERCISES

1. A department store manager is interested in the number of complaints received by the customer service department about the quality of electrical products sold by the store. Records over a 10-week period yield the data shown in the table.

WEEK	1	2	3	4	5
NUMBER OF COMPLAINTS	13	15	8	16	8
WEEK	6	7	8	9	10
NUMBER OF COMPLAINTS	4	21	11	3	15

(a) Find the mean number of weekly complaints for this population.

(b) Find the median number of weekly complaints for this population.

2. A company owns twelve commercially zoned parcels of land. The assessment rates (in percentages) assigned to these in 1994 were

$$21 \quad 22 \quad 27 \quad 36 \quad 22 \quad 29$$

$$22 \quad 23 \quad 22 \quad 28 \quad 36 \quad 33$$

For this population:

(a) Find the mean percentage assessment rate.

(b) Find the median of these percentage rates.

(c) Find the mode of these percentage assessment rates.

3. The ten business economists in a sample were asked to predict the percentage growth in the consumer price index over the next year. The forecasts were

$$3.6 \quad 3.1 \quad 3.9 \quad 3.7 \quad 3.5$$

$$3.7 \quad 3.4 \quad 3.0 \quad 3.6 \quad 3.4$$

(a) Find the sample mean prediction.

(b) Find the sample median.

4. A sample of eight students, living in campus dormitories, were asked to rate on a scale from one (poor) to seven (excellent) the quality of dormitory food service. The ratings were

$$2 \quad 4 \quad 2 \quad 3 \quad 5 \quad 4 \quad 3 \quad 2$$

(a) Find the sample mean rating.

(b) Find the sample median.

5. A corporation recruiting business graduates was particularly interested in hiring numerate graduates. To check on the numeracy of applicants, a test of fifty questions was developed. In a pilot study, this test was administered to a sample of ten recent business graduates, resulting in the following numbers of correct answers:

$$42 \quad 29 \quad 21 \quad 37 \quad 40$$

$$33 \quad 38 \quad 26 \quad 39 \quad 47$$

(a) Find the sample mean number of correct answers.

(b) Find the median for this sample.

6. A department store chain has ten stores in a state. After a review of sales records, it was found that compared with the same period last year, the following percentage increases in dollar sales had been achieved over the Christmas period this year:

10.2	3.1	5.9	7.0	3.7
2.9	6.8	7.3	8.2	4.3

For this population:
(a) Find the mean percentage increase in dollar sales.
(b) Find the median.

7. A sample of twelve senior executives found the following results for percentage of total compensation derived from bonus payments:

15.8	7.3	28.4	18.2	15.0	24.7
13.1	10.2	29.3	34.7	16.9	25.3

(a) Find the sample median.
(b) Find the sample mean.

8. Develop a realistic business example in which the most appropriate measure of central tendency is
(a) The mean.
(b) The median.
(c) The mode.

9. Refer to the data of Exercise 1 on weekly complaints received by a store's customer service department over a 10-week period.
(a) Find the population variance and standard deviation.
(b) Find the mean absolute deviation.
(c) Find the range.
(d) Find the interquartile range.

10. Refer to the percentage assessments data of Exercise 2.
(a) Find the population variance and standard deviation.
(b) Find the mean absolute deviation.
(c) Find the range.
(d) Find the interquartile range.

11. Refer to the data of Exercise 3 on a sample of ten forecasts of the percentage growth in the consumer price index.
(a) Find the sample variance and standard deviation.
(b) Find the interquartile range.

12. The data of Exercise 4 show ratings of dormitory food service given by a sample of eight students.
(a) Find the sample variance and standard deviation.
(b) Find the interquartile range.

13. Refer to the data of Exercise 5 on a sample of ten test scores.
(a) Find the sample variance and standard deviation.
(b) Find the mean absolute deviation.
(c) Find the interquartile range.

14. The data of Exercise 6 show percentage sales increases for ten stores.
(a) Find the population variance and standard deviation.

(b) Find the range.

(c) Find the interquartile range.

15. Refer to the data of Exercise 7 on bonus payments as a percentage of total compensation for a sample of twelve senior executives.

(a) Find the sample standard deviation.

(b) Find the interquartile range.

16. A sample of twelve business statistics students found the following figures for number of hours spent studying the course material in the week before the final exam:

$$12 \quad 7 \quad 4 \quad 16 \quad 21 \quad 5$$

$$9 \quad 3 \quad 11 \quad 14 \quad 10 \quad 6$$

(a) Find the sample mean.

(b) Find the sample median.

(c) Find the sample variance and standard deviation.

(d) Find the interquartile range.

17. Consider the following four populations:

(a) 1, 2, 3, 4, 5, 6, 7, 8

(b) 1, 1, 1, 1, 8, 8, 8, 8

(c) 1, 1, 4, 4, 5, 5, 8, 8

(d) –6, –3, 0, 3, 6, 9, 12, 15

All of these populations have the same mean. *Without doing the calculations,* arrange the populations according to the magnitudes of their variances, from smallest to largest. Then check your intuition by calculating the four population variances.

18. An auditor finds that the values of a corporation's accounts receivable have mean $295 and standard deviation $63.

(a) Find a range in which it can be guaranteed that 60% of these values lie.

(b) Find a range in which it can be guaranteed that 80% of these values lie.

19. In one year, earnings growth of the 500 largest U.S. corporations averaged 9.2%; the standard deviation was 3.5%.

(a) Find a range in which it can be guaranteed that 84% of these earnings growth figures lie.

(b) Using the rule of thumb, find a range in which it can be estimated that approximately 68% of these earnings growth figures lie.

20. Tires of a particular brand have lifetimes with mean 29,000 miles and standard deviation 3,000 miles.

(a) Find a range in which it can be guaranteed that 75% of the lifetimes of tires of this brand lie.

(b) Using the rule of thumb, find a range in which it can be estimated that approximately 95% of the lifetimes of tires of this brand lie.

2.4 GROUPED DATA AND HISTOGRAMS

When a data set of interest contains only a few observations, the presentation of numerical measures of central location and dispersion, together with a plot such as Figure 2.1, typically provides an adequate summary. The purpose of including the plot is to give a visual impression of the distribution of the observations. However, most data sets met in practice contain many observations, and it is generally desirable to obtain a clearer picture of the distribution of such data.

To illustrate the methods to be examined in this section, Table 2.5 shows inflation-adjusted annual percentage returns on common stocks over a period of 30 years. To summarize these data, we could certainly calculate the mean and variance. However, our objective here is to provide additional visual feel for the information they contain.

The task of interpreting the data of Table 2.5 might be made somewhat easier by reducing the amount of information that must be absorbed, possibly by *grouping* the observations. We could subdivide the range of the data and count the number of returns in each subinterval. This has been done in Table 2.6, which shows the number of values between −39.95 and −19.95, the number between −19.95 and .05, and so on. This tabulation allows us rather easily to see simple facts that cannot be absorbed so readily from Table 2.5. For example, there are twice as many positive real returns as negative ones, 60% of all returns are positive but less than 40.05%, and so on.

The subintervals into which the data are broken down are called **classes,** and the numbers of observations in each class are called **frequencies.** For any particular class, the **cumulative frequency** is the total number of observations in that and previous classes. For example, from Table 2.6 we see that twenty-one of the thirty returns are less than 20.05%.

Tabular information of this sort can also be represented pictorially, using a diagram called a **histogram.** The histogram corresponding to Table 2.6 is shown in Figure 2.7. The class boundaries are marked along a horizontal scale. On top of each class interval is drawn a rectangle, the area of which is proportional to the frequency in that class. Since the class intervals are all of the same width (20%) in this example, the heights of the rectangles also are proportional to the frequencies. The histogram allows us to form a quick and reliable visual impression of the proportions of observations falling in particular ranges.

Now, Table 2.6 quotes the actual number of observations in each class, whereas our instinct is to think in terms of the *proportion* of observations in each class. It seems desirable, then, that these proportions, or **relative frequencies,** be shown. In addition, we often want to consider the proportion of observations that are either in that or one of the earlier classes. These proportions are called **cumulative relative frequencies.** These two modifications are easily incorporated, as can be seen in Table 2.7.

The relative frequencies are obtained by dividing the frequencies by the total number of observations. In drawing a histogram with equal class widths, we can use relative frequency rather than frequency along the vertical axis, the picture otherwise

TABLE 2.5 Inflation-adjusted annual percentage returns on common stocks over a 30-year period

−3.2	17.4	−13.4	−9.9	20.4	15.1
2.7	−1.6	41.0	20.8	6.1	−21.8
20.9	53.4	10.3	15.1	−13.8	−34.8
24.6	31.1	−1.0	10.3	−1.5	28.3
17.2	3.6	26.0	−13.0	10.6	18.2

TABLE 2.6 A subdivision of the inflation-adjusted returns of Table 2.5 into classes

INFLATION-ADJUSTED RETURNS (CLASSES)	NUMBER OF YEARS (FREQUENCIES)	CUMULATIVE FREQUENCIES
−39.95% to −19.95%	2	2
−19.95% to .05%	8	10
.05% to 20.05%	11	21
20.05% to 40.05%	7	28
40.05% to 60.05%	2	30

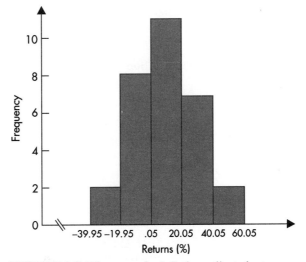

FIGURE 2.7 Histogram for inflation-adjusted returns on common stocks, using the classification of Table 2.6

TABLE 2.7 Classification of inflation-adjusted returns, showing relative frequencies and cumulative relative frequencies

CLASSES	FREQUENCIES (f_i)	RELATIVE FREQUENCIES (f_i/N)	CUMULATIVE RELATIVE FREQUENCIES
−39.95% to −19.95%	2	$2/30$	$2/30$
−19.95% to .05%	8	$8/30$	$10/30$
.05% to 20.05%	11	$11/30$	$21/30$
20.05% to 40.05%	7	$7/30$	$28/30$
40.05% to 60.05%	2	$2/30$	1
Sums $N = 30$		1	

being unchanged, as shown in Figure 2.8. We see, for example, that 7/30 of all the returns are between 20.05% and 40.05%.

The cumulative relative frequencies are the cumulated sums of the relative frequencies. Thus, for the first class, the cumulative relative frequency is the same as the relative frequency. For subsequent classes, the cumulative relative frequency is obtained by adding the relative frequency for the class to the cumulative relative frequency of the previous class. The interpretation of these quantities is straightforward and often valuable. For example, 21/30 of all yields are in the class .05%–20.05% or in one of the previous classes; more succinctly, 21/30 of all yields are less than 20.05%. The information contained in the cumulative relative frequencies can also be presented pictorially, as in Figure 2.9. Unlike the histogram, the areas of the rectangles drawn over the class intervals here are proportional to the *cumulative* relative frequencies.

The accompanying box summarizes the terminology and notation introduced thus far.

Definitions and Notation

Suppose that a set of N numerical observations is subdivided into K classes. Then:

(i) The numbers of observations falling into each of these classes are called **frequencies** and are denoted $f_1, f_2, \ldots, f_K$. Since N is the total number of observations, we must have

$$\sum_{i=1}^{K} f_i = N$$

FIGURE 2.8 Histogram for inflation-adjusted returns on common stocks, scaled in terms of relative frequencies

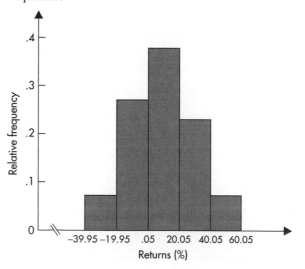

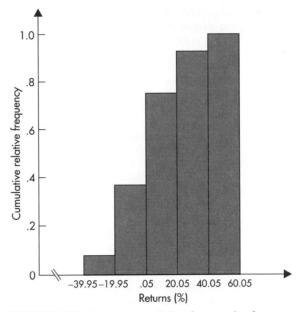

FIGURE 2.9 Cumulative relative frequencies for inflation-adjusted returns on common stocks

(ii) The proportions of observations falling into each of the classes are called **relative frequencies.** Hence, the relative frequency for the ith class is f_i/N.

(iii) The proportion of all the observations that are less than the upper boundary of the ith class is called the **cumulative relative frequency** of that class. This proportion is given by $(f_1/N + f_2/N + \cdots + f_i/N) = (f_1 + f_2 + \cdots + f_i)/N$.

In any practical application, the objective of constructing a histogram is to bring out the interesting and important features of the data, and the most critical question, almost inevitably, is how much detail to include. Presentation of too little detail can mask important characteristics, while, at the other extreme, these can be lost in a mass of detail. The best guide is common sense, although it is possible to set out a few general guidelines:

1. The range of possible observations should be subdivided into *nonoverlapping* classes so that any particular observation must fall into one, but only one, of these classes. This may be accomplished by specifying the class boundaries in units on a finer grid than the data. For example, the percentage returns on common stocks in Table 2.5 are given to the nearest tenth of a percent. Thus, using values such as 20.05%, 40.05%, and so on, as class boundaries in Table 2.6 and Figure 2.7 ensures that each observation will fall strictly within one of the classes rather than on a boundary.

2. In general, because of the resulting ease of interpretation, it is preferable to have all class intervals of equal width. Thus, in our example, the range of possible values was broken down into five intervals, each of width 20%. On occasion, however, this principle must be abandoned. If a data set is such that many observations fall into a relatively narrow part of the

range, while others are widely dispersed, it may be desirable to have narrow classes where the bulk of the observations lie and broader ones elsewhere. If this is done, it is important to remember that it is the *areas,* rather than the heights, of the rectangles of the histogram that must be proportional to the frequencies. In Example 2.9, we will illustrate the construction of a histogram when class widths are not all the same.

3. It is important to ensure that the midpoints of the class intervals are representative of the values of the class members. For example, many items in stores are priced at $19.99, $29.99, and so on. If we divide the range of prices into intervals from $10 to $20, $20 to $30, etc., it is likely that a preponderance of prices in each class will be near its upper boundary. A better solution would be to have classes from $15.50 to $25.50, $25.50 to $35.50, and so on. One reason for having class midpoints be representative of their members' values is that the histogram will present a more reliable visual picture. Also, as we will see in the next section, measures of central tendency and dispersion are often calculated from grouped data. These calculations rely on an assumption that the class midpoints are representative.

4. Often, the most difficult decision is the number of classes to include. If too few classes are employed, the resulting coarse classification can obscure important aspects of the data. If there are too many classes, a choppy and uneven picture, which is difficult to interpret, can result. It is generally felt that at least five, but no more than twenty, classes should be used. To some extent, the more observations, the more classes it is reasonable to include. The subdivision of, say, twenty observations into ten to fifteen classes will inevitably lead to many empty or near-empty classes. This is less likely to be a problem if we have 200 observations. Even with this factor taken into consideration, the choice will often not be clear-cut. It is a good idea, in such circumstances, to try one or two possibilities and see which of the resulting histograms appears to present the truest and clearest picture.

EXAMPLE 2.9

The accompanying table shows nonaudit fees as a proportion of total auditor remuneration for 692 Australian companies that were charged nonaudit fees.[4]

NONAUDIT FEE ⎯⎯⎯⎯⎯⎯⎯⎯⎯⎯ TOTAL AUDITOR REMUNERATION	NUMBER OF COMPANIES
.00 – .05	84
.05 – .10	113
.10 – .15	112
.15 – .20	85
.20 – .25	77
.25 – .30	58
.30 – .40	75
.40 – .50	48
.50 – 1.00	40

Find the relative frequencies and cumulative relative frequencies, and draw the histogram.

---

[4] The data are given by J. R. Francis and B. M. Pollard, "An investigation of nonaudit fees in Australia," *Abacus, 15* (1979), 136–44, published by Sydney University Press.

The fact that the class intervals are not of equal width does not affect the calculations for the relative frequencies and cumulative relative frequencies, which are shown in the next table.

CLASSES		f_i	RELATIVE FREQUENCIES	CUMULATIVE RELATIVE FREQUENCIES
.00– .05		84	$84/692$	$84/692$
.05– .10		113	$113/692$	$197/692$
.10– .15		112	$112/692$	$309/692$
.15– .20		85	$85/692$	$394/692$
.20– .25		77	$77/692$	$471/692$
.25– .30		58	$58/692$	$529/692$
.30– .40		75	$75/692$	$604/692$
.40– .50		48	$48/692$	$652/692$
.50–1.00		40	$40/692$	1
	Sums	692	1	

The quantities in this table are interpreted in the usual way. Thus, a proportion $113/692$, or 16.3%, of all these companies had nonaudit fee as a proportion of total auditor remuneration in the range .05 to .10. Again, a proportion $309/692$, or 44.7%, had nonaudit fee as a proportion less than .15 of total auditor remuneration.

In constructing the histogram, it is crucial to keep in mind that it is the *areas* of the rectangles drawn over the class intervals that must be proportional to their frequencies. Since each of the first six classes has width .05, we can draw rectangles of heights 84, 113, 112, 85, 77, and 58 over these class intervals. The next two classes are of width .10 — that is, twice the width of the first six classes. Thus, in order for their areas to be proportional to the frequencies, the rectangles drawn over these class intervals should have heights that are one-half of the corresponding frequencies—that is, 37.5 and 24. Finally, the last class has width .50, ten times the width of each of the first six classes. It follows that the height of the rectangle drawn over this last class interval should be one-tenth of the class frequency—that is, 4. The completed histogram is shown in Figure 2.10. The reason that we make the areas of these rectangles proportional to the frequencies is that visually we associate area with size.

STEM-AND-LEAF DIAGRAMS

An alternative to the histogram for the presentation of data grouped into classes is the stem-and-leaf diagram. In its most straightforward form, this involves grouping the data according to their leading digits while listing the final digits separately for each member of a class. To illustrate, consider the thirty inflation-adjusted annual returns on common stock of Table 2.5. To begin, we round these to the nearest integer, so, for example, the first four values on the first row are –3, 17, –13, and –10. The stem-and-leaf diagram that results is then

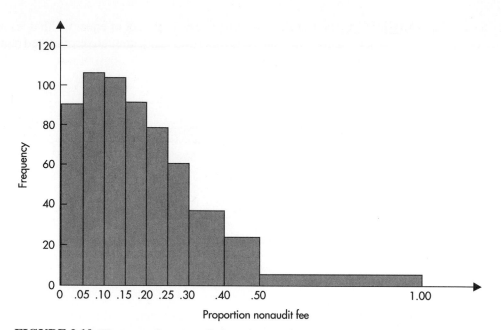

FIGURE 2.10 Histogram for nonaudit fee as proportion of total auditor remuneration, using the data of Example 2.9

```
-3  |  5
-2  |  2
-1  |  4   3   2   0
-0  |  3   3   2   1
 0  |  3   4   6
 1  |  0   0   1   5   5   7   7   8
 2  |  0   1   1   5   6   8
 3  |  1
 4  |  1
 5  |  3
```

The numbers to the left of the vertical line are the leading digits; to the right we insert the final digits of all numbers in the class. For example, rounding to the nearest integer, there are six returns in the range 20% to 29%: 20, 21, 21, 25, 26, and 28.

Like the histogram, the stem-and-leaf diagram provides a visual impression of the numbers of observations in the classes. However, it has the further advantage of providing more detail. Thus, not only do we see that six values are in the 20s, but we can also read their individual magnitudes, to the nearest integer.

If the straightforward procedure just described is insufficiently informative because the groupings are too coarse, further elaboration is possible by subdividing some or all of the classes. For example, the values in the range 20–24 can be listed separately from those in the range 25–29, using two lines instead of one in the diagram.

2.5 NUMERICAL SUMMARY OF GROUPED DATA

A histogram provides a very convenient visual summary of a large set of numerical observations. However, an investigator will frequently want, in addition to this picture, some numerical summary measures of central tendency and dispersion. When the original data are available, this can be accomplished using the procedures discussed in Sections 2.2 and 2.3. Given modern computing resources, this typically provides only a modest computational burden, even for very large data sets. However, it sometimes happens that only grouped data, rather than the raw values, are available. In that case, it will not be possible to determine precisely the values of such quantities as the mean and variance. It is then desirable to have methods for estimating these measures from the recorded group frequencies. Such estimates are also useful if a quick approximation is wanted, even when all the data are available. In this section, we will discuss procedures for finding numerical summary measures based only on grouped data.

MEAN AND VARIANCE FOR DATA WITH MULTIPLE-OBSERVATION VALUES

Suppose that the data are such that only a few different observation values, which may occur repeatedly, are possible. For example, a publisher receives from a printer a copy of a 500-page textbook. The page proofs are carefully read, and the number of errors on each page is recorded, producing the data shown in Table 2.8.

Suppose that we want to find the mean and variance of the number of errors per page for this population. The data presented here are simply a special case, in which there happen to be multiple-observation values, of the general data sets considered in Sections 2.2 and 2.3. Thus, no new principles are involved in computing these numerical summary measures. We simply have 102 observations taking the value 0, 138 taking the value 1, 140 taking the value 2, and so on.

The mean number of errors per page is just the total number of errors divided by the number of pages. The total number of errors is

$$(102)(0) + (138)(1) + (140)(2) + (79)(3) + (33)(4) + (8)(5) = 827$$

TABLE 2.8 Number of errors found in a textbook of 500 pages

NUMBER OF ERRORS	NUMBER OF PAGES
0	102
1	138
2	140
3	79
4	33
5	8
Sum	500

Thus, the mean number of errors is

$$\mu = \frac{827}{500} = 1.654$$

Hence, the mean for this population is 1.654 errors per page.

The variance of the number of errors per page is the average of the squared discrepancies of all the observations from their mean. Now, we have 102 discrepancies of $(0 - 1.654)$, 138 discrepancies of $(1 - 1.654)$, and so on. Therefore, the sum of all squared discrepancies is

$$(102)(0 - 1.654)^2 + (138)(1 - 1.654)^2 + (140)(2 - 1.654)^2$$
$$+ (79)(3 - 1.654)^2 + (33)(4 - 1.654)^2 + (8)(5 - 1.654)^2 = 769.1420$$

Thus, the population variance is

$$\sigma^2 = \frac{769.1420}{500} = 1.5383$$

Hence, the standard deviation is

$$\sigma = \sqrt{\sigma^2} = \sqrt{1.5383} = 1.240$$

The data have a standard deviation of 1.240 errors per page.

We can now consider the general case, in which there are K possible observation values, $m_1, m_2 \ldots, m_K$, and the number of occurrences are, respectively, $f_1, f_2, \ldots, f_K$. The formulas for both the population and sample cases are presented in the box.

Mean and Variance for Multiple-Observation Values

Suppose that a data set contains observation values, $m_1, m_2, \ldots, m_K$, occurring with frequencies, $f_1, f_2, \ldots, f_K$, respectively.

(i) For a *population* of N observations, so that

$$N = \sum_{i=1}^{K} f_i$$

the **mean** is

$$\mu = \frac{\sum_{i=1}^{K} f_i m_i}{N}$$

and the **variance** is

$$\sigma^2 = \frac{\sum_{i=1}^{K} f_i (m_i - \mu)^2}{N} = \frac{\sum_{i=1}^{K} f_i m_i^2}{N} - \mu^2$$

(ii) For a *sample* of n observations, so that

$$n = \sum_{i=1}^{K} f_i$$

the **mean** is

$$\bar{x} = \frac{\sum_{i=1}^{K} f_i m_i}{n}$$

and the **variance** is

$$s^2 = \frac{\sum_{i=1}^{K} f_i (m_i - \bar{x})^2}{n-1} = \frac{\sum_{i=1}^{K} f_i m_i^2 - n\bar{x}^2}{n-1}$$

The arithmetic is most conveniently set out in tabular form. For the data on errors in a textbook, this is done in Table 2.9. Note that we will compute the variance using the alternative, computationally efficient formula.

Reading directly from the table, we have

$$\sum_{i=1}^{K} f_i = N = 500 \qquad \sum_{i=1}^{K} f_i m_i = 827 \qquad \sum_{i=1}^{K} f_i m_i^2 = 2{,}137$$

Thus, the population mean is

$$\mu = \frac{\sum_{i=1}^{K} f_i m_i}{N} = \frac{827}{500} = 1.654$$

as before. For the variance, we find

$$\sigma^2 = \frac{\sum_{i=1}^{K} f_i m_i^2}{N} - \mu^2 = \frac{2{,}137}{500} - (1.654)^2 = 1.5383$$

confirming our previous calculations.

TABLE 2.9 Calculations for the mean and variance of data on errors found in textbook

m_i	f_i	$f_i m_i$	$f_i m_i^2$
0	102	0	0
1	138	138	138
2	140	280	560
3	79	237	711
4	33	132	528
5	8	40	200
Sums	500	827	2,137

MEAN AND VARIANCE FOR GROUPED DATA

Suppose that an investigator has available only data grouped into classes, such as the information in Table 2.6 on inflation-adjusted returns of common stocks. Given only this information, we want to obtain estimates of the mean and variance. We will not, of course, be able to find the precise values of these summary measures if the raw data are unavailable. For example, from Table 2.6 we know that seven of the returns are between 20.05% and 40.05%. However, we do not know where in this range these seven returns lie. In order to make further progress, some approximation is needed. Since the exact location is a particular class of all its members is unknown, one obvious possibility is to proceed as if they were all located at the midpoint of the class interval. Thus, we would take each of the seven returns between 20.05% and 40.05% to have the value 30.05%. If this is done, we are in the position of having multiple-observation values and can proceed to calculate their mean and variance exactly as described above. When employed in this way, the class midpoints are often referred to as **class marks.**

Approximate Mean and Variance for Grouped Data

Suppose that we have data grouped into K classes, with frequencies $f_1, f_2, \ldots, f_K$. If the midpoints of these classes are $m_1, m_2, \ldots, m_K$, the mean and variance of the grouped data are estimated by using the formulas for multiple-observation values given previously.

The calculations for estimating the mean and variance of the inflation-adjusted returns on common stocks, when grouped as in Table 2.6, are set out in Table 2.10. Once the class midpoints have been located, the computations proceed precisely as for multiple-observation values.

From the table, we find

$$\sum_{i=1}^{K} f_i = N = 30 \qquad \sum_{i=1}^{K} f_i m_i = 281.5 \qquad \sum_{i=1}^{K} f_i m_i^2 = 15{,}028.075$$

TABLE 2.10 Calculations for mean and variance of grouped inflation-adjusted returns on common stocks

CLASSES	MIDPOINTS m_i	FREQUENCIES f_i	$f_i m_i$	$f_i m_i^2$
−39.95% to −19.95%	−29.95	2	−59.90	1,794.0050
−19.95% to .05%	−9.95	8	−79.60	792.0200
.05% to 20.05%	10.05	11	110.55	1,111.0275
20.05% to 40.05%	30.05	7	210.35	6,321.0175
40.05% to 60.05%	50.05	2	100.10	5,010.0050
Sums		30	281.50	15,028.0750

The population mean is then estimated by

$$\mu = \frac{\sum_{i=1}^{K} f_i m_i}{N} = \frac{281.5}{30} = 9.383$$

Thus, on rounding, the mean return over this 30-year period is estimated as 9.4%.
Next, we estimate the population variance by

$$\sigma^2 = \frac{\sum_{i=1}^{K} f_i m_i^2}{N} - \mu^2 = \frac{15,028.075}{30} - (9.383)^2 = 412.8952$$

The population standard deviation is obtained by taking the square root:

$$\sigma = \sqrt{\sigma^2} = \sqrt{412.8952} = 20.320$$

Therefore, on rounding, the standard deviation of these returns is estimated as 20.3%.
A word of caution is in order. If one or another of the extreme classes is much wider than the others, it is particularly important that the midpoint of that class be representative of its members' values, in order to obtain reasonably good estimates of the mean and variance.

EXAMPLE
2.10

A sample of 20 batches of a chemical was tested for concentration of impurities. The results obtained were

PERCENTAGE IMPURITIES	0–2	2–4	4–6	6–8	8–10
BATCHES	2	3	6	5	4

Find the sample mean and standard deviation of these percentage impurity levels. The computations are set out in the following table.

CLASSES	m_i	f_i	$f_i m_i$	$f_i m_i^2$
0–2	1	2	2	2
2–4	3	3	9	27
4–6	5	6	30	150
6–8	7	5	35	245
8–10	9	4	36	324
		Sums 20	112	748

From this table, then,

$$\sum_{i=1}^{K} f_i = n = 20 \qquad \sum_{i=1}^{K} f_i m_i = 112 \qquad \sum_{i=1}^{K} f_i m_i^2 = 748$$

The sample mean is estimated by

$$\bar{x} = \frac{\sum\limits_{i=1}^{K} f_i m_i}{n} = \frac{112}{20} = 5.6$$

Since these are sample data, the variance is estimated by

$$s^2 = \frac{\sum\limits_{i=1}^{K} f_i m_i^2 - n\bar{x}^2}{n - 1} = \frac{748 - (20)(5.6)^2}{19} = 6.3579$$

Hence, the sample standard deviation is estimated as

$$s = \sqrt{s^2} = \sqrt{6.3579} = 2.52$$

Therefore, for this sample, the mean impurity concentration is estimated to be 5.6%, and the sample standard deviation is estimated to be 2.52%.

MEDIAN AND INTERQUARTILE RANGE FOR GROUPED DATA

In Section 2.2, we defined the median as the middle value when the observations are arranged in ascending order. Now, if we have available only data grouped into classes, so that the original observation values are unknown, we will not be able to arrange them in ascending order. Still, we can do part of that job. Referring to the returns on common stocks in Table 2.7, we know that the two smallest returns are in the class −39.95% to −19.95%, the eight next smallest are in the class −19.95% to .05%, the eleven next smallest in the class .05% to 20.05%, and so on.

Now, since there are thirty observations in all for this data set, the median is the average of the fifteenth and sixteenth values when these observations are arranged in ascending order. How can we estimate what, for example, this fifteenth observation is? In fact, we know quite a bit about it. It is in the class .05% to 20.05% and is, moreover, the fifth value of the eleven observations in that class.

We see, then, that the estimation of the median, and similarly that of the other quartiles, boils down to estimating, for example, the location of the fifth observation when the eleven observations in a particular class are arranged in ascending order. We do not have enough information to answer such questions with certainty, but we can achieve a reasonable approximation by assuming that within a class, the observations are equispaced. To see how this is done in practice, consider the simple example illustrated in Figure 2.11, where each of three consecutive classes, 0–10, 10–20, and 20–30, contains five observations. The width of each class interval is ten units, and dividing this by 5 suggests that if the observations are to be equispaced, they should be separated by two units. This can be achieved, as illustrated in the figure, by placing the first observation one unit after the lower boundary of the class and ending with the last observation one unit before the upper boundary. Thus, for the middle class, the five observations are placed at 11, 13, 15, 17, and 19.

FIGURE 2.11 Illustration of the assumed spacings of observations within classes in the estimation of the quartiles for grouped data

This simple illustration suggests a general rule:

Estimating the Position of an Observation in a Class

Suppose that a class, with lower boundary L and upper boundary U, contains f observations. If these observations were to be arranged in ascending order, the jth is estimated by

$$L + (j - \tfrac{1}{2}) \frac{(U - L)}{f}$$

for $j = 1, 2, \ldots, f$.

We will illustrate this rather forbidding-looking formula by estimating the median and other quartiles of the inflation-adjusted returns on common stocks. As a first step, we retabulate the data in Table 2.11. Here we show the cumulative frequencies, that is, the total number of observations up to and including those of the corresponding class.

Since there are thirty observations, the median is, as we have already noted, the average of the fifteenth and sixteenth when they are arranged in ascending order. To begin, we will estimate the location of the fifteenth observation. Clearly, from the cumulative frequencies, this is the fifth observation in the class .05 to 20.05, which contains eleven observations in total. Thus, in our notation,

$$j = 5 \qquad f = 11 \qquad L = .05 \qquad U = 20.05$$

The location of the fifth of these observations is illustrated in Figure 2.12. The class width

$$U - L = 20.05 - .05 = 20$$

TABLE 2.11 Classification of inflation-adjusted returns, showing cumulative frequencies

CLASSES	FREQUENCIES	CUMULATIVE FREQUENCIES
−39.95% to −19.95%	2	2
−19.95% to .05%	8	10
.05% to 20.05%	11	21
20.05% to 40.05%	7	28
40.05% to 60.05%	2	30
Sums	30	

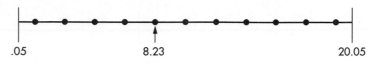

is divided by the number of observations, $f = 11$, so

$$\frac{U - L}{f} = \frac{20}{11}$$

To locate the fifth observation, we count half a step for the first and one step for each of the next four, so we have

$$(j - \tfrac{1}{2}) = (5 - \tfrac{1}{2}) = 4\tfrac{1}{2}$$

of these steps to add to the lower limit, $L = .05$. We therefore have

$$L + (j - \tfrac{1}{2})\frac{(U - L)}{f} = .05 + (4\tfrac{1}{2})\frac{20}{11} = 8.23$$

Thus, we estimate this observation to be 8.23%.

Similarly, the sixteenth observation is the sixth one in this class, so that we now have $j = 6$, with everything else as before. Our estimate is therefore

$$L + (j - \tfrac{1}{2})\frac{(U - L)}{f} = .05 + (5\tfrac{1}{2})\frac{20}{11} = 10.05$$

The median, then, is the average of the fifteenth and sixteenth observations, so

$$\text{Median} = \frac{8.23 + 10.05}{2} = 9.14$$

Thus, our estimate of the median inflation-adjusted return is 9.14%.

In Section 2.3, we defined the first and third quartiles. Since there are $N = 30$ observations, we have

$$\frac{N + 1}{4} = \frac{31}{4} = 7\tfrac{3}{4}$$

Hence, the first quartile is three-quarters of the way from the seventh observation to the eighth. From Table 2.11, we see that the seventh observation is the fifth value in the class -19.95% to $.05\%$. In our notation then

$$j = 5 \qquad f = 8 \qquad L = -19.95 \qquad U = .05$$

The seventh observation is then estimated by

$$L + (j - \tfrac{1}{2})\frac{U - L}{f} = -19.95 + (4\tfrac{1}{2})\frac{20}{8} = -8.7$$

Similarly, the eighth observation is the sixth value in the same class, so now, with $j = 6$, we have

$$L + (j - \tfrac{1}{2})\frac{U - L}{f} = -19.95 + (5\tfrac{1}{2})\frac{20}{8} = -6.2$$

Since the first quartile is three-quarters of the way from the seventh observation to the eighth, we have

$$\text{First quartile} = -8.7 + \tfrac{3}{4}[-6.2 - (-8.7)] = -6.825$$

To locate the third quartile, we have

$$\frac{3(N + 1)}{4} = \frac{93}{4} = 23\tfrac{1}{4}$$

Therefore, when the observations are arranged in ascending order, the third quartile is one-quarter of the way from the twenty-third to the twenty-fourth.

Looking at Table 2.11, we see that the twenty-third observation is the second value in the class 20.05% to 40.05%, which contains seven observations. We have then

$$j = 2 \qquad f = 7 \qquad L = 20.05 \qquad U = 40.05$$

Thus, the twenty-third observation is estimated by

$$L + (j - \tfrac{1}{2})\frac{U - L}{f} = 20.05 + (1\tfrac{1}{2})\frac{20}{7} = 24.336$$

Similarly, the twenty-fourth observation is the third value in this same class, so, with $j = 3$, we estimate it by

$$L + (j - \tfrac{1}{2})\frac{U - L}{f} = 20.05 + (2\tfrac{1}{2})\frac{20}{7} = 27.193$$

Hence, since the third quartile is one-quarter of the way from the twenty-third observation to the twenty-fourth, we have

$$\text{Third quartile} = 24.336 + \tfrac{1}{4}[27.193 - 24.336] = 25.050$$

Finally, then, the interquartile range is the difference between the third and first quartiles, so

$$\text{Interquartile range} = 25.050 - (-6.825) = 31.875$$

Thus, if the interquartile range is to be used as a measure of dispersion, we estimate it by 31.875%.

MODAL CLASS

When the raw data are available, we saw in Section 2.2 that an occasionally used measure of central tendency is the mode, which is defined as the most frequently occurring value. A similar concept can be defined when the data are grouped.

> **Definition**
>
> For grouped data, the **modal class** is the class with the highest frequency.

For the inflation-adjusted returns on common stock, grouped as in Table 2.6, the modal class is .05% to 20.05%; that is, more of the returns are in this class than in any other.

SKEWNESS

In much applied work, only measures of central tendency and dispersion—typically the mean and standard deviation—are calculated. Thus, a very large set of data is often reduced to just two numbers. For many real data sets, such extreme parsimony is justifiable, and little more would be learned through the calculation of further summary measures. However, it can certainly happen that valuable insight into the form of the population distribution is lost when the data are reduced to just a measure of central tendency and one of dispersion. We will now illustrate one possibility of this sort.

Consider the three histograms of Figure 2.13. The histogram in part (a) of the figure depicts a situation in which the data are distributed **symmetrically** about their central value. Extremely large observations are no more likely than extremely small ones. By contrast, the histogram in part (b) of the figure has a very long tail to the right, with a far more abrupt cutoff to the left. Such distributions, which are said to be **skewed to the right,** have the characteristic that their mean exceeds their median. Distributions of population income or wealth generally have this shape. A large proportion of the population have relatively modest incomes, but the incomes of, say, the

FIGURE 2.13 (a) Symmetric distribution

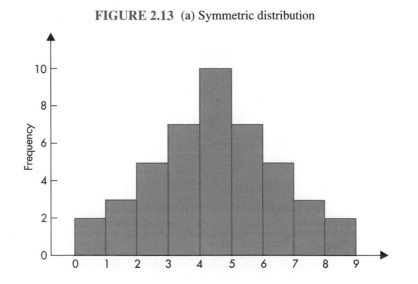

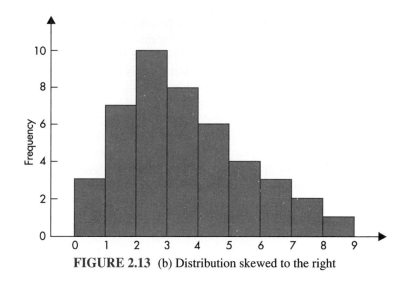

FIGURE 2.13 (b) Distribution skewed to the right

highest 10% of all earners, extend over a considerable range. The histogram in part (c) of Figure 2.13 depicts the opposite situation. Here, the distribution is **skewed to the left,** so the lowest observations extend over a wide range but the highest do not.

The property of skewness can be of considerable interest in the characterization of a distribution of observations. However, the mean and standard deviation contain no information about the skewness of a distribution. The most straightforward way to detect skewness is through inspection of the histogram. Indeed, we have already seen one example of a skewed distribution. It is quite clear from Figure 2.10 that the distri-

FIGURE 2.13 (c) Distribution skewed to the left

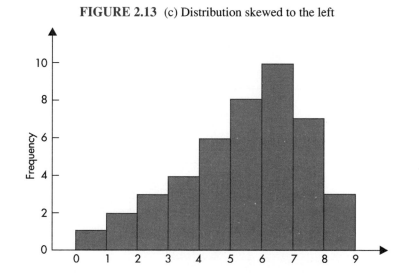

bution of nonaudit fees as a proportion of total auditor remuneration is quite severely skewed to the right. Indeed, for the bulk of the companies, this proportion is relatively modest (less than .20 for 394 of the 692 companies). Yet, for an appreciable number of companies, the proportion is considerably higher.

Although it is possible to find a numerical summary measure to indicate the direction and extent of the skewness of a set of observations, the details need not detain us here. Our objective, rather, has been to indicate the value of drawing a histogram and the potential for the histogram to reveal interesting and important information that would be missed if only a mean and standard deviation were calculated. Viewed in this light, the histogram is an important pictorial tool for summarizing data. In the following section, we will discuss other graphical methods that can be of value in understanding and presenting numerical information of different types.

EXERCISES

21. The accompanying table shows test scores of the forty students in a class. Construct an appropriate histogram to summarize these data.

54	56	56	59	60
62	62	66	67	68
68	70	70	73	73
73	75	77	78	79
79	81	81	82	83
83	85	86	86	88
89	89	90	90	91
93	93	94	95	98

22. The accompanying table shows the percentage decreases in share values for the twenty-five largest U.S. common stock mutual funds on Friday, November 13, 1989. Construct an appropriate histogram to summarize these data.

4.7	4.7	4.0	4.7	3.0
4.4	5.0	3.3	3.8	6.4
3.3	3.6	4.7	4.4	5.4
3.0	4.9	5.2	4.2	3.3
4.1	6.0	5.8	4.9	3.8

23. The accompanying table shows percentage returns for the twenty-five largest U.S. common stock mutual funds for 1989, through Thursday, November 12, 1989.

(a) Construct a histogram to summarize these data.

(b) Draw a stem-and-leaf diagram to summarize these data.

38.0	24.5	21.5	30.8	20.3
24.0	29.6	19.4	25.6	39.5
13.3	28.0	30.8	32.9	30.3
19.9	24.6	32.3	24.7	18.7
36.8	31.2	50.9	30.7	20.3

24. The following table shows the percentage of worker unionization in the fifty states. Construct an appropriate histogram to summarize the data.

STATE	WORKERS UNIONIZED (%)	STATE	WORKERS UNIONIZED (%)
Alabama	19.2	Montana	24.1
Alaska	26.2	Nebraska	15.3
Arizona	13.8	Nevada	22.9
Arkansas	15.0	New Hampshire	13.3
California	23.7	New Jersey	23.0
Colorado	15.2	New Mexico	12.1
Connecticut	21.9	New York	39.2
Delaware	21.7	North Carolina	6.5
Florida	11.7	North Dakota	14.7
Georgia	13.6	Ohio	29.5
Hawaii	32.1	Oklahoma	13.5
Idaho	14.3	Oregon	23.1
Illinois	31.5	Pennsylvania	34.2
Indiana	29.3	Rhode Island	27.1
Iowa	19.2	South Carolina	6.7
Kansas	12.8	South Dakota	10.3
Kentucky	22.4	Tennessee	17.7
Louisiana	16.0	Texas	11.0
Maine	18.3	Utah	13.0
Maryland	21.0	Vermont	17.5
Massachusetts	24.4	Virginia	12.7
Michigan	34.6	Washington	33.1
Minnesota	24.4	West Virginia	36.8
Mississippi	12.4	Wisconsin	27.8
Missouri	30.0	Wyoming	14.9

25. Draw a stem-and-leaf diagram to summarize the test scores of Exercise 21.

26. The forty students in a class rated the instructor on a scale from one (poor) to five (excellent). The results are shown in the table.

RATING	1	2	3	4	5
NUMBER OF STUDENTS	1	7	15	10	7

(a) Find the mean rating.
(b) Find the median of these ratings.
(c) What is the modal rating?
(d) Find the variance and standard deviation for this population of ratings.

27. A sample of fifty personal property insurance policies found the following numbers of claims over the past 2 years.

NUMBER OF CLAIMS	0	1	2	3	4	5	6
NUMBER OF POLICIES	21	13	5	4	2	3	2

(a) Find the mean number of claims per policy.
(b) Find the sample median number of claims.
(c) Find the modal number of claims for this sample.
(d) Find the sample variance and standard deviation.

28. Refer to the data of Exercise 21, which provide test scores of a class of forty students.
(a) Based on the data groupings used in constructing your histogram, estimate
   (i) The population mean.
   (ii) The population standard deviation.
   (iii) The median for this population.
   (iv) The interquartile range for this population.
(b) Using the raw data of Exercise 21, compute directly the four population summary statistics estimated in part (a), and discuss the quality of these estimates.

29. Refer to the data of Exercise 23 on percentage returns for the twenty-five largest U.S. common stock mutual funds.
(a) Based on the data grouping used in constructing your histogram:
   (i) Estimate the mean for these percentage returns.
   (ii) Estimate the population standard deviation for these percentage returns.
   (iii) Estimate the median percentage return.
   (iv) Estimate the interquartile range for these percentage returns.
(b) Now calculate the mean and standard deviation directly from the twenty-five observations and compare them with your answers in (a).

30. Refer to the data of Exercise 24 on the percentage of unionization in the fifty states.
(a) Based on the data grouping used in constructing your histogram:
   (i) Estimate the mean of these unionization rates.
   (ii) Estimate the population standard deviation for these rates.
   (iii) Estimate the median unionization percentage.
   (iv) Estimate the interquartile range of these percentages.
(b) Now calculate the mean and standard deviation directly from the fifty observations and compare them with your answers in (a).

31. A corporation with new positions to fill was anxious to interview business majors on the campuses of twenty large Midwestern universities. The table shows the number of business majors from these campuses requesting interviews with the corporation.

NUMBER OF STUDENTS	.5–10.5	10.5–20.5	20.5–30.5	30.5–40.5
NUMBER OF CAMPUSES	2	4	9	5

(a) Draw the histogram.
(b) Find the relative frequencies.

(c) Find the cumulative frequencies.

(d) Find the cumulative relative frequencies.

(e) Estimate the population mean number of students per campus requesting interviews.

(f) Estimate the population variance number of students per campus requesting interviews.

(g) Estimate the population standard deviation.

(h) Estimate the population median.

(i) Estimate the interquartile range.

(j) Which is the modal class?

32. For a random sample of twenty-five students from a large class, the accompanying table shows the amounts of time spent studying for a test.

STUDY TIME (HOURS)	0–4	4–8	8–12	12–16	16–20
NUMBER OF STUDENTS	3	7	8	5	2

(a) Draw the histogram.

(b) Find the relative frequencies.

(c) Find the cumulative relative frequencies and draw the corresponding histogram.

(d) Estimate the sample mean study time.

(e) Estimate the sample standard deviation.

(f) In which class is the sample median?

(g) Which is the modal class?

33. An educational psychologist presented a task to a sample of twenty-five young children. The table shows the times spent on the task, before completing or abandoning it, by these children.

TIME (MINUTES)	0–5	5–10	10–15	15–20	20–25
NUMBER OF CHILDREN	4	7	8	4	2

(a) Draw the histogram.

(b) Find the relative frequencies for this sample.

(c) Estimate the sample mean time spent.

(d) Estimate the sample variance and standard deviation of time spent.

34. A sample of twenty financial analysts was asked to provide forecasts of earnings per share of a corporation for next year. The results are summarized in the following table.

FORECAST ($ per share)	9.95–10.45	10.45–10.95	10.95–11.45	11.45–11.95	11.95–12.45
NUMBER OF ANALYSTS	2	8	6	3	1

(a) Draw the histogram.

(b) Find the sample relative frequencies.

(c) Find the sample cumulative frequencies.
(d) Find and interpret the sample cumulative relative frequencies.
(e) Estimate the sample mean forecast.
(f) Estimate the sample variance and standard deviation of the forecasts.
(g) Estimate the sample median of the forecasts.
(h) Estimate the sample interquartile range.
(i) Which is the modal class for this sample?

35. A sample was taken of flights arriving at a major airport to study the problem of air traffic delays. The table shows numbers of minutes late for a sample of 100 flights.

MINUTES LATE	0–10	10–20	20–30	30–40	40–50	50–60
NUMBER OF FLIGHTS	29	23	17	14	11	6

(a) Draw the histogram.
(b) Find the sample relative frequencies.
(c) Find and interpret the sample cumulative relative frequencies.
(d) Estimate the sample mean number of minutes late.
(e) Estimate the sample variance and standard deviation.
(f) Estimate the sample median number of minutes late.
(g) Estimate the interquartile range.
(h) Which is the modal class for this sample?

36. During a winter flu epidemic, waiting times at a student health center were longer than usual. The accompanying table summarizes the distribution of waiting times for a sample of twenty students who visited the health center in this period.

WAITING TIME (HOURS)	0–1	1–2	2–3	3–4
NUMBER OF STUDENTS	6	9	4	1

(a) Draw the histogram.
(b) Find the sample relative frequencies.
(c) Find and interpret the sample cumulative relative frequencies.
(d) Estimate the sample mean waiting time.
(e) Estimate the sample variance and standard deviation of waiting times.
(f) Estimate the sample median waiting time.
(g) Estimate the sample interquartile range.
(h) What is the modal class for this sample?

37. For a sample of fifty new full-size cars, fuel consumption figures were obtained and summarized in the accompanying table.

FUEL CONSUMPTION (MILES PER GALLON)	14–16	16–18	18–20	20–22	22–24
NUMBER OF CARS	3	6	13	20	8

(a) Draw the histogram.

(b) Find the sample relative frequencies.

(c) Find and interpret the sample cumulative relative frequencies.

(d) Estimate the sample mean fuel consumption.

(e) Estimate the sample standard deviation of fuel consumption.

(f) Estimate the sample median fuel consumption.

(g) Estimate the sample interquartile range.

(h) What is the modal class for this sample?

38. For households in a large town, the following information on incomes is available.

HOUSEHOLD INCOME ($)	RELATIVE FREQUENCY
10,000–15,000	.20
15,000–20,000	.18
20,000–25,000	.14
25,000–30,000	.12
30,000–40,000	.14
40,000–50,000	.14
50,000–60,000	.08

(a) Draw the histogram.

(b) Estimate the population mean household income.

(c) Estimate the population standard deviation of household incomes.

(d) Estimate the population median income.

(e) Compare your estimates in parts (b) and (d) and comment on their difference.

2.6 SOME OTHER GRAPHICAL METHODS

The presentation of numerical information is often most conveniently and attractively achieved through the use of graphs and charts. These have the advantage that features of data are more easily absorbed visually than through the contemplation of a numerical tabulation. In this section, we will briefly outline a few of the graphical techniques in common use.

(i) BAR CHARTS

Bar charts provide a convenient way to see the relative sizes of numerical quantities that are distributed either spatially or over time. For example, Table 2.12 shows the numbers of visitors to the United States in 1992 from three countries. This information is presented visually in the bar chart of Figure 2.14. The chart is drawn so that the height of the rectangle representing each country is proportional to the number of visitors from that country. The information in charts of this sort can be quickly and easily

TABLE 2.12 Numbers of visitors to the United States in 1992

COUNTRY OF ORIGIN	NUMBER (MILLIONS)
Japan	3.7
United Kingdom	2.8
Germany	1.7

TABLE 2.13 Percentage of U.S. married women, with children under age six, in the labor force

YEAR	1960	1965	1970	1975	1980	1985	1990
PERCENTAGE	19	23	30	37	45	53	59

assimilated. Such charts are often used to report business and economic information—for example, in corporate reports and in the financial press.

The same approach can be used to illustrate the movement over time of a quantity. Table 2.13 shows the percentage of U.S. married women, with children under age six, who were in the labor force, in seven years. The same information is depicted in the bar chart of Figure 2.15. It is easier to form a quick and reliable impression of changes over time from visual inspection of the bar chart than by looking at the numbers themselves.

An interesting and useful extension to the simple bar chart can be drawn when components of individual categories are also of interest. For example, Table 2.14 on page 56 shows acreage of rain forest in three continents for two years. This information can be shown in a bar chart by breaking down the total acreage for each year so that the three components are distinguished by differences in shading, as shown in

FIGURE 2.14 Bar chart for numbers of visitors to the United States in 1992 from three countries

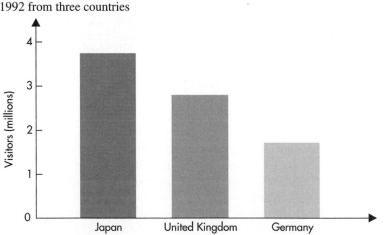

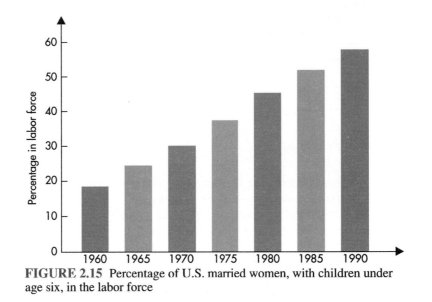

FIGURE 2.15 Percentage of U.S. married women, with children under age six, in the labor force

Figure 2.16. This kind of chart is often called a *component bar chart,* and allows us to make visual comparisons of both the totals and the individual components. In this example, it appears that the fall in acreage of rain forest over the decade was fairly uniform over the three continents.

FIGURE 2.16 Acreage of rain forest in 1980 and 1990

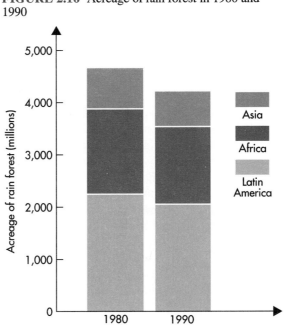

TABLE 2.14 Acreage of rain forest (millions)

	1980	1990
Latin America	2,279	2,074
Africa	1,606	1,482
Asia	767	679

(ii) TIME PLOTS

As an alternative to a bar chart, the progression of a numerical quantity through time can also be illustrated by graphing its value against time. Measuring time along the horizontal axis and the numerical quantity of interest along the vertical axis yields a point on the graph for each observation. Joining points adjacent in time by straight lines then produces a time plot, which provides an easily read visual impression of the historical record.

To illustrate, Table 2.15 shows average Scholastic Assessment Test mathematics scores for the period 1973–1993. The corresponding time plot is shown in Figure 2.17. From the figure, we can see scores falling through 1980–1981, followed by a recovery, so that 1993 provided the highest average score since 1974.

Time plots such as this certainly provide a convenient view of a historical record. It is tempting to try to extrapolate visual patterns into the future from casual examination of such plots. However, experience suggests that this can be a very unreliable strategy for predicting the future. The difficulty is that, when viewed on a time plot, chance variability can give the impression of a systematic pattern. A time plot alone is an inadequate basis for forecasting. As will be discussed in Chapter 17, a more thorough analysis of the data is desirable when prediction is the goal.

(iii) PIE CHARTS

Pie charts are used to depict the division of a whole into its constituent parts. For example, it was estimated[5] that of all computer crimes in the United States, 44% involve theft of money, 16% involve theft of information or programs, 16% involve damage to software, 12% involve alteration of data, 10% involve theft of service, and 2% involve trespass.

This breakdown is pictured in the pie chart of Figure 2.18. The circle (or "pie") represents total computer crimes, and the segments (or "pieces of the pie") cut from its center depict shares of that total. The pie is constructed so that the area of each segment is proportional to the corresponding number of crimes. Pie charts are easily

---

[5] S. Shahabuddin, "Computer security problems and control techniques," *American Business Review, 7,* no. 1 (1989), 14–22.

TABLE 2.15 Average Scholastic Assessment Test mathematics scores

YEAR	SCORE	YEAR	SCORE	YEAR	SCORE
1973	481	1980	466	1987	476
1974	480	1981	466	1988	476
1975	472	1982	467	1989	476
1976	472	1983	468	1990	476
1977	470	1984	471	1991	474
1978	468	1985	475	1992	476
1979	467	1986	475	1993	478

drawn. Beginning at the center of the circle, the total of 360° is subdivided to determine the angle cut off at the center by each segment. For example, for "alteration of data," this angle is the proportion .12 of 360°, or 43.2°.

Pie charts are another example of the value of graphical representation of data, where visual comparison of areas forms a very convenient way for assessing the relative magnitudes of numbers.

(iv) *SCATTER PLOTS*

Often we want to look at the relationship, if any, between a pair of numerical variables. For example, Table 2.16 shows consumer price inflation and long-term interest

FIGURE 2.17 Average Scholastic Assessment Test mathematics scores

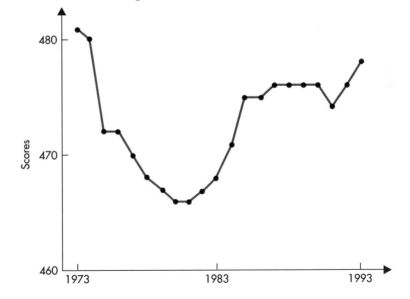

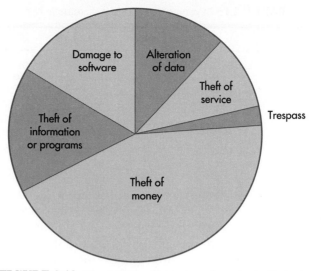

FIGURE 2.18 Pie chart for computer crimes in the United States

rates in the twelve countries of the European Community in 1992. We would expect interest rates to be highest in those countries where inflation is highest, and a glance at the numbers in the table indicates that this is so. To obtain a fuller picture of the relationship between these two quantities, we have graphed the data on the scatter plot of Figure 2.19. It appears from this graph that, for the eight countries with the lowest levels of interest rates and inflation, there is little relationship between these two variables. However, the four countries with the highest inflation rates also have the highest interest rates. One of these (Greece) stands out as having higher levels of both inflation and interest rates than the others.

Scatter plots such as Figure 2.19 can provide a pictorial view of the relationship between a pair of numerical variables. Statistical techniques to be discussed in Chapters 12–14 allow a more detailed analysis of this type of data.

TABLE 2.16 Consumer price inflation and long-term interest rates

COUNTRY	INFLATION (%)	INTEREST RATES (%)	COUNTRY	INFLATION (%)	INTEREST RATES (%)
France	2.8	8.6	Greece	15.9	22.5
Germany	4.5	7.9	Ireland	3.0	9.4
Italy	5.5	13.1	Luxembourg	3.2	7.9
United Kingdom	3.7	9.1	Netherlands	3.7	8.1
Belgium	2.4	8.6	Portugal	8.9	16.1
Denmark	2.0	9.8	Spain	5.9	12.6

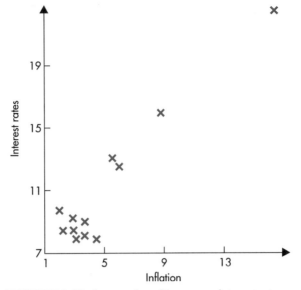

FIGURE 2.19 Scatter plot of long-term interest rates and inflation

(v) *BOX-AND-WHISKER PLOTS*

The box-and-whisker plot is a useful tool in the graphical summary of a batch of data. We will illustrate by looking again at the inflation rates, given in Table 2.16, for the twelve countries of the European Community.

The median inflation rate for these countries is 3.7%, while the first and third quartiles are 2.85% and 5.8%, respectively. A feature of these data is that the inflation rate of 15.9% for Greece is very much higher than the rates for the other countries. With the exception of this value, all inflation rates range from 2.0% to 8.9%.

This information is summarized in the plot of Figure 2.20. The scale shows inflation rates. The rectangle (or "box") is drawn so that its lower and upper boundaries correspond to the first and third quartiles. A line at the value of the median is drawn in the interior of the box. The exceptional value for Greece is shown separately, while lines run from the edges of the box to dashed lines (or "whiskers") drawn at the levels of the largest and smallest of the remaining observations.

Box-and-whisker plots are useful in allowing a visual comparison of two or more batches of data. To illustrate, Table 2.17 shows the final examination scores of the fifteen sophomores, fifteen juniors, and fifteen seniors in a statistics class. The medians and first and third quartiles of these three batches of scores are set out in Table 2.18. Then, Figure 2.21 shows side-by-side box-and-whisker plots of the scores of these three groups of students. In this particular example, there appear to be no ex-

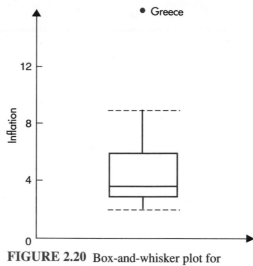

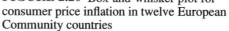

FIGURE 2.20 Box-and-whisker plot for consumer price inflation in twelve European Community countries

treme outlying observations in any of the batches. The whiskers in the plots are then for the highest and lowest scores. From the figure, it is clear that, while the seniors achieved the highest median score, their scores exhibit considerably more variability than those of the other groups. Also notable is the relative success of the juniors in avoiding many very low scores.

TABLE 2.17 Final examination scores

SOPHOMORES		JUNIORS		SENIORS	
47	72	56	76	43	80
52	72	59	80	48	80
52	78	59	83	50	83
57	81	61	83	55	85
63	81	67	84	61	89
64	86	69	90	67	91
69	91	73	94	72	97
71		76		78	

TABLE 2.18 Summary statistics for examination scores

	SOPHOMORES	JUNIORS	SENIORS
First Quartile	57	61	55
Median	71	76	78
Third Quartile	81	83	85

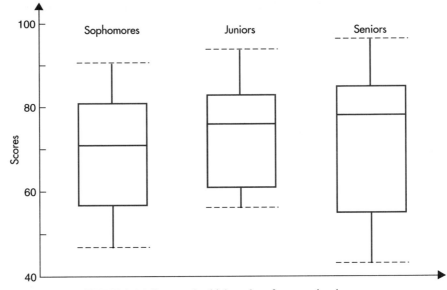

FIGURE 2.21 Box-and-whisker plots for examination scores

2.7 LYING WITH STATISTICS[6]

We have now considered several procedures that might be appropriate for summarizing and presenting numerical information. Used sensibly and carefully, these can be excellent tools for extracting the essential information from what would otherwise be an indigestible mass of numbers. Unfortunately, however, it is not invariably the case that an attempt at data summarization is carried out either sensibly or carefully. In such circumstances, one can easily be misled by the manner in which the summary is presented. The statistician's art involves drawing from data as clear and accurate a picture as possible. Improper use of the various techniques can produce a distorted picture, yielding a false impression. It is possible to "lie with statistics" without being deliberately dishonest. In this section, we present six suggestions for how to do so, the intent being not to encourage their use but to caution against their dangers.

(i) EMOTIVE AND LOADED STATEMENTS

Numbers, in and of themselves, contain no value judgments. Data simply provide factual material, which could, of course, be useful on one side or another of a particular

---

[6] The title of this section is inspired by D. Huff and I. Geis, *How to Lie with Statistics* (New York: Norton, 1954). This delightful little book is essential reading for anyone with a serious interest in the presentation of statistical information. Also see H. Wainer, "How to display data badly," *American Statistician, 38* (1984), 137–47, and D. S. Christensen and A. Larkin, "Criteria for high intensity graphics," *Journal of Managerial Issues, 4* (1992), 130–53.

argument. However, it is possible, through simple verbal tricks of presentation, to color the numbers in a suggestive manner. Suppose that a census of blue-collar production workers in a particular plant reveals their mean annual income to be $25,000. This fact can be presented as

"The mean annual income for these employees is $25,000."

A union representative might report the same information as

"The mean annual income for these employees is only $25,000."

The injection of the word *only* into this sentence clarifies nothing. Rather, it carries the suggestion—certainly unwarranted in the absence of further information—that the average income is unduly low.

A more colorful, and more extreme, example is the following statement.[7]

"If all the nation's federal bureaucrats were laid end to end, they would reach from New York City to beyond Las Vegas."

The purpose of such a statement is not to present numerical information but to convey the impression that the number of federal bureaucrats is very large. The reader is encouraged to deduce that there are "too many" such government employees. Here the underlying numerical information is obscured by the spurious appeal to the irrelevant fact that, in the unlikely event that these people were to be laid end to end, a considerable distance would be covered. Only by working backwards can we extract the fact that there are 2.1 million federal white-collar employees.

(ii) *INADEQUATE NUMERICAL SUMMARIES*

The reduction of a vast amount of data to one or two summary measures, intended to carry as much information as possible, is often necessary. Without such summary statistics, interpretation would frequently be impossible. Still, the process can be taken too far. If too little summary information is provided, a false impression can be created.

An example of this type of distortion concerns the population density in Washoe County, Nevada, which has an average 13.5 people per square mile.[8] In fact, 80% of the inhabitants of this county live in Reno and Sparks, where there are, respectively, 4,362 and 6,155 people per square mile. The remainder of Washoe County—99.8% of

---

[7] This is based on a total of 2.1 million federal white-collar employees. Assuming an average height of 5 feet 9 inches gives a total distance of 2,287 miles.

[8] This illustration is given by J. W. Tukey in "Methodology and the statistician's responsibility for both accuracy and relevance," *Journal of the American Statistical Association, 74* (1979), 786–93.

its area—has 2.66 people per square mile. The average population density for this county, then, tells us very little. The great majority of its inhabitants live in parts that are substantially more densely populated, while the overwhelming majority of the area is much more sparsely populated than the average. Yet, presented with just the mean number of people per square mile, we might jump to the erroneous conclusion of uniformity of population density in this county.

(iii) CHOICE OF SCALE FOR TIME PLOTS

Figure 2.17, which for convenience is reproduced as Figure 2.22(a), shows average Scholastic Assessment Test mathematics scores over a period of eleven years. This picture suggests quite wide fluctuations in average scores. Precisely the same information is graphed in Figure 2.22(b), but now with a much coarser scale on the vertical axis. The resulting picture is much flatter, suggesting considerably less variability in average scores over time.

By selecting a particular scale of measurement, one can, in a time plot, create an impression either of relative stability or of substantial fluctuations over time. There is no "correct" choice of scale for any particular plot. Rather, the conclusion from examples such as this is that looking at the shape of the plot alone is inadequate for obtaining a clear picture of the data. It is also necessary to keep in mind the scale on which the measurements are made.

FIGURE 2.22 Time plots of average Scholastic Assessment Test mathematics scores

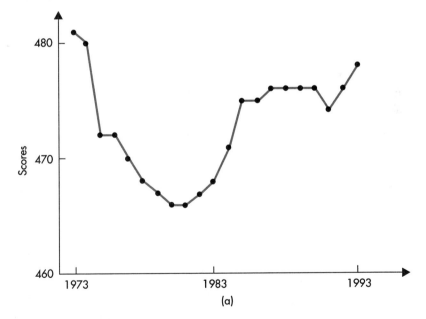

(a)

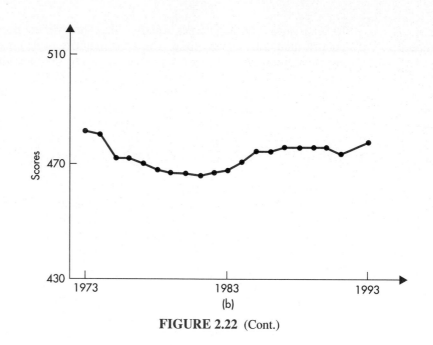

FIGURE 2.22 (Cont.)

(iv) IMPROPER GRAPHICAL SIZE COMPARISONS

From Table 2.12, we see that there were 1.7 million visitors to the United States from Germany and 3.7 million from Japan. Then, the number of visitors from Japan is approximately 2.2 times the number from Germany. One simple possibility to illustrate this might be by drawing a 1-unit square to depict numbers from Germany and a 2.2-unit square to represent numbers from Japan, as in Figure 2.23(a). However, a casual look at this picture suggests a multiple of considerably more than 2.2 to 1 in the relative sizes. This is so because we visually associate size with area. Since the square for Japan has area $(2.2)^2 = 4.84$ times that for Germany, the impression created is that the number of visitors from Japan is almost five times the number from Germany.

It is simple to put matters right. The area for the Japan square should be 2.2 times the area of the Germany square. Therefore, as in Figure 2.23(b), the sides of the Japan square should be of length $\sqrt{2.2} = 1.48$ units. This latter figure now gives the correct visual impression of the relative numbers of visitors from the two countries.

This same point is important to keep in mind when constructing histograms in situations where the classes are not all of equal width. In Example 2.9 we looked at some data on nonaudit fees as a proportion of total auditor remuneration. Correctly drawn, as in Figure 2.10, the *areas* of the rectangles over the class intervals should be proportional to the frequencies. For convenience, Figure 2.10 is reproduced as Figure 2.24(a). Now, suppose instead, as in Figure 2.24(b), the histogram is (incorrectly) drawn so that the *heights* of the rectangles over the class intervals are proportional to the frequencies. The change is quite dramatic. Visual inspection of this latter figure gives the mistaken impression of a very large proportion of observations in the highest classes.

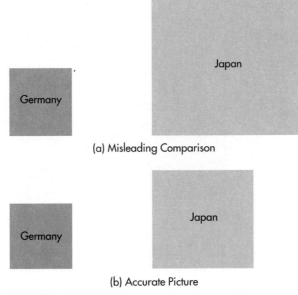

(a) Misleading Comparison

(b) Accurate Picture

FIGURE 2.23 Visitors to the United States from two countries

FIGURE 2.24 Histograms for nonaudit fee as proportion of total auditor remuneration in Australia drawn correctly (a), with areas proportional to frequencies, and drawn incorrectly (b), with heights proportional to frequencies.

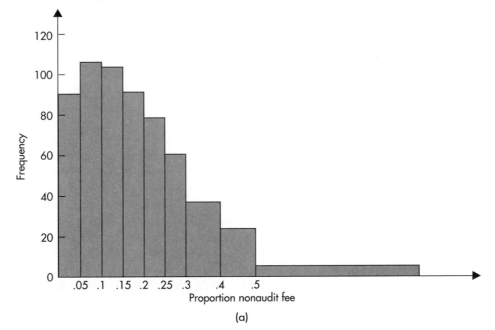

(a)

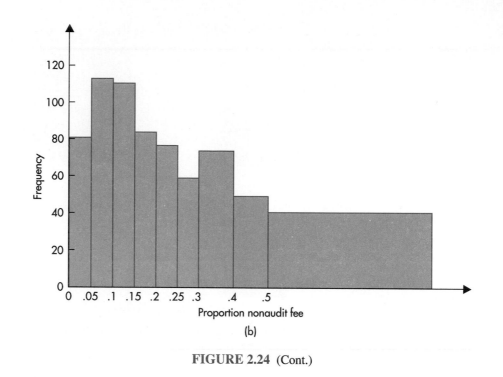

FIGURE 2.24 (Cont.)

(v) *COINCIDENCES THAT REALLY ARE JUST THAT*

It often happens that we are told of a conjunction of events and are invited to conclude that this conjunction is "too much of a coincidence" to be coincidental. My own favorite is the "Super Bowl Stock Market Predictor Theory." According to this "theory," if a member of the old American Football League wins the Super Bowl, the outlook for the stock market is bearish, whereas if an original National Football League member wins, the outlook is bullish. This simple rule correctly predicted the overall direction of the stock market in twenty-three of the years following the first twenty-six Super Bowls.

One should react with skepticism to this theory. The notion that the outcome of a football game could influence the direction of the stock market is implausible, and it remains implausible even given the evidence of its apparent success as a predictor. This evidence can be put into better perspective when one considers just how many people—amateurs and professionals—look for indicators of future trends in the stock market. How many possible correlates had been looked at before this particular one was discovered? Probably hundreds, possibly thousands! An appropriate attitude might be to argue that among the very many that have been tried, this one seems to be a fairly close correlate of past behavior. However, a look at how well this *single* predictor performs over the next few years would allow a fair assessment as to whether the record of the first twenty-six years really was coincidental!

"Two out of three beer drinkers prefer Blast to Schlush." How should one react to this statement? If the opinions of 3,000 beer drinkers had been solicited and a preference was expressed for Blast by about 2,000 of them, this would provide substantial evidence in favor of the contention that Blast is preferred by a majority of drinkers. However, if only three drinkers had been questioned and it turned out that two of them preferred Blast, we would be much less impressed. Rather, we would believe it quite likely that for three other drinkers, the position could be reversed or that all would prefer Schlush.

On the basis of a very small sample, it is extremely dangerous to generalize about a population. Such samples may contain insufficient evidence to allow a conclusion with a reasonable level of certainty. As we will see in subsequent chapters, generalization from a sample to conclusions about a population becomes more precise as the amount of sample evidence increases. Very small samples may tell us little, if anything, about the wider population.

EXERCISES

39. The following are gross box office revenues, in millions of dollars, for eight movies:

☐ E.T.—the Extra-Terrestrial	$399.8
☐ Return of the Jedi	$263.0
☐ Raiders of the Lost Ark	$242.3
☐ Beverly Hills Cop	$234.7
☐ The Empire Strikes Back	$223.0
☐ Ghostbusters	$220.8
☐ Back to the Future	$208.2
☐ Indiana Jones and the Temple of Doom	$179.8

Draw a bar chart to represent this information.

40. It has been estimated that average annual U.S. household spending is $607 on women's clothes and $345 on men's clothes. Draw a bar chart showing this information.

41. It was estimated that in the 1992–93 school year, 3.4 million high school boys and 1.9 million high school girls in the United States played sports. Draw a bar chart showing this information.

42. A recent estimate suggested that, in the United States, 43,000 deaths per year of women are caused by breast cancer, and 90,000 deaths per year of women are caused by diabetes. Draw a bar chart showing this information.

43. Over a period of thirteen years, average annual returns (in U.S. dollars) on stock markets in different countries were: Japan 18.0%, United Kingdom 17.9%, Germany 15.1%, United States 14.1%, Canada 7.7%. Draw a bar chart showing this information.

44. In 1986, there were 50.2 births per thousand girls aged 15–19 in the United States. For 1991, the comparable figure was 62.1. Draw a bar chart showing this information.

45. In 1987, there were 13,144 white and 1,190 minority graduates from U.S. medical schools. The comparable figures for 1992 were 11,525 and 1,273, respectively. Show this information on a component bar chart.

46. In 1987, there were 19,152 men and 602 women in prisons in Illinois. The comparable figures for 1992 were 29,089 and 1,226, respectively. Show this information on a component bar chart.

47. The accompanying table shows, for selected years, interest payments on the U.S. national debt, as a percentage of gross domestic product. Draw a time plot of these data and verbally interpret the resulting picture.

YEAR	1948	1952	1956	1960	1964	1968
INTEREST	2.1	1.7	1.6	1.8	1.7	1.7
YEAR	1972	1976	1980	1984	1988	1992
INTEREST	1.9	2.2	2.8	4.2	4.5	5.0

48. The accompanying table shows percentage changes in the Consumer Price Index in the United States over a period of ten years. Draw a time plot of these data and verbally interpret the resulting picture.

YEAR	1983	1984	1985	1986	1987
% CHANGE C.P.I.	3.8	3.9	3.8	1.1	4.4
YEAR	1988	1989	1990	1991	1992
% CHANGE C.P.I.	4.4	4.6	6.1	3.1	2.9

49. The accompanying table shows the number of loans to exporters from the U.S. Small Business Administration over a period of six years. Draw a time plot of these data and verbally interpret the resulting picture.

YEAR	1987	1988	1989	1990	1991	1992
LOANS	58	116	112	137	348	617

50. A recent estimate of U.S. federal budget spending showed that 46% was to entitlements, 18% to defense, 15% was grants to states and localities, 14% was interest on debt, 6% was for other federal operations, and 1% was deposit insurance. Construct a pie chart to show this information.

51. It has been estimated that, of all U.S. business travel costs, 46% are on airfares, 23% on lodging, 11% on meals, 8% on car rentals, and 12% on other expenses. Construct a pie chart to show this information.

52. Of all alcohol advertising expenditures in the United States, 71% are on beer, 20% on distilled spirits, 7% on wine, and 2% on low-alcohol beverages. Construct a pie chart to show this information.

53. (a) Draw a box-and-whisker plot for the data of Exercise 24 on the unionization rate in the fifty states.
    (b) Ignoring Alaska and Hawaii, divide the country into five geographic regions. Draw on the same scale separate box-and-whisker plots for unionization in each region.

54. Draw a box-and-whisker plot for the data of Exercise 22, which shows percentage decreases in share values for the twenty-five largest U.S. common stock mutual funds on Friday, November 13, 1989.

55. Draw a box-and-whisker plot for the data of Exercise 23, which shows percentage returns for the twenty-five largest U.S. common stock mutual funds for 1989, through Thursday, November 12, 1989.

56. Refer again to the mutual funds data in Exercises 22 and 23. The two tables are arranged to coincide, so that information about any particular mutual fund is in the same location in each of the two tables. Draw a scatter plot illustrating this information and discuss its features.

57. From a local newspaper, obtain information on the advertised selling prices of homes in your area. Draw a box-and-whisker plot summarizing this information.

58. The accompanying table shows both higher education expenditures and public welfare expenditures as a percentage of total expenditures for each of the fifty states. Write an essay on these data. Use any numerical or graphical summary measures that you think are appropriate for the extraction of information contained in the data.

STATE	HIGHER EDUCATION	PUBLIC WELFARE	STATE	HIGHER EDUCATION	PUBLIC WELFARE
Alabama	15.4	13.5	Montana	9.7	9.3
Alaska	8.5	5.6	Nebraska	17.0	12.4
Arizona	16.7	5.6	Nevada	10.3	6.4
Arkansas	12.0	14.8	New Hampshire	13.4	14.9
California	9.2	11.0	New Jersey	6.6	10.1
Colorado	20.0	7.5	New Mexico	14.8	9.3
Connecticut	8.7	18.1	New York	5.1	6.4
Delaware	17.3	11.1	North Carolina	13.6	11.0
Florida	8.8	9.5	North Dakota	16.2	8.8
Georgia	12.0	14.2	Ohio	11.8	11.8
Hawaii	12.7	13.8	Oklahoma	16.1	16.8
Idaho	12.7	10.8	Oregon	11.8	13.1
Illinois	8.3	19.8	Pennsylvania	5.5	19.2
Indiana	17.2	8.8	Rhode Island	9.8	20.8
Iowa	13.9	14.4	South Carolina	15.1	10.7
Kansas	14.7	16.2	South Dakota	15.5	13.7
Kentucky	12.0	13.9	Tennessee	14.6	14.7
Louisiana	11.3	13.1	Texas	17.0	12.7
Maine	9.1	19.5	Utah	19.6	10.3
Maryland	8.8	13.8	Vermont	15.7	14.1
Massachusetts	5.9	23.9	Virginia	15.4	10.3
Michigan	11.3	19.8	Washington	15.1	13.7
Minnesota	12.7	10.3	West Virginia	9.7	9.3
Mississippi	11.3	14.3	Wisconsin	13.2	12.4
Missouri	12.2	16.2	Wyoming	11.4	5.3

59. Turn to the current day's issue of *The Wall Street Journal*. Discuss the procedures that are used therein for the graphical summarization of numerical information. Do the methods used present clear pictures? Can you suggest any alternative or additional graphical methods that might have been used?

60. Obtain the annual report of a major U.S. corporation. Describe the graphical techniques for data presentation used in the report and suggest any improvements that might be made.

61. Collect data on any business or economic phenomenon of interest to you. Provide a graphical summary that gives a clear and accurate picture of these data. Can you now produce a *misleading* graphical summary?

REVIEW EXERCISES

62. Explain what can be learned about a population from each of the following measures.
(a) The mean
(b) The median
(c) The standard deviation
(d) The interquartile range

63. If the standard deviation of a population is zero, what can you say about the members of that population?

64. (a) Two populations each contain two members. The means of the two populations are the same, as are their standard deviations. Are the numerical values of the members of the first population necessarily the same as those of the second?

(b) Two populations each contain three members. The means of these two populations are the same, as are their standard deviations. Are the numerical values of the members of the first population necessarily the same as those of the second?

65. Draw two histograms to represent two populations with a common mean but with the standard deviation of the first population larger than that of the second.

66. Shown below are percentage returns of the ten largest U.S. general stock mutual funds over a one-year period, ending September 17, 1993.

27.9	11.6	17.6	26.6	15.6
12.4	22.4	18.5	22.9	25.0

For this population:
(a) Find the mean.
(b) Find the median.
(c) Find the variance.
(d) Find the standard deviation.
(e) Find the range.
(f) Find the interquartile range.

67. A sample of ten gas stations in a large city showed the following prices (in cents) for a gallon of regular unleaded gas for self-service customers.

96	99	104	98	103	107	103	96	99	98

(a) Find the mean.
(b) Find the median.
(c) Find the variance.
(d) Find the standard deviation.
(e) Find the range.
(f) Find the interquartile range.

68. The accompanying table shows the accumulated years of service before voluntary resignation of 355 managerial, professional, and technical employees of a large oil company.

YEARS OF SERVICE	NUMBER OF EMPLOYEES	YEARS OF SERVICE	NUMBER OF EMPLOYEES
0–1	4	8–9	11
1–2	41	9–10	7
2–3	67	10–11	14
3–4	82	11–12	6
4–5	28	12–13	14
5–6	43	13–14	5
6–7	14	14–15	2
7–8	17		

Data from G. F. Dreher, "The role of performance in the turnover process," *Academy of Management Journal, 25* (1982), 137–47.

For this sample:

(a) Draw the histogram.
(b) Estimate the mean.
(c) Estimate the variance.
(d) Estimate the standard deviation.
(e) Estimate the median.
(f) Estimate the interquartile range.

69. A company manufactures nails, which are sold in packages. For a sample of forty packages, the following numbers of nails were found in the packages.

NUMBER OF NAILS	18	19	20	21	22
NUMBER OF PACKAGES	4	9	15	10	2

For this sample:
(a) Find the mean number of nails per package.
(b) Find the median.
(c) Find the mode.
(d) Find the variance.
(e) Find the standard deviation.

70. Let $x_1, x_2, \ldots, x_N$ denote the N observations in a population with mean μ. Let K be any number. Show that

$$\sum_{i=1}^{N} (x_i - K)^2 = \sum_{i=1}^{N} (x_i - \mu)^2 + N(K - \mu)^2$$

Hence, deduce that the value of K for which $\sum_{i=1}^{N} (x_i - K)^2$ is smallest is $K = \mu$.

71. For a sample of twenty-five local companies, the accompanying table shows percentage change in output over the last three months, grouped into classes.

PERCENTAGE CHANGE	0–2	2–4	4–6	6–8	8–10
NUMBER OF COMPANIES	3	4	8	7	3

For this sample:

(a) Draw the histogram.

(b) Find and interpret the cumulative relative frequencies.

(c) Estimate the mean percentage change in output.

(d) Estimate the median.

(e) Find the modal class.

(f) Estimate the variance.

(g) Estimate the standard deviation.

(h) Estimate the interquartile range.

72. The accompanying table shows percentage returns over 5 years of fifty-five corporate bond funds.

97.9	91.3	69.0	83.6	63.0	86.3	121.3	73.8	90.4	76.6
99.7	91.4	82.7	94.3	45.9	86.5	90.3	85.6	83.6	81.7
83.5	93.7	91.3	83.1	79.6	106.3	92.4	77.4	79.2	85.3
96.6	94.5	88.3	74.2	77.5	71.5	82.8	81.5	92.1	94.7
62.9	74.6	83.0	77.6	87.3	82.1	62.6	84.2	69.5	75.1
83.1	77.3	79.2	98.1	57.4					

(a) Represent these data with a histogram.

(b) Represent these data with a stem-and-leaf diagram.

(c) Draw a box-and-whisker plot for these data.

73. Draw a box-and-whisker plot to represent the data of Exercise 66 on returns of mutual funds.

74. The accompanying table shows the most important applications cited in a survey of personal computer users in small businesses. Construct a pie chart to illustrate these findings.

AREA	CITATIONS (%)	AREA	CITATIONS (%)
Accounting	32	Point of sale	4
Word processing	16	Telecommunications	1
Spreadsheet applications	13	Others	22
Database management	12		

Data from F. Farhoomand and G. P. Hrycyk, "The feasibility of computers in the small business environment," *American Journal of Small Business, 9,* no. 4 (1985), 15–22.

75. In 1992, revenues, in billions of dollars, for the largest media companies in three countries were 13.07 for Time Warner (U.S.), 8.41 for Bertelsmann (Germany), and 7.16 for Sony (Japan). Draw a bar chart illustrating this information.

76. In the United States, 63% of all physicians are specialists, as are 48% in Canada, 47% in Belgium, 46% in Germany, and 37% in the United Kingdom. Draw a bar chart illustrating this information.

77. The accompanying table shows annual percentage changes in philanthropic giving in the United States over a period of twelve years. Draw a time plot of these data and verbally interpret the resulting picture.

YEAR	1981	1982	1983	1984	1985	1986
% CHANGE GIVING	13.9	7.0	6.8	8.8	6.4	14.7

YEAR	1987	1988	1989	1990	1991	1992
% CHANGE GIVING	7.6	9.0	8.8	4.4	4.5	6.4

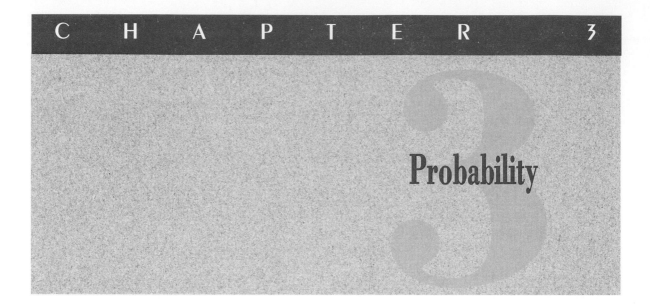

CHAPTER 3

Probability

3.1 INTRODUCTION

In Chapter 1, we stressed the importance of the problem of making inferences about a population, based on observations drawn from a sample. The sample is taken in order to gain knowledge of the population but will typically not produce certain knowledge. For example, a product may be test-marketed in a limited number of retail outlets to get an assessment of consumer reaction. The results are used to form a judgment of the likely demand if the product were to be marketed nationally. Of course, based on this sample information, it is impossible to know *exactly* the reaction of the whole population; any measure of that reaction will inevitably involve *uncertainty*.

Although it is not possible, on the basis of a sample, to derive certain knowledge about a population, it may be possible to make precise statements *about the nature of our uncertainty*. Such statements are couched in the language of **probability,** which is therefore a concept of fundamental importance in statistical inference. It is also a notion frequently met in everyday life. For example, the "probability of precipitation" is an important element in daily weather forecasts, investment decisions are based on the investor's assessment of probable future returns, and a baseball fan will use information such as past records and starting pitchers to form a judgment of the probability of a team's winning a particular game.

In this chapter, a formal structure is developed for making probability statements, and some basic results are derived. For purposes of exposition it is often simplest to illustrate the concepts by reference to simple games of chance, although their applicability is far broader and will be demonstrated in subsequent chapters.

In order to make statements about an uncertain environment, we need to develop a language. One can think of probability as the language in which we discuss uncertainty. Before we can communicate with one another in this language, we need to acquire a common vocabulary. Moreover, as in any other language, rules of grammar are needed so that clear statements can be made with our vocabulary. It will be necessary, therefore, to introduce a good deal of new terminology and to become acquainted with the manipulation of these terms in the production of probability statements.

3.2 RANDOM EXPERIMENT, OUTCOMES, EVENTS

Suppose that a process that could lead to two or more different outcomes is to be observed and there is uncertainty beforehand as to which outcome will occur. Some examples are the following:

1. A coin is thrown.
2. A die is rolled.
3. A consumer is asked which of two products he or she prefers.
4. An item from a set of accounts is examined by an auditor.
5. The daily change in an index of stock market prices is observed.
6. A batch of a chemical produced by a particular process is tested to determine whether it contains more than an allowable percentage of impurity.

Each of these examples involves a **random experiment.**

Definition

A **random experiment** is a process leading to at least two possible outcomes with uncertainty as to which will occur.

In each of the first three experiments listed, it is possible to specify what outcomes might arise. If a coin is thrown, the result will be either "head" or "tail." If a die is rolled, the result will be one of the numbers 1, 2, 3, 4, 5, or 6. A consumer might indicate a preference for one of the products or no preference. In each case, the different possible outcomes, called **basic outcomes,** have been listed. The set of all these outcomes exhausts the possibilities and is called the **sample space** of the random experiment.

Definition

The possible outcomes of a random experiment are called the **basic outcomes,** and the set of all basic outcomes is called the **sample space.**

Notice that basic outcomes are defined in such a way that no two can occur simultaneously; moreover, the random experiment must necessarily lead to the occurrence of one of the basic outcomes. The symbol S will be used to denote the sample space.

EXAMPLE 3.1
A die is rolled. The basic outcomes are the numbers 1, 2, 3, 4, 5, 6. Thus, the sample space is

$$S = [1, 2, 3, 4, 5, 6]$$

Here we see that there are six basic outcomes. No two can occur together, and one of them must occur.

EXAMPLE 3.2
An investor follows the stock market and is particularly interested in the Dow-Jones industrial index. Consider the following two outcomes:

"At the close of trading today, the Dow-Jones index will be higher than at yesterday's close."

"At the close of trading today, the Dow-Jones index will not be higher than at yesterday's close."

One or the other of these outcomes must occur, but they cannot occur simultaneously. Therefore, these two outcomes together constitute a sample space.

Frequently, interest is not in the basic outcomes themselves but in some subset of all the outcomes in the sample space. For example, if a die is rolled, an event that might be of interest is whether the resulting number is even—a result that will occur if one of the basic outcomes 2, 4, or 6 arises. Such sets of basic outcomes are called **events.**

Definition

An **event** is a set of basic outcomes from the sample space, and it is said to **occur** if the random experiment gives rise to one of its constituent basic outcomes.

In many applications, we are concerned simultaneously with two or more events. For example, if a die is thrown, two events that might be considered are "Number resulting is even" and "Number resulting is at least 4." One possibility is that all the events of interest might occur; this will be the case if the basic outcome of the random experiment belongs to all these events. The set of basic outcomes belonging to every event in a group of events is called the **intersection** of these events.

Definition

Let A and B be two events in the sample space S. Their **intersection,** denoted $A \cap B$, is the set of all basic outcomes in S that belong to both A and B. Hence, the intersection $A \cap B$ occurs if and only if both A and B occur.

More generally, given K events $E_1, E_2, \ldots, E_K$, their intersection, $E_1 \cap E_2 \cdots \cap E_K$, is the set of all basic outcomes that belong to every $E_i (i = 1, 2, \ldots, K)$.

A useful pictorial mechanism for thinking about intersections and other set relations is the *Venn diagram.* Figure 3.1 shows diagrams for pairs of sets A and B. In part (a) of the figure, the rectangle S represents the sample space, while two closed figures denote the two events A and B. So, for example, a basic outcome belonging to A will be inside the corresponding figure. The shaded area where the figures intersect is $A \cap B$. Clearly, a basic outcome will be in $A \cap B$ if and only if it is in both A and B. Thus, in rolling a die, the outcomes 4 and 6 both belong to the two events "Even number results" and "Number at least 4 results."

It is possible that events A and B have no common basic outcomes, in which case the figures will not intersect, as in part (b) of Figure 3.1. Such events are said to be **mutually exclusive.** For example, if a set of accounts is audited, the events "Less than 5% contain material errors" and "More than 10% contain material errors" are mutually exclusive.

Definition

If the events A and B have no common basic outcomes, they are called **mutually exclusive** and their intersection $A \cap B$ is said to be the **empty set.** It follows, then, that $A \cap B$ cannot occur.

More generally, the K events $E_1, E_2, \ldots, E_K$ are said to be mutually exclusive if every pair of them is a pair of mutually exclusive events—that is, if $E_i \cap E_j$ is the empty set for all $i \neq j$.

FIGURE 3.1 Venn diagrams for the intersection of events A and B: (a) $A \cap B$ is the shaded area; (b) A and B are mutually exclusive

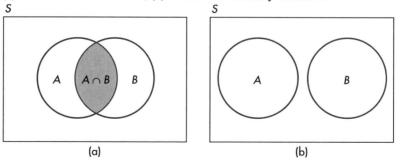

(a)   (b)

When considering jointly several events, another possibility of interest is that at least one of them will occur. This will happen if the basic outcome of the random experiment belongs to at least one of the events. The set of basic outcomes belonging to at least one of the events is called their **union.** For example, in the die throw experiment, the outcomes 2, 4, 5, and 6 all belong to at least one of the events "Even number results" or "Number at least 4 results."

Definition

Let A and B be two events in the sample space S. Their **union,** denoted $A \cup B$, is the set of all basic outcomes in S that belong to at least one of these two events. Hence, the union $A \cup B$ occurs if and only if either A or B (or both) occurs.

More generally, given K events $E_1, E_2, \ldots, E_K$, their union, $E_1 \cup E_2 \cup \cdots \cup E_K$, is the set of all basic outcomes belonging to at least one of these K events.

The union of a pair of events is illustrated in the Venn diagram in Figure 3.2, from which it is clear that a basic outcome will be in $A \cup B$ if and only if it is in either A or B (or both).

A case of special interest concerns a collection of several events whose union is the whole sample space S. Since every basic outcome is always contained in S, it follows that every outcome of the random experiment will be in at least one of this collection of events. These events are then said to be **collectively exhaustive.** For example, if a die is thrown, the events "Result is at least 3" and "Result is at most 5" are together collectively exhaustive—at least one of these two events must occur.

Definition

Let $E_1, E_2, \ldots, E_K$ be K events in the sample space S. If $E_1 \cup E_2 \cup \cdots \cup E_K = S$, these K events are said to be **collectively exhaustive.**

Using the terminology just introduced, it follows that the set of all basic outcomes contained in a sample space are both mutually exclusive and collectively exhaustive. We have already noted that these outcomes are such that one must occur, but no more than one can simultaneously occur.

Next, let A be an event, and suppose our interest is that A not occur. This will happen if the basic outcome of the random experiment lies in S (as it must) but *not* in A. The set of basic outcomes belonging to the sample space but not to a particular event is called the **complement** of that event and is denoted $\overline{A}$. Clearly, the events A and $\overline{A}$ are mutually exclusive (no basic outcome can belong to both) and collectively exhaustive (every basic outcome must belong to one or the other). The complement of the event A is illustrated in the Venn diagram in Figure 3.3.

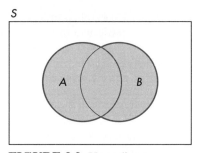

FIGURE 3.2 Venn diagram for the union of events *A* and *B*; $A \cup B$ is the shaded area

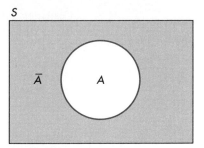

FIGURE 3.3 Venn diagram for the complement of event *A*; $\overline{A}$ is the shaded area

---

Definition

Let *A* be an event in the sample space *S*. The set of basic outcomes of a random experiment belonging to *S* but not to *A* is called the **complement** of *A* and is denoted $\overline{A}$.

We have now met three important concepts—the intersection, the union, and the complement. All will be important in our subsequent discussions of probability. The following examples should serve to make these ideas more concrete.

EXAMPLE 3.3

A die is rolled. Let *A* be the event "Number resulting is even" and *B* be the event "Number resulting is at least 4." Then

$$A = [2, 4, 6] \qquad \text{and} \qquad B = [4, 5, 6]$$

The complements of these events are respectively

$$\overline{A} = [1, 3, 5] \qquad \text{and} \qquad \overline{B} = [1, 2, 3]$$

The intersection of *A* and *B* is the event "Number resulting is both even and at least 4," so

$$A \cap B = [4, 6]$$

The union of *A* and *B* is the event "Number resulting is either even or at least 4, or both," and so

$$A \cup B = [2, 4, 5, 6]$$

Note also that the events *A* and $\overline{A}$ are mutually exclusive, since their intersection is the empty set, and collectively exhaustive, since their union is the sample space *S*; that is

$$A \cup \overline{A} = [1, 2, 3, 4, 5, 6] = S$$

The same statements also apply for the events *B* and $\overline{B}$.

EXAMPLE
3.4

Consider the observation of the Dow-Jones industrial average over two consecutive days. We will designate the four basic outcomes as follows:

O_1: Dow-Jones average rises on both days.
O_2: Dow-Jones average rises on the first day but does not rise on the second day.
O_3: Dow-Jones average does not rise on the first day but rises on the second day.
O_4: Dow-Jones average does not rise on either day.

Clearly, one of these outcomes must occur, but not more than one can occur at the same time. We can therefore write the sample space as $S = [O_1, O_2, O_3, O_4]$.

Now, let us consider the two events.

A: Dow-Jones average rises on the first day.
B: Dow-Jones average rises on the second day.

We see that the event A occurs if either basic outcome O_1 or O_2 occurs, so we can write $A = [O_1, O_2]$. Similarly, we have $B = [O_1, O_3]$.

The intersection of A and B is the event "Dow-Jones average rises on the first day and rises on the second day." This is the set of all basic outcomes belonging to both A and B, so $A \cap B = [O_1]$.

The union of A and B is the event "Dow-Jones average rises on at least one of the two days." This is the set of all basic outcomes belonging to either A or B, or both. It follows that $A \cup B = [O_1, O_2, O_3]$.

Finally, the complement of A is the event "Dow-Jones average does not rise on the first day." This is the set of all basic outcomes in the sample space S that do not belong to A. Hence, $\overline{A} = [O_3, O_4]$.

It is also possible to examine other unions or intersections involving event complements. To illustrate, the intersection of the events $\overline{A}$ and B is shown in Figure 3.4. This intersection contains all outcomes that are in both $\overline{A}$ (that is, not in A) and B. In Example 3.3, the intersection of these two events is $\overline{A} \cap B = [5]$, as the only outcome that is both "not even" and "at least 4" is 5.

We now introduce three results involving unions and intersections of events. These will be employed in Section 3.6 to develop some probability rules.

(i) Let A and B be two events. Then the events $A \cap B$ and $\overline{A} \cap B$ are mutually exclusive, and their union is B, as illustrated in the Venn diagram in Figure 3.5. Clearly

$$(A \cap B) \cup (\overline{A} \cap B) = B$$

(ii) Let A and B be two events. The events A and $\overline{A} \cap B$ are mutually exclusive, and their union is $A \cup B$. Again, this result can best be seen from inspection of the Venn diagram, shown in Figure 3.6. It is clear from this figure that

$$A \cup (\overline{A} \cap B) = A \cup B$$

(iii) Let $E_1, E_2, \ldots, E_K$ be K mutually exclusive and collectively exhaustive events, and let A be some other event. Then the K events $E_1 \cap A, E_2 \cap A, \ldots, E_K \cap A$ are mutually exclusive, and their union is A.

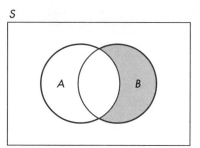

FIGURE 3.4 Venn diagram for the intersection of $\overline{A}$ and B; $\overline{A} \cap B$ is the shaded area

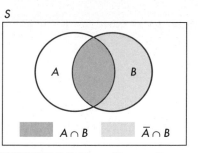

FIGURE 3.5 Venn diagram for $A \cap B$ and $\overline{A} \cap B$

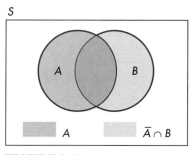

FIGURE 3.6 Venn diagram for A and $\overline{A} \cap B$

To see the truth of the third statement, consider the Venn diagram in Figure 3.7. The large rectangle denoting the whole sample space is subdivided into smaller rectangles, depicting the K mutually exclusive and collectively exhaustive events E_1, E_2, ..., E_K. The event A is represented by the closed figure. We see that the events comprised of the intersection of A and each of the E_i are indeed mutually exclusive and that their union is simply the event A. We can therefore write

$$(E_1 \cap A) \cup (E_2 \cap A) \cup \cdots \cup (E_K \cap A) = A$$

FIGURE 3.7 Venn diagram for $A \cap E_1$, $A \cap E_2$, ..., $A \cap E_K$

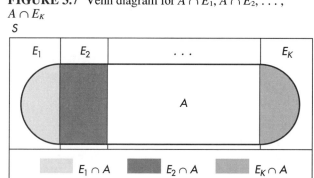

EXAMPLE
3.5

The truth of results (i) and (ii) is established for the die-rolling experiment of Example 3.3. As before, let

$$A = [2, 4, 6] \qquad B = [4, 5, 6] \qquad \overline{A} = [1, 3, 5]$$

Then

$$A \cap B = [4, 6] \qquad \text{and} \qquad \overline{A} \cap B = [5]$$

Then $A \cap B$ and $\overline{A} \cap B$ are mutually exclusive, and their union is

$$B = [4, 5, 6]$$

Also, A and $\overline{A} \cap B$ are mutually exclusive, and their union is

$$A \cup B = [2, 4, 5, 6]$$

EXAMPLE
3.6

The truth of result (iii) is established for another die-rolling example. Define

$$A = [2, 4, 6] \qquad E_1 = [1, 2] \qquad E_2 = [3, 4] \qquad E_3 = [5, 6]$$

so that E_1, E_2, E_3 are mutually exclusive and collectively exhaustive. Then

$$E_1 \cap A = [2] \qquad E_2 \cap A = [4] \qquad E_3 \cap A = [6]$$

Clearly, these three events are mutually exclusive, and their union is

$$(E_1 \cap A) \cup (E_2 \cap A) \cup (E_3 \cap A) = [2, 4, 6] = A$$

EXAMPLE
3.7

A problem often faced in market research is that some of the questions we would like to ask are so sensitive that many subjects will either refuse to reply or will give a dishonest answer. One way of attacking this problem is through the method of *randomized response*.[1] This technique involves pairing the sensitive question with a nonsensitive question. For instance, we might have the following pair:

(a) Have you purposely shoplifted in the last 12 months?
(b) Have you made a purchase from a catalog in the last 12 months?

Subjects are asked to flip a coin and then to answer question (a) if the result is "head" and (b) otherwise. Since the investigator cannot *know* which question is answered, it is hoped that honest responses will be obtained in this way. The nonsensitive question is one for which the investigator already has information about the population under study. Thus, in our example, the investigator knows what proportion of the population made a purchase from a catalog in the last 12 months. (Later in this chapter we will see how the responses can be analyzed to produce the information required.)

---

[1] See, for example, M. D. Geurts, "Using a randomized response research design to eliminate nonresponse biases in business research," *Journal of Academy of Marketing Science, 8* (1980), 83–90.

Now, we define the following events:

A: Subject answers "yes."
E_1: Subject answers sensitive question.
E_2: Subject answers nonsensitive question.

Clearly, the events E_1 and E_2 are mutually exclusive and collectively exhaustive. Thus, the conditions of result (iii) are satisfied, and it follows that the events

$A \cap E_1$: Subject both responds "yes" and has answered the sensitive question

and

$A \cap E_2$: Subject both responds "yes" and has answered the nonsensitive question

are mutually exclusive. Furthermore, their union must be the event A; that is

$$A = (A \cap E_1) \cup (A \cap E_2)$$

3.3 WHAT IS PROBABILITY?

Suppose that a random experiment is to be carried out and we are interested in the chance of a particular event's occurring. The concept of probability is intended to provide a numerical measure for the likelihood of an event's occurrence. Probability is measured on a scale from 0 to 1. At the extremes of this range, a probability of 0 implies that the event is impossible (it is certain not to occur), whereas a probability of 1 implies that the event is certain to occur. For uncertain events, we want to attach a probability between 0 and 1 such that the more likely the event is to occur, the higher the probability. In practice, such ideas are frequently met. It is known that rain is more likely under certain meteorological conditions than others. An experienced manager may judge that one product is more likely to achieve substantial market penetration than another.

To take a very simple example, suppose a coin is thrown. The statement "The probability that a head results is ½" may be viewed through two distinct ideas—*relative frequency* and *subjective probability*.

RELATIVE FREQUENCY

Suppose that a random experiment can be replicated in such a way that, after each trial, it is possible to return to the initial state and repeat the experiment so that the resulting outcome is unaffected by previous outcomes. For example, a coin or die can be thrown repeatedly in this way.

If some number N of experiments is conducted and the event A occurs in N_A of them (N_A clearly depending on N), we have

$$\text{Proportion of occurrences of } A \text{ in } N \text{ trials} = \frac{N_A}{N}$$

Now, if N is very large, we would not expect much variation in the proportion N_A/N as N increases; that is, the proportion of occurrences of A will remain approximately constant. This notion underlies the **relative frequency** concept of probability.

Definition

Let N_A be the number of occurrences of event A in N repeated trials. Then, under the **relative frequency** concept of probability, the probability that A occurs is the limit of the ratio N_A/N as the number of trials N becomes infinitely large.

Under this definition, if we say "The probability of a head resulting from a single throw of a coin is ½," we mean that if the coin is thrown repeatedly, the proportion of heads resulting will get very close to ½ as the number of trials gets very large.

The relative frequency notion provides a convenient framework for thinking about probability, but it does involve conceptual difficulties. These are illustrated, in increasing order of magnitude, in the following examples.

1. Do we really have to throw a coin a very large number of times before concluding that the probability of a head resulting is ½? Certainly, this could be done, but it would be a very tedious business indeed if all probability assessments had to be made in this fashion. One way around the difficulty is to regard repeated experimentation as a purely abstract notion, without requiring that the experiments actually be carried out. For example, it might be reasonable to conclude that the coin appears to be perfectly fair, so the two outcomes, "head" and "tail," are equally likely. Hence, one might reasonably infer that if the coin were thrown repeatedly, the proportion of heads would approach ½. (Notice that in deciding that "head" and "tail" are equally likely, we have introduced an element of subjectivity.) More generally, suppose that a random experiment can lead to n mutually exclusive and collectively exhaustive possible basic outcomes, where each basic outcome is equally likely. If the event A occurs in n_A of these outcomes, it would be inferred that the probability of A occurring is n_A/n. For example, if a fair die is rolled, there are six basic outcomes, each equally likely. The event "an even number results" involves three of these outcomes, so its probability is ³⁄₆ = ½. Unfortunately, it is not always the case that the sample space of an experiment is made up of equally likely basic outcomes.

2. A meteorologist announces that the probability of rain today is .7. Now, once today has ended, it is impossible to go back to its beginning and start again from the same initial conditions. However, in assessing a probability for rain, the meteorologist could argue that meteorological conditions essentially the same as those prevailing at the time the forecast was made had been experienced many times in the past and rain had resulted on 70% of those occasions. Thus, a long-run frequency interpretation of the meteorologist's probability statement could still be made. Similarly, we might reasonably assert that the probability that the Dow-Jones index will close higher than yesterday is ½, because historically the market has risen on 50% of all trading days.

3. The 1996 Kentucky Derby is to be run. A bettor is interested in a particular horse and concludes that the probability that it will win the race is .4. In contrast to example 2, essentially similar races involving essentially similar horses will not have been run frequently in the past, and certainly the bettor's probability judgment will not have been based on such a notion. It

seems more reasonable to suggest that taking various relevant factors (such as past performance of the horse) into account, the bettor has formed a personal subjective judgment as to the chance of the horse winning, and this is reflected in the probability statement. In a similar vein, corporate executives must often face decisions as to whether to make potentially lucrative investments in countries that have unstable political climates. Either formally or informally, it is necessary to enter into the decision-making process some assessment of the likelihood of a revolution, resulting in the nationalization of the corporation's assets and the receipt of unfavorable compensation terms for such a take-over. Such an assessment must surely be subjective.

SUBJECTIVE PROBABILITY

An alternative view, which does not depend on the notion of repeatable experiments, regards probability as a personal subjective concept, expressing an individual's degree of belief about the chance that an event will occur. One way to understand this idea is in terms of *fair bets*.

For example, if I assert that the probability of a head resulting from the throw of a coin is ½, what I have in mind is that the coin appears to be perfectly fair and that the throw is just as likely to produce a head as a tail. In assessing this subjective probability, I am not necessarily thinking in terms of repeated experimentation but am concerned with only a single throw of the coin. My subjective probability assessment implies that I would view as fair a bet in which I had to pay $1 if the result was tail and would receive $1 if the result was head. If I were to receive more than $1 if the throw yielded a head, I would regard the bet as in my favor. Similarly, if I believe that the probability of a horse's winning a particular race is .4, I am asserting the personal view that there is a 40–60 chance of its winning. Given this belief, I would regard as fair a bet in which I lost $2 if the horse did not win and gained $3 if it did.

It should be emphasized that subjective probabilities are personal; there is no requirement that different individuals considering the same event should arrive at the same probabilities. In the coin-throwing example, most people will conclude that the appropriate probability for a head is ½. However, an individual with more information about the coin in question might believe otherwise. In the example of the horse race, it is likely that two bettors will reach different subjective probabilities. They may not, for example, have the same information, and even if they do, they might not interpret it in the same way. It is certainly clear that individual investors do not all hold the same views on the likely future behavior of the stock market! Their subjective probabilities might be thought of as depending on the knowledge they have and the way they interpret it.

3.4 PROBABILITY AND ITS POSTULATES

It is necessary to develop a framework in which probabilities can be assessed or manipulated. In order to do this, we first set down three rules (or postulates) that probabilities will be required to obey and show that these requirements are "reasonable."

Let S denote the sample space of a random experiment, O_i the basic outcomes, and A an event. Then, using the notation $P(A)$ for "probability event A occurs," we have the requirements stated in the box.

---

1. If A is any event in the sample space S

$$0 \leq P(A) \leq 1$$

2. Let A be an event in S, and let O_i denote the basic outcomes. Then

$$P(A) = \sum_{A} P(O_i)$$

where the notation implies that the summation extends over all the basic outcomes in A.

3. $$P(S) = 1$$

The first postulate simply requires that a probability lie between 0 and 1. The second postulate can be motivated in terms of relative frequencies. Suppose that a random experiment is repeated N times. Let N_i be the number of times the basic outcome O_i occurs and N_A the number of times event A occurs. Then, since the basic outcomes are mutually exclusive, N_A is just the sum of N_i for all the basic outcomes in A; that is

$$N_A = \sum_{A} N_i$$

and on dividing by the number of trials N, we obtain

$$\frac{N_A}{N} = \sum_{A} \frac{N_i}{N}$$

But under the relative frequency concept of probability, N_A/N tends to $P(A)$, and each N_i/N tends to $P(O_i)$ as N becomes infinitely large. Thus, the second postulate can be seen as a logical requirement when probability is viewed in this way. The third postulate can be paraphrased as "When a random experiment is to be carried out, something has to happen." Replacing A by the sample space S in the second postulate gives

$$P(S) = \sum_{S} P(O_i)$$

where the summation extends over all the basic outcomes in the sample space. But since $P(S) = 1$ by the third postulate, it follows that

---

$$\sum_{S} P(O_i) = 1 \qquad\qquad (3.4.1)$$

That is, the sum of the probabilities for all the basic outcomes in the sample space is 1.

CONSEQUENCES OF THE POSTULATES

We now list and illustrate some immediate consequences of the three postulates.

(i) If the sample space S consists of n equally likely basic outcomes, $O_1, O_2, \ldots, O_n$, then each of these has probability $1/n$; that is

$$P(O_i) = \frac{1}{n} \qquad (i = 1, 2, \ldots, n)$$

The first consequence follows from Eq. (3.4.1): If $P(O_i)$ is the same for each basic outcome and $\sum_{i=1}^{n} P(O_i) = 1$, then $P(O_i) = 1/n$ for each outcome. For example, if a fair die is rolled, the probability for each of the six basic outcomes is ⅙.

(ii) If the sample space S consists of n equally likely basic outcomes and the event A consists of n_A of these outcomes, then

$$P(A) = \frac{n_A}{n}$$

This follows from consequence (i) and the second postulate. Every basic outcome has probability $1/n$ and, by postulate 2, $P(A)$ is just the sum of the probabilities (each $1/n$) of the n_A basic outcomes in A. For example, if a fair die is rolled and A is the event "Even number results," there are $n = 6$ basic outcomes, and $n_A = 3$ of these are in A. Hence, $P(A) = ⅜ = ½$. Notice that this result agrees with our intuitive reasoning in Section 3.3.

(iii) Let A and B be *mutually exclusive* events. Then the probability of their union is the sum of their individual probabilities; that is

$$P(A \cup B) = P(A) + P(B)$$

More generally, if $E_1, E_2, \ldots, E_K$ are mutually exclusive events

$$P(E_1 \cup E_2 \cup \cdots \cup E_K) = P(E_1) + P(E_2) + \cdots + P(E_K)$$

This result is a consequence of the second postulate. The probability of the union of A and B is

---

$$P(A \cup B) = \sum_{A \cup B} P(O_i) \qquad\qquad (3.4.2)$$

---

where the summation extends over all the basic outcomes in $A \cup B$. But since A and B are mutually exclusive, no basic outcome can belong to both, so the right-hand side of Eq. (3.4.2) can be broken down into the sum of two parts:

$$\sum_{A \cup B} P(O_i) = \sum_{A} P(O_i) + \sum_{B} P(O_i)$$

The right-hand side of this equation is just $P(A) + P(B)$, by postulate 2. The more general result follows through similar reasoning.

(iv) If $E_1, E_2, \ldots, E_K$ are collectively exhaustive events, the probability of their union is

$$P(E_1 \cup E_2 \cup \cdots \cup E_K) = 1$$

Since the events are collectively exhaustive, their union is the whole sample space S, and the result follows from the third postulate.

EXAMPLE 3.8

A charitable organization sells 1,000 lottery tickets. There are ten major prizes and 100 minor prizes, all of which must be won. The process for choosing winners is such that, at the outset, each ticket has an equal chance of winning a major prize, and each has an equal chance of winning a minor prize. No ticket can win more than one prize. What is the probability of winning a major prize with a single ticket? What is the probability of winning a minor prize? What is the probability of winning *some* prize?

Of the 1,000 tickets, ten will win major prizes, 100 will win minor prizes, and 890 will win no prize. Our single ticket can be regarded as one selected from the 1,000. Let A be the event "Selected ticket wins major prize." Since there are 1,000 equally likely outcomes, ten of which correspond to event A, we have

$$P(A) = \frac{10}{1,000} = .01$$

Similarly, for event B, "Selected ticket wins minor prize," it follows that

$$P(B) = \frac{100}{1,000} = .10$$

Now, the event "Ticket wins some prize" is simply the union of the events A and B. Moreover, since only one prize per ticket is permitted, these events are mutually exclusive. It follows that the probability required is

$$P(A \cup B) = P(A) + P(B) = .01 + .10 = .11$$

EXAMPLE 3.9

In Example 3.4, we considered the course of the Dow-Jones average over two days and defined the four basic outcomes

O_1:   Average rises on both days.
O_2:   Average rises on first day but does not rise on second day.
O_3:   Average does not rise on first day but does rise on second day.
O_4:   Average does not rise on either day.

It is reasonable to assert that these four basic outcomes are equally likely. In that case, what is the probability that the market will rise on at least one of the two days?

The event of interest, "Market rises on at least one of the two days," contains three of the four basic outcomes—O_1, O_2, O_3. Since the basic outcomes are all equally likely, it follows that the probability of this event is ¾.

**EXAMPLE
3.10**

In the early stages of the development of the Hibernia oil site in the Atlantic Ocean, the Petroleum Directorate of Newfoundland estimated the probability to be .1 that economically recoverable reserves exceeded 2 billion barrels. The probability for reserves in excess of 1 billion barrels was estimated to be .5. Given this information, what is the estimated probability of reserves between 1 and 2 billion barrels?

Let A be the event "reserves exceed 2 billion barrels," and B the event "reserves between 1 and 2 billion barrels." These events are mutually exclusive, and their union, $A \cup B$, is the event "reserves exceed 1 billion barrels." We therefore have

$$P(A) = .1 \qquad P(A \cup B) = .5$$

Then, since A and B are mutually exclusive

$$P(B) = P(A \cup B) - P(A) = .5 - .1 = .4$$

EXERCISES

1. A corporation takes delivery of some new machinery that must be installed and checked before it becomes operational. The accompanying table shows a manager's probability assessment for the number of days required before the machinery becomes operational.

NUMBER OF DAYS	3	4	5	6	7
PROBABILITY	.08	.24	.41	.20	.07

Let A be the event "It will be more than 4 days before the machinery becomes operational" and B the event "It will be less than 6 days before the machinery becomes available."
(a) Find the probability of event A.
(b) Find the probability of event B.
(c) Describe the event that is the complement of event A.
(d) Find the probability of the complement of event A.
(e) Describe the event that is the intersection of events A and B.

(f) Find the probability of the intersection of events A and B.

(g) Describe the event that is the union of events A and B.

(h) Find the probability of the union of events A and B.

(i) Are events A and B mutually exclusive?

(j) Are events A and B collectively exhaustive?

2. A fund manager is considering investment in the stock of a health care provider. The manager's assessment of probabilities for rates of return on this stock over the next year are summarized in the accompanying table. Let A be the event "Rate of return will be more than 10%" and B the event "Rate of return will be negative."

RATE OF RETURN	Less than −10%	−10% to 0%	0% to 10%	10% to 20%	More than 20%
PROBABILITY	.04	.14	.28	.33	.21

(a) Find the probability of event A.

(b) Find the probability of event B.

(c) Describe the event that is the complement of A.

(d) Find the probability of the complement of A.

(e) Describe the event that is the intersection of A and B.

(f) Find the probability of the intersection of A and B.

(g) Describe the event that is the union of A and B.

(h) Find the probability of the union of A and B.

(i) Are A and B mutually exclusive?

(j) Are A and B collectively exhaustive?

3. A manager has available a pool of eight employees who could be assigned to a project-monitoring task. Four of the employees are women and four are men. Two of the men are brothers. The manager is to make the assignment at random, so that each of the eight employees is equally likely to be chosen. Let A be the event "Chosen employee is a man" and B the event "Chosen employee is one of the brothers."

(a) Find the probability of A.

(b) Find the probability of B.

(c) Find the probability of the intersection of A and B.

(d) Find the probability of the union of A and B.

4. In Section 3.4, we saw that *if a pair of events are mutually exclusive*, the probability of their union is the sum of their individual probabilities. However, this is *not* the case for events that are not mutually exclusive. Verify this assertion by considering the events A and B of Exercise 1.

5. A department store manager has monitored the numbers of complaints received per week about poor service. The probabilities for numbers of complaints in a week, established by this review, are shown in the table. Let A be the event "There will be at least one complaint in a week," and B the event "There will be less than 10 complaints in a week."

NUMBER OF COMPLAINTS	0	1–3	4–6	7–9	10–12	More than 12
PROBABILITY	.14	.39	.23	.15	.06	.03

    (a) Find the probability of *A*.
    (b) Find the probability of *B*.
    (c) Find the probability of the complement of *A*.
    (d) Find the probability of the union of *A* and *B*.
    (e) Find the probability of the intersection of *A* and *B*.
    (f) Are *A* and *B* mutually exclusive?
    (g) Are *A* and *B* collectively exhaustive?

6. A corporation receives a particular part in shipments of 100. Research has indicated the probabilities shown in the accompanying table for numbers of defective parts in a shipment.

NUMBER DEFECTIVE	0	1	2	3	More than 3
PROBABILITY	.29	.36	.22	.10	.03

    (a) What is the probability there will be less than three defective parts in a shipment?
    (b) What is the probability there will be more than one defective part in a shipment?
    (c) The five probabilities in the table sum to one. Why must this be so?

3.5 PERMUTATIONS AND COMBINATIONS

A practical difficulty that sometimes arises in computing the probability of an event is counting the numbers of basic outcomes in the sample space and the event of interest. For some problems, the use of *permutations* or *combinations* can be helpful.

    We begin with the problem of *ordering*. Suppose that we have some number *x* of objects that are to be placed in order. Each object may be used only once. How many different sequences are possible? We can view this problem as a requirement to place one of the objects in each of *x* boxes arranged in a row, as illustrated in Figure 3.8. Beginning with the first box, there are *x* different ways to fill it. Once an object is put in that box, there are $(x - 1)$ objects remaining, and so $(x - 1)$ ways to fill the second

FIGURE 3.8 The orderings of *x* objects

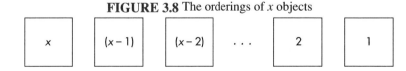

box. That is, for each of the x ways to place an object in the first box, there are $(x - 1)$ possible ways to fill the second box, so the first two boxes can be filled in a total of $x(x - 1)$ ways. Given that the first two boxes are filled, there are now $(x - 2)$ ways of filling the third box, so the first three boxes can be filled in a total of $x(x - 1)(x - 2)$ ways. Finally, when we arrive at the last box there is only one object left to put in it. Hence, the total number of possible orderings is $x(x - 1)(x - 2) \cdots (2)(1)$, which for notational convenience is written $x!$ (read "x factorial").[2]

The number of possible orderings of x objects is

$$x(x - 1)(x - 2) \cdots (2)(1) = x!$$

EXAMPLE
3.11

The three letters A, B, C can be arranged in $3! = 6$ different orders:

ABC   ACB   BAC   BCA   CAB   CBA

This example is illustrated in the *tree diagram* of Figure 3.9. We begin at the intersection on the left-hand side of the figure by choosing one of the three letters to fill the first position. Following each of the emerging branches, we then have two possibilities for filling the second position. For example, if the letter A is in the first position, either B or C must be placed in the second position. Finally, once the first two positions have

FIGURE 3.9 Tree diagram for Example 3.11

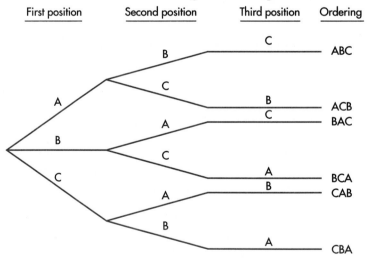

---

[2] We have defined $x!$ for positive integers x. Also, we define $0! = 1$.

been filled, there is just one letter available to put in the final position. On the right-hand side of the figure, we show the six possible orderings achieved in this way.

EXAMPLE 3.12

A consumer is asked to rank, in order of preference, the taste of five brands of beer. If the consumer is in fact indifferent among these brands, what is the probability that a specific ordering will be selected by chance?

There are $5! = 120$ different possible orderings. Thus, the probability of selecting any particular one, if each is equally likely to be picked, is $\frac{1}{120}$.

Suppose now that we have a number n of objects with which the x ordered boxes could be filled (with $n > x$). Each object may be used only once. The number of possible orderings is called the number of **permutations** of x objects chosen from n and is denoted by the symbol $_nP_x$. Now, we can argue precisely as before, except that there will be n ways to fill the first box, $(n - 1)$ ways to fill the second box, and so on, until we come to the final box. At this point there will be $(n - x + 1)$ objects left, each of which could be placed in that box, as illustrated in Figure 3.10. Thus, the total number of permutations is

$$_nP_x = n(n - 1)(n - 2) \cdots (n - x + 1)$$

A more convenient expression is obtained by multiplying and dividing by $(n - x)(n - x - 1) \cdots (2)(1) = (n - x)!$ giving

$$_nP_x = \frac{n(n - 1)(n - 2) \cdots (n - x + 1)(n - x)(n - x - 1) \cdots (2)(1)}{(n - x)(n - x - 1) \cdots (2)(1)}$$

$$= \frac{n!}{(n - x)!}$$

Definition

The number of **permutations**, $_nP_x$, of x objects chosen from n is the number of possible arrangements when x objects are to be selected from a total of n and arranged in order. This number is

$$_nP_x = \frac{n!}{(n - x)!}$$

FIGUREL 3.10 The permutations of x objects chosen from n

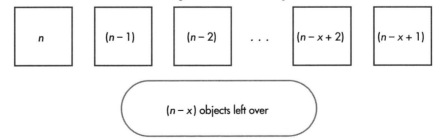

EXAMPLE
3.13

Suppose that two letters are to be selected from A, B, C, D, E and arranged in order. The number of permutations, with $n = 5$ and $x = 2$, is $n!/(n - x)! = 5!/3! = 20$. These are

AB	AC	AD	AE	BC
BA	CA	DA	EA	CB
BD	BE	CD	CE	DE
DB	EB	DC	EC	ED

We illustrate this example in the tree diagram of Figure 3.11. At the left-hand intersection, there are five possible letters to put in the first position. Now, following any of

FIGURE 3.11 Tree diagram for Example 3.13

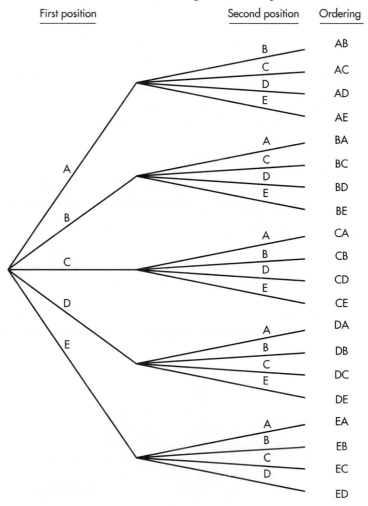

the emerging branches, we have four letters from which to fill the second position. For instance, if A is in the first position, then B, C, D, or E can be placed in the second position. Thus, we see on the right-hand side of the figure that there are twenty possible permutations.

EXAMPLE 3.14

Refer to Example 3.12, where five beers are ranked in order of preference. What is the probability that an individual who is truly indifferent will select a specific ordering for the first three places?

The number of permutations is $_5P_3 = 5!/(5 - 3)! = 5!/2! = 60$. Thus, the probability of selecting any one of these, if each is equally likely, is $1/60$.

Finally, suppose that we are interested in the number of different ways that x objects can be selected from n (where no object may be chosen more than once) but are not concerned about the order. Notice in Example 3.13 that the entries in the second and fourth rows are just rearrangements of those directly above them and may therefore be ignored. There are thus ten possibilities for selecting two objects from a group of five. The number of possible selections is called the number of **combinations** and is denoted $_nC_x$, where x objects are to be chosen from n. To find this number, note first that the number of possible permutations is $_nP_x$. However, many of these will be rearrangements of the same x objects and so are irrelevant. In fact, since x objects can be ordered in $x!$ ways, we are concerned with only a proportion $1/x!$ of the permutations; that is, the number of combinations is

$$_nC_x = \frac{_nP_x}{x!} = \frac{n!}{x!(n - x)!}$$

Definition

The number of **combinations,** $_nC_x$, of x objects chosen from n is the number of possible selections that can be made. This number is

$$_nC_x = \frac{n!}{x!(n - x)!}$$

EXAMPLE 3.15

A personnel officer has eight candidates to fill four positions. Five candidates are men, and three are women. If, in fact, every combination of candidates is equally likely to be chosen, what is the probability that no women will be hired?

First, the total number of possible combinations of four candidates chosen from eight is

$$_8C_4 = \frac{8!}{4!4!} = 70$$

Now, in order for no women to be hired, it follows that the four successful candidates must come from the available five men. The number of such combinations is

$$_5C_4 = \frac{5!}{4!1!} = 5$$

Therefore, if at the outset each of the seventy possible combinations was equally likely to be chosen, the probability that one of the five all-male combinations would be selected is $\frac{5}{70} = \frac{1}{14}$.

3.6 PROBABILITY RULES

It is often the case that our interest centers on some compound of events, such as the union or intersection. In this section, we will develop rules for computing probabilities for compound events of this kind.

First, let A be an event in the sample space S. We have noted already that A and its complement $\overline{A}$ are mutually exclusive and collectively exhaustive. Hence, by consequence (iii) of Section 3.4, since A and $\overline{A}$ are mutually exclusive

$$P(A \cup \overline{A}) = P(A) + P(\overline{A})$$

and by consequence (iv) of that section, since A and $\overline{A}$ are collectively exhaustive

$$P(A \cup \overline{A}) = 1$$

Putting these equations together yields

$$P(A) + P(\overline{A}) = 1 \qquad \text{or} \qquad P(\overline{A}) = 1 - P(A)$$

so that the probability that an event does *not* occur is 1 minus the probability that it *does* occur. For example, when a die is rolled, the probability of getting a 2 is $\frac{1}{6}$, so the probability that the result is not 2 is $1 - \frac{1}{6} = \frac{5}{6}$. The value of this result lies in the fact that it may be easier to find directly the probability of the complement of an event of interest.

Let A be an event and $\overline{A}$ its complement. Then

$$P(\overline{A}) = 1 - P(A)$$

EXAMPLE 3.16

In Example 3.15, five men and three women were candidates for four positions. Assuming again that every combination is equally likely to be chosen, what is the probability that at least one woman will be selected?

Let A be the event "No women are selected." The event "At least one woman is selected" is then $\overline{A}$, the complement of A. In Example 3.15, we found $P(A) = \frac{1}{14}$.

Therefore, the required probability is

$$P(\overline{A}) = 1 - P(A) = 1 - \frac{1}{14} = \frac{13}{14}$$

Now let A and B be two events. In Section 3.4, we showed that if A and B are mutually exclusive, the probability of their union is the sum of their individual probabilities. We now want to find the probability of the union when the events are not mutually exclusive. Two results derived in Section 3.2 will be used. First, the events $(A \cap B)$ and $(\overline{A} \cap B)$ are mutually exclusive, and their union is B. Hence

$$P(B) = P(A \cap B) + P(\overline{A} \cap B) \qquad\qquad (3.6.1)$$

Also, the events A and $(\overline{A} \cap B)$ are mutually exclusive, and their union is $A \cup B$, so

$$P(A \cup B) = P(A) + P(\overline{A} \cap B) \qquad\qquad (3.6.2)$$

Eliminating $P(\overline{A} \cap B)$ from Eqs. (3.6.1) and (3.6.2) then gives

$$P(A \cup B) = P(A) + P(B) - P(A \cap B)$$

This is called the **addition rule of probabilities.** Notice that the rule implies that the probability of a union is *not* the sum of the individual probabilities, unless the events are mutually exclusive; that is, unless the probability of the intersection is zero.

Addition Rule of Probabilities

Let A and B be two events. The probability of their union is

$$P(A \cup B) = P(A) + P(B) - P(A \cap B)$$

EXAMPLE 3.17

A hamburger chain found that 75% of all customers use mustard, 80% use ketchup, and 65% use both. What is the probability that a particular customer will use at least one of these?

Let A be the event "Customer uses mustard" and B the event "Customer uses ketchup." From the statement of the example, we then have

$$P(A) = .75 \qquad P(B) = .80 \qquad P(A \cap B) = .65$$

The probability required is

$$P(A \cup B) = P(A) + P(B) - P(A \cap B)$$
$$= .75 + .80 - .65 = .90$$

Suppose that we are interested in a pair of events A and B and are given the extra piece of information that event B has occurred. A question of interest then is, what is the probability that A occurs, *given that B has occurred?* This type of problem can be approached through the notion of **conditional probability.** The basic idea is that the chance of any event's occurring is likely to depend on whether or not other events occur. For example, a manufacturer planning to introduce a new brand may test-market the product in a few selected stores. This manufacturer is likely to be much more confident about the brand's success in the wider market if it is well accepted in the test market than if it is not. The firm's assessment of the probability of high sales will therefore be conditioned by the test market outcome.

Again, if I knew that interest rates were going to fall over the next year, I would be far more bullish about the stock market than if I believed that interest rates would rise. Once more, my probabilistic assessment of the likely course of stock prices is conditioned by what I know, or believe, about interest rates. We must therefore be concerned about the probability of occurrence of a particular event, given the occurrence of another.

Definition

Let A and B be two events. The **conditional probability** of event A, given event B, denoted $P(A|B)$, is defined as

$$P(A|B) = \frac{P(A \cap B)}{P(B)}$$

provided that $P(B) > 0$. Similarly, the conditional probability of B given A is defined as

$$P(B|A) = \frac{P(A \cap B)}{P(A)}$$

provided that $P(A) > 0$.

This definition can be motivated in terms of relative frequencies. Suppose that a random experiment is repeated N times, with N_B occurrences of event B and $N_{A \cap B}$ occurrences of A and B together. Then the proportion of times that A occurs, *when B has occurred,* is $N_{A \cap B}/N_B$, and one can think of the conditional probability of A given B as the limit of this proportion as the number of replications of the experiment becomes infinitely large. But

$$\frac{N_{A \cap B}}{N_B} = \frac{N_{A \cap B}/N}{N_B/N}$$

and, as N becomes large, the numerator and denominator of the right-hand side of this expression approach $P(A \cap B)$ and $P(B)$, respectively. The definition of conditional probability is thus compatible with the relative frequency concept.

EXAMPLE
3.18

Refer to Example 3.17. If 75% of the chain's customers use mustard, 80% use ketchup, and 65% use both, what are the probabilities that a ketchup user uses mustard and that a mustard user uses ketchup?

Let A be the event "Customer uses mustard" and B the event "Customer uses ketchup" so that $P(A) = .75$, $P(B) = .80$, and $P(A \cap B) = .65$. The probability that a ketchup user uses mustard is the conditional probability of event A, given event B; that is

$$P(A|B) = \frac{P(A \cap B)}{P(B)} = \frac{.65}{.80} = .8125$$

In the same way, the probability that a mustard user uses ketchup is

$$P(B|A) = \frac{P(A \cap B)}{P(A)} = \frac{.65}{.75} = .8667$$

An immediate consequence of the definition of conditional probability is the **multiplication rule of probabilities,** which expresses the probability of an intersection in terms of probabilities for individual events and conditional probabilities.

Multiplication Rule of Probabilities

Let A and B be two events. The probability of their intersection is

$$P(A \cap B) = P(A|B)P(B)$$

Also,

$$P(A \cap B) = P(B|A)P(A)$$

The following example illustrates an interesting application of the multiplication rule of probabilities and ties together some of the ideas introduced in previous sections of this chapter.

EXAMPLE
3.19

In Example 3.7, we briefly met the *randomized response* approach for the solicitation of honest answers to sensitive questions in surveys. In a survey of this kind carried out in Hawaii by Geurts,[3] each respondent was faced with the following two questions:

(a) Is the last digit of your Social Security number odd?

(b) Do you believe there should be fewer Caucasian professors in the College of Business at the University of Hawaii?

Respondents were asked first to flip a coin and then to answer question (a) if the result was "head" and (b) otherwise. Thirty-seven percent of all respondents gave the an-

---

[3] Geurts, "Using a randomized response research design."

swer "yes." What is the probability that a respondent who was answering the sensitive question (b) replied "yes"?

Let us define the following events:

A: Respondent answers "yes."
E_1: Respondent answers question (a).
E_2: Respondent answers question (b).

We now summarize the given information. First, since 37% of all respondents answered "yes," it follows that $P(A) = .37$. Further, since the question answered is determined by the flip of a coin, the probability that either question will be answered is .5—that is, $P(E_1) = .5$ and $P(E_2) = .5$.

We also know something about the answers to question (a). Since half of all Social Security numbers have an odd last digit, it must be that the probability of a "yes" answer, *given that question (a) has been answered,* is .5—that is, $P(A|E_1) = .5$.

However, what we require is $P(A|E_2)$, the conditional probability of a "yes" response, given that question (b) was answered. To obtain this probability, we make use of two results from previous sections. First, since the events E_1 and E_2 are mutually exclusive and collectively exhaustive, we know that the two intersections $E_1 \cap A$ and $E_2 \cap A$ are mutually exclusive and that their union is A. It therefore follows that the sum of the probabilities of these two intersections is the probability of A, so

$$P(A) = P(E_1 \cap A) + P(E_2 \cap A)$$

Next, we use the multiplication rule, which in this context implies

$$P(E_1 \cap A) = P(A|E_1)P(E_1) \qquad \text{and} \qquad P(E_2 \cap A) = P(A|E_2)P(E_2)$$

We therefore have

$$P(A) = P(A|E_1)P(E_1) + P(A|E_2)P(E_2)$$

Substituting known values in this equation gives

$$.37 = (.5)(.5) + P(A|E_2)(.5)$$

We can now solve for the required conditional probability:

$$P(A|E_2) = \frac{.37 - .25}{.5} = .24$$

Hence, we estimate that 24% of the surveyed population believes there should be fewer Caucasian professors in the College of Business at the University of Hawaii.

Notice in general that the probability of an intersection of two events is *not* equal to the product of the individual event probabilities. However, a special case of considerable practical importance arises when this is in fact so. The events are then said to be **statistically independent.**

Definition

Let A and B be two events. These events are said to be **statistically independent** if and only if

$$P(A \cap B) = P(A)P(B)$$

It follows from the multiplication rule that equivalent conditions are

(i) $P(A|B) = P(A)$ (if $P(B) > 0$)

(ii) $P(B|A) = P(B)$ (if $P(A) > 0$)

More generally, the events $E_1, E_2, \ldots, E_K$ are statistically independent if and only if

$$P(E_1 \cap E_2 \cap \cdots \cap E_K) = P(E_1)P(E_2) \cdots P(E_K)$$

The logical basis for this definition of statistical independence is best seen in terms of conditional probabilities and is perhaps most appealing from a subjective view of probability. Suppose that I believe that the probability that event A will occur is $P(A)$. I am now given the extra piece of information that event B has occurred. If this does not change my view about the likelihood of occurrence of A, my conditional probability assessment $P(A|B)$ will be the same as $P(A)$. I will have concluded that knowledge of the occurrence of B is of no use in determining whether or not A will occur; that is, A is no more or less likely to occur when B does than otherwise. Thus, this definition of statistical independence agrees with a commonsense notion of "independence." In what follows, where the sense is clear, we will drop the word *statistical* and refer to events as being *independent*. (As a trivial example, the events "Dow-Jones average will rise" and "Rain will fall in Austin, Texas" are independent. Whatever I believe about the likelihood of the latter will not influence my judgment of the chances of the former.)

It is often required to check, using the definition, whether or not a pair of events are independent. The method is illustrated in the following example.

EXAMPLE
3.20

It is estimated that 48% of all bachelor's degrees are obtained by women and that 17.5% of all bachelor's degrees are in business. Also, 4.7% of all bachelor's degrees go to women majoring in business. Are the events "Bachelor's degree holder is a woman" and "Bachelor's degree in business" statistically independent?

Let A and B denote these respective events. Then

$$P(A) = .48 \qquad P(B) = .175 \qquad P(A \cap B) = .047$$

Since

$$P(A)P(B) = (.48)(.175) = .084 \neq P(A \cap B)$$

these events are not independent. The dependence can be seen from the conditional probability

$$P(A|B) = \frac{P(A \cap B)}{P(B)} = \frac{.047}{.175} = .269$$

Thus, only 26.9% of business degrees go to women, whereas women constitute 48% of all degree recipients.

It is important to distinguish between the terms *mutually exclusive* and *independent*. A pair of events are mutually exclusive if they cannot jointly occur—that is, if the probability of their intersection is 0. Independent events are characterized by the fact that the probability of their intersection is the product of their individual probabilities. For example, consider the two events, "The stock market will rise today" and "It will rain in Austin, Texas today." We can certainly agree that these are independent events; however, they are not mutually exclusive, as both could occur.

In some circumstances, independence can be deduced, or at least reasonably inferred, from the nature of a random experiment, and the probabilities for intersections can then be calculated as the product of individual probabilities. This is particularly useful in the case of repeated trials.

EXAMPLE 3.21

It is known that 90% of all personal computers of a particular model will operate for at least 1 year before requiring repair. A manager purchases three of these computers. What is the probability that all three will work for 1 year before any repair is needed?

Let E_i ($i = 1, 2, 3$) be the events "The ith computer works for at least 1 year before repair is needed." If the computers are operated independently, it is reasonable to assume independence of the events E_i. Hence, the required probability is

$$P(E_1 \cap E_2 \cap E_3) = P(E_1)P(E_2)P(E_3) = (.9)^3 = .729$$

EXAMPLE 3.22

Assume that the probability that the Dow-Jones average will rise over any given trading day is .5 and that the course of the stock market in any day is independent of what has happened on previous days. What is the probability that the Dow-Jones average will rise over every one of four consecutive trading days? What is the probability that the average will fall or remain constant on at least one of these days?

Let $E_i (i = 1, 2, 3, 4)$ be the events "Dow-Jones average rises on the ith day." Then, by our assumptions, $P(E_i) = \frac{1}{2}$, and these events are independent. Hence, the probability that the market will rise on all four days is

$$P(E_1 \cap E_2 \cap E_3 \cap E_4) = P(E_1)P(E_2)P(E_3)P(E_4) = \left(\frac{1}{2}\right)^4 = \frac{1}{16}$$

Further, the event "Dow-Jones average will fall or remain constant on at least one of these days" is simply the complement of the event whose probability we have just found. Its probability is therefore

$$1 - P(E_1 \cap E_2 \cap E_3 \cap E_4) = 1 - \frac{1}{16} = \frac{15}{16}$$

We conclude this section with two examples to illustrate a useful technique—finding the probability of the complement of an event as a first step in deducing the probability for that event.

EXAMPLE 3.23

How many people must there be in a group so that there is a 50% chance that at least one pair of them has the same birthday? To make the problem manageable, we assign all those born on February 29 to March 1 and assume that all 365 possible birthdays occur equally often in the population at large. (These simplifications have only very small effects on the numerical results.)

Let M be the number of people in the group and A the event "At least one pair has a common birthday." Now, to find the probability of A directly would be very tedious, since we would have to take into account the possibility of more than one pair of matching birthdays. It is more straightforward to find the probability of the complement $\overline{A}$—the event "All M people have different birthdays."

First, since there are 365 possible birthdays for each individual, and each can be associated with every possible birthday of other individuals, the total number of equally likely distinct arrangements for M people is 365^M. Next, we ask how many of these outcomes are contained in the event $\overline{A}$—that is, how many involve the M individuals' all having different birthdays. This is precisely the same as asking in how many ways M birthdays can be selected from 365 possible birthdays and arranged in order. This is just the number of permutations, $_{365}P_M$. Hence, the probability that all M birthdays will be different is

$$P(\overline{A}) = \frac{_{365}P_M}{365^M} = \frac{365!}{365^M(365-M)!}$$

$$= \frac{(364)(363)\cdots(366-M)}{365^{M-1}} \qquad \text{(for } M \geq 2)$$

Having evaluated the probability of the complement, we obtain the required probability as follows:

$$P(A) = 1 - P(\overline{A}) = 1 - \frac{(364)(363)\cdots(366-M)}{365^{M-1}}$$

Some values of this probability for specific numbers of people M are shown in the table

M	10	20	22	23	30	40	60
$P(A)$	.117	.411	.476	.507	.706	.891	.994

Therefore, if there are at least twenty-three people in the group, it is more likely than not that there will be at least one pair of matching birthdays. This probability rises fairly sharply as the group size increases, until, with sixty people in the group, the probability of finding a match is very high indeed.

At first sight, this result may be counterintuitive. After all, the probability that any given pair of individuals will have the same birthday is very small ($\frac{1}{365}$). However, for a group of twenty or more people, the number of possible matches becomes quite large, so although the event "At least one match" is the union of unlikely events, there are so many of them that, when considered together, they yield a high probability for the union.

EXAMPLE 3.24

In a promotion for United Airlines, customers and potential customers were given vouchers. A $\frac{1}{325}$ proportion of these were worth a free round-trip ticket anywhere United flies. How many vouchers would an individual have needed to collect in order to have a 50% chance of winning at least one free trip?

The event A of interest is "At least one free trip is won from M vouchers." Again, it is easiest to find first the probability of the complement $\overline{A}$—the event "No free trips are won with M vouchers."

The probability of a win with a single voucher is $\frac{1}{325}$, so the probability that this voucher will not win is $\frac{324}{325}$. If the individual has M vouchers, the event that none of these wins is just the intersection of the events "No win" for each of the M vouchers. Moreover, these events are independent, so

$$P(\overline{A}) = \left(\frac{324}{325} \right)^M$$

Hence, the probability of at least one win is

$$P(A) = 1 - P(\overline{A}) = 1 - \left(\frac{324}{325} \right)^M$$

In order for $P(A)$ to be at least .5, the individual needs at least $M = 225$ vouchers.

Again, this result might appear counterintuitive. At first sight, one might guess that if the probability of a win for a single voucher was $\frac{1}{325}$, then 163 vouchers would be enough to ensure a 50% chance of a win. However, one would be implicitly assuming that the probability of a union was the sum of the individual probabilities, neglecting to subtract for double counting in the intersections (which in this case would involve more than one win from the M vouchers).

EXERCISES

7. A company knows that a rival is about to bring out a competing product. It believes that this rival has three possible packaging plans (superior, normal, cheap) in mind and that all are equally likely. Also, there are three equally likely possible marketing strategies (intense media advertising, price discounts, and use of a coupon to reduce the price of future purchases). What is the probability that the rival will employ superior packaging in conjunction with an intense media advertising campaign? Assume that packaging plans and marketing strategies are determined independently.

8. A financial analyst was asked to evaluate earnings prospects for seven corporations over the next year, and to rank them in order of predicted earnings growth rates.
   (a) How many different rankings are possible?
   (b) If, in fact, a specific ordering is simply guessed, what is the probability that this guess will turn out to be correct?

9. A company has fifty sales representatives. It decides that the most successful representative during the previous year will be awarded a January vacation in Hawaii, while the second most successful will win a vacation in Las Vegas. The other representatives will be required to attend a conference on modern sales methods in Buffalo. How many outcomes are possible?

10. A securities analyst claims that given a specific list of six common stocks, it is possible to predict, in the correct order, the three that will perform best during the coming year. What is the probability of making the correct selection by chance?

11. A student committee has six members—four undergraduates and two graduate students. A subcommittee of three members is to be chosen randomly, so that each possible combination of three of the six students is equally likely to be selected. What is the probability that there will be no graduate students on the subcommittee?

12. Baseball's American League East has five teams. You are required to predict, in order, the top three teams at the end of the season. Ignoring the possibility of ties, calculate the number of different predictions you could make. What is the probability of making the correct prediction by chance?

13. A manager has four assistants—John, George, Mary, and Jean—to assign to four tasks. Each assistant will be assigned to one of the tasks, one assistant to each task.

    (a) How many different arrangements of assignments are possible?

    (b) If assignments are made at random, what is the probability that Mary will be assigned to a specific task?

14. The senior management of a corporation has decided that in the future, it wishes to divide its advertising budget between two agencies. Eight agencies are currently being considered for this work. How many different choices of two agencies are possible?

15. You are one of seven female candidates auditioning for two parts—the heroine and her best friend—in a play. Before the auditions, you know nothing of the other candidates, and assume all candidates have equal chances for either part.

    (a) How many distinct choices are possible for casting the two parts?

    (b) In how many of the possibilities in (a) would you be chosen to play the heroine?

    (c) In how many of the possibilities in (a) would you be chosen to play the best friend?

    (d) Use the results in (a) and (b) to find the probability you will be chosen to play the heroine. Indicate a more direct way of finding this probability.

    (e) Use the results in (a), (b), and (c) to find the probability you will be chosen to play one of the two parts. Indicate a more direct way of finding this probability.

16. A work crew for a building project is to be made up of two craftsmen and four laborers selected from a total of five craftsmen and six laborers available.

    (a) How many different combinations are possible?

    (b) The brother of one of the craftsmen is a laborer. If the crew is selected at random, what is the probability that both brothers will be selected?

    (c) What is the probability that neither brother will be selected?

17. A mutual fund company has six funds that invest in the U.S. market, and four that invest in foreign markets. A customer wants to invest in two U.S. funds and two foreign funds.

    (a) How many different sets of funds from this company could the investor choose?

    (b) Unknown to this investor, one of the U.S. funds and one of the foreign funds will seriously under-perform next year. If the investor selects funds for purchase at random, what is the probability that at least one of the chosen funds will seriously under-perform next year?

18. It was estimated that 30% of all seniors on a campus were seriously concerned about employment prospects, 25% were seriously concerned about grades, and 20% were seriously concerned about both. What is the probability that a randomly chosen senior from this campus is seriously concerned about at least one of these two things?

19. A music store owner finds that 30% of customers entering the store ask an assistant for help and that 20% make a purchase before leaving. It was also found that 15% of all customers both ask for assistance and make a purchase. What is the probability that a customer does at least one of these two things?

20. Refer to the information in Exercise 19, and consider the two events "Customer asks for assistance" and "Customer makes purchase." In answering the following questions, provide reasons expressed in terms of probabilities of relevant events.

(a) Are the two events mutually exclusive?

(b) Are the two events collectively exhaustive?

(c) Are the two events statistically independent?

21. A local public-action group solicits donations by telephone. For a particular list of prospects, it was estimated that for any individual, the probability was .05 of an immediate donation by credit card, .25 of no immediate donation but a request for further information through the mail, and .7 of no expression of interest. Mailed information is sent to all people requesting it, and it is estimated that 20% of these people will eventually donate. An operator makes a sequence of calls, the outcomes of which can be assumed to be independent.

(a) What is the probability that no immediate credit card donation will be received until at least four unsuccessful calls have been made?

(b) What is the probability that the first call leading to any donation (either immediately or eventually after a mailing) is preceded by at least four unsuccessful calls?

22. A mail-order firm considers three possible foul-ups in filling an order:

> A: The wrong item is sent.
> B: The item is lost in transit.
> C: The item is damaged in transit.

Assume that event A is independent of both B and C and that events B and C are mutually exclusive. The individual event probabilities are $P(A) = .02$, $P(B) = .01$, and $P(C) = .04$. Find the probability that at least one of these foul-ups occurs for a randomly chosen order.

23. A coach recruits for a college team a star player who is currently a high school senior. In order to play next year, the senior must both complete high school with adequate grades and pass a standardized test. The coach estimates that the probability the athlete will fail to obtain adequate high school grades is .02, the probability the athlete will not pass the standardized test is .15, and that these are independent events. According to these estimates, what is the probability this recuit will be eligible to play in college next year?

24. Market research in a particular city indicated that during a week 18% of all adults watch a television program oriented to business and financial issues, 12% read a publication oriented to these issues, and 10% do both.

(a) What is the probability that an adult in this city, who watches a television program oriented to business and financial issues, reads a publication oriented to these issues?

(b) What is the probability that an adult in this city, who reads a publication oriented to business and financial issues, watches a television program oriented to these issues?

25. An inspector examines items coming from an assembly line. A review of her record reveals that she accepts only 8% of all defective items. It was also found that 1% of all items from the assembly line are both defective and accepted by the inspector. What is the probability that a randomly chosen item from this assembly line is defective?

26. An analyst is presented with lists of four stocks and five bonds. He is asked to predict, in order, the two stocks that will yield the highest return over the next year and the two bonds that will have the highest return over the next year. Suppose that these predictions are made randomly and independently of each other. What is the probability that the analyst will be successful in at least one of the two tasks?

27. A bank classifies borrowers as high-risk or low-risk. Only 15% of its loans are made to those in the high-risk category. Of all its loans, 5% are in default, and 40% of those in default are to high-risk borrowers. What is the probability that a high-risk borrower will default?

28. A conference began at noon with two parallel sessions. The session on portfolio management was attended by 40% of the delegates, while the session on chartism was attended by 50%. The evening session consisted of a talk titled, "Is the random walk dead?" This was attended by 80% of all delegates.

(a) If attendance at the sessions on portfolio management and chartism are mutually exclusive, what is the probability that a randomly chosen delegate attended at least one of these sessions?

(b) If attendance at the portfolio management and evening sessions are statistically independent, what is the probability that a randomly chosen delegate attended at least one of these sessions?

(c) Of those attending the chartism session, 75% also attended the evening session. What is the probability that a randomly chosen delegate attended at least one of these two sessions?

29. A stock market analyst claims expertise in picking stocks that will outperform the corresponding industry norms. This analyst is presented with a list of five high-technology stocks and a list of five airline stocks, and she is invited to nominate, in order, the three stocks that will do best on each of these two lists over the next year. The analyst claims that success in just one of these two tasks would be a substantial accomplishment. If, in fact, the choices were made randomly and independently, what would be the probability of success in at least one of the two tasks merely by chance? Given this result, what do you think of the analyst's claim?

30. A quality control manager found that 30% of worker-related problems occurred on Mondays, and that 20% occurred in the last hour of a day's shift. It was also found that 4% of worker-related problems occurred in the last hour of Monday's shift.

(a) What is the probability that a worker-related problem that occurs on a Monday does not occur in the last hour of the day's shift?

(b) Are the events "Problem occurs on Monday" and "Problem occurs in the last hour of the day's shift" statistically independent?

31. A corporation was concerned about the basic educational skills of its workers and decided to offer a selected group of them separate classes in reading and practical mathematics. Forty percent of these workers signed up for the reading classes, and 50% for the practical mathematics classes. Of those signing up for the reading classes, 30% signed up for the mathematics classes.

(a) What is the probability that a randomly selected worker signed up for both classes?

(b) What is the probability that a randomly selected worker who signed up for the mathematics classes also signed up for the reading classes?

(c) What is the probability that a randomly chosen worker signed up for at least one of these two classes?

(d) Are the events "Signs up for reading classes" and "Signs up for mathematics classes" statistically independent?

32. A lawn care service makes telephone solicitations, seeking customers for the coming season. A review of the records indicated that 15% of these solicitations produced new customers, and that, of these new customers, 80% had used some rival service in the previous year. It was also estimated that, of all solicitation calls made, 60% were to people who had used a rival service the previous year. What is the probability that a call to a person who used a rival service the previous year will produce a new customer for the lawn care service?

33. An editor may use all, some, or none of three possible strategies to enhance the sales of a book:

    A: An expensive prepublication promotion
    B: An expensive cover design
    C: A bonus for sales representatives who meet predetermined sales levels

In the past, these three strategies have been applied simultaneously to only 2% of the company's books. Twenty percent of the books have had expensive cover designs, and of these, 80% have had expensive prepublication promotion. A rival editor learns that a new book is to have both expensive prepublication promotion and cover design and now wants to know how likely it is that a bonus scheme for sales representatives will be introduced. Compute the probability of interest to the rival editor.

3.7   BIVARIATE PROBABILITIES

In this section, we introduce a class of problems that can be handled using the material developed previously. However, they are sufficiently important to be treated separately.

The general setup is as follows. A random experiment is to be conducted, and interest centers on two distinct sets of events that could occur. We label these A_1, A_2, ..., A_h and B_1, B_2, ..., B_k. The events A_i are mutually exclusive and collectively exhaustive, as are the events B_j. However, any A_i event can occur jointly with any B_j event, so that the intersections $A_i \cap B_j$ can occur. These intersections can be regarded as the basic outcomes of the random experiment. Two sets of events, considered jointly in this way, are often called *bivariate,* and the probabilities are referred to as **bivariate probabilities.** The setup is illustrated in Table 3.1. If probabilities can be attached to all of the events $A_i \cap B_j$, then the whole probability structure of the random experiment is known and other probabilities of interest can be calculated.

As an example, a potential advertiser will want to know not only the likely size of the viewing audience for a particular television show but also the relevant characteristics of that audience. Thus, families may be categorized (corresponding to the A_i categorization) as to whether they regularly, occasionally, or never watch a particular series and also (corresponding to the B_j) according to low, middle, or high income. Then the nine possible cross-classifications can be set out as in Table 3.1, with $h = 3$

TABLE 3.1 Outcomes for bivariate events

	B_1	B_2	$\cdots$	B_k
A_1	$A_1 \cap B_1$	$A_1 \cap B_2$	$\cdots$	$A_1 \cap B_k$
A_2	$A_2 \cap B_1$	$A_2 \cap B_2$	$\cdots$	$A_2 \cap B_k$
.				
.				
.				
A_h	$A_h \cap B_1$	$A_h \cap B_2$	$\cdots$	$A_h \cap B_k$

and $k = 3$. An alternative way to view this breakdown of the population into these nine distinct groups is through the use of a *tree diagram,* as shown in Figure 3.12. Beginning at the left with the whole population of families, there are three distinct branches according to the frequency with which the show is watched. Each of these branches has three sub-branches, corresponding to the three income categories. Therefore, there are nine sub-branches in all, each associated with one of the possible viewing-income event intersections.

As a first step, probabilities for the event intersections are required. Values for the television viewing example, obtained from survey results, are given in the body of Table 3.2. For example, it was found that 10% of families in the survey have high incomes and occasionally watch the series. In equating proportions of the survey members and probabilities in this way, we are tacitly invoking the relative frequency concept of probability, assuming that the survey is sufficiently large that proportions can be approximated as probabilities. On this basis, the probability that a family chosen at

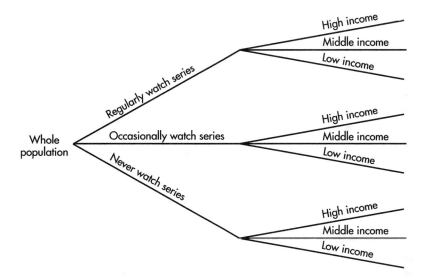

FIGURE 3.12 Tree diagram of events for the television viewing-income example

TABLE 3.2 Probabilities for the television viewing-income example

VIEWING FREQUENCY	INCOME			TOTALS
	HIGH	MIDDLE	LOW	
Regular	.04	.13	.04	.21
Occasional	.10	.11	.06	.27
Never	.13	.17	.22	.52
Totals	.27	.41	.32	1.00

random from the population has a high income and occasionally watches the show is .10; that is

$$P(\text{Occasionally watch} \cap \text{High income}) = .10$$

Definitions

In the context of bivariate probabilities, the intersection probabilities $P(A_i \cap B_j)$ are called **joint probabilities.** The probabilities for individual events, $P(A_i)$ or $P(B_j)$, are called **marginal probabilities.**

Given the joint probabilities, suppose that we require the marginal probabilities. Consider the general setup in Table 3.1, where interest is in the event A_i. Now A_i is the union of the mutually exclusive events $A_i \cap B_1, A_i \cap B_2, \ldots, A_i \cap B_k$. [This result was formally established in Section 3.2 as result (iii).] Hence, by the addition rule for mutually exclusive events [established in Section 3.4 as result (iii)], the probability of event A_i is just the sum of the intersection probabilities for those intersections involving A_i—that is

$$P(A_i) = P(A_i \cap B_1) + P(A_i \cap B_2) + \cdots + P(A_i \cap B_k)$$

Thus, when the intersection probabilities are cross-tabulated, the individual event probabilities for the A_i are just the row totals. From an analogous argument, the probabilities for the B_j are the column totals.

For the television viewing-income example, it follows that the probability that a randomly chosen individual occasionally watches the show is

$$P(\text{Occasionally watch}) = P(\text{Occasionally watch} \cap \text{High income})$$
$$+ P(\text{Occasionally watch} \cap \text{Middle income})$$
$$+ P(\text{Occasionally watch} \cap \text{Low income})$$
$$= .10 + .11 + .06 = .27$$

Similarly

$$P(\text{Regularly watch}) = .21 \qquad \text{and} \qquad P(\text{Never watch}) = .52$$

and

$$P(\text{High income}) = .27 \qquad P(\text{Middle income}) = .41$$
$$P(\text{Low income}) = .32$$

Marginal probabilities can also be deduced directly from tree diagrams, as in Figure 3.13, in which the branches and sub-branches are the same events as in Figure 3.12. Beginning on the right-hand side of the figure, the joint probabilities can be entered immediately on the nine sub-branches. The marginal probabilities for each of the three viewing frequency events can then be entered on the main branches by

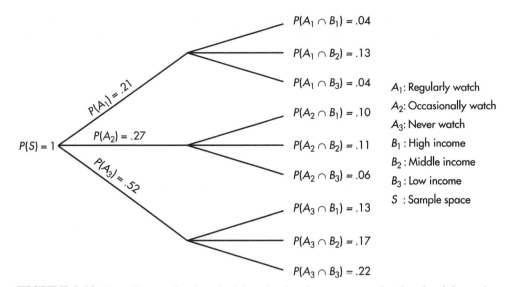

P(S) = 1

P(A₁) = .21
P(A₂) = .27
P(A₃) = .52

$P(A_1 \cap B_1) = .04$
$P(A_1 \cap B_2) = .13$
$P(A_1 \cap B_3) = .04$
$P(A_2 \cap B_1) = .10$
$P(A_2 \cap B_2) = .11$
$P(A_2 \cap B_3) = .06$
$P(A_3 \cap B_1) = .13$
$P(A_3 \cap B_2) = .17$
$P(A_3 \cap B_3) = .22$

A_1: Regularly watch
A_2: Occasionally watch
A_3: Never watch
B_1 : High income
B_2 : Middle income
B_3 : Low income
S : Sample space

FIGURE 3.13 Tree diagram for the television viewing-income example, showing joint and marginal probabilities

adding the probabilities on the corresponding sub-branches. This approach is particularly useful when there are more than two attributes of interest. For example, the advertiser might be interested also in the age of the head of the household or whether there are children in the household.

Since the events $A_1, A_2, \ldots, A_h$ are mutually exclusive and collectively exhaustive, their marginal probabilities must sum to 1. The same is true of the events $B_1, B_2, \ldots, B_k$. For the television viewing-income example, this is illustrated in Table 3.2, where the row and column totals both sum to 1, and in the tree diagram of Figure 3.13, where the sum of the probabilities on the main branches is also 1. It also follows that the joint probabilities summed over all event combinations add to 1.

In many applications, the conditional probabilities are of more interest than the marginal probabilities. For example, an advertiser will be less concerned with the total size of the viewing audience for a show than with the chance that a family that is likely to be in the market for a particular product is watching. The conditional probabilities can be obtained by direct application of the definition of conditional probability introduced in Section 3.6. Thus, the probability of A_i given B_j is

$$P(A_i | B_j) = \frac{P(A_i \cap B_j)}{P(B_j)}$$

for any pair of events A_i and B_j. Similarly

$$P(B_j | A_i) = \frac{P(A_i \cap B_j)}{P(A_i)}$$

Once the joint and marginal probabilities are known, the conditional probabilities then follow. For example, the probability that a randomly chosen family occasionally watches the show given that its income is in the middle range is

$$P(\text{Occasionally watch}|\text{Middle income}) = \frac{P(\text{Occasionally watch} \cap \text{Middle income})}{P(\text{Middle income})}$$

$$= \frac{.11}{.41} = .27$$

Other conditional probabilities of viewing frequency given income level can be found in the same way and are given in Table 3.3.

The probabilities for income levels given viewing frequencies can also be found. For example, the probability that a randomly chosen family has middle income given that they occasionally watch the show is

$$P(\text{Middle income}|\text{Occasionally watch}) = \frac{P(\text{Occasionally watch} \cap \text{Middle income})}{P(\text{Occasionally watch})}$$

$$= \frac{.11}{.27} = .41$$

The conditional probabilities for income levels given viewing frequencies are displayed in Table 3.4.

TABLE 3.3 Conditional probabilities of viewing frequencies given income levels

VIEWING FREQUENCY	INCOME		
	HIGH	MIDDLE	LOW
Regular	.15	.32	.12
Occasional	.37	.27	.19
Never	.48	.41	.69

TABLE 3.4 Conditional probabilities of income levels given viewing frequencies

VIEWING FREQUENCY	INCOME		
	HIGH	MIDDLE	LOW
Regular	.19	.62	.19
Occasional	.37	.41	.22
Never	.25	.33	.42

We can also check whether or not a pair of events are statistically independent. In general, the events A_i and B_j are independent if and only if their joint probability is the product of their marginal probabilities; that is, if

$$P(A_i \cap B_j) = P(A_i)P(B_j)$$

In our example, for the events "Occasionally watch" and "High income," we have from Table 3.2

$$P(\text{Occasionally watch} \cap \text{High income}) = .10$$

and

$$P(\text{Occasionally watch}) = .27 \qquad P(\text{High income}) = .27$$

The product of the marginal probabilities is .0729, which differs from the joint probability .10. Hence, the two events are not statistically independent.

A case of particular interest arises when every event A_i is independent of every event B_j, in which case the two *attributes* are said to be **independent.** Here we have just established that viewing frequency and income are *not* independent.

Definition

Let A and B be a pair of attributes, each broken down into mutually exclusive and collectively exhaustive event categories, respectively denoted $A_1, A_2, \ldots, A_h$ and $B_1, B_2, \ldots, B_k$. If every event A_i is statistically independent of every event B_j, the attributes A and B are said to be **independent.**

In many practical applications, the joint probabilities will not be known precisely. A problem of considerable importance arises when a sample is available from a population, allowing estimates to be made of the joint probabilities, and it is required to test, on the basis of this sample evidence, whether or not a pair of attributes are independent of one another. A procedure for carrying out such a test will be introduced in Chapter 11.

3.8 BAYES' THEOREM

In this section, we introduce a mechanism for the modification of probability assessments when additional information becomes available. To illustrate, suppose that an investor is interested in a particular stock and forms a judgment about the likely profitability of an investment in it. If the investor then learns that the stock is being recommended by an expert analyst, he or she might modify this original judgment, depending on his or her faith in the analyst's ability.

Let A and B be two events with respective probabilities $P(A)$ and $P(B)$. The multiplication rule of probabilities gives

$$P(A \cap B) = P(A|B)P(B) \qquad (3.8.1)$$

and also

$$P(A \cap B) = P(B|A)P(A) \qquad (3.8.2)$$

Since the left-hand sides of Eqs. (3.8.1) and (3.8.2) are the same, so must be the right-hand sides, so that

$$P(B|A)P(A) = P(A|B)P(B)$$

Dividing through this equation by $P(A)$, assuming that probability is not zero, gives Bayes' theorem.[4]

Bayes' Theorem

Let A and B be two events. Then

$$P(B|A) = \frac{P(A|B)P(B)}{P(A)} \qquad (3.8.3)$$

The most interesting interpretation of Bayes' theorem is in terms of subjective probabilities. Suppose that an individual is interested in the event B and forms a subjective view of the probability that B will occur; in this context, the probability $P(B)$ is called a **prior** probability. If then the individual acquires an additional piece of information—namely, that event A has occurred—this may cause a modification of the initial judgment as to the likelihood of the occurrence of B. Since A is known to have happened, the relevant probability for B is now the conditional probability of B given A and is termed the **posterior** probability. Viewed in this way, Bayes' theorem can be thought of as a mechanism for updating a prior probability to a posterior probability when the additional information that event A has occurred becomes available. The theorem then states that the updating is accomplished through multiplication of the prior probability by $P(A|B)/P(A)$.

That people form and subsequently modify subjective probability assessments is common experience. An important aspect of an auditor's work is to determine

---

[4] The theorem is named for its discoverer, an English clergyman, the Reverend Thomas Bayes (1702–1761).

whether or not the account balances are correct. Before examining a particular account, the auditor will have formed some view, based on experience from earlier audits, of the probability that it is in error. However, if the balance is found to be substantially different from what might be expected on the basis of the last few years' figures, the auditor will feel that the probability of an error is higher and therefore give the account particularly close attention. Here, the prior probability has been updated in the light of additional information.

EXAMPLE 3.25 In examining past records of a corporation's account balances, an auditor finds that 15% of them have contained errors. Of those balances in error, 60% were regarded as unusual values based on historical figures. Of all the account balances, 20% were unusual values. If the figure for a particular balance appears unusual on this basis, what is the probability that it is in error?

Denoting the events of interest as "Error" and "Unusual value," we have

$$P(\text{Error}) = .15 \qquad \text{and} \qquad P(\text{Unusual value}) = .20$$

and

$$P(\text{Unusual value} \mid \text{Error}) = .60$$

Invoking Bayes' theorem, we obtain

$$P(\text{Error} \mid \text{Unusual value}) = \frac{P(\text{Unusual value} \mid \text{Error})P(\text{Error})}{P(\text{Unusual value})}$$

$$= \frac{(.60)(.15)}{.20} = .45$$

Thus, given the information that the account balance appears unusual, the probability that it is in error is modified from the prior .15 to the posterior .45.

Bayes' theorem is often expressed in a different but equivalent form. Let $E_1, E_2, \ldots, E_K$ be K mutually exclusive and collectively exhaustive events and let A be some other event. For some i, we want to find the conditional probability of E_i given A. This can be obtained directly from Bayes' theorem by setting B in Eq. (3.8.3) equal to E_i. However, the denominator on the right-hand side of that equation can be expressed in terms of conditional probabilities for A given the E_j and probabilities of the individual E_j. We have seen in Section 3.2 that the events $E_1 \cap A, E_2 \cap A, \ldots, E_K \cap A$ are mutually exclusive and that their union is A. It then follows [see result (iii) in Section 3.4] that the probability of A is

$$P(A) = P(E_1 \cap A) + P(E_2 \cap A) + \cdots + P(E_K \cap A) \qquad (3.8.4)$$

Furthermore, from the multiplication rule of probabilities

$$P(E_j \cap A) = P(A \mid E_j)P(E_j) \qquad (j = 1, 2, \ldots, K)$$

so substituting into Eq. (3.8.4) yields

$$P(A) = P(A|E_1)P(E_1) + P(A|E_2)P(E_2)$$
$$+ \cdots + P(A|E_K)P(E_K)$$

(3.8.5)

Finally, the restatement of Bayes' theorem is obtained by substituting E_i for B and the right-hand side of Eq. (3.8.5) for $P(A)$ in Eq. (3.8.3).

Bayes' Theorem (Alternative Statement)

Let $E_1, E_2, \ldots, E_K$ be K mutually exclusive and collectively exhaustive events and let A be some other event. The conditional probability of E_i given A can be expressed as

$$P(E_i|A) = \frac{P(A|E_i)P(E_i)}{P(A|E_1)P(E_1) + P(A|E_2)P(E_2) + \cdots + P(A|E_K)P(E_K)}$$

The advantage of this restatement of the theorem lies in the fact that the probabilities it involves are often precisely those that are directly available. As will be seen in Chapter 19, an important application of this result is in statistical decision making.

EXAMPLE 3.26

A publisher sends advertising material for an accounting text to 80% of all professors teaching the appropriate accounting course. Thirty percent of the professors who received this material adopted the book, as did 10% of the professors who did not receive the material. What is the probability that a professor who adopts the book has received the advertising material?

Let "Receives" denote the event that a professor receives the advertising material and "Does not receive" denote the complement of that event. Then

$$P(\text{Receives}) = .80 \qquad P(\text{Does not receive}) = 1 - .80 = .20$$

Also

$$P(\text{Adopts}|\text{Receives}) = .30 \qquad P(\text{Adopts}|\text{Does not receive}) = .10$$

We require the conditional probability of having received the advertising material given that the book is adopted. By Bayes' theorem this is

$$P(\text{Receives}|\text{Adopts}) = \frac{P(\text{Adopts}|\text{Receives})P(\text{Receives})}{P(\text{Adopts}|\text{Receives})P(\text{Receives})}$$
$$+ P(\text{Adopts}|\text{Does not receive})P(\text{Does not receive})$$

$$= \frac{(.30)(.80)}{(.30)(.80) + (.10)(.20)} = .923$$

EXAMPLE
3.27

A stock market analyst examined the prospects of the shares of a large number of corporations. When the performance of these stocks was investigated one year later, it turned out that 25% performed much better than the market average, 25% much worse, and the remaining 50% about the same as the average. Forty percent of the stocks that turned out to do much better than the market were rated "good buys" by the analyst, as were 20% of those that did about as well as the market and 10% of those that did much worse. What is the probability that a stock rated a "good buy" by the analyst performed much better than the market average?

Define the following events:

E_1: Stock performs much better than the market average.
E_2: Stock performs about the same as market average.
E_3: Stock performs much worse than market average.
A: Stock is rated "good buy" by the analyst.

From the statement of the example, we have the probabilities

$$P(E_1) = .25 \qquad P(E_2) = .50 \qquad P(E_3) = .25$$

and the conditional probabilities

$$P(A|E_1) = .4 \qquad P(A|E_2) = .2 \qquad P(A|E_3) = .1$$

It is required to find the probability that a stock performs much better than the market average, given that it was rated a "good buy" by the analyst. This is the conditional probability $P(E_1|A)$, which is obtained from Bayes' theorem as follows:

$$P(E_1|A) = \frac{P(A|E_1)P(E_1)}{P(A|E_1)P(E_1) + P(A|E_2)P(E_2) + P(A|E_3)P(E_3)}$$

$$= \frac{(.4)(.25)}{(.4)(.25) + (.2)(.50) + (.1)(.25)} = .444$$

EXERCISES

34. A survey carried out for a supermarket classified customers according to whether their visits to the store are frequent or infrequent and to whether they often, sometimes, or never purchase generic products. The accompanying table gives the proportions of people surveyed in each of the six joint classifications.

FREQUENCY OF VISIT	PURCHASE OF GENERIC PRODUCTS		
	OFTEN	SOMETIMES	NEVER
Frequent	.12	.48	.19
Infrequent	.07	.06	.08

(a) What is the probability that a customer is both a frequent shopper and often purchases generic products?

(b) What is the probability that a customer who never buys generic products visits the store frequently?

(c) Are the events "Never buys generic products" and "Visits the store frequently" independent?

(d) What is the probability that a customer who infrequently visits the store often buys generic products?

(e) Are the events "Often buys generic products" and "Visits the store infrequently" independent?

(f) What is the probability that a customer frequently visits the store?

(g) What is the probability that a customer never buys generic products?

(h) What is the probability that a customer either frequently visits the store or never buys generic products, or both?

35. A consulting organization predicts whether corporations' earnings for the coming year will be unusually low, unusually high, or normal. Before deciding whether to continue purchasing these forecasts, a stockbroker compares past predictions with actual outcomes. The accompanying table shows proportions in the nine joint classifications.

OUTCOME	PREDICTION		
	UNUSUALLY HIGH	NORMAL	UNUSUALLY LOW
Unusually high	.23	.12	.03
Normal	.06	.22	.08
Unusually low	.01	.06	.19

(a) What proportion of predictions have been for unusually high earnings?

(b) What proportion of outcomes were for unusually high earnings?

(c) If a firm were to have unusually high earnings, what is the probability that the consulting organization would correctly predict this event?

(d) If the organization predicted unusually high earnings for a corporation, what is the probability that these would materialize?

(e) What is the probability that a corporation for which unusually high earnings had been predicted will have unusually low earnings?

36. Subscribers to a local newspaper were asked whether they regularly, occasionally, or never read the business section, and also whether they had traded common stocks (or shares in a mutual fund) over the last year. The table given here shows proportions of subscribers in six joint classifications.

TRADED STOCKS	READ BUSINESS SECTION		
	REGULARLY	OCCASIONALLY	NEVER
Yes	.18	.10	.04
No	.16	.31	.21

(a) What is the probability that a randomly chosen subscriber never reads the business section?

(b) What is the probability that a randomly chosen subscriber has traded stocks over the last year?

(c) What is the probability that a subscriber who never reads the business section has traded stocks over the last year?

(d) What is the probability that a subscriber who traded stocks over the last year never reads the business section?

(e) What is the probability that a subscriber who does not regularly read the business section traded stocks over the last year?

37. A corporation regularly takes deliveries of a particular sensitive part from three subcontractors. It found that the proportion of parts that are good or defective from the total received were as shown in the following table.

PART	SUBCONTRACTOR		
	A	B	C
Good	.27	.30	.33
Defective	.02	.05	.03

(a) If a part is chosen randomly from all those received, what is the probability that it is defective?

(b) If a part is chosen randomly from all those received, what is the probability it is from subcontractor B?

(c) What is the probability that a part from subcontractor B is defective?

(d) What is the probability that a randomly chosen defective part is from subcontractor B?

(e) Is the quality of a part independent of the source of supply?

(f) In terms of quality, which of the three subcontractors is most reliable?

38. In a survey of students in a business statistics class, students were asked what grade they expected in the course, and also whether they worked additional problems beyond those assigned by the instructor. The table gives proportions of students in each of eight joint classifications.

WORKED PROBLEMS	EXPECTED GRADE			
	A	B	C	BELOW C
Yes	.12	.06	.12	.02
No	.13	.21	.26	.08

(a) Find the probability that a randomly chosen student from this class worked additional problems.

(b) Find the probability that a randomly chosen student from this class expects an A.

(c) Find the probability that a randomly chosen student who worked additional problems expects an A.

(d) Find the probability that a randomly chosen student who expects an A worked additional problems.

(e) Find the probability that a randomly chosen student who worked additional problems expects a grade below B.

(f) Are working additional problems and expected grade statistically independent?

39. The accompanying table shows proportions of computer salespeople classified according to marital status and whether they left their jobs or stayed over a period of one year.[5]

MARITAL STATUS	STAYED	LEFT
Married	.64	.13
Single	.17	.06

(a) What is the probability that a randomly chosen salesperson was married?

(b) What is the probability that a randomly chosen computer salesperson left his or her job within the year?

(c) What is the probability that a randomly chosen single salesperson left his or her job within the year?

(d) What is the probability that a randomly chosen salesperson who stayed in the job over the year was married?

40. The accompanying table shows proportions of adults in nonmetropolitan areas, categorized as to whether they were readers or nonreaders of newspapers and whether or not they voted in the last election.[6]

VOTED	READERS	NONREADERS
Yes	.63	.13
No	.14	.10

(a) What is the probability that a randomly chosen adult from this population voted?

(b) What is the probability that a randomly chosen adult from this population read newspapers?

(c) What is the probability that a randomly chosen adult who did not read newspapers, from this population, did not vote?

41. A campus student club distributed material about membership to new students attending an orientation meeting. Of those receiving this material, 40% were men and 60% were women. Subsequently, it was found the 7% of the men and 9% of the women who received this material joined the club.

(a) Find the probability that a randomly chosen new student who receives the membership material will join the club.

(b) Find the probability that a randomly chosen new student who joins the club after receiving the membership material is a woman.

---

[5] These estimates are based on information given by E. F. Fern, R. A. Avila, and D. Grewal, "Salesforce turnover: Those who left and those who stayed," *Industrial Marketing Management, 18* (1989), 1–9.

[6] These estimates are based on information given by J. R. Lynn, "Newspaper ad impact in nonmetropolitan markets," *Journal of Advertising Research, 21,* no. 4 (1981), 13–19.

42. An analyst attempting to predict a corporation's earnings next year believes that the corporation's business is quite sensitive to the level of interest rates. She believes that if average rates in the next year are more than 1% higher than this year, the probability of significant earnings growth is .1. If average rates next year are more than 1% lower than this year, the probability of significant earnings growth is estimated to be .8. Finally, if average interest rates next year are within 1% of this year's rates, the probability for significant earnings growth is put at .5. The analyst estimates that the probability is .25 that rates next year will be more than 1% higher than this year, and .15 that they will be more than 1% lower than this year.

    (a) What is the estimated probability that both interest rates will be 1% higher and significant earnings growth will result?

    (b) What is the probability this corporation will experience significant earnings growth?

    (c) If the corporation exhibits significant earnings growth, what is the probability that interest rates will have been more than 1% lower than in the current year?

43. Forty-two percent of blue-collar employees in a corporation were in favor of a modified health care plan, and 22% of the corporation's blue-collar employees favored a proposal to change the work schedule. Thirty-four percent of those favoring the health plan modification favored the work schedule change.

    (a) What is the probability that a randomly selected blue-collar employee is in favor of both the modified health care plan and the changed work schedule?

    (b) What is the probability that a randomly chosen blue-collar employee is in favor of at least one of the two changes?

    (c) What is the probability that a blue-collar employee favoring the work schedule change also favors the modified health plan?

44. The grades of a freshman college class, obtained at the end of their first year of college, were analyzed. Seventy percent of the students in the top quarter of the college class had graduated in the upper 10% of their high school class, as had 50% of the students in the middle half of the college class and 20% of the students in the bottom quarter of the college class.

    (a) What is the probability that a randomly chosen freshman graduated in the upper 10% of his or her high school class?

    (b) What is the probability that a randomly chosen freshman who graduated in the upper 10% of his or her high school class will be in the top quarter of the college class?

    (c) What is the probability that a randomly chosen freshman who did not graduate in the upper 10% of his or her high school class will not be in the top quarter of the college class?

45. Before books aimed at preschool children are marketed, reactions are obtained from a panel of preschool children. These reactions are categorized as "favorable," "neutral," or "unfavorable." Subsequently, books sales are categorized as "high," "moderate," or "low," according to the norms of this market. Similar panels have evaluated 1,000 books in the past. The accompanying table shows their reactions and the resulting market performance of the books.

SALES	PANEL REACTION		
	FAVORABLE	NEUTRAL	UNFAVORABLE
High	173	101	61
Moderate	88	211	70
Low	42	113	141

(a) If the panel reaction is favorable, what is the probability that sales will be high?

(b) If the panel reaction is unfavorable, what is the probability that sales will be low?

(c) If the panel reaction is neutral or better, what is the probability that sales will be low?

(d) If sales are low, what is the probability that the panel reaction was neutral or better?

46. A manufacturer produces boxes of candy, each containing ten pieces. Two machines are used for this purpose. After a large batch has been produced, it is discovered that one of the machines, which produces 40% of the total output, has a fault that has led to the introduction of an impurity into 10% of the pieces of candy it makes. From a single box of candy, one piece is selected at random and tested. If that piece contains no impurity, what is the probability that the box from which it came was produced by the faulty machine?

47. A student feels that 70% of his college courses have been enjoyable and the remainder have been boring. He has access to student evaluations of professors and finds that 60% of his enjoyable courses and 25% of his boring courses have been taught by professors who had previously received strong positive evaluations from their students. Next semester the student decides to take three courses, all from professors who have received strongly positive student evaluations. Assume that his reactions to the three courses are independent of one another.

(a) What is the probability that he will find all three courses enjoyable?

(b) What is the probability that he will find at least one of the courses enjoyable?

REVIEW EXERCISES

48. Suppose that you have an intelligent friend who has not studied probability. How would you explain to your friend the distinction between mutually exclusive events and independent events? Illustrate your answer with suitable examples.

49. State, with reasons, whether each of the following statements is true or false:

(a) The complement of the union of two events is the intersection of their complements.

(b) The sum of the probabilities of collectively exhaustive events must equal 1.

(c) The number of combinations of x objects chosen from n is equal to the number of combinations of $(n - x)$ objects chosen from n, where $1 \le x \le (n - 1)$.

(d) If A and B are two events, the probability of A given B is the same as the probability of B given A if the probability of A is the same as the probability of B.

(e) If an event and its complement are equally likely to occur, the probability of that event must .5.

(f) If A and B are independent, then $\overline{A}$ and $\overline{B}$ must be independent.

(g) If A and B are mutually exclusive, then $\overline{A}$ and $\overline{B}$ must be mutually exclusive.

50. Explain carefully the meaning of conditional probability. Why is this concept important in discussing the chance of an event's occurrence?

51. "Bayes' theorem is important, as it provides a rule for moving from a prior probability to a posterior probability." Elaborate on this statement so that it would be well understood by a fellow student who has not yet studied probability.

52. State, with reasons, whether each of the following statements is true or false:

(a) The probability of the union of two events cannot be less than the probability of their intersection.

(b) The probability of the union of two events cannot be more than the sum of their individual probabilities.

(c) The probability of the intersection of two events cannot be greater than either of their individual probabilities.

(d) An event and its complement are mutually exclusive.

(e) The individual probabilities of a pair of events cannot sum to more than 1.

(f) If a pair of events are mutually exclusive, they must also be collectively exhaustive.

(g) If a pair of events are collectively exhaustive, they must also be mutually exclusive.

53. Distinguish among joint probability, marginal probability, and conditional probability. Provide examples to make the distinctions clear.

54. State, giving reasons, whether each of the following claims is true or false:

(a) The conditional probability of A given B must be at least as large as the probability of A.

(b) An event must be independent of its complement.

(c) The probability of A given B must be at least as large as the probability of the intersection of A and B.

(d) The probability of the intersection of two events cannot exceed the product of their individual probabilities.

(e) The posterior probability of any event must be at least as large as its prior probability.

55. Show that the probability of the union of the events A and B can be written

$$P(A \cup B) = P(A) + P(B)[1 - P(A \mid B)]$$

56. An insurance company estimated that 30% of all automobile accidents were partly caused by weather conditions, and that 20% of all automobile accidents involved bodily injury. Further, of those accidents that involved bodily injury, 40% were partly caused by weather conditions.

(a) What is the probability that a randomly chosen accident both was partly caused by weather conditions and involved bodily injury?

(b) Are the events "partly caused by weather conditions" and "involved bodily injury" independent?

(c) If a randomly chosen accident was partly caused by weather conditions, what is the probability that it involved bodily injury?

(d) What is the probability that a randomly chosen accident both was not partly caused by weather conditions and did not involve bodily injury?

57. A company places a rush order for wire of two thicknesses. Consignments of each thickness are to be sent immediately when they are available. Previous experience suggests that the probability is .8 that at least one of these consignments will arrive within a week. It is also estimated that if the thinner wire arrives within a week, the probability is .4 that the thicker wire will also arrive within a week. Further, it is estimated that if the thicker wire arrives within a week, the probability is .6 that the thinner wire will also arrive within a week.

(a) What is the probability that the thicker wire will arrive within a week?

(b) What is the probability that the thinner wire will arrive within a week?

(c) What is the probability that both consignments will arrive within a week?

58. Based on a survey of students on a large campus, it was estimated that 35% of the students drink at least once a week in campus bars, and that 40% of all students have grade-point averages of B or better. Further, of those who drink at least once a week in campus bars, 30% have a B average or better.

(a) What is the probability that a randomly chosen student both drinks at least once a week in campus bars and has a B average or better?

(b) What is the probability that a randomly chosen student, who has a B average or better, drinks at least once a week in campus bars?

(c) What is the probability that a randomly chosen student has at least one of the characteristics "drinks at least once a week in campus bars" or "B average or better"?

(d) What is the probability that a randomly chosen student, who does not have a B average or better, does not drink at least once a week in campus bars?

(e) Are the events "drinks at least once a week in campus bars" and "B average or better" independent?

(f) Are the events "drinks at least once a week in campus bars" and "B average or better" mutually exclusive?

(g) Are the events "drinks at least once a week in campus bars" and "B average or better" collectively exhaustive?

59. In a campus restaurant, it was found that 35% of all customers order hot meals and that 50% of all customers are students. Further, 25% of all customers who are students order hot meals.

(a) What is the probability that a randomly chosen customer is both a student and orders a hot meal?

(b) If a randomly chosen customer orders a hot meal, what is the probability that he or she is a student?

(c) What is the probability that a randomly chosen customer both does not order a hot meal and is not a student?

(d) Are the events "customer orders a hot meal" and "customer is a student" independent?

(e) Are the events "customer orders a hot meal" and "customer is a student" mutually exclusive?

(f) Are the events "customer orders a hot meal" and "customer is a student" collectively exhaustive?

60. It is known that 20% of all farms in a state exceed 160 acres, and that 60% of all farms in that state are owned by persons over 50 years old. Of all farms in the state exceeding 160 acres, 55% are owned by persons over 50 years old.

(a) What is the probability that a randomly chosen farm in this state both exceeds 160 acres and is owned by a person over 50 years old?

(b) What is the probability that a farm in this state is either bigger than 160 acres or is owned by a person over 50 years old (or both)?

(c) What is the probability that a farm in this state, owned by a person over 50 years old, exceeds 160 acres?

(d) Are size of farm and age of owners in this state statistically independent?

61. In a large corporation, 80% of the employees are men and 20% are women. The highest levels of education obtained by the employees are graduate training for 10% of the men, undergraduate training for 30% of the men, and high school training for 60% of the men. The highest levels of education obtained are also graduate training for 15% of the women, undergraduate training for 40% of the women, and high school training for 45% of the women.

(a) What is the probability that a randomly chosen employee will be a man with only a high school education?

(b) What is the probability that a randomly chosen employee will have graduate training?

(c) What is the probability that a randomly chosen employee who has graduate training is a man?

(d) Are sex and level of education of employees in this corporation statistically independent?

(e) What is the probability that a randomly chosen employee who has not had graduate training is a woman?

62. A large corporation organized a ballot for all its workers on a new bonus plan. It was found that 65% of all night-shift workers favored the plan and that 40% of all women workers favored the plan. Also, 50% of all employees are night-shift workers, and 30% of all employees are women. Finally, 20% of the night-shift workers are women.

(a) What is the probability that a randomly chosen employee is a woman in favor of the plan?

(b) What is the probability that a randomly chosen employee is either a woman or a night-shift worker (or both)?

(c) Is employee sex independent of whether the night-shift is worked?

(d) What is the probability that a woman employee is a night-shift worker?

(e) If 50% of all male employees favor the plan, what is the probability that a randomly chosen employee both does not work the night-shift and does not favor the plan?

63. A jury of twelve members is to be selected from a panel consisting of eight men and eight women.

(a) How many different jury selections are possible?

(b) If the choice is made randomly, what is the probability that a majority of the jury members will be men?

64. A consignment of twelve electronic components contains one component that is faulty. Two components are chosen randomly from this consignment for testing.

(a) How many different combinations of two components could be chosen?

(b) What is the probability that the faulty component will be one of the two components chosen for testing?

65. Of 100 patients with a certain disease, ten were chosen at random to undergo a drug treatment that increases the cure rate from 50% for those not given the treatment to 75% for those given the drug treatment.

(a) What is the probability that a randomly chosen patient both was cured and was given the drug treatment?

(b) What is the probability that a patient who was cured had been given the drug treatment?

(c) What is the probability that a specific group of ten patients was chosen to undergo the drug treatment? (Leave your answer in terms of factorials.)

66. Subscriptions to *American History Illustrated* are classified as gift, previous renewal, direct mail, or subscription service.[7] In January 1979, 8% of expiring subscriptions were gift; 41%, previous renewal; 6%, direct mail; and 45% subscription service. The percentages of renewals in these four categories were 81%, 79%, 60%, and 21%, respectively. In February 1979, 10% of expiring subscriptions were gift; 57%, previous renewal; 24%, direct mail; and 9% subscription service. The percentages of renewals were 80%, 76%, 51%, and 14%, respectively.

(a) Find the probability that a randomly chosen subscription expiring in January 1979 was renewed.

(b) Find the probability that a randomly chosen subscription expiring in February 1979 was renewed.

(c) Verify that the probability in part (b) is higher than that in part (a). Do you believe that the editors of *American History Illustrated* should view the change from January to February as a positive or negative development?

67. In a large city, 8% of the inhabitants have contracted a particular disease. A test for this disease is positive in 80% of people who have the disease and is negative in 80% of people who do not have the disease. What is the probability that a person for whom the test result is positive has the disease?

68. A life insurance salesman finds that of all the sales he makes, 70% are to people who already own policies. He also finds that of all contacts for which no sale is made, 50% already own life insurance policies. Furthermore, 40% of all contacts result in sales. What is the probability that a sale will be made to a contact who already owns a policy?

---

[7] This example is adapted from C. H. Wagner, "Simpson's paradox in real life," *American Statistician, 36* (1982), 46–48.

69. A professor finds that she awards a final grade of A to 20% of the students. Of those who obtain a final grade of A, 70% obtained an A in the midterm examination. Also, 10% of students who failed to obtain a final grade of A earned an A in the midterm exam. What is the probability that a student with an A on the midterm examination will obtain a final grade of A?

70. The accompanying table shows, for 1,000 forecasts of earnings per share made by financial analysts, the numbers of forecasts and outcomes in particular categories (compared with the previous year).

OUTCOME	FORECAST		
	IMPROVEMENT	ABOUT THE SAME	WORSE
Improvement	210	82	66
About the same	106	153	75
Worse	75	84	149

(a) Find the probability that if the forecast is for a worse performance in earnings, this outcome will result.

(b) If the forecast is for an improvement in earnings, find the probability that this outcome fails to result.

71. A dean has found that 62% of entering freshmen and 78% of junior college transfers eventually graduate. Of all entering students, 73% are freshmen, and the remainder are junior college transfers.

(a) What is the probability that a randomly chosen entering student is a freshman who will eventually graduate?

(b) Find the probability that a randomly chosen entering student will eventually graduate.

(c) What is the probability that a randomly chosen entering student is either a freshman or will eventually graduate, or both?

(d) Are the events "Eventually graduates" and "Enters as junior college transfer" statistically independent?

72. A market research group specializes in providing assessments of the prospects of sites for new clothing stores in shopping centers. The group assesses prospects as either good, fair, or poor. The records of requests for assessments made to this group were examined, and it was found that for all stores that turned out to be successful, the assessment was good for 70%, fair for 20%, and poor for 10%. For all stores that turned out to be unsuccessful, the assessment was good for 20%, fair for 30%, and poor for 50%. It is also known that 60% of new clothing stores are successful and 40% are unsuccessful.

(a) For a randomly chosen store, what is the probability that prospects will be assessed as good?

(b) If prospects for a store are assessed as good, what is the probability that it will be successful?

(c) Are the events "Prospects assessed as good" and "Store is successful" statistically independent?

(d) Suppose that five stores are chosen at random. What is the probability that at least one of them will be successful?

73. A restaurant manager classifies customers as well dressed, moderately dressed, or poorly dressed, and finds 50%, 40%, and 10% respectively of all customers fall into these categories. The manager found that wine was ordered by 70% of the well dressed, by 50% of the moderately dressed, and by 30% of the poorly dressed customers.

(a) What is the probability that a randomly chosen customer orders wine?

(b) If wine is ordered, what is the probability that the person ordering was well dressed?

(c) If wine is ordered, what is the probability that the person ordering was not well dressed?

74. A record store owner assesses customers entering the store as high school age, college age, or older, and finds 30%, 50%, and 20% respectively of all customers fall into these categories. The owner also found that purchases were made by 20% of high school age customers, by 60% of college age customers, and by 80% of older customers.

(a) What is the probability that a randomly chosen customer entering the store will make a purchase?

(b) If a randomly chosen customer makes a purchase, what is the probability that this customer is high school age?

(c) If a randomly chosen customer makes a purchase, what is the probability that this customer is not high school age?

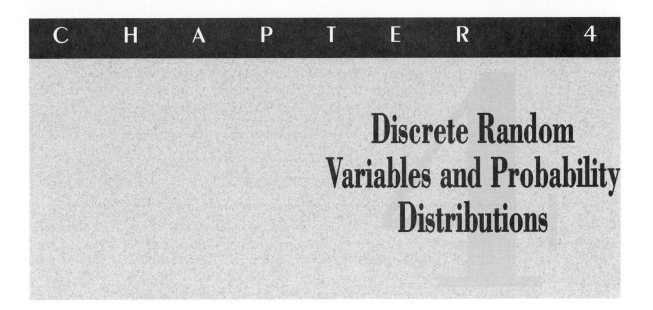

CHAPTER 4

Discrete Random Variables and Probability Distributions

4.1 RANDOM VARIABLES

Suppose that a random experiment is to be carried out and that numerical values can be attached to the possible outcomes. In experiments such as throwing a die or measuring a family's income, the outcomes are naturally in numerical form. When this is not the case, it may still be useful and meaningful to attach numbers to the outcomes, particularly in experiments where only two outcomes are possible. For example, a component produced by an industrial process might be classified as "defective" or "not defective." We could attach the value 1 to the former possibility and 0 to the latter.

Before the random experiment is carried out, there will be uncertainty as to the outcome, and, as we have seen in Chapter 3, this uncertainty can be quantified in terms of probability statements. When the outcomes are numerical values, these probabilities can be conveniently summarized through the notion of a **random variable.**

Definition

A **random variable** is a variable that takes on numerical values determined by the outcome of a random experiment.

It is important to distinguish between a random variable and the possible values it can take. Notationally, we do this by using capital letters, such as X, to denote the random variable and the corresponding lowercase x to denote a possible value. For example, prior to the result's being observed in the throw of a die, the random variable X can be used to denote the outcome. This random variable can take the specific values $x = 1, x = 2, \ldots, x = 6$, each with probability ⅙.

A further important distinction is between **discrete** and **continuous** random variables. The die throw provides an example of the former; there are only six possible outcomes, and a probability can be attached to each.

Definition

A random variable is **discrete** if it can take on no more than a countable number of values.

It follows from the definition that any random variable that can take on only a finite number of values is discrete. For example, the number of heads resulting from ten throws of a coin is a discrete random variable. Even if the number of possible outcomes is infinite but countable, the random variable is discrete. An example is the number of throws of a coin needed before a head first appears. The possible outcomes are $1, 2, 3, \ldots$, and a probability can be attached to each. (A discrete random variable that can take a countably infinite number of values will be discussed in Section 4.7.) Here are some other examples of discrete random variables:

1. The number of defective items in a sample of twenty items from a large shipment
2. The number of customers arriving at a check-out counter in an hour
3. The number of errors detected in a corporation's accounts
4. The number of claims on a medical insurance policy in a particular year

By contrast, suppose that we are interested in the day's high temperature. The random variable, temperature, is measured on a continuum and so is said to be **continuous.**

Definition

A random variable is **continuous** if it can take any value in an interval.

For continuous random variables, one cannot attach probabilities to specific values. For example, the probability that today's high temperature will be precisely 77.236° Fahrenheit is 0. It will certainly not be *precisely* that figure. However, probabilities may be determined for ranges, so that one could attach a probability to the event "Today's high temperature will be between 75 and 80°." Here are some other examples of continuous random variables:

1. The income in a year for a family
2. The amount of oil imported into the United States in a particular month
3. The change in the price of a share of IBM common stock in a month
4. The time that elapses between the installation of a new component and its failure
5. The percentage of impurity in a batch of chemicals

The distinction that has been made between discrete and continuous random variables may appear rather artificial. After all, rarely is anything actually measured on a continuum. For example, the day's high temperature cannot be reported more precisely than the measuring instrument allows. Moreover, a family's income in a year will be some integer number of cents. However, when measurements can be made on such a fine scale that differences between adjacent values are of no significance, it is convenient to act as if they had truly been made on a continuum. For example, the difference between a family income of \$35,276.21 and \$35,276.22 is of very little significance, and the attachment of probabilities to each would be a tedious and worthless exercise.

For practical purposes, we will treat as discrete all random variables for which probability statements about the individual possible outcomes have worthwhile meaning; all other random variables will be regarded as continuous. Because of this distinction, it is convenient to treat these two classes separately. Discrete random variables are discussed in this chapter; continuous random variables will be treated in Chapter 5.

4.2 PROBABILITY DISTRIBUTIONS FOR DISCRETE RANDOM VARIABLES

Suppose that X is a discrete random variable and that x is one of its possible values. The probability that the random variable X takes the specific value x is denoted $P(X = x)$. The **probability distribution** of a random variable is a representation of the probabilities for all the possible outcomes. This representation might be algebraic, graphical, or tabular. For discrete random variables, one simple procedure is to list the probabilities of all possible outcomes, according to the values of x.

Definition

The **probability function,** $P_X(x)$, of a discrete random variable X expresses the probability that X takes the value x, as a function of x. That is

$$P_X(x) = P(X = x)$$

where the function is evaluated at all possible values of x.

Because the probability function takes nonzero values only at discrete points x, it is sometimes called a **probability mass function.** Once the probabilities have been calculated, the function can easily be graphed.

EXAMPLE 4.1

A die is rolled. Let the random variable X denote the number resulting. Since $P(X = 1) = P(X = 2) = \cdots = P(X = 6) = \frac{1}{6}$, the probability function is

$$P_X(x) = P(X = x) = \frac{1}{6} \qquad \text{for } x = 1, 2, 3, \ldots, 6$$

The function takes the value 0 for all other values of x, which cannot occur. The probability function is graphed in Figure 4.1, where spikes of height ⅙ represent probability masses at the points $x = 1, x = 2, \ldots, x = 6$.

EXAMPLE 4.2

A roulette wheel contains thirty-eight slots, numbered 00, 0, 1, 2, . . . , 36. One possible bet is on the event "Odd number results," so that a player making this bet would win in eighteen of the thirty-eight possible outcomes. Since there are eighteen odd numbers

$$P(\text{Odd number results}) = \frac{18}{38} = \frac{9}{19}$$

If a player makes a bet in which he or she loses \$1 if an odd number does not result and wins \$1 if it does, we can denote the player's gain (in dollars) by the random variable X, where

$$X = \begin{cases} -1 & \text{if an odd number does not result} \\ 1 & \text{if an odd number results} \end{cases}$$

Then $P(X = 1) = 9/19$, and hence $P(X = -1) = 10/19$; so the probability function of the random variable X is

$$P_X(x) = \begin{cases} \dfrac{10}{19} & \text{for } x = -1 \\ \dfrac{9}{19} & \text{for } x = 1 \end{cases}$$

This function is graphed in Figure 4.2.

The probability function of a discrete random variable must satisfy the two conditions given in the box.

Properties of Probability Functions of Discrete Random Variables

Let X be a discrete random variable with probability function $P_X(x)$. Then

(i) $P_X(x) \geq 0$ for any value x

(ii) The individual probabilities sum to 1; that is

$$\sum_x P_X(x) = 1$$

where the notation indicates summation over all possible values x.

Property (i) merely states that probabilities cannot be negative. Property (ii) follows from the fact that the events "$X = x$," for all possible values x, are mutually exclusive and collectively exhaustive. The probabilities for these events must therefore sum to 1. That this is in fact so for Examples 4.1 and 4.2 can be verified directly. It is simply a way of saying that when a random experiment is to be carried out, something must happen.

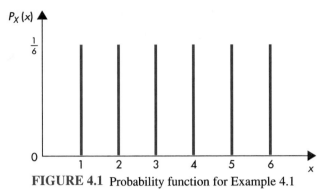

FIGURE 4.1 Probability function for Example 4.1

Another representation of discrete probability distributions is also useful.

Definition

The **cumulative probability function,** $F_X(x_0)$, of a random variable X expresses the probability that X does not exceed the value x_0, as a function of x_0. That is

$$F_X(x_0) = P(X \leq x_0)$$

where the function is evaluated at all values x_0.

For discrete random variables, the cumulative probability function is sometimes called the **cumulative mass function.** It can be seen from the definition that, as x_0 increases, the cumulative probability function will change values only at those points x_0 that can be taken by the random variable with positive probability. Its evaluation at these points can be carried out in terms of the probability function.

FIGURE 4.2 Probability function for Example 4.2

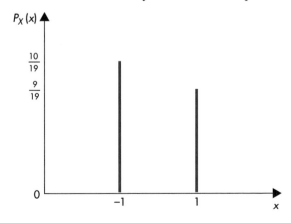

> **Relationship Between Probability Function and Cumulative Probability Function**
>
> Let X be a random variable with probability function $P_X(x)$ and cumulative probability function $F_X(x_0)$. Then
>
> $$F_X(x_0) = \sum_{x \le x_0} P_X(x)$$
>
> where the notation implies that summation is over all possible values x that are less than or equal to x_0.

The result in the box follows since the event "$X \le x_0$" is the union of the mutually exclusive events "$X = x$" for every x less than or equal to x_0. The probability of the union is then the sum of these individual event probabilities.

EXAMPLE 4.3

In the die-throwing experiment in Example 4.1, where the random variable X denotes the number observed, we have the probability function

$$P_X(x) = \frac{1}{6} \qquad \text{for } x = 1, 2, \ldots, 6$$

Now, if x_0 is some number less than 1, X cannot be less than x_0, so

$$F_X(x_0) = P(X \le x_0) = 0 \qquad \text{for } x_0 < 1$$

If x_0 is greater than or equal to 1 but strictly less than 2, the only way for X to be less than or equal to x_0 is if $X = 1$. Hence

$$F_X(x_0) = P(X \le x_0) = P_X(1) = \frac{1}{6} \qquad \text{for } 1 \le x_0 < 2$$

If x_0 is greater than or equal to 2 but strictly less than 3, X is less than or equal to x_0 if and only if either $X = 1$ or $X = 2$, so

$$F_X(x_0) = P(X \le x_0) = P_X(1) + P_X(2) = \frac{1}{3} \qquad \text{for } 2 \le x_0 < 3$$

Continuing in this way, we see that if x_0 is any number greater than or equal to 6, X will certainly be less than x_0, so

$$F_X(x_0) = P(X \le x_0) = \sum_{x=1}^{6} P_X(x) = 1 \qquad \text{for } x_0 \ge 6$$

The cumulative probability function may then be written as

$$F_X(x_0) = \begin{cases} 0 & \text{if } x_0 < 1 \\ \dfrac{j}{6} & \text{if } j \le x_0 < j + 1 \qquad (j = 1, 2, \ldots, 5) \\ 1 & \text{if } x_0 \ge 6 \end{cases}$$

This function is plotted in Figure 4.3, from which it can be seen that the cumulative probability function increases in steps until the value 1 is attained.

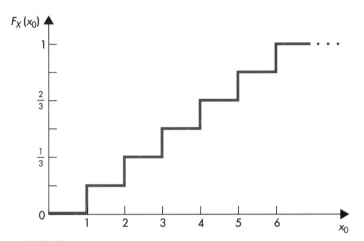

FIGURE 4.3 Cumulative probability function for Example 4.3

For discrete random variables, the cumulative probability function is always in the form of a step function beginning at 0 and ending at 1. These properties are expressed formally in the accompanying box.

Properties of Cumulative Probability Functions for Discrete Random Variables

Let X be a discrete random variable with cumulative probability function $F_X(x_0)$. Then

   (i) $0 \leq F_X(x_0) \leq 1$ for every number x_0
  (ii) If x_0 and x_1 are two numbers with $x_0 < x_1$, then

$$F_X(x_0) \leq F_X(x_1)$$

Property (i) simply states that a probability cannot be less than 0 or greater than 1. Property (ii) implies that the probability that a random variable does not exceed some number cannot be more than the probability that it does not exceed any larger number.

4.3 EXPECTATIONS FOR DISCRETE RANDOM VARIABLES

The probability distribution contains all the information about the probability properties of a random variable, and graphical inspection of this distribution can certainly be valuable. However, it is frequently desirable to have some numerical summary measures of the distribution's characteristics.

In order to obtain a measure of the center of a probability distribution, we introduce here the notion of the **expectation** of a random variable. In our discussion of sets of numerical observations in Chapter 2, we often found it convenient to compute the mean as a measure of central location. The **expected value** is the corresponding measure of central location for a random variable. Before introducing its definition, it is convenient to dismiss a superficially attractive alternative measure.

Consider the following example: A review of textbooks in a segment of the business area found that 81% of all pages of text were error-free, 17% of all pages contained one error, and the remaining 2% contained two errors. If we let the random variable X denote the number of errors on a page chosen at random from one of these books, we see that its possible values are 0, 1, and 2, with probability function

$$P_X(0) = .81 \qquad P_X(1) = .17 \qquad P_X(2) = .02$$

Now, one possible measure of the central location of a random variable might be the simple average of the values it can take. In our example, the possible numbers of errors on a page are 0, 1, and 2. Their average is, then, one error. However, a moment's reflection will convince the reader that this is an absurd measure of central location. In calculating this average, we have paid no attention to the fact that 81% of all pages contain no errors, while only 2% contain two errors. In order to obtain a sensible measure of central location, it is desirable to *weight* the various possible outcomes by the probabilities of their occurrence.

Definition

The **expected value,** $E(X)$, of a discrete random variable X is defined as

$$E(X) = \sum_x xP_X(x)$$

where the notation indicates that summation extends over all possible values x.
The expected value of a random variable is called its **mean** and is denoted μ_X.

The definition of expected value can be motivated in terms of long-run relative frequencies. Suppose that a random experiment is repeated N times and that the event "$X = x$" occurs in N_x of these trials. The average of the values taken by the random variable over all N trials will then be the sum of xN_x/N over all possible values x. Now, as the number of replications N becomes infinitely large, the ratio N_x/N tends to the probability of the occurrence of the event "$X = x$"—that is, to $P_X(x)$. Hence, the quantity xN_x/N tends to $xP_X(x)$. Thus, the expected value can be viewed as the long-run average value that a random variable would take over a large number of trials. Recall that in Chapter 2, we used the word *mean* for the average of a set of numerical observations. The foregoing justifies the use of the same term for the expectation of a random variable.

EXAMPLE 4.4

The probability function for the number of errors, X, on pages from business textbooks is

$$P_X(0) = .81 \qquad P_X(1) = .17 \qquad P_X(2) = .02$$

Find the mean number of errors per page.
We have

$$\mu_X = E(X) = \sum_x xP_X(x)$$

$$= (0)(.81) + (1)(.17) + (2)(.02) = .21$$

We thus conclude that over a large number of pages, we would expect to find an average of .21 error per page. Figure 4.4 shows the probability function, with the location of the mean indicated.

The notion of expectation is not restricted to the random variable itself but can be applied to any function of the random variable. For example, a contractor may be uncertain of the time required to complete a contract. This uncertainty could be represented by a random variable whose possible values are the numbers of days elapsing from the beginning to the completion of work on the contract. However, the contractor's primary concern is not with the time taken but rather with the cost of fulfilling the contract. This cost will be a function of the time taken, so in determining expected cost, it is necessary to find the expectation of a function of the random variable "Time to completion."

Definition

Let X be a discrete random variable with probability function $P_X(x)$, and let $g(X)$ be some function of X. Then the **expected value,** $E[g(X)]$, of that function is defined as

$$E[g(X)] = \sum_x g(x)P_X(x)$$

The definition of $E[g(X)]$ can be motivated in precisely the same way as the previous one. That is, the expectation can be thought of as the average value that $g(X)$ would take over a very large number of repeated trials.

In Chapter 2, one useful measure of the spread of a set of numerical observations was found to be the *variance,* the average of the squared discrepancies of the observations from their mean. In the same way, this notion can be used to measure dispersion in the probability distribution of a random variable. In defining the vari-

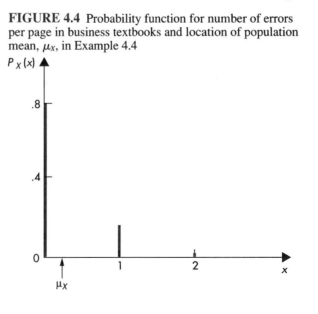

FIGURE 4.4 Probability function for number of errors per page in business textbooks and location of population mean, μ_X, in Example 4.4

ance of a random variable, a weighted average of the squares of its possible discrepancies about the mean is formed; the weight associated with $(x - \mu_x)^2$ is the probability that the random variable takes the value x. The variance can then be viewed as the average value that will be taken by the function $(X - \mu_x)^2$ over a very large number of repeated trials.

Definition

Let X be a discrete random variable. The expectation of the squared discrepancy about the mean $(X - \mu_x)^2$ is called the **variance,** denoted σ_x^2 and given by

$$\sigma_x^2 = E[(X - \mu_x)^2] = \sum_x (x - \mu_x)^2 P_x(x)$$

The **standard deviation,** σ_X, is the positive square root of the variance.

Taking the square root of the variance to obtain the standard deviation yields a quantity in the original units of measurement, as noted in Chapter 2.

When the probability function is known, the mean and variance of a random variable can be computed through direct application of the definitions.

In some practical applications, an alternative but equivalent formula for the variance is preferable for computational purposes. That the alternative formula is indeed equivalent to the formula given in the definition can be verified algebraically.[1] It can be conveniently remembered as the expectation of the square less the square of the expectation of X.

Variance of a Discrete Random Variable (Alternative Formula)

The variance of a discrete random variable X can be expressed as

$$\sigma_x^2 = E(X^2) - \mu_x^2$$
$$= \sum_x x^2 P_x(x) - \mu_x^2$$

---

[1] Begin with the original definition of variance:

$$\sigma_x^2 = \sum_x (x - \mu_x)^2 P_x(x) = \sum_x (x^2 - 2\mu_x x + \mu_x^2) P_x(x)$$

$$= \sum_x x^2 P_x(x) - 2\mu_x \sum_x x P_x(x) + \mu_x^2 \sum_x P_x(x)$$

But we have seen that $\sum_x x P_x(x) = \mu_x$ and $\sum_x P_x(x) = 1$, so

$$\sigma_x^2 = \sum_x x^2 P_x(x) - 2\mu_x^2 + \mu_x^2$$

$$= \sum_x x^2 P_x(x) - \mu_x^2$$

**EXAMPLE
4.5**

Suppose that the probability function for the number of errors, X, on pages from business textbooks is

$$P_X(0) = .81 \qquad P_X(1) = .17 \qquad P_X(2) = .02$$

In Example 4.4, we found the mean number of errors per page to be $\mu_X = .21$.

To obtain the variance, we first find the expectation of the squares; that is

$$E(X^2) = \sum_x x^2 P_X(x) = (0)^2(.81) + (1)^2(.17) + (2)^2(.02) = .25$$

The variance is then

$$\sigma_X^2 = E(X^2) - \mu_X^2 = .25 - (.21)^2 = .2059$$

Finally, the standard deviation of the number of errors per page is

$$\sigma_X = \sqrt{\sigma_X^2} = \sqrt{.2059} = .45$$

The concept of variance can be very useful in comparing the dispersions of probability distributions. Consider, for example, viewing as a random variable the return over a year on an investment. Two investments may have the same expected returns but will still differ in an important way if the variances of these returns are substantially different. A higher variance indicates that returns substantially different from the mean are more likely than if the variance of returns is small. In this context, then, variance of return can be associated with the concept of the riskiness of an investment—the higher the variance, the greater the risk.

We have defined the expectation of a function of a random variable X. The linear function $a + bX$, where a and b are constant fixed numbers, is of particular interest. Let X be a random variable that takes the value x with probability $P_X(x)$, and consider a new random variable Z, defined by

$$Z = a + bX$$

When the random variable X takes the specific value x, Z must take the value $a + bx$. We frequently require the mean and variance of such variables. These quantities are given in the box.

Let X be a random variable with mean μ_X and variance σ_X^2, and let a and b be any constant fixed numbers. Define the random variable $Z = a + bX$. Then, the mean and variance of Z are

$$\mu_Z = E(a + bX) = a + b\mu_X \qquad (4.3.1)$$

and

$$\sigma_Z^2 = \text{Var}(a + bX) = b^2\sigma_X^2 \qquad (4.3.2)$$

so that the standard deviation of Z is

$$\sigma_Z = |b|\sigma_X$$

To verify these results, note that it follows from the definition of expectation that if Z takes values $a + bx$ with probabilities $P_X(x)$, its mean is

$$E(Z) = \mu_Z = \sum_x (a + bx)P_X(x)$$

$$= a \sum_x P_X(x) + b \sum_x xP_X(x)$$

Then, since the first summation on the right-hand side of this equation is 1 [by property (ii) of Section 4.2] and the second summation is, by definition, the mean of X, we have

$$E(Z) = a + b\mu_X$$

as in Eq. (4.3.1). Further, the variance of Z is, by definition

$$\sigma_Z^2 = E[(Z - \mu_Z)^2] = \sum_x [(a + bx) - \mu_Z]^2 P_X(x)$$

Substituting $a + b\mu_X$ for μ_Z then gives

$$\sigma_Z^2 = \sum_x (bx - b\mu_X)^2 P_X(x) = b^2 \sum_x (x - \mu_X)^2 P_X(x)$$

and, since the summation on the right-hand side of this equation is, by definition, the variance of X, the result (4.3.2) follows.

EXAMPLE 4.6

A contractor is interested in the total cost of a project on which he intends to bid. He estimates that materials will cost $25,000 and that his labor costs will be $900 per day. If the project takes X days to complete, the total labor costs will be $900X$ dollars, and the total cost of the project (in dollars) will be

$$C = 25,000 + 900X$$

The contractor forms subjective probability assessments of likely completion times for the project, as indicated in the table.

COMPLETION TIME X (DAYS)	10	11	12	13	14
PROBABILITY	.1	.3	.3	.2	.1

The mean and variance for completion time X can then be found directly as

$$\mu_X = E(X) = \sum_x xP_X(x)$$

$$= (10)(.1) + (11)(.3) + (12)(.3) + (13)(.2) + (14)(.1) = 11.9 \text{ days}$$

and

$$\sigma_X^2 = E[(X - \mu_X)^2] = \sum_x (x - \mu_X)^2 P_X(x)$$

$$= (10 - 11.9)^2(.1) + (11 - 11.9)^2(.3) + \cdots + (14 - 11.9)^2(.1) = 1.29$$

The mean and variance of total cost C can now be obtained using Eqs. (4.3.1) and (4.3.2). The expected cost is

$$\mu_C = E(25,000 + 900X) = 25,000 + 900\mu_X$$

$$= 25{,}000 + (900)(11.9) = \$35{,}710$$

and the variance is

$$\sigma_C^2 = \text{Var}(25{,}000 + 900X) = (900)^2\sigma_X^2$$

$$= (810{,}000)(1.29) = 1{,}044{,}900$$

so the standard deviation is

$$\sigma_C = \sqrt{\sigma_C^2} = \$1{,}022.20$$

The following special cases of results (4.3.1) and (4.3.2) are of interest:

(i) By setting $b = 0$ in these equations, it follows that for any constant a

$$E(a) = a \qquad \text{and} \qquad \text{Var}(a) = 0$$

Thus, if a random variable always takes the value a, it will have mean a and variance 0.

(ii) Setting $a = 0$ in these equations, we have, for any constant b

$$E(bX) = b\mu_X \qquad \text{and} \qquad \text{Var}(bX) = b^2\sigma_X^2$$

Thus, if a random variable is multiplied by any constant, the mean is multiplied by the same constant, and the variance is multiplied by the square of that constant.

(iii) Setting $a = -\mu_X/\sigma_X$ and $b = 1/\sigma_X$, we have

$$Z = a + bX = \frac{X - \mu_X}{\sigma_X}$$

so that

$$E\left(\frac{X - \mu_X}{\sigma_X}\right) = -\frac{\mu_X}{\sigma_X} + \frac{1}{\sigma_X}\mu_X = 0$$

and

$$\text{Var}\left(\frac{X - \mu_X}{\sigma_X}\right) = \frac{1}{\sigma_X^2}\sigma_X^2 = 1$$

Thus, subtracting from a random variable its mean and dividing by its standard deviation yields a random variable with mean 0 and standard deviation 1.

EXERCISES

1. An automobile dealer calculates the proportion of new cars sold that have been returned various numbers of times for the correction of defects during the warranty period. The results are shown in the table.

NUMBER OF RETURNS	0	1	2	3	4
PROPORTION	.28	.36	.23	.09	.04

(a) Draw the probability function.
(b) Calculate and draw the cumulative probability function.

2. A company specializes in installing and servicing central heating furnaces. In the pre-winter period, service calls may result in an order for a new furnace. The table shows estimated probabilities for numbers of new furnace orders generated in this way in the last two weeks of September.

NUMBER OF ORDERS	0	1	2	3	4	5
PROBABILITY	.10	.14	.26	.28	.15	.07

   (a) Draw the probability function.
   (b) Calculate and draw the cumulative probability function.
   (c) Find the probability that at least three orders will be generated in this period

3. A corporation produces packages of paper clips. The number of clips per package varies, as indicated in the accompanying table.

NUMBER OF CLIPS	47	48	49	50	51	52	53
PROPORTION OF PACKAGES	.04	.13	.21	.29	.20	.10	.03

   (a) Draw the probability function.
   (b) Calculate and draw the cumulative probability function.
   (c) What is the probability that a randomly chosen package will contain between 49 and 51 clips (inclusive)?
   (d) Two packages are chosen at random. What is the probability that at least one of them contains at least fifty clips?

4. A municipal bus company has started operations in a new subdivision. Records were kept on the numbers of riders from this subdivision on the early-morning service. The accompanying table shows proportions over all weekdays.

NUMBER OF RIDERS	0	1	2	3	4	5	6	7
PROPORTION	.02	.12	.23	.31	.19	.08	.03	.02

   (a) Draw the probability function.
   (b) Calculate and draw the cumulative probability function.
   (c) What is the probability that on a randomly chosen weekday, there will be at least four riders from the subdivision on this service?
   (d) Two weekdays are chosen at random. What is the probability that on both these days there will be fewer than three riders from the subdivision on this service?

5. (a) A very large shipment of parts contains 10% defectives. Two parts are chosen at random from the shipment and checked. Let the random variable X denote the number of defectives found. Find the probability function of this random variable.
   (b) A shipment of twenty parts contains two defectives. Two parts are chosen at random from the shipment and checked. Let the random variable Y denote the number of defectives found. Find the probability function of this random variable. Explain why your answer is different from that of part (a).

6. A student needs to know details of a class assignment that is due the next day, and decides to call fellow class members for this information. She believes that, for any particular call, the probability of obtaining the necessary information is .40. She decides to continue call-

ing class members until the information is obtained. Let the random variable X denote the number of calls needed to obtain the information.

(a) Find the probability function of X.

(b) Find the cumulative probability function of X.

(c) Find the probability that at least three calls are required.

7. Refer to Example 4.2. A player makes a bet in which he or she loses $1 if an odd number does not result and wins $1 if it does. Let the random variable X denote the player's gain (in dollars). Find the mean and standard deviation of X.

8. Refer to the information in Exercise 1. Find the mean and variance of the number of returns of an automobile for corrections for defects during the warranty period.

9. Refer to the information in Exercise 2. Find the mean and standard deviation of the number of orders for new furnaces in this period of two weeks.

10. Refer to the information in Exercise 3.

(a) Find the mean and standard deviation of the number of paper clips per package.

(b) The cost (in cents) of producing a package of clips is $16 + 2X$, where X is the number of clips in the package. The revenue from selling the package, however many clips it contains, is $1.50. If profit is defined as the difference between revenue and cost, find the mean and standard deviation of profit per package.

11. Refer to the information in Exercise 4.

(a) Find the mean and standard deviation of the number of riders from this subdivision on this service on a weekday.

(b) If the cost of a ride is 50 cents, find the mean and standard deviation of the total payments of riders from this subdivision on this service on a weekday.

12. Refer to the information in Exercise 5.

(a) Find the mean and variance of the random variable X in part (a).

(b) Find the mean and variance of the random variable Y in part (b).

13. A college basketball player, who sinks 75% of his free throws, comes to the line to shoot a "one and one" (if the first shot is successful, he is allowed a second shot, but no second shot is taken if the first is missed; one point is scored for each successful shot). Assume that the outcome of the second shot, if any, is independent of that of the first. Find the expected number of points resulting from the "one and one." Compare this with the expected number of points from a "two-shot foul," where a second shot is allowed irrespective of the outcome of the first.

14. A professor teaches a large class, and has scheduled an examination for 7:00 P.M. in a different classroom. She estimates the probabilities in the table for the number of students who will call her at home, in the hour before the examination, asking in which classroom it will be held.

NUMBER OF CALLS	0	1	2	3	4	5
PROBABILITY	.10	.15	.19	.26	.19	.11

Find the mean and standard deviation of the number of calls.

15. Students in a large accounting class were asked to rate the course on a scale from 1 (poor) to 5 (excellent). The accompanying table shows proportions of students rating the course in each category.

RATING	1	2	3	4	5
PROPORTION	.07	.19	.28	.30	.16

Find the mean and standard deviation of the ratings.

16. A store owner stocks an out-of-town newspaper, which is sometimes requested by a small number of customers. Each copy of this newspaper costs him 70 cents, and he sells them for 90 cents each. Any copies left over at the end of the day have no value and are destroyed. Any requests for copies that cannot be met because stocks have been exhausted are considered by the store owner as a loss of 5 cents in goodwill. The probability distribution of the number of requests for the newspaper in a day is shown in the accompanying table. If the store owner defines total daily profit as total revenue from newspaper sales, less total cost of newspapers ordered, less goodwill loss from unsatisfied demand, how many copies per day should he order to maximize expected profit?

NUMBER OF REQUESTS	0	1	2	3	4	5
PROBABILITY	.12	.16	.18	.32	.14	.08

17. A factory manager is considering whether to replace a temperamental machine. A review of past records indicates the following probability distribution for the number of breakdowns of this machine in a week.

NUMBER OF BREAKDOWNS	0	1	2	3	4
PROBABILITY	.10	.26	.42	.16	.06

   (a) Find the mean and standard deviation of the number of weekly breakdowns.
   (b) It is estimated that each breakdown costs the company $1,500 in lost output. Find the mean and standard deviation of the weekly cost to the company from breakdown of this machine.

18. An investor is considering three strategies for a $1,000 investment. The probable returns are estimated as follows:

STRATEGY 1 □ A profit of $10,000 with probability .15 and a loss of $1,000 with probability .85

STRATEGY 2 □ A profit of $1,000 with probability .50, a profit of $500 with probability .30, and a loss of $500 with probability .20

STRATEGY 3 □ A certain profit of $400

Which strategy has the highest expected profit? Would you necessarily advise the investor to adopt this strategy?

4.4 JOINTLY DISTRIBUTED DISCRETE RANDOM VARIABLES

In Section 3.7, we discussed joint probabilities. We now consider the case where we wish to examine two or more, possibly related, discrete random variables. As for a single random variable, the probabilities for all possible outcomes can be summarized in a probability function, where we now need to define the probabilities that the random variables of interest simultaneously take specific values.

Definition

Let X and Y be a pair of discrete random variables. Their **joint probability function** expresses the probability that simultaneously X takes the specific value x and Y takes the value y, as a function of x and y. The notation used is $P_{X,Y}(x, y)$, so

$$P_{X,Y}(x, y) = P(X = x \cap Y = y)$$

More generally, if $X_1, X_2, \ldots, X_K$ are K discrete random variables, their joint probability function is

$$P_{X_1, X_2, \ldots, X_K}(x_1, x_2, \ldots, x_K) = P(X_1 = x_1 \cap X_2 = x_2 \cap \cdots \cap X_K = x_K)$$

To illustrate, consider a pair of random variables X and Y, measuring, respectively, a consumer's satisfaction with food stores in a particular town and the number of years residence in that town. Suppose that X can take values 1, 2, 3, or 4, ranging from low to high satisfaction levels, and that Y takes the value 1 if the consumer has lived in the town less than six years and 2 otherwise. The main body of Table 4.1 shows the eight joint probabilities for X and Y. These constitute the joint probability function for this pair of random variables.[2] Thus, for instance

$$P_{X,Y}(1, 1) = .04 \qquad \text{and} \qquad P_{X,Y}(1, 2) = .07$$

Hence, for example, the probability is .07 that a randomly chosen consumer both has satisfaction level 1 and has lived in the town more than six years.

When dealing with jointly distributed random variables, we are frequently interested in the probability functions for the individual random variables.

TABLE 4.1 Probabilities for consumer satisfaction (X) and time in residence (Y)

Y	X				
	1	2	3	4	TOTALS
1	.04	.14	.23	.07	.48
2	.07	.17	.23	.05	.52
Totals	.11	.31	.46	.12	1.00

Definition

Let X and Y be a pair of jointly distributed random variables. In this context the probability function of the random variable X is called its **marginal probability function** and is obtained by summing the joint probabilities over all possible values; that is,

$$P_X(x) = \sum_y P_{X,Y}(x, y)$$

---

[2] These probabilities are estimated from results reported in J. A. Miller, "Store satisfaction and aspiration theory," *Journal of Retailing, 52* (Fall 1976), 65–84.

Similarly, the marginal probability function of the random variable Y is

$$P_Y(y) = \sum_x P_{X,Y}(x, y)$$

More generally, if $X_1, X_2, \ldots, X_K$ are K jointly distributed discrete random variables, the marginal probability function of any one of them is obtained by summing the joint probabilities over all possible combinations of values of all the others.

The marginal probabilities for the random variables X and Y of Table 4.1 can be read from the row and column totals. For consumer satisfaction, the marginal probability function is

$$P_X(1) = .11 \qquad P_X(2) = .31 \qquad P_X(3) = .46 \qquad P_X(4) = .12$$

Thus, for instance, the probability is .11 that a randomly chosen consumer has satisfaction level 1. Similarly, for time in residence in the town

$$P_Y(1) = .48 \qquad P_Y(2) = .52$$

so the probability is .48 that a randomly chosen consumer has lived in the town less than six years.

We have already seen that the marginal probabilities must sum to 1; it follows that the joint probabilities necessarily sum to 1. Further, since any probability must be nonnegative, joint probability functions must have the properties given in the box.

Properties of Joint Probability Functions of Discrete Random Variables

Let X and Y be discrete random variables with joint probability function $P_{X,Y}(x, y)$. Then

(i) $P_{X,Y}(x, y) \geq 0$ for any pair of values x and y.
(ii) The sum of the joint probabilities $P_{X,Y}(x, y)$ over all possible pairs of values must be 1.

The conditional probability function of one random variable, given specified values of another, is the collection of conditional probabilities, which can be found in exactly the manner described in Section 3.7.

Definition

Let X and Y be a pair of jointly distributed discrete random variables. The **conditional probability function** of the random variable Y, given that the random variable X takes the value x, expresses the probability that Y takes the value y, as a function of y, when the value x is specified for X. This is denoted $P_{Y|X}(y|x)$, so by the definition of conditional probability

---

$$P_{Y|X}(y|x) = \frac{P_{X,Y}(x, y)}{P_X(x)}$$

Similarly, the conditional probability function of X, given $Y = y$, is

$$P_{X|Y}(x|y) = \frac{P_{X,Y}(x, y)}{P_Y(y)}$$

To illustrate, consider again the information in Table 4.1. The conditional probability that time in residence Y takes the value 1, given that consumer satisfaction X takes the value 2, is

$$P_{Y|X}(1|2) = P(Y = 1|X = 2) = \frac{P(X = 2 \cap Y = 1)}{P(X = 2)} = \frac{P_{X,Y}(2, 1)}{P_X(2)}$$

$$= \frac{.14}{.31} = .45$$

That is, the probability that a consumer will have resided less than six years in the town given that the satisfaction level is 2 is .45. The conditional probability function of Y given X is displayed in Table 4.2.

TABLE 4.2 Conditional probabilities for time in residence (Y) given consumer satisfaction (X)

Y	X			
	1	2	3	4
1	.36	.45	.50	.58
2	.64	.55	.50	.42

Similarly, we can find the conditional probability function for consumer satisfaction given time in residence. The probability that X takes the value 4, given that Y takes the value 2, is

$$P_{X|Y}(4|2) = P(X = 4|Y = 2) = \frac{P(X = 4 \cap Y = 2)}{P(Y = 2)} = \frac{P_{X,Y}(4, 2)}{P_Y(2)}$$

$$= \frac{.05}{.52} = .10$$

Therefore, the probability that a consumer will have the highest satisfaction level, given that he or she has been resident at least six years in the town, is .10. The conditional probability function of X given Y is shown in Table 4.3.

In Chapter 3, we discussed the idea of independence of events. This concept extends directly to random variables.

The random variables X and Y are said to be **independent** if and only if their joint probability function is the product of their marginal probability functions, that is, if and only if

$$P_{X,Y}(x, y) = P_X(x)P_Y(y)$$

for all possible pairs of values x and y.

More generally, the K random variables $X_1, X_2, \ldots, X_K$ are independent if and only if

$$P_{X_1,X_2,\ldots,X_K}(x_1, x_2, \ldots, x_K) = P_{X_1}(x_1)P_{X_2}(x_2) \cdots P_{X_K}(x_K)$$

From the definition of conditional probability functions, it follows that if the random variables X and Y are independent, then the conditional probability function of Y given X is the same as the marginal probability function of Y; that is

$$P_{Y|X}(y|x) = P_Y(y)$$

Similarly, it follows that

$$P_{X|Y}(x|y) = P_X(x)$$

For the example of Table 4.1, we have

$$P_{X,Y}(1, 1) = .04 \qquad P_X(1) = .11 \qquad P_Y(1) = .48$$

so

$$P_X(1)P_Y(1) = (.11)(.48) = .05$$

Since this differs from $P_{X,Y}(1, 1)$, the two random variables are not independent. It follows that there is some relationship between the time of residence in a town and the level of satisfaction with its food stores. This can be seen from Table 4.3, from which we find, for example, that the probability is .15 that a consumer who has lived less than six years in the town will have the highest satisfaction level. The corresponding probability is only .10 for consumers who have been residents more than six years.

As in the case of a single random variable, the joint probability distribution of a set of random variables can also be represented through their joint cumulative probability function.

TABLE 4.3 Conditional probabilities for consumer satisfaction (X) given time in residence (Y)

Y	X			
	1	2	3	4
1	.08	.29	.48	.15
2	.13	.33	.44	.10

Definition

The **joint cumulative probability function,** $F_{X,Y}(x_0, y_0)$, of a pair of discrete random variables X and Y expresses the probability that simultaneously X does not exceed the value x_0 and Y does not exceed the value y_0, as a function of x_0 and y_0. That is

$$F_{X,Y}(x_0, y_0) = P(X \leq x_0 \cap Y \leq y_0)$$

where the function is evaluated at all values x_0 and y_0. This can be written

$$F_{X,Y}(x_0, y_0) = \sum_{x \leq x_0} \sum_{y \leq y_0} P_{X,Y}(x, y)$$

where the notation implies that summation extends over all pairs of values of x and y that the random variables can take that simultaneously satisfy $x \leq x_0$ and $y \leq y_0$.

For the example of Table 4.1, consider $F_{X,Y}(2, 1)$—that is, the probability that both $X \leq 2$ and $Y \leq 1$. This is

$$F_{X,Y}(2, 1) = P_{X,Y}(1, 1) + P_{X,Y}(2, 1) = .04 + .14 = .18$$

Hence, the probability is .18 that a randomly chosen consumer will both have lived less than six years in the town and have satisfaction level at most 2.

In the preceding section, we defined the expectation of a function of a single random variable. This definition can be extended to functions of several random variables.

Definition

Let X and Y be a pair of discrete random variables with joint probability function $P_{X,Y}(x, y)$. The **expectation** of any function $g(X, Y)$ of these random variables is defined as

$$E[g(X, Y)] = \sum_{x} \sum_{y} g(x,y) P_{X,Y}(x, y)$$

More generally, if the K random variables $X_1, X_2, \ldots, X_K$ have joint probability function $P_{X_1, X_2, \ldots, X_K}(x_1, x_2, \ldots, x_K)$, then the expectation of the function $g(X_1, X_2, \ldots, X_K)$ is

$$E[g(X_1, X_2, \ldots, X_K)] = \sum_{x_1} \sum_{x_2} \cdots \sum_{x_K} g(x_1, \ldots, x_K) P_{X_1, \ldots, X_K}(x_1, \ldots, x_K)$$

An important application of the expectation of a function of random variables is to the **covariance.** Suppose that X and Y are a pair of random variables that are not statistically independent. We would like some measure of the nature and strength of the relationship between them. This is rather difficult to achieve, since they could conceivably be related in any number of ways. To simplify matters, we restrict attention to the possibility of linear association. For example, a high value of X might be associated on the average with a high value of Y and a low value of X with a low value of Y in such a way that, to a good approximation, a straight line might be drawn through the associated values when plotted on a graph. Suppose that the random variable X has mean μ_X and Y has mean μ_Y, and consider the product $(X - \mu_X)(Y - \mu_Y)$. If high values of X tend to be associated with high values of Y and low values of X with low values of Y, we would expect this product to be positive, and the stronger the association, the larger the expectation of $(X - \mu_X)(Y - \mu_Y)$. By contrast, if high values of X are associated with low values of Y and low X with high Y, the expected value for this product would be negative. An expectation of 0 for $(X - \mu_X)(Y - \mu_Y)$ would imply an absence of linear association between X and Y. Thus, as a measure of linear association in the population, we are led to an examination of the expected value of $(X - \mu_X)(Y - \mu_Y)$.[3]

Definition

Let X be a random variable with mean μ_X, and let Y be a random variable with mean μ_Y. The expected value of $(X - \mu_X)(Y - \mu_Y)$ is called the **covariance** between X and Y, denoted $\text{Cov}(X, Y)$. For discrete random variables

$$\text{Cov}(X, Y) = E[(X - \mu_X)(Y - \mu_Y)] = \sum_x \sum_y (x - \mu_X)(y - \mu_Y)P_{X,Y}(x, y)$$

An equivalent expression[4] is

$$\text{Cov}(X, Y) = E(XY) - \mu_X\mu_Y = \sum_x \sum_y xyP_{X,Y}(x, y) - \mu_X\mu_Y$$

To illustrate, we evaluate the covariance between consumer satisfaction and time in residence, using the joint probabilities in Table 4.1. First, the means of these two random variables are

$$\mu_X = E(X) = \sum_x xP_X(x) = (1)(.11) + (2)(.31) + (3)(.46) + (4)(.12) = 2.59$$

and

$$\mu_Y = E(Y) = \sum_y yP_Y(y) = (1)(.48) + (2)(.52) = 1.52$$

The expectation of the product of X and Y is

$$E(XY) = \sum_x \sum_y xyP_{X,Y}(x, y)$$

$$= (1)(1)(.04) + (1)(2)(.07) + (2)(1)(.14) + (2)(2)(.17)$$
$$+ (3)(1)(.23) + (3)(2)(.23) + (4)(1)(.07) + (4)(2)(.05)$$
$$= 3.89$$

---

[3] This measure is not free from interpretational difficulties. In particular, it is not independent of the units in which X and Y are measured. We return to this subject in Chapter 12.

[4] This follows since

$$\sum_x \sum_y (x - \mu_X)(y - \mu_Y)P_{X,Y}(x, y) = \sum_x \sum_y (xy - \mu_Y x - \mu_X y + \mu_X\mu_Y)P_{X,Y}(x, y)$$

$$= \sum_x \sum_y xyP_{X,Y}(x, y) - \mu_Y \sum_x \sum_y xP_{X,Y}(x, y) - \mu_X \sum_x \sum_y yP_{X,Y}(x, y) + \mu_X\mu_Y$$

$$= \sum_x \sum_y xyP_{X,Y}(x, y) - \mu_Y \sum_x xP_X(x) - \mu_X \sum_y yP_Y(y) + \mu_X\mu_Y$$

$$= \sum_x \sum_y xyP_{X,Y}(x, y) - \mu_X\mu_Y$$

Finally, the covariance is

$$\text{Cov}(X, Y) = E(XY) - \mu_X\mu_Y = 3.89 - (2.59)(1.52) = -.05$$

This negative value for the covariance indicates some tendency for high values of consumer satisfaction to be associated with a low period of time in residence in the town—that is, a *negative association* between this pair of random variables. Again, this property can be seen from the conditional probabilities of Table 4.3. Consumers who have lived longest in the town are more likely than others to have low satisfaction levels and less likely to have high levels of satisfaction with food stores.

As might be expected, the notions of covariance and statistical independence are not unrelated.

Covariance and Statistical Independence

If a pair of random variables are statistically independent, the covariance between them is 0. However, the converse is not necessarily true.

The reason a covariance of 0 does not necessarily imply statistical independence is that covariance is designed to measure linear association, and it is possible that this quantity may not detect other types of dependency. As an extreme example, suppose that the random variable X has probability function

$$P_X(-1) = \frac{1}{4} \qquad P_X(0) = \frac{1}{2} \qquad P_X(1) = \frac{1}{4}$$

and let the random variable Y be defined as

$$Y = X^2$$

Thus, knowledge of the value taken by X implies knowledge of the value taken by Y, and hence, these two random variables are certainly not independent. We know that whenever $X = 0$, then $Y = 0$, and that if X is either -1 or 1, then $Y = 1$. Hence, the joint probability function of X and Y is

$$P_{X,Y}(-1, 1) = \frac{1}{4} \qquad P_{X,Y}(0, 0) = \frac{1}{2} \qquad P_{X,Y}(1, 1) = \frac{1}{4}$$

with the probability of any other combination of values being equal to 0. It is then straightforward to verify that

$$E(X) = 0 \qquad E(Y) = \frac{1}{2} \qquad E(XY) = 0$$

and hence that the covariance between X and Y is 0.

To conclude our discussion of joint distributions, we consider the mean and variance of a random variable that can be written as the sum or difference of other random variables.

Sums and Differences of Random Variables

Let X and Y be a pair of random variables with means μ_X and μ_Y and variances σ_X^2 and σ_Y^2. The following properties hold:

(i) The expected value of their sum is the sum of their expected values:

$$E(X + Y) = \mu_X + \mu_Y$$

(ii) The expected value of their difference is the difference between their expected values:

$$E(X - Y) = \mu_X - \mu_Y$$

(iii) If the covariance between X and Y is 0, the variance of their sum is the sum of their variances:

$$\mathrm{Var}(X + Y) = \sigma_X^2 + \sigma_Y^2$$

(iv) If the covariance between X and Y is 0, the variance of their difference is the *sum* of their variances:

$$\mathrm{Var}(X - Y) = \sigma_X^2 + \sigma_Y^2$$

Let $X_1, X_2, \ldots, X_K$ be K random variables with means $\mu_1, \mu_2, \ldots, \mu_K$ and variances $\sigma_1^2, \sigma_2^2, \ldots, \sigma_K^2$. The following properties hold:

(v) The expected value of their sum is

$$E(X_1 + X_2 + \cdots + X_K) = \mu_1 + \mu_2 + \cdots + \mu_K$$

(vi) If the covariance between every pair of these random variables is 0, the variance of their sum is

$$\mathrm{Var}(X_1 + X_2 + \cdots + X_K) = \sigma_1^2 + \sigma_2^2 + \cdots + \sigma_K^2$$

Notice that the results (iii), (iv), and (vi) require that the covariances between random variables be zero. More generally, if the covariance between the random variables X and Y is $\mathrm{Cov}(X, Y)$, it can be shown that

$$\mathrm{Var}(X + Y) = \sigma_X^2 + \sigma_Y^2 + 2\,\mathrm{Cov}(X, Y)$$

and

$$\mathrm{Var}(X - Y) = \sigma_X^2 + \sigma_Y^2 - 2\,\mathrm{Cov}(X, Y)$$

EXAMPLE 4.7

An investor has \$1,000 to invest and two investment opportunities, each requiring a minimum of \$500. The profit per \$100 from the first can be represented by a random variable, X, having the following probability function:

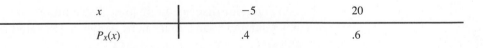

x	-5	20
$P_X(x)$	.4	.6

The profit per $100 from the second is given by the random variable Y, whose probability function is

y	0	25
$P_Y(y)$	.6	.4

The random variables X and Y are independent.

The investor has the following three possible strategies:

(a) $1,000 in the first investment
(b) $1,000 in the second investment
(c) $500 in each investment

Find the mean and variance of the profit from each strategy.

The random variable X has mean

$$\mu_X = E(X) = \sum xP_X(x) = (-5)(.4) + (20)(.6) = \$10$$

and variance

$$\sigma_X^2 = E[(X - \mu_X)^2] = \sum (x - \mu_X)^2 P_X(x)$$
$$= (-5 - 10)^2(.4) + (20 - 10)^2(.6) = 150$$

Hence, the mean profit from strategy (a) is

$$E(10X) = 10E(X) = \$100$$

and the variance is

$$\text{Var}(10X) = 100 \text{ Var}(X) = 15,000$$

The random variable Y has mean

$$\mu_Y = E(Y) = \sum yP_Y(y) = (0)(.6) + (25)(.4) = \$10$$

and variance

$$\sigma_Y^2 = E[(Y - \mu_Y)^2] = \sum (y - \mu_Y)^2 P_Y(y)$$
$$= (0 - 10)^2(.6) + (25 - 10)^2(.4) = 150$$

Therefore, strategy (b) has mean profit

$$E(10Y) = 10E(Y) = \$100$$

and variance

$$\text{Var}(10Y) = 100 \text{ Var}(Y) = 15,000$$

Now, the return from strategy (c) is $5X + 5Y$, which has mean

$$E(5X + 5Y) = E(5X) + E(5Y) = 5E(X) + 5E(Y) = \$100$$

Thus, all three strategies have the same expected profit. However, since X and Y are independent, and hence have covariance 0, the variance of the return from strategy (c) is

$$\text{Var}(5X + 5Y) = \text{Var}(5X) + \text{Var}(5Y) = 25\sigma_X^2 + 25\sigma_Y^2 = 7,500$$

This is smaller than the variances of the other strategies, reflecting the decrease in risk that follows from diversification in an investment portfolio. This investor should certainly prefer strategy (c), since it yields the same expected return as the other two, but with lower risk.

In the remaining sections in this chapter, we will discuss some specific discrete probability distributions that have important applications in the business area.

EXERCISES

19. A researcher suspected that the number of between-meals snacks eaten by students in a day during final examinations week might depend on the number of tests a student had to take on that day. The accompanying table shows joint probabilities, estimated from a survey.

NUMBER OF SNACKS (Y)	NUMBER OF TESTS (X)			
	0	1	2	3
0	.07	.09	.06	.01
1	.07	.06	.07	.01
2	.06	.07	.14	.03
3	.02	.04	.16	.04

(a) Find the probability function of X and hence the mean number of tests taken by students on that day.
(b) Find the probability function of Y and hence the mean number of snacks eaten by students on that day.
(c) Find, and interpret, the conditional probability function of Y, given $X = 3$.
(d) Find the covariance between X and Y.
(e) Are number of snacks and number of tests independent of each other?

20. A real estate agent is interested in the relationship between the number of lines in a newspaper advertisement for an apartment and the volume of enquiries from potential renters. Let volume of enquiries be denoted by the random variable X, with the value 0 for little interest, 1 for moderate interest, and 2 for heavy interest. The real estate agent estimated the joint probability function shown in the accompanying table.

NUMBER OF LINES (Y)	VOLUME OF ENQUIRIES (X)		
	0	1	2
3	.09	.14	.07
4	.07	.23	.16
5	.03	.10	.11

(a) Find the joint cumulative probability function at $X = 1$, $Y = 4$, and interpret your result.

(b) Find and interpret the conditional probability function for Y, given $X = 0$.

(c) Find and interpret the conditional probability function for X, given $Y = 5$.

(d) Find and interpret the covariance between X and Y.

(e) Are number of lines in the advertisement and volume of enquiries independent of one another?

21. The accompanying table shows, for credit card holders with one to three cards, the joint probabilities for number of cards owned (X) and number of credit purchases made in a week (Y).

NUMBER OF CARDS (X)	NUMBER OF PURCHASES IN WEEK (Y)				
	0	1	2	3	4
1	.08	.13	.09	.06	.03
2	.03	.08	.08	.09	.07
3	.01	.03	.06	.08	.08

(a) For a randomly chosen person from this group, what is the probability function for number of purchases made in the week?

(b) For a person in this group who has three cards, what is the probability function for number of purchases made in the week?

(c) Are the number of cards owned and number of purchases made statistically independent?

22. A market researcher wants to determine whether a new model of a personal computer, which had been advertised on a late-night talk show, had achieved more brand name recognition among people who watched the show regularly than among people who did not. After conducting a survey, it was found that 15% of all people both watched the show regularly and could correctly identify the product. Also, 16% of all people regularly watched the show and 45% of all people could correctly identify the product. Define a pair of random variables as follows:

$$X = \begin{cases} 1 & \text{if regularly watch the show} \\ 0 & \text{otherwise} \end{cases}$$

$$Y = \begin{cases} 1 & \text{if product correctly identified} \\ 0 & \text{otherwise} \end{cases}$$

(a) Find the joint probability function of X and Y.

(b) Find the conditional probability function of Y, given $X = 1$.

(c) Find and interpret the covariance between X and Y.

23. A college bookseller makes calls at the offices of professors and forms the impression that professors are more likely to be away from their offices on Friday than any other working day. A review of the records of calls, one-fifth of which are on Fridays, indicates that for 16% of Friday calls, the professor is away from the office, while this occurs for only 12% of calls on every other working day. Define the random variables as follows:

$$X = \begin{cases} 1 & \text{if call is made on a Friday} \\ 0 & \text{otherwise} \end{cases}$$

$$Y = \begin{cases} 1 & \text{if professor is away from the office} \\ 0 & \text{otherwise} \end{cases}$$

(a) Find the joint probability function of X and Y.

(b) Find the conditional probability function of Y, given $X = 0$.

(c) Find the marginal probability functions of X and Y.

(d) Find and interpret the covariance between X and Y.

24. A restaurant manager receives occasional complaints about the quality of both the food and the service. The marginal probability functions for the number of weekly complaints in each category are shown in the accompanying table. If complaints about food and service are independent of each other, find the joint probability function.

NUMBER OF FOOD COMPLAINTS	PROBABILITY	NUMBER OF SERVICE COMPLAINTS	PROBABILITY
0	.12	0	.18
1	.29	1	.38
2	.42	2	.34
3	.17	3	.10

25. Refer to the information in Exercise 24. Find the mean and standard deviation of the total number of complaints received in a week. Having reached this point, you are concerned that numbers of food and service complaints may not be independent of each other. However, you have no information about the nature of their dependence. What can you now say about the mean and standard deviation of the total number of complaints received in a week?

26. A company has five representatives covering large territories and ten representatives covering smaller territories. The probability distributions for the numbers of orders received by each of these types of representatives in a day are shown in the accompanying table. Assuming that the number of orders received by any representative is independent of the number received by any other, find the mean and standard deviation of the total number of orders received by the company in a day.

NUMBER OF ORDERS (LARGE TERRITORY)	PROBABILITY	NUMBER OF ORDERS (SMALLER TERRITORY)	PROBABILITY
0	.08	0	.18
1	.16	1	.26
2	.28	2	.36
3	.32	3	.13
4	.10	4	.07
5	.06		

27. From the results given in Section 4.4, it follows that for any pair of random variables X and Y, the variance of $(X - Y)$ is the same as the variance of $(Y - X)$. Explain why you would expect this to be so. [Note: $(Y - X) = -(X - Y)$.]

4.5 THE BINOMIAL DISTRIBUTION

Suppose that a random experiment can give rise to just two possible mutually exclusive and collectively exhaustive outcomes, which for convenience we will label "success" and "failure." Let p denote the probability of success, so that the probability of failure is $(1 - p)$. Now define the random variable X so that X takes the value 1 if the outcome of the experiment is success and 0 otherwise. The probability function of this random variable is then

$$P_X(0) = (1 - p) \qquad P_X(1) = p$$

This distribution is known as the **Bernoulli distribution.** Its mean and variance can be found by direct application of the definitions in Section 4.3. The mean of a Bernoulli random variable is

$$\mu_X = E(X) = \sum_x xP_X(x) = (0)(1 - p) + (1)(p) = p$$

and the variance is

$$\sigma_X^2 = E[(X - \mu_X)^2] = \sum_x (x - \mu_X)^2 P_X(x)$$

$$= (0 - p)^2(1 - p) + (1 - p)^2 p = p(1 - p)$$

EXAMPLE 4.8

An insurance broker believes that for a particular contact, the probability of making a sale is .4. If the random variable X is defined to take the value 1 if a sale is made and 0 otherwise, then X has a Bernoulli distribution with probability of success p equal to .4; that is, the probability function of X is

$$P_X(0) = .6 \qquad P_X(1) = .4$$

The mean of this distribution is $p = .4$, and the variance is

$$\sigma_X^2 = p(1 - p) = (.4)(.6) = .24$$

An important generalization of the Bernoulli distribution concerns the case where a random experiment, with two possible outcomes, is repeated several times. Suppose again that the probability of a success resulting in a single trial is p and that n independent trials are carried out, so that the result of any one trial has no influence on the outcome of any other. The number of successes X resulting from these n trials could be any whole number from 0 to n, and we are interested in the probability of obtaining exactly $X = x$ successes in n trials.

We develop the result in two stages. First, observe that the n trials will result in a sequence of n outcomes, each of which must be either success (S) or failure (F). One sequence with x successes and $(n - x)$ failures is

$$S, S, \ldots, S, \qquad F, F, \ldots, F$$

$$\underbrace{}_{x \text{ times}} \qquad \underbrace{}_{(n - x) \text{ times}}$$

In words, the first x trials result in success, while the remainder result in failure. Now, the probability of success in a single trial is p, and the probability of failure is $(1 - p)$. Since the n trials are independent of one another, the probability of any particular sequence of outcomes is, by the multiplication rule of probabilities (Section 3.6), equal to the product of the probabilities for the individual outcomes. Thus, the probability of observing the specific sequence of outcomes described above is

$$\underbrace{p \bullet p \bullet \cdots \bullet p \bullet}_{x \text{ times}} \quad \underbrace{(1 - p) \bullet (1 - p) \bullet \cdots \bullet (1 - p)}_{(n - x) \text{ times}} = p^x(1 - p)^{n-x}$$

This line of argument establishes that the probability of observing *any specific sequence* involving x successes and $(n - x)$ failures is $p^x(1 - p)^{n-x}$.

Our original interest concerned the determination not of the probability of occurrence of a particular sequence but of the probability of precisely x successes, regardless of the order of the outcomes. There are several sequences in which x successes could be arranged among $(n - x)$ failures. In fact, the number of such possibilities is just the number of combinations of x objects chosen from n, since we can select any x locations from a total of n in which to place the successes. Therefore, as follows from Section 3.5

$$\text{Number}^5 \text{ of sequences involving } x \text{ successes in } n \text{ trials} = {}_nC_x = \frac{n!}{x!(n - x)!}$$

Moreover, these sequences are mutually exclusive, since no two of them can occur at the same time.

We have now shown that the event "x successes result from n trials" can occur in ${}_nC_x$ mutually exclusive ways, each with probability $p^x(1 - p)^{n-x}$. Therefore, by the addition rule of probabilities (Section 3.6), the probability required is the sum of these ${}_nC_x$ individual probabilities; that is

$$P(x \text{ successes in } n \text{ trials}) = \frac{n!}{x!(n - x)!} p^x(1 - p)^{n-x}$$

The Binomial Distribution

Suppose that a random experiment can result in two possible mutually exclusive and collectively exhaustive outcomes, "success" and "failure," and that p is the probability of a success resulting in a single trial. If n independent trials are carried out, the distribution of the number of successes X resulting is called the **binomial distribution.** Its probability function is

$$P_X(x) = \frac{n!}{x!(n - x)!} p^x(1 - p)^{n-x} \qquad \text{for } x = 0, 1, 2, \ldots, n$$

---

[5] Note that in this expression, we define $0! = 1$.

**EXAMPLE
4.9**

Suppose now that the insurance broker of Example 4.8 has five contacts, and she believes that for each, the probability of making a sale is .4. The distribution of the number of sales X is then binomial, with $n = 5$ and $p = .4$; that is

$$P_X(x) = \frac{5!}{x!(5 - x)!} \, (.4)^x(.6)^{5-x} \qquad \text{for } x = 0, 1, \ldots, 5$$

The probabilities for numbers of successes (sales made) are

$$P(0 \text{ successes}) = P_X(0) = \frac{5!}{0! \, 5!} \, (.4)^0(.6)^5 = (.6)^5 = .078$$

$$P(1 \text{ success}) = P_X(1) = \frac{5!}{1! \, 4!} \, (.4)^1(.6)^4 = (5)(.4)(.6)^4 = .259$$

$$P(2 \text{ successes}) = P_X(2) = \frac{5!}{2! \, 3!} \, (.4)^2(.6)^3 = (10)(.4)^2(.6)^3 = .346$$

$$P(3 \text{ successes}) = P_X(3) = \frac{5!}{3! \, 2!} \, (.4)^3(.6)^2 = (10)(.4)^3(.6)^2 = .230$$

$$P(4 \text{ successes}) = P_X(4) = \frac{5!}{4! \, 1!} \, (.4)^4(.6)^1 = (5)(.4)^4(.6) = .077$$

$$P(5 \text{ successes}) = P_X(5) = \frac{5!}{5! \, 0!} \, (.4)^5(.6)^0 = (.4)^5 = .010$$

The probability function is graphed in Figure 4.5. The shape is rather typical of binomial probabilities when p is neither very large nor very small. At the extremes (0 and 5 successes), the probabilities are quite low, since in either case only one possible sequence of outcomes could give rise to this event. The probabilities peak toward the center of the distribution (the location of the peak depending on p), where the number of possible sequences is higher.

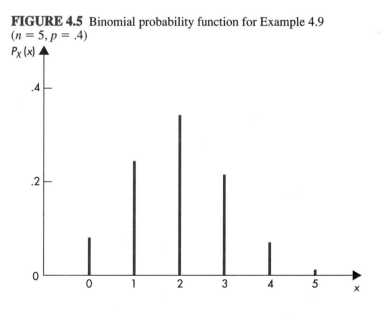

FIGURE 4.5 Binomial probability function for Example 4.9 $(n = 5, p = .4)$

To find the mean and variance of the binomial distribution, it is convenient to return to the Bernoulli distribution. Consider n independent trials, each with probability of success p, and let $X_i = 1$ if the ith trial results in success and 0 otherwise. The random variables $X_1, X_2, \ldots, X_n$ are therefore n independent Bernoulli variables, each with probability of success p. Moreover, the total number of successes X is

$$X = X_1 + X_2 + \cdots + X_n$$

That is to say, the binomial random variable can be expressed as the sum of independent Bernoulli random variables. Now, since we have already found the mean and variance for the Bernoulli random variable, the results of Section 4.4 can be used to find the mean and variance of the binomial distribution. Recall that for a Bernoulli variable

$$E(X_i) = p \qquad \text{and} \qquad \text{Var}(X_i) = p(1 - p) \qquad \text{for } i = 1, 2, \ldots, n$$

Then, for the binomial distribution

$$E(X) = E(X_1 + X_2 + \cdots + X_n) = E(X_1) + E(X_2) + \cdots + E(X_n) = np$$

Since the Bernoulli random variables are independent, the covariance between any pair of them is zero, and

$$\text{Var}(X) = \text{Var}(X_1 + X_2 + \cdots + X_n)$$
$$= \text{Var}(X_1) + \text{Var}(X_2) + \cdots + \text{Var}(X_n) = np(1 - p)$$

Mean and Variance of Binomial Distribution

Let X be the number of successes in n independent trials, each with probability of success p. Then X follows a binomial distribution with mean

$$\mu_X = E(X) = np$$

and variance

$$\sigma_X^2 = E[(X - \mu_X)^2] = np(1 - p)$$

EXAMPLE 4.10

Refer to Example 4.9. For the insurance broker who makes five contacts, each with probability of a sale of .4, the mean (or expected) number of sales is

$$\mu_X = np = (5)(.4) = 2$$

and the variance is

$$\sigma_X^2 = np(1 - p) = (5)(.4)(.6) = 1.2$$

so the standard deviation for the number of sales is

$$\sigma_X = \sqrt{1.2} = 1.10$$

Given our knowledge of the form of the binomial probability function, it is straightforward to find the probability that the number of successes falls in some specified range. Since the events "0 successes," "1 success," etc., are mutually exclusive, the required probability is just the sum of the probabilities over all numbers of successes in that range.

EXAMPLE 4.11
Refer to Example 4.9. What is the probability that the number of successes will be between 2 and 4 (inclusive)? We require

$$P(2 \le X \le 4) = P(X = 2) + P(X = 3) + P(X = 4)$$
$$= P_X(2) + P_X(3) + P_X(4)$$

which, using the results of Example 4.9, is

$$.346 + .230 + .077 = .653$$

What is the probability of at least one success? We could find

$$P(X \ge 1) = P_X(1) + P_X(2) + P_X(3) + P_X(4) + P_X(5)$$

directly, but this is unnecessarily tedious. The probabilities for any discrete distribution sum to 1, so

$$P(X \ge 1) = 1 - P(X = 0) = 1 - P_X(0) = 1 - .078 = .922$$

Unless the number of trials n is very small, the calculation of binomial probabilities is likely to be extremely burdensome. However, in real-world applications, the computations can readily be carried out on an electronic computer or with a programmed calculator. Moreover, as will be seen in Section 4.7 and in the next chapter, when the number of trials n is quite large, the required probabilities can be obtained through convenient approximations to the binomial distribution. In order to facilitate problem solving, Table 1 in the Appendix lists binomial probabilities for values of n up to 20 and selected values of p up to and including $p = .5$. For higher values of p, use the following rule:[6]

☐ P[x successes in n trials when probability of success in a single trial is p] = $P[(n - x)$ successes in n trials when probability of success in a single trial is $(1 - p)$].

☐ To illustrate, the probability of seven successes in twelve trials where $p = .6$ is the same as the probability of five successes in twelve trials with $p = .4$. That is, setting $x = 7$, $n = 12$, and $p = .6$ in the formula yields $P[7$ successes in 12 trials when probability of success in a single trial is .6$] = P[5$ successes in 12 trials when probability of success in a single trial is .4$]$.

☐ This can be read directly from Table 1 as .2270. This value is obtained by locating, from the first two columns of the table, the row corresponding to $n = 12$ and $x = 5$; we then locate the required probability in the column corresponding to $p = .40$.

EXAMPLE 4.12
Invitations to dinner are sent to twenty delegates attending a convention, and it is believed that for each delegate invited, the probability of an acceptance is .9. If it is assumed that decisions to accept these invitations are made independently, what is the probability that at most seventeen acceptances will be received?

Let the random variable X denote the number of acceptances. Then X has a binomial distribution, with $n = 20$ and $p = .9$. We require

$$P(X \le 17) = 1 - P(X = 18) - P(X = 19) - P(X = 20)$$

---

[6] The truth of this rule can be seen by reversing x and $(n - x)$ in the binomial probability function.

$$= 1 - P_X(18) - P_X(19) - P_X(20)$$

Now, with $n = 20$, the probability of eighteen successes for $p = .9$ is the same as the probability of two successes for $p = .1$. From Table 1 of the Appendix, we find $P_X(18) = .2852$. Similarly, we find $P_X(19) = .2702$, and $P_X(20) = .1216$. Thus, the probability of at most seventeen acceptances is

$$P(X \leq 17) = 1 - .2852 - .2702 - .1216 = .323$$

An important application of the binomial distribution is in **acceptance sampling.** When a firm receives a very large shipment of goods from a manufacturer, it has to decide, based on information about the quality of those goods, whether to accept delivery. Typically, a thorough inspection of the whole consignment would be prohibitively expensive, so a small random sample[7] is selected and examined. Based on the results of this examination, a decision is made as to whether to accept the shipment. It is possible to calculate, for any particular decision rule of this kind, the probability of accepting a shipment with any given proportion of defectives. This is so, since if p is the proportion of defectives in the shipment and n is the number sampled,[8] the number of defectives X in the sample follows the binomial distribution with probability function

$$P_X(x) = \frac{n!}{x! \, (n-x)!} \, p^x(1-p)^{n-x} \qquad \text{for } x = 0, 1, 2, \ldots, n$$

The following example illustrates how the probabilities for accepting delivery can be calculated.

EXAMPLE 4.13

A company receiving a very large shipment of items decides to accept delivery if, in a random sample of twenty items, not more than one is defective. Thus, the shipment is accepted if the number of defectives is either zero or one, so that if $P_X(x)$ is the probability function for the number X of defectives in the sample, we have

$$P(\text{Shipment accepted}) = P_X(0) + P_X(1)$$

Suppose that the proportion of defectives in the shipment is $p = .1$. For $n = 20$, we find directly from Table 1 of the Appendix that the probabilities for zero and one defectives in the sample are, respectively, $P_X(0) = .1216$ and $P_X(1) = .2702$. Hence, with this decision rule, the probability that the company accepts delivery is

$$P(\text{Shipment accepted}) = .1216 + .2702 = .3918$$

Similarly, if 20% of the items in the shipment are defective—that is, if $p = .2$—then

$$P(\text{Shipment accepted}) = .0115 + .0576 = .0691$$

and for $p = .3$

$$P(\text{Shipment accepted}) = .0008 + .0068 = .0076$$

---

[7] By a **random sample** of n items, it is meant that the sample is selected in such a way that every set of n items in the shipment is equally likely to be chosen. This concept will be more thoroughly explored in Chapter 6.
[8] We are assuming that the number of items n in the sample is a very small proportion of the total number in the shipment. In the next section, we will see how it is possible to proceed if this assumption is not appropriate.

As can be seen from Example 4.13, the higher the proportion of defectives in the shipment, the less likely is acceptance of the delivery. We can graph the probability of acceptance against the proportion of defectives in the shipment, as in Figure 4.6. This allows acceptance probabilities to be read off for any proportion of defective items.

Of course, any number of curves relating acceptance probabilities to proportion of defectives in a shipment can be constructed by choosing different sample sizes n and different rules for determining acceptance. In this way, a company is able to choose a scheme with the desired balance between the costs of accepting shipments with particular proportions of defectives and of carrying out the checks on quality.

4.6 THE HYPERGEOMETRIC DISTRIBUTION

In Example 4.13, we considered a situation in which a sample of items from a very large consignment was to be checked for defectives. By assuming that the number sampled was extremely small relative to the total number of items in the consignment, we were able to approach the problem through use of the binomial distribution. However, in cases where the number of sample members is not a very small proportion of the total number of items in the population, the binomial distribution is inappropriate. The reason is that in such circumstances, the sample outcomes for individual items will not be independent of one another. To illustrate, suppose that a consignment contains ten items, three of which are defective. If one of these is chosen at random, the probability that it is defective is simply 3/10. Now, suppose that a second item is to be chosen. If the first was defective, then the remaining nine would contain two defectives, so the probability that the second item is defective, given that the first was defective, would be 2/9. The probability that the second item is defective given that the first was not defective would, by a similar argument, be 3/9. Hence, the events "First item defective" and "Second item defective" are not statistically independent. Recall that for the distribution of the number of successes in n trials to be bi-

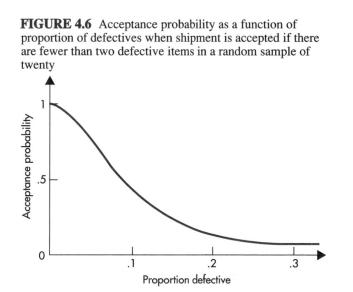

FIGURE 4.6 Acceptance probability as a function of proportion of defectives when shipment is accepted if there are fewer than two defective items in a random sample of twenty

nomial, it is necessary that the outcomes of these trials be independent of one another. As we have seen, this will not be the case when sampling from a small population of items. If the total number of items in the population is very large relative to the number to be sampled, the extent of any dependencies will be so trivial that they can be ignored, and the binomial distribution can safely be used. However, this is not so when the number of population items is not very large.

We can, nevertheless, find the appropriate probability distribution in situations of this kind. In general, suppose that a group of N objects, each of which can be labeled "success" or "failure," contains S successes and $(N - S)$ failures. A random sample of n objects is chosen from this group, and we require the probability that the sample contains x successes. First, the number of possible different samples of n objects that could be drawn from a total of N is the number of combinations

$$_NC_n = \frac{N!}{n! \, (N - n)!}$$

The number of possible ways of getting the x successes in the sample from a total of S successes is

$$_SC_x = \frac{S!}{x! \, (S - x)!}$$

Since the sample contains x successes, it must also contain $(n - x)$ failures, and the number of ways of choosing these from a total of $(N - S)$ failures is

$$_{N-S}C_{n-x} = \frac{(N - S)!}{(n - x)! \, (N - S - n + x)!}$$

The total number of samples of n objects containing exactly x successes and $(n - x)$ failures is, therefore

$$_SC_x{}_{N-S}C_{n-x} = \frac{S!}{x! \, (S - x)!} \, \frac{(N - S)!}{(n - x)! \, (N - S - n + x)!}$$

Finally, since the number of possible samples is $_NC_n$, the probability of obtaining x successes in the sample is

$$P(x \text{ successes}) = \frac{_SC_x{}_{N-S}C_{n-x}}{_NC_n} = \frac{\dfrac{S!}{x! \, (S - x)!} \cdot \dfrac{(N-S)!}{(n-x)! \, (N-S-n+x)!}}{\dfrac{N!}{n! \, (N - n)!}}$$

The Hypergeometric Distribution

Suppose that a random sample of n objects is chosen from a group of N objects, S of which are successes. The distribution of the number of successes X in the sample is called the **hypergeometric distribution.** Its probability function is

$$P_X(x) = \frac{_SC_x{}_{N-S}C_{n-x}}{_NC_n} = \frac{\dfrac{S!}{x! \, (S - x)!} \cdot \dfrac{N-S)!}{(n-x)! \, (N-S-n+x)!}}{\dfrac{N!}{n! \, (N - n)!}}$$

where x can take integer values ranging from the larger of 0 and $[n - (N - S)]$ to the smaller of n and S.

The mean and variance of this distribution are

$$\mu_X = E(X) = np$$

and

$$\sigma_X^2 = E[(X - \mu_X)^2] = \left(\frac{N - n}{N - 1}\right) np(1 - p)$$

where $p = S/N$ is the proportion of successes in the population.

If the sample size n is very small relative to the total number of items, N, the hypergeometric probabilities are very close to binomial probabilities, and the binomial distribution may be used rather than the hypergeometric. In this case, $(N - n)/(N - 1)$ is very close to 1, so the variance of the hypergeometric distribution is close to $np(1 - p)$, the variance of the binomial distribution.

EXAMPLE
4.14

A company receives a shipment of twenty items. Because inspection of each individual item is expensive, it has a policy of checking a random sample of six items from such a shipment, accepting delivery if no more than one sampled item is defective. What is the probability that a shipment with five defective items will be accepted?

If we identify "defective" with "success" in this example, the shipment contains $N = 20$ items, $S = 5$ of which are successes. A sample of $n = 6$ items is selected. Then the number of successes X in the sample has a hypergeometric distribution with probability function

$$P_X(x) = \frac{{}_SC_x \, {}_{N-S}C_{n-x}}{{}_NC_n} = \frac{{}_5C_x \, {}_{15}C_{6-x}}{{}_{20}C_6}$$

$$= \frac{\dfrac{5!}{x! \, (5 - x)!} \cdot \dfrac{15!}{(6 - x)! \, (9 + x)!}}{\dfrac{20!}{6! \, 14!}}$$

The shipment is accepted if the sample contains either zero or one success (defective), so the probability of its acceptance is

$$P(\text{Shipment accepted}) = P_X(0) + P_X(1)$$

The probability of no defectives in the sample is

$$P_X(0) = \frac{\dfrac{5!}{0! \, 5!} \cdot \dfrac{15!}{6! \, 9!}}{\dfrac{20!}{6! \, 14!}} = .129$$

(Recall that $0! = 1$.) The probability of one defective in the sample is

$$P_X(1) = \frac{\dfrac{5!}{1!\,4!} \cdot \dfrac{15!}{5!\,10!}}{\dfrac{20!}{6!\,14!}} = .387$$

Therefore, the probability that the shipment of twenty items containing five defectives is accepted using this procedure is

$$P(\text{Shipment accepted}) = P_X(0) + P_X(1) = .129 + .387 = .516$$

4.7 THE POISSON DISTRIBUTION

Consider the following random variables:

- ☐ The number of fatal traffic accidents in a city in a particular week
- ☐ The number of telephone calls arriving at a corporation's switchboard in the fifteen minutes before noon on a given day
- ☐ The number of replacement orders for a part received by a firm in a week
- ☐ The number of times a piece of equipment fails during a 3-month period
- ☐ The number of strikes at a plant in a year

Each of these five random variables can be characterized as the number of occurrences of a certain event in a given period of time. Experience indicates that for a wide range of problems of this kind, the *Poisson probability distribution* well represents the probability structure of the random variable.

Consider the situation illustrated in Figure 4.7, where time is measured along the horizontal line, and we are interested in the period beginning at time 0 and ending at time t. Occurrences of events along the time axis are indicated by ●●●, so in this illustration, six events occur in the relevant time period. Suppose that the following assumptions can be made:

1. For any small time interval, represented by a small segment of the time axis between 0 and t in Figure 4.7, the probability that one event will occur in this interval is approximately proportional to the length of the interval.
2. The probability of two or more occurrences in such an interval is negligibly small compared to the probability of one occurrence.
3. The numbers of occurrences in any nonoverlapping time intervals are independent of one another.

If these assumptions hold, it can be shown that the probability of x occurrences in the interval between 0 and t is

$$P(x \text{ occurrences}) = \frac{e^{-\lambda}\lambda^x}{x!}$$

FIGURE 4.7 Illustration of random occurrences ● of an event over time

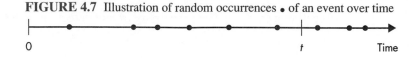

where λ is the mean number of occurrences in the interval from 0 to t and $e = 2.71828 \ldots$ is the base of the natural logarithms. (Table 2 in the Appendix gives values of $e^{-\lambda}$ for values of λ from 0 to 10.) The distribution with these probabilities is called the **Poisson distribution.**

The Poisson Distribution

The random variable X is said to follow the **Poisson distribution** if it has probability function

$$P_X(x) = \frac{e^{-\lambda}\lambda^x}{x!} \qquad \text{for } x = 0, 1, 2, \ldots$$

where λ is any number with $\lambda > 0$.
    The mean of this distribution is

$$\mu_X = E(X) = \lambda$$

and the variance is

$$\sigma_X^2 = E[(X - \mu_X)^2] = \lambda$$

The shape of the Poisson probability function depends on the mean, λ. Figure 4.8 shows probability functions for $\lambda = .5, 1, 2,$ and 4.

EXAMPLE 4.15

Research has indicated[9] that for a typical plant with 2,000 employees in Britain, the number of strikes in a year can be represented by a Poisson distribution with mean $\lambda = .4$. The probability function for the number of strikes X in a year is then

FIGURE 4.8 Probability functions for the Poisson distribution

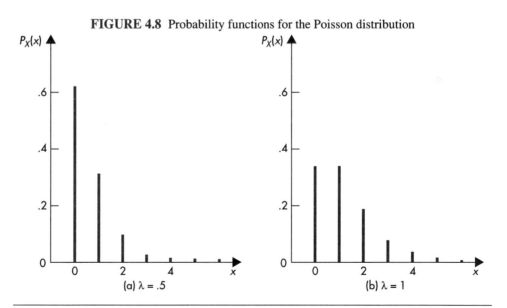

(a) $\lambda = .5$ (b) $\lambda = 1$

---

[9] This example is adapted from S. J. Prais, "The strike-proneness of large plants in Britain," *Journal of the Royal Statistical Society A, 141* (1978), 368–84.

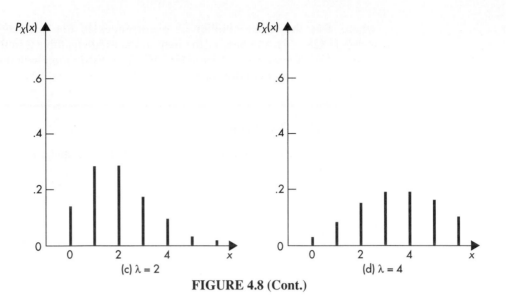

FIGURE 4.8 (Cont.)

$$P_X(x) = \frac{e^{-.4}(.4)^x}{x!} \qquad \text{for } x = 0, 1, 2, \ldots$$

We can now calculate probabilities for particular numbers of strikes in a year, using (from Table 2 in the Appendix) $e^{-.4} = .6703$.

The probability of no strikes is

$$P(0 \text{ strikes}) = P_X(0) = \frac{e^{-.4}(.4)^0}{0!} = \frac{(.6703)(1)}{1} = .6703$$

Similarly

$$P(1 \text{ strike}) = P_X(1) = \frac{e^{-.4}(.4)^1}{1!} = \frac{(.6703)(.4)}{1} = .2681$$

$$P(2 \text{ strikes}) = P_X(2) = \frac{e^{-.4}(.4)^2}{2!} = \frac{(.6703)(.16)}{2} = .0536$$

$$P(3 \text{ strikes}) = P_X(3) = \frac{e^{-.4}(.4)^3}{3!} = \frac{(.6703)(.064)}{6} = .0071$$

$$P(4 \text{ strikes}) = P_X(4) = \frac{e^{-.4}(.4)^4}{4!} = \frac{(.6703)(.0256)}{24} = .0007$$

These probabilities could then be used to find the probability that the number of strikes falls in any given range. For example, the probability of more than one strike in a year is

$$P(\text{More than 1 strike}) = 1 - P(0 \text{ strikes}) - P(1 \text{ strike})$$

$$= 1 - P_X(0) - P_X(1)$$

$$= 1 - .6703 - .2681 = .0616$$

EXAMPLE
4.16

The Poisson distribution has been found to be particularly useful in *waiting line,* or *queuing,* problems. Customers arrive at a photocopying machine at an average rate of two every 5 minutes. In practice, it is often possible to represent *arrival processes* of this sort by a Poisson distribution. Assuming this to be the case here, we will let X denote the number of arriving customers in a 5-minute period, so that X has a Poisson distribution with mean $\lambda = 2$, and probability function

$$P_X(x) = \frac{e^{-2}(2)^x}{x!} \qquad \text{for } x = 0, 1, 2, \ldots$$

[This is the probability function graphed in Figure 4.8(c).] Using (from Table 2 of the Appendix) $e^{-2} = .135335$, the probabilities for numbers of arrivals in a 5-minute period are

$$P(0 \text{ arrivals}) = P_X(0) = \frac{e^{-2}(2)^0}{0!} = \frac{(.135335)(1)}{1} = .1353$$

$$P(1 \text{ arrival}) = P_X(1) = \frac{e^{-2}(2)^1}{1!} = \frac{(.135335)(2)}{1} = .2707$$

$$P(2 \text{ arrivals}) = P_X(2) = \frac{e^{-2}(2)^2}{2!} = \frac{(.135335)(4)}{2} = .2707$$

and so on. Thus, for example, the probability of more than two arrivals in a 5-minute period is

$$P(X > 2) = 1 - P_X(0) - P_X(1) - P_X(2)$$
$$= 1 - .1353 - .2707 - .2707 = .3233$$

As we have seen, the Poisson distribution arises naturally in the characterization of the number of occurrences of an event in a period of time. This distribution also has a further use. In Section 4.5, we saw that if the number of trials n is very large, the computation of probabilities for the binomial random variable could be very tedious. Since such probabilities are frequently required in practice, it is convenient to have available easily computed approximations to them when n is large. The Poisson distribution can be used for this purpose when the number of trials n is large, but at the same time the probability p of a success in any single trial is very small, so that np is of only moderate size.[10] (The approximation to be presented here is generally satisfactory if $np \leq 7$.)

The following situations would satisfy these conditions:

1. An insurance company will hold a large number of life policies on individuals of any particular age, and the probability that a single policy will result in a claim during the year is very low. The distribution of the number of claims is binomial, with large n and very small p.
2. A company may have a large number of machines working on a process simultaneously. If the probability that any one of them will break down in a single day is small, the distribution of the number of daily breakdowns is binomial, with large n and small p.

---

[10] In Chapter 5, we present an approximation to the binomial distribution that is appropriate for larger values of np.

In such cases, the binomial distribution can be well approximated by the Poisson distribution with mean $\lambda = np$. That is, the mean, λ, of the approximating Poisson distribution is fixed at the value of the known mean, np, of the binomial distribution being approximated.

Poisson Approximation to the Binomial Distribution

Let X be the number of successes resulting from n independent trials, each with probability of success p. The distribution of the number of successes X is binomial, with mean np. However, if the number of trials n is large and np is of only moderate size (preferably $np \leq 7$), this distribution can be well approximated by the Poisson distribution with mean $\lambda = np$. The probability function of the approximating distribution is then

$$P_X(x) = \frac{e^{-np}(np)^x}{x!} \qquad \text{for } x = 0, 1, 2, \ldots$$

EXAMPLE 4.17

An analyst predicted that 3.5% of all small corporations would file for bankruptcy in the coming year. For a random sample of 100 small corporations, estimate the probability that at least three will file for bankruptcy in the next year, assuming that the analyst's prediction is correct.

The distribution of the number X of filings for bankruptcy is binomial, with $n = 100$ and $p = .035$, so the mean of the distribution is

$$\mu_X = np = (100)(.035) = 3.5$$

We will use the Poisson distribution, with mean $\lambda = 3.5$, to approximate our binomial distribution. The probability function of the number X of bankruptcy filings is then approximated by

$$P_X(x) = \frac{e^{-3.5}(3.5)^x}{x!} \qquad \text{for } x = 0, 1, 2, \ldots$$

Thus, using $e^{-3.5} = .030197$ from Table 2 of the Appendix, we have

$$P_X(0) = \frac{e^{-3.5}(3.5)^0}{0!} = \frac{(.030197)(1)}{1} = .0302$$

$$P_X(1) = \frac{e^{-3.5}(3.5)^1}{1!} = \frac{(.030197)(3.5)}{1} = .1057$$

$$P_X(2) = \frac{e^{-3.5}(3.5)^2}{2!} = \frac{(.030197)(12.25)}{2} = .1850$$

Therefore, the probability of at least three filings for bankruptcy from these 100 corporations is

$$P(X \geq 3) = 1 - P_X(0) - P_X(1) - P_X(2)$$

$$= 1 - .0302 - .1057 - .1850 = .679$$

(The reader is invited to speculate on the formidability of the task of computing this probability directly from the probability function of the binomial distribution. In fact, to three decimal places, this yields .684. Our approximation here is satisfactorily close to the exact probability.)

EXERCISES

28. A production manager knows that 5% of components produced by a particular manufacturing process have some defect. Six of these components, whose characteristics can be assumed to be independent of each other, were examined.

    (a) What is the probability that none of these components has a defect?

    (b) What is the probability that one of these components has a defect?

    (c) What is the probability that at least two of these components have a defect?

29. A politician believes that 25% of all macroeconomists in senior positions would strongly support a proposal he wishes to advance. Suppose that this belief is correct and that five senior macroeconomists are approached at random.

    (a) What is the probability that at least one of the five would strongly support the proposal?

    (b) What is the probability that a majority of the five would strongly support the proposal?

30. A public interest group hires students to solicit donations by telephone. After a brief training period, students make calls to potential donors and are paid on a commission basis. Experience indicates that early on, these students tend to have only modest success, and that 70% of them give up their jobs in their first 2 weeks of employment. The group hires six students, who can be viewed as a random sample.

    (a) What is the probability that at least two of the six will give up in the first 2 weeks?

    (b) What is the probability that at least two of the six will not give up in the first 2 weeks?

31. Suppose that the probability is .5 that the value of the U.S. dollar will rise against the Japanese yen over any given week, and that the outcome in one week is independent of that in any other week. What is the probability that the value of the U.S. dollar will rise against the Japanese yen in a majority of weeks over a period of 7 weeks?

32. A company installs new central heating furnaces, and has found that for 15% of all installations a return visit is needed to make some modifications. Six installations were made in a particular week. Assume independence of outcomes for these installations.

    (a) What is the probability that a return visit was needed in all of these cases?

    (b) What is the probability that a return visit was needed in none of these cases?

    (c) What is the probability that a return visit was needed in more than one of these cases?

33. The Cubs are to play a series of five games in St. Louis against the Cardinals. For any one game, it is estimated that the probability of a Cubs win is .4. The outcomes of the five games are independent of one another.

    (a) What is the probability that the Cubs will win all five games?

    (b) What is the probability that the Cubs will win a majority of the five games?

    (c) If the Cubs win the first game, what is the probability that they will win a majority of the five games?

    (d) Before the series begins, what is the expected number of Cubs' wins in these five games?

    (e) If the Cubs win the first game, what is the expected number of Cubs' wins in the five games?

34. A small commuter airline flies planes that can seat up to eight passengers. The airline has determined that the probability that a ticketed passenger will not show up for a flight is .2. For each flight, the airline sells tickets to the first ten people placing orders. The probability distribution for the number of tickets sold per flight is shown in the accompanying table. For what proportion of the airline's flights does the number of ticketed passengers showing up exceed the number of available seats? (Assume independence between number of tickets sold and the probability that a ticketed passenger will show up.)

NUMBER OF TICKETS	6	7	8	9	10
PROBABILITY	.25	.35	.25	.10	.05

35. Following a touchdown, a college football coach has the option to elect to attempt a "2-point conversion"; that is, 2 additional points are scored if the attempt is successful, and none if it is unsuccessful. The coach believes that the probability is .4 that his team will be successful in any attempt, and that outcomes of different attempts are independent of each other. In a particular game, the team scored four touchdowns and 2-point conversion attempts were made each time.

  (a) What is the probability that at least two of these attempts were successful?
  (b) Find the mean and standard deviation of the total number of points resulting from these four attempts.

36. An automobile dealer mounts a new promotional campaign, in which it is promised that purchasers of new automobiles may, if dissatisfied for any reason, return them within two days of purchase and receive a full refund. It is estimated that the cost to the dealer of such a refund is $250. The dealer estimates that 15% of all purchasers will indeed return automobiles and obtain refunds. Suppose that fifty automobiles are purchased during the campaign period.

  (a) Find the mean and standard deviation of the number of these automobiles that will be returned for refunds.
  (b) Find the mean and standard deviation of the total refund costs that will accrue as a result of these fifty purchases.

37. A family of mutual funds maintains a service that allows clients to switch money among accounts through a telephone call. It was estimated that 3.2% of callers either got a busy signal or were kept on hold so long that they hung up. Fund management assesses any failure of this sort as a $10 goodwill loss. Suppose that 2,000 calls were attempted over a particular period.

  (a) Find the mean and standard deviation of the number of callers who either got a busy signal or hung up after being kept on hold.
  (b) Find the mean and standard deviation of the total goodwill loss to the mutual fund company from these 2,000 calls.

38. We have seen that, for a binomial distribution with n trials, each with probability of success p, the mean is

$$\mu_X = np$$

Verify this result for the data of Example 4.9 by calculating the mean direct from

$$\mu_X = \sum x P_X(x)$$

showing that, for the binomial distribution, the two formulas produce the same answer.

39. A campus finance officer finds that for all parking tickets issued, fines on 78% are paid. The fine is $2. In the most recent week, 620 parking tickets have been issued.

  (a) Find the mean and standard deviation of the number of these tickets for which the fines will be paid.
  (b) Find the mean and standard deviation of the amount of money that will be obtained from the payment of these fines.

40. A company receives a very large shipment of components. A random sample of sixteen of these components are checked, and the shipment is accepted if fewer than two of these components are defective. What is the probability of accepting a shipment containing:

(a) 5% defectives?

(b) 15% defectives?

(c) 25% defectives?

41. The following two acceptance rules are being considered for determining whether to take delivery of a large shipment of components:

(i) A random sample of ten components is checked, and the shipment is accepted only if none of them is defective.

(ii) A random sample of twenty components is checked, and the shipment is accepted only if not more than one of them is defective.

Which of these acceptance rules has the smaller probability of accepting a shipment containing 20% defectives?

42. A company receives large shipments of parts from two sources. Seventy percent of the shipments come from a supplier whose shipments typically contain 10% defectives, while the remainder are from a supplier whose shipments typically contain 20% defectives. A manager receives a shipment but does not know the source. A random sample of twenty items from this shipment is tested, and one of the parts is found to be defective. What is the probability that this shipment came from the more reliable supplier? [*Hint:* Use Bayes' theorem.]

43. A company receives a shipment of sixteen items. A random sample of four items is selected, and the shipment is rejected if any of these items proves to be defective.

(a) What is the probability of accepting a shipment containing four defective items?

(b) What is the probability of accepting a shipment containing two defective items?

(c) What is the probability of rejecting a shipment containing one defective item?

44. A committee of eight members is to be formed from a group of eight men and eight women. If the choice of committee members is made randomly, what is the probability that precisely half of these members will be women?

45. A bond analyst was given a list of twelve corporate bonds. From that list, she selected three whose ratings she felt were in danger of being downgraded in the next year. In actuality, a total of four of the twelve bonds on the list had their ratings downgraded in the next year. Suppose that the analyst had simply chosen three bonds randomly from this list. What is the probability that at least two of the chosen bonds would be among those whose ratings were to be downgraded in the next year?

46. A bank executive is presented with loan applications from ten people. The profiles of the applicants are similar, except that five are minorities and five are nonminorities. In the end, the executive approved six of the applications. If these six approvals had been chosen at random from the ten applications, what is the probability that less than half the approvals would be of applications involving minorities?

47. Customers arrive at a busy check-out counter at an average rate of three per minute. If the distribution of arrivals is Poisson, find the probability that in any given minute there will be two or fewer arrivals.

48. The number of accidents in a production facility has a Poisson distribution with mean 2.6 per month.

(a) For a given month, what is the probability there will be fewer than two accidents?

(b) For a given month, what is the probability there will be more than three accidents?

49. A professor receives, on average, 4.2 telephone calls from students the day before a final examination. If the distribution of calls is Poisson, what is the probability of receiving at least three of these calls on such a day?

50. Records indicate that on average, 3.2 breakdowns per day occur on an urban highway during the morning rush hour. Assume that the distribution is Poisson.

(a) Find the probability that on any given day, there will be fewer than two breakdowns on this highway during the early morning rush hour.

(b) Find the probability that on any given day, there will be more than four breakdowns on this highway during the early morning rush hour.

51. The Internal Revenue Service reported that 5.5% of all taxpayers filling out the 1040 short form make mistakes. If 100 of these forms are chosen at random, what is the probability that fewer than three of them contain errors? Use the Poisson approximation to the binomial distribution.

52. A corporation has 250 personal computers. The probability that any one of them will require repair in a given week is .01. Find the probability that fewer than four of the personal computers will require repair in a particular week. Use the Poisson approximation to the binomial distribution.

53. An insurance company holds fraud insurance policies on 6,000 firms. In any given year, the probability that any single policy will result in a claim is .001. Find the probability that at least three claims are made in a given year. Use the Poisson approximation to the binomial distribution.

54. A state has a law requiring motorists to carry insurance. It was estimated that, despite this law, 7.5% of all motorists in the state are uninsured. A random sample of 60 motorists was taken. Use the Poisson approximation to the binomial distribution to estimate the probability that at least three of the motorists in this sample are uninsured. Also, indicate what calculations would be needed to find this probability exactly if the Poisson approximation was not used.

REVIEW EXERCISES

55. Explain carefully, with an illustrative example, what is meant by the expected value of a random variable. Why is this concept important?

56. As an investment adviser, you tell a client that an investment in a mutual fund has (over the next year) a higher expected return than an investment in the money market. The client then asks the following questions:
    (a) Does that imply that the mutual fund will certainly yield a higher return than the money market?
    (b) Does it follow that I should invest in the mutual fund rather than in the money market?
    How would you reply?

57. Develop a realistic business example (other than those in the text and in other exercises) in which each of the following probability distributions would be appropriate.
    (a) The binomial distribution
    (b) The hypergeometric distribution
    (c) The Poisson distribution

58. Explain what can be learned from each of the following:
    (a) A graph of the probability function of a random variable
    (b) A graph of the cumulative probability function of a random variable
    (c) The standard deviation of a random variable
    (d) The covariance between a pair of random variables

59. A contractor estimates the probabilities for the number of days required to complete a certain type of construction project as follows:

TIME (DAYS)	1	2	3	4	5
PROBABILITY	.05	.20	.35	.30	.10

    (a) What is the probability that a randomly chosen project will take less than 3 days to complete?

(b) Find the expected time to complete a project.

(c) Find the standard deviation of time required to complete a project.

(d) The contractor's project cost is made up of two parts—a fixed cost of $20,000, plus $2,000 for each day taken to complete the project. Find the mean and standard deviation of total project cost.

(e) If three projects are undertaken, what is the probability that at least two of them will take at least 4 days to complete, assuming independence of individual project completion times?

60. A car salesman estimates the following probabilities for the number of cars that he will sell in the next week.

NUMBER OF CARS	0	1	2	3	4	5
PROBABILITY	.10	.20	.35	.16	.12	.07

(a) Find the expected number of cars that will be sold in the week.

(b) Find the standard deviation of the number of cars that will be sold in the week.

(c) The salesman receives for the week a salary of $250, plus an additional $300 for each car sold. Find the mean and standard deviation of his total salary for the week.

(d) What is the probability that the salesman's salary for the week will be more than $1,000?

61. A multiple-choice test has nine questions. For each question, there are four possible answers from which to select. One point is awarded for each correct answer, and points are not subtracted for incorrect answers. The instructor awards a bonus point if the student spells his or her name correctly. A student who has not studied for this test decides to choose at random an answer for each question.

(a) Find the expected number of correct answers for the student on these nine questions.

(b) Find the standard deviation of the number of correct answers for the student on these nine questions.

(c) The student spells his name correctly.

(i) Find the expected total score on the test for this student.

(ii) Find the standard deviation of his total score on the test.

62. Develop realistic examples of pairs of random variables for which you would expect to find:

(a) Positive covariance

(b) Negative covariance

(c) Zero covariance

63. A long-distance taxi service owns four vehicles. These are of different ages and have different repair records. The probabilities that on any given day, each vehicle will be available for use are .95, .90, .90, and .80. Whether one vehicle is available is independent of whether any other vehicle is available.

(a) Find the probability function for the number of vehicles available for use on a given day.

(b) Find the expected number of vehicles available for use on a given day.

(c) Find the standard deviation of the number of vehicles available for use on a given day.

64. Students in a college were classified according to years in school (X) and number of visits to a museum in the last year ($Y = 0$ for no visits, $= 1$ for one visit, $= 2$ for more than one visit). The joint probabilities in the accompanying table were estimated for these random variables.

NUMBER OF VISITS (Y)	YEARS IN SCHOOL (X)			
	1	2	3	4
0	.07	.05	.03	.02
1	.13	.11	.17	.15
2	.04	.04	.09	.10

(a) Find the probability that a randomly chosen student has not visited a museum in the last year.

(b) Find the means of the random variables X and Y.

(c) Find and interpret the covariance between the random variables X and Y.

65. A basketball team's star 3-point shooter takes six 3-point shots in a game. Historically, he makes 40% of all 3-point shots attempted. Answer the following questions about the outcome of the six 3-point shots taken in this game, stating at the outset what assumptions you have made.

(a) Find the probability that at least two shots were made.

(b) Find the probability that exactly three shots were made.

(c) Find the mean and standard deviation of the number of shots made.

(d) Find the mean and standard deviation of the total number of points scored as a result of these shots.

66. It is estimated that 55% of the freshmen entering a particular college will graduate from that college in four years.

(a) For a random sample of five entering freshmen, what is the probability that exactly three will graduate in four years?

(b) For a random sample of five entering freshmen, what is the probability that a majority will graduate in four years?

(c) Eighty entering freshmen are chosen at random. Find the mean and standard deviation of the proportion of these eighty who will graduate in four years.

67. The World Series of baseball is to be played by team A and team B. The first team to win four games wins the series. Suppose that team A is the better team, in the sense that the probability is .6 that team A will win any specific game. Assume also that the result of any game is independent of that of any other.

(a) What is the probability that team A will win the series?

(b) What is the probability that a seventh game will be needed to determine the winner?

(c) Suppose that, in fact, each team wins two of the first four games.

  (i) What is the probability that team A will win the series?

  (ii) What is the probability that a seventh game will be needed to determine the winner?

68. Using detailed cash flow information, a financial analyst claims to be able to spot companies that are likely candidates for bankruptcy. The analyst is presented with information on the past records of fifteen companies and told that in fact five of these have failed. He selects as candidates for failure five companies from the group of fifteen. In fact, three of the five companies selected by the analyst were among those that failed. Evaluate the financial analyst's performance on this test of his ability to detect failed companies.

69. A team of five analysts is about to examine the earnings prospects of twenty corporations. Each of the five analysts will study four of the corporations. These analysts are not equally competent. In fact, one of them is a star, having an excellent record of anticipating changing trends. Ideally, management would like to allocate to this analyst the four corporations whose earnings will deviate most from past trends. However, lacking this information, management allocates corporations to analysts randomly. What is the probability that at

least two of the four corporations whose earnings will deviate most from past trends are allocated to the star analyst?

70. On the average, 2.4 customers per minute arrive at an airline check-in desk during the peak period. Assume that the distribution of arrivals is Poisson.

   (a) What is the probability that there will be no arrivals in a minute?

   (b) What is the probability that there will be more than three arrivals in a minute?

71. A recent estimate suggested that of all individuals and couples reporting income in excess of $200,000, 6.5% either paid no federal tax or paid tax at an effective rate of less than 15%. A random sample of 100 of those reporting income in excess of $200,000 was taken. What is the probability that more than two of the sample members either paid no federal tax or paid tax at an effective rate of less than 15%?

72. A company has two assembly lines, each of which stalls an average of 2.4 times per week, according to a Poisson distribution. Assume that the performances of these assembly lines are independent of one another. What is the probability that at least one line stalls at least once in any given week?

73. A coin is thrown three times, and interest is in the number, X, of heads resulting.

   (a) Find the probability function of the random variable X.

   (b) Find the mean and standard deviation of the random variable X.

   (c) Consider a game in which you gain $2 if either one or three heads result, you lose $4 if two heads result, and there is no gain or loss if no heads result. Let the random variable Y, which can take the values -4, 0, or 2, denote your gain from this game. Find the probability function, the mean, and the standard deviation of the random variable Y.

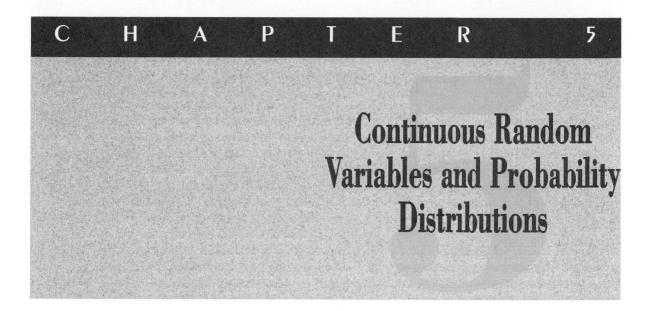

CHAPTER 5

Continuous Random Variables and Probability Distributions

5.1 CONTINUOUS RANDOM VARIABLES

In this chapter, we will analyze probability statements about random variables that can take any value on a continuum. Measures of time, distance, or temperature fit naturally into this category. In such cases, the probability that the random variable takes a single specific value—for instance, the probability that a car will travel precisely 27.236 miles on a gallon of gasoline—is 0. It is also convenient to regard as continuous essentially discrete random variables that are measured on such a fine grid that the probability of occurrence of any specific value is trivially small. For instance, in a study of the total debt incurred by students while attending four-year colleges, it is certainly true that the total debt for any given student will be some integer number of cents. However, the probability that a randomly chosen student will have debts totaling precisely $9,274.57 is sufficiently small that the random variable of interest can be treated as if it were continuous.

Although the assessment of probabilities for individual values of continuous random variables is meaningless, we may well be interested in the probability that such a variable lies in some given range. For example, the probability that a car travels between 27 and 28 miles on a gallon of gasoline or the probability that a randomly chosen student has incurred debts between $9,000 and $10,000 may be useful quantities to evaluate. Therefore, in characterizing probability distributions for continuous random variables, a natural place to begin (by analogy with our discussion of discrete random variables) is with the idea of cumulative probability. This will provide us with a measure of the probability that a random variable does not exceed any specific value.

179

5.2 PROBABILITY DISTRIBUTIONS FOR CONTINUOUS RANDOM VARIABLES

As in Chapter 4, we let X be a random variable and x a specific value that it could take. Here we call the probability that X does not exceed x the **cumulative distribution function.** This is analogous to the cumulative probability function of Chapter 4.

Definition

The **cumulative distribution function** $F_X(x)$ of a continuous random variable X expresses the probability that X does not exceed the value x, as a function of x; that is

$$F_X(x) = P(X \le x)$$

To illustrate the ideas involved, we introduce a random variable that has a particularly simple probability structure. As one example of its use, suppose that a road tunnel is precisely 1 mile long and that we are concerned with vehicle breakdowns in the tunnel. Let the random variable X denote the distance into the tunnel, measured in miles from one of its entrances, at which a breakdown occurs, and suppose that for a stretch of the tunnel of fixed length, the probability of breakdown is identical to that for any other stretch of the same length. Then the distribution of X, for a particular breakdown, is said to be **uniform** in the range 0 to 1. The cumulative distribution function for this random variable is

$$F_X(x) = \begin{cases} 0 & \text{if } x \le 0 \\ x & \text{if } 0 < x < 1 \\ 1 & \text{if } x \ge 1 \end{cases}$$

This function, which between $x = 0$ and $x = 1$ is a straight line, is graphed in Figure 5.1. Using this function, we see that the probability that any breakdown occurs in the first ¼ mile of the tunnel is

$$P\left(X \le \frac{1}{4}\right) = F_X\left(\frac{1}{4}\right) = \frac{1}{4}$$

Now, suppose we want to measure the probability that a continuous random variable falls in a specified range. Let the endpoints of the range of interest be $X = a$ and $X = b$, with $b > a$, so that we require $P(a < X < b)$.[1] If X is less than b, then it is either less than a or it lies between a and b. Moreover, since this latter pair of events are mutually exclusive

$$P(X < b) = P(X < a) + P(a < X < b)$$

Hence, from the definition of the cumulative distribution function

$$F_X(b) = F_X(a) + P(a < X < b)$$

---

[1] Note that for continuous random variables, it does not matter whether we write "less than," as in $P(X < b)$, or "less than or equal to," as in $P(X \le b)$, because the probability that X is precisely equal to b is 0.

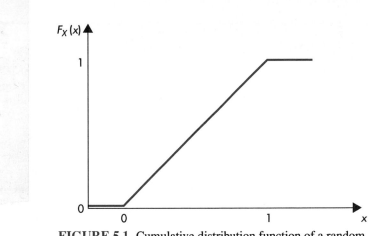

FIGURE 5.1 Cumulative distribution function of a random variable distributed uniformly in the range 0 to 1

Thus, the probability that a random variable takes a value in a particular range can be obtained from the cumulative distribution function, as described in the box.

Range Probabilities and the Cumulative Distribution Function

Let X be a continuous random variable with cumulative distribution function $F_X(x)$, and let a and b be two possible values of X, with $a < b$. The probability that X lies between a and b is

$$P(a < X < b) = F_X(b) - F_X(a) \qquad (5.2.1)$$

For the random variable that is distributed uniformly in the range 0 to 1, the cumulative distribution function in that range is $F_X(x) = x$. Therefore, if a and b are two numbers between 0 and 1, with $a < b$

$$P(a < X < b) = F_X(b) - F_X(a) = b - a$$

For example, if a breakdown occurs, the probability that it happens between ¼ and ¾ mile into the tunnel (that is, $a = \frac{1}{4}$, $b = \frac{3}{4}$) is

$$P\left(\frac{1}{4} < X < \frac{3}{4}\right) = \frac{3}{4} - \frac{1}{4} = \frac{1}{2}$$

We have seen that the probability that a continuous random variable lies between any two values can be expressed in terms of its cumulative distribution function. This function therefore contains all the information about the probability structure of the random variable. However, for many purposes, a different function is more useful. In Chapter 4, we discussed the probability function for discrete random variables, which expresses the probability that a discrete random variable takes any specific value. This concept is not directly relevant in the case of continuous random variables, since here the probability of any specific value arising is 0. However, a related function, called the **probability density function,** can be constructed for continuous random variables, allowing for graphical interpretation of their probability structure.

Let X be a continuous random variable, and let x be any number lying in the range of values this random variable can take. The **probability density function,** $f_X(x)$, of the random variable is a function with the following properties:

(i) $f_X(x) \geq 0$ for all values of x

(ii) Suppose this density function is graphed. Let a and b be two possible values of the random variable X, with $a < b$. Then the probability that X lies between a and b is the area under the density function between these points.

To illustrate property (ii), Figure 5.2 shows the plot of an arbitrary probability density function for some continuous random variable. Two possible values, a and b, are shown, and the shaded area under the curve between these points is the probability that the random variable lies in the interval between them.[2]

To see a specific probability density function, we return to the case of a random variable having a uniform distribution in the range 0 to 1. We introduced this distribution to represent the distance into a 1-mile-long tunnel of vehicle breakdowns, where it could be assumed that the probability of a breakdown in any stretch of the tunnel of fixed length is the same as that in any other stretch of the same length. Given this assumption, the shape of the appropriate probability density function can be deduced. Suppose that the complete 1-mile interval is divided into a large number of small subintervals of equal length. Since the probability of a breakdown is the same in each of these subintervals, and since probability corresponds to area under the density function, it follows that the value of the probability density function must be constant throughout the whole range from 0 to 1. Moreover, since, if a breakdown occurs, it must do so between 0 and 1 miles into the tunnel, it follows that the total area under the density function in this range is 1. Hence, the probability density function of this random variable is simply the unit square graphed in Figure 5.3. The uniformity of the

FIGURE 5.2 The shaded area is the probability that the random variable X lies between a and b

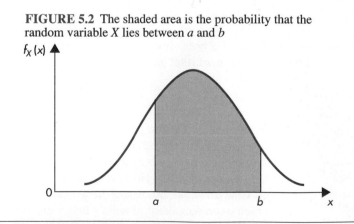

[2] Readers with a knowledge of calculus will recognize that the probability that a random variable lies in a given range is the *integral* of the probability density function between the endpoints of the range; that is

$$P(a < X < b) = \int_a^b f_X(x)\, dx$$

density along the range of possible values gives the distribution its name. This probability density function can be written algebraically as

$$f_X(x) = \begin{cases} 1 & \text{for } 0 < x < 1 \\ 0 & \text{for all other values of } x \end{cases}$$

We can now use this density function to find the probability that the random variable falls in any specified range. The calculation of the probability that a given breakdown occurs between ¼ and ¾ mile into the tunnel is illustrated in Figure 5.4. Since the height of the density function is $f_X(x) = 1$, the area under the curve between these two points is ½, which is the required probability. This is precisely the conclusion reached earlier from consideration of the cumulative distribution function.

We have seen that the probability that a random variable lies between a pair of values is the area under the probability density function between those values. Two special cases of this result are of considerable importance. First, since the random variable must take *some* value—that is, it certainly lies between minus infinity and plus infinity—it follows that the total area under the probability density function is 1. (This is analogous to the requirement for discrete random variables that the individual event probabilities sum to 1.) Second, if we let $F_X(x_0)$ be the cumulative distribution function evaluated at x_0, this is just the probability that the random variable does not exceed x_0; that is

$$F_X(x_0) = P(X \le x_0)$$

which we now see is the area under the probability density function to the left of x_0.

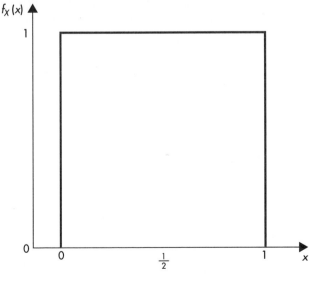

FIGURE 5.3 Probability density function of a random variable distributed uniformly in the range 0 to 1

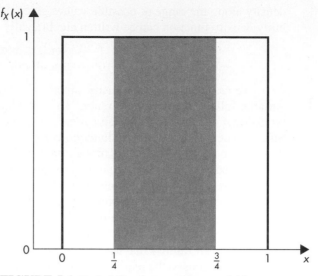

FIGURE 5.4 Probability that a random variable, distributed uniformly in the range 0 to 1, lies between ¼ and ¾; the shaded area is the probability, equal to ½

Areas Under Continuous Probability Density Functions

Let X be a continuous random variable with probability density function $f_X(x)$ and cumulative distribution function $F_X(x)$. Then the following properties hold:

(i) The total area under the curve $f_X(x)$ is 1.[3]

(ii) The area under the curve $f_X(x)$ to the left of x_0 is $F_X(x_0)$, where x_0 is any value that the random variable can take.[4]

The two results stated in the box are illustrated for the uniform distribution in Figure 5.5. In part (a) of the figure, it can be seen that the area under the probability density function is 1, as it is simply the area of a square whose sides are of length 1. Part (b) of the figure shows the cumulative distribution function, evaluated at x_0, as the area of a rectangle of height 1 and width x_0. Hence, we have $F_X(x_0) = x_0$.

---

[3] Formally, in integral calculus notation

$$\int_{-\infty}^{\infty} f_X(x)\, dx = 1$$

[4] The cumulative distribution function is thus the integral

$$F_X(x_0) = \int_{-\infty}^{x_0} f_X(x)\, dx$$

It therefore follows that the probability density function is the derivative of the cumulative distribution function; that is

$$f_X(x) = \frac{dF_X(x)}{dx}$$

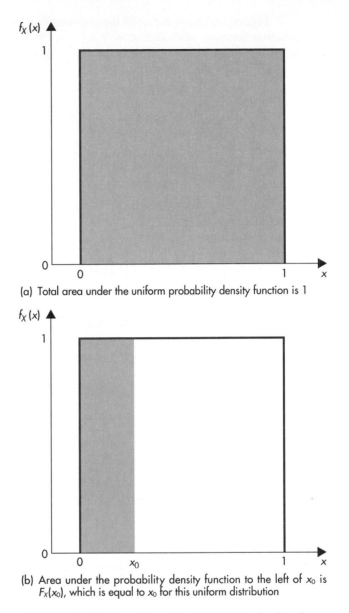

(a) Total area under the uniform probability density function is 1

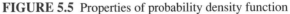

(b) Area under the probability density function to the left of x_0 is $F_X(x_0)$, which is equal to x_0 for this uniform distribution

FIGURE 5.5 Properties of probability density function

EXAMPLE 5.1

A repair team is responsible for a stretch of oil pipeline 2 miles long. The distance (in miles) along this stretch at which any fracture arises can be represented by a uniformly distributed random variable, with probability density function

$$f_X(x) = \begin{cases} .5 & \text{for } 0 < x < 2 \\ 0 & \text{for all other values of } x \end{cases}$$

Find the cumulative distribution function and the probability that any given fracture occurs between .5 mile and 1.5 miles along this stretch of pipeline.

PROBABILITY DISTRIBUTIONS FOR CONTINUOUS RANDOM VARIABLES **185**

Figure 5.6 shows a plot of the probability density function. The cumulative distribution function evaluated at x_0, $F_X(x_0)$, is the probability that the random variable takes a value less than x_0. This is the shaded area shown in the graph—a rectangle of height .5 and width x_0. Thus

$$F_X(x_0) = .5x_0 \qquad \text{for } 0 < x_0 < 2$$

To find the probability that a particular fracture arises between .5 mile and 1.5 miles along the pipeline, we have

$$P(.5 < X < 1.5) = F_X(1.5) - F_X(.5)$$
$$= (.5)(1.5) - (.5)(.5) = .5$$

This result can also be deduced from the area under the probability density function between $x = .5$ and $x = 1.5$.

5.3 EXPECTATIONS FOR CONTINUOUS RANDOM VARIABLES

In Section 4.3, we introduced the ideas of the expectation of a discrete random variable X and the expectation of a function of that random variable. These concepts extend to the case where the random variable is continuous, though the fact that here the probability of any specific value is 0 necessitates some modification in the method of evaluating expectations, as indicated in the box.

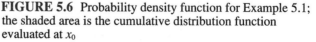

Expectations for Continuous Random Variables

Suppose that a random experiment leads to an outcome that can be represented by a continuous random variable. If N independent replications of this experiment are carried out, then the **expected value** of the random variable is the average of the values taken, as the

FIGURE 5.6 Probability density function for Example 5.1; the shaded area is the cumulative distribution function evaluated at x_0

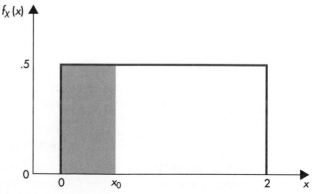

number N of replications becomes infinitely large. The expected value of a random variable X is denoted $E(X)$.

Similarly, if $g(X)$ is any function of the random variable X, then the expected value of this function is the average value taken by the function over repeated independent trials, as the number of trials becomes infinitely large.[5] This expectation is denoted $E[g(X)]$.

In the next box, some important specific expected values are defined in precisely the same manner as for discrete random variables.

Definitions

Let X be a continuous random variable.

(i) The **mean** of X, denoted μ_X, is defined as the expected value of X; that is

$$\mu_X = E(X)$$

(ii) The **variance** of X, denoted σ_X^2, is defined as the expectation of the squared discrepancy, $(X - \mu_X)^2$, of the random variable from its mean; that is

$$\sigma_X^2 = E[(X - \mu_X)^2]$$

An alternative but equivalent expression is

$$\sigma_X^2 = E(X^2) - \mu_X^2$$

(iii) The **standard deviation** of X, σ_X, is the square root of the variance.

The mean and variance are two pieces of summary information about a probability distribution. The mean provides a measure of the center of the probability distribution. A physical interpretation is as follows: Cut out the graph of a probability density function. The point along the x-axis at which this figure exactly balances on one's finger is the mean of the distribution. For example, the graph of the probability density function of the uniform distribution in Figure 5.3 is perfectly symmetric about $x = \frac{1}{2}$, so $\mu_X = \frac{1}{2}$ is the mean of this random variable. In the example about vehicle breakdowns in a 1-mile-long tunnel, a mean breakdown distance of $\frac{1}{2}$ mile from the tunnel entrance can be interpreted as a statement that over a very large number of breakdowns, the average distance into the tunnel will be $\frac{1}{2}$ mile.

The variance—or its square root, the standard deviation—gives a measure of the spread (or dispersion) of a probability distribution about its center. To illustrate, consider a uniform distribution in the range 0 to 1 and a second distribution that is uni-

---

[5] Formally, using integral calculus, we express the expected value of the random variable X by

$$E(X) = \int_{-\infty}^{\infty} x f_X(x)\, dx$$

and the expected value of the function $g(X)$ by

$$E[g(X)] = \int_{-\infty}^{\infty} g(x) f_X(x)\, dx$$

Notice that in forming these expectations, the integral plays the same role as the summation operator in the discrete case.

form on the range of ¼ to ¾. The probability density functions of these two distributions are graphed in Figure 5.7. For the second distribution, shown in part (b) of the figure, the probability density function is

$$f_X(x) = \begin{cases} 2 & \text{for } \dfrac{1}{4} < x < \dfrac{3}{4} \\ 0 & \text{for all other values of } x \end{cases}$$

This is a proper density function, since the area under the curve is 1. Both distributions are centered on $x = \frac{1}{2}$, which is the mean in each case. However, the density of the distribution of part (a) is more disperse about this mean than that of part (b). This is reflected in the fact that the former distribution has the larger variance.[6]

In Section 4.3, we showed how means and variances could be found for linear functions of discrete random variables. In fact, the same results are true for continuous random variables, as summarized in the box.

Let X be a continuous random variable with mean μ_X and variance σ_X^2, and let a and b be any constant fixed numbers. Define the random variable Z as

$$Z = a + bX$$

Then the mean and variance of Z are

$$\mu_Z = E(a + bX) = a + b\mu_X$$

and

$$\sigma_Z^2 = \text{Var}(a + bX) = b^2\sigma_X^2$$

so the standard deviation of Z is

$$\sigma_Z = |b|\sigma_X$$

As a special case of these results, the random variable

$$Z = \frac{X - \mu_X}{\sigma_X}$$

has mean 0 and variance 1.

EXAMPLE
5.2

A homeowner estimates that within the range of likely temperatures, her January heating bill Y, in dollars, will be

$$Y = 290 - 5T$$

where T is the average temperature in the month, in degrees Fahrenheit. If average January temperature can be represented by a random variable with mean 24°F and standard deviation 4°F, find the mean and standard deviation of this homeowner's January heating bill.

The random variable T has mean and standard deviation

$$\mu_T = 24 \qquad \sigma_T = 4$$

---

[6] In fact, the variances are $\frac{1}{12}$ for the distribution of part (a) and $\frac{1}{48}$ for that of part (b).

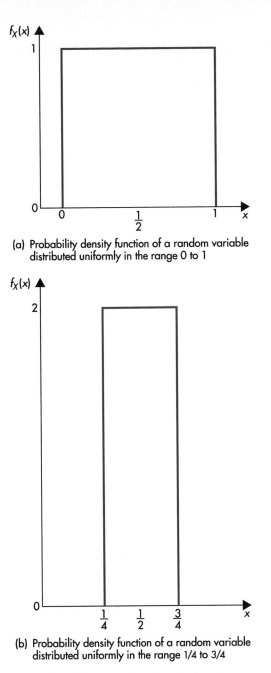

(a) Probability density function of a random variable distributed uniformly in the range 0 to 1

(b) Probability density function of a random variable distributed uniformly in the range 1/4 to 3/4

FIGURE 5.7 Probability density functions for two uniformly distributed random variables

Therefore, the expected heating bill is

$$\mu_Y = 290 - 5\mu_T$$
$$= 290 - (5)(24) = \$170$$

The standard deviation for this bill is

$$\sigma_Y = |-5|\sigma_T = (5)(4) = \$20$$

EXPECTATIONS FOR CONTINUOUS RANDOM VARIABLES   189

5.4 JOINTLY DISTRIBUTED CONTINUOUS RANDOM VARIABLES

Section 4.4 introduced joint distributions for discrete random variables. Many of the concepts and results discussed there extend quite naturally to the case of continuous random variables.

Definitions

Let $X_1, X_2, \ldots, X_K$ be continuous random variables.

(i) Their **joint cumulative distribution function,** $F_{X_1, X_2, \ldots, X_K}(x_1, x_2, \ldots, x_K)$ expresses the probability that simultaneously X_1 is less than x_1, X_2 is less than x_2, and so on; that is

$$F_{X_1, X_2, \ldots, X_K}(x_1, x_2, \ldots, x_K) = P(X_1 < x_1 \cap X_2 < x_2 \cap \cdots \cap X_K < x_K)$$

(ii) The cumulative distribution functions $F_{X_1}(x_1)$, $F_{X_2}(x_2)$, $\ldots$, $F_{X_K}(x_K)$ of the individual random variables are called their **marginal distribution functions.** For any i, $F_{X_i}(x_i)$ is the probability that the random variable X_i does not exceed the specific value x_i.

(iii) The random variables are **independent** if and only if

$$F_{X_1, X_2, \ldots, X_K}(x_1, x_2, \ldots, x_K) = F_{X_1}(x_1) F_{X_2}(x_2) \cdots F_{X_K}(x_K)$$

The notion of statistical independence here is precisely the same as in the discrete case. Independence of a set of random variables implies that the probability distribution of any one of them is unaffected by the values taken by the others. Thus, for example, the assertion that consecutive daily changes in the price of a share of common stock are independent of one another implies that information about past price changes is of no value in assessing what is likely to happen tomorrow.

The notion of expectation extends to functions of jointly distributed continuous random variables. As in the case of discrete random variables, an important quantity of this kind is the **covariance,** which is used in assessing linear association between a pair of random variables.

Definition

Let X and Y be a pair of continuous random variables, with respective means μ_X and μ_Y. The expected value of $(X - \mu_X)(Y - \mu_Y)$ is called the **covariance** between Y and X. That is

$$\text{Cov}(X, Y) = E[(X - \mu_X)(Y - \mu_Y)]$$

An alternative but equivalent expression is

$$\text{Cov}(X, Y) = E(XY) - \mu_X \mu_Y$$

If the random variables X and Y are independent, then the covariance between them is 0. However, the converse is not necessarily true.

The results in Section 4.4 on means and variances of sums and differences of discrete random variables also hold for continuous random variables. For convenience, they are repeated here.

Sums and Differences of Random Variables

Let $X_1, X_2, \ldots, X_K$ be K random variables with means $\mu_1, \mu_2, \ldots, \mu_K$ and variances $\sigma_1^2, \sigma_2^2, \ldots, \sigma_K^2$. The following properties hold:

(i) The mean of their sum is the sum of their means; that is

$$E(X_1 + X_2 + \cdots + X_K) = \mu_1 + \mu_2 + \cdots + \mu_K$$

(ii) If the covariance between every pair of these random variables is 0, then the variance of their sum is the sum of their variances; that is

$$\text{Var}(X_1 + X_2 + \cdots + X_K) = \sigma_1^2 + \sigma_2^2 + \cdots + \sigma_K^2$$

Let X and Y be a pair of random variables with means μ_X and μ_Y and variances σ_X^2 and σ_Y^2. The following properties hold:

(iii) The mean of their difference is the difference of their means; that is

$$E(X - Y) = \mu_X - \mu_Y$$

(iv) If the covariance between X and Y is 0, then the variance of their difference is the *sum* of their variances; that is

$$\text{Var}(X - Y) = \sigma_X^2 + \sigma_Y^2$$

The results (ii) and (iv) hold only if the covariance between the random variables is zero. More generally, if X and Y are a pair of random variables with variances σ_X^2 and σ_Y^2, and covariance $\text{Cov}(X, Y)$, it can be shown that

$$\text{Var}(X + Y) = \sigma_X^2 + \sigma_Y^2 + 2\text{Cov}(X, Y)$$

and

$$\text{Var}(X - Y) = \sigma_X^2 + \sigma_Y^2 - 2\text{Cov}(X, Y)$$

EXAMPLE 5.3

A contractor is uncertain of the precise total costs for either materials or labor for a project. It is believed that materials costs can be represented by a random variable with mean \$100,000 and standard deviation \$10,000. Labor costs are \$1,500 a day, and the number of days needed to complete the project can be represented by a random variable with mean 80 and standard deviation 12. Assuming that materials and labor costs are independent, what are the mean and standard deviation of total project cost (materials plus labor)?

Let the random variables X_1 and X_2 denote, respectively, materials and labor costs. Then, X_1 has mean $\mu_1 = 100,000$ and standard deviation $\sigma_1 = 10,000$. For the random variable X_2

$$\mu_2 = (1,500)(80) = 120,000 \qquad \text{and} \qquad \sigma_2 = (1,500)(12) = 18,000$$

Since total project cost is $X_1 + X_2$, we have mean cost

$$\mu_1 + \mu_2 = 100{,}000 + 120{,}000 = \$220{,}000$$

and since X_1 and X_2 are independent, the variance of their sum is

$$\sigma_1{}^2 + \sigma_2{}^2 = (10{,}000)^2 + (18{,}000)^2 = 424{,}000{,}000$$

Taking the square root, we find the standard deviation to be \$20,591.

EXAMPLE 5.4

Like Example 4.7, this example illustrates the reduction in risk that can follow from the diversification of investments. An investor has \$1,000, which can be allocated in any proportions to two alternative investments. The returns per dollar on these investments will be denoted by the random variables X and Y. It will be assumed that these random variables have the same mean, μ, and the same variance, σ^2, and that they are independent of one another. Suppose that the investor chooses to allocate \$$\alpha$ to the first investment, so that \$$(1{,}000 - \alpha)$ is allocated to the second. We now compare the merits of alternative allocations.

The total return on the investment is

$$R = \alpha X + (1{,}000 - \alpha)Y$$

This random variable has expected value

$$E(R) = \alpha E(X) + (1{,}000 - \alpha)E(Y)$$
$$= \alpha\mu + (1{,}000 - \alpha)\mu = \$1{,}000\mu$$

This expected return is the same whatever choice of α is made.

The variance of the total return is

$$Var(R) = \alpha^2 Var(X) + (1{,}000 - \alpha)^2 Var(Y)$$
$$= \alpha^2\sigma^2 + (1{,}000 - \alpha)^2\sigma^2$$
$$= (2\alpha^2 - 2{,}000\alpha + 1{,}000{,}000)\sigma^2$$

Notice that, if either $\alpha = 0$ or $\alpha = 1{,}000$, so that the entire \$1,000 is allocated to just one of the investments, the variance of total return is $1{,}000{,}000\sigma^2$. However, if \$500 is allocated to each investment, so that $\alpha = 500$, the variance of total return is $500{,}000\sigma^2$. (This is the smallest possible value in this example.) Thus, by spreading the investment this way, as compared with allocating everything to just one of the possibilities, the investor can achieve the same expected return, but a much smaller variance—that is, a much lower level of risk.

EXERCISES

1. An analyst has available two forecasts, F_1 and F_2, of earnings per share of a corporation next year. He intends to form a compromise forecast as a weighted average of the two individual forecasts. In forming the compromise forecast, weight X will be given to the first forecast and weight $(1 - X)$ to the second, so that the compromise forecast is $XF_1 + (1 - X)F_2$. The analyst wants to choose a value between 0 and 1 for the weight X, but he is quite uncertain of what will be the best choice. Suppose that what eventually emerges as the best possible choice of the weight X can be viewed as a random variable uniformly distributed between 0 and 1, having probability density function

$$f_X(x) = \begin{cases} 1 & \text{for } 0 < x < 1 \\ 0 & \text{for all other values of } x \end{cases}$$

(a) Draw the probability density function.

(b) Find and draw the cumulative distribution function.

(c) Find the probability that the best choice of the weight X is less than .25.

(d) Find the probability that the best choice of the weight X is more than .75.

(e) Find the probability that the best choice of the weight X is between .2 and .8.

2. The jurisdiction of a rescue team includes emergencies occurring on a stretch of river that is four miles long. Experience has shown that the distance along this stretch, measured in miles from its northernmost point, at which an emergency occurs can be represented by a uniformly distributed random variable over the range 0 to 4 miles. Then, if X denotes the distance (in miles) of an emergency from the northernmost point of this stretch of river, its probability density function is

$$f_X(x) = \begin{cases} .25 & \text{for } 0 < x < 4 \\ 0 & \text{for all other } x \end{cases}$$

(a) Draw the probability density function.

(b) Find and draw the cumulative distribution function.

(c) Find the probability that a given emergency arises within 1 mile of the northernmost point of this stretch of river.

(d) The rescue team's base is at the midpoint of this stretch of river. Find the probability that a given emergency arises more than 1.5 miles from this base.

3. The incomes of all families in a particular suburb can be represented by a continuous random variable. It is known that the median income for all families in this suburb is $60,000 and that 40% of all families in the suburb have incomes above $72,000.

(a) For a randomly chosen family, what is the probability that income will be between $60,000 and $72,000?

(b) Given no further information, what can be said about the probability that a randomly chosen family has income below $65,000?

4. At the beginning of winter, a homeowner estimates that the probability is .4 that her total heating bill for the three winter months will be less than $380. She also estimates that the probability is .6 that the total bill will be less than $460.

(a) What is the probability that the total bill will be between $380 and $460?

(b) Given no further information, what can be said about the probability that the total bill will be less than $400?

5. An author receives from a publisher a contract, according to which she is to be paid a fixed sum of $10,000, plus $1.50 for each copy of her book sold. Her uncertainty about total sales of the book can be represented by a random variable with mean 30,000 and standard deviation 8,000. Find the mean and standard deviation of the total payments she will receive.

6. A contractor submits a bid on a project, for which more research and development work needs to be done. It is estimated that the total cost of satisfying the project specifications will be $20 million, plus the cost of the further research and development work. The contractor views the cost of this work as a random variable with mean $4 million and standard deviation $1 million. The contractor wishes to submit a bid such that his expected profit will be 10% of his expected costs. What should be the bid? If this bid is accepted, what will be the standard deviation of the profit made on the project?

7. A charitable organization solicits donations by telephone. Employees are paid $60 plus 20% of the money their calls generate each week. The amount of money generated in a week can be viewed as a random variable with mean $700 and standard deviation $130. Find the mean and standard deviation of an employee's total pay in a week.

8. A salesman receives an annual salary of $6,000, plus 8% of the value of the orders he takes. The annual value of these orders can be represented by a random variable with

mean $600,000 and standard deviation $180,000. Find the mean and standard deviation of the salesman's annual income.

9. An investor plans to divide $200,000 between two investments. The first yields a certain profit of 10%, while the second yields a profit with expected value 18% and standard deviation 6%. If the investor divides the money equally between these two investments, find the mean and standard deviation of the total profit.

10. A homeowner has installed a new energy-efficient furnace. It is estimated that, over a year, the new furnace will reduce energy costs by an amount that can be regarded as a random variable with mean $200 and standard deviation $60. Stating any assumptions you need to make, find the mean and standard deviation of total energy cost reductions over a period of 5 years.

11. A consultant is beginning work on three projects. The expected profits from these projects are $50,000, $72,000, and $40,000. The associated standard deviations are $10,000, $12,000, and $9,000. Assuming independence of outcomes, find the mean and standard deviation of the consultant's total profit from these three projects.

12. Continuing Example 5.4, assume the same specifications as that example, except that now we no longer assume that the random variables X and Y are independent of one another. Denote by C the covariance between these random variables. Show now that the variance of total return is

$$\text{Var}(R) = (2\alpha^2 - 2,000\alpha + 1,000,000)\sigma^2 + 2\alpha(1,000 - \alpha)C$$

Show that the choice of $\alpha = 500$ is less risky than the choice of $\alpha = 0$, provided $C < \sigma^2$ (as it must be). For what values of C does diversification most reduce risk?

13. A consultant has three sources of income—from teaching short courses, from selling computer software, and from advising on projects. His expected annual incomes from these sources are $20,000, $25,000, $15,000, and the respective standard deviations are $2,000, $5,000, $4,000. Assuming independence, find the mean and standard deviation of his total annual income.

14. Five inspectors are employed to check the quality of components produced on an assembly line. For each inspector, the number of components that can be checked in a shift can be represented by a random variable with mean 120 and standard deviation 16. Let X represent the number of components checked by an inspector in a shift. Then the total number checked is $5X$, which has mean 600 and standard deviation 80. What is wrong with this argument? Assuming that inspectors' performances are independent of one another, find the mean and standard deviation of the total number of components checked in a shift.

15. It is estimated that in normal highway driving, the number of miles that can be covered by automobiles of a particular model on 1 gallon of gasoline can be represented by a random variable with mean 28 and standard deviation 2.4. Sixteen of these cars, each with 1 gallon of gasoline, are driven independently under highway conditions. Find the mean and standard deviation of the average number of miles that will be achieved by these cars.

5.5 THE NORMAL DISTRIBUTION

In this section, we introduce a continuous distribution that plays a central role in a very large body of statistical analysis. For example, suppose that a big group of students takes a test. A large proportion of their scores are likely to be concentrated about the mean, and the numbers of scores in ranges of a fixed width are likely to "tail off" away from the mean. If the average score on the test is 60, we would expect to find, for instance, more students with scores in the range 55–65 than in the range 85–95. These considerations suggest a probability density function that peaks at the mean and tails off at its extremities. One distribution with these properties is the **normal distribution,** whose probability density function is shown in Figure 5.8. As can be seen, this density function is *bell-shaped*.

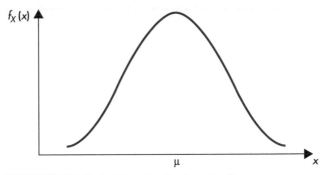

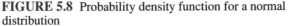

FIGURE 5.8 Probability density function for a normal distribution

---

Probability Density Function of the Normal Distribution

If the random variable X has probability density function

$$f_X(x) = \frac{1}{\sqrt{2\pi\sigma^2}}\, e^{-(x-\mu)^2/2\sigma^2} \qquad \text{for } -\infty < x < \infty$$

where μ and σ^2 are any number such that $-\infty < \mu < \infty$ and $0 < \sigma^2 < \infty$ and where e and π are physical constants, $e = 2.71828\ldots$ and $\pi = 3.14159\ldots$, then X is said to follow a **normal distribution.**

It can be seen from the definition that there is not a single normal distribution but a whole family of distributions, resulting from different specifications of μ and σ^2. These two parameters have very convenient interpretations.

Some Properties of the Normal Distribution

Suppose that the random variable X follows a normal distribution with parameters μ and σ^2. The following properties hold:

(i) The mean of the random variable is μ; that is

$$E(X) = \mu$$

(ii) The variance of the random variable is σ^2; that is

$$\text{Var}(X) = E[(X - \mu)^2] = \sigma^2$$

(iii) The shape of the probability density function is a symmetric bell-shaped curve (see Figure 5.8) centered on the mean μ.

It follows from these properties that given the mean and variance of a normal random variable, an individual member of the family of normal distributions is specified. This allows use of a convenient notation.

Now, the mean of any distribution provides a measure of central location, while the variance gives a measure of spread or dispersion about the mean. Thus, the values taken by the parameters μ and σ^2 have different effects on the probability density function of a normal random variable. Figure 5.9(a) shows probability density functions for two normal distributions with a common variance but different means. It can be seen that increasing the mean while holding the variance fixed shifts the density function but does not alter its shape. In Figure 5.9(b), the two density functions are of

FIGURE 5.9 Effects of μ and σ^2 on the probability density function of a normal random variable

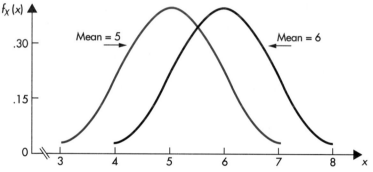

(a) Probability density functions for two normal distributions with means 5 and 6; each distribution has variance 1

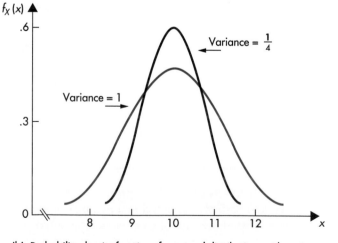

(b) Probability density functions for normal distributions with variances 1/4 and 1; each distribution has mean 10

normal random variables with a common mean but different variances. Each is symmetric about the common mean, but that with the larger variance is more disperse.

An extremely important practical question concerns the determination of probabilities from a specified normal distribution. As a first step in determining probabilities, we introduce the cumulative distribution function.

Cumulative Distribution Function of the Normal Distribution

Suppose that X is a normal random variable with mean μ and variance σ^2; that is, $X \sim N(\mu, \sigma^2)$. Then the **cumulative distribution function** $F_X(x_0)$ is

$$F_X(x_0) = P(X \leq x_0)$$

This is the area under the probability density function to the left of x_0, as illustrated in Figure 5.10. As for any proper density function, the total area under the curve is 1; that is

$$F_X(\infty) = 1$$

There is no simple algebraic expression for calculating the cumulative distribution function of a normally distributed random variable.[7] The general shape of the cumulative distribution function is shown in Figure 5.11.

We have already seen that for *any* continuous random variable, probabilities can be expressed in terms of the cumulative distribution function.

Range Probabilities for Normal Random Variables

Let X be a normal random variable with cumulative distribution function $F_X(x)$, and let a and b be two possible values of X, with $a < b$. Then

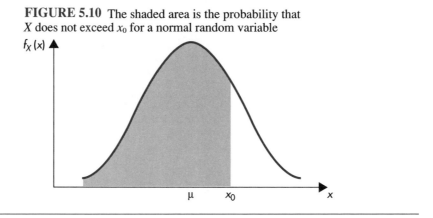

FIGURE 5.10 The shaded area is the probability that X does not exceed x_0 for a normal random variable

---

[7] That is to say that the integral

$$F_X(x_0) = \int_{-\infty}^{x_0} \frac{1}{\sqrt{2\pi\sigma^2}}\, e^{-(x-\mu)^2/2\sigma^2}\, dx$$

does not have a simple algebraic form.

$$P(a < X < b) = F_X(b) - F_X(a)$$

The probability is the area under the corresponding probability density function between a and b, as illustrated in Figure 5.12.

Any required probability can be obtained from the cumulative distribution function. However, a crucial difficulty remains because there does not exist a convenient formula for determining the cumulative distribution function. In principle, for any specific normal distribution, probabilities could be obtained by numerical methods using an electronic computer. However, it would be enormously tedious if we had to carry out such an operation for every normal distribution we encountered. Fortunately, probabilities for *any* normal distribution can always be expressed in terms of probabilities for a *single* normal distribution for which the cumulative distribution function has been evaluated and tabulated. We now introduce the particular distribution that is used for this purpose.

The Standard Normal Distribution

Let Z be a normal random variable with mean 0 and variance 1; that is

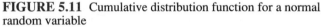

FIGURE 5.11 Cumulative distribution function for a normal random variable

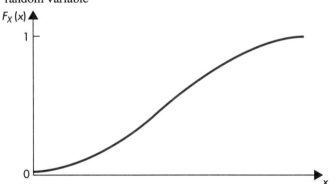

FIGURE 5.12 The shaded area is the probability that X lies between a and b for a normal random variable

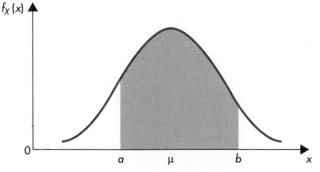

$$Z \sim N(0, 1)$$

Then Z is said to follow the **standard normal distribution.**

If the cumulative distribution function of this random variable is denoted $F_Z(z)$, and $a*$ and $b*$ are two numbers with $a* < b*$, then

$$P(a* < Z < b*) = F_Z(b*) - F_Z(a*)$$

The cumulative distribution function of the standard normal distribution is tabulated in Table 3 in the Appendix. This table gives values of

$$F_Z(z) = P(Z \le z)$$

for nonnegative values of z. For example

$$F_Z(1.25) = .8944$$

Thus, the probability is .8944 that the standard normal random variable takes a value less than 1.25. Values of the cumulative distribution function for negative values of z can be inferred from the symmetry of the probability density function. Let z_0 be any positive number, and suppose that we require

$$F_Z(-z_0) = P(Z \le -z_0)$$

As illustrated in Figure 5.13, because the density function of the standard normal random variable is symmetric about its mean, 0, the area under the curve to the left of $-z_0$ is the same as the area under the curve to the right of z_0; that is

$$P(Z \le -z_0) = P(Z \ge z_0)$$

Moreover, since the total area under the curve is 1

$$P(Z \ge z_0) = 1 - P(Z \le z_0) = 1 - F_Z(z_0)$$

Hence, it follows that

$$F_Z(-z_0) = 1 - F_Z(z_0)$$

FIGURE 5.13 Probability density function for the standard normal random variable Z; the shaded areas, which are equal, show the probability that Z does not exceed $-z_0$ and the probability that Z is greater than z_0

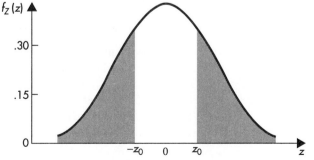

For example

$$P(Z \leq -1.25) = F_Z(-1.25) = 1 - F_Z(1.25) = 1 - .8944 = .1056$$

EXAMPLE
5.5

If Z is a standard normal random variable, find $P(-.50 < Z < .75)$. The required probability is

$$P(-.50 < Z < .75) = F_Z(.75) - F_Z(-.50)$$
$$= F_Z(.75) - [1 - F_Z(.50)]$$

Then, using Table 3 of the Appendix, we obtain

$$P(-.50 < Z < .75) = .7734 - (1 - .6915) = .4649$$

We now show how probabilities for any normal random variable can be expressed in terms of those for the standard normal random variable. Let the random variable X be normally distributed with mean μ and variance σ^2. We saw in Section 5.3 that subtracting the mean and dividing by the standard deviation yields a random variable Z that has mean 0 and variance 1. It can also be shown that if X is normally distributed, so is Z. Hence, Z has a standard normal distribution. Suppose, then, that we require the probability that X lies between the numbers a and b. This is equivalent to $(X - \mu)/\sigma$ lying between $(a - \mu)/\sigma$ and $(b - \mu)/\sigma$, so that the probability of interest is

$$P(a < X < b) = P\left(\frac{a - \mu}{\sigma} < \frac{X - \mu}{\sigma} < \frac{b - \mu}{\sigma}\right)$$
$$= P\left(\frac{a - \mu}{\sigma} < Z < \frac{b - \mu}{\sigma}\right)$$

Finding Range Probabilities for Normal Random Variables

Let X be a normal random variable with mean μ and variance σ^2. Then the random variable $Z = (X - \mu)/\sigma$ has a standard normal distribution; that is, $Z \sim N(0,1)$.

It follows that if a and b are any numbers with $a < b$, then

$$P(a < X < b) = P\left(\frac{a - \mu}{\sigma} < Z < \frac{b - \mu}{\sigma}\right)$$
$$= F_Z\left(\frac{b - \mu}{\sigma}\right) - F_Z\left(\frac{a - \mu}{\sigma}\right)$$

where Z is the standard normal random variable and $F_Z(z)$ denotes its cumulative distribution function.

The result is illustrated in Figure 5.14. Part (a) of the figure shows the probability density function of a normal random variable X with mean $\mu = 3$ and standard deviation $\sigma = 2$. The shaded area shows the probability that X lies between 4 and 6. This is the same as the probability that a standard normal random variable lies between $(4 - \mu)/\sigma$ and $(6 - \mu)/\sigma$, that is, between .5 and 1.5. This probability is the shaded area under the standard normal curve in Figure 5.14(b).

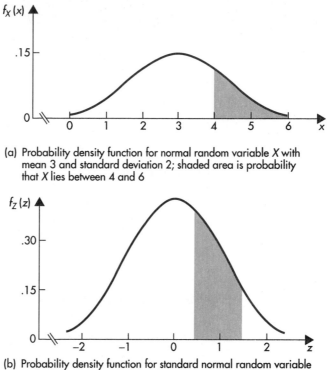

(a) Probability density function for normal random variable X with mean 3 and standard deviation 2; shaded area is probability that X lies between 4 and 6

(b) Probability density function for standard normal random variable Z; shaded area is probability that Z lies between .5 and 1.5 and is equal to shaded area in part (a)

FIGURE 5.14 Finding range probabilities for normal random variables

EXAMPLE 5.6

If $X \sim N(15, 16)$, find the probability that X is larger than 18. This probability is

$$P(X > 18) = P\left(Z > \frac{18 - \mu}{\sigma}\right)$$

$$= P\left(Z > \frac{18 - 15}{4}\right)$$

$$= P(Z > .75)$$

$$= 1 - P(Z < .75)$$

$$= 1 - F_Z(.75)$$

From Table 3 in the Appendix, $F_Z(.75)$ is .7734, so

$$P(X > 18) = 1 - .7734 = .2266$$

EXAMPLE 5.7

If X is normally distributed with mean 3 and standard deviation 2, find $P(4 < X < 6)$.

We have

$$P(4 < X < 6) = P\left(\frac{4 - \mu}{\sigma} < Z < \frac{6 - \mu}{\sigma}\right)$$

$$= P\left(\frac{4 - 3}{2} < Z < \frac{6 - 3}{2}\right)$$

$$= P(.5 < Z < 1.5)$$

$$= F_Z(1.5) - F_Z(.5)$$

$$= .9332 - .6915 = .2417$$

These are the calculations illustrated in Figure 5.14.

EXAMPLE
5.8

A company produces lightbulbs whose lifetimes follow a normal distribution with mean 1,200 hours and standard deviation 250 hours. If a lightbulb is chosen randomly from the company's output, what is the probability that its lifetime will be between 900 and 1,300 hours?

Let X represent lifetime in hours. Then

$$P(900 < X < 1,300) = P\left(\frac{900 - \mu}{\sigma} < Z < \frac{1,300 - \mu}{\sigma}\right)$$

$$= P\left(\frac{900 - 1,200}{250} < Z < \frac{1,300 - 1,200}{250}\right)$$

$$= P(-1.2 < Z < .4)$$

$$= F_Z(.4) - F_Z(-1.2)$$

$$= .6554 - (1 - .8849) = .5403$$

Hence, the probability is approximately .54 that a lightbulb will last between 900 and 1,300 hours.

EXAMPLE
5.9

A very large group of students obtains test scores that are normally distributed with mean 60 and standard deviation 15. What proportion of the students obtained scores between 85 and 95?

Let X denote the test score. Then we have

$$P(85 < X < 95) = P\left(\frac{85 - \mu}{\sigma} < Z < \frac{95 - \mu}{\sigma}\right)$$

$$= P\left(\frac{85 - 60}{15} < Z < \frac{95 - 60}{15}\right)$$

$$= P(1.67 < Z < 2.33)$$

$$= F_Z(2.33) - F_Z(1.67)$$

$$= .9901 - .9525 = .0376$$

That is, 3.76% of the students obtained scores in the range 85 to 95.

EXAMPLE 5.10

For the test scores of Example 5.9, find the cutoff point for the top 10% of all students.

We have previously found probabilities corresponding to cutoff points. Here we need the cutoff point corresponding to a particular probability. The position is illustrated in Figure 5.15, which shows the probability density function of a normally distributed random variable with mean 60 and standard deviation 15. Let the number b denote the minimum score needed to be in the highest 10%. Then, the probability is .10 that the score of a randomly chosen student exceeds the number b. This probability is shown as the shaded area in Figure 5.15. If X denotes the test scores, then the probability that X exceeds b is .1, so

$$.1 = P(X > b)$$
$$= P\left(Z > \frac{b - \mu}{\sigma}\right)$$
$$= P\left(Z > \frac{b - 60}{15}\right)$$

Hence, it follows that

$$.9 = P\left(Z < \frac{b - 60}{15}\right)$$
$$= F_Z\left(\frac{b - 60}{15}\right)$$

Now, from Table 3 of the Appendix, if $F_Z(z) = .9$, then $z = 1.28$. Therefore, we have

$$\frac{b - 60}{15} = 1.28$$

so

$$b = 79.2$$

The conclusion is that 10% of the students obtain scores higher than 79.2.

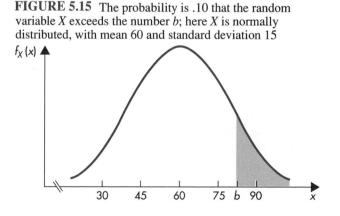

FIGURE 5.15 The probability is .10 that the random variable X exceeds the number b; here X is normally distributed, with mean 60 and standard deviation 15

In Examples 5.9 and 5.10, if the scores awarded on the test were integers, the distribution of scores would be inherently discrete. Nevertheless, the normal distribution can typically provide an adequate approximation in such circumstances. We will see later in this chapter that the normal distribution can often be employed as an approximation to discrete distributions. As a preliminary, we introduce in the next section a result that provides strong justification for the emphasis given to the normal distribution in this book.

EXERCISES

16. Let the random variable Z follow a standard normal distribution.
    (a) Find P($Z < 1.20$)
    (b) Find $P(Z > 1.33)$
    (c) Find $P(Z < -1.70)$
    (d) Find $P(Z > -1.00)$
    (e) Find $P(1.20 < Z < 1.33)$
    (f) Find $P(-1.70 < Z < 1.20)$
    (g) Find $P(-1.70 < Z < -1.00)$

17. Let the random variable Z follow a standard normal distribution.
    (a) The probability is .70 that Z is less than what number?
    (b) The probability is .25 that Z is less than what number?
    (c) The probability is .2 that Z is greater than what number?
    (d) The probability is .6 that Z is greater than what number?

18. It is known that amounts of money spent on textbooks in a year by students on a particular campus follow a normal distribution with mean $380 and standard deviation $50.
    (a) What is the probability that a randomly chosen student will spend less than $400 on textbooks in a year?
    (b) What is the probability that a randomly chosen student will spend more than $360 on textbooks in a year?
    (c) Draw a graph to illustrate why the answers to parts (a) and (b) are the same.
    (d) What is the probability that a randomly chosen student will spend between $300 and $400 on textbooks in a year?
    (e) You want to find a range of dollar spending on textbooks in a year that includes 80% of all students on this campus. Explain why any number of such ranges could be found, and find the shortest one.

19. Anticipated consumer demand for a product next month can be represented by a normal random variable with mean 1,200 units and standard deviation 100 units.
    (a) What is the probability that sales will exceed 1,000 units?
    (b) What is the probability that sales will be between 1,100 and 1,300 units?
    (c) The probability is .10 that sales will be more than how many units?

20. The tread life of a particular brand of tire has a normal distribution with mean 35,000 miles and standard deviation 4,000 miles.
    (a) What proportion of these tires have tread lives of more than 38,000 miles?
    (b) What proportion of these tires have tread lives of less than 32,000 miles?
    (c) What proportion of these tires have tread lives between 32,000 and 38,000 miles?
    (d) Draw a graph of the probability density function of tread lives, illustrating
        (i) Why the answers to (a) and (b) are the same.
        (ii) Why the answers to (a), (b), and (c) sum to one.

21. An investment portfolio contains stocks of a large number of corporations. Over the last year the rates of return on these corporate stocks followed a normal distribution, with mean 12.2%, and standard deviation 7.2%.

   (a) For what proportion of these corporations was the rate of return higher than 20%?

   (b) For what proportion of these corporations was the rate of return negative?

   (c) For what proportion of these corporations was the rate of return between 5% and 15%?

22. A company produces bags of a chemical, and it is concerned about impurity content. It is believed that the weights of impurities per bag are normally distributed, with mean 12.2 grams, and standard deviation 2.8 grams. A bag is chosen at random.

   (a) What is the probability that it contains less than 10 grams of impurities?

   (b) What is the probability that it contains more than 15 grams of impurities?

   (c) What is the probability that it contains between 12 and 15 grams of impurities?

   (d) It is possible, without doing the detailed calculations, to deduce which of the answers to (a) and (b) will be the larger. How?

23. A contractor regards the cost of fulfilling a particular contract as a normally distributed random variable with mean $500,000 and standard deviation $50,000.

   (a) What is the probability that the cost of fulfilling the contract will be between $460,000 and $540,000?

   (b) The probability is .2 that the contract will cost less than how much to fulfill?

   (c) Find the shortest range such that the probability is .95 that the cost of fulfilling the contract will fall in this range.

24. Scores on a test follow a normal distribution. What is the probability that a randomly selected student will achieve a score that exceeds the mean score by more than 1.5 standard deviations?

25. A new television series is to be shown. A broadcasting executive feels that his uncertainty about the rating which the show will receive in its first month can be represented by a normal distribution with mean 18.2 and standard deviation 1.6. According to this executive, the probability is .1 that the rating will be less than what number?

26. A broadcasting executive is reviewing the prospects for a new television series. According to her judgment, the probability is .25 that the show will achieve a rating higher than 17.8, and the probability is .15 that it will achieve a rating higher than 19.2. If the executive's uncertainty about the rating can be represented by a normal distribution, what are the mean and variance of that distribution?

27. Scores on an examination taken by a very large group of students are normally distributed with mean 700 and standard deviation 120.

   (a) An A is awarded for a score higher than 820. What proportion of all students obtain an A?

   (b) A B is awarded for scores between 730 and 820. An instructor has a section of 100 students, who can be viewed as a random sample of all students in the large group. Find the expected number of students in this section who will obtain a B.

   (c) It is decided to give a failing grade to the 5% of students with the lowest scores. What is the minimum score needed to avoid a failing grade?

28. I am considering two alternative investments. In both cases, I am unsure about the percentage return but believe that my uncertainty can be represented by normal distributions with the means and standard deviations shown in the accompanying table. I want to make the investment that is more likely to produce a return of at least 10%. Which should I choose?

	MEAN	STANDARD DEVIATION
Investment A	10.4	1.2
Investment B	11.0	4.0

29. A company can purchase raw material from either of two suppliers and is concerned about the amounts of impurity the material contains. A review of the records for each supplier indicates that the percentage impurity levels in consignments of the raw material follow normal distributions with the means and standard deviations given in the table. The company is particularly anxious that the impurity level in a consignment not exceed 5% and wants to purchase from the supplier more likely to meet that specification. Which supplier should be chosen?

	MEAN	STANDARD DEVIATION
Supplier A	4.4	.4
Supplier B	4.2	.6

30. An instructor has found that times spent by students on a particular homework assignment follow a normal distribution with mean 150 minutes and standard deviation 40 minutes.
   (a) The probability is .9 that a randomly chosen student spends more than how many minutes on this assignment?
   (b) The probability is .8 that a randomly chosen student spends less than how many minutes on this assignment?
   (c) Two students are chosen at random. What is the probability that at least one of them spends at least two hours on this assignment?

31. A company services copiers. A review of its records shows that the time taken for a service call can be represented by a normal random variable with mean 75 minutes and standard deviation 20 minutes.
   (a) What proportion of service calls take less than one hour?
   (b) What proportion of service calls take more than 90 minutes?
   (c) Sketch a graph to show why the answers to parts (a) and (b) are the same.
   (d) The probability is .1 that a service call takes more than how many minutes?

32. Scores on an achievement test are known to be normally distributed, with mean 420 and standard deviation 80.
   (a) For a randomly chosen person taking this test, what is the probability of a score between 400 and 480?
   (b) What is the minimum score needed in order to be in the top 10% of all people taking the test?
   (c) For a randomly chosen individual, state, without doing the calculations, in which of the following ranges his or her score is most likely to be: 400–440, 440–480, 480–520, 520–560.
   (d) In which of the ranges listed in (c) is the individual's score least likely to be?
   (e) Two people taking the test are chosen at random. What is the probability that at least one of them scores more than 500 points?

33. It is estimated that the times a well-known rock band, the Living Ingrates, spends on-stage at their concerts follow a normal distribution with mean 200 minutes and standard deviation 20 minutes.
   (a) What proportion of concerts played by this band last between 180 and 200 minutes?
   (b) An audience member smuggles a tape recorder with reel-to-reel tapes with capacity 245 minutes into a Living Ingrates concert. What is the probability that this capacity will be insufficient to record the entire concert?
   (c) If the standard deviation of concert time was only 15 minutes, state, without doing the calculations, whether the probability that a concert would last more than 245 minutes

would be larger than, smaller than, or the same as that found in (b). Sketch a graph to illustrate your answer.

(d) The probability is .1 that a Living Ingrates concert will last less than how many minutes? (Assume, as originally, that the population standard deviation is 20 minutes.)

34. An economics test is taken by a large group of students. The test scores are normally distributed with mean 70, and the probability that a randomly chosen student receives a score less than 85 is .9332. Four students are chosen at random. What is the probability that at least one of them scores more than 80 points on this test?

5.6 THE CENTRAL LIMIT THEOREM

Many random variables met in practice can be characterized as either the sum or the average of a fairly large number of independent random variables. Let $X_1, X_2, \ldots, X_n$ be n independent random variables having identical distributions with mean μ and variance σ^2. Denote their sum by

$$X = X_1 + X_2 + \cdots + X_n$$

We have seen in Sections 4.4 and 5.4 that the mean of a sum is the sum of the means and that, for independent random variables, the variance of the sum is the sum of the variances. Hence, the mean and variance of X are

$$E(X) = n\mu \qquad \text{Var}(X) = n\sigma^2$$

Now, for any random variable, subtracting the mean and dividing by the standard deviation yields a random variable with mean 0 and variance 1, so the random variable

$$Z = \frac{X - E(X)}{\sqrt{\text{Var}(X)}} = \frac{X - n\mu}{\sqrt{n\sigma^2}}$$

has mean 0 and variance 1. Dividing the numerator and denominator of this expression by n yields

$$Z = \frac{\overline{X} - \mu}{\sigma/\sqrt{n}}$$

where

$$\overline{X} = \frac{X_1 + X_2 + \cdots + X_n}{n} = \frac{X}{n}$$

is the average of the X_i.

So far this is not new. The crucial additional information, provided by the **central limit theorem,** is that *whatever the distribution of the X_i* (provided that σ^2 is finite), as the number of terms n in the sum becomes large, the distribution of Z tends to the standard normal.

Central Limit Theorem

Let $X_1, X_2, \ldots, X_n$ be n independent random variables having identical distributions with

---

mean μ and variance σ^2. Denote by X and $\overline{X}$, respectively, the sum and average of these random variables. As n becomes large, the distribution of

$$Z = \frac{X - n\mu}{\sqrt{n\sigma^2}} = \frac{\overline{X} - \mu}{\sigma/\sqrt{n}}$$

tends to the standard normal.

The central limit theorem has a substantial impact on the practice of statistics. Many practical problems involve sums or averages of random variables, and in these circumstances, by virtue of this theorem, the normal distribution very often provides a satisfactory approximation of the true distribution.

The result has a remarkably wide range of applicability. It states that *whatever* the common distribution of a set of independent random variables, provided that their variance is finite, the sum or average of a moderately large number of them will be a random variable with a distribution close to the normal. To illustrate, in Sections 5.2 and 5.3, we introduced the uniform distribution. The density function of this random variable is certainly very different in shape from that of a normal random variable. Nevertheless, the average of a moderately large number of independent uniformly distributed random variables has a distribution close to the normal. Figure 5.16 shows the shapes of the probability density functions of the averages of one, two, and ten independent uniform random variables. In part (a) of the figure, for $n = 1$, we see the familiar uniform density function. Part (b) shows the density function, which is triangular in shape, for the average of $n = 2$ of these random variables. Then, with as few as $n = 10$ values in the average, we find in part (c) a probability density function whose shape is already very similar to that of a normal distribution.

The uniform distribution is symmetric about its mean. However, the central limit theorem applies also to asymmetric distributions. To illustrate, Figure 5.17(a) shows such a distribution.[8] The shape of its probability density function is very different from that of the normal distribution. Parts (b) and (c) of the figure show the probability density functions for the averages of $n = 4$ and $n = 10$ independent observations from this distribution. As can be seen, when there are ten values in the average, the shape of the density function is quite close to that of the standard normal random variable.

The validity of the central limit theorem is not restricted to sums of continuous random variables. It extends also to discrete random variables. In the following section, we will see how the theorem can be exploited to allow us to obtain good approximations of range probabilities for random variables following binomial and Poisson distributions.

In Chapter 6, we will begin our discussion of the important statistical problem of making inference about a population, based on results from a sample. Many of the quantities calculated from sample data are sums or averages. Thus, the central limit theorem becomes relevant and provides a validity for many of the techniques used for approaching this class of problems.

---

[8] This is the chi-square distribution with one degree of freedom. We will meet this distribution again in Section 6.4.

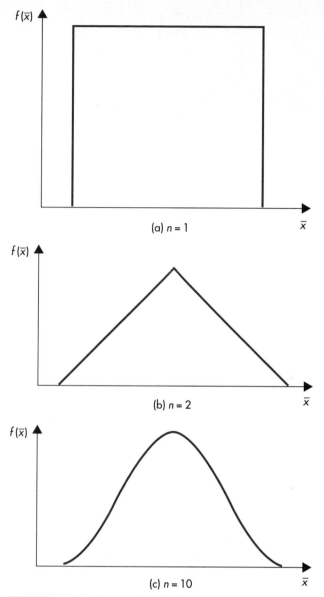

FIGURE 5.16 Shapes of probability density functions for the average of n independent uniformly distributed random variables

5.7 THE NORMAL DISTRIBUTION AS AN APPROXIMATION TO THE BINOMIAL AND POISSON DISTRIBUTIONS

In Chapter 4, we introduced the binomial and Poisson distributions and showed how probabilities for these random variables can be calculated. It emerged that in cases where the number of binomial trials was large and where the mean of the Poisson dis-

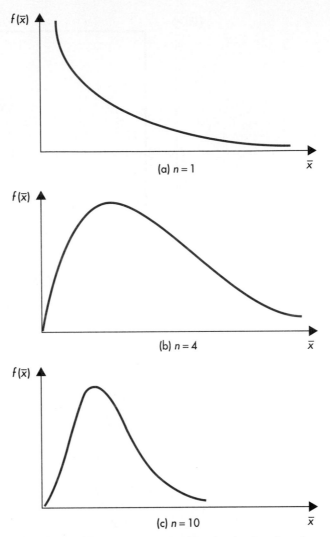

FIGURE 5.17 Shapes of probability density functions for the average of n independent random variables from the chi-square distribution with one degree of freedom

tribution was large, these computations constituted a formidable burden. Fortunately, as a consequence of the central limit theorem, considerable computational simplification can be achieved through a normal approximation to these distributions. We will discuss and illustrate these approximations.

NORMAL APPROXIMATION TO THE BINOMIAL DISTRIBUTION

If n independent trials, each with probability of success p, are carried out, then the number X of successes resulting has a binomial distribution with mean and variance

$$E(X) = np \qquad \text{Var}(X) = np(1 - p)$$

We saw in Section 4.5 that the random variable X could be written as the sum of n independent Bernoulli random variables; that is

$$X = X_1 + X_2 + \cdots + X_n$$

where the random variable X_i takes the value 1 if the outcome of the ith trial is "success," and 0 otherwise, with respective probabilities p and $1 - p$.

Now, this is precisely the setup in which the central limit theorem is applicable. It therefore follows that if the number of trials n is large, the distribution of the random variable

$$Z = \frac{X - E(X)}{\sqrt{\text{Var}(X)}} = \frac{X - np}{\sqrt{np(1 - p)}}$$

is approximately standard normal.

The importance of this result lies in the ease with which it allows us to find, for large n, the probability that the number of successes lies in some given range. Suppose that we want to know the probability that the number of successes will be between a and b, inclusive. We then have

$$P(a \leq X \leq b) = P\left(\frac{a - np}{\sqrt{np(1 - p)}} \leq \frac{X - np}{\sqrt{np(1 - p)}} \leq \frac{b - np}{\sqrt{np(1 - p)}} \right)$$

$$= P\left(\frac{a - np}{\sqrt{np(1 - p)}} \leq Z \leq \frac{b - np}{\sqrt{np(1 - p)}} \right)$$

If the number of trials n is large, the distribution of Z can be well approximated by the standard normal so that the above probability can be found using the methods of Section 5.5.

If the number of trials n is only of moderate size, a worthwhile improvement to this approximation can be achieved. We are here approximating a discrete distribution by a continuous one. While the binomial random variable can take on only integer values, the normal random variable is defined on a continuum. To allow for this distinction, a *continuity correction* can be applied to the previous formula, replacing a and b by $(a - .5)$ and $(b + .5)$, respectively. We then have

$$P(a \leq X \leq b) \approx P\left(\frac{a - .5 - np}{\sqrt{np(1 - p)}} \leq Z \leq \frac{b + .5 - np}{\sqrt{np(1 - p)}} \right)$$

To see the rationale for this modification, suppose that we seek the probability that the number of successes is both greater than or equal to 10 and less than or equal to 15. Since the actual number of successes must be an integer, the probability required is the same as the probability that the number of successes is both greater than or equal to 9.001 and less than or equal to 15.999. As a compromise between these two extremes, we employ a range with end-points 9.5 and 15.5.

Approximating Binomial Probabilities Using the Normal Distribution

Let X be the number of successes resulting from n independent trials, each with probability of success p. If n is large, and provided p is not very small or very large,[9] then to a good approximation

$$P(a \leq X \leq b) \approx P\left(\frac{a - np}{\sqrt{np(1 - p)}} \leq Z \leq \frac{b - np}{\sqrt{np(1 - p)}}\right)$$

or, using the continuity correction

$$P(a \leq X \leq b) \approx P\left(\frac{a - .5 - np}{\sqrt{np(1 - p)}} \leq Z \leq \frac{b + .5 - np}{\sqrt{np(1 - p)}}\right)$$

where Z is a standard normal distribution.[10]

EXAMPLE
5.11

A salesman makes initial telephone contact with potential customers in an effort to assess whether a follow-up visit to their homes is likely to be worthwhile. His experience suggests that 40% of initial contacts lead to follow-up visits. If he contacts 100 people by telephone, what is the probability that between forty-five and fifty home visits will result?

Let X be the number of follow-up visits. Then X has a binomial distribution with $n = 100$ and $p = .4$. Approximating the required probability without using the continuity correction gives

$$P(45 \leq X \leq 50) \approx P\left[\frac{45 - (100)(.4)}{\sqrt{(100)(.4)(.6)}} \leq Z \leq \frac{50 - (100)(.4)}{\sqrt{(100)(.4)(.6)}}\right]$$

$$= P(1.02 \leq Z \leq 2.04)$$

$$= F_Z(2.04) - F_Z(1.02)$$

$$= .9793 - .8461 = .1332$$

This probability is shown as an area under the standard normal curve in Figure 5.18.

If the continuity correction is used in approximating this binomial probability, we have

$$P(45 \leq X \leq 50) \approx P\left[\frac{44.5 - (100)(.4)}{\sqrt{(100)(.4)(.6)}} \leq Z \leq \frac{50.5 - (100)(.4)}{\sqrt{(100)(.4)(.6)}}\right]$$

$$= P(.92 \leq Z \leq 2.14)$$

$$= F_Z(2.14) - F_Z(.92)$$

$$= .9838 - .8212 = .1626$$

The two approximations here yield results that are quite close. For most purposes, the simpler approximation would be adequate in this case. (In fact, to 4 decimal places, the exact probability here is .1621.)

---

[9] In such a case, the Poisson approximation to the binomial distribution should be used (see Section 4.7).

[10] The simpler approximation is generally satisfactory for $n \geq 50$, while for $20 \leq n < 50$, it is preferable to use the continuity correction. In fact, the quality of the approximation depends also on p; it is quite reliable when $np(1 - p) > 9$.

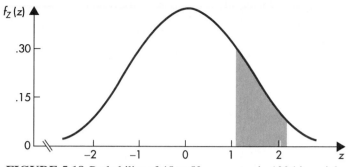

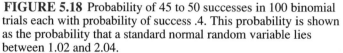

FIGURE 5.18 Probability of 45 to 50 successes in 100 binomial trials each with probability of success .4. This probability is shown as the probability that a standard normal random variable lies between 1.02 and 2.04.

NORMAL APPROXIMATION TO THE POISSON DISTRIBUTION

Let the random variable X denote the number of occurrences of an event in a particular interval of time and denote by λ the expected, or mean, number of occurrences in that time interval. Then X obeys the Poisson distribution discussed in Section 4.7, with mean and variance

$$E(X) = \lambda \qquad \text{and} \qquad \text{Var}(X) = \lambda$$

Consider now the situation in which the mean number of occurrences, λ, is large. Suppose that the time interval of interest is broken down into subintervals of equal width, as in Figure 5.19. Then the total number of occurrences is the sum of the numbers of occurrences in each subinterval. Thus, we see that when the mean of the Poisson distribution is large, the total number of occurrences can be viewed as the sum of a moderately large number of random variables, each of which represents the number of occurrences in a subinterval of the time period. Hence, invoking the central limit theorem, we conclude that when λ is large, the distribution of the random variable

$$Z = \frac{X - E(X)}{\sqrt{\text{Var}(X)}} = \frac{X - \lambda}{\sqrt{\lambda}}$$

is approximately standard normal.

As in the case of the binomial distribution, this result can be used to approximate probabilities. Here again, if λ is of only moderate size, a continuity correction will be desirable.

FIGURE 5.19 Occurrences (•) in the interval from 0 to t broken down into subintervals of equal width

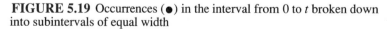

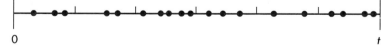

> **Approximating Poisson Probabilities Using the Normal Distribution**
>
> Let X be a Poisson random variable with mean λ. If λ is large, then to a good approximation
>
> $$P(a \le X \le b) \approx P\left(\frac{a - \lambda}{\sqrt{\lambda}} \le Z \le \frac{b - \lambda}{\sqrt{\lambda}} \right)$$
>
> or, using the continuity correction
>
> $$P(a \le X \le b) \approx P\left(\frac{a - .5 - \lambda}{\sqrt{\lambda}} \le Z \le \frac{b + .5 - \lambda}{\sqrt{\lambda}} \right)$$
>
> where Z has a standard normal distribution.

EXAMPLE 5.12

A consumer advice center receives, on average, twenty-five calls per day, and the distribution can be assumed to be Poisson. Estimate the probability that the number of calls received in a given day will be between twenty and thirty.

Let X be the number of calls received, so that X has a Poisson distribution with mean $\lambda = 25$. Approximating the Poisson distribution by the normal distribution, without the continuity correction, yields

$$P(20 \le X \le 30) \approx P\left(\frac{20 - 25}{\sqrt{25}} \le Z \le \frac{30 - 25}{\sqrt{25)}} \right)$$

$$= P(-1 \le Z \le 1)$$

$$= F_Z(1) - F_Z(-1)$$

$$= .8413 - (1 - .8413) = .6826$$

If the continuity correction is used in approximating the Poisson probability, we obtain

$$P(20 \le X \le 30) \approx P\left(\frac{19.5 - 25}{\sqrt{25}} \le Z \le \frac{30.5 - 25}{\sqrt{25}} \right)$$

$$= P(-1.1 \le Z \le 1.1)$$

$$= F_Z(1.1) - F_Z(-1.1)$$

$$= .8643 - (1 - .8643) = .7286$$

The two approximations are fairly close, both suggesting that on about 70% of all days between twenty and thirty calls will be received. It is preferable to use the continuity correction for smaller values of λ than this, while if λ is at least forty the simpler approximation should work very well.

EXERCISES

35. A car rental company has determined that the probability a car will need service work in any given month is .2. The company has 900 cars.

    (a) What is the probability that more than 200 cars will require service work in a particular month?

(b) What is the probability that fewer than 175 cars will need service work in a given month?

(Use the normal approximation to the binomial distribution, without the continuity correction.)

36. It is known that 10% of all the items produced by a particular manufacturing process are defective. From the very large output of a single day, 400 items are selected at random.
    (a) What is the probability that at least thirty-five of the selected items are defective?
    (b) What is the probability that between forty and fifty of the selected items are defective?
    (c) What is the probability that between thirty-four and forty-eight of the selected items are defective?
    (d) Without doing the calculations, state which of the following ranges of defectives has the highest probability: 37–39, 39–41, 41–43, 43–45, 45–47.

(Use the normal approximation to the binomial distribution, without the continuity correction.)

37. A sample of 100 blue-collar employees at a large corporation is taken to assess their attitudes on a proposed new work schedule. If 60% of all blue-collar employees at this corporation favor the new schedule, what is the probability that less than 50 of the sample members will be in favor?

(Use the normal approximation to the binomial distribution, without the continuity correction.)

38. Suppose that half of all students in campus dormitories are dissatisfied with the food service. A random sample of forty students was taken.
    (a) What is the probability that more than fifteen students in the sample were dissatisfied with the food service?
    (b) What is the probability that the number of students in the sample who were dissatisfied with the food service was between 18 and 22 (inclusive)?

(Use the normal approximation to the binomial distribution, with the continuity correction.)

39. A hospital finds that 25% of its bills are at least one month in arrears. A random sample of forty-five bills was taken.
    (a) What is the probability that less than ten bills in the sample were at least one month in arrears?
    (b) What is the probability that the number of bills in the sample at least one month in arrears was between twelve and fifteen (inclusive)?

(Use the normal approximation to the binomial distribution, with the continuity correction.)

40. The tread life of a brand of tire can be represented (as in Exercise 20) by a normal distribution with mean 35,000 miles and standard deviation 4,000 miles. A sample of 100 of these tires is taken. What is the probability that more than 25 of them have tread lives of more than 38,000 miles?

(Use the normal approximation to the binomial distribution, without the continuity correction.)

41. Bags of a chemical produced by a company have (as in Exercise 22) impurity weights that can be represented by a normal distribution with mean 12.2 grams, and standard deviation 2.8 grams. A random sample of 400 of these bags is taken. What is the probability that at least 100 of them contain less than 10 grams of impurities?

42. In the hour before noon, a busy corporation switchboard receives an average of fifty-five calls.
    (a) What is the probability that more than seventy calls will be received during this hour?
    (b) What is the probability that fewer than fifty calls will be received during this hour?
    (c) What is the probability that between fifty and seventy calls will be received during this hour?

(Use the normal approximation to the Poisson distribution, without the continuity correction.)

43. A campus clinic receives walk-in patients at an average rate of thirty per hour, during the midday hours.
   (a) Find the probability that there will be fewer than twenty-five walk-in patients in a particular midday hour.
   (b) Find the probability that there will be more than forty walk-in patients in a particular midday hour.
   (c) Find the probability that there will be between twenty-five and thirty walk-in patients in a particular midday hour.

   (Use the normal approximation to the Poisson distribution, with and without the continuity correction, and compare your answers.)

44. A firm receives, on average, twenty-two replacement orders per week for a particular part. If it begins the week with a stock of twenty-five of these parts, what is the probability that this stock will be exhausted by the end of the week?

   (Use the normal approximation to the Poisson distribution, with and without the continuity correction, and compare your answers.)

5.8   THE EXPONENTIAL DISTRIBUTION

We conclude this chapter by introducing a continuous distribution, the **exponential distribution,** that has been found to be particularly useful in attacking *waiting-line,* or *queuing,* problems. Where *service times* for customers are uncertain, this uncertainty can often be closely represented by the exponential distribution. The exponential distribution differs in two important ways from the normal distribution: It is restricted to random variables that can take only positive values, and its probability density function is not symmetric about its mean. The properties of the exponential distribution are summarized in the box.

The Exponential Distribution

If the random variable X cannot take negative values and has probability density function

$$f_X(x) = \frac{e^{-x/\mu}}{\mu} \qquad \text{for } x \geq 0$$

where μ is any positive number and $e = 2.71828\ldots$, then X is said to follow an **exponential distribution.**
   The cumulative distribution function is

$$F_X(x) = 1 - e^{-x/\mu} \qquad \text{for } x \geq 0$$

The distribution has mean μ and variance μ^2.

EXAMPLE 5.13

Service of customers at a library information desk follows an exponential distribution, with mean service time 5 minutes. What is the probability that a customer service will take longer than 10 minutes?
   Let X denote service time, in minutes. Then, the probability density function is

$$f_X(x) = \frac{e^{-x/5}}{5} \qquad \text{for } x \geq 0$$

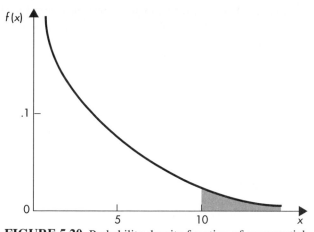

FIGURE 5.20 Probability density function of exponential distribution with mean 5; shaded area is $P(X > 10)$

This function is graphed in Figure 5.20, where the required probability, $P(X > 10)$, is shown. This probability is

$$P(X > 10) = 1 - P(X < 10)$$

$$= 1 - F_X(10)$$

$$= 1 - (1 - e^{-10/5})$$

$$= e^{-2} = .135335$$

from Table 2 of the Appendix.

The exponential distribution is related to the Poisson distribution of Section 4.7. Specifically, if the number of occurrences of an event in a time interval follows a Poisson distribution with mean λ, it can be shown that the time between successive occurrences of the event follows an exponential distribution with mean $\mu = 1/\lambda$. In Example 4.15, we considered a typical industrial plant in Britain with 2,000 employees for which the number of strikes in a year could be represented by a Poisson distribution with mean $\lambda = .4$. Then, the time X, in years, between successive strikes has an exponential distribution with mean $1/.4 = 2.5$ years. For example, the probability that the time between successive strikes is less than 2 years is

$$P(X < 2) = F_X(2) = 1 - e^{-(.4)(2)}$$

$$= 1 - e^{-.8}$$

$$= 1 - .449329 = .550671$$

EXERCISES

45. A professor sees students during regular office hours. Times spent with students follow an exponential distribution with mean 10 minutes.

(a) Find the probability that a given student spends less than 20 minutes with the professor.

(b) Find the probability that a given student spends more than 5 minutes with the professor.

(c) Find the probability that a given student spends between 10 and 15 minutes with the professor.

46. Times to gather preliminary information from arrivals at an outpatients clinic follow an exponential distribution with mean 15 minutes. Find the probability, for a randomly chosen arrival, that more than 18 minutes will be required.

47. It is known that for a laboratory computing system, the number of system failures during a month has a Poisson distribution with mean .8. The system has just failed. Find the probability that at least 2 months will elapse before a further failure.

48. Suppose that the time between successive occurrences of an event follows an exponential distribution with mean $1/\lambda$ minutes. Assume that an event occurs.

(a) Show that the probability that more than 3 minutes elapses before the occurrence of the next event is $e^{-3\lambda}$.

(b) Show that the probability that more than 6 minutes elapses before the occurrence of the next event is $e^{-6\lambda}$.

(c) Using the results of (a) and (b), show that if 3 minutes has already elapsed, the probability that a further 3 minutes will elapse before the next occurrence is $e^{-3\lambda}$. Explain your answer in words.

REVIEW EXERCISES

49. Explain verbally what can be learned from each of the following:
(a) The cumulative distribution function of a continuous random variable
(b) The probability density function of a continuous random variable
(c) The mean of a continuous random variable
(d) The standard deviation of a continuous random variable
(e) The covariance between a pair of continuous random variables

50. "In the real world, measurements on any quantity of interest are almost invariably made on a discrete scale. Therefore, the study of continuous random variables is only of academic interest and has no practical value." Comment on this statement.

51. Answer the following questions:
(a) Why is it necessary to use tables to find probabilities for the normal distribution?
(b) Why is it necessary to tabulate probabilities for only one of the infinite number of normal distributions?
(c) Why is the normal distribution important in the study of statistics?

52. "Many quantities we measure—such as height, weight, and distance—are necessarily positive. It therefore follows that the mean of a sample of observations on such a quantity must also be positive. However, the normal distribution supposes a range of values from minus infinity to plus infinity. Thus, in spite of the central limit theorem, the normal distribution cannot possibly be appropriate for such sample means." Comment on this statement.

53. In practice, we find probabilities for any normal distribution based on probabilities for the standard normal distribution. Suppose that you had available tables of probabilities for the normal distribution with mean 1 and standard deviation 10, rather than tables for the standard normal distribution. Could these tables be used to find probabilities for any other normal distribution? If so, explain how.

54. A consultant knows that it will cost her $10,000 to fulfill a particular contract. The contract is to be put out for bids, and she believes that the lowest bid, excluding her own, can

be represented by a distribution that is uniform between $8,000 and $20,000. Therefore, if the random variable X denotes the lowest of all other bids (in thousands of dollars), its probability density function is

$$f_X(x) = \begin{cases} 1/12 & \text{for } 8 < x < 20 \\ 0 & \text{for all other values of } x \end{cases}$$

(a) What is the probability that the lowest of the other bids will be less than the consultant's cost estimate of $10,000?

(b) If the consultant submits a bid of $12,000, what is the probability that she will secure the contract?

(c) The consultant decides to submit a bid of $12,000. What is her expected profit from this strategy?

(d) If the consultant wants to submit a bid so that her expected profit is as high as possible, discuss how she should go about making this choice.

55. The ages of a group of executives attending a convention are uniformly distributed between 35 and 65 years. If X denotes ages in years, the probability density function is

$$f_X(x) = \begin{bmatrix} \dfrac{1}{30} & \text{for } 35 < x < 65 \\ 0 & \text{for all other values of } x \end{bmatrix}$$

(a) Draw the probability density function for this random variable X.

(b) Find and draw the cumulative distribution function for this random variable.

(c) Find the probability that the age of a randomly chosen executive in this group is between 40 and 50 years.

(d) Find the mean age of the executives in the group.

56. The random variable X has probability density function

$$f_X(x) = \begin{cases} x & \text{for } 0 < x < 1 \\ 2 - x & \text{for } 1 < x < 2 \\ 0 & \text{for all other values of } x \end{cases}$$

(a) Draw the probability density function for this random variable.

(b) Show that the density function has the properties of a proper probability density function.

(c) Find the probability that this random variable takes a value between .5 and 1.5.

57. An investor puts $2,000 into a deposit account with a fixed rate of return of 10% per annum. A second sum of $1,000 is invested in a fund with expected rate of return of 16% and standard deviation of 8% per annum.

(a) Find the expected value of the total amount of money this investor will have after a year.

(b) Find the standard deviation of the total amount after a year.

58. A hamburger stand sells burgers for $1.45 each. Daily sales have a distribution with mean 530 and standard deviation 69.

(a) Find the mean daily total revenues from the sale of hamburgers.

(b) Find the standard deviation of total revenues from the sale of hamburgers.

(c) Daily costs (in dollars) are given by

$$C = 100 + .95X$$

where X is the number of hamburgers sold. Find the mean and standard deviation of daily profits from sales.

59. An analyst forecasts corporate earnings, and her record is evaluated by comparing actual earnings with predicted earnings. Define

Actual earnings = Predicted earnings + Forecast error

If the predicted earnings and forecast error are independent of each other, show that the variance of predicted earnings is less than the variance of actual earnings.

60. Let X_1 and X_2 be a pair of random variables. Show that the covariance between the random variables $(X_1 + X_2)$ and $(X_1 - X_2)$ is 0 if and only if X_1 and X_2 have the same variance.

61. Grade point averages of students on a large campus follow a normal distribution with mean 2.6 and standard deviation .5.

   (a) One student is chosen at random from this campus. What is the probability that student has a grade point average higher than 3.0?

   (b) One student is chosen at random from this campus. What is the probability that student has a grade point average between 2.25 and 2.75?

   (c) What is the minimum grade point average needed for a student's grade point average to be among the highest 10% on this campus?

   (d) A random sample of 400 students is chosen from this campus. What is the probability that at least 80 of these students have grade point averages higher than 3.0?

   (e) Two students are chosen at random from this campus. What is the probability that at least one of them has a grade point average higher than 3.0?

62. A company services home air conditioners. It is known that times for service calls follow a normal distribution with mean 60 minutes and standard deviation 10 minutes.

   (a) What is the probability that a single service call takes more than 65 minutes?

   (b) What is the probability that a single service call takes between 50 and 70 minutes?

   (c) The probability is .025 that a single service call takes more than how many minutes?

   (d) Find the shortest range of times that includes 50% of all service calls.

   (e) A random sample of four service calls is taken. What is the probability that exactly two of them take more than 65 minutes?

63. It has been found that times taken by people to complete a particular tax form follow a normal distribution with mean 100 minutes and standard deviation 30 minutes.

   (a) What is the probability that a randomly chosen person takes less than 85 minutes to complete this form?

   (b) What is the probability that a randomly chosen person takes between 70 and 130 minutes to complete this form?

   (c) Five percent of all people take more than how many minutes to complete this form?

   (d) Two people are chosen at random. What is the probability that at least one of them takes more than an hour to complete this form?

   (e) Four people are chosen at random. What is the probability that exactly two of them take longer than an hour to complete this form?

   (f) For a randomly chosen person, state in which of the following ranges (expressed in minutes) time to complete the form is most likely to lie.

$$70\text{–}90 \qquad 90\text{–}110 \qquad 110\text{–}130 \qquad 130\text{–}150$$

   (g) For a randomly chosen person, state in which of the following ranges (expressed in minutes) time to complete the form is least likely to lie.

$$70\text{–}90 \qquad 90\text{–}110 \qquad 110\text{–}130 \qquad 130\text{–}150$$

64. A pizza delivery service delivers to a campus dormitory. Delivery times follow a normal distribution with mean 20 minutes and standard deviation 4 minutes.

   (a) What is the probability that a delivery will take between 15 and 25 minutes?

   (b) The service does not charge for the pizza if delivery takes more than 30 minutes. What is the probability of getting a free pizza from a single order?

   (c) During final exams week, a student plans to order pizza five consecutive evenings. Assume that these delivery times are independent of each other. What is the probability that the student will get at least one free pizza?

   (d) Find the shortest range of times that includes 40% of all deliveries from this service.

(e) For a single delivery, state in which of the following ranges (expressed in minutes) delivery time is most likely to lie.

$$18\text{–}20 \qquad 19\text{–}21 \qquad 20\text{–}22 \qquad 21\text{–}23$$

(f) For a single delivery, state in which of the following ranges (expressed in minutes) delivery time is least likely to lie.

$$18\text{–}20 \qquad 19\text{–}21 \qquad 20\text{–}22 \qquad 21\text{–}23$$

65. A video rental chain estimates that annual expenditures of members on rentals follow a normal distribution with mean $100. It was also found that 10% of all members spend more than $130 in a year. What percentage of members spend more than $140 in a year?

66. It is estimated that amounts of money spent on gasoline by customers at a gas station follow a normal distribution with standard deviation $2.50. It was also found that 10% of all customers spend more than $15. What percentage of customers spend less than $10?

67. A market research organization has found that 40% of all supermarket shoppers refuse to cooperate when questioned by its pollsters. If 1,000 shoppers are approached, what is the probability that less than 500 will refuse to cooperate?

68. An organization that gives regular seminars on sales motivation methods determines that 60% of its clients have attended previous seminars. From a sample of 400 clients, what is the probability that more than half have attended previous seminars?

69. An emergency towing service receives an average of seventy calls per day for assistance. For any given day, what is the probability that fewer than fifty calls will be received?

70. In a large department store, a customer complaints office handles an average of six complaints per hour about quality of service. The distribution is Poisson.

   (a) What is the probability that in any hour exactly six complaints will be received?

   (b) What is the probability that more than 20 minutes will elapse between successive complaints?

   (c) What is the probability that less than 5 minutes will elapse between successive complaints?

   (d) The store manager observes the complaints office for a 30-minute period, during which no complaints are received. She concludes that a talk she gave to her staff on the theme "the customer is always right" has obviously had a beneficial effect. Suppose that in fact the talk had no effect. What is the probability of the manager's observing a period of 30 minutes or longer with no complaints?

71. A Chicago radio station believes that 40% of its listeners are younger than 25 years of age. Six hundred listeners are chosen at random.

   (a) If the station's belief is correct, what is the probability that more than 260 of these listeners are younger than 25?

   (b) If the station's belief is correct, the probability is .6 that more than how many of these 600 listeners are younger than 25?

72. It is estimated that major league baseball game times-to-completion follow a normal distribution with mean 132 minutes and standard deviation 12 minutes.

   (a) What proportion of all games last between 120 minutes and 150 minutes?

   (b) Thirty-three percent of all games last longer than how many minutes?

   (c) What proportion of games last less than 120 minutes?

   (d) If 100 games are chosen at random, what is the probability that at least twenty-five of these games last less than 120 minutes?

73. A management consultant found that the amount of time per day spent by executives performing tasks that could equally well be done by subordinates followed a normal distribution with mean 2.4 hours. It was also found that 10% of executives spent over 3.5 hours per day on tasks of this type. For a random sample of 400 executives, find the probability that more than 80 spend more than 3 hours per day on tasks of this type.

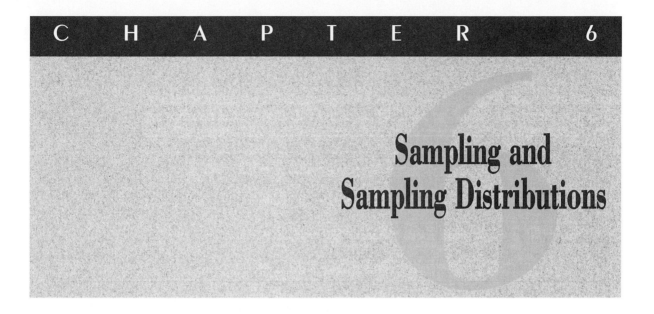

CHAPTER 6

Sampling and Sampling Distributions

6.1 SAMPLING FROM A POPULATION

In much of the remainder of this volume, we will be occupied with a class of problems that involve an attempt to say something about the properties of a large group of objects, given information on a relatively small subset of them. The larger parent group is referred to as a **population,** and the subset of population members is called a **sample.**

Here are some examples of populations that might be of interest:

1. The incomes of all families living in the city of Chicago
2. The annual yields of all stocks traded on the New York Stock Exchange
3. The costs of all claims for automobile accident insurance coverage received by a company in a given year
4. The annual repair costs of all cars of a particular model
5. The errors in a large collection of accounts receivable

In particular, we might be interested in learning about specific characteristics, or *attributes*, of these populations. For example, we might want to make an *inference* about the mean or variance of the population distribution of family incomes in Chicago or about the proportion of all families in the city with annual incomes below $15,000.

The major motivation for examining a sample rather than the whole population is that the collection of complete information on the latter would typically be prohibitively expensive. Even in circumstances where sufficient resources seem available to contact the whole population, it may well be preferable to devote these resources to just a subset of the population in the hope that such a concentration of effort will produce more accurate measurements. It is well known, for example, that the decennial census of the U.S. population produces an undercount in which certain groups are seriously underrepresented.[1]

If a sample is to be taken from a population, the eventual aim is to make statements that have some validity for the population at large. Therefore, it is important that the sample be representative of the population. Suppose, for instance, that a marketing manager wants to assess reactions to a new food product. It would be unwise of him to restrict his survey to his circle of friends or to people living in his immediate neighborhood. Such groups are very unlikely to reflect the spectrum of views of the population at large and may well be heavily weighted toward one end of that spectrum. To avoid problems of this kind and to allow valid inference about a population based on a sample, it is important that the principle of **randomness** be embodied in the sample selection procedure. The most straightforward way of achieving this is to design the selection mechanism in such a way that every sample of the same size is equally likely to be chosen.

Simple Random Sampling

Suppose that it is required to select a sample of *n* objects from a population of *N* objects. A **simple random sampling** procedure is one in which every possible sample of *n* objects is equally likely to be chosen. This method is in such common use that the adjective *simple* is generally dropped, and the resulting sample is called a **random sample.**

The process of simple random sampling can be thought of as follows: Suppose that the *N* population members are put into a (very large) hat and mixed thoroughly. A random sample is then obtained by pulling out *n* of them. In practice, this is not necessary (even if it were feasible); tables of **random numbers,** such as those given in Table 4 in the Appendix, can be used to achieve the same objective. If the *N* population members are labeled 1 through *N*, we can begin at some arbitrary point in the table and read off numbers until a sample of *n* members has been identified. The tables are constructed in such a way that this process has the properties of simple random sampling. One possible, but very tedious, way of constructing a table of random numbers would be to place ten balls, numbered 0 through 9, in a bag. After shaking thoroughly, draw a ball and record the number on it. Then replace this ball and repeat the process. We can continue in this fashion to obtain random numbers of as many digits as are required. This process has the properties that each possible number is equally likely to be chosen and successive choices are independent of one another. In practice, random numbers can be generated much more rapidly using an electronic computer with mechanisms that effectively mimic the process just described.

In this and the next few chapters, we will focus on methods for analyzing sample results, with the objective of gaining information about the population. We will concentrate on samples that have been selected through simple random sampling schemes. However, this is by no means the only procedure available for choosing sample members, and in some circumstances alternative sampling schemes may be preferable. We postpone a more thorough discussion of methods of sample selection

---

[1] See, for instance, H. Hogan, "The 1990 post-enumeration survey: An overview," *American Statistician, 46* (1992), 261–269.

until Chapter 18, where the use of random number tables will also be more fully described.

The principle of randomness in the selection of the sample members provides some protection against the sample's being unrepresentative of the population, in the sense that on the average, if the population were repeatedly sampled in this fashion, no particular subgroup would be over-represented in the sample. Moreover, through the concept of a **sampling distribution,** it allows us to determine the probability that the particular sample obtained will be, to any specified degree, unrepresentative.

On the basis of sample information, our objective is to make *inferences* about the parent population. The distribution of all the values of interest in this population can be represented by a random variable. It would be too ambitious to attempt to describe the whole population distribution based on a small random sample of observations. However, we may well be able to make quite firm inferences about important characteristics of the population distribution. For example, we may want to make statements about its mean and variance. As an illustration, given a random sample of fuel consumption of twenty cars of a particular model, one can make inferential statements about the mean and variance of fuel consumption for all cars of that model. This inference will be based on just the sample information, so we are naturally led to ask such questions as "If the fuel consumption of all cars of a particular model, in miles per gallon, has mean 25 and standard deviation 2, what is the probability that for a random sample of twenty such cars, the average fuel consumption will be less than 24 miles per gallon?" In asking this question, we are implicitly assuming that inferences about the population mean will be based on the sample average, or mean.

It is important to distinguish between population attributes and the corresponding sample quantities. In the example of the preceding paragraph, the population fuel consumption of all automobiles of a particular model has a distribution with a specific mean. This mean, which is an attribute of the population, is a fixed (but unknown) number. In attempting to make inferences about this attribute, a random sample is drawn from the population, and the sample mean is found. Since from sample to sample, different values would result for the sample mean, this quantity can be regarded as a random variable, which has a probability distribution. This distribution of possible sample outcomes provides a basis for inferential statements about the population. Our objective in this chapter is to examine the properties of **sampling distributions** of this sort.

Statistics and Sampling Distributions

Suppose that a random sample is drawn from a population and that an inference about some characteristic of the population distribution is to be made. This inference is based on some **statistic,** a particular function of the sample information. The **sampling distribution** of this statistic is the probability distribution of the values it could take over all possible samples of the same number of observations drawn from the population.

To illustrate the important concept of a sampling distribution, let us consider the position of a supervisor with six employees, whose experiences (in terms of years on the job) are

$$2 \quad 4 \quad 6 \quad 6 \quad 7 \quad 8$$

Four of these employees are to be chosen randomly and assigned to a particular work shift. The mean number of years of experience for all six employees is

$$\frac{2 + 4 + 6 + 6 + 7 + 8}{6} = 5.5$$

Our interest now is the mean number of years of experience of the particular four employees assigned to the work shift. These can be regarded as a simple random sample of four values, chosen from a population of six. Fifteen possible samples could be selected. Table 6.1 shows the possible samples and associated sample means. Samples such as (2, 4, 6, 7) occur twice because there are two employees in the population with 6 years of work experience.

TABLE 6.1 Possible samples of four observations, and sample means, from the population 2, 4, 6, 6, 7, 8

SAMPLE	SAMPLE MEAN	SAMPLE	SAMPLE MEAN
2, 4, 6, 6	4.50	2, 6, 7, 8	5.75
2, 4, 6, 7	4.75	2, 6, 7, 8	5.75
2, 4, 6, 8	5.00	4, 6, 6, 7	5.75
2, 4, 6, 7	4.75	4, 6, 6, 8	6.00
2, 4, 6, 8	5.00	4, 6, 7, 8	6.25
2, 4, 7, 8	5.25	4, 6, 7, 8	6.25
2, 6, 6, 7	5.25	6, 6, 7, 8	6.75
2, 6, 6, 8	5.50		

Now, since each of the fifteen possible samples is equally likely to be selected, the probability is $\frac{1}{15}$ that any specific sample will be selected. Using this information, we can determine the probability that any particular value will result for the sample mean. For example, we see from Table 6.1 that three of the possible samples have mean 5.75. Hence, it follows that the probability is $\frac{3}{15}$ that the four employees assigned to the work shift have an average of 5.75 years experience. In this way, we can find probabilities for every possible sample mean. The collection of these probabilities constitutes the sampling distribution of the sample mean.

Perhaps the simplest way to describe this sampling distribution is through its probability function. Denoting the sample mean by $\overline{X}$, we have

$$P(\overline{X} = 4.50) = P_{\overline{X}}(4.50) = \frac{1}{15} \qquad P(\overline{X} = 5.75) = P_{\overline{X}}(5.75) = \frac{3}{15}$$

$$P_{\overline{X}}(4.75) = \frac{2}{15} \qquad P_{\overline{X}}(6.00) = \frac{1}{15}$$

$$P_{\overline{X}}(5.00) = \frac{2}{15} \qquad P_{\overline{X}}(6.25) = \frac{2}{15}$$

$$P_{\overline{X}}(5.25) = \frac{2}{15} \qquad P_{\overline{X}}(6.75) = \frac{1}{15}$$

$$P_{\overline{X}}(5.50) = \frac{1}{15}$$

This probability function is graphed in Figure 6.1. Notice that while the numbers of years of experience for the six workers range from 2 to 8, the possible values for the sample mean have a much more restricted range—from 4.50 to 6.75. Moreover, the preponderance of values lie in the central portion of this range.

In the next section, we consider the sampling distribution of the sample mean for sampling from more general populations.

6.2 SAMPLING DISTRIBUTION OF THE SAMPLE MEAN

Suppose that a random sample of n observations is drawn from a population with mean μ_X and variance σ_X^2 and that the sample members are denoted $X_1, X_2, \ldots, X_n$. Before the sample is observed, there will be uncertainty about the outcomes. This uncertainty is characterized by viewing each of the sample members as a random variable having mean μ_X and variance σ_X^2. Assume for now that our primary interest is in making inferences about the population mean μ_X. An obvious place to start is with the average of the sample values.

Definition

Let $X_1, X_2, \ldots, X_n$ be a random sample from a population. The average value

$$\overline{X} = \frac{1}{n} \sum_{i=1}^{n} X_i$$

of these observations is called the **sample mean.**

FIGURE 6.1 Probability function of sampling distribution for means of samples of four observations from the population 2, 4, 6, 6, 7, 8

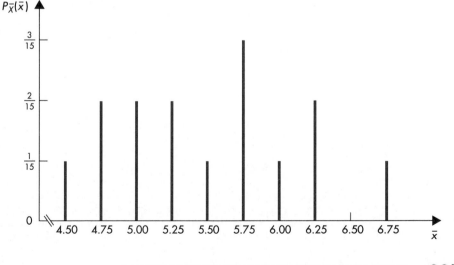

We need to consider the sampling distribution of the random variable $\overline{X}$.[2] First, we determine the mean of this distribution. In Sections 4.4 and 5.4, it was seen that for discrete and continuous random variables, the expectation of a sum is the sum of expectations, so

$$E\left(\sum_{i=1}^{n} X_i\right) = E(X_1) + E(X_2) + \cdots + E(X_n)$$

Since each random variable X_i has mean μ_X, we can write

$$E\left(\sum_{i=1}^{n} X_i\right) = n\mu_X$$

Now, the sample mean is just the sum of the sample members multiplied by $1/n$, so its expected value is

$$E(\overline{X}) = E\left(\frac{1}{n} \sum_{i=1}^{n} X_i\right) = \frac{1}{n} E\left(\sum_{i=1}^{n} X_i\right) = \frac{n\mu_X}{n} = \mu_X$$

Thus, the mean of the sampling distribution of the sample mean is the population mean. This conclusion states that if samples of n observations are repeatedly and independently drawn from a population, then as the number of samples taken becomes very large, the average of the sample means becomes very close to the true population mean. This result is an important consequence of random sampling and represents the protection this form of sampling affords against the sample's being unrepresentative of the population. Of course, the mean obtained from any *particular* sample could be either much higher or much lower than the population mean. However, *on the average,* there is no reason to expect a value that is either higher or lower than the population value.

EXAMPLE 6.1

We confirm this result for the example of Table 6.1, in which we considered a population of years of experience figures for six employees:

2   4   6   6   7   8

The mean of this population is simply the average of these six values; that is, $\mu_X = 5.5$.

We found that the probability distribution of the sample mean, for samples of four observations from this population, could be represented by the following probability function:

$$P_{\overline{X}}(4.50) = \frac{1}{15} \qquad P_{\overline{X}}(4.75) = \frac{2}{15} \qquad P_{\overline{X}}(5.00) = \frac{2}{15}$$

$$P_{\overline{X}}(5.25) = \frac{2}{15} \qquad P_{\overline{X}}(5.50) = \frac{1}{15} \qquad P_{\overline{X}}(5.75) = \frac{3}{15}$$

$$P_{\overline{X}}(6.00) = \frac{1}{15} \qquad P_{\overline{X}}(6.25) = \frac{2}{15} \qquad P_{\overline{X}}(6.75) = \frac{1}{15}$$

---

[2] As in Chapters 4 and 5, we distinguish between a random variable and specific values it can take. Thus, when the sample is drawn, we might observe the specific values $x_1, x_2, \ldots, x_n$, with mean $\overline{x} = \sum_{i=1}^{n} x_i/n$. In this context, $\overline{x}$ is a single specific realization of the random variable $\overline{X}$.

Thus, the expected value of the sample mean is

$$E(\overline{X}) = \sum \overline{x} P_{\overline{x}}(\overline{x})$$

$$= (4.50)\left(\frac{1}{15}\right) + (4.75)\left(\frac{2}{15}\right) + \cdots + (6.75)\left(\frac{1}{15}\right) = 5.5$$

which is the population mean, μ_X.

It has been established, then, that the distribution of the sample mean is centered on the population mean. It is also of interest to determine how close the sample mean is likely to be to the population mean. For instance, suppose that a random sample of twenty cars of a particular model yielded average fuel consumption of 24 miles per gallon. How good an approximation might this be to the mean consumption figure for the whole population of such cars? Questions of this kind depend on the spread, or *variance*, in the sampling distribution of $\overline{X}$.

If the number of population members is very large compared to the number in the sample, then an implication of simple random sampling is that the distributions of the individual sample members are independent of one another. Recalling from Sections 4.4 and 5.4 that in this case, the variance of a sum is the sum of the variances, we have

$$\text{Var}\left(\sum_{i=1}^{n} X_i\right) = \text{Var}(X_1) + \text{Var}(X_2) + \cdots + \text{Var}(X_n)$$

Since each X_i has variance of σ_X^2, it follows that

$$\text{Var}\left(\sum_{i=1}^{n} X_i\right) = n\sigma_X^2$$

It then follows that the variance of the sample mean is

$$\text{Var}(\overline{X}) = \text{Var}\left(\frac{1}{n}\sum_{i=1}^{n} X_i\right) = \frac{1}{n^2}\text{Var}\left(\sum_{i=1}^{n} X_i\right) = \frac{n\sigma_X^2}{n^2} = \frac{\sigma_X^2}{n}$$

The variance of the sampling distribution of $\overline{X}$ thus decreases as the sample size n increases. In effect, this says that the more observations in the sample, the more concentrated is the sampling distribution of the sample mean about the population mean. In other words, the larger the sample, the more certain will be our inference about the population mean. This is to be expected: The more information we obtain from a population, the more we are likely to learn about characteristics (such as the mean) of that population. The variance of the sample mean is denoted $\sigma_{\overline{X}}^2$, and the corresponding standard deviation, called the **standard error** of $\overline{X}$, is given by

$$\sigma_{\overline{X}} = \frac{\sigma_X}{\sqrt{n}}$$

If the number of sample members n is not a very small fraction of the number of population numbers N, it is no longer the case that the individual sample members are distributed independently of one another. For example, since a population member cannot be included more than once in the sample, the probability of any specific population member's being the second value chosen in the sample will depend on what the first chosen sample member was. The argument leading to the derivation of the

variance of the sample mean given in the preceding paragraph then no longer holds. In fact, it can be shown that the appropriate expression[3] is

$$\text{Var}(\overline{X}) = \frac{\sigma_X^2}{n} \cdot \frac{N - n}{N - 1}$$

The term $(N - n)/(N - 1)$ is often called a *finite population correction factor.*

So far, we have found expressions for the mean and variance of the sampling distribution of $\overline{X}$. Fortunately, for most applications, this is all that is required to characterize that distribution completely. If the parent population distribution is normal, it is possible to show that the sample mean also has a normal distribution. If the sample size is a small proportion of the population size, then subtracting the mean and dividing by the standard error yields a random variable

$$Z = \frac{\overline{X} - \mu_X}{\sigma_{\overline{X}}} = \frac{\overline{X} - \mu_X}{\sigma_X \sqrt{n}} \qquad (6.2.1)$$

that has a standard normal distribution. Moreover, by virtue of the central limit theorem, *even if the population distribution is not normal* but the sample size n is moderately large, the distribution of $\overline{X}$ will still be very close to normal, so that the quantity (6.2.1) is, to a very close approximation, distributed as standard normal.

The results of this section are summarized in the box.

Sampling Distribution of $\overline{X}$

Let $\overline{X}$ denote the mean of a random sample of n observations from a population with mean μ_X and variance σ_X^2. Then

(i) The sampling distribution of $\overline{X}$ has mean μ_X; that is

$$E(\overline{X}) = \mu_X$$

(ii) The sampling distribution of $\overline{X}$ has standard deviation

$$\sigma_{\overline{X}} = \frac{\sigma_X}{\sqrt{n}}$$

This quantity is called the **standard error** of $\overline{X}$.

(iii) If the number n of sample members is not a small proportion of the number N of population members, then the standard error of $\overline{X}$ is

$$\sigma_{\overline{X}} = \frac{\sigma_X}{\sqrt{n}} \sqrt{\frac{N - n}{N - 1}}$$

(iv) If the population distribution is normal, then the random variable

$$Z = \frac{\overline{X} - \mu_X}{\sigma_{\overline{X}}}$$

has a standard normal distribution.

---

[3] We encountered this phenomenon in Chapter 4. The variance of the hypergeometric distribution is $(N - n)/(N - 1)$ times that of the binomial distribution.

(v) If the population distribution is not normal and the sample size n is moderately large, then it follows from the central limit theorem that, to a close approximation, the result (iv) continues to hold.

Figure 6.2 shows the sampling distribution of the sample mean for sample sizes $n = 25$ and $n = 100$ from a normal population. It can be seen that each distribution is centered on the population mean but that as the sample size increases, the distribution becomes more concentrated about that mean, reflecting the fact that the standard error of the sample mean is a decreasing function of the number of observations in the sample. Thus, as we would expect, the probability that the sample mean differs from the population mean by some fixed amount decreases as the sample size increases.

We now illustrate the ideas of this section with some specific examples, based on sampling from a normally distributed population.

EXAMPLE 6.2

Suppose that annual percentage salary increases for the chief executive officers of all mid-size corporations are normally distributed with mean 12.2% and standard deviation 3.6%. A random sample of nine observations from this population of percentage salary increases is taken. What is the probability that the sample mean will be less than 10%?

We have

$$\mu_X = 12.2 \qquad \sigma_X = 3.6 \qquad n = 9$$

Let $\overline{X}$ denote the sample mean. Then we need to find

$$P(\overline{X} < 10) = P\left(\frac{\overline{X} - \mu_X}{\sigma_{\overline{X}}} < \frac{10 - \mu_X}{\sigma_{\overline{X}}}\right) = P\left(Z < \frac{10 - \mu_X}{\sigma_{\overline{X}}}\right)$$

where the standard error of the sampling distribution of the sample mean is

$$\sigma_{\overline{X}} = \frac{\sigma_X}{\sqrt{n}} = \frac{3.6}{\sqrt{9}} = 1.2$$

FIGURE 6.2 Probability density functions for the sample means of samples of 25 and 100 observations from a normal distribution with mean 100 and standard deviation 5

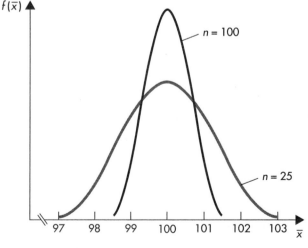

Hence, the required probability is

$$P(\overline{X} < 10) = P\left(Z < \frac{10 - 12.2}{1.2}\right)$$

$$= P(Z < -1.83)$$

where the random variable Z has a standard normal distribution. Therefore, using Table 3 of the Appendix

$$P(\overline{X} < 10) = F_Z(-1.83)$$

$$= 1 - F_Z(1.83)$$

$$= 1 - .9664 = .0336$$

We conclude then that the probability is only .0336 that the sample mean will be less than 10%.

EXAMPLE 6.3

A manufacturer claims that the life of its spark plugs is normally distributed with mean 36,000 miles and standard deviation 4,000 miles. For a random sample of sixteen of these plugs, the average life was found to be 34,500 miles. If the manufacturer's claim is correct, what would be the probability of finding a sample mean this small or smaller?

If $\overline{X}$ denotes the sample mean, then the probability of interest is

$$P(\overline{X} < 34,500) = P\left(\frac{\overline{X} - \mu_X}{\sigma_{\overline{X}}} < \frac{34,500 - \mu_X}{\sigma_{\overline{X}}}\right)$$

where $\mu_X = 36,000$ is the assumed population mean and

$$\sigma_{\overline{X}} = \frac{\sigma_X}{\sqrt{n}} = \frac{4,000}{4} = 1,000$$

Then

$$P(\overline{X} < 34,500) = P\left(Z < \frac{34,500 - 36,000}{1,000}\right)$$

$$= P(Z < -1.5)$$

where Z has a standard normal distribution.

Figure 6.3(a) shows the probability density function of $\overline{X}$, the shaded area being the probability that the sample mean is less than 34,500. In Figure 6.3(b), the same probability is indicated on the graph of the probability density function of the standard normal distribution. The probability is

$$P(\overline{X} < 34,500) = F_Z(-1.5)$$

$$= 1 - F_Z(1.5)$$

$$= 1 - .9332 = .0668$$

from Table 3 of the Appendix.

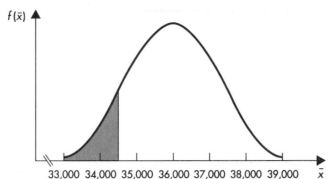

FIGURE 6.3 (a) Probability that sample mean is less than 34,500 in samples of 16 observations from normal distribution with mean 36,000 and standard deviation 4,000; sample mean has normal distribution with mean 36,000 and standard deviation 1,000

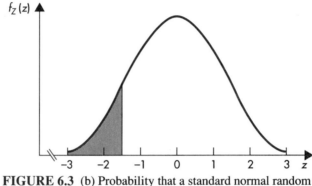

FIGURE 6.3 (b) Probability that a standard normal random variable is less than -1.5

This result suggests that if the manufacturer's claim is correct, the probability of observing such a low value for the sample mean would be quite small. The observed result then casts some doubt on the claim. In Chapter 9, we will discuss a general framework for testing such claims, or hypotheses, on the basis of sample evidence.

6.3 SAMPLING DISTRIBUTION OF A SAMPLE PROPORTION

We saw in Section 4.5 that if n independent trials, each with probability of success p, are carried out, then the total number of successes, X, obeys a binomial distribution. A common problem arises when the parameter p is unknown. For instance, we may want to determine the proportion of an electorate intending to vote for a particular candidate for office or the proportion of a magazine's readership likely to be in the market for a specific product. In cases of this kind, it is natural to base inference on the proportion of successes in a sample taken from the relevant population.

Definition

Let X be the number of successes in a binomial sample of n observations, where the probability of success is p. (In most applications, the parameter p is the proportion of members of a large population possessing a characteristic of interest.) Then the proportion of successes

$$\hat{p}_x = \frac{X}{n}$$

in the sample is called the **sample proportion.**[4]

The mean and variance of the sampling distribution of the sample proportion can be easily deduced from the mean and variance of the number of successes, which we found in Section 4.5 to be

$$E(X) = np \qquad \text{Var}(X) = np(1 - p)$$

It then follows that

$$E(\hat{p}_x) = E\left(\frac{X}{n}\right) = \frac{1}{n} E(X) = p$$

That is, the mean of the sample proportion is the proportion p of "successes" in the population. Its variance is

$$\text{Var}(\hat{p}_x) = \text{Var}\left(\frac{X}{n}\right) = \frac{1}{n^2} \text{Var}(X) = \frac{p(1 - p)}{n}$$

Again, the standard deviation of the sample proportion, which is the square root of the variance, is called its **standard error.**

If the number, N, of individuals in the population is not very large compared with the number of sample members, a **finite population correction** is needed in the expression for the variance of the sample proportion. The variance is then

$$\text{Var}(\hat{p}_x) = \frac{p(1 - p)}{n} \cdot \frac{N - n}{N - 1}$$

We saw in Section 5.7 that as a consequence of the central limit theorem, the distribution of the number of successes is approximately normal for large sample sizes. The same is true of the proportion of successes. It follows that by subtracting from the sample proportion its mean, p, and dividing by its standard error, we obtain a random variable with a standard normal distribution.

Sampling Distribution of the Sample Proportion

Let $\hat{p}_x$ be the proportion of successes in a random sample of n observations from a population in which the proportion of successes is p. Then

---

[4] Again we distinguish between a random variable and its possible specific realizations. We might, for example, observe x successes in a specific sample, in which case the observed sample proportion would be $\hat{p}_x = x/n$. Then $\hat{p}_x$ is a particular realization of the random variable $\hat{p}_x$.

(i) The sampling distribution of $\hat{p}_X$ has mean p; that is

$$E(\hat{p}_X) = p$$

(ii) The sampling distribution of $\hat{p}_X$ has standard deviation

$$\sigma_{\hat{p}} = \sqrt{\frac{p(1-p)}{n}}$$

The quantity $\sigma_{\hat{p}}$ is called the **standard error** of $\hat{p}_X$.

(iii) If the number n of the sample members is not a small proportion of the number N of population members, then the standard error of $\hat{p}_X$ is

$$\sigma_{\hat{p}} = \sqrt{\frac{p(1-p)}{n}} \sqrt{\frac{N-n}{N-1}}$$

(iv) If the sample size is large,[5] the random variable

$$Z = \frac{\hat{p}_X - p}{\sigma_{\hat{p}}}$$

is approximately distributed as standard normal.

Notice that for fixed p, the standard error of the sample proportion decreases as the sample size increases. This implies that for increasing sample size, the distribution of $\hat{p}_X$ becomes more concentrated about its mean, as illustrated in Figure 6.4. The implication is that for any particular population proportion, the probability that the sample and population proportions will differ by any fixed amount decreases as the number of sample members increases. In other words, if we take a bigger sample from a population, our inference about the proportion of population members that possess some particular characteristic becomes more firm.

When the sample size is large, the normal approximation to the binomial distribution provides a very convenient procedure for calculating the probability that a sample proportion lies in some given range. This is illustrated in the following examples.

EXAMPLE 6.4

A random sample of 250 homes was taken from a large population of older homes to estimate the proportion of such homes in which the electric wiring was unsafe. Suppose that, in fact, 30% of all homes in this population have unsafe wiring. Find the probability that the proportion of homes in the sample with unsafe wiring is between .25 and .35.

We have

$$p = .30 \qquad n = 250$$

Denote by $\hat{p}_X$ the proportion of homes in the sample with unsafe wiring. We then require

$$P(.25 < \hat{p}_X < .35) = P\left(\frac{.25 - p}{\sigma_{\hat{p}}} < \frac{\hat{p}_X - p}{\sigma_{\hat{p}}} < \frac{.35 - p}{\sigma_{\hat{p}}} \right)$$

$$= P\left(\frac{.25 - p}{\sigma_{\hat{p}}} < Z < \frac{.35 - p}{\sigma_{\hat{p}}} \right)$$

---

[5] In general, the approximation is satisfactory for samples of fifty or more observations. The quality of the approximation depends also on p: ideally, we should have $np(1-p) > 9$.

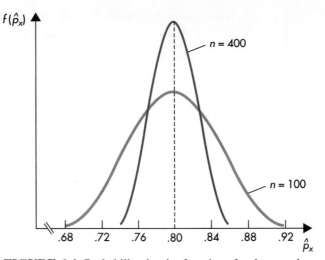

FIGURE 6.4 Probability density functions for the sample proportions in samples of 100 and 400 observations when the population proportion is .8

where the standard error of the sampling distribution of the sample proportion is

$$\sigma_{\hat{p}} = \sqrt{\frac{p(1-p)}{n}} = \sqrt{\frac{(.30)(.70)}{250}} = .029$$

The required probability is then

$$P(.25 < \hat{p}_X < .35) = P\left(\frac{.25 - .30}{.029} < Z < \frac{.35 - .30}{.029}\right)$$

$$= P(-1.72 < Z < 1.72)$$

where, to a good approximation, the random variable Z has a standard normal distribution. Therefore we have, using Table 3 of the Appendix

$$P(.25 < \hat{p}_X < .35) = F_Z(1.72) - F_Z(-1.72)$$

$$= F_Z(1.72) - [1 - F_Z(1.72)]$$

$$= .9573 - (1 - .9573) = .9146$$

Thus, the sample proportion will fall in this range for about 91.5% of samples of 250 observations from this population.

EXAMPLE 6.5
It has been estimated that 43% of business graduates believe that a course in business ethics is very important for imparting ethical values to students.[6] Find the probability that more than one-half of a random sample of 80 business graduates have this belief.

We are given

$$n = 80 \qquad p = .43$$

---

[6] F. R. David, L. M. Anderson and K. W. Lawrimore, "Perspectives on business ethics in management education," *S.A.M. Advanced Management Journal*, 55, no. 4 (1990), 26–32.

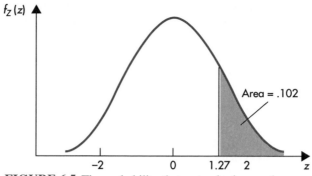

FIGURE 6.5 The probability that a standard normal random variable exceeds 1.27. This is the probability that the sample proportion exceeds .50, for a sample of 80 observations when the population proportion is .43.

Denoting by $\hat{p}_x$ the sample proportion, the probability required is

$$P(\hat{p}_x > .50) = P\left(\frac{\hat{p}_x - p}{\sigma_{\hat{p}}} > \frac{.50 - p}{\sigma_{\hat{p}}}\right)$$

$$= P\left(Z > \frac{.50 - p}{\sigma_{\hat{p}}}\right)$$

The standard error of the sampling distribution of the sample proportion is

$$\sigma_{\hat{p}} = \sqrt{\frac{p(1-p)}{n}} = \sqrt{\frac{(.43)(.57)}{80}} = .055$$

Then

$$P(\hat{p}_x > .50) = P\left(Z > \frac{.50 - .43}{.055}\right) = P(Z > 1.27)$$

The random variable Z has a distribution that is approximately standard normal. Therefore, using Table 3 of the Appendix, we find

$$P(\hat{p}_x > .50) = P(Z > 1.27)$$

$$= 1 - P(Z < 1.27)$$

$$= 1 - F_Z(1.27)$$

$$= 1 - .8980 = .1020$$

Thus, the probability is approximately .1 of finding more than one-half of the sample members with this belief. This probability is shown as the shaded area under the standard normal density curve in Figure 6.5.

EXERCISES

1. When a production process is operating correctly, the resistance in ohms of electrical components produced has a normal distribution with mean 92.0 and standard deviation 3.6. A random sample of four components was taken.

(a) Find the mean of the sampling distribution of the sample mean resistance.

(b) Find the variance of the sample mean.

(c) Find the standard error of the sample mean.

(d) What is the probability that the sample mean exceeds 93.0 ohms?

2. The lifetimes of lightbulbs produced by a particular manufacturer have mean 1,200 hours and standard deviation 400 hours. The population distribution is normal. Suppose that you purchase nine bulbs, which can be regarded as a random sample from the manufacturer's output.

(a) What is the mean of the sample mean lifetime?

(b) What is the variance of the sample mean?

(c) What is the standard error of the sample mean?

(d) What is the probability that, on average, these nine lightbulbs have lifetimes of less than 1,050 hours?

3. The fuel consumption, in miles per gallon, of all cars of a particular model has mean 25 and standard deviation 2. The population distribution can be assumed to be normal. A random sample of these cars is taken.

(a) Find the probability that sample mean fuel consumption will be less than 24 miles per gallon if

   (i) a sample of one observation is taken.

   (ii) a sample of four observations is taken.

   (iii) a sample of sixteen observations is taken.

(b) Explain why the three answers in (a) differ in the way they do. Draw a graph to illustrate your reasoning.

4. The mean selling price of new homes in a city over a year was $115,000. The population standard deviation was $25,000. A random sample of 100 new homes sales from this city was taken.

(a) What is the probability that the sample mean selling price was more than $110,000?

(b) What is the probability that the sample mean selling price was between $113,000 and $117,000?

(c) What is the probability that the sample mean selling price was between $114,000 and $116,000?

(d) Without doing the calculations, state in which of the following ranges the sample mean selling price is most likely to lie:

$113,000–$115,000, $114,000–$116,000, $115,000–$117,000, $116,000–$118,000

(e) Suppose that, after you had done the above calculations, a friend asserted that the population distribution of selling prices of new homes in this city was almost certainly not normal. How would you respond?

5. Candidates for employment at a city fire department are required to take a written aptitude test. Scores on this test are normally distributed with mean 280 and standard deviation 60. A random sample of nine test scores was taken.

(a) What is the standard error of the sample mean score?

(b) What is the probability that the sample mean score is less than 270?

(c) What is the probability that the sample mean score is more than 250?

(d) Suppose that the population standard deviation is in fact 40 rather than 60. Without doing the calculations, state how this would change your answers to (a), (b), and (c). Illustrate your conclusions with appropriate graphs.

6. A random sample of sixteen junior managers in the offices of corporations in a large city center was taken in order to estimate average daily commuting times for all such managers. Suppose that the population times have a normal distribution with mean 87 minutes and standard deviation 22 minutes.

(a) What is the standard error of the sample mean commuting time?

(b) What is the probability that the sample mean is less than 100 minutes?

(c) What is the probability that the sample mean is more than 80 minutes?

(d) What is the probability that the sample mean is outside the range 85 to 95 minutes?

(e) Suppose that a second (independent) random sample, of fifty junior managers, is taken. Without doing the calculations, state whether the probabilities in parts (b), (c), and (d) would be higher, lower, or the same for the second sample. Sketch graphs to illustrate your answers.

7. A company produces breakfast cereal. The true mean weight of the contents of boxes of its cereal is 20 ounces, and the standard deviation is .6 ounce. The population distribution of weights is normal. Suppose that you purchase four boxes, which can be regarded as a random sample of all those produced.

(a) What is the standard error of the sample mean weight?

(b) What is the probability that, on average, the contents of these four boxes will weigh less than 19.7 ounces?

(c) What is the probability that, on average, the contents of these four boxes will weigh more than 20.6 ounces?

(d) What is the probability that, on average, the contents of these four boxes will weigh between 19.5 and 20.5 ounces?

(e) Two of the four boxes are chosen at random. What is the probability that, on average, the contents of these two boxes will weigh between 19.5 and 20.5 ounces?

8. Assume that the standard deviation of monthly rents paid by students in a particular town is $40. A random sample of 100 students was taken to estimate the mean monthly rent paid by the whole student population.

(a) What is the standard error of the sample mean monthly rent?

(b) What is the probability that the sample mean exceeds the population mean by more than $5?

(c) What is the probability that the sample mean is more than $4 below the population mean?

(d) What is the probability that the sample mean differs from the population mean by more than $3?

9. Times spent studying by students in the week before final exams follow a normal distribution with standard deviation 8 hours. A random sample of 4 students was taken in order to estimate the mean study time for the population of all students.

(a) What is the probability that the sample mean exceeds the population mean by more than 2 hours?

(b) What is the probability that the sample mean is more than 3 hours below the population mean?

(c) What is the probability that the sample mean differs from the population mean by more than 4 hours?

(d) Suppose that a second (independent) random sample of ten students was taken. Without doing the calculations, state whether the probabilities in (a), (b), and (c) would be higher, lower, or the same for the second sample.

10. An industrial process produces batches of a chemical whose impurity levels follow a normal distribution with standard deviation 1.6 grams per hundred grams of the chemical. A random sample of 100 batches is selected in order to estimate the population mean impurity level.

(a) The probability is .05 that the sample mean impurity level exceeds the population mean by how much?

(b) The probability is .10 that the sample mean impurity level is below the population mean by how much?

(c) The probability is .15 that the sample mean impurity level differs from the population mean by how much?

11. The price-earnings ratios for all companies whose shares are traded on the New York Stock Exchange follow a normal distribution with standard deviation 3.8. A random sam-

ple of these companies is selected in order to estimate the population mean price-earnings ratio.

  (a) How large a sample is necessary in order to ensure that the probability that the sample mean differs from the population mean by more than 1.0 is less than .10?

  (b) Without doing the calculations, state whether a larger or smaller sample than that in part (a) would be required to guarantee that the probability that the sample mean differs from the population mean by more than 1.0 is less than .05.

  (c) Without doing the calculations, state whether a larger or smaller sample than that in part (a) would be required to guarantee that the probability that the sample mean differs from the population mean by more than 1.5 is less than .10.

12. The number of hours spent studying by students on a large campus in the week before final exams follows a normal distribution with standard deviation 8.4 hours. A random sample of these students is taken to estimate the population mean number of hours studying.

  (a) How large a sample is needed to ensure that the probability that the sample mean differs from the population mean by more than 2.0 hours is less than .05?

  (b) Without doing the calculations, state whether a larger or smaller sample than that in part (a) would be required to guarantee that the probability that the sample mean differs from the population mean by more than 2.0 hours is less than .10.

  (c) Without doing the calculations, state whether a larger or smaller sample than that in part (a) would be required to guarantee that the probability that the sample mean differs from the population mean by more than 1.5 hours is less than .05.

13. In Table 6.1 and Example 6.1, we considered samples of $n = 4$ observations from a population of $N = 6$ values of years on the job for employees. The population mean is $\mu_X = 5.5$ years.

  (a) Confirm from the six population values that the population variance is

$$\sigma_X^2 = \frac{47}{12}$$

  (b) Confirm, following the approach of Example 6.1, that the variance of the sampling distribution of the sample mean is

$$\sigma_{\bar{X}}^2 = \sum (\bar{x} - \mu_X)^2 \, P_{\bar{X}}(\bar{x}) = \frac{47}{120}$$

  (c) Verify for this example that

$$\sigma_{\bar{X}}^2 = \frac{\sigma_X^2}{n} \cdot \frac{N - n}{N - 1}$$

14. In taking a sample of n observations from a population of N members, the variance of the sampling distribution of the sample mean is

$$\sigma_{\bar{X}}^2 = \frac{\sigma_X^2}{n} \cdot \frac{N - n}{N - 1}$$

The quantity $\frac{(N - n)}{(N - 1)}$ is called the "finite population correction factor."

  (a) To get some feeling for possible magnitudes of the finite population correction factor, calculate it for samples of $n = 20$ observations from populations of $N = 20, 40, 100, 1,000,$ and $10,000$ members.

  (b) Explain why the result for $N = 20$, found in part (a), is precisely what one should expect on intuitive grounds.

  (c) Given the results in part (a), discuss the practical significance of using the finite population correction factor for samples of 20 observations from populations of different sizes.

15. A town has 500 real estate agents. The mean value of the properties sold in a year by these agents is \$800,000, and the standard deviation is \$300,000. A random sample of 100 agents is selected, and the value of the properties they sold in a year is recorded.

   (a) What is the standard error of the sample mean?

   (b) What is the probability that the sample mean exceeds \$825,000?

   (c) What is the probability that the sample mean exceeds \$780,000?

   (d) What is the probability that the sample mean is between \$790,000 and \$820,000?

16. An economics course was taken by 250 students. Each member of a random sample of 50 of these students was asked to estimate the amount of time he or she spent on the previous week's assignment. Suppose that the population standard deviation is 30 minutes.

   (a) What is the probability that the sample mean exceeds the population mean by more than 2.5 minutes?

   (b) What is the probability that the sample mean is more than 5 minutes below the population mean?

   (c) What is the probability that the sample mean differs from the population mean by more than 10 minutes?

17. For an audience of 600 people attending a concert, the average time on the journey to the concert was 32 minutes, and the standard deviation was 10 minutes. A random sample of 150 audience members was taken.

   (a) What is the probability that the sample mean journey time was more than 31 minutes?

   (b) What is the probability that the sample mean journey time was less than 33 minutes?

   (c) Draw a graph to illustrate why the answers to (a) and (b) are the same.

   (d) What is the probability that the sample mean journey time was not between 31 and 33 minutes?

18. In 1992, Canadians voted in a referendum on a new constitution. In the province of Quebec, 42.4% of those who voted were in favor of the new constitution. A random sample of 100 voters from the province was taken.

   (a) What is the mean of the sample proportion in favor of a new constitution?

   (b) What is the variance of the sample proportion?

   (c) What is the standard error of the sample proportion?

   (d) What is the probability that the sample proportion is bigger than .5?

19. According to the Internal Revenue Service, 75% of all tax returns lead to a refund. A random sample of 100 tax returns is taken.

   (a) What is the mean of the sample proportion of returns leading to refunds?

   (b) What is the variance of the sample proportion?

   (c) What is the standard error of the sample proportion?

   (d) What is the probability that the sample proportion exceeds .8?

20. A record store owner finds that 20% of customers entering her store make a purchase. One morning 180 people, who can be regarded as a random sample of all customers, enter the store.

   (a) What is the mean of the sample proportion of customers making a purchase?

   (b) What is the variance of the sample proportion?

   (c) What is the standard error of the sample proportion?

   (d) What is the probability that the sample proportion is less than .15?

21. An administrator for a large group of hospitals believes that of all patients, 30% will generate bills that become at least 2 months overdue. A random sample of 200 patients is taken.

   (a) What is the standard error of the sample proportion that will generate bills that become at least 2 months overdue?

   (b) What is the probability that the sample proportion is less than .25?

   (c) What is the probability that the sample proportion is more than .33?

(**d**) What is the probability that the sample proportion is between .27 and .33?

22. A corporation receives 120 applications for positions from recent college graduates in business. Assuming that these applicants can be viewed as a random sample of all such graduates, what is the probability that between 35% and 45% of them are women if 40% of all recent college graduates in business are women?

23. A charity has found that 42% of donors from last year will donate again this year. A random sample of 300 donors from last year was taken.

    (**a**) What is the standard error of the sample proportion who will donate again this year?

    (**b**) What is the probability that more than half these sample members will donate again this year?

    (**c**) What is the probability that the sample proportion is between .40 and .45?

    (**d**) Without doing the calculations, state in which of the following ranges the sample proportion is more likely to lie: .39–.41, .41–.43, .43–.45, .45–.47.

24. A corporation is considering a new issue of convertible bonds. Management believes that the offer terms will be found attractive by 20% of all its current stockholders. Suppose that this belief is correct. A random sample of 130 current stockholders is taken.

    (**a**) What is the standard error of the sample proportion who find this offer attractive?

    (**b**) What is the probability that the sample proportion is more than .15?

    (**c**) What is the probability that the sample proportion is between .18 and .22?

    (**d**) Suppose that a sample of 500 current stockholders had been taken. Without doing the calculations, state whether the probabilities in (b) and (c) would have been higher, lower, or the same as those found.

25. A store has determined that 30% of all lawn mower purchasers will also purchase a service agreement. In one month, 280 lawn mowers are sold to customers who can be regarded as a random sample of all purchasers.

    (**a**) What is the standard error of the sample proportion of those who will purchase a service agreement?

    (**b**) What is the probability that the sample proportion will exceed .25?

    (**c**) What is the probability that the sample proportion will be less than .32?

    (**d**) Without doing the calculations, state in which of the following ranges the sample proportion is most likely to be: .29–.31, .30–.32, .31–.33, .32–.34.

26. A random sample of 100 voters is taken to estimate the proportion of a state's electorate in favor of an increase in the level of gasoline tax to provide additional revenue for highway repairs. What is the largest value that the standard error of the sample proportion in favor of this measure can take?

27. In Exercise 26, suppose that it is decided that a sample of 100 voters is too small to provide a sufficiently reliable estimate of the population proportion. It is required instead that the probability that the sample proportion differs from the population proportion (whatever its value) by more than .03 should not exceed .05. How large a sample is needed to guarantee that this requirement is met?

28. A company wants to estimate the proportion of people who are likely purchasers of electric shavers who watch the nationally telecast baseball playoffs. A random sample obtained information from 120 people who were identified as likely purchasers of electric shavers. Suppose that the proportion of likely purchasers of electric shavers in the population who watch the telecast is .25.

    (**a**) The probability is .10 that the sample proportion watching the telecast exceeds the population proportion by how much?

    (**b**) The probability is .05 that the sample proportion is lower than the population proportion by how much?

    (**c**) The probability is .30 that the sample proportion differs from the population proportion by how much?

29. Suppose that 50% of all adult Americans believe that a major overhaul of the nation's health care delivery system is essential. What is the probability that more than 56% of a random sample of 150 adult Americans would hold this belief?

30. Suppose that 50% of all adult Americans believe that federal budget deficits at recent levels cause long-term harm to the nation's economy. What is the probability that more than 58% of a random sample of 250 adult Americans would hold this belief?

31. A journalist wanted to learn the views of the chief executive officers of the 500 largest U.S. corporations on program trading of stocks. In the time available, it was only possible to contact a random sample of eight-one of these chief executive officers. If 55% of all the population members believe that program trading should be banned, what is the probability that less than half the sample members hold this view?

32. A small college has an entering freshman class of 528 students. Of these, 211 have brought their own personal computers to campus. A random sample of 120 entering freshmen was taken.
   (a) What is the standard error of the sample proportion bringing their own personal computers to campus?
   (b) What is the probability that the sample proportion is less than .33?
   (c) What is the probability that the sample proportion is between .40 and .50?

33. A manufacturing plant has 438 blue-collar employees. Of this group, 239 are concerned about future health care benefits. A random sample of 80 of these employees was questioned to estimate the population proportion concerned about future health care benefits.
   (a) What is the standard error of the sample proportion who are concerned?
   (b) What is the probability that the sample proportion is less than .5?
   (c) What is the probability that the sample proportion is between .5 and .6?

34. The annual percentage salary increases for the chief executive officers of all midsize corporations are normally distributed with mean 12.2% and standard deviation 3.6%. A random sample of eighty-one of these chief executive officers was taken. What is the probability that more than half the sample members had salary increases of less than 10%?

6.4 SAMPLING DISTRIBUTION OF THE SAMPLE VARIANCE

In Section 6.2, we considered the problem of making an inference about the mean of a population, based on sample information. We now turn our attention to the population variance.

Suppose that a random sample of n observations is drawn from a population with unknown mean μ_X and unknown variance σ_X^2, the sample members being denoted as $X_1, X_2, \ldots, X_n$. Now, the population variance is the expectation

$$\sigma_X^2 = E[(X - \mu_X)^2]$$

so an obvious quantity to look at would be the average of $(X_i - \mu_X)^2$ over the n sample members. However, the population mean μ_X is unknown, so in practice this quantity cannot be calculated. It is natural then to replace the unknown μ_X by the sample mean $\overline{X}$ and to consider the average of $(X_i - \overline{X})^2$. In fact, as we noted in Chapter 2, the sample variance is defined as

$$s_X^2 = \frac{1}{n-1} \sum_{i=1}^{n} (X_i - \overline{X})^2$$

Definition

Let $X_1, X_2, \ldots, X_n$ be a random sample from a population. The quantity

$$s_X^2 = \frac{1}{n-1} \sum_{i=1}^{n} (X_i - \overline{X})^2$$

is called the **sample variance.**[7] Its square root, s_X, is called the **sample standard deviation.**

At first sight, the use of $(n-1)$ rather than n as the divisor in our definition of the sample variance may be rather surprising. The motivation for this formulation is that if the sample variance is defined in this way, it can be shown that the mean of its sampling distribution is the true population variance;[8] that is

$$E(s_X^2) = \sigma_X^2$$

The conclusion that the expected value of the sample variance is the population variance is quite general. However, in order to characterize further the sampling distribution, we need to know more about the underlying population distribution. In many practical applications, the assumption that the population distribution is normal is not unreasonable. In this case, it can be shown that the random variable

$$\frac{(n-1)s_X^2}{\sigma_X^2} = \frac{\sum_{i=1}^{n}(X_i - \overline{X})^2}{\sigma_X^2}$$

has a distribution known as the χ^2 **distribution (chi-square distribution) with $(n-1)$ degrees of freedom.**[9]

The chi-square family of distributions is frequently employed in statistical analysis. The distributions are defined only for positive values of a random variable, which is appropriate in the present context since a sample variance cannot be negative. The density function, which is illustrated in Figure 6.6, is asymmetric. A specific member of the chi-square family is characterized by a single parameter, referred to as the number of *degrees of freedom*, for which the symbol ν is typically used. If a random variable has a χ^2 distribution with ν degrees of freedom, it will be denoted χ_ν^2. The mean and variance of this distribution are equal to the number of degrees of freedom and twice the number of degrees of freedom, respectively; that is

$$E(\chi_\nu^2) = \nu \qquad \text{and} \qquad \text{Var}(\chi_\nu^2) = 2\nu$$

In the present context, the random variable $(n-1)s_X^2/\sigma_X^2$ has a $\chi_{(n-1)}^2$ distribution, so its mean is

---

[7] Again we distinguish between the random variable s_X^2 and specific values it can take. Thus, if the actual sample observed is $x_1, x_2, \ldots, x_n$, then the realization of s_X^2 is

$$s_x^2 = \frac{1}{n-1} \sum_{i=1}^{n} (x_i - \overline{x})^2$$

[8] The result is established in Appendix A6.1 at the end of this chapter. Note that it is only true if the number of sample members is a small proportion of the number of population members.

[9] The chi-square distribution with ν degrees of freedom is the distribution of the sum of squares of ν independent standard normal random variables.

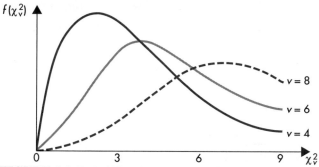

FIGURE 6.6 Probability density functions of the chi-square distribution with $\nu = 4, 6$, and 8 degrees of freedom

$$E\left[\frac{(n-1)s_X^2}{\sigma_X^2}\right] = (n-1)$$

Hence, we have

$$\frac{(n-1)}{\sigma_X^2}E(s_X^2) = (n-1)$$

so

$$E(s_X^2) = \sigma_X^2$$

as before. To get the variance of s_X^2, we have

$$\text{Var}\left[\frac{(n-1)s_X^2}{\sigma_X^2}\right] = 2(n-1)$$

Hence

$$\frac{(n-1)^2}{\sigma_X^4}\text{Var}(s_X^2) = 2(n-1)$$

so

$$\text{Var}(s_X^2) = \frac{2\sigma_X^4}{(n-1)}$$

The properties of the χ^2 distribution can therefore be used to find the variance of the sampling distribution of the sample variance.[10]

The parameter ν of the χ^2 distribution is known as the number of **degrees of freedom.** To understand this terminology, let us look at the sample variance. It involves the sum of the squares of the quantities

$$(X_1 - \overline{X}), (X_2 - \overline{X}), \ldots, (X_n - \overline{X})$$

Thus, these n pieces of information are employed to calculate the sample variance. However, they are not *independent* pieces of information, since they must sum to 0 (as follows from the definition of $\overline{X}$). Hence, if we know any $(n-1)$ of the $(X_i - \overline{X})$, we can calculate the other one from the first $(n-1)$. For example, since

---

[10] Remember that this result holds only when the parent population is normal.

$$\sum_{i=1}^{n} (X_i - \overline{X}) = 0$$

it follows that

$$X_n - \overline{X} = -\sum_{i=1}^{n-1} (X_i - \overline{X})$$

The n quantities $(X_i - \overline{X})$ are equivalent to a set of $(n - 1)$ independent pieces of information. The situation can be thought of as follows: We want to make an inference about the unknown σ_X^2. If the population mean μ_X were known, this inference could be based on the sum of squares of

$$(X_1 - \mu_X), (X_2 - \mu_X), \ldots, (X_n - \mu_X)$$

These quantities are independent of one another, and we would say that we have n degrees of freedom for the estimation of σ_X^2. However, since the unknown population mean must be replaced in practice by its estimate $\overline{X}$, one of these degrees of freedom is used up, and we are left with the equivalent of $(n - 1)$ independent observations for use in making inferences about the population variance. It is then said that $(n - 1)$ degrees of freedom are available.

We frequently need to find values of the cumulative distribution function for a χ^2 random variable. Such problems are often phrased in terms of the determination of cutoff points corresponding to particular specified probabilities. For instance, if a random variable has a χ_{10}^2 distribution, we may require the number K for which

$$P(\chi_{10}^2 < K) = .90$$

or, equivalently

$$P(\chi_{10}^2 > K) = .10$$

The distribution function of the chi-square random variable is tabulated in Table 5 in the Appendix in such a way that these cutoff points can be read directly. For the χ_{10}^2 random variable, it can be seen from Table 5 that if $P(\chi_{10}^2 > K) = .10$, then $K = 15.99$. This probability is shown as an area under the density function of the random variable in Figure 6.7.

Sampling Distribution of the Sample Variance

Let s_X^2 denote the sample variance for a random sample of n observations from a population with a variance σ_X^2. Then

(i) The sampling distribution of s_X^2 has mean σ_X^2; that is

$$E(s_X^2) = \sigma_X^2$$

(ii) The variance of the sampling distribution of s_X^2 depends on the underlying population distribution. If that distribution is normal, then

$$\text{Var}(s_X^2) = \frac{2\sigma_X^4}{n - 1}$$

(iii) If the population distribution is normal, then $\dfrac{(n-1)s_X^2}{\sigma_X^2}$ is distributed as $\chi^2_{(n-1)}$.

Suppose that we take a random sample from a population and want to make some inferential statements about the population variance. Given an assumption of normality in the underlying population, the chi-square distribution can be used, as illustrated in the following examples.

EXAMPLE
6.6

When a production process is operating correctly, the resistance in ohms of components produced has a normal distribution with standard deviation 3.6. A random sample of four components was taken. What is the probability that the sample variance is bigger than 30?

We have

$$n = 4 \qquad \sigma_X = 3.6 \qquad \sigma_X^2 = (3.6)^2 = 12.96$$

The required probability is

$$P(s_X^2 > 30) = P\left(\frac{(n-1)s_X^2}{\sigma_X^2} > \frac{30(n-1)}{\sigma_X^2}\right)$$

$$= P\left(\chi_3^2 > \frac{(30)(3)}{12.96}\right)$$

$$= P\left(\chi_3^2 > 6.94\right)$$

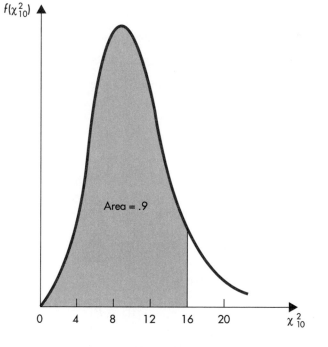

FIGURE 6.7 Probability (.9) that a chi-square random variable with 10 degrees of freedom is less than 15.99

$f(\chi_{10}^2)$

Area = .9

0   4   8   12   16   20 χ_{10}^2

From Table 5 of the Appendix, we find

$$P(\chi_3^2 > 6.25) = .10 \qquad P(\chi_3^2 > 7.81) = .05$$

Then, since 6.94 is between 6.25 and 7.81, the probability we require must be between .05 and .10; that is

$$.05 < P(s_X^2 > 30) < .10$$

The table does not allow us to find the precise probability, though computer programs for this purpose are widely available. Notice also that the sample variance is bigger than 30 if and only if the sample standard deviation is bigger than $\sqrt{30} = 5.48$. The probabilities of these two events are therefore the same. It follows that

$$.05 < P(s_X > 5.48) < .10$$

EXAMPLE 6.7   A manufacturer of canned peas is concerned that the mean weight of the product be close to the advertised weight. In addition, he does not want too much variability in the weights of the cans of peas; otherwise, a large proportion will differ markedly from the advertised weight. Assume that the population distribution of weights is normal. If a random sample of twenty cans is checked, find the numbers K_1 and K_2 such that

$$P\left(\frac{s_X^2}{\sigma_X^2} < K_1\right) = .05 \qquad \text{and} \qquad P\left(\frac{s_X^2}{\sigma_X^2} > K_2\right) = .05$$

We have

$$.05 = P\left(\frac{s_X^2}{\sigma_X^2} < K_1\right) = P\left[\frac{(n-1)s_X^2}{\sigma_X^2} < (n-1)K_1\right]$$

$$= P[\chi_{(n-1)}^2 < (n-1)K_1]$$

where $n = 20$ is the sample size and $\chi_{(n-1)}^2$ is a chi-square random variable with $(n-1) = 19$ degrees of freedom. Then

$$.05 = P(\chi_{19}^2 < 19K_1) \qquad \text{or} \qquad .95 = P(\chi_{19}^2 > 19K_1)$$

From Table 5 in the Appendix, we therefore have

$$19K_1 = 10.12$$

so

$$K_1 = .533$$

The conclusion, then, is that the probability is .05 that the sample variance will be less than 53.3% of the population variance.

We also require the number K_2 such that

$$.05 = P\left(\frac{s_X^2}{\sigma_X^2} > K_2\right)$$

Equivalently, we have

$$.05 = P\left[\frac{(n-1)s_X^2}{\sigma_X^2} > (n-1)K_2\right]$$

$$= P[\chi^2_{(n-1)} > (n-1)K_2]$$

Hence, since $n = 20$

$$.05 = P(\chi_{19}^2 > 19K_2)$$

Then, from Table 5, it follows that

$$19K_2 = 30.14$$

so

$$K_2 = 1.586$$

This implies that the probability is .05 that the sample variance will be more than 58.6% bigger than the population variance.

These probabilities are shown in Figure 6.8 as areas under the probability density function of the χ_{19}^2 distribution.

It should be emphasized that the technique of these examples is less universally applicable in practice than are those of earlier sections of this chapter. The assumption that the distribution of the population being sampled is normal is more critical here. We have seen how probability statements can be made about both the sample mean and sample variance when sampling from a normal distribution. However, the latter will typically be far more affected than the former by any departures from normality in the distribution being sampled. In making probability statements about the sample mean, the central limit theorem ensures that for moderately large samples, modest departures from normality in the sampled population have only minor influence on the validity of any derived probability statements. As a result, we say that an inference based on the sample mean is *robust* to departures from

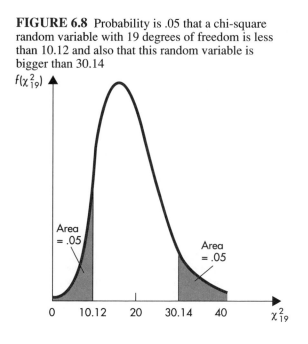

FIGURE 6.8 Probability is .05 that a chi-square random variable with 19 degrees of freedom is less than 10.12 and also that this random variable is bigger than 30.14

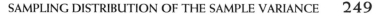

assumed normality in the parent population, whereas an inference based on the sample variance is not.

Nevertheless, it often happens in practice that the population variance is of direct interest to an investigator. It must be kept in mind that if only a moderate number of sample observations are available, serious departures from normality in the parent population can severely invalidate the conclusions of analyses based on the technique described in this section. The cautious analyst will therefore be rather tentative in making inferences in these circumstances.

EXERCISES

35. A process produces batches of a chemical whose impurity concentrations follow a normal distribution with variance 1.75. A random sample of twenty of these batches is chosen. Find the probability that the sample variance exceeds 3.10.

36. Monthly rates of return on the shares of a particular common stock are independent of one another and normally distributed with a standard deviation of 1.7 A sample of 12 months is taken.

(a) Find the probability that the sample standard deviation is less than 2.5.

(b) Find the probability that the sample standard deviation is bigger than 1.0.

37. It is believed that first-year salaries for newly qualified accountants follow a normal distribution with standard deviation $2,500. A random sample of sixteen observations was taken.

(a) Find the probability that the sample standard deviation is more than $3,000.

(b) Find the probability that the sample standard deviation is less than $1,500.

38. A mathematics test of 100 multiple choice questions is to be given to all freshmen entering a large university. Initially, in a pilot study, the test was given to a random sample of twenty freshmen. Suppose that, for the population of all entering freshmen, the distribution of number of correct answers would be normal with variance 250.

(a) What is the probability that the sample variance would be less than 100?

(b) What is the probability that the sample variance would be more than 500?

39. In a large city it was found that summer electricity bills for single family homes followed a normal distribution with standard deviation $100. A random sample of 25 bills was taken.

(a) Find the probability that the sample standard deviation is less than $75.

(b) Find the probability that the sample standard deviation is more than $150.

40. Numbers of hours spent watching television by students in the week before final exams have a normal distribution with standard deviation 4.5 hours. A random sample of thirty students was taken.

(a) Is the probability more than .95 that the sample standard deviation exceeds 3.5 hours?

(b) Is the probability more than .95 that the sample standard deviation is less than 6 hours?

41. In Table 6.1, we considered the fifteen possible samples of four observations from a population of $N = 6$ values of years on the job for employees. The population variance for these six values is

$$\sigma_X^2 = \frac{47}{12}$$

For each of the fifteen possible samples, calculate the sample variance. Find the average of these fifteen sample variances, thus confirming that the expected value of the sample variance is not equal to the population variance when the number of sample members is not a small proportion of the number of population members. [In fact, as you can verify here, $E(s_X^2) = N\sigma_X^2/(N - 1)$.]

42. A production process manufactures electronic components with timing signals whose duration follows a normal distribution. A random sample of six components was taken, and the durations of their timing signals were measured.

   (a) The probability is .05 that the sample variance is bigger than what percentage of the population variance?

   (b) The probability is .10 that the sample variance is less than what percentage of the population variance?

43. A random sample of ten stock market mutual funds was taken. Suppose that rates of returns on the population of all stock market mutual funds follow a normal distribution.

   (a) The probability is .10 that the sample variance is bigger than what percentage of the population variance?

   (b) Find any pair of numbers, a and b, to complete the following sentence. The probability is .95 that the sample variance is between $a\%$ and $b\%$ of the population variance.

   (c) Suppose that a sample of twenty mutual funds had been taken. Without doing the calculations, indicate how this would change your answer to part (b).

44. Each member of a random sample of fifteen business economists was asked to predict the rate of inflation for the coming year. Assume that the predictions for the whole population of business economists follow a normal distribution with standard deviation 1.8%.

   (a) The probability is .01 that the sample standard deviation is bigger than what number?

   (b) The probability is .025 that the sample standard deviation is smaller than what number?

   (c) Find any pair of numbers such that the probability that the sample standard deviation lies between these numbers is .90.

45. A precision instrument is checked by making twelve readings on the same quantity. The population distribution of readings is normal.

   (a) The probability is .95 that the sample variance is more than what percentage of the population variance?

   (b) The probability is .90 that the sample variance is more than what percentage of the population variance?

   (c) Determine any pair of appropriate numbers a and b to complete the following sentence: The probability is .95 that the sample variance is between $a\%$ and $b\%$ of the population variance.

46. A drug company produces pills containing an active ingredient. The company is concerned about the mean weight of this ingredient per pill, but it also requires that the variance (in squared milligrams) be no more than 1.5. A random sample of twenty pills is selected, and the sample variance is found to be 2.05. How likely is it that a sample variance this high or higher would be found if the population variance is in fact 1.5? Assume that the population distribution is normal.

47. A manufacturer has been purchasing raw materials from a supplier whose consignments have a variance of 15.4 (in squared pounds) in impurity levels. A rival supplier claims that he can supply consignments of this raw material with the same mean impurity level but with lower variance. For a random sample of twenty-five consignments from the second supplier, the variance in impurity levels was found to be 12.2. What is the probability of observing a value this low or lower for the sample variance if, in fact, the true population variance is 15.4? Assume that the population distribution is normal.

REVIEW EXERCISES

48. What is meant by the statement that the sample mean has a sampling distribution?

49. An investor is considering six different money market funds. The average number of days to maturity for these funds is

41   39   35   35   33   38

Two of these funds are to be chosen at random.

    (a) How many possible samples of two funds are there?

    (b) List all possible samples.

    (c) Find the probability function of the sampling distribution of the sample mean.

    (d) Verify directly that the mean of the sampling distribution of the sample mean is equal to the population mean.

50. Of what relevance is the central limit theorem to the sampling distribution of the sample mean?

51. Refer to Exercise 49. Find the probability function of the sampling distribution of the sample proportion of funds with average maturity more than 36 days for samples of two observations. Also verify directly that the mean of the sampling distribution of the sample proportion is equal to the population proportion.

52. The scores of all applicants taking an aptitude test required by a law school have a normal distribution with mean 420 and standard deviation 100. A random sample of twenty-five scores is taken.

    (a) Find the probability that the sample mean score is bigger than 450.

    (b) Find the probability that the sample mean score is between 400 and 450.

    (c) The probability is .10 that the sample mean score is bigger than what number?

    (d) The probability is .10 that the sample mean score is less than what number?

    (e) The probability is .05 that the sample standard deviation of the scores is bigger than what number?

    (f) The probability is .05 that the sample standard deviation of the scores is less than what number?

    (g) If a sample of fifty test scores had been taken, would the probability of a sample mean score bigger than 450 be smaller than, larger than, or the same as the correct answer to part (a)? It is not necessary to do the detailed calculations here. Sketch a graph to illustrate your reasoning.

53. A company services home air conditioners. It has been found that times for service calls follow a normal distribution with mean 60 minutes and standard deviation 10 minutes. A random sample of four service calls was taken.

    (a) What is the probability that the sample mean service time is more than 65 minutes?

    (b) The probability is .10 that the sample mean service time is less than how many minutes?

    (c) The probability is .10 that the sample standard deviation of service times is more than how many minutes?

    (d) The probability is .10 that the sample standard deviation of service times is less than how many minutes?

    (e) What is the probability that more than two of these calls take more than 65 minutes?

54. In a particular year, the percentage rates of returns of U.S. common stock mutual funds had a normal distribution with mean 14.8 and standard deviation 6.3. A random sample of nine of these mutual funds was taken.

    (a) What is the probability that the sample mean percentage rate of return is more than 19.0?

    (b) What is the probability that the sample mean percentage rate of return is between 10.6 and 19.0?

    (c) The probability is .25 that the sample mean percentage return is less than what number?

    (d) The probability is .10 that the sample standard deviation of percentage return is more than what number?

    (e) If a sample of twenty of these funds was taken, state whether the probability of a sample mean percentage rate of return of more than 19.0 would be smaller than, bigger than, or the same as the correct answer to (a). Sketch a graph to illustrate your reasoning.

55. The lifetimes of a certain electronic component are known to be normally distributed with a mean of 1,600 hours and a standard deviation of 400 hours.

   (a) For a random sample of sixteen components, find the probability that the sample mean is more than 1,500 hours.

   (b) For a random sample of sixteen components, the probability is .15 that the sample mean lifetime is more than how many hours?

   (c) For a random sample of sixteen components, the probability is .10 that the sample standard deviation lifetime is more than how many hours?

   (d) For a random sample of 121 components, find the probability that less than half the sampled components have lifetimes of more than 1,500 hours.

56. Refer to Appendix A6.1 in order to derive the mean of the sampling distribution of the sample variance for a sample of n observations from a population of N members, when the population variance is σ_x^2. By appropriately modifying the argument in Appendix A6.1, show that

$$E(s_x^2) = N\sigma_x^2/(N - 1)$$

Note the intuitive plausibility of this result when $n = N$.

57. It has been found that times taken by people to complete a particular tax form follow a normal distribution with mean 100 minutes and standard deviation 30 minutes. A random sample of nine people who have completed this tax form was taken.

   (a) What is the probability that the sample mean time taken is more than two hours?

   (b) The probability is .20 that the sample mean time taken is less than how many minutes?

   (c) The probability is .05 that the sample standard deviation of time taken is more than how many minutes?

   (d) The probability is .05 that the sample standard deviation of time taken is less than how many minutes?

58. It was found that 80% of seniors at a particular college had accepted a job offer before graduation. For those accepting offers, salary distribution was normal with mean $29,000 and standard deviation $4,000.

   (a) For a random sample of sixty seniors, what is the probability that less than 70% have accepted job offers?

   (b) For a random sample of six seniors, what is the probability that less than 70% have accepted job offers?

   (c) For a random sample of six seniors who have accepted job offers, what is the probability that the average salary is more than $30,000?

   (d) A senior is chosen at random. What is the probability that he or she has accepted a job offer with a salary of more than $30,000?

59. Plastic bags used for packaging produce are manufactured so that the breaking strengths of the bags are normally distributed with a standard deviation of 1.8 pounds per square inch. A random sample of sixteen bags is selected.

   (a) The probability is .01 that the sample standard deviation of breaking strengths exceeds what number?

   (b) The probability is .15 that the sample mean exceeds the population mean by how much?

   (c) The probability is .05 that the sample mean differs from the population mean by how much?

60. A quality control manager was concerned about variability in the amount of active ingredient in pills produced by a particular process. A random sample of 21 pills was taken. What is the probability that the sample variance of the amount of active ingredient was more than twice the population variance?

61. A sample of 100 students is to be taken to determine which of two brands of beer is preferred in a blind taste test. Suppose that, in the whole population of students, 50% would prefer brand A.

(a) What is the probability that more than 60% of the sample members prefer brand A?

(b) What is the probability that between 45% and 55% of the sample members prefer brand A?

(c) Suppose that a sample of only ten students was available. Indicate how the method of calculation of probabilities would differ, compared with your solutions to (a) and (b).

62. Scores on a particular test, taken by a large group of students, follow a normal distribution with standard deviation 40 points. A random sample of sixteen scores was taken to estimate the population mean score. Let $\overline{X}$ denote the sample mean. What is the probability that the interval $(\overline{X} - 10)$ to $(\overline{X} + 10)$ contains the true population mean?

63. A manufacturer of liquid detergent claims that the mean weight of liquid in containers sold is at least 30 ounces. It is known that the population distribution of weights is normal with standard deviation 1.3 ounces. In order to check the manufacturer's claim, a random sample of sixteen containers of detergent is examined. The claim will be questioned if the sample mean weight is less than 29.5 ounces. What is the probability that the claim will be questioned if in fact the population mean weight is 30 ounces?

64. In a particular year, 40% of home sales were partially financed by the seller. A random sample of 250 sales is examined.

(a) The probability is .8 that the sample proportion is bigger than what amount?

(b) The probability is .9 that the sample proportion is smaller than what amount?

(c) The probability is .7 that the sample proportion differs from the population proportion by how much?

65. A candidate for office intends to campaign in a state if her initial support level exceeds 30% of the voters. A random sample of 300 voters is taken, and it is decided to campaign if the sample proportion supporting the candidate exceeds .28.

(a) What is the probability of a decision to campaign if in fact the initial support level is 20%?

(b) What is the probability of a decision not to campaign if in fact the initial support level is 40%?

66. It is known that the incomes of subscribers to a particular magazine have a normal distribution with standard deviation $6,600. A random sample of twenty-five subscribers is taken.

(a) What is the probability that the sample standard deviation of their incomes is bigger than $4,000?

(b) What is the probability that the sample standard deviation of their incomes is less than $8,000?

67. Batches of chemical are manufactured by a production process. Samples of twenty batches from a production run are selected for testing. If the standard deviation of the percentage impurity contents in the sampled batches exceeds 2.5%, the production process is thoroughly checked. Assume that the population distribution of percentage impurity concentrations is normal. What is the probability that the production process will be thoroughly checked if the population standard deviation of percentage impurity concentrations is 2%?

APPENDIX A6.1

In this appendix, we will show that the mean of the sampling distribution of the sample variance is the population variance. We begin by finding the expectation of the sum of squares of the sample members about their mean; that is, the expectation of

$$\sum_{i=1}^{n} (X_i - \overline{X})^2 = \sum_{i=1}^{n} [(X_i - \mu_X) - (\overline{X} - \mu_X)]^2$$

$$= \sum_{i=1}^{n} [(X_i - \mu_X)^2 - 2(\overline{X} - \mu_X)(X_i - \mu_X) + (\overline{X} - \mu_X)^2]$$

$$= \sum_{i=1}^{n} (X_i - \mu_X)^2 - 2(\overline{X} - \mu_X) \sum_{i=1}^{n} (X_i - \mu_X) + \sum_{i=1}^{n} (\overline{X} - \mu_X)^2$$

$$= \sum_{i=1}^{n} (X_i - \mu_X)^2 - 2n(\overline{X} - \mu_X)^2 + n(\overline{X} - \mu_X)^2$$

$$= \sum_{i=1}^{n} (X_i - \mu_X)^2 - n(\overline{X} - \mu_X)^2$$

Taking expectations then gives

$$E\left[\sum_{i=1}^{n} (X_i - \overline{X})^2\right] = E\left[\sum_{i=1}^{n} (X_i - \mu_X)^2\right] - nE[(\overline{X} - \mu_X)^2]$$

$$= \sum_{i=1}^{n} E[(X_i - \mu_X)^2] - nE[(\overline{X} - \mu_X)^2]$$

Now, the expectation of each $(X_i - \mu_X)^2$ is the population variance σ_X^2, and the expectation of $(\overline{X} - \mu_X)^2$ is the variance of the sample mean—that is, σ_X^2/n. Hence, we have

$$E\left[\sum_{i=1}^{n} (X_i - \overline{X})^2\right] = n\sigma_X^2 - \frac{n\sigma_X^2}{n} = (n - 1)\sigma_X^2$$

Finally, for the expected value of the sample variance, we have

$$E(s_X^2) = E\left[\frac{1}{n - 1} \sum_{i=1}^{n} (X_i - \overline{X})^2\right]$$

$$= \frac{1}{n - 1} E\left[\sum_{i=1}^{n} (X_i - \overline{X})^2\right]$$

$$= \frac{1}{n - 1} (n - 1)\sigma_X^2 = \sigma_X^2$$

This is the result we set out to establish.

CHAPTER 7

Point Estimation

7.1 INTRODUCTION

In this chapter, we begin to explore the possibility of making inferential statements about a population, based on the information contained in a random sample. We will focus attention on specific characteristics, or **parameters,** of the population. Parameters of interest might include the population mean or variance, or the proportion of population members possessing some specific attribute. For example, we may want to make inferences about

1. The mean income of all families in a particular neighborhood
2. The variation in the impurity levels in batches of a manufactured chemical
3. The proportion of a corporation's employees favoring the introduction of a modified bonus scheme

Any inference drawn about the population will, of necessity, be based on sample **statistics**—that is, on functions of the sample information. The choice of appropriate statistics will depend on which population parameter is of interest. The true parameter will be unknown, and one objective of sampling could be to estimate its value.

Definitions

An **estimator** of a population parameter is a random variable that depends on the sample information and whose realizations provide approximations to this unknown parameter. A specific realization of that random variable is called an **estimate.**

257

To clarify the distinction between the terms *estimator* and *estimate*, consider the estimation of the mean income of all families in a neighborhood, based on a random sample of twenty families. It seems reasonable to base our conclusions on the sample mean income, so we say that the *estimator* of the population mean is the sample mean. Suppose that, having obtained the sample, we find that the average income of the families in the sample is $49,356. Then the *estimate* of the population mean family income is $49,356. Notationally, we have already made this distinction, using $\overline{X}$ to denote the random variable and $\overline{x}$ a specific realization.

In discussing the estimation of an unknown population parameter, two possibilities must be considered. First, we could compute from the sample a single number as "representative," or perhaps "most representative." The estimate $49,356 for the neighborhood mean family income is an example of such an estimate. Alternatively, we could try to find an interval, or range, that we are fairly sure contains the true parameter. In this chapter, we consider the first type of estimation problem, postponing until Chapter 8 a discussion of interval estimation.

Definitions

A **point estimator** of a population parameter is a function of the sample information that yields a single number. The corresponding realization is called the **point estimate** of the parameter.

In the neighborhood family income example, the parameter to be estimated is the population mean family income. The point estimator used is the sample mean, and the resulting point estimate is $49,356.

For purposes of illustration, we will discuss in this chapter four point estimators, all of which were met in Chapter 6. These are the sample mean, variance, standard deviation, and proportion. Table 7.1 summarizes the notation we have used.

TABLE 7.1 Notation for population parameters, point estimators, and estimates

POPULATION PARAMETER	ESTIMATOR	ESTIMATE
Mean (μ_X)	$\overline{X}$	$\overline{x}$
Variance (σ_X^2)	s_X^2	s_X^2
Standard deviation (σ_X)	s_X	s_X
Proportion (p)	$\hat{p}_X$	$\hat{p}_X$

EXAMPLE 7.1

Price-earnings ratios for a random sample of ten stocks traded on the New York Stock Exchange on a particular day were

$$10 \quad 16 \quad 5 \quad 10 \quad 12 \quad 8 \quad 4 \quad 6 \quad 5 \quad 4$$

Find point estimates of the population mean, variance, and standard deviation, and proportion of stocks in the population for which the price-earnings ratio exceeded 8.5.

To find the first three of these sample quantities, we show the calculations in tabular form:

i	x_i	x_i^2
1	10	100
2	16	256
3	5	25
4	10	100
5	12	144
6	8	64
7	4	16
8	6	36
9	5	25
10	4	16
Sums	80	782

We then have

$$n = 10 \qquad \sum x_i = 80 \qquad \sum x_i^2 = 782$$

Hence, the sample mean is

$$\bar{x} = \frac{1}{n} \sum x_i = \frac{80}{10} = 8$$

which is our point estimate of the population mean.

A point estimate of the population variance is provided by

$$s_x^2 = \frac{1}{n-1} \left(\sum x_i^2 - n\bar{x}^2 \right)$$

$$= \frac{782 - (10)(8)^2}{9} = 15.78$$

For the population standard deviation, the point estimate is

$$s_x = \sqrt{s_x^2} = \sqrt{15.78} = 3.97$$

Finally, in the sample, the number of stocks for which the price-earnings ratio exceeds 8.5 is $x = 4$. Hence, our point estimate of the population proportion is

$$\hat{p}_x = \frac{x}{n} = \frac{4}{10} = .4$$

For the specific estimation problems discussed in this section, the choice of point estimator has been based mainly on intuitive plausibility. In the remainder of this chapter, we consider various desirable properties of point estimators. This provides a framework within which a particular choice can be evaluated and alternatives examined. At the outset it must be stated that no single mechanism exists for the determination of a uniquely "best" point estimator in all circumstances. What is available instead is a set of criteria under which particular estimators can be evaluated. We will see that for most general purposes, the sample mean, variance, standard deviation, and proportion provide satisfactory estimators of the corresponding population quantities. However, in subsequent chapters, we will meet estimation problems for which the choice of an appropriate point estimator is rather less obvious.

7.2 UNBIASED ESTIMATORS AND THEIR EFFICIENCY

In this discussion, we will denote by θ a parameter to be estimated and by $\hat{\theta}$ the corresponding point estimator. As we saw in Chapter 6, it is sometimes possible to find the sampling distribution of the random variable $\hat{\theta}$. That estimator is said to be **unbiased** if the mean of its sampling distribution is the unknown parameter θ.

Definitions

The estimator $\hat{\theta}$ is said to be an **unbiased estimator** of the parameter θ if the mean of the sampling distribution of $\hat{\theta}$ is θ; that is

$$E(\hat{\theta}) = \theta$$

We say that the corresponding point estimate is obtained through an **unbiased estimation procedure.**

It follows from the notion of expectation that if the sampling procedure is repeated many times, then *on the average*, the value obtained for an unbiased estimator will be equal to the population parameter. It seems reasonable to assert that, all other things being equal, unbiasedness is a desirable property in a point estimator. Figure 7.1 shows the sampling distributions of two estimators, one unbiased and one not.

For three of the estimators being considered, we saw in Chapter 6 that

$$E(\overline{X}) = \mu_X \qquad E(s_X^2) = \sigma_X^2 \qquad E(\hat{p}_X) = p$$

Thus, we can say that the sample mean, variance, and proportion are unbiased estimators of the corresponding population parameters. It is for this reason that in defining the sample variance, we divided the sum of squared discrepancies from the sample mean by $(n - 1)$ rather than n. The former produces an unbiased estimator; the latter does not. The mean of the sampling distribution of the sample standard deviation is *not* equal to the population standard deviation. Hence, the sample standard deviation is not an unbiased estimator of the population standard deviation.

FIGURE 7.1 Probability density functions for the estimators $\hat{\theta}_1$ and $\hat{\theta}_2$, $\hat{\theta}_1$ being an unbiased estimator of θ and $\hat{\theta}_2$ not

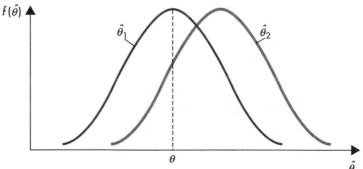

EXAMPLE 7.2

Refer to the results in Example 7.1. We can now state that the estimates of the population mean, variance, and proportion of stocks for which the price-earnings ratio exceeded 8.5

$$\bar{x} = 8 \qquad s_x^2 = 15.78 \qquad \hat{p}_x = .4$$

are obtained through unbiased estimation procedures. However, the estimate of the population standard deviation, $s_x = 3.97$, is not obtained through an unbiased estimation procedure.

An estimator that is not unbiased is said to be **biased.** The extent of the **bias** is the difference between the mean of the estimator and the true parameter.

Definition

Let $\hat{\theta}$ be an estimator of θ. The **bias** in $\hat{\theta}$ is defined as the difference between its mean and θ; that is

$$\text{Bias}(\hat{\theta}) = E(\hat{\theta}) - \theta$$

It follows that the bias of an unbiased estimator is 0.

In many practical problems, different unbiased estimators can be obtained, and some method of choosing among them needs to be found. In this situation, it is natural to prefer the estimator whose distribution is most closely concentrated about the population parameter being estimated. Values of such an estimator are less likely to differ, by any fixed amount, from the parameter being estimated than are those of its competitors. Using variance as a measure of concentration, we introduce the concept of **efficiency** of an estimator as a criterion for preferring one estimator over another.

Definitions

Let $\hat{\theta}_1$ and $\hat{\theta}_2$ be two unbiased estimators of θ, based on the same number of sample observations. Then

(i) $\hat{\theta}_1$ is said to be **more efficient** than $\hat{\theta}_2$ if

$$\text{Var}\ (\hat{\theta}_1) < \text{Var}\ (\hat{\theta}_2)$$

(ii) The **relative efficiency** of one estimator with respect to the other is the ratio of their variances; that is

$$\text{Relative efficiency} = \frac{\text{Var} (\hat{\theta}_2)}{\text{Var} (\hat{\theta}_1)}$$

Figure 7.2 shows the sampling distributions of two unbiased estimators. Clearly, $\hat{\theta}_1$ is the more efficient.

EXAMPLE 7.3

Let $X_1, X_2, \ldots, X_n$ be a random sample from a normal distribution with mean μ_X and variance $\sigma_X{}^2$. The sample mean, $\overline{X}$, is an unbiased estimator of the population mean, with variance

$$\text{Var} (\overline{X}) = \frac{\sigma_X{}^2}{n}$$

As an alternative estimator, we could use the median of the sample observations. It can be shown that this estimator is also unbiased for μ_X and that its variance is

$$\text{Var} (\text{Median}) = \frac{\pi}{2} \cdot \frac{\sigma_X{}^2}{n} \approx \frac{1.57\, \sigma_X{}^2}{n}$$

The sample mean is more efficient than the median, the relative efficiency of the mean with respect to the median being

$$\text{Relative efficiency} = \frac{\text{Var} (\text{Median})}{\text{Var} (\overline{X})} = 1.57$$

The variance of the sample median is 57% higher than that of the sample mean. Here, in order for the sample median to have as small a variance as the sample mean, it would have to be based on 57% more observations. In Chapter 2, we noted that one advantage of the median over the mean is that it gives far less weight to extreme observations. We now see, in terms of its relative inefficiency, a potential disadvantage in using the sample median as a measure of central location.

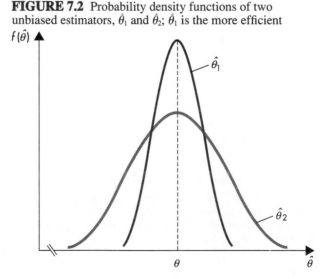

FIGURE 7.2 Probability density functions of two unbiased estimators, $\hat{\theta}_1$ and $\hat{\theta}_2$; $\hat{\theta}_1$ is the more efficient

In some estimation problems,[1] the point estimator with the smallest variance among a group of unbiased estimators is sought. In a few relatively simple cases, it is possible to find the most efficient of *all* unbiased estimators for a parameter.

Definition

If $\hat{\theta}$ is an unbiased estimator of θ, and no other unbiased estimator has smaller variance, then $\hat{\theta}$ is said to be the **most efficient** or **minimum variance unbiased estimator** of θ.

Specific examples of minimum variance unbiased estimators include

1. The sample mean when sampling from a normal distribution
2. The sample variance when sampling from a normal distribution
3. The binomial sample proportion

The use of minimum variance unbiased estimators is appealing. However, it is not always possible to find such estimators.

EXERCISES

1. A random sample of eight batches of chemical were tested for impurity concentration. The percentage impurity levels found in this sample were

    3.2   4.3   2.1   2.8   3.2   3.6   4.0   3.8

    (a) Find the sample mean, variance, and standard deviation. Find the sample proportion of batches with impurity level greater than 3.75%.
    (b) For what population quantities have estimates based on unbiased estimation procedures been found in part (a)?

2. A random sample of eight homes in a particular suburb had the following selling prices (in thousands of dollars):

    92   83   112   127   109   96   102   90

    (a) Find the sample mean, variance, and standard deviation.
    (b) For what population quantities have estimates based on an unbiased estimation procedure been found in part (a)?
    (c) Use an unbiased estimation procedure to find a point estimate of the variance of the sample mean.
    (d) Use an unbiased estimator to estimate the proportion of homes in this suburb selling for less than $92,500.

3. Students in a large economics class rated the course on a scale from 1 (poor) to 5 (excellent). A random sample of ten ratings provided the following values:

    3   3   4   3   5   2   4   4   4   5

    (a) Find the sample mean, variance, and standard deviation. Also find the sample proportion of ratings higher than 3.
    (b) For what population quantities have estimates based on unbiased estimation procedures been found in part (a)?

---

[1] The most important examples of this type will be discussed in Chapters 12 and 13.

(c) Using an unbiased estimation procedure, find a point estimate of the variance of the sample mean.

4. Let X_1 and X_2 be a random sample of two observations from a population with mean μ and variance σ^2. Consider the following three point estimators of μ:

$$\overline{X} = \frac{1}{2}X_1 + \frac{1}{2}X_2 \qquad \hat{\mu}^{(1)} = \frac{1}{4}X_1 + \frac{3}{4}X_2 \qquad \hat{\mu}^{(2)} = \frac{1}{3}X_1 + \frac{2}{3}X_2$$

(a) Show that all three estimators are unbiased.

(b) Which of these estimators is the most efficient?

(c) Find the relative efficiency of $\overline{X}$ with respect to each of the other two estimators.

5. A random sample of sixteen families in the Elm Park subdivision showed a mean annual income of $69,200, and the sample standard deviation was $6,200. An independent random sample of ten families in the Cherry Hills subdivision showed a mean annual income of $86,700, and the sample standard deviation was $9,400. Let μ_1 and σ_1^2 denote the population mean and variance for incomes in Elm Park and μ_2 and σ_2^2 the population mean and variance for incomes in Cherry Hills.

(a) Use an unbiased estimation procedure to find a point estimate of $(\mu_2 - \mu_1)$, the difference between the population means.

(b) Let $\overline{X}_1$ and $\overline{X}_2$ denote the two sample means. Using an unbiased estimation procedure, find a point estimate of the variance of $(\overline{X}_2 - \overline{X}_1)$.

6. Let X_1, X_2, and X_3 be a random sample from a population with mean μ and variance σ^2. Consider the following two point estimators of μ:

$$\hat{\mu}^{(1)} = \frac{X_1 + 2X_2 + 3X_3}{6} \qquad \hat{\mu}^{(2)} = \frac{X_1 + 4X_2 + X_3}{6}$$

(a) Show that both estimators are unbiased.

(b) Which estimator is the more efficient?

(c) Find the relative efficiency.

(d) Find an unbiased estimator of the population mean that is more efficient than either of these estimators.

7. Let X_1, X_2, X_3, and X_4 be a random sample from a population with mean μ and variance σ^2. Consider the following two estimators of μ:

$$\hat{\mu}^{(1)} = \frac{X_1 + 2X_2 + 3X_3 + 4X_4}{10} \qquad \hat{\mu}^{(2)} = \frac{X_1 + 4X_2 + 4X_3 + X_4}{10}$$

(a) Show that both estimators are unbiased.

(b) Which estimator is the more efficient?

(c) Find the relative efficiency.

(d) Find an unbiased estimator of the population mean that is more efficient than either of these estimators.

8. Let θ be a population parameter, and $\hat{\theta}^{(1)}$ and $\hat{\theta}^{(2)}$ two unbiased estimators of that parameter. Show that for any number, α, the estimator $\alpha\hat{\theta}^{(1)} + (1 - \alpha)\hat{\theta}^{(2)}$ is unbiased for θ. Hence deduce that if two unbiased estimators of a population parameter exist, then infinitely many exist.

9. A random sample of 100 voters found sixty-eight concerned about the federal budget deficit and sixty-two who were opposed to federal taxes on gasoline. Forty-two of the sample members were both concerned about the federal budget deficit and opposed to federal taxes on gasoline.

(a) Use an unbiased estimation procedure to estimate the population proportion of voters who are both concerned about the federal budget deficit and opposed to federal taxes on gasoline.

(b) Use an unbiased estimation procedure to estimate the proportion of voters concerned about the federal budget deficit who are opposed to federal taxes on gasoline.

10. On a college campus, 480 men and 370 women live in dormitories. Of a random sample of sixty men, twenty-four were satisfied with dormitory food. Of a random sample of sixty women, thirty-two were satisfied with dormitory food. Using an unbiased estimation procedure, find a point estimate of the percentage of all students living in dormitories on this campus who are satisfied with dormitory food.

11. A random sample of 100 voters in a city found sixty-two in favor of an immediate reduction in property taxes. An independent random sample of 200 voters from the same population found 102 in favor of extending the services of the public library system. Let p_1 denote the population proportion favoring property tax reduction and p_2 the proportion favoring extending public library services.

   (a) Use an unbiased estimation procedure to find a point estimate of $(p_1 - p_2)$, the difference between the two population proportions.

   (b) If $\hat{p}_1$ and $\hat{p}_2$ denote the two sample proportions, find the variance of $(\hat{p}_1 - \hat{p}_2)$.

12. A random sample of twenty bond market professionals was taken. Of these sample members, seven believed that a portfolio of low-grade corporate bonds represented a good investment over the next year. In an independent random sample of twelve bond market professionals, six believed that long-term government bonds represented a good investment over the next year. Let p_1 denote the population proportion of bond market professionals believing low-grade corporate bonds to be a good investment, and p_2 the population proportion believing long-term government bonds to be a good investment.

   (a) Use an unbiased estimation procedure to find a point estimate of $(p_1 - p_2)$, the difference between the two population proportions.

   (b) If $\hat{p}_1$ and $\hat{p}_2$ denote the two sample proportions, find an expression for the variance of $(\hat{p}_1 - \hat{p}_2)$.

13. A random sample of sixty account balances contained four with at least one serious error and ten with at least one minor error. Two of the balances contained at least one serious and one minor error. Use an unbiased estimation procedure to find a point estimate of the proportion of all balances in the population containing no errors.

14. Let X be the number of successes in n independent trials, each with probability of success p. Find an unbiased estimator of the variance of the sample proportion of successes.

7.3   CHOICE OF POINT ESTIMATOR

The problem that often arises in practice of how to choose an appropriate point estimator for a population parameter is by no means straightforward and, moreover, involves considerable mathematical intricacy beyond the scope of this text. We are able to make only a few brief comments on this important question.

   In Section 7.2, we saw that an attractive possibility is to choose the most efficient of all unbiased estimators, or perhaps the most efficient of a broad group of unbiased estimators. However, for two reasons, this approach does not constitute a sufficient prescription for all point estimation problems arising in practice.

   First, although, all other things being equal, unbiasedness in a point estimator is a desirable property, on occasion all other things may not be equal. There are estimation problems for which no unbiased estimator is very satisfactory and for which there may be much to be gained from the sacrifice of accepting a little bias. One measure of the expected closeness of an estimator $\hat{\theta}$ to a parameter θ is its **mean squared error**—the expectation of the squared difference between the estimator and the parameter, that is

$$\text{MSE}(\hat{\theta}) = E[(\hat{\theta} - \theta)^2]$$

It can be shown that

$$\text{MSE}(\hat{\theta}) = \text{Var}(\hat{\theta}) + [\text{Bias}(\hat{\theta})]^2$$

which suggests the possibility of obtaining a smaller mean squared error in moving from an unbiased to a biased estimator, provided that this achieves a sufficiently large reduction in estimator variance. It is tempting to conclude that a sensible procedure for choosing a point estimator is to seek the estimator with the smallest mean squared error. However, this approach is unworkable, as the mean squared error of an estimator will typically depend on the unknown parameter θ. On some occasions, it is possible to show that one estimator has a smaller mean squared error than another for *all* possible values of the parameter θ. The inferior estimator is then said to be **inadmissible.** The comparison of point estimators in this way has, on occasion, been useful in suggesting superior estimation procedures.

A second difficulty in using minimum variance unbiasedness as the criterion for estimator choice is that it will very often be impossible to determine such estimators. Indeed, for a great many important problems, it is not possible to find expressions for even the mean or variance of possible estimators for any finite number of sample observations. In this circumstance, the comparison of estimators in terms of bias, efficiency, or mean squared error is infeasible.

Perhaps surprisingly, even when it is difficult to characterize the sampling distribution of a point estimator for a finite number of sample observations, it is very often easier to characterize the distribution as the number of sample observations becomes infinitely large. This fact has driven statisticians to look at the limiting behavior of point estimators as the number of sample observations approaches infinity. Let θ be a parameter to be estimated and $\hat{\theta}_n$ a point estimator based on a sample of n observations. Since we are concerned about the "closeness" of the estimator to the parameter, consider the probability that $\hat{\theta}_n$ differs from θ by less than some positive amount ϵ, that is

$$P[|\hat{\theta}_n - \theta| < \epsilon]$$

If for any positive ϵ, however small, this probability approaches 1 as the sample size n approaches infinity, the estimator is said to be **consistent.** Loosely speaking, the use of a consistent estimator with an infinite amount of sample information would give the correct result. Conversely, an inconsistent estimator would not yield the correct result, even if it were based on an infinite amount of sample information. For this reason, inconsistency in a point estimator is regarded as undesirable.

Not all unbiased estimators are consistent, and by no means are all consistent estimators unbiased. For example, in sampling from a normal population, the sample standard deviation is consistent for the population standard deviation (as are the sample mean and variance for the corresponding population parameters). Also, the sample proportion is a consistent estimator of the population proportion.

For many estimation problems, it will be possible to find different consistent estimators, and some method of choosing among them is required. It is often possible to show for a consistent estimator that as the number of sample observations becomes infinitely large, the distribution of $n^{-1/2}(\hat{\theta}_n - \theta)$ approaches the normal. Then, paralleling our discussion of efficiency in Section 7.2, it is natural to look for the consistent estimator for which the variance of this limiting distribution is smallest. Such estimators are called **best asymptotic normal.** In fact, there exists a procedure, known as the **maximum likelihood method,** for finding point estimators that can be shown under very general conditions to yield best asymptotic normal estimators. This approach is often quite easy to apply and, because of its optimality property, is perhaps more widely used in attacking new estimation problems than any other procedure. Although we will not again emphasize the point, many estimators met in later chapters of this book are maximum likelihood or close approximations to maximum likelihood estimators.

These considerations by no means exhaust the possibilities that statisticians have when approaching point estimation problems. For example, in some instances, it may be important to guard against the influence on an estimator of the odd unusual extreme observation, a point that echoes our discussion in Chapter 2 on an advantage of the median over the mean as a measure of central location.

REVIEW EXERCISES

15. Of what practical value is the concept of efficiency in evaluating the merits of a point estimator?

16. Let $\hat{\theta}_1$ be an unbiased estimator of θ_1, and $\hat{\theta}_2$ an unbiased estimator of θ_2.
    (a) Show that $(\hat{\theta}_1 + \hat{\theta}_2)$ is an unbiased estimator of $(\theta_1 + \theta_2)$.
    (b) Show that $(\hat{\theta}_1 - \hat{\theta}_2)$ is an unbiased estimator of $(\theta_1 - \theta_2)$.

17. A random sample of ten economists produced the following forecasts for percentage growth in real gross domestic product in the next year:

2.2	2.8	3.0	2.5	2.4	2.6	2.5	2.4	2.7	2.6

    Use unbiased estimation procedures to find point estimates for each of the following:
    (a) The population mean.
    (b) The population variance.
    (c) The variance of the sample mean.
    (d) The population proportion of economists predicting growth of at least 2.5% in real gross domestic product.
    (e) The variance of the sample proportion of economists predicting growth of at least 2.5% in real gross domestic product.

18. A random sample of twelve blue-collar employees in a large manufacturing plant found the following figures for number of hours overtime worked in the last month:

22	16	28	12	18	36	23	11	41	29	26	31

    Use an unbiased estimation procedure to find point estimates for each of the following:
    (a) The population mean.
    (b) The population variance.
    (c) The variance of the sample mean.
    (d) The population proportion of blue-collar employees working more than thirty hours overtime in this plant in the last month.
    (e) The variance of the sample proportion of blue-collar employees working more than thirty hours overtime in this plant in the last month.

19. Let $X_1, X_2, \ldots, X_n$ be a random sample from a population with mean μ and variance σ^2. Also, let $c_1, c_2, \ldots, c_n$ be any set of fixed numbers, and consider the estimator of μ

    $$\hat{\mu} = c_1 X_1 + c_2 X_2 + \cdots + c_n X_n$$

    (a) Show that $\hat{\mu}$ is an unbiased estimator of μ if and only if

$$c_1 + c_2 + \cdots + c_n = 1$$

(b) Show that the variance of $\hat{\mu}$ is

$$\text{Var}(\hat{\mu}) = \sigma^2(c_1^2 + c_2^2 + \cdots + c_n^2) = \sigma^2 \sum_{i=1}^{n} c_i^2$$

(c) Show that if $\hat{\mu}$ is an unbiased estimator of μ

$$\sum_{i=1}^{n} c_i^2 = \sum_{i=1}^{n} [(c_i - n^{-1}) + n^{-1}]^2$$

$$= \sum_{i=1}^{n} (c_i - n^{-1})^2 + n^{-1}$$

Note that, if we are free to choose the numbers c_i, this expression is minimized by setting

$$c_i = n^{-1} \quad \text{for} \quad i = 1, 2, \ldots, n$$

(d) Using the results in (a)–(c), show that of all estimators of the form $\hat{\mu}$, the sample mean is the most efficient.

20. Let $X_1, X_2, \ldots, X_n$ be a random sample from a population with mean μ and variance σ^2. Also, let $\overline{X}$ be the sample mean.

(a) Show that

$$\hat{\sigma}_1^2 = \sum_{i=1}^{n} (X_i - \mu)^2/n$$

is an unbiased estimator of σ^2.

(b) Show that

$$\hat{\sigma}_2^2 = \sum_{i=1}^{n} (X_i - \overline{X})^2/n$$

is a biased estimator of σ^2, and find the bias. (Use the fact that the sample variance is known to be unbiased for σ^2.)

21. There are some estimation problems for which no unbiased estimator can be found. For example, if a sample of one observation is drawn from a population with mean μ and variance σ^2, we have an unbiased estimator of μ but cannot find an unbiased estimator of σ^2. Explain why this conclusion is plausible.

22. A large statistics class was taken by both business and liberal arts majors. A random sample of ten business majors obtained the following scores on the final examination:

62	57	85	59	64	63	71	58	77	72

An independent random sample of eight liberal arts majors obtained the following scores:

73	79	73	62	51	60	57	59

(a) Use an unbiased estimation procedure to obtain a point estimate of the difference in the population mean scores between business and liberal arts majors.

(b) Use an unbiased estimation procedure to obtain a point estimate of the difference between the population proportion of business majors with scores over 70 and the population proportion of liberal arts majors with scores over 70.

23. A random sample of ten X-cars achieved the following fuel consumption figures, in miles per gallon:

27.2	27.2	26.8	26.9	25.3
26.0	26.4	25.7	28.1	25.7

An independent random sample of twelve Y-cars achieved the following results:

24.2	24.3	25.3	24.8	25.1	25.0
24.9	23.9	26.0	26.1	26.0	26.3

(a) Use an unbiased estimation procedure to obtain a point estimate of the difference in population mean fuel consumption between X-cars and Y-cars.

(b) Use an unbiased estimation procedure to obtain a point estimate of the difference between the population proportion of X-cars achieving more than 25.5 miles per gallon and the population proportion of Y-cars achieving more than 25.5 miles per gallon.

24. A random sample, $X_1, X_2, \ldots, X_n$, of n observations is taken from a population with mean μ and variance of σ^2. Consider the following estimator of μ:

$$\hat{\mu} = \frac{2}{n(n+1)} (X_1 + 2X_2 + 3X_3 + \cdots + nX_n)$$

(a) Show that $\hat{\mu}$ is an unbiased estimator of μ.

(b) Find the efficiency of $\hat{\mu}$ relative to $\overline{X}$, the sample mean.

$$\left[Hint: \sum_{i=1}^{n} i = \frac{n(n+1)}{2} \quad \text{and} \quad \sum_{i=1}^{n} i^2 = \frac{n(n+1)(2n+1)}{6} \right]$$

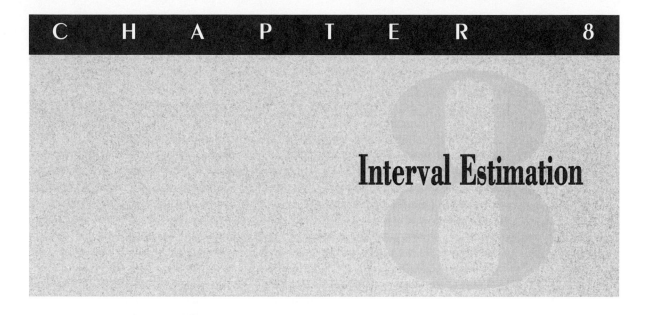

CHAPTER 8

Interval Estimation

8.1 CONFIDENCE INTERVALS

In the preceding chapter, we considered the point estimation of an unknown population parameter—that is, the production of a single number that in some sense is a "good bet." For most practical problems, a point estimate alone is inadequate. For instance, suppose that a check on a random sample of parts from a large shipment leads to the estimate that 10% of all the parts are defective. Faced with this figure, a manager is likely to ask such questions as "Can I be fairly sure that the true percentage of defectives is between 5% and 15%?" or "Does it then seem very likely that between 9% and 11% of all the parts are defective?" Questions of this kind seek information beyond that contained in a single point estimate; they are asking about the reliability of that estimate. More directly, the quest is for an **interval estimate,** a range of values in which the quantity to be estimated appears likely to lie.

In sampling from a population, we would expect, all other things being equal, to obtain more secure knowledge about that population from a relatively large sample than we would from a small sample. However, this factor is not reflected in point estimates. For example, our point estimate of the proportion of defective parts in a shipment would be the same if we observed one defective in a sample of ten parts as if we observed 100 defectives in a sample of 1,000 parts. As we will see, increased precision in our information about population parameters *is* reflected in interval estimates; specifically, the larger the sample size, the shorter, all other things being equal, will be the interval estimates that reflect our uncertainty about a parameter's true value.

An **interval estimator** for a population parameter is a rule for determining (based on sample information) a range, or interval, in which the parameter is likely to fall. The corresponding estimate is called an **interval estimate.**

So far, we have described interval estimators as being "likely" or "very likely" to contain the true, but unknown, population parameter. To make our discussion more precise, it is necessary to phrase such terms as probability statements. Let us denote by θ the parameter to be estimated. Suppose that a random sample has been taken and that based on the sample information, it is possible to find two random variables, A and B, with A less than B. If these random variables have the property that the probability that both A is less than θ and B is bigger than θ is .9, we can write

$$P(A < \theta < B) = .9$$

The interval from A to B is then said to be a 90% confidence interval estimator for θ. If the specific sample realizations of the random variables A and B are denoted a and b, then the interval from a to b is called a 90% **confidence interval** for θ. According to the frequency concept of probability, we can interpret such intervals as follows: If the population is repeatedly sampled and intervals calculated in this fashion, then 90% of the intervals would contain the unknown parameter.

More generally, we can define confidence intervals of any required probability content less than 1. Suppose that the random variables A and B are such that

$$P(A < \theta < B) = 1 - \alpha$$

where α is any number between 0 and 1. (In the example of the preceding paragraph, $1 - \alpha = .9$, so $\alpha = .1$.) Then, if the population is repeatedly sampled and this interval is calculated, a proportion $(1 - \alpha)$, or $100(1 - \alpha)\%$, of those intervals will contain θ. A confidence interval calculated in this way is called a $100(1 - \alpha)\%$ confidence interval for θ.

Definitions

Let θ be an unknown parameter. Suppose that on the basis of sample information, we can find random variables A and B such that

$$P(A < \theta < B) = 1 - \alpha$$

If the specific sample realizations of A and B are denoted a and b, then the interval from a to b is called a **$100(1 - \alpha)\%$ confidence interval** for θ. The quantity $(1 - \alpha)$ is called the **probability content,** or **level of confidence,** of the interval.

If the population was repeatedly sampled a very large number of times, the parameter θ would be contained in $100(1 - \alpha)\%$ of intervals calculated this way. The confidence interval calculated in this manner is written

$$a < \theta < b$$

In the remainder of this chapter, we will develop and illustrate procedures for finding confidence intervals in several common types of estimation problems. Further examples of interval estimation will be given in subsequent chapters.

8.2 CONFIDENCE INTERVALS FOR THE MEAN OF A NORMAL DISTRIBUTION: POPULATION VARIANCE KNOWN

Let us assume that a random sample is taken from a normal distribution with an unknown mean and a *known* variance and that the objective is to find a confidence interval for the population mean. This problem is somewhat unrealistic, because rarely (if ever) will a population variance be precisely known and yet the mean be unknown. It does sometimes happen, however, that similar populations have been sampled so often in the past that the variance of the population of interest can be assumed known to a very close approximation on the basis of past experience. Further, as we will see later in this section, if a sufficiently large sample is available, the procedures developed for the case where the population variance is known can be used if that variance has to be estimated from the sample. Nevertheless, the chief virtue in beginning with this problem is that it allows a fairly straightforward exposition of the procedures involved in finding confidence intervals.

Denote by $X_1, X_2, \ldots, X_n$ a random sample of n observations from a normal population with unknown mean μ and known variance σ^2, and let $\overline{X}$ be the sample mean. Then confidence intervals for the population mean are based on the result that the random variable

$$Z = \frac{\overline{X} - \mu}{\sigma/\sqrt{n}}$$

has a standard normal distribution.

Suppose that we want to find a 90% confidence interval for the population mean. Now, from the cumulative distribution function of the standard normal random variable, given in Table 3 of the Appendix, we find that

$$P(Z < 1.645) = F_Z(1.645) = .95$$

It therefore follows that

$$P(Z > 1.645) = .05$$

Also, since the density function of the standard normal random variable is symmetric about its mean, 0, it follows that

$$P(Z < -1.645) = .05$$

The probability that Z is between -1.645 and 1.645 is therefore

$$P(-1.645 < Z < 1.645) = 1 - P(Z > 1.645) - P(Z < -1.645)$$

$$= 1 - .05 - .05 = .90$$

These probability calculations are illustrated in Figure 8.1.

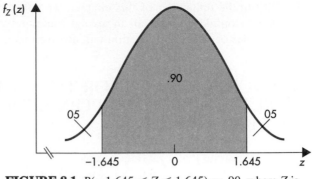

FIGURE 8.1 $P(-1.645 < Z < 1.645) = .90$, where Z is a standard normal random variable

So far, then, we have shown that the probability is .9 that a standard normal random variable lies between the numbers -1.645 and 1.645. We now convert this probability statement into a confidence interval for the population mean as follows:

$$
\begin{aligned}
.90 &= P(-1.645 < Z < 1.645) \\
&= P\left(-1.645 < \frac{\overline{X} - \mu}{\sigma/\sqrt{n}} < 1.645\right) \\
&= P\left(\frac{-1.645\sigma}{\sqrt{n}} < \overline{X} - \mu < \frac{1.645\sigma}{\sqrt{n}}\right) \\
&= P\left(\overline{X} - \frac{1.645\sigma}{\sqrt{n}} < \mu < \overline{X} + \frac{1.645\sigma}{\sqrt{n}}\right)
\end{aligned}
$$

Therefore, the probability is .9 that the random interval from $(\overline{X} - 1.645\sigma/\sqrt{n})$ to $(\overline{X} + 1.645\sigma/\sqrt{n})$ contains the population mean μ. Thus, from our definition of confidence intervals, it follows that the interval from $(\bar{x} - 1.645\sigma/\sqrt{n})$ to $(\bar{x} + 1.645\sigma/\sqrt{n})$ is a 90% confidence interval for μ, where $\bar{x}$ is the specific value observed for the sample mean. For simplicity, this interval is written

$$
\bar{x} - \frac{1.645\sigma}{\sqrt{n}} < \mu < \bar{x} + \frac{1.645\sigma}{\sqrt{n}}
$$

EXAMPLE 8.1

A random sample of sixteen observations from a normal population with standard deviation 6 had mean 25. Find a 90% confidence interval for the population mean, μ.

We have

$$
\bar{x} = 25 \qquad \sigma = 6 \qquad n = 16
$$

The 90% confidence interval is given by

$$
\bar{x} - \frac{1.645\sigma}{\sqrt{n}} < \mu < \bar{x} + \frac{1.645\sigma}{\sqrt{n}}
$$

so that we have

$$25 - \frac{(1.645)(6)}{\sqrt{16}} < \mu < 25 + \frac{(1.645)(6)}{\sqrt{16}}$$

or

$$22.5325 < \mu < 27.4675$$

We now pause to consider the proper interpretation of confidence intervals in terms of Example 8.1. In that example, we found, based on a sample of sixteen observations, a 90% confidence interval for the unknown population mean running from 22.5325 to 27.4675. Now, this particular sample is just one of many that might have been drawn from the population. Suppose that we were to start over again, taking a second sample of sixteen observations. It is virtually certain that the mean of the second sample will differ from that of the first. Accordingly, if a 90% confidence interval is calculated from the results of the second sample, it will differ from that found in Example 8.1. We can imagine taking a very large number of independent random samples of sixteen observations from this population and, from each sample result, calculating a 90% confidence interval. The probability content of the interval implies that 90% of intervals found in this manner contain the true population mean. It is in this sense that we can say that we have a "90% confidence" in our interval estimate.

This position is illustrated in Figure 8.2. Part (a) of the figure shows the sampling distribution of the sample mean of n observations from a normal population with mean μ and standard deviation σ. This sampling distribution is normal, with mean μ and standard deviation $\sigma/\sqrt{n}$. A confidence interval for the population mean will be based on the observed value of the sample mean—that is, on an observation drawn from our sampling distribution. Part (b) of Figure 8.2 shows a sequence of 90% confidence intervals, obtained from independent samples taken from the population. The centers of these intervals, which are just the observed sample means, will often be quite close to the population mean, μ. However, some may differ quite substantially. We are assured that 90% of a large number of these intervals will contain the population mean.

We now turn to the general case of finding confidence intervals with any required probability content. To do so, we introduce a new notation.

Notation

Let Z be a standard normal random variable and α be any number such that $0 < \alpha < 1$. We then denote by z_α the number for which

$$P(Z > z_\alpha) = \alpha$$

This notation is illustrated in Figure 8.3, from which it is clear how z_α can be found from tables of the cumulative distribution function of the standard normal random variable. Since $P(Z > z_\alpha) = \alpha$, it follows that

$$F_Z(z_\alpha) = P(Z < z_\alpha) = 1 - \alpha$$

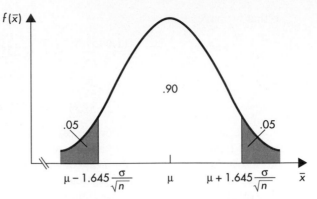

(a) Sampling distribution of sample mean of n observations from a normal distribution with mean μ and variance σ^2

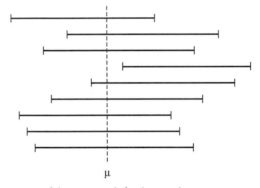

(b) Some 90% confidence intervals for the population mean

FIGURE 8.2 Interpretation of a 90% confidence interval

as illustrated in Figure 8.3. Therefore, for any specified α, z_α can be determined from Table 3 in the Appendix. For example, if $\alpha = .025$, then

$$1 - \alpha = .975$$

so

$$F_Z(z_\alpha) = F_Z(z_{.025}) = .975$$

and from the table

$$z_{.025} = 1.96$$

Therefore

$$P(Z > 1.96) = .025$$

Table 8.1 shows values of z_α corresponding to some α values that are frequently used in finding confidence intervals. The reader can verify these quantities from Table 3 of the Appendix.

Now, suppose that a $100(1 - \alpha)\%$ confidence interval is required for the population mean. Using the notation just established, we have

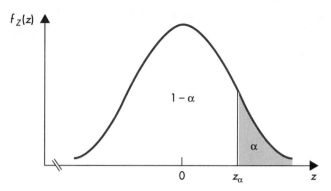

FIGURE 8.3 $P(Z > z_\alpha) = \alpha$, where Z is a standard normal random variable

$$P(Z > z_{\alpha/2}) = \frac{\alpha}{2}$$

and so, by the symmetry of the standard normal density function about its mean of 0

$$P(Z < -z_{\alpha/2}) = \frac{\alpha}{2}$$

It therefore follows that

$$P(-z_{\alpha/2} < Z < z_{\alpha/2}) = 1 - \frac{\alpha}{2} - \frac{\alpha}{2} = 1 - \alpha$$

These probability calculations are illustrated in Figure 8.4.

We have found a range of values of the standard normal random variable with a specified probability content. This information can now be used to develop a confidence interval of the same probability content for the population mean. Using exactly the same line of argument as employed in developing the 90% interval, we have

$$1 - \alpha = P(-z_{\alpha/2} < Z < z_{\alpha/2})$$

$$= P\left(-z_{\alpha/2} < \frac{\overline{X} - \mu}{\sigma/\sqrt{n}} < z_{\alpha/2}\right)$$

$$= P\left(\frac{-z_{\alpha/2}\sigma}{\sqrt{n}} < \overline{X} - \mu < \frac{z_{\alpha/2}\sigma}{\sqrt{n}}\right)$$

$$= P\left(\overline{X} - \frac{z_{\alpha/2}\sigma}{\sqrt{n}} < \mu < \overline{X} + \frac{z_{\alpha/2}\sigma}{\sqrt{n}}\right)$$

TABLE 8.1 Values of z_α, from table of the standard normal cumulative distribution function

α		.005	.01	.025	.05	.10
z_α		2.575	2.33	1.96	1.645	1.28

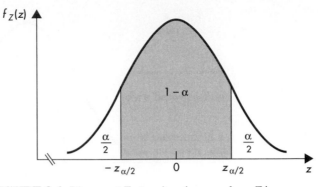

FIGURE 8.4 $P(-z_{\alpha/2} < Z < z_{\alpha/2}) = 1 - \alpha$, where Z is a standard normal random variable

It follows from the definition of confidence intervals that if $\bar{x}$ is the specific value observed for the sample mean, then a $100(1 - \alpha)\%$ confidence interval for the population mean is given by

$$\bar{x} - \frac{z_{\alpha/2}\sigma}{\sqrt{n}} < \mu < \bar{x} + \frac{z_{\alpha/2}\sigma}{\sqrt{n}}$$

Confidence Intervals for the Mean of a Normal Population: Population Variance Known

Suppose that we have a random sample of n observations from a normal distribution with mean μ and variance σ^2. If σ^2 is known, and the observed sample mean is $\bar{x}$, then a $100(1 - \alpha)\%$ confidence interval for the population mean is given by

$$\bar{x} - \frac{z_{\alpha/2}\sigma}{\sqrt{n}} < \mu < \bar{x} + \frac{z_{\alpha/2}\sigma}{\sqrt{n}}$$

where $z_{\alpha/2}$ is that number for which

$$P(Z > z_{\alpha/2}) = \frac{\alpha}{2}$$

and the random variable Z has a standard normal distribution.

The interpretation of these general confidence intervals corresponds to that for the specific 90% interval. If samples of n observations are drawn repeatedly and independently from the population and $100(1 - \alpha)\%$ confidence intervals are calculated using the formula given in the box, then over a very large number of repeated trials, $100(1 - \alpha)\%$ of these intervals will contain the true population mean.

EXAMPLE 8.2

A process produces bags of refined sugar. The weights of the contents of these bags are normally distributed with standard deviation 1.2 ounces. The contents of a random sample of twenty-five bags had mean weight 19.8 ounces. Find a 95% confidence interval for the true mean weight for all bags of sugar produced by the process.

Since a 95% confidence interval is required, we have

$$100(1 - \alpha) = 95$$

so

$$\alpha = .05$$

Hence

$$z_{\alpha/2} = z_{.025}$$

and we require that number $z_{.025}$ for which

$$P(Z > z_{.025}) = .025$$

Hence

$$P(Z < z_{.025}) = F_Z(z_{.025}) = .975$$

where $F_Z(z)$ is the cumulative distribution function of the standard normal random variable. Then, from Table 3 in the Appendix, it follows that

$$z_{.025} = 1.96$$

The 95% confidence interval for the population mean μ is

$$\bar{x} - \frac{z_{\alpha/2}\sigma}{\sqrt{n}} < \mu < \bar{x} + \frac{z_{\alpha/2}\sigma}{\sqrt{n}}$$

where

$$\bar{x} = 19.8 \qquad z_{\alpha/2} = 1.96 \qquad \sigma = 1.2 \qquad n = 25$$

Hence, the required confidence interval is

$$19.8 - \frac{(1.96)(1.2)}{\sqrt{25}} < \mu < 19.8 + \frac{(1.96)(1.2)}{\sqrt{25}}$$

or

$$19.33 < \mu < 20.27$$

Hence, the 95% confidence interval for the true mean weight ranges from 19.33 to 20.27 ounces.

We now pause to consider the general nature of confidence intervals for the mean of a normal population, when the variance is known. The results that follow provide some insight into the structure of interval estimation. Many extend also to other interval estimation problems.

We have seen that a $100(1 - \alpha)\%$ confidence interval for the population mean is

$$\bar{x} - \frac{z_{\alpha/2}\sigma}{\sqrt{n}} < \mu < \bar{x} + \frac{z_{\alpha/2}\sigma}{\sqrt{n}}$$

As might be expected, the sample mean $\bar{x}$ is at the center of this interval. The width, w, of the interval—that is, the distance between its endpoints—is

$$w = \frac{2z_{\alpha/2}\sigma}{\sqrt{n}}$$

It can be seen, then, that the width of the confidence interval is determined by its probability content, the population standard deviation, and the number of sample observations. In particular, the following results hold:

1. For a given probability content and sample size, *the bigger the population standard deviation* σ, *the wider the confidence interval for the population mean.* This is intuitively plausible since, all other things being equal, the more disperse the population distribution is about its mean, the more uncertain will be our inference about that mean. This extra uncertainty is reflected in wider confidence intervals.

2. For a given probability content and population standard deviation, *the bigger the sample size n, the narrower the confidence interval for the population mean.* Again, this conclusion accords with intuition. The more information we obtain from a population, the more precise should be our inference about its mean. This extra precision is reflected in narrower confidence intervals.

3. For a given population standard deviation and sample size, *the bigger the probability content* $(1 - \alpha)$, *the wider the confidence interval for the population mean.* For example, a 99% confidence interval will be wider than a 95% confidence interval based on the same information. This result follows since the larger $(1 - \alpha)$ is, the smaller will be α, and hence the bigger will be $z_{\alpha/2}$. In effect, we pay for an increased certainty in probability statements through a reduced definitiveness in those statements. This is reflected in wider confidence intervals for population parameters, as the probability content is increased.

These results are illustrated in Figure 8.5 for the data of Example 8.2. This figure illustrates, for the same sample mean, the effect on the confidence interval of increases in the sample size, the population standard deviation, and the probability content of the interval.

In developing confidence intervals for the mean in this section, we introduced two requirements that limit the range of applicability of these interval estimates in practical problems—namely, that the population distribution is normal and that the variance of this population is known. However, if the sample size is large, neither re-

FIGURE 8.5 The effects of sample size n, population standard deviation σ, and probability content $(1 - \alpha)$ on confidence intervals for the mean of a normal distribution; in each case the sample mean is 19.80

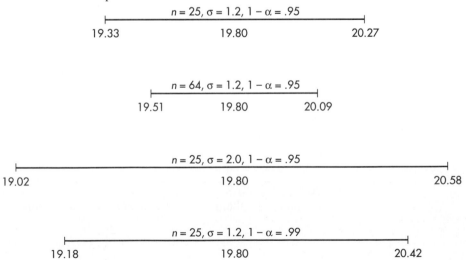

quirement is critical. In this case, by virtue of the central limit theorem, the confidence intervals described in this section remain appropriate to a sufficiently good approximation even when the population distribution is not normal. Moreover, when the sample size is large, the sample standard deviation will be a sufficiently good estimator of the population standard deviation to allow us to use the former in place of the latter without affecting very much the probability content of the intervals. Thus, we can compute intervals in exactly the manner described previously, substituting the sample standard deviation for the population standard deviation.

Confidence Intervals for the Population Mean: Large Sample Sizes

Suppose we have a sample of n observations from a distribution with mean μ. Denote the observed sample mean and standard deviation by $\bar{x}$ and s_x. Then if n is large,[1] to a good approximation, a $100(1 - \alpha)\%$ confidence interval for μ is given by

$$\bar{x} - \frac{z_{\alpha/2}s_x}{\sqrt{n}} < \mu < \bar{x} + \frac{z_{\alpha/2}s_x}{\sqrt{n}}$$

This approximation will typically remain adequate even if the population distribution is not normal.

Thus, if the sample size is large, we can relax two of the assumptions made earlier and consequently broaden considerably the range of applicability of our results, as illustrated in the following example.

EXAMPLE
8.3

A random sample of 172 accounting students was asked to rate the importance of particular job characteristics on a scale from one (not important) to five (extremely important).[2] For "job security," the sample mean rating was 4.38 and the sample standard deviation was .70. Find a 99% confidence interval for the population mean.

Since the observation values must be integers between one and five, the population distribution is certainly not normal. Nevertheless, thanks to the central limit theorem, for a sample of this size the sampling distribution of the sample mean will be very close to normal, which justifies the following calculations. We compute the interval

$$\bar{x} - \frac{z_{\alpha/2}s_x}{\sqrt{n}} < \mu < \bar{x} + \frac{z_{\alpha/2}s_x}{\sqrt{n}}$$

where

$$\bar{x} = 4.38 \qquad s_x = .70 \qquad n = 172$$

and $z_{\alpha/2}$ is the number for which

$$P(Z > z_{\alpha/2}) = \alpha/2$$

---

[1] As a rule of thumb, we will consider $n = 30$ observations or more to constitute a "large" sample. However, it should not be inferred that the approximation is virtually perfect for sample size 30 and absolutely awful for sample size 29. Rather, the quality of this approximation gradually improves with increasing sample size.

[2] Results given by P. Bundy and D. Norris, "What accounting students consider important in the job selection process," *Journal of Applied Business Research*, 8, no. 2 (1992), 1–6.

Then, for a 99% confidence interval

$$\alpha/2 = .005 \qquad \text{and} \qquad z_{\alpha/2} = 2.575$$

from Table 3 of the Appendix.

The required 99% confidence interval for the population mean is

$$4.38 - \frac{(2.575)(.70)}{\sqrt{172}} < \mu < 4.38 + \frac{(2.575)(.70)}{\sqrt{172}}$$

which is

$$4.24 < \mu < 4.52$$

Thus, our 99% confidence interval for the population mean rating runs from 4.24 to 4.52.

8.3   THE STUDENT'S t DISTRIBUTION

In the preceding section, we derived confidence intervals for the mean of a normal population when the population variance was known. It was noted that the assumption of known population variance could be relaxed when the sample size was large. We will now deal with the case, of considerable practical importance, where the population variance is unknown and the sample size is not large. To do so, it is necessary to introduce a new class of probability distributions.

The development of Section 8.2 was based on the fact that the random variable

$$Z = \frac{\overline{X} - \mu}{\sigma/\sqrt{n}} \tag{8.3.1}$$

has a standard normal distribution. In the case where the population standard deviation is unknown, this result cannot be used directly. It is natural in such circumstances to consider the random variable obtained by replacing the unknown σ in Eq. (8.3.1) by the sample standard deviation, s_X, giving

$$t = \frac{\overline{X} - \mu}{s_X/\sqrt{n}}$$

This random variable does not follow a standard normal distribution. However, its distribution is known and is in fact a member of a family of distributions called **Student's t.**[3]

---

[3] This result was published in 1908 by W. S. Gosset. Gosset was employed by Guinness Breweries in Ireland, which forbade the publication of scientific research by its employees. His research appeared under the pseudonym "Student," and this name is now given to the distribution.

Student's _t_ Distribution

Given a random sample of _n_ observations, with mean $\overline{X}$ and standard deviation s_X, from a normal population with mean μ, the random variable

$$t = \frac{\overline{X} - \mu}{s_X/\sqrt{n}}$$

follows the **Student's _t_ distribution with $(n - 1)$ degrees of freedom.**[4]

A specific member of the family of Student's _t_ distributions is characterized by the number of degrees of freedom, for which we will use the parameter ν. A Student's _t_ random variable with ν degrees of freedom will be denoted t_ν. The shape of the Student's _t_ distribution is rather similar to that of the standard normal. Both distributions have mean 0, and the probability density functions of both are symmetric about their means. However, the density function of the Student's _t_ has larger dispersion (reflected in a larger variance) than the standard normal. This can be seen in Figure 8.6, which shows density functions for the standard normal and the Student's _t_ distribution with 3 degrees of freedom. The additional dispersion in the Student's _t_ distribution arises as a result of the extra uncertainty caused by replacing the known population standard deviation by its sample estimator. As the number of degrees of freedom increases, the Student's _t_ becomes increasingly similar to the standard normal. For large degrees of freedom, the two distributions are virtually identical. This is intuitively

FIGURE 8.6 Probability density functions of the standard normal and the Student's _t_ distribution with 3 degrees of freedom

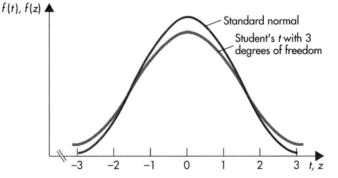

---

[4] Note that the number of degrees of freedom here corresponds to that quantity for the chi-square distribution based on the same sample size, as in Section 6.4. Formally, the Student's _t_ random variable with ν degrees of freedom is defined as

$$t_\nu = \frac{Z}{\sqrt{\chi_\nu^2/\nu}}$$

where Z is a standard normal random variable, χ_ν^2 is a chi-square random variable with ν degrees of freedom, and Z and χ_ν^2 are independent.

reasonable and follows from the fact that for a large sample, the sample standard deviation is a very precise estimator of the population standard deviation.

In order to base inferences about a population mean on the Student's t distribution, we need probabilities associated with that distribution. To describe these probabilities, some further notation is required, as presented in the box and illustrated in Figure 8.7.

Notation

A random variable having the Student's t distribution with ν degrees of freedom will be denoted t_ν. We define as $t_{\nu,\alpha}$ the number for which

$$P(t_\nu > t_{\nu,\alpha}) = \alpha$$

In the typical application, we will need to find the value $t_{\nu,\alpha}$ corresponding to a specified probability α. These quantities can be read directly from Table 6 in the Appendix. To illustrate, suppose that we want to find the number that is exceeded with probability .1 by a Student's t random variable with 15 degrees of freedom. That is

$$P(t_{15} > t_{15,.1}) = .1$$

Reading directly from the table, we have

$$t_{15,.1} = 1.341$$

We will now use the Student's t distribution to compute confidence intervals for the mean of a normal population. Paralleling our discussion of the standard normal distribution in Section 8.2, we have

$$P(t_\nu > t_{\nu,\alpha/2}) = \frac{\alpha}{2}$$

Furthermore, as a result of the symmetry of the density function of the Student's t distribution about its mean of 0

$$P(t_\nu < -t_{\nu,\alpha/2}) = \frac{\alpha}{2}$$

FIGURE 8.7 $P(t_\nu > t_{\nu,\alpha}) = \alpha$, where t_ν is a Student's t random variable with ν degrees of freedom

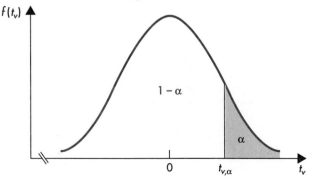

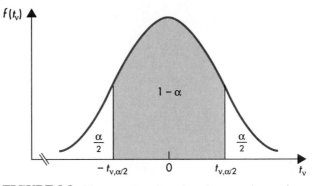

FIGURE 8.8 $P(-t_{\nu,\alpha/2} < t_\nu < t_{\nu,\alpha/2}) = 1 - \alpha$, where t_ν is a Student's t random variable with ν degrees of freedom

Finally, since probabilities for mutually exclusive and collectively exhaustive events must sum to 1, it follows that

$$P(-t_{\nu,\alpha/2} < t_\nu < t_{\nu,\alpha/2}) = 1 - P(t_\nu > t_{\nu,\alpha/2}) - P(t_\nu < -t_{\nu,\alpha/2})$$

$$= 1 - \frac{\alpha}{2} - \frac{\alpha}{2} = 1 - \alpha$$

These probabilities are shown in Figure 8.8, which corresponds to Figure 8.4 for the standard normal distribution.

8.4 CONFIDENCE INTERVALS FOR THE MEAN OF A NORMAL POPULATION: POPULATION VARIANCE UNKNOWN

We can now use the Student's t distribution to derive confidence intervals for the mean of a normal population when the variance is unknown, using an argument similar to that of Section 8.2.

Assume that a random sample of n observations is available from a normal population with mean μ and unknown variance and that confidence intervals for the population mean are required.

Let $\overline{X}$ and s_X^2 denote the sample mean and variance. Then, from Section 8.3, we know that the random variable

$$t_{n-1} = \frac{\overline{X} - \mu}{s_X/\sqrt{n}}$$

follows a Student's t distribution with $(n - 1)$ degrees of freedom.

Suppose that a $100(1 - \alpha)\%$ confidence interval for the population mean is required. Following precisely the same line of reasoning used to obtain the confidence intervals of Section 8.2, we have

$$1 - \alpha = P(-t_{n-1,\alpha/2} < t_{n-1} < t_{n-1,\alpha/2})$$

$$= P\left(-t_{n-1,\alpha/2} < \frac{\overline{X} - \mu}{s_X/\sqrt{n}} < t_{n-1,\alpha/2}\right)$$

$$= P\left(\frac{-t_{n-1,\alpha/2}s_X}{\sqrt{n}} < \overline{X} - \mu < \frac{t_{n-1,\alpha/2}s_X}{\sqrt{n}}\right)$$

$$= P\left(\overline{X} - \frac{t_{n-1,\alpha/2}s_X}{\sqrt{n}} < \mu < \overline{X} + \frac{t_{n-1,\alpha/2}s_X}{\sqrt{n}}\right)$$

Therefore, from our definition of confidence intervals, it follows that if $\overline{x}$ and s_x are the specific values observed for the sample mean and standard deviation, then a $100(1 - \alpha)\%$ confidence interval for the population mean is given by

$$\overline{x} - \frac{t_{n-1,\alpha/2}s_x}{\sqrt{n}} < \mu < \overline{x} + \frac{t_{n-1,\alpha/2}s_x}{\sqrt{n}}$$

Confidence Intervals for the Mean of a Normal Population: Population Variance Unknown

Suppose that we have a random sample of n observations from a normal distribution with mean μ and unknown variance. If the observed sample mean and standard deviation are, respectively, $\overline{x}$ and s_x, then a $100(1 - \alpha)\%$ confidence interval for the population mean is given by

$$\overline{x} - \frac{t_{n-1,\alpha/2}s_x}{\sqrt{n}} < \mu < \overline{x} + \frac{t_{n-1,\alpha/2}s_x}{\sqrt{n}}$$

where $t_{n-1,\alpha/2}$ is the number for which

$$P(t_{n-1} > t_{n-1,\alpha/2}) = \frac{\alpha}{2}$$

and the random variable t_{n-1} has a Student's t distribution with $(n - 1)$ degrees of freedom.

We now illustrate the use of the Student's t distribution in finding confidence intervals for the mean of a normal population when only a moderate number of sample observations are available.

EXAMPLE 8.4

A random sample of six cars from a particular model year had the following fuel consumption figures, in miles per gallon:

$$18.6 \qquad 18.4 \qquad 19.2 \qquad 20.8 \qquad 19.4 \qquad 20.5$$

Find a 90% confidence interval for the population mean fuel consumption for cars of this model year, assuming that the population distribution is normal.

As a first step, we must find the sample mean and variance, which can be conveniently calculated from the accompanying table.

i	x_i	x_i^2
1	18.6	345.96
2	18.4	338.56
3	19.2	368.64
4	20.8	432.64
5	19.4	376.36
6	20.5	420.25
Sums	116.9	2,282.41

The sample mean is then

$$\bar{x} = \frac{1}{n} \sum x_i = \frac{1}{6}(116.9) = 19.4833$$

and the sample variance is

$$s_x^2 = \frac{1}{(n-1)} \left(\sum x_i^2 - n\bar{x}^2 \right)$$

$$= \frac{1}{5} [2{,}282.41 - (6)(19.4833)^2] = .96$$

so the sample standard deviation is

$$s_x = \sqrt{.96} = .98$$

Given the assumption that the population distribution is normal, we can construct confidence intervals for the population mean as

$$\bar{x} - \frac{t_{n-1,\alpha/2} s_x}{\sqrt{n}} < \mu < \bar{x} + \frac{t_{n-1,\alpha/2} s_x}{\sqrt{n}}$$

where

$$\bar{x} = 19.48 \qquad s_x = .98 \qquad n = 6$$

Also, since $n - 1 = 5$ and a 90% confidence interval is needed, we have $\alpha = .1$, so $\alpha/2 = .05$ and

$$t_{n-1,\alpha/2} = t_{5,.05} = 2.015$$

from Table 6 in the Appendix. The 90% confidence interval for the population mean fuel consumption is then

$$19.48 - \frac{(2.015)(.98)}{\sqrt{6}} < \mu < 19.48 + \frac{(2.015)(.98)}{\sqrt{6}}$$

or

$$18.67 < \mu < 20.29$$

Thus, our 90% confidence interval for the population mean fuel consumption for these cars ranges from 18.67 to 20.29 miles per gallon.

Rather than presenting just a single confidence interval, it is sometimes convenient to calculate a sequence of confidence intervals of differing probability contents. Taken together, these allow us to form a clearer picture about likely values of the population parameter being estimated. Figure 8.9 shows also the 80%, 95%, and 99% confidence intervals calculated from the data of Example 8.4. Notice that the intervals increase in width with increasing probability content, as we would expect.

EXAMPLE 8.5

In a study of the effects of mergers in the motor carrier industry,[5] a random sample of seventeen merged carriers was examined, and their increase in the growth rate of truckload tons of revenue freight in the postmerger period, compared with the premerger period, was measured. For each of these sample carriers, a nonmerged firm with similar location and size characteristics was examined for comparison. The difference between the increased growth rate for the merged firm and the corresponding nonmerged firm was calculated. The sample values had mean .105 and standard deviation .440. Find a 95% confidence interval for the population mean, assuming that the population distribution is normal.

Confidence intervals for the population mean may be found from

$$\bar{x} - \frac{t_{n-1,\alpha/2}S_x}{\sqrt{n}} < \mu < \bar{x} + \frac{t_{n-1,\alpha/2}S_x}{\sqrt{n}}$$

FIGURE 8.9 80%, 90%, 95%, and 99% confidence intervals for population mean fuel consumption from the data of Example 8.4

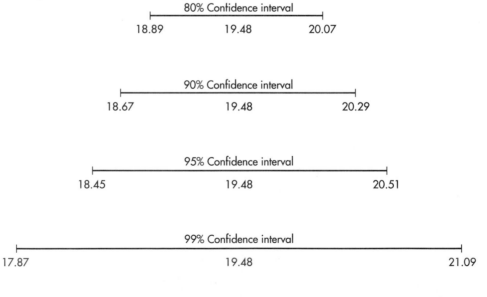

	80% Confidence interval	
18.89	19.48	20.07

	90% Confidence interval	
18.67	19.48	20.29

	95% Confidence interval	
18.45	19.48	20.51

	99% Confidence interval	
17.87	19.48	21.09

[5] Described in R. P. Boisjoly and T. M. Corsi, "The economic implications of less-than-truckload motor carrier mergers," *Journal of Economics and Business*, *33* (1980), 13–20.

where, in this example

$$\bar{x} = .105 \qquad s_x = .440 \qquad n = 17$$

Since $n - 1 = 16$ and we require a 95% confidence interval, then $\alpha = .05$ and we have

$$t_{n-1,\alpha/2} = t_{16,.025} = 2.120$$

from Table 6 of the Appendix. Thus, the 95% confidence interval for the population mean is

$$.105 - \frac{(2.120)(.440)}{\sqrt{17}} < \mu < .105 + \frac{(2.120)(.440)}{\sqrt{17}}$$

or

$$-.121 < \mu < .331$$

The 95% confidence interval for the population mean difference in increased growth rates between merged and nonmerged firms ranges from $-.121$ to .331. Notice that this interval for the population mean difference includes 0, suggesting that the data do not strongly contradict the conclusion of no difference between merged and nonmerged firms, on the average.

EXERCISES

1. A college admissions officer for an M.B.A. program has determined that historically, candidates have undergraduate grade point averages that are normally distributed with standard deviation .45. A random sample of twenty-five applications from the current year is taken, yielding a sample mean grade point average of 2.90.
   (a) Find a 95% confidence interval for the population mean.
   (b) Based on these sample results, a statistician computes for the population mean a confidence interval running from 2.81 to 2.99. Find the probability content associated with this interval.

2. A process producing bricks is known to give an output whose weights are normally distributed with standard deviation .12 pound. A random sample of sixteen bricks from today's output had mean weight 4.07 pounds.
   (a) Find a 99% confidence interval for the mean weight of all bricks produced this day.
   (b) Without doing the calculations, state whether a 95% confidence interval for the population mean would be wider than, narrower than, or the same width as that found in (a).
   (c) It is decided that tomorrow a sample of twenty bricks will be taken. Without doing the calculations, state whether a correctly calculated 99% confidence interval for the mean weight of tomorrow's output would be wider than, narrower than, or the same width as that found in (a).
   (d) In fact, the population standard deviation for today's output is .15 pound. Without doing the calculations, state whether a correctly calculated 99% confidence interval for the mean weight of today's output would be wider than, narrower than, or the same width as that found in (a).

3. A production manager knows that historically, the amounts of impurities in bags of a chemical follow a normal distribution with standard deviation 3.8 grams. A random sample of nine bags of the chemical yielded the following amounts of impurities in grams.

   18.2   13.7   15.9   17.4   21.8   16.6   12.3   18.8   16.2

(a) Find a 90% confidence interval for the population mean weight of impurities.

(b) Without doing the calculations, state whether a 95% confidence interval for the population mean would be wider than, narrower than, or the same as that found in (a).

4. A personnel manager has found that historically, the scores on aptitude tests given to applicants for entry-level positions follow a normal distribution with standard deviation 32.4 points. A random sample of nine test scores from the current group of applicants had mean 187.9 points.

(a) Find an 80% confidence interval for the population mean score of the current group of applicants.

(b) Based on these sample results, a statistician found for the population mean a confidence interval running from 165.8 to 210.0 points. Find the probability content of this interval.

5. A random sample of 1,562 undergraduates enrolled in marketing courses was asked to respond on a scale from one (strongly disagree) to seven (strongly agree) to the statement: "Most advertising insults the intelligence of the average consumer."[6] The sample mean response was 3.92 and the sample standard deviation was 1.57. Find a 95% confidence interval for the population mean response.

6. A random sample of 541 consumers was asked to respond on a scale from one (strongly disagree) to five (strongly agree) to the statement: "A seller should be liable for a defective product even when he has exercised all possible care in its sale and manufacture."[7] The sample mean response was 3.81 and the sample standard deviation was 1.34.

(a) Find a 90% confidence interval for the population mean response.

(b) Without doing the calculations, state whether an 80% confidence interval for the population mean would be wider than, narrower than, or the same as the answer to (a).

7. A random sample of 457 Japanese manufacturing managers was asked to respond on a scale from one (strongly agree) to 5 (strongly disagree) to the statement: "Reducing defective goods in customer deliveries means higher cost."[8] The sample mean response was 3.59 and the sample standard deviation was 1.045. Based on these results, a confidence interval running from 3.49 to 3.69 was calculated for the population mean. Find the probability content of this interval.

8. The cloze readability procedure is designed to measure the effectiveness of a written communication. (A score of 57% or more on the cloze test demonstrates adequate understanding of the written material.) A random sample of 352 certified public accountants was asked to read financial report messages.[9] The sample mean cloze score was 60.41% and the sample standard deviation was 11.28%. Find a 90% confidence interval for the population mean score, and comment on your result.

9. A random sample of 174 marketing research professionals was asked to respond on a scale from one (strongly agree) to seven (strongly disagree) to the statement: "I sometimes use research techniques that guarantee the obtaining of results my client/boss desires."[10] The sample mean response was 6.06 and the sample standard deviation was 1.43.

(a) Based on these results, a confidence interval running from 5.96 to 6.16 was calculated for the population mean. Find the probability content of this interval.

---

[6] Data from J. C. Andrews, "The dimensionality of beliefs toward advertising in general," *Journal of Advertising*, *18*, no. 1 (1989), 26–35.

[7] J. DeConinck and J. Kopf, "Consumers' attitudes toward product liability reform," *American Business Review*, *10*, no. 2 (1992), 78–83.

[8] S. J. Daniel and W. D. Reitsparger, "Linking quality strategy with management control systems: empirical evidence from Japanese industry," *Accounting, Organizations and Society*, *16* (1991), 601–18.

[9] Reported in A. H. Adelberg, "A methodology for measuring the understandability of financial report messages," *Journal of Accounting Research*, *17* (1979), 565–92.

[10] I. P. Akaah, "Organizational culture and ethical research behavior," *Journal of the Academy of Marketing Science*, *21* (1993), 59–63.

(b) Compare the result of this exercise with Exercise 7. The two confidence intervals have the same width, but their probability contents are quite different. What factors account for this difference?

10. A retail clothing store is interested in the expenditures on clothes of college students in the first month of the school year. For a random sample of nine students, the mean expenditure was $157.82, and the sample standard deviation was $38.89. Assuming that the population distribution is normal, find a 95% confidence interval for the population mean expenditure.

11. There is concern about the speed of automobiles traveling over a particular stretch of highway. For a random sample of seven automobiles, radar indicated the following speeds, in miles per hour:

$$79 \quad 73 \quad 68 \quad 77 \quad 86 \quad 71 \quad 69$$

(a) Find the sample mean and variance.

(b) Assuming a normal population distribution, find a 95% confidence interval for the mean speed of all automobiles travelling over this stretch of highway.

12. A clinic offers a weight reduction program. A review of its records found the following weight losses, in pounds, for a random sample of ten of its patients at the conclusion of the program.

$$18.2 \quad 25.9 \quad 6.3 \quad 11.8 \quad 15.4$$
$$20.3 \quad 16.8 \quad 19.5 \quad 12.3 \quad 17.2$$

Assume the population distribution is normal.

(a) Find a 99% confidence interval for the population mean.

(b) Without doing the calculations, state whether a 90% confidence interval for the population mean would be wider than, narrower than, or the same as that found in (a).

13. Scores obtained by a large group of students taking a test are known to be normally distributed. A random sample of twenty-five test scores yielded the following statistics:

$$\sum_{i=1}^{25} x_i = 1,508 \qquad \sum_{i=1}^{25} x_i^2 = 95,628$$

(a) Find the sample mean and variance.

(b) Find a 90% confidence interval for the population mean.

14. A population has a normal distribution with unknown mean and unknown variance. Based on the material of Section 8.4, it is possible, given a random sample of two observations, to find confidence intervals for the population mean. However, this is not possible for a sample of one observation. Explain why this is to be expected.

15. A business school placement officer wants to estimate the mean annual salaries of the school's former students 5 years after graduation. A random sample of twenty-five such graduates found a sample mean of $42,740 and a sample standard deviation of $4,780. Assuming that the population distribution is normal, find a 90% confidence interval for the population mean.

16. A manufacturer of electronic games is considering their installation in campus bars. In a pilot study of the potential profitability of this enterprise, games were placed for one week in ten randomly chosen college bars. Denoting by x_i weekly profits in dollars, the following sample results were found:

$$\sum_{i=1}^{10} x_i = 1,120 \qquad \sum_{i=1}^{10} (x_i - \bar{x})^2 = 5,184$$

(a) Stating any assumptions you need to make, find an 80% confidence interval for mean weekly profits for all campus bars.

(b) Without doing the calculations, state whether a 90% confidence interval for the population mean would be wider than, narrower than, or the same as that found in part (a).

17. A car rental company is interested in the amount of time its vehicles are out of operation for repair work. A random sample of nine cars showed that over the past year, the numbers of days each had been inoperative were

$$16 \quad 10 \quad 21 \quad 22 \quad 8 \quad 17 \quad 19 \quad 14 \quad 19$$

Stating any assumptions you need to make, find a 90% confidence interval for the mean number of days in a year that all vehicles in the company's fleet are out of operation.

8.5 CONFIDENCE INTERVALS FOR THE POPULATION PROPORTION (LARGE SAMPLES)

Suppose now that we are interested in the proportion of population members possessing some specific attribute. For example, we might want to estimate the proportion of all adult Americans in favor of handgun control legislation. If a random sample is taken from the population, a natural point estimator of the population proportion is provided by the sample proportion. In this section, we derive confidence intervals for the population proportion.

Using the binomial setup, we let $\hat{p}_X$ denote the proportion of "successes" in n independent trials, each with probability of success p. In Section 6.3, we saw that if the number n of sample members is large, then the random variable

$$Z = \frac{\hat{p}_X - p}{\sqrt{p(1 - p)/n}} \qquad (8.5.1)$$

has, to a close approximation, a standard normal distribution. Unfortunately, this result is not quite sufficient to allow us to find confidence intervals for the population proportion, as the denominator of Eq. (8.5.1) involves the unknown p. However, if the sample size is large, we can obtain a good approximation if we replace p by its point estimator $\hat{p}_X$ in this denominator; that is

$$\sqrt{\frac{p(1 - p)}{n}} \approx \sqrt{\frac{\hat{p}_X(1 - \hat{p}_X)}{n}}$$

Hence, for large sample sizes, the distribution of the random variable

$$Z = \frac{\hat{p}_X - p}{\sqrt{\hat{p}_X(1 - \hat{p}_X)/n}}$$

is approximately standard normal. This result can then be used to obtain confidence intervals for the population proportion.

As before, we define $z_{\alpha/2}$ as the number for which

$$P(Z > z_{\alpha/2}) = \frac{\alpha}{2}$$

where the random variable Z follows a standard normal distribution. Then

$$1 - \alpha = P(-z_{\alpha/2} < Z < z_{\alpha/2})$$

$$= P\left(-z_{\alpha/2} < \frac{\hat{p}_x - p}{\sqrt{\hat{p}_x(1 - \hat{p}_x)/n}} < z_{\alpha/2}\right)$$

$$= P\left(-z_{\alpha/2}\sqrt{\frac{\hat{p}_x(1 - \hat{p}_x)}{n}} < \hat{p}_x - p < z_{\alpha/2}\sqrt{\frac{\hat{p}_x(1 - \hat{p}_x)}{n}}\right)$$

$$= P\left(\hat{p}_x - z_{\alpha/2}\sqrt{\frac{\hat{p}_x(1 - \hat{p}_x)}{n}} < p < \hat{p}_x + z_{\alpha/2}\sqrt{\frac{\hat{p}_x(1 - \hat{p}_x)}{n}}\right)$$

It therefore follows that if the observed sample proportion is $\hat{p}_x$, an approximate $100(1 - \alpha)\%$ confidence interval for the population proportion is

$$\hat{p}_x - z_{\alpha/2}\sqrt{\frac{\hat{p}_x(1 - \hat{p}_x)}{n}} < p < \hat{p}_x + z_{\alpha/2}\sqrt{\frac{\hat{p}_x(1 - \hat{p}_x)}{n}}$$

Confidence Intervals for the Population Proportion (Large Samples)

Let $\hat{p}_x$ denote the observed proportion of "successes" in a random sample of n observations from a population with a proportion p of successes. Then, if n is large, a $100(1 - \alpha)\%$ confidence interval for the population proportion is given by

$$\hat{p}_x - z_{\alpha/2}\sqrt{\frac{\hat{p}_x(1 - \hat{p}_x)}{n}} < p < \hat{p}_x + z_{\alpha/2}\sqrt{\frac{\hat{p}_x(1 - \hat{p}_x)}{n}}$$

where $z_{\alpha/2}$ is the number for which

$$P(Z > z_{\alpha/2}) = \frac{\alpha}{2}$$

and the random variable Z has a standard normal distribution.[11]

Confidence intervals for the population proportion are centered on the sample proportion. Also, it can be seen that all other things being equal, the larger the sample size n, the narrower the confidence interval. This reflects the increasing precision of the information about the population proportion obtained as the sample size becomes larger.

EXAMPLE 8.6

A random sample of 344 industrial buyers was asked: "What is your firm's policy for purchasing personnel to follow on accepting gifts from vendors?" For eighty-three of these buyers, either the policy was for each buyer to make his or her own decision, or there was no policy (so that, in effect, buyers were left to make their own decisions).[12] Find a 90% confidence interval for the population proportion of all buyers who make their own decisions on accepting gifts from vendors.

---

[11] Confidence intervals formed in this way are generally quite reliable when based on samples of $n = 40$ or more observations.

[12] Reported by M. M. Bird, "Gift-giving and gift-taking in industrial companies," *Industrial Marketing Management, 18* (1989), 91–94.

If p denotes the true population proportion and $\hat{p}_x$ the sample proportion, then confidence intervals for the population proportion are obtained from

$$\hat{p}_x - z_{\alpha/2} \sqrt{\frac{\hat{p}_x(1 - \hat{p}_x)}{n}} < p < \hat{p}_x + z_{\alpha/2} \sqrt{\frac{\hat{p}_x(1 - \hat{p}_x)}{n}}$$

where, for a 90% confidence interval, $\alpha = .10$, so that

$$\alpha/2 = .05 \qquad \text{and} \qquad z_{\alpha/2} = z_{.05} = 1.645$$

from Table 3 of the Appendix. We then have

$$n = 344 \qquad \hat{p}_x = 83/344 = .241 \qquad z_{\alpha/2} = 1.645$$

Therefore, a 90% confidence interval for the population proportion is

$$.241 - 1.645 \sqrt{\frac{(.241)(.759)}{344}} < p < .241 + 1.645 \sqrt{\frac{(.241)(.759)}{344}}$$

or

$$.203 < p < .279$$

Hence, the interval ranges from 20.3% to 27.9% of the population of all industrial buyers. Figure 8.10 also shows 80%, 95%, and 99% confidence intervals for the population proportion. As always, the greater the probability content, the wider is the confidence interval based on the same data.

EXAMPLE 8.7

A random sample of 142 company recruiters on college campuses was asked what role grades play in the consideration of a candidate. Of these sample members, 87

FIGURE 8.10 80%, 90%, 95%, and 99% confidence intervals for a population proportion based on data from Example 8.6

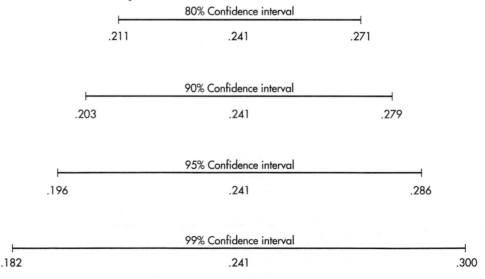

answered "critical," "extremely important," or "very important."[13] Find a 95% confidence interval for the population proportion of company recruiters with this view.

For a 95% confidence interval, $\alpha = .05$, so $z_{\alpha/2} = z_{.025} = 1.96$ from Table 3 of the Appendix. We then have

$$n = 142 \qquad \hat{p}_x = 87/142 = .613 \qquad z_{\alpha/2} = 1.96$$

Substituting these values into the general formula gives the 95% confidence interval

$$.613 - 1.96 \sqrt{\frac{(.613)(.387)}{142}} < p < .613 + 1.96 \sqrt{\frac{(.613)(.387)}{142}}$$

or

$$.533 < p < .693$$

Therefore, a 95% confidence interval for the percentage of recruiters viewing grades as critical, extremely important, or very important runs from 53.3% to 69.3%.

This interval is rather wide, reflecting imprecision in our knowledge about the population proportion. Narrower confidence intervals can be obtained by taking larger samples. In Section 8.9, we will see how to determine the sample size to achieve a confidence interval of specific width.

8.6 CONFIDENCE INTERVALS FOR THE VARIANCE OF A NORMAL POPULATION

In Sections 8.2 and 8.4, we saw how to obtain interval estimates for the population mean. On occasion, interval estimates are also required for the variance of a population. As might be expected, such estimates are based on the sample variance.

Suppose that we have a sample of n observations from a normal population with variance σ^2 and that the sample variance is denoted s_X^2. In Section 6.4, we saw that the random variable

$$\chi^2_{n-1} = \frac{(n-1)s_X^2}{\sigma^2}$$

follows a chi-square distribution with $(n-1)$ degrees of freedom. This result forms the basis for the derivation of confidence intervals for the population variance when sampling from a normal distribution.

In order to develop the formula for calculating confidence intervals for the variance, an additional notation is needed, as described in the box and illustrated in Figure 8.11.

---

[13] This information was reported by R. M. Schramm and R. N. Dortch, "An analysis of effective resumé content, format, and appearance, based on college recruiter perceptions," *Bulletin of the Association of Business Communication*, *54*, no. 3 (1991), 18–23.

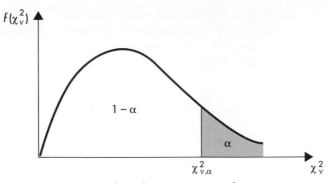

FIGURE 8.11 $P(\chi_\nu^2 > \chi_{\nu,\alpha}^2) = \alpha$, where χ_ν^2 is a chi-square random variable with ν degrees of freedom

---

Notation

A random variable having the chi-square distribution with ν degrees of freedom will be denoted χ_ν^2. We define as $\chi_{\nu,\alpha}^2$ the number for which

$$P(\chi_\nu^2 > \chi_{\nu,\alpha}^2) = \alpha$$

For a specified probability α, we will need to find the corresponding number $\chi_{\nu,\alpha}^2$. This can be achieved from the values of the cumulative distribution function of the chi-square random variable given in Table 5 in the Appendix. For instance, suppose we need the number that is exceeded with probability .05 by a chi-square random variable with 6 degrees of freedom; that is

$$P(\chi_6^2 > \chi_{6,.05}^2) = .05$$

Then, we have from Table 5 of the Appendix

$$\chi_{6,.05}^2 = 12.59$$

Using the notation just defined, we can write

$$P(\chi_\nu^2 > \chi_{\nu,\alpha/2}^2) = \frac{\alpha}{2}$$

Similarly, we define $\chi_{\nu,1-\alpha/2}^2$ so that

$$P(\chi_\nu^2 > \chi_{\nu,1-\alpha/2}^2) = 1 - \frac{\alpha}{2}$$

and hence,

$$P(\chi_\nu^2 < \chi_{\nu,1-\alpha/2}^2) = \frac{\alpha}{2}$$

It therefore follows that

$$P(\chi_{\nu,1-\alpha/2}^2 < \chi_\nu^2 < \chi_{\nu,\alpha/2}^2) = 1 - \frac{\alpha}{2} - \frac{\alpha}{2} = 1 - \alpha$$

This probability is illustrated in Figure 8.12.

To illustrate, suppose that we want to find a pair of numbers such that the probability that a chi-square random variable with 6 degrees of freedom lying between these numbers is .9. Then

$$1 - \alpha = .9 \qquad \text{and} \qquad \alpha = .1$$

so

$$P(\chi^2_{6,.95} < \chi^2_6 < \chi^2_{6,.05}) = .9$$

We determined previously that $\chi^2_{6,.05} = 12.59$. From Table 5 of the Appendix we see that

$$\chi^2_{6,.95} = 1.64$$

Thus, the probability is .9 that this chi-square random variable lies between 1.64 and 12.59.

To find confidence intervals for the population variance, we have for the chi-square distribution with $(n - 1)$ degrees of freedom

$$1 - \alpha = P(\chi^2_{n-1,1-\alpha/2} < \chi^2_{n-1} < \chi^2_{n-1,\alpha/2})$$

$$= P\left(\chi^2_{n-1,1-\alpha/2} < \frac{(n-1)s_X^2}{\sigma^2} < \chi^2_{n-1,\alpha/2}\right)$$

$$= P\left[\frac{(n-1)s_X^2}{\chi^2_{n-1,\alpha/2}} < \sigma^2 < \frac{(n-1)s_X^2}{\chi^2_{n-1,1-\alpha/2}}\right]$$

Therefore, if s_x^2 is the specific value observed for the sample variance, it follows that a $100(1 - \alpha)\%$ confidence interval for the population variance is given by

$$\frac{(n-1)s_x^2}{\chi^2_{n-1,\alpha/2}} < \sigma^2 < \frac{(n-1)s_x^2}{\chi^2_{n-1,1-\alpha/2}}$$

FIGURE 8.12 $P(\chi^2_{\nu,1-\alpha/2} < \chi^2_\nu < \chi^2_{\nu,\alpha/2}) = 1 - \alpha$, where χ^2_ν is a chi-square random variable with ν degrees of freedom

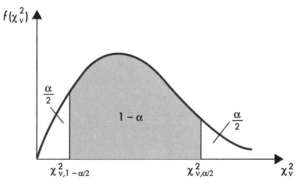

Confidence Intervals for the Variance of a Normal Population

Suppose that we have a random sample of n observations from a normal population with variance σ^2. If the observed sample variance is s_x^2, then a $100(1 - \alpha)\%$ confidence interval for the population variance is given by

$$\frac{(n - 1)s_x^2}{} < \sigma^2 < \frac{(n - 1)s_x^2}{}$$

where $\chi_{n-1,\alpha/2}^2$ is the number for which

$$P(\chi_{n-1}^2 > \chi_{n-1,\alpha/2}^2) = \frac{\alpha}{2}$$

and $\chi_{n-1,1-\alpha/2}^2$ is the number for which

$$P(\chi_{n-1}^2 < \chi_{n-1,1-\alpha/2}^2) = \frac{\alpha}{2}$$

and the random variable χ_{n-1}^2 obeys a chi-square distribution with $(n - 1)$ degrees of freedom.

EXAMPLE 8.8

A random sample of fifteen pills for headache relief showed a standard deviation of .8% in the concentration of the active ingredient. Find a 90% confidence interval for the population variance for these pills.

We have

$$n = 15 \quad \text{and} \quad s_x^2 = (.8)^2 = .64$$

Since a 90% confidence interval is wanted, we have $\alpha = .1$, and from Table 5 of the Appendix

$$\chi_{n-1,\alpha/2}^2 = \chi_{14,.05}^2 = 23.68 \quad \text{and} \quad \chi_{n-1,1-\alpha/2}^2 = \chi_{14,.95}^2 = 6.57$$

The 90% confidence interval for the population variance is given by

$$\frac{(n - 1)s_x^2}{\chi_{n-1,\alpha/2}^2} < \sigma^2 < \frac{(n - 1)s_x^2}{\chi_{n-1,1-\alpha/2}^2}$$

Substitution yields

$$\frac{(14)(.64)}{23.68} < \sigma^2 < \frac{(14)(.64)}{6.57}$$

so

$$.378 < \sigma^2 < 1.364$$

Our 90% confidence interval for the population variance in concentration of the active ingredient therefore ranges from .378 to 1.364.

Since the standard deviation is the square root of the variance, we can take square roots to obtain a 90% confidence interval for the population standard deviation. We have, then, for this interval

$$.61 < \sigma < 1.17$$

Hence, our 90% confidence interval for the population standard deviation in the percentage concentration of the active ingredient in these pills runs from .61% to 1.17%.

We conclude this section with the warning that it is dangerous to follow the procedure just demonstrated when the population distribution is not normal. The validity of the interval estimator for the variance depends far more critically on the assumption of normality than does that of the interval estimator for the population mean, developed in Section 8.4.

EXERCISES

18. In October 1992, ownership of the San Francisco Giants baseball team was considering a sale of the franchise that would lead to a move to St. Petersburg, Florida. A random sample of 610 San Francisco Bay Area taxpayers, carried out by *The San Francisco Examiner*, contained 50.7% who would be disappointed by this move. Find a 99% confidence interval for the population proportion of Bay Area taxpayers with this feeling.

19. A random sample was taken of 189 National Basketball Association games in which the score was not tied after one quarter. In 132 of these games, the team leading after one quarter won the game.[14]

   (a) Find a 90% confidence interval for the population proportion of all occasions on which the team leading after one quarter wins the game.

   (b) Without doing the calculations, state whether a 95% confidence interval for the population proportion would be wider than or narrower than that found in part (a).

20. Of a random sample of 323 union members, 47.9% agreed or strongly agreed with the statement: "Union workers should refuse to work when a nonunion worker is sent to the job."[15] Based on this information, a statistician calculated, for the percentage of all union members with this view, a confidence interval running from 45.8% to 50.0%. Find the level of confidence associated with this interval.

21. Of a random sample of 134 auditors employed by major auditing firms, 82 said that, on receiving new audit business, they always enquired of the predecessor auditor the reason for the change of auditors.[16] Find a 95% confidence interval for the population proportion.

22. Of a random sample of 95 small manufacturing firms, 29 indicated improvements in quality as the most important action taken to revitalize products or improve competitive performance.[17]

   (a) Find a 99% confidence interval for the population proportion.

   (b) Without doing the calculations, state whether a 90% confidence interval for the population proportion would be wider than, narrower than, or the same as that found in (a).

23. A random sample was taken of 96 foreign manufacturers, with direct investment in the United States, who use independent U.S. industrial distributors. Of these sample members, 32 said the distributors were rarely or never capable of performing the advice and technical support function.[18] Find an 80% confidence interval for the population proportion.

---

[14] H. Cooper, K. M. DeNeve, and F. Mosteller, "Predicting professional sports game outcomes from intermediate game scores," *Chance*, 5, no. 3 (1992), 18–22.

[15] S. Chang and L. Robinson, "Perceptions of labor unions by union members and their potential employers," *Mid-American Journal of Business*, 5, no. 2 (1990), 25–30.

[16] J. C. Lambert, S. J. Lambert, and T. G. Calderon, "Communication between successor and predecessor auditors," *Auditing: A Journal of Practice and Theory*, 10, no. 1 (1991), 97–109.

[17] W. Davig and S. Brown, "Incremental decision making in small manufacturing firms," *Journal of Small Business Management*, 30, no. 2 (1992), 53–60.

[18] B. Rosenbloom and T. L. Larsen, "How foreign firms view their U.S. distributors," *Industrial Marketing Management*, 21 (1992), 93–101.

24. Of a random sample of 198 marketing students, 98 rated a case of resumé inflation as unethical.[19] Based on this information, a statistician computed for the population proportion a confidence interval running from .445 to .545. What is the probability content of this interval?

25. A random sample of fifteen financial analysts' forecasts of next year's earnings per share for General Motors Corporation was taken. The sample standard deviation was $.880. Find a 95% confidence interval for the variance of predicted earnings per share for all analysts.

26. Using the data of Exercise 11, find an 80% confidence interval for the population variance of the speeds of all automobiles travelling over this stretch of highway.

27. Using the data of Exercise 12, find a 90% confidence interval for the population standard deviation of weight losses for patients of the clinic's weight reduction program.

28. Using the data of Exercise 13, find a 95% confidence interval for the population standard deviation of all test scores of the group of students.

29. The confidence intervals for the population variance described in this section are *not* centered on the sample variance. Explain graphically why this is so.

30. Given the same sample information, it is possible (in principle) to obtain narrower confidence intervals, of the same probability content, for the population variance than those found in this section. Explain graphically why this is so.

31. A psychologist wants to estimate the variance of employee test scores. A random sample of eighteen scores had sample standard deviation 10.4. Find a 90% confidence interval for the population variance. What assumption, if any, have you made in calculating this interval estimate?

32. A manufacturer is concerned about the variability of the levels of impurity contained in consignments of raw material from a supplier. A random sample of fifteen consignments showed a standard deviation of 2.36% in the concentration of impurity levels. Assume a normal population distribution.

    (a) Find a 95% confidence interval for the population variance.

    (b) Would a 99% confidence interval for this variance be wider or narrower than that found in part (a)?

33. A manufacturer bonds a plastic coating to a metal surface. A random sample of nine observations on the thicknesses of this coating is taken from a week's output. The sample thicknesses (in millimeters) were as follows:

| 19.8 | 21.2 | 18.6 | 20.4 | 21.6 | 19.8 | 19.9 | 20.3 | 20.8 |

Assuming that the population distribution is normal, find a 90% confidence interval for the population variance.

8.7 CONFIDENCE INTERVALS FOR THE DIFFERENCE BETWEEN THE MEANS OF TWO NORMAL POPULATIONS

An important problem in statistical inference deals with the comparison of two population means. As one illustration, a company might receive shipments of a chemical from two suppliers and be concerned about the difference between the mean levels of impurity present in the chemicals from the two sources of supply. As another exam-

---

[19] P. A. Dabholkar and J. J. Kellaris, "Toward understanding marketing students' ethical judgment of controversial personal selling practices," *Journal of Business Research*, 24 (1992), 313–29.

ple, a farmer may consider the use of two alternative fertilizers, his interest being in the difference between the resulting mean crop yields per acre.

To compare population means, a random sample is drawn from the two populations, and an inference about the difference between population means is based on the sample results. The appropriate method for analyzing this information depends on the procedure used in selecting the samples. We will consider the following two very common sampling schemes:

1. MATCHED PAIRS □ In this scheme, the sample members are chosen in pairs, one from each population. The idea is that, apart from the factor under study, the members of these pairs should resemble one another as closely as possible so that the comparison of interest can be made directly. For instance, suppose that we want to measure the effectiveness of a speed-reading course. One possible approach would be to record the number of words per minute read by a sample of students before taking the course and compare with results *for the same students* after completing the course. In this case, each pair of observations consists of "before" and "after" measurements on a single student.

2. INDEPENDENT SAMPLES □ In this scheme, samples are drawn independently from the two populations of interest so that the membership of one sample is not influenced by that of another. In the example of the company that receives shipments of a chemical from two suppliers, we might choose independent random samples of batches from each supplier and measure the impurity levels of each batch sampled.

Whichever sampling method is used, our objective in this section is to obtain confidence intervals for the difference between the two population means.

CONFIDENCE INTERVALS BASED ON MATCHED PAIRS

Suppose, in general, that we obtain a random sample of n matched pairs of observations, denoted $(x_1, y_1), (x_2, y_2), \ldots, (x_n, y_n)$, from populations with means μ_X and μ_Y. Thus, $x_1, x_2, \ldots, x_n$ denote the observations from the population with mean μ_X, and $y_1, y_2, \ldots, y_n$ the matched sampled values from the population with the mean μ_Y. Table 8.2 shows fuel consumption figures obtained for a random sample of eight cars from each of two different models. The sample cars were paired, and each member of a particular pair was driven over the same route by the same driver so that variability between drivers and routes could be eliminated from the comparisons. The table also

TABLE 8.2 Fuel consumption, in miles per gallon, recorded for matched pairs of cars

i	X-CARS x_i	Y-CARS y_i	DIFFERENCES d_i	d_i^2
1	19.4	19.6	−.2	.04
2	18.8	17.5	1.3	1.69
3	20.6	18.4	2.2	4.84
4	17.6	17.5	.1	.01
5	19.2	18.0	1.2	1.44
6	20.9	20.0	.9	.81
7	18.3	18.8	−.5	.25
8	20.4	19.2	1.2	1.44
		Sums	6.2	10.52

shows the differences, d_i, between the figures. These differences represent a random sample from a population whose mean is $(\mu_X - \mu_Y)$, the difference between the population means for the two car models.

From the information in the table, the sample mean and variance of the differences in fuel consumption can be calculated. We have, for the mean

$$\bar{d} = \frac{1}{n} \sum_{i=1}^{n} d_i = \frac{1}{8} (6.2) = .775$$

and, for the variance

$$s_d^2 = \frac{1}{n-1} \left(\sum_{i=1}^{n} d_i^2 - n\bar{d}^2 \right)$$

$$= \frac{1}{7}[10.52 - (8)(.775)^2] = .816$$

so the observed sample standard deviation is

$$s_d = \sqrt{.816} = .903$$

We are now in the position of requiring a confidence interval for a population mean $(\mu_X - \mu_Y)$, given a random sample (the values of the differences d_i) from that population. If the population distribution is assumed to be normal, the procedure developed in Section 8.4 is immediately applicable because the differences in matched pairs constitute a random sample from a population whose mean is the quantity we are trying to estimate.

Confidence Intervals for Difference Between Means: Matched Pairs

Suppose that we have a random sample of n matched pairs of observations from distributions with means μ_X and μ_Y. Let $\bar{d}$ and s_d denote the observed sample mean and standard deviation for the n differences $d_i = x_i - y_i$. If the population distribution of the differences is assumed to be normal, then a $100(1 - \alpha)\%$ confidence interval for $(\mu_X - \mu_Y)$ is given by

$$\bar{d} - \frac{t_{n-1,\alpha/2}s_d}{\sqrt{n}} < \mu_X - \mu_Y < \bar{d} + \frac{t_{n-1,\alpha/2}s_d}{\sqrt{n}}$$

where $t_{n-1,\alpha/2}$ is the number for which

$$P(t_{n-1} > t_{n-1,\alpha/2}) = \frac{\alpha}{2}$$

and the random variable t_{n-1} has a Student's t distribution with $(n-1)$ degrees of freedom.

In the fuel consumption example, we have found

$$\bar{d} = .775 \qquad s_d = .903 \qquad n = 8$$

For a 99% confidence interval, $\alpha = .01$, so

$$t_{n-1,\alpha/2} = t_{7,.005} = 3.499$$

from Table 6 in the Appendix. Hence, we obtain the 99% confidence interval for the difference between the population means on substituting in

$$\overline{d} - \frac{t_{n-1,\alpha/2}s_d}{\sqrt{n}} < \mu_X - \mu_Y < \overline{d} + \frac{t_{n-1,\alpha/2}s_d}{\sqrt{n}}$$

that is

$$.775 - \frac{(3.499)(.903)}{\sqrt{8}} < \mu_X - \mu_Y < .775 + \frac{(3.499)(.903)}{\sqrt{8}}$$

or

$$-.342 < \mu_X - \mu_Y < 1.892$$

We therefore find that based on the data of Table 8.2, a 99% confidence interval for the difference in population mean fuel consumption for these two types of automobile ranges from $-.342$ to 1.892 miles per gallon. Since the interval includes 0, the sample evidence against the conjecture that the population means are the same is not extremely strong.

CONFIDENCE INTERVALS BASED ON INDEPENDENT SAMPLES

We now consider the case where independent samples, not necessarily of equal size, are taken from the two populations of interest. Suppose that we have a random sample of n_x observations from a population with mean μ_X and variance σ_X^2 and an independent random sample of n_y observations from a population with mean μ_Y and variance σ_Y^2. Let the respective sample means be $\overline{X}$ and $\overline{Y}$.

As a first step, we examine the situation where the two population distributions are normal with known variances. Since the object of interest is the difference between the two population means, it is natural to base inference on the difference between the corresponding sample means. This random variable has mean

$$E(\overline{X} - \overline{Y}) = E(\overline{X}) - E(\overline{Y}) = \mu_X - \mu_Y$$

and, since the samples are independent, variance

$$\text{Var}(\overline{X} - \overline{Y}) = \text{Var}(\overline{X}) + \text{Var}(\overline{Y}) = \frac{\sigma_X^2}{n_x} + \frac{\sigma_Y^2}{n_y}$$

Furthermore, it can be shown that its distribution is normal. It therefore follows that the random variable

$$Z = \frac{(\overline{X} - \overline{Y}) - (\mu_X - \mu_Y)}{\sqrt{\dfrac{\sigma_X^2}{n_x} + \dfrac{\sigma_Y^2}{n_y}}}$$

has a standard normal distribution. An argument parallel to that of Section 8.2 can then be used to obtain confidence intervals for the difference between the population means. Since this interval requires knowledge of the true population variances, it is rarely of much direct use. However, as was the case in Section 8.2, its range of applicability is greatly extended when the sample sizes are large, as indicated in the box.

> ### Confidence Intervals for Difference Between Means: Independent Samples (Known Variances or Large Sample Sizes)
>
> Suppose that we have independent random samples of n_x and n_y observations from normal distributions with means μ_X and μ_Y and variances σ_X^2 and σ_Y^2. If the observed sample means are $\bar{x}$ and $\bar{y}$, then a $100(1 - \alpha)\%$ confidence interval for $(\mu_X - \mu_Y)$ is given by
>
> $$(\bar{x} - \bar{y}) - z_{\alpha/2} \sqrt{\frac{\sigma_X^2}{n_x} + \frac{\sigma_Y^2}{n_y}} < \mu_X - \mu_Y < (\bar{x} - \bar{y}) + z_{\alpha/2} \sqrt{\frac{\sigma_X^2}{n_x} + \frac{\sigma_Y^2}{n_y}}$$
>
> where $z_{\alpha/2}$ is the number for which
>
> $$P(Z > z_{\alpha/2}) = \frac{\alpha}{2}$$
>
> and the random variable Z has a standard normal distribution.
>
> If the sample sizes n_x and n_y are large,[20] then to a good approximation, a $100(1 - \alpha)\%$ confidence interval for $(\mu_X - \mu_Y)$ is obtained by replacing the population variances in the previous expression by the corresponding observed sample variances s_x^2 and s_y^2. For large sample sizes, this approximation will typically remain adequate even if the population distributions are not normal.

EXAMPLE 8.9

For a random sample of ninety-six smokers, the mean amount of short-term absenteeism from work was 2.15 hours per month, and the sample standard deviation was 2.09 hours per month. For an independent random sample of 206 employees who had never smoked, the mean amount of absenteeism was 1.69 hours per month, and the sample standard deviation was 1.91 hours per month.[21] Find a 99% confidence interval for the difference between the two population means.

For the smokers, we have

$$\bar{x} = 2.15 \qquad n_x = 96 \qquad s_x = 2.09$$

and for those who never smoked

$$\bar{y} = 1.69 \qquad n_y = 206 \qquad s_y = 1.91$$

Since the sample sizes are large, we can use the sample variances in place of the unknown population variances in the formula given in the box. Confidence intervals for the difference between the population means then take the form

$$(\bar{x} - \bar{y}) - z_{\alpha/2} \sqrt{\frac{s_x^2}{n_x} + \frac{s_y^2}{n_y}} < \mu_X - \mu_Y < (\bar{x} - \bar{y}) + z_{\alpha/2} \sqrt{\frac{s_x^2}{n_x} + \frac{s_y^2}{n_y}}$$

where, for a 99% interval

$$z_{\alpha/2} = z_{.005} = 2.575$$

---

[20] Thirty observations in each sample are generally adequate for this approximation.

[21] Reported in M. R. Manning, J. S. Osland, and A. Osland, "Work-related consequences of smoking cessation," *Academy of Management Journal, 32* (1989), 606–21.

The required interval is then

$$(2.15 - 1.69) - 2.575 \sqrt{\frac{(2.09)^2}{96} + \frac{(1.91)^2}{206}} < \mu_X - \mu_Y$$

$$< (2.15 - 1.69) + 2.575 \sqrt{\frac{(2.09)^2}{96} + \frac{(1.91)^2}{206}}$$

which is

$$-.19 < \mu_X - \mu_Y < 1.11$$

Since 0 is inside the 99% confidence interval for the difference in population means, the evidence in the data against the conjecture that the mean absentee rates for the two groups is the same is not overwhelming.

EXAMPLE 8.10

Independent random samples of professors and chief executive officers were asked to evaluate the relevance to managerial practice of strategic management research over the past decade on a scale from one (declined substantially) to five (improved substantially).[22] The sample of 321 professors produced a mean rating of 3.01, and sample standard deviation 1.09. For the sample of 94 chief executive officers, the mean rating was 2.88 and the sample standard deviation was 1.01. Denoting by μ_X the population mean for professors and by μ_Y the population mean for chief executive officers, find a 95% confidence interval for $(\mu_X - \mu_Y)$.

Again, since the sample sizes are large, we can use the sample variances in place of the population variances and obtain intervals from

$$(\bar{x} - \bar{y}) - z_{\alpha/2} \sqrt{\frac{s_x^2}{n_x} + \frac{s_y^2}{n_y}} < \mu_X - \mu_Y < (\bar{x} - \bar{y}) + z_{\alpha/2} \sqrt{\frac{s_x^2}{n_x} + \frac{s_y^2}{n_y}}$$

where

$$n_x = 321 \qquad \bar{x} = 3.01 \qquad s_x = 1.09$$
$$n_y = 94 \qquad \bar{y} = 2.88 \qquad s_y = 1.01$$

and for a 95% confidence interval

$$z_{\alpha/2} = z_{.025} = 1.96$$

The interval is then

$$(3.01 - 2.88) - 1.96 \sqrt{\frac{(1.09)^2}{321} + \frac{(1.01)^2}{94}} < \mu_X - \mu_Y$$

$$< (3.01 - 2.88) + 1.96 \sqrt{\frac{(1.09)^2}{321} + \frac{(1.01)^2}{94}}$$

or

$$-.11 < \mu_X - \mu_Y < .37$$

[22] S. A. Zahra and J. A. Pearce, "Priorities of CEOs and strategic management professors for future academic research," *Journal of Managerial Issues*, 4 (1992), 171–89.

This interval includes zero, indicating an absence of strong evidence that the population means are different. Figure 8.13 shows this confidence interval, together with 80%, 90%, and 99% confidence intervals for the difference in the population means.

We now have to consider the case where the sample sizes are not large, and a confidence interval is needed for the difference between the means of two normal populations based on independent random samples from the two populations. In fact, when the population variances are unknown, there is considerable difficulty in attacking this general problem. However, in one special case, where it can be assumed that the two population variances are equal,[23] a fairly straightforward method is available.

Suppose again that we have independent random samples of n_x and n_y observations from normal populations with means μ_X and μ_Y and that the populations have a common (unknown) variance σ^2. Inference about the population means is, as before, based on the difference $(\overline{X} - \overline{Y})$ between the two sample means. This random variable has a normal distribution with mean $(\mu_X - \mu_Y)$ and variance

$$\text{Var} \, (\overline{X} - \overline{Y}) = \text{Var} \, (\overline{X}) + \text{Var} \, (\overline{Y})$$

$$= \frac{\sigma^2}{n_x} + \frac{\sigma^2}{n_y}$$

$$= \sigma^2 \left(\frac{1}{n_x} + \frac{1}{n_y} \right)$$

FIGURE 8.13 80%, 90%, 95%, and 99% confidence intervals for difference in population means based on the data of Example 8.10

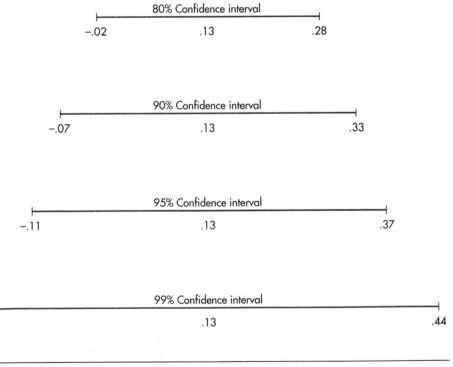

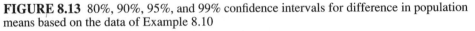

---

[23] We will see in Chapter 9 how the data can be used to check this assumption.

$$= \sigma^2 \left(\frac{n_x + n_y}{n_x n_y} \right)$$

It therefore follows that the random variable

$$Z = \frac{(\overline{X} - \overline{Y}) - (\mu_X - \mu_Y)}{\sqrt{\sigma^2 \left(\dfrac{n_x + n_y}{n_x n_y} \right)}} \tag{8.7.1}$$

has a standard normal distribution. However, this result cannot be used as it stands because the unknown population variance is involved. Since this variance is common to the two populations, the two sets of sample information can be pooled together to estimate it. The estimator used is

$$s^2 = \frac{(n_x - 1)s_X^2 + (n_y - 1)s_Y^2}{(n_x + n_y - 2)}$$

where s_X^2 and s_Y^2 are the two sample variances.

Replacing the unknown σ^2 by its estimator s^2 in Eq. (8.7.1) gives the random variable

$$t = \frac{(\overline{X} - \overline{Y}) - (\mu_X - \mu_Y)}{s \sqrt{\dfrac{n_x + n_y}{n_x n_y}}}$$

It can be shown that this random variable obeys the Student's t distribution with $(n_x + n_y - 2)$ degrees of freedom. Given this result, confidence intervals for the difference between the population means can be obtained through an argument similar to that used in Section 8.4.

Confidence Intervals for Difference Between the Means of Two Normal Populations: Independent Samples, Population Variances Equal

Suppose that we have independent random samples of n_x and n_y observations from normal distributions with means μ_X and μ_Y and a common variance. If the observed sample means and variances are $\overline{x}$, $\overline{y}$ and s_x^2, s_y^2, then a $100(1 - \alpha)\%$ confidence interval for $(\mu_X - \mu_Y)$ is given by

$$(\overline{x} - \overline{y}) - t_{n_x + n_y - 2, \alpha/2} s \sqrt{\frac{n_x + n_y}{n_x n_y}} < \mu_X - \mu_Y < (\overline{x} - \overline{y}) + t_{n_x + n_y - 2, \alpha/2} s \sqrt{\frac{n_x + n_y}{n_x n_y}}$$

where

$$s^2 = \frac{(n_x - 1)s_x^2 + (n_y - 1)s_y^2}{(n_x + n_y - 2)}$$

and $t_{n_x + n_y - 2, \alpha/2}$ is the number for which

$$P(t_{n_x + n_y - 2} > t_{n_x + n_y - 2, \alpha/2}) = \frac{\alpha}{2}$$

where the random variable $t_{n_x + n_y - 2}$ has a Student's t distribution with $(n_x + n_y - 2)$ degrees of freedom.

EXAMPLE 8.11

In a study of the effects of planning on the financial performance of banks,[24] a random sample of six "partial formal planners" showed mean annual percentage increase in net income of 9.972 and a standard deviation of 7.470. An independent random sample of nine banks with no formal planning system had a mean annual percentage increase in net income of 2.098 and a standard deviation of 10.834. Assuming that the two population distributions are normal with the same variance, find a 90% confidence interval for the difference between their means.

We have, with x referring to the "partial formal planners" and y to those with no formal planning

$$n_x = 6 \qquad \bar{x} = 9.972 \qquad s_x = 7.470$$
$$n_y = 9 \qquad \bar{y} = 2.098 \qquad s_y = 10.834$$

The estimate of the common population variance is then

$$s^2 = \frac{(n_x - 1)s_x^2 + (n_y - 1)s_y^2}{(n_x + n_y - 2)}$$
$$= \frac{(5)(7.470)^2 + (8)(10.834)^2}{13} = 93.693$$

so

$$s = \sqrt{93.693} = 9.680$$

The interval required is of the form

$$(\bar{x} - \bar{y}) - t_{n_x + n_y - 2, \alpha/2}s \sqrt{\frac{n_x + n_y}{n_x n_y}} < \mu_X - \mu_Y < (\bar{x} - \bar{y}) + t_{n_x + n_y - 2, \alpha/2}s \sqrt{\frac{n_x + n_y}{n_x n_y}}$$

where, for a 90% confidence interval, $\alpha = .10$, so

$$t_{n_x + n_y - 2, \alpha/2} = t_{13, .05} = 1.771$$

from Table 6 of the Appendix.

Hence, the 90% confidence interval for the difference between the population mean percentage increases in net incomes is

$$(9.972 - 2.098) - (1.771)(9.680) \sqrt{\frac{6 + 9}{54}}$$

$$< \mu_X - \mu_Y < (9.972 - 2.098) + (1.771)(9.680) \sqrt{\frac{6 + 9}{54}}$$

---

[24] Reported in D. R. Wood and R. L. La Forge, "The impact of comprehensive planning on financial performance," *Academy of Management Journal*, 22 (1979), 516–26.

or

$$-1.161 < \mu_X - \mu_Y < 16.909$$

Our 90% confidence interval for the difference between population mean annual percentage increases in net income for these two groups of banks includes 0. This suggests that the evidence in the data against the conjecture that the two population means are the same is not strong.

8.8 CONFIDENCE INTERVALS FOR THE DIFFERENCE BETWEEN TWO POPULATION PROPORTIONS (LARGE SAMPLES)

In Section 8.5, we derived confidence intervals for a single population proportion. Often, we are interested in comparing two proportions. For instance, we might want to compare the proportion of football players who succeed in graduating with the proportion of nonathletes who graduate. In this section, we show how to obtain confidence intervals for the difference between population proportions when independent large samples are taken from the two populations.

Suppose that a random sample of n_x observations from a population with proportion p_X of "successes" yields sample proportion $\hat{p}_X$ and that an independent random sample of n_y observations from a population with proportion p_Y of "successes" produces sample proportion $\hat{p}_Y$. Since our concern is with the population difference $(p_X - p_Y)$, it is natural to examine the random variable $(\hat{p}_X - \hat{p}_Y)$. This has mean

$$E(\hat{p}_X - \hat{p}_Y) = E(\hat{p}_X) - E(\hat{p}_Y) = p_X - p_Y$$

and, since the samples are taken independently, variance

$$\text{Var}\ (\hat{p}_X - \hat{p}_Y) = \text{Var}\ (\hat{p}_X) + \text{Var}\ (\hat{p}_Y) \qquad (8.8.1)$$
$$= \frac{p_X(1 - p_X)}{n_x} + \frac{p_Y(1 - p_Y)}{n_y}$$

Furthermore, if the sample sizes are large, the distribution of this random variable is approximately normal, so subtracting its mean and dividing by its standard deviation gives a standard normal random variable. Moreover, for large sample sizes, this approximation remains good when the unknown population proportions in Eq. (8.8.1) are replaced by the corresponding sample quantities. Thus, to a good approximation, the random variable

$$Z = \frac{(\hat{p}_X - \hat{p}_Y) - (p_X - p_Y)}{\sqrt{\dfrac{\hat{p}_X(1 - \hat{p}_X)}{n_x} + \dfrac{\hat{p}_Y(1 - \hat{p}_Y)}{n_y}}}$$

has a standard normal distribution.

This result allows the derivation of confidence intervals for the difference between the two population proportions when the same sample sizes are large, as shown in the box.

Confidence Intervals for the Difference Between Population Proportions (Large Samples)

Let $\hat{p}_x$ denote the observed proportion of successes in a random sample of n_x observations from a population with proportion p_X successes, and let $\hat{p}_y$ denote the proportion of successes observed in an independent random sample from a population with proportion p_Y successes. Then, if the sample sizes are large,[25] a $100(1 - \alpha)\%$ confidence interval for $(p_X - p_Y)$ is given by

$$(\hat{p}_x - \hat{p}_y) - z_{\alpha/2} \sqrt{\frac{\hat{p}_x(1 - \hat{p}_x)}{n_x} + \frac{\hat{p}_y(1 - \hat{p}_y)}{n_y}}$$

$$< p_X - p_Y < (\hat{p}_x - \hat{p}_y) + z_{\alpha/2} \sqrt{\frac{\hat{p}_x(1 - \hat{p}_x)}{n_x} + \frac{\hat{p}_y(1 - \hat{p}_y)}{n_y}}$$

where $z_{\alpha/2}$ is the number for which

$$P(Z > z_{\alpha/2}) = \frac{\alpha}{2}$$

and the random variable Z has a standard normal distribution.

We now illustrate this procedure with two examples.

EXAMPLE 8.12

In a survey of client-sponsored projects (CSPs) in college marketing courses, faculty members who used CSPs were presented with the statement "CSPs are too time-consuming for faculty." Of a sample of ninety-two CSP users in schools accredited by the American Assembly of Collegiate Schools of Business, forty-nine agreed with this statement. Of an independent sample of eighty-six CSP users in nonaccredited schools, thirty-six agreed with the statement.[26] If the respective population proportions are denoted p_X and p_Y, find a 90% confidence interval for $(p_X - p_Y)$.

From the sample information, we have

$$n_x = 92 \qquad \hat{p}_x = \frac{49}{92} = .533 \qquad n_y = 86 \qquad \hat{p}_y = \frac{36}{86} = .419$$

For a 90% confidence interval, $\alpha = .10$, so

$$z_{\alpha/2} = z_{.05} = 1.645$$

Substituting these values into the formula for the confidence interval gives

$$(.533 - .419) - 1.645 \sqrt{\frac{(.533)(.467)}{92} + \frac{(.419)(.581)}{86}}$$

---

[25] This approximation is generally adequate if there are at least forty observations in each sample.

[26] Reported in V. Vincent and G. de los Santos, "Combining theory and practice in college marketing courses," *Business Forum*, *14*, no. 1 (1989), 25–28.

$$< p_X - p_Y < (.533 - .419) + 1.645 \sqrt{\frac{(.533)(.467)}{92} + \frac{(.419)(.581)}{86}}$$

or

$$-.008 < p_X - p_Y < .236$$

Since the difference 0 is just inside this 90% confidence interval, the evidence in these data against the conjecture that the two population proportions are the same is not very strong.

EXAMPLE 8.13

Independent random samples of male and female senior accounting students were taken. Of 120 men, 107 expected to be working full time ten years later. Of 141 women, 73 had this expectation.[27] Find a 95% confidence interval for the difference between the two population proportions.

The sample values are

$$n_x = 120 \qquad \hat{p}_x = 107/120 = .892 \qquad n_y = 141 \qquad \hat{p}_y = 73/141 = .518$$

For a 95% confidence interval, $\alpha = .05$, and so

$$z_{\alpha/2} = z_{.025} = 1.96$$

The required interval is therefore

$$(.892 - .518) - 1.96 \sqrt{\frac{(.892)(.108)}{120} + \frac{(.518)(.482)}{141}} < p_X - p_Y$$

$$< (.892 - .518) + 1.96 \sqrt{\frac{(.892)(.108)}{120} + \frac{(.518)(.482)}{141}}$$

or

$$.275 < p_X - p_Y < .473$$

The fact that zero is well outside this range suggests strongly that in the population of senior accounting students, men are more likely than women to expect to be working full time in ten years.

EXERCISES

34. A random sample of ten pairs of identical houses was chosen in a large midwestern city, and a passive solar heating system was installed in one member of each pair. The total fuel bills (in dollars) for three winter months for these homes were then determined as shown in the accompanying table. Assuming normal population distributions, find a 90% confidence interval for the difference between the two population means.

---

[27] R. J. Maupin, "Gender roles in transition: career and family expectations of accounting students," *Mid-American Journal of Business*, 8 (1993), 33–37.

PAIR	WITHOUT PASSIVE SOLAR	WITH PASSIVE SOLAR	PAIR	WITHOUT PASSIVE SOLAR	WITH PASSIVE SOLAR
1	485	452	6	386	380
2	423	386	7	426	395
3	515	502	8	473	411
4	425	376	9	454	415
5	653	605	10	496	441

35. A random sample of six salespersons who had attended a motivational course on sales techniques was monitored in the 3 months before and the 3 months after the course. The table shows the values of sales, in thousands of dollars, generated by these six salespersons in the two periods. Assuming that the population distributions are normal, find an 80% confidence interval for the difference between the two population means.

SALESPERSON	BEFORE COURSE	AFTER COURSE
1	212	237
2	282	291
3	203	191
4	327	341
5	165	192
6	198	180

36. For a random sample of forty accounting students in a class using group learning techniques, the mean examination score was 322.12, and the sample standard deviation was 54.53. For an independent random sample of sixty-one students in the same course but in a class not using group learning techniques, the sample mean and standard deviation of the scores were 304.61 and 62.61, respectively.[28] Find a 95% confidence interval for the difference between the two population mean scores.

37. In a survey of practicing certified public accountants on women in the accounting profession, sample members were asked to respond on a scale from one (strongly disagree) to five (strongly agree) to the statement: "Women are equally acceptable to clients as are men to perform work on engagements." For a random sample of 172 female accountants, the mean response was 3.483, and the sample standard deviation was .970. For an independent random sample of 186 male accountants, the sample mean and standard deviation of responses were 3.435 and .894, respectively.[29] Find a 95% confidence interval for the difference between the two population means.

38. Recent business graduates currently employed in full-time positions were surveyed. Family backgrounds were self-classified as relatively high or low socioeconomic status.[30] For a random sample of 138 high socioeconomic status recent business graduates, mean

[28] Reported in S. M. Lightner, "Accounting education and participating group dynamics," *Collegiate News and Views*, *35*, no. 1 (1981), 5–9.

[29] Data given in M. W. Trapp, R. H. Hermanson, and D. H. Turner, "Current perceptions of issues related to women employed in public accounting," *Accounting Horizons*, *3*, no. 1 (1989), 71–85.

[30] W. Whitely, T. W. Dougherty, and G. F. Dreher, "Relationship of career mentoring and socioeconomic origin to managers' and professionals' early career progress," *Academy of Management Journal*, *34* (1991), 331–51.

total compensation was \$36,558 and the sample standard deviation was \$11,624. For an independent random sample of 266 low socioeconomic status recent business graduates, mean total compensation was \$37,499 and the sample standard deviation was \$16,521. Find a 90% confidence interval for the difference between the two population means.

39. For a random sample of 190 firms that revalued their fixed assets, the mean ratio of debt to tangible assets was .517 and the sample standard deviation was .148. For an independent random sample of 417 firms that did not revalue their fixed assets,[31] the mean ratio of debt to tangible assets was .489 and the sample standard deviation was .159. Find a 99% confidence interval for the difference between the two population means.

40. A researcher intends to estimate the effect of a drug on the scores of human subjects performing a task of psychomotor coordination. The members of a random sample of nine subjects were given the drug prior to testing. Their mean score was 9.78, and the sample variance was 17.64. An independent random sample of ten subjects was used as a control group and given a placebo prior to testing. The mean score in this control group was 15.10, and the sample variance was 27.01. Assuming that the population distributions are normal with equal variances, find a 90% confidence interval for the difference between the population mean scores.

41. A company sends a random sample of twelve of its salespeople to a course designed to increase their motivation and hence, presumably, their effectiveness. In the following year, these people generated sales with an average value of \$435,000 and a sample standard deviation of \$56,000. During the same period, an independently chosen random sample of fifteen salespeople who had not attended the course obtained sales with average value \$408,000 and standard deviation \$43,000. Assuming that the two population distributions are normal and have the same variance, find a 95% confidence interval for the difference between their means.

42. Students in an introductory economics class are assigned to quiz sections conducted by teaching assistants. For one teaching assistant, the twenty-one students in the quiz section obtained a mean score of 72.1 on the final examination, and a standard deviation of 11.3. For a second teaching assistant, the eighteen students in the section obtained a mean score on the final exam of 73.8, and a standard deviation of 10.6. Assuming that these data can be regarded as independent random samples from normal populations with a common variance, find an 80% confidence interval for the difference between the population means.

43. Of a random sample of 112 large retailers, 70 used regression as a method of forecasting. Of an independent random sample of 135 small retailers, 65 used regression as a method of forecasting.[32] Find a 95% confidence interval for the difference between the two population proportions.

44. Of a random sample of 1,203 business students in 1979, 20.2% said that teaching as a career was very unappealing. Of an independent random sample of 1,203 business students in 1989, 13.2% had this reaction to teaching as a career.[33] Find a 99% confidence interval for the difference between the population proportions regarding teaching as very unappealing in the two years.

45. Of a random sample of 154 physicians, 59.0% viewed hospital advertising as a poor or very poor idea. Of an independent random sample of 310 consumers, 24.2% had this view.[34] Find a 95% confidence interval for the difference between the two population proportions with this view of hospital advertising.

---

[31] P. Brown, H. Y. Izan, and A. L. Loh, "Fixed asset revaluations and managerial incentives," *Abacus, 28* (1992), 36–57.

[32] R. T. Peterson, "Forecasting practices in retail industry," *Journal of Business Forecasting Methods and Systems, 12*, no. 1 (1993), 11–14. We will discuss regression in Chapters 12–14.

[33] W. R. Swinyard, F. W. Langrehr, and S. M. Smith, "The appeal of retailing as a career: a decade later," *Journal of Retailing, 67* (1991), 451–65.

[34] J. A. Bell and C. R. Vitaska, "Who likes hospital advertising—consumer or physician?" *Journal of Health Care Marketing, 12*, no. 2 (1992), 2–7.

46. A random sample of 100 men contained sixty-one in favor of a state constitutional amendment to retard the rate of growth of property taxes. An independent random sample of 100 women contained fifty-four in favor of this amendment. The confidence interval

$$.04 < p_X - p_Y < .10$$

was calculated for the difference between the population proportions. What is the probability content of this interval?

47. Supermarket shoppers were observed, and questioned immediately after putting an item in the cart. Of a random sample of 570 choosing a product at the regular price, 308 claimed to check price at the point of choice. Of an independent random sample of 232 choosing a product at a special price, 157 made this claim.[35] Find a 90% confidence interval for the difference between the two population proportions.

8.9 ESTIMATING THE SAMPLE SIZE

So far, we have developed methods for finding confidence intervals for a population parameter on the basis of the information contained in a given sample. Following such a process, an investigator may believe that the resulting confidence interval is too wide, reflecting an undesirable amount of uncertainty about the parameter being estimated. Typically, the only way to obtain a narrower interval with a given probability content is to take a larger sample.

In some circumstances, the investigator may be able to fix in advance the width of the confidence interval, choosing a sample size big enough to guarantee that width. In this section, we show how the sample size can be chosen in this way for two interval estimation problems. Similar procedures can be employed to solve other problems.

INTERVALS FOR THE MEAN OF A NORMAL DISTRIBUTION:
POPULATION VARIANCE KNOWN

If a random sample of n observations is taken from a normal population with mean μ and known variance σ^2, it was seen in Section 8.2 that a $100(1 - \alpha)\%$ confidence interval for the population mean is provided by

$$\bar{x} - \frac{z_{\alpha/2}\sigma}{\sqrt{n}} < \mu < \bar{x} + \frac{z_{\alpha/2}\sigma}{\sqrt{n}}$$

where $\bar{x}$ is the observed sample mean and $z_{\alpha/2}$ is the appropriate cutoff point of the standard normal distribution. This interval is centered on the sample mean and extends a distance

$$L = \frac{z_{\alpha/2}\sigma}{\sqrt{n}} \tag{8.9.1}$$

---

[35] P. R. Dickson and A. G. Sawyer, "The price knowledge and search of supermarket shoppers," *Journal of Marketing, 54,* no. 3 (1990), 42–53.

on each side of the sample mean, so that L is half the width of the interval. Suppose, now, that the investigator wants to fix L in advance. From Eq. (8.9.1) we have

$$\sqrt{n} = \frac{z_{\alpha/2}\sigma}{L}$$

and by squaring both sides of this equation, we obtain

$$n = \frac{z_{\alpha/2}^2 \sigma^2}{L^2}$$

This choice of the sample size ensures that the confidence interval extends a distance L on each side of the sample mean.

Sample Size for Confidence Intervals for the Mean of a Normal Distribution: Population Variance Known

Suppose that we take a random sample from a normal population with known variance σ^2. Then a $100(1 - \alpha)\%$ confidence interval for the population mean extends a distance L on each side of the sample mean, if the number of observations is

$$n = \frac{z_{\alpha/2}^2 \sigma^2}{L^2}$$

where $z_{\alpha/2}$ is the number for which

$$P(Z > z_{\alpha/2}) = \frac{\alpha}{2}$$

and Z has a standard normal distribution.

Of course, the number of sample observations must necessarily be an integer. If the number n resulting from the sample size formula is not an integer, we *round up* to the next whole number in order to guarantee that our confidence interval does not exceed the required width.

EXAMPLE 8.14

The lengths of metal rods produced by an industrial process are normally distributed with standard deviation 1.8 millimeters. Based on a random sample of nine observations from this population, the 99% confidence interval

$$194.65 < \mu < 197.75$$

was found for the population mean length. Suppose that a production manager believes that the interval is too wide for practical use and instead requires a 99% confidence interval extending no further than .50 mm on each side of the sample mean. How large a sample is needed to achieve such an interval?

We have

$$L = .50 \qquad \sigma = 1.8 \qquad z_{\alpha/2} = z_{.005} = 2.575$$

Hence, the required sample size is

$$n = \frac{z_{\alpha/2}^2 \sigma^2}{L^2}$$

$$= \frac{(2.575)^2 (1.8)^2}{(.5)^2} = 85.93$$

Therefore, to satisfy the manager's requirement, a sample of at least eighty-six observations is needed. This large increase in the sample size represents the additional cost of achieving the higher precision in the estimate of the true mean, reflected in a narrower confidence interval.

INTERVALS FOR THE POPULATION PROPORTION

In Section 8.5, we saw that based on a random sample of n observations, a $100(1 - \alpha)\%$ confidence interval for the population proportion p is given by

$$\hat{p}_x - z_{\alpha/2} \sqrt{\frac{\hat{p}_x (1 - \hat{p}_x)}{n}} < p < \hat{p}_x + z_{\alpha/2} \sqrt{\frac{\hat{p}_x (1 - \hat{p}_x)}{n}}$$

where $\hat{p}_x$ is the observed sample proportion. This interval is centered on the sample proportion and extends a distance

$$L = z_{\alpha/2} \sqrt{\frac{\hat{p}_x (1 - \hat{p}_x)}{n}}$$

on each side of the sample proportion. Now, this result cannot be used directly to determine the sample size necessary to obtain a confidence interval of some specified width, since it involves the sample proportion, which will not be known at the outset. However, whatever the outcome, $\hat{p}_x (1 - \hat{p}_x)$ cannot be bigger than .25, its value when the sample proportion is .5. Thus, the largest possible value for L is L_*, given by

$$L_* = z_{\alpha/2} \sqrt{\frac{.25}{n}} = \frac{.5 z_{\alpha/2}}{\sqrt{n}} \qquad (8.9.2)$$

Suppose, then, that an investigator wants to choose a sufficiently large sample size to *guarantee* that the confidence interval extends no more than L_* on each side of the sample proportion. From Eq. (8.9.2), we have

$$\sqrt{n} = \frac{.5 z_{\alpha/2}}{L_*}$$

and squaring yields

$$n = \frac{.25 z_{\alpha/2}^2}{L_*^2}$$

This provides the required sample size.

> **Sample Size for Confidence Intervals for the Population Proportion**
>
> Suppose that we take a random sample from a population. Then a $100(1 - \alpha)\%$ confidence interval for the population proportion, extending a distance of *at most* L_* on each side of the sample proportion, can be guaranteed if the number of sample observations is
>
> $$n = \frac{.25z_{\alpha/2}^2}{L_*^2}$$

EXAMPLE 8.15

In Example 8.7, we calculated a 95% confidence interval for the proportion of company recruiters who viewed grades as very important in the consideration of a candidate. Based on 142 observations, the interval obtained was

$$.533 < p < .693$$

Suppose, instead, we want to ensure that a 95% confidence interval for the population proportion extends no further than .06 on each side of the sample proportion. How large a sample must be taken?

We have

$$L_* = .06 \qquad \text{and} \qquad z_{\alpha/2} = z_{.025} = 1.96$$

Thus, the number of sample observations needed is

$$n = \frac{.25z_{\alpha/2}^2}{L_*^2} = \frac{.25(1.96)^2}{(.06)^2} = 266.78$$

To be sure of achieving this narrower confidence interval, we see that a minimum of 267 sample observations is required.

MEDIA REPORTS OF OPINION SURVEYS

The media frequently report the results of surveys of the opinions of the population, or some subset of the population, on issues of current interest. Typically these reports give estimates of the percentage of population members holding particular views. These reports often end with a statement like: "There is a plus or minus 3% sampling error," or "The poll has a 3% margin of error." Although not explicitly stated, the "sampling error" or "margin of error" refers to the width of 95% confidence intervals. Specifically, these intervals are the sample percentage, plus or minus the advertised sampling error or margin of error; that is, in our notation, the number L_*, expressed as a percentage.

To illustrate, an opinion survey during the 1992 presidential election campaign reported the views of a sample of 1,065 U.S. citizens of voting age. The poll was said to have "a 3% margin of error." The implication is that a 95% confidence interval for the population percentage holding a particular opinion is the sample percentage plus or minus at most 3%. To see this, we have from Eq. (8.9.2)

$$L_* = \frac{.5z_{\alpha/2}}{\sqrt{n}} = \frac{(.5)(1.96)}{\sqrt{1,065}} = .030$$

or, in percentages, 3.0%. In practice, the sample size was chosen to achieve this result.

EXERCISES

48. Using the information in Exercise 1, find the number of sample observations necessary to obtain a 95% confidence interval for the population mean grade point average extending .05 point on each side of the sample mean.

49. Using the information in Exercise 2, find the sample size needed so that a 90% confidence interval for the population mean weight of bricks extends an amount .01 on each side of the sample mean.

50. Using the information in Exercise 3, find the number of sample observations required for a 99% confidence interval for the population mean amount of impurities to extend .5 gram on each side of the sample mean.

51. A research group wants to estimate the proportion of consumers who claim, all else equal, that they would purchase a domestically made product rather than a foreign competitor. It is required that a 95% confidence interval for the population proportion extends at most .04 on either side of the sample proportion. How large a sample is needed to be sure this requirement is met?

52. A politician wants to estimate the proportion of constituents favoring a controversial piece of proposed legislation. Suppose that a 99% confidence interval that extends at most .05 on each side of the sample proportion is required. How many sample observations are needed?

53. An investigator wants to compare two population proportions and intends to take independent random samples of the same size from each population. She wants to be sure that a 90% confidence interval for the difference between the two population proportions extends no further than .05 on each side of the difference between the sample proportions. How large a sample should she take from each population?

REVIEW EXERCISES

54. Based on independent random samples from the two populations, an investigator found a 95% confidence interval for the difference between mean fuel consumption for X-cars and for Y-cars, running from .6 to 1.9 miles per gallon. Does this imply that the probability is .95 that the true difference in mean fuel consumption lies between .6 and 1.9 miles per gallon? If not, provide a valid interpretation of the interval estimate.

55. A brewing company knows that the quantities of beer in its cans have a normal distribution with standard deviation .2 ounce.

    (a) A random sample of twenty-five cans was taken, and using the sample results, a statistician found a confidence interval for the population mean ranging from 11.98 ounces to 12.12 ounces. What is the level of confidence associated with this interval?

    (b) A manager of the brewing company asserts that he requires a 99% confidence interval for the population mean extending at most .07 ounce on either side of the sample mean. How many sample observations are needed to achieve this objective?

56. A random sample of 595 packaging professionals was asked to assess on a scale from one (completely unethical) to seven (completely ethical) the practice of packaging a store brand to closely resemble a national brand.[36] The sample mean response was 3.38 and the sample standard deviation was 1.80.

    (a) Find a 90% confidence interval for the population mean.

    (b) Without doing the calculations, state whether a 99% confidence interval for the population mean would be wider than, narrower than, or the same as the interval found in (a).

---

[36] P. F. Bone and R. J. Corey, "Ethical dilemmas in packaging: beliefs of packaging professionals," *Journal of Macromarketing*, *12*, no. 1 (1992), 45–54.

57. The numbers of requests for seats on a particular airline flight for midweek days can be assumed to be normally distributed. A random sample of eighty-one observations on numbers of requests for this flight was taken. The sample mean number of requests for seats was 112, and the sample standard deviation was 36. Also, of these eighty-one flights, thirty arrived at their destination more than 15 minutes late.

(a) Find a 95% confidence interval for the population mean number of requests for seats on this flight.

(b) Find a 95% confidence interval for the population variance of number of requests for seats.

(c) Find a 95% confidence interval for the population proportion of all such flights arriving more than 15 minutes late at their destination.

58. A random sample of sixteen tires of a particular brand found a sample mean of 32.0 thousand miles for lifetime, and a sample standard deviation of 6.4 thousand miles. Assume that the population distribution is normal.

(a) Find a 90% confidence interval for the population mean, in thousands of miles.

(b) Find a 90% confidence interval for the population standard deviation, in thousands of miles.

59. Suppose that time spent, in hours, by students studying for a test has a normal distribution. A random sample of six students found the following results for hours spent studying

$$12.2 \qquad 18.4 \qquad 23.1 \qquad 11.7 \qquad 8.2 \qquad 24.0$$

(a) Find the sample mean and sample variance.

(b) Find a 99% confidence interval for the population mean.

(c) Find a 99% confidence interval for the population variance.

(d) Without doing the calculations, state whether a 90% confidence interval for the population mean would be wider than or narrower than that found in (b).

60. (a) Explain the relevance of the central limit theorem to interval estimation for a population mean.

(b) In Section 8.7, we discussed two different procedures for finding confidence intervals for the difference between population means. Explain why two different procedures are needed, and provide realistic examples where each would be appropriate.

61. In order to estimate the mean value of the purchases of card holders in a month, a credit card company takes a random sample of twelve monthly statements and obtains the following amounts in dollars:

91.21	98.26	143.62	65.93	95.08	159.11
34.27	127.26	211.87	53.91	139.53	87.80

Assuming that the population distribution is normal, find a 90% confidence interval for the mean monthly value of purchases of all card holders.

62. In a random sample of 1,158 newly promoted executives, 47.9% rated a statistics course as very important or somewhat important as part of the preparation for a career in general management.[37]

(a) Find a 99% confidence interval for the population proportion of all newly promoted executives holding this view.

(b) Based on the sample information, a statistician computed a confidence interval for the population proportion running from .458 to .500. What is the probability content of this interval?

---

[37] If you don't believe this, see H. W. Hildebrandt, F. A. Bond, E. L. Miller, and A. W. Swinyard, "An executive appraisal of courses which best prepare one for general management," *Journal of Business Communication*, *19*, no. 1, (1982), 5–15.

63. Of a random sample of 177 people who claimed to be able to correctly identify the official credit card sponsor of the 1988 Calgary Winter Olympic Games, 106 correctly nominated Visa.[38] Find a 90% confidence interval for the population proportion of those making this claim who could in fact do so.

64. Of a random sample of 113 American consumers, 57 claimed to own an American-made television set.[39]

    (a) Find a 95% confidence interval for the population proportion of all American consumers who would make this claim.

    (b) Without doing the calculations, state whether a 90% confidence interval for the population proportion would be wider than, narrower than, or the same as the interval found in (a).

65. Of a random sample of 87 firms with employee stock ownership plans, 54 said that the primary motivation for setting up such a plan was tax-related.[40]

    (a) Find a 90% confidence interval for the population proportion of all such firms with this primary motivation.

    (b) Without doing the calculations, state whether a 95% confidence interval for the population proportion would be wider than, narrower than, or the same as the interval found in (a).

66. Of a random sample of 151 marketing executives in consumer goods manufacturing, 76.0% said that brand identification held by incumbents was an important or extremely important barrier to entering a new market.[41] Based on this information a statistician computed, for the population proportion with this view, the confidence interval

$$.720 < p < .800$$

Find the probability content of this interval.

67. The performances of a random sample of ten stocks traded on the New York Stock Exchange were examined. The following figures are the rates of returns for these stocks over the last year.

12.61	8.20	16.28	9.73	3.10
13.12	7.20	6.35	−1.89	4.20

    (a) Find a 95% confidence interval for the population standard deviation, and state any assumptions that you have made.

    (b) Without doing the calculations, state whether a 99% confidence interval for the population standard deviation would be narrower or wider than that found in part (a).

68. A random sample of twelve middle managers was sent to an intensive business school summer session on modern techniques. The job performance appraisal scores given by their immediate superiors in the year before and the year after this session are shown in the accompanying table. Stating any assumptions you need to make, find a 95% confidence interval for the difference between the population mean appraisal scores before and after attendance at this business school summer session.

[38] Reported in D. M. Sandler and D. Shani, "Olympic sponsorship versus ambush marketing: Who gets the gold?" *Journal of Advertising Research*, 29, no. 4 (1989), 9–14.

[39] G. A. Pitman and S. T. Choe, "Attitudinal variations toward Japanese investment in the United States," *S.A.M. Advanced Management Journal*, 54, no. 3 (1989), 15–18.

[40] S. B. Block, "The advantages and disadvantages of ESOPs: A long-range analysis," *Journal of Small Business Management*, 29, no. 1 (1991), 15–21.

[41] F. Karakaya and M. J. Stahl, "Underlying dimensions of barriers to market entry in consumer goods markets," *Journal of Academy of Marketing Science*, 20 (1992), 275–78.

BEFORE	69	54	82	67	60	73
AFTER	73	50	83	78	56	74
BEFORE	75	78	64	72	70	63
AFTER	74	87	69	72	77	75

69. Candidates for employment in a large corporation must take a written aptitude test and complete an interview with a personnel manager. After the interview, the personnel manager grades each candidate on a scale from 0 to 100. To check the consistency, in the aggregate, of the scores of personnel managers, a random sample of ten pairs of candidates was selected. The pairing was arranged so that within each pair, the two candidates obtained identical scores on the written aptitude test. Candidates in each pair were then interviewed by one of two personnel managers, John Doe and Jean Ray. The grades awarded following these interviews are shown in the accompanying table.

JOHN DOE	80	65	87	64	73	78	83	91	84	83
JEAN RAY	74	63	91	65	64	71	69	90	79	87

(a) Stating any assumptions that you have made, find a 90% confidence interval for the difference between the population mean scores awarded by Doe and Ray.

(b) Without doing the calculations, state whether a 99% confidence interval for the difference in the population means would be narrower or wider than that found in part (a).

70. A random sample of ten department store credit accounts of customers who had these accounts for over a year showed the following charges (in dollars) at the end of a month:

58.36   43.97   65.18   62.39   17.97

47.62   63.21   75.91   51.70   18.23

For an independent random sample of eight new credit customers, charges at the end of the same month were as follows:

21.72   43.81   29.21   27.96   37.83   23.64   16.25   31.93

Stating carefully any assumptions you make, find a 90% confidence interval for the difference between the two population means.

71. A random sample of eight presidents of manufacturing corporations yielded the following results for number of months in the position:

96   71   144   62   31   18   56   92

For an independent random sample of six bank presidents, the corresponding figures were as follows:

71   173   94   111   135   87

Stating carefully any assumptions you make, find a 95% confidence interval for the difference between the two population means.

72. Samples of patients were asked to assess satisfaction with health care systems on a scale from one (very satisfied) to four (very dissatisfied).[42] For a random sample of 879 health maintenance organization (H.M.O.) members, the mean satisfaction level was 1.48, and the sample standard deviation was .68. For an independent random sample of 801 non-H.M.O. members, the mean satisfaction level was 1.86 and the sample standard deviation

---

[42] A. L. Dolinsky and R. K. Caputo, "The role of health care attributes and demographic characteristics in the determination of health care satisfaction," *Journal of Health Care Marketing*, *10*, no. 4 (1990), 31–39.

was .80. Find a 95% confidence interval for the difference between the two population means.

73. Of a random sample of 569 males in introductory college accounting classes, 90 dropped the class. Of an independent random sample of 517 females in these classes, 85 dropped the class.[43] Find a 90% confidence interval for the difference in the population proportions of males and females who drop introductory college accounting classes.

74. Of a random sample of 69 Canadian industrial firms, 43 did market research in-house. Of an independent random sample of 69 Canadian consumer goods firms, 30 did market research in-house.[44] Find a 95% confidence interval for the difference between the population proportions of these two types of firms that do market research in-house.

75. Samples of Small Business Center clients considering starting a business were questioned. Of a random sample of 94 males, 50 received assistance in business planning. Of an independent random sample of 68 females, 40 received assistance in business planning.[45] Find a 99% confidence interval for the difference between the population proportion of male and female clients who received assistance in business planning.

76. In Exercise 64, we found a confidence interval for the proportion of American consumers who believe they own an American-made television set. How many sample observations would be needed to be sure that a 95% confidence interval for the population proportion extends no more than .05 on each side of the sample proportion?

[43] V. L. Carpenter, S. Friar, and M. G. Lipe, "Evidence on the performance of accounting students: race, gender, and expectations," *Issues in Accounting Education*, 8 (1993), 1–17.

[44] M. L. Ripley, "Why industrial advertising is often done in-house," *Industrial Marketing Management*, 21 (1992), 331–34.

[45] J. J. Chrisman, A. L. Carsrud, J. DeCastro, and L. Herron, "A comparison of assistance needs of male and female pre-venture entrepreneurs," *Journal of Business Venturing*, 5 (1990), 235–48.

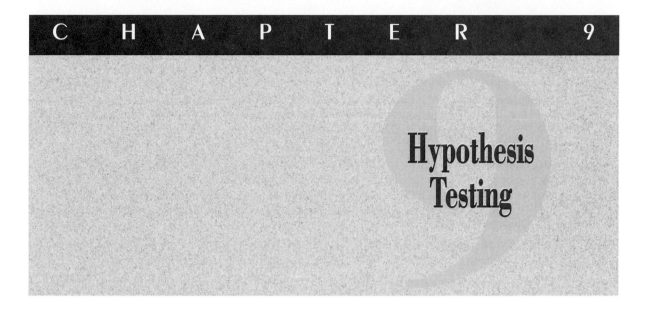

Hypothesis Testing

9.1 CONCEPTS OF HYPOTHESIS TESTING

When a sample is drawn from a population, the evidence obtained can be used to make inferential statements about the characteristics of the population. As we have seen, one possibility is to estimate the unknown population parameters through the calculation of point estimates or confidence intervals. Alternatively, the sample information can be employed to assess the validity of some conjecture, or **hypothesis,** that an investigator has formed about the population. Consider the following examples of situations of this kind.

1. A manufacturer who produces boxes of cereal claims that, on average, the contents weigh at least 20 ounces. To check this claim, the contents of a random sample of boxes can be weighed, and an inference can be based on the sample results.

2. A company receiving a large shipment of parts may want to accept delivery only if no more than 5% of the parts are defective. The decision on whether to take delivery might be based on a check of a random sample of these parts.

3. An instructor is interested in the value of regularly administered quizzes in a statistics course. She uses these quizzes in one section of the course but not in another. At the end of the course, she compares the average performances of students in the two sections on the final examination to check her hypothesis that the quizzes raise average performance.

4. A political scientist wants to know if a tax reform proposal appeals equally to men and women. To check if this is so, he obtains the opinions of randomly selected samples of males and females.

The examples given here have a common theme. A hypothesis is formed about some population, and conclusions about the merits of this hypothesis are to be based on sample information. In this section, we introduce a general framework for approaching such problems. Specific procedures are then developed in the following sections.

To keep our discussion quite general, let us denote the population parameter of interest (for example, the population mean, variance, or proportion) by θ. Suppose that some hypothesis has been formed about this parameter and that this hypothesis will be believed unless sufficient contrary evidence is produced. This can be thought of as a *maintained hypothesis*. In the language of statistical hypothesis testing, it is called a **null hypothesis.** For example, we might, in the absence of evidence to dispute it, believe the manufacturer's claim that, on average, the contents of its boxes of cereal weigh at least 20 ounces. When sample information is collected, this hypothesis is put in jeopardy, or *tested*. If the hypothesis is not true, then some alternative must be true, and in carrying out a hypothesis test, the investigator formulates an **alternative hypothesis** against which the null hypothesis is tested. For the cereal manufacturer, we could test the null hypothesis that the mean contents weight is at least 20 ounces against the alternative hypothesis that the mean weight is less than 20 ounces. The null hypothesis will be denoted H_0 and the alternative hypothesis H_1.

A hypothesis, whether null or alternative, might specify just a single value, say θ_0, for the population parameter θ. In that case, the hypothesis is said to be **simple.** A convenient shorthand notation would read, for example

$$H_0: \theta = \theta_0$$

for "The null hypothesis is that the population parameter θ is equal to the specific value θ_0." For instance, the political scientist in our earlier example might begin his investigation with the simple null hypothesis that the difference between the proportions of men and women in the population who favor the tax reform proposal is 0.

A hypothesis may also specify a *range* of values for the unknown population parameter. Such a hypothesis is said to be **composite** and will hold true for more than one value of the population parameter. For instance, the null hypothesis that the mean weight of boxes of cereal is at least 20 ounces is composite. The hypothesis is true for *any* population mean weight greater than or equal to 20 ounces.

In many applications, a simple null hypothesis, say, $H_0: \theta = \theta_0$, is tested against a composite alternative. In some cases, only alternatives on one side of the null hypothesis are of interest. For example, we might want to test this null hypothesis against the alternative hypothesis that the true value of θ is bigger than θ_0, which we can write

$$H_1: \theta > \theta_0$$

Conversely, the alternative of interest might be

$$H_1: \theta < \theta_0$$

Such alternative hypotheses are called **one-sided alternatives.** Another possibility is that we want to test this simple null hypothesis against the very general alternative that the true value of θ is something other than θ_0, that is

$$H_1: \theta \neq \theta_0$$

This is referred to as a **two-sided alternative.**

The specification of appropriate null and alternative hypotheses is problem-dependent. To illustrate, we return to our earlier examples:

1. Let θ denote the population mean weight (in ounces) of cereal per box. The null hypothesis is that this mean is at least 20 ounces, so we have the composite null hypothesis

$$H_0: \theta \geq 20$$

The obvious alternative is that the true mean weight is less than 20 ounces, that is

$$H_1: \theta < 20$$

2. A company intends to accept delivery of parts unless it has evidence to suspect that more than 5% are defective. Let θ denote the population proportion of defectives. The null hypothesis here is that this proportion is at most .05, that is

$$H_0: \theta \leq .05$$

On the basis of sample information, this hypothesis is tested against the alternative

$$H_1: \theta > .05$$

The null hypothesis, then, is that the shipment of parts is of adequate quality overall, while the alternative is that it is not.

3. Suppose an instructor conjectures that the regular administration of quizzes in class makes no difference to the average scores on the final examination. Let θ denote the difference between the population mean scores for sections with and without regular quizzes. The null hypothesis is then the simple null hypothesis

$$H_0: \theta = 0$$

However, she may suspect the possibility that quizzes lead to an increase in average performance and thus would want to test the null hypothesis against the alternative hypothesis

$$H_1: \theta > 0$$

4. A political scientist might hold, as a working hypothesis, the view that the tax reform proposal is equally appealing to men and women. If θ is the difference between the two population proportions in favor of the proposal, then the null hypothesis is

$$H_0: \theta = 0$$

If the political scientist has no good reason to suspect that the bulk of support comes from one population rather than the other, this null hypothesis would be tested against the two-sided alternative hypothesis

$$H_1: \theta \neq 0$$

Having specified a null and alternative hypothesis and collected sample information, a decision concerning the null hypothesis must be made. The two possibilities are to **accept** the null hypothesis or to **reject** it in favor of the alternative. In order to reach one of these conclusions, some **decision rule,** based on the sample evidence, has to be formulated. In subsequent sections, we will discuss specific decision rules, noting for now only that their general form is often fairly obvious. Suppose, for instance, that a random sample of ten boxes of cereal is taken and their contents are weighed. If the sample mean weight is much less than 20 ounces, we might suspect the validity of the null hypothesis that the population mean is at least 20 ounces. The decision rule would then involve the rejection of this null hypothesis if the sample mean was "too low." Thus, in testing a null hypothesis about a population mean, it is plausible that our conclusion will be based on the value observed for the sample mean. All other things being equal, the greater the difference between the sample mean and the values postulated by the null hypothesis for the population mean, the more suspicious we would be of the truth of that hypothesis.

If all that is available is a sample from a population, then the population parameters will not be precisely known. Accordingly, it *cannot be known for sure* whether a null hypothesis is true or false. Therefore, whatever decision rule is adopted, there is some chance of reaching an erroneous conclusion about the population parameter of interest. In fact, as indicated in Table 9.1, either of two possible kinds of error could be made. There are two possible states of nature—either the null hypothesis is true or it is false. One error that could be made, called a **Type I error,** is the rejection of a true null hypothesis. If the decision rule is such that the probability of rejecting the null hypothesis when it is true is α, then α is said to be the **significance level** of the test. Since the null hypothesis must either be accepted or rejected, it follows that the probability of accepting the null hypothesis when it is true is $(1 - \alpha)$. The other possible error, called a **Type II error,** arises when a false null hypothesis is accepted. Suppose that for a particular decision rule, the probability of making such an error when the null hypothesis is false is denoted β. Then, the probability of rejecting a false null hypothesis is $(1 - \beta)$, which is called the **power** of the test.

We will illustrate these ideas by reference to one of our earlier examples. Consider again the problem of the political scientist trying to determine whether a tax reform proposal appeals equally to men and women. The null hypothesis is that *in the population*, the proportion of men in favor of this proposal is the same as the proportion of women. This null hypothesis is to be tested against the alternative that the two population proportions differ. In order to test the null hypothesis, independent random samples of men and women are taken, and the views of the sample members are solicited. It is natural to base inference about the null hypothesis on the difference between the *sample proportions* of men and women in favor of the proposal. If this difference is large, the null hypothesis of equality of the *population proportions* would be rejected; otherwise, this null hypothesis would be accepted. Let $\hat{p}_x$ denote the sample proportion of men and $\hat{p}_y$ the sample proportion of women in favor of the tax reform proposal. Then, a possible decision rule is

$$\text{Reject } H_0 \text{ if} \qquad (\hat{p}_x - \hat{p}_y) > .05 \qquad \text{or} \qquad (\hat{p}_x - \hat{p}_y) < -.05$$

Now, suppose that, in fact, the null hypothesis that the two population proportions favoring the proposal are equal is true. It nevertheless could happen that the sample proportions differ by more than .05, so according to our decision rule, the null hypoth-

TABLE 9.1 States of nature and decisions on null hypothesis, with associated probabilities of making the decisions, given the particular states of nature

DECISIONS ON NULL HYPOTHESIS	STATES OF NATURE	
	NULL HYPOTHESIS TRUE	NULL HYPOTHESIS FALSE
ACCEPT	Correct decision Probability $= 1 - \alpha$	Type II error Probability $= \beta$
REJECT	Type I error Probability $= \alpha$ (α is called **significance level**)	Correct decision Probability $= 1 - \beta$ ($1 - \beta$ is called **power**)

esis would be rejected. In that case, a Type I error would have been made. The probability of this occurring (when the null hypothesis is true) is the significance level α. By contrast, suppose that the null hypothesis is false and that, in fact, the population proportions of men and women in favor of the proposal are not the same. It may still be the case that the two sample proportions differ by less than .05. Then, according to our decision rule, the null hypothesis would be accepted, and a Type II error would have been made. The probability of making such an error will depend on just how different the two population proportions are. We would be less likely, for given sample sizes, to accept the null hypothesis if 80% of men and 20% of women favored the proposal than if these percentages were 55% and 45%.

Ideally, of course, we would like to have the probabilities of both types of error be as small as possible. However, there is clearly a trade-off between the two. Once a sample has been taken, any adjustment to the decision rule that makes it less likely to reject a true null hypothesis will inevitably render it more likely to accept this hypothesis when it is false. Specifically, suppose that we want to test, on the basis of a random sample, the null hypothesis that the true mean weight of the contents of boxes of cereal is at least 20 ounces. Given a specific sample size—say, $n = 30$ observations—we might adopt the decision rule that the null hypothesis is rejected if the sample mean weight is less than 18.5 ounces. Now, it is easy to find a decision rule for which the probability of Type I error is lower. If we modify our decision rule to "Reject null hypothesis if sample mean weight is less than 18 ounces," this objective will have been achieved. However, there is a price to be paid. Using the modified decision rule, we will be more likely to accept the null hypothesis, whether it is true or false. Thus, in decreasing the Type I error probability, we have increased the Type II error probability. The only way of simultaneously lowering both error probabilities would be to obtain more information about the true population mean, by taking a larger sample. Typically what is done in practice is to fix at some desired level the probability of making a Type I error; that is, the significance level is fixed. This then determines the appropriate decision rule, which in turn determines the probability of a Type II error. This sequence is illustrated in Figure 9.1.

To illustrate this sequence, consider again the problem of testing, based on a sample of thirty observations, whether the true mean weight of boxes of cereal is at least 20 ounces. Given a decision rule, we could determine the probabilities of Type I and Type II errors associated with the test. However, in fact, we proceed by first fixing the Type I error probability. Suppose, for example, that we want to ensure that the probability of rejecting the null hypothesis when it is true is at most .05. We can do this by choosing an appropriate number, K, in the decision rule "Reject the null hypothesis if the sample mean is less than K ounces." (We will discuss in the next section how this can be done.) Once the number K is chosen, the Type II error probabilities can be computed, using procedures to be discussed in Section 9.9.

We have seen that since the decision rule is determined by the particular significance level chosen, the concept of power plays no direct part in the decision as to whether to reject a null hypothesis. However, calculations of power, stemming from

FIGURE 9.1 Consequences of fixing the significance level of a test

Investigator chooses significance level (probability of Type I error) → Decision rule is determined → Probability of Type II error follows

particular significance-level choices, provide the investigator with valuable information about the properties of the decision rule. Often an investigator has some flexibility in the choice of the number of sample observations to take. For a given significance level, the bigger the sample size, the higher will be the power of the test. In deciding how big the sample should be, the analyst must balance the benefits from increased power against the costs of acquiring additional sample information. Another important use of power calculations arises when we have available two or more possible tests for analyzing the same problem. If the decision rules associated with these tests are determined so that each has the same significance level, for a given sample size, then it is natural to prefer the procedure with the smallest probability of Type II error—that is, the procedure with the highest power.

In Sections 9.2–9.8, we show how, for given significance levels, decision rules can be formulated for some important classes of hypothesis-testing problems. We will return in Section 9.9 to a consideration of the power of a test.

For convenience, the new terminology introduced in this section is summarized in the box.

Some Hypothesis-Testing Terminology

NULL HYPOTHESIS (H_0): A maintained hypothesis that is held to be true unless sufficient evidence to the contrary is obtained

ALTERNATIVE HYPOTHESIS (H_1): A hypothesis against which the null hypothesis is tested and which will be held to be true if the null is held false

SIMPLE HYPOTHESIS: A hypothesis that specifies a single value for a population parameter of interest

COMPOSITE HYPOTHESIS: A hypothesis that specifies a range of values for a population parameter

ONE-SIDED ALTERNATIVE: An alternative hypothesis involving all possible values of a population parameter on either one side or the other of (that is, either greater than or less than) the value specified by a simple null hypothesis

TWO-SIDED ALTERNATIVE: An alternative hypothesis involving all possible values of a population parameter other than the value specified by a simple null hypothesis

HYPOTHESIS TEST DECISIONS: A *decision rule* is formulated, leading the investigator to either *accept* or *reject* the null hypothesis on the basis of sample evidence

TYPE I ERROR: The rejection of a true null hypothesis

TYPE II ERROR: The acceptance of a false null hypothesis

SIGNIFICANCE LEVEL: The probability of rejecting a null hypothesis that is true (This probability is sometimes expressed as a percentage, so a test of significance level α is referred to as a $100\alpha\%$-level test.)

POWER: The probability of rejecting a null hypothesis that is false

---

The terms *accept* and *reject* for the possible decisions about a null hypothesis are commonly used in formal summaries of the outcomes of particular tests. However, these terms do not adequately reflect the asymmetry of the status of the null and alternative hypotheses or the consequences of a procedure in which the significance level is fixed and the probability of a Type II error is not controlled. As we have already noted, the null hypothesis has the status of a maintained hypothesis—a hypothesis that will be held true *unless the data contain sufficient contrary evidence*. Moreover, in fixing a significance level, generally at some small probability, we are ensuring that the chance is low that a true null hypothesis will be rejected. In such a setup, we are not likely with only a modest amount of data to be in a position to reject a null hypothesis unless it is wildly in error. As we have seen, as the number of sample observations increases, so does the chance of our being able to detect a false null hypothesis. Thus, in "accepting" a null hypothesis, we are not necessarily saying a great deal in its favor. A more accurate, though more pedantic, statement of the position might be "The data available do not provide enough evidence for rejection of the null hypothesis, given that we want to fix at α the probability of rejecting a null hypothesis that is true." For this reason, some writers prefer the phrase "The null hypothesis is not rejected" rather than "The null hypothesis is accepted." We will continue to use "accept" as an efficient way of expressing this idea, but it is important that this interpretation of the phrase be kept in mind. The position is rather similar to that prevailing in a court of law, where the defendant is, at the outset, deemed innocent, and the burden is on the prosecution to present sufficiently strong contrary evidence to secure a verdict of guilty. In the classical hypothesis-testing framework, the null hypothesis is, in the same sense, initially held to be true. The burden of persuading us otherwise rests on the sample data.

In the following sections of this chapter, we will present tests of a number of specific hypotheses.

9.2 TESTS OF THE MEAN OF A NORMAL DISTRIBUTION: POPULATION VARIANCE KNOWN

We introduce the methodology of classical hypothesis testing by considering the case where a random sample of n observations, $X_1, X_2, \ldots, X_n$, from a normal distribution with mean μ and variance σ^2, is available. The objective is to test hypotheses about the unknown population mean. Initially it will be assumed that the population variance is known. Later we will see that this assumption and that of normality can be relaxed when the number of sample observations is large.

We begin with the problem of testing the simple null hypothesis that the population mean is equal to some specified value, μ_0. This hypothesis is denoted

$$H_0: \mu = \mu_0$$

Suppose that the alternative hypothesis of interest is that the population mean exceeds this specified value; that is

$$H_1: \mu > \mu_0$$

It is natural to base tests of the population mean on the sample mean $\overline{X}$. In particular, one would doubt the truth of the null hypothesis, as opposed to this alternative, if the observed sample mean was greatly in excess of μ_0. We require the format of a test with some preassigned significance level α. That is, we want a decision rule such that the probability of rejecting the null hypothesis, when it is in fact true, is α. The basis for such a test lies in the fact that the random variable

$$Z = \frac{\overline{X} - \mu}{\sigma/\sqrt{n}}$$

follows a standard normal distribution; that is, the sampling distribution of the sample mean is normal, with mean μ and standard deviation $\sigma/\sqrt{n}$. When the null hypothesis is true, μ is equal to μ_0, so the random variable

$$Z = \frac{\overline{X} - \mu_0}{\sigma/\sqrt{n}} \qquad (9.2.1)$$

then has a standard normal distribution. Now, the null hypothesis is to be rejected if the sample mean greatly exceeds the value μ_0 hypothesized for the population mean. Thus, H_0 will be rejected if a high value for the random variable (9.2.1) is observed. We want to fix at α the probability of rejecting the null hypothesis when it is true. As in Chapter 8, we denote by z_α the number for which

$$P(Z > z_\alpha) = \alpha$$

It then follows that when the null hypothesis is true, the probability that the random variable (9.2.1) is bigger than z_α is α. Hence, denoting the observed sample mean by $\bar{x}$, suppose that we adopt the following decision rule:

$$\text{Reject } H_0 \text{ if} \qquad \frac{\bar{x} - \mu_0}{\sigma/\sqrt{n}} > z_\alpha$$

Then, the probability of rejecting H_0 when it is true will be α, so α is the significance level of the test based on this decision rule. This situation is illustrated in Figure 9.2, which shows the sampling distribution of the random variable (9.2.1) when the null hypothesis is true through a graph of its probability density function. The figure shows the value z_α, which is such that the probability of its being exceeded, when the null hypothesis is true, is the significance level α of the test. It follows that the probability

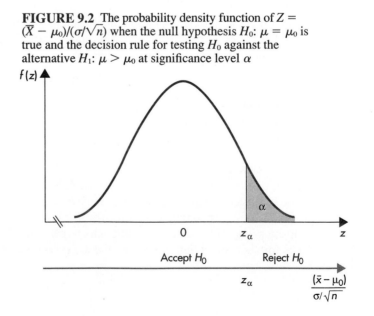

FIGURE 9.2 The probability density function of $Z = (\overline{X} - \mu_0)/(\sigma/\sqrt{n})$ when the null hypothesis H_0: $\mu = \mu_0$ is true and the decision rule for testing H_0 against the alternative H_1: $\mu > \mu_0$ at significance level α

of a sample result in the corresponding rejection region, shown as the shaded area in the figure, must be α when the null hypothesis is correct.

A Test of the Mean of a Normal Population: Population Variance Known

Suppose that we have a random sample of n observations from a normal population with mean μ and known variance σ^2. If the observed sample mean is $\bar{x}$, then a test with significance level α of the null hypothesis

$$H_0: \mu = \mu_0$$

against the alternative

$$H_1: \mu > \mu_0$$

is obtained from the decision rule

$$\text{Reject } H_0 \text{ if } \frac{\bar{x} - \mu_0}{\sigma/\sqrt{n}} > z_\alpha$$

where z_α is the number for which

$$P(Z > z_\alpha) = \alpha$$

and Z is a standard normal random variable.

EXAMPLE 9.1

When a process producing ball bearings is operating correctly, the weights of the ball bearings have a normal distribution with mean 5 ounces and standard deviation .1 ounce. An adjustment has been made to the process, and the plant manager suspects that this has raised the mean weight of ball bearings produced, leaving the standard deviation unchanged. A random sample of sixteen ball bearings is taken, and their mean weight is found to be 5.038 ounces. Test at significance levels .05 and .10 (that is, at 5% and 10% levels) the null hypothesis that the population mean weight is 5 ounces against the alternative that it is bigger.

Denoting by μ the population mean weight (in ounces), we want to test

$$H_0: \mu = \mu_0 = 5$$

against

$$H_1: \mu > 5$$

The decision rule is to reject H_0 in favor of H_1 if

$$\frac{\bar{x} - \mu_0}{\sigma/\sqrt{n}} > z_\alpha$$

From the statement of the example, we have

$$\bar{x} = 5.038 \qquad \mu_0 = 5 \qquad \sigma = .1 \qquad n = 16$$

so

$$\frac{\bar{x} - \mu_0}{\sigma/\sqrt{n}} = \frac{5.038 - 5}{.1/\sqrt{16}} = 1.52$$

For a 5%-level test, we find from Table 3 in the Appendix

$$z_{.05} = 1.645$$

Since 1.52 does not exceed 1.645, we fail to reject the null hypothesis at the 5% level of significance; that is, the null hypothesis is accepted at this significance level. In other words, if we use a test that ensures that the probability of rejecting the null hypothesis when it is in fact true is .05, the sample data do not contain enough evidence to allow rejection of that hypothesis.

For a 10%-level test, we have

$$z_{.10} = 1.28$$

Since 1.52 is bigger than 1.28, the null hypothesis is rejected at the 10% level of significance. To this extent, then, there is some evidence in the data to suggest that the true mean weight exceeds 5 ounces.

Let us pause to consider what is meant by the rejection of a null hypothesis. In Example 9.1, the hypothesis that the population mean weight is 5 ounces was rejected by a test with significance level .1. This certainly does not mean that we have *proved* that the true mean exceeds 5 ounces. Given only sample information, it will never be possible to be *certain* about a population parameter. Rather, we might view the data as having cast some doubt on the truth of the null hypothesis. If that hypothesis were true, then the observed value

$$\frac{\bar{x} - \mu_0}{\sigma/\sqrt{n}} = 1.52$$

would represent a single observation drawn from a standard normal distribution. In testing hypotheses, we are really asking how likely it would be to observe such an extreme value if the null hypothesis were in fact true. In Example 9.1, we saw that the probability of observing a value bigger than 1.28 is .1. Hence, in rejecting the null hypothesis, we are saying either that the null hypothesis is false or that we have observed an unlikely event—one that would occur only with the probability specified by the significance level. This is the sense in which the sample information has aroused doubt about the null hypothesis.

Notice that in Example 9.1, the null hypothesis was rejected at significance level .10 but was not rejected at the lower .05 level. In lowering the significance level, we are reducing the probability of rejecting a true null hypothesis and therefore modifying the decision rule to make it less likely that the null hypothesis will be rejected whether or not it is true. Obviously, the lower the significance level at which a null hypothesis can be rejected, the greater the doubt cast on its truth. Rather than testing hypotheses at preassigned levels of significance, investigators often determine the smallest level of significance at which a null hypothesis can be rejected.

Definition

The smallest significance level at which a null hypothesis can be rejected is called the **probability value,** or *p*-**value,** of the test.[1]

---

[1] In the last few years, it has become increasingly important to understand this concept. All modern statistical computer programs routinely produce *p*-values, and indeed some pocket calculators allow their computation. In consequence, *p*-values are now very frequently reported in applied studies.

In Example 9.1, we found

$$\frac{\bar{x} - \mu_0}{\sigma/\sqrt{n}} = 1.52$$

Therefore, according to our decision rule, the null hypothesis is rejected for any significance level α for which z_α is less than 1.52. From Table 3 in the Appendix, we find that when z_α is 1.52, α is equal to .0643. This, then, is the **p-value** of the test. The implication is that the null hypothesis can be rejected at all levels of significance higher than 6.43%. This is illustrated in Figure 9.3, which shows the correspondence between the significance level of the test, α, and the corresponding value z_α, which enters the decision rule.

Suppose that in place of the simple null hypothesis, we had wanted to test the composite null hypothesis

$$H_0: \mu \leq \mu_0$$

against the alternative

$$H_1: \mu > \mu_0$$

at significance level α. For the decision rule developed in the case of the simple null hypothesis, we saw that if the population mean is precisely μ_0, then the probability of rejecting the null hypothesis is α. For this same decision rule, if the true population mean is anything less than μ_0, we would be even less likely to reject the null hypothesis. Hence, use of this decision rule in the present context *guarantees* a probability of *at most* α of rejecting the composite null hypothesis when it is true.

A Test of the Mean of a Normal Distribution (Variance Known): Composite Null and Alternative Hypotheses

The appropriate procedure for testing, at significance level α, the null hypothesis

$$H_0: \mu \leq \mu_0$$

against the alternative hypothesis

$$H_1: \mu > \mu_0$$

is precisely the same as when the null hypothesis is $H_0: \mu = \mu_0$.

Consider now the problem of testing the simple null hypothesis

FIGURE 9.3 Rejection regions for testing $H_0: \mu = \mu_0$ against $H_1: \mu > \mu_0$ for significance levels .10, .0643, and .05

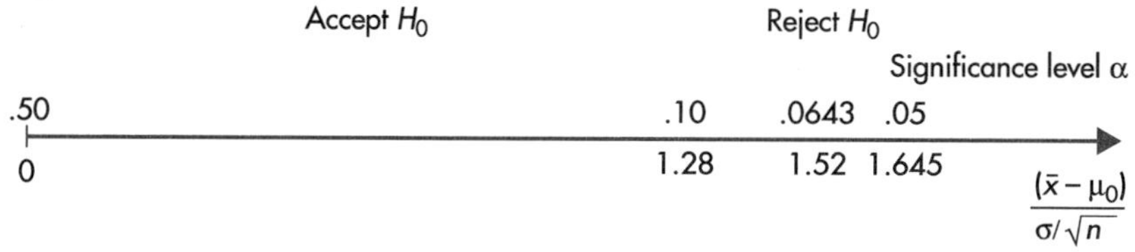

$$H_0: \mu = \mu_0$$

against the composite alternative that the true mean is *less than* μ_0, that is

$$H_1: \mu < \mu_0$$

In this circumstance, doubt would be cast on the null hypothesis if the sample mean were a good deal *lower* than the hypothesized population mean. Once again, if the null hypothesis were true, the random variable of (9.2.1) would follow a standard normal distribution. To achieve a test with significance level α, we only need to note that

$$P(Z < -z_\alpha) = \alpha$$

if Z is a standard normal random variable. Hence, if $\bar{x}$ is the observed sample mean, the appropriate decision rule is

$$\text{Reject } H_0 \text{ if } \qquad \frac{\bar{x} - \mu_0}{\sigma/\sqrt{n}} < -z_\alpha$$

This is illustrated in Figure 9.4, which should be compared with Figure 9.2. Clearly, the former is simply the mirror image of the latter.

Using an analogous argument to that developed earlier, we can see that this decision rule continues to be appropriate if in place of the simple null hypothesis, we have the composite hypothesis

$$H_0: \mu \geq \mu_0$$

with the same alternative hypothesis.

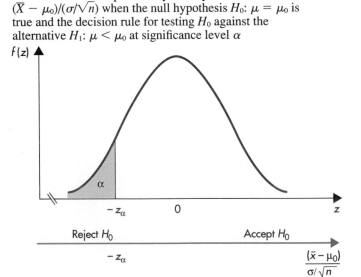

FIGURE 9.4 The probability density function of $Z = (\bar{X} - \mu_0)/(\sigma/\sqrt{n})$ when the null hypothesis $H_0: \mu = \mu_0$ is true and the decision rule for testing H_0 against the alternative $H_1: \mu < \mu_0$ at significance level α

Tests of the Mean of a Normal Distribution: Population Variance Known

Suppose that we have a random sample of n observations from a normal population with mean μ and known variance σ^2. If the observed sample mean is $\bar{x}$, a test with significance level α of either null hypothesis

$$H_0: \mu = \mu_0 \qquad \text{or} \qquad H_0: \mu \geq \mu_0$$

against the alternative

$$H_1: \mu < \mu_0$$

is obtained from the decision rule

$$\text{Reject } H_0 \text{ if} \qquad \frac{\bar{x} - \mu_0}{\sigma/\sqrt{n}} < -z_\alpha$$

We now consider the test of the null hypothesis

$$H_0: \mu = \mu_0$$

against the two-sided alternative

$$H_1: \mu \neq \mu_0$$

It is assumed here that the investigator has no strong reason for suspecting departures on one side rather than the other side of the hypothesized population mean. The null hypothesis would then be doubted if the observed sample mean were either much higher *or* much lower than μ_0. Once again, if the null hypothesis is true, the random variable (9.2.1) has a standard normal distribution. To obtain a test with significance level α, note that under the null hypothesis

$$P(Z > z_{\alpha/2}) = \frac{\alpha}{2} \qquad \text{and} \qquad P(Z < -z_{\alpha/2}) = \frac{\alpha}{2}$$

Hence, the probability that Z either exceeds $z_{\alpha/2}$ or is less than $-z_{\alpha/2}$ is α. It therefore follows that a test of level α is obtained from the decision rule

$$\text{Reject } H_0 \text{ if } \frac{\bar{x} - \mu_0}{\sigma/\sqrt{n}} \text{ is either bigger than } z_{\alpha/2} \text{ or less than } -z_{\alpha/2}$$

This is illustrated in Figure 9.5, from which we see that the region of sample outcomes for which the null hypothesis is rejected is divided into two parts. The upper part of the region corresponds to observed values of the sample mean greatly in excess of the hypothesized population mean, and the lower part corresponds to values of the sample mean that are substantially below μ_0.

Test for the Mean of a Normal Distribution Against Two-Sided Alternative: Population Variance Known

Suppose that we have a random sample of n observations from a normal population with mean μ and known variance σ^2. If the observed sample mean is $\bar{x}$, then a test with significance level α of the null hypothesis

---

$$H_0: \mu = \mu_0$$

against the two-sided alternative

$$H_1: \mu \neq \mu_0$$

is obtained from the decision rule

Reject H_0 if $\quad \dfrac{\bar{x} - \mu_0}{\sigma/\sqrt{n}} > z_{\alpha/2} \quad$ or $\quad \dfrac{\bar{x} - \mu_0}{\sigma/\sqrt{n}} < -z_{\alpha/2}$

The reader has probably noticed the similarity between the developments of procedures for determining confidence intervals and testing hypotheses. A review of the material in Section 8.2 will clarify the relationship: The null hypothesis $H_0: \mu = \mu_0$ is rejected against the two-sided alternative $H_1: \mu \neq \mu_0$ at significance level α *if and only if* the $100(1 - \alpha)\%$ confidence interval for μ does not contain μ_0. This relationship holds for most such tests developed in subsequent sections of this chapter.

EXAMPLE
9.2

A drill, as part of an assembly-line operation, is used to drill holes in sheet metal. When the drill is functioning properly, the diameters of these holes have a normal distribution with mean 2 inches and standard deviation .06 inch. Periodically, to check that the drill is functioning properly, the diameters of a random sample of holes are measured. Assume that the standard deviation does not vary. A random sample of nine measurements yielded mean diameter 1.95 inches. Test the null hypothesis that the population mean is 2 inches against the alternative that it is not. Use a 5% significance level, and also find the *p*-value of the test.

Let μ denote the population mean diameter (in inches). Then, we require to test

$$H_0: \mu = \mu_0 = 2$$

against

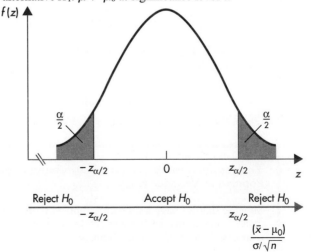

FIGURE 9.5 The probability density function of $Z = (\bar{X} - \mu_0)/(\sigma/\sqrt{n})$ when the null hypothesis $H_0: \mu = \mu_0$ is true and the decision rule for testing H_0 against the alternative $H_1: \mu \neq \mu_0$ at significance level α

$$H_1: \mu \neq 2$$

The decision rule is to reject H_0 in favor of H_1 if

$$\frac{\bar{x} - \mu_0}{\sigma/\sqrt{n}} > z_{\alpha/2} \qquad \text{or} \qquad \frac{\bar{x} - \mu_0}{\sigma/\sqrt{n}} < -z_{\alpha/2}$$

We have

$$\bar{x} = 1.95 \qquad \mu_0 = 2 \qquad \sigma = .06 \qquad n = 9$$

and so

$$\frac{\bar{x} - \mu_0}{\sigma/\sqrt{n}} = \frac{1.95 - 2}{.06/\sqrt{9}} = -2.50$$

For a 5%-level test, $\alpha = .05$, and $z_{\alpha/2} = z_{.025} = 1.96$. Then, since -2.50 is less than -1.96, the null hypothesis is rejected at the 5% significance level.

In fact, according to the decision rule, the null hypothesis will be rejected for any significance level α for which $-z_{\alpha/2}$ is bigger than -2.50. From Table 3 in the Appendix, we see that when $z_{\alpha/2}$ is 2.50, $\alpha/2$ is equal to .0062. Hence, $\alpha = .0124$. This is the p-value of the test, implying that the null hypothesis can be rejected against the two-sided alternative at any level of significance greater than 1.24%. This certainly casts substantial doubt on the hypothesis that the drill is functioning correctly. What we have found is that if the null hypothesis were true, the probability would be only .0124 of finding a sample mean this far or farther from two inches.

Until now we have dealt only with the (generally unrealistic) case where the population variance is known. However, if the available number of sample observations is large, the tests can readily be modified to deal with an important class of practical problems. As in Section 8.2, we are indebted to the central limit theorem, which allows us to conclude that for large samples, the sampling distribution of the sample mean will be approximately normal, even though the population distribution is not normal.

Tests for the Mean: Large Sample Sizes

Suppose that we have a random sample of n observations from a population with mean μ and variance σ^2. If the sample size n is large,[2] the test procedures developed for the case where the population variance is known can be employed when it is unknown, replacing σ^2 by the observed sample variance s_x^2. Moreover, these procedures remain approximately valid even if the population distribution is not normal.

EXAMPLE 9.3

A random sample of 541 consumers was asked to respond on a scale from one (strongly disagree) to five (strongly agree) to the assertion that a limit should be placed on the amount of punitive damages awarded for product liability.[3] The sample

---

[2] This approximation is generally satisfactory for samples of thirty or more observations.
[3] J. DeConinck and J. Kopf, "Consumers' attitudes toward product liability reform," *American Business Review*, 10, no. 2 (1992), 78–83.

mean response was 3.68 and the sample standard deviation was 1.21. Suppose that a population mean response of 3.75 or more is taken as broad general support for the assertion. Test the null hypothesis that the population mean is at least 3.75 against the alternative that it is less than 3.75.

We want to test the null hypothesis

$$H_0: \mu \geq \mu_0 = 3.75$$

against the alternative

$$H_1: \mu < 3.75$$

The decision rule is to reject H_0 in favor of H_1 if

$$\frac{\bar{x} - \mu_0}{s_x/\sqrt{n}} < -z_\alpha$$

Here we have

$$\bar{x} = 3.68 \qquad \mu_0 = 3.75 \qquad s_x = 1.21 \qquad n = 541$$

and hence

$$\frac{\bar{x} - \mu_0}{s_x/\sqrt{n}} = \frac{3.68 - 3.75}{1.21/\sqrt{541}} = -1.35$$

According to the decision rule, the null hypothesis is rejected for any significance level α for which $-z_\alpha$ is bigger than -1.35. From Table 3 of the Appendix, we see that when z_α is 1.35, α is equal to .0885. Therefore, the probability of observing a sample mean of 3.68 or less, if the population mean is 3.75, would be .0885. The null hypothesis can be rejected at significance levels above 8.85%, so there is moderately strong evidence against that hypothesis. The conclusion of the test is illustrated in Figure 9.6, which shows the distribution of the decision rule criterion when the popu-

FIGURE 9.6 Conclusion of the test in Example 9.3: the null hypothesis $H_0: \mu \geq \mu_0$ is rejected against the alternative $H_1: \mu < \mu_0$ at significance levels greater than .0885.

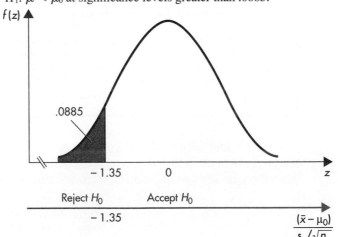

lation mean is 3.75. Also illustrated is the lower-tail area probability corresponding to the observed value, -1.35, of the test statistic.

9.3 TESTS OF THE MEAN OF A NORMAL DISTRIBUTION: POPULATION VARIANCE UNKNOWN

In this section, we again consider the problem where a random sample of n observations is taken from a normal population and it is required to test hypotheses about the population mean μ. However, the population variance is no longer assumed known. If the sample size is not large, the procedures discussed at the end of Section 9.2 are no longer appropriate. Nevertheless, valid tests can be derived, based on a result discussed in Sections 8.3 and 8.4. It was seen there that if the sample mean and variance are denoted $\overline{X}$ and $s_x{}^2$, the random variable

$$t_{n-1} = \frac{\overline{X} - \mu}{s_x/\sqrt{n}}$$

follows a Student's t distribution with $(n-1)$ degrees of freedom. Using precisely the line of argument adopted in Section 9.2, with the Student's t distribution now playing the same role as the standard normal distribution, we can obtain valid tests, as indicated in the box.

Tests of the Mean of a Normal Distribution: Population Variance Unknown

Suppose that we have a random sample of n observations from a normal population with mean μ. If the observed sample mean and standard deviation are $\overline{x}$ and s_x, then the following tests have significance level α:

(i) To test either null hypothesis

$$H_0: \mu = \mu_0 \qquad \text{or} \qquad H_0: \mu \leq \mu_0$$

against the alternative

$$H_1: \mu > \mu_0$$

the decision rule is

$$\text{Reject } H_0 \text{ if} \qquad \frac{\overline{x} - \mu_0}{s_x/\sqrt{n}} > t_{n-1,\alpha}$$

(ii) To test either null hypothesis

$$H_0: \mu = \mu_0 \qquad \text{or} \qquad H_0: \mu \geq \mu_0$$

against the alternative

$$H_1: \mu < \mu_0$$

the decision rule is

$$\text{Reject } H_0 \text{ if} \qquad \frac{\overline{x} - \mu_0}{s_x/\sqrt{n}} < -t_{n-1,\alpha}$$

(iii) To test the null hypothesis

$$H_0: \mu = \mu_0$$

against the two-sided alternative

$$H_1: \mu \neq \mu_0$$

the decision rule is

Reject H_0 if $\qquad \dfrac{\bar{x} - \mu_0}{s_x/\sqrt{n}} > t_{n-1,\alpha/2} \qquad$ or $\qquad \dfrac{\bar{x} - \mu_0}{s_x/\sqrt{n}} < -t_{n-1,\alpha/2}$

Here, $t_{n-1,\alpha}$ is the number for which

$$P(t_{n-1} > t_{n-1,\alpha}) = \alpha$$

where the random variable t_{n-1} follows a Student's t distribution with $(n-1)$ degrees of freedom.

Figure 9.7 illustrates the setup of the test against a two-sided alternative. The probability density function is now that of the Student's t distribution, and this figure is the analogue of Figure 9.5, which related to the case where the population variance was known. In an obvious way, tests against one-sided alternative hypotheses can be viewed pictorially in a manner analogous to Figures 9.2 and 9.4.

EXAMPLE 9.4

A retail chain knows that on average, sales in its stores are 20% higher in December than in November. For the current year, a random sample of six stores was selected. Their percentage December sales increases were found to be

$$19.2 \qquad 18.4 \qquad 19.8 \qquad 20.2 \qquad 20.4 \qquad 19.0$$

FIGURE 9.7 The probability density function of $t_{n-1} = \dfrac{(\bar{X} - \mu_0)}{s_x/\sqrt{n}}$ when the null hypothesis $H_0: \mu = \mu_0$ is true and the decision rule for testing H_0 against the alternative $H_1: \mu \neq \mu_0$ at significance level α

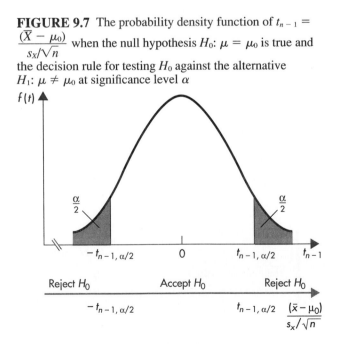

Assuming a normal population distribution, test the null hypothesis that the true mean percentage sales increase is 20, against the two-sided alternative, at the 10% significance level.

Letting μ denote the population mean percentage increase in sales in December, we want to test the null hypothesis

$$H_0: \mu = \mu_0 = 20$$

against the alternative

$$H_1: \mu \neq 20$$

The decision rule is to reject H_0 in favor of H_1 if

$$\frac{\bar{x} - \mu_0}{s_x/\sqrt{n}} > t_{n-1,\alpha/2} \qquad \text{or} \qquad \frac{\bar{x} - \mu_0}{s_x/\sqrt{n}} < -t_{n-1,\alpha/2}$$

The sample mean and variance are obtained by using the computations in the accompanying table.

	x_i	x_i^2
	19.2	368.64
	18.4	338.56
	19.8	392.04
	20.2	408.04
	20.4	416.16
	19.0	361.00
Sums	117.0	2,284.44

We have for the sample mean

$$\bar{x} = \frac{\sum x_i}{n} = \frac{117}{6} = 19.5$$

and for the sample variance

$$s_x^2 = \frac{\sum x_i^2 - n\bar{x}^2}{n-1} = \frac{2,284.44 - (6)(19.5)^2}{5} = .588$$

so the sample standard deviation is

$$s_x = \sqrt{.588} = .767$$

We then have

$$\frac{\bar{x} - \mu_0}{s_x/\sqrt{n}} = \frac{19.5 - 20}{.767/\sqrt{6}} = -1.597$$

Since a test of significance level $\alpha = .10$ is required, we have from Table 6 of the Appendix

$$t_{n-1,\alpha/2} = t_{5,.05} = 2.015$$

Thus, since -1.597 lies between -2.015 and 2.015, the null hypothesis that the true mean percentage increase is 20 is accepted at the 10% level. The evidence in the data against this hypothesis is not particularly strong.

EXERCISES

1. A manufacturer of detergent claims that the contents of boxes sold weigh on average at least 16 ounces. The distribution of weights is known to be normal, with standard deviation .4 ounce. A random sample of sixteen boxes yielded a sample mean weight of 15.84 ounces. Test at the 10% significance level the null hypothesis that the population mean weight is at least 16 ounces.

2. A company which receives shipments of batteries tests a random sample of nine of them before agreeing to take a shipment. The company is concerned that the true mean lifetime for all batteries in the shipment should be at least 50 hours. From past experience, it is safe to conclude that the population distribution of lifetimes is normal, with standard deviation 3 hours. For one particular shipment, the mean lifetime for a sample of nine batteries was 48.2 hours. Test at the 10% level the null hypothesis that the population mean lifetime is at least 50 hours.

3. A pharmaceutical manufacturer is concerned about the impurity concentration in pills, and it is anxious that this concentration not exceed 3%. It is known that from a particular production run, impurity concentrations follow a normal distribution with standard deviation .4%. A random sample of sixty-four pills from a production run was checked, and the sample mean impurity concentration was found to be 3.07%.
   (a) Test at the 5% level the null hypothesis that the population mean impurity concentration is 3% against the alternative that it is more than 3%.
   (b) Find the p-value for this test.
   (c) Suppose that the alternative hypothesis had been two-sided rather than one-sided (with null hypothesis H_0: $\mu = 3$). State, without doing the calculations, whether the p-value of the test would be higher than, lower than, or the same as that found in (b). Sketch a graph to illustrate your reasoning.
   (d) In the context of this problem, explain why a one-sided alternative hypothesis is more appropriate than a two-sided alternative.

4. A manufacturer claims that through the use of a fuel additive, automobiles should achieve on average an additional 3 miles per gallon of gas. A random sample of 100 automobiles was used to evaluate this product. The sample mean increase in miles per gallon achieved was 2.4 and the sample standard deviation was 1.8 miles per gallon. Test the null hypothesis that the population mean is at least 3 miles per gallon. Find the p-value of this test, and interpret your findings.

5. A random sample of 1,562 undergraduates enrolled in marketing courses was asked to respond on a scale from one (strongly disagree) to seven (strongly agree) to the proposition: "Advertising helps raise our standard of living."[4] The sample mean response was 4.27 and the sample standard deviation was 1.32. Test at the 1% level, against a two-sided alternative, the null hypothesis that the population mean is 4.

6. A random sample of 76 percentage changes in promised pension benefits of single employer plans after the establishment of the Pension Benefit Guarantee Corporation was observed.[5] The sample mean percentage change was .078 and the sample standard deviation was .201. Find and interpret the p-value of a test of the null hypothesis that the population mean percentage change is 0, against a two-sided alternative.

---

[4] See J. C. Andrews, "The dimensionality of beliefs toward advertising in general," *Journal of Advertising*, *18*, no. 1 (1989), 26–35.

[5] G. R. Niehaus, "The PBGC's flat fee schedule, moral hazard and promised pension benefits," *Journal of Banking and Finance*, *14* (1990), 55–68.

7. A random sample of 172 accounting students was asked to rate on a scale from one (not important) to five (extremely important) starting salary as a job characteristic.[6] The sample mean rating was 3.31 and the sample standard deviation was .70. Test at the 1% significance level the null hypothesis that the population mean rating is at most 3.0 against the alternative that it is bigger than 3.0.

8. A random sample of 170 people was provided with a prediction problem.[7] Each sample member was given, in two ways, the task of projecting the next value of an economic variable. The previous twenty values were presented both as numbers and as points on a graph. Subjects were asked to predict the next value, as a number and as a point on the graph. The absolute prediction errors were measured. The sample then consisted of 170 differences in absolute forecast errors (numerical minus graphical). The sample mean of these differences was -2.91 and the sample standard deviation was 11.33. Find and interpret the p-value of a test of the null hypothesis that the population mean difference is 0, against the alternative that it is negative. (The alternative can be viewed as the hypothesis that, in the aggregate, people are more successful at graphical than numerical prediction.)

9. The accounts of a corporation show that on average accounts receivable are $125.32. An auditor checked a random sample of sixteen of these accounts. The sample mean was $131.78 and the sample standard deviation was $25.41. Assume that the population distribution is normal. Test at the 5% significance level against a two-sided alternative the null hypothesis that the population mean is $125.32.

10. On the basis of a random sample, the null hypothesis

$$H_0: \mu = \mu_0$$

is tested against the alternative

$$H_1: \mu > \mu_0$$

and the null hypothesis is accepted at the 5% significance level.

   (a) Does this necessarily imply that μ_0 is contained in the 95% confidence interval for μ?
   (b) Does this necessarily imply that μ_0 is contained in the 90% confidence interval for μ, if the observed sample mean is bigger than μ_0?

11. A company selling franchises advertises that operators obtain, on average during the first year, a yield of 10% on their initial investments. A random sample of ten of these franchises produced the following yields for the first year of operation:

   6.1   9.2   11.5   8.6   12.1   3.9   8.4   10.1   9.4   8.9

   Assuming that population yields are normally distributed, test the company's claim.

12. A process that produces bottles of shampoo, when operating correctly, produces bottles whose contents weigh, on average, 20 ounces. A random sample of nine bottles from a single production run yielded the following contents weights (in ounces):

   21.4   19.7   19.7   20.6   20.8   20.1   19.7   20.3   20.9

   Assuming that the population distribution is normal, test at the 5% level against a two-sided alternative the null hypothesis that the process is operating correctly.

13. A statistics instructor is interested in the ability of students to assess the difficulty of a test they have taken. This test was taken by a large group of students, and the average score was 78.5. A random sample of eight students was asked to predict this average score. Their predictions were:

   72   83   78   65   69   77   81   71

---

[6] P. Bundy and D. Norris, "What accounting students consider important in the job selection process," *Journal of Applied Business Research*, 8, no. 2 (1992), 1–6.

[7] J. M. Carey and E. M. White, "The effects of graphical versus numerical response on the accuracy of graph-based forecasts," *Journal of Management*, 17 (1991), 77–96.

Assuming a normal distribution, test the null hypothesis that the population mean prediction would be 78.5. Use a two-sided alternative and a 10% significance level.

14. A beer distributor claims that a new display, featuring a life-size picture of a well-known athlete, will increase product sales in supermarkets by an average of 50 cases in a week. For a random sample of twenty supermarkets, the average sales increase was 41.3 cases and the sample standard deviation was 12.2 cases. Test at the 5% level the null hypothesis that the population mean sales increase is at least 50 cases, stating any assumption you make.

15. In contract negotiations, a company claims that a new incentive scheme has resulted in average weekly earnings of at least $400 for all production workers. A union representative takes a random sample of fifteen workers and finds that their weekly earnings have an average of $381.35 and a standard deviation of $48.60. Assume a normal distribution.

(a) Test the company's claim.

(b) If the same sample results had been obtained from a random sample of fifty employees, could the company's claim be rejected at a lower significance level than in part (a)?

9.4 TESTS OF THE VARIANCE OF A NORMAL DISTRIBUTION

In this section, we develop procedures for testing the population variance σ^2, based on a random sample of n observations from a normal population.

It is natural to base these tests on the sample variance s_X^2. The basis for developing particular tests lies in the fact that the random variable

$$\chi^2_{n-1} = \frac{(n-1)s_X^2}{\sigma^2}$$

follows a chi-square distribution with $(n-1)$ degrees of freedom.[8] If the null hypothesis is that the population variance is equal to some specified value σ_0^2, that is

$$H_0: \sigma^2 = \sigma_0^2$$

then when this hypothesis is true, the random variable

$$\chi^2_{n-1} = \frac{(n-1)s_X^2}{\sigma_0^2} \qquad (9.4.1)$$

obeys a chi-square distribution with $(n-1)$ degrees of freedom. Tests of hypotheses about the variance of a normal population are then based on the sample value observed for the quantity (9.4.1). If the alternative hypothesis is that the true variance exceeds σ_0^2, we would be suspicious of the null hypothesis if the observed sample variance was much bigger than σ_0^2. Hence, the null hypothesis would be rejected if a high value of (9.4.1) was observed. Conversely, if the alternative is that the population variance is less than the value specified by the null hypothesis, the null hypothesis would be rejected for low values of (9.4.1). Finally, for the two-sided alternative that

---

[8] Once again, we caution that the validity of this result rests crucially on the assumption that the population distribution is normal.

the population variance differs from σ_0^2, we would want to reject the null hypothesis on observing either unusually high or unusually low values of (9.4.1).

The rationale for the development of appropriate tests now follows the same pattern as in Section 9.2. As a preliminary, we recall a notation introduced in Section 8.5. We denote by $\chi_{\nu,\alpha}^2$ that number that is exceeded with probability α by a chi-square random variable with ν degrees of freedom. Hence

$$P(\chi_\nu^2 > \chi_{\nu,\alpha}^2) = \alpha$$

It then follows that

$$P(\chi_\nu^2 < \chi_{\nu,1-\alpha}^2) = \alpha$$

and that

$$P(\chi_\nu^2 > \chi_{\nu,\alpha/2}^2 \quad \text{or} \quad \chi_\nu^2 < \chi_{\nu,1-\alpha/2}^2) = \alpha$$

These probabilities are shown in Figure 9.8. Tests for the normal variance then follow as indicated in the box.

Tests of the Variance of a Normal Population

Suppose that we have a random sample of n observations from a normal population with variance σ^2. If the observed sample variance is s_x^2, then the following tests have significance level α:

(i) To test either null hypothesis

$$H_0: \sigma^2 = \sigma_0^2 \quad \text{or} \quad H_0: \sigma^2 \leq \sigma_0^2$$

against the alternative

$$H_1: \sigma^2 > \sigma_0^2$$

the decision rule is

$$\text{Reject } H_0 \text{ if } \frac{(n-1)s_x^2}{\sigma_0^2} > \chi_{n-1,\alpha}^2$$

(ii) To test either null hypothesis

$$H_0: \sigma^2 = \sigma_0^2 \quad \text{or} \quad H_0: \sigma^2 \geq \sigma_0^2$$

against the alternative

$$H_1: \sigma^2 < \sigma_0^2$$

the decision rule is

$$\text{Reject } H_0 \text{ if } \frac{(n-1)s_x^2}{\sigma_0^2} < \chi_{n-1,1-\alpha}^2$$

(iii) To test the null hypothesis

$$H_0: \sigma^2 = \sigma_0^2$$

against the two-sided alternative

$$H_1: \sigma^2 \neq \sigma_0^2$$

the decision rule is

$$\text{Reject } H_0 \text{ if } \frac{(n-1)s_x^2}{\sigma_0^2} > \chi_{n-1,\alpha/2}^2 \qquad \text{or} \qquad \frac{(n-1)s_x^2}{\sigma_0^2} < \chi_{n-1,1-\alpha/2}^2$$

Here $\chi_{n-1,\alpha}^2$ is the number for which

$$P(\chi_{n-1}^2 > \chi_{n-1,\alpha}^2) = \alpha$$

where the random variable χ_{n-1}^2 follows a chi-square distribution with $(n-1)$ degrees of freedom.

The decision rule for the test against the two-sided alternative is illustrated in Figure 9.9.

EXAMPLE 9.5

In order to meet established standards, it is important that the variance of the percentage impurity levels in consignments of a chemical not exceed 4. A random sample of twenty consignments had a sample variance of 5.62 in impurity level percentage. Test the null hypothesis that the population variance is no more than 4.

Let σ^2 denote the population variance of impurity concentrations. The null hypothesis

$$H_0: \sigma^2 \leq \sigma_0^2 = 4$$

is to be tested against

$$H_1: \sigma^2 > 4$$

Based on the assumption that the population distribution is normal, the decision rule, for a test of significance level α, is to reject H_0 in favor of H_1 if

$$\frac{(n-1)s_x^2}{\sigma_0^2} > \chi_{n-1,\alpha}^2$$

From the statement of the example, we have

$$s_x^2 = 5.62 \qquad n = 20 \qquad \sigma_0^2 = 4$$

Hence

$$\frac{(n-1)s_x^2}{\sigma_0^2} = \frac{(19)(5.62)}{4} = 26.695$$

FIGURE 9.8 Some probabilities for the chi-square distribution

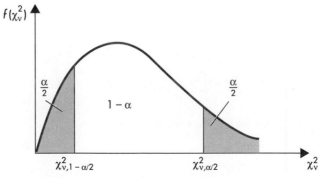

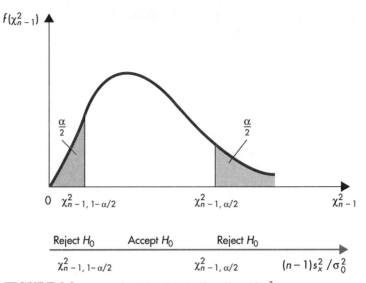

FIGURE 9.9 The probability density function of $\chi^2_{n-1} = (n-1)s_x^2/\sigma_0^2$ when the null hypothesis H_0: $\sigma^2 = \sigma_0^2$ is true and the decision rule for testing H_0 against the alternative H_1: $\sigma^2 \neq \sigma_0^2$ at significance level α

For a 10%-level test, $\alpha = .10$, and we see from Table 5 in the Appendix that the corresponding cutoff point of the chi-square distribution with $(n - 1) = 19$ degrees of freedom is

$$\chi^2_{19,.10} = 27.20$$

Therefore, since 26.695 is not bigger than 27.20, the null hypothesis cannot be rejected at the 10% level. Hence, the data do not contain particularly strong evidence against the hypothesis that the population variance in impurity level percentages is at most 4.

9.5 TESTS OF THE POPULATION PROPORTION (LARGE SAMPLES)

In many practical problems, we want to test hypotheses about the proportion of members of a large population possessing some particular attribute. Inference about the population proportion is based on the proportion of individuals in a random sample who possess the attribute of interest.

Denoting by p the population proportion and by $\hat{p}_x$ the proportion in a random sample of n observations, we know that if the sample size is large, then to a good approximation the random variable

$$Z = \frac{\hat{p}_x - p}{\sqrt{p(1 - p)/n}}$$

has a standard normal distribution. That the sampling distribution for the sample proportion is approximately normal when the sample size is large follows, as we have noted in previous chapters, as a result of the central limit theorem.

If the null hypothesis is that the population proportion is equal to some specific value p_0, it follows that when this hypothesis is true, the random variable

$$Z = \frac{\hat{p}_x - p_0}{\sqrt{p_0(1 - p_0)/n}}$$

follows a standard normal distribution. We can now deduce appropriate tests for the population proportion, as described in the box.

Tests of the Population Proportion (Large Sample Sizes)

Suppose that we have a random sample of n observations from a population, a proportion p of whose members possess a particular attribute. Then, if the number of sample observations is large[9] and the observed sample proportion is $\hat{p}_x$, the following tests have significance level α:

(i) To test either null hypothesis

$$H_0: p = p_0 \qquad \text{or} \qquad H_0: p \leq p_0$$

against the alternative

$$H_1: p > p_0$$

the decision rule is

$$\text{Reject } H_0 \text{ if } \frac{\hat{p}_x - p_0}{\sqrt{p_0(1 - p_0)/n}} > z_\alpha$$

(ii) To test either null hypothesis

$$H_0: p = p_0 \qquad \text{or} \qquad H_0: p \geq p_0$$

against the alternative

$$H_1: p < p_0$$

the decision rule is

$$\text{Reject } H_0 \text{ if } \frac{\hat{p}_x - p_0}{\sqrt{p_0(1 - p_0)/n}} < -z_\alpha$$

(iii) To test the null hypothesis

$$H_0: p = p_0$$

against the two-sided alternative

$$H_1: p \neq p_0$$

the decision rule is

$$\text{Reject } H_0 \text{ if } \frac{\hat{p}_x - p_0}{\sqrt{p_0(1 - p_0)/n}} > z_{\alpha/2} \qquad \text{or} \qquad \frac{\hat{p}_x - p_0}{\sqrt{p_0(1 - p_0)/n}} < -z_{\alpha/2}$$

---

[9] The approximations implied here are generally adequate for samples of forty or more observations.

Here, as previously, z_α is the number for which

$$P(Z > z_\alpha) = \alpha$$

where the random variable Z has a standard normal distribution.

The decision rule for the second of these tests is illustrated in Figure 9.10.

EXAMPLE
9.6

Of a random sample of 802 supermarket shoppers, 378 were able to state the correct price of an item immediately after putting it into the cart.[10] Test at the 10% level the null hypothesis that at least one-half of all shoppers are able to state the correct price, against the alternative that the population proportion is less than one-half. Also, find the p-value of this test.

Let p denote the population proportion of supermarket shoppers able to state the correct price in these circumstances. We want to test the null hypothesis

$$H_0: p \geq p_0 = .50$$

against the alternative

$$H_1: p < .50$$

The decision rule is to reject the null hypothesis in favor of the alternative if

$$\frac{\hat{p}_x - p_0}{\sqrt{p_0(1 - p_0)/n}} < -z_\alpha$$

FIGURE 9.10 The probability density function of $Z = \dfrac{\hat{p}_x - p_0}{\sqrt{p_0(1 - p_0)/n}}$ when the null hypothesis $H_0: p = p_0$ is true and the decision rule for testing H_0 against the alternative $H_1: p < p_0$ at significance level α

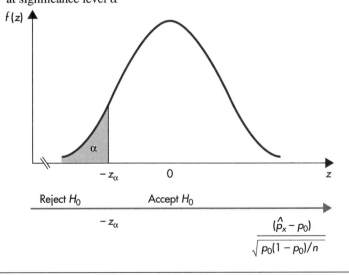

[10] P. R. Dickson and A. G. Sawyer, "The price knowledge and search of supermarket shoppers," *Journal of Marketing*, *54*, no. 3 (1990), 42–53.

In this example, we have

$$p_0 = .50 \qquad n = 802 \qquad \hat{p}_x = 378/802 = .471$$

For a 10% level test, $\alpha = .10$, so that

$$z_\alpha = z_{.10} = 1.28$$

The test statistic is then

$$\frac{\hat{p}_x - p_0}{\sqrt{p_0(1 - p_0)/n}} = \frac{.471 - .50}{\sqrt{(.50)(.50)/802}} = -1.64$$

Since -1.64 is less than -1.28, the null hypothesis is rejected at the 10% level.

From Table 3 of the Appendix, we see that, if $z_\alpha = 1.64$, then $\alpha = (1 - .9495) = .0505$. This is the p-value of the test. The null hypothesis can be rejected at all significance level above 5.05%. The data, then, strongly suggest that less than one-half of shoppers can correctly state the price of an item immediately after putting it into a supermarket cart.

EXERCISES

16. At the insistence of a government inspector, a new safety device is installed in an assembly-line operation. After the installation of this device, a random sample of eight days output gave the following results for numbers of finished components produced:

   618　　660　　638　　625　　571　　598　　639　　582

   Management is concerned about the variability of daily output and views as undesirable any variance above 500. Test at the 10% significance level the null hypothesis that the population variance for daily output does not exceed 500.

17. Plastic sheets produced by a machine are periodically monitored for possible fluctuations in thickness. If the true variance in thicknesses exceeds 2.25 square millimeters, there is cause for concern about product quality. Thickness measurements for a random sample of ten sheets produced in a particular shift were taken, giving the following results (in millimeters):

   226　　226　　232　　227　　225

   228　　225　　228　　229　　230

   (a) Find the sample variance.
   (b) Test at the 5% significance level the null hypothesis that the population variance is at most 2.25.

18. One way to evaluate the effectiveness of a teaching assistant is to examine the scores achieved by his or her students in an examination at the end of the course. Obviously, the mean score is of interest. However, the variance also contains useful information—some teachers have a style that works very well with more able students but is unsuccessful with less able or poorly motivated students. A professor sets a standard examination at the end of each semester for all sections of a course. The variance of the scores on this test is typically very close to 300. A new teaching assistant has a class of thirty students, whose test scores had variance 480. Regarding these students' test scores as a random sample from a normal population, test against a two-sided alternative the null hypothesis that the population variance of their scores is 300.

19. A company produces electric devices operated by a thermostatic control. The standard deviation of the temperature at which these controls actually operate should not exceed 2.0° Fahrenheit. For a random sample of twenty of these controls, the sample standard devia-

tion of operating temperatures was 2.36° Fahrenheit. Stating any assumptions you need to make, test at the 5% level the null hypothesis that the population standard deviation is 2.0 against the alternative that it is bigger.

20. An instructor has decided to introduce a greater component of independent study into an intermediate macroeconomics course, as a way of motivating students to work independently and think more carefully about the course material. A colleague cautions that a possible consequence may be increased variability in student performance. However, the instructor responds that she would expect less variability. From her records, she found that in the past, student scores on the final exam for this course followed a normal distribution with standard deviation 18.2 points. For a class of twenty-five students using the new approach, the standard deviation of scores on the final exam was 15.3 points. Assuming that these twenty-five students can be viewed as a random sample of all those who might be subjected to the new approach, test the null hypothesis that the population standard deviation is at least 18.2 points against the alternative that it is lower.

21. Of a sample of 361 owners of retail service and business firms which had gone into bankruptcy, 105 reported having no professional assistance prior to opening the business.[11] Test the null hypothesis that at most 25% of all members of this population had no professional assistance before opening the business.

22. In a random sample of 998 adults in the U.S., 17.3% of sample members indicated some measure of disagreement with the statement: "Capitalism is more than an economic system—it is a complex of institutions, attitudes and culture." Test at the 5% level the null hypothesis that at least 25% of all U.S. adults would disagree with this statement.[12]

23. In a random sample of 160 business school graduates, seventy-two sample members indicated some measure of agreement with the statement: "A reputation for ethical conduct is less important for a manager's chances for promotion than a reputation for making money for the firm."[13] Test the null hypothesis that one-half of all business school graduates would agree with this statement against a two-sided alternative. Find and interpret the p-value of the test.

24. Of a random sample of 199 audit partners in U.S. accounting firms, 104 indicated some measure of agreement with the statement: "Cash flow from operations is a valid measure of profitability."[14] Test at the 10% significance level against a two-sided alternative the null hypothesis that one-half of the members of this population would agree with this statement. Also, find and interpret the p-value of this test.

25. A random sample of fifty chief executive officers of small companies was asked about expectations in job interviews. Of these sample members, twenty-eight agreed that the interviewer usually expects the interviewee to have learned as much as possible about the company beforehand.[15] Test the null hypothesis that one-half of all interviewers have this expectation against the alternative that the population proportion is bigger than one-half.

26. Of a random sample of 172 minority small business owners, 118 said that personal savings was the most important source of initial financing.[16] Test the null hypothesis that personal savings is the most important source of initial financing for 75% of minority small business owners against the alternative that the population percentage is less than 75%.

---

[11] D. B. Bradley and H. L. Saunders, "A seven year strategic marketing profile of retail and service business bankruptcy," *Journal of Applied Business Research, 5*, no. 2 (1989), 69–79.

[12] Data from R. A. Peterson, G. Albaum, and G. Kozmetsky, "Capitalism and business: Public perceptions," *Business Horizons, 32*, no. 4 (1989), 63–66.

[13] Reported in M. M. Dolecheck, J. Caldwell, and C. C. Dolecheck, "Ethical perceptions and attitudes of business personnel," *American Business Review, 6*, no. 1 (1988), 47–54.

[14] J. E. McEnroe, "Cash flow accounting revisited: a note on a partial replication of the Lee study," *Abacus, 25* (1989), 56–60.

[15] B. Wells and N. Spinks, "Interviewing: What small companies say," *Bulletin of the Association of Business Communication, 55*, no. 2 (1992), 18–22.

[16] H. D. Feldman, C. S. Koberg, and T. J. Dean, "Minority small business owners and their paths to ownership," *Journal of Small Business Management, 29*, no. 4 (1991), 12–27.

27. A random sample of 202 college accounting faculty members was questioned. Of these sample members, 140 felt there was a need for more ethics coverage in accounting courses.[17] Test the null hypothesis that at least 75% of all college accounting faculty members hold this view.

9.6 TESTS FOR THE DIFFERENCE BETWEEN TWO MEANS

In this section, we examine the case where random samples are available from two populations, and the quantity of interest is the difference between the two population means. In developing procedures for testing hypotheses, the appropriate methodology once again depends on the manner in which the samples are taken. As in Section 8.7, we need to consider separately the cases of matched pairs and independent samples.

TESTS BASED ON MATCHED PAIRS

Here we assume that a random sample of n matched pairs of observations is obtained from populations with means μ_X and μ_Y. The actual sample observations will be denoted $(x_1, y_1), (x_2, y_2), \ldots, (x_n, y_n)$.

In a study aimed at assessing the relationship between a subject's brain activity while watching a television commercial and the subject's subsequent ability to recall the contents of the commercial, the data in Table 9.2 were obtained.[18] Subjects were shown commercials for two brands of each of ten products. For each commercial, the ability to recall 24 hours later was measured, and each member of a pair of commercials was then designated "high-recall" or "low-recall." The table shows an index of the total amount of brain activity of subjects while watching these commercials.

If μ_X denotes the population mean brain activity for the high-recall commercials and μ_Y the population mean for the low-recall commercials, then the differences d_i represent a random sample of ten observations from a population with mean $(\mu_X - \mu_Y)$. If the population distribution of these differences can be assumed normal, the methods of Section 9.3 are immediately applicable for testing hypotheses about $(\mu_X - \mu_Y)$. For this particular example, a natural test is of the null hypothesis of no difference in mean brain activity levels

$$H_0: \mu_X - \mu_Y = 0$$

against the alternative that, on average, brain activity is greater for the high-recall commercials, that is

$$H_1: \mu_X - \mu_Y > 0$$

More generally, we can test the hypothesis that the difference $(\mu_X - \mu_Y)$ is equal to any specified value D_0 using the procedure given in the box.

---

[17] E. Milam and F. McNair, "An examination of accounting faculty perceptions of the importance of ethics coverage in accounting courses," *Business and Professional Ethics Journal*, *11*, no. 2 (1992), 57–71.

[18] V. Appel, S. Weinstein, and C. Weinstein, "Brain activity and recall of TV advertising," *Journal of Advertising Research*, *19*, no. 4 (1979), 7–15.

TABLE 9.2 Brain activities of subjects watching ten pairs of television commercials

PRODUCT	HIGH RECALL	LOW RECALL		DIFFERENCES	
i	x_i	y_i		d_i	d_i^2
1	137	53		84	7,056
2	135	114		21	441
3	83	81		2	4
4	125	86		39	1,521
5	47	34		13	169
6	46	66		-20	400
7	114	89		25	625
8	157	113		44	1,936
9	57	88		-31	961
10	144	111		33	1,089
			Sums	210	14,202

Tests of the Difference Between Population Means: Matched Pairs

Suppose that we have a random sample of n matched pairs of observations from distributions with means μ_X and μ_Y. Let $\bar{d}$ and s_d denote the observed sample mean and standard deviation for the n differences $(x_i - y_i)$. If the population distribution of the differences is normal, then the following tests have significance level α:

(i) To test either null hypothesis

$$H_0: \mu_X - \mu_Y = D_0 \qquad \text{or} \qquad H_0: \mu_X - \mu_Y \leq D_0$$

against the alternative

$$H_1: \mu_X - \mu_Y > D_0$$

the decision rule is

$$\text{Reject } H_0 \text{ if } \frac{\bar{d} - D_0}{s_d/\sqrt{n}} > t_{n-1,\alpha}$$

(ii) To test either null hypothesis

$$H_0: \mu_X - \mu_Y = D_0 \qquad \text{or} \qquad H_0: \mu_X - \mu_Y \geq D_0$$

against the alternative

$$H_1: \mu_X - \mu_Y < D_0$$

the decision rule is

$$\text{Reject } H_0 \text{ if } \frac{\bar{d} - D_0}{s_d/\sqrt{n}} < -t_{n-1,\alpha}$$

(iii) To test the null hypothesis

$$H_0: \mu_X - \mu_Y = D_0$$

against the two-sided alternative

$$H_1: \mu_X - \mu_Y \neq D_0$$

the decision rule is

$$\text{Reject } H_0 \text{ if } \frac{\overline{d} - D_0}{s_d/\sqrt{n}} < -t_{n-1,\alpha/2} \qquad \text{or} \qquad \frac{\overline{d} - D_0}{s_d/\sqrt{n}} > t_{n-1,\alpha/2}$$

Here $t_{n-1,\alpha}$ is the number for which

$$P(t_{n-1} > t_{n-1,\alpha}) = \alpha$$

where the random variable t_{n-1} follows a Student's t distribution with $(n-1)$ degrees of freedom.

When we want to test the null hypothesis that the two population means are equal, we set $D_0 = 0$ in the formulas.

We now return to our example of brain activity of subjects watching television commercials; from Table 9.2, the sample mean of the differences is

$$\overline{d} = \frac{1}{n} \sum_{i=1}^{n} d_i = \frac{1}{10}(210) = 21$$

The sample variance is

$$s_d^2 = \frac{1}{n-1}\left(\sum_{i=1}^{n} d_i^2 - n\overline{d}^2\right)$$

$$= \frac{1}{9}[14{,}202 - (10)(21)^2] = 1{,}088$$

so the sample standard deviation is

$$s_d = \sqrt{1{,}088} = 32.98$$

We want to test the null hypothesis

$$H_0: \mu_X - \mu_Y = D_0 = 0$$

against the alternative

$$H_1: \mu_X - \mu_Y > 0$$

The test is based on

$$\frac{\overline{d} - D_0}{s_d/\sqrt{n}} = \frac{21}{32.98/\sqrt{10}} = 2.014$$

This quantity must be compared with tabulated values of the Student's t distribution with $(n-1) = 9$ degrees of freedom. From Table 6 of the Appendix, we have for 5%-level and 2.5%-level tests

$$t_{9,.05} = 1.833 \qquad \text{and} \qquad t_{9,.025} = 2.262$$

Hence, the null hypothesis of equality of the population means can be rejected at the 5%-level, but not at the 2.5%-level of significance. We see then that the data of Table 9.2 contain much evidence suggesting that on the average, brain activity is higher for the high-recall than for the low-recall group. If, in fact, the mean brain activity were the same for these two groups, then the probability of finding a sample result as extreme as or more extreme than that actually obtained would be between .025 and .05.

Suppose now that we have a random sample of n_x observations from a normal population with mean μ_X and variance σ_X^2 and an independent random sample of n_y observations from a normal population with mean μ_Y and variance σ_Y^2.

In Section 8.7, we saw that if the sample means are denoted $\overline{X}$ and $\overline{Y}$, then the random variable

$$Z = \frac{(\overline{X} - \overline{Y}) - (\mu_X - \mu_Y)}{\sqrt{\dfrac{\sigma_X^2}{n_x} + \dfrac{\sigma_Y^2}{n_y}}}$$

has a standard normal distribution. If the two population variances are known, tests for the difference between the population means can be based on this result, using the same arguments as before. Moreover (thanks to the central limit theorem), if the two sample sizes are large, the result continues to hold to a good approximation when the sample variances replace the population variances, even when the population distributions are not normal. This allows the derivation of tests of wide applicability, as summarized in the box.

Tests for the Difference Between Population Means: Independent Samples (Known Variances or Large Sample Sizes)

Suppose that we have independent random samples of n_x and n_y observations from normal distributions with means μ_X and μ_Y and variances σ_X^2 and σ_Y^2. If the observed sample means are $\overline{x}$ and $\overline{y}$, then the following tests have significance level α.

(i) To test either null hypothesis

$$H_0: \mu_X - \mu_Y = D_0 \qquad \text{or} \qquad H_0: \mu_X - \mu_Y \leq D_0$$

against the alternative

$$H_1: \mu_X - \mu_Y > D_0$$

the decision rule is

$$\text{Reject } H_0 \text{ if } \frac{\overline{x} - \overline{y} - D_0}{\sqrt{\dfrac{\sigma_X^2}{n_x} + \dfrac{\sigma_Y^2}{n_y}}} > z_\alpha$$

(ii) To test either null hypothesis

$$H_0: \mu_X - \mu_Y = D_0 \qquad \text{or} \qquad H_0: \mu_X - \mu_Y \geq D_0$$

against the alternative

$$H_1: \mu_X - \mu_Y < D_0$$

the decision rule is

$$\text{Reject } H_0 \text{ if } \frac{\overline{x} - \overline{y} - D_0}{\sqrt{\dfrac{\sigma_X^2}{n_x} + \dfrac{\sigma_Y^2}{n_y}}} < -z_\alpha$$

(iii) To test the null hypothesis

$$H_0: \mu_X - \mu_Y = D_0$$

---

against the two-sided alternative

$$H_1: \mu_X - \mu_Y \neq D_0$$

the decision rule is

$$\text{Reject } H_0 \text{ if } \frac{\bar{x} - \bar{y} - D_0}{\sqrt{\dfrac{\sigma_X^2}{n_x} + \dfrac{\sigma_Y^2}{n_y}}} < -z_{\alpha/2} \quad \text{or} \quad \frac{\bar{x} - \bar{y} - D_0}{\sqrt{\dfrac{\sigma_X^2}{n_x} + \dfrac{\sigma_Y^2}{n_y}}} > z_{\alpha/2}$$

If the sample sizes n_x and n_y are large,[19] then to a good approximation, tests of significance level α for the difference between population means are obtained by replacing the population variances by the sample variances, s_x^2 and s_y^2. For large sample sizes, these approximations remain good even when the population distributions are not normal.

EXAMPLE 9.7

A survey of practicing certified public accountants on attitudes to women in the profession was carried out.[20] Survey respondents were asked to react on a scale from one (strongly disagree) to five (strongly agree) to the statement: "Women in public accounting are given the same job assignments as men." For a sample of 186 male accountants, the mean response was 4.059 and the sample standard deviation was .839. For an independent random sample of 172 female accountants, the mean response was 3.680 and the sample standard deviation was .966. Test the null hypothesis that the two population means are equal against the alternative that the true mean is higher for male accountants.

Let μ_X and μ_Y denote the respective population means for male and female accountants. We want to test the null hypothesis

$$H_0: \mu_X - \mu_Y = 0$$

against the alternative

$$H_1: \mu_X - \mu_Y > 0$$

The decision rule is to reject H_0 in favor of H_1 if

$$\frac{\bar{x} - \bar{y}}{\sqrt{(s_x^2/n_x) + (s_y^2/n_y)}} > z_\alpha$$

In this example

$$n_x = 186 \qquad \bar{x} = 4.059 \qquad s_x = .839$$
$$n_y = 172 \qquad \bar{y} = 3.680 \qquad s_y = .966$$

so that

$$\frac{\bar{x} - \bar{y}}{\sqrt{(s_x^2/n_x) + (s_y^2/n_y)}} = \frac{4.059 - 3.680}{\sqrt{[(.839)^2/186] + [(.966)^2/172]}} = 3.95$$

Referring to Table 3 of the Appendix, it can be seen that such an extreme sample result would be highly unlikely if the null hypothesis of equality of the two population means were indeed true. For instance, for a .01%-level test, $\alpha = .0001$, so $z_\alpha = z_{.0001} = 3.75$. Since 3.95 is bigger than 3.75, the null hypothesis is rejected even at such a

---

[19] This approximation is generally satisfactory when each sample contains at least thirty observations.
[20] M. W. Trapp, R. H. Hermanson and D. H. Turner, "Current perceptions of issues related to women employed in public accounting," *Accounting Horizons*, 3, no. 1 (1989), 71–85.

low significance level. These data contain overwhelming evidence suggesting that the population mean response is higher for males than for females—that is, that on the average, males feel more strongly than females in the profession that women are given the same job assignments as men.

We will now treat the case where the sample sizes are not large. If it can be assumed that the two population variances are equal, then tests can be based on the result (given in Section 8.7) that the random variable

$$t = \frac{(\overline{X} - \overline{Y}) - (\mu_X - \mu_Y)}{s\sqrt{\dfrac{n_x + n_y}{n_x n_y}}}$$

has a Student's t distribution with $(n_x + n_y - 2)$ degrees of freedom, where

$$s^2 = \frac{(n_x - 1)s_X^2 + (n_y - 1)s_Y^2}{(n_x + n_y - 2)}$$

is an estimator of the common variance. The appropriate hypothesis tests on the difference between the population means are given in the box.

Tests for the Difference Between the Means of Two Normal Populations: Independent Samples, Population Variances Equal

Suppose that we have independent random samples of n_x and n_y observations from normal distributions with means μ_X and μ_Y and a common variance. If the observed sample variances are s_x^2 and s_y^2, an estimate of the common population variance is provided by

$$s^2 = \frac{(n_x - 1)s_x^2 + (n_y - 1)s_y^2}{n_x + n_y - 2}$$

Then, if the observed sample means are $\overline{x}$ and $\overline{y}$, the following tests have significance level α:

(i) To test either null hypothesis

$$H_0: \mu_X - \mu_Y = D_0 \qquad \text{or} \qquad H_0: \mu_X - \mu_Y \leq D_0$$

against the alternative

$$H_1: \mu_X - \mu_Y > D_0$$

the decision rule is

$$\text{Reject } H_0 \text{ if } \frac{\overline{x} - \overline{y} - D_0}{s\sqrt{\dfrac{n_x + n_y}{n_x n_y}}} > t_{n_x + n_y - 2, \alpha}$$

(ii) To test either null hypothesis

$$H_0: \mu_X - \mu_Y = D_0 \qquad \text{or} \qquad H_0: \mu_X - \mu_Y \geq D_0$$

against the alternative

$$H_1: \mu_X - \mu_Y < D_0$$

the decision rule is

$$\text{Reject } H_0 \text{ if } \frac{\bar{x} - \bar{y} - D_0}{s\sqrt{\dfrac{n_x + n_y}{n_x n_y}}} < -t_{n_x + n_y - 2, \alpha}$$

(iii) To test the null hypothesis

$$H_0: \mu_X - \mu_Y = D_0$$

against the two-sided alternative

$$H_1: \mu_X - \mu_Y \neq D_0$$

the decision rule is

$$\text{Reject } H_0 \text{ if } \frac{\bar{x} - \bar{y} - D_0}{s\sqrt{\dfrac{n_x + n_y}{n_x n_y}}} < -t_{n_x + n_y - 2, \alpha/2}$$

$$\text{or } \frac{\bar{x} - \bar{y} - D_0}{s\sqrt{\dfrac{n_x + n_y}{n_x n_y}}} > t_{n_x + n_y - 2, \alpha/2}$$

Here $t_{n_x + n_y - 2, \alpha}$ is the number for which

$$P(t_{n_x + n_y - 2} > t_{n_x + n_y - 2, \alpha}) = \alpha$$

where $t_{n_x + n_y - 2}$ has a Student's t distribution with $(n_x + n_y - 2)$ degrees of freedom.

EXAMPLE 9.8

A study attempted to assess the effect of the presence of a moderator on the number of ideas generated by a group.[21] Groups of four members, with or without moderators, were observed. For a random sample of four groups with a moderator, the mean number of ideas generated per group was 78.0, and the sample standard deviation was 24.4. For an independent random sample of four groups without a moderator, the mean number of ideas generated was 63.5, and the sample standard deviation was 20.2. Assuming that the population distributions are normal with equal variances, test the null hypothesis that the population means are equal against the alternative that the true mean is higher for groups with a moderator.

Let μ_X and μ_Y denote the respective population means for groups with and without a moderator. Then the objective is to test the null hypothesis

$$H_0: \mu_X - \mu_Y = 0$$

against the alternative

$$H_1: \mu_X - \mu_Y > 0$$

The decision rule is to reject H_0 in favor of H_1 if

$$\frac{\bar{x} - \bar{y}}{s\sqrt{\dfrac{n_x + n_y}{n_x n_y}}} > t_{n_x + n_y - 2, \alpha}$$

For these data, we have

---

[21] E. F. Fern, "The use of focus groups for idea generations: The effects of group size, acquaintance-ship, and moderator on response quantity and quality," *Journal of Marketing Research*, *19* (1982), 1–13.

$$\bar{x} = 78.0 \qquad s_x = 24.4 \qquad n_x = 4$$
$$\bar{y} = 63.5 \qquad s_y = 20.2 \qquad n_y = 4$$

Thus, the common population variance is estimated by

$$s^2 = \frac{(n_x - 1)s_x^2 + (n_y - 1)s_y^2}{n_x + n_y - 2}$$

$$= \frac{(3)(24.4)^2 + (3)(20.2)^2}{4 + 4 - 2} = 501.7$$

so that the common standard deviation is estimated by

$$s = \sqrt{501.7} = 22.4$$

Then, the test statistic is

$$\frac{\bar{x} - \bar{y}}{s\sqrt{\dfrac{n_x + n_y}{n_x n_y}}} = \frac{78.0 - 63.5}{22.4\sqrt{\dfrac{8}{16}}} = .915$$

For a 10%-level test, from Table 6 of the Appendix

$$t_{n_x + n_y - 2, .10} = t_{6, .10} = 1.440$$

Thus, since .915 does not exceed 1.440, the null hypothesis of equality of population means cannot be rejected against the one-sided alternative at the 10% significance level. The sample data do not contain strong evidence suggesting that on average, more ideas will be generated by groups with moderators. However, for such small sample sizes, we cannot expect great power in the test, so quite large differences in the population means would be needed to reject the null hypothesis at low significance levels.

The test in Example 9.8 is based on an assumption that the two population variances are equal. It is in fact possible to develop tests that are valid when this assumption does not hold; however, these will not be discussed further here.

9.7 TESTS FOR THE DIFFERENCE BETWEEN TWO POPULATION PROPORTIONS (LARGE SAMPLES)

We turn now to the problem of comparing two population proportions. As in Section 8.8, suppose that a random sample of n_x observations from a population with proportion p_X "successes" gives a sample proportion $\hat{p}_X$ and that an independent random sample of n_y observations from a population with proportion p_Y "successes" yields sample proportion $\hat{p}_Y$.

In Section 8.8, we saw that if the numbers of sample observations are large, then to a very good approximation, the random variable

$$Z = \frac{(\hat{p}_X - \hat{p}_Y) - (p_X - p_Y)}{\sqrt{\dfrac{p_X(1 - p_X)}{n_x} + \dfrac{p_Y(1 - p_Y)}{n_y}}}$$

has a standard normal distribution, by virtue of the central limit theorem.

Suppose that we want to test the hypothesis that the population proportions p_X and p_Y are equal. If their common value is denoted p_0, then we have under this hypothesis that

$$
\begin{aligned}
Z &= \frac{(\hat{p}_X - \hat{p}_Y)}{\sqrt{\dfrac{p_0(1 - p_0)}{n_x} + \dfrac{p_0(1 - p_0)}{n_y}}} \\[2em]
&= \frac{\hat{p}_X - \hat{p}_Y}{\sqrt{p_0(1 - p_0)\left(\dfrac{n_x + n_y}{n_x n_y}\right)}}
\end{aligned}
\tag{9.7.1}
$$

follows to a good approximation a standard normal distribution.

Finally, the unknown common proportion p_0 in expression (9.7.1) can be estimated by the pooled estimator $\hat{p}_0$, given by

$$
\hat{p}_0 = \frac{n_x \hat{p}_X + n_y \hat{p}_Y}{n_x + n_y}
$$

Replacing the unknown p_0 by $\hat{p}_0$ in (9.7.1) gives a random variable that has a distribution close to the standard normal, provided the sample sizes are large. This result forms the basis for our tests, as indicated in the box.

Testing the Equality of Two Population Proportions (Large Samples)

Let $\hat{p}_x$ denote the proportion of successes in a random sample of n_x observations from a population with proportion p_X successes and $\hat{p}_y$ the proportion of successes observed in an independent random sample of n_y observations from a population with proportion p_Y successes. If it is hypothesized that the population proportions are equal, an estimate of the common proportion is given by

$$
\hat{p}_0 = \frac{n_x \hat{p}_x + n_y \hat{p}_y}{n_x + n_y}
$$

Then, if the sample sizes are large,[22] the following tests have significance level α:

(i) To test either null hypothesis

$$H_0: p_X - p_Y = 0 \qquad \text{or} \qquad H_0: p_X - p_Y \leq 0$$

against the alternative

$$H_1: p_X - p_Y > 0$$

the decision rule is

---

[22] The approximation is generally adequate if each sample contains at least forty observations.

$$\text{Reject } H_0 \text{ if } \frac{\hat{p}_x - \hat{p}_y}{\sqrt{\hat{p}_0(1 - \hat{p}_0)\left(\dfrac{n_x + n_y}{n_x n_y}\right)}} > z_\alpha$$

(ii) To test either null hypothesis

$$H_0: p_X - p_Y = 0 \qquad \text{or} \qquad H_0: p_X - p_Y \geq 0$$

against the alternative

$$H_1: p_X - p_Y < 0$$

the decision rule is

$$\text{Reject } H_0 \text{ if } \frac{\hat{p}_x - \hat{p}_y}{\sqrt{\hat{p}_0(1 - \hat{p}_0)\left(\dfrac{n_x + n_y}{n_x n_y}\right)}} < -z_\alpha$$

(iii) To test the null hypothesis

$$H_0: p_X - p_Y = 0$$

against the alternative

$$H_1: p_X - p_Y \neq 0$$

the decision rule is

$$\text{Reject } H_0 \text{ if } \frac{\hat{p}_x - \hat{p}_y}{\sqrt{\hat{p}_0(1 - \hat{p}_0)\left(\dfrac{n_x + n_y}{n_x n_y}\right)}} < -z_{\alpha/2}$$

$$\text{or} \quad \frac{\hat{p}_x - \hat{p}_y}{\sqrt{\hat{p}_0(1 - \hat{p}_0)\left(\dfrac{n_x + n_y}{n_x n_y}\right)}} > z_{\alpha/2}$$

EXAMPLE 9.9

Of a random sample of 203 British trade magazine advertisements, fifty-two were humorous. Of an independent random sample of 270 American trade magazine advertisements, fifty-six were humorous.[23] Test against a two-sided alternative the null hypothesis that the proportions of all British and American trade magazine advertisements that are humorous are the same.

Let p_X and p_Y denote the population proportions of humorous British and American advertisements, respectively. Then, we want to test the null hypothesis

$$H_0: p_X - p_Y = 0$$

against the alternative

$$H_1: p_X - p_Y \neq 0$$

The decision rule is to reject H_0 in favor of H_1 if

---

[23] L. S. McCullogh and R. K. Taylor, "Humor in American, British, and German ads," *Industrial Marketing Management*, 22 (1993), 17–28.

$$\frac{\hat{p}_x - \hat{p}_y}{\sqrt{\hat{p}_0(1 - \hat{p}_0)\left(\dfrac{n_x + n_y}{n_x n_y}\right)}} < -z_{\alpha/2} \quad \text{or} \quad > z_{\alpha/2}$$

In this example, we have

$$n_x = 203 \qquad \hat{p}_x = 52/203 = .256 \qquad n_y = 270 \qquad \hat{p}_y = 56/270 = .207$$

Then, the estimate of the common proportion under the null hypothesis is

$$\hat{p}_0 = \frac{n_x \hat{p}_x + n_y \hat{p}_y}{n_x + n_y} = \frac{(203)(.256) + (270)(.207)}{203 + 270} = .228$$

The test statistic is then

$$\frac{\hat{p}_x - \hat{p}_y}{\sqrt{\hat{p}_0(1 - \hat{p}_0)\left(\dfrac{n_x + n_y}{n_x n_y}\right)}} = \frac{.256 - .207}{\sqrt{(.228)(.772)\left(\dfrac{203 + 270}{(203)(270)}\right)}} = 1.26$$

The value of $\alpha/2$ corresponding to $z_{\alpha/2} = 1.26$ is, from Table 3 of the Appendix, $\alpha/2 = .1038$. Therefore, the p-value of the test against the two-sided alternative is .2076. The null hypothesis that the population proportions of humorous advertisements are the same can be rejected at significance levels greater than 20.76%. This reflects just a moderate amount of evidence in the data against the null hypothesis.

EXERCISES

28. A college placement officer wants to determine whether male and female business graduates receive, on average, different salary offers for their first position after graduation. The placement officer randomly selected eight pairs of business graduates in such a way that the qualifications, interests, and backgrounds of the members of any pair were as similar as possible. The major difference was that one member of each pair was male and one was female. The accompanying table shows the highest salary offer received by each sample member at the end of the recruiting round. Assuming that the distributions are normal, test the null hypothesis that the population means are equal against the alternative that the true mean for males is higher than for females.

PAIR	HIGHEST SALARY OFFER (IN DOLLARS)	
	MALE	FEMALE
1	26,200	22,600
2	24,700	23,600
3	28,400	29,300
4	21,700	22,300
5	28,600	26,200
6	29,300	25,900
7	28,300	28,500
8	24,300	21,300

29. An agency offers students preparation courses for an achievement test. As part of an experiment to evaluate the merits of the course, twelve students were chosen and divided into six

pairs, in such a way that the two members of any pair had similar academic records. Before taking the test, one member of each pair was assigned at random to take the preparation course, while the other member took no course. The achievement test scores are shown in the accompanying table. Assuming that the differences in scores follow a normal distribution, test at the 5% level the null hypothesis that the two population means are equal, against the alternative that the true mean is higher for students taking the preparation course.

STUDENT PAIR	COURSE	NO COURSE
1	82	75
2	73	71
3	59	52
4	48	46
5	69	70
6	93	83

30. In a study comparing state-chartered and federally chartered credit unions, a sample of 145 matched pairs of credit unions was formed. Each pair contained one state-chartered and one federally chartered credit union. The pairings were made in such a way that the two members were as similar as possible in regard to such factors as size and age.[24] The ratio of total loans outstanding to total assets was calculated for each of the credit unions. For this ratio, the sample mean difference (federally chartered minus state-chartered) was .0518, and the sample standard deviation of the differences was .3055. Test against a two-sided alternative the null hypothesis that the two population means are equal.

31. The MATWES procedure was designed to measure attitudes toward women as managers. High scores indicate negative attitudes and low scores indicate positive attitudes. Independent random samples were taken of 151 male M.B.A. students and 108 female M.B.A. students.[25] For the former group, the sample mean and standard deviation MATWES scores were 85.8 and 19.3, while the corresponding figures for the latter group were 71.5 and 12.2. Test the null hypothesis that the two population means are equal against the alternative that the true mean MATWES score is higher for male than for female M.B.A. students.

32. For a random sample of 125 Japanese entrepreneurs,[26] the mean number of job changes was 1.91 and the sample standard deviation was 1.32. For an independent random sample of 86 Japanese corporate managers, the mean number of job changes was .21 and the sample standard deviation was .53. Test the null hypothesis that the population means are equal against the alternative that the mean number of job changes is higher for Japanese entrepreneurs than for Japanese corporate managers.

33. A political science professor is interested in comparing the characteristics of students who do and do not vote in national elections. For a random sample of 114 students who claimed to have voted in the last presidential election, she found a mean grade point average of 2.71 and standard deviation .64. For an independent random sample of 123 students who did not vote, the mean grade point average was 2.79, and the standard deviation was .56. Test against a two-sided alternative the null hypothesis that the population means are equal.

34. Auditors are greatly concerned by the possibility of fraud, and its detection. It was conjectured that auditors might be helped in the evaluation of the chances of fraud by a "red flags questionnaire"; that is, a list of potential symptoms of fraud to be assessed. To evaluate

[24] T. Kohers and S. M. Rao, "The choice of regulatory regime and its effect on financial profile: A study of credit union chartering," *American Business Review*, 6, no. 2 (1988), 38–45.

[25] P. Dubno, "Attitudes toward women executives: A longitudinal approach," *Academy of Management Journal*, 28 (1985), 235–39.

[26] T. Ohe, S. Honjo, and I. C. MacMillan, "Japanese entrepreneurs and corporate managers: a comparison," *Journal of Business Venturing*, 5 (1990), 163–76.

this possibility, samples of mid-level auditors from C.P.A. firms were presented with audit information from a fraud case, and they were asked to evaluate the chance of material fraud, on a scale from zero to 100.[27] A sample of thirty-three auditors used the red flags questionnaire. Their mean assessment was 36.21, and the sample standard deviation was 22.93. For an independent sample of thirty-six auditors not using the red flags questionnaire, the sample mean and standard deviation were respectively 47.56 and 27.56. Assuming that the two population distributions are normal with equal variances, test against a two-sided alternative the null hypothesis that the population means are equal.

35. Initial public offerings prospectuses were examined.[28] In a random sample of seventy prospectuses in which earnings forecasts were disclosed, the mean debt-to-equity ratio prior to the offering issue was 3.97, and the sample standard deviation was 6.14. For an independent random sample of fifty-one prospectuses in which earnings forecasts were not disclosed, the mean debt-to-equity ratio was 2.86, and the sample standard deviation was 4.29. Test against a two-sided alternative the null hypothesis that population mean debt-to-equity ratios are the same for disclosers and nondisclosers of earnings forecasts.

36. A publisher is interested in the effects on sales of college texts of expensive three-color cover designs. The publisher is planning to bring out twenty texts in the business area and randomly chooses ten of them to have expensive cover designs. The remaining ten are produced with plain covers. For those with expensive cover designs, first-year sales averaged 9,254, and the sample standard deviation was 2,107. For the books with plain cover designs, average first-year sales were 8,167, and the sample standard deviation was 1,681. Assuming that the two population distributions are normal with the same variance, test the null hypothesis that the population means are equal against the alternative that the true mean is higher for books with expensive cover designs.

37. In 1980, a random sample of 1,556 people were asked to respond to the statement: "Capitalism must be altered before any significant improvements in human welfare can be realized."[29] Of these sample members, 38.4% agreed with the statement. When the same statement was presented to a random sample of 1,108 people in 1989, 52.0% agreed. Test the null hypothesis that the population proportions agreeing with this statement were the same in the two years, against the alternative that a higher proportion agreed in 1989.

38. Residential phone users were surveyed one year after access to carriers other than ATT became available for long-distance service.[30] Of a random sample of 368 ATT users, ninety-two said they were attempting to learn more about their options, as did thirty-seven of an independent random sample of 116 users of alternate carriers. Test at the 5% significance level, against a two-sided alternative, the null hypothesis that the two population proportions are the same.

39. Employees of a supermarket chain, facing a shutdown, were surveyed on a prospective employee ownership plan. Some employees pledged $5,000 to this plan, putting up $200 immediately, while others indicated that they did not intend to pledge. Of a random sample of 175 pledgers, seventy-eight had already been laid off, while 208 of a random sample of 604 nonpledgers had already been laid off.[31] Test at the 5% level, against a two-sided alternative, the null hypothesis that the population proportions already laid off were the same for pledgers as for nonpledgers.

40. Of a random sample of 381 investment-grade corporate bonds, 191 had sinking funds. Of an independent random sample of 166 speculative-grade corporate bonds, 145 had sinking

[27] K. V. Pincus, "The efficacy of a red flags questionnaire for assessing the possibility of a fraud," *Accounting, Organizations and Society*, *14* (1989), 153–63.

[28] P. M. Clarkson, A. Dontoh, G. Richardson, and S. E. Sefcik, "The voluntary inclusion of earnings forecasts in IPO prospectuses," *Contemporary Accounting Research*, *8* (1992), 601–26.

[29] R. A. Peterson, G. Kozmetsky, and G. Albaum, "The public's attitude toward capitalism: 1980–89," *Business Horizons*, *34*, no. 5 (1991), 59–63.

[30] J. F. Snyder, P. T. Nelson, and C. C. Morris, "The end of the telecommunication monopoly: Subsequent residential customer choice among long distance carriers," *Southern Business Review*, *17*, no. 2 (1991), 40–54.

[31] Data from A. Hochner and C. S. Granrose, "Sources of motivation to choose employee ownership as an alternative to job loss," *Academy of Management Journal*, *28* (1985), 860–75.

funds.[32] Test against a two-sided alternative the null hypothesis that the two population proportions are equal.

41. Independent random samples of consumers were asked about satisfaction with their vehicles in two slightly different ways.[33] The options available for answer were the same in the two cases. When asked how *satisfied* they were with their vehicles, 138 of 240 sample members opted for "very satisfied." When asked how *dissatisfied* they were with their vehicles, 128 of 240 sample members opted for "very satisfied." Test at the 5% level, against the obvious one-sided alternative, the null hypothesis that the two population proportions are equal.

42. Of a random sample of 1,200 people in the United States, 480 had a positive attitude toward lawyers.[34] Of an independent random sample of 1,000 Canadians, 790 had a positive attitude toward lawyers. Test at the 1% significance level the null hypothesis that the population proportions are equal, against the alternative that a higher proportion of Canadians have a positive attitude toward lawyers.

9.8 TESTING THE EQUALITY OF THE VARIANCES OF TWO NORMAL POPULATIONS

One of the tests developed in Section 9.6 for the comparison of population means depends on an assumption of equality of the two population variances. Although in many practical applications such an assumption is reasonable, it is prudent to use the available data to test its validity. In addition, it sometimes happens when comparing population distributions that the population variances are of interest in their own right and that we wish to compare them.

In this section, we consider the problem when independent random samples from two normal populations are available and it is required to test the equality of the population variances. To develop such a test, another probability distribution must be introduced. Let s_X^2 be the sample variance for a random sample of n_x observations from a normal population with variance σ_X^2 and s_Y^2 be the sample variance from an independent random sample of n_y observations from a normal population with variance σ_Y^2. Then the random variable

$$F = \frac{s_X^2/\sigma_X^2}{s_Y^2/\sigma_Y^2} \qquad (9.8.1)$$

follows a distribution known as the **F distribution.**[35] This family of distributions is widely used in statistical analysis. A particular member of the family is distinguished by two values—the degrees of freedom associated with the numerator and with the denominator. In the present context, recall that the number of degrees of freedom

---

[32] M. W. Marr and J. P. Ogden, "Market imperfections and the choices of maturity and call provisions in corporate debt," *Journal of Business Research*, 19 (1989), 17–31.

[33] R. A. Peterson and W. R. Wilson, "Measuring consumer satisfaction: fact and artifact," *Journal of Academy of Marketing Science*, 20 (1992), 61–71.

[34] K. L. Hooks, "Professionalism and self-interest: a critical view of the expectations gap," *Critical Perspectives in Accounting*, 3 (1991), 109–36.

[35] Formally, the F distribution is defined as the distribution followed by the ratio of two independent chi-square random variables, each divided by its associated degrees of freedom.

associated with the sample variance s_X^2 is $(n_x - 1)$ and that with s_Y^2 is $(n_y - 1)$. The random variable (9.8.1), then, has an F distribution with numerator degrees of freedom $(n_x - 1)$ and denominator degrees of freedom $(n_y - 1)$.

The F distribution has an asymmetric probability density function, defined only for nonnegative values. This density function is illustrated in Figure 9.11.

The F Distribution

Suppose that independent random samples of n_x and n_y observations are taken from two normal populations with variances σ_X^2 and σ_Y^2. If the sample variances are s_X^2 and s_Y^2, then the random variable

$$F = \frac{s_X^2/\sigma_X^2}{s_Y^2/\sigma_Y^2}$$

has an **F distribution** with numerator degrees of freedom $(n_x - 1)$ and denominator degrees of freedom $(n_y - 1)$.

An F distribution with numerator degrees of freedom ν_1 and denominator degrees of freedom ν_2 will be denoted F_{ν_1,ν_2}. We denote by $F_{\nu_1,\nu_2,\alpha}$ the number for which

$$P(F_{\nu_1,\nu_2} > F_{\nu_1,\nu_2,\alpha}) = \alpha$$

The cutoff points $F_{\nu_1,\nu_2,\alpha}$, for α equal to .05 and .01, are provided in Table 7 of the Appendix. For example, for 10 numerator degrees of freedom and 20 denominator degrees of freedom, we see from the table

$$F_{10,20,.05} = 2.35 \qquad \text{and} \qquad F_{10,20,.01} = 3.37$$

Hence

$$P(F_{10,20} > 2.35) = .05 \qquad \text{and} \qquad P(F_{10,20} > 3.37) = .01$$

FIGURE 9.11 Probability density function of the F distribution with 6 numerator degrees of freedom and 4 denominator degrees of freedom; the probability is α that

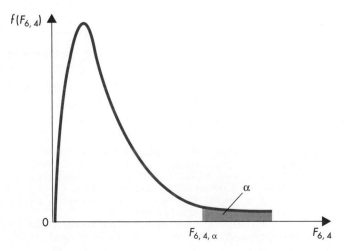

In practical applications, provided we arrange matters so that the larger sample variance appears in the numerator, these are the only cutoff points necessary to test the hypothesis of equality of population variances. When the population variances are equal, it follows from (9.8.1) that the random variable

$$F = \frac{s_X^2}{s_Y^2}$$

obeys an F_{n_x-1,n_y-1} distribution. Appropriate hypothesis tests are described in the box.

Tests for the Equality of the Variances of Two Normal Populations

Let s_x^2 and s_y^2 be observed sample variances from independent random samples of n_x and n_y observations from normal populations with variances σ_X^2 and σ_Y^2. If s_x^2 is bigger than s_y^2, then the following tests have significance level α:

(i) To test either null hypothesis

$$H_0: \sigma_X^2 = \sigma_Y^2 \qquad \text{or} \qquad H_0: \sigma_X^2 \leq \sigma_Y^2$$

against the alternative

$$H_1: \sigma_X^2 > \sigma_Y^2$$

the decision rule is

$$\text{Reject } H_0 \text{ if } \frac{s_x^2}{s_y^2} > F_{n_x-1,n_y-1,\alpha}$$

(ii) To test the null hypothesis

$$H_0: \sigma_X^2 = \sigma_Y^2$$

against the two-sided alternative

$$H_1: \sigma_X^2 \neq \sigma_Y^2$$

the decision rule is

$$\text{Reject } H_0 \text{ if } \frac{s_x^2}{s_y^2} > F_{n_x-1,n_y-1,\alpha/2}$$

where s_x^2 is the larger of the two sample variances.
Here, $F_{n_x-1,n_y-1,\alpha}$ is the number for which

$$P(F_{n_x-1,n_y-1} > F_{n_x-1,n_y-1,\alpha}) = \alpha$$

where F_{n_x-1,n_y-1} has an F distribution with numerator degrees of freedom $(n_x - 1)$ and denominator degrees of freedom $(n_y - 1)$.

EXAMPLE 9.10

For a random sample of seventeen newly issued AAA-rated industrial bonds, the variance of maturities (in years squared) was 123.35. For an independent random sample of eleven newly issued CCC-rated industrial bonds,[36] the variance of maturi-

---

[36] M. W. Marr and J. P. Ogden, "Market imperfections and the choices of maturity and call provisions in corporate debt," *Journal of Business Research, 19* (1989), 17–31.

ties was 8.02. If the respective population variances are denoted σ_X^2 and σ_Y^2, test the null hypothesis

$$H_0: \sigma_X^2 = \sigma_Y^2$$

against the two-sided alternative

$$H_1: \sigma_X^2 \neq \sigma_Y^2$$

Assume that the two population distributions are normal.

The decision rule is to reject H_0 in favor of H_1 if

$$\frac{s_x^2}{s_y^2} > F_{n_x - 1, n_y - 1, \alpha/2}$$

We have the data

$$n_x = 17 \qquad s_x^2 = 123.35 \qquad n_y = 11 \qquad s_y^2 = 8.02$$

where we have ensured that the larger of the sample variances is denoted s_x^2. Then the test statistic is

$$\frac{s_x^2}{s_y^2} = \frac{123.35}{8.02} = 15.38$$

Since the degrees of freedom are $(n_x - 1) = 16$ and $(n_y - 1) = 10$, we have, from interpolation in Table 7 of the Appendix

$$F_{16,10,.01} = 4.53$$

As the alternative hypothesis is two-sided, this is the appropriate critical value for testing at the 2%-level. Clearly, 15.38 is much bigger than 4.53, and the null hypothesis is easily rejected. There is very strong evidence that variances in maturities are different for these two types of bonds.

9.9 MEASURING THE POWER OF A TEST

In Sections 9.2–9.8, we have concentrated on the development of tests at a particular significance level. That is, we have developed decision rules for which the probability of making a Type I error—rejecting the null hypothesis when it is true—is fixed at some preassigned value. As noted in Section 9.1, a decision rule of this kind will necessarily imply some probability of making a Type II error—accepting a null hypothesis that is false. Moreover, it is often important to know what are the probabilities of making this kind of error, so that if a null hypothesis is accepted, we will have an assessment of how likely such a decision would be when that hypothesis is false.

In this section, we consider for the first time the characteristics of some of our tests when the null hypothesis is not true. In particular, we show how the power can be calculated for tests of the mean of a normal distribution when the variance is known and for tests of the population proportion.

TESTS OF THE MEAN OF A NORMAL DISTRIBUTION: POPULATION VARIANCE KNOWN

Suppose, using the procedures of Section 9.2, that we test the null hypothesis that the mean of a normal population is equal to some specific value μ_0. The probability, β, of making a Type II error will depend on the true population mean. This probability can be found as follows:

(i) From the decision rule of the test, determine the range of values of the sample mean leading to acceptance of the null hypothesis.

(ii) For the value μ_1 of interest of the population mean, find the probability that the sample mean will lie in the acceptance region determined in (i) for samples of n observations from a population with mean μ_1.

To illustrate, in Example 9.1, given a random sample of sixteen observations, we tested the null hypothesis that the true mean weight of ball bearings was 5 ounces against the alternative that the true mean was bigger than 5 ounces, at the 5% significance level. The population distribution was assumed to be normal, with standard deviation .1 ounce. Thus, we tested

$$H_0: \mu = \mu_0$$

against

$$H_1: \mu > \mu_0$$

through the decision rule

$$\text{Reject } H_0 \text{ if } \frac{\bar{x} - \mu_0}{\sigma/\sqrt{n}} > z_\alpha$$

with

$$\mu_0 = 5 \qquad n = 16 \qquad \sigma = .1 \qquad z_\alpha = z_{.05} = 1.645$$

Hence, the null hypothesis is rejected if

$$\frac{\bar{x} - 5}{.1/4} > 1.645$$

or

$$\bar{x} > 1.645(.1/4) + 5 = 5.041$$

Conversely, the null hypothesis will be accepted if

$$\bar{x} \leq 5.041$$

We have thus established, in line with (i), that the test procedure will lead to acceptance of the null hypothesis if the sample mean weight does not exceed 5.041 ounces.

Suppose now that we want to determine the probability that the null hypothesis will be accepted if the true mean weight is 5.05 ounces. In effect, we are asking for the probability that the sample mean does not exceed 5.041 for a random sample of sixteen observations from a normal population with mean $\mu_1 = 5.05$ and standard deviation .1. This is

$$P(\overline{X} \le 5.041) = P\left(Z \le \frac{5.041 - \mu_1}{\sigma/\sqrt{n}}\right)$$

$$= P\left(Z \le \frac{5.041 - 5.05}{.1/4}\right)$$

$$= P(Z \le -.36)$$

$$= 1 - .6406 = .3594$$

Thus, we have established that with this decision rule, the probability β of the Type II error involved in accepting the null hypothesis when the true mean is 5.05 ounces is .3594. The power of the test for this value of the population mean is then

$$1 - \beta = .6406$$

These power calculations are illustrated in Figure 9.12, which shows the probability density functions of the sample mean when the population mean is 5 and 5.05.

FIGURE 9.12 Sampling distributions of sample mean for sixteen observations with $\sigma = .1$ with (a) $\mu = 5$, (b) $\mu = 5.05$; figure shows calculation of power $1 - \beta$, corresponding to significance level $\alpha = .05$ for testing H_0: $\mu = 5$ against H_1: $\mu > 5$; power is evaluated at $\mu = 5.05$

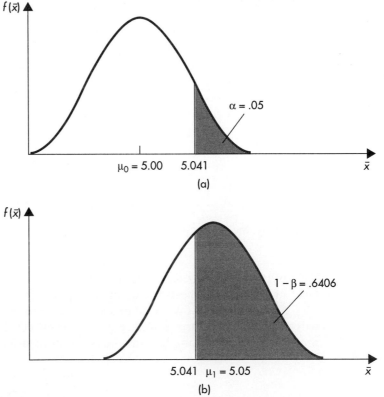

In part (a), we see that when the population mean is 5, the probability that the sample mean exceeds 5.041 is .05, the significance level of the test. Part (b) of the figure shows the density function of the sampling distribution of the sample mean when the population mean is 5.05. It differs from part (a) of the figure in being shifted to the right by an amount .05—the difference between the means 5.05 and 5. The shaded area in this figure shows the probability that the sample mean exceeds 5.041 when the population mean is 5.05. This is the power, evaluated at this point, as calculated previously.

Similar calculations yield the powers of the test for any value μ_1 of the population mean. Figure 9.13 graphs power as a function of the mean μ.

Note that the power function has the following features:

1. Everything else being equal, the farther the true mean μ_1 from the hypothesized mean μ_0, the greater the power of the test. This is illustrated in Figure 9.13; it means that we are more likely to detect large than small discrepancies from the hypothesized mean.

2. Everything else being equal, the smaller the significance level of the test, the smaller the power. In other words, reducing the probability of a Type I error will increase the probability of a Type II error.

3. Everything else being equal, the larger the population variance, the lower the power of the test. We are less likely to detect small departures from the hypothesized mean when there is greater variability in the population.

4. Everything else being equal, the larger the sample size, the greater the power of the test. Again, this is intuitively plausible. The more information obtained from the population, the greater the chance of detecting any departure from the null hypothesis. This is illustrated in Figure 9.14. Together with the power function for samples of $n = 16$ observations, this figure shows also the power functions for the same test based on $n = 4$ and $n = 9$ observations. Note that for every value of the population mean higher than the hypothesized mean, the greater the number of observations, the greater the probability of rejecting the null hypothesis.

Using arguments similar to those given previously, we can also calculate the power of a test against the two-sided alternative hypothesis. However, rather than pursuing that case here, we will illustrate these calculations for tests on a population proportion.

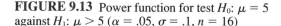

FIGURE 9.13 Power function for test H_0: $\mu = 5$ against H_1: $\mu > 5$ ($\alpha = .05$, $\sigma = .1$, $n = 16$)

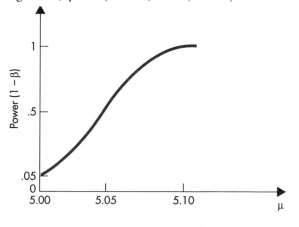

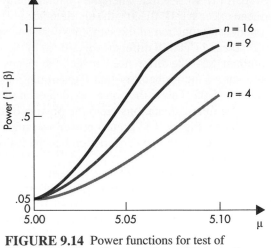

FIGURE 9.14 Power functions for test of H_0: $\mu = 5$ against H_1: $\mu > 5$ ($\alpha = .05$, $\sigma = .1$), shown for sample sizes 4, 9, 16

TESTS OF THE POPULATION PROPORTION (LARGE SAMPLES)

Using the approach of Section 9.5, we can test the null hypothesis that the proportion of population members having a particular attribute is some specific amount p_0. The probability, β, of making a Type II error for any given population proportion is found as follows:

(i) From the test decision rule, find the range of values of the sample proportion leading to acceptance of the null hypothesis.

(ii) For the value p_1 of interest of the population proportion, find the probability that the sample proportion will be in the acceptance range determined in (i) for samples of n observations when the population proportion is p_1.

For example, forecasts of corporate earnings per share are made on a regular basis by many financial analysts. In a random sample of 600 forecasts, it was found that 382 of these forecasts exceeded the actual outcome for earnings.[37] Suppose that we want to test against a two-sided alternative the null hypothesis that the population proportion of forecasts that are higher than actual outcomes is .50. (This is the hypothesis we would expect to be true if there were no overall tendency for financial analysts to be either unduly optimistic or unduly pessimistic about earnings prospects.) We will test this hypothesis at the 5% significance level. The aim is to test

$$H_0: p = p_0 = .50$$

against

$$H_1: p \neq p_0$$

The decision rule is

---

[37] Data from R. M. Barefield and E. E. Comiskey, "The accuracy of analysts' forecasts of earnings per share," *Journal of Business Research*, *3* (1975), 241–52.

Reject H_0 if $\dfrac{\hat{p}_x - p_0}{\sqrt{\dfrac{p_0(1 - p_0)}{n}}} > z_{\alpha/2}$ or $\dfrac{\hat{p}_x - p_0}{\sqrt{\dfrac{p_0(1 - p_0)}{n}}} < -z_{\alpha/2}$

where

$$p_0 = .50 \qquad n = 600 \qquad z_{\alpha/2} = z_{.025} = 1.96$$

Thus, the null hypothesis is rejected if

$$\dfrac{\hat{p}_x - .50}{\sqrt{\dfrac{(.50)(.50)}{600}}} > 1.96 \qquad \text{or} \qquad \dfrac{\hat{p}_x - .50}{\sqrt{\dfrac{(.50)(.50)}{600}}} < -1.96$$

Equivalently, H_0 is rejected if

$$\hat{p}_x > .50 + 1.96 \sqrt{\dfrac{(.50)(.50)}{600}} = .50 + .040 = .54$$

or $\hat{p}_x < .50 - .040 = .46$

Therefore, the null hypothesis will be accepted if

$$.46 \leq \hat{p}_x \leq .54$$

In fact, the sample proportion is

$$\hat{p}_x = 382/600 = .637$$

so the null hypothesis is rejected at the 5% level.

Suppose now that we want to find the probability that with this decision rule, the null hypothesis would be accepted if the true population proportion was .55. Then, we are asking for the probability that the sample proportion lies between .46 and .54 for a random sample of 600 observations when the population proportion is $p_1 = .55$. This is

$$P(.46 \leq \hat{p}_x \leq .54) = P \left[\dfrac{.46 - p_1}{\sqrt{\dfrac{p_1(1 - p_1)}{n}}} \leq Z \leq \dfrac{.54 - p_1}{\sqrt{\dfrac{p_1(1 - p_1)}{n}}} \right]$$

$$= P \left[\dfrac{.46 - .55}{\sqrt{\dfrac{(.55)(.45)}{600}}} \leq Z \leq \dfrac{.54 - .55}{\sqrt{\dfrac{(.55)(.45)}{600}}} \right]$$

$$= P(-4.43 \leq Z \leq -.49)$$

$$= .3121$$

Thus, given the decision rule, the probability β of the Type II error involved in accepting the null hypothesis when the true proportion is .55 is .3121. The power of the test for this value of the population proportion is

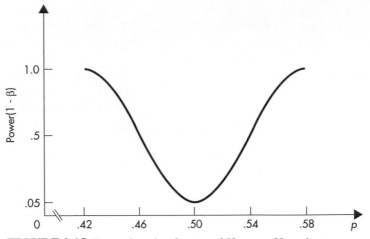

FIGURE 9.15 Power function for test of H_0: $p = .50$ against H_1: $p \neq .50$ ($\alpha = .05$, $n = 600$)

$$1 - \beta = .6879$$

Similarly, this probability can be calculated for any population proportion p_1. Figure 9.15 shows the power function for this example. Because the alternative hypothesis is two-sided, the power function differs in shape from that of Figure 9.13. Here we are considering possible values of the population proportion on either side of the hypothesized value, .50. As we see, the probability of rejecting the null hypothesis when it is false increases the farther the true population proportion is from the hypothesized value.

9.10 SOME COMMENTS ON HYPOTHESIS TESTING

Classical hypothesis testing methods are probably used more frequently in empirical investigations than any other statistical technique. The relative simplicity of the procedures, together with the frequency of real-world problems for which competing hypotheses exist, render hypothesis testing extremely appealing. Nevertheless, some caution is necessary in interpreting test results.

Perhaps of paramount concern is the crucial role played by the null hypothesis in the hypothesis-testing framework. In a typical investigation, the significance level—that is, the probability of rejecting the null hypothesis when it is true—will be set at some low level. Evidence is then gathered from the population to put this hypothesis in jeopardy. However, we might fail to reject a drastically false null hypothesis simply because very little sample information is available or because the test employed has low power. This may be perfectly appropriate if the null hypothesis is indeed special and the investigator is, for some reason, reluctant to abandon it. Such might be the case, for example, if rejection of a null hypothesis would lead to costly modifications in a production process. However, the special status of the null hypothesis is very often neither warranted nor appropriate. In such circumstances, a more symmetric treatment of competing hypotheses would be desirable. One obvious possibility would be to take into account the actual costs (if they could be quantified) of making both Type I errors and Type II errors in deciding between competing hypotheses. Considerations of this sort are embedded in statistical decision theory, which will be discussed in Chapter 19.

On some occasions, very large amounts of sample information are available, and the opposite problem arises—the null hypothesis is put in very considerable jeopardy indeed. It is then important to distinguish between the use of the word *significant*, as it is used in statistical significance testing, compared with its dictionary definition. Suppose that very large numbers of households are sampled from two cities. The analysis might contain a statement such as "The difference between the sample average annual incomes for the two cities is $2.37; this is significant." Presumably what is meant is that the null hypothesis of equality of the population means can, on the basis of such large samples, be rejected at the usual significance levels. Nevertheless, the best estimate available of the difference between the population mean annual incomes is a mere $2.37, which is of no practical significance whatever!

The tests developed in this chapter have typically been based on an assumption about the underlying population distribution. Often, we have assumed that distribution to be normal. When such an assumption fails to hold, the procedures are not strictly valid. Specifically, the true significance levels will differ from those derived on the basis of the normality assumption. Since it is difficult to believe that any population distribution is *precisely* normal, it is important to ask how badly the significance levels might be affected by nonnormality in the parent population. If the effect is relatively small, the tests are said to be *robust* to departures from normality. Generally speaking, it is known that tests on population means are robust.[38] However, tests (such as those of Section 9.8) that compare population variances are not. In the next chapter, we will discuss some tests that do not depend for their validity on specific assumptions about the population distribution.

EXERCISES

43. It is hypothesized that the more expert a group of people examining a corporation's financial report, the more variable will be their predictions about its future. Independent random samples, each of thirty individuals, from groups of different levels of expertise were chosen.[39] The "low-expertise" group consisted of people who had just completed their first intermediate accounting course. Members of the "high-expertise" group had completed undergraduate studies and were employed by reputable C.P.A. firms. The sample members were asked to predict the next period's operating net cash flow of a company on the basis of its annual financial report. For the low-expertise group, the sample variance was 451.770, while for the high-expertise group it was 1,614.208. Test the null hypothesis that the two population variances are equal against the alternative that the true variance is higher for the high-expertise group.

44. It is hypothesized that the market share of a corporation should vary more in an industry with active price competition than in one with duopoly and tacit collusion. In a study of the steam turbine generator industry,[40] it was found that in 4 years of active price competition,

[38] However, the tests for equality of population means based on independent samples, discussed in Section 9.6, become rather less robust when the two sample sizes are not equal.

[39] D. Snowball, "Some effects of accounting expertise and information load. An empirical study," *Accounting, Organizations and Society*, 5 (1980), 323–38.

[40] B. T. Allen, "Tacit collusion and market sharing: The case of steam turbine generators," *Industrial Organization Review*, 4 (1976), 48–57.

the variance of General Electric's market share was 114.09. In the following 7 years, in which there was duopoly and tacit collusion, this variance was 16.08. Assume that the data can be regarded as an independent random sample from two normal distributions. Test at the 5%-level the null hypothesis that the two population variances are equal against the alternative that the variance of market share is higher in years of active price competition.

45. In Exercise 34, it was assumed that population variances for assessments of the chance of material fraud were the same for auditors using a red flags questionnaire as for auditors not using this questionnaire. Test this assumption against a two-sided alternative hypothesis.

46. In Exercise 36, it was assumed that population variances were equal for first-year sales of textbooks with plain and expensive cover designs. Test this assumption against a two-sided alternative.

47. In Example 9.8, we tested the hypothesis that the mean numbers of ideas generated were the same for groups with and without a moderator. This test was based on the assumption that the two population variances were equal. Test this assumption against the alternative that the population variance is higher for groups with a moderator.

48. Refer to Exercise 2. Find the power of a 10%-level test when the true mean lifetime of batteries is 49 hours.

49. Refer to Exercise 3(a). Find the probability of a 5%-level test rejecting the null hypothesis when the true mean impurity concentration is 3.10%.

50. Refer to Exercise 5. Find the probability of a 1%-level test accepting the null hypothesis when the true mean response is 3.95.

51. Refer to Example 9.6. Find the power of a 10% level test if in fact 45% of supermarket shoppers are able to state the correct price of an item immediately after putting it into the cart.

52. Refer to Exercise 22. Find the probability of rejecting the null hypothesis with a 5% level test if in fact 20% of all U.S. adults would disagree with the statement.

53. Refer to Exercise 24. Find the probability of accepting the null hypothesis with a 10% level test if in fact 60% of all audit partners agree that cash flow from operations is a valid measure of profitability.

54. A fast-food chain tests each day that the average weight of its "two-pounders" is at least 32 ounces. The alternative hypothesis is that the average weight is less than 32 ounces, indicating that new processing procedures are needed. The weights of two-pounders can be assumed to be normally distributed, with a standard deviation of 3 ounces. The decision rule adopted is to reject the null hypothesis if the sample mean weight is less than 30.8 ounces.

    (a) If random samples of $n = 36$ two-pounders are selected, what is the probability of a Type I error, using this decision rule?

    (b) If random samples of $n = 9$ two-pounders are selected, what is the probability of a Type I error, using this decision rule? Explain why your answer differs from that in part (a).

    (c) Suppose that the true mean weight is 31 ounces. If random samples of thirty-six two-pounders are selected, what is the probability of a Type II error, using this decision rule?

55. A wine producer claims that the proportion of its customers who cannot distinguish its product from frozen grape juice is at most .10. The producer decides to test this null hypothesis against the alternative that the true proportion is more than .10. The decision rule adopted is to reject the null hypothesis if the sample proportion who cannot distinguish between these two flavors exceeds .14.

    (a) If a random sample of 100 customers is chosen, what is the probability of a Type I error, using this decision rule?

    (b) If a random sample of 400 customers is selected, what is the probability of a Type I error, using this decision rule? Explain, in words and graphically, why your answer differs from that in part (a).

(c) Suppose that the true proportion of customers who cannot distinguish between these flavors is .20. If a random sample of 100 customers is selected, what is the probability of a Type II error?

(d) Suppose that instead of the given decision rule, it is decided to reject the null hypothesis if the sample proportion of customers who cannot distinguish between the two flavors exceeds .16. A random sample of 100 customers is selected.

  (i) Without doing the calculations, state whether the probability of a Type I error will be higher than, lower than, or the same as that in part (a).

  (ii) If the true proportion is .20, will the probability of a Type II error be higher than, lower than, or the same as that in part (c)?

REVIEW EXERCISES

56. Explain carefully the distinction between each of the following pairs of terms:
   (a) Null and alternative hypotheses
   (b) Simple and composite hypotheses
   (c) One-sided and two-sided alternatives
   (d) Type I and Type II errors
   (e) Significance level and power

57. A statistician tests the null hypothesis that the proportion of men favoring a tax reform proposal is the same as the proportion of women. Based on sample data, the null hypothesis is rejected at the 5% significance level. Does this imply that the probability is at least .95 that the null hypothesis is false? If not, provide a valid probability statement.

58. Carefully explain what is meant by the p-value of a test, and discuss the use of this concept in hypothesis testing.

59. A random sample of ten students found the following figures, in hours, for time spent studying in the week before final exams.

| 28 | 57 | 42 | 35 | 61 | 39 | 55 | 46 | 49 | 38 |

Assume that the population distribution is normal.
   (a) Find the sample mean and standard deviation.
   (b) Test at the 5% significance level the null hypothesis that the population mean is 40 hours against the alternative that it is higher.
   (c) Test at the 5% significance level against a two-sided alternative the null hypothesis that the population standard deviation is 10 hours.

60. State whether each of the following is true or false.
   (a) The significance level of a test is the probability that the null hypothesis is false.
   (b) A Type I error occurs when a true null hypothesis is rejected.
   (c) A null hypothesis is rejected at the .025 level, but is accepted at the .01 level. This means that the p-value of the test is between .01 and .025.
   (d) The power of a test is the probability of accepting a null hypothesis that is true.
   (e) If a null hypothesis is rejected against an alternative at the 5%-level, then using the same data, it must be rejected against that alternative at the 1%-level.
   (f) If a null hypothesis is rejected against an alternative at the 1%-level, then using the same data it must be rejected against that alternative at the 5%-level.
   (g) The p-value of a test is the probability that the null hypothesis is true.

61. A process produces cable for the local telephone company. When the process is operating correctly, cable diameter follows a normal distribution with mean 1.6 inches and standard deviation .05 inch. A random sample of sixteen pieces of cable found diameters with mean 1.615 inches and sample standard deviation .086 inches.

(a) Assuming that the population standard deviation is .05 inch, test at the 10%-level against a two-sided alternative the null hypothesis that the population mean is 1.6 inches. Find also the lowest level of significance at which this null hypothesis can be rejected against the two-sided alternative.

(b) Test at the 10%-level the null hypothesis that the population standard deviation is .05 inch against the alternative that it is bigger.

62. When operating normally, a manufacturing process produces tablets for which the mean weight of the active ingredient is 5 grams, and the standard deviation is .025 gram. For a random sample of twelve tablets, the following weights of active ingredient (in grams) were found:

| 5.01 | 4.96 | 5.03 | 4.98 | 4.98 | 4.95 |
| 5.00 | 5.00 | 5.03 | 5.01 | 5.04 | 4.95 |

(a) Without assuming that the population variance is known, test the null hypothesis that the population mean weight of active ingredient per tablet is 5 grams. Use a two-sided alternative and a 5% significance level. State any assumptions that you make.

(b) Stating any assumptions that you make, test the null hypothesis that the population standard deviation is .025 gram against the alternative hypothesis that the population standard deviation exceeds .025 gram. Use a 5% significance level.

63. An insurance company employs agents on a commission basis. It claims that in their first year, agents will earn a mean commission of at least $40,000 and that the population standard deviation is no more than $6,000. A random sample of nine agents found, for commission in the first year,

$$\sum_{i=1}^{9} x_i = 333 \quad \text{and} \quad \sum_{i=1}^{9} (x_i - \bar{x})^2 = 312$$

where x_i are measured in thousands of dollars and the population distribution can be assumed to be normal.

(a) Test at the 5%-level the null hypothesis that the population mean is at least $40,000.

(b) Test at the 10% significance level the null hypothesis that the population standard deviation is at most $6,000.

64. Supporters claim that a new windmill can generate an average of at least 800 kilowatts of power per day. Daily power generation for the windmill is assumed to be normally distributed with a standard deviation of 120 kilowatts. A random sample of 100 days is taken to test this claim against the alternative hypothesis that the true mean is less than 800 kilowatts. The claim will be accepted if the sample mean is 776 kilowatts or more and rejected otherwise.

(a) What is the probability α of a Type I error using the decision rule if the population mean is in fact 800 kilowatts per day?

(b) What is the probability β of a Type II error using this decision rule if the population mean is in fact 740 kilowatts per day?

(c) Suppose that the same decision rule is used, but with a sample of 200 days rather than 100 days.

  (i) Would the value of α be larger than, smaller than, or the same as that found in (a)?

  (ii) Would the value of β be larger than, smaller than, or the same as that found in (b)?

(d) Suppose that a sample of 100 observations was taken but that the decision rule was changed so that the claim would be accepted if the sample mean was at least 765 kilowatts.

  (i) Would the value of α be larger than, smaller than, or the same as that found in (a)?

  (ii) Would the value of β be larger than, smaller than, or the same as that found in (b)?

65. Of a random sample of 545 accountants engaged in preparing city operating budgets for use in planning and control, 117 indicated that estimates of cash flow were the most difficult element of the budget to derive.[41]

  (a) Test at the 5%-level the null hypothesis that at least 25% of all accountants find cash flow the most difficult estimates to derive.

  (b) Based on the procedure used in (a), what is the probability that the null hypothesis would be rejected if the true percentage of those finding cash flow estimates most difficult was:

  (i) 20%

  (ii) 25%

  (iii) 30%

66. A random sample of 104 executives from large U.S. corporations was questioned on future developments in the business environment.[42] Of those sample members, fifty indicated some measure of agreement with the statement: "Firms will concentrate their efforts more on cash flow than on profits." What is the lowest level of significance at which the null hypothesis, which states that the true proportion of all such executives who would agree with this statement is one-half, can be rejected against a two-sided alternative?

67. In a random sample of ninety-nine National Football League games, the home team won fifty-seven games.[43] Test the null hypothesis that the home team wins one-half of all games against the alternative that the home team wins a majority of games.

68. Of a random sample of 150 business graduates, fifty agreed or strongly agreed that employees are often rewarded for unethical business behavior.[44] Test at the 5%-level the null hypothesis that at most 25% of all business graduates would be in agreement with this assertion.

69. Of a random sample of 142 company recruiters on college campuses, thirty-nine indicated that on average they spent sixty seconds or less studying each resumé.[45] Test the null hypothesis that at most 20% of all company recruiters spend this little time studying resumés.

70. In an agricultural experiment, two expensive high-yield varieties of corn are to be tested and the yield improvements measured. The experiment is arranged so that each variety is planted in one of each of ten pairs of similar plots. The data shown in the accompanying table are the percentage yield increases obtained for these two varieties. Stating any assumptions you make, test at the 10% significance level the null hypothesis that the two population mean percentage yield increases are the same. Use a two-sided alternative hypothesis.

PLOT	VARIETY A	VARIETY B	PLOT	VARIETY A	VARIETY B
1	12.6	10.5	6	16.1	14.0
2	9.2	8.1	7	12.3	10.1
3	6.4	6.2	8	11.3	13.6
4	9.8	10.1	9	12.2	9.8
5	15.3	12.2	10	14.1	13.4

[41] C. T. Cox, H. M. Nix, and H. Wichmann, "Responsibility accounting and operational control for government units," *Accounting Horizons*, *3*, no. 2 (1989), 38–48.

[42] S. H. Akhter and G. R. Laczniak, "The future U.S. business environment with strategic marketing implications for European exporters," *European Journal of Marketing*, *23*, no. 5 (1989), 58–74.

[43] H. Cooper, K. M. DeNeve, and F. Mosteller, "Predicting professional sports game outcomes from intermediate game scores," *Chance*, *5*, no. 3 (1992), 18–22.

[44] F. R. David, L. M. Anderson, and K. W. Lawrimore, "Perspectives on business ethics in management education," *S.A.M. Advanced Management Journal*, *55*, no. 4 (1990), 26–32.

[45] R. M. Schramm and R. M. Dortch, "An analysis of effective resumé content, format, and appearance based on college recruiter perceptions," *Bulletin of the Association of Business Communication*, *54*, no. 3 (1991), 18–23.

71. Two financial analysts were asked to predict earnings per share for a random sample of twelve corporations over the coming year. The quality of their forecasts was evaluated in terms of absolute percentage forecast error, defined as

$$100 \cdot \frac{|\text{Actual} - \text{Predicted}|}{\text{Actual}}$$

The absolute percentage forecast errors made are shown in the accompanying table. Stating any assumptions you make, test against a two-sided alternative the null hypothesis that the population mean absolute percentage forecast errors are the same for these two financial analysts.

CORPORATION	ANALYST A	ANALYST B	CORPORATION	ANALYST A	ANALYST B
1	12.3	7.3	7	5.2	3.1
2	15.4	12.1	8	4.1	0.6
3	5.3	7.4	9	5.3	5.5
4	9.2	8.1	10	4.1	2.8
5	8.6	11.3	11	3.6	4.3
6	14.2	12.3	12	5.6	1.7

72. In a study of short-term absenteeism from work of ex-smokers,[46] a random sample of thirty-four recent ex-smokers found a mean absenteeism of 2.21 days per month and a sample standard deviation of 2.21 days per month. For an independent random sample of eighty-six long-term ex-smokers, mean absenteeism was 1.47 days per month and the sample standard deviation was 1.69 days per month. Find the lowest level of significance at which the null hypothesis of equality of the two population means can be rejected against a two-sided alternative.

73. Independent random samples of practicing public accountants and college accounting faculty were asked to respond on a scale from one (strongly disagree) to seven (strongly agree) to the statement: "Grades in advanced accounting are good indicators of students' analytical skills."[47] For a sample of seventy practicing public accountants, the mean response was 4.4, and the sample standard deviation was 1.3. For a sample of 106 accounting faculty, the mean response was 5.3, and the sample standard deviation was 1.4.

    (a) Test at the 5% significance level the null hypothesis that the population mean response for practicing public accountants would be at most 4.0.

    (b) Test at the 5% significance level the null hypothesis that the population means are equal, against the alternative that the population mean response is higher for accounting faculty than for practicing public accountants.

74. Independent random samples of bachelors and masters degree holders in accounting, whose initial job was with a "big eight" firm, and who subsequently moved to industry, were questioned.[48] For a sample of forty-four bachelors degree holders, the mean number of months before the first job change was 35.02, and the sample standard deviation was 18.20. For a sample of 68 masters degree holders, the mean number of months before the first job change was 36.34, and the sample standard deviation was 18.94. Test at

---

[46] M. R. Manning, J. S. Osland, and A. Osland, "Work-related consequences of smoking cessation," *Academy of Management Journal*, *32* (1989), 606–21.

[47] J. L. Armitage, "Academicians' and practitioners' views on the context and importance of the advanced financial accounting course," *Journal of Accounting Education*, *9* (1991), 327–39.

[48] L. A. Deppe, J. M. Smith, and J. D. Stice, "The debate over post-baccalaureate education: one university's experience," *Issues in Accounting Education*, *7* (1992), 18–36.

the 10% significance level, against a two-sided alternative, the null hypothesis that the population mean numbers of months before the first job change are the same for the two groups.

75. A study was aimed at assessing the effects of the size and characteristics of groups on the generation of ideas.[49] To assess the influence of group size, groups of four and eight members were compared. For a random sample of four 4-member groups, the mean number of ideas generated per group was 78.0, and the sample standard deviation was 24.4. For an independent random sample of four 8-member groups, the mean number of ideas generated per group was 114.7, and the sample standard deviation was 14.6. (In each case, the groups had a moderator.) Stating any assumptions that you need to make, test at the 1%-level the null hypothesis that the population means are the same against the alternative that the mean is higher for eight-member groups.

76. The *fog index* is used to measure the reading difficulty of a written text. The index is calculated through the following steps:

   (i) Find the average number of words per sentence.

   (ii) Find the percentage of words with three or more syllables.

   (iii) The fog index is then 40% of the sum of (i) and (ii).

   A random sample[50] of six advertisements taken from Scientific American had the following fog indices:

   | 15.75 | 11.55 | 11.16 | 9.92 | 9.23 | 8.20 |

   An independent random sample of six advertisements from Sports Illustrated had the following fog indices:

   | 9.17 | 8.44 | 6.10 | 5.78 | 5.58 | 5.36 |

   Stating any assumptions you need to make, test at the 5%-level the null hypothesis that the population mean fog indices are the same against the alternative that the true mean is higher for Scientific American than for Sports Illustrated.

77. From the report described in Exercise 76, the fog indices for a random sample of six advertisements in *People Weekly* were as follows:

   | 9.50 | 8.60 | 8.59 | 6.50 | 4.79 | 4.29 |

   For an independent random sample of six advertisements in *Newsweek*, the fog indices were as follows:

   | 10.21 | 9.66 | 7.67 | 5.12 | 4.88 | 3.12 |

   Stating any assumptions you need to make, test against a two-sided alternative the null hypothesis that the two population mean fog indices are the same.

78. Independent random samples of insider and outsider corporate directors were asked to respond on a scale from one (strongly disagree) to four (strongly agree) to the statement: "The threat and actuality of takeovers of publicly held companies provide discipline for boards and managers to maximize the value of the company to shareholders."[51] For a sample of 202 insiders, the mean response was 2.83, and the sample standard deviation was .89. For a sample of 291 outsiders, the mean response was 3.00, and the sample standard deviation was .67. Test the null hypothesis that the population means are equal, against the alternative that the mean is higher for outsiders.

---

[49] E. F. Fern, "The use of focus groups for idea generation: The effects of group size, acquaintanceship, and moderator on response quantity and quality," *Journal of Marketing Research, 19* (1982), 1–13.

[50] Reported in F. K. Shuptrine and D. D. McVicker, "Readability levels of magazine advertisements," *Journal of Advertising Research, 21,* no. 5 (1981), 45–50.

[51] H. D. Dewhirst and J. Wang, "Boards of directors and hostile takeovers," *Journal of Managerial Issues, 4* (1992), 269–87.

79. Independent random samples of cosmetic and reconstructive plastic surgery patients were asked to assess the quality of service on a scale from one (low) to seven (high).[52] (These patients had received breast implants.) For a sample of eighty-three cosmetic patients, the mean rating was 6.543, and the sample standard deviation was .649. For a sample of fifty-four reconstructive patients, the mean rating was 6.733, and the sample standard deviation was .425. Test against a two-sided alternative the null hypothesis that the population mean ratings for these two types of patient are the same.

80. Of a random sample of 148 marketing majors, seventy-five rated a sense of humor as a very important trait to their career performance.[53] This same view was held by eighty-one of an independent random sample of 178 accounting majors.

   (a) Test at the 5%-level of significance the null hypothesis that at least one-half of all accounting majors rate a sense of humor as very important.

   (b) Test at the 5%-level of significance, against a two-sided alternative, the null hypothesis that the population proportions of marketing and accounting majors who rate a sense of humor as very important are the same.

81. In a study aimed at finding early warning signals of business failure, a random sample of twenty-three failed retail firms showed mean returns on assets 3 years previously was .058 and sample standard deviation .055. An independent random sample of twenty-three successful retail firms showed mean return of .146 and standard deviation .058 for the same period.[54] Assume that the two population distributions are normal with equal standard deviations. Test at the .5% significance level the null hypothesis that the population mean returns on assets are the same against the alternative that the true mean is higher for successful firms.

82. Random samples of employees in mid-sized plants where the employer provides a training program were drawn.[55] Of a sample of sixty-seven employees who had not completed high school, eleven had participated in a training program provided by their current employer. Of an independent random sample of 113 employees who had completed high school but had not attended college, twenty-seven had participated. Test at the 1% significance level the null hypothesis that the participation rates are the same for the two groups, against the alternative that the rate is lower for those who have not completed high school.

83. Of a random sample of sixty-nine industrial firms, forty-seven did public relations in-house, as did forty of an independent random sample of sixty-nine consumer goods firms.[56] Find and interpret the p-value of a test of equality of the population proportions against a two-sided alternative.

84. Independent random samples were taken of male and female clients of Small Business Development Centers.[57] These clients were considering starting a business. Of ninety-four male clients, fifty-three actually started a business venture, as did forty-seven of sixty-eight female clients. Find and interpret the p-value of a test of equality of the population proportions against the alternative that the proportion of female clients actually starting a business is higher than the proportion of male clients.

---

[52] E. Babakus, S. J. Remington, G. H. Lucas, and C. G. Carnell, "Issues in the practice of cosmetic surgery: consumers' use of information and perceptions of service quality," *Journal of Health Care Marketing*, *11*, no. 3 (1991), 12–18.

[53] H. P. Rogers, C. M. Kochuny, and A. Ogbuehi, "Ethical inclinations of tomorrow's marketers," *Journal of Marketing Education*, *15* (1993), 11–19.

[54] S. Sharma and V. Mahajan, "Early warning indicators of business failure," *Journal of Marketing*, *44*, no. 4 (1980), 80–89.

[55] A. G. Holtmann and T. L. Idson, "Employer size and on-the-job training decisions," *Southern Economic Journal*, *58* (1991), 339–55.

[56] M. L. Ripley, "Why industrial advertising is often done in-house," *Industrial Marketing Management*, *21* (1992), 331–34.

[57] J. J. Chrisman, A. L. Carsrud, J. DeCastro, and L. Herron, "A comparison of assistance needs of male and female pre-venture entrepreneurs," *Journal of Business Venturing*, *5* (1990), 235–48.

85. Using the data of Exercise 76, test against a two-sided alternative the null hypothesis that the population standard deviation of the fog index of advertisements in *Scientific American* is the same as the population standard deviation of the fog index of advertisements in *Sports Illustrated*.

86. Based on the material of Section 9.8, can you use the data of Exercise 71 to test the null hypothesis of equality of population variances for absolute percentage forecast errors for the two analysts?

Some Nonparametric Tests

10.1 INTRODUCTION

In Chapter 9, several hypothesis tests that depended on the assumption of normality for population distributions were introduced. Frequently, the assumption of normality is reasonable. Moreover, by virtue of the central limit theorem, many of these test procedures remain approximately valid when applied to large samples even if the population distribution is not normal. However, it is often the case in practical applications that a normality assumption is not tenable. In these circumstances, it is desirable to base inference on tests that are valid over a wide range of distributions of the parent population. Such tests are called **nonparametric,** or **distribution-free.**

In this chapter, we describe nonparametric tests that are appropriate for analyzing some of the problems we have already met. Other nonparametric tests will be discussed in subsequent chapters. Although they do require certain assumptions, such as independent sample observations, nonparametric tests are generally valid *whatever* the population distribution. That is to say, tests can be developed that have the required significance levels, no matter what the distribution of the population members. It is not our intention here to attempt to describe the wide array of such tests that are available. Rather, our objective is the more modest one of providing a flavor of the methods used. In this chapter, we will discuss nonparametric procedures for testing the equality of the centers of two population distributions. These tests are nonparametric alternatives to the tests discussed in Section 9.6.

10.2 THE SIGN TEST

The simplest nonparametric test to carry out is the **sign test.** It is used for testing hypotheses about the central location of a population distribution and is most frequently employed in analyzing data from matched pairs.

Table 10.1 shows the results of a taste comparison experiment. A manufacturer of baked beans was contemplating a new recipe for the sauce used in its product. A random sample of eight individuals was chosen, and each was asked to rate on a scale from 1 to 10 the taste of the original and the proposed new product. The scores are shown in the table. Also shown are the differences in the scores for every taster and the signs of these differences. Thus, a + is assigned if the original product is preferred, a − if the new product is preferred, and 0 if the two products are rated equally. In this particular experiment, two tasters preferred the original product and five the new; one rated them equal.

The null hypothesis of interest is that in the population at large, there is no overall tendency to prefer one product over the other. In assessing this hypothesis, we compare the numbers expressing a preference for each product, discarding those who rated the products equally. In the present example then, the effective sample size is reduced to 7, and the only sample information on which our test is based is that two of the seven tasters preferred the original product.

The null hypothesis can be viewed as the hypothesis that the population median of the differences is 0 (which would be true, for example, if the differences came from a population whose distribution was symmetric about a mean of 0). If this hypothesis were true, our sequence of + and − differences could be regarded as a random sample from a population in which the probabilities for + and − were each .5. In that case, the observations would constitute a random sample from a binomial population in which the probability of + was .5. Thus, if p denotes the true proportion of +'s in the population, the null hypothesis is simply

$$H_0: \quad p = .5$$

We may want to test this hypothesis against either a one-sided or a two-sided alternative. Suppose that in the taste preference example, the alternative of interest is

TABLE 10.1 Taster ratings for baked beans

TASTER	RATING		DIFFERENCE	SIGN OF DIFFERENCE
	ORIGINAL PRODUCT	NEW PRODUCT		
A	6	8	−2	−
B	4	9	−5	−
C	5	4	1	+
D	8	7	1	+
E	3	9	−6	−
F	6	9	−3	−
G	7	7	0	0
H	5	9	−4	−

that in the population, the majority of preferences are for the new product. This alternative is expressed as

$$H_1: \quad p < .5$$

In testing the null hypothesis against this alternative, we ask, What is the probability of observing a sample result as extreme as or more extreme than that found if the null hypothesis were in fact true? If we denote by $P(x)$ the probability of observing x "successes" (+'s) in $n = 7$ binomial trials, each with probability of success .5, the probability of observing two or fewer +'s is

$$P(0) + P(1) + P(2) = .0078 + .0547 + .1641$$

$$= .2266$$

from Table 1 in the Appendix. Therefore, if we adopt the decision rule "Reject H_0 if two or fewer +'s occur in the sample," the probability is .2266 that the null hypothesis will be rejected when it is in fact true. Hence, such a test has significance level 22.66%, and in the present example, the null hypothesis can be rejected at this level. It is also important to ask at what level we fail to reject the null hypothesis. Had the decision rule required no + or one + for rejection, H_0 would not have been rejected. The significance level for this test is

$$P(0) + P(1) = .0625$$

Thus, the null hypothesis is not rejected by a 6.25%-level test.

We now summarize our findings about these data. The null hypothesis that in the population at large, as many people prefer the original product as the new is rejected against the alternative that the majority of the population prefer the new product, using a test with significance level 22.66%. However, the null hypothesis cannot be rejected using a test with significance level 6.25%. Thus, these data contain a modest amount of evidence against the hypothesis of population equality of preferences, but by no means an overwhelming amount. This could be a consequence of our having such a small number of sample observations.

Finally, we need to consider the case where the alternative hypothesis is two-sided, that is, where

$$H_1: \quad p \neq .5$$

In our example, this is the hypothesis that there is an overall preference in the population for either one of the products. If alternatives on each side of the null hypothesized value are treated symmetrically, a decision rule that would lead to rejection of the null hypothesis for these data is "Reject H_0 if either two or fewer or five or more +'s occur in the sample." The significance level for this test is

$$P(0) + P(1) + P(2) + P(5) + P(6) + P(7) = 2[P(0) + P(1) + P(2)] = .4532$$

since the probability function of the binomial distribution is symmetric for $p = .5$. The null hypothesis will not be rejected by the rule "Reject H_0 if either one or fewer or six or more +'s occur in the sample." This test has significance level

$$P(0) + P(1) + P(6) + P(7) = 2[P(0) + P(1)] = .1250$$

Hence, for a 12.5%-level test, the null hypothesis that half the population members with a preference prefer the new product is not rejected against a two-sided alternative.

The Sign Test

The **sign test** can be used to test the null hypothesis that a population median is 0. Suppose that a random sample is taken from the population, and the observations equal to 0 are discarded, leaving n observations. The null hypothesis to be tested is that the proportion p of nonzero observations in the population that are positive is .5; that is

$$H_0: \quad p = .5$$

The test is then based on the fact that the number of positive observations in the sample has a binomial distribution (with $p = .5$ under the null hypothesis).

If the number of sample observations is large, the normal approximation to the binomial distribution can be used to carry out the sign test. Once again, this is a consequence of the central limit theorem.

The Sign Test: Large Samples

If the number n of nonzero sample observations is large,[1] the sign test is based on the normal approximation to the binomial. The test of

$$H_0: \quad p = .5$$

is then precisely that described in Section 9.5.

EXAMPLE
10.1

A random sample of 100 children was asked to compare two new ice cream flavors—peanut butter ripple and bubblegum surprise. Fifty-six sample members preferred peanut butter ripple, forty preferred bubblegum surprise, and four expressed no preference. Test against a two-sided alternative the null hypothesis that there is no overall preference in this population for one flavor over the other.

If p is the population proportion of all children expressing a preference who favor peanut butter ripple we want to test

$$H_0: \quad p = .5$$

against

$$H_1: \quad p \neq .5$$

---

[1] This approximation is adequate for samples of more than twenty observations. (This sample size is generally sufficient for using the normal approximation when testing the null hypothesis that the binomial probability is .5; however, as we noted in Chapter 9, larger sample sizes are desirable for more extreme values of this parameter.)

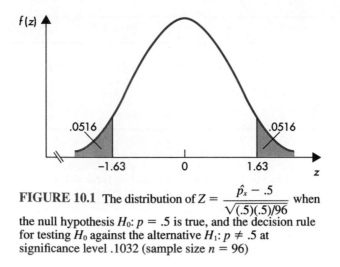

FIGURE 10.1 The distribution of $Z = \dfrac{\hat{p}_x - .5}{\sqrt{(.5)(.5)/96}}$ when the null hypothesis H_0: $p = .5$ is true, and the decision rule for testing H_0 against the alternative H_1: $p \neq .5$ at significance level .1032 (sample size $n = 96$)

Since four children gave no preference, we are left with $n = 96$ sample members. The sample proportion preferring peanut butter ripple is

$$\hat{p}_x = \frac{56}{96} = .583$$

For a test of significance level α, the decision rule (see Section 9.5) is

$$\text{Reject } H_0 \text{ if } \frac{\hat{p}_x - .5}{\sqrt{(.5)(.5)/n}} < -z_{\alpha/2} \quad \text{or} \quad \frac{\hat{p}_x - .5}{\sqrt{(.5)(.5)/n}} > z_{\alpha/2}$$

Here we have

$$\frac{\hat{p}_x - .5}{\sqrt{(.5)(.5)/n}} = \frac{.583 - .5}{\sqrt{(.5)(.5)/96}} = 1.63$$

From Table 3 of the Appendix, we find that if $z_{\alpha/2} = 1.63$, $\alpha/2 = .0516$, so $\alpha = .1032$. Hence, the null hypothesis can be rejected at all significance levels greater than 10.32% If the null hypothesis that as many children prefer peanut butter ripple as prefer bubblegum surprise were true, the chance of observing a sample outcome as extreme as or more extreme than that actually obtained would be a little higher than 1 in 10. These data, then, contain a modest amount of evidence against that hypothesis.

This test is illustrated in Figure 10.1, which shows tail area probabilities of the standard normal distribution corresponding to the upper and lower 5.16% of the total area under the probability density function.

EXERCISES

1. A random sample of twelve financial analysts was asked to predict the percentage increases in the prices of two common stocks over the next year. The results obtained are shown in the table. Use the sign test to test the null hypothesis that for the population of analysts, there is no overall preference for one stock over the other.

ANALYST	STOCK 1	STOCK 2	ANALYST	STOCK 1	STOCK 2
A	6.8	7.1	G	9.3	10.1
B	9.8	12.3	H	1.0	2.7
C	2.1	5.3	I	−.2	1.3
D	6.2	6.8	J	9.6	9.8
E	7.1	7.2	K	12.0	12.0
F	6.5	6.2	L	6.3	8.9

2. An organization offers a program designed to increase the level of comprehension achieved by students when reading technical material quickly. Each member of a random sample of ten students was given 30 minutes to read an article. A test of the level of comprehension achieved was then administered. This process was repeated after these students had completed the program. The accompanying table shows comprehension scores before and after completion of the program. Use the sign test to test the null hypothesis that for this population, there is no overall improvement in comprehension levels following completion of the program.

STUDENT	BEFORE	AFTER	STUDENT	BEFORE	AFTER
A	62	69	F	53	61
B	63	72	G	49	63
C	84	80	H	58	59
D	70	70	I	83	87
E	60	69	J	92	98

3. A sample of eleven grocery store managers in stores having electronic coupon programs were asked if their customers have a positive attitude about electronic coupons.[2] Seven managers answered "yes," and four answered "no." Test against a two-sided alternative the null hypothesis that, for the population of managers, responses would be equally divided between "yes" and "no."

4. A sample of sixty corporations buying back franchises was examined.[3] Of these cases, returns on common stock around the buy-back announcement date were positive thirty-nine times, negative eighteen times, and zero three times. Test the null hypothesis that positive and negative returns are equally likely against the alternative that positive returns are more likely.

5. Of a random sample of 130 voters, forty-four favored a state tax increase to raise funding for education, sixty-eight opposed the tax increase, and eighteen expressed no opinion. Test against a two-sided alternative the null hypothesis that voters in the state are evenly divided on the issue of this tax increase.

6. A random sample of sixty professional economists was asked to predict whether next year's inflation rate would be higher than, lower than, or about the same as in the current year. The results are shown in the following table. Test the null hypothesis that the profession is evenly divided on the question.

[2] See D. R. Hoffman, A. F. Ketcham and F. A. Taylor, "Electronic coupons: A double-barreled sales promotion technique," *Mid-American Journal of Business*, 7 (1992), no. 1, 42–48.

[3] Results due to J. A. Brickley, F. H. Dark and M. S. Weisbach, "An agency perspective on franchising," *Financial Management*, 20 (1991), no. 1, 27–35.

PREDICTION	NUMBER
Higher	20
Lower	29
About the same	11

10.3 THE WILCOXON TEST

We saw in Section 10.2 that the sign test provides an easy test procedure for comparing populations when a sample of matched pairs is available. One difficulty with the test is that it takes account of only a very limited amount of information—namely, the signs of the differences. For example, in Table 10.1, the sign test takes account only of which product is preferred, ignoring the strengths of the preferences. When the sample size is small, it might be suspected therefore that the test would not be very powerful. In fact, it is possible to take some account not only of the signs but also of the magnitudes of the differences between matched pairs and still achieve a test that is distribution-free. The **Wilcoxon test** provides a method of incorporating information about the relative sizes of the differences. Like very many nonparametric tests, it is based on *ranks*.

To illustrate, Table 10.2 extends the calculations of Table 10.1 for the data on the ratings of two baked bean products.

The test statistic for the Wilcoxon test is calculated as follows:

1. As in the sign test, differences of 0 are ignored, so in this example, the effective number of sample observations is seven.
2. The nonzero absolute differences are then ranked in ascending order of magnitude. If two or more values are equal, they are assigned the average of the next available ranks. In our example, the two smallest absolute differences are equal. The rank assigned them is therefore the average of ranks 1 and 2—that is, 1.5. The next value is assigned rank 3, and so on. Proceeding in this way, we rank all differences.
3. The ranks for positive and negative differences are summed separately. The smaller of these sums is the Wilcoxon statistic T. From Table 10.2, the two sums in this case are 3 and 25, so $T = 3$.

TABLE 10.2 Calculation of Wilcoxon test statistic for taste preference data

TASTER	DIFFERENCE		RANK (+)	RANK (−)
A	−2			3
B	−5			6
C	1		1.5	
D	1		1.5	
E	−6			7
F	−3			4
G	0			
H	−4			5
		Sums	3	25

We will now suppose, as if often reasonable, that the population distribution of the paired differences is symmetric. The null hypothesis to be tested is that the center of this distribution is 0. In our example, then, we are assuming that differences in the ratings of the two products have a symmetric distribution, and we want to test whether that distribution is centered on 0—that is, no difference between ratings. We would be suspicious of the null hypothesis if the sum of the ranks for positive differences was very different from that for negative differences. Hence, the null hypothesis will be rejected for low values of the statistic T. Cutoff points for the distribution of this random variable are given in Table 8 of the Appendix for tests against a one-sided alternative that the population distribution of the paired differences is specified either to be centered on some number bigger than 0 or to be centered on some number less than 0. In our example, we might want to take the alternative hypothesis that the new product tends to be preferred over the original. This would imply that the distribution of the paired differences in ratings is centered on some number less than 0. From Table 8, we see that for a sample size of $n = 7$, the cutoff points are 3 for a 2.5%-level test and 4 for a 5%-level test. Hence, the null hypothesis is rejected against the one-sided alternative at the 5% level and is just rejected at the 2.5% level. The evidence against the hypothesis that the population differences in ratings for these products is centered on 0 is quite strong. It appears likely that overall, ratings are higher for the new product.

If the alternative hypothesis is two-sided—that is, that the population differences are centered on some number other than 0—the appropriate significance levels are twice those for the one-sided alternative. Hence, for these data, the null hypothesis is rejected against a two-sided alternative at the 10% level and is just rejected at the 5% level of significance.

Notice that using the additional information provided by the ranks allows the rejection of the null hypothesis at a much lower level of significance than was possible for the sign test.

The Wilcoxon Test

The **Wilcoxon test** can be employed when a random sample of matched pairs of observations is available. We assume that the population distribution of the differences in matched pairs is symmetric, and we want to test the null hypothesis that this distribution is centered on 0. Discarding pairs for which the difference is 0, we rank the remaining n absolute differences in ascending order. The sums of the ranks corresponding to positive and negative differences are calculated, and the smaller of these sums is the Wilcoxon test statistic T. The null hypothesis is rejected if T is less than or equal to the value in Table 8 of the Appendix.

When the number n of nonzero differences in the sample is large,[4] the normal distribution provides a good approximation to the distribution of the Wilcoxon statistic T under the null hypothesis. It can be shown that when the null hypothesis that the population differences are centered on 0 is true, the mean and variance of this distribution are

---

[4] The approximation is adequate for twenty or more observations.

$$E(T) = \mu_T = \frac{n(n + 1)}{4}$$

and

$$\text{Var }(T) = \sigma_T^2 = \frac{n(n + 1)(2n + 1)}{24}$$

Then, for large n, the distribution of the random variable

$$Z = \frac{T - \mu_T}{\sigma_T}$$

is approximately standard normal, and tests can be based on this result, as indicated in the box.

The Wilcoxon Test: Large Samples

If the number n of nonzero differences is large and T is the observed value of the Wilcoxon statistic, the following tests have significance level α:

(i) If the alternative hypothesis is one-sided, reject the null hypothesis if

$$\frac{T - \mu_T}{\sigma_T} < -z_\alpha$$

(ii) If the alternative hypothesis is two-sided, reject the null hypothesis if

$$\frac{T - \mu_T}{\sigma_T} < -z_{\alpha/2}$$

EXAMPLE 10.2

A study compared firms with and without sophisticated postaudit procedures.[5] A sample of thirty-one matched pairs of firms was examined. For each firm the ratio of market valuation to replacement cost of assets was computed as a measure of firm performance. In each of the thirty-one pairs, one firm employed sophisticated postaudit procedures, and the other did not. The thirty-one differences in ratios were calculated, and the absolute differences ranked. The smaller of the rank sums, 189, was for those pairs where the ratio was higher for the firm without sophisticated postaudit procedures. Test the null hypothesis that the distribution of differences in ratios is centered on 0 against the alternative that the ratio of market valuation to replacement cost of assets tends to be lower for firms without sophisticated postaudit procedures.

Given a sample of $n = 31$ pairs, the Wilcoxon statistic has, under the null hypothesis, mean

$$\mu_T = \frac{n(n + 1)}{4} = \frac{(31)(32)}{4} = 248$$

---

[5] This example is adapted from results given in M. D. Myers, L. A. Gordon and M. M. Hamer, "Postauditing capital assets and firm performance: an empirical investigation," *Managerial and Decision Economics*, *12* (1991), 317–27.

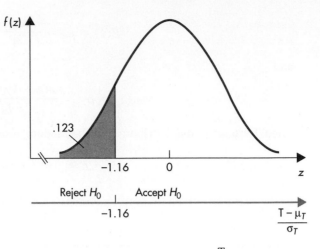

FIGURE 10.2 The distribution of $Z = \dfrac{T - \mu_T}{\sigma_T}$ when the null hypothesis that the distribution of the paired differences is centered on 0 is true, and the decision rule for testing against a one-sided alternative at significance level .123.

and variance

$$\sigma_T{}^2 = \frac{n(n + 1)(2n + 1)}{24} = \frac{(31)(32)(63)}{24} = 2{,}604$$

so that the standard deviation is

$$\sigma_T = 51.03$$

If T is the observed value of the statistic, the null hypothesis is rejected against the one-sided alternative if

$$\frac{T - \mu_T}{\sigma_T} < -z_\alpha$$

Here, $T = 189$, and

$$\frac{T - \mu_T}{\sigma_T} = \frac{189 - 248}{51.03} = -1.16$$

The value of α corresponding to $z_\alpha = 1.16$ is, from Table 3 of the Appendix, $(1 - .8770) = .123$. Then the null hypothesis can be rejected at all significance levels greater than 12.3%. The data contain modest evidence suggesting better performance for corporations with sophisticated postaudit procedures, but that evidence is not overwhelmingly strong. The test is illustrated in Figure 10.2.

10.4 THE MANN-WHITNEY TEST

In Section 10.3, we saw how the central locations of two population distributions could be compared when a random sample of matched pairs was available. In this section, we introduce a test for the same problem when *independent random samples* are taken from the two populations.

Table 10.3 shows the numbers of hours per week students claim to spend studying for introductory finance and accounting courses. The data are from independent random samples of ten finance students and twelve accounting students.

Our null hypothesis is that the central locations of the two population distributions are identical. As a first step in testing this hypothesis, the two samples are pooled and the observations are ranked in ascending order, ties being treated in the same way as previously. These ranks are shown in Table 10.3. Now, if the null hypothesis were true, we would expect the average ranks for the two samples to be quite close. In this particular example, the average rank for the finance students is 9.35, while that for the accounting students is 13.29. As usual, when testing hypotheses, we want to know how likely a discrepancy of this magnitude would be if the null hypothesis were true.

We note that it is not necessary to calculate both rank sums, for if we know one, we can deduce the other. In our example, for instance, the ranks must sum to the sum of the integers 1 through 22—that is, to 253. Thus, any test of our hypothesis can be based on just one of the rank sums.

In general, suppose that n_1 observations are available from the first population and n_2 from the second, and let R_1 denote the sum of the ranks of the observations from the first population. The **Mann-Whitney test statistic** is then defined as

$$U = n_1 n_2 + \frac{n_1(n_1 + 1)}{2} - R_1$$

In testing the null hypothesis that the central locations of the two population distributions are the same, we assume that apart from any possible differences in central location, the two population distributions are identical. It can be shown, then, that if the null hypothesis is true, the random variable U has mean

$$E(U) = \mu_U = \frac{n_1 n_2}{2}$$

and variance

TABLE 10.3 Number of hours per week spent studying for introductory finance and accounting courses

FINANCE	(RANK)	ACCOUNTING	(RANK)
10	(10)	13	(17.5)
6	(2)	17	(22)
8	(4.5)	14	(19)
10	(10)	12	(15.5)
12	(15.5)	10	(10)
13	(17.5)	9	(7)
11	(13)	15	(20)
9	(7)	16	(21)
5	(1)	11	(13)
11	(13)	8	(4.5)
		9	(7)
		7	(3)
Rank sum	93.5	Rank sum	159.5

$$\text{Var} (U) = \sigma_U{}^2 = \frac{n_1 n_2 (n_1 + n_2 + 1)}{12}$$

Furthermore, under the null hypothesis, the distribution of U approaches the normal quite rapidly as the number of sample observations increases.[6] Hence, for moderately large sample sizes, the distribution of the random variable

$$Z = \frac{U - \mu_U}{\sigma_U}$$

is well approximated by the standard normal. This allows tests to be carried out in a straightforward manner, as described in the box.

The Mann-Whitney Test

Suppose that we have independent random samples of n_1 and n_2 observations from two populations. If the sample observations are pooled and ranked, with R_1 denoting the sum of the ranks for the first population, the Mann-Whitney test statistic is

$$U = n_1 n_2 + \frac{n_1 (n_1 + 1)}{2} - R_1$$

It is assumed that the two population distributions are identical, apart from any possible differences in central location. In testing the null hypothesis that the two population distributions have the same central location, the following tests have significance level α:

(i) If the alternative is the one-sided hypothesis that the location of population 1 is higher than that of population 2, the decision rule is

$$\text{Reject } H_0 \text{ if } \quad \frac{U - \mu_U}{\sigma_U} < -z_\alpha$$

(ii) If the alternative is the one-sided hypothesis that the location of population 1 is lower than that of population 2, the decision rule is

$$\text{Reject } H_0 \text{ if } \quad \frac{U - \mu_U}{\sigma_U} > z_\alpha$$

(iii) If the alternative is the two-sided hypothesis that the two population distributions differ, the decision rule is

$$\text{Reject } H_0 \text{ if } \quad \frac{U - \mu_U}{\sigma_U} < -z_{\alpha/2} \quad \text{ or } \quad \frac{U - \mu_U}{\sigma_U} > z_{\alpha/2}$$

We now return to the example introduced in this section. Suppose that we want to test the null hypothesis that the central locations of the distributions of study times are identical against the two-sided alternative. For these data, we have

$$n_1 = 10 \qquad n_2 = 12 \qquad R_1 = 93.5$$

so the value observed for the Mann-Whitney statistic is

---

[6] The approximation is adequate if each sample contains ten or more observations.

$$U = n_1 n_2 + \frac{n_1(n_1 + 1)}{2} - R_1$$

$$= (10)(12) + \frac{(10)(11)}{2} - 93.5 = 81.5$$

Under the null hypothesis, the distribution of the statistic has mean

$$\mu_U = \frac{n_1 n_2}{2} = \frac{(10)(12)}{2} = 60$$

and variance

$$\sigma_U{}^2 = \frac{n_1 n_2(n_1 + n_2 + 1)}{12} = \frac{(10)(12)(23)}{12} = 230$$

The decision rule is to reject the null hypothesis if

$$\frac{U - \mu_U}{\sigma_U} < -z_{\alpha/2} \qquad \text{or} \qquad \frac{U - \mu_U}{\sigma_U} > z_{\alpha/2}$$

Here

$$\frac{U - \mu_U}{\sigma_U} = \frac{81.5 - 60}{\sqrt{230}} = 1.42$$

Now, from Table 3 of the Appendix, the value of $\alpha/2$ corresponding to a value 1.42 for $z_{\alpha/2}$ is .0778, so the corresponding α is .1556. Hence, the null hypothesis can be rejected against the two-sided alternative at levels higher than 15.56%, as indicated in Figure 10.3. Thus, these data do not contain terribly strong evidence against the

FIGURE 10.3 The distribution of $Z = \dfrac{U - \mu_U}{\sigma_U}$ when the null hypothesis that the central locations of the two population distributions are identical is true, and the decision rule for testing this hypothesis against the two-sided alternative at significance level .1556

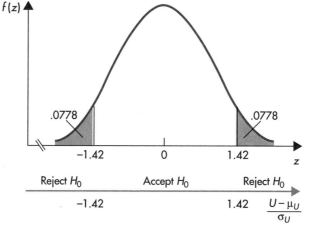

hypothesis that the central locations of the distributions of study times in accounting and finance are the same. There is not very strong support for the conclusion that on the whole, students spend more time studying for one of these subjects than the other.

EXAMPLE 10.3

In a study designed to compare the performance of firms that give management forecasts of earnings with those that do not, independent random samples of eighty firms from each of the populations were taken.[7] The variability of the growth rate of earnings over the previous ten periods was measured for each of the 160 firms, and these variabilities were ranked. The sum of the ranks for firms not disclosing management earnings forecasts was 7,287. Test against a two-sided alternative the null hypothesis that the central locations of the population distributions of earnings variabilities are the same for these two types of firms.

Since we have $n_1 = 80$, $n_2 = 80$, and $R_1 = 7,287$, the calculated value of the Mann-Whitney statistic is

$$U = n_1 n_2 + \frac{n_1(n_1 + 1)}{2} - R_1 = (80)(80) + \frac{(80)(81)}{2} - 7,287 = 2,353$$

Under the null hypothesis, the Mann-Whitney statistic has mean

$$\mu_U = \frac{n_1 n_2}{2} = \frac{(80)(80)}{2} = 3,200$$

and variance

$$\sigma_U^2 = \frac{n_1 n_2 (n_1 + n_2 + 1)}{12} = \frac{(80)(80)(161)}{12} = 85,867$$

The decision rule is to reject the null hypothesis against a two-sided alternative if

$$\frac{U - \mu_U}{\sigma_U} < -z_{\alpha/2} \qquad \text{or} \qquad \frac{U - \mu_U}{\sigma_U} > z_{\alpha/2}$$

Here, we have

$$\frac{U - \mu_U}{\sigma_U} = \frac{2,353 - 3,200}{\sqrt{85,867}} = -2.89$$

From Table 3 of the Appendix, we see that the value of $\alpha/2$ corresponding to a value 2.89 for $z_{\alpha/2}$ is .0019, so α is .0038. Hence, the null hypothesis can be rejected at all levels higher than .38%. These data, then, present very strong evidence against the hypothesis that the central locations of the distributions of population variabilities in earnings growth rates are the same for firms that give management earnings forecasts as for those that do not. On the contrary, it appears that in the aggregate, there is more variability in earnings for one group of firms than for the other.

Now, if we had been given the actual data rather than just the ranks, we could have carried out a test of the null hypothesis using the methods of Section 9.6. However, using the Mann-Whitney test, we have found that the null hypothesis can be rejected *without having to make the assumption of population normality.*

---

[7] This example is adapted from results given in B. Jaggi and P. Grier, "A comparative analysis of forecast disclosing and nondisclosing firms," *Financial Management*, 9, no. 2 (1980), 38–43.

10.5 DISCUSSION

The nonparametric tests discussed in this chapter represent a very small subset of the nonparametric procedures in current use. We will meet some other distribution-free tests in later chapters.

It is instructive to compare the tests of this chapter with those of Section 9.6, where we considered the problem of testing the equality of two population means, *assuming the population distributions to be normal*. The tests developed in this chapter can be regarded also as tests of this null hypothesis, but assuming only that the two population distributions have the same shape. This brings out the major advantage of nonparametric methods: They are appropriate under a wide range of assumptions about the underlying population distributions.

Nonparametric methods also have the following advantages:

1. They are often computationally more straightforward, so that the tests can be carried out quite rapidly. This is particularly true of the sign test.
2. The data available to the investigator may be of the natural form for these tests. For example, if all that was known in a product comparison study was which product is preferred, the sign test would be immediately applicable. In many practical situations, data are available only in the form of ranks, leading naturally to such procedures as the Wilcoxon test or the Mann-Whitney test.
3. Just as the mean is greatly susceptible to influence by extreme outlying observations, so are inferences based on the *t* tests of Section 9.6. By contrast, tests based on ranks give far less weight to odd outlying sample values.

Of course, when the assumption of normality in the population is at least approximately true, one would expect tests based on the assumption to be more powerful than tests based on rankings, since the latter discard some of the information in the data. In fact, however, at least in samples of moderate size, tests such as the Wilcoxon and Mann-Whitney are only a little less powerful than the competing *t* tests when the population distributions are normal. For this reason, together with their broader applicability, these nonparametric tests are very popular. Moreover, when the population distribution differs markedly from the normal, nonparametric tests can have much more power than the corresponding normal-theory tests.

However, nonparametric methods are rather difficult to extend to problems that involve complex model building. For this reason, the traditional procedures of Chapter 9, whose development is far more straightforward, remain in the mainstream of statistical analysis.

EXERCISES

7. Use the Wilcoxon test to analyze the data of Exercise 1. Discuss your findings.
8. A random sample of ten students were asked to rate, in a blind taste test, the quality of two brands of beer, one domestic and one imported. Ratings were on a scale from one (poor) to ten (excellent). The accompanying table gives the results. Use the Wilcoxon test to test the null hypothesis that the distribution of the paired differences is centered on 0 against the alternative that the imported brand is preferred by the population of all student beer drinkers.

STUDENT	DOMESTIC	IMPORTED	STUDENT	DOMESTIC	IMPORTED
A	2	6	F	4	8
B	3	5	G	3	9
C	7	6	H	4	6
D	8	8	I	5	4
E	7	5	J	6	9

9. Sixteen freshmen on a college campus were grouped into eight pairs, in such a way that the two members of any pair were as similar as possible in academic backgrounds—as measured by high school class rank and achievement test scores—and also in social backgrounds. The major difference within pairs was that one student was from in state and the other from out of state. At the end of the first year of college, grade point averages of these students were recorded, yielding the results shown in the table. Use the Wilcoxon test to analyze the data. Discuss the implications of the test results.

PAIR	IN STATE	OUT OF STATE	PAIR	IN STATE	OUT OF STATE
A	3.4	2.8	E	3.9	3.7
B	3.0	3.1	F	2.3	2.8
C	2.4	2.7	G	2.6	2.6
D	3.8	3.3	H	3.7	3.3

10. A random sample of forty business majors who had just completed introductory courses in both statistics and accounting was asked to rate each in terms of level of interest, on a scale from one (very uninteresting) to ten (very interesting). The forty differences in the pairs of ratings were calculated and the absolute differences ranked. The smaller of the rank sums, which was for those finding accounting the more interesting, was 281. Test the null hypothesis that the population of business majors would rate these courses equally against the alternative that the statistics course is viewed as the more interesting.

11. A consultant is interested in the impact of the introduction of a total quality management program on job satisfaction of employees. A random sample of thirty employees was asked to assess level of satisfaction on a scale from one (very dissatisfied) to ten (very satisfied) three months before the introduction of the program. These same sample members were asked to make this assessment again three months after the introduction of the program. The thirty differences in the pairs of ratings were calculated and the absolute differences ranked. The smaller of the rank sums, which was for those more satisfied before the introduction of the program, was 169. What can be concluded from these findings?

12. A random sample of eighty owners of videocassette recorders was taken. Each sample member was asked to assess the amounts of time in a month spent watching material he or she had recorded from television broadcasts and on watching purchased or rented commercially recorded tapes. The eighty differences in times spent were then calculated and their absolute values ranked. The smaller of the rank sums, which was for material recorded from television, was 1,502. Discuss the implications of these sample results.

13. A corporation interviews both marketing and finance majors for general management positions. A random sample of ten marketing majors and an independent random sample of fourteen finance majors were subjected to intensive interviewing and testing by a team of the corporation's senior managers. The candidates were then ranked from 1 (most suitable for employment) to 24, as shown in the accompanying table. Test the null hypothesis that overall, the corporation's senior management has no preference between marketing and finance majors against the alternative that finance majors are preferred.

1. finance	9. marketing	17. marketing
2. finance	10. marketing	18. marketing
3. marketing	11. finance	19. finance
4. finance	12. finance	20. finance
5. finance	13. marketing	21. finance
6. marketing	14. finance	22. marketing
7. finance	15. finance	23. marketing
8. marketing	16. finance	24. finance

14. A random sample of fifteen male students and an independent random sample of fifteen female students were asked to write essays at the conclusion of a writing course. Those essays were then ranked from 1 (best) to 30 (worst) by a professor. The following rankings resulted.

MALE:	26	24	15	16	8	29	12	6	18
	11	13	19	10	28	7			

FEMALE:	22	2	17	25	14	21	5	30	3
	9	4	1	27	23	20			

Test the null hypothesis that, in the aggregate the two sexes are equally ranked, against a two-sided alternative.

15. A newsletter rates mutual funds. Independent random samples of ten funds with the highest rating and ten funds with the lowest rating were chosen. The following figures are percentage rates of return achieved by these twenty funds in the next year.

HIGHEST RATED:	8.1	12.7	13.9	2.3	16.1	5.4	7.3
	9.8	14.3	4.1				

LOWEST RATED:	3.5	14.0	11.1	4.7	6.2	13.3	7.0
	7.3	4.6	10.0				

Test the null hypothesis of no difference between the central locations of population distributions of rates of return against the alternative that the highest rated funds tended to achieve higher rates of return than lowest rated funds.

16. A random sample of fifty students was asked what salary the college should be prepared to pay to attract the right individual to coach the football team. An independent random sample of fifty faculty members was asked the same question. The 100 salary figures were then pooled and ranked in order (with rank 1 assigned to the lowest salary). The sum of the ranks for faculty members was 2,024. Test the null hypothesis that there is no difference between the central locations of the distributions of salary proposals of students and faculty members against the alternative that in the aggregate, students would propose a higher salary to attract a football coach.

17. The time taken in days from year-end for a random sample of 120 Australian companies with clean audit reports to release a preliminary profit report was compared with the time taken for an independent random sample of eighty-six companies whose reports had a "subject to" qualification.[8] The times taken for the 206 companies were pooled and

---

[8] Results reported in G. P. Whittred, "Audit qualification and the timeliness of corporate annual reports," *Accounting Review*, 55 (1980), 563–77.

ranked, with shortest time assigned rank 1. The sum of the ranks for companies with a "subject to" qualification was 9,686. Test the null hypothesis that the central locations of the two population distributions are identical against the alternative that companies with "subject to" qualifications tend to take longer to produce their preliminary profit reports.

18. Starting salaries of M.B.A. graduates from two leading business schools were compared. Independent random samples of thirty students from each school were taken, and the sixty starting salaries were pooled and ranked. The sum of the ranks for students from one of these schools was 1,243. Test the null hypothesis that the central locations of the population distributions are identical.

REVIEW EXERCISES

19. What does it mean to say that a test is nonparametric? What are the relative advantages of such tests?

20. Construct a realistic example of a statistical problem in the business area where you would prefer the use of a nonparametric test to the alternative parametric test.

21. In a random sample of twelve analysts, seven believed that automobile sales in the United States were likely to be significantly higher next year than in the present year, two believed that sales would be significantly lower, and the others anticipated that next year's sales would be roughly the same as those in the current year. What can you conclude from these data?

22. In a random sample of sixteen exchange rate analysts, eight believed that the Japanese yen would be an excellent investment this year, five believed that it would be a poor investment, and three had no strong opinion on the question. What conclusions can be drawn from these data?

23. Of a random sample of 100 college students, thirty-five expected to achieve a higher standard of living than their parents, forty-three expected a lower standard of living, and twenty-two expected about the same standard of living as their parents. Do these data present strong evidence that, for the population of students, more expect a lower standard of living, compared with their parents, than expect a higher standard of living?

24. Of a random sample of 120 business school professors, forty-eight believed students' analytical skills had improved over the last decade, thirty-five believed these skills had deteriorated, and thirty-seven saw no discernible change. Evaluate the strength of the sample evidence suggesting that, for all business school professors, more believe that analytical skills have improved than believe that these skills have deteriorated.

25. A random sample of ten corporate analysts was asked to rate, on a scale from 1 (very poor) to 10 (very high), the prospects for their own corporations and for the economy at large in the current year. The results obtained are shown in the accompanying table. Using the Wilcoxon test, discuss the proposition that in the aggregate, corporate analysts are more optimistic about the prospect for their own companies than for the economy at large.

ANALYST	OWN CORPORATION	ECONOMY AT LARGE	ANALYST	OWN CORPORATION	ECONOMY AT LARGE
1	8	8	6	6	9
2	7	5	7	7	7
3	6	7	8	5	2
4	5	4	9	4	6
5	8	4	10	9	6

26. Nine pairs of hypothetical profiles were constructed for business school graduates applying for general management positions. Within each pair, these profiles were identical, except that one candidate was male and the other female. For interviews for employment of these graduates, evaluations on a scale of 1 (low) to 10 (high) were made of the candidates' suitability for employment. The results are shown in the accompanying table. Analyze these data using the Wilcoxon test.

INTERVIEW	MALE	FEMALE	INTERVIEW	MALE	FEMALE
1	8	8	6	9	9
2	9	10	7	5	3
3	7	5	8	4	5
4	4	7	9	6	2
5	8	8			

27. A study compared firms with and without an audit committee.[9] For samples of firms of each type, the extent of directors' ownership was measured as number of shares owned by the board as a proportion of the total number of shares issued. In the sample, directors' ownership was, overall, higher for firms without an audit committee. To test for statistical significance, the Mann-Whitney U statistic was calculated. Then, $(U - \mu_U)/\sigma_U$ was found to be 2.01. What can you conclude from this result?

28. A stock market analyst produced at the beginning of the year a list of stocks to buy and another list of stocks to sell. For a random sample of ten stocks from the "buy list," percentage returns over the year were as follows:

$$9.6 \quad 5.8 \quad 13.8 \quad 17.2 \quad 11.6$$
$$4.2 \quad 3.1 \quad 11.7 \quad 13.9 \quad 12.3$$

For an independent random sample of ten stocks from the "sell list," percentage returns over the year were as follows:

$$-2.7 \quad 6.2 \quad 8.9 \quad 11.3 \quad 2.1$$
$$3.9 \quad -2.4 \quad 1.3 \quad 7.9 \quad 10.2$$

Use the Mann-Whitney test to interpret these data.

29. For a random sample of twelve graduates in business from a technical college, the starting salaries accepted for employment on graduation (in thousands of dollars) were the following:

$$26.2 \quad 29.3 \quad 31.3 \quad 28.7 \quad 27.4 \quad 25.1$$
$$26.0 \quad 27.2 \quad 27.5 \quad 29.8 \quad 32.6 \quad 34.6$$

For an independent random sample of ten graduates from a state university, the corresponding figures were as follows:

$$25.3 \quad 28.2 \quad 29.2 \quad 27.1 \quad 26.8$$
$$26.5 \quad 30.7 \quad 31.3 \quad 26.3 \quad 24.9$$

Analyze the data using the Mann-Whitney test, and comment on the results.

30. The data of Exercise 29 could have been analyzed using one of the tests discussed in Chapter 9. Which one? Which test would you prefer to use in this particular case? Why?

---

[9] M. E. Bradbury, "The incentives for voluntary audit committee formation," *Journal of Accounting and Public Policy, 9* (1990), 19–36.

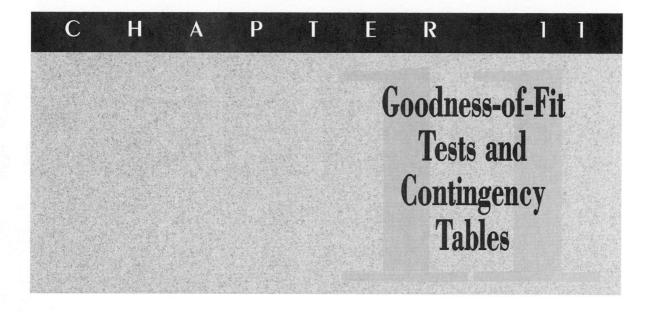

CHAPTER 11

Goodness-of-Fit Tests and Contingency Tables

11.1 GOODNESS-OF-FIT TESTS

In this chapter, we discuss some tests that require comparison of test statistics with tabulated values of the chi-square distribution. We begin by illustrating the most straightforward test of this type with a numerical example. A study observed a random sample of thirty-three subjects purchasing three soft drinks.[1] Of these subjects, fifteen selected three different varieties, ten selected two of one variety and one of a second, and eight selected all three of the same variety. This information is displayed in Table 11.1, which lists the numbers of sample members in each of three possible categories.

More generally, we may have a random sample of n observations that can be classified according to K categories. If the numbers of observations falling into each category are $O_1, O_2, \ldots, O_K$, the setup is as shown in Table 11.2.

The sample data are to be used to test a null hypothesis specifying the probabilities that an observation falls in each of the categories. In our example, the null hypothesis (H_0) might be that a randomly chosen subject is equally likely to select one, two, or three different varieties. This null hypothesis, then, specifies that the probability is one-third that a sample observation falls into each of the three categories. To test this hypothesis, it is natural to compare the sample numbers *observed* with what would be *expected* if the null hypothesis were true. In our example, given a total of thirty-three sample observations, the expected number of subjects in each category under the null hypothesis would be $(33)(1/3) = 11$. This information is summarized in Table 11.3.

---

[1] I. Simonson, "The effect of purchase quantity and timing on variety-seeking behavior," *Journal of Marketing Research*, 27 (1990), 150–62.

TABLE 11.1 Number of varieties selected in purchase of three soft drinks

CATEGORY (NUMBER OF VARIETIES)	1	2	3	Total
NUMBER OF SUBJECTS	8	10	15	33

TABLE 11.2 Classification of n observations into K categories

CATEGORY	1	2	$\cdots$	K	Total
NUMBER OF OBSERVATIONS	O_1	O_2	$\cdots$	O_K	n

TABLE 11.3 Observed and expected number of varieties selected in purchase of three soft drinks

CATEGORY (NUMBER OF VARIETIES)	1	2	3	Total
OBSERVED NUMBER OF SUBJECTS	8	10	15	33
PROBABILITY (UNDER H_0)	1/3	1/3	1/3	1
EXPECTED NUMBER OF SUBJECTS (UNDER H_0)	11	11	11	33

More generally, where there are K categories, suppose that the null hypothesis specifies $p_1, p_2, \ldots, p_K$ for the probabilities that an observation falls into the categories. We assume that these possibilities are mutually exclusive and collectively exhaustive—that is, each sample observation must belong to one of the categories and cannot belong to more than one. In that case, the hypothesized probabilities must sum to 1, that is

$$p_1 + p_2 + \cdots + p_K = 1$$

Then, if there are n sample observations, the expected numbers in each category, under the null hypothesis, will be

$$E_i = np_i \qquad (i = 1, 2, \ldots, K)$$

This is shown in Table 11.4.

We have a null hypothesis about the population that specifies the probabilities that a sample observation will fall into each possible category. The sample observations are to be used to check this hypothesis. If the numbers of sample values observed in each category are very close to those expected if the null hypothesis were true, this fact would lend support to that hypothesis. We might, in such circumstances,

TABLE 11.4 Observed and expected numbers for n observations and K categories

CATEGORY	1	2	$\cdots$	K	Total
OBSERVED NUMBER	O_1	O_2	$\cdots$	O_K	n
PROBABILITY (UNDER H_0)	p_1	p_2	$\cdots$	p_K	1
EXPECTED NUMBER (UNDER H_0)	$E_1 = np_1$	$E_2 = np_2$	$\cdots$	$E_K = np_K$	n

say that the data provide a close *fit* to the assumed population distribution of probabilities. Our tests of the null hypothesis are based on an assessment of the closeness of this fit and are generally referred to as **goodness-of-fit tests.**

Now, in order to test the null hypothesis, it is natural to look at the magnitudes of the discrepancies between what is observed and what is expected. The larger these discrepancies in absolute value, the more suspicious we are of the null hypothesis. It can be shown that when the null hypothesis is true and the sample size is moderately large,[2] the random variable associated with

$$\chi^2 = \sum_{i=1}^{K} \frac{(O_i - E_i)^2}{E_i} \tag{11.1.1}$$

has, to a good approximation, a chi-square distribution with $(K - 1)$ degrees of freedom. Intuitively, the number of degrees of freedom follows from the fact that the O_i must sum to n. Hence, if we know the number of sample members n and the numbers of observations falling in any $(K - 1)$ of the categories, we necessarily know the number in the Kth category. We will want to reject the null hypothesis when the observed numbers differ substantially from the expected numbers—that is, for unusually large values of the statistic (11.1.1). The appropriate test is given in the box.

A Goodness-of-Fit Test

Suppose that we are given a random sample of n observations, each of which can be classified into exactly one of K categories. Denote the observed numbers in each category by $O_1, O_2, \ldots, O_K$. If a null hypothesis (H_0) specifies probabilities $p_1, p_2, \ldots, p_K$ for an observation falling into each of these categories, the expected numbers in the categories, under H_0, would be

$$E_i = np_i \qquad (i = 1, 2, \ldots, K)$$

A test, of significance level α, of H_0 against the alternative that the specified probabilities are not correct is based on the decision rule

$$\text{Reject } H_0 \text{ if } \sum_{i=1}^{K} \frac{(O_i - E_i)^2}{E_i} > \chi^2_{K-1,\alpha}$$

where $\chi^2_{K-1,\alpha}$ is the number for which

$$P(\chi^2_{K-1} > \chi^2_{K-1,\alpha}) = \alpha$$

and the random variable χ^2_{K-1} follows a chi-square distribution with $(K - 1)$ degrees of freedom.

To illustrate this test, consider again the data of Table 11.3, on number of varieties of soft drink selected. Our null hypothesis is that the probabilities are the same for the three categories. The test of this hypothesis is based on

---

[2] The approximation works well if each of the expected values (E_i) is at least 5.

$$\chi^2 = \sum_{i=1}^{3} \frac{(O_i - E_i)^2}{E_i}$$

$$= \frac{(8 - 11)^2}{11} + \frac{(10 - 11)^2}{11} + \frac{(15 - 11)^2}{11} = 2.364$$

There are $K = 3$ categories, so the degrees of freedom associated with the chi-square distribution are $K - 1 = 2$. From Table 5 of the Appendix, we find

$$\chi^2_{2,.10} = 4.61$$

Therefore, according to our decision rule, which is illustrated in Figure 11.1, the null hypothesis cannot be rejected at the 10% significance level. These data do not contain strong evidence against the hypothesis that a randomly chosen subject is equally likely to select one, two, or three different varieties.

EXAMPLE 11.1

A gas company has determined from past experience that at the end of winter, 80% of its accounts are fully paid, 10% are 1 month in arrears, 6% are 2 months in arrears, and 4% are more than 2 months in arrears. At the end of this winter, the company checked a random sample of 400 of its accounts, finding 287 to be fully paid, 49 to be 1 month in arrears, 30 to be 2 months in arrears, and 34 to be more than 2

FIGURE 11.1 The distribution of $\chi_2^2 = \sum_{i=1}^{3} (O_i - E_i)^2/E_i$ when

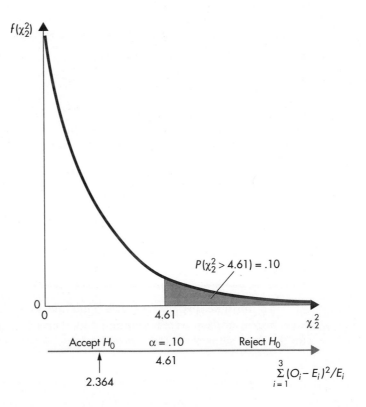

months in arrears. Do these data suggest that the pattern of previous years is still being followed this winter?

Under the null hypothesis that the proportions in the present winter conform to the historical record, the respective probabilities for the four categories are .8, .1, .06, and .04. Under that hypothesis, the expected numbers of accounts in each category, for a random sample of 400 accounts, would be

$$400(.8) = 320 \qquad 400(.1) = 40 \qquad 400(.06) = 24 \qquad 400(.04) = 16$$

Thus, we have the observed and expected numbers shown in the table.

NUMBER OF MONTHS IN ARREARS	0	1	2	More than 2	Total
OBSERVED NUMBER	287	49	30	34	400
PROBABILITY (UNDER H_0)	.80	.10	.06	.04	1
EXPECTED NUMBER (UNDER H_0)	320	40	24	16	400

The test of the null hypothesis (H_0) is based on

$$\chi^2 = \sum_{i=1}^{4} \frac{(O_i - E_i)^2}{E_i}$$

$$= \frac{(287 - 320)^2}{320} + \frac{(49 - 40)^2}{40} + \frac{(30 - 24)^2}{24} + \frac{(34 - 16)^2}{16} = 27.178$$

Here there are $K = 4$ categories, so the degrees of freedom are $K - 1 = 3$. From Table 5 of the Appendix, we have

$$\chi^2_{3,.005} = 12.84$$

Since 27.178 is much bigger than 12.84, the null hypothesis is very clearly rejected, even at the .5% significance level. Certainly these data provide considerable evidence to suspect that the pattern of payments of gas bills this year differs from the historical norm. Inspection of the numbers in the table shows that more accounts are in arrears over a longer time period than is usually the case.

We conclude this section with a word of caution: The figures used in calculating the test statistic (11.1.1) must be the *observed* and *expected numbers* in each category. It is not correct, for example, to use instead the percentages of sample members in each category.

EXERCISES

1. A professor is planning to use a new book for a financial accounting course and is considering three possibilities: *Financial Accounting Made Easy*, *Financial Accounting Without Tears*, and *Financial Accounting for Profit and Pleasure*. He contacted a random sample of sixty students who had already taken his course and asked each to review the three books, indicating a first preference. The results obtained are shown in the table. Test the null hypothesis that for this population, first preferences are evenly distributed over the three books.

BOOK	Made Easy	Without Tears	Profit and Pleasure
NUMBER OF FIRST PREFERENCES	17	25	18

2. A random sample of sixty-five mutual funds whose performance ranked in the top 25% of all funds in 1979–83 was selected.[3] Their performance was observed over the next five years. In this later period, eleven of the sample funds ranked in the top 25% of all funds, seventeen in the second 25%, eighteen in the third 25%, and nineteen in the bottom 25%. Test the null hypothesis that a randomly chosen top 25% fund from 1979–83 is equally likely to fall into each of the four possible categories (performance quartiles) over the following five years.

3. A random sample of 502 consumers were asked about the importance of price as a factor in choosing a hospital.[4] Sample members were asked to select "not important," "important," or "very important" as an answer. Respective numbers selecting these answers were 169, 136, and 197. Test the null hypothesis that a randomly chosen consumer is equally likely to select each of these three answers.

4. Production records indicate that in normal operation for a certain electronic component, 93% have no faults, 5% have one fault, and 2% have more than one fault. For a random sample of 500 of these components from a week's output, 458 were found to have no faults, thirty to have one fault, and twelve to have more than one fault. Test at the 5% level the null hypothesis that the quality of the output from this week conforms to the usual pattern.

5. A charity solicits donations by telephone. It has been found that 60% of all calls result in a refusal to donate; 30% result in a request for more information through the mail, with a promise to at least consider donating; and 10% generate an immediate credit card donation. For a random sample of 100 calls made in the current week, sixty-five resulted in a refusal to donate, thirty-one in a request for more information through the mail, and four in an immediate credit card donation. Test at the 10%-level the null hypothesis that the usual pattern of outcomes is being followed in the current week.

6. A campus administrator has found that 60% of all students view courses as very useful, 20% as somewhat useful, and 20% as worthless. Of a random sample of 100 students taking business courses, sixty-eight found the course in question very useful, eighteen somewhat useful, and fourteen worthless. Test the null hypothesis that the population distribution for business courses is the same as that for all courses.

11.2 GOODNESS-OF-FIT TESTS: POPULATION PARAMETERS UNKNOWN

In Section 11.1, we tested the hypothesis that data are generated by a *fully specified* probability distribution. The null hypothesis in this test specifies the probability that a sample observation will fall in any category. However, it often happens that we want to test the hypothesis that data are generated by some distribution, such as the binomial, the Poisson, or the normal, without assuming the parameters of that distribution to be known. In these circumstances, the available data can be used to estimate the unknown population parameters. The test procedure of Section 11.1 is then applicable, but the number of degrees of freedom for the chi-square test is reduced by one for each population parameter that has been estimated.

---

[3] M. L. Troutman, "The Steinbrenner syndrome and the challenge of manager selection," *Financial Analysts Journal*, *47* (1991), no. 2, 37–44.

[4] C. M. Fisher and C. J. Anderson, "Hospital advertising: Does it influence consumers?" *Journal of Health Care Marketing*, *10* (1990), no. 4, 40–46.

We will illustrate this approach by testing whether a set of data is generated by the Poisson distribution. One procedure for attempting to resolve questions of disputed authorship is to count the number of occurrences of particular words in blocks of text. These can be compared with results from passages whose authorship is known; often this comparison can be achieved through the assumption that the number of occurrences follows a Poisson distribution. An example of this type of research involves the study of *The Federalist Papers*.[5] For a sample of 262 blocks of text (each approximately 200 words in length) from this source, the mean number of occurrences of the word *may* was .66. Table 11.5 shows the observed frequencies of occurrence of this word in the 262 sampled blocks of text. Our aim is to test the null hypothesis that the population distribution of occurrences is Poisson, without assuming prior knowledge of the mean of this distribution.

Recall from Section 4.7 that if the Poisson distribution is appropriate, the probability of x occurrences is

$$P(x) = \frac{e^{-\lambda}\lambda^x}{x!} \tag{11.2.1}$$

where λ is the mean number of occurrences. Although this population mean is unknown, it can be estimated by the sample mean .66. It is then possible, by substituting .66 for λ in (11.2.1), to estimate the probability for any number of occurrences under the null hypothesis that the population distribution is Poisson. For example, the probability of two occurrences is

$$P(2) = \frac{e^{-0.66}(.66)^2}{2!}$$

$$= \frac{(.5169)(.66)^2}{2} = .1126$$

Similarly, the probabilities for zero and one occurrence can be found, so the probability of three or more occurrences is

$$P(X \geq 3) = 1 - P(0) - P(1) - P(2)$$

These probabilities are shown in the second row of Table 11.6.

TABLE 11.5 Occurrences of the word *may* in 262 blocks of text in *The Federalist Papers*

NUMBER OF OCCURRENCES	0	1	2	3 or more
OBSERVED FREQUENCY	156	63	29	14

[5] Data from F. Mosteller and D. L. Wallace, *Inference and Disputed Authorship: The Federalist*, © 1964, Addison-Wesley, Reading, Mass., tables 2.3 and 2.4. Reprinted with permission.

TABLE 11.6 Observed and expected frequencies for *The Federalist Papers* data

NUMBER OF OCCURRENCES	0	1	2	3 or more	Total
OBSERVED FREQUENCIES (O_i)	156	63	29	14	262
PROBABILITIES (p_i)	.5169	.3412	.1126	.0293	1
EXPECTED FREQUENCIES (E_i) UNDER H_0	135	89	30	8	262

Then, exactly as before, the expected frequencies under the null hypothesis are obtained from

$$E_i = np_i$$

Thus, for example, the expected frequency of two occurrences of the word *may* in 262 blocks of text is $(262)(.1126) = 30$. The bottom row of Table 11.6 shows these expected frequencies.

The test statistic is then

$$\sum_{i=1}^{4} \frac{(O_i - E_i)^2}{E_i} = \frac{(156 - 135)^2}{135} + \frac{(63 - 89)^2}{89} + \frac{(29 - 30)^2}{30} + \frac{(14 - 8)^2}{8}$$
$$= 15.396$$

Since there are four categories, and one parameter has been estimated, the appropriate number of degrees of freedom for the test is 2. From Table 5 of the Appendix, we find

$$\chi^2_{2,.005} = 10.60$$

Thus, the null hypothesis that the population distribution is Poisson can be rejected at the .5% significance level. The evidence in the data against that hypothesis is, then, very strong indeed.

Goodness-of-Fit Tests When Population Parameters Are Estimated

Suppose that a null hypothesis specifies category probabilities that depend on the estimation (from the data) of m unknown population parameters. The appropriate test of the null hypothesis is precisely as in Section 11.1, except that the number of degrees of freedom for the chi-square random variable is $(K - m - 1)$, where K is the number of categories.

A TEST OF NORMALITY

The normal distribution plays an important part in statistics, and many practical procedures rely for their validity, or for particular optimality properties, on an assumption that sample data are from a normal distribution. The normality assumption can be tested through an adaptation of the procedure just described. However, here we describe a test that is both easier to carry out and likely to be more powerful.

Suppose that we have a sample $x_1, x_2, \ldots, x_n$ of n observations from a population. Our approach is based on checking whether these data reflect two characteristics of the normal distribution. First is that the distribution is symmetric about its mean—

in the terminology of Section 2.5, that it is skewed neither to the left nor to the right. Using sample information, *skewness* of a population is estimated by

$$\text{Skewness} = \frac{\sum_{i=1}^{n}(x_i - \bar{x})^3/n}{s^3}$$

where $\bar{x}$ and s are the sample mean and standard deviation, respectively. The important part of this expression is the numerator; the denominator serves the purpose of standardization, making units of measurement irrelevant. Positive skewness will result if a distribution is skewed to the right, since average cubed discrepancies about the mean would be positive. Skewness will be negative for distributions skewed to the left and 0 for distributions, such as the normal, that are symmetric about their mean.

Since there are any number of symmetric distributions, a further characteristic is required to distinguish the normal distribution. In computing the sample variance, squared discrepancies about the mean are used, while skewness is based on cubed discrepancies about the mean. The next logical step is to look at fourth powers of these discrepancies, leading to the sample *kurtosis*, defined as

$$\text{Kurtosis} = \frac{\sum_{i=1}^{n}(x_i - \bar{x})^4/n}{s^4}$$

Kurtosis provides a measure of the weight in the tails of a probability density function: It is known that for the normal distribution, the population kurtosis is 3.

The sample skewness and kurtosis are readily computed from data; indeed, these statistics are standard output in many statistical computing packages. The *Bowman-Shelton test* for normality is based on the closeness to 0 of the sample skewness and the closeness to 3 of the sample kurtosis. The test statistic is

$$B = n\left[\frac{(\text{Skewness})^2}{6} + \frac{(\text{Kurtosis} - 3)^2}{24}\right] \qquad (11.2.2)$$

It is known that as the number of sample observations becomes very large, this statistic has, under the null hypothesis that the population distribution is normal, a chi-square distribution with 2 degrees of freedom. The null hypothesis is, of course, rejected for large values of the test statistic.

Unfortunately, the chi-square approximation to the distribution of (11.2.2) is close only for a very large sample sizes. Table 11.7 shows significance points appropriate for a range of sample sizes for tests at the 5% and 10% levels.[6] The recommended procedure, then, is to calculate the statistic (11.2.2) and reject the null hypothesis of normality if the test statistic exceeds the appropriate value tabulated in Table 11.7.

---

[6] These figures are from A. K. Bera and C. M. Jarque, "An efficient large-sample test for normality of observations and regression residuals," *Working Papers in Economics and Econometrics, 40*, Australian National University (1981). Significance points for other sample sizes can be obtained by interpolation in the table.

TABLE 11.7 Significance points of the Bowman-Shelton statistic

SAMPLE SIZE n	10% POINT	5% POINT	SAMPLE SIZE n	10% POINT	5% POINT
20	2.13	3.26	200	3.48	4.43
30	2.49	3.71	250	3.54	4.51
40	2.70	3.99	300	3.68	4.60
50	2.90	4.26	400	3.76	4.74
75	3.09	4.27	500	3.91	4.82
100	3.14	4.29	800	4.32	5.46
125	3.31	4.34	∞	4.61	5.99
150	3.43	4.39			

To illustrate this test, a sample of 278 daily rates of return on a live hog futures contract[7] had skewness .04033 and kurtosis 3.15553. To test the null hypothesis that the true distribution for these rates of return is normal, we find for the statistic (11.2.2)

$$B = 278\left[\frac{(.04033)^2}{6} + \frac{(.15553)^2}{24} \right] = .36$$

Comparison of this result with the significance points in Table 11.7 certainly provides little ground for questioning the hypothesis that the population distribution is normal.

EXERCISES

7. The number of times a machine broke down each week was observed over a period of 100 weeks, giving the results shown in the accompanying table. It was found that the average number of breakdowns per week over this period was 2.1. Test the null hypothesis that the population distribution of breakdown is Poisson.

NUMBER OF BREAKDOWNS	0	1	2	3	4	5 or more
NUMBER OF WEEKS	10	24	32	23	6	5

8. In a period of 100 minutes, there were a total of 190 arrivals at a highway toll booth. The accompanying table shows the frequency of arrivals per minute over this period. Test the null hypothesis that the population distribution is Poisson.

NUMBER OF ARRIVALS IN MINUTE	0	1	2	3	4 or more
OBSERVED FREQUENCY	10	26	35	24	5

9. A random sample of fifty students were asked to estimate how much money they spent on textbooks in a year. The sample skewness of these amounts was found to be .83 and the sample kurtosis was 3.98. Test at the 10%-level the null hypothesis that the population distribution of amounts spent is normal.

---

[7] Data from C. F. Lee and R. M. Leuthold, "Investment horizon, risk, and return in commodity futures markets: An empirical analysis with daily data," *Quarterly Review of Economics and Business*, *23*, no. 3 (1983), 6–18.

10. A random sample of one hundred measurements of the resistance of electronic components produced in a period of one week was taken. The sample skewness was .63 and the sample kurtosis was 3.85. Test the null hypothesis that the population distribution is normal.

11. The sample skewness and kurtosis are employed to test population normality. Explain why the sample mean and sample variance would be inadequate for this purpose.

11.3 CONTINGENCY TABLES

In this section, we show how the test of Section 11.1 can be extended to deal with a problem to which we alluded briefly in Section 3.7. Suppose that a sample is taken from a population, each of whose members can be uniquely cross-classified according to a pair of attributes. The hypothesis to be tested is of no association or dependence in the population between possessions of these attributes.

To illustrate, Table 11.8 contains information on 513 photographs in annual reports of airline firms.[8] The photographs were of non-flight crew employees, and the subjects in the photographs were either male only or female only. The photographs were classified according to the gender of the subjects and also according to the roles portrayed by the subjects. The table shows numbers of observations in each of six possible cross-classifications. For example, 256 of the photographs were of males actively engaged in work. For convenience, row and column totals are also given in the table.

The null hypothesis to be tested is of no association between the attributes—in this case, that there is no association between subjects' gender and role portrayed in the photographs. This null hypothesis would imply that, in the population, the proportion of photographs showing subjects actively engaged in work would be the same for male as for female subjects.

More generally, suppose we are concerned with two attributes, A and B. We assume that there are r categories for A and c categories for B, so a total of rc cross-classifications is possible. The number of sample observations belonging to both the ith category of A and the jth category of B will be denoted O_{ij}, as shown in Table 11.9.

This tabulation is called an $r \times c$ **contingency table.** In this terminology, Table 11.8 is a 3×2 contingency table. For convenience, we have added to Table 11.9 the row and column totals, denoted respectively $R_1, R_2, \ldots, R_r$, and $C_1, C_2, \ldots, C_c$.

TABLE 11.8 Cross-classification of annual report photographs by gender and roles portrayed by subjects

ROLES PORTRAYED	SUBJECTS IN PHOTOGRAPH		
	MALE ONLY	FEMALE ONLY	TOTALS
Actively engaged in work	256	74	330
In nonrecognizable role	41	42	83
Not engaged in apparent occupation	66	34	100
Totals	363	150	513

[8] Data from C. J. Anderson and G. Imperia, "The corporate annual report: a photo analysis of male and female portrayals," *Journal of Business Communication*, 29 (1992), 113–28.

To test the null hypothesis of no association between the attributes, we again ask how many observations we would expect to find in each cross-classification if that hypothesis were true. This question becomes meaningful when the row and column totals are taken to be *fixed*. Consider, then, the joint classification corresponding to the *i*th row and *j*th column of the table. There are a total of C_j observations in the *j*th column, and given no association, we would expect these to be distributed among the rows in proportion to the total number of observations in each row. Thus, we would expect a proportion R_i/n of these C_j observations to be in the *i*th row. Hence, the estimated expected numbers of observations in the cross-classifications are

$$\hat{E}_{ij} = \frac{R_i C_j}{n} \qquad (i = 1, 2, \ldots, r; j = 1, 2, \ldots, c)$$

For example, if there were no association between gender and role played in the photographs in Table 11.8, we would expect, since 363 of 513 photographs are of males only, a proportion 363/513 of the 330 photographs with subjects actively engaged in work to be of males only; that is

$$\hat{E}_{11} = \frac{(330)(363)}{513} = 233.5$$

The other expected numbers are calculated in the same way. They are shown in Table 11.10 alongside the corresponding observed numbers.

Our test of the null hypothesis of no association is based on the magnitudes of the discrepancies between the observed numbers and those that would be expected if that hypothesis were true. The test is similar to that of Section 11.1. It can be shown that under the null hypothesis, for moderately large sample sizes,[9] the random variable associated with

$$\chi^2 = \sum_{i=1}^{r} \sum_{j=1}^{c} \frac{(O_{ij} - \hat{E}_{ij})^2}{\hat{E}_{ij}} \qquad (11.3.1)$$

TABLE 11.9 Cross-classification of *n* observations in an $r \times c$ contingency table

ATTRIBUTE A	ATTRIBUTE B				
	1	2	$\cdots$	c	TOTALS
1	O_{11}	O_{12}	$\cdots$	O_{1c}	R_1
2	O_{21}	O_{22}	$\cdots$	O_{2c}	R_2
$\vdots$	$\vdots$	$\vdots$	$\cdots$	$\vdots$	$\vdots$
r	O_{r1}	O_{r2}	$\cdots$	O_{rc}	R_r
Totals	C_1	C_2	$\cdots$	C_c	n

[9] The approximation works well if each of the estimated expected numbers ($\hat{E}_{ij}$) is at least 5.

TABLE 11.10 Observed (and estimated expected) numbers in each cross-classification for photographs in airline annual reports

ROLES PORTRAYED	SUBJECTS IN PHOTOGRAPH	
	MALE ONLY	FEMALE ONLY
Actively engaged in work	256 (233.5)	74 (96.5)
In nonrecognizable role	41 (58.7)	42 (24.3)
Not engaged in apparent occupation	66 (70.8)	34 (29.2)

has, to a good approximation, a chi-square distribution with $(r - 1)(c - 1)$ degrees of freedom. The double summation in expression (11.3.1) implies that summation extends over all rc cells of the table. The number of degrees of freedom follows from regarding the row and column totals as fixed. If these are known and the $(r - 1)(c - 1)$ entries corresponding to the first $(r - 1)$ rows and $(c - 1)$ columns are also known, the remaining entries in the table can be deduced. Clearly, the null hypothesis of no association will be rejected for large absolute discrepancies between observed and expected numbers—that is, for high values of (11.3.1). The test procedure is given in the box.

A Test of Association in Contingency Tables

Suppose that a sample of n observations is cross-classified, according to two attributes, in an $r \times c$ contingency table. Denote by O_{ij} the number of observations in the cell that is in the ith row and jth column. If the null hypothesis is

H_0: No association between the two attributes in the population

the estimated expected number of observations in this cell, under H_0, is

$$\hat{E}_{ij} = \frac{R_i C_j}{n}$$

where R_i and C_j are the corresponding row and column totals. A test of significance level α is based on the following decision rule:

$$\text{Reject } H_0 \text{ if } \sum_{i=1}^{r} \sum_{j=1}^{c} \frac{(O_{ij} - \hat{E}_{ij})^2}{\hat{E}_{ij}} > \chi^2_{(r-1)(c-1),\alpha}$$

Returning to our example, we find

$$\sum_{i=1}^{3} \sum_{j=1}^{2} \frac{(O_{ij} - \hat{E}_{ij})^2}{\hat{E}_{ij}} = \frac{(256 - 233.5)^2}{233.5} + \frac{(74 - 96.5)^2}{96.5}$$

$$+ \frac{(41 - 58.7)^2}{58.7} + \frac{(42 - 24.3)^2}{24.3}$$

$$+ \frac{(66 - 70.8)^2}{70.8} + \frac{(34 - 29.2)^2}{29.2} = 26.8$$

Here there are $r = 3$ rows and $c = 2$ columns in the table, so the appropriate number of degrees of freedom is

$$(r - 1)(c - 1) = (3 - 1)(2 - 1) = 2$$

From Table 5 of the Appendix, we find

$$\chi^2_{2,.005} = 10.60$$

Therefore, the null hypothesis of no association is very clearly rejected, even at the .5% significance level. The evidence against this hypothesis is overwhelming. The cause of rejection can be seen from Table 11.10. Women are far less likely to be portrayed actively engaged in work than are men.

EXAMPLE 11.2

In a sample of small businesses, firms were classified according to age and also according to the percentage of debt in their capital structure.[10] Numbers of firms in each of eight categories are shown in the table. Test the null hypothesis of no association between firm age and debt as a percentage of capital structure.

PERCENTAGE DEBT	OLDER FIRMS	NEWER FIRMS
0–25	19	29
26–50	13	10
51–75	7	11
76–100	4	32

The preliminary calculations are set out in the following table. The expected numbers are shown in parentheses, following the corresponding observed numbers.

PERCENTAGE DEBT	OLDER FIRMS	NEWER FIRMS	TOTALS
0–25	19 (16.5)	29 (31.5)	48
26–50	13 (7.9)	10 (15.1)	23
51–75	7 (6.2)	11 (11.8)	18
76–100	4 (12.4)	32 (23.6)	36
Totals	43	82	125

Given the row and column totals, the expected values under the null hypothesis of no association are found from

$$\hat{E}_{ij} = \frac{R_i C_j}{n}$$

For instance, the expected number of older firms with 26–50% debt is

$$\hat{E}_{21} = \frac{R_2 C_1}{n} = \frac{(23)(43)}{125} = 7.9$$

---

[10] H. E. Van Auken and B. M. Doran, "Small business capitalization patterns," *Journal of Applied Business Research*, 5, no. 2 (1989), 15–22.

The test of the null hypothesis of no association is based on

$$\sum_{i=1}^{4} \sum_{j=1}^{2} \frac{(O_{ij} - \hat{E}_{ij})^2}{\hat{E}_{ij}} = \frac{(19 - 16.5)^2}{16.5} + \cdots + \frac{(32 - 23.6)^2}{23.6} = 14.43$$

Since there are $r = 4$ rows and $c = 2$ columns in the contingency table, the number of degrees of freedom associated with the test is

$$(r - 1)(c - 1) = (4 - 1)(2 - 1) = 3$$

From Table 5 of the Appendix, we find

$$\chi^2_{3,.005} = 12.84$$

Hence, the null hypothesis of no association between firm age and debt as a percentage of capital structure can be rejected at the .5% level. The evidence in the data against that hypothesis is quite overwhelming.

It should be noted, as was the case for the goodness-of-fit tests of earlier sections, that the figures used in calculating the statistic 11.3.1 must be the *actual numbers* observed and not, for example, percentages of the total.

EXERCISES

12. A sample of twenty women planning to send a "thinking of you" card and a sample of twenty women planning to send a wedding card were asked about important attributes in choosing a card.[11] The table shows numbers mentioning pictures as an important attribute. Test at the 10% level the null hypothesis of no association between type of greeting card and whether pictures are important in the choice of card.

TYPE OF CARD	PICTURES IMPORTANT	
	YES	NO
Thinking of You	12	8
Wedding	14	6

13. Suppose that in a 2×2 contingency table, the numbers observed are denoted a, b, c, d, as indicated in the following table:

			TOTALS
	a	b	$a + b$
	c	d	$c + d$
TOTALS	$a + c$	$b + d$	n

---

[11] See B. A. Walker and J. C. Olson, "Mean-end chains: Connecting products with self," *Journal of Business Research*, 22 (1991), 111–18. Used by permission of Elsevier Science Publishing Co., Inc. copyright 1991.

Show that the test statistic of Eq. (11.3.1) can be written

$$\chi^2 = \frac{n(ad - bc)^2}{(a + b)(a + c)(b + d)(c + d)}$$

14. A sample of 165 firms filing for bankruptcy were classified according to whether the prior audit opinion was qualified or unqualified, and also according to the time from year-end to the bankruptcy filing date.[12] The results are shown in the table. Test the null hypothesis of no association between audit opinion and time to filing.

TIME TO FILING	AUDIT OPINION	
	QUALIFIED	UNQUALIFIED
12 Months or less	61	28
More than 12 months	32	44

15. A sample of 3,262 corporate dividend changes were investigated.[13] These were classified as increases or decreases in dividends, and also as to whether the dividend announcement was made before or after the earnings announcement. Using the data in the accompanying table, test the null hypothesis of no association between the direction of the dividend change and the timing of the announcement.

EARLIER ANNOUNCEMENT	DIVIDEND CHANGE	
	INCREASE	DECREASE
Dividend	1,210	32
Earnings	1,960	61

16. A sample of multi-unit department stores was categorized according to size (as measured by number of employees) and whether or not there was a formal marketing plan. The table shows numbers in each category.[14] Test at the 1% level the null hypothesis of no association between size and marketing plan, based on the data in the accompanying table.

EMPLOYEES	FORMAL PLAN	NO FORMAL PLAN
Less than 100	13	10
100 to 500	18	12
More than 500	32	6

---

[12] D. B. Kennedy and W. H. Shaw, "Evaluating financial distress resolution using prior audit opinions," *Contemporary Accounting Research*, 8 (1991), 97–114.

[13] J. W. Wansley, C. F. Sirmans, J. D. Shilling, and Y. J. Lee, "Dividend change announcement effects and earnings volatility and timing," *Journal of Financial Research*, 14 (1991), 37–49.

[14] See J. B. Mason, M. L. Mayer, and A. Koh, "Functional marketing plan development in department store retailing," *Journal of the Academy of Marketing Science*, 13, no. 3 (1985), 161–82.

17. A sample of firms with impaired assets were classified according to whether discretionary write-downs of these assets were taken and also according to whether there was evidence of subsequent merger or acquisition activity.[15] Using the data in the accompanying table, test the null hypothesis of no association between these attributes

WRITE-DOWN	MERGER OR ACQUISITION ACTIVITY	
	YES	NO
Yes	28	39
No	20	47

18. A sample of corporate chief executive officers was asked to rate both corporate level financial performance and corporate level strategy. The results are shown in the accompanying table.[16] Test at the 1% level the null hypothesis of no association between the two sets of ratings.

STRATEGY	FINANCIAL PERFORMANCE		
	LOW	MEDIUM	HIGH
Low	15	25	18
Medium	30	52	23
High	23	49	61

19. The accompanying table shows information on fifty-five forecasts of inflation rate.[17] Forecasts were classified as to whether or not inflation was predicted to accelerate. It was also noted whether or not the actual outcome was for accelerated inflation. Test the null hypothesis of no association between forecasts and outcomes.

OUTCOME	FORECAST	
	ACCELERATION	NO ACCELERATION
Acceleration	18	11
No Acceleration	6	20

20. A sample of 201 computer salespeople was followed over a year to assess factors involved in job changes.[18] The accompanying table classifies these people according to whether they were married or single and whether they left their jobs or stayed for the year. Test at

[15] L. J. Zucca and D. R. Campbell, "A closer look at discretionary writedowns of impaired assets," *Accounting Horizons*, 6 (1992), no. 3, 30–41.
[16] Data from M. Leontiades and A. Tezel, "CEOs' perceptions of strategy consultants," *Business Forum*, *14*, no. 1 (1989), 51–53.
[17] See H. O. Stekler and M. H. Schnader, "Evaluating predictions of change: an application to inflation forecasts," *Applied Financial Economics*, *1* (1991), 135–37. Used by permission of Chapman & Hall Ltd, Uk.
[18] E. F. Fern, R. A. Avila, and D. Grewal, "Salesforce turnover: Those who left and those who stayed," *Industrial Marketing Management*, *18* (1989), 1–9.

the 5% level the null hypothesis of no association between marital status and whether computer salespeople leave their jobs.

MARITAL STATUS	STAYED	LEFT
Married	128	27
Single	34	12

21. Users and nonusers of legal services were asked to respond to the proposition that "professionals should display prices for typical services being advertised." The results obtained are shown in the accompanying table.[19] Test the null hypothesis that in the population at large, users and nonusers of legal services would not differ in their responses to this proposition.

	RESPONSE		
	AGREE OR STRONGLY AGREE	NO OPINION	DISAGREE OR STRONGLY DISAGREE
Users	76	16	25
Nonusers	242	36	33

REVIEW EXERCISES

22. A random sample of thirty sportswriters was asked to nominate which of three graduating college senior guards had the best professional prospects. These guards came, respectively, from a "big power" college program, a small state school, and a small private school. The following table shows the number of nominations. Test the null hypothesis that for the population of sportswriters, nominations are evenly distributed over these three players.

	BIG POWER	STATE SCHOOL	PRIVATE SCHOOL
Number of nominations	12	11	7

23. It is known that on a particular campus, 62% of all students are undergraduates, 23% are in professional schools, and 15% are in graduate school. A sample of eighty students attending a concert was taken. Of these sample members, fifty-four were undergraduates, seventeen were in professional schools, and nine were in graduate school. Test the null hypothesis that the distribution of students attending the concert was the same as the distribution of students on campus.

---

[19] See R. E. Hite and E. Kiser, "Consumers' attitudes toward lawyers with regard to advertising professional services," *Journal of the Academy of Marketing Science*, 13 (1985), 321–39.

24. An admissions dean has noted that historically, 75% of all applicants for a college program are from in-state, 15% are from neighboring states, and 10% are from other states. For a random sample of 100 applicants for the current year, seventy were from in-state, twenty-one were from neighboring states, and nine were from other states. Test the null hypothesis that applications in the current year follow the usual pattern.

25. The number of customers arriving at a supermarket checkout counter over a period of 200 minutes was recorded, yielding the results shown in the table. The average number of customers per minute was 2.3. Test the null hypothesis that the population distribution is Poisson.

NUMBER OF CUSTOMERS IN MINUTE	0	1	2	3	4	5 or more
OBSERVED FREQUENCY	16	50	51	44	28	11

26. A sample of 300 daily rates of return on shares of a common stock was obtained. The sample skewness was .47 and the sample kurtosis was 3.86. Test the null hypothesis that the population distribution of daily rates of return of this stock is normal.

27. A study assessed the reactions of firms to qualified audit opinions.[20] The accompanying table shows, for samples of firms that did and did not receive qualified opinions, the numbers that switched auditors in the following year. Test at the 1% significance level the null hypothesis that the switching of auditors is independent of whether a qualified opinion has been given.

	OPINION RECEIVED	
	QUALIFIED	UNQUALIFIED
Switched	141	227
Did not switch	991	8,051

28. In the study in Exercise 27, a random sample of 273 firms that had received qualified opinions was taken. The accompanying table shows the numbers of qualified opinions received by these firms in the following year for firms that did and did not switch auditors. What can be learned from these data?

	OPINION RECEIVED NEXT YEAR	
	QUALIFIED	UNQUALIFIED
Switched	103	29
Did not switch	100	41

29. For a sample of seventy-six firms that switched auditors following qualified reports, it was noted whether the auditor subsequent to the switch was a "Big Eight" firm or a non-Big Eight firm, and also whether the type of report subsequent to the switch was qualified or

---

[20] C. W. Chow and S. J. Rice, "Qualified audit opinions and auditor switching," *Accounting Review*, *57* (1982), 326–35.

unqualified. The results are shown in the accompanying table.[21] Test the null hypothesis of no association.

	TYPE OF AUDITOR	
TYPE OF REPORT	BIG EIGHT	NON-BIG EIGHT
Qualified	7	24
Unqualified	14	31

30. The accompanying table shows, for independent random samples of men and women, the numbers who watch television for more or less than 2½ hours per day.[22] Test at the 10% level the null hypothesis of no relationship between a person's sex and the amount of television watched.

	HOURS TELEVISION PER DAY	
	LESS THAN 2½	2½ OR MORE
Men	18	10
Women	17	13

31. The accompanying table shows responses to the statement: "I think companies should not fire employees who test positive for drugs." Respondents were also classified according to political party affiliation.[23] Test the null hypothesis of no association between response to this statement and party affiliation.

PARTY	RESPONSE	
	AGREED	DID NOT AGREE
Democrat	37	23
Republican	39	49

32. Forecasts of corporate earnings that differed from actual outcomes were examined.[24] In these cases the percentage of insider directors on the board was recorded. Test the null hypothesis of no association between the direction of forecast errors and the extent of insider control of the board, using the data in the accompanying table.

---

[21] Data from A. T. Craswell, "The association between qualified opinions and auditor switches," *Accounting and Business Research*, *19* (1988), 23–31.

[22] Data from B. W. Becker and P. E. Connor, "Personal values of the heavy user of mass media," *Journal of Advertising Research*, *21*, no. 5 (1981), 37–43.

[23] Data from S. Chawla, D. Elmuti, Y. Kathawala, and Z. Khan, "The relationship of an individual's classification with their opinion on drug testing," *American Business Review*, *10* (1992), no. 1, 1–7.

[24] See T. G. Calderon and S. A. Fisher, "Impact of management and insider control on the accuracy of management forecasts," *American Business Review*, *10* (1992), no. 1, 41–45.

FORECAST ERROR	PERCENTAGE INSIDER DIRECTORS ON BOARD	
	LESS THAN 22%	AT LEAST 22%
Actual > Forecast	8	6
Forecast > Actual	14	23

33. Samples of Anglos and Hispanics, aged 16–24, in the same areas of the southwestern United States, were asked their weekly alcohol consumption.[25] The accompanying table shows numbers in various categories for number of drinks per week. Test the null hypothesis of no association between ethnicity and level of alcohol consumption.

ETHNICITY	NUMBER OF DRINKS			
	0–1	2–4	5–10	MORE THAN 10
Anglo	19	45	27	28
Hispanic	25	47	29	13

34. Two brands of lemon/lime liquid dishwashing detergents—Sunlight and Palmolive—were monitored for fifty-two weeks.[26] For each week it was recorded, for each brand, whether or not manufacturer trade deals were available. The accompanying table shows the number of weeks in each of four possible categories. What can be concluded from these data?

SUNLIGHT	PALMOLIVE	
	NO DEAL	DEAL
No Deal	16	21
Deal	12	3

35. A sample of electric companies whose first mortgage bonds experienced a rating change by Moody's was examined.[27] These companies were classified according to whether the change was up or down and also according to whether there was a new debt issue. The findings are shown in the accompanying table. Test the null hypothesis of no association between the direction of a rating change and the issue of new debt.

---

[25] L. T. Patterson, G. G. Hunnicutt, and M. A. Stutts, "Young adults' perceptions of warnings and risks associated with alcohol consumption," *Journal of Public Policy and Marketing*, *11* (1992), no. 1, 96–103.

[26] See R. Lal, "Manufacturer trade deals and retail price promotions," *Journal of Marketing Research*, *27* (1990), 428–44.

[27] See S. B. Bhandari, J. J. Chrisman, and A. R. Rubash, "Rating changes and new bond issues: Some new insights," *American Business Review*, *3* (1985), 35–43.

RATING CHANGE	NEW DEBT ISSUE	
	NO	YES
Down	18	37
Up	12	6

36. Firms that changed chief executive officers were classified[28] as failing if bankruptcy followed within 3 years or not failing and were compared as to whether the new chief executive officer was a corporate insider or an outsider. The results are shown in the accompanying table. Test the null hypothesis of no association between these categorizations.

SUCCESSOR	FAILING	
	YES	NO
Insider	21	14
Outsider	39	11

[28] See K. B. Schwarz and K. Menon, "Executive succession in failing firms," *Academy of Management Journal*, *28* (1985), 680–86.

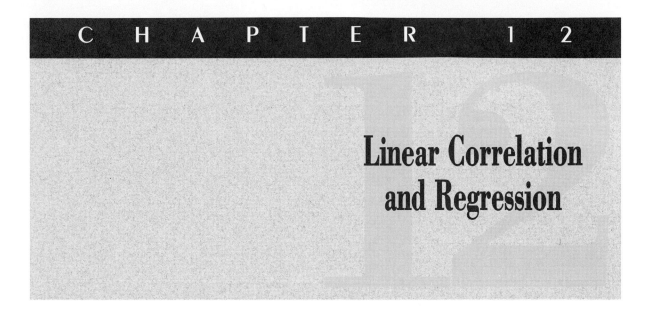

Linear Correlation and Regression

12.1 CORRELATION

To this point, we have dealt almost exclusively with problems of inference about a single random variable or independent random variables. Very often, however, in business and economic applications, interest is focused on the *relationships* between two or more random variables. In this chapter, we will consider the case where a pair of random variables is under study, extending our results to the more general case in Chapter 13.

In principle, there are any number of ways in which a pair of random variables might be related to each other, and before much progress can be made, it is helpful to postulate some functional form for their relationship. It is often reasonable to conjecture, as a good approximation, that the association is linear. Thus, if the pair of random variables X and Y is being considered, joint observations on this pair will tend to be clustered around a straight line, as in the graph of Figure 12.1. We do not mean to imply that the relationships studied here need necessarily be very strong, as would be the case if observations on a pair of random variables were very tightly clustered around a straight line. In practice, many relationships that we want to analyze will be rather weak, as is the one depicted in Figure 12.1. Then, in order to learn about such relations, we will need more sophisticated techniques than graphical inspection. Nevertheless, the plotting of a graph is a desirable preliminary to the more detailed analysis that follows. Although the assumption that any association that might exist between random variables can be characterized as linear is very convenient, and frequently realistic, it is only an assumption. One benefit from making plots is that they might provide an indication of any serious departures from linearity in the association between random variables. Looked at in this light, Figure 12.1 provides no indication

427

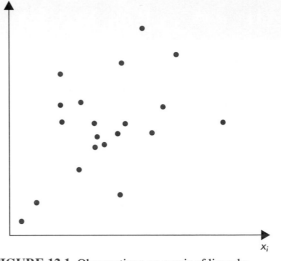

FIGURE 12.1 Observations on a pair of linearly related random variables

that the association between these two particular random variables is anything other than linear.

In this section, we are concerned with measuring the *strength* of the linear association between a pair of random variables. Let X and Y be a pair of random variables, with means μ_X and μ_Y and variances σ_X^2 and σ_Y^2. As a measure of the association between these quantities, we introduced in Sections 4.4 and 5.4 the **covariance,** defined as

$$\text{Cov}(X, Y) = E[(X - \mu_X)(Y - \mu_Y)]$$

If there is positive association between the random variables, so that high values of X tend to be associated with high values of Y and low X with low Y (as in Figure 12.1), the covariance is positive. When there is negative association, so that high values of X are associated with low values of Y and low X with high Y, the covariance is negative. If there is no linear association between X and Y, their covariance is 0.

As it stands, however, the covariance is of little use in assessing the strength of the relation between a pair of random variables, as its value depends on the units in which they are measured. Ideally, we would like a pure, scale-free measure. Fortunately, such a measure is easily obtained by dividing the covariance by the product of the individual standard deviations. The quantity resulting is called the **correlation coefficient.**

The Correlation Coefficient

Let X and Y be a pair of random variables, with means μ_X and μ_Y and variances σ_X^2 and σ_Y^2. A measure of the strength of their linear association is provided by the **correlation coefficient,** ρ, defined as

$$\rho = \text{Corr}(X, Y) = \frac{\text{Cov}(X, Y)}{\sigma_X \sigma_Y} = \frac{E[(X - \mu_X)(Y - \mu_Y)]}{\sqrt{E[(X - \mu_X)^2]E[(Y - \mu_Y)^2]}} \qquad (12.1.1)$$

It can be shown that the correlation must lie between -1 and 1; that is

$$-1 \le \rho \le 1$$

with the following interpretations:

(i) A correlation of -1 implies perfect negative linear association.
(ii) A correlation of 1 implies perfect positive linear association.
(iii) A correlation of 0 implies no linear association.
(iv) The larger in absolute value the correlation, the stronger the linear association between the random variables.

The implication of the value of the correlation coefficient is illustrated in Figure 12.2, which displays plots of random samples of observations from joint distributions for which the correlations are $-1.0, -.8, -.4, 0, .4, .8, 1.0$. The two extreme cases exhibit perfect linear association, while for the other cases, the higher in absolute value the correlation, the more closely the observations cluster about a straight line.

The correlation coefficient ρ is a population quantity that will be unknown in practice and must be estimated from data. To illustrate, Table 12.1 contains data relating to an advertising promotion run in seventeen magazines. These advertisements were to promote tourism in South Carolina, and readers were invited to write for additional literature. The two variables to be related are

X: Cost of advertisement and circulation (in thousands of dollars)
Y: Return-on-inquiry cost

FIGURE 12.2 Samples of observations from joint distributions with different correlations

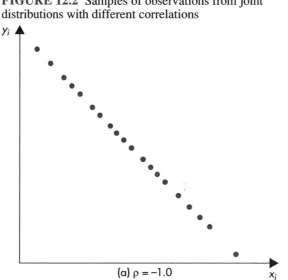

(a) $\rho = -1.0$

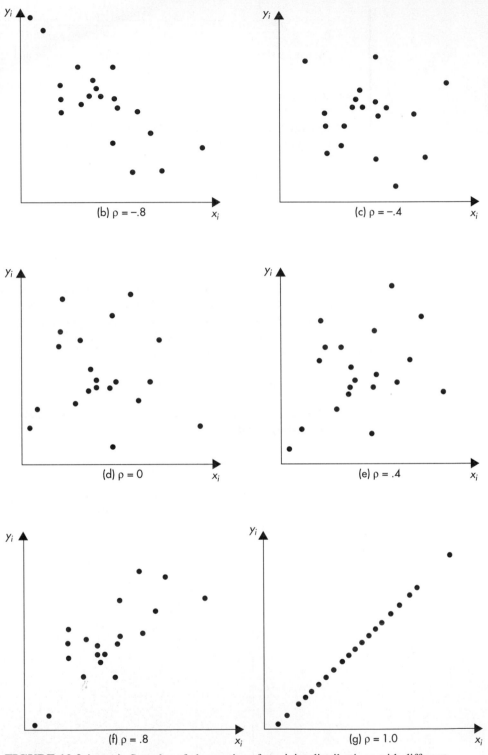

FIGURE 12.2 (cont.) Samples of observations from joint distributions with different correlations

TABLE 12.1 Data on cost of advertisement and circulation (x) and return-on-inquiry cost (y)

x_i	y_i	x_i	y_i	x_i	y_i
4.07	17.41	9.87	35.95	1.61	21.93
2.51	22.25	1.27	61.81	1.52	31.29
1.25	106.84	1.80	48.36	3.10	88.31
14.67	14.41	1.50	78.74	3.32	92.70
16.02	24.18	1.68	66.42	3.07	59.06
3.81	29.73	2.72	121.95		

Source: Data from A. G. Woodside and D. M. Reid, "Is CPM related to the advertising effectiveness of magazines?" *Journal of Business Research*, 3 (1975), 323–34. Copyright 1975 by Elsevier Science Publishing Co., Inc. Reprinted by permission of the publisher.

where the latter is defined as

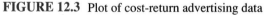

$$Y = \frac{\text{Estimated revenue from inquiries } - \text{ Cost of advertisement}}{\text{Cost of advertisement}}$$

The data are plotted in Figure 12.3, from which it appears that the relationship between cost and return is negative, with high levels of one tending to be associated with low values of the other.

In general, suppose that a sample contains n pairs of observations, denoted $(x_1, y_1), (x_2, y_2), \ldots, (x_n, y_n)$ and that these data are to be used to estimate the population correlation ρ. As usual, estimates of population standard deviations are provided by the corresponding sample standard deviations

$$s_x = \sqrt{\frac{1}{n-1} \sum_1^n (x_i - \bar{x})^2} \qquad \text{and} \qquad s_y = \sqrt{\frac{1}{n-1} \sum_1^n (y_i - \bar{y})^2}$$

Similarly, an estimate of the covariance is given by

FIGURE 12.3 Plot of cost-return advertising data

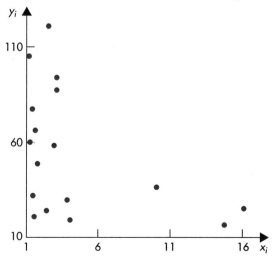

$$\text{Estimated Cov}(X, Y) = \frac{1}{n-1} \sum_{1}^{n} (x_i - \bar{x})(y_i - \bar{y})$$

The population correlation is then estimated by substituting sample estimates for the corresponding population values in formula (12.1.1).

The Sample Correlation Coefficient

Let $(x_1, y_1), (x_2, y_2), \ldots, (x_n, y_n)$ denote a random sample of n pairs of observations on the random variables X and Y. An estimate of the population correlation between X and Y is provided by the **sample correlation coefficient**

$$r = \frac{\frac{1}{n-1} \sum_{1}^{n} (x_i - \bar{x})(y_i - \bar{y})}{s_x s_y} = \frac{\sum_{1}^{n} (x_i - \bar{x})(y_i - \bar{y})}{\sqrt{\sum_{1}^{n} (x_i - \bar{x})^2 \sum_{1}^{n} (y_i - \bar{y})^2}}$$

An equivalent expression, often computationally simpler, is

$$r = \frac{\sum_{1}^{n} x_i y_i - n \bar{x} \bar{y}}{\sqrt{\left(\sum_{1}^{n} x_i^2 - n \bar{x}^2 \right) \left(\sum_{1}^{n} y_i^2 - n \bar{y}^2 \right)}}$$

The calculation of the sample correlation for the advertising data is set out in Table 12.2. The sample means are

$$\bar{x} = \frac{73.79}{17} = 4.3406 \qquad \text{and} \qquad \bar{y} = \frac{921.34}{17} = 54.1965$$

TABLE 12.2 Calculation of sample correlation for the data of Table 12.1

x_i	y_i	x_i^2	y_i^2	$x_i y_i$
4.07	17.41	16.5649	303.1081	70.8587
2.51	22.25	6.3001	495.0625	55.8475
1.25	106.84	1.5625	11,414.7856	133.5500
14.67	14.41	215.2089	207.6481	211.3947
16.02	24.18	256.6404	584.6724	387.3636
3.81	29.73	14.5161	883.8729	113.2713
9.87	35.95	97.4169	1,292.4025	354.8265
1.27	61.81	1.6129	3,820.4761	78.4987
1.80	48.36	3.2400	2,338.6896	87.0480
1.50	78.74	2.2500	6,199.9876	118.1100
1.68	66.42	2.8224	4,411.6164	111.5856
2.72	121.95	7.3984	14,871.8025	331.7040
1.61	21.93	2.5921	480.9249	35.3073
1.52	31.29	2.3104	979.0641	47.5608
3.10	88.31	9.6100	7,798.6561	273.7610
3.32	92.70	11.0224	8,593.2900	307.7640
3.07	59.06	9.4249	3,488.0836	181.3142
73.79	921.34	660.4933	68,164.1430	2,899.7659

Hence, the sample correlation is

$$r = \frac{\sum_1^n x_i y_i - n\overline{xy}}{\sqrt{\left(\sum_1^n x_i^2 - n\overline{x}^2\right)\left(\sum_1^n y_i^2 - n\overline{y}^2\right)}}$$

$$= \frac{2{,}899.7659 - (17)(4.3406)(54.1965)}{\sqrt{[660.4933 - (17)(4.3406)^2][68{,}164.143 - (17)(54.1965)^2]}}$$

$$= -.441$$

The sample correlation, $-.441$, indicates a mild negative relationship between cost and return for the magazine advertisements. The fact that the estimated correlation coefficient is negative indicates that high values of cost tend to be associated with low values of return. However, since a correlation of 0 implies no linear association and a value of -1 is equivalent to perfect negative linear association, the value found for the sample correlation here does not suggest a terribly strong association between cost and return.

The sample correlation coefficient is useful as a descriptive measure of the strength of linear association in a sample. It can also be used as the basis of a test of the hypothesis of no linear association in the population between a pair of random variables; that is

$$H_0: \quad \rho = 0$$

This particular null hypothesis, of no (linear) relationship between a pair of random variables, is often of great interest to an investigator. Of course, if we estimate the correlation, we will almost inevitably obtain some value other than 0, whether or not a relationship exists. What we are asking is how likely we are to find sample correlations that differ by particular amounts from 0 when in fact there is no linear association between the random variables under study.

It can be shown that when this null hypothesis is true and the random variables have a joint normal distribution,[1] the random variable corresponding to

$$t = \frac{r}{\sqrt{(1 - r^2)/(n - 2)}}$$

follows a Student's t distribution with $(n - 2)$ degrees of freedom. The appropriate tests are then derived as indicated in the box.

Test for Zero Population Correlation

Let r be the sample correlation coefficient, calculated from a random sample of n pairs of observations from a joint normal distribution. The following tests of the null hypothesis

$$H_0: \quad \rho = 0$$

---

[1] This is equivalent to requiring that every linear combination of the random variables X and Y have a normal distribution.

have significance level α:

(i) To test H_0 against the alternative

$$H_1: \quad \rho > 0$$

the decision rule is

$$\text{Reject } H_0 \text{ if } \quad \frac{r}{\sqrt{(1 - r^2)/(n - 2)}} > t_{n-2, \alpha}$$

(ii) To test H_0 against the alternative

$$H_1: \quad \rho < 0$$

the decision rule is

$$\text{Reject } H_0 \text{ if } \quad \frac{r}{\sqrt{(1 - r^2)/(n - 2)}} < -t_{n-2, \alpha}$$

(iii) To test H_0 against the two-sided alternative

$$H_1: \quad \rho \neq 0$$

the decision rule is

$$\text{Reject } H_0 \text{ if } \quad \frac{r}{\sqrt{(1 - r^2)/(n - 2)}} < -t_{n-2, \alpha/2}$$

or

$$\frac{r}{\sqrt{(1 - r^2)/(n - 2)}} > t_{n-2, \alpha/2}$$

Here, $t_{n-2, \alpha}$ is the number for which

$$P(t_{n-2} > t_{n-2, \alpha}) = \alpha$$

where the random variable t_{n-2} follows a Student's t distribution with $(n - 2)$ degrees of freedom.

Returning to the advertising cost-return example, we will test the hypothesis of no population correlation against the two-sided alternative. The test is based on

$$\frac{r}{\sqrt{(1 - r^2)/(n - 2)}} = \frac{-.441}{\sqrt{[1 - (-.441)^2]/(17 - 2)}} = -1.903$$

Since $n = 17$, there are $(n - 2) = 15$ degrees of freedom, so from Table 6 of the Appendix, appropriate points of comparison for 10%- and 5%-level tests against the two-sided alternative are, respectively

$$t_{15, .05} = 1.753 \qquad \text{and} \qquad t_{15, .025} = 2.131$$

Hence, according to our decision rule, these data allow rejection of the null hypothesis of no population correlation against the two-sided alternative at the 10% but not at the 5% level of significance. Although the data contain some evidence suggesting that there is an association between costs and returns, the indications against the hypothesis of no (linear) association between these variables are only moderately strong.

EXAMPLE
12.1

A survey of political risk analysts produced mean political risk scores for forty-nine countries—the higher the score, the more politically risky the country is considered.[2] The sample correlation between political risk score and inflation for these countries was found to be .43. Test the null hypothesis of no population correlation between political riskiness and inflation against the alternative of positive correlation.

Denoting by ρ the population correlation, we want to test

$$H_0: \quad \rho = 0$$

against

$$H_1: \quad \rho > 0$$

using the sample information

$$n = 49 \qquad r = .43$$

The test is based on

$$\frac{r}{\sqrt{(1 - r^2)/(n - 2)}} = \frac{.43}{\sqrt{[1 - (.43)^2]/(49 - 2)}} = 3.265$$

Since there are $(n - 2) = 47$ degrees of freedom, we have from interpolation in Table 6 of the Appendix

$$t_{47,.005} = 2.689$$

Therefore, the null hypothesis of no population correlation can be rejected against the alternative that the true correlation is positive at the .5% significance level. These data, then, contain very strong evidence of positive (linear) association between inflation and experts' judgments of political riskiness of countries.

A TEST FOR THE EQUALITY OF VARIANCES: MATCHED PAIRS

At first sight, the heading of this subsection appears to be misplaced. In Section 9.8 we discussed a test of the equality of two population variances. That test is valid *when independent random samples from the two populations are available*. However, as we saw in Section 9.6, in some applications the available sample data consists of *matched pairs* of observations from the two populations. In Section 9.6, a test of the equality of population means was developed for this case. The results of the present section can be exploited to develop a test of the equality of population variances, based on a sample of matched pairs, provided the population distributions are normal.

Let X and Y be a pair of random variables, with variances σ_X^2 and σ_Y^2. Our test is based on the fact that the correlation between $(X - Y)$ and $(X + Y)$ is zero if and only if σ_X^2 and σ_Y^2 are equal. The test procedure then requires the calculation of the corresponding sample correlation. Tests against one-sided alternatives follow from noting that a positive correlation between $(X - Y)$ and $(X + Y)$ occurs if $\sigma_X^2 > \sigma_Y^2$, and a negative correlation if $\sigma_X^2 < \sigma_Y^2$.

---

[2] Data from J. L. Mumpower, S. Livingston, and T. J. Lee, "Expert judgements of political riskiness," *Journal of Forecasting*, 6 (1987), 51-65.

TABLE 12.3 Calculations for a test of the equality of variances of brain activities

x_i	y_i	$x_i - y_i$	$x_i + y_i$
137	53	84	190
135	114	21	249
83	81	2	164
125	86	39	211
47	34	13	81
46	66	−20	112
114	89	25	203
157	113	44	270
57	88	−31	145
144	111	33	255

To illustrate the test, consider again the data on brain activities of subjects watching ten pairs of television commercials. Observations for high recall commercials (x_i) and low recall commercials (y_i) are given in Table 9.2, and reproduced in the first two columns of Table 12.3.

In the third and fourth columns of Table 12.3 we have calculated ($x_i - y_i$) and ($x_i + y_i$). Our test is based on the sample correlation of these two sets of values. In fact, that sample correlation is

$$r = .535$$

Since there are $n = 10$ pairs of observations, the test statistic is

$$\frac{r}{\sqrt{(1 - r^2)/(n - 2)}} = \frac{.535}{\sqrt{[1 - (.535)^2]/(10 - 2)}} = 1.791$$

We shall test the null hypothesis of equality of population variances against the two-sided alternative. From Table 6 of the Appendix, we find

$$t_{8,.10} = 1.397 \qquad t_{8,.05} = 1.860$$

It follows that the null hypothesis can be rejected against the two-sided alternative at the 20% level, but not at the 10% level. The data therefore contain just a moderate amount of evidence against the null hypothesis.

12.2 RANK CORRELATION

The sample correlation coefficient of Section 12.1 can be seriously affected by odd extreme observations. Moreover, tests based on it rely for their validity on an assumption of normality. A measure of correlation that is not susceptible to serious influence by extreme values and on which valid tests can be based for very general population distributions is obtained through the use of *ranks*, as in Chapter 10. The resulting test will then be nonparametric. In Table 12.4, we illustrate the calculation of this coefficient for the advertising cost-return data of Section 12.1.

The x_i and y_i observations are first ranked in ascending order. **Spearman's rank correlation coefficient** is then calculated as the sample correlation between the *ranks* of x_i and y_i, using the formula of Section 12.1. However, if there are no ties in the

TABLE 12.4 Rank correlation calculations for data of Table 12.1

x_i	RANK (x_i)	y_i	RANK (y_i)	$d_i = \text{RANK}(x_i) - \text{RANK}(y_i)$	d_i^2
4.07	14	17.41	2	12	144
2.51	8	22.25	4	4	16
1.25	1	106.84	16	-15	225
14.67	16	14.41	1	15	225
16.02	17	24.18	5	12	144
3.81	13	29.73	6	7	49
9.87	15	35.95	8	7	49
1.27	2	61.81	11	-9	81
1.80	7	48.36	9	-2	4
1.50	3	78.74	13	-10	100
1.68	6	66.42	12	-6	36
2.72	9	121.95	17	-8	64
1.61	5	21.93	3	2	4
1.52	4	31.29	7	-3	9
3.10	11	88.31	14	-3	9
3.32	12	92.70	15	-3	9
3.07	10	59.06	10	0	0
				Sum	1,168

rankings of the x_i and no ties in the rankings of the y_i, it can be shown that the computationally simpler expression

$$r_s = 1 - \frac{6 \sum_{1}^{n} d_i^2}{n(n^2 - 1)}$$

is equivalent, where the d_i are the differences in ranks. Thus, since there are no ties in our advertising data, we have from Table 12.4

$$r_s = 1 - \frac{(6)(1,168)}{(17)[(17)^2 - 1]} = -.431$$

In this particular case, note that the rank correlation coefficient is remarkably close to the ordinary sample correlation coefficient found for these data in Section 12.1.

Spearman's rank correlation coefficient can be used to test the null hypothesis of no association between a pair of random variables. Its distribution under that hypothesis is known, and cutoff points are given in Table 9 of the Appendix. Specifically, for various sample sizes n, the tabulated values are the numbers $r_{s,\alpha}$ that are exceeded with probability α by the rank correlation when the null hypothesis is true.

Spearman's Rank Correlation Test

Suppose that we have a random sample $(x_1, y_1), \ldots, (x_n, y_n)$ of n pairs of observations. If the x_i and y_i are each ranked in ascending order and the sample correlation of these ranks is calculated, the resulting coefficient is called **Spearman's rank correlation coefficient.** If there are no tied ranks, an equivalent formula for computing this coefficient is

---

$$r_s = 1 - \frac{6 \sum_1^n d_i^2}{n(n^2 - 1)}$$

where the d_i are the differences of the ranked pairs.

The following tests of the null hypothesis H_0 of no association in the population have significance level α:

(i) To test against the alternative of positive association, the decision rule is

Reject H_0 if $r_s > r_{s,\alpha}$

(ii) To test against the alternative of negative association, the decision rule is

Reject H_0 if $r_s < -r_{s,\alpha}$

(iii) To test against the two-sided alternative of some association, the decision rule is

Reject H_0 if $r_s < -r_{s,\alpha/2}$ or $r_s > r_{s,\alpha/2}$

Here, $r_{s,\alpha}$ is the cutoff point of the distribution of the Spearman coefficient, given in Table 9 of the Appendix.

For the advertising cost-return example, we will test the null hypothesis of no association in the population against the two-sided alternative. Since there are seventeen pairs of observations, we find from Table 9 of the Appendix that cutoff points for 10%- and 5%-level tests are, respectively

$$r_{s,.05} = .412 \quad \text{and} \quad r_{s,.025} = .490$$

Since the calculated value of the Spearman coefficient is $-.431$, the null hypothesis of no association can be rejected against the two-sided alternative, according to the decision rule, at the 10% significance level but not at the 5% level. We reached the same conclusion for these data in Section 12.1. However, we have now been able to do so without an assumption of population normality. There is, then, some gain in using the rank correlations here, since our conclusions are no longer conditioned on an assumption about the population distribution.

EXERCISES

1. An instructor in a statistics course set a final examination and also required the students to do a data analysis project. For a random sample of ten students, the scores obtained are shown in the table. Find the sample correlation between the examination and project scores.

EXAMINATION	81	62	74	78	93	69	72	83	90	84
PROJECT	76	71	69	76	87	62	80	75	92	79

2. The accompanying table shows percentage changes (x_i) in the Dow-Jones index over the first five trading days of each of thirteen years, and also the corresponding percentage changes (y_i) in the index over the whole year.

x_i	y_i	x_i	y_i	x_i	y_i
1.5	14.9	−1.6	27.7	1.4	27.0
.2	−9.2	−1.3	22.6	1.5	−4.3
−.1	19.6	5.6	2.3	−4.7	20.3
2.8	20.3	−1.4	11.9	1.1	4.2
2.2	−3.7				

(a) Calculate the sample correlation.

(b) Test at the 10% significance level, against a two-sided alternative, the null hypothesis that the population correlation is 0.

3. A college administers for all its courses a student evaluation questionnaire. For a random sample of twelve courses, the accompanying table shows both average student ratings of the instructor (on a scale from 1 to 5), and average expected grades of the students (on a scale from $A = 4$ to $E = 0$).

INSTRUCTOR RATING	2.8	3.7	4.4	3.6	4.7	3.5
EXPECTED GRADE	2.6	2.9	3.3	3.2	3.1	2.8
INSTRUCTOR RATING	4.1	3.2	4.9	4.2	3.8	3.3
EXPECTED GRADE	2.7	2.4	3.5	3.0	3.4	2.5

(a) Find the sample correlation between the instructor ratings and expected grades.

(b) Test at the 10% significance level the hypothesis that the population correlation coefficient is zero against the alternative that it is positive.

4. In the advertising study discussed in Section 12.1, the following results were also found:

x_i	y_i	x_i	y_i	x_i	y_i
7.70	141.77	1.57	98.61	4.18	95.83
4.17	96.97	3.63	179.18	6.09	196.67
1.52	163.92	1.57	125.19	3.09	275.97
10.04	154.70	4.65	171.81	3.08	289.59
6.02	151.61	2.97	200.23	1.76	105.71
4.81	147.82	.98	120.49		

x_i = Cost of advertisement ÷ Number of inquiries received
y_i = Revenue from inquiries ÷ Number of inquiries received

Find the sample correlation, and test against a two-sided alternative the null hypothesis that the population correlation is 0.

5. In the study of forty-nine countries discussed in Example 12.1, the sample correlation between the experts' political riskiness score and the infant mortality rate in these countries was .75. Test the null hypothesis of no correlation between these quantities against the alternative of positive correlation.

6. For a random sample of 353 college faculty, the correlation between annual raises and teaching evaluations was found to be .11.[3] Test the null hypothesis that these quantities are uncorrelated in the population against the alternative that the population correlation is positive.

7. The sample correlation for sixty-eight pairs of quarterly returns on common stocks in the United States and Germany was found to be .51.[4] Test the null hypothesis that the population correlation is 0, against the alternative that it is positive.

8. Refer to Exercise 28 of Chapter 9. Test against a two-sided alternative the null hypothesis of equality of population variances of salary offers to males and females.

9. Refer to the data of Exercise 2. Find Spearman's rank correlation coefficient, and use it to test, against a two-sided alternative, the null hypothesis of no association between the performance of the Dow Jones index in the first five days of a year and the performance of the index in the whole year.

10. Refer to the data of Exercise 4. Find Spearman's rank correlation coefficient, and use it to test, against a two-sided alternative, the null hypothesis of no association in the population between this pair of random variables.

11. Some products or services cause more shopping difficulty than others. The table given here shows rankings of twenty-four products and services, in order of shopping difficulty as perceived by men and women.[5] Find Spearman's rank correlation coefficient, and test the null hypothesis of no association against the alternative of positive association.

PRODUCT OR SERVICE	ORDER OF SHOPPING DIFFICULTY	
	MEN	WOMEN
Auto repairs	2	1
Automobiles	4	2
Home improvement	1	3
Clothing and footwear	13	4
Household furnishings	5	5
Household appliances	7	6
Housing and real estate	6	7
Home entertainment	8	8
Life insurance	3	9
Household moving	9	10
Sporting goods	17	11
Groceries	19	12
Photographic equipment	12	13
Auto insurance	10	14
Children's toys	15	15
Home gardening supplies	18	16
Legal services	11	17
Dry cleaning	23	18
Stationery supplies	20	19
Travel agency services	16	20
Drugs and pharmaceuticals	21	21
Jewelry	14	22
Financial services	22	23
Personal care	24	24

12. Multinational corporations frequently transfer from one division to another goods and services across international boundaries. They have much flexibility in the pricing of the transferred items. A study of large U.S. and Japanese multinational corporations was

---

[3] L. R. Gomez-Mejia and D. R. Balkin, "Determinants of faculty pay: an agency theory perspective," *Academy of Management Journal, 35* (1992), 921–55.

[4] J. E. Hunter and T. D. Coggin, "An analysis of the diversification benefit from international equity investment," *Journal of Portfolio Management, 17,* no. 1 (1990), 33–36.

[5] J. D. Claxton and J.R.B. Ritchie, "Consumer prepurchase shopping problems: A focus on the retailing component," *Journal of Retailing, 55,* no. 3 (1979), 24–43.

aimed at determining the relative importance of twenty variables that might be considered in formulating international transfer pricing policies.[6] Rankings for these variables are shown in the accompanying table.

(a) Compute Spearman's rank correlation coefficient. (Notice that there are tied ranks.)

(b) Test the hypothesis of no association against the alternative of positive association.

VARIABLE	RANKING	
	UNITED STATES	JAPANESE
Overall profit to company	1	1
Restrictions imposed by foreign countries on repatriation of profits or dividends	2	4
Competitive position of subsidiaries in foreign countries	3	2
Differentials in tax rates and tax legislation among countries	4	14
Performance evaluation of foreign subsidiaries	5	5
Rate of customs duties and customs legislation	6	9.5
Import restrictions imposed by foreign countries	7	12
Need to maintain adequate cash flows in foreign subsidiaries	8.5	7
Maintaining good relations with host governments	8.5	9.5
Restrictions on royalty or management fees that can be charged against foreign subsidiaries	10	11
Rules of financial reporting for foreign subsidiaries	11	15
Devaluation and revaluation in countries where company has operations	12	3
Rates of inflation in foreign countries	13	8
Volume of industrial transfers	14	18
Need of subsidiaries in foreign countries to seek local funds	15	16
Antidumping legislation in foreign countries	16	13
Interests of local partners of foreign subsidiaries	17	6
Domestic government requirements on foreign investments	18	20
Risk of expropriation in foreign countries	19	17
Antitrust legislation of foreign countries	20	19

12.3 THE LINEAR REGRESSION MODEL

We use correlation to provide a measure of the strength of any linear association between a pair of random variables. The random variables are treated perfectly symmetrically, and it is a matter of indifference whether we speak of "the correlation between X and Y" or "the correlation between Y and X." In the remainder of this chapter, we

---

[6] R.Y.W. Tang and K. H. Chan, "Environmental variables of international transfer pricing: A Japan–United States comparison," *Abacus, 15* (1979), 3–12.

will continue to discuss the linear relationship between a pair of variables, but in terms of the *dependency* of one on the other. The symmetry of our previous discussion is now removed. Rather, the concept here is that, given that the random variable X takes a specific value, we expect a response in the random variable Y. That is, the value taken by X influences the value of Y. This can be thought of as a dependence of Y on X.

To illustrate, Table 12.5 and Figure 12.4 show twenty-two annual values for retail sales per household and disposable income per household (in constant dollars).[7] We would expect expenditures on retail sales to depend on available income. Specifically, in years when income is relatively high, high retail sales would be expected. That this pattern generally emerges is clear from the plot of the data in Figure 12.4.

The objective of regression analysis is to *model* this relationship. At the outset, two problems must be faced. First, in typical business and economic applications, the precise functional form of any underlying relation will not be known. In the context of our example, we expect high income to lead to high sales, but we know very little more than that. In such circumstances, it is sensible to begin by postulating as simple a structure as seems plausible. For a great many problems, it is reasonable to assume a **linear** model, at least in the range of interest.[8]

Our concern, then, is with the value taken by the random variable Y, when the random variable X takes a specific value. For example, we may be interested in the value of retail sales per household in a year in which disposable income per household is $12,000. Now, we do not know, and will not know, *precisely* what value would result for sales in a particular instance in which disposable income was $12,000. In reality, the relationship between the quantities will not be exact, so it is not reasonable to think of just a single possible sales level resulting from a particular value for disposable income. Rather, it is more realistic to conceive of a *distribution* of possible sales levels resulting from each possible level of disposable income. In the terminology of Chapters 4 and 5, we might reasonably think of the *conditional distribution* of sales when disposable income has some specific value such as $12,000. A crucial charac-

TABLE 12.5 Data on disposable income per household (x) and retail sales per household (y), in constant dollars

YEAR	x_i	y_i	YEAR	x_i	y_i
1	9,098	5,492	12	11,307	5,907
2	9,138	5,540	13	11,432	6,124
3	9,094	5,305	14	11,449	6,186
4	9,282	5,507	15	11,697	6,224
5	9,229	5,418	16	11,871	6,496
6	9,347	5,320	17	12,018	6,718
7	9,525	5,538	18	12,523	6,921
8	9,756	5,692	19	12,053	6,471
9	10,282	5,871	20	12,088	6,394
10	10,662	6,157	21	12,215	6,555
11	11,019	6,342	22	12,494	6,755

[7] These data are taken from N. K. Dhalla, "Short-term forecasts of advertising expenditures," *Journal of Advertising Research, 19,* no. 1 (1979), 7–14.

[8] The analyst should, however, be prepared to abandon this assumption if it is strongly contradicted by the data.

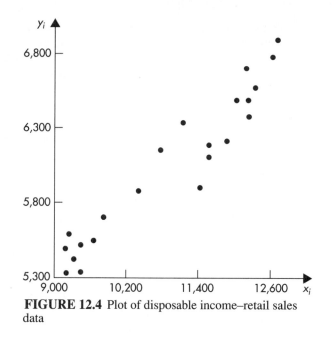

FIGURE 12.4 Plot of disposable income–retail sales data

teristic of this distribution, in the present context, is its mean, or expected value. Therefore, we can reasonably ask what would be the **expected value,** or average level, of retail sales per household in years in which disposable income per household was $12,000. In general, we will denote by $E(Y|X = x)$ the expected value of the random variable Y, when the random variable X takes the specific value x. Our assumption of linearity is the assumption that this conditional expectation depends linearly on x.

We are concerned with the expected value of the random variable Y, when X takes a specific value x. The assumption of linearity then implies that this expectation can be written

$$E(Y|X = x) = \alpha + \beta x \qquad (12.3.1)$$

where the fixed numbers α and β determine a specific straight line. Each of these numbers has a simple interpretation—one extremely important, the other typically much less so. Suppose that retail sales are related to disposable income through the equation

$$E(Y|X = x) = 2{,}000 + .4x \qquad (12.3.2)$$

so that, in Eq. (12.3.1), $\alpha = 2{,}000$ and $\beta = .4$. Now, substituting $x = 0$ in (12.3.1) gives

$$E(Y|X = 0) = \alpha$$

so that α emerges as the expected value of the **dependent variable** Y when the **independent variable** X takes the value 0. Although theoretically correct, this interpretation must not always be taken seriously. The implication for our example would be that if disposable income were \$0, retail sales per household would be expected to be \$2,000. However, we have no interest in the case of \$0 disposable income, since it will never arise. It is important to remember that the assumption of linearity should not be stretched too far. We have observations on disposable income in a range from roughly \$9,000 to \$12,500 per household, and although linearity in this range seems not unreasonable, it would be dangerous to extrapolate our conclusions very far outside that range. Thus, the assertion that expected retail sales per household would be \$2,000 in a year in which disposable income per household was \$0 would imply a belief that our assumption of linearity held true well beyond the boundaries of the \$9,000 to \$12,500 income range. Since we have no observational experience outside of this range, such a belief would be unsupported by our data.

We now return to Eq. (12.3.1). Suppose that X is increased by 1 unit, from x to $(x + 1)$. Then we have

$$E(Y|X = x + 1) = \alpha + \beta(x + 1)$$

so that

$$E(Y|X = x + 1) - E(Y|X = x) = \alpha + \beta(x + 1) - (\alpha + \beta x) = \beta$$

Thus, β, the **slope** of the line, is the expected increase in Y for a 1-unit increase in X. If the relation (12.3.2) held for this disposable income–retail sales data, the implication would be that for each \$1 increase in disposable income per household, a \$.40 increase in retail sales per household would be expected. We have already seen that the objective of regression is to describe, or model, the dependence of one variable on another. One way to think of such dependence is in terms of the change in the dependent variable, Y, resulting from a change in the independent variable, X. As we have just seen, each unit increase in X results in an expected change β in Y. Thus, if β is positive, an increase in X leads to an expected increase in Y, while if β is negative, an increase in X leads to an expected decrease in Y. In each case, the magnitude of the expected change in the dependent variable is a multiple β of the change in the independent variable.

A further problem is that no hypothesized theoretical relation will hold *exactly* in the real world, as we have already suggested. The data points in Figure 12.4 do not all lie on a single straight line (or any other convenient simple curve we might draw). Suppose that the independent variable takes the value x_i. Let Y_i denote the corresponding dependent variable, whose expected value would be

$$E(Y_i|X = x_i) = \alpha + \beta x_i \qquad (12.3.3)$$

In practice, the observed value of Y_i would almost invariably deviate somewhat from this expectation. If the discrepancy is denoted by the random variable ϵ_i—which should, by virtue of (12.3.3), have mean 0—then we can write

$$\epsilon_i = Y_i - E(Y_i|X = x_i) = Y_i - (\alpha + \beta x_i)$$

or

$$Y_i = \alpha + \beta x_i + \epsilon_i \qquad\qquad (12.3.4)$$

Equation (12.3.4) is called the **population (or true) regression line** of Y on X.

The Population Regression Line

Suppose that we are interested in the relation of a dependent variable Y to an independent variable X. If the random variable X takes specific values x_i, the **population regression line** expresses the corresponding values Y_i as

$$Y_i = \alpha + \beta x_i + \epsilon_i$$

where α and β are constants and ϵ_i is a random variable with mean 0.

Thus, the response of retail sales to a particular value, say x_i, of disposable income will be the sum of two parts—an expectation $(\alpha + \beta x_i)$ reflecting their systematic relationship and a discrepancy (ϵ_i) from the expectation. One can think of the discrepancy or **error term** ϵ_i, as embodying the multitude of factors *other than disposable income* that influence retail sales.

The regression model we have just described is illustrated in Figure 12.5, which shows a line representing the linear relationship between the expected value of the dependent variable and the value taken by the independent variable. For each different possible value of the independent variable, the value of the dependent variable can be

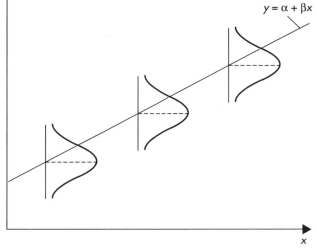

FIGURE 12.5 Illustration of the population regression model; shown are probability density functions of the dependent variable for given values x of the independent variable.

represented by a random variable whose mean lies on the regression line. We represent this in the figure by drawing a series of probability density functions for the dependent variable, given values of the independent variable. The regression line traces out the means of these distributions. For any given value x_i, the deviation of the dependent variable Y_i from the regression line is the discrepancy or error term ϵ_i. The density functions drawn in Figure 12.5 can be regarded as probability density functions of the random variables ϵ_i when each of these density functions is centered on 0.

12.4 LEAST SQUARES ESTIMATION

The population regression line introduced in Section 12.3 is a valuable theoretical construct. However, in practical applications, one will never be able to determine it *precisely*. Instead, it will be necessary to obtain an *estimate* from whatever data are available.

Suppose that we have n pairs of observations $(x_1, y_1), (x_2, y_2), \ldots, (x_n, y_n)$. We would like to find the straight line that best fits these points, in some sense. In other words, we would like to find estimates of the unknown coefficients α and β of the population regression line. An obvious approach would be through visual inspection of the plotted points. One might, after a little trial and error, be able to draw a line that passes reasonably near every point. However, a more formal approach that has attractive features is available.

Consider, as possible estimates of α and β, the numbers a and b, so that the estimated line is

$$y = a + bx$$

To determine how good an estimate this is, we need some measure of the distance of the points (x_i, y_i) from this line. Figure 12.6 shows, for a single point, how this dis-

FIGURE 12.6 Distance $e_i = y_i - (a + bx_i)$ from point (x_i, y_i) to the line $y = a + bx$

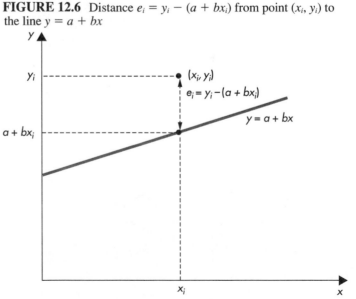

tance is measured. For the value x_i the corresponding y value on our line is $(a + bx_i)$, while the value actually observed for the dependent variable is y_i. The discrepancy between the two is therefore

$$e_i = y_i - (a + bx_i) \qquad\qquad (12.4.1)$$

At first sight, it may seem surprising that we did not take the shortest distance from the point to the line. Recall that our objective is to use the independent variable to explain the behavior of the dependent variable. The discrepancy e_i therefore reflects departure of the dependent variable from the value $(a + bx_i)$ predicted by the postulated line. To illustrate, consider the first observations on disposable income and retail sales in Table 12.5. These are

$$x_1 = 9{,}098 \qquad \text{and} \qquad y_1 = 5{,}492$$

Consider also the possible line

$$y = 2{,}000 + .4x$$

that is, the line with values

$$a = 2{,}000 \qquad \text{and} \qquad b = .4$$

for the intercept and slope. The value predicted by this line for retail sales, when disposable income is 9,098, is

$$a + bx_1 = 2{,}000 + (.04)(9{,}098) = 5{,}639.2$$

The discrepancy e_1 between the actual value y_1 and the value predicted by this line is

$$e_1 = y_1 - (a + bx_1)$$
$$= 5{,}492 - 5{,}639.2 = -147.2$$

Now, for any reasonable candidate as an estimate of the true regression line, some of the observed data points will be above the estimated line and some below. Hence, some of the e_i of (12.4.1) will be positive and some negative. If we want to penalize equally positive and negative values of the same magnitude, one way to achieve this is to work with the *squares* of the e_i. The sum of squared discrepancies from the points to the line is

$$SS = \sum_{i=1}^{n} e_i^2 = \sum_{i=1}^{n} (y_i - a - bx_i)^2$$

The method of **least squares** selects, as an estimate of the population regression line, that line for which this sum of squares is smallest.

Least Squares Estimation and the Sample Regression Line

Let $(x_1, y_1), (x_2, y_2), \ldots, (x_n, y_n)$ be a sample of n pairs of observations on a process with population regression line

$$Y_i = \alpha + \beta x_i + \epsilon_i$$

The **least squares estimates** of the coefficients α and β are the values a and b for which the sum of squared discrepancies

$$SS = \sum_{i=1}^{n}(y_i - a - bx_i)^2$$

is a minimum. It can be shown[9] that the resulting estimates are

$$b = \frac{\sum_{1}^{n}(x_i - \bar{x})(y_i - \bar{y})}{\sum_{1}^{n}(x_i - \bar{x})^2} = \frac{\sum_{1}^{n}x_i y_i - n\bar{x}\bar{y}}{\sum_{1}^{n}x_i^2 - n\bar{x}^2}$$

and

$$a = \bar{y} - b\bar{x}$$

where $\bar{x}$ and $\bar{y}$ are the respective sample means.

The line

$$y = a + bx$$

is called the **sample regression line** of Y on X.

The calculation of the sample regression line for the retail sales–disposable income data follows from the computations of Table 12.6, from which we have

$$\sum x_i = 237{,}579 \qquad \sum y_i = 132{,}933$$

$$\sum x_i y_i = 1{,}448{,}555{,}000 \qquad \sum x_i^2 = 2{,}599{,}715{,}000$$

Hence, the sample means are

$$\bar{x} = \frac{\sum x_i}{n} = \frac{237{,}579}{22} = 10{,}799.0 \qquad \text{and} \qquad \bar{y} = \frac{\sum y_i}{n} = \frac{132{,}933}{22} = 6{,}042.4$$

The least squares estimates of the coefficients of the population regression line are therefore

$$b = \frac{\sum x_i y_i - n\bar{x}\bar{y}}{\sum x_i^2 - n\bar{x}^2}$$

$$= \frac{1{,}448{,}555{,}000 - (22)(10{,}799.0)(6{,}042.4)}{2{,}599{,}715{,}000 - (22)(10{,}799.0)^2} = .3815$$

and

$$a = \bar{y} - b\bar{x} = 6{,}042.4 - (.3815)(10{,}799.0) = 1{,}923$$

The sample, or estimated, regression line is therefore

$$y = 1{,}923 + .3815x$$

Recalling the interpretation of the slope of the regression line, we are estimating that each \$1 increase in disposable income per household leads, on average, to an increase of \$.3815 in retail sales per household. Figure 12.7 shows the least squares estimated

---

[9] The result is most easily derived using calculus. Refer to Appendix A12.1 at the end of this chapter.

TABLE 12.6 Calculations for the sample regression of retail sales per household on disposable income per household ($x_i y_i$ and x_i^2 rounded to nearest thousand)

	x_i	y_i	$x_i y_i$	x_i^2
	9,098	5,492	49,966,000	82,774,000
	9,138	5,540	50,625,000	85,503,000
	9,094	5,305	48,244,000	82,701,000
	9,282	5,507	51,116,000	86,156,000
	9,229	5,418	50,003,000	85,174,000
	9,347	5,320	49,726,000	87,366,000
	9,525	5,538	52,749,000	90,726,000
	9,756	5,692	55,531,000	95,180,000
	10,282	5,871	60,366,000	105,720,000
	10,662	6,157	65,646,000	113,678,000
	11,019	6,342	69,882,000	121,418,000
	11,307	5,907	66,790,000	127,848,000
	11,432	6,124	70,010,000	130,691,000
	11,449	6,186	70,824,000	131,080,000
	11,697	6,224	72,802,000	136,820,000
	11,871	6,496	77,114,000	140,921,000
	12,018	6,718	80,737,000	144,432,000
	12,523	6,921	86,672,000	156,826,000
	12,053	6,471	77,995,000	145,275,000
	12,088	6,394	77,291,000	146,120,000
	12,215	6,555	80,069,000	149,206,000
	12,494	6,755	84,397,000	156,100,000
Sums	237,579	132,933	1,448,555,000	2,599,715,000

FIGURE 12.7 Disposable income-retail sales data and least squares estimated regression line, $y = 1,923 + .3815x$

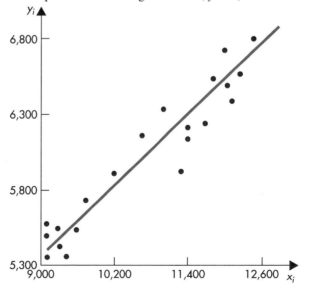

regression line, together with the twenty-two data points. The estimated regression line seems to give a good visual fit to these data points.

The arithmetic calculations involved in obtaining these estimates are already rather tedious. However, for more complicated regression problems, the computational burden can be enormously higher. In practice, this presents no great problem, since computer packages have been developed to perform regression calculations. (We will discuss such packages in Chapter 13.) Also, some pocket calculators have built-in programs for linear regression calculations.

12.5 STANDARD ASSUMPTIONS FOR THE LINEAR REGRESSION MODEL

The least squares method was presented in Section 12.4 as a plausible procedure to use to estimate a population regression line. It is not invariably the case that the least squares estimates are the most appropriate. However, given certain assumptions, it can be shown that least squares estimates possess desirable properties. These standard assumptions are generally taken to hold, unless the available data or theoretical subject matter considerations suggest otherwise. In this section, we introduce these assumptions; an important consequence of them is discussed in Section 12.6.

Standard Assumptions of the Linear Regression Model

Denote the population regression line by

$$Y_i = \alpha + \beta x_i + \epsilon_i$$

and assume that n pairs of observations are available. The following standard assumptions are often made:

1. Either the x_i are fixed numbers (set, for example, by an experimenter), or they are realizations of random variables X_i that are independent of the error terms ϵ_i. In the latter case, inference is carried out conditionally on the observed x_i.
2. The error terms ϵ_i are random variables with mean 0, that is

$$E(\epsilon_i) = 0 \qquad (i = 1, 2, \ldots, n)$$

3. The random variables ϵ_i all have the same variance, say σ_ϵ^2, so that

$$E(\epsilon_i^2) = \sigma_\epsilon^2 \qquad (i = 1, 2, \ldots, n)$$

4. The random variables ϵ_i are not correlated with one another, so that

$$E(\epsilon_i \epsilon_j) = 0 \text{ for all } i \neq j$$

The first of these assumptions is generally, with justification, taken to be true, although in some advanced econometric work it is untenable. (The assumption fails to hold, for example, when the x_i cannot be measured precisely or when the regression equation is part of a system of interdependent equations.) Henceforth, however, we will take this assumption as given.

Assumptions 2–4 concern the error terms ϵ_i in the regression equation—that is, the differences between the Y_i and their conditional expectations $(\alpha + \beta x_i)$. The expected discrepancy is 0, and all discrepancies are assumed to have the same variance. Thus, we do not expect the magnitudes of the error terms to be higher for some observations than for others. Finally, it is assumed that the discrepancies are not correlated with one another. Thus, for example, the occurrence of a large positive discrepancy at one observation point does not help us predict the values of any of the other error terms. Assumptions 2–4 will be satisfied if the error terms ϵ_i can be viewed as a random sample from a population with mean zero.

In the remainder of this chapter, it will be taken that these assumptions hold. The possibility of their breakdown will be considered in Chapter 14.

12.6 THE GAUSS-MARKOV THEOREM

In this section, we present a justification for the use of least squares in the estimation of a population regression line. Suppose that we have available n pairs of sample observations $(x_1, y_1), (x_2, y_2), \ldots, (x_n, y_n)$. Any number of possible estimates of the parameters α and β could be constructed. One possibility is to restrict attention to quantities that are linear functions of the y_i—that is, estimates of the general form

$$c_1 y_1 + c_2 y_2 + \cdots + c_n y_n$$

where the c_i are numbers that do not depend on the y_i. There is a sense in which, from this broad range of potential estimates, the least squares estimates are the most appealing, as discussed in the box.

The Gauss-Markov Theorem

Denote the population regression line by

$$Y_i = \alpha + \beta x_i + \epsilon_i$$

and assume that n pairs of observations are available. Suppose, further, that assumptions 1–4 of Section 12.5 hold.

Then, of all possible estimators of α and β that are linear in the Y_i and unbiased, the least squares estimators (that is, the random variables corresponding to the least squares estimates a and b of Section 12.4) have the smallest variances.

Further, if d_0 and d_1 are any fixed numbers, and we want to estimate

$$d_0 \alpha + d_1 \beta$$

then the estimator corresponding to

$$d_0 a + d_1 b$$

has the smallest variance in the class of all estimators that are linear in the Y_i and unbiased. (This result is useful when using the regression line to obtain predictions of the dependent variable.)

By virtue of this theorem, least squares estimators are said to be **best linear unbiased estimators (BLUE).**

The Gauss-Markov theorem provides a powerful motivation for estimating the parameters of a regression model by least squares. Recalling from Chapter 7 the definition of the efficiency of a point estimator, we see that the method of least squares yields the most efficient estimators from a wide class of unbiased estimators. It should be emphasized, however, that this result depends on the assumptions of Section 12.5 and does not necessarily hold if these assumptions break down. In the remainder of this chapter, we continue to explore the properties of the least squares estimation method when those assumptions are true.

The technique of regression analysis is perhaps the most commonly applied statistical tool in business and economics. The result of this section, though briefly stated, is therefore of great practical importance. Regression models are, in practice, generally estimated by the method of least squares. In Section 12.4, we introduced this technique as a sensible procedure for fitting a straight line to a set of data points. However, it is not difficult to think of other sensible ways of accomplishing the same objective. What distinguishes the method of least squares is the fact, following from the Gauss-Markov theorem, that the resulting estimators have desirable statistical properties.

12.7 THE EXPLANATORY POWER OF A LINEAR REGRESSION EQUATION

A regression equation can be viewed as an attempt to employ information on an independent variable, X, to *explain* the behavior of a dependent variable, Y. In this section, we develop a measure of the degree to which this attempt has been successful for the sample data. The observations on the dependent variable will exhibit a certain amount of *variability* within the sample. In essence, we are asking here what *proportion* of that variability can be explained by the linear dependence of Y on X.

For the sample values, the estimated regression can be written

$$y_i = a + bx_i + e_i$$

or

$$y_i = \hat{y}_i + e_i \qquad (12.7.1)$$

where

$$\hat{y}_i = a + bx_i$$

The quantity $\hat{y}_i$ is the value of the dependent variable predicted by the regression line, and the **residual** e_i is the difference between the observed and predicted values. Therefore, the residual represents the part of the behavior of the dependent variable in the sample that cannot be explained by its linear relationship with the independent variable. For the disposable income-retail sales data, the three quantities in Eq. (12.7.1) are tabulated in the first three columns of Table 12.7.

TABLE 12.7 Actual and predicted values for retail sales per household and residuals from its linear regression on income per household

y_i	$\hat{y}_i = a + bx_i$ $= 1,923 +$ $0.3815x_i$	$e_i = y_i - \hat{y}_i$	$y_i - \bar{y}$ $= y_i - 6,042.4$	$\hat{y}_i - \bar{y}$ $= \hat{y}_i - 6,042.4$
5,492	5,394	98	−550.4	−648.4
5,540	5,409	131	−502.4	−633.4
5,305	5,392	−87	−737.4	−650.4
5,507	5,464	43	−535.4	−578.4
5,418	5,444	−26	−624.4	−598.4
5,320	5,489	−169	−722.4	−553.4
5,538	5,557	−19	−504.4	−485.4
5,692	5,645	47	−350.4	−397.4
5,871	5,846	25	−171.4	−196.4
6,157	5,991	166	114.6	−51.4
6,342	6,127	215	299.6	84.6
5,907	6,237	−330	−135.4	194.6
6,124	6,284	−160	81.6	241.6
6,186	6,291	−105	143.6	248.6
6,224	6,385	−161	181.6	342.6
6,496	6,452	44	453.6	409.6
6,718	6,508	210	675.6	465.6
6,921	6,701	220	878.6	658.6
6,471	6,521	−50	428.6	478.6
6,394	6,535	−141	351.6	492.6
6,555	6,583	−28	512.6	540.6
6,755	6,689	66	712.6	646.6

For our present purpose, a small modification of Eq. (12.7.1) is useful. We can think of the sample variability of the dependent variable in terms of deviations from its sample mean. Subtracting $\bar{y}$ from each side of Eq. (12.7.1), we can write

$$(y_i - \bar{y}) = (\hat{y}_i - \bar{y}) + e_i \qquad (12.7.2)$$

or

Observed deviation from sample mean

$\qquad$ = Predicted deviation from sample mean + Residual

The first two quantities in Eq. (12.7.2) are tabulated, for our data, in the two rightmost columns of Table 12.7.

Now, it can be shown that if we square both sides of Eq. (12.7.2) and sum over the sample index i, the result is

$$\sum_{i=1}^{n} (y_i - \bar{y})^2 = \sum_{i=1}^{n} (\hat{y}_i - \bar{y})^2 + \sum_{i=1}^{n} e_i^2 \qquad (12.7.3)$$

Equation (12.7.3) has a valuable interpretation. The quantity on its left-hand side represents the total variability in the sample of the dependent variable about its mean. This is decomposed into two parts. The first term on the right-hand side of (12.7.3) represents the part of the variability that is explained by the regression, while the second term represents unexplained variability. The equation can therefore be expressed as

Total sample variability = Explained variability + Unexplained variability

In a sense, the higher the proportion of the sample variability explained, the stronger the explanatory power of the regression.

Sum of Squares Decomposition and the Coefficient of Determination

Suppose that a linear regression equation is fitted by least squares to n pairs of observations, yielding

$$y_i = a + bx_i + e_i = \hat{y}_i + e_i \qquad (i = 1, 2, \ldots, n)$$

where a and b are the least squares estimates of the intercept and slope of the population regression and e_i are the **residuals** from the fitted regression line.

We define the following quantities (where $\bar{y}$ is the sample mean for the dependent variable):

$$\text{TOTAL SUM OF SQUARES:} \quad SST = \sum_{i=1}^{n}(y_i - \bar{y})^2$$

$$\text{REGRESSION SUM OF SQUARES:} \quad SSR = \sum_{i=1}^{n}(\hat{y}_i - \bar{y})^2$$

$$\text{ERROR SUM OF SQUARES:} \quad SSE = \sum_{i=1}^{n} e_i^2$$

It can be shown that

$$SST = SSR + SSE$$

The **coefficient of determination,** R^2, of the fitted regression is defined as

$$R^2 = \frac{SSR}{SST} = 1 - \frac{SSE}{SST}$$

This is the proportion of the sample variability of the dependent variable explained by its linear relationship with the independent variable. It can further be shown that R^2 is the square of the sample correlation coefficient defined in Section 12.1.[10]

It follows from its definition as the proportion of sample variability explained that

$$0 \le R^2 \le 1$$

and that the higher R^2 is, the greater is the explanatory power of the regression.

---

[10] Here we use the notation R^2, rather than the equivalent r^2, because the use of the coefficient of determination extends naturally to the case of multiple regression, to be discussed in the next chapter.

For our example, the sums of squares of the elements in columns 3 and 4 of Table 12.7 are, respectively

$$\text{SSE} = \sum_{i=1}^{n} e_i^2 = 435{,}799 \qquad \text{and} \qquad \text{SST} = \sum_{i=1}^{n} (y_i - \bar{y})^2 = 5{,}397{,}560$$

The coefficient of determination is, therefore

$$R^2 = 1 - \frac{\text{SSE}}{\text{SST}} = 1 - \frac{435{,}799}{5{,}397{,}560} = .92$$

This result implies that 92% of the sample variability in retail sales per household is explained by its linear dependence on income per household. We could therefore conclude that in using disposable income per household as the independent variable, we have been rather successful in explaining variability in retail sales per household.

EXERCISES

13. A company sets different prices for a particular stereo system in eight different regions of the country. The accompanying table shows the numbers of units sold and the corresponding prices (in hundreds of dollars).

SALES	420	380	350	400	440	380	450	420
PRICE	5.5	6.0	6.5	6.0	5.0	6.5	4.5	5.0

(a) Plot these data, and estimate the linear regression of sales on price.

(b) What effect would you expect a \$100 increase in price to have on sales?

14. Refer to the data of Exercise 2 on percentage change (x) in the Dow-Jones index over the first five trading days of the year, and percentage change (y) in the index over the whole year.

(a) Estimate the linear regression of y on x.

(b) Provide interpretations of the intercept and slope of the sample regression line.

15. On Friday, November 13, 1989, prices on the New York Stock Exchange fell steeply; the Standard and Poors 500-share index was down 6.1% on that day. The accompanying table shows the percentage *losses* (y) of the twenty-five largest mutual funds on November 13, 1989. Also shown are the percentage *gains* (x), assuming reinvested dividends and capital gains, for these same funds for 1989, through November 12.

y	x	y	x	y	x
4.7	38.0	6.4	39.5	4.2	24.7
4.7	24.5	3.3	23.3	3.3	18.7
4.0	21.5	3.6	28.0	4.1	36.8
4.7	30.8	4.7	30.8	6.0	31.2
3.0	20.3	4.4	32.9	5.8	50.9
4.4	24.0	5.4	30.3	4.9	30.7
5.0	29.6	3.0	19.9	3.8	20.3
3.3	19.4	4.9	24.6		
3.8	25.6	5.2	32.3		

(a) Estimate the linear regression of November 13 losses on pre-November 13, 1989, gains.

(b) Interpret the slope of the sample regression line.

16. For a period of 11 years, the figures in the accompanying table were found for annual change in unemployment rate and annual change in mean employee absence rate due to own illness.[11]

YEAR	CHANGE IN UNEMPLOYMENT RATE	CHANGE IN MEAN EMPLOYEE ABSENCE RATE DUE TO OWN ILLNESS
1	−.2	+.2
2	−.1	+.2
3	+1.4	+.2
4	+1.0	−.4
5	−.3	−.1
6	−.7	+.2
7	+.7	−.1
8	+2.9	−.8
9	−.8	+.2
10	−.7	+.2
11	−1.0	+.2

(a) Estimate the linear regression of change in mean employee absence rate due to own illness on change in unemployment rate.

(b) Interpret the estimated slope of the regression line.

17. For a sample of twenty monthly observations, a financial analyst wants to regress the percentage rate of return (Y) of the common stock of a corporation on the percentage rate of return (X) of the S. and P. 500 index. The following information is available:

$$\sum_{i=1}^{20} y_i = 22.6 \qquad \sum_{i=1}^{20} x_i = 25.4 \qquad \sum_{i=1}^{20} x_i^2 = 145.7 \qquad \sum_{i=1}^{20} x_i y_i = 150.5$$

(a) Estimate the linear regression of Y on X.

(b) Interpret the slope of the sample regression line.

(c) Interpret the intercept of the sample regression line.

18. A corporation administers an aptitude test to all new sales representatives. Management is interested in the extent to which this test is able to predict their eventual success. The accompanying table records average weekly sales (in thousands of dollars) and aptitude test scores for a random sample of eight representatives.

WEEKLY SALES	10	12	28	24	18	16	15	12
TEST SCORE	55	60	85	75	80	85	65	60

(a) Estimate the linear regression of weekly sales on aptitude test scores.

(b) Interpret the estimated slope of the regression line.

---

[11] Reprinted by permission of the publisher from "The effects of unemployment and the business cycle on absenteeism," by J. P. Leigh, *Journal of Economics and Business*, *37* (1985), 159–70. Copyright 1985 by the Elsevier Science Publishing Co., Inc.

19. It was hypothesized that the number of bottles of an imported premium beer sold per evening in the restaurants of a city depends linearly on the average costs of meals in the restaurants. The following results were obtained for a sample of $n = 17$ restaurants, of approximately equal size, where

y = Number of bottles sold per evening
x = Average cost, in dollars, of a meal

$$\bar{x} = 25.5 \qquad \bar{y} = 16.0 \qquad \frac{\sum_{i=1}^{n}(x_i - \bar{x})^2}{n-1} = 350 \qquad \frac{\sum_{i=1}^{n}(x_i - \bar{x})(y_i - \bar{y})}{n-1} = 180$$

(a) Find the sample regression line.
(b) Interpret the slope of the sample regression line.
(c) Is it possible to provide a meaningful interpretation of the intercept of the sample regression line? Explain.

20. Let the sample regression line be

$$y_i = a + bx_i + e_i = \hat{y}_i + e_i \qquad (i = 1, 2, \ldots, n)$$

and let $\bar{x}$ and $\bar{y}$ denote the sample means for the independent and dependent variables, respectively.

(a) Show that

$$e_i = y_i - \bar{y} - b(x_i - \bar{x})$$

(b) Using the result in part (a), show that

$$\sum_{i=1}^{n} e_i = 0$$

(c) Using the result in part (a), show that

$$\sum_{i=1}^{n} e_i^2 = \sum_{i=1}^{n}(y_i - \bar{y})^2 - b^2 \sum_{i=1}^{n}(x_i - \bar{x})^2$$

(d) Show that

$$\hat{y}_i - \bar{y} = b(x_i - \bar{x})$$

(e) Using the results in parts (c) and (d), show that

$$\text{SST} = \text{SSR} + \text{SSE}$$

(f) Using the result in part (a), show that

$$\sum_{i=1}^{n} e_i(x_i - \bar{x}) = 0$$

21. Let

$$R^2 = \frac{\text{SSR}}{\text{SST}}$$

denote the coefficient of determination for the sample regression line.

(a) Using part (d) of Exercise 20, show that

$$R^2 = b^2 \frac{\sum_{i=1}^{n}(x_i - \bar{x})^2}{\sum_{i=1}^{n}(y_i - \bar{y})^2}$$

(b) Using the result in part (a), show that the coefficient of determination is equal to the square of the sample correlation between X and Y.

   (c) Let b be the slope of the least squares regression of Y on X, b^* the slope of the least squares regression of X on Y, and r the sample correlation between X and Y. Show that

   $$b \cdot b^* = r^2$$

22. Find and interpret the coefficient of determination for the regression of stereo system sales on price, using the data of Exercise 13.

23. Find and interpret the coefficient of determination for the regression of the percentage change in the Dow-Jones index in a year on the percentage change in the index over the first five trading days of the year, continuing the analysis of Exercise 14. Compare your answer with the sample correlation found for these data in Exercise 2.

24. Find the proportion of the sample variability in mutual fund percentage losses on November 13, 1989, explained by their linear dependence on 1989 percentage gains through November 12, based on the data of Exercise 15.

25. Refer to the data on unemployment rate and employee absence rate in Exercise 16.

   (a) Find the predicted values, $\hat{y}_i$, and the residuals, e_i, for the least squares regression of change in mean employee absence rate due to own illness on change in unemployment rate.

   (b) Find the sums of squares SST, SSR, and SSE, and verify that

   $$SST = SSR + SSE$$

   (c) Using the results in part (b), find and interpret the coefficient of determination.

26. For the problem in Exercise 17, use

   $$\sum_{i=1}^{20} y_i^2 = 196.2$$

   to find the coefficient of determination for the regression of the rate of return of the corporation's common stock on the rate of return of the *S. and P.* 500 index. [*Hint:* Use the result in part (a) of Exercise 21.]

27. Refer to the data on weekly sales and aptitude test scores achieved by sales representatives given in Exercise 18.

   (a) Find the predicted values, $\hat{y}_i$, and residuals, e_i, for the least squares regression of weekly sales on aptitude test scores.

   (b) Find the sums of squares SST, SSR, and SSE, and verify that

   $$SST = SSR + SSE$$

   (c) Using the results in part (b), find and interpret the coefficient of determination.

   (d) Find directly the sample correlation coefficient between sales and aptitude test scores, and verify that its square is equal to the coefficient of determination.

28. In the study discussed in Exercise 6, we saw that for a sample of 353 college faculty, the correlation was .11 between annual raises and teaching evaluations. What would be the coefficient of determination of a regression of annual raises on teaching evaluations for this sample? Interpret your result.

12.8 CONFIDENCE INTERVALS AND HYPOTHESIS TESTS

In studying the population regression line

$$Y_i = \alpha + \beta x_i + \epsilon_i$$

we have produced point estimates, through the method of least squares, of the unknown parameters α and β. In addition, we have seen that given certain assumptions, the least squares estimators have desirable properties by virtue of the Gauss-Markov theorem. However, point estimation is rarely by itself sufficient for a thorough analysis of data. It is natural, for example, in the present context to ask how reliable are the estimates that have been obtained. In this section, we consider the problems of finding confidence intervals for and testing hypotheses about the population regression parameters.

To begin, we note in the box an important use of the quantity SSE, introduced in Section 12.7.

Estimation of the Error Variance

Suppose that the population regression line is

$$Y_i = \alpha + \beta x_i + \epsilon_i$$

and that assumptions 1–4 of Section 12.5 hold. Let σ_ϵ^2 denote the common variance of the error terms ϵ_i. An unbiased estimate[12] of σ_ϵ^2 is provided by

$$s_e^2 = \frac{\sum\limits_{i=1}^{n} e_i^2}{n-2} = \frac{SSE}{n-2}$$

In the next box, we consider the sampling distribution of the least squares estimator of the slope of the population regression line.

Sampling Distribution of the Least Squares Estimator

Let b denote the least squares estimate of the slope β of the population regression line. If assumptions 1–4 of Section 12.5 hold, the estimator corresponding to b is unbiased for β and has variance.

$$\sigma_b^2 = \frac{\sigma_\epsilon^2}{\sum\limits_{i=1}^{n}(x_i - \bar{x})^2} = \frac{\sigma_\epsilon^2}{\sum x_i^2 - n\bar{x}^2}$$

An unbiased estimate of σ_b^2 is provided by

$$s_b^2 = \frac{s_e^2}{\sum\limits_{i=1}^{n}(x_i - \bar{x})^2} = \frac{s_e^2}{\sum x_i^2 - n\bar{x}^2}$$

In the disposable income-retail sales example, we have

$$s_e^2 = \frac{SSE}{n-2} = \frac{435,799}{22-2} = 21,789.95$$

---

[12] It is natural to use the least squares residuals, e_i, as proxies for the unknown ϵ_i. Intuitively, the reason for division by $(n-2)$ is that 2 degrees of freedom are "lost" through the necessity to estimate the unknown parameters α and β.

Also, we found in Section 12.4, that

$$\bar{x} = 10{,}799 \qquad \text{and} \qquad \sum_{i=1}^{n} x_i^2 = 2{,}599{,}715{,}000$$

Hence

$$s_b^2 = \frac{21{,}789.95}{[2{,}599{,}715{,}000 - (22)(10{,}799)^2]} = .0006388$$

so the estimated standard deviation of the least squares estimator of the slope of the population regression line is

$$s_b = \sqrt{s_b^2} = .0253$$

In the overwhelming majority of practical applications, the major focus of interest is on the slope rather than on the intercept of the regression line. Accordingly, we will concentrate on that quantity in what follows, noting here that inference about the intercept can be carried out in an analogous fashion by substituting for β, b, and s_b^2 the quantities, α, a, and s_a^2, where

$$s_a^2 = s_e^2 \left(\frac{1}{n} + \frac{\bar{x}^2}{\sum x_i^2 - n\bar{x}^2} \right)$$

Up to this point, we have not required specific distributional assumptions about the population errors ϵ_i. However, in order to take inference further, something more definite has to be assumed. Almost invariably, unless strong contrary evidence is available, these errors are taken to obey a normal distribution. Given this additional assumption, we can develop confidence intervals and hypothesis tests. Moreover, as a result of the central limit theorem, the procedures remain approximately valid for a wide range of nonnormal error distributions. The main result, from which appropriate confidence intervals and tests immediately follow, is stated in the box.

Basis for Inference About the Population Regression Slope

Let β be a population regression slope and b its least squares estimate based on n pairs of sample observations. Then, if assumptions 1–4 of Section 12.5 hold, and if it can also be assumed that the errors ϵ_i are normally distributed, the random variable corresponding to

$$t = \frac{b - \beta}{s_b}$$

is distributed as Student's t with $(n - 2)$ degrees of freedom.

Confidence intervals for the slope β of the population regression line can then be derived through a line of argument used repeatedly in Chapter 8, as summarized in the next box.

For the regression of retail sales on disposable income, we have already found

$$n = 22 \qquad b = .3815 \qquad s_b = .0253$$

If a 99% confidence interval for β is required, we have $1 - \alpha = .99$, and so, from Table 6 of the Appendix

$$t_{n - 2,\alpha/2} = t_{20,.005} = 2.845$$

Hence, the 99% confidence interval is

$$.3815 - (2.845)(.0253) < \beta < .3815 + (2.845)(.0253)$$

or

$$.3095 < \beta < .4535$$

Thus, in the context of our problem, the 99% confidence interval for the expected increase in retail sales per household resulting from a $1 increase in disposable income per household runs from $.3095 to $.4535. Figure 12.8 shows also the 90% and 95% confidence intervals for the population regression slope, calculated from these data.

FIGURE 12.8 90%, 95%, and 99% confidence intervals for the population regression slope for regression of retail sales on disposable income

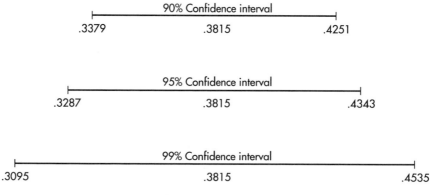

Following the same kind of reasoning used frequently in Chapter 9, we can readily develop tests of the hypothesis that the population regression slope β is equal to some specified value β_0. The procedure is described in the box.

Tests of the Population Regression Slope

If the regression errors ϵ_i are normally distributed and assumptions 1–4 of Section 12.5 hold, the following tests have significance level α:

(i) To test either null hypothesis

$$H_0: \quad \beta = \beta_0 \qquad \text{or} \qquad H_0: \quad \beta \leq \beta_0$$

against the alternative

$$H_1: \quad \beta > \beta_0$$

the decision rule is

$$\text{Reject } H_0 \text{ if } \quad \frac{b - \beta_0}{s_b} > t_{n-2,\alpha}$$

(ii) To test either null hypothesis

$$H_0: \quad \beta = \beta_0 \qquad \text{or} \qquad H_0: \quad \beta \geq \beta_0$$

against the alternative

$$H_1: \quad \beta < \beta_0$$

the decision rule is

$$\text{Reject } H_0 \text{ if } \quad \frac{b - \beta_0}{s_b} < -t_{n-2,\alpha}$$

(iii) To test the null hypothesis

$$H_0: \quad \beta = \beta_0$$

against the two-sided alternative

$$H_1: \quad \beta \neq \beta_0$$

the decision rule is

$$\text{Reject } H_0 \text{ if } \quad \frac{b - \beta_0}{s_b} > t_{n-2,\alpha/2} \qquad \text{or} \qquad \frac{b - \beta_0}{s_b} < -t_{n-2,\alpha/2}$$

A special case of some practical interest arises when the value hypothesized for the regression slope is 0. The population regression line is

$$Y_i = \alpha + \beta x_i + \epsilon_i$$

so on setting β equal to 0, we have

$$Y_i = \alpha + \epsilon_i$$

This implies that *irrespective of the value taken by the independent variable*, the dependent variable will be a random variable with mean α and variance σ_ϵ^2. Thus, the expected value of the dependent variable will not be (linearly) affected by the value of the independent variable. In other words, variability in the dependent variable cannot at all be explained by a linear relation with the independent variable.

To illustrate, we test for the retail sales–disposable income data the null hypothesis

$$H_0: \quad \beta = 0$$

This is the hypothesis that income does not (linearly) influence sales. The alternative of interest is that an increase in income leads to an expected increase in sales; that is

$$H_1: \quad \beta > 0$$

We have

$$n = 22 \qquad b = .3815 \qquad s_b = .0253 \qquad \beta_0 = 0$$

so

$$\frac{b - \beta_0}{s_b} = \frac{.3815 - 0}{.0253} = 15.08$$

From Table 6 of the Appendix, for $n - 2 = 20$ degrees of freedom, we find

$$t_{20,.005} = 2.845$$

Hence, the null hypothesis that the population regression slope is 0 is very clearly rejected against the alternative that it is positive at the .5% significance level. Thus, we see that the evidence in these data against the hypothesis that a change in disposable income per household does not induce a change in expected retail sales per household is overwhelming. The data point very strongly to the conclusion that an increase in disposable income leads to an expected increase in retail sales, as one might reasonably believe.

We have now developed, under normality assumptions, two tests of the hypothesis of no linear association between a pair of random variables. In Section 12.1, such a test was based on the sample correlation coefficient, whereas the test just illustrated is based on the least squares estimate of the slope of the regression line. In fact, no contradiction in conclusions can arise from these two tests. It is possible to show that precisely the same test statistic emerges whichever route is followed, making the two tests equivalent. The distinction between linear regression and correlation analysis lies not in the formal procedures for testing for lack of association but in the interpretation of any association. The correlation model does not postulate a *direction* for any dependence between random variables. But in estimating the regression model for our data in this chapter, we have implicitly assumed that changes in disposable income per household lead to changes in retail sales per household, rather than the converse.

12.9 PREDICTION

One important use of regression is in the computation of *predictions*, or forecasts, for the dependent variable, conditional on an assumed value for the independent variable. Suppose that the independent variable is equal to some specified value, x_{n+1}, and that the linear relationship between dependent and independent variables continues to hold. The corresponding value of the dependent variable will then be

$$Y_{n+1} = \alpha + \beta x_{n+1} + \epsilon_{n+1} \qquad (12.9.1)$$

which, given x_{n+1}, has expectation

$$E(Y_{n+1} \mid x_{n+1}) = \alpha + \beta x_{n+1} \qquad (12.9.2)$$

Two distinct prediction problems are of interest:

1. We may want to estimate the *actual value* that will result for Y_{n+1} in Eq. (12.9.1).
2. We might want to estimate the conditional expectation $E(Y_{n+1}|x_{n+1})$ of (12.9.2)—that is, the *average value* of the dependent variable when the independent variable is fixed at x_{n+1}.

Provided that the assumptions of Section 12.5 continue to hold, the same point estimate results for either problem. It is natural to replace the unknown α and β by their least squares estimates, a and b. Hence, $(\alpha + \beta x_{n+1})$ is estimated by $(a + bx_{n+1})$. We know from the Gauss-Markov theorem that the corresponding estimator is best linear unbiased. Thus, for both problems, an appropriate point estimate under our assumptions is

$$\hat{Y}_{n+1} = a + bx_{n+1}$$

This follows, since we know nothing useful, in the present context, about the random variable ϵ_{n+1} of (12.9.1) except that its mean is 0. In the absence of any other relevant information, then, the best we can do is to use 0 as its point estimate.

However, confidence intervals are usually wanted along with the point estimates, and at this point the two problems become distinct. This is because there will be uncertainty about the value to be taken by the random variable ϵ_{n+1}, which appears in (12.9.1) but not in (12.9.2). The appropriate procedures are summarized in the box.

Confidence Intervals for Predictions

Suppose that the population regression model

$$Y_i = \alpha + \beta x_i + \epsilon_i \qquad (i = 1, \ldots, n + 1)$$

holds, that the assumptions of Section 12.5 hold, and that the ϵ_i are normally distributed. Let a and b be the least squares estimates of α and β, based on (x_1, y_1), (x_2, y_2), . . . , (x_n, y_n). Then it can be shown that the following are $100(1 - \alpha)\%$ confidence intervals:

(i) For the prediction of the actual value resulting for Y_{n+1}, the interval is

$$\hat{Y}_{n+1} \pm t_{n-2,\alpha/2} \sqrt{\left[1 + \frac{1}{n} + \frac{(x_{n+1} - \bar{x})^2}{\sum\limits_{i=1}^{n} x_i^2 - n\bar{x}^2} \right] s_e^2} \qquad (12.9.3)$$

(ii) For the prediction of the conditional expectation, $E(Y_{n+1} \mid x_{n+1})$, the interval is

$$\hat{Y}_{n+1} \pm t_{n-2,\alpha/2} \sqrt{\left[\frac{1}{n} + \frac{(x_{n+1} - \bar{x})^2}{\sum_{i=1}^{n} x_i^2 - n\bar{x}^2} \right] s_e^2} \qquad (12.9.4)$$

Here

$$\bar{x} = \frac{\sum_{i=1}^{n} x_i}{n} \qquad \text{and} \qquad \hat{Y}_{n+1} = a + bx_{n+1}$$

To illustrate these procedures, consider again the retail sales–disposable income example. Suppose that we are interested in the prediction of retail sales per household in a year in which disposable income per household is \$12,000. Thus

$$x_{n+1} = 12,000$$

For point prediction, we then have

$$\hat{Y}_{n+1} = a + bx_{n+1}$$

$$= 1,923 + (.3815)(12,000) = 6,501$$

Thus, we estimate sales of \$6,501 when income is \$12,000. We have earlier found

$$n = 22 \qquad \bar{x} = 10,799 \qquad \sum_{i=1}^{n} x_i^2 = 2,599,715,000 \qquad s_e^2 = 21,789.95$$

Hence

$$\sqrt{\left[1 + \frac{1}{n} + \frac{(x_{n+1} - \bar{x})^2}{\sum_{i=1}^{n} x_i^2 - n\bar{x}^2} \right] s_e^2}$$

$$= \sqrt{\left[1 + \frac{1}{22} + \frac{(12,000 - 10,799)^2}{2,599,715,000 - (22)(10,799)^2} \right] (21,789.95)}$$

$$= 153.954$$

Similarly, we find

$$\sqrt{\left[\frac{1}{n} + \frac{(x_{n+1} - \bar{x})^2}{\sum_{i=1}^{n} x_i^2 - n\bar{x}^2} \right] s_e^2} = 43.725$$

Suppose that 95% confidence intervals are required for the predictions, so that $\alpha = .05$ and

$$t_{n-2,\alpha/2} = t_{20,.025} = 2.086$$

Then, for a prediction of the actual value resulting for retail sales in a year when disposable income is \$12,000, we have the 95% interval

$$6,501 \pm (2.086)(153.954)$$

or

$$6,501 \pm 321$$

Thus, the 95% confidence interval for sales in a year in which income is $12,000 runs from $6,180 to $6,822.

For the confidence interval for the expected value of retail sales when disposable income is $12,000, we have

$$6,501 \pm (2.086)(43.725)$$

or

$$6,501 \pm 91$$

Hence, the 95% confidence interval runs from $6,410 to $6,592.

The distinction between these two interval estimation problems is illustrated in Figures 12.9 and 12.10. Each figure shows the estimated regression line for our retail sales–disposable income data. Also shown in Figure 12.9 is a probability density function representing our uncertainty about the value that retail sales will take in any specific year in which disposable income is $12,000. The probability density function in Figure 12.10 represents our uncertainty about *expected*, or average, retail sales in years when disposable income is $12,000. Now, we would be far more uncertain about sales in a single specific year than about average sales, and this is reflected in the shapes of the two density functions. Although both are centered on a retail sales figure of $6,501, the density function in Figure 12.9 is far more dispersed about this value. This additional uncertainty is reflected in wider confidence intervals for a specific value of retail sales than for expected retail sales.

FIGURE 12.9 Least squares estimated regression line of retail sales on disposable income; the probability density function represents our uncertainty about actual retail sales when disposable income is $12,000

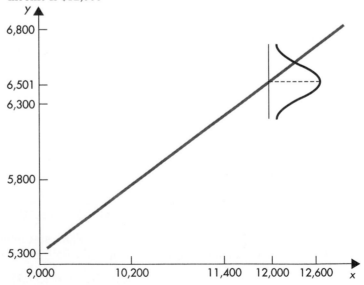

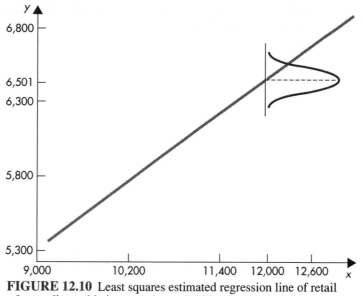

FIGURE 12.10 Least squares estimated regression line of retail sales on disposable income; the probability density function represents our uncertainty about expected, or average, retail sales when disposable income is $12,000

A study of the general forms of the confidence intervals (12.9.3) and (12.9.4) provides some insight. Keeping in mind that the wider the confidence interval, the greater the uncertainty surrounding the point forecast, we can make four observations from these formulas:

1. All other things being equal, the larger the sample size n, the narrower the confidence interval. This reflects the fact that the more sample information is available, the more sure will be our inference.

2. All other things being equal, the larger s_e^2 is, the wider is the confidence interval. Again, this is to be expected, since s_e^2 is an estimate of σ_ϵ^2, the variance of the regression errors ϵ_i. Since these errors

$$\epsilon_i = Y_i - \alpha - \beta x_i$$

represent the discrepancy between the observed values of the dependent variables and their expectations given the independent variables, the bigger the magnitude of this discrepancy is, the more imprecise will be our inference.

3. Consider now the quantity $(\sum x_i^2 - n\bar{x}^2)$. This is simply a multiple of the sample variance of the observations on the independent variable. A large variance implies that we have information for a wide range of values of this variable, which allows more precise estimates of the population regression line and correspondingly narrower confidence intervals.

4. Finally, we see that the larger $(x_{n+1} - \bar{x})^2$ is, the wider are the confidence intervals for the predictions. That is, our inference becomes more uncertain the farther x_{n+1} is from the sample mean of the independent variable. This, too, is a plausible conclusion. If our sample data are centered on $\bar{x}$, we would expect to be able to be more definitive about our inference when the independent variable is relatively close to this central value than when it is some distance away.

Suppose, now, referring to the data of Table 12.5, that you are asked to predict retail sales per household in a year in which disposable income per household is

$30,000. In principle, you could routinely follow the procedures of this section and produce point and interval forecasts. However, to do so would be extremely rash. The available data do suggest, *within the income range observed*, a linear relationship between expected sales and income. However, we have no observed experience of what happens when income is as high as $30,000. It would be an act of pure faith to assume that our linear relationship continues to hold for such high income levels. It might, of course, but this certainly should not be inferred from the data. If, indeed, the assumed relation does break down, forecasts based on the assumption that it holds can be wildly in error. The point is that it is unwise to extrapolate an estimated linear regression very far outside the range of the independent variable for which we have sample data.

EXERCISES

29. Consider the linear regression of stereo system sales on price, based on the data of Exercise 13.
   (a) Use an unbiased estimation procedure to find an estimate of the variance of the error terms in the population regression.
   (b) Use an unbiased estimation procedure to find an estimate of the variance of the least squares estimator of the slope of the population regression line.
   (c) Find a 90% confidence interval for the slope of the population regression line.
30. Continue the analysis of Exercise 14 of the regression of the percentage change in the Dow-Jones index in a year on the percentage change in the index over the first five trading days of the year.
   (a) Use an unbiased estimation procedure to find a point estimate of the variance of the error terms in the population regression.
   (b) Use an unbiased estimation procedure to find a point estimate of the variance of the least squares estimator of the slope of the population regression line.
   (c) Find and interpret a 95% confidence interval for the slope of the population regression line.
   (d) Test at the 10% significance level, against a two-sided alternative, the null hypothesis that the slope of the population regression line is 0.
   (e) Compare your test in part (d) with the test of zero correlation in part (b) of Exercise 2.
31. Consider the model for mutual fund losses on November 13, 1989, based on the data of Exercise 15.
   (a) Use an unbiased estimation procedure to obtain a point estimate of the variance of the error terms in the population regression.
   (b) Use an unbiased estimation procedure to obtain a point estimate of the variance of the least squares estimator of the slope of the population regression line.
   (c) Find 90%, 95%, and 99% confidence intervals for the slope of the population regression line.
32. A fast-food chain decided to carry out an experiment to assess the influence of advertising expenditure on sales. Different relative changes in advertising expenditure, compared to the previous year, were made in eight regions of the country, and resulting changes in sales levels were observed. The accompanying table shows the results.

INCREASE IN ADVERTISING EXPENDITURE (%)	0	4	14	10	9	8	6	1
INCREASE IN SALES (%)	2.4	7.2	10.3	9.1	10.2	4.1	7.6	3.5

(a) Estimate by least squares the linear regression of increase in sales on increase in advertising expenditure.

(b) Find a 90% confidence interval for the slope of the population regression line.

33. A liquor wholesaler is interested in assessing the effect of the price of a premium scotch whiskey on the quantity sold. The results in the accompanying table on price, in dollars, and sales, in cases, were obtained from a sample of 8 weeks of sales records.

PRICE	19.2	20.5	19.7	21.3	20.8	19.9	17.8	17.2
SALES	25.4	14.7	18.6	12.4	11.1	15.7	29.2	35.2

Find a 95% confidence interval for the expected change in sales resulting from a $1 increase in price.

34. Using the data of Exercise 16, test against a two-sided alternative the null hypothesis that change in mean employee absence rate due to own illness does not depend linearly on change in unemployment rate.

35. A sample of twenty-five blue-collar employees at a production plant was taken. Each employee was asked to assess his or her own job satisfaction (x), on a scale from 1 to 10. In addition, the number of days absent (y) from work during the last year were found for these employees. The sample regression line

$$y = 13.6 - 1.2x$$

was estimated by least squares for these data. Also found were

$$\bar{x} = 6.0 \qquad \sum_{i=1}^{25}(x_i - \bar{x})^2 = 130.0 \qquad SSE = 80.6$$

(a) Test at the 1% significance level against the appropriate one-sided alternative the null hypothesis that job satisfaction has no linear effect on absenteeism.

(b) A particular employee has job satisfaction level 4. Find a 90% confidence interval for the number of days this employee would be absent from work in a year.

36. Doctors are interested in the relationship between the dosage of a medicine and the time required for a patient's recovery. The following table shows, for a sample of five patients, dosage levels (in grams) and recovery times (in hours). These patients have similar characteristics except for medicine dosages.

DOSAGE LEVEL	1.2	1.0	1.5	1.2	1.4
RECOVERY TIME	25	40	10	27	16

(a) Estimate the linear regression of recovery time on dosage level.

(b) Find and interpret a 90% confidence interval for the slope of the population regression line.

(c) Would the sample regression derived in part (a) be useful in predicting recovery time for a patient given 2.5 grams of this drug? Explain your answer.

37. For the stock rate-of-return problem of Exercises 17 and 26 it was found that

$$\sum_{i=1}^{20} y_i^2 = 196.2$$

(a) Test the null hypothesis that the slope of the population regression line is 0 against the alternative that it is positive.

(**b**) Test against a two-sided alternative the null hypothesis that the slope of the population regression line is 1.

38. Using the data of Exercise 18, test the null hypothesis that representatives' weekly sales are not linearly related to their aptitude test scores against the alternative that there is positive association.

39. Refer to the data of Exercise 15. Test against a two-sided alternative the null hypothesis that mutual fund losses on Friday, November 13, 1989, did not depend linearly on previous gains in 1989.

40. Denote by r the sample correlation between a pair of random variables.

(**a**) Show that

$$\frac{1 - r^2}{n - 2} = \frac{s_e^2}{\text{SST}}$$

(**b**) Using the result in part (a), show that

$$\frac{r}{\sqrt{(1 - r^2)/(n - 2)}} = \frac{b}{s_e/\sqrt{\sum(x_i - \bar{x})^2}}$$

(**c**) Using the result in part (b), deduce that the test of the null hypothesis of 0 population correlation, given in Section 12.1, is the same as the test of 0 population regression slope, given in Section 12.8.

41. For the problem of Exercise 19, on sales of premium beer in restaurants, it was found that

$$\frac{\sum(y_i - \bar{y})^2}{n - 1} = 250$$

Test against a two-sided alternative the null hypothesis that the slope of the population regression line is 0.

42. For a sample of 74 monthly observations, the regression of the percentage return on gold (y) against the percentage change in the consumer price index (x) was estimated.[13] The sample regression line, obtained through least squares, was

$$y = -.003 + 1.11x$$

The estimated standard deviation of the slope of the population regression line was 2.31. Test the null hypothesis that the slope of the population regression line is 0 against the alternative that the slope is positive.

43. Refer to the data of Exercise 33. Test at the 5% level against the appropriate one-sided alternative the null hypothesis that sales do not depend linearly on price for this premium scotch whiskey.

44. Refer to the data of Exercise 13.

(**a**) Find a point estimate for the volume of sales when the price of the stereo system is $480 in a given region.

(**b**) If the price of the system is set at $480, find 95% confidence intervals for the *actual* volume of sales in a particular region and the *expected* number of sales in that region.

45. Continue the analysis of Exercise 14. If the Dow-Jones index increases by 1.0% in the first five trading days of a year, find 90% confidence intervals for the *actual*, and also for the *expected*, percentage changes in the index over the whole year. Discuss the distinction between these intervals.

46. Refer to the data in Exercise 16. For a year in which there is no change in the unemployment rate, find a 90% confidence interval for the *actual*, and also for the *expected*, change in mean employee absence rate due to own illness.

---

[13] M. Ratner, "Inflation, currency devaluation, and the price of gold," *American Business Review*, *10*, no. 1 (1992), 93–97.

47. Use the data of Exercises 17 and 26 to find 90% and 95% confidence intervals for the expected return on the corporation's stock when the rate of return on the S. and P. 500 index is 1%.

48. A new sales representative for the corporation of Exercise 18 scores 70 on the aptitude test. Find 80% and 90% confidence intervals for the value of weekly sales he will achieve.

REVIEW EXERCISES

49. What is meant by the statement that a pair of random variables are positively correlated? Give examples of pairs of random variables for which you would expect
   (**a**) Positive correlation
   (**b**) Negative correlation
   (**c**) Zero correlation

50. In this chapter, we discussed two measures of correlation—the sample correlation coefficient r and Spearman's rank correlation coefficient. Discuss the circumstances in which each measure might be appropriate.

51. A random sample of five sets of observations on a pair of random variables yielded the results given in the table.

y_i	4	1	0	1	4
x_i	-2	-1	0	1	2

   (**a**) Find the sample correlation coefficient.
   (**b**) In light of the fact that each y_i value is the square of the corresponding x_i value, comment on your answer in part (a).

52. For a random sample of fifty-three specialty stores in a chain, the correlation between annual dollar sales per square foot of floor space and annual dollar rent per square foot of floor space was found to be .37.[14] Test the null hypothesis that these two quantities are uncorrelated in the population against the alternative that the population correlation is positive.

53. For a random sample of 526 firms, the sample correlation between the proportion of a firm's directors who are outsiders and a risk-adjusted measure of return on the firm's stock was found to be .1398.[15] Test against a two-sided alternative the null hypothesis that the population correlation is zero.

54. For a sample of sixty-six months, the correlation between the returns on U.S. and Japanese 5-year bonds was found to be .293.[16] Test the null hypothesis that the population correlation is 0 against the alternative that it is positive.

55. Refer to Exercise 71 of Chapter 9. Test against a two-sided alternative the null hypothesis that the variances of absolute percentage forecast errors are the same for the two financial analysts.

56. The accompanying table shows, for a random sample of twenty long-term-growth mutual funds, percentage return over a period of 12 months and total assets (in millions of dollars).

---

[14] P. M. Anderson, "Association of shopping center anchors with performance of a nonanchor specialty chain's store," *Journal of Retailing, 61*, no. 2 (1985), 61–74.

[15] M. H. Schellenberger, D. D. Wood, and A. Tashakori, "Board of director composition, shareholder wealth, and dividend policy," *Journal of Management, 15* (1989), 457–67.

[16] S. Hauser and A. Levy, "Optimal forward coverage of international fixed income portfolios," *Journal of Portfolio Management, 17*, no. 4 (1991), 54–59.

RETURN	ASSETS	RETURN	ASSETS	RETURN	ASSETS
29.3	300	16.0	421	12.9	75
27.6	70	15.5	99	11.3	610
23.7	3,004	15.2	756	9.9	264
22.3	161	15.0	730	7.9	27
22.0	827	14.4	436	6.7	71
19.6	295	14.0	143	3.3	719
17.6	29	13.7	117		

(a) Calculate Spearman's rank correlation coefficient.

(b) Carry out a nonparametric test of the null hypothesis of no association in the population against a two-sided alternative.

(c) Discuss the advantages of a nonparametric test for these data.

57. In a study of the motives for patronage of a used merchandise outlet, the rankings of motives were obtained from samples of light and heavy shoppers, as indicated in the accompanying table.[17] Calculate Spearman's rank correlation coefficient, and test against the alternative of positive association the null hypothesis of no association between patronage motives of light and heavy shoppers.

	LIGHT SHOPPERS	HEAVY SHOPPERS
Price	1	1
Adventure, treasure hunting	2	4
Quality	3	2
Location	4	3
Salespeople	5	5
Cleanliness	6	6

58. A study was carried out on the perceptions of problems arising in relationships between advertising agencies and their clients.[18] Agencies were asked the extent to which various agency characteristics caused problems. The table given here shows average responses on a scale from 1 (seldom a problem) to 4 for agency-client relationships lasting less than and more than 10 years.

	LENGTH OF RELATIONSHIP	
	LESS THAN 10 YEARS	MORE THAN 10 YEARS
High personnel turnover	2.21	1.80
Failure to meet deadlines	2.14	2.04
Poor communications	2.14	2.05
Poor follow-through	2.07	1.81
Understanding	2.00	1.81
Lack of cost-consciousness	2.00	2.10
Tendency not to listen	1.95	1.86
Inexperienced account personnel	1.93	1.76
Tendency to be defensive	1.79	1.62
Unstructured procedures	1.50	2.00
Inflexible procedures	1.43	1.57
Too much politics	1.20	1.80

[17] U. Yavas and G. Riecken, "Heavy, medium, light shoppers, and nonshoppers of a used merchandise outlet," *Journal of Business Research*, *9* (1981), 243–53. Copyright 1981 by Elsevier Science Publishing Co., Inc. Reprinted by permission of the publisher.

[18] M. R. Hotz, J. K. Ryans, and W. L. Shanklin, "Agency-client relationships as seen by influentials on both sides," *Journal of Advertising*, *11*, no. 1 (1982), 37–44.

(a) Calculate Spearman's rank correlation coefficient.

(b) Carry out against a two-sided alternative a nonparametric test of the null hypothesis of no association.

59. For a random sample of 192 male employees, a sample correlation of $-.18$ was found between age and a measure of willingness to relocate.[19] Given only this information, derive all the conclusions you can about the regression of willingness to relocate on age.

60. Based on a sample of n observations, $(x_1, y_1), (x_2, y_2), \ldots, (x_n, y_n)$, the sample regression of y on x is calculated. Show that the sample regression line passes through the point $(x = \bar{x}, y = \bar{y})$, where $\bar{x}$ and $\bar{y}$ are the sample means.

61. A company routinely administers an aptitude test to all new management trainees. At the end of the first year with the company, these trainees are graded by their immediate supervisors. For a random sample of twelve trainees, the results shown in the accompanying table were obtained.

APTITUDE SCORE	84	79	92	53	65	82
SUPERVISOR'S GRADE	76	75	81	72	68	88
APTITUDE SCORE	87	75	77	76	69	88
SUPERVISOR'S GRADE	79	81	70	83	62	86

(a) Estimate the regression of supervisor's grade on aptitude score.

(b) Interpret the slope of the sample regression line.

(c) Is it possible to give a useful interpretation of the intercept of the sample regression line? Explain.

(d) Find and interpret the coefficient of determination for this regression.

(e) Test against the obvious one-sided alternative the null hypothesis that the slope of the population regression line is 0.

(f) Find a 95% confidence interval for the supervisor's grade that would be obtained by a particular trainee who had an aptitude score of 70.

62. An attempt was made to evaluate the forward rate as a predictor of the spot rate in the Canadian treasury bill market.[20] For a sample of seventy-nine quarterly observations, the estimated linear regression.

$$y = .00027 + .7916x$$

was obtained, where

$y = $ Actual change in the spot rate
$x = $ Change in the spot rate predicted by the forward rate

The coefficient of determination was .097, and the estimated standard deviation of the estimator of the slope of the population regression line was .2759.

(a) Interpret the slope of the estimated regression line.

(b) Interpret the coefficient of determination.

(c) Test the null hypothesis that the slope of the population regression line is 0 against the alternative that the true slope is positive, and interpret your result.

(d) Test against a two-sided alternative the null hypothesis that the slope of the population regression line is 1, and interpret your result.

---

[19] S. Gould and L. E. Penley, "A study of the correlates of willingness to relocate," *Academy of Management Journal*, 28 (1985), 472–78.

[20] Reported in S. B. Park, "Spot and forward rates in the Canadian treasury bill market," *Journal of Financial Economics*, 10 (1982), 107–14.

63. The table shows, for eight brands of instant coffee, purchases per buyer (y) and the percentage buying in a year (x).[21]

y	3.6	3.3	2.8	2.6	2.7	2.9	2.0	2.6
x	24	21	22	22	18	13	9	6

(a) Estimate the regression of purchases per buyer on percentage buying.
(b) Interpret the slope of the estimated regression line.
(c) Find and interpret the coefficient of determination.
(d) Find and interpret a 90% confidence interval for the slope of the population regression line.
(e) Find a 90% confidence interval for expected purchases per buyer for a brand for which the percentage buying is 20.

64. For a sample of 306 students in a basic business communications course, the sample regression line

$$y = 58.813 + .2875x$$

was obtained.[22] Here

y = Final student score at the end of the course
x = Score on a diagnostic writing skills test given at the beginning of the course

The coefficient of determination was .1158, and the estimated standard deviation of the estimator of the slope of the population regression line was .04566.

(a) Interpret the slope of the sample regression line.
(b) Interpret the coefficient of determination.
(c) The information given allows the null hypothesis that the slope of the population regression is 0 to be tested against the alternative that it is positive in two different ways. Carry out these tests and show that they reach the same conclusion.

65. Based on a sample of thirty observations, the population regression model

$$Y_i = \alpha + \beta x_i + \epsilon_i$$

was estimated. The least squares estimates obtained were

$$a = 10.1 \quad \text{and} \quad b = 8.4$$

The regression and error sums of squares were

$$SSR = 128 \quad \text{and} \quad SSE = 286$$

(a) Find and interpret the coefficient of determination.
(b) Test at the 10% significance level against a two-sided alternative the null hypothesis that β is 0.
(c) Find

$$\sum_{i=1}^{30}(x_i - \bar{x})^2$$

---

[21] A.S.C. Ehrenberg, G. J. Goodhardt, and T. P. Bariuse, "Double jeopardy revisited," *Journal of Marketing*, *54*, no. 3 (1990), 82–91.

[22] V. Richerson and K. Sutrick, "The relationship between scores on a diagnostic writing skills-test and success in a basic business communication course," *Bulletin of the Association of Business Communication*, *55*, no. 3 (1992), 102–7.

66. Based on a sample of twenty-five observations, the population regression model

$$Y_i = \alpha + \beta x_i + \epsilon_i$$

was estimated. The least squares estimates obtained were

$$a = 15.6 \qquad \text{and} \qquad b = 1.3$$

The total and error sums of squares were

$$\text{SST} = 268 \qquad \text{and} \qquad \text{SSE} = 204$$

(a) Find and interpret the coefficient of determination.

(b) Test against a two-sided alternative at the 5% significance level the null hypothesis that the slope of the population regression line is 0.

(c) Find a 95% confidence interval for β.

67. An analyst believes that the only important determinant of banks' return on assets (Y) is the ratio of loans to deposits (x). For a random sample of twenty banks, the sample regression line

$$Y = .97 + .47x$$

was obtained, with coefficient of determination .720.

(a) Find the sample correlation between return on assets and the ratio of loans to deposits.

(b) Test against a two-sided alternative at the 5% level the null hypothesis of no linear association between return on assets and the ratio of loans to deposits.

(c) Find

$$\frac{s_e}{\sqrt{\sum(x_i - \bar{x})^2}}$$

68. Comment on the following statement:

If a regression of the yield per acre of corn on the quantity of fertilizer used were estimated, using fertilizer quantities in the range typically used by farmers, the slope of the estimated regression line would certainly be positive. However, it is well known that if an enormously high amount of fertilizer were to be used, corn yield would be very low. Therefore, regression equations are not of much use in forecasting.

APPENDIX A12.1

In this appendix, we derive the least squares estimates of the population regression parameters. We want to find the values a and b for which the sum of squared discrepancies

$$SS = \sum_{i=1}^{n}(y_i - a - bx_i)^2 \qquad (A12.1.1)$$

is as small as possible.

As a first step, we keep b in Eq. (A12.1.1) constant and differentiate[23] with respect to a, giving

$$\frac{\partial SS}{\partial a} = -2\sum_{i=1}^{n}(y_i - a - bx_i)$$

$$= -2\left(\sum y_i - na - b\sum x_i\right)$$

Since this derivative must be 0 for a minimum, we have

$$\sum y_i - na - b\sum x_i = 0$$

Hence, dividing through by n yields

$$a = \bar{y} - b\bar{x}$$

Substituting this expression for a in Eq. (A12.1.1) gives

$$SS = \sum_{i=1}^{n}[(y_i - \bar{y}) - b(x_i - \bar{x})]^2$$

Differentiating this expression with respect to b then gives

$$\frac{\partial SS}{\partial b} = -2\sum_{i=1}^{n}(x_i - \bar{x})[(y_i - \bar{y}) - b(x_i - \bar{x})]$$

$$= -2[\sum(x_i - \bar{x})(y_i - \bar{y}) - b\sum(x_i - \bar{x})^2]$$

This derivative must be 0 for a minimum, and so we have

$$\sum(x_i - \bar{x})(y_i - \bar{y}) = b\sum(x_i - \bar{x})^2$$

Hence,

$$b = \frac{\sum(x_i - \bar{x})(y_i - \bar{y})}{\sum(x_i - \bar{x})^2}$$

---

[23] Here we are using the concept of **partial differentiation.** The partial derivative of SS with respect to a is denoted $\partial SS/\partial a$ and is obtained by differentiating SS with respect to a, treating other variables as constant. The sum of squares SS is a minimum with respect to a and b when both partial derivatives, $\partial SS/\partial a$ and $\partial SS/\partial b$, are 0.

Multiple Regression

13.1 THE MULTIPLE REGRESSION MODEL

In the linear regression model of Chapter 12, the behavior of a *single* independent variable was employed to explain the behavior of a dependent variable. In this chapter, our objective remains the construction of a model to explain, as much as possible, variability in some dependent variable in which we are interested. However, we now admit the possibility of several relevant independent variables, or *multiple influences*. To illustrate, suppose that we want to explain the variability through the years of profit margins of savings and loan associations. It is reasonable to conjecture that, all other things being equal, profit margins will be positively related to net revenues per deposit dollar; that is, the higher net revenues are, the higher profit margins will be. Another possibility is that profit margins will fall due to increased competition, all other things being equal, as the number of savings and loan offices increases. We therefore seek a model in which the dependent variable, profit margin (Y), is related to the pair of independent variables, net revenues (X_1) and number of savings and loan offices (X_2). In order to build a model of this relationship, we require data on these three quantities. Table 13.1 shows twenty-five annual sets of observations.[1]

At the outset, we are again faced with the difficulty that an infinite number of possible functional forms are available to describe the relationship of interest. Once more, it is convenient to consider the appropriateness of the linear form. In Chapter 12, when relating a dependent variable to a single independent variable, we constructed a model in which the expected value of the dependent variable was related linearly to the value of the independent variable. Once again, our interest is in the ex-

---

[1] Data from L. J. Spellman, "Entry and profitability in a rate-free savings and loan market," *Quarterly Review of Economics and Business*, *18*, no. 2 (1978), 87–95.

TABLE 13.1 Data on percentage net revenues per deposit dollar (x_1), number of offices (x_2), and percentage profit margin (y) for savings and loan associations

YEAR	x_{1i}	x_{2i}	y_i	YEAR	x_{1i}	x_{2i}	y_i
1	3.92	7,298	0.75	14	3.78	6,672	0.84
2	3.61	6,855	0.71	15	3.82	6,890	0.79
3	3.32	6,636	0.66	16	3.97	7,115	0.70
4	3.07	6,506	0.61	17	4.07	7,327	0.68
5	3.06	6,450	0.70	18	4.25	7,546	0.72
6	3.11	6,402	0.72	19	4.41	7,931	0.55
7	3.21	6,368	0.77	20	4.49	8,097	0.63
8	3.26	6,340	0.74	21	4.70	8,468	0.56
9	3.42	6,349	0.90	22	4.58	8,717	0.41
10	3.42	6,352	0.82	23	4.69	8,991	0.51
11	3.45	6,361	0.75	24	4.71	9,179	0.47
12	3.58	6,369	0.77	25	4.78	9,318	0.32
13	3.66	6,546	0.78				

pected value of the dependent variable, but this is now conditioned by the values taken by all the independent variables. For example, in the context of our savings and loan problem, we might ask what value would be expected for percentage profit margin in a year in which percentage net revenues per deposit dollar were 4.0 and there were 8,000 offices. Again, we need a convenient notation for such a concept. For the case where a dependent variable, Y, is related to a pair of independent variables, X_1 and X_2, we will use $E(Y|X_1 = x_1, X_2 = x_2)$ to represent the expected value of the dependent variable when the independent variables take the respective values x_1 and x_2. Our assumption of linearity, within this context, implies that this conditional expected value is of the form.

$$E(Y|X_1 = x_1, X_2 = x_2) = \alpha + \beta_1 x_1 + \beta_2 x_2 \qquad (13.1.1)$$

where the numbers α, β_1, and β_2 must be estimated from data.

More generally, we may want to relate a dependent variable, Y, to K independent variables, $X_1, X_2, \ldots, X_K$. Then, if X_1 takes the value x_1, X_2 takes the value x_2, and so on, the generalization of Eq. (13.1.1) gives the expected value of the dependent variable as

$$\begin{aligned} E(Y|X_1 = x_1, X_2 = x_2, \ldots, X_K = x_K) \\ = \alpha + \beta_1 x_1 + \beta_2 x_2 + \cdots + \beta_K x_K \end{aligned} \qquad (13.1.2)$$

where $E(Y|X_1 = x_1, X_2 = x_2, \ldots, X_K = x_K)$ denotes the expected value of the dependent variable when the independent variables take the specific values $x_1, x_2, \ldots, x_K$, and where the fixed numbers $\alpha, \beta_1, \beta_2, \ldots, \beta_K$ determine the nature of the relationship. These numbers have straightforward interpretations. First, if each of the independent variables is set to 0, it follows from (13.1.2) that

$$E(Y|X_1 = 0, X_2 = 0, \ldots, X_K = 0) = \alpha$$

Thus, α is the expected value of the dependent variable when every independent variable takes the value 0. Frequently this interpretation is of no practical interest since the point at which all independent variables are 0 is of no concern and indeed may be meaningless. (For example, we have no interest in the case where the number of savings and loan offices is 0.) Moreover, while the assumed model form may be reasonable in the region of observed values of the independent variables, it would be unduly optimistic to assume validity of the model very far outside that region.

The interpretation of the coefficients $\beta_1, \beta_2, \ldots, \beta_K$ is extremely important. Referring to Eq. (13.1.2), suppose that one of the independent variables, say X_1, is increased by 1 unit from x_1 to $(x_1 + 1)$, *while the values of the other independent variables are held constant*. Then we have

$$E(Y|X_1 = x_1 + 1, X_2 = x_2, \ldots, X_K = x_K) = \alpha + \beta_1(x_1 + 1) + \beta_2 x_2 + \cdots + \beta_K x_K$$

Hence, using Eq. (13.1.2), we have

$$E(Y|X_1 = x_1 + 1, X_2 = x_2, \ldots, X_K = x_K) - E(Y|X_1 = x_1, X_2 = x_2, \ldots, X_K = x_K)$$

$$= \alpha + \beta_1(x_1 + 1) + \beta_2 x_2 + \cdots + \beta_K x_K - (\alpha + \beta_1 x_1 + \beta_2 x_2 + \cdots + \beta_K x_K) = \beta_1$$

It therefore follows that β_1 is the expected increase in Y resulting from a 1-unit increase in X_1 when the values of the other independent variables remain constant. In general, the coefficient β_j is the expected increase in the dependent variable resulting from a 1-unit increase in the independent variable X_j when the values of the other independent variables are held constant. The quantities β_j, called **partial regression coefficients,** provide separate measures of the influences of the independent variables on the dependent variable when all other relevant factors remain unchanged.

Returning to our savings and loan example, suppose that the true relationship is

$$E(Y|X_1 = x_1, X_2 = x_2) = 1.5 + .2x_1 - .00025x_2$$

The coefficient on x_1 implies that an increase of 1 unit in net revenues leads to an expected increase of .2 in the percentage profit margin of savings and loan associations when the number of savings and loan offices remains fixed. Similarly, the coefficient on x_2 implies that, holding net revenues fixed, an increase of 1 in the number of savings and loan offices leads to an expected increase of $-.00025$—that is, to an expected *decrease* of .00025—in percentage profit margin. To use more realistic numbers, an increase of 1,000 in the number of savings and loan offices, with net revenues held fixed, leads to an expected decrease of .25 in percentage profit margins. These partial regression coefficients are illustrated in Figure 13.1

Figure 13.1(a) shows the relationship between expected profit margin and net revenues when the number of savings and loan offices is fixed at 8,000. This relation slopes upward, indicating that an increase in net revenues leads to an expected increase in profit margins when the number of offices remains unchanged. Part (b) of the figure depicts the relation between expected profit margin and the number of offices when percentage net revenues per deposit dollar are fixed at 4. The downward-

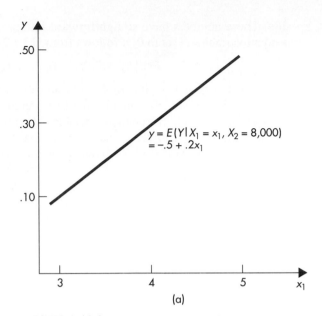

FIGURE 13.1 Postulated model $E(Y|X_1 = x_1, X_2 = x_2)$ $= 1.5 + .2x_1 - .00025x_2$, where

Y = Percentage profit margin for savings and loan associations
X_1 = Percentage net revenues per deposit dollar
X_2 = Number of savings and loan offices

(a) When number of offices is fixed at 8,000, substituting $x_2 = 8{,}000$ gives

$$E(Y|X_1 = x_1, X_2 = 8{,}000) = -.5 + .2x_1$$

sloping relation indicates that an increase in the number of offices leads to an expected decrease in profit margins when net revenues per deposit dollar remain unchanged.

We extend the graphical illustration of this population regression in Figure 13.2. Part (a) of the figure shows the dependence of expected profit margin on net revenues for three different numbers of savings and loan offices—7,000, 7,500, and 8,000. Notice that the straight lines depicting these relations are parallel to one another. This reflects the fact that according to our model, an increase in net revenues, with the number of offices held constant, leads to the same increase in expected profit margin, whatever the fixed value of the number of offices. Notice also that the higher the number of offices, the lower the line relating expected profit margin to net revenues. This says that for any given value of net revenues, the greater the number of offices, the smaller the expected profit margins. This is precisely the interpretation of the partial regression coefficient on number of offices that we noted earlier.

Part (b) of Figure 13.2 shows the relationship between expected profit margins and the number of savings and loan offices for three different values of percentage net revenues per deposit dollar—3.5, 4.0, and 4.5. Again the three lines are parallel. Also, we see that the higher net revenues, the higher the line relating expected profit margin

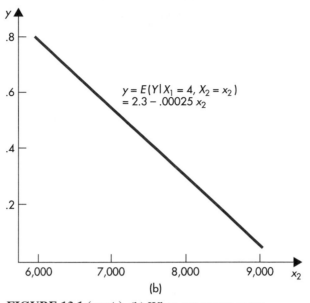

FIGURE 13.1 (cont.) (b) When net revenues per deposit dollar are fixed at 4%, substituting $x_1 = 4$ gives

$$E(Y|X_1 = 4, X_2 = x_2) = 2.3 - .00025x_2$$

FIGURE 13.2 Postulated model $E(Y|X_1 = x_1, X_2 = x_2) = 1.5 + .2x_1 - .00025x_2$ (a) Relationship between expected Y and x_1, with x_2 fixed at 7,000, 7,500, and 8,000

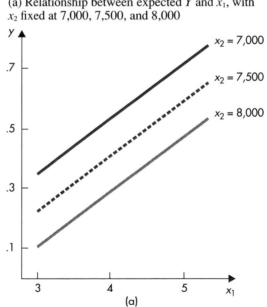

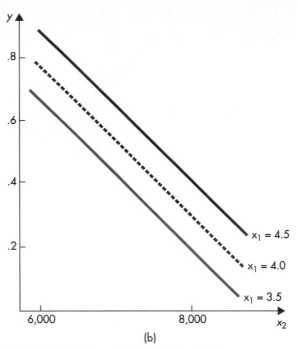

FIGURE 13.2 (cont.) (b) Relationship between
expected Y and x_2, with x_1 fixed at 3.5, 4.0, and 4.5

to the number of offices. This is to be expected since, as we have already seen, for any
fixed number of offices, an increase in net revenues leads to an expected increase in
profit margin.

When, as in the present example, the multiple regression involves only two independent variables, a further graphical description of the model is available. The relationship can be viewed as three-dimensional, as in Figure 13.3. This figure shows
the regression function as a plane in three-dimensional space and is the multiple regression analog of the line in two-dimensional space used to represent the relation between a dependent variable and a single independent variable. For each pair of possible values of the independent variables, the expected value of the dependent variable
is a point on this plane. As we have drawn it, Figure 13.3 shows the situation in our
savings and loan example. An increase in X_1 leads, all other things being equal, to an
expected increase in the dependent variable, while an increase in X_2 leads, all else remaining the same, to an expected decrease in the dependent variable.

To complete our model, it is necessary to add an error term, in acknowledgment
of the fact that in the real world, no postulated relationship will hold precisely.
Suppose that the K independent variables take the specific values $x_{1i}, x_{2i}, \ldots, x_{Ki}$.
Then, if the corresponding value of the dependent variable is denoted Y_i, its expectation is

$$E(Y_i | X_1 = x_{1i}, X_2 = x_{2i}, \ldots, X_K = x_{Ki})$$

$$= \alpha + \beta_1 x_{1i} + \beta_2 x_{2i} + \cdots + \beta_K x_{Ki}$$

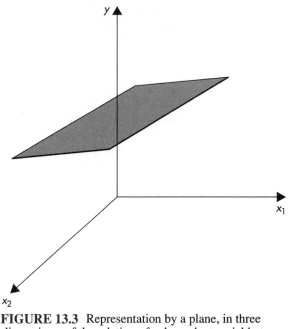

FIGURE 13.3 Representation by a plane, in three dimensions, of the relation of a dependent variable to a pair of independent variables

Now, let the random variable ϵ_i denote the discrepancy between Y_i and its expected value given the independent variables, so that

$$\epsilon_i = Y_i - E(Y_i | X_1 = x_{1i}, X_2 = x_{2i}, \ldots, X_K = x_{Ki})$$
$$= Y_i - (\alpha + \beta_1 x_{1i} + \beta_2 x_{2i} + \cdots + \beta_K x_{Ki})$$

Hence, we can write

$$Y_i = \alpha + \beta_1 x_{1i} + \beta_2 x_{2i} + \cdots + \beta_K x_{Ki} + \epsilon_i$$

The Population Multiple Regression

Suppose that we are interested in the relation of a dependent variable Y to K independent variables, $X_1, X_2, \ldots, X_K$. If the independent variables take the specific values $x_{1i}, x_{2i}, \ldots, x_{Ki}$, then the **population multiple regression** expresses the corresponding value of the dependent variable, Y_i, as

$$Y_i = \alpha + \beta_1 x_{1i} + \beta_2 x_{2i} + \cdots + \beta_K x_{Ki} + \epsilon_i$$

where $\alpha, \beta_1, \beta_2, \ldots, \beta_K$ are constants and ϵ_i is a random variable with mean 0.

For our savings and loan example, where there are two independent variables, the population multiple regression is

$$Y_i = \alpha + \beta_1 x_{1i} + \beta_2 x_{2i} + \epsilon_i$$

Thus, for particular values, x_{1i} and x_{2i}, of net revenues and number of savings and loan offices, the corresponding profit margin is the sum of two parts—an expectation $(\alpha + \beta_1 x_{1i} + \beta_2 x_{2i})$ and a discrepancy, or error term, ϵ_i. The error term can be regarded as the amalgamation of the influences of the multitude of factors (other than net revenues and number of offices) that affect profit margins. We illustrate the population regression model for the case of a pair of independent variables in Figure 13.4. This figure shows the regression plane, relating the expected value of the dependent variable to the values of the independent variables, exactly as in Figure 13.3. Also, marked by a large dot, is a possible observation point, representing the value of the dependent variable that actually occurs for given values of the independent variables. Now, such observations will not lie precisely on the regression plane. The difference between observed and expected values of the dependent variable is represented by the error term, ϵ_i. If, as drawn in Figure 13.4, the observation point is above the regression plane, this error term will be positive. For observations below the regression plane, the error term is negative. On average, these error terms are 0.

We note that the simple linear regression model developed in Chapter 12 is merely the special case of the multiple regression model with just a single independent variable. Our analysis of the multiple regression model will, accordingly, run along lines similar to those of the earlier chapter.

FIGURE 13.4 An observation point, distance ϵ_i along the y-axis, from the regression plane showing the relation between the expected value of the dependent variable and the values taken by a pair of independent variables

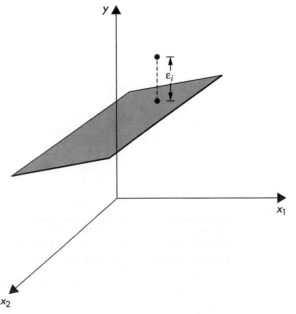

13.2 LEAST SQUARES ESTIMATION

The principle of least squares estimation of the parameters of the population multiple regression is identical to that in the simple linear regression case. Once again, we seek an estimated equation that is as close as possible to the observed data, in the sense of minimizing the sum of squared discrepancies.

Suppose that we have n sets of joint observations on the K independent variables and the dependent variable. These observation points can be denoted as follows:

$$(x_{11}, x_{21}, \ldots, x_{K1}, y_1)$$

$$(x_{12}, x_{22}, \ldots, x_{K2}, y_2)$$

.

.

.

$$(x_{1n}, x_{2n}, \ldots, x_{Kn}, y_n)$$

Referring to Table 13.1, we see for the savings and loan example that there are two independent variables and $n = 25$ observation points, which, in the specified format, would be depicted

$$(x_{11}, x_{21}, y_1) = (3.92, 7{,}298, .75)$$

$$(x_{12}, x_{22}, y_2) = (3.61, 6{,}855, .71)$$

.

.

.

$$(x_{1n}, x_{2n}, y_n) = (4.78, 9{,}318, .32)$$

Given these data, our problem is to find estimates of the unknown parameters α, β_1, $\beta_2, \ldots, \beta_K$ of the population multiple regression model.

Consider, as possible estimates of these unknown parameters, the numbers a, b_1, $b_2, \ldots, b_K$, so that the estimated model is

$$\hat{y} = a + b_1x_1 + b_2x_2 + \cdots + b_Kx_K$$

Then, for the observed values of the independent variables, the values predicted for the dependent variable by this estimated model are

$$(a + b_1x_{1i} + b_2x_{2i} + \cdots + b_Kx_{Ki})$$

whereas the values actually observed are y_i. Hence, the discrepancies between the observed and predicted outcomes for the dependent variable are

$$e_i = y_i - (a + b_1x_{1i} + b_2x_{2i} + \cdots + b_Kx_{Ki}) \qquad (i = 1, 2, \ldots, n)$$

Precisely as for the linear regression model, the least squares estimates are the numbers $a, b_1, b_2, \ldots, b_K$ for which the sum of squared discrepancies

$$SS = \sum_{i=1}^{n} e_i^2 = \sum_{i=1}^{n} (y_i - a - b_1 x_{1i} - b_2 x_{2i} - \cdots - b_K x_{Ki})^2$$

is as small as possible.

Least Squares Estimation and the Sample Multiple Regression

Let $(x_{11}, x_{21}, \ldots, x_{K1}, y_1)$, $(x_{12}, x_{22}, \ldots, x_{K2}, y_2)$, $\ldots$, $(x_{1n}, x_{2n}, \ldots, x_{Kn}, y_n)$ be a sample of n sets of observations on a process with population multiple regression

$$Y_i = \alpha + \beta_1 x_{1i} + \beta_2 x_{2i} + \cdots + \beta_K x_{Ki} + \epsilon_i$$

The **least squares estimates** of the coefficients $\alpha, \beta_1, \beta_2, \ldots, \beta_K$ are the values, $a, b_1, b_2, \ldots, b_K$, for which the sum of squared discrepancies

$$SS = \sum_{i=1}^{n} (y_i - a - b_1 x_{1i} - b_2 x_{2i} - \cdots - b_K x_{Ki})^2 \tag{13.2.1}$$

is a minimum.
   The equation

$$y = a + b_1 x_1 + b_2 x_2 + \cdots + b_K x_K$$

represents the **sample multiple regression** of Y on $X_1, X_2, \ldots, X_K$.

Unless the number, K, of independent variables is very small, expressions for the computation of the least squares estimates can be extremely cumbersome.[2] For the interested reader, some algebraic details are included in Appendix A13.1 at the end of this chapter. Fortunately, from a practical point of view, this matter need not detain us here. The fitting of regression models is such a commonly used tool in so many branches of applied statistics that computer packages for performing the necessary arithmetic have long been widely available. A fuller discussion of such packages will be postponed until additional concepts have been developed. It is sufficient to note for the present that the operation involved in computing the least squares estimates is the minimization of the sum of squared discrepancies in Eq. (13.2.1).
   Based on the data in Table 13.1, the least squares estimates of the parameters of the regression of savings and loan profit margins on net revenues and number of offices were found to be

$$a = 1.565 \qquad b_1 = .237 \qquad b_2 = -.000249$$

The sample multiple regression is therefore

$$y = 1.565 + .237 x_1 - .000249 x_2$$

We therefore estimate that for a fixed number of offices, an increase of 1 in percentage net revenues leads to an expected increase of .237 in percentage profit margin.

---

[2] In fact, algebraically manageable expressions can be achieved through the use of matrix algebra. That approach, however, is beyond the scope of this text.

Similarly, we estimate that for a fixed level of net revenues, an increase of 1,000 in the number of offices leads to an expected decrease of .249 in percentage profit margin.

When, as in the present example, the regression model contains two independent variables, the least squares estimates can be computed through a moderate amount of arithmetic effort, without recourse to a computer program. The details are set out in Appendix A13.1.

13.3 STANDARD ASSUMPTIONS FOR THE MULTIPLE REGRESSION MODEL

Before continuing our discussion of the practice of regression analysis, we introduce in the box some assumptions that are reasonable in many applications. When these assumptions do hold, a powerful justification for the use of least squares estimation exists.

Standard Assumptions

Denote the population multiple regression by

$$Y_i = \alpha + \beta_1 x_{1i} + \beta_2 x_{2i} + \cdots + \beta_K x_{Ki} + \epsilon_i$$

and assume that n sets of observations are available. The following standard assumptions are often made:

1. Either the $x_{1i}, x_{2i}, \ldots, x_{Ki}$ are fixed numbers, or they are realizations of random variables $X_{1i}, X_{2i}, \ldots, X_{Ki}$, which are independent of the error terms ϵ_i. In the latter case, inference is carried out conditionally on the observed $x_{1i}, x_{2i}, \ldots, x_{Ki}$.

2. The error terms ϵ_i are random variables with mean 0, that is

$$E(\epsilon_i) = 0 \qquad (i = 1, 2, \ldots, n)$$

3. The random variables ϵ_i all have the same variance, say σ_ϵ^2, so that

$$E(\epsilon_i^2) = \sigma_\epsilon^2 \qquad (i = 1, 2, \ldots, n)$$

4. The random variables ϵ_i are not correlated with one another, so that

$$E(\epsilon_i \epsilon_j) = 0 \text{ for all } i \neq j$$

5. It is not possible to find a set of numbers, $c_0, c_1, c_2, \ldots, c_K$, such that

$$c_0 + c_1 x_{1i} + c_2 x_{2i} + \cdots + c_K x_{Ki} = 0$$

for every $i = 1, 2, \ldots, n$.

The first four assumptions are essentially the same as those made in Section 12.5 for the linear regression model. The purpose of assumption 5 is to exclude from consideration certain pathological cases in which unique least squares estimates do not exist. To illustrate, suppose that we are interested in explaining the variability in rates charged for shipping corn. One obvious explanatory variable would be the distance that the shipment is to travel. We can measure distance in any convenient units. However, there is clearly no point in including in the regression two separate measures of distance, such as distance in miles (x_1) and distance in kilometers (x_2). These two independent variables are really just alternative measures of the same quantity, distance, and it would be foolish to try to assess their *separate* effects. It is this kind of situation that is excluded by the fifth assumption. As a practical matter, it will be safe to assume (provided the regression model is sensibly specified) that assumption 5 is not violated.

In the remainder of this chapter, we will take it that all of the standard assumptions hold, and in the next chapter we will deal with the consequences of their breakdown.

13.4 THE GAUSS-MARKOV THEOREM

In this section, we extend the result of Section 12.6. Suppose that we want to use the observations $(x_{11}, x_{21}, \ldots, x_{K1}, y_1), (x_{12}, x_{22}, \ldots, x_{K2}, y_2), \ldots, (x_{1n}, x_{2n}, \ldots, x_{Kn}, y_n)$ to estimate the parameters of the multiple regression model. As in Section 12.6, we restrict attention to estimates that are linear functions of the y_i—that is, to estimates of the form

$$c_1 y_1 + c_2 y_2 + \cdots + c_n y_n$$

where the c_i are numbers that do not depend on the y_i. The Gauss-Markov theorem asserts that of all possible estimates of this type, the least squares estimates are best, in a sense, as described in the box.

The Gauss-Markov Theorem

Denote the population multiple regression by

$$Y_i = \alpha + \beta_1 x_{1i} + \beta_2 x_{2i} + \cdots + \beta_K x_{Ki} + \epsilon_i$$

and assume that n sets of observations are available. Suppose, further, that assumptions 1–5 of Section 13.3. hold.

Then, of all possible estimators of $\alpha, \beta_1, \beta_2, \ldots, \beta_K$, which are linear in the Y_i and unbiased, the least squares estimators (that is, the random variables corresponding to the least squares estimates $a, b_1, b_2, \ldots, b_K$ of Section 13.2) have the smallest variances.

Further, if $d_0, d_1, d_2, \ldots, d_K$ are any fixed numbers and we want to estimate

$$d_0 \alpha + d_1 \beta_1 + d_2 \beta_2 + \cdots + d_K \beta_K$$

the estimator corresponding to

$$d_0 a + d_1 b_1 + d_2 b_2 + \cdots + d_K b_K$$

has the smallest variance in the class of all estimators that are linear in the Y_i and unbiased.

By virtue of this theorem, least squares estimators are said to be **best linear unbiased estimators (BLUE).**

Now, in certain circumstances, it may be entirely reasonable to prefer a biased estimator to the best available unbiased estimator. Nevertheless, the Gauss-Markov theorem gives a strong justification for the use of the least squares method of estimation and provides the bulk of the theoretical support for the broad popularity of this procedure in practical applications. The Gauss-Markov theorem asserts that from a very wide class of unbiased estimators, the least squares estimators are the most efficient. Thus, exactly as in our discussion of simple linear regression in Chapter 12, the Gauss-Markov theorem elevates the status of the method of least squares from an apparently sensible method for obtaining point estimates to a procedure for generating point estimators with optimal statistical properties.

We hasten to add that the method of least squares is not invariably the best approach to the problem of estimating the coefficients of a regression model. We have seen that there is strong justification for using this approach when the standard assumptions of Section 13.3 hold. However, if one or more of these assumptions break down, alternative estimators may be preferable. (This will be discussed in the next chapter.) Indeed, if an assumption is seriously violated, least squares estimators can be very poor indeed, and inference based on them can be quite misleading.

13.5 THE EXPLANATORY POWER OF A MULTIPLE REGRESSION EQUATION

The purpose of regression analysis is to use the independent variables to explain the behavior of the dependent variable. Variability in the dependent variable can, in part, be explained by its linear association with the independent variables. In this section, we discuss a measure of the proportion of the variability, in the sample, of the dependent variable that is explained by the estimated multiple regression.

For the sample, the estimated regression is written

$$y_i = a + b_1 x_{1i} + b_2 x_{2i} + \cdots + b_K x_{Ki} + e_i$$

Alternatively, we may write

$$y_i = \hat{y}_i + e_i \qquad (13.5.1)$$

where

$$\hat{y}_i = a + b_1 x_{1i} + b_2 x_{2i} + \cdots + b_K x_{Ki}$$

is the value of the dependent variable predicted by the regression and the **residual** e_i is the difference between the observed and predicted value. For the savings and loan data, the three quantities in Eq. (13.5.1) are given in the first three columns of Table 13.2.

As in Section 12.7, we subtract the sample mean of the dependent variable from each side of Eq. (13.5.1), giving

$$(y_i - \bar{y}) = (\hat{y}_i - \bar{y}) + e_i \qquad (13.5.2)$$

TABLE 13.2 Actual values, predicted values, and residuals for savings and loan regression

y_i	$\hat{y}_i = a + b_1 x_{1i} + b_2 x_{2i}$ $= 1.565 + .237 x_{1i}$ $- .000249 x_{2i}$	e_i $= y_i - \hat{y}_i$	$y_i - \bar{y}$ $= y_i - .674$	$\hat{y}_i - \bar{y}$ $= \hat{y}_i - .674$
.75	.677	.073	.076	.003
.71	.714	−.004	.036	.040
.66	.699	−.039	−.014	.025
.61	.673	−.063	−.064	−.001
.70	.684	.016	.026	.010
.72	.708	.012	.046	.034
.77	.740	.030	.096	.066
.74	.759	−.019	.066	.085
.90	.795	.105	.226	.121
.82	.794	.026	.146	.120
.75	.799	−.049	.076	.125
.77	.828	−.058	.096	.154
.78	.802	−.022	.106	.128
.84	.800	.040	.166	.126
.79	.755	.035	.116	.081
.70	.734	−.034	.026	.060
.68	.705	−.025	.006	.031
.72	.693	.027	.046	.019
.55	.635	−.085	−.124	−.039
.63	.613	.017	−.044	−.061
.56	.570	−.010	−.114	−.104
.41	.480	−.070	−.264	−.194
.51	.438	.072	−.164	−.236
.47	.396	.074	−.204	−.278
.32	.378	−.058	−.354	−.296
Sum 16.86				

which can be interpreted as

Observed deviation from sample mean

$\qquad\qquad$ = Predicted deviation from sample mean + Residual

For our example, the sample mean for the dependent variable is

$$\bar{y} = \frac{\sum y_i}{n} = \frac{16.86}{25} = .674$$

Using this value, we have computed the first two terms of Eq. (13.5.2) for the savings and loan data in the final two columns of Table 13.2.

It can be shown that squaring both sides of Eq. (13.5.2) and summing over the index i yields

$$\sum_{i=1}^{n} (y_i - \bar{y})^2 = \sum_{i=1}^{n} (\hat{y}_i - \bar{y})^2 + \sum_{i=1}^{n} e_i^2$$

This is precisely the sum of squares decomposition obtained in Section 12.7, and it is interpreted here in an analogous fashion, as indicated in the box.

From Table 13.2, we find (on summing the squares of the elements of the third and fourth columns) that, for our savings and loan example

$$SSE = \sum\limits_{i=1}^{n} e_i^2 = .0623 \qquad \text{and} \qquad SST = \sum\limits_{i=1}^{n} (y_i - \bar{y})^2 = .4640$$

The coefficient of determination is, therefore

$$R^2 = 1 - \frac{SSE}{SST} = 1 - \frac{.0623}{.4640} = .87$$

Thus, in this sample, 87% of the variability in savings and loan associations' profit margins is explained by their linear association with net revenues and number of offices.

If the regression sum of squares is needed, we do not have to go to the trouble of summing the squares of the terms in the final column of Table 13.2. Rather, we can obtain this quantity through

$$SSR = SST - SSE$$

so that, for our example

$$SSR = .4640 - .0623 = .4017$$

The sum of squared errors is also useful in estimating the variance of the error terms in the population regression model, as described in the box.

Estimation of the Error Variance

Suppose that the population regression model is

$$Y_i = \alpha + \beta_1 x_{1i} + \beta_2 x_{2i} + \cdots + \beta_K x_{Ki} + \epsilon_i$$

and that assumptions 1–5 of Section 13.3 hold. Let σ_ϵ^2 denote the common variance of the error terms ϵ_i. Then an unbiased estimate of σ_ϵ^2 is provided by[3]

$$s_e^2 = \frac{\sum_{i=1}^{n} e_i^2}{n - K - 1} = \frac{SSE}{n - K - 1}$$

The major use of the coefficient of determination is as a descriptive statistic that provides a measure of the success of the independent variables in explaining the behavior of the dependent variable. While it can certainly be valuable in this context, its use can be criticized in circumstances where the number, K, of independent variables is not a small proportion of the number, n, of data points. In this case the model can appear to fit the data rather well, even when in truth the independent variables are not strongly linked to the dependent variable. As a trivial example, we can fit perfectly a straight line to just two points. In order to alleviate this problem somewhat, a modified measure of the strength of the regression relation is sometimes calculated. Essentially, the idea is that in the expression

$$R^2 = 1 - \frac{SSE}{SST}$$

some compensation for the inevitable reduction in the sum of squared errors occasioned by the addition of more independent variables (relevant or not) to the regression equation can be achieved by dividing each of the sums of squares by their appropriate number of degrees of freedom. We have already seen that in order to obtain an unbiased estimate of the error variance, SSE should be divided by $(n - K - 1)$. Further, division of SST by $(n - 1)$ provides an unbiased estimate of the variance of the dependent variable when the observations constitute a random sample. The introduction of these modifications produces an **adjusted, or corrected, coefficient of determination.**

---

[3] Intuitively, the reason for division by $(n - K - 1)$ is that $(K + 1)$ degrees of freedom are "lost" in the estimation of the unknown population parameters $\alpha, \beta_1, \beta_2, \ldots, \beta_K$.

Suppose that a multiple regression relates a dependent variable to K independent variables. The **adjusted (or corrected) coefficient of determination**, $\overline{R}^2$, is defined as

$$\overline{R}^2 = 1 - \frac{\text{SSE}/(n - K - 1)}{\text{SST}/(n - 1)}$$

For our example

$$n = 25 \qquad K = 2 \qquad \text{SSE} = .0623 \qquad \text{SST} = .4640$$

The adjusted coefficient of determination is therefore

$$\overline{R}^2 = 1 - \frac{.0623/22}{.4640/24} = .85$$

In this particular case, the adjustment is very minor. More severe adjustments result when the number of independent variables is a larger proportion of the number of sample points.

PARTIAL CORRELATION

The partial regression coefficients, β_i, measure the expected changes in the dependent variable resulting from a unit increase in one of the independent variables *when the other independent variables remain unchanged*. In this sense, the partial regression coefficients describe the *separate* impacts of the independent variables on the dependent variable. They do not, however, provide a direct measure of the *strengths* of these relationships, since their numerical values depend on the units in which the variables are measured. In Section 12.1 we saw how the correlation coefficient provides a measure of the strength of the linear association between a pair of random variables. Here we show how this concept can be extended to give a measure of the strength of the linear association between a dependent variable, Y, and an independent variable, X_1, given that the other independent variables, $X_2, X_3, \ldots, X_K$, remain unchanged.

The population **partial correlation** between Y and X_1 given $X_2, X_3 \ldots, X_K$, is the correlation between Y and X_1 for given constant values of $X_2, X_3, \ldots, X_K$. This quantity is estimated from sample data as follows:

1. Fit by least squares the regression with dependent variable Y and independent variables $X_2, X_3, \ldots, X_K$.
2. Fit by least squares the regression with dependent variable X_1 and independent variables $X_2, X_3, \ldots, X_K$.
3. Compute the sample correlation between the residuals from the regressions in steps 1 and 2. The purpose of steps 1 and 2 is to remove the effects of $X_2, X_3, \ldots, X_K$ on Y and X_1 before computing the sample correlation.

The arithmetic involved in finding sample partial correlations can be very tedious; however, these quantities are routinely calculated by most regression computer packages. For the data of Table 13.1, the sample partial correlation between percentage profit margin and percentage net revenues per deposit dollar, given that the number of offices is fixed, is .67. The sample partial correlation between percentage profit margin and number of offices, given fixed net revenues per deposit dollar, is $-.86$.

The main use of the sample partial correlation is as a descriptive statistic, providing an estimate of the strength of the relationship, its interpretation paralleling that of the ordinary sample correlation. Thus, our findings for the savings and loan data indicate two fairly strong relationships, with a positive partial linear association between profit margin and net revenues and a negative association between profit margin and number of offices; the dependence of profit margin on number of offices appears to be particularly strong. The square of a partial correlation is sometimes called the *partial R^2*. Thus, the partial R^2 between profit margins and net revenues, given a fixed number of offices, is $(.67)^2 = .45$. This implies an estimate that, if the number of offices remained constant, 45% of the remaining variability in profit margin would be explained by its linear dependence on net revenues.

To the extent that there are multiple influences on a dependent variable, making a multiple regression more appropriate than a simple linear regression, the partial correlation rather than the simple correlation of Section 12.1 is the appropriate measure of the strengths of the relationships involved. Indeed, use of the latter can be quite misleading. For example, the sample correlation between profit margin and net revenue is *negative* (in fact, it is $-.70$), though, as we have seen, once the movement of number of offices over the sample period is factored out, a moderately strong *positive* association is revealed.

A word of caution must be added. On occasion, sample data can be very uninformative about the *separate* effects of dependent variables on an independent variable. In that case, sample partial correlations that are quite small in magnitude will result. Thus, while a sample partial correlation close to 0 is likely to be obtained when there is a truly weak relationship, it could also be no more than a reflection of uninformative data. We will return to this point in Section 14.6.

MULTIPLE CORRELATION

We have seen that, in the context of a multiple regression, the ordinary sample correlations between the dependent variable and each of the independent variables are inappropriate and can be quite misleading. The sample partial correlations are more appropriately in the spirit of assessing the strength of the relationship between the dependent variable and an independent variable, when the values of the other independent variables are held fixed.

Another generalization of the sample correlation is also sometimes calculated. If we view the problem as explaining, or predicting, the dependent variable, we have from the sample the observations $y_i (i = 1, \ldots, n)$, and the corresponding predictions $\hat{y}_i$. The sample correlation between these two quantities is called the *coefficient of multiple correlation*. It provides a measure of the strength of the relationship, in the sample, between the dependent variable and its predictions from the sample regression model.

In fact, the coefficient of multiple correlation is just the positive square root of the coefficient of determination. In our savings and loan example, then, the coefficient of multiple correlation is

$$R = \sqrt{R^2} = \sqrt{.87} = .93$$

The coefficient of multiple correlation provides a measure of the overall strength of a regression relationship analogous to the measure of strength of association between a pair of random variables provided by the ordinary sample correlation coefficient. Indeed, in the case of simple linear regression, the coefficient of multiple correlation is just the absolute value of the sample correlation between the dependent and independent variables.

EXERCISES

1. An aircraft company wanted to predict the number of worker-hours necessary to finish the design of a new plane. Relevant explanatory variables were thought to be the plane's top speed, its weight, and the number of parts it had in common with other models built by the company. A sample of twenty-seven of the company's planes was taken, and the following model estimated:

$$Y_i = \alpha + \beta_1 x_{1i} + \beta_2 x_{2i} + \beta_3 x_{3i} + \epsilon_i$$

where

Y_i = Design effort, in millions of worker-hours
x_{1i} = Plane's top speed, in Mach number
x_{2i} = Plane's weight, in tons
x_{3i} = Percentage number of parts in common with other models

The estimated partial regression coefficients were

$$b_1 = .661 \qquad b_2 = .065 \qquad b_3 = -.018$$

Interpret these estimates

2. In a study of the influence of financial institutions on share prices in the United Kingdom, quarterly data over a period of 12 years were analyzed.[4] The postulated model was

$$Y_i = \alpha + \beta_1 x_{1i} + \beta_2 x_{2i} + \epsilon_i$$

where

Y_i = Change over the quarter in the *Financial Times* stock price index
x_{1i} = Change over the quarter in equity purchases by financial institutions
x_{2i} = Change over the quarter in equity sales by financial institutions

The estimated partial regression coefficients were

$$b_1 = .057 \qquad \text{and} \qquad b_2 = -.065$$

Interpret these estimates.

3. The following model was fitted to a sample of thirty families in order to explain household milk consumption:

$$Y_i = \alpha + \beta_1 x_{1i} + \beta_2 x_{2i} + \epsilon_i$$

---

[4] R. Dobbins and S. F. Witt, "Stock market prices and sector activity," *Journal of Business, Finance and Accounting,* 7 (1980), 261–76.

where

Y_i = Milk consumption, in quarts per week
x_{1i} = Weekly income, in hundreds of dollars
x_{2i} = Family size

The least squares estimates of the regression parameters were

$$a = -.025 \qquad b_1 = .052 \qquad b_2 = 1.14$$

(a) Interpret the estimates b_1 and b_2.
(b) Is it possible to provide a meaningful interpretation of the estimate a?

4. The following model was fitted to a sample of twenty-five students using data obtained at the end of their freshman year in college. The aim was to explain students' weight gains.

$$Y_i = \alpha + \beta_1 x_{1i} + \beta_2 x_{2i} + \beta_3 x_{3i} + \epsilon_i$$

where

Y_i = Weight gained, in pounds, during freshman year
x_{1i} = Average number of meals eaten per week
x_{2i} = Average number of hours exercise per week
x_{3i} = Average number of beers consumed per week

The least squares estimates of the regression parameters were

$$a = 7.35 \qquad b_1 = .653 \qquad b_2 = -1.345 \qquad b_3 = .613$$

(a) Interpret the estimates b_1, b_2, and b_3.
(b) Is it possible to provide a meaningful interpretation of the estimate a?

5. In the study of Exercise 1, where the least squares estimates were based on twenty-seven sets of sample observations, the total sum of squares and regression sum of squares were found to be

$$\text{SST} = 3.881 \qquad \text{and} \qquad \text{SSR} = 3.549$$

(a) Find and interpret the coefficient of determination.
(b) Find the error sum of squares.
(c) Find the corrected coefficient of determination.
(d) Find and interpret the coefficient of multiple correlation.

6. In the study of Exercise 3, where the least squares estimates were based on thirty sets of sample observations, the total sum of squares and regression sum of squares were found to be

$$\text{SST} = 162.1 \qquad \text{and} \qquad \text{SSE} = 88.2$$

(a) Find and interpret the coefficient of determination.
(b) Find the corrected coefficient of determination.
(c) Find and interpret the coefficient of multiple correlation.

7. In the study of Exercise 4, twenty-five observations were used to calculate the least squares estimates. The regression sum of squares and error sum of squares were found to be

$$\text{SSR} = 79.2 \qquad \text{and} \qquad \text{SSE} = 45.9$$

(a) Find and interpret the coefficient of determination.
(b) Find the corrected coefficient of determination.
(c) Find and interpret the coefficient of multiple correlation.

8. Refer to the savings and loan association data given in Table 13.1.
   (a) Estimate by least squares the regression of profit margin on number of offices.
   (b) Estimate by least squares the regression of net revenues on number of offices.
   (c) Estimate by least squares the regression of profit margin on net revenues.
   (d) Estimate by least squares the regression of number of offices on net revenues.
   (e) Based on the results in parts (a) and (b), verify that the sample partial correlation between profit margin and net revenues for a given number of offices is .67.
   (f) Based on the results in parts (c) and (d), verify that the sample partial correlation between profit margin and number of offices for a given level of net revenues is $-.86$.

13.6 CONFIDENCE INTERVALS AND HYPOTHESIS TESTS FOR INDIVIDUAL REGRESSION PARAMETERS

Up to this stage, we have discussed point estimation of the parameters of the multiple regression model

$$Y_i = \alpha + \beta_1 x_{1i} + \beta_2 x_{2i} + \cdots + \beta_K x_{Ki} + \epsilon_i$$

In this section, we extend our results to develop confidence intervals and tests of hypotheses.

The least squares estimators are unbiased for the corresponding population parameters. Expressions for the variances of these estimators can be derived, but their precise algebraic forms are rather complicated. However, multiple regression computer packages routinely calculate unbiased estimates, s_a^2, $s_{b_1}^2$, $s_{b_2}^2$, ..., $s_{b_K}^2$, for the variances of the least squares estimators of the population parameters. In fact, it is more usual to report the square roots of these quantities, the estimated standard deviations, or **standard errors.** For the savings and loan data, the values

$$s_a = .079 \qquad s_{b_1} = .0555 \qquad s_{b_2} = .0000320$$

were obtained. Thus, for example, the standard deviation of the sampling distribution of the least squares estimator of β_1 is estimated by .0555.

In reporting estimated regressions, it is common practice to include these standard deviations in parentheses beneath the corresponding estimated parameters and also to include either the coefficient of determination or the adjusted coefficient. Thus, the savings and loan example results would be reported as

$$y = 1.565 + .237x_1 - .000249x_2 \qquad R^2 = .87$$

$$(.079) \quad (.0555) \quad (.0000320)$$

The reader is cautioned, however, that this convention is not universal. Some authors report the ratios of estimated coefficients to their estimated standard deviations instead of the estimated standard deviations. Also, the estimated standard deviation, s_a, of the intercept term is frequently omitted.

At this point, in order to make further progress, an assumption about the distribution of the population error terms, ϵ_i, is needed. It is common practice to assume that their distribution is normal and to base inferences on this assumption. In fact, by virtue of the central limit theorem, the resulting confidence intervals and hypothesis tests are not very seriously affected by moderate departures from normality in the distribution of the error terms. Moreover, the central limit theorem provides, in many circumstances, some justification for the assumption that the error terms are normal. We might think of the error term in the population regression model as representing the sum of the influences on the dependent variable of a multitude of factors not specifically accounted for in the list of independent variables. Individually, none of these factors should exert a strong influence, as such influential factors should be included among the independent variables. However, their joint effect may be nontrivial. Thus, since the error term is made up of the sum of a large number of components of this sort, the central limit theorem suggests that its distribution will often be close to normal. The main result, on which inference about the parameters of the population multiple regression model is based, is stated in the box.

Basis for Inference About the Population Regression Parameters

Let the population regression model be

$$Y_i = \alpha + \beta_1 x_{1i} + \beta_2 x_{2i} + \cdots + \beta_K x_{Ki} + \epsilon_i$$

Let $a, b_1, b_2, \ldots, b_K$ be the least squares estimates of the population parameters and s_a, $s_{b_1}, s_{b_2}, \ldots, s_{b_K}$ the estimated standard deviations of the least squares estimators. Then, if assumptions 1–5 of Section 13.3 hold and if the error terms ϵ_i are normally distributed, the random variables corresponding to

$$t_a = \frac{a - \alpha}{s_a}$$

and

$$t_{b_i} = \frac{b_i - \beta_i}{s_{b_i}} \qquad (i = 1, 2, \ldots, K)$$

are distributed as Student's t with $(n - K - 1)$ degrees of freedom.

Typically, interest is in the partial regression coefficients, β_i, rather than the intercept, α. Accordingly, we will concentrate on the former, noting that inference about the latter proceeds along similar lines.

Confidence intervals for the β_i can be derived using familiar arguments. The procedure is summarized in the next box.

Confidence Intervals for the Partial Regression Coefficients

If the population regression errors, ϵ_i, are normally distributed and assumptions 1–5 of Section 13.3 hold, then $100(1 - \alpha)\%$ confidence intervals for the partial regression coefficients, β_i, are given by

$$b_i - t_{n - K - 1, \alpha/2} s_{b_i} < \beta_i < b_i + t_{n - K - 1, \alpha/2} s_{b_i}$$

---

where $t_{n-K-1,\alpha/2}$ is the number for which

$$P(t_{n-K-1} > t_{n-K-1,\alpha/2}) = \frac{\alpha}{2}$$

and the random variable t_{n-K-1} follows a Student's t distribution with $(n - K - 1)$ degrees of freedom.

For the savings and loan regression, we have found

$$n = 25 \qquad b_1 = .237 \qquad s_{b_1} = .0555 \qquad b_2 = -.000249 \qquad s_{b_2} = .0000320$$

To obtain 99% confidence intervals for β_1 and β_2, we have from Table 6 of the Appendix

$$t_{n-K-1,\alpha/2} = t_{22,.005} = 2.819$$

Hence, the 99% confidence interval for β_1 is

$$.237 - (2.819)(.0555) < \beta_1 < .237 + (2.819)(.0555)$$

or

$$.081 < \beta_1 < .393$$

Thus, the 99% confidence interval for the expected increase in savings and loan profit margins resulting from a 1-unit increase in net revenues, given a fixed number of offices, runs from .081 to .393. The 99% confidence interval for β_2 is

$$-.000249 - (2.819)(.0000320) < \beta_2 < -.000249 + (2.819)(.0000320)$$

or

$$-.000339 < \beta_2 < -.000159$$

Therefore, the 99% confidence interval for the expected *decrease* in savings and loan profit margins resulting from an increase of 1,000 offices, for a fixed level of net revenues, runs from .159 to .339.

Tests of hypotheses about individual regression parameters can also be obtained. We consider in the box the hypothesis that the parameter β_i is equal to some specific value $\beta_{i,0}$.

Tests of Hypotheses for the Partial Regression Coefficients

If the regression errors, ϵ_i, are normally distributed and assumptions 1–5 of Section 13.3 hold, then the following tests have significance level α:

(i) To test either null hypothesis

$$H_0: \quad \beta_i = \beta_{i,0} \qquad \text{or} \qquad H_0: \quad \beta_i \leq \beta_{i,0}$$

against the alternative

$$H_1: \quad \beta_i > \beta_{i,0}$$

the decision rule is

$$\text{Reject } H_0 \text{ if } \frac{b_i - \beta_{i,0}}{s_{b_i}} > t_{n-K-1,\alpha}$$

(ii) To test either null hypothesis

$$H_0: \quad \beta_i = \beta_{i,0} \qquad \text{or} \qquad H_0: \quad \beta_i \geq \beta_{i,0}$$

against the alternative

$$H_1: \quad \beta_i < \beta_{i,0}$$

the decision rule is

$$\text{Reject } H_0 \text{ if } \frac{b_i - \beta_{i,0}}{s_{b_i}} < -t_{n-K-1,\alpha}$$

(iii) To test the null hypothesis

$$H_0: \quad \beta_i = \beta_{i,0}$$

against the two-sided alternative

$$H_1: \quad \beta_i \neq \beta_{i,0}$$

the decision rule is

$$\text{Reject } H_0 \text{ if } \frac{b_i - \beta_{i,0}}{s_{b_i}} > t_{n-K-1,\alpha/2} \qquad \text{or} \qquad \frac{b_i - \beta_{i,0}}{s_{b_i}} < -t_{n-K-1,\alpha/2}$$

An important special case arises when the hypothesized value for an individual parameter is 0. In this case, all else being equal, the expected value of the dependent variable will not be affected by a change in the corresponding independent variable. For example, suppose that in the regression

$$Y_i = \alpha + \beta_1 x_{1i} + \beta_2 x_{2i} + \cdots + \beta_K x_{Ki} + \epsilon_i$$

the true value of the parameter β_1 is 0. The implication is that given that $X_2, \ldots, X_K$ are also to be used, information on X_1 contributes nothing further, at least within a linear framework, toward explaining the behavior of the dependent variable.

We will test, for the savings and loan data, the hypothesis

$$H_0: \quad \beta_1 = 0$$

It has already been noted that a reasonable conjecture is that, all else being equal, an increase in net revenues might be expected to lead to an increase in profit margins. Hence, the appropriate alternative hypothesis is

$$H_1: \quad \beta_1 > 0$$

The test is based on

$$\frac{b_1 - \beta_{1,0}}{s_{b_1}} = \frac{.237 - 0}{.0555} = 4.27$$

From Table 6 of the Appendix, we have for $(n - K - 1) = 22$ degrees of freedom

$$t_{22,.005} = 2.819$$

Thus, the null hypothesis that net revenues do not contribute toward explaining the behavior of profit margins, given that number of offices is also used as an explanatory variable, is clearly rejected, even at the .5% significance level.

Next we test, using these data, the hypothesis

$$H_0: \quad \beta_2 = 0$$

In fact, it is suspected that, all else remaining the same, an increase in the number of offices will lead, on the average, to a decrease in the profit margins of savings and loan associations. Thus, as an alternative hypothesis, we employ

$$H_1: \quad \beta_2 < 0$$

The test is based on

$$\frac{b_2 - \beta_{2,0}}{s_{b_2}} = \frac{-.000249 - 0}{.0000320} = -7.78$$

Comparing this with tabulated values of Student's t for 22 degrees of freedom, we see that the null hypothesis that the number of offices does not contribute toward explaining the behavior of profit margins, given that net revenues are also used as an explanatory variable, is very clearly rejected at the .5% significance level.

EXAMPLE 13.1

A study was conducted to determine factors influencing urban property tax rates. For a sample of twenty U.S. cities with population between 100,000 and 200,000,[5] the following regression was estimated:

$$y = 1.79 + .000567x_1 + .0183x_2 - .000191x_3 \qquad R^2 = .71$$

$$(.000139) \quad (.0082) \quad (.000446)$$

where

$y =$ Effective property tax rate (actual levies divided by market value of the tax base)
$x_1 =$ Number of housing units per square mile
$x_2 =$ Percentage of total city revenue represented by grants from state and federal governments
$x_3 =$ Median per capita personal income, in dollars

The figures in parentheses beneath the least squares parameter estimates are the corresponding estimated standard errors.

The estimates have the following implications:

(i) All else being equal, an increase of 1 in the number of housing units per square mile leads to an expected increase of .000567 in the effective property tax rate.

(ii) All else being equal, an increase of 1 in the percent of total city revenue represented by grants from state and federal governments leads to an expected increase of .0183 in the effective property tax rate.

---

[5] C. J. Stokes, "Do urban tax rates converge?" *American Journal of Economics and Sociology*, 44 (1985), 29–38.

(iii)   All else being equal, an increase of \$1 in median per capita personal income leads to an expected decrease of .000191 in the effective property tax rate.

(iv)   Taken together, these three independent variables explain 71% of the variability in effective property tax rates in this sample.

We now find confidence intervals for β_2, the expected increase in the effective property tax rate when government revenue share increases by 1 percentage point and the other two independent variables remain constant. The appropriate intervals, based on the usual assumptions, take the form

$$b_2 - t_{n-K-1,\alpha/2}s_{b_2} < \beta_2 < b_2 + t_{n-K-1,\alpha/2}s_{b_2}$$

where

$$n = 20 \qquad K = 3 \qquad b_2 = .0183 \qquad s_{b_2} = .0082$$

For a 95% confidence interval, $\alpha/2 = .025$, so from Table 6 of the Appendix

$$t_{n-K-1,\alpha/2} = t_{16,.025} = 2.120$$

The interval is therefore

$$.0183 - (2.120)(.0082) < \beta_2 < .0183 + (2.120)(.0082)$$

or

$$.0009 < \beta_2 < .0357$$

Thus, our 95% confidence interval for the expected increase in effective property tax rate resulting, all other things being equal, from a 1-percentage-point increase in government revenue share runs from .0009 to .0357. Figure 13.5 shows also 80%, 90%, and 99% confidence intervals.

FIGURE 13.5 80%, 90%, 95%, and 99% confidence intervals for β_2, the slope of the partial regression of effective property tax rate on percentage government revenue share, using the data of Example 13.1

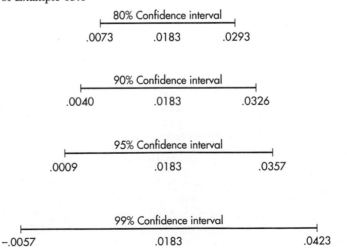

EXAMPLE 13.2

The following regression model[6] was fitted to data on thirty-one stock repurchase cash tender offers—offers by corporations repurchasing large blocks of their own outstanding shares:

$$y = .69 + 4.70x_1 + .00041x_2 - .72x_3 + .023x_4 \qquad R^2 = .72$$

$$(.651) \quad (.00128) \quad (.353) \quad (.0185)$$

where

> y = Tender premium, as a percentage of closing market price 1 week prior to offer date
> x_1 = Soliciting fee per share, as a percentage of closing market price 1 week prior to offer date (this provides a measure of the perceived degree of difficulty in obtaining the shares)
> x_2 = Percentage of shares sought
> x_3 = Relative monthly change in the Dow-Jones industrial average
> x_4 = Volume of shares traded as a percentage of those outstanding

The figures in brackets under the least squares parameter estimates are the corresponding estimated standard deviations.

The reported estimates have the following implications:

(i) All else being equal, an increase of 1 unit in the soliciting fee per share leads to an expected increase of 4.70 in the tender premium.

(ii) All else being equal, an increase of 1 in the percentage of shares sought leads to an expected increase of .00041 in the tender premium.

(iii) All else being equal, an increase of 1 unit in the relative monthly change of the Dow-Jones industrial average leads to an expected decrease of .72 in the tender premium.

(iv) All else being equal, an increase of 1 unit in the volume of shares traded leads to an expected increase of .023 in the tender premium. The authors of the study note that this result is surprising since, if trading volume is high, the corporation would be able to purchase more of the required shares on the open market and hence would presumably not need to offer such a high tender premium. This would suggest, contrary to the above findings, that, all else being equal, the higher the volume of shares traded, the lower the tender premium.

(v) Taken together, these four independent variables explain 72% of the variability in tender premiums in this sample.

We want to test the null hypothesis

$$H_0: \quad \beta_3 = 0$$

This is the hypothesis that given that the other independent variables are included in the regression, the relative monthly change in the Dow-Jones industrial average contributes nothing further toward explaining variability in tender premiums. The authors of the study note that for this variable, a case could be made for either a positive or negative relationship with cash tender premium. Therefore, we will test the null hypothesis against the two-sided alternative

$$H_1: \quad \beta_3 \neq 0$$

---

[6] Reported in K. R. Ferris, A. Melnik, and A. Rappaport, "Factors influencing the pricing of stock repurchase tenders," *Quarterly Review of Economics and Business*, *18*, no. 1 (1978), 31–39.

The test is based on

$$\frac{b_3 - \beta_{3,0}}{s_{b_3}} = \frac{-.72 - 0}{.353} = -2.040$$

Here we have $(n - K - 1) = (31 - 4 - 1) = 26$ degrees of freedom. From Table 6 in the Appendix

$$t_{26,.05} = 1.706 \qquad \text{and} \qquad t_{26,.025} = 2.056$$

Thus, the null hypothesis can be rejected against a two-sided alternative at the 10% but not at the 5% significance level. These data, then, contain moderately strong evidence against the hypothesis that, all else being equal, the relative monthly change in the Dow-Jones industrial average does not influence the tender premium.

We now test the null hypothesis

$$H_0: \quad \beta_4 = 0$$

that given that the other independent variables are used, the inclusion of volume of shares traded in the regression contributes nothing more toward explaining variability in tender premiums. Again we test against the two-sided alternative:

$$H_1: \quad \beta_4 \neq 0$$

The test is based on

$$\frac{b_4 - \beta_{4,0}}{s_{b_4}} = \frac{.023 - 0}{.0185} = 1.243$$

FIGURE 13.6 The probability density function of $t = b_4/s_{b_4}$ when the null hypothesis $H_0: \beta_4 = 0$ is true. (The distribution is the Student's t with 26 degrees of freedom in this case.) Illustrated is the test of the null hypothesis that β_4, the slope of the partial regression of tender premium on volume of shares traded, is 0, based on the data of Example 13.2. The alternative hypothesis is $\beta_4 \neq 0$, and the significance level is .20

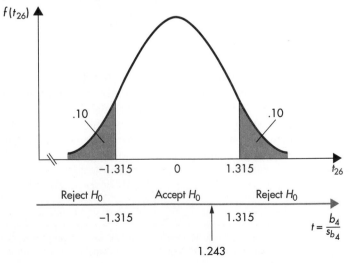

For $(n - K - 1) = 26$ degrees of freedom, we find from Table 6 of the Appendix

$$t_{26,.10} = 1.315$$

Hence, the null hypothesis cannot be rejected against a two-sided alternative at the 20% significance level. This test is illustrated in Figure 13.6. We noted earlier that the sign of the least squares estimate b_4 was the opposite of what one would have expected on the basis of subject matter theory. However, it now emerges that the data contain little evidence to contradict the hypothesis that the population parameter β_4 is in fact 0. In such circumstances, common practice is to omit variables such as x_4 from the regression model and to reestimate the other parameters.

The hypothesis tests discussed in this section are tests on the *individual* regression parameters. We may also want to test the hypothesis that, *simultaneously*, two or more of these parameters are 0. Tests of such hypotheses will be discussed in the next section.

13.7 TESTS ON SETS OF REGRESSION PARAMETERS

In Section 13.6, we showed how to perform tests on individual regression parameters. It is often the case that one must test hypotheses that specify values for some or all of these parameters. Consider once again the model

$$Y_i = \alpha + \beta_1 x_{1i} + \beta_2 x_{2i} + \cdots + \beta_K x_{Ki} + \epsilon_i \qquad (13.7.1)$$

We begin by examining the rather pessimistic null hypothesis that *all* the partial regression coefficients are 0, that is

$$H_0: \quad \beta_1 = \beta_2 = \cdots = \beta_K = 0 \qquad (13.7.2)$$

If this hypothesis were true, the regression model (13.7.1) would reduce to

$$Y_i = \alpha + \epsilon_i$$

implying that *whatever the values of the independent variables*, the expected value of the dependent variable would be a constant number, α. This null hypothesis, then, implies that taken as a group, the independent variables do not (linearly) influence the dependent variable. If this were the case, the attempt to explain the behavior of the dependent variable through the regression model would be regarded as a failure.

The basis of a test of this null hypothesis is provided by the sum of squares decomposition

$$SST = SSR + SSE \qquad (13.7.3)$$

introduced in Section 13.5. Recall that Eq. (13.7.3) expresses the total sample variability of the dependent variable as the sum of two parts. The first, SSR, is the part of total variability due to the regression on the independent variables, while the second, SSE, is the part of total variability that cannot be explained by the regression. Hence, if the null hypothesis that the independent variables do not (linearly) affect the dependent variable were true, we would expect SSR to be relatively small compared with SSE. Therefore, the larger the ratio of SSR to SSE, the less inclined would we be to believe the null hypothesis. In fact, in forming an appropriate test statistic, it is necessary to divide each of these sums of squares by their corresponding degrees of freedom. We have already seen that the degrees of freedom associated with SSE are $(n - K - 1)$. Also, since there are K partial regression coefficients, $\beta_1, \beta_2, \ldots, \beta_K$, there are K degrees of freedom associated with SSR.

It can be shown that when the null hypothesis (13.7.2) is true, the random variable corresponding to

$$F = \frac{\text{SSR}/K}{\text{SSE}/(n - K - 1)} \qquad (13.7.4)$$

follows an F distribution[7] with numerator degrees of freedom K and denominator degrees of freedom $(n - K - 1)$. The null hypothesis would be in doubt if the regression sum of squares was large compared with the error sum of squares. Hence, the null hypothesis would be rejected for large values of the test statistic (13.7.4).

A Test on All the Parameters of a Regression Model

Consider the multiple regression model

$$Y_i = \alpha + \beta_1 x_{1i} + \beta_2 x_{2i} + \cdots + \beta_K x_{Ki} + \epsilon_i$$

and the null hypothesis

$$H_0: \quad \beta_1 = \beta_2 = \cdots = \beta_K = 0$$

A test of H_0 against the alternative

$$H_1: \quad \text{At least one } \beta_i \neq 0$$

at significance level α is based on the decision rule

$$\text{Reject } H_0 \text{ if } \frac{\text{SSR}/K}{\text{SSE}/(n - K - 1)} > F_{K, n - K - 1, \alpha}$$

where $F_{K, n - K - 1, \alpha}$ is the number for which

$$P(F_{K, n - K - 1} > F_{K, n - K - 1, \alpha}) = \alpha$$

and the random variable $F_{K, n - K - 1}$ follows an F distribution with numerator degrees of freedom K and denominator degrees of freedom $(n - K - 1)$.

---

[7] The F distribution was introduced in Section 9.8. Cutoff points for this distribution are given in Table 7 of the Appendix.

The test can also be based directly on the coefficient of determination, R^2, since[8]

$$\frac{SSR/K}{SSE/(n-K-1)} = \frac{n-K-1}{K} \cdot \frac{R^2}{1-R^2}$$

To illustrate this test, consider, for the savings and loan association example, the null hypothesis

$$H_0: \quad \beta_1 = \beta_2 = 0$$

This is the hypothesis that, taken together, net revenues and number of offices do not (linearly) affect profit margins. For these data, we have found

$$n = 25 \qquad K = 2 \qquad SSE = .0623 \qquad SST = .4640$$

Hence, by subtraction

$$SSR = SST - SSE = .4640 - .0623 = .4017$$

The test of the null hypothesis is then based on

$$\frac{SSR/K}{SSE/(n-K-1)} = \frac{.4017/2}{.0623/22} = 70.92$$

From Table 7 of the Appendix, we find for a 1% level test

$$F_{K,n-K-1,\alpha} = F_{2,22,.01} = 5.72$$

Thus, the null hypothesis is very clearly rejected at the 1% significance level. The evidence against the null hypothesis that, taken together, net revenues per deposit dollar and number of offices do not linearly influence percentage profit margins of savings and loan associations is overwhelming.

The calculations for this particular test are sometimes set out in a table called an **analysis of variance** table.[9] Table 13.3 shows the analysis of variance for the savings and loan data. The table lists the three sums of squares and the corresponding degrees of freedom. The mean squares are the sums of squares divided by the associated degrees of freedom, and the ratio of these mean squares is given in the final column as the F ratio on which the test is based.

The logic behind the analysis of variance can be seen as follows. The error mean square is

$$s_e^2 = \frac{SSE}{n-K-1}$$

---

[8] This follows, as

$$R^2 = \frac{SSR}{SST} = 1 - \frac{SSE}{SST}$$

and hence

$$\frac{R^2}{1-R^2} = \frac{SSR/SST}{SSE/SST} = \frac{SSR}{SSE}$$

[9] We will discuss the analysis of variance in greater detail in Chapter 15.

TABLE 13.3 Analysis of variance for savings and loan regression

SOURCES OF VARIATION	SUMS OF SQUARES	DEGREES OF FREEDOM	MEAN SQUARES	F RATIO
Regression	.4017	2	.20085	70.92
Error	.0623	22	.0028318	
Total	.4640	24		

As we saw in Section 13.5, this provides an unbiased estimate of σ_ϵ^2, the variance of the errors in the population regression model. It can further be shown that the regression mean square provides an unbiased estimate of the quantity

$$\sigma_\epsilon^2 + \frac{\sum_{i=1}^{n} [\beta_1(x_{1i} - \bar{x}_1) + \beta_2(x_{2i} - \bar{x}_2) + \cdots + \beta_K(x_{Ki} - \bar{x}_K)]^2}{K}$$

where $\bar{x}_j$ denotes the sample mean of the observations on the jth independent variable. Therefore, when the null hypothesis that all of the β_j are 0 is correct, the regression and error mean squares have the same expected value. However, when that hypothesis is not true, the expected value of the regression mean square exceeds that of the error mean square.

EXAMPLE 13.3

For the data of Example 13.2 we will test the null hypothesis that the four independent variables, taken together, do not linearly affect the tender premium.

The null hypothesis, then, is

$$H_0: \quad \beta_1 = \beta_2 = \beta_3 = \beta_4 = 0$$

For these data, we have

$$n = 31 \qquad K = 4 \qquad R^2 = .72$$

The test of H_0 is based on

$$\frac{n - K - 1}{K} \cdot \frac{R^2}{1 - R^2} = \frac{26}{4} \cdot \frac{.72}{.28} = 16.7$$

From Table 7 of the Appendix, for a test at the 1% level, we have

$$F_{K, n-K-1, \alpha} = F_{4, 26, .01} = 4.14$$

The null hypothesis is therefore very clearly rejected at the 1% significance level. The evidence against the hypothesis that, taken together, the four independent variables do not linearly affect tender premiums is overwhelming.

TEST ON A SUBSET OF THE REGRESSION PARAMETERS

So far, we have developed tests of hypotheses for individual regression parameters and for all the parameters taken together. As a final point, we note that it is also possible to test hypotheses about some subset of these parameters. Suppose that there are K independent variables and we are interested in the possibility that the coefficients on the first K_1 of them are 0. We denote the independent variables $X_1, X_2, \ldots, X_{K_1}, X_{K_1 + 1}, \ldots, X_K$, so the regression model is

$$Y_i = \alpha + \beta_1 x_{1i} + \cdots + \beta_{K_1} x_{K_1 i} + \beta_{K_1 + 1} x_{K_1 + 1, i} \qquad (13.7.5)$$
$$+ \cdots + \beta_K x_{Ki} + \epsilon_i$$

and the null hypothesis to be tested is

$$H_0: \quad \beta_1 = \beta_2 = \cdots = \beta_{K_1} = 0$$

If true, this hypothesis implies that given that $X_{K_1 + 1}, \ldots, X_K$ are to be used, the addition of the independent variables $X_1, X_2, \ldots, X_{K_1}$ contributes nothing further toward explaining the behavior of the dependent variable. The test of this hypothesis is carried out by also estimating the regression of Y on $X_{K_1 + 1}, \ldots, X_K$ only, that is

$$Y_i = \alpha^* + \beta^*_{K_1 + 1} x_{K_1 + 1, i} + \cdots + \beta^*_K x_{Ki} + \epsilon_i^* \qquad (13.7.6)$$

where the purpose of the symbol * is to indicate that the quantities in (13.7.6) will differ from the corresponding values in (13.7.5) if the null hypothesis is false. Now, if H_0 is in fact true, we would not expect the sum of squared errors, SSE, from the full regression model (13.7.5) to differ much from the sum of squared errors, SSE*, from the regression model (13.7.6). The test is based on the difference between these quantities, and on the fact that when the null hypothesis is true, the statistic

$$F = \frac{(SSE^* - SSE)/K_1}{SSE/(n - K - 1)}$$

follows an F distribution with numerator degrees of freedom K_1 and denominator degrees of freedom $(n - K - 1)$. The null hypothesis is rejected for large values of this test statistic.

A Test on a Subset of the Regression Parameters

To test the null hypothesis

$$H_0: \beta_1 = \beta_2 = \cdots = \beta_{K_1} = 0$$

let SSE denote the sum of squared errors when the dependent variable is regressed on all the independent variables, and SSE* the sum of squared errors when the dependent variable is regressed on $X_{K_1 + 1}, \ldots, X_K$. A test of H_0 against the alternative

$$H_1: \text{At least one } \beta_i \neq 0 \qquad (i = 1, 2, \ldots, K_1)$$

at significance level α is based on the decision rule

$$\text{Reject } H_0 \text{ if } \frac{(SSE^* - SSE)/K_1}{SSE/(n - K - 1)} > F_{K_1, n - K - 1, \alpha}$$

EXAMPLE
13.4

A fast-food franchise operates in twenty regions of the country. It was believed that sales in these regions were likely to be influenced by promotional expenditures. Accordingly, a linear regression model was fitted to twenty pairs of observations. The dependent variable was the percentage increase in sales per outlet over the previous year, and the independent variable was percentage change in promotional expenditures. The sum of squared errors from this fitted regression was found to be 78.21. An economist consulted by the franchise claimed that two other factors would also influence sales. Following the economist's advice, the franchise estimated a multiple regression equation. The dependent variable was defined as before. In addition to the independent variable previously used, two further variables—the percentage change in regional unemployment rates and the percentage change in the number of outlets in the regions—were included. It was found that the sum of squared errors from this fitted multiple regression model was 66.73.

Test the null hypothesis that given that promotional expenditures are used, unemployment and the number of outlets contribute nothing further toward explaining variability in sales.

The regression model here is

$$Y_i = \alpha + \beta_1 x_{1i} + \beta_2 x_{2i} + \beta_3 x_{3i} + \epsilon_i$$

where

Y_i = Percentage increase in sales
x_{1i} = Percentage change in unemployment
x_{2i} = Percentage change in number of outlets
x_{3i} = Percentage change in promotional expenditures

The null hypothesis to be tested is

$$H_0: \quad \beta_1 = \beta_2 = 0$$

In the notation established previously, we have

$$n = 20 \qquad K_1 = 2 \qquad K = 3 \qquad SSE^* = 78.21 \qquad SSE = 66.73$$

Our test is based on

$$\frac{(SSE^* - SSE)/K_1}{SSE/(n - K - 1)} = \frac{(78.21 - 66.73)/2}{66.73/16} = 1.38$$

From Table 7 of the Appendix, we find, for a 5% level test

$$F_{K_1, n - K - 1, \alpha} = F_{2,16,.05} = 3.63$$

Thus, the null hypothesis that unemployment and the number of outlets contribute nothing further to explaining sales is not rejected by a 5%-level test. There is no strong case for adding this pair of variables to the regression.

13.8 PREDICTION

As in the case of the linear regression model, an important use of the multiple regression model is in the prediction of values of the dependent variable for specified values of the set of independent variables. Suppose that the K independent variables are equal to the particular values $x_{1,n+1}, x_{2,n+1}, \ldots, x_{K,n+1}$. Assume further that the regression model continues to hold, so that the corresponding value for the dependent variable is

$$Y_{n+1} = \alpha + \beta_1 x_{1,n+1} + \beta_2 x_{2,n+1} + \cdots + \beta_K x_{K,n+1} + \epsilon_{n+1} \qquad (13.8.1)$$

where ϵ_{n+1} is a random variable with mean 0. We want to predict the value that Y_{n+1} will actually take. An obvious choice of predictor is obtained by replacing the unknown parameters, $\alpha, \beta_1, \beta_2, \ldots, \beta_K$, in (13.8.1) by their least squares estimates, $a, b_1, b_2, \ldots, b_K$, and the random variable ϵ_{n+1} by its expected value, 0.

Prediction from Multiple Regressions

Suppose that the population regression model

$$Y_i = \alpha + \beta_1 x_{1i} + \beta_2 x_{2i} + \cdots + \beta_K x_{Ki} + \epsilon_i \qquad (i = 1, 2, \ldots, n+1)$$

holds and that the assumptions of Section 13.3 are valid. Let $a, b_1, \ldots, b_K$ be the least squares estimates of $\alpha, \beta_1, \beta_2, \ldots, \beta_K$, based on $(x_{11}, x_{21}, \ldots, x_{K1}, y_1), (x_{12}, x_{22}, \ldots, x_{K2}, y_2), \ldots, (x_{1n}, x_{2n}, \ldots, x_{Kn}, y_n)$. Then, given $x_{1,n+1}, x_{2,n+1}, \ldots, x_{K,n+1}$, the best linear unbiased predictor of Y_{n+1} is, by virtue of the Gauss-Markov theorem

$$\hat{Y}_{n+1} = a + b_1 x_{1,n+1} + b_2 x_{2,n+1} + \cdots + b_K x_{K,n+1}$$

Returning once more to the savings and loan example, suppose that we want to predict profit margins in a year in which net revenue is 4.50 and there are 9,000 offices. In our notation

$$x_{1,n+1} = 4.50 \qquad \text{and} \qquad x_{2,n+1} = 9,000$$

Our optimal point predictor of profit margins is therefore

$$\hat{Y}_{n+1} = a + b_1 x_{1,n+1} + b_2 x_{2,n+1}$$
$$= 1.565 + (.237)(4.50) - (.000249)(9000) = .39$$

Thus, in a year in which net revenues per deposit dollar are 4.50 and the number of offices is 9,000, we predict a value .39 for percentage profit margin of savings and loan associations.

Given the further assumption that the error terms, ϵ_i, are normally distributed, formulas can be developed for calculating confidence intervals for predictions from regression models. These formulas are, in general, rather complicated. However, many multiple regression computer packages have the facility for computing interval forecasts for predictions.

EXERCISES

9. In the study of Exercise 1, the estimated standard errors were

$$s_{b_1} = .099 \qquad s_{b_2} = .032 \qquad s_{b_3} = .0023$$

   (a) Find 90% and 95% confidence intervals for β_1.
   (b) Find 95% and 99% confidence intervals for β_2.
   (c) Test against a two-sided alternative the null hypothesis that, all else being equal, the plane's weight has no linear influence on its design effort.
   (d) The error sum of squares for this regression was .332. Using the same data, a simple linear regression of design effort on percentage number of common parts was fitted, yielding error sum of squares 3.311. Test at the 1% level the null hypothesis that taken together, top speed and weight contribute nothing in a linear sense to explanation of design effort, given that percentage number of common parts is also used as an explanatory variable.

10. In the study of Exercise 3, where the sample regression was based on thirty observations, the estimated standard errors were

$$s_{b_1} = .023 \qquad s_{b_2} = .35$$

   (a) Test against the appropriate one-sided alternative the null hypothesis that for fixed family size, milk consumption does not depend linearly on income.
   (b) Find 90%, 95%, and 99% confidence intervals for β_2.

11. In the study of Exercise 4, where the sample regression was based on twenty-five observations, the estimated standard errors were

$$s_{b_1} = .189 \qquad s_{b_2} = .565 \qquad s_{b_3} = .243$$

   (a) Test against the appropriate one-sided alternative the null hypothesis that, all else being equal, hours of exercise do not linearly influence weight gain.
   (b) Test against the appropriate one-sided alternative the null hypothesis that, all else being equal, beer consumption does not linearly influence weight gain.
   (c) Find 90%, 95%, and 99% confidence intervals for β_1.

12. Refer to the data of Example 13.1.
   (a) Test against a two-sided alternative the null hypothesis that, all else being equal, median per capita personal income has no influence on the effective property tax rate.
   (b) Test the null hypothesis that, taken together, the three independent variables do not linearly influence the effective property tax rate.

13. Refer to the data of Example 13.2.
   (a) Find 95% and 99% confidence intervals for the expected change in tender premium resulting from a 1-unit increase in soliciting fee per share, as a percentage of closing market price, when the values of all other independent variables remain unchanged.
   (b) Test the null hypothesis that, all else being equal, percentage of shares sought does not influence the tender premium, against the alternative that, the higher is the percentage of shares sought, the higher is the tender premium.

14. In a study of revenue generated by state lotteries,[10] the following regression equation was fitted to data from twenty-nine states with lotteries:

$$y = -31.323 + .04045x_1 + .8772x_2 - 365.01x_3 - 9.9298x_4 \qquad R^2 = .51$$

$$(.00755) \quad (.3107) \quad (263.88) \quad (3.4520)$$

---

[10] J. R. Davis, J. E. Filer, and D. L. Moak, "The lottery as an alternative source of state revenue," *Atlantic Economic Journal, 20*, no. 2 (1992), 1–10.

where

> y = Dollars of net revenue per capita per year generated by the lottery
> x_1 = Mean per capita personal income of the state
> x_2 = Number of hotel, motel, inn, and resort rooms per thousand of population
> x_3 = State spendable revenue per capita per year generated by parimutual betting, racing, and other legalized gambling
> x_4 = Percentage of the state's border contiguous with a state or states with a lottery

The numbers in parentheses below the coefficient estimates are the corresponding estimated standard errors.

(a) Interpret the estimated coefficient on x_1.

(b) Find and interpret a 95% confidence interval for the coefficient on x_2 in the population regression.

(c) Test the null hypothesis that the coefficient on x_3 in the population regression is 0, against the alternative that this coefficient is negative. Interpret your findings.

15. A study was conducted to determine whether certain features could be used to explain variability in the prices of air conditioners.[11] For a sample of nineteen air conditioners, the following regression was estimated:

$$y = -68.236 + .0023x_1 + 19.729x_2 + 7.653x_3 \qquad R^2 = .84$$

$$(.005) \qquad (8.992) \qquad (3.082)$$

where

> y = Price (in dollars)
> x_1 = Rating of air conditioner, in BTU per hour
> x_2 = Energy efficiency ratio
> x_3 = Number of settings

The figures in parentheses beneath the coefficient estimates are the corresponding estimated standard errors.

(a) Find a 95% confidence interval for the expected increase in price resulting from an additional setting when the values of the rating and the energy efficiency ratio remain fixed.

(b) Test the null hypothesis that, all else being equal, the energy efficiency ratio of air conditioners does not affect their price against the alternative that the higher the energy efficiency ratio, the higher the price.

16. In a study of the demand for imports in Jamaica,[12] the following model was fitted to 19 years of data:

$$y = -58.9 + .20x_1 - .10x_2 \qquad \overline{R}^2 = .96$$

$$(.0092) \ (.084)$$

where

> y = Quantity of imports
> x_1 = Personal consumption expenditures
> x_2 = Price of imports ÷ Domestic prices

---

[11] B. T. Ratchford, "The value of information for selected appliances," *Journal of Marketing Research, 17* (1980), 14–25.

[12] J. Gafar, "Devaluation and the balance of payments adjustment in a developing economy: An analysis relating to Jamaica," *Applied Economics, 13* (1981), 151–65.

The figures in parentheses beneath the coefficient estimates are their estimated standard errors.

(a) Find a 95% confidence interval for β_1.

(b) Test against the appropriate one-sided alternative the null hypothesis that $\beta_2 = 0$.

17. In a study of foreign holdings in U.S. banks,[13] the following sample regression was obtained, based on fourteen annual observations.

$$y = -3.248 + .101x_1 - .244x_2 + .057x_3 \qquad R^2 = .93$$

$$(.023) \quad (.080) \quad (.00925)$$

where

y = Year-end share of assets in U.S. bank subsidiaries held by foreigners, as a percentage of total assets

x_1 = Annual change, in billions of dollars, in foreign direct investment in the U.S. (excluding finance, insurance, and real estate)

x_2 = Bank price-earnings ratio

x_3 = Index of the exchange value of the dollar

The figures in brackets below coefficient estimates are estimated standard errors.

(a) Find a 90% confidence interval for β_1 and interpret your result.

(b) Test the null hypothesis that β_2 is zero, against the alternative that it is negative, and interpret your result.

(c) Test the null hypothesis that β_3 is zero, against the alternative that it is positive, and interpret your result.

18. In a study of differences in levels of community demand for police officers,[14] the following sample regression was obtained, based on data from thirty-nine towns in Delaware County, Pennsylvania.

$$y = -.00232 - .00024x_1 - .00002x_2 + .00034x_3 + .48122x_4 + .04950x_5$$

$$(.00010) \quad (.000018) \quad (.00012) \quad (.77954) \quad (.01172)$$

$$-.00010x_6 + .00645x_7 \qquad \overline{R}^2 = .3572$$

$$(.00005) \quad (.00306)$$

where

y = Number of full-time police officers per capita

x_1 = Maximum base salary of police officers, in thousands of dollars

x_2 = Percentage of population that is black

x_3 = Estimated per capita income, in thousands of dollars

x_4 = Population density

x_5 = Amount of intergovernmental grants per capita, in thousands of dollars

x_6 = Number of miles from center city Philadelphia

x_7 = Percentage of population that is male and between 12 and 21 years of age

The figures in brackets beneath coefficient estimates are estimated standard errors.

[13] C. W. Hultman and L. R. McGee, "Factors affecting the foreign banking presence in the U.S.," *Journal of Banking and Finance, 12* (1989), 383–96.

[14] E. J. Mathias and C. E. Zech, "The community demand for police officers," *American Journal of Economics and Sociology, 44* (1985), 401–10.

(a) Find and interpret a 99% confidence interval for β_5.

(b) Test against a two-sided alternative the null hypothesis that β_4 is 0, and interpret your result.

(c) Test against a two-sided alternative the null hypothesis that β_7 is 0, and interpret your result.

19. Suppose that a dependent variable is related to K independent variables through a multiple regression model. Let R^2 denote the coefficient of determination and $\overline{R}^2$ the corrected coefficient. Suppose that n sets of observations are used to fit the regression.

(a) Show that

$$\overline{R}^2 = \frac{(n-1)R^2 - K}{n-K-1}$$

(b) Show that

$$R^2 = \frac{(n-K-1)\overline{R}^2 + K}{n-1}$$

(c) Show that the statistic for testing the null hypothesis that all the partial regression coefficients are 0 can be written

$$\frac{SSR/K}{SSE/(n-K-1)} = \frac{n-K-1}{K} \cdot \frac{\overline{R}^2 + A}{1 - \overline{R}^2}$$

where

$$A = \frac{K}{n-K-1}$$

20. Refer to the study on aircraft design effort of Exercises 1 and 5.

(a) Test the null hypothesis

$$H_0: \quad \beta_1 = \beta_2 = \beta_3 = 0$$

(b) Set out the analysis of variance table for the fitted regression.

21. For the study on the influence of financial institutions on share prices of Exercise 2, forty-eight quarterly observations were used, and the corrected coefficient of determination was found to be $\overline{R}^2 = .463$. Test the null hypothesis

$$H_0: \quad \beta_1 = \beta_2 = 0$$

22. Refer to the study on milk consumption, described in Exercises 3 and 6.

(a) Test the null hypothesis

$$H_0: \quad \beta_1 = \beta_2 = 0$$

(b) Set out the analysis of variance table.

23. Refer to the study on weight gains, described in Exercises 4 and 7.

(a) Test the null hypothesis

$$H_0: \quad \beta_1 = \beta_2 = \beta_3 = 0$$

(b) Set out the analysis of variance table.

24. Refer to Exercise 14. Test the null hypothesis that, taken together, the four independent variables do not linearly influence revenue generated by state lotteries.

25. Refer to Exercise 15. Test the null hypothesis that, taken together, the three independent variables do not linearly influence the price of air conditioners.

26. Refer to the study of Exercise 16. Test the null hypothesis that taken together, consumption expenditures and the relative price of imports do not linearly affect the demand for imports in Jamaica.

27. Refer to the study on the determinants of community demand for police officers discussed in Exercise 18. Test the null hypothesis

$$H_0: \quad \beta_1 = \beta_2 = \beta_3 = \beta_4 = \beta_5 = \beta_6 = \beta_7 = 0$$

and interpret your findings.

28. A dependent variable is regressed on K independent variables, using n sets of sample observations. We denote by SSE the error sum of squares and by R^2 the coefficient of determination for this estimated regression. We want to test the null hypothesis that K_1 of these independent variables, taken together, do not linearly affect the dependent variable, given that the other $(K - K_1)$ independent variables are also to be used. Suppose that the regression is reestimated, with the K_1 independent variables of interest excluded. Let SSE* denote the error sum of squares and R_*^2 the coefficient of determination for this regression. Show that the statistic for testing our null hypothesis, introduced in Section 13.7, can be expressed as

$$\frac{(SSE^* - SSE)/K_1}{SSE/(n - K - 1)} = \frac{R^2 - R_*^2}{1 - R^2} \cdot \frac{n - K - 1}{K_1}$$

29. In the study of Exercises 3 and 6 on milk consumption, a third independent variable— number of preschool children in the household—was added to the regression model. The sum of squared errors when this augmented model was estimated by least squares was found to be 83.7. Test the null hypothesis that, all other things being equal, number of preschool children in the household does not linearly affect milk consumption.

30. Using the information in Exercise 4, predict the weight gain for a freshman who eats an average of twenty meals per week, exercises an average of 10 hours per week, and consumes an average of six beers per week.

31. Using the information in Exercise 3, predict the weekly milk consumption of a family of four with an income of $600 per week.

32. For the regression on aircraft design effort of Exercise 1, the estimated intercept was

$$a = .578$$

Predict design effort for a plane with top speed Mach 1.0, weighing 7 tons, and having 50% of its parts in common with other models.

33. A real estate agent hypothesizes that in her town, the selling price of a house in dollars (y) depends on its size in square feet of floor space (x_1), the lot size in square feet (x_2), the number of bedrooms (x_3), and the number of bathrooms (x_4). For a random sample of twenty house sales, the following least squares estimated model was obtained:

$$y = 1998.5 + 22.352x_1 + 1.4686x_2 + 6767.3x_3 + 2701.1x_4 \qquad R^2 = .9843$$

$$(2.5543) \quad (1.4492) \quad (1820.8) \quad (1996.2)$$

The figures in parentheses are estimated standard errors.

(a) Interpret in the context of this model the estimated coefficient on x_2.

(b) Interpret the coefficient of determination.

(c) Assuming that the model is correctly specified, test at the 5% level against the appropriate one-sided alternative the null hypothesis that, all else being equal, selling price does not depend on number of bathrooms.

(d) Estimate the selling price of a house with 1,250 square feet of floor space, on a lot of 4,700 square feet, with three bedrooms and 1 1/2 bathrooms.

13.9 COMPUTER PACKAGES FOR REGRESSION CALCULATIONS

As we have already noted, multiple regression analysis calculations are almost invariably carried out on an electronic computer. Indeed, without this aid, the arithmetic involved would be formidably difficult if the model contained more than a very small number of independent variables.

Most modern computing facilities have available prewritten program packages for carrying out regression analyses, and such packages are available for use on personal computers. The user need only supply the data and specify the model that is to be fitted. All these packages produce the basic information we have discussed in this chapter and generally contain options to allow the production of much more numerical and graphical output.

Table 13.4 shows part of the output from a standard regression package, the Statistical Analysis System (SAS) program, used in the analysis of our savings and loan data. The upper half of the table shows the analysis of variance for the fitted regression. This reproduces the information in Table 13.3, but with the "Regression" source of variation referred to as MODEL. The final row of this table contains the sum of the degrees of freedom and sums of squares for the model and error. The coefficient of determination, R-SQUARE, is also shown in the upper portion of the output.

The lower half of the table shows the least squares parameter estimates and their estimated standard errors. The ratios of these estimates to their standard errors are labeled T FOR H0: PARAMETER = 0 and are the statistics discussed in Section 13.6 for testing the null hypotheses that the population regression parameters are 0.

Table 13.5 shows part of the output from a second package, the MINITAB program, used to perform the savings and loan regression. The output of the MINITAB program begins with a summary of the least squares estimated regression model. Next, the coefficient estimates, together with their associated standard errors and t ratios, are shown. The ST. DEV. OF Y ABOUT REGRESSION LINE is an estimate of the standard deviation of the error terms, ϵ_i, in the population regression. Thus, it provides an estimate of the standard deviation of the unexplained part of the dependent variable. Here, we have

TABLE 13.4 Part of output of SAS program for savings and loan regression

DEPENDENT VARIABLE: Y PROFIT MARGIN

SOURCE	DF	SUM OF SQUARES	MEAN SQUARE	F VALUE	R-SQUARE
MODEL	2	.4017	.20085	70.92	.866
ERROR	22	.0623	.0028318		
CORRECTED TOTAL	24	.4640			

PARAMETER	ESTIMATE	T FOR H0: PARAMETER = 0	STD. ERROR OF ESTIMATE
INTERCEPT	1.565		
X1	.237	4.27	.0555
X2	−.000249	−7.78	.0000320

TABLE 13.5 Part of output of MINITAB program for savings and loan regression

THE REGRESSION EQUATION IS
Y = 1.565 + .237 X 1 − .000249 X 2

	COEFFICIENT	ST. DEV. OF COEF.	T-RATIO = COEF/S.D.
	1.565		
X1	.237	.0555	4.27
X2	−.000249	.000032	−7.78

THE ST. DEV. OF Y ABOUT REGRESSION LINE IS S = .0532
WITH (25-3) = 22 DEGREES OF FREEDOM

R-SQUARED = 86.6 PERCENT
R-SQUARED = 85.4 PERCENT, ADJUSTED FOR D.F.

ANALYSIS OF VARIANCE

DUE TO	DF	SS	MS = SS/DF
REGRESSION	2	.4017	.20085
RESIDUAL	22	.0623	.0028318
TOTAL	24	.4640	

ST. DEV. OF Y ABOUT REGRESSION LINE

$$= s_e$$
$$= \sqrt{\frac{SSE}{n - K - 1}}$$
$$= \sqrt{\frac{.0623}{22}} = .0532$$

The coefficient of determination, R^2, is shown next, followed by the adjusted coefficient, $\overline{R}^2$. Finally, the analysis of variance table is displayed.

As a final example, Table 13.6 shows part of the output from the Statistical Package for the Social Sciences (SPSS) program for our savings and loan data. Many of the quantities reported by the SPSS program correspond in an obvious way to those reported by the other programs. The STANDARD ERROR is s_e, the estimated standard deviation of the error terms of the population regression model. Instead of reporting the t ratios, the SPSS program gives F values, which are in fact the squares of the t ratios.

Obviously, the development of multiple regression computer packages has greatly eased the arithmetic burden involved in regression computations. Largely as a result of this factor, the technique is now extremely widely used. This is not entirely an unmixed blessing. Perhaps because the procedure is so easy to carry out, regression analyses based on an inadequate amount of forethought are frequently reported. In fact, there are a number of pitfalls involved in the analysis of data through this technique. Some of these will be discussed in Chapter 14.

TABLE 13.6 Part of output of SPSS program for savings and loan regression

DEPENDENT VARIABLE .. Y PROFIT MARGIN

MULTIPLE R	.930
R SQUARE	.866
ADJUSTED R SQUARE	.854
STANDARD ERROR	.0532

ANALYSIS OF VARIANCE

	DF	SUM OF SQUARES	MEAN SQUARE	F
REGRESSION	2	.4017	.20085	70.92
RESIDUAL	22	.0623	.0028318	

VARIABLE	B	STD. ERROR B	F
X1	.237	.0555	18.23
X2	-.000249	.0000320	60.53
(CONSTANT)	1.565		

34. In order to assess the effect in a state of banks' economic power on their political power, the following model was hypothesized and fitted to data from all fifty states.[15]

$$Y = \alpha + \beta_1 x_1 + \beta_2 x_2 + \beta_3 x_3 + \beta_4 x_4 + \beta_5 x_5 + \epsilon$$

where

Y = Ratio of bank provisions for state and local taxes (in thousands of dollars) to total state and local tax revenues (in millions of dollars)

x_1 = 3-Bank organization state concentration ratio (a measure of the concentration of banking resources)

x_2 = Per capita income in the state (in thousands of dollars)

x_3 = Ratio of nonfarm income to the sum of farm and nonfarm income

x_4 = Ratio of banks' net after-tax income to banks' assets (multiplied by 1,000)

x_5 = Average of banks' assets (divided by 10,000)

Part of the computer output from the estimated regression is shown here. Write a report summarizing the findings of this study.

| | | R-SQUARE | |
| | | .515 | |

PARAMETER	ESTIMATE	T FOR H0: PARAMETER = 0	STD. ERROR OF ESTIMATE
INTERCEPT	10.60	2.41	4.40
X1	−.90	−.69	1.31
X2	.14	.50	.28
X3	−11.85	−2.83	4.18
X4	.080	.50	.160
X5	.100	5.00	.020

35. The subjects of a random sample of ninety-three freshmen at the University of Illinois were asked to rate on a scale from 1 (low) to 10 (high) their overall opinion of residence hall life. They were also asked to rate their levels of satisfaction with roommates, with the floor, with the hall, and with the resident adviser. (Information on satisfaction with the room itself was obtained, but this was later discarded as it provided no useful additional power in explaining overall opinion.) The following model was estimated:

$$Y = \alpha + \beta_1 x_1 + \beta_2 x_2 + \beta_3 x_3 + \beta_4 x_4 + \epsilon$$

where

Y = Overall opinion of residence hall

x_1 = Satisfaction with roommates

x_2 = Satisfaction with floor

x_3 = Satisfaction with hall

x_4 = Satisfaction with resident adviser

---

[15] Adapted from C. A. Glassman, "The impact of banks' statewide economic power on their political power: An empirical analysis," *Atlantic Economic Journal*, 19, no. 2 (1981), 53–56.

Use the accompanying portion of the computer output from the estimated regression to write a report summarizing the findings of this study.

DEPENDENT VARIABLE: Y OVERALL OPINION

SOURCE	DF	SUM OF SQUARES	MEAN SQUARE	F VALUE	R-SQUARE
MODEL	4	37.016	9.2540	9.958	.312
ERROR	88	81.780	.9293		
CORRECTED TOTAL	92	118.79			

PARAMETER	ESTIMATE	T FOR H0: PARAMETER = 0	STD. ERROR OF ESTIMATE
INTERCEPT	3.950	5.84	.676
X1	.106	1.69	.063
X2	.122	1.70	.072
X3	.092	1.75	.053
X4	.169	2.64	.064

36. The following model[16] was fitted to forty-seven monthly observations in an attempt to explain the difference between secondary market certificate of deposit rates and Treasury bill rates:

$$Y = \alpha + \beta_1 x_1 + \beta_2 x_2 + \epsilon$$

where

Y = Secondary market certificate of deposit rate less Treasury bill rate
x_1 = Treasury bill rate
x_2 = Ratio of loans and investments to capital

Use the part of the computer output from the estimated regression shown here to write a report summarizing the findings of this analysis.

	R-SQUARE .730		
PARAMETER	ESTIMATE	T FOR H0: PARAMETER = 0	STD. ERROR OF ESTIMATE
INTERCEPT	−5.559	−4.14	1.343
X1	.186	5.64	.033
X2	.450	2.08	.216

37. [*This problem requires either the material in Appendix A13.1 or a computer program to carry out the multiple regression computations.*] The accompanying table gives 10 years

[16] Adapted from I. H. Giddy, "Moral hazard and Central Bank rescues in an international context," *Financial Review*, 15, no. 2 (1980), 50–56.

of annual data on traffic death rates per 100 million vehicle miles (y), total travel in billion vehicle miles (x_1), and the average speed in miles per hour of all vehicles (x_2). Compute the multiple regression of y on x_1 and x_2, and write a report discussing your findings.

y	x_1	x_2	y	x_1	x_2
5.2	738	52.6	5.7	930	57.3
5.3	767	53.8	5.5	962	58.0
5.4	805	55.8	5.4	1,016	59.0
5.6	847	55.9	5.2	1,071	60.0
5.5	889	56.4	4.9	1,121	59.2

38. [*This problem requires a computer program to carry out the multiple regression calculations.*] The table shows, for the fifty states in the United States, percentage of females that are in the labor force (y), median household personal income (x_1), mean years of education completed by females (x_2), and the unemployment rate of women (x_3). Compute the multiple regression of y on x_1, x_2, and x_3, and write a report on your findings.

y	x_1	x_2	x_3	y	x_1	x_2	x_3
61.0	17,306	12.5	6.3	65.3	20,951	12.6	6.5
63.8	17,747	12.6	4.7	59.9	22,897	12.6	7.7
58.5	18,840	12.3	7.6	63.9	25,881	12.6	6.2
52.6	22,456	12.5	6.4	57.4	25,372	12.5	5.8
54.1	19,128	12.4	6.1	56.8	17,916	12.4	5.8
57.4	17,217	12.4	5.5	58.3	20,824	12.5	6.5
55.7	18,679	12.5	8.5	63.1	18,046	12.5	4.8
66.6	19,107	12.6	4.0	62.2	17,505	12.5	4.1
60.2	17,842	12.4	6.2	59.9	16,088	12.5	3.8
62.7	16,392	12.5	3.6	63.4	17,852	12.6	2.6
60.4	18,511	12.6	4.4	60.7	20,349	12.5	5.0
62.8	22,080	12.5	5.9	64.0	19,976	12.4	6.0
44.2	14,174	12.2	9.1	60.5	16,642	12.2	5.7
59.5	15,420	12.1	6.0	57.4	17,364	12.2	5.2
54.6	18,880	12.5	7.6	52.9	15,539	12.1	7.3
53.9	16,352	12.2	6.6	51.8	15,567	12.2	7.6
54.1	13,343	12.2	8.9	53.6	14,753	12.2	7.5
52.7	15,143	12.2	7.8	54.3	15,827	12.5	6.2
58.7	17,305	12.4	6.7	60.8	16,043	12.6	6.4
57.8	15,401	12.6	5.8	61.8	17,118	12.7	5.0
63.3	19,440	12.8	4.8	54.8	14,844	12.6	6.5
55.6	16,401	12.7	5.0	61.2	14,529	12.8	5.0
61.6	19,175	12.6	4.7	59.3	19,442	12.7	5.4
58.4	17,592	12.7	6.5	56.0	20,952	12.7	7.1
64.9	21,932	12.8	6.9	61.7	21,306	12.7	2.8

39. [*This problem requires a computer program to carry out the multiple regression computations.*] The table shows twelve annual observations on real money per capita (y), real income per capita (x_1), and interest rates (x_2) in Germany. Compute the multiple regression of y on x_1 and x_2, and write a report on your findings.

y	x_1	x_2	y	x_1	x_2
1,762	13,091	9.6	2,408	14,968	7.9
1,856	12,391	10.3	2,373	14,481	8.6
2,010	12,905	8.4	2,190	14,034	10.0
2,025	13,207	7.5	2,272	14,022	8.1
2,186	13,881	5.7	2,390	14,554	8.1
2,453	14,702	6.7	2,483	14,852	7.2

40. [*This problem requires a computer program to carry out the multiple regression computations.*] The table shows percentage manufacturing growth (y), percentage agricultural growth (x_1), percentage exports growth (x_2), and percentage rate of inflation (x_3) in forty-eight developing countries. Compute the multiple regression of y on x_1, x_2, and x_3, and write a report on your findings.

y	x_1	x_2	x_3	y	x_1	x_2	x_3
1.3	3.4	−2.7	13.0	4.1	2.3	8.7	9.5
1.0	1.4	−6.0	10.5	−5.0	1.2	−2.0	1.1
.4	.1	−3.6	15.9	2.1	2.7	5.6	11.2
4.9	1.8	13.6	3.2	7.7	3.0	2.0	8.9
9.8	5.6	27.3	5.4	9.3	3.3	6.2	7.5
−2.1	2.2	2.6	5.2	−1.7	2.0	−1.7	18.2
2.0	2.3	−9.5	8.7	5.8	4.7	−.2	2.1
5.8	3.0	4.4	1.4	3.9	−3.9	−2.5	3.4
5.2	2.9	9.2	3.0	5.6	3.9	6.4	13.9
−1.1	−2.3	−6.3	14.9	6.9	1.3	11.6	6.4
.2	.3	12.0	20.3	−4.6	.8	−9.8	21.5
1.1	1.4	−7.2	19.8	−2.6	1.7	−6.6	6.7
−12.0	4.8	−5.5	8.6	1.1	3.9	3.8	7.7
−1.6	−.4	−2.5	11.3	4.6	3.0	−3.5	8.6
2.9	−.6	5.4	7.5	−3.4	7.9	−7.9	45.4
.5	1.9	1.6	19.0	−.6	2.5	2.0	11.5
2.2	−3.5	4.7	1.9	8.2	1.9	3.8	7.8
8.0	3.1	19.9	37.3	4.1	.9	1.3	5.6
6.5	3.3	−.6	8.9	12.6	7.9	11.7	3.8
.2	.1	8.4	29.5	4.1	2.8	−.9	9.9
7.8	5.3	10.4	8.1	.6	2.8	−2.1	23.3
2.5	2.3	4.9	22.6	2.0	.5	−3.1	33.5
−.2	3.1	7.9	20.2	0.0	.4	6.9	32.6
6.1	10.3	−19.0	−1.3	−2.6	−1.3	3.4	7.7

REVIEW EXERCISES

41. The method of least squares is used far more often than any alternative procedure to estimate the parameters of a multiple regression model. Explain the basis for this method of estimation, and discuss why its use is so widespread.

42. It is common practice to compute an analysis of variance table in conjunction with an estimated multiple regression. Carefully explain what can be learned from such a table.

43. State whether each of the following statements is true or false.

(a) The error sum of squares must be smaller than the regression sum of squares.

(b) Instead of carrying out a multiple regression, we can get the same information from simple linear regressions of the dependent variable on each independent variable.

(c) The coefficient of determination cannot be negative.

(d) The adjusted coefficient of determination cannot be negative.

(e) The coefficient of multiple correlation is the square root of the coefficient of determination.

44. If an additional independent variable, however irrelevant, is added to a multiple regression model, a smaller sum of squared errors will result. Explain why this is so, and discuss the consequences for the interpretation of the coefficient of determination.

45. A dependent variable is regressed on two independent variables. It is possible that the hypotheses $\beta_1 = 0$ and $\beta_2 = 0$ cannot be rejected at low significance levels, yet the hypothesis $\beta_1 = \beta_2 = 0$ can be rejected at a very low significance level. In what circumstances might this result arise?

46. [*This exercise requires the material in Appendix A13.1.*] Suppose that the regression model

$$Y_i = \alpha + \beta_1 x_{1i} + \beta_2 x_{2i} + \epsilon_i$$

is estimated by least squares. Show that the residuals, e_i, from the fitted model sum to 0.

47. A study was conducted to assess the influence of various factors on the start of new firms in the electronics components industry in urban areas.[17] For a sample of seventy standard metropolitan statistical areas, the following model was estimated:

$$y = -59.31 + 4.983x_1 + 2.198x_2 + 3.816x_3 - .310x_4$$

$$(1.156) \quad (.210) \quad (2.063) \quad (.330)$$

$$-.886x_5 + 3.215x_6 + .085x_7 \qquad R^2 = .766$$

$$(3.055) \quad (1.568) \quad (.354)$$

where

y = New business starts in the industry
x_1 = Population, in millions
x_2 = Industry size
x_3 = Measure of economic quality of life
x_4 = Measure of political quality of life
x_5 = Measure of environmental quality of life
x_6 = Measure of health and educational quality of life
x_7 = Measure of social quality of life

The figures in parentheses beneath the coefficient estimates are their estimated standard errors.

(a) Interpret the estimated partial regression coefficients.

(b) Interpret the coefficient of determination.

(c) Find a 90% confidence interval for the increase in new business starts resulting from a 1-unit increase in the economic quality of life, with all other variables unchanged.

(d) Test against a two-sided alternative at the 5% significance level the null hypothesis that, all else remaining equal, the environmental quality of life does not influence new business starts.

---

[17] J. M. Pennings, "The urban quality of life and entrepreneurship," *Academy of Management Journal*, 25 (1982), 63–79.

(e) Test against a two-sided alternative at the 5% significance level the null hypothesis that, all else remaining equal, the health and educational quality of life does not influence new business starts.

(f) Test the null hypothesis that taken together, these seven independent variables do not influence new business starts.

48. A survey research group conducts regular studies of households through mail questionnaires and is concerned about the factors influencing the response rate. In an experiment, thirty sets of questionnaires were mailed to potential respondents. The regression model fitted to the resulting data set was

$$Y = \alpha + \beta_1 x_1 + \beta_2 x_2 + \epsilon$$

where

Y = Percentage of responses received
x_1 = Number of questions asked
x_2 = Length of questionnaire, in number of words

Part of the SAS computer output from the estimated regression is shown here.

		R-SQUARE .637	
PARAMETER	ESTIMATE	T FOR H0: PARAMETER = 0	STD. ERROR OF ESTIMATE
INTERCEPT	74.3652		
X1	−1.8345	−2.89	.6349
X2	−.0162	−1.78	.0091

(a) Interpret the estimated partial regression coefficients.

(b) Interpret the coefficient of determination.

(c) Test at the 1% significance level the null hypothesis that taken together, the two independent variables do not linearly influence the response rate.

(d) Find and interpret a 99% confidence interval for β_1.

(e) Test the null hypothesis

$$H_0: \quad \beta_2 = 0$$

against the alternative

$$H_1: \quad \beta_2 < 0$$

and interpret your findings.

49. A consulting group offers courses in financial management for executives. At the end of these courses, participants are asked to provide overall ratings of the value of the course. To assess the impact of various factors on ratings, the model

$$Y = \alpha + \beta_1 x_1 + \beta_2 x_2 + \beta_3 x_3 + \epsilon$$

was fitted for twenty-five such courses, where

y = Average rating by participants of the course

x_1 = Percentage of course time spent in group discussion sessions

x_2 = Amount of money (in dollars) per course member spent on the preparation of subject matter material

x_3 = Amount of money per course member spent on the provision of non-course-related material (food, drinks, etc.)

Part of the SAS computer output for the fitted regression is shown here.

		R-SQUARE .579	
PARAMETER	ESTIMATE	T FOR H0: PARAMETER = 0	STD. ERROR OF ESTIMATE
INTERCEPT	42.9712		
X1	.3817	1.89	.2018
X2	.5172	2.64	.1957
X3	.0753	1.09	.0693

(a) Interpret the estimated partial regression coefficients.

(b) Interpret the coefficient of determination.

(c) Test at the 5% level the null hypothesis that taken together, the three independent variables do not linearly influence the course rating.

(d) Find and interpret a 90% confidence interval for β_1.

(e) Test the null hypothesis

$$H_0: \quad \beta_2 = 0$$

against the alternative

$$H_1: \quad \beta_2 > 0$$

and interpret your result.

(f) Test at the 10% significance level the null hypothesis

$$H_0: \quad \beta_3 = 0$$

against the alternative

$$H_1: \quad \beta_3 \neq 0$$

and interpret your result.

50. [*This exercise requires a computer program to carry out the multiple regression computations.*] At the end of classes, professors are rated by their students on a scale from 1 (poor) to 5 (excellent). Students are also asked what course grades they expect, and these are coded as A = 4, B = 3, and so on. In the table we show, for a random sample of twenty classes, ratings of professors, average expected grades, and the numbers of students in the classes. Compute the multiple regression of rating on expected grade and number of students, and write a report on your findings.

RATING	EXPECTED GRADE	NUMBER OF STUDENTS	RATING	EXPECTED GRADE	NUMBER OF STUDENTS
4.1	3.4	45	3.5	3.0	40
3.4	3.1	52	4.0	3.5	29
3.3	3.0	47	3.6	3.3	38
3.0	2.8	63	3.1	3.1	67
4.7	3.7	20	3.3	3.3	61
4.6	3.5	32	4.5	3.9	50
3.0	2.9	51	2.8	2.9	63
4.6	3.7	32	3.7	3.2	47
4.6	3.5	21	3.8	3.4	51
3.6	3.2	33	3.9	3.4	31

51. Based on a sample of sixty-four observations, the following model[18] was estimated by least squares:

$$y = -16.528 + 28.729x_1 + .022x_2 - .023x_3 - .054x_4$$
$$- .077x_5 + .411x_6 + .349x_7 + .028x_8 \qquad R^2 = .467$$

where

y = Index of direct labor efficiency in production plant
x_1 = Ratio of overtime hours to straight-time hours worked by all production workers
x_2 = Average number of hourly workers in the plant
x_3 = Percentage of employees involved in some quality-of-worklife program
x_4 = Number of grievances filed per 100 workers
x_5 = Disciplinary action rate
x_6 = Absenteeism rate for hourly workers
x_7 = Salaried workers' attitudes, from low (dissatisfied) to high, as measured by questionnaire
x_8 = Percentage of hourly employees submitting at least one suggestion in a year to the plant's suggestion program

Also obtained by least squares from these data was the fitted model

$$y = 9.062 - 10.944x_1 - .320x_2 + .019x_3 \qquad R^2 = .242$$

The variables x_4, x_5, x_6, x_7, x_8 are measures of the performance of a plant's industrial relations system. Test at the 1% level the null hypothesis that they contribute nothing to explaining direct labor efficiency, given that x_1, x_2, x_3 are also to be used.

52. Based on 107 students' scores on the first examination in a course on managerial cost accounting, the following model[19] was estimated by least squares:

$$y = 2.178 + .469x_1 + 3.369x_2 + 3.054x_3 \qquad R^2 = .686$$
$$(.090) \qquad (.456) \qquad (1.457)$$

[18] H. C. Katz, T. A. Kochan, and M. R. Weber, "Assessing the effects of industrial relations systems and efforts to improve the quality of working life on organizational effectiveness," *Academy of Management Journal, 28* (1985), 509–26.
[19] M. E. Ibrahim, "Effort-expectation and academic performance in managerial cost accounting," *Journal of Accounting Education, 7* (1989), 57–68.

where

y = Student's actual score on the examination
x_1 = Student's expected score on the examination
x_2 = Hours per week spent working on the course
x_3 = Student's grade point average

(a) Interpret the estimate of β_1.
(b) Find and interpret a 95% confidence interval for β_2.
(c) Test against a two-sided alternative the null hypothesis that β_3 is 0, and interpret your result.
(d) Interpret the coefficient of determination.
(e) Test the null hypothesis $\beta_1 = \beta_2 = \beta_3 = 0$.
(f) Find and interpret the coefficient of multiple correlation.
(g) Predict the score of a student who expects a score of 80, works 8 hours per week on the course, and has a grade point average of 3.0.

53. Based on 25 years of annual data, an attempt was made to explain savings in India.[20] The model fitted was

$$Y_i = \alpha + \beta_1 x_{1i} + \beta_2 x_{2i} + \epsilon_i$$

where

Y = Change in real deposit rate
x_1 = Change in real per capita income
x_2 = Change in real interest rate

The least squares parameter estimates (with standard errors in parentheses) were:

$$b_1 = .0974 \ (.0215) \qquad b_2 = .374 \ (.209)$$

The corrected coefficient of determination was

$$\overline{R}^2 = .91$$

(a) Find and interpret a 99% confidence interval for β_1.
(b) Test against the alternative that it is positive the null hypothesis that β_2 is 0.
(c) Find the coefficient of determination.
(d) Test the null hypothesis $\beta_1 = \beta_2 = 0$.
(e) Find and interpret the coefficient of multiple correlation.

54. Based on data on 2,679 college basketball players, the following model was fitted:[21]

$$Y_i = \alpha + \beta_1 x_{1i} + \beta_2 x_{2i} + \cdots + \beta_9 x_{9i} + \epsilon_i$$

where

Y = Minutes played in season
x_1 = Field goal percentage
x_2 = Free throw percentage
x_3 = Rebounds per minute
x_4 = Points per minute

---

[20] S. Ghatak and D. Deadman, "Money, prices and stabilization policies in some developing countries," *Applied Economics, 21* (1989), 853–65.
[21] R. C. Clement and R. E. McCormick, "Coaching team production," *Economic Inquiry, 27* (1989), 287–304.

x_5 = Fouls per minute
x_6 = Steals per minute
x_7 = Blocked shots per minute
x_8 = Turnovers per minute
x_9 = Assists per minute

The least squares parameter estimates (with standard errors in parentheses) were:

$a = 358.848$ (44.695) $b_1 = .6742$ (.0639) $b_2 = .2855$ (.0388)

$b_3 = 303.81$ (77.73) $b_4 = 504.95$ (43.26) $b_5 = -3923.5$ (120.6)

$b_6 = 480.04$ (224.9) $b_7 = 1350.3$ (212.3) $b_8 = -891.67$ (180.87)

$b_9 = 722.95$ (110.98)

The coefficient of determination was

$$R^2 = .5239$$

(a) Find and interpret a 90% confidence interval for β_6.
(b) Find and interpret a 99% confidence interval for β_7.
(c) Test against the alternative that it is negative the null hypothesis that β_8 is 0. Interpret your result.
(d) Test against the alternative that it is positive the null hypothesis that β_9 is 0. Interpret your result.
(e) Interpret the coefficient of determination.
(f) Find and interpret the coefficient of multiple correlation.

55. Based on data from sixty-three countries, the following model[22] was estimated by least squares:

$$y = .058 - .052x_1 - .005x_2 \qquad R^2 = .17$$

$$(.019) \quad (.042)$$

where

y = Growth rate in real gross domestic product
x_1 = Real income per capita
x_2 = Average tax rate, as a proportion of gross national product

(a) Test against a two-sided alternative the null hypothesis that β_1 is 0. Interpret your result.
(b) Test against a two-sided alternative the null hypothesis that β_2 is 0. Interpret your result.
(c) Interpret the coefficient of determination.
(d) Find and interpret the coefficient of multiple correlation.

56. The following regression model was fitted to data on sixty U.S. male professional golfers:[23]

$$y = 164{,}683 + 341.10x_1 + 170.02x_2 + 495.19x_3 - 4.23x_4$$

$$(100.59) \quad (167.18) \quad (305.48) \quad (90.0)$$

$$-136{,}040x_5 - 35{,}549x_6 + 202.52x_7 \qquad \overline{R}^2 = .516$$

$$(25{,}634) \quad (16{,}240) \quad (106.20)$$

[22] R. B. Koester and R. C. Kormendi, "Taxation, aggregate activity, and economic growth: Cross-country evidence on some supply-side hypotheses," *Economic Inquiry*, 27 (1989), 367–86.

[23] S. Shmanske, "Human capital formation in professional sports: evidence from the P.G.A. tour," *Atlantic Economic Journal*, 20, no. 3 (1992), 66–80.

where figures in brackets are estimated standard errors, and

y = Winnings per tournament, in dollars
x_1 = Average length of drive, in yards
x_2 = Percentage times drive ends in fairway
x_3 = Percentage times green reached in regulation
x_4 = Percentage times par saved after hitting into sandtrap
x_5 = Average number of putts taken on greens reached in regulation
x_6 = Average number of putts taken on greens not reached in regulation
x_7 = Number of years golfer has been a professional

Write a report summarizing what can be learned from these results.

APPENDIX A13.1

In Section 13.2, we defined the least squares estimates of the parameters of the multiple regression model as the values $a, b_1, b_2, \ldots, b_K$ for which the sum of squared discrepancies

$$SS = \sum_{i=1}^{n} (y_i - a - b_1 x_{1i} - b_2 x_{2i} - \cdots - b_K x_{Ki})^2$$

is a minimum. It can be shown[24] that this minimization problem leads to the values $b_1, b_2, \ldots, b_K$, which are the solutions of the K equations

$$\sum(x_{1i} - \bar{x}_1)(y_i - \bar{y}) = b_1\sum(x_{1i} - \bar{x}_1)^2 + b_2\sum(x_{1i} - \bar{x}_1)(x_{2i} - \bar{x}_2)$$
$$+ \cdots + b_K\sum(x_{1i} - \bar{x}_1)(x_{Ki} - \bar{x}_K)$$

$$\sum(x_{2i} - \bar{x}_2)(y_i - \bar{y}) = b_1\sum(x_{2i} - \bar{x}_2)(x_{1i} - \bar{x}_1) + b_2\sum(x_{2i} - \bar{x}_2)^2$$
$$+ \cdots + b_K\sum(x_{2i} - \bar{x}_2)(x_{Ki} - \bar{x}_K)$$

$$\vdots \qquad \qquad \vdots$$

$$\sum(x_{Ki} - \bar{x}_K)(y_i - \bar{y}) = b_1\sum(x_{Ki} - \bar{x}_K)(x_{1i} - \bar{x}_1) + b_2\sum(x_{Ki} - \bar{x}_K)(x_{2i} - \bar{x}_2)$$
$$+ \cdots + b_K\sum(x_{Ki} - \bar{x}_K)^2$$

and that the intercept estimate a is given by

$$a = \bar{y} - b_1\bar{x}_1 - b_2\bar{x}_2 - \cdots - b_K\bar{x}_K$$

where $\bar{x}_1, \bar{x}_2, \ldots, \bar{x}_K$ are the sample means of the independent variables.

The preceding equations are called the **normal equations.** The arithmetic involved in their solution is quite tedious. However, if there are only two independent variables, hand calculation is not too burdensome. In that case we have

$$\sum(x_{1i} - \bar{x}_1)(y_i - \bar{y}) = b_1\sum(x_{1i} - \bar{x}_1)^2 + b_2\sum(x_{1i} - \bar{x}_1)(x_{2i} - \bar{x}_2)$$
$$\sum(x_{2i} - \bar{x}_2)(y_i - \bar{y}) = b_1\sum(x_{2i} - \bar{x}_2)(x_{1i} - \bar{x}_1) + b_2\sum(x_{2i} - \bar{x}_2)^2$$

The solution of this pair of equations is

$$b_1 = \frac{\sum(x_{2i} - \bar{x}_2)^2\sum(x_{1i} - \bar{x}_1)(y_i - \bar{y}) - \sum(x_{1i} - \bar{x}_1)(x_{2i} - \bar{x}_2)\sum(x_{2i} - \bar{x}_2)(y_i - \bar{y})}{\sum(x_{1i} - \bar{x}_1)^2\sum(x_{2i} - \bar{x}_2)^2 - \left[\sum(x_{1i} - \bar{x}_1)(x_{2i} - \bar{x}_2)\right]^2}$$

and

$$b_2 = \frac{\sum(x_{1i} - \bar{x}_1)^2\sum(x_{2i} - \bar{x}_2)(y_i - \bar{y}) - \sum(x_{1i} - \bar{x}_1)(x_{2i} - \bar{x}_2)\sum(x_{1i} - \bar{x}_1)(y_i - \bar{y})}{\sum(x_{1i} - \bar{x}_1)^2\sum(x_{2i} - \bar{x}_2)^2 - \left[\sum(x_{1i} - \bar{x}_1)(x_{2i} - \bar{x}_2)\right]^2}$$

---

[24] The result follows by setting to 0 the partial derivatives of SS with respect to $a, b_1, b_2, \ldots, b_K$.

Finally, the estimate of the intercept is

$$a = \bar{y} - b_1\bar{x}_1 - b_2\bar{x}_2$$

We will use these formulas to calculate least squares estimates for the parameters of the savings and loan model. Using the data of Table 13.1, we calculate

$$\sum x_{1i} = 96.34 \qquad \sum x_{2i} = 181,083 \qquad \sum y_i = 16.86$$

$$\sum x_{1i}^2 = 379.2928 \qquad \sum x_{2i}^2 = 1,335,795,900 \qquad \sum x_{1i}x_{2i} = 710,932.32$$

$$\sum x_{1i}y_i = 63.6124 \qquad \sum x_{2i}y_i = 119,215.94$$

The sample means are, therefore

$$\bar{x}_1 = \frac{\sum x_{1i}}{n} = \frac{96.34}{25} = 3.8536$$

$$\bar{x}_2 = \frac{\sum x_{2i}}{n} = \frac{181,083}{25} = 7,243.32$$

$$\bar{y} = \frac{\sum y_i}{n} = \frac{16.86}{25} = .6744$$

The quantities required in the calculation of the least squares estimates are, then

$$\sum(x_{1i} - \bar{x}_1)^2 = \sum x_{1i}^2 - n\bar{x}_1^2 = 379.2928 - (25)(3.8536)^2 = 8.03698$$

$$\sum(x_{2i} - \bar{x}_2)^2 = \sum x_{2i}^2 - n\bar{x}_2^2 = 1,335,795,900 - (25)(7,243.32)^2 = 24,153,800$$

$$\sum(x_{1i} - \bar{x}_1)(x_{2i} - \bar{x}_2) = \sum x_{1i}x_{2i} - n\bar{x}_1\bar{x}_2$$
$$= 710,932.32 - (25)(3.8536)(7,243.32) = 13,110.88$$

$$\sum(x_{1i} - \bar{x}_1)(y_i - \bar{y}) = \sum x_{1i}y_i - n\bar{x}_1\bar{y} = 63.6124 - (25)(3.8536)(.6744)$$
$$= -1.359296$$

$$\sum(x_{2i} - \bar{x}_2)(y_i - \bar{y}) = \sum x_{2i}y_i - n\bar{x}_2\bar{y} = 119,215.94 - (25)(7,243.32)(.6744)$$
$$= -2,906.43$$

We can now use the formulas to compute the least squares estimates:

$$b_1 = \frac{(24,153,800)(-1.359296) - (13,110.88)(-2,906.43)}{(8.03698)(24,153,800) - (13,110.88)^2} = .237$$

and

$$b_2 = \frac{(8.03698)(-2,906.43) - (13,110.88)(-1.359296)}{(8.03698)(24,153,800) - (13,110.88)^2} = -.000249$$

Finally, the intercept term is estimated by

$$a = \bar{y} - b_1\bar{x}_1 - b_2\bar{x}_2 = .6744 - (.237)(3.8536) - (-.000249)(7,243.32)$$
$$= 1.565$$

When the regression model contains only two independent variables, manageable expressions can also be obtained for the estimated standard deviations of the least squares estimators, discussed in Section 13.6. For the estimated variances, it can be shown that

$$s_{b_1}^2 = \frac{s_e^2 \sum(x_{2i} - \bar{x}_2)^2}{\sum(x_{1i} - \bar{x}_1)^2 \sum(x_{2i} - \bar{x}_2)^2 - [\sum(x_{1i} - \bar{x}_1)(x_{2i} - \bar{x}_2)]^2}$$

and

$$s_{b_2}^2 = \frac{s_e^2 \sum(x_{1i} - \bar{x}_1)^2}{\sum(x_{1i} - \bar{x}_1)^2 \sum(x_{2i} - \bar{x}_2)^2 - [\sum(x_{1i} - \bar{x}_1)(x_{2i} - \bar{x}_2)]^2}$$

where

$$s_e^2 = \frac{\text{SSE}}{n - K - 1}$$

is the estimate of the variance of the error terms ϵ_i in the population regression. For the savings and loan association data, we have

$$s_e^2 = \frac{.0623}{22} = .0028318$$

Hence

$$s_{b_1}^2 = \frac{(.0028318)(24{,}153{,}800)}{(8.03698)(24{,}153{,}800) - (13{,}110.88)^2} = .003077$$

so by taking square roots, we obtain

$$s_{b_1} = .0555$$

Also

$$s_{b_2}^2 = \frac{(.0028318)(8.03698)}{(8.03698)(24{,}153{,}800) - (13{,}110.88)^2} = .0000000010238$$

and so

$$s_{b_2} = .0000320$$

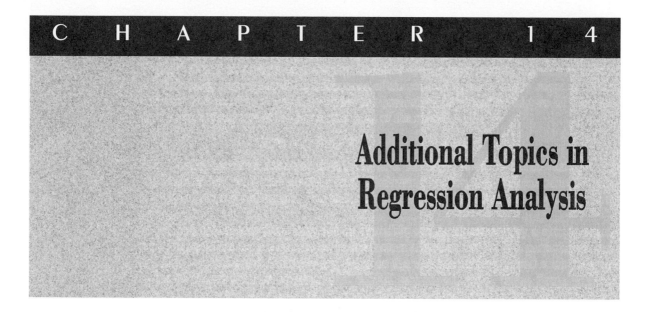

Additional Topics in Regression Analysis

14.1 MODEL-BUILDING METHODOLOGY

The technique of regression analysis has been discussed in Chapters 12 and 13. The purpose of fitting a regression equation is to use information on the independent variables to explain the behavior of the dependent variable. Subsequently, the estimated regression model might be employed to derive predictions of the dependent variable. In the development of a regression equation, a rich variety of alternative specifications is possible, and a number of problems may arise. In this chapter, we will consider some of the issues that occur in practical model building.

As a prelude, a general strategy for the construction of statistical models, such as a regression equation, is outlined. We live in an extremely complex world. No one really believes that the behavior of business and economic variables can be *precisely* described by a simple equation or system of equations. Nevertheless, it may be possible to find a relatively simple formal model that provides a sufficiently close representation of the complex reality to provide useful insights. The art of model building is to recognize the impossibility of accounting for the myriad individual influences on a variable of interest and to try, rather, to pick out the most influential factors. Next, it is necessary to formulate a model to depict the interaction of these factors. The goal is to achieve a model that is sufficiently simple to allow convenient interpretation but not so oversimplified that important influences are ignored.

The process of statistical model building is problem-specific. Just what is, and can be, done will depend on what is known about the behavior of the quantities under study and on what data are available. It is, however, possible to make some generalizations about the various stages of a model-building exercise.

Figure 14.1 shows schematically the steps involved in statistical modeling. We will consider these in turn.

535

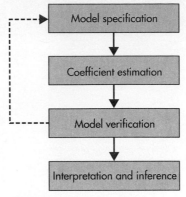

FIGURE 14.1 The stages of
statistical model building

(i) MODEL SPECIFICATION

The initial problem is to specify a formal algebraic model that might provide a convenient, useful, and reasonably accurate description of the system under study. The regression equations of Chapters 12 and 13 have postulated a linear relationship between the expected value of a dependent variable and the values taken by independent variables. Often this formulation will provide an adequate description of the underlying reality. However, this is by no means invariably the case. In Sections 14.2–14.4, we will discuss certain elaborations and modifications of the multiple regression model.

It is important to keep in mind that any assumptions about the properties of the random variables involved in a statistical model constitute part of the postulated model specification. For example, in working with regression models to this point, we have assumed that the error terms all have the same variance and are uncorrelated with one another. Any inference derived from the estimated regression equation depends for its validity on these assumptions being appropriate.

(ii) COEFFICIENT ESTIMATION

A statistical model, once specified, typically involves a number of unknown coefficients, or **parameters.** The next stage of the model-building exercise is to employ available data in the estimation of these coefficients. Both point estimates and interval estimates may be obtained. Thus, in the multiple regression model

$$Y_i = \alpha \; + \; \beta_1 x_{1i} + \beta_2 x_{2i} + \cdots + \beta_K x_{Ki} + \epsilon_i \qquad (14.1.1)$$

observations on the dependent and independent variables are used to estimate the coefficients $\alpha, \beta_1, \beta_2, \ldots, \beta_K$.

The appropriate method of estimation depends on the model specification. We have seen that given certain assumptions about the statistical properties of the error terms ϵ_i of (14.1.1), the method of least squares is appropriately used to estimate the partial regression coefficients. However, as we will see, if these assumptions fail to hold, least squares estimators can be quite inefficient. In general, the Gauss-Markov theorem, which provides a strong justification for the use of least squares, holds only when these assumptions are true.

(iii) MODEL VERIFICATION

In postulating a model, an investigator incorporates insights into the behavior of the underlying system. However, in translating these into algebraic form, certain simplifications and assumptions, which in the event might prove untenable, will have been made. Accordingly, it is important to check the adequacy of the model.

Having estimated a regression equation, an analyst may find that the estimates achieved simply do not make sense, given what is known or strongly suspected about the system under study. For instance, suppose that an estimated model suggests that, holding all other relevant factors fixed, the demand for imported cars *increases* as their price increases. Certainly such a conclusion runs counter to elementary economic theory and to common sense. When a least squares point estimate has the "wrong" sign, the problem is usually caused by insufficient data to allow much precision in the estimator. In our illustration, it is likely that, all else being equal, at least a modest negative relationship exists between the demand for imported automobiles and their price; however, this can be masked by sampling error in the coefficient estimates. More seriously, it sometimes occurs that coefficient estimates with the "wrong" sign appear to differ significantly from 0 at the usual levels. It is likely, in such circumstances, that the cause of this phenomenon is a faulty model specification. The investigator should then give further thought to the original specification. Perhaps an important explanatory variable has been overlooked, or possibly the assumed functional form of the relationship is inappropriate. Certainly, checking the plausibility of the estimated model is an important ingredient of model verification.

It is also important to check the assumptions made about the statistical properties of the random variables in the model. In the regression equation (14.1.1), it is often assumed initially that the error terms ϵ_i all have the same variance and are uncorrelated with one another. In Sections 14.7 and 14.8, we will see how these assumptions can be checked, on the basis of evidence provided by the available data.

Any checks on the adequacy of a model may lead the analyst to conjecture an alternative specification. For that reason, we have connected the verification stage to the specification stage with a dashed arrow in Figure 14.1. Viewed in this way, model building can be thought of as an iterative process of specification, estimation, and verification, the process being continued until an apparently satisfactory model is achieved.

(iv) INTERPRETATION AND INFERENCE

Once a model has been constructed, it can be used to learn something about the system under study. In regression analysis, this may involve finding confidence intervals for the model parameters, testing hypotheses of interest, or forecasting future values of the dependent variable, given assumed values of the independent variables. It is important to recognize that inference of this sort is based on the assumption of an appropriate model specification. The more severe are any specification errors, the less reliable, in general, is any inference derived from the fitted model.

14.2 DUMMY VARIABLES

It often happens that factors that are not directly quantifiable exert an important influence on the behavior of a dependent variable of interest. For example, the sale of many products will fluctuate according to the time of year, exports will be affected by dock strikes, and the rate of wage inflation will be influenced by government-mandated controls. Often such factors can be taken into account in a regression model through the introduction of *dummy variables.*

To illustrate the ideas involved, we will consider a study on the taxable capacity of less developed countries.[1] It was believed that tax revenues (Y) as a percentage of gross national product would depend on exports (x_1) as a percentage of gross national product and on per capita income (x_2). However, it was further suspected that tax revenues would be lower in countries that participated in some form of economic integration (such as a free trade area, customs union, or common market) than in those that did not. To allow for the influence of this last factor, another independent variable (x_3) is created. This variable is constructed so that it takes the value 1 for countries that take part in some form of economic integration and 0 for countries that do not. The postulated multiple regression model is then

$$Y_i = \alpha + \beta_1 x_{1i} + \beta_2 x_{2i} + \beta_3 x_{3i} + \epsilon_i \qquad (14.2.1)$$

where

Y_i = Tax revenue as a percentage of gross national product in country i
x_{1i} = Exports as a percentage of gross national product in country i
x_{2i} = Income per capita (in U.S. dollars) in country i
$x_{3i} = \begin{cases} 1 & \text{if country } i \text{ participated in some form of economic integration} \\ 0 & \text{otherwise} \end{cases}$

Variables such as x_{3i} in Eq. (14.2.1) are called **dummy variables.** The interpretation of β_1 and β_2 in (14.2.1) is precisely the same as in regression models that do not contain dummy variables. Thus, β_2 is the expected increase in tax revenues (as a percentage of gross national product) resulting from a 1-unit increase in income per capita, with the values of the other independent variables held constant. To interpret β_3, notice that there are just two possibilities for the dummy variable. For countries participating in a form of economic integration, x_{3i} takes the value 1, and Eq. (14.2.1) becomes

---

[1] T. V. Truong and D. N. Gash, "Less developed countries' taxable capacity and economic integration: A cross-sectional analysis," *Review of Economics and Statistics, 61* (1979), 312–16.

$$Y_i = \alpha + \beta_1 x_{1i} + \beta_2 x_{2i} + \beta_3 + \epsilon_i$$

Similarly, for the other countries, since x_{3i} takes the value 0, Eq. (14.2.1) may be written

$$Y_i = \alpha + \beta_1 x_{1i} + \beta_2 x_{2i} + \epsilon_i$$

Hence, we see that for fixed levels of exports and income per capita, β_3 is the difference between expected tax revenues (as a percentage of gross national product) in countries that participate in some form of economic integration and in those that do not.

Dummy Variables

Suppose it is believed that a dependent variable can be influenced by some factor that might be in one of two states, A or B. This factor is taken into account by adding to the regression a **dummy variable**—an independent variable defined to take the value 1 when this factor is in state A and 0 otherwise.

The partial regression coefficient on the dummy variable is the difference between the expected values of the dependent variable when the factor is in state A or B and all other variables are held constant.

Regression equations involving dummy variables can be estimated by least squares, exactly as in Chapter 13. When the model (14.2.1) was fitted to data on forty-three less developed countries, the estimated equation resulting was

$$y = 9.188 + .315x_1 + .00286x_2 - 3.664x_3 \qquad R^2 = .503$$

$$(1.646) \quad (.061) \quad (.00272) \quad (1.412)$$

Thus, taken together, the three independent variables explain 50.3% of the variability in the dependent variable for this sample of countries. Table 14.1 shows part of the computer output for the fitted regression relationship.

Based on the estimated equation, our point estimate is that for given levels of exports and income per capita, expected tax revenues as a percentage of gross national product are lower by 3.664 in countries that participate in some form of economic integration than in those that do not. This result is illustrated in Figure 14.2, which shows the estimated relation between tax revenues and exports for a given level of income per capita. There are two possible relations—one for countries participating in

TABLE 14.1 Part of output from SAS program for tax revenues example

		R-SQUARE .503	
PARAMETER	ESTIMATE	T FOR H0: PARAMETER = 0	STD. ERROR OF ESTIMATE
INTERCEPT	9.188	5.58	1.646
X1	.315	5.16	.061
X2	.00286	1.05	.00272
X3	−3.664	−2.60	1.412

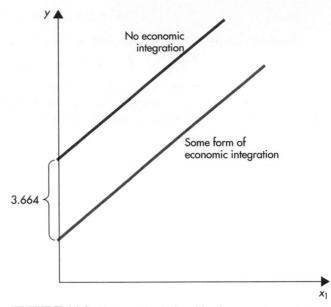

FIGURE 14.2 Estimated relationships between tax revenues as percentage of gross national product (y) and exports as percentage of gross national product (x_1) for a fixed level of income per capita

some form of integration and one for those that do not. These relationships are shown as two parallel lines, indicating that for each level of exports the expected tax revenues are higher by 3.664 in the latter group than in the former.

Confidence intervals for and tests of hypotheses about the model parameters can be obtained in the usual way when dummy variables are included in a regression model. Referring to the model (14.2.1), we will test the null hypothesis

$$H_0: \quad \beta_3 = 0$$

against the alternative

$$H_1: \quad \beta_3 < 0$$

using the data on forty-three less developed countries. The null hypothesis is that, all else being equal, expected tax revenues in countries that participate in some form of economic integration are the same as in those that do not. The alternative hypothesis is that expected tax revenues are lower in countries participating in some form of economic integration.

The test is based on the ratio of the estimated coefficient to its estimated standard error, that is

$$\frac{b_3}{s_{b_3}} = \frac{-3.664}{1.412} = -2.595$$

as can also be read directly from Table 14.1. Since there are forty-three observations and three independent variables, we have

$$n = 43 \qquad \text{and} \qquad K = 3$$

and the appropriate comparison is with the tabulated Student's t cut-off point, $-t_{n-K-1,\alpha}$. From Table 6 of the Appendix, we have

$$-t_{39,.01} \approx -2.423 \qquad \text{and} \qquad -t_{39,.005} \approx -2.704$$

Hence, the null hypothesis can be rejected at the 1% level but not at the .5% level of significance. The evidence in favor of the alternative, that tax revenues are higher in the absence of participation in a form of economic integration, is very strong.

So far, we have discussed qualitative variables with just two classes; for example, a country either participates in some form of economic integration or it does not. However, on occasion, qualitative variables with three or more classes may be thought to be relevant in explaining the behavior of a dependent variable. This situation can be handled by introducing several dummy variables, the number required being one less than the number of classes. Suppose that we again want to explain some measure of the economic performance of a developing country. We may believe that the geographic location of the country is relevant. A sample of developing countries might be separated into three classes:

1. Countries in Asia.
2. Countries in Africa.
3. Countries in Central or South America.

To allow for these three possibilities, two dummy variables are required:

$x_{1i} = 1$ if country is in class 1, 0 otherwise
$x_{2i} = 1$ if country is in class 2, 0 otherwise

These can be incorporated into the regression together with other relevant independent variables. Care is needed in interpreting the partial regression coefficients on such dummy variables. For example, the coefficient on x_{1i} in this example is the difference, all else being equal, in expectations of the dependent variable between countries in class 1 and those in class 3. (Notice that the comparison is always with the class for which no dummy variable has been directly introduced.)

14.3 LAGGED DEPENDENT VARIABLES

The subject matter of this section is relevant when time series data are analyzed—that is, when measurements on the quantities of interest are taken through time. We might, for instance, have annual, quarterly, or monthly observations. To make the point notationally transparent, we will index the observations by the subscript t, denoting time, rather than the subscript i that we have previously used. Thus, a regression model in which the value taken by the independent variable is influenced only by the values taken by K independent variables in the same time period will be written

$$Y_t = \alpha + \beta_1 x_{1t} + \beta_2 x_{2t} + \cdots + \beta_K x_{Kt} + \epsilon_t$$

In many applications involving time series data, an elaboration of this model is desirable. The value Y_t taken by the dependent variable in time period t is often related also to the value taken by this variable in the previous time period—that is, to Y_{t-1}. The value of a dependent variable in an earlier time period is called a **lagged dependent variable.**

Regressions Involving Lagged Dependent Variables

Consider the following regression model linking a dependent variable, Y, and K independent variables, $x_1, x_2, \ldots, x_K$:

$$Y_t = \alpha + \beta_1 x_{1t} + \beta_2 x_{2t} + \cdots + \beta_K x_{Kt} + \gamma Y_{t-1} + \epsilon_t$$

where $\alpha, \beta_1, \beta_2, \ldots, \beta_K, \gamma$ are fixed coefficients. If data are generated by this model:

(i) An increase of 1 unit in the independent variable x_j in time period t, with all other independent variables held fixed, leads to an expected increase in the dependent variable of β_j in period t, $\beta_j \gamma$ in period $(t + 1)$, $\beta_j \gamma^2$ in period $(t + 2)$, $\beta_j \gamma^3$ in period $(t + 3)$, and so on. The total expected increase over all current and future time periods is $\beta_j/(1 - \gamma)$.

(ii) The coefficients $\alpha, \beta_1, \beta_2, \ldots, \beta_K, \gamma$ can be estimated by least squares in the usual manner.

(iii) Confidence intervals and hypothesis tests for the regression coefficients are obtained precisely as for the ordinary multiple regression model. (Strictly speaking, when the regression equation contains lagged dependent variables, these procedures are only approximately valid. The quality of the approximation improves, all other things being equal, as the number of sample observations increases.)

To illustrate the calculation of regression estimates and inference based on the fitted regression equation when the model includes lagged dependent variables, we consider a model intended to explain local advertising expenditure per household.[2] Table 14.2 gives twenty-three annual observations on this quantity.

TABLE 14.2 Data on local advertising expenditures per household in the United States (in 1972 dollars)

YEAR	ADVERTISING	YEAR	ADVERTISING
0	115.80	12	132.27
1	117.66	13	134.69
2	115.62	14	138.62
3	110.79	15	136.15
4	119.22	16	144.17
5	120.78	17	154.03
6	110.20	18	161.39
7	110.86	19	157.72
8	114.06	20	145.37
9	120.87	21	152.73
10	127.03	22	155.70
11	132.08		

---

[2] From N. K. Dhalla, "Short-term forecasts of advertising expenditures," *Journal of Advertising Research, 19*, no. 1 (1979), 7–14.

It was believed that local advertising per household would depend on retail sales per household. (Data for this latter variable are given in Table 12.5.) Also, since advertisers may be unwilling or unable to adjust their plans to sudden changes in the level of retail sales, the value of local advertising expenditures per household in the previous year was added to the model. Thus, advertising expenditures in the current year are related to retail sales (x_t) in the current year and advertising expenditures (Y_{t-1}) in the previous year. The model to be fitted is, then

$$Y_t = \alpha + \beta x_t + \gamma Y_{t-1} + \epsilon_t$$

where

Y_t = Local advertising per household in year t
x_t = Retail sales per household in year t

In Table 14.3, the data are set out in the appropriate form for least squares estimation. The y_t are the observations on the dependent variable. For the purposes of carrying through the regression calculations, the lagged dependent variable, y_{t-1}, is treated simply as a second independent variable. Thus, the regression is computed as the regression of the dependent variable y_t on the pair of "independent variables," y_{t-1} and x_t.

In this event, the estimated regression obtained is

$$y_t = -41.87 + .0185 x_t + .480 y_{t-1} \qquad (14.3.1)$$
$$(.0028) \quad (.086)$$

where, as usual, the figures in parentheses beneath the coefficient estimates are the corresponding estimated standard errors.

Part of the SAS computer output for the estimated regression is shown in Table 14.4. Notice that in presenting the regression results, we have not given the value of the coefficient of determination, R^2. Although this coefficient is frequently reported in practice, its interpretation is problematic and can lead to misleading conclusions. For

TABLE 14.3 Data on local advertising expenditures per household (y_t) and retail sales per household (x_t)

YEAR	y_t	y_{t-1}	x_t	YEAR	y_t	y_{t-1}	x_t
1	117.66	115.80	5,492	12	132.27	132.08	5,907
2	115.62	117.66	5,540	13	134.69	132.27	6,124
3	110.79	115.62	5,305	14	138.62	134.69	6,186
4	119.22	110.79	5,507	15	136.15	138.62	6,224
5	120.78	119.22	5,418	16	144.17	136.15	6,496
6	110.20	120.78	5,320	17	154.03	144.17	6,718
7	110.86	110.20	5,538	18	161.39	154.03	6,921
8	114.06	110.86	5,692	19	157.72	161.39	6,471
9	120.87	114.06	5,871	20	145.37	157.72	6,394
10	127.03	120.87	6,157	21	152.73	145.37	6,555
11	132.08	127.03	6,342	22	155.70	152.73	6,755

TABLE 14.4 Part of output from SAS program for local advertising expenditures example

PARAMETER	ESTIMATE	T FOR H0: PARAMETER = 0	STD. ERROR OF ESTIMATE
INTERCEPT	−41.87		
X1	.0185	6.61	.0028
X2	.480	5.58	.086

example, a high value for R^2 in the present context would *not* necessarily indicate a strong relationship between local advertising and retail sales. Rather, it is a well-known empirical fact that the time plots of many business and economic time series exhibit a rather smooth evolutionary pattern through time. This fact alone is enough to ensure a high value for the coefficient of determination when a lagged dependent variable is included in the regression model. As a practical matter, the reader is advised to pay relatively little attention to the value of R^2 for such models.

The estimated regression equation (14.3.1) can be interpreted as follows. Suppose that retail sales per household increase by \$1 in the current year. The expected impact on local advertising per household is an increase of \$.0185 in the current year, a further increase of

$$(.480)(.0185) = \$.0089$$

next year, a further increase of

$$(.480)^2(.0185) = \$.0043$$

in 2 years, and so on. The total effect on all future advertising expenditure per household is an expected increase of

$$\frac{.0185}{1 - .480} = \$.0356$$

Thus, we see that the expected effect of an increase in sales is an immediate increase in advertising expenditure, a further smaller increase in the following year, a yet smaller increase 2 years ahead, and so on. This is illustrated in Figure 14.3, from which we see that as time goes on, the effect of an increase in sales in the current year on advertising in distant future years becomes negligible.

As we have already mentioned, no new principles are involved in finding confidence intervals for or testing hypotheses about the partial regression coefficients. To illustrate, we will find a 95% confidence interval for the coefficient β on x_t—that is, the expected increase in the same year in local advertising expenditure per household resulting from a 1-unit increase in retail sales per household. From Eq. (14.3.1), we have

$$b = .0185 \quad \text{and} \quad s_b = .0028$$

Since there are $n = 22$ observations and $K = 2$ "independent variables" (including the lagged dependent variable), we have from the tabulated Student's t distribution, for a 95% interval

$$t_{n-K-1,\alpha/2} = t_{19,.025} = 2.093$$

Therefore, the 95% confidence interval for β is

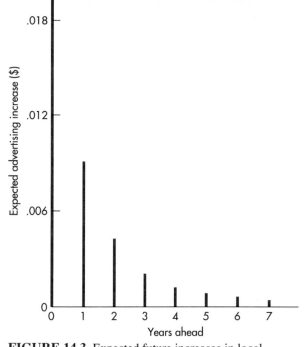

FIGURE 14.3 Expected future increases in local advertising per household

$$b - t_{n-K-1,\alpha/2}s_b < \beta < b + t_{n-K-1,\alpha/2}s_b$$

that is

$$.0185 - (2.093)(.0028) < \beta < .0185 + (2.093)(.0028)$$

or

$$.0126 < \beta < .0244$$

Thus, if retail sales per household increase by $1 in the current year, the 95% confidence interval for the expected increase in local advertising expenditures per household this year runs from $.0126 to $.0244.

Finally, we test the null hypothesis that the coefficient, γ, on the lagged dependent variable is 0. The null hypothesis

$$H_0: \quad \gamma = 0$$

implies that any increase in sales would affect advertising expenditures in the current year only, not also in future years. We will test against the alternative

$$H_1: \quad \gamma > 0$$

The test is based on the least squares estimate, c, of γ and the corresponding estimated standard error s_c. Here we have, from the estimated regression (14.3.1)

$$c = .480 \qquad \text{and} \qquad s_c = .086$$

As usual, the test statistic is the ratio of the coefficient estimate to its standard error; that is

$$\frac{c}{s_c} = \frac{.480}{.086} = 5.581$$

as can be read directly from the printout in Table 14.4. From the tabulated Student's t distribution, we find

$$t_{19,.005} = 2.861$$

Hence, the null hypothesis is very clearly rejected, even at the .5% significance level. This implies quite strongly the desirability of including the lagged dependent variable in this regression model if the only other independent variable to be used is the current level of retail sales per household.

EXERCISES

1. The following model was fitted to eight annual sets of observations from 1972 to 1979, in an attempt to explain Organization of Petroleum Exporting Countries (OPEC) pricing behavior.[3]

$$y = .37x_1 + 5.22x_2$$

$$(.029) \quad (.50)$$

where

y = Difference between OPEC price in the current year and OPEC price in the previous year, in dollars per barrel
x_1 = Difference between spot price in the current year and OPEC price in the previous year
x_2 = Dummy variable taking the value 1 in 1974 and 0 otherwise, to represent the specific effect of the oil embargo of that year

Interpret verbally and graphically the estimated coefficient on the dummy variable.

2. The following model was fitted, to explain the selling prices of houses, to a sample of 815 sales.[4]

$$y = -1264 + 48.18x_1 + 3382x_2 - 1859x_3 + 3219x_4 + 2005x_5 \qquad \overline{R}^2 = .86$$

$$(0.91) \quad (515) \quad (488) \quad (947) \quad (768)$$

where

y = Selling price of house, in dollars
x_1 = Square footage of living area
x_2 = Size of garage, in number of cars

---

[3] W. D. Nordhaus, "Oil and economic performance in industrial countries," *Brookings Papers on Economic Activity* (1980), 341–88.

[4] B. A. Newsome, "Adjusting comparable sales for vinyl siding," *The Appraisal Journal, 59* (1991), 92–5.

x_3 = Age of house, in years

x_4 = Dummy variable taking the value 1 if the house has a fireplace, and 0 otherwise

x_5 = Dummy variable taking the value 1 if the house has brick siding and 0 if it has vinyl siding

(a) Interpret the estimated coefficient on x_4.

(b) Interpret the estimated coefficient on x_5.

(c) Find a 95% confidence interval for the impact of a fireplace on selling price, all other things equal.

(d) Test the null hypothesis that type of siding has no impact on selling price, against the alternative that, all other things equal, houses with brick siding have a higher selling price than houses with vinyl siding.

3. The following model was fitted to data on thirty-two large bank holding companies.[5]

$$y = 7.62 - .016x_1 + 1.23x_2 \qquad R^2 = .37$$

$$(.008) \qquad (.496)$$

where

y = Price-earnings ratio

x_1 = Size of total bank assets, in billions of dollars

x_2 = Dummy variable, taking the value 1 for regional banks, and 0 for money center banks

(a) Interpret the estimated coefficient on the dummy variable.

(b) Test against a two-sided alternative the null hypothesis that the true coefficient on the dummy variable is 0.

(c) Test at the 5% significance level the null hypothesis $\beta_1 = \beta_2 = 0$, and interpret your result.

4. A law school dean wanted to assess the importance of factors that might help in predicting success in law school. For a random sample of fifty students, data were obtained when they graduated from law school, and the following model was fitted:

$$Y_i = \alpha + \beta_1 x_{1i} + \beta_2 x_{2i} + \beta_3 x_{3i} + \epsilon_i$$

where

Y_i = Score reflecting overall performance while in law school

x_{1i} = Undergraduate grade point average

x_{2i} = Score on Law School Admission Test

x_{3i} = Dummy variable taking the value 1 if the student's letters of recommendation are unusually strong and 0 otherwise

Use the portion of the computer output from the estimated regression shown here to write a report summarizing the findings of this study.

---

[5] W. B. Harrison and D. R. Wood, "The development of a bank classification scheme through discriminant analysis," *Atlantic Economic Journal, 17*, no. 1 (1989), 35–46.

SOURCE	DF	SUM OF SQUARES	MEAN SQUARE	F VALUE	R-SQUARE
MODEL	3	641.04	213.68	8.48	.356
ERROR	46	1159.66	25.21		
CORRECTED TOTAL	49	1800.70			

PARAMETER	ESTIMATE	T FOR H0: PARAMETER = 0	STD. ERROR OF ESTIMATE
INTERCEPT	6.512		
X1	3.502	1.45	2.419
X2	.491	4.59	.107
X3	10.327	2.45	4.213

5. The following model was fitted to data on fifty states.[6]

$$y = 13{,}472 + 547x_1 + 5.48x_2 + 493x_3 + 32.7x_4 + 5{,}793x_5 - 3{,}100x_6 \qquad R^2 = .54$$

$$(124.3) \quad (1.858) \quad (208.9) \quad (234) \quad (2{,}897) \quad (1{,}761)$$

where

y = Annual salary of the chief justice of the state supreme court
x_1 = Average annual salary of lawyers, in thousands of dollars
x_2 = Number of bills enacted in previous legislative session
x_3 = Number of due process reviews by state courts that resulted in overturn of legislation in previous forty years
x_4 = Length of term of the chief justice of the state supreme court
x_5 = Dummy variable, taking value 1 if justices of the state supreme court can be removed from office by the governor, judicial review board, or majority vote of the supreme court, and 0 otherwise
x_6 = Dummy variable, taking value 1 if supreme court justices are elected on partisan ballots, and 0 otherwise

(a) Interpret the estimated coefficient on the dummy variable x_5.
(b) Interpret the estimated coefficient on the dummy variable x_6.
(c) Test at the 5% level the null hypothesis that the true coefficient on the dummy variable x_5 is 0, against the alternative that it is positive.
(d) Test at the 5% level the null hypothesis that the true coefficient on the dummy variable x_6 is 0, against the alternative that it is negative.
(e) Find and interpret a 95% confidence interval for the parameter β_1.

6. [*This problem requires a computer program to carry out the multiple regression computations.*] In a student survey of twenty-seven undergraduates at the University of Illinois, the accompanying results were obtained on grade point average (y), number of hours per week spent on studying (x_1), average number of hours spent preparing for tests (x_2), number of hours per week spent in bars (x_3), whether students take notes or mark highlights when reading texts ($x_4 = 1$ if yes, 0 if no), and average number of credit hours taken per semester (x_5). Estimate the regression of grade point average on the five independent variables, and write a report on your findings.

---

[6] G. M. Anderson, W. F. Shughart, and R. D. Tollison, "On the incentives of judges to enforce legislative wealth transfers," *Journal of Law and Economics*, 32 (1989), 215–28.

y	x_1	x_2	x_3	x_4	x_5
4.8	25	5	6	1	16
4.3	22	2	1	1	15
3.8	9	3	4	0	15
3.8	15	2	8	1	17
4.2	15	3	4	0	15
4.3	30	5	3	1	13
3.8	20	6	7	1	17
4.3	10	3	5	1	19
4.0	30	2	6	1	19
3.8	20	6	6	0	15
3.1	10	4	7	0	16
3.9	18	3	5	1	15
3.2	10	3	4	0	16
4.9	18	3	4	0	17
4.4	12	2	4	1	16
4.5	12	1	4	0	17
4.6	10	10	3	1	17
4.0	28	1	4	0	15
3.7	15	4	6	1	14
3.5	12	2	7	0	17
2.8	28	4	6	1	15
4.3	10	8	5	1	15
5.0	25	4	5	1	19
3.0	25	1	4	1	16
4.1	30	3	6	1	18
4.1	25	3	7	1	17
4.6	25	4	7	1	15

7. A consulting group offers courses in financial management for executives. At the end of these courses, participants are asked to provide overall ratings of the value of the course. For a sample of twenty-five courses, the following regression was estimated by least squares.

$$y = 42.97 + .38x_1 + .52x_2 + .08x_3 + 6.21x_4 \qquad R^2 = .569$$

$$(.29) \quad (.21) \quad (.11) \quad (3.59)$$

where

   $y =$ Average rating by participants of the course
   $x_1 =$ Percentage of course time spent in group discussion sessions
   $x_2 =$ Money, in dollars, per course member spent on preparing course material
   $x_3 =$ Money, in dollars, per course member spent on food and drinks
   $x_4 =$ Dummy variable, taking the value 1 if a visiting guest lecturer is brought in, and 0 otherwise

(a) Interpret the estimated coefficient on x_4.
(b) Test against the alternative that it is positive the null hypothesis that the true coefficient on x_4 is 0.
(c) Interpret the coefficient of determination, and use it to test the null hypothesis that, taken as a group, the four independent variables do not linearly influence the dependent variable.
(d) Find and interpret a 95% confidence interval for β_2.

8. A regression model was estimated to compare performances of students taking a micro-economics principles course—either as a standard fourteen-week course, or as an intensive three-week-course. The following model was estimated from observations on 350 students.[7]

$$y = -.7052 + 1.4170\, x_1 + 2.1624 x_2 + .8680 x_3 + 1.0845 x_4$$

$$(0.4568) \quad (0.3287) \quad (.4393) \quad (0.3766)$$

$$+ .4694 x_5 + .0038 x_6 + .0484 x_7 \qquad R^2 = .344$$

$$(.0628) \quad (.0094) \quad (.0776)$$

where

$y =$ Score on a standardized test of understanding of college economics after taking the course

$x_1 =$ Dummy variable taking the value 1 if the three-week course was taken, and 0 if the fourteen-week course was taken

$x_2 =$ Student's grade point average

$x_3 =$ Dummy variable taking the value 0 or 1, depending on which of two teachers had taught the course

$x_4 =$ Dummy variable taking the value 1 if the student is male, and 0 if female

$x_5 =$ Score on a standardized test of understanding of college economics before taking the course

$x_6 =$ Number of semester credit hours the student had completed

$x_7 =$ Age of student

Write a report discussing what can be learned from this fitted regression.

9. A market researcher is interested in the average amount of money per year spent by college students on clothing. From 25 years of annual data the following estimated regression was obtained through least squares.

$$y_t = 50.72 + .142 x_{1t} + .027 x_{2t} + .432 y_{t-1}$$

$$(.047) \quad (.021) \quad (.136)$$

where

$y =$ Expenditure per student, in dollars, on clothes

$x_1 =$ Disposable income per student, in dollars, after the payment of tuition, fees, room and board

$x_2 =$ Index of advertising, aimed at the student market, on clothes

(a) Test at the 5% level, against the obvious one-sided alternative, the null hypothesis that, all else being equal, advertising does not affect expenditures on clothes in this market.

(b) Find a 95% confidence interval for the coefficient on x_1 in the population regression.

(c) With advertising held fixed, what would be the expected impact over time of a $1 increase in disposable income per student on clothing expenditure?

10. [*This problem requires either the material in Appendix A13.1 or a computer program to carry out the multiple regression computations.*] In Chapter 12, using the data of Table 12.5, we estimated the regression model

---

[7] L. J. Van Scyoc and J. Gleason, "Traditional or intensive course lengths? A comparison of outcomes in economics learning," *Journal of Economic Education*, *24* (1993), 15–22.

$$Y_t = \alpha + \beta x_t + \epsilon_t$$

where

Y_t = Retail sales per household
x_t = Disposable income per household

Use these same data to estimate the regression model

$$Y_t = \alpha + \beta x_t + \gamma Y_{t-1} + \epsilon_t$$

and test the null hypothesis that $\gamma = 0$.

11. [*This problem requires a computer program to carry out the multiple regression computations.*] The table shows twenty-eight quarterly observations from the United Kingdom[8] on the quantity of money in million pounds (y), income in million pounds (x_1), and the local authority interest rate (x_2). Estimate the model

$$Y_t = \alpha + \beta_1 x_{1t} + \beta_2 x_{2t} + \gamma Y_{t-1} + \epsilon_t$$

and write a report on your findings.

y	x_1	x_2	y	x_1	x_2
17,602.5	14,744	.0805	17,965.1	15,950	.0582
17,746.9	14,516	.0828	18,651.9	15,957	.0482
17,769.0	14,815	.0781	19,352.7	16,031	.0480
17,909.1	14,900	.0738	20,446.1	16,295	.0513
17,855.0	14,829	.0798	20,835.3	16,151	.0762
17,470.8	14,900	.0914	21,827.4	16,803	.0791
17,352.0	14,980	.0957	22,375.2	17,528	.1009
17,481.6	15,085	.0922	23,217.0	17,301	.0919
17,240.2	14,973	.0910	24,011.6	17,503	.1173
17,467.2	15,359	.0813	24,975.2	17,455	.1411
17,619.7	15,362	.0754	24,736.3	16,620	.1566
17,683.8	15,540	.0718	23,407.3	17,779	.1333
17,954.1	15,404	.0753	23,560.7	18,040	.1313
17,734.9	15,649	.0666	23,421.2	17,827	.1263

12. [*This problem requires a computer program to carry out the multiple regression computations.*] The accompanying table shows data,[9] collected over a period of 25 years, on the market return (x) of the Standard and Poor's 500 stocks and the percentage (y) of portfolios in common stocks at market value at the end of the year for noninsurance private pension funds. Estimate the regression model

$$Y_t = \alpha + \beta x_t + \gamma Y_{t-1} + \epsilon_t$$

and write a report on your findings.

---

[8] T. C. Mills, "The functional form of the UK demand for money," *Applied Statistics*, 27 (1978), 52–57.
[9] From W. S. Bauman and C. M. McLaren, "An asset allocation model for active portfolios," *Journal of Portfolio Management*, 8, no. 2 (1982), 76–86.

YEAR	y	x	YEAR	y	x	YEAR	y	x
1	30	31.6	10	52	16.5	18	73	19.0
2	32	6.6	11	55	12.5	19	68	−14.7
3	30	−10.8	12	53	−10.1	20	56	−26.5
4	38	43.4	13	59	24.0	21	60	37.2
5	43	12.0	14	63	11.1	22	62	23.8
6	43	.5	15	63	−8.5	23	56	−7.2
7	49	26.9	16	62	4.0	24	53	6.6
8	45	−8.7	17	68	14.3	25	55	18.7
9	49	22.8						

13. [*This problem requires a computer program to carry out the multiple regression computations.*] The accompanying table[10] shows twenty quarterly observations on income (y) and money supply (x) in Canada. Estimate the model

$$Y_t = \alpha + \beta x_t + \gamma Y_{t-1} + \epsilon_t$$

and write a report on your findings.

y	x	y	x	y	x
116,652	42,011	153,560	56,512	191,592	74,544
120,392	43,313	157,328	59,243	195,600	77,300
124,572	44,808	161,740	60,783	201,204	80,021
132,624	47,324	168,732	63,738	204,160	83,482
139,656	50,094	173,980	66,338	210,780	85,868
145,320	52,117	182,744	68,694	214,712	87,911
150,164	54,253	190,172	72,238		

14. [*This problem requires a computer program to carry out the multiple regression computations.*] The accompanying table shows twenty annual observations[11] on the first confinement resulting in a live birth of the current marriage (y) and the number of first marriages (for females) in the previous year (x) in Australia. Estimate the model

$$Y_t = \alpha + \beta x_t + \gamma Y_{t-1} + \epsilon_t$$

and write a report on your findings.

---

[10] Data from C. Hsiao, "Autoregressive modeling of Canadian money and income data," *Journal of the American Statistical Association*, 74 (1979), 553–60.

[11] Data from J. McDonald, "Modeling demographic relationships: An analysis of forecast functions for Australian births," *Journal of the American Statistical Association*, 76 (1981), 782–92.

y	x	y	x	y	x
65,792	63,488	68,581	72,833	95,418	105,235
65,431	65,471	70,197	77,670	91,683	106,337
66,717	65,956	73,462	84,850	85,707	102,106
66,890	65,902	76,127	87,110	86,248	99,950
70,177	67,077	81,341	90,608	81,543	98,031
68,310	68,609	85,650	96,553	78,086	90,010
69,130	70,849	88,412	102,186		

14.4 NONLINEAR MODELS

In our discussion of regression modeling so far, we have assumed that the relationship between a dependent variable and a set of independent variables is *linear*. The assumption of linearity frequently provides a useful and easily analyzed approximation of a far more complex reality, at least within relevant ranges of the independent variables. However, on many occasions, it is both necessary and desirable to abandon the linearity assumption. Often, subject matter theory, data, or both will suggest that the appropriate formulation is *nonlinear*. The difficulty lies in the fact that once our horizons are expanded in this way, an infinity of nonlinear functional forms is possible. Moreover, in business and economic applications, only very rarely does subject matter theory postulate a specific credible functional form. Nevertheless, nonlinear models are built on occasion, and frequently this can be achieved through only minor modifications of the techniques we have discussed so far.

To illustrate, consider the case of a dependent variable, Y, and a single independent variable, X_1. The linear regression model of Chapter 12 is

$$Y_i = \alpha + \beta x_{1i} + \epsilon_i$$

One possible alternative to this model is to postulate **quadratic** dependence—that is, the dependence of Y on both X and X^2. The model then is

$$Y_i = \alpha + \beta_1 x_{1i} + \beta_2 x_{1i}^2 + \epsilon_i \qquad (14.4.1)$$

But this is simply a multiple regression equation involving three unknown coefficients, α, β_1, and β_2. These can be estimated by least squares, using precisely the procedures described in Chapter 13. The model is simply treated as one relating the dependent variable to a pair of "independent variables," x_{1i} and x_{1i}^2. To make the point transparent, we can write Eq. (14.4.1) as

$$Y_i = \alpha + \beta_1 x_{1i} + \beta_2 x_{2i} + \epsilon_i$$

where

$$x_{2i} = x_{1i}^2$$

Confidence intervals and hypothesis tests for the parameters β_1 and β_2 of the model (14.4.1) are obtained in the usual way. In particular, the desirability of employing the quadratic rather than the linear form can be checked by testing the null hypothesis that $\beta_2 = 0$. If that hypothesis were indeed correct, (14.4.1) would simplify to the linear model.

A more common alternative to the linear model in business and economic applications is the **log linear model.** In this formulation, a linear relationship is postulated not between the variables themselves but between their *logarithms*. With just a single independent variable, this model is written

$$\log Y_i = \alpha + \beta \log x_i + \epsilon_i$$

Such models are easily estimated by least squares and analyzed through the methods described in Chapter 12. All that is necessary is to take logarithms of the observations on the dependent and independent variables first and proceed with these quantities through the remainder of the analysis.

The log linear model depicts a curvilinear relationship between the values of the dependent and independent variables, as illustrated in Figure 14.4. Part (a) of this figure shows the case where an increase in the independent variable leads to an expected increase in the dependent variable, while part (b) shows an increase in the former leading to an expected decrease in the latter. One way to recognize the possibility that a log linear specification might be appropriate is to graph the data and check whether one of the curvilinear forms of Figure 14.4 seems, from a visual perspective, to provide a better representation of the relationship than a linear form.

The log linear model can be extended to the case of several independent variables. As we note in the box, interpretation of the model parameters is somewhat different in this model than in the multiple regression model of Chapter 13.

The Log Linear Model

Suppose that a dependent variable Y is related to K independent variables, $X_1, X_2, \ldots, X_K$. If the independent variables take the specific values $x_{1i}, x_{2i}, \ldots, x_{Ki}$, the population **log linear model** is of the form

$$\log Y_i = \alpha + \beta_1 \log x_{1i} + \beta_2 \log x_{2i} + \cdots + \beta_K \log x_{Ki} + \epsilon_i$$

where $\alpha, \beta_1, \beta_2, \ldots, \beta_K$ are constants and ϵ_i is a random variable with mean 0.

The coefficient β_j is the expected *percentage* increase in the dependent variable, resulting from a *1%* increase in the independent variable X_j, when the values of all the other independent variables are held fixed.

The interpretation of the coefficients of the log linear model points up a feature that makes this formulation attractive in some applications. If, whatever its value, a 1% increase in the value of an independent variable is expected to lead to a fixed *percentage* increase in the dependent variable, the log linear model is likely to be the preferred functional form.

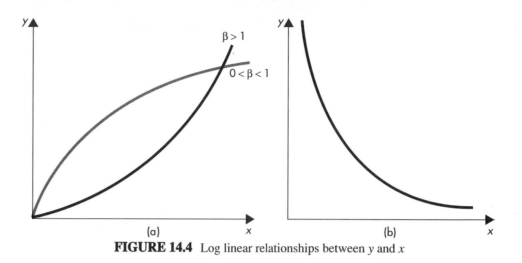

FIGURE 14.4 Log linear relationships between y and x

EXAMPLE 14.1

In a study of credit unions,[12] the following regression was fitted to eighty-seven quarterly observations:

$$\log y = .47 + .31 \log x_1 + .47 \log x_2 \qquad \overline{R}^2 = .86$$

$$(.13) \qquad (.21)$$

where

$y = $ Output of loans
$x_1 = $ Expenditure on capital equipment
$x_2 = $ Salaries and wages paid to employees

The figures in parentheses under the least squares parameter estimates are the corresponding estimated standard errors.

The reported estimates of the partial regression coefficients have the following interpretations:

(i) For a fixed salaries and wages bill, a 1% increase in capital equipment expenditure leads to an expected .31% increase in loan output.

(ii) For a fixed capital expenditure, a 1% increase in the salaries and wages bill leads to an expected .47% increase in loan output.

Confidence intervals for the regression coefficients can be obtained in the usual way. To illustrate, we find a 95% confidence interval for β_1. This interval takes the form

$$b_1 - t_{n - K - 1, .025} s_{b_1} < \beta_1 < b_1 + t_{n - K - 1, .025} s_{b_1}$$

where

---

[12] From Y. L. Mahajan, "A macroeconometric model of the credit unions," *Atlantic Economic Journal*, *9*, no. 2 (1981), 40–48.

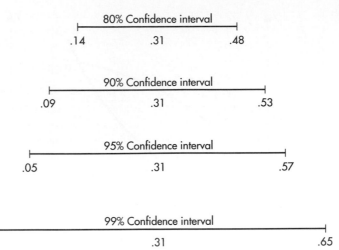

FIGURE 14.5 80%, 90%, 95%, and 99% confidence intervals for expected percentage increase in loan output of credit unions resulting from a 1% increase in capital expenditure with a fixed salaries and wages bill

$$n = 87 \qquad K = 2 \qquad b_1 = .31 \qquad s_{b_1} = .13$$

From Table 6 of the Appendix, we find, on interpolation

$$t_{84,.025} \approx 1.99$$

Our confidence interval is then

$$.31 - (1.99)(.13) < \beta_1 < .31 + (1.99)(.13)$$

or

$$.05 < \beta_1 < .57$$

Thus, the 95% confidence interval for the expected percentage increase in loan output following from a 1% increase in capital expenditure, with salaries and wages bill remaining fixed, runs from .05% to .57%. Figure 14.5 shows also 80%, 90%, and 99% confidence intervals.

14.5 SPECIFICATION BIAS

The specification of a statistical model that adequately depicts real-world behavior is a delicate and difficult task. Certainly no simple model can describe perfectly the precise nature of the actual determinants of a quantity of interest. The objective of model building is to attempt to discover a straightforward formulation that is not too drastically at variance with the complex underlying reality. While simplicity of model form is certainly an advantage, substantial divergence of the model from actuality can result in seriously erroneous conclusions about the behavior of the system under study.

One important aspect of model formulation, briefly discussed in Section 14.4, is the appropriate specification of the functional form linking the dependent and independent variables. If the assumed form differs substantially from the true form, any conclusions drawn from the estimated model will be of dubious value. Another important part of model specification concerns the assumptions made about the statistical properties of the error terms in a regression equation. In our analyses so far, we have assumed that these errors all have the same variance and are uncorrelated with one another. If these assumptions are in fact true, we have seen that the least squares method and the inferential procedures flowing from it provide a convenient procedure for learning about the process under study. However, if these assumptions are seriously violated, this is no longer necessarily the case. This aspect of model specification will be considered in greater detail in Sections 14.7 and 14.8.

In the present section, we will discuss one specific form of model misspecification and highlight its potential consequences. In formulating a regression model, an investigator attempts to relate the dependent variable of interest to all its *important* determinants. Thus, if the linear model is adopted as the appropriate form, one wants to include among the independent variables all quantities that might markedly influence the dependent variable of interest. In formulating the regression model

$$Y_i = \alpha + \beta_1 x_{1i} + \beta_2 x_{2i} + \cdots + \beta_K x_{Ki} + \epsilon_i$$

it is implicitly assumed that the set of independent variables, $X_1, X_2, \ldots, X_K$, contains *all* quantities that significantly affect the behavior of the dependent variable, Y. Certainly, in any practical problem, there will be other factors that also affect the dependent variable. The joint influence of these factors is absorbed within the error term, ϵ_i. It is, however, potentially of very great importance that no important explanatory variable be omitted from the list of independent variables.

Except in the very special (and rare) case where omitted variables are uncorrelated with the independent variables included in the regression model, very serious consequences can follow from this type of misspecification. In particular, the least squares estimates will generally be biased, and the usual inferential statements derived from confidence intervals or tests of hypotheses can be seriously misleading.

To illustrate this particular type of specification bias, we will consider further an example used in Chapter 13. Table 13.1 gives 25 years of annual data on the percentage profit margin (y) of savings and loan associations, their percentage net revenues per deposit dollar (x_1), and the number of offices (x_2). In Sections 13.2 and 13.6 we found the estimated regression equation linking profits to revenues and number of offices to be

$$y = 1.565 + .237x_1 - .000249x_2 \qquad R^2 = .87 \qquad (14.5.1)$$
$$(.079) \quad (.0555) \quad (.0000320)$$

One conclusion that follows from this analysis is that for a fixed number of offices, a 1-unit increase in net revenues per deposit dollar leads to an expected *increase* of .237 unit in profit margin.

Now, suppose that our only interest is in the effect of net revenues on profit margins. One approach to this problem might be to estimate the regression of profit margin on net revenue, using these twenty-five pairs of observations. Such an analysis, in fact, yields the fitted model

$$y = 1.326 - .169x_1 \qquad R^2 = .50 \qquad\qquad (14.5.2)$$
$$(.139) \quad (.036)$$

Comparing the fitted models (14.5.1) and (14.5.2), we immediately notice that one consequence of ignoring the number of offices in the analysis is a substantial reduction in R^2, the proportion of the variability in the dependent variable explained by the regression.

There is, however, a more serious consequence. The fitted model (14.5.2) implies that an increase of 1 unit in percentage net revenues per deposit dollar leads to an expected *decrease* of .169 unit in the percentage profit margin. Moreover, comparing the coefficient estimate with its estimated standard error, we see that the null hypothesis of no linear relation between these variables is comfortably rejected against the alternative that an increase in net revenues leads to an expected *decrease* in profit margins. But such a conclusion is surely counterintuitive! While it is not completely beyond the realm of possibility, we would certainly expect, all else being equal, to find high net revenues associated with high profit margins. But over the 25-year period for which the model (14.5.2) was estimated, all else was *not* equal. In particular, another potentially important variable—the number of savings and loan offices— changed markedly over this period. When this relevant variable is incorporated into the regression analysis, in (14.5.1), an opposite conclusion is reached. It now emerges, as we might have predicted, that the association between profits and net revenues is positive, once the influence of the number of offices is taken into account.

This example rather nicely illustrates the point. If an important explanatory variable is not included in the regression model, any conclusions drawn about the effects of other independent variables can be seriously misleading. In this particular case, we have seen that adding a relevant variable could well alter the impression of a significant negative association to the conclusion of significant positive association. Further insight can be gained from casual inspection of the data in Table 13.1. Over the latter part of the period, at least, profit margins fell and net revenues rose, suggesting a negative association between these variables. However, a further look at the data reveals an increase in the number of offices over this same period, suggesting the possibility that this factor could be the cause of the declining profit margins. The only legitimate way to disentangle the separate effects of the two independent variables on the dependent variable is to model them jointly in a regression equation. This example illustrates the importance of using the multiple regression model rather than simple linear regression equations when there is more than one relevant independent variable.

14.6 MULTICOLLINEARITY

If a regression model is correctly specified, the least squares estimates are, in the sense of the Gauss-Markov theorem, the best that can be achieved. Nevertheless, in some circumstances, they may not be very good!

To illustrate, consider again the savings and loan association example of Chapter 13. In this particular study, we observed twenty-five pairs of annual values of net revenues per deposit dollar and the number of savings and loan offices, together with the corresponding profit margins. These data were then used to estimate, through a multiple regression model, the separate effects of the two independent variables on profit margins. Imagine, now, that you wanted to study this problem but were in the fortunate position of the laboratory scientist, able to *design the experiment*. That is, rather than taking what nature happened to give, suppose that you were free to choose twenty-five pairs of values for the independent variables and to observe the effects of your choices on profit margins. The best possible choice depends somewhat on the objectives of the analysis and involves the interesting statistical topic of **design of experiments.** Since in business and economic applications we are rarely in the position of being able to select a design, we will not pursue this question further. It is, however, instructive to ask what the *worst* choices you could possibly make are.

If you could choose pairs of values for net revenues (x_1) and number of offices (x_2), what would be the silliest choices you could make? One obvious answer is to select the same pair of values each time for the independent variables. Clearly, if all twenty-five experiments were run with net revenues set at 3.0 and the number of offices at 7,000, we could not learn anything about the influence of these factors on profit margins. Only by varying the independent variables is it possible to learn about their effect on the dependent variable.

The following choice is almost equally absurd:

x_{1i}	3.0	3.1	3.2	3.3	3.4	3.5
x_{2i}	8,000	7,900	7,800	7,700	7,600	7,500

and so on. The values of the independent variables are now changed from one experimental run to the next, but they are changed in unison. Indeed, these values can be represented as points on a (downward-sloping) straight line, as in Figure 14.6(a). [An essentially similar situation arises if the data points lie on an upward-sloping straight line, as in part (b) of the figure.] Thus, in the particular design given in the table, whenever x_1 is increased, x_2 is decreased by a proportionate amount. To see the futility of such a choice, suppose that you observe that an increase in net revenues, together with the associated decrease in number of offices, leads to an increase in profit margins. To what would you attribute this rise in profit margin? Was it in fact caused by revenue growth, by the decrease in the number of offices, or by some combination of the two? The short answer is that it is impossible to tell! If we want to assess the separate effects of the independent variables, it is essential that they not move in unison through the experiment.

In fact, in the extreme case of the example just given, if we attempted to estimate the coefficients β_1 and β_2 of the regression

$$Y_i = \alpha + \beta_1 x_{1i} + \beta_2 x_{2i} + \epsilon_i \qquad (14.6.1)$$

by least squares, we would find it impossible to do so. This is because β_1 and β_2 are measures of the *separate* effects of the independent variables, and the data cannot

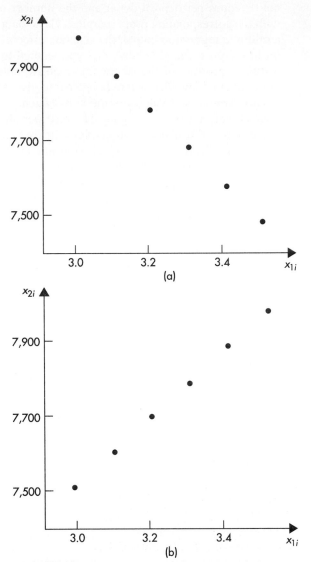

FIGURE 14.6 Two designs with perfect multicollinearity

possibly contain any useful information about these quantities. The fifth of the standard assumptions for a multiple regression analysis, set out in Section 13.3, is designed to exclude cases of this sort.

This, then, is clearly a very bad choice of design. A slightly less extreme case is illustrated in Figure 14.7. Here, the design points do not lie on single straight lines but are very close to doing so. In this situation, the experimental results are able to provide *some* information about the separate influences of the independent variables, but not very much. It will now be possible to calculate least squares point estimates of β_1 and β_2 in (14.6.1), but these will be very imprecise. This imprecision will be reflected in very large standard errors for the estimated coefficients, suggesting statistical in-

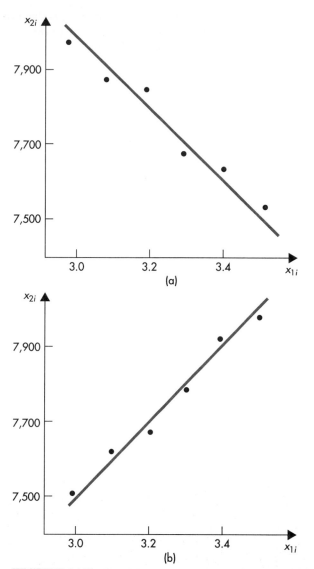

FIGURE 14.7 Illustrations of designs with multicollinearity

significance even when the relationships involved are quite strong. This phenomenon is referred to as **multicollinearity.**

In the vast majority of practical cases involving business and economic applications, we are not able to design the experiments. Rather, we are constrained to work with the particular experimental design that fate has given us. In this context, then, multicollinearity is a problem arising not from our own bad choice of design but from the one with which we must work. More generally, in regression equations involving several independent variables, the multicollinearity problem arises from patterns of strong intercorrelations among the independent variables—the case, in fact, where assumption 5 of Section 13.3 is close to being violated. Perhaps the most frustrating aspect of the problem, which can be summarized as having data that are not very informative about the parameters of interest, is that typically little can be done about it.[13] It is, however, still important to be aware of the problem and to watch for its occurrence. A clear indication of the likely presence of multicollinearity occurs when, taken as a group, a set of independent variables appears to exert considerable influence on the dependent variable, but when looked at separately, through tests of hypotheses, all appear individually to be insignificant. It would certainly be unwise in these circumstances to jump to the conclusion that a particular independent variable did not affect the dependent variable. Rather, it is preferable to acknowledge that the group as a whole is clearly influential but the data are not sufficiently informative to allow the disentangling, with any precision, of its members' separate effects.

EXERCISES

15. In a study of the determinants of household expenditures on vacation travel, data were obtained from a sample of 2,246 households.[14] The model estimated was

$$\log y = -4.054 + 1.1556 \log x_1 - .4408 \log x_2 \qquad R^2 = .168$$
$$ (.0546) \qquad\quad (.0490)$$

where

y = Expenditure on vacation travel
x_1 = Total annual consumption expenditure
x_2 = Number of members in household

The figures in parentheses beneath the coefficient estimates are the corresponding estimated standard errors.

(a) Interpret the estimated partial regression coefficients.
(b) Interpret the coefficient of determination.
(c) All else being equal, find a 95% confidence interval for the percentage increase in expenditure on vacation travel resulting from a 1% increase in total annual consumption expenditure.
(d) Assuming that the model is correctly specified, test at the 1% significance level the null hypothesis that, all else being equal, number of members in household does not affect expenditure on vacation travel against the alternative that the greater the number of household members, the lower vacation travel expenditure.

16. The following model was estimated for a sample of 322 supermarkets in large metropolitan areas.[15]

$$\log y = 2.921 + .680 \log x \qquad R^2 = .19$$
$$ (.077)$$

where

---

[13] One possible approach, which we cannot discuss in detail here, is to abandon least squares in favor of procedures that yield biased estimators whose variances may be much smaller than those of least squares estimators.

[14] R. P. Hagermann, "The determinants of household vacation travel: Some empirical evidence," *Applied Economics*, *13* (1981), 225–34.

[15] J. M. MacDonald and P. E. Nelson, "Do the poor still pay more? Food price variations in large metropolitan areas," *Journal of Urban Economics*, *30* (1991), 344–59.

y = Store size

x = Median income in zip code area in which store is located

(a) Interpret the estimated coefficient on log x.

(b) Test the null hypothesis that income has no impact on store size against the alternative that higher income tends to be associated with larger store size.

17. An agricultural economist believes that the amount of beef consumed (y) in tons in a year in the United States depends on the price of beef (x_1) in dollars per pound, the price of pork (x_2) in dollars per pound, the price of chicken (x_3) in dollars per pound, and income per household (x_4) in thousands of dollars. The following sample regression was obtained through least squares, using thirty annual observations:

$$\log y = -.024 - .529 \log x_1 + .217 \log x_2 + .193 \log x_3 + .416 \log x_4 \qquad R^2 = .683$$

$$\qquad\qquad (.168) \qquad\quad (.103) \qquad\quad (.106) \qquad\quad (.163)$$

(a) Interpret the coefficient on log x_1.

(b) Interpret the coefficient on log x_2.

(c) Test at the 1% significance level the null hypothesis that the coefficient on log x_4 in the population regression is 0, against the alternative that it is positive.

(d) Test the null hypothesis that the four variables (log x_1, log x_2, log x_3, log x_4) do not, as a set, have any linear influence on log y.

(e) The economist is also concerned that over the years, increasing awareness of the effects of heavy red meat consumption on health may have influenced the demand for beef. If this is indeed the case, how would this influence your view of the original estimated regression?

18. [*This problem requires a computer program to carry out the regression calculations.*] The accompanying table shows German real imports (y), real private consumption (x_1), and real exchange rate (x_2), in terms of U.S. dollars per mark, over a period of 31 years. Estimate the model

$$\log Y_t = \alpha + \beta_1 \log x_{1t} + \beta_2 \log x_{2t} + \epsilon_t$$

and write a report on your findings.

y_t	x_{1t}	x_{2t}	y_t	x_{1t}	x_{2t}
527	1,718	4.17	2,799	6,325	2.36
560	1,833	4.00	2,967	6,831	2.11
619	2,047	4.00	3,071	7,289	1.83
665	2,167	3.98	3,661	7,851	1.73
739	2,336	3.98	4,253	8,408	1.96
868	2,575	4.01	4,650	8,840	2.26
909	2,751	3.98	4,756	9,150	2.38
890	2,826	4.00	4,804	9,590	2.72
1,004	3,007	4.00	5,306	10,009	3.15
1,198	3,309	3.69	5,718	10,368	2.46
1,380	3,689	3.65	5,278	10,670	1.94
1,549	4,094	3.27	5,249	11,089	1.58
1,672	4,522	3.20	5,646	11,515	1.78
1,884	4,953	2.70	6,435	12,210	1.70
2,351	5,337	2.41	7,187	13,212	1.49
2,412	5,853	2.62			

19. [*This problem requires a computer program to carry out the regression calculations.*] The accompanying table shows twenty-five annual observations[16] on sales (y) and advertising expenditure (x), both in thousands of dollars, of Lydia E. Pinkham. Estimate the model

$$\log Y_t = \alpha + \beta \log x_t + \gamma \log Y_{t-1} + \epsilon_t$$

and write a report on your findings.

y	x	y	x	y	x
1,103	339	2,637	1,145	1,896	964
1,266	562	2,177	1,012	1,684	811
1,473	745	1,920	836	1,633	789
1,423	749	1,910	941	1,657	802
1,767	862	1,984	981	1,569	770
2,161	1,034	1,787	974	1,390	639
2,336	1,054	1,689	766	1,387	644
2,602	1,164	1,866	920	1,289	564
2,518	1,102				

20. For a random sample of fifty observations, an economist estimated the regression model

$$\log Y_i = \alpha + \beta_1 \log x_{1i} + \beta_2 \log x_{2i} + \beta_3 \log x_{3i} + \beta_4 \log x_{4i} + \epsilon_i$$

where

Y_i = Gross revenue from a medical practice
x_{1i} = Average number of hours worked by physicians in the practice
x_{2i} = Number of physicians in the practice
x_{3i} = Number of allied health personnel (such as nurses) employed in the practice
x_{4i} = Number of rooms used in the practice

Use the portion of the computer output shown here to write a report on these results.

		R-SQUARE .927	
PARAMETER	ESTIMATE	T FOR H0: PARAMETER = 0	STD. ERROR OF ESTIMATE
INTERCEPT	2.347		
LOG X1	.239	3.27	.073
LOG X2	.673	8.31	.081
LOG X3	.279	6.64	.042
LOG X4	.082	1.61	.051

21. For a sample of thirty-five industries, an economist estimated the regression model

$$\log Y_i = \alpha + \beta_1 \log x_{1i} + \beta_2 \log x_{2i} + \epsilon_i$$

[16] Data from G. M. Erickson, "Using ridge regression to estimate directly lagged effects in marketing," *Journal of the American Statistical Association*, 76 (1981), 766–73, and K. S. Palda, *The Measurement of Cumulative Advertising Effects* (Englewood Cliffs, N.J.: Prentice Hall, 1964).

where

> Y_i = Industry concentration ratio, measured by the percentage of output accounted for by the largest four firms in the industry
>
> x_{1i} = Amount of capital required for entry into the industry, as measured by the size of a single efficient plant
>
> x_{2i} = Measure of economies of scale in the industry, measured by the ratio of average plant size for the largest firms (those that account for 50% of industry output) to the total output in the industry

Part of the computer output is shown here. Write a report on these results.

| | | R-SQUARE .825 | |
| | | | |
PARAMETER	ESTIMATE	T FOR H0: PARAMETER = 0	STD. ERROR OF ESTIMATE
INTERCEPT	3.621		
LOG X1	.234	3.55	.066
LOG X2	.267	3.18	.084

22. [*This problem requires a computer program to carry out the regression calculations.*] The accompanying table shows twenty-nine annual observations on private consumption (y) and disposable income (x) in Thailand. Fit the regression model

$$\log Y_t = \alpha + \beta \log x_t + \gamma \log Y_{t-1}$$

and write a report on your findings.

y_t	x_t	y_t	x_t	y_t	x_t
170	179	360	377	580	731
181	195	394	421	618	773
196	204	404	434	652	827
213	216	427	453	663	856
233	247	462	495	693	901
252	264	491	541	761	978
267	285	527	596	831	1,093
278	307	554	623	919	1,206
333	343	557	656	1,003	1,296
336	359	564	695		

23. Suppose that a regression relationship is given by

$$Y_i = \alpha + \beta_1 x_{1i} + \beta_2 x_{2i} + \epsilon_i$$

If the simple linear regression of Y_i on x_{1i} is estimated from a sample of n observations, the resulting slope estimate will generally be biased for β_1. However, in the special case where the sample correlation between the x_{1i} and x_{2i} is 0, this will not be so. In fact, in that case, the same estimate results whether or not x_{2i} is included in the regression equation.

(a) Explain verbally why this statement is true.

(b) Show algebraically, using material in Appendix A13.1, that this statement is true.

24. An economist wants to estimate a regression equation relating demand for a product (y) to its price (x_1) and income (x_2). It is to be based on 12 years of quarterly data. However, it is known that demand for this product is seasonal—that is, it is higher at certain times of the year than at others.

(a) One possibility for accounting for seasonality is to estimate the model

$$Y_t = \alpha + \beta_1 x_{1t} + \beta_2 x_{2t} + \beta_3 x_{3t} + \beta_4 x_{4t} + \beta_5 x_{5t} + \beta_6 x_{6t} + \epsilon_t$$

where $x_{3t}, x_{4t}, x_{5t}, x_{6t}$ are dummy variables, with

$x_{3t} = 1$ in first quarter of each year, 0 otherwise
$x_{4t} = 1$ in second quarter of each year, 0 otherwise
$x_{5t} = 1$ in third quarter of each year, 0 otherwise
$x_{6t} = 1$ in fourth quarter of each year, 0 otherwise

Explain why this model cannot be estimated by least squares.

(b) A model that can be estimated is

$$Y_t = \alpha + \beta_1 x_{1t} + \beta_2 x_{2t} + \beta_3 x_{3t} + \beta_4 x_{4t} + \beta_5 x_{5t} + \epsilon_t$$

Interpret the coefficients on the dummy variables in this model.

25. In the regression model

$$Y_i = \alpha + \beta_1 x_{1i} + \beta_2 x_{2i} + \epsilon_i$$

the extent of any multicollinearity can be evaluated by finding the correlation between x_{1i} and x_{2i} in the sample. Explain why this is so.

26. An economist estimates the regression model

$$Y_i = \alpha + \beta_1 x_{1i} + \beta_2 x_{2i} + \epsilon_i$$

The estimates of the parameters β_1 and β_2 are not very large, compared with their respective standard errors. But the size of the coefficient of determination indicates quite a strong relationship between the dependent variable and the pair of independent variables. Having obtained these results, the economist strongly suspects the presence of multicollinearity. Since his chief interest is in the influence of x_1 on the dependent variable, he decides that he will avoid the problem of multicollinearity by regressing Y on x_1 alone. Comment on this strategy.

27. Refer to Exercise 55 of Chapter 13. The independent variable x_1, real income per capita, was dropped from the model, and the regression of growth rate in real gross domestic product on x_1, average tax rate, was estimated. This yielded the fitted model

$$y = .060 - .074x_2 \qquad R^2 = .072$$
$$(.034)$$

Comment on this result.

14.7 HETEROSCEDASTICITY

The least squares estimation method and the inferential procedures based on it are based on certain assumptions, discussed in Section 13.3. When these assumptions hold, the methods discussed in Chapter 13 provide a powerful set of tools for practical analysis of data in many fields. However, when one or more of the assumptions break down, least squares estimation of the coefficients of a regression model can be inefficient, and the inferences drawn could be badly misleading.

In Section 14.5, one possible difficulty—specification bias—was considered. We saw that if important explanatory variables are omitted from a regression model, any inference drawn about the influences of the remaining variables is suspect. In this and the next section, we will consider the possibility of violation of two of the standard assumptions about the error terms, ϵ_i, of the model

$$Y_i = \alpha + \beta_1 x_{1i} + \beta_2 x_{2i} + \cdots + \beta_K x_{Ki} + \epsilon_i$$

Specifically, we have assumed that these error terms all have the same variance and are uncorrelated with one another. In the following section, we will examine the possibility of correlated errors. For the moment, we consider the assumption of fixed variance.

That this assumption may not be plausible can be illustrated by a simple example. Suppose that we are interested in the factors affecting output in a particular industry. Data are collected from several firms on the volume of output and such determinants as the quantities of labor and capital employed. Now, these firms will not generally be of the same size, and it might be expected that for the firms with the highest outputs, the error terms from the postulated model will, on average, be larger than those for the smallest firms. Thus, the error variances will not be the same for all firms but rather an increasing function of firm size.

Models in which the error terms do not all have the same variance are said to exhibit **heteroscedasticity.** When this phenomenon is present, least squares is not the most efficient procedure for estimating the coefficients of the regression model. Moreover, the usual procedures for deriving confidence intervals and tests of hypotheses for these coefficients are no longer valid. It is therefore extremely important to have techniques for detecting the presence of heteroscedasticity. Most of the approaches in common use check the assumption of constant error variance against some plausible alternative. It may be, for instance, that the size of the error variance is an increasing function of the size of one or another of the independent variables. Another possibility is that the error variance depends on the expected value of the dependent variable—that is, on $(\alpha + \beta_1 x_{1i} + \cdots + \beta_K x_{Ki})$.

Now, let $a, b_1, b_2, \ldots, b_K$ be the usual least squares estimates of the coefficients $\alpha, \beta_1, \beta_2, \ldots, \beta_K$. Natural estimates of the expected values of the dependent variables, given the independent variables, are provided by

$$\hat{y}_i = a + b_1 x_{1i} + b_2 x_{2i} + \cdots + b_K x_{Ki}$$

Similarly, the error terms ϵ_i are estimated by the **residuals**

$$e_i = y_i - \hat{y}_i$$

Graphical techniques for detecting heteroscedasticity are frequently of value. In practice, a series of graphs in which the residuals e_i are plotted against the individual independent variables or against the expected values $\hat{y}_i$ can be examined. To illustrate, consider Figure 14.8, which shows possible plots of e_i against the independent variable x_{1i}. In part (a) of the figure, we see that the magnitudes of the errors tend to increase with increasing x_i. This suggests that the error variances are not constant. By contrast, in part (b) of the figure, there appears to be no systematic relationship. In this latter case, then, there is no evidence to suggest the absence of constant error variance.

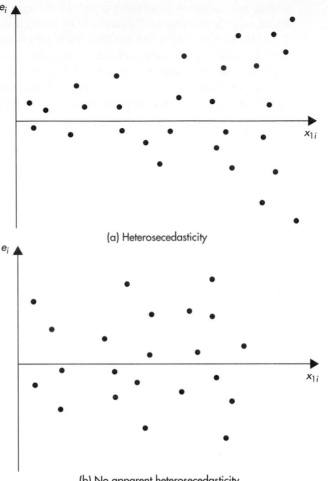

(a) Heterosecedasticity

(b) No apparent heterosecedasticity

FIGURE 14.8 Plots of residuals against an independent variable

In Chapter 13, we related savings and loan association profit margins to net revenues per deposit dollar (x_1) and number of offices (x_2) through the model

$$Y_i = \alpha + \beta_1 x_{1i} + \beta_2 x_{2i} + \epsilon_i$$

The coefficients of this model were estimated by least squares, with the implicit assumption that the error terms all have the same variance. We will now check this assumption. Figure 14.9 shows the plots of the residuals from the least squares regression against the two independent variables. (The independent variables are tabulated in Table 13.1 and the residuals in Table 13.2.) From these two graphs, there appears to be no systematic relationship between the magnitudes of the residuals and the values of either independent variable.

In Figure 14.10, the residuals from the least squares regression are plotted against the predicted values, $\hat{y}_i$, of the dependent variable. (The values $\hat{y}_i$ for the fitted regression are given in Table 13.2.) Once again, there appears to be no strong relationship between the magnitudes of the residuals and the sizes of the predicted values of

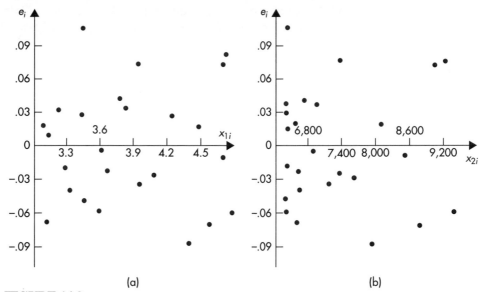

FIGURE 14.9 Plots of residuals against the independent variables for savings and loan data

the dependent variables. Taken together, then, for these particular data, Figures 14.9 and 14.10 do not suggest the presence of heteroscedasticity.

In the remainder of this section, we will consider more formal procedures for detecting heteroscedasticity and for estimating the coefficients of regression models when it is strongly suspected that the assumption of constant error variances is untenable. In fact, a multitude of such procedures exist, tailored to meet the myriad of ways

FIGURE 14.10 Plot of e_i against $\hat{y}_i$ for savings and loan data

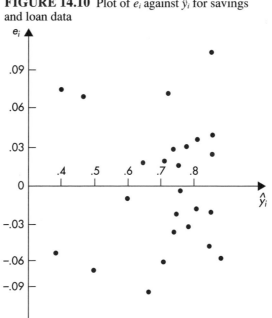

in which departures from this assumption might occur. We will deal here with a single possibility, which commonly arises in practice. Specifically, we will entertain the alternative hypothesis that the variance of the regression error terms, ϵ_i, depends on the expected value of the dependent variable, given the values of the independent variables. The test procedure is specified in the box.

A Test for Heteroscedasticity

Consider a regression model

$$Y_i = \alpha + \beta_1 x_{1i} + \beta_2 x_{2i} + \cdots + \beta_K x_{Ki} + \epsilon_i$$

linking a dependent variable to K independent variables and based on n sets of observations. Let $a, b_1, b_2, \ldots, b_K$ be the usual least squares estimates of the coefficients of this model, so the predicted values of the dependent variable are

$$\hat{y}_i = a + b_1 x_{1i} + b_2 x_{2i} + \cdots + b_K x_{Ki}$$

and the residuals from the fitted model are

$$e_i = y_i - \hat{y}_i$$

To test the null hypothesis that the error terms, ϵ_i, all have the same variance against the alternative that their variances depend on the expected values

$$\alpha + \beta_1 x_{1i} + \beta_2 x_{2i} + \cdots + \beta_K x_{Ki}$$

we estimate a simple linear regression. In this regression, the dependent variable is the square of the residual—that is, e_i^2—and the independent variable is the predicted value, $\hat{y}_i$.

Let R^2 be the coefficient of determination *of this auxiliary regression*. Then, for a test of significance level α, the null hypothesis is rejected if nR^2 is bigger than $\chi_{1,\alpha}^2$ where $\chi_{1,\alpha}^2$ is the number exceeded with probability α by a chi-square random variable with 1 degree of freedom.

We will carry out this test for the savings and loan example. The quantities employed in the auxiliary regression are tabulated in Table 14.5. The predicted values $\hat{y}_i$ are taken directly from Table 13.2, and the e_i^2 are the squares of the residuals e_i, also given in Table 13.2.

TABLE 14.5 Quantities required for a test of heteroscedasticity in the savings and loan regression

e_i^2	$\hat{y}_i$	e_i^2	$\hat{y}_i$	e_i^2	$\hat{y}_i$
.005329	.677	.000676	.794	.000729	.693
.000016	.714	.002401	.799	.007225	.635
.001521	.699	.003364	.828	.000289	.613
.003969	.673	.000484	.802	.000100	.570
.000256	.684	.001600	.800	.004900	.480
.000144	.708	.001225	.755	.005184	.438
.000900	.740	.001156	.734	.005476	.396
.000361	.759	.000625	.705	.003364	.378
.011025	.795				

When the regression of these squared residuals on the predicted values is estimated by least squares, we obtain

$$e^2 = .00470 - .00328\hat{y} \qquad R^2 = .027$$

$$(.00408)$$

Part of the SAS computer output for this auxiliary regression is shown in Table 14.6.

Since there are $n = 25$ sets of observations, the test is based on

$$nR^2 = (25)(.027) = .675$$

From Table 5 of the Appendix, we find, for a 10% level test

$$\chi^2_{1,.10} = 2.71$$

Therefore, the null hypothesis that the error terms in the regression of profit margins on net revenues and number of offices all have the same variance cannot be rejected at this level. This formal test confirms our impression from Figures 14.9 and 14.10 that there is little evidence in these data to suggest that heteroscedasticity is a serious problem here.

When it is strongly suspected that the regression errors do not all have the same variance, least squares estimation may not be the most appropriate procedure. Several alternatives can be used, the choice depending on how the error variances are thought to behave. Here, we briefly mention one possibility. Suppose that the variance of the error terms is directly proportional to the square of the expected value of the dependent variable, given the independent variables, that is

$$\text{Var}(\epsilon_i) \infty (\alpha + \beta_1 x_{1i} + \beta_2 x_{2i} + \cdots + \beta_K x_{Ki})^2$$

Also assume that the dependent variable can only take positive values. When this particular form is assumed, a simple two-stage procedure is used to estimate the parameters of the regression model. At the first stage, the model is estimated by least squares in the usual way, and the predicted values, $\hat{y}_i$, of the dependent variable are recorded. At the second stage, we estimate the regression equation

$$\frac{Y_i}{\hat{y}_i} = \alpha\frac{1}{\hat{y}_i} + \beta_1\frac{x_{1i}}{\hat{y}_i} + \beta_2\frac{x_{2i}}{\hat{y}_i} + \cdots + \beta_K\frac{x_{Ki}}{\hat{y}_i} + u_i \qquad (14.7.1)$$

TABLE 14.6 Part of the output from the SAS program for auxiliary regression for testing for heteroscedasticity in the savings and loan model

		R-SQUARE .027	
PARAMETER	ESTIMATE	T FOR H0: PARAMETER = 0	STD. ERROR OF ESTIMATE
INTERCEPT	.00470		
YHAT	−.00328	−.80	.00408

where u_i is an error term that will have approximately constant variance. Thus, Eq. (14.7.1) represents a regression model in which the dependent variable is $Y_i/\hat{y}_i$ and the independent variables are $1/\hat{y}_i, x_{1i}/\hat{y}_i, x_{2i}/\hat{y}_i, \ldots, x_{Ki}/\hat{y}_i$. (Notice that there is no intercept term.) The coefficients of (14.7.1) are then estimated by least squares, the resulting estimates of $\alpha, \beta_1, \beta_2, \ldots, \beta_K$ being retained.

The appearance of heteroscedastic errors can result if a linear regression model is estimated in circumstances where a log linear model is appropriate. The analyst might then, when heteroscedasticity is indicated, consider the possibility of reestimating the model in logarithmic form, particularly if subject matter theory suggests that such a specification would not be unreasonable. Essentially, taking logarithms will dampen the influence of large observations. Often the resulting model will appear to be free from heteroscedasticity. This approach is often appropriate when the data under study are time series of economic variables, such as consumption, income, and money, that tend to grow exponentially over time.

14.8 AUTOCORRELATED ERRORS

We will now examine the possibility of the failure of the assumption that the error terms in a regression model are uncorrelated with one another. In situations where the data analyzed consist of a random sample from some population, this assumption is quite justifiable. However, for another extremely important class of regression problems, it must be regarded as somewhat suspect. When time series data are analyzed, the error term represents the amalgam of all factors (apart from the independent variables) that influence the behavior of the dependent variable, and hence some correlation between errors might be anticipated. The behavior of these factors in the current time period might be quite similar to their behavior in the previous time period, suggesting the possibility of a positive correlation between errors close together in time.

To emphasize that the subject matter of this section is restricted to time series data, we will, as in Section 14.3, subscript observations by t and write the regression model as

$$Y_t = \alpha + \beta_1 x_{1t} + \beta_2 x_{2t} + \cdots + \beta_K x_{Kt} + \epsilon_t \qquad (14.8.1)$$

We have assumed that the error terms, ϵ_t, of such models are not correlated with one another. The consequences of proceeding with the usual least squares analysis when this assumption does not hold can be very serious indeed. In particular, the usual inferential statements based on confidence intervals or hypothesis tests for the model parameters might be badly misleading.

It is therefore critically important in regressions involving time series data to test the hypothesis that the error terms are not correlated with one another. The possibility that they are correlated through time is referred to as the problem of **autocorrelated errors.** When approaching this problem, it can be useful to have in mind some specific plausible autocorrelation structure. One appealing possibility is that the error ϵ_t in time period t is quite strongly correlated with the error ϵ_{t-1} in the previous time period, rather less strongly correlated with the error ϵ_{t-2} two time periods earlier, and so on, so that the correlation between error terms separated by a considerable period of time is relatively weak. Let us denote by ρ the correlation between error terms in adjacent time periods, so that

$$\text{Corr}(\epsilon_t, \epsilon_{t-1}) = \rho$$

where, since ρ is a correlation coefficient, it will be less than 1 in absolute value. (In most applications, it will be reasonable to take this correlation to be either 0 or positive.) A particularly simple formulation, in which the correlation between error terms decreases the farther apart they are in time, is to have

$$\text{Corr}(\epsilon_t, \epsilon_{t-2}) = \rho^2$$

$$\text{Corr}(\epsilon_t, \epsilon_{t-3}) = \rho^3$$

and so on. Thus, for errors separated by j units of time, we have

$$\text{Corr}(\epsilon_t, \epsilon_{t-j}) = \rho^j \qquad (j = 1, 2, 3, \ldots) \qquad (14.8.2)$$

Suppose, for example, that the correlation between adjacent errors is .5 and that the autocorrelation structure 14.8.2 holds. We then have

$$\text{Corr}(\epsilon_t, \epsilon_{t-1}) = .5$$

$$\text{Corr}(\epsilon_t, \epsilon_{t-2}) = (.5)^2 = .25$$

$$\text{Corr}(\epsilon_t, \epsilon_{t-3}) = (.5)^3 = .125$$

$$\text{Corr}(\epsilon_t, \epsilon_{t-4}) = (.5)^4 = .0625$$

.

.

.

We see then that the correlation between errors far apart in time is relatively weak, while that between errors closer to one another in time is possibly quite strong.

Now, if we assume that the errors ϵ_t all have the same variance, it is possible to show that the autocorrelation structure (14.8.2) corresponds to the model

$$\epsilon_t = \rho\epsilon_{t-1} + u_t \qquad (14.8.3)$$

where the random variable u_t has mean 0, has constant variance, and is not autocorrelated. Equation (14.8.3) depicts the **first-order autoregressive model** of autocorrelated behavior. Looking at this equation, we see that the value taken by the error at time t, ϵ_t, depends on its value in the previous time period (the strength of that dependence being determined by the correlation coefficient ρ) and on a second random term, u_t. This model is illustrated in Figure 14.11, which shows time plots of errors

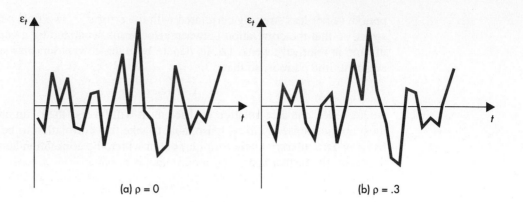

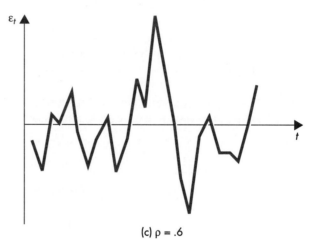

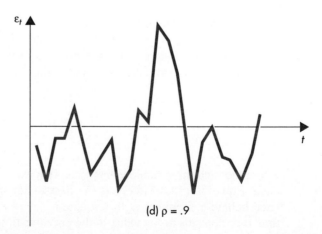

FIGURE 14.11 Time plots of residuals from regressions whose error terms follow a first-order autoregressive process

generated by the model (14.8.3) for values of $\rho = 0, .3, .6, .9$. The case $\rho = 0$ corresponds to no autocorrelation in the errors. In part (a) of the figure, it can be seen that there is no apparent pattern in the progression through time of the errors. The value taken by one does not influence the values of others. As we move from relatively weak autocorrelation ($\rho = .3$) to quite strong autocorrelation ($\rho = .9$), in parts (b), (c), and (d), it emerges that the pattern through time of the errors becomes increasingly less jagged, so that in part (d) of the figure, it is quite clear that an error is likely to be relatively close in value to its immediate neighbor.

Examination of Figure 14.11 suggests that graphical methods might be useful in detecting the presence of autocorrelated errors. Ideally, we would like to plot the errors ϵ_t of model (14.8.1) against time. However, since the actual errors will be unknown, estimates of them are obtained as the residuals, e_t, when the model is estimated by least squares. Thus, for practical purposes, it is the time plot of these residuals that is examined. Figure 14.12 shows the time plot of the residuals from our savings and loan regression. (These residuals are set out in Table 13.2.)

Looking at the time plot in Figure 14.12, one does not get the impression of any strong autocorrelation in the residuals. They do not follow the kind of smooth path through time depicted in Figure 14.11(d). On this evidence alone, then, our suspicions of autocorrelated errors would not be terribly strong. However, since the problem is so important, it is desirable to have a more formal test of the hypothesis of no autocorrelation in the errors of a regression model.

The test that is most often used is the **Durbin-Watson test** and is based on the residuals, e_t, from the least squares estimated regression. The test statistic calculated is

$$d = \frac{\sum_{t=2}^{n}(e_t - e_{t-1})^2}{\sum_{t=1}^{n}e_t^2}$$

FIGURE 14.12 Time plot of residuals from savings and loan regression

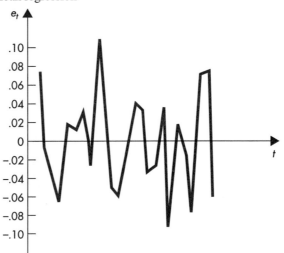

The computations needed to find this test statistic for the savings and loan regression are set out in Table 14.7. From this table, we find

$$\sum_{t=2}^{25}(e_t - e_{t-1})^2 = .121615 \qquad \text{and} \qquad \sum_{t=1}^{25}e_t^2 = .062319$$

Hence, the test statistic for this regression is

$$d = \frac{.121615}{.062319} = 1.95$$

When regressions involving time series data are reported, it is common practice to include among the summary information the calculated Durbin-Watson statistic. Our savings and loan regression would therefore be reported as

$$y = 1.565 + .237x_1 - .000249x_2 \qquad R^2 = .87 \qquad d = 1.95$$

$$(.079) \quad (.0555) \quad (.0000320)$$

Now, the Durbin-Watson statistic can be written approximately as

$$d = 2(1 - r) \tag{14.8.4}$$

TABLE 14.7 Durbin-Watson statistic computations for the savings and loan regression

t	e_t	e_t^2	$e_t - e_{t-1}$	$(e_t - e_{t-1})^2$
1	.073	.005329		
2	−.004	.000016	−.077	.005929
3	−.039	.001521	−.035	.001225
4	−.063	.003969	−.024	.000576
5	.016	.000256	.079	.006241
6	.012	.000144	−.004	.000016
7	.030	.000900	.018	.000324
8	−.019	.000361	−.049	.002401
9	.105	.011025	.124	.015376
10	.026	.000676	−.079	.006241
11	−.049	.002401	−.075	.005625
12	−.058	.003364	−.009	.000081
13	−.022	.000484	.036	.001296
14	.040	.001600	.062	.003844
15	.035	.001225	−.005	.000025
16	−.034	.001156	−.069	.004761
17	−.025	.000625	.009	.000081
18	.027	.000729	.052	.002704
19	−.085	.007225	−.112	.012544
20	.017	.000289	.102	.010404
21	−.010	.000100	−.027	.000729
22	−.070	.004900	−.060	.003600
23	.072	.005184	.142	.020164
24	.074	.005476	.002	.000004
25	−.058	.003364	−.132	.017424
	Sums	.062319		.121615

where r is the sample estimate of the correlation, ρ, between adjacent errors.[17] Therefore, if the errors are not autocorrelated, we would expect the value of d to be quite close to 2. Positive autocorrelation in the errors, by contrast, would tend to produce a positive value for the sample correlation, r, and hence a value for d that is lower than 2. There is a theoretical difficulty involved in basing tests for autocorrelated errors on the Durbin-Watson statistic. The problem is that the actual sampling distribution of d, even when the hypothesis of no autocorrelation is true, depends on the particular values of the independent variables. It is obviously infeasible to tabulate the distribution for every possible set of values of the independent variables. Fortunately, it is known that whatever the independent variables, the distribution of d lies between that of two other random variables, whose percentage points can be tabulated. For tests of significance levels 1% and 5%, cutoff points for these random variables are tabulated in Table 10 of the Appendix. For various combinations of n and K, these tables give values d_L and d_U. The null hypothesis of no autocorrelation is rejected against the alternative of positive autocorrelation in the errors if the calculated d is less than d_L. The null hypothesis is accepted if d is bigger than d_U, while if d lies between d_L and d_U, the test is inconclusive. This is illustrated in Figure 14.13.

To illustrate, we will test the null hypothesis of no autocorrelation in the errors of the savings and loan model, against the alternative that these errors are positively autocorrelated, at the 5% level of significance. In this model, we have

$$n = 25 \quad \text{and} \quad K = 2$$

so, from Table 10

$$d_L = 1.21 \quad \text{and} \quad d_U = 1.55$$

Since the calculated d, 1.95, is bigger than d_U, the null hypothesis of no autocorrelation in the errors is accepted, confirming our visual impression from Figure 14.12. This test is shown in Figure 14.14.

The detection of autocorrelated errors in regression analysis is so important that most modern regression computer packages offer the calculation of the Durbin-Watson test statistic as an option. If such a package is available, it is not necessary to carry out the computations of Table 14.7.

FIGURE 14.13 Decision rule for carrying out Durbin-Watson d test of null hypothesis, H_0, of no autocorrelation in regression errors

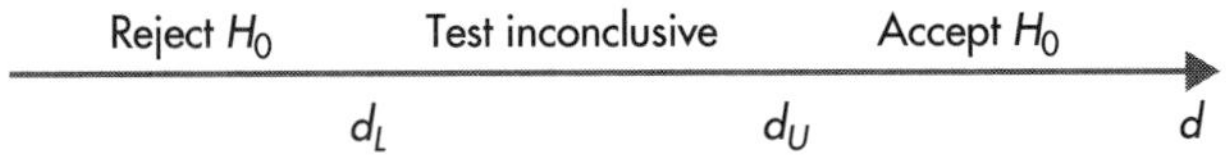

---

[17] This follows since

$$d = \frac{\sum\limits_{t=2}^{n} (e_t - e_{t-1})^2}{\sum\limits_{t=1}^{n} e_t^2} = \frac{\sum\limits_{t=2}^{n} e_t^2}{\sum\limits_{t=1}^{n} e_t^2} + \frac{\sum\limits_{t=2}^{n} e_{t-1}^2}{\sum\limits_{t=1}^{n} e_t^2} - 2\frac{\sum\limits_{t=2}^{n} e_t e_{t-1}}{\sum\limits_{t=1}^{n} e_t^2}$$

The first two terms on the right-hand side of this expression are very close to 1, while the ratio of sums in the final term provides an estimate, r, of the correlation between ϵ_t and ϵ_{t-1}.

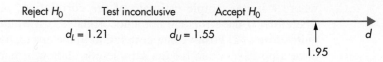

Reject H_0 Test inconclusive   Accept H_0

$d_L = 1.21$ $d_U = 1.55$ 1.95 d

FIGURE 14.14 Test of null hypothesis, H_0, of no autocorrelation in the errors of the savings and loan regression model

---

The Durbin-Watson Test

Consider the regression model

$$Y_t = \alpha + \beta_1 x_{1t} + \beta_2 x_{2t} + \cdots + \beta_K x_{Kt} + \epsilon_t$$

based on n sets of observations. We contemplate the possibility that the error terms ϵ_t are autocorrelated according to

$$\text{Corr}(\epsilon_t, \epsilon_{t-j}) = \rho^j \qquad (j = 1, 2, 3, \ldots)$$

or, equivalently, that the ϵ_t can be represented by the process

$$\epsilon_t = \rho \epsilon_{t-1} + u_t$$

where u_t is not autocorrelated.

The test of the null hypothesis of no autocorrelation

$$H_0: \quad \rho = 0$$

is based on the Durbin-Watson statistic

$$d = \frac{\sum\limits_{t=2}^{n}(e_t - e_{t-1})^2}{\sum\limits_{t=1}^{n} e_t^2}$$

where the e_t are the residuals when the regression equation is estimated by least squares.

When the alternative hypothesis is of positive autocorrelation in the errors, that is

$$H_1: \quad \rho > 0$$

the decision rule is as follows:

Reject H_0 if $d < d_L$

Accept H_0 if $d > d_U$

Test inconclusive if $d_L < d < d_U$

where d_L and d_U are tabulated for values of n and K and for significance levels of 1% and 5% in Table 10 of the Appendix.

Occasionally, one wants to test against the alternative of negative autocorrelation, that is

$$H_1: \quad \rho < 0$$

The appropriate test is precisely the same as for the alternative of positive autocorrelation, except that it is based on the statistic $(4 - d)$ rather than d. This quantity is then compared with tabulated d_L and d_U.

EXAMPLE
14.2

A student wanted to run a regression model to explain variability in the birth rate in the United States. She believed that relevant explanatory variables might be the percentage of women in the labor market, the unemployment rate, and the divorce rate. An attempt was also made, through the use of dummy variables, to take into account the effects of wars. The model was fitted using the 30 years of annual data shown in Table 14.8. The equation obtained by least squares estimation was

$$y = 4.30 - .0477x_1 - .0389x_2 - .0094x_3 - .321x_4 + .0205x_5$$

$$(.0155) \quad (.0233) \quad (.0166) \quad (.077) \quad (.0905)$$

$$R^2 = .73 \qquad d = .55$$

where

y = Birth rate
x_1 = Percentage of women in the labor force
x_2 = Percentage of labor force unemployed
x_3 = Divorce rate
x_4 = Dummy variable taking value 1 during war years, 0 otherwise
x_5 = Dummy variable taking value 1 in the 3 years following the first year of peace after a war, 0 otherwise

TABLE 14.8 Data for birth rate regression of Example 14.2

y_t	x_{1t}	x_{2t}	x_{3t}	x_{4t}	x_{5t}
2.03	25.4	9.9	17	1	0
2.22	26.7	4.7	18	1	0
2.27	29.1	1.9	23	1	0
2.12	29.2	1.2	28	1	0
2.04	29.2	1.9	30	1	0
2.41	27.8	3.9	27	0	0
2.66	27.4	3.9	24	0	1
2.49	28.0	3.8	23	0	1
2.45	28.3	5.9	25	0	1
2.41	28.8	5.3	23	1	0
2.49	29.3	3.3	24	1	0
2.51	29.4	3.0	25	1	0
2.50	29.2	2.9	25	1	0
2.53	29.4	5.5	25	0	0
2.50	30.2	4.4	25	0	1
2.52	31.0	4.1	24	0	1
2.53	31.2	4.3	25	0	1
2.45	31.5	6.8	25	0	0
2.40	31.7	5.5	26	0	0
2.37	32.3	5.5	27	0	0
2.33	32.6	6.7	26	0	0
2.24	32.7	5.5	26	0	0
2.17	33.2	5.7	26	0	0
2.10	33.6	5.2	26	0	0
1.94	34.0	4.5	27	1	0
1.84	34.6	3.8	27	1	0
1.78	35.1	3.8	27	1	0
1.75	35.5	3.6	28	1	0
1.78	36.3	3.5	30	1	0
1.84	36.7	4.9	33	1	0

We want to test the null hypothesis of no autocorrelation in the errors of the regression equation against the alternative of positive autocorrelation. Here we have

$$n = 30 \quad \text{and} \quad K = 5$$

Thus, from Table 10 of the Appendix, for a 1% level test, the points for comparison with the calculated Durbin-Watson statistic are

$$d_L = .88 \quad \text{and} \quad d_U = 1.61$$

Since the calculated test statistic, $d = .55$, is below the lower bound, d_L, the null hypothesis of no autocorrelation in the errors can be rejected at the 1% significance level. These data, then, cast considerable doubt on the validity of the assumption that the error terms are uncorrelated with one another.

It is perplexing that the Durbin-Watson test can yield an inconclusive result, as, whatever the case, some decision on how to proceed must be made. Since the consequences of ignoring autocorrelated errors can be so serious, it is preferable to treat an inconclusive result in the same way as a rejection of the null hypothesis of no autocorrelation. The regression model can then be reestimated, using the procedure described below.

ESTIMATION OF REGRESSIONS WITH AUTOCORRELATED ERRORS

When, as in Example 14.2, it appears likely that the regression errors are autocorrelated, least squares estimates and inferences based on them can be very unreliable. In these circumstances, it is preferable to use an alternative estimator. To motivate the estimation procedure to be used, we write the regression

$$Y_t = \alpha + \beta_1 x_{1t} + \beta_2 x_{2t} + \cdots + \beta_K x_{Kt} + \epsilon_t \qquad (14.8.5)$$

so that at time $(t - 1)$ we have

$$Y_{t-1} = \alpha + \beta_1 x_{1,t-1} + \beta_2 x_{2,t-1} + \cdots + \beta_K x_{K,t-1} + \epsilon_{t-1} \qquad (14.8.6)$$

Multiplying through Eq. (14.8.6) by ρ, the correlation between adjacent errors, gives

$$\rho Y_{t-1} = \alpha\rho + \beta_1 \rho x_{1,t-1} + \beta_2 \rho x_{2,t-1} + \cdots + \beta_K \rho x_{K,t-1} + \rho\epsilon_{t-1} \qquad (14.8.7)$$

Subtracting Eq. (14.8.7) from (14.8.5) then gives

$$Y_t - \rho Y_{t-1} = \alpha(1 - \rho) + \beta_1(x_{1t} - \rho x_{1,t-1})$$
$$+ \beta_2(x_{2t} - \rho x_{2,t-1}) + \cdots + \beta_K(x_{Kt} - \rho x_{K,t-1}) + u_t \qquad (14.8.8)$$

where, as in (14.8.3)

$$u_t = \epsilon_t - \rho\epsilon_{t-1}$$

and the random variable u_t has constant variance and is not autocorrelated. Equation (14.8.8) can therefore be regarded as a regression model linking the dependent variable $(Y_t - \rho Y_{t-1})$ to the K independent variables $(x_{1t} - \rho x_{1,t-1}), \ldots, (x_{Kt} - \rho x_{K,t-1})$. The parameters of this model are precisely the same as those of the original model (14.8.5), except that the intercept term in (14.8.8) is $\alpha(1 - \rho)$ rather than α. There is, however, one very important difference between the models (14.8.5) and (14.8.8). In the former, the error terms ϵ_t are autocorrelated, so least squares estimation of the model parameters is inappropriate. However, since the errors, u_t, of (14.8.8) are not autocorrelated, the usual least squares inferential procedures, when applied to this model, are perfectly valid.

The foregoing discussion suggests that the problem of autocorrelated errors can be circumvented by estimating by least squares a regression equation with dependent variable $(Y_t - \rho Y_{t-1})$ and independent variables $(x_{1t} - \rho x_{1,t-1}), \ldots, (x_{Kt} - \rho x_{K,t-1})$. Unfortunately, this is not possible in practice, since the true value of ρ will be unknown. However, we can replace ρ by its sample estimate r, which, by virtue of (14.8.4), an be found directly from the Durbin-Watson statistic as

$$r = 1 - \frac{d}{2}$$

The procedure is described in the box.

Estimation of Regression Models with Autocorrelated Errors

Suppose that we want to estimate the parameters of the regression model

$$Y_t = \alpha + \beta_1 x_{1t} + \beta_2 x_{2t} + \cdots + \beta_K x_{Kt} + \epsilon_t$$

when the error term ϵ_t is autocorrelated.

This can be accomplished in two stages, as follows:

(i) Estimate the model by least squares, obtaining the Durbin-Watson statistic, d, and hence the estimate

$$r = 1 - \frac{d}{2}$$

of the autocorrelation parameter.

> (ii) Estimate by least squares a second regression in which the dependent variable is $(Y_t - rY_{t-1})$ and the independent variables are $(x_{1t} - rx_{1,t-1}), \ldots, (x_{Kt} - rx_{K,t-1})$. The parameters $\beta_1, \beta_2, \ldots, \beta_K$ are estimated by the estimated partial regression coefficients from this second model. An estimate of α is obtained by dividing by $(1 - r)$ the estimated intercept for the second model. Hypothesis tests and confidence intervals for the β_i can be carried out using the standard methods on the output of the second regression.

In Example 14.2, we estimated by least squares a regression model seeking to explain variability in birth rates in the United States. The possibility of autocorrelation in the errors of that model was strongly indicated by the Durbin-Watson statistic

$$d = .55$$

We now want to reestimate the model parameters, allowing for the presence of auto-correlated errors. First, the sample autocorrelation is

$$r = 1 - \frac{d}{2} = 1 - \frac{.55}{2} = .725$$

Next, we must construct new variables for a second regression. The dependent variable for this regression is $(Y_t - rY_{t-1})$. Referring to Table 14.8, we find

$$y_2 - ry_1 = 2.22 - (.725)(2.03) = .748$$

$$y_3 - ry_2 = 2.27 - (.725)(2.22) = .661$$

and so on. The new independent variables are found in the same way, so, for example.

$$x_{1,2} - rx_{1,1} = 26.7 - (.725)(25.4) = 8.285$$

$$x_{1,3} - rx_{1,2} = 29.1 - (.725)(26.7) = 9.743$$

In this way, the new variables can be computed, as summarized in Table 14.9. The resulting estimated regression was

$$(y_t - ry_{t-1}) = 1.383 - .0667(x_{1,t} - rx_{1,t-1}) - .0083(x_{2,t} - rx_{2,t-1})$$
$$\phantom{(y_t - ry_{t-1}) = 1.383} (.0203) \phantom{- .0667(x_{1,t} - rx_{1,t-1})} (.0133)$$
$$- .0200(x_{3,t} - rx_{3,t-1}) - .106(x_{4,t} - rx_{4,t-1}) + .0322(x_{5,t} - rx_{5,t-1})$$
$$(.0109) \phantom{- .0200(x_{3,t} - rx} (.0617) \phantom{- .106(x_{4,t} - rx_{4,t-1})} (.0526)$$

Now, the intercept term in the original regression is estimated by

$$\frac{1.383}{1 - r} = \frac{1.383}{1 - .725} = 5.029$$

The estimated model is therefore

$$y = 5.029 - .0667x_1 - .0083x_2 - .0200x_3 - .106x_4 + .0322x_5$$
$$ (.0203) \quad (.0133) \quad (.0109) \quad (.0617) \quad (.0526)$$

TABLE 14.9 Variables used for estimating birth rate regression, allowing for autocorrelated errors

$y_t - ry_{t-1}$	$x_{1t} - rx_{1,t-1}$	$x_{2t} - rx_{2,t-1}$	$x_{3t} - rx_{3,t-1}$	$x_{4t} - rx_{4,t-1}$	$x_{5t} - rx_{5,t-1}$
.748	8.285	−2.478	5.675	.275	0
.661	9.743	−1.508	9.950	.275	0
.474	8.103	−.178	11.325	.275	0
.503	8.030	1.030	9.700	.275	0
.931	6.630	2.523	5.250	−.725	0
.913	7.245	1.073	4.425	0	1
.562	8.135	.973	5.600	0	.275
.645	8.000	3.145	8.325	0	.275
.634	8.283	1.023	4.875	1	−.725
.743	8.420	−.543	7.325	.275	0
.705	8.158	.608	7.600	.275	0
.680	7.885	.725	6.875	.275	0
.718	8.230	3.398	6.875	−.725	0
.666	8.885	.413	6.875	0	1
.708	9.105	.910	5.875	0	.275
.703	8.725	1.328	7.600	0	.275
.616	8.880	3.683	6.875	0	.725
.624	8.863	.570	7.875	0	0
.630	9.318	1.513	8.150	0	0
.612	9.183	2.713	6.425	0	0
.551	9.065	.643	7.150	0	0
.546	9.493	1.713	7.150	0	0
.527	9.530	1.068	7.150	0	0
.418	9.640	.730	8.150	1	0
.434	9.950	.538	7.425	.275	0
.446	10.015	1.045	7.425	.275	0
.460	10.053	.845	8.425	.275	0
.511	10.563	.890	9.700	.275	0
.550	10.383	2.363	11.250	.275	0

Given the estimated model, confidence intervals for and tests of hypotheses about the individual regression parameters can be carried out in the usual way. To illustrate, we will test the null hypothesis that, all else being equal, the percentage of women in the labor force (x_1) does not influence the birth rate. That is the hypothesis

$$H_0: \quad \beta_1 = 0$$

This will be tested against the alternative

$$H_1: \quad \beta_1 < 0$$

The test is based on

$$\frac{b_1}{s_{b_1}} = \frac{-.0667}{.0203} = -3.286$$

In the second regression, we have $n = 29$ observations and $K = 5$ independent variables. Thus, for a .5%-level test

$$-t_{n-K-1,\alpha} = -t_{23,.005} = -2.807$$

The null hypothesis can therefore be rejected at this level.

CONSEQUENCES OF AUTOCORRELATED ERRORS

The consequences of proceeding with the ordinary least squares analysis of a regression model that has autocorrelated errors can be extremely severe. If the presence of autocorrelated errors is ignored, three consequences result:

1. The least squares estimators of the parameters of the regression model are likely to be inefficient. Generally, superior estimators will be obtained if autocorrelated errors are taken into account.
2. Forecasts of future values of the dependent variable, obtained through the standard analysis, will be unnecessarily inefficient.
3. The usual inferential statements based on confidence intervals or tests of hypotheses can be badly misleading.

AUTOCORRELATED ERRORS IN MODELS WITH LAGGED DEPENDENT VARIABLES

When a regression model contains lagged dependent variables, the consequences of proceeding with the usual least squares inferential procedures in the presence of autocorrelated errors can be even more severe than for other regression models. In this situation, the least squares parameter estimators are not consistent.[18] Unfortunately, for lagged dependent variable models, the previously discussed procedures for testing for autocorrelated errors and estimation in the presence of autocorrelated errors are not valid. Here, we briefly introduce appropriate procedures.

Consider the model

$$Y_t = \alpha + \beta_1 x_{1t} + \beta_2 x_{2t} + \cdots + \beta_K x_{Kt} + \gamma Y_{t-1} + \epsilon_t \qquad (14.8.9)$$

Suppose that this model is fitted to n sets of sample observations by least squares. Let d be the usual Durbin-Watson statistic, with

$$r = 1 - \frac{d}{2}$$

and let s_c denote the estimated standard deviation of the estimated coefficient γ on the lagged dependent variable. Our null hypothesis is that the autoregressive parameter ρ is 0. A test of this hypothesis, approximately valid in large samples, is based on **Durbin's h statistic**

$$h = r\sqrt{n/(1 - ns_c^2)} \qquad (14.8.10)$$

---

[18] The property of consistency of an estimator was discussed in Section 7.3.

Under the null hypothesis, the statistic has a distribution that is well approximated in large samples by the standard normal. Thus, for example, the null hypothesis of no autocorrelation is rejected against the alternative that ρ is positive at the 5% level if the statistic (14.8.10) exceeds 1.645.

If the autoregressive error model is

$$u_t = \epsilon_t - \rho\epsilon_{t-1}$$

then, using (14.8.9), we can write, corresponding to (14.8.8)

$$Y_t - \rho Y_{t-1} = \alpha(1 - \rho) + \beta_1(x_{1t} - \rho x_{1,t-1}) + \cdots$$
$$+ \beta_K(x_{Kt} - \rho x_{K,t-1}) + \gamma(Y_{t-1} - \rho Y_{t-2}) + u_t \qquad (14.8.11)$$

One possible approach to parameter estimation, which requires only an ordinary least squares estimation program, is to substitute in turn in (14.8.11) possible values of ρ—say, .1, .3, .5, .7, and .9. Then the regression of $(Y_t - \rho Y_{t-1})$ on $(x_{1t} - \rho x_{1,t-1})$, ..., $(x_{Kt} - \rho x_{K,t-1})$, $(Y_{t-1} - \rho Y_{t-2})$ is fitted by least squares for each possible ρ value. The value of ρ chosen is that for which the resulting sum of squared errors is smallest. Inference about the β_i is then based on the corresponding fitted regression (14.8.11).

14.9 SUMMARY

In this chapter we have tried to show that regression modeling involves much more than the routine exercise described in Chapters 12 and 13. In practice, much art is involved in successful model building, and care must be taken. In particular, important explanatory variables should not be ignored. Some important factors may require the use of dummy variables. Further possibilities that may need to be taken into account in model specification include the use of lagged dependent variables and the consideration of nonlinear models, such as the log linear form.

As we have seen, it is also very important to check, as far as possible, any assumptions made about the behavior of the error terms in a regression model. Tests for heteroscedasticity and autocorrelated errors can be carried out, and if either of these problems appears to be present, the regression model should be reestimated.

These considerations by no means exhaust the possible circumstances in which a departure from the standard regression treatment is desirable. They are, however, among the most important in business and economic applications, and a great many well-executed practical studies involve at least one of them.

EXERCISES

28. In Chapter 12, the regression of retail sales per household on disposable income per household was estimated by least squares. The data are given in Table 12.5, and Table 12.7 shows the residuals and the predicted values of the dependent variable.

(a) Graphically check for heteroscedasticity in the regression errors.

(b) Check for heteroscedasticity by using a formal test.

29. Refer to Exercise 4. Let e_i denote the residuals from the fitted regression and $\hat{y}_i$ the in-sample predicted values of the dependent variable. The least squares regression of e_i^2 on $\hat{y}_i$ has coefficient of determination .032. What can you conclude from this finding?

30. In Exercise 38 of Chapter 13, a regression explaining the percentage of females in the labor force was fitted to data from fifty states.

   (a) Graphically check for heteroscedasticity in the regression errors.

   (b) Use a formal test to check for heteroscedasticity.

31. In a regression based on thirty annual observations, U.S. farm income was related to four independent variables—grain exports, federal government subsidies, population, and a dummy variable for bad weather years. The model was fitted by least squares, resulting in a Durbin-Watson statistic of 1.29. The regression of e_i^2 on $\hat{y}_i$ yielded a coefficient of determination of .043.

   (a) Test for heteroscedasticity.

   (b) Test for autocorrelated errors.

32. Consider the regression model

$$Y_i = \alpha + \beta_1 x_{1i} + \beta_2 x_{2i} + \cdots + \beta_K x_{Ki} + \epsilon_i$$

   Show that if

$$\text{Var}(\epsilon_i) = K x_i^2 \qquad (K > 0)$$

   then

$$\text{Var}\left(\frac{\epsilon_i}{x_i}\right) = K$$

   Discuss the possible relevance of this result in treating a form of heteroscedasticity.

33. Refer to Exercise 7. Let e_i denote the residuals from the fitted regression and $\hat{y}_i$ the in-sample predicted values. The least squares regression of e_i^2 on $\hat{y}_i$ has coefficient of determination .087. What can you conclude from this finding?

34. Refer to Exercise 53 of Chapter 13 explaining the change in the real deposit rate in India. The Durbin-Watson statistic for the fitted regression model was 1.71. Test the null hypothesis of no autocorrelated errors against the alternative of positive autocorrelation.

35. Refer to Exercise 18 on German real imports. What can be concluded from the Durbin-Watson statistic for the fitted regression?

36. Refer to Exercise 17 on beef consumption. The Durbin-Watson statistic for the fitted regression model was 1.72. Test the null hypothesis of no autocorrelated errors against the alternative of positive autocorrelation.

37. Refer to the regression, in Chapter 12, of retail sales per household on disposable income per household.

   (a) Calculate the Durbin-Watson d statistic.

   (b) Test the null hypothesis of no autocorrelation in the regression errors.

   (c) If necessary, reestimate the model allowing for autocorrelated errors.

38. A factory operator hypothesizes that her unit output costs (y) depend on wage rate (x_1), other input costs (x_2), overhead costs (x_3), and advertising expenditures (x_4). A series of twenty-four monthly observations were obtained, and a least squares estimate of the model yielded the following results:

$$y_t = .75 + .24x_{1t} + .56x_{2t} - .32x_{3t} + .23x_{4t}$$

$$(.07) \quad (.12) \quad (.23) \quad (.05)$$

$$R^2 = .79 \qquad d = .85$$

   The figures in parentheses below the estimated coefficients are their estimated standard errors.

   What can you conclude from these results?

39. The accompanying table shows, for a consumer goods corporation, 20 consecutive years of data on sales (y) and advertising (x).

y	x	y	x	y	x
102	61	109	58	220	86
92	45	109	61	251	102
93	53	115	54	273	136
98	54	133	75	318	148
93	53	198	61	335	161
105	55	222	86	344	180
118	52			292	185

(a) Estimate the regression

$$Y_t = \alpha + \beta x_t + \epsilon_t$$

(b) Check for autocorrelated errors in this model.

(c) If necessary, reestimate the model, allowing for autocorrelated errors.

40. The omission of an important independent variable from a time series regression model can result in the appearance of autocorrelated errors. In Section 14.5, we estimated the model

$$Y_t = \alpha + \beta_1 x_{1t} + \epsilon_t$$

relating profit margins to net revenues for our savings and loan data. Carry out a Durbin-Watson test on the residuals from this model. What can you infer from the results?

41. Refer to Exercise 9 on money spent by students on clothing. The Durbin-Watson statistic for the fitted regression model was 1.82. Test the null hypothesis of no autocorrelated errors against the alternative of positive autocorrelation.

REVIEW EXERCISES

42. Write brief reports, including examples, explaining the use of each of the following in specifying regression models:

(a) Dummy variables.

(b) Lagged dependent variables.

(c) The logarithmic transformation.

43. In Section 14.2, we discussed the fitting of the model

$$Y = \alpha + \beta_1 x_1 + \beta_2 x_2 + \beta_3 x_3 + \epsilon$$

where

Y = Tax revenues as a percentage of gross national product in a country
x_1 = Exports as a percentage of gross national product in the country
x_2 = Income per capita in the country
x_3 = Dummy variable taking the value 1 if the country participates in some form of economic integration, 0 otherwise

This provides a means of allowing for the effects on tax revenue of participation in some form of economic integration. Another possibility would be to estimate the regression

$$Y = \alpha + \beta_1 x_1 + \beta_2 x_2 + \epsilon$$

separately for countries that did and did not participate in some form of economic integration. Explain how these approaches to the problem differ.

44. Discuss the following statement: "In many practical regression problems, multicollinearity is so severe that it would be best to run separate simple linear regressions of the dependent variable on each independent variable."

45. Explain the nature of and the difficulties caused by each of the following:

(a) Heteroscedasticity

(b) Autocorrelated errors

46. The following model was fitted to data on 90 United Kingdom electronics companies.[19]

$$y = .819 + 2.11x_1 + .96x_2 - .059x_3 + 5.87x_4 + .00226x_5 \qquad \overline{R}^2 = .410$$

$$(1.79) \quad (1.94) \quad (.144) \quad (4.08) \quad (.00115)$$

where figures in brackets are estimated standard errors, and

y = Share price
x_1 = Earnings per share
x_2 = Funds flow per share
x_3 = Dividends per share
x_4 = Book value per share
x_5 = A measure of growth

(a) Test at the 10% level the null hypothesis that the coefficient on x_1 is zero in the population regression, against the alternative that the true coefficient is positive.

(b) Test at the 10% level the null hypothesis that the coefficient on x_2 is zero in the population regression, against the alternative that the true coefficient is positive.

(c) The variable x_1 was dropped from the model, and the regression of y on (x_2, x_3, x_4, x_5) was estimated. The estimated coefficient on x_2 was then 3.10, with standard error .68. Next, the variable x_2 was dropped from the original model, and the regression of y on (x_1, x_3, x_4, x_5) was estimated. The estimated coefficient on x_1 was 2.95, with standard error .63. How can these results be reconciled with the conclusions of parts (a) and (b)?

47. The following model was fitted to data from twenty-eight less developed countries in 1987 in order to explain the market value of their debt at that time.[20]

$$y = 77.2 - 9.6x_1 - 17.2x_2 - .15x_3 + 2.2x_4 \qquad R^2 = .84$$

$$(8.0) \quad (2.73) \quad (.056) \quad (1.0)$$

where

y = Secondary market price, in dollars, in 1987 of $100 of country's debt
x_1 = 1 if U.S. bank regulators have mandated write-down for the country's assets on books of U.S. banks, 0 otherwise
x_2 = 1 if country suspended interest payments in 1987, 2 if the country suspended interest payments before 1987 and was still in suspension, and 0 otherwise

[19] J. Board, B. Rees, and C. Sutcliffe, "Measuring the incremental information content of multiple accounting signals: a note on the use of the singular value decomposition," *Journal of Business, Finance and Accounting, 19* (1992), 447–54.
[20] J. Sachs and H. Huizinga, "U.S. commercial banks and the developing-country debt crisis," *Brookings Papers on Economic Activity* (1987), 555–601.

x_3 = Debt to gross national product ratio

x_4 = Rate of real gross national product growth, 1980–85.

(a) Interpret the estimated coefficient on x_1.

(b) Test the null hypothesis that, all else being equal, debt to gross national product ratio does not linearly influence the market value of a country's debt against the alternative that the higher this ratio the lower is the value of the debt.

(c) Interpret the coefficient of determination.

(d) The specification of the dummy variable x_2 is unorthodox. An alternative would be to replace x_2 by the pair of variables (x_5, x_6), defined as:

x_5 = 1 if country suspended interest payments in 1987, 0 otherwise

x_6 = 1 if country suspended interest payments before 1987 and was still in suspension, 0 otherwise

Compare the implications of these two alternative specifications.

48. An attempt was made to construct a regression model explaining student scores in intermediate economics courses.[21] The population regression model assumed was

$$Y = \alpha + \beta_1 x_1 + \beta_2 x_2 + \cdots + \beta_7 x_7 + \epsilon$$

where

Y = Total student score in intermediate economics courses

x_1 = Mathematics score on scholastic aptitude test

x_2 = Verbal score on scholastic aptitude test

x_3 = Grade in college algebra (A = 4, B = 3, C = 2, D = 1)

x_4 = Grade in college principles of economics course

x_5 = Dummy variable taking the value 1 if student is female, and 0 if male

x_6 = Dummy variable taking the value 1 if instructor is male, and 0 if female

x_7 = Dummy variable taking the value 1 if student and instructor are the same gender, and 0 otherwise.

This model was fitted to data on 262 students. Below we report t-ratios, so that t_i is the ratio of the estimate of β_i to its associated estimated standard error. These ratios are

$$t_1 = 4.69 \qquad t_2 = 2.89 \qquad t_3 = .46 \qquad t_4 = 4.90$$

$$t_5 = .13 \qquad t_6 = -1.08 \qquad t_7 = .88$$

The objective of this study was to assess the impact of the gender of student and instructor on performance. Write a brief report outlining what has been learned about this issue.

49. The following regression was fitted by least squares to thirty-two annual observations on time series data:

$$\log y_t = 4.52 - .62 \log x_{1t} + .92 \log x_{2t} + .61 \log x_{3t} + .16 \log x_{4t}$$

$$(.28) \qquad\qquad (.38) \qquad\qquad (.21) \qquad\qquad (.12)$$

$$\overline{R}^2 = .638 \qquad d = .61$$

where

[21] C. Waldauer, V. G. Duggal, and M. L. Williams, "Gender differences in economic knowledge: a further extension of the analysis," *Quarterly Review of Economics and Finance*, *32*, no. 4 (1992), 138–43.

y_t = Quantity of U.S. wheat exported
x_{1t} = Price of U.S. wheat on world market
x_{2t} = Quantity of U.S. wheat harvested
x_{3t} = Measure of income in countries importing U.S. wheat
x_{4t} = Price of barley on world market

(a) Interpret the estimated coefficient on $\log x_{1t}$ in the context of the assumed model.

(b) Test at the 5% level the null hypothesis that, all else being equal, income in importing countries has no effect on U.S. wheat exports against the alternative that higher income leads to higher expected exports. (Ignore, for now, the Durbin-Watson d statistic.)

(c) What null hypothesis can be tested by the d statistic? Carry out this test for the present problem, using a 1% significance level.

(d) In view of your finding in part (c), comment on your conclusion in part (b). How might you proceed to test the null hypothesis of part (b)?

50. The following regression was fitted by least squares to thirty annual observations on time series data:

$$\log y_t = 4.31 + .27 \log x_{1t} + .53 \log x_{2t} - .82 \log x_{3t}$$

$$(.17) \qquad (.21) \qquad (.30)$$

$$\overline{R}^2 = .615 \qquad d = .49$$

where

y_t = Number of business failures
x_{1t} = Rate of unemployment
x_{2t} = Short-term interest rate
x_{3t} = Value of new business orders placed

(a) Interpret the estimated coefficient on $\log x_{3t}$ in the context of the assumed model.

(b) What null hypothesis can be tested by the d statistic? Carry out this test for the present problem, using a 1% significance level.

(c) Given your result in part (b), is it possible to test, with the information given, the null hypothesis that, all else being equal, short-term interest rates do not influence business failures?

(d) Estimate the correlation between adjacent error terms in the regression model.

51. A stockbroker is interested in the factors influencing the rate of return on the common stock of banks. For a sample of thirty banks the following regression was estimated by least squares:

$$y = 2.37 + .84x_1 + .15x_2 - .13x_3 + 1.67x_4 \qquad R^2 = .317$$

$$(.39) \quad (.12) \quad (.09) \quad (1.97)$$

where

y = Percentage rate of return on common stock of bank
x_1 = Percentage rate of growth of bank's earnings
x_2 = Percentage rate of growth of bank's assets
x_3 = Loan losses as percentage of bank's assets
x_4 = 1 if bank head office is in New York City, and 0 otherwise

(a) Interpret the estimated coefficient on x_4.

(b) Interpret the coefficient of determination and use it to test the null hypothesis that, taken as a group, the four independent variables do not linearly influence the dependent variable.

(c) Let e_i denote the residuals from the fitted regression and $\hat{y}_i$ the in-sample predicted values of the dependent variable. The least squares regression of e_i^2 on $\hat{y}_i$ yielded coefficient of determination .082. What can be concluded from this finding?

52. A market researcher is interested in the average amount of money per year spent by students on entertainment. From 30 years of annual data, the following regression was estimated by least squares:

$$y_t = 40.93 + .253x_t + .546y_{t-1} \qquad d = 1.86$$

$$(.106) \quad (.134)$$

where

y_t = Expenditure per student, in dollars, on entertainment
x_t = Disposable income per student, in dollars, after payment of tuition, fees, room and board

(a) Find a 95% confidence interval for the coefficient on x_t in the population regression.

(b) What would be the expected impact over time of a $1 increase in disposable income per student on entertainment expenditure?

(c) Test the null hypothesis of no autocorrelation in the errors against the alternative of positive autocorrelation.

53. A local public utility would like to be able to predict a dwelling unit's average monthly electricity bill. The company statistician estimated by least squares the following regression model:

$$Y_i = \alpha + \beta_1 x_{1i} + \beta_2 x_{2i} + \epsilon_i$$

where

Y = Average monthly electricity bill, in dollars
x_1 = Average bimonthly automobile gasoline bill, in dollars
x_2 = Number of rooms in dwelling unit

From a sample of twenty-five dwelling units, the statistician obtained the following output from the SAS program:

PARAMETER	ESTIMATE	T FOR H0: PARAMETER = 0	STD. ERROR OF ESTIMATE
INTERCEPT	−10.8030		
X1	−.0247	−.956	.0259
X2	10.9409	18.517	.5909

(a) Interpret, in the context of the problem, the least squares estimate of β_2.

(b) Test against a two-sided alternative the null hypothesis

$$H_0: \quad \beta_1 = 0$$

(c) The statistician is concerned about the possibility of multicollinearity. What information is needed to assess the potential severity of this problem?

(d) It is suggested that household income is an important determinant of size of electricity bill. If this is so, what can you say about the regression estimated by the statistician?

(e) Given the fitted model, the statistician obtains the predicted electricity bills, $\hat{y}$, and the residuals, e. He then regresses e^2 on $\hat{y}$, finding that the regression has a coefficient of determination of .0470. Interpret this finding.

54. The accompanying table shows fifteen annual observations from Indonesia on total government tax revenues, other than from oil (y), national income (x_1), and the value added by oil as a percentage of gross domestic product (x_2). Estimate by least squares the regression

$$\log Y_t = \alpha + \beta_1 \log x_{1t} + \beta_2 \log x_{2t} + \epsilon_t$$

Write a report summarizing your findings, including a test for autocorrelated errors.

YEAR	y	x_1	x_2	YEAR	y	x_1	x_2
1	177.9	2,507	4.7	9	1,586.7	17,097	18.9
2	245.4	3,071	5.3	10	1,957.4	20,371	19.2
3	287.3	3,367	8.0	11	2,437.2	28,452	21.8
4	360.1	4,109	10.8	12	3,201.4	40,473	25.7
5	585.5	6,069	12.3	13	3,584.8	48,590	24.0
6	796.5	9,505	22.2	14	4,247.9	53,799	19.6
7	993.9	11,266	19.7	15	4,912.5	62,550	19.4
8	1,270.7	14,028	18.9				

55. The accompanying table shows twenty-two annual observations from the Federal Republic of Germany on percentage change in wages and salaries (y), productivity growth (x_1), and the rate of inflation (x_2) as measured by the gross national product price deflator. Estimate by least squares the regression

$$Y_t = \alpha + \beta_1 x_{1t} + \beta_2 x_{2t} + \epsilon_t$$

Write a report summarizing your findings, including a test for heteroscedasticity and a test for autocorrelated errors.

YEAR	y	x_1	x_2	YEAR	y	x_1	x_2
1	9.0	3.5	4.5	12	12.0	5.0	6.1
2	6.0	2.8	3.0	13	12.5	2.3	6.9
3	8.9	6.3	3.1	14	8.5	1.5	7.1
4	9.0	4.5	3.8	15	5.9	6.0	3.1
5	7.1	3.1	3.8	16	6.8	2.9	3.7
6	3.2	1.5	1.1	17	5.6	2.8	3.9
7	6.5	7.6	2.3	18	4.8	2.6	3.9
8	9.1	6.7	3.6	19	6.7	.9	4.8
9	14.6	4.2	7.5	20	5.5	.6	4.3
10	11.9	2.7	8.0	21	4.0	.7	4.8
11	9.4	3.5	6.3	22	3.3	3.1	3.2

56. The accompanying table shows thirty-five quarterly observations from Japan on quantity of imports (y), ratio of import prices to domestic prices (x_1), and real gross national product (x_2). Estimate by least squares the regression

$$\log Y_t = \alpha + \beta_1 \log x_{1t} + \beta_2 \log x_{2t} + \gamma \log Y_{t-1} + \epsilon_t$$

Write a report summarizing your findings, including a test for autocorrelated errors.

y	x_1	x_2	y	x_1	x_2	y	x_1	x_2
78.7	.8450	77.3	94.5	.6150	89.4	97.0	1.0010	102.1
80.4	.8264	78.2	95.0	.5487	90.4	93.6	1.0214	103.0
84.0	.8391	79.7	102.1	.5447	91.6	101.1	.9787	103.0
80.9	.8484	81.2	104.2	.5970	92.9	103.3	.9663	104.1
86.5	.8188	82.4	106.7	.6695	94.5	96.7	.9895	105.6
89.7	.7986	83.1	105.8	.7916	95.5	92.1	1.0391	106.5
91.7	.8060	83.8	108.2	.9323	96.6	95.1	1.0459	106.9
89.8	.7886	85.3	98.0	1.5067	97.9	94.1	.9364	107.1
89.7	.7611	86.9	104.0	1.0494	98.3	95.5	.8975	108.3
88.5	.7345	87.0	96.6	.9781	99.5	94.6	.9190	109.9
91.3	.6854	88.4	100.8	.9427	100.0	108.2	.8878	110.8
90.6	.6608	88.4	97.9	.9449	101.5			

57. A study was conducted on the worker-hour costs of Federal Deposit Insurance Corporation (FDIC) examinations of banks.[22] Data were obtained on ninety-one such examinations. Some of these were conducted by the FDIC alone, some jointly with state examiners. Examiners rated banks' management as good, satisfactory, fair, or unsatisfactory. The model estimated was

$$\log y = 2.41 + .3674 \log x_1 + .2217 \log x_2 + .0803 \log x_3$$
$$ (.0477) \qquad (.0628) \qquad (.0287)$$
$$- .1755 x_4 + .2799 x_5 + .5634 x_6 - .2572 x_7 \qquad R^2 = .766$$
$$(.2905) \quad (.1044) \quad (.1657) \quad (.0787)$$

where

y = FDIC examiner worker-hours
x_1 = Total assets of bank
x_2 = Total number of offices in bank
x_3 = Ratio of classified loans to total loans for bank
x_4 = 1 if management rating was "good," 0 otherwise
x_5 = 1 if management rating was "fair," 0 otherwise
x_6 = 1 if management rating was "unsatisfactory," 0 otherwise
x_7 = 1 if examination was conducted jointly with the state, 0 otherwise

The figures in parentheses beneath coefficient estimates are the associated estimated standard errors.

Write a report on these results.

---

[22] R. J. Miller, "Examination of man-hour cost for independent, joint, and divided examination programs," *Journal of Bank Research, 11* (1980), 28–35.

58. The accompanying table[23] shows, for a period of 20 years, data from Great Britain on days of incapacity due to sickness per person at risk (y), the male unemployment rate (x_1), the ratio of sickness benefits to earnings (x_2), and the real wage rate (x_3). Estimate the model

$$\log Y_t = \alpha + \beta_1 \log x_{1t} + \beta_2 \log x_{2t} + \beta_3 \log x_{3t} + \epsilon_t$$

and write a report on your findings. Include in your analysis a check on the possibility of autocorrelated errors and, if necessary, a correction for this problem.

YEAR	y	x_1	x_2	x_3	YEAR	y	x_1	x_2	x_3
1	12.2	1.5	.367	1.190	11	13.5	2.0	.446	1.362
2	12.2	1.2	.394	1.216	12	13.9	1.8	.493	1.355
3	11.7	1.3	.371	1.250	13	14.1	2.0	.686	1.364
4	11.9	1.7	.355	1.267	14	15.1	3.2	.732	1.383
5	12.1	2.4	.440	1.273	15	15.4	3.4	.728	1.407
6	12.3	2.5	.419	1.299	16	15.8	3.3	.710	1.406
7	11.9	1.9	.395	1.318	17	15.4	3.6	.727	1.454
8	12.1	1.9	.443	1.329	18	15.0	4.7	.779	1.501
9	12.8	2.5	.430	1.321	19	15.7	5.1	.737	1.593
10	12.9	3.1	.474	1.342	20	16.2	3.6	.706	1.660

[23] From R. B. Thomas, "Wages, sickness benefits, and absenteeism," *Journal of Economic Studies, 7,* no. 1 (1980), 51–61, © M.C.B. Publications Limited, Bradford, United Kingdom.

Analysis of Variance

15.1   COMPARISON OF SEVERAL POPULATION MEANS

In Section 9.6, we saw how to test the hypothesis of equality of two population means. In fact, two distinct tests were developed, the appropriate test depending on the **experimental design**—that is, the mechanism employed in the generation of sample observations. Specifically, our tests assumed either paired observations or independent random samples. This distinction is important, and to clarify it, we pause to consider a simple illustration. Suppose that it is our objective to compare the fuel consumption recorded for two different makes of automobile, A-cars and B-cars. We could randomly select ten people to drive these cars over a specified distance, each driver being assigned to a car of each type, so that any particular driver will drive both an A-car and a B-car. The twenty resulting fuel consumption figures obtained will consist of ten pairs, each pair corresponding to a single driver. This is the **matched pairs** design, and its attraction lies in its ability to produce a comparison between the quantities of interest (in this case, fuel consumption for the two types of car) while making allowance for the possible importance of an additional relevant factor (individual driver differences). Thus, if a significant difference between the performance of A-cars and B-cars is found, we have some assurance that this is not a result of differences in driver behavior. An alternative design would be to take twenty drivers and randomly assign ten of them to A-cars and ten to B-cars (though, in fact, there is no need to have equal numbers of trials for each type of car). The twenty resulting fuel consumption figures would then constitute a pair of **independent random samples** of ten observations each on A-cars and B-cars.

For these two types of design, we discussed in Section 9.6 appropriate procedures for testing the null hypothesis of equality of a pair of population means. In this chapter, our aim is to extend these procedures to the development of tests for the equality of several population means. Suppose, for example, that our study was to include a third make of automobile, the C-car. The null hypothesis of interest would then be that the population mean fuel consumption is the same for all three makes of car. We will see how tests for such hypotheses can be constructed, beginning with the case where independent random samples are taken. In Section 15.4, the extension of the test based on matched pairs will be discussed.

Suppose that of twenty drivers, seven are randomly assigned to A-cars, seven to B-cars, and six to C-cars. Table 15.1 shows the figures obtained at the completion of these trials.

Now, since our objective is the comparison of population means, an obvious starting place is the calculation of the sample means. From Table 15.1, we obtain for these data:

$$\text{Sample mean for A-cars} = \frac{146.3}{7} = 20.9$$

$$\text{Sample mean for B-cars} = \frac{162.4}{7} = 23.2$$

$$\text{Sample mean for C-cars} = \frac{137.4}{6} = 22.9$$

Naturally, these sample means are not all the same. As always, however, when testing hypotheses, we are interested in the likelihood of such differences arising by chance if in fact the null hypothesis were true. If it is concluded that such discrepancies would be very unlikely to arise by chance, considerable skepticism about the truth of the null hypothesis would arise.

To clarify the issues involved, consider Figure 15.1, which depicts two hypothetical sets of data. The sample means in part (a) of the figure are precisely the same as those in part (b). The crucial difference is that in the former, the observations are tightly clustered about their respective sample means, while in the latter, there is much greater dispersion. Visual inspection of part (a) suggests very strongly the conjecture that the data in fact arise from three populations with different means. Looking at part (b) of the figure, by contrast, we would not be terribly surprised to learn that these data came from a common population.

TABLE 15.1 Fuel consumption figures from three independent random samples, in miles per gallon

	A-CARS	B-CARS	C-CARS
	22.2	24.6	22.7
	19.9	23.1	21.9
	20.3	22.0	23.3
	21.4	23.5	24.1
	21.2	23.6	22.1
	21.0	22.1	23.4
	20.3	23.5	—
Sums	146.3	162.4	137.4

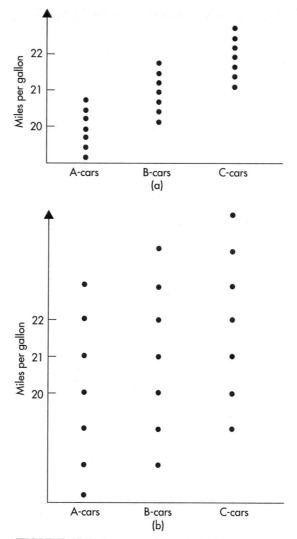

FIGURE 15.1 Two sets of sample fuel
consumption data on three makes of automobile

This illustration serves to point out the very essence of the test for equality of population means. The critical factor is the *variability* involved in the data. If the variability *around* the sample means is small compared with the variability *among* the sample means, as in Figure 15.1(a), we would be inclined to doubt the null hypothesis that the population means are equal. If, as in Figure 15.1(b), the variability around the sample means is large compared with the variability among them, the evidence against this null hypothesis is rather flimsy. This being the case, it seems reasonable to expect that an appropriate test will be based on estimates of variance. This is indeed the case, and for this reason the general technique employed is referred to as the **analysis of variance.**

15.2 ONE-WAY ANALYSIS OF VARIANCE

The problem introduced in Section 15.1 can be treated quite generally. Suppose that we want to compare the means of K populations, *each of which is assumed to have the same variance*. Independent random samples of $n_1, n_2, \ldots, n_K$ observations are taken from these populations. We will use the symbol x to denote the actual sample values and will index this with a double subscript, so that x_{ij} denotes the jth observation on the ith population. Then, using the format of Table 15.1, we can display the sample data as in Table 15.2.

The procedure for testing the equality of population means in this setup is called **one-way analysis of variance,** a terminology that will become clearer when we discuss other analysis of variance models.

The Framework for One-Way Analysis of Variance

Suppose that we have independent random samples of $n_1, n_2, \ldots, n_K$ observations from K populations. If the population means are denoted $\mu_1, \mu_2, \ldots, \mu_K$, **the one-way analysis of variance** framework is designed to test the null hypothesis

$$H_0: \quad \mu_1 = \mu_2 = \cdots = \mu_K$$

In this section, we will develop a test of the null hypothesis that the K population means are equal, given independent random samples from those populations. The obvious first step is to calculate the sample means for the K groups of observations. These sample means will be denoted $\bar{x}_1, \bar{x}_2, \ldots, \bar{x}_K$. Formally, then

$$\bar{x}_i = \frac{\sum_{j=1}^{n_i} x_{ij}}{n_i} \qquad (i = 1, 2, \ldots, K)$$

where n_i denotes the number of sample observations in group i. In this notation, we have already found for the data of Table 15.1

$$\bar{x}_1 = 20.9 \qquad \bar{x}_2 = 23.2 \qquad \bar{x}_3 = 22.9$$

TABLE 15.2 Sample observations from independent random samples of K populations

POPULATION			
1	2	$\ldots$	K
x_{11}	x_{21}		x_{K1}
x_{12}	x_{22}		x_{K2}
.	.		.
.	.		.
.	.		.
x_{1n_1}	x_{2n_2}		x_{Kn_K}

Now, the null hypothesis of interest specifies that the K populations have a common mean. A logical step, then, is to form an estimate of that common mean from the sample data. A sensible choice for such an estimate is the *overall mean* of the sample observations. This is just the sum of all of the sample values, divided by their total number. If we let n denote the total number of sample observations, then

$$n = \sum_{i=1}^{K} n_i$$

so in our example, $n = 20$. The overall mean of the sample observations can then be expressed as

$$\bar{x} = \frac{\sum_{i=1}^{K} \sum_{j=1}^{n_i} x_{ij}}{n}$$

where the double summation notation indicates that we sum over all groups and over all observations within each group—that is, we sum all of the available observations. An equivalent expression is

$$\bar{x} = \frac{\sum_{i=1}^{K} n_i \bar{x}_i}{n}$$

For the fuel consumption data of Table 15.1, the overall mean is

$$\bar{x} = \frac{(7)(20.9) + (7)(23.2) + (6)(22.9)}{20} = 22.305$$

Hence, if in fact the population mean fuel consumption is the same for A-cars, B-cars, and C-cars, we estimate that common mean to be 22.305 miles per gallon.

As indicated in Section 15.1, the test of equality of population means is based on a comparison of two types of variability exhibited by the sample members. The first is variability about the individual sample means within the K groups of observations. It is convenient to refer to this as **within-groups variability.** Second, we are interested in the variability among the K group means. This is called **between-groups variability.** We now seek measures, based on the sample data, of these two types of variability.

To begin, consider variability within the groups. To measure variability in the first group, we calculate the sum of squared deviations of the observations about their sample mean $\bar{x}_1$, that is

$$SS_1 = \sum_{j=1}^{n_1} (x_{1j} - \bar{x}_1)^2$$

Similarly, for the second group, whose sample mean is $\bar{x}_2$, we calculate

$$SS_2 = \sum_{j=1}^{n_2} (x_{2j} - \bar{x}_2)^2$$

and so on. The total within-groups variability, denoted SSW, is then the sum of these sums of squares over all K groups, that is

$$SSW = SS_1 + SS_2 + \cdots + SS_K$$

or

$$SSW = \sum_{i=1}^{K} \sum_{j=1}^{n_i} (x_{ij} - \bar{x}_i)^2$$

For the data on fuel consumption, we have

$$SS_1 = (22.2 - 20.9)^2 + (19.9 - 20.9)^2 + \cdots + (20.3 - 20.9)^2 = 3.76$$

$$SS_2 = (24.6 - 23.2)^2 + (23.1 - 23.2)^2 + \cdots + (23.5 - 23.2)^2 = 4.96$$

$$SS_3 = (22.7 - 22.9)^2 + (21.9 - 22.9)^2 + \cdots + (23.4 - 22.9)^2 = 3.46$$

The within-groups sum of squares is therefore

$$SSW = SS_1 + SS_2 + SS_3 = 3.76 + 4.96 + 3.46 = 12.18$$

Next, we need a measure of variability between groups. A natural measure is based on the discrepancies between the individual group means and the overall mean. In fact, as before, these discrepancies are squared, giving

$$(\bar{x}_1 - \bar{x})^2, (\bar{x}_2 - \bar{x})^2, \ldots, (\bar{x}_K - \bar{x})^2$$

In computing the total between-groups sum of squares, SSG, we weight each squared discrepancy by the number of sample observations in the corresponding group (so that most weight is given to the squared discrepancies in groups with most observations), giving

$$SSG = \sum_{i=1}^{K} n_i (\bar{x}_i - \bar{x})^2$$

Thus, for our fuel consumption data

$$SSG = (7)(20.9 - 22.305)^2 + (7)(23.2 - 22.305)^2 + (6)(22.9 - 22.305)^2$$

$$= 21.5495$$

Another sum of squares is often calculated. This is the sum of squared discrepancies of *all* the sample observations about their *overall* mean. This is called the **total sum of squares** and is expressed as

$$SST = \sum_{i=1}^{K} \sum_{j=1}^{n_i} (x_{ij} - \bar{x})^2$$

In fact, it can be shown that the total sum of squares is the sum of the within-groups and between-groups sums of squares, that is

$$SST = SSW + SSG$$

Hence, for the fuel consumption data, we have

$$SST = 12.18 + 21.5495 = 33.7295$$

In the box, we summarize the results obtained so far.

The decomposition of the total sum of squares into the sum of two components—within-groups and between-groups sums of squares—provides the basis for the analysis of variance test of equality of group population means. We can view this decomposition as expressing the total variability of all the sample observations about their overall mean as the sum of variability within groups and variability between groups. Schematically, this is shown in Figure 15.2.

Our test of the equality of population means is based on the assumption that the K populations have a common variance. If the null hypothesis that the population means are all the same is true, each of the sums of squares, SSW and SSG, can be used as the basis for an estimate of the common population variance. To obtain these estimates, the sums of squares must be divided by the appropriate number of degrees of freedom.

First, it can be shown that an unbiased estimate of the population variance results if SSW is divided by $(n - K)$. The resulting estimate is called the **within-groups mean square,** denoted MSW, so that

$$\text{MSW} = \frac{\text{SSW}}{n - K}$$

FIGURE 15.2 Sum of squares decomposition for one-way analysis of variance

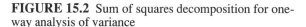
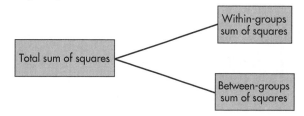

For our data, we have

$$\text{MSW} = \frac{12.18}{20 - 3} = .7165$$

If the population means are equal, another unbiased estimate of the population variance is obtained by dividing SSG by $(K - 1)$. The resulting quantity is called the **between-groups mean square,** denoted MSG, and hence

$$\text{MSG} = \frac{\text{SSG}}{K - 1}$$

For the fuel consumption data

$$\text{MSG} = \frac{21.5495}{3 - 1} = 10.7748$$

When the population means are *not* equal, the between-groups mean square does *not* provide an unbiased estimate of the common population variance. Rather, the expected value of the corresponding random variable exceeds the common population variance, as it also carries information about the squared differences of the true population means.

If the null hypothesis were true, we would now be in possession of two unbiased estimates of the same quantity, the common population variance. It would be reasonable to expect these estimates to be quite close to each other. The greater the discrepancy between these two estimates, all else being equal, the stronger would be our suspicion that the null hypothesis is not true. The test of the null hypothesis is based on the ratio of mean squares

$$F = \frac{\text{MSG}}{\text{MSW}} \tag{15.2.1}$$

If this ratio is quite close to 1, there would be little cause to doubt the null hypothesis of equality of population means. However, if the variability between groups is large compared to the variability within groups, we would, as already noted, suspect the null hypothesis to be false. This is the case where a value considerably larger than 1 arises for the ratio (15.2.1). The null hypothesis is rejected for large values of this ratio.

A formal test follows from the fact that if the null hypothesis of equality of population means is true, the random variable corresponding to (15.2.1) follows the *F* distribution (discussed in Section 9.8) with numerator degrees of freedom $(K - 1)$ and denominator degrees of freedom $(n - K)$, assuming the population distributions to be normal.

Hypothesis Test for One-Way Analysis of Variance

Suppose that we have independent random samples of $n_1, n_2, \ldots, n_K$ observations from K populations. Denote by n the total sample size, so that

$$n = n_1 + n_2 + \cdots + n_K$$

We define the **mean squares** as follows:

$$\text{WITHIN-GROUPS: MSW} = \frac{\text{SSW}}{n - K}$$

$$\text{BETWEEN-GROUPS: MSG} = \frac{\text{SSG}}{K - 1}$$

The null hypothesis to be tested is that the K population means are equal, that is

$$H_0: \quad \mu_1 = \mu_2 = \cdots = \mu_K$$

We make the following additional assumptions:

(i) The population variances are equal.
(ii) The population distributions are normal.

A test of significance level α is provided by the decision rule

$$\text{Reject } H_0 \text{ if } \quad \frac{\text{MSG}}{\text{MSW}} > F_{K - 1, n - K, \alpha}$$

where $F_{K - 1, n - K, \alpha}$ is the number for which

$$P(F_{K - 1, n - K} > F_{K - 1, n - K, \alpha}) = \alpha$$

and the random variable $F_{K - 1, n - K}$ follows an F distribution with numerator degrees of freedom $(K - 1)$ and denominator degrees of freedom $(n - K)$.

For the fuel consumption data, we find

$$\frac{\text{MSG}}{\text{MSW}} = \frac{10.7748}{.7165} = 15.04$$

The numerator and denominator degrees of freedom are, respectively, $(K - 1) = 2$ and $(n - K) = 17$. Thus, for a 1%-level test, from Table 7 of the Appendix, we have

$$F_{2,17,.01} = 6.11$$

Hence, these data allow us to reject, at the 1% significance level, the null hypothesis that population mean fuel consumption is the same for all three types of automobile.

The computations involved in carrying out this test are very conveniently summarized in a **one-way analysis of variance table.** The general form of the table is set out in Table 15.3. For the fuel consumption data, the analysis of variance is set out in Table 15.4. Note that in some expositions, the within-groups sum of squares is referred to as the **error sum of squares.**

EXAMPLE 15.1

The *fog index* is used to measure the reading difficulty of a written text: The higher the value of the index, the more difficult the reading level. Independent random samples of six advertisements were taken from *Scientific American*, *Fortune*, and *New*

TABLE 15.3 General format of one-way analysis of variance table

SOURCE OF VARIATION	SUMS OF SQUARES	DEGREES OF FREEDOM	MEAN SQUARES	F RATIO
Between groups	SSG	$K - 1$	$MSG = \dfrac{SSG}{K - 1}$	$\dfrac{MSG}{MSW}$
Within groups	SSW	$\underline{n - K}$	$MSW = \dfrac{SSW}{n - K}$	
Total	SST	$n - 1$		

Yorker magazines, and the fog indices for the eighteen advertisements were measured, as recorded in the table.[1]

SCIENTIFIC AMERICAN	FORTUNE	NEW YORKER
15.75	12.63	9.27
11.55	11.46	8.28
11.16	10.77	8.15
9.92	9.93	6.37
9.23	9.87	6.37
8.20	9.42	5.66

From these data we can derive the analysis of variance table:

SOURCE OF VARIATION	SUMS OF SQUARES	DEGREES OF FREEDOM	MEAN SQUARES	F RATIO
Between groups	48.5288	2	24.2644	6.97
Within groups	52.2173	15	3.4812	
Total	100.7461	17		

TABLE 15.4 One-way analysis of variance table for fuel consumption data

SOURCE OF VARIATION	SUMS OF SQUARES	DEGREES OF FREEDOM	MEAN SQUARES	F RATIO
Between groups	21.5495	2	10.7748	15.04
Within groups	12.1800	17	.7165	
Total	33.7295	19		

---

[1] Data from F. K. Shuptrine and D. D. McVicker, "Readability levels of magazine advertisements," *Journal of Advertising Research*, *21*, no. 5 (1981), 45–50. The details of the construction of the fog index are set out in Exercise 76 of Chapter 9.

To test the null hypothesis that the population mean fog indices are the same, the computed F ratio in the analysis of variance table must be compared with tabulated values of the F distribution with $(2, 15)$ degrees of freedom. From Table 7 of the Appendix, we find

$$F_{2,15,.01} = 6.36$$

Thus, the null hypothesis of equality of the three population mean fog indices is rejected at the 1% significance level. The evidence in the data against this hypothesis is very strong.

POPULATION MODEL FOR ONE-WAY ANALYSIS OF VARIANCE

It is instructive to view the one-way analysis of variance model in a different light. Let the random variable X_{ij} denote the jth observation from the ith population, and let μ_i stand for the mean of this population. Then, X_{ij} can be viewed as the sum of two parts—its mean and a random variable ϵ_{ij} having mean 0. Therefore, we can write

$$X_{ij} = \mu_i + \epsilon_{ij} \qquad (15.2.2)$$

Now, because independent random samples are taken, the random variables ϵ_{ij} will be uncorrelated with one another. Moreover, given our assumption that the population variances are all the same, it follows that the ϵ_{ij} all have the same variances. Hence, these random variables satisfy the standard assumptions (see Section 13.3) imposed on the error terms of a multiple regression model. Thus, Eq. (15.2.2) can be viewed as such a model, with unknown parameters $\mu_1, \mu_2, \ldots, \mu_K$. The null hypothesis of interest

$$H_0: \quad \mu_1 = \mu_2 = \cdots = \mu_K$$

is a test on these parameters, facilitated by the further assumption of normality.

The model (15.2.2) can be written in a slightly different manner. Let μ denote the overall mean of the K combined populations and G_i the discrepancy between the population mean for the ith group and this overall mean, so that

$$G_i = \mu_i - \mu \qquad \text{or} \qquad \mu_i = \mu + G_i$$

Substituting into Eq. (15.2.2) then gives

$$X_{ij} = \mu + G_i + \epsilon_{ij}$$

so that an observation is made up of the sum of an overall mean μ, a group-specific term G_i, and a random error ϵ_{ij}. Then our null hypothesis is that every population mean μ_i is the same as the overall mean, or

$$H_0: \quad G_1 = G_2 = \cdots = G_K = 0$$

This population model and some of the assumptions are illustrated in Figure 15.3. For each type of car, actual fuel consumption recorded in any trial can be represented by a normally distributed random variable. The population means of fuel consumption, μ_1, μ_2, and μ_3, for A-cars, B-cars, and C-cars, respectively, determine the centers of these distributions. According to our assumption, these population distribu-

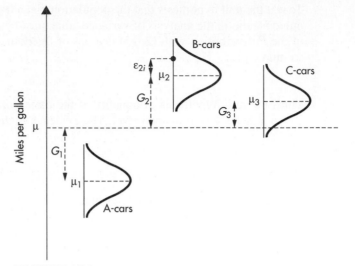

FIGURE 15.3 Illustration of the population model for the one-way analysis of variance

tions must have the same variance. The figure also shows the mean μ of the three combined populations and the differences G_i between the individual population means and the overall mean. Finally, for B-cars, we have marked by a dot the jth sample observation. The random variable ϵ_{2j} is then the difference between the observed value and the corresponding population mean. Thus, we can think of the observed value as the sum of three parts—the overall mean μ, the difference G_2 between the population mean fuel consumption for B-cars and the overall mean, and the discrepancy (due to sampling variability) of the observed value and the mean of the population from which it is drawn.

15.3 THE KRUSKAL-WALLIS TEST

As we have already noted, the one-way analysis of variance test of Section 15.2 generalizes to the multipopulation case the t test for comparing two population means when independent random samples are available. The test is based on an assumption that the underlying population distributions are normal. In Section 10.4, we introduced the Mann-Whitney test, a nonparametric test that is valid for the comparison of the central locations of two populations based on independent random samples, even when the population distributions are not normal. It is also possible to develop a nonparametric alternative to the one-way analysis of variance test. This is known as the **Kruskal-Wallis test,** employed when an investigator has strong grounds for suspecting that the parent population distributions may be markedly different from the normal.

Like the majority of the nonparametric tests we have already encountered, the Kruskal-Wallis test is based on the *ranks* of the sample observations. We will illustrate the computation of the test statistic by reference to the fuel consumption data of Table 15.1. The sample values are all pooled together and ranked in ascending order, as in Table 15.5, using the average of adjacent ranks in the case of ties.

TABLE 15.5 Fuel consumption figures (in miles per gallon) and ranks from three independent random samples

A-CARS	RANK	B-CARS	RANK	C-CARS	RANK
22.2	11	24.6	20	22.7	12
19.9	1	23.1	13	21.9	7
20.3	2.5	22.0	8	23.2	14
21.4	6	23.5	16.5	24.1	19
21.2	5	23.6	18	22.1	9.5
21.0	4	22.1	9.5	23.4	15
20.3	2.5	23.5	16.5		
Rank sums	32		101.5		76.5

The test is based on the sums of the ranks $R_1, R_2, \ldots, R_K$, for the K samples. In the fuel consumption example

$$R_1 = 32 \qquad R_2 = 101.5 \qquad R_3 = 76.5$$

Now, the null hypothesis to be tested is that the three population means are the same. We would be suspicious of that hypothesis if there were substantial differences among the average ranks for the K samples. In fact, our test is based on the statistic

$$W = \frac{12}{n(n+1)} \sum_{i=1}^{K} \frac{R_i^2}{n_i} - 3(n+1) \qquad (15.3.1)$$

where n_i are the sample sizes in the K groups and n is the total number of sample observations. The null hypothesis would be in doubt if a large value for (15.3.1) were observed. The basis for the test follows from the fact that unless the sample sizes are very small, the random variable corresponding to the test statistic has, under the null hypothesis, a distribution that is well approximated by the χ^2 distribution with $(K - 1)$ degrees of freedom.

The Kruskal-Wallis Test

Suppose that we have independent random samples of $n_1, n_2, \ldots, n_K$ observations from K populations. Let

$$n = n_1 + n_2 + \cdots + n_K$$

denote the total number of sample observations. Denote by $R_1, R_2, \ldots, R_K$ the sums of ranks for the K samples when the sample observations are pooled together and ranked in ascending order. The test of the null hypothesis, H_0, of equality of the population means is based on the statistic

$$W = \frac{12}{n(n+1)} \sum_{i=1}^{K} \frac{R_i^2}{n_i} - 3(n+1)$$

A test of significance level α is given by the decision rule

$$\text{Reject } H_0 \text{ if } \quad W > \chi^2_{K-1,\alpha}$$

where $\chi^2_{K-1,\alpha}$ is the number that is exceeded with probability α by a χ^2 random variable with $(K-1)$ degrees of freedom.

This test procedure is approximately valid provided that the sample contains at least five observations from each population.

For our fuel consumption data, we find

$$W = \frac{12}{(20)(21)} \left[\frac{(32)^2}{7} + \frac{(101.5)^2}{7} + \frac{(76.5)^2}{6} \right] - (3)(21) = 11.10$$

Here, we have $(K-1) = 2$ degrees of freedom, so for a .5% significance level test, we find from Table 5 of the Appendix

$$\chi^2_{2,.005} = 10.60$$

Hence, the null hypothesis that the population mean fuel consumption is the same for the three types of automobiles can be rejected even at the .5% significance level. Of course, we also rejected this hypothesis using the analysis of variance test of Section 15.2. However, here we have been able to do so without imposing the assumption of normality of the population distributions.

EXAMPLE 15.2

Independent random samples of 101 lower-class, 112 middle-class, and ninety-six upper-class women were asked to rate, on a scale from 1 to 7, the importance they attached to brand name when purchasing soft drinks.[2] The value of the Kruskal-Wallis statistic for this study was reported as 25.22. Test the null hypothesis that the population mean ratings are the same for these three populations.

The calculated test statistic is

$$W = 25.22$$

Since there are $K = 3$ groups, we have for a .5%-level test

$$\chi^2_{K-1,\alpha} = \chi^2_{2,.005} = 10.60$$

Thus, the null hypothesis that the three population mean ratings are the same is very clearly rejected on the evidence of this sample, even at the .5% level of significance.

EXERCISES

1. A manufacturer of diet soda is considering three alternative can colors—red, yellow, and blue. To check whether such considerations have any effect on sales, sixteen stores of approximately equal size are chosen. Red cans are sent to six of these stores, yellow cans to five others, and blue cans to the remaining five. After a few days, a check is made on the number of sales in each store. The results (in tens of cans) shown in the table were obtained.

---

[2] P. E. Murphy, "The effect of social class on brand and price consciousness for supermarket products," *Journal of Retailing*, 55, no. 2 (1978), 33–42.

RED	YELLOW	BLUE
43	52	61
52	37	29
59	38	38
76	64	53
61	74	79
81		

(a) Calculate the within-groups, between-groups, and total sums of squares.

(b) Complete the analysis of variance table, and test the null hypothesis that the population mean sales levels are the same for all three can colors.

2. An instructor has a class of twenty-three students. At the beginning of the semester, each student is randomly assigned to one of four teaching assistants—Smiley, Haydon, Alleline, or Bland. The students are encouraged to meet with their assigned teaching assistant to discuss difficult course material. At the end of the semester, a common examination is administered. The scores obtained by students working with these teaching assistants are shown in the accompanying table.

SMILEY	HAYDON	ALLELINE	BLAND
72	78	80	79
69	93	68	70
84	79	59	61
76	97	75	74
64	88	82	85
	81	68	63

(a) Calculate the within-groups, between-groups, and total sums of squares.

(b) Complete the analysis of variance table, and test the null hypothesis of equality of population mean scores for the four teaching assistants.

3. Three suppliers provide parts in shipments of 500 units. Random samples of six shipments from each of the three suppliers were carefully checked, and the numbers of parts not conforming to standards were recorded. These numbers are listed in the table.

SUPPLIER A	SUPPLIER B	SUPPLIER C
28	22	33
37	27	29
34	29	39
29	20	33
31	18	37
33	30	38

(a) Set out the analysis of variance table for these data.

(b) Test the null hypothesis that the population mean numbers of parts per shipment not conforming to standards are the same for all three suppliers.

4. A corporation is trying to decide which of three makes of automobile to order for its fleet—domestic, Japanese, or European. Five cars of each type were ordered, and after 10,000 miles of driving, the operating cost per mile of each was assessed. The accompanying results in cents per mile were obtained.

DOMESTIC	JAPANESE	EUROPEAN
18.0	20.1	19.3
17.6	15.6	17.4
15.4	16.1	15.1
19.1	15.3	18.6
16.9	15.4	16.1

(a) Set out the analysis of variance table for these data.
(b) Test the null hypothesis that the population mean operating costs per mile are the same for these three types of car.

5. Random samples of seven freshmen, seven sophomores, and seven juniors taking a business statistics class were drawn. The accompanying table shows scores on the final examination.

FRESHMEN	SOPHOMORES	JUNIORS
82	71	64
93	62	73
61	85	87
74	94	91
69	78	56
70	66	78
53	71	87

(a) Set out the analysis of variance table.
(b) Test the null hypothesis that the three population mean scores are equal.

6. Samples of four salespeople from each of four regions were asked to predict percentage increases in sales volume for their territories in the next twelve months. The predictions are shown in the accompanying table.

WEST	MIDWEST	SOUTH	EAST
6.8	7.2	4.2	9.0
4.2	6.6	4.8	8.0
5.4	5.8	5.8	7.2
5.0	7.0	4.6	7.6

(a) Set out the analysis of variance table.
(b) Test the null hypothesis that the four population mean predictions are equal.

7. Independent random samples of six assistant professors, four associate professors, and five full professors were asked to estimate the amount of time outside the classroom spent on teaching responsibilities in the last week. Results, in hours, are shown in the accompanying table.

	ASSISTANT	ASSOCIATE	FULL
	7	15	11
	12	12	7
	11	15	6
	15	8	9
	9		7
	14		

(a) Set out the analysis of variance table.

(b) Test the null hypothesis that the three population mean times are equal.

8. Two tutoring services offer crash courses in preparation for the C.P.A. exam. To check on the effectiveness of these services, fifteen students were chosen. Five students were randomly assigned to service A, five were assigned to service B, and the remaining five took no crash course. Their scores on the examination, expressed as percentages, are given in the table.

	SERVICE A COURSE	SERVICE B COURSE	NO COURSE
	79	74	72
	74	69	71
	92	87	81
	67	81	61
	85	64	63

(a) Set out the analysis of variance table.

(b) Test the null hypothesis that the three population mean scores are the same.

9. In the study of Example 15.1, independent random samples of six advertisements from *True Confessions*, *People Weekly*, and *Newsweek* were taken. The fog indices for these advertisements are given in the accompanying table. Test the null hypothesis that the population mean fog indices are the same for advertisements in these three magazines.

TRUE CONFESSIONS	*PEOPLE WEEKLY*	*NEWSWEEK*
12.89	9.50	10.21
12.69	8.60	9.66
11.15	8.59	7.67
9.52	6.50	5.12
9.12	4.79	4.88
7.04	4.29	3.12

10. For the one-way analysis of variance model, we write the jth observation from the ith group as

$$X_{ij} = \mu + G_i + \epsilon_{ij}$$

where μ is the overall mean, G_i is the effect specific to the ith group, and ϵ_{ij} is a random error for the jth observation from the ith group. Consider the data of Example 15.1.

(a) Estimate μ.

(b) Estimate G_i for each of the three magazines.

(c) Estimate ϵ_{32}, the error term corresponding to the second observation (8.28) for *New Yorker*.

11. Use the model for the one-way analysis of variance for the data of Exercise 9.

(a) Estimate μ.

(b) Estimate G_i for each of the three magazines.

(c) Estimate ϵ_{13}, the error term corresponding to the third observation (11.15) for *True Confessions*.

12. For the data of Exercise 1, use the Kruskal-Wallis test to test the null hypothesis that the population mean sales levels are identical for the three can colors.

13. Using the data of Exercise 2, perform a Kruskal-Wallis test of the null hypothesis that the population mean test scores are the same for students assigned to the four teaching assistants.

14. Using the data of Exercise 3, carry out a test of the null hypothesis of equality of the three population mean numbers of parts per shipment not conforming to standards without assuming normality of population distributions.

15. For the data of Exercise 4, test the null hypothesis that the population mean operating costs per mile are the same for all three types of automobile, without assuming normal population distributions.

16. Using the data of Exercise 5, carry out a nonparametric test of the null hypothesis of equality of the population mean examination scores for freshmen, sophomores, and juniors.

17. Based on the data of Exercise 6, use the Kruskal-Wallis method to test the null hypothesis of equality of population mean sales growth predictions for the four regions.

18. Refer to Exercise 7. Without assuming normal population distributions, test the null hypothesis that population mean times spent on teaching responsibilities are the same for assistant, associate, and full professors.

19. Based on the data of Exercise 8, perform the Kruskal-Wallis test of the null hypothesis of equal population mean scores on the C.P.A. exam for students using no tutoring service and those using services A and B.

20. Independent random samples of 101 lower-class women, 112 middle-class women, and ninety-six upper-class women were asked to rate, on a scale from 1 to 7, the importance attached to brand name when purchasing paper towels.[3] The value of the Kruskal-Wallis statistic obtained was .17.

(a) What null hypothesis can be tested using this information?

(b) Carry out this test.

---

[3] Ibid.

15.4 TWO-WAY ANALYSIS OF VARIANCE: ONE OBSERVATION PER CELL, RANDOMIZED BLOCKS

Although our primary interest lies in the analysis of one particular feature of an experiment, we may suspect that a second factor could exert an important influence on the outcome. In the earlier sections of this chapter, we discussed an experiment in which the objective was to compare the fuel consumption of three types of automobile. Data were collected from three independent random samples of trials and analyzed through a one-way analysis of variance. It was assumed that the variability in the sample data was due to two causes—genuine differences between the performance characteristics of the three types of car, and random variation. In fact, we might suspect that part of the observed random variability could be explained by differences in driver habits. Now, if in some way this last factor could be isolated, the amount of random variability in the experiment would be reduced accordingly. This might in turn make it easier to detect differences in the performance of the automobiles. In other words, by designing an experiment to account for differences in driver characteristics, we hope to achieve a more powerful test of the null hypothesis that population mean fuel consumption is the same for all types of automobiles.

In fact, it is quite straightforward to design an experiment in such a way that the influence of a second factor of this kind can be taken into account. Suppose, once again, that we have three makes of automobile (say, α-cars, β-cars, and γ-cars) whose fuel economies we wish to compare. We will consider an experiment in which six trials are to be run with each type of car. If these trials are conducted using six drivers, each of whom drives a car of all three types, it will be possible, since every car will have been tested by every driver, to extract from the results information about driver variability as well as information about differences among the three types of car. The additional variable—in this case, drivers—is sometimes called a **blocking variable.** The experiment is said to be arranged in **blocks;** in our example, there would be six blocks, one for each driver.

This kind of blocked design can be used to obtain information about two factors simultaneously. For example, suppose that we want to compare fuel economy obtained not only by different types of automobile but also by different types of drivers. In particular, we may be interested in the effect of driver age on fuel economy. To do this, drivers can be subdivided into age categories. We might use the following six age classes (in years):

1. 25 and under
2. 26–35
3. 36–45
4. 46–55
5. 56–65
6. Over 65

Then, we can arrange our experiment so that an automobile from each group is driven by a driver from each age class. In this way, in addition to testing the hypothesis that population mean fuel consumption is the same for each automobile type, we can also test the hypothesis that population mean fuel consumption is the same for each age class.

In fact, whether a car of each type is driven by each of six drivers or a car of each type is driven by a driver from each of six age classes, the procedure for testing equality of population mean fuel consumption for the automobile types is the same. In this section, we will use the latter design for purposes of illustration.

Table 15.6 gives results for an experiment involving three automobile types and six driver age classes. The comparison of automobile types is the main focus of interest, and driver ages are used as a blocking variable.

This kind of design is called a **randomized blocks design.** The randomization arises because we randomly select one driver from the first age class to drive an α-car, one driver from the second age class to drive an α-car, and so on. This procedure is repeated for each of the other driver classes and for each of the cars. If possible, the trials should be carried out in random order rather than block by block.

Suppose that we have K groups and that there are H blocks. We will use x_{ij} to denote the sample observation corresponding to the ith group and the jth block. Thus, the sample data may be set out as in Table 15.7. Notice that the format here is simply an extension of the experimental form used for the paired observations test of Section 9.6, where we had only two groups. Thus, the development of this section extends the paired t test of Section 9.6 to allow us to test the equality of several population means.

To develop a test of the hypothesis that the population means are the same for all K groups, we require the sample means for these groups. For the mean of the ith group, we use the notation $\bar{x}_{i\cdot}$, so

$$\bar{x}_{i\cdot} = \frac{\sum_{j=1}^{H} x_{ij}}{H} \qquad (i = 1, 2, \ldots, K)$$

From Table 15.6, we obtain

$$\bar{x}_{1\cdot} = \frac{148.2}{6} = 24.7 \qquad \bar{x}_{2\cdot} = \frac{143.4}{6} = 23.9 \qquad \bar{x}_{3\cdot} = \frac{151.2}{6} = 25.2$$

TABLE 15.6 Sample observations on fuel consumption recorded for three types of automobile driven by six drivers

DRIVER CLASSES		AUTOMOBILES		
	α-CARS	β-CARS	γ-CARS	SUMS
1	25.1	23.9	26.0	75.0
2	24.7	23.7	25.4	73.8
3	26.0	24.4	25.8	76.2
4	24.3	23.3	24.4	72.0
5	23.9	23.6	24.2	71.7
6	24.2	24.5	25.4	74.1
Sums	148.2	143.4	151.2	442.8

TABLE 15.7 Sample observations on K groups and H blocks

BLOCK	GROUP			
	1	2	$\ldots$	K
1	x_{11}	x_{21}	$\ldots$	x_{K1}
2	x_{12}	x_{22}	$\ldots$	x_{K2}
.	.	.		.
.	.	.		.
.	.	.		.
H	x_{1H}	x_{2H}	$\ldots$	x_{KH}

We are also interested in the differences in the population block means. Hence, we require the sample means for the H blocks. We use $\bar{x}_{\cdot j}$ to denote the sample mean for the jth block, so

$$\bar{x}_{\cdot j} = \frac{\sum_{i=1}^{K} x_{ij}}{K} \qquad (j = 1, 2, \ldots, H)$$

For the fuel consumption data of Table 15.6, we have

$$\bar{x}_{\cdot 1} = \frac{75.0}{3} = 25.0 \qquad \bar{x}_{\cdot 2} = \frac{73.8}{3} = 24.6 \qquad \bar{x}_{\cdot 3} = \frac{76.2}{3} = 25.4$$

$$\bar{x}_{\cdot 4} = \frac{72.0}{3} = 24.0 \qquad \bar{x}_{\cdot 5} = \frac{71.7}{3} = 23.9 \qquad \bar{x}_{\cdot 6} = \frac{74.1}{3} = 24.7$$

Finally, we require the overall mean of the sample observations. If n denotes the total number of observations, then

$$n = HK$$

and the sample mean of all the observations is

$$\bar{x} = \frac{\sum_{i=1}^{K}\sum_{j=1}^{H} x_{ij}}{n} = \frac{\sum_{i=1}^{K} \bar{x}_{i\cdot}}{K} = \frac{\sum_{j=1}^{H} \bar{x}_{\cdot j}}{H}$$

For the data of Table 15.6

$$\bar{x} = \frac{442.8}{18} = 24.6$$

Before proceeding to consider the form of an appropriate test for the hypothesis of interest, it is useful to examine the population model that is implicitly being assumed. Let the random variable X_{ij} correspond to the observation for the ith group and jth block. This value is then regarded as the sum of the following four components:

1. An "overall" mean, μ
2. A parameter G_i, which is specific to the ith group and measures the discrepancy between the mean for that group and the overall mean

3. A parameter B_j, which is specific to the jth block and measures the discrepancy between the mean for that block and the overall mean

4. A random variable ϵ_{ij}, which represents experimental error, or that part of the observation not explained by either the overall mean or the group or block membership

We can therefore write

$$X_{ij} = \mu + G_i + B_j + \epsilon_{ij} \qquad (15.4.1)$$

The error term ϵ_{ij} is taken to obey the standard assumptions of the multiple regression model. In particular, then, we assume independence and equality of variances.

It is now convenient to write (15.4.1) as

$$X_{ij} - \mu = G_i + B_j + \epsilon_{ij} \qquad (15.4.2)$$

Now, given sample data, the overall mean μ is estimated by the overall sample mean $\bar{x}$, so an estimate of the left-hand side of (15.4.2) is provided by $(x_{ij} - \bar{x})$. The difference G_i between the population mean for the ith group and the overall population mean is estimated by the corresponding difference in sample means, $(\bar{x}_{i\cdot} - \bar{x})$. Similarly, B_j is estimated by $(\bar{x}_{\cdot j} - \bar{x})$. Finally, by subtraction, we estimate the error term by

$$(x_{ij} - \bar{x}) - (\bar{x}_{i\cdot} - \bar{x}) - (\bar{x}_{\cdot j} - \bar{x}) = x_{ij} - \bar{x}_{i\cdot} - \bar{x}_{\cdot j} + \bar{x}$$

Thus, corresponding to Eq. (15.4.2), we have for the sample members

$$(x_{ij} - \bar{x}) = (\bar{x}_{i\cdot} - \bar{x}) + (\bar{x}_{\cdot j} - \bar{x}) + (x_{ij} - \bar{x}_{i\cdot} - \bar{x}_{\cdot j} + \bar{x}) \qquad (15.4.3)$$

To illustrate, consider the fuel consumption recorded by a driver from the third class with an α-car. From Table 15.6

$$x_{13} = 26.0$$

The term on the left-hand side of Eq. (15.4.3) is

$$x_{13} - \bar{x} = 26.0 - 24.6 = 1.4$$

For the group (automobile) effect, we have

$$\bar{x}_{1\cdot} - \bar{x} = 24.7 - 24.6 = .1$$

(Notice that this term will result whenever the α-car is driven.) For the block (driver) effect, we have

$$\bar{x}_{\cdot 3} - \bar{x} = 25.4 - 24.6 = .8$$

Finally, the error term is

$$x_{13} - \bar{x}_1. - \bar{x}._3 + \bar{x} = 26.0 - 24.7 - 25.4 + 24.6 = .5$$

Thus, corresponding to Eq. (15.4.3), we have for this observation

$$1.4 = .1 + .8 + .5$$

We can interpret this equation as follows: When a driver from the third age class tested the α-car, she used 1.4 miles per gallon more than the average for all cars and drivers. Of this amount, it is estimated that .1 is due to the automobile, .8 to the driver age class, and the remaining .5 mile per gallon to other factors, which we put down to chance variability or experimental error.

Now, if both sides of Eq. (15.4.3) are squared and summed over all n sample observations, it can be shown that the result is

$$\sum_{i=1}^{K} \sum_{j=1}^{H} (x_{ij} - \bar{x})^2 = H \sum_{i=1}^{K} (\bar{x}_i. - \bar{x})^2 + K \sum_{j=1}^{H} (\bar{x}._j - \bar{x})^2 + \sum_{i=1}^{K} \sum_{j=1}^{H} (x_{ij} - \bar{x}_i. - \bar{x}._j + \bar{x})^2$$

This equation expresses the total sample variability of the observations about their overall mean as the sum of variabilities due to differences among groups, differences among blocks, and error, respectively. It is on this sums of squares decomposition that the analysis of experiments of this type is based. The analysis is called **two-way analysis of variance,** as the data are categorized in two ways, according to groups and blocks.

We illustrate this important sum of squares decomposition in Figure 15.4. Notice, by contrast with the decomposition for the one-way analysis of variance, that the total sum of squares of the sample observations about their overall mean is here broken down into *three* components. The extra component arises because of our ability to extract from the data information about differences among blocks.

For the fuel consumption data of Table 15.6, we find

$$SST = (25.1 - 24.6)^2 + (24.7 - 24.6)^2 + \cdots + (25.4 - 24.6)^2 = 11.88$$

$$SSG = 6[(24.7 - 24.6)^2 + (23.9 - 24.6)^2 + (25.2 - 24.6)^2] = 5.16$$

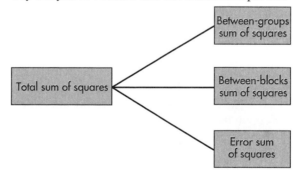

FIGURE 15.4 Sum of squares decomposition for two-way analysis of variance with one observation per cell

---

Sums of Squares Decomposition for Two-Way Analysis of Variance

Suppose that we have a sample of observations with x_{ij} denoting the observation in the ith group and jth block. Suppose also that there are K groups and H blocks, for a total of

$$n = KH$$

observations. Denote the group sample means by $\bar{x}_{i\cdot}$ ($i = 1, 2, \ldots, K$), the block sample means by $\bar{x}_{\cdot j}$ ($j = 1, 2, \ldots, H$), and the overall sample mean by $\bar{x}$.

We define the following **sums of squares:**

$$\text{TOTAL: SST} = \sum_{i=1}^{K} \sum_{j=1}^{H} (x_{ij} - \bar{x})^2$$

$$\text{BETWEEN-GROUPS: SSG} = H \sum_{i=1}^{K} (\bar{x}_{i\cdot} - \bar{x})^2$$

$$\text{BETWEEN-BLOCKS: SSB} = K \sum_{j=1}^{H} (\bar{x}_{\cdot j} - \bar{x})^2$$

$$\text{ERROR: SSE} = \sum_{i=1}^{K} \sum_{j=1}^{H} (x_{ij} - \bar{x}_{i\cdot} - \bar{x}_{\cdot j} + \bar{x})^2$$

Then

$$\text{SST} = \text{SSG} + \text{SSB} + \text{SSE}$$

$$\text{SSB} = 3[(25.0 - 24.6)^2 + (24.6 - 24.6)^2 + \cdots + (24.7 - 24.6)^2] = 4.98$$

and so, by subtraction

$$\text{SSE} = \text{SST} - \text{SSG} - \text{SSB} = 11.88 - 5.16 - 4.98 = 1.74$$

From this point, the tests associated with the two-way analysis of variance proceed in a similar fashion to the one-way analysis of Section 15.2. First, the mean squares are obtained by dividing each sum of squares by the appropriate number of degrees of freedom. For the total sum of squares, the degrees of freedom are 1 less than the total number of observations, that is, $(n - 1)$. For the sum of squares between groups, the degrees of freedom are 1 less than the number of groups, or $(K - 1)$. Similarly, for the sum of squares between blocks, the number of degrees of freedom is $(H - 1)$. Hence, by subtraction, the degrees of freedom associated with the sum of squared errors are

$$(n - 1) - (K - 1) - (H - 1) = n - K - H + 1$$
$$= KH - K - H + 1$$
$$= (K - 1)(H - 1)$$

The null hypothesis that the population group means are equal can then be tested through the ratio of the mean square for groups to the mean square error. Very often, a blocking variable is included in the analysis simply to reduce variability due to experimental error. However, sometimes the hypothesis that the block population means are equal is also of interest. This can be tested through the ratio of the mean square for blocks to the mean square error. As in the case of the one-way analysis of variance, the relevant standard for comparison is obtained from a tail probability of the F distribution. The procedures are described in the box.

Hypothesis Tests for Two-Way Analysis of Variance

Suppose that we have a sample observation for each group-block combination in a design containing K groups and H blocks. Define the following mean squares:

$$\text{BETWEEN-GROUPS: MSG} = \frac{\text{SSG}}{K - 1}$$

$$\text{BETWEEN-BLOCKS: MSB} = \frac{\text{SSB}}{H - 1}$$

$$\text{ERROR: MSE} = \frac{\text{SSE}}{(K - 1)(H - 1)}$$

We assume that the error terms ϵ_{ij} in the model (15.4.1) are independent of one another and have the same variance. It is further assumed that these errors are normally distributed. Then:

(i) A test of significance level α of the null hypothesis H_0 that the K population group means are all the same is provided by the decision rule

$$\text{Reject } H_0 \text{ if } \quad \frac{\text{MSG}}{\text{MSE}} > F_{K-1,(K-1)(H-1),\alpha}$$

(ii) A test of significance level α of the null hypothesis H_0 that the H population block means are all the same is provided by the decision rule

$$\text{Reject } H_0 \text{ if } \quad \frac{\text{MSB}}{\text{MSE}} > F_{H-1,(K-1)(H-1),\alpha}$$

Here, $F_{\nu_1,\nu_2,\alpha}$ is the number exceeded with probability α by a random variable following an F distribution with numerator degrees of freedom ν_1 and denominator degrees of freedom ν_2.

For the fuel consumption data, the mean squares are

$$\text{MSG} = \frac{\text{SSG}}{K - 1} = \frac{5.16}{2} = 2.58$$

$$\text{MSB} = \frac{\text{SSB}}{H - 1} = \frac{4.98}{5} = .996$$

$$\text{MSE} = \frac{\text{SSE}}{(K - 1)(H - 1)} = \frac{1.74}{10} = .174$$

To test the null hypothesis that the population mean fuel consumption is the same for all three types of automobile, we require

$$\frac{MSG}{MSE} = \frac{2.58}{.174} = 14.83$$

For a 1%-level test, we have for comparison, from Table 7 of the Appendix

$$F_{K-1,(K-1)(H-1),\alpha} = F_{2,10,.01} = 7.56$$

Therefore, on the evidence of these data, the hypothesis of equal mean population performances for the three types of automobile is clearly rejected at the 1% significance level.

In this particular example, the null hypothesis of equality of the population block means is the hypothesis that population values of mean fuel consumption are the same for each driver age class. The test is based on

$$\frac{MSB}{MSE} = \frac{.996}{.174} = 5.72$$

For a 1%-level test, we have, from Table 7 of the Appendix

$$F_{H-1,(K-1)(H-1),\alpha} = F_{5,10,.01} = 5.64$$

Hence, the null hypothesis of equal population means for the six driver age classes is also rejected at the 1% significance level.

Once again, it is very convenient to summarize the computations in tabular form. The general setup for the **two-way analysis of variance table** is shown in Table 15.8. For the fuel consumption data, this analysis of variance is set out in Table 15.9. The numbers of degrees of freedom are determined by the numbers of groups and blocks. The mean squares are obtained by dividing the sums of squares by their associated degrees of freedom. The mean square error is then the denominator in the calculation of the two F ratios on which our tests are based.

TABLE 15.8 General format of two-way analysis of variance table

SOURCE OF VARIATION	SUMS OF SQUARES	DEGREES OF FREEDOM	MEAN SQUARES	F RATIOS
Between groups	SSG	$K-1$	$MSG = \dfrac{SSG}{K-1}$	$\dfrac{MSG}{MSE}$
Between blocks	SSB	$H-1$	$MSB = \dfrac{SSB}{H-1}$	$\dfrac{MSB}{MSE}$
Error	SSE	$(K-1)(H-1)$	$MSE = \dfrac{SSE}{(K-1)(H-1)}$	
Total	SST	$n-1$		

TABLE 15.9 Two-way analysis of variance table for automobile miles per gallon data

SOURCE OF VARIATION	SUMS OF SQUARES	DEGREES OF FREEDOM	MEAN SQUARES	F RATIOS
Automobiles	5.16	2	2.580	14.83
Drivers	4.98	5	.996	5.72
Error	1.74	10	.174	
Total	11.88	17		

EXERCISES

21. Four financial analysts were asked to predict earnings growth over the coming year for five oil companies. Their forecasts, as projected percentage increases in earnings, are given in the accompanying table.

OIL COMPANY	ANALYST			
	A	B	C	D
1	8	12	7	13
2	9	9	8	12
3	12	10	9	10
4	11	10	10	12
5	9	8	10	14

(a) Set out the two-way analysis of variance table.
(b) Test the null hypothesis that the population mean growth forecasts are the same for all oil companies.

22. An agricultural experiment designed to assess differences in yields of corn for four different varieties, using three different fertilizers, produced the results (in bushels per acre) shown in the table.

FERTILIZER	VARIETY			
	A	B	C	D
1	86	88	77	84
2	92	91	81	93
3	75	80	83	79

(a) Set out the two-way analysis of variance table.
(b) Test the null hypothesis that the population mean yields are identical for all four varieties of corn.
(c) Test the null hypothesis that population mean yields are the same for all three brands of fertilizer.

23. A company has test-marketed three new types of soup in selected stores over a period of 1 year. The table records sales achieved (in thousands of dollars) for each of the three soups in each quarter of the year.

QUARTER	SOUP		
	A	B	C
1	47	57	65
2	63	63	76
3	79	67	54
4	52	50	49

(a) Set out the two-way analysis of variance table.

(b) Test the null hypothesis that population mean sales are the same for all three types of soup.

24. A diet soda manufacturer wants to compare the effects on sales of three can colors—red, yellow, and blue. Four regions are selected for the test, and three stores are randomly chosen from each region, each to display one color of cans. The accompanying table shows sales (in tens of cans) at the end of the experimental period.

REGION	CAN COLOR		
	RED	YELLOW	BLUE
East	47	52	60
South	56	54	52
Midwest	49	63	55
West	41	44	48

(a) Set out the appropriate analysis of variance table.

(b) Test the null hypothesis that population mean sales are the same for each can color.

25. An instructor in an economics class is considering three different texts. She is also considering three types of examinations—multiple choice, essays, and a mix of multiple choice and essays. During the year she teaches nine sections of the course, and randomly assigns a text–examination type combination to each section. At the end of the course, she obtained students evaluations for each section. These ratings are shown in the accompanying table.

EXAMINATION	TEXT		
	A	B	C
Multiple choice	4.8	5.3	4.9
Essays	4.6	5.0	4.3
Mix	4.6	5.1	4.8

(a) Set out the analysis of variance table.

(b) Test the null hypothesis of equality of population mean ratings for the three texts.

(c) Test the null hypothesis of equality of population mean ratings for the three examination types.

26. In Eq. (15.4.2) we introduced for the two-way analysis of variance the population model

$$X_{ij} - \mu = G_i + B_j + \epsilon_{ij}$$

For the data of Exercise 24, obtain sample estimates for each term on the right-hand side of this equation for the East region–red can combination.

27. For the data of Exercise 25, obtain sample estimates for each term on the right-hand side of Eq. (15.4.2) for the text C–multiple choice combination.

28. Four real estate agents were asked to appraise the values of ten houses in a particular neighborhood. The appraisals were expressed in thousands of dollars, with the results shown in the table.

SOURCE OF VARIATION	SUMS OF SQUARES
Between agents	268
Between houses	1,152
Error	2,352

(a) Complete the analysis of variance table.

(b) Test the null hypothesis that mean assessments are the same for these four real estate agents.

29. Four brands of fertilizer were evaluated. Each brand was applied to each of six plots of land containing soils of different types. Percentage increases in corn yields were then measured for the twenty-four brand-soil type combinations. The results obtained are summarized in the accompanying table.

SOURCE OF VARIATION	SUMS OF SQUARES
Between fertilizers	135.6
Between soil types	81.7
Error	111.3

(a) Complete the analysis of variance table.

(b) Test the null hypothesis that mean yield increases are the same for the four fertilizers.

(c) Test the null hypothesis that mean yield increases are the same for the six soil types.

30. Three television pilot shows for potential situation comedy series were shown to audiences in four regions of the country—the East, the South, the Midwest, and the West Coast. Based on audience reactions, a score (on a scale from 0 to 100) was obtained for each show. The sums of squares between groups (shows) and between blocks (regions) were found to be

$$\text{SSG} = 95.2 \quad \text{and} \quad \text{SSB} = 69.5$$

and the error sum of squares was

$$SSE = 79.3$$

Set out the analysis of variance table, and test the null hypothesis that the population mean scores for audience reactions are the same for all three shows.

31. Suppose that in the two-way analysis of variance setup with one observation per cell, there are just two groups. Show that in this case, the F ratio for testing the equality of the group population means is precisely the square of the test statistic discussed in Section 9.6 for testing equality of population means, given a sample of matched pairs. Hence, deduce that the two tests are equivalent in this particular case.

15.5 TWO-WAY ANALYSIS OF VARIANCE: MORE THAN ONE OBSERVATION PER CELL

In the two-way analysis of variance layout of Section 15.4, we can view the tabulated raw data (as in Tables 15.6 and 15.7) as being broken down into cells, where each cell refers to a particular group–block combination. Thus, for example, the results obtained when a driver from the fourth age class drives a β-car constitute a single cell. A feature of the design analyzed in Section 15.4 is that each cell contains just a single sample observation. Thus, a driver from the fourth age class tests a β-car only once.

In this section, we consider the possibility of **replicating** the experiment, so that, for example, β-cars would be driven by more than one driver from the fourth age class. The data resulting from such a design would then involve more than just a single observation per cell. There are two major advantages in extending the sample in this way. First, the more sample data that are available, the more precise will be the resulting estimates and the more surely will we be able to distinguish differences among the population means. Second, a design with more than one observation per cell allows the isolation of a further source of variability—the **interaction** between groups and blocks. Such interactions occur when differences in group effects are not distributed uniformly across blocks. For example, drivers who achieve better than average fuel consumption figures may be considerably more successful in getting better fuel economy than other drivers when driving an α-car than when driving a β-car. Thus, this better than average performance is not uniformly spread over all types of cars but rather is more manifest in some types than others. This possibility of driver–car interaction can be taken into account in an analysis based on more than one observation per cell.

To illustrate the kind of data that can be analyzed, Table 15.10 contains results on fuel consumption recorded for drivers from five age classes with three types of automobile—X-cars, Y-cars, and Z-cars. The three observations in each cell refer to independent trials by drivers from a given age class with automobiles of a particular type.

To denote the individual sample observations, we require a triple subscript, so x_{ijl} will denote the lth observation in the ijth cell, that is, the lth observation in the cell corresponding to the ith group and the jth block. As before, we will let K denote the number of groups and H the number of blocks. We denote by L the number of observations per cell. Hence, in the example of Table 15.10, $K = 3$, $H = 5$, and $L = 3$. This notation is illustrated in Table 15.11.

Based on the results of an experiment of this type, there are three null hypotheses that can be tested: no difference between group means, no difference between

TABLE 15.10 Sample observations on fuel consumption recorded for three types of automobile driven by five drivers; three observations per cell

DRIVER CLASSES	AUTOMOBILES								
	X-CARS			Y-CARS			Z-CARS		
1	25.0	25.4	25.2	24.0	24.4	23.9	25.9	25.8	25.4
2	24.8	24.8	24.5	23.5	23.8	23.8	25.2	25.0	25.4
3	26.1	26.3	26.2	24.6	24.9	24.9	25.7	25.9	25.5
4	24.1	24.4	24.4	23.9	24.0	23.8	24.0	23.6	23.5
5	24.0	23.6	24.1	24.4	24.4	24.1	25.1	25.2	25.3

block means, and no group–block interaction. In order to carry out these tests, we will again calculate various sample means, defined and calculated as follows.

(i) GROUP MEANS

The mean of *all* the sample observations in the *i*th group is denoted $\bar{x}_{i\cdot\cdot}$, so

$$\bar{x}_{i\cdot\cdot} = \frac{\sum\limits_{j=1}^{H} \sum\limits_{l=1}^{L} x_{ijl}}{HL}$$

From Table 15.10, we find

$$\bar{x}_{1\cdot\cdot} = \frac{25.0 + 25.4 + \cdots + 23.6 + 24.1}{15} = 24.86$$

$$\bar{x}_{2\cdot\cdot} = \frac{24.0 + 24.4 + \cdots + 24.4 + 24.1}{15} = 24.16$$

$$\bar{x}_{3\cdot\cdot} = \frac{25.9 + 25.8 + \cdots + 25.2 + 25.3}{15} = 25.10$$

TABLE 15.11 Sample observations on K groups and H blocks; L observations per cell

BLOCK	GROUP			
	1	2	$\ldots$	K
1	$x_{111}\ x_{112}\ \ldots\ x_{11L}$	$x_{211}\ x_{212}\ \ldots x_{21L}$	$\ldots$	$x_{K11}\ x_{K12}\ \ldots\ x_{K1L}$
2	$x_{121}\ x_{122}\ \ldots\ x_{12L}$	$x_{221}\ x_{222}\ \ldots x_{22L}$		$x_{K21}\ x_{K22}\ \ldots\ x_{K2L}$
.	.	.		.
.	.	.		.
.	.	.		.
H	$x_{1H1}\ x_{1H2}\ \ldots\ x_{1HL}$	$x_{2H1}\ x_{2H2}\ \ldots\ x_{2HL}$	$\ldots$	$x_{KH1}\ x_{KH2}\ \ldots\ x_{KHL}$

(ii) BLOCK MEANS

The mean of all the sample observations in the jth block is denoted $\bar{x}_{\cdot j \cdot}$, so

$$\bar{x}_{\cdot j \cdot} = \frac{\sum\limits_{i=1}^{K} \sum\limits_{l=1}^{L} x_{ijl}}{KL}$$

For the data of Table 15.10, we have

$$\bar{x}_{\cdot 1 \cdot} = \frac{25.0 + 25.4 + \cdots + 25.8 + 25.4}{9} = 25.00$$

$$\bar{x}_{\cdot 2 \cdot} = \frac{24.8 + 24.8 + \cdots + 25.0 + 25.4}{9} = 24.53$$

$$\bar{x}_{\cdot 3 \cdot} = \frac{26.1 + 26.3 + \cdots + 25.9 + 25.5}{9} = 25.57$$

$$\bar{x}_{\cdot 4 \cdot} = \frac{24.1 + 24.4 + \cdots + 23.6 + 23.5}{9} = 23.97$$

$$\bar{x}_{\cdot 5 \cdot} = \frac{24.0 + 23.6 + \cdots + 25.2 + 25.3}{9} = 24.47$$

(iii) CELL MEANS

To check the possibility of group–block interactions, it is necessary to calculate the sample mean for each cell. Let $\bar{x}_{ij\cdot}$ denote the sample mean for the (i, j)th cell. Then

$$\bar{x}_{ij\cdot} = \frac{\sum\limits_{l=1}^{L} x_{ijl}}{L}$$

Hence we find, for the data of Table 15.10

$$\bar{x}_{11\cdot} = \frac{25.0 + 25.4 + 25.2}{3} = 25.2$$

$$\bar{x}_{12\cdot} = \frac{24.8 + 24.8 + 24.5}{3} = 24.7$$

and similarly

	$\bar{x}_{13\cdot} = 26.2$	$\bar{x}_{14\cdot} = 24.3$	$\bar{x}_{15\cdot} = 23.9$	
$\bar{x}_{21\cdot} = 24.1$	$\bar{x}_{22\cdot} = 23.7$	$\bar{x}_{23\cdot} = 24.8$	$\bar{x}_{24\cdot} = 23.9$	$\bar{x}_{25\cdot} = 24.3$
$\bar{x}_{31\cdot} = 25.7$	$\bar{x}_{32\cdot} = 25.2$	$\bar{x}_{33\cdot} = 25.7$	$\bar{x}_{34\cdot} = 23.7$	$\bar{x}_{35\cdot} = 25.2$

(iv) OVERALL MEAN

We denote the mean of all the sample observations by $\bar{x}$, so

$$\bar{x} = \frac{\sum\limits_{i=1}^{K} \sum\limits_{j=1}^{H} \sum\limits_{l=1}^{L} x_{ijl}}{KHL}$$

For our data, this quantity is simplest to calculate as the average of the three group sample means, giving

$$\bar{x} = \frac{24.86 + 24.16 + 25.10}{3} = 24.71$$

Now, to get a feeling for the analysis, it is convenient to think in terms of the assumed population model. Let X_{ijl} denote the random variable corresponding to the lth observation in the ijth cell. Then, the model assumed in our analysis is

$$X_{ijl} = \mu + G_i + B_j + I_{ij} + \epsilon_{ijl} \qquad (15.5.1)$$

The first three terms on the right-hand side of Eq. (15.5.1) are precisely the same as those in Eq. (15.4.1). As before, they represent an overall mean, a group-specific factor, and a block-specific factor. The next term I_{ij} represents the effect of being in the ijth cell, given that the overall, group, and block effects are already accounted for. If there were no group–block interaction, this term would be 0. Its presence in the model allows us to check for interaction. Finally, the error term ϵ_{ijl} is a random variable representing experimental error.

We will rewrite Eq. (15.5.1) as

$$X_{ijl} - \mu = G_i + B_j + I_{ij} + \epsilon_{ijl} \qquad (15.5.2)$$

From Eq. (15.5.2), it is seen that the total sum of squares can be decomposed as the sum of four terms, representing variability due to groups, blocks, interaction between groups and blocks, and error.

Without providing detailed derivations, we state in the box the decomposition on which the tests are based.

Two-Way Analysis of Variance: Several Observations per Cell

Suppose that we have a sample of observations on K groups and H blocks, with L observations per cell. Let x_{ijl} denote the lth observation in the cell for the ith group and jth block. Let $\bar{x}$ denote the overall sample mean, $\bar{x}_{i\cdot\cdot}$ the group sample means, $\bar{x}_{\cdot j\cdot}$ the block sample means, and $\bar{x}_{ij\cdot}$ the cell sample means.

Then, we define the following sums of squares and associated degrees of freedom:

SUMS OF SQUARES		DEGREES OF FREEDOM
Total:	$SST = \sum_i \sum_j \sum_l (x_{ijl} - \bar{x})^2$	$KHL - 1$
Between-Groups:	$SSG = HL \sum_{i=1}^{K} (\bar{x}_{i..} - \bar{x})^2$	$K - 1$
Between-Blocks:	$SSB = KL \sum_{j=1}^{H} (\bar{x}_{.j.} - \bar{x})^2$	$H - 1$
Interaction:	$SSI = L \sum_{i=1}^{K} \sum_{j=1}^{H} (\bar{x}_{ij.} - \bar{x}_{i..} - \bar{x}_{.j.} + \bar{x})^2$	$(K - 1)(H - 1)$
Error:	$SSE = \sum_i \sum_j \sum_l (x_{ijl} - \bar{x}_{ij.})^2$	$KH(L - 1)$

Then

$$SST = SSG + SSB + SSI + SSE$$

Division of the component sums of squares by their corresponding degrees of freedom yields the mean squares MSG, MSB, MSI, and MSE.

Tests of the hypotheses of no effects for groups, blocks, and interaction are based on the respective F ratios

$$\frac{MSG}{MSE} \qquad \frac{MSB}{MSE} \qquad \frac{MSI}{MSE}$$

The tests are carried out with reference to the F distributions with the corresponding numerator and denominator degrees of freedom. Their validity rests on the assumption that the ϵ_{ijl} in model (15.5.1) behave as a random sample from a normal distribution.

Figure 15.5 depicts the decomposition of the total sum of squares of the sample observations about their overall mean as the sum of four components. It differs from Figure 15.4 in that, as the experiment is replicated, we are now able to isolate an interaction sum of squares.

As before, the calculations involved can be conveniently summarized in an analysis of variance table. The general form of the table when there are L observations per cell in a two-way analysis of variance is shown in Table 15.12.

In fact, formulas that are computationally simpler exist for the calculation of the various sums of squares. Nevertheless, the arithmetic involved is still rather tedious. We will not go into further detail here, but will simply quote in Table 15.13 the results of the calculations for our data. In practice, analysis of variance computations are typically carried out through a prewritten program package on an electronic computer. Thus, considerations of arithmetic complexity rarely impose any constraint on practical analyses.

The degrees of freedom in Table 15.13 follow from the fact that for these data, we have

$$K = 3 \qquad H = 5 \qquad L = 3$$

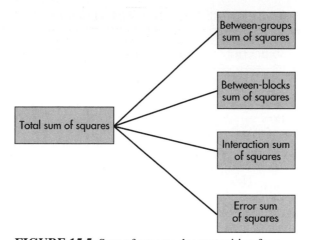

FIGURE 15.5 Sum of squares decomposition for a two-way analysis of variance with more than one observation per cell

The mean squares are obtained by dividing the sums of squares by their associated degrees of freedom. Finally, the F ratios follow from dividing, in turn, each of the first three mean squares by the error mean square.

Using the material in Table 15.13, we can test the three null hypotheses of interest. To begin, we test the null hypothesis that the population mean fuel consumption is the same for X-cars, Y-cars, and Z-cars. The test is based on the calculated F ratio 92.46. From Table 7 in the Appendix, we find, for 1%-level test with numerator and denominator degrees of freedom 2 and 30, respectively

$$F_{2,30,.01} = 5.39$$

Hence, the null hypothesis of equality of the population means for automobile types is overwhelmingly rejected at the 1% significance level.

TABLE 15.12 General format of the two-way analysis of variance table with L observations per cell

SOURCE OF VARIATION	SUMS OF SQUARES	DEGREES OF FREEDOM	MEAN SQUARES	F RATIOS
Between groups	SSG	$K - 1$	$\text{MSG} = \dfrac{\text{SSG}}{K - 1}$	$\dfrac{\text{MSG}}{\text{MSE}}$
Between blocks	SSB	$H - 1$	$\text{MSB} = \dfrac{\text{SSB}}{H - 1}$	$\dfrac{\text{MSB}}{\text{MSE}}$
Interaction	SSI	$(K - 1)(H - 1)$	$\text{MSI} = \dfrac{\text{SSI}}{(K - 1)(H - 1)}$	$\dfrac{\text{MSI}}{\text{MSE}}$
Error	SSE	$KH(L - 1)$	$\text{MSE} = \dfrac{\text{SSE}}{KH(L - 1)}$	
Total	SST	$KHL - 1$		

TABLE 15.13 Two-way analysis of variance table for fuel consumption data of Table 15.10

SOURCE OF VARIATION	SUMS OF SQUARES	DEGREES OF FREEDOM	MEAN SQUARES	F RATIOS
Automobiles	7.1565	2	3.5783	92.46
Drivers	13.1517	4	3.2879	84.96
Interaction	6.6045	8	.8256	21.33
Error	1.1600	30	.0387	
Total	28.0727	44		

Next, we test the null hypothesis that the population mean fuel consumption is the same for all five driver age classes. From Table 15.13, the test is based on the calculated F ratio 84.96. Hence, the numerator and denominator degrees of freedom are 4 and 30, so for a 1%-level test

$$F_{4,30,.01} = 4.02$$

The null hypothesis of equality of population means for these driver age classes is very clearly rejected at the 1% significance level.

Finally, we test the null hypothesis of no interaction between drivers and automobile type. This test is based on the calculated F ratio 21.33. Since the numerator and denominator degrees of freedom are 8 and 30, respectively, we have, from Table 7 in the Appendix

$$F_{8,30,.01} = 3.17$$

The null hypothesis of no interaction between car and driver type is very clearly rejected at the 1% level of significance.

The evidence of our data points very firmly to the following three conclusions:

1. Average fuel consumption is not the same for X-cars, Y-cars, and Z-cars.
2. The average performance levels are not the same for all driver classes.
3. The differences in driver performance are not spread evenly over all three types of automobile. Rather, compared with other drivers, a driver from a particular age class is likely to do relatively better in one automobile type than in another.

Computer programs for carrying out analysis of variance calculations are now widely available, so the computational burden involved in analyzing the models of this chapter, and more complex models, need not be severe. Table 15.14 shows part of the output from one prewritten package, the Statistical Package for the Social Sciences (SPSS) program, for our fuel consumption data. The output contains all of the information in our Table 15.13, with the error source labeled RESIDUAL. In addition, the total of the two main sums of squares is shown as MAIN EFFECTS, together with the associated degrees of freedom, mean square, and F ratio. Similarly, the sum of the MAIN EFFECTS and 2-WAY INTERACTIONS sums of squares is designated EXPLAINED sum of squares. This, too, is displayed, together with its degrees of freedom and the associated mean square and F ratio.

TABLE 15.14 Part of SPSS analysis of variance program output for fuel consumption data

SOURCE OF VARIATION	SUM OF SQUARES	DF	MEAN SQUARE	F
MAIN EFFECTS	20.3082	6	3.3847	87.46
AUTOMOBILES	7.1565	2	3.5783	92.46
DRIVERS	13.1517	4	3.2879	84.96
2-WAY INTERACTIONS	6.6045	8	.8256	21.33
AUTOMOBILES–DRIVERS	6.6045	8	.8256	21.33
EXPLAINED	26.9127	14	1.9223	49.67
RESIDUAL	1.1600	30	.0387	
TOTAL	28.0727	44	.6380	

EXAMPLE 15.3

So far in this section, we have assumed that the number of observations in each cell is the same. However, this restriction is not necessary and may, on occasion, be inconvenient for an investigator. In fact, the formulas for the computation of sums of squares can be modified to allow for unequal cell contents. We will not be concerned here with the technical details of the calculation of appropriate sums of squares. Generally, an investigator will have available a computer package for this purpose. Rather, our interest lies in the analysis of the results.

A study was designed to compare the satisfaction levels of introverted and extroverted workers performing stimulating and nonstimulating tasks.[4] Thus, for the purpose of this study, there are two worker types and two task types, giving four combinations. The sample mean satisfaction levels reported by workers in these four combinations were as follows:

Introverted worker, nonstimulating task (16 observations):   2.78

Extroverted worker, nonstimulating task (15 observations):   1.85

Introverted worker, stimulating task (17 observations):   3.87

Extroverted worker, stimulating task (19 observations):   4.12

The following table shows the calculated sums of squares and associated degrees of freedom. Complete the analysis of variance table, and analyze the results of this experiment.

---

[4] J. S. Kim, "Relationships of personality to perceptual and behavioral responses in stimulating and nonstimulating tasks," *Academy of Management Journal*, 23 (1980), 307–19.

SOURCE OF VARIATION	SUMS OF SQUARES	DEGREES OF FREEDOM
Task	62.04	1
Worker type	.06	1
Interaction	1.85	1
Error	23.31	63
Total	87.26	66

Once again, the mean squares are obtained from division of the sums of squares by their associated degrees of freedom. The F ratios then follow from division of the task, worker type, and interaction mean squares by the error mean square. The analysis of variance table may now be completed as shown.

SOURCE OF VARIATION	SUMS OF SQUARES	DEGREES OF FREEDOM	MEAN SQUARES	F RATIOS
Task	62.04	1	62.04	167.68
Worker type	.06	1	.06	.16
Interaction	1.85	1	1.85	5.00
Error	23.31	63	.37	
Total	87.26	66		

The analysis of variance table can be used as the basis for testing three null hypotheses. For the null hypothesis of equal mean population satisfaction levels with the two types of task, the calculated F ratio is 167.68. We have numerator degrees of freedom 1 and denominator degrees of freedom 63, so from Table 7 of the Appendix, for a 1%-level test

$$F_{1,63,.01} = 7.07$$

Hence, the null hypothesis of equal population mean satisfaction levels for stimulating and nonstimulating tasks is very clearly rejected. This result is not surprising. We would naturally expect workers to be more satisfied when performing stimulating rather than nonstimulating tasks.

Next, we test the null hypothesis that the population mean satisfaction levels are the same for introverted and extroverted workers. Here, the calculated F ratio is .16. Again, the degrees of freedom are 1 and 63, so for a 5%-level test

$$F_{1,63,.05} = 4.00$$

The null hypothesis of equal mean levels of satisfaction for introverted and extroverted workers cannot be rejected at the 5% level of significance.

In many studies, the interaction term is not, in itself, of any great importance. The main reason for including it in the analysis is to "soak up" some of the variability in the data, rendering any differences between population means easier to detect. However, in this particular study, the interaction is of major interest. The null hypothesis of no interaction between task and worker type in determining worker satisfaction levels is tested through the calculated F ratio 5.00. Once again, the numerator and denominator degrees of freedom are 1 and 63, respectively. Hence, comparison with the tabulated values of the F distribution reveals that the null hypothesis of no interaction can be rejected at the 5% level but not at the 1% level of significance.

EXERCISES

32. The scores given by judges to competitors in the figure skating events of the 1980 Winter Olympics were analyzed.[5] For the ladies' figure skating competition, there were twenty-two contestants and nine judges. Each contestant was assessed by each judge in seven subevents. The scores given can thus be treated in the framework of a two-way analysis of variance with 198 contestant-judge cells, seven observations per cell. The sums of squares are given in the table.

SOURCE OF VARIATION	SUMS OF SQUARES
Between contestants	364.50
Between judges	.81
Interaction	4.94
Error	1,069.94

(a) Complete the analysis of variance table.

(b) Carry out the associated F tests, and interpret your findings.

33. Refer to Exercise 32. Twelve pairs were entered in the ice-dancing competition. Once again, there were nine judges, and contestants were assessed in seven subevents. The sums of squares between groups (pairs of contestants) and between blocks (judges) were found to be

$$SSG = 60.10 \quad \text{and} \quad SSB = 1.65$$

while the interaction and error sums of squares were

$$SSI = 3.35 \quad \text{and} \quad SSE = 31.61$$

Analyze these results, and verbally interpret the conclusions.

34. A psychologist is working with three types of aptitude tests that may be given to prospective management trainees. In deciding how to structure the testing process, an important issue is the possibility of interaction between test takers and test type. If there were no interaction, only one type of test would be needed. Three tests of each type are given to members of each of four groups of subject type. These were distinguished by ratings of poor, fair, good, and excellent in preliminary interviews. The scores obtained are listed in the following table.

---

[5] G. Fenwick and S. Chatterjee, "Perception, preference, and patriotism: An exploratory analysis of the 1980 Winter Olympics," *American Statistician, 35* (1981), 170–73.

SUBJECT TYPE	TEST TYPE								
	PROFILE FIT			MINDBENDER			PSYCH OUT		
Poor	65	68	62	69	71	67	75	75	78
Fair	74	79	76	72	69	69	70	69	65
Good	64	72	65	68	73	75	78	82	80
Excellent	83	82	84	78	78	75	76	77	75

(a) Set up the analysis of variance table.

(b) Test the null hypothesis of no interaction between subject type and test type.

35. Random samples of two freshmen, two sophomores, two juniors, and two seniors each from four dormitories were asked to rate on a scale from 1 (poor) to 10 (excellent) the quality of dormitory environment for studying. The results are shown in the table.

YEAR	DORMITORY							
	A		B		C		D	
Freshman	7	5	8	6	9	8	9	9
Sophomore	6	8	5	5	7	8	8	9
Junior	5	4	7	6	6	7	7	8
Senior	7	4	6	8	7	5	6	7

(a) Set up the analysis of variance table.

(b) Test the null hypothesis that the population mean ratings are the same for the four dormitories.

(c) Test the null hypothesis that the population mean ratings are the same for the four student years.

(d) Test the null hypothesis of no interaction between student year and dormitory ratings.

36. In some experiments with several observations per cell, the analyst is prepared to assume that there is no interaction between groups and blocks. Any apparent interaction found is then attributed to random error. When such an assumption is made, the analysis is carried out in the usual way, except that what were previously the interaction and error sums of squares are added together to form a new error sum of squares. Similarly, the corresponding degrees of freedom are also added. If the assumption of no interaction is correct, this approach has the advantage of providing more error degrees of freedom and hence more powerful tests of the equality of group and block means. For the study of Exercise 35, suppose that we now make the assumption of no interaction between dormitories and student years.

(a) State, in words, what is implied by this assumption.

(b) Given this assumption, set up the new analysis of variance table.

(c) Test the null hypothesis that the mean ratings are the same for all four dormitories.

(d) Test the null hypothesis that the mean ratings are the same for all four student years.

37. Refer to Exercise 22. Having carried out the experiment to compare mean yields per acre of four varieties of corn and three brands of fertilizer, an agricultural researcher suggested that there might be some interaction between variety and fertilizer. To check this possibility, another set of trials was carried out, producing the yields in the table.

FERTILIZER	VARIETY			
	A	B	C	D
1	80	88	73	88
2	94	91	79	93
3	81	78	83	83

(a) What would be implied by an interaction between variety and fertilizer?

(b) Combine the data from the two sets of trials and set up an analysis of variance table.

(c) Test the null hypothesis that the mean yield is the same for all four varieties of corn.

(d) Test the null hypothesis that the mean yield is the same for all three brands of fertilizer.

(e) Test the null hypothesis of no interaction between variety of corn and brand of fertilizer.

38. Refer to Exercise 24. Suppose that a second store for each region–can color combination is added to the study, yielding the results shown in the following table. Amalgamating these results with those of Exercise 24, carry out the analysis of variance calculations and discuss your findings.

REGION	CAN COLOR		
	RED	YELLOW	BLUE
East	45	50	54
South	49	51	58
Midwest	43	60	50
West	38	49	44

39. Having carried out the study of Exercise 25, the instructor decided to replicate the study the following year. The results obtained are shown in the table. Amalgamating these results with those of Exercise 25, carry out the analysis of variance calculations and discuss your findings.

EXAMINATION	TEXT		
	A	B	C
Multiple choice	4.7	5.1	4.8
Essays	4.4	4.6	4.0
Mix	4.5	5.3	4.9

REVIEW EXERCISES

40. Carefully distinguish between the one-way analysis of variance framework and the two-way analysis of variance framework. Give examples different from those discussed in the text and exercises of business problems for which each might be appropriate.

41. Carefully explain what is meant by the interaction effect in the two-way analysis of variance with more than one observation per cell. Give examples of this effect in business-related problems.

42. In Exercise 8 of Chapter 8 we considered a study to assess the readability of financial report messages.[6] The technique for assessing the effectiveness of the written message is called the *cloze readability procedure*. Financial reports were given to independent random samples from three groups—certified public accountants, chartered financial analysts, and commercial bank loan officer trainees. The cloze procedure was then administered, and the scores for the sample members were recorded. The null hypothesis of interest is that the population mean scores for the three groups are identical. Test this hypothesis given the information in the accompanying table.

SOURCE OF VARIATION	SUMS OF SQUARES	DEGREES OF FREEDOM
Between groups	5,156	2
Within groups	120,802	1,005
Total	125,967	1,007

43. In an experiment designed to assess aids to the success of interviews of subordinates carried out by managers, interviewers were randomly assigned to one of three interview modes—feedback, feedback and goal setting, and control. For the feedback mode, interviewers had the opportunity to examine and discuss their subordinates' reactions to previous interviews. In the feedback-and-goal-setting mode, managers were encouraged to set goals for the forthcoming interview. For the control group, interviews were carried out in the usual way, without feedback or goal setting. After the interviews were completed, the satisfaction levels of the subordinates with the interviews were assessed.[7] For the forty-five people in the feedback group, the mean satisfaction level was 13.98. The forty-nine people in the feedback-and-goal-setting group had a mean satisfaction level of 15.12, while the forty-one control group members had a mean satisfaction level of 13.07. The F ratio computed from the data was 4.12.

(a) Set out the complete analysis of variance table.

(b) Test the null hypothesis that the population mean satisfaction levels are the same for all three types of interview.

44. A study classified each of 134 managers into one of four groups, based on observation and an interview.[8] The sixty-two managers in group A were categorized as having high levels of stimulation and support and average levels of public spirit. The fifty-two managers in group B had low stimulation, average support, and high public spirit. Group C contained seven managers, with average stimulation, low support, and low public spirit. The thirteen managers in group D were assessed as low on all three criteria. Salary levels for these four groups were compared. The sample means were 7.87 for group A, 7.47 for group B, 5.14 for group C, and 3.69 for group D. The F ratio calculated from these data was 25.60.

(a) Set out the complete analysis of variance table.

---

[6] A. H. Adelberg, "A methodology for measuring the understandability of financial report messages," *Journal of Accounting Research*, 17 (1979), 565–92.

[7] W. F. Nemeroff and J. Cosentino, "Utilizing feedback and goal setting to increase performance appraisal interviewer skills of managers," *Academy of Management Journal*, 22 (1979), 516–26.

[8] D. C. Pheysey, "Managers occupational histories, organizational environments, and climates for management development," *Journal of Management Studies*, 14 (1977), 58–79.

(**b**) Test the null hypothesis that the population mean salaries are the same for managers in these four groups.

45. In a study[9] to estimate the effects of smoking on absenteeism, employees were classed as continuous smokers, recent ex-smokers, long-term ex-smokers, and those who never smoked. Samples of ninety-six, thirty-four, eighty-six, and 206 members of these groups were taken. Sample mean numbers of hours per month of short-term absenteeism were found to be 2.15, 2.21, 1.47, and 1.69, respectively. The F ratio calculated from these data was 2.56.

(**a**) Set out the complete analysis of variance table.

(**b**) Test the null hypothesis of equality of the four population mean absenteeism rates.

46. Lower Michigan has had restrictions on price advertising for alcoholic beverages. However, for a period, these restrictions were lifted. Data were collected on total brewed beverage sales over three periods of time—under restricted price advertising, with restrictions lifted, and after the reimposition of restrictions.[10] The accompanying table shows sums of squares and degrees of freedom. Assuming that the usual requirements for the analysis of variance are met—in particular that sample observations are independent of one another—test the null hypothesis of equality of mean sales in these three time periods.

SOURCE OF VARIATION	SUMS OF SQUARES	DEGREES OF FREEDOM
Between groups	11,438.3028	2
Within groups	109,200.0000	15
Total	120,638.3028	17

47. Independent random samples of the selling prices of houses in four districts were taken. The selling prices (in thousands of dollars) are shown in the accompanying table. Test the null hypothesis that population mean selling prices are the same in all four districts.

DISTRICT A	DISTRICT B	DISTRICT C	DISTRICT D
73	85	97	61
63	59	86	67
89	84	76	84
75	70	78	67
70	80	76	69

48. For the data of Exercise 47, use the Kruskal-Wallis test to test the null hypothesis that the population mean selling prices of houses are the same in the four districts.

[9] M. R. Manning, J. S. Osland, and A. Osland, "Work-related consequences of smoking cessation," *Academy of Management Journal*, 32 (1989), 606–21.

[10] G. B. Wilcox, "The effect of price advertising on alcoholic beverage sales," *Journal of Advertising Research*, 25, no. 5 (1985), 33–38. Reprinted from the *Journal of Advertising Research*. © Copyright 1985 by the Advertising Research Foundation, Inc.

49. A study[11] was aimed at assessing work schedule satisfaction levels, on a scale from 1 (very dissatisfied) to 7 (very satisfied), of hospital employees who were either job-sharers, full-time, or part-time. For a sample of twenty-five job-sharers, the mean satisfaction level was 6.60; for a sample of twenty-four full-time employees, the mean satisfaction level was 5.37; for a sample of twenty part-time employees, the mean satisfaction level was 5.20. The F ratio calculated from these data was 6.62.

(a) Set out the complete analysis of variance table.

(b) Test the null hypothesis of equality of the three population mean satisfaction levels.

50. Consider the one-way analysis of variance setup.

(a) Show that the within-groups sum of squares can be written

$$SSW = \sum_{i=1}^{K} \sum_{j=1}^{n_i} x_{ij}^2 - \sum_{i=1}^{K} n_i \bar{x}_i^2$$

(b) Show that the between-groups sum of squares can be written

$$SSG = \sum_{i=1}^{K} n_i \bar{x}_i^2 - n\bar{x}^2$$

(c) Show that the total sum of squares can be written

$$SST = \sum_{i=1}^{K} \sum_{j=1}^{n_i} x_{ij}^2 - n\bar{x}^2$$

51. Consider the two-way analysis of variance setup, with one observation per cell.

(a) Show that the between-groups sum of squares can be written

$$SSG = H \sum_{i=1}^{K} \bar{x}_{i\cdot}^2 - n\bar{x}^2$$

(b) Show that the between-blocks sum of squares can be written

$$SSB = K \sum_{j=1}^{H} \bar{x}_{\cdot j}^2 - n\bar{x}^2$$

(c) Show that the total sum of squares can be written

$$SST = \sum_{i=1}^{K} \sum_{j=1}^{H} x_{ij}^2 - n\bar{x}^2$$

(d) Show that the error sum of squares can be written

$$SSE = \sum_{i=1}^{K} \sum_{j=1}^{H} x_{ij}^2 - H \sum_{i=1}^{K} \bar{x}_{i\cdot}^2 - K \sum_{j=1}^{H} \bar{x}_{\cdot j}^2 + n\bar{x}^2$$

52. Information on consumer perceptions of three brand types—national, private, and generic—were obtained from a random sample of 125 consumers.[12] The sums of squares for these perception measures are given in the accompanying table. Complete the analysis of variance table, and test the null hypothesis that the population mean perception levels are the same for all three brand types.

---

[11] J. G. Pesek and C. McGee, "An analysis of job sharing, full-time and part-time work arrangements: One hospital's experience," *American Business Review*, 7, no. 2 (1989), 34–40.

[12] Data from J. A. Bellizzi, H. F. Krueckeberg, J. R. Hamilton, and W. S. Martin, "Consumer perceptions of national, private, and generic brands," *Journal of Retailing*, 57, no. 4 (1981), 56–70.

SOURCE OF VARIATION	SUMS OF SQUARES
Between consumers	37,571.5
Between brands	32,987.3
Error	55,710.7

53. Three real estate agents were each asked to assess the values of five houses in a neighborhood. The results, in thousands of dollars, are set out in the table. Set out the analysis of variance table, and test the null hypothesis that population mean valuations are the same for the three real estate agents.

HOUSE	AGENT		
	A	B	C
1	210	218	226
2	192	190	198
3	183	187	185
4	227	223	237
5	242	240	237

54. Students were classified according to three parental income groups and also according to three possible score ranges in the SAT examination. One student was chosen randomly from each of the nine cross-classifications, and the grade point average of each sample member at the end of the sophomore year was recorded. The results are shown in the accompanying table.

SAT SCORE	INCOME GROUP		
	HIGH	MODERATE	LOW
Very high	3.7	3.6	3.6
High	3.4	3.5	3.2
Moderate	2.9	2.8	3.0

(a) Set out the analysis of variance table.
(b) Test the null hypothesis that the population mean grade point averages are the same for all three income groups.
(c) Test the null hypothesis that the population mean grade point averages are the same for all three SAT score groups.

55. For the two-way analysis of variance model with one observation per cell, write the observation from the ith group and jth block as

$$X_{ij} = \mu + G_i + B_j + \epsilon_{ij}$$

Refer to Exercise 53 and consider the observation on agent B and house 1 ($x_{21} = 218$).

(a) Estimate μ.

(b) Estimate, and interpret, G_2.

(c) Estimate, and interpret, B_1.

(d) Estimate ϵ_{21}.

56. Refer to Exercise 54 and consider the observation on moderate income group and high SAT score ($x_{22} = 3.5$).

(a) Estimate μ.

(b) Estimate G_2.

(c) Estimate B_2.

(d) Estimate ϵ_{22}.

57. Consider the two-way analysis of variance setup, with L observations per cell.

(a) Show that the between-groups sum of squares can be written

$$\text{SSG} = HL \sum_{i=1}^{K} \bar{x}_{i..}^2 - HKL\bar{x}^2$$

(b) Show that the between-blocks sum of squares can be written

$$\text{SSB} = KL \sum_{j=1}^{H} \bar{x}_{.j.}^2 - HKL\bar{x}^2$$

(c) Show that the error sum of squares can be written

$$\text{SSE} = \sum_{i=1}^{K} \sum_{j=1}^{H} \sum_{l=1}^{L} x_{ijl}^2 - L \sum_{i=1}^{K} \sum_{j=1}^{H} \bar{x}_{ij.}^2$$

(d) Show that the total sum of squares can be written

$$\text{SST} = \sum_{i=1}^{K} \sum_{j=1}^{H} \sum_{l=1}^{L} x_{ijl}^2 - HKL\bar{x}^2$$

(e) Show that the interaction sum of squares can be written

$$\text{SSI} = L \sum_{i=1}^{K} \sum_{j=1}^{H} \bar{x}_{ij.}^2 - HL \sum_{i=1}^{K} \bar{x}_{i..}^2 - KL \sum_{j=1}^{H} \bar{x}_{.j.}^2 + HKL\bar{x}^2$$

58. Purchasing agents were given information about a dictation system and asked to assess its quality.[13] The information given was identical except for two factors—price and country of origin. For price, there were three possibilities: $605, $495, or no price given. For country of origin, there were also three possibilities: United States, Brazil, or no country given. Part of the analysis of variance table for the quality assessments of the purchasing agents is shown here. Complete the analysis of variance table and provide a full analysis of these data.

---

[13] Reported in D. R. Lambert, "Price as a quality cue in industrial buying," *Journal of Academy of Marketing Science*, 9 (1981), 227–38; © 1981; reprinted by permission of the Academy of Marketing Science.

SOURCE OF VARIATION	SUMS OF SQUARES	DEGREES OF FREEDOM
Between prices	.178	2
Between countries	4.365	2
Interaction	1.262	4
Error	93.330	99

59. In the study of Exercise 58, information on the dictation system was also shown to M.B.A. students. Part of the analysis of variance table for their quality assessments is shown here. Complete the analysis of variance table and provide a full analysis of these data.

SOURCE OF VARIATION	SUMS OF SQUARES	DEGREES OF FREEDOM
Between prices	.042	2
Between countries	15.319	2
Interaction	2.235	4
Error	70.414	50

60. Having carried out the study of Exercise 54, the investigator decided to take an independent random sample of one student from each of the nine income-SAT score categories. The grade point averages found are given in the accompanying table.

SAT SCORE	INCOME GROUP		
	HIGH	MODERATE	LOW
Very high	3.9	3.7	3.8
High	3.2	3.6	3.4
Moderate	2.7	3.0	2.8

(a) Set out the analysis of variance table.

(b) Test the null hypothesis that the population mean grade point averages are the same for all three income groups.

(c) Test the null hypothesis that the population mean grade point averages are the same for all three SAT score groups.

(d) Test the null hypothesis of no interaction between income group and SAT score.

61. [*This exercise requires a computer program to carry out the analysis of variance computations.*] An experiment was carried out to test the effects on yields of five varieties of corn and five types of fertilizer. For each variety–fertilizer combination, six plots were used and the yields recorded, with the results shown in the table.

FERTILIZER	VARIETY				
	A	B	C	D	E
1	75 77 79 83 85 78	74 67 73 65 79 80	93 90 87 82 86 88	79 83 87 88 86 90	72 77 79 83 78 86
2	80 72 76 73 70 74	71 69 75 62 77 83	84 88 90 79 83 80	77 82 84 87 82 83	70 75 80 80 74 81
3	85 87 80 79 87 80	76 73 77 70 83 80	88 94 89 86 89 93	81 86 90 90 87 88	77 83 87 79 86 88
4	80 79 82 77 85 80	74 77 69 78 74 76	86 87 90 85 83 88	80 77 90 84 80 88	79 85 88 80 87 82
5	75 79 86 82 79 83	75 80 84 80 72 77	92 88 89 94 86 90	82 78 85 86 82 89	80 87 90 83 86 83

(a) Test the null hypothesis that the population mean yields are the same for all five varieties of corn.

(b) Test the null hypothesis that the population mean yields are the same for all five brands of fertilizer.

(c) Test the null hypothesis of no interaction between variety and fertilizer.

Statistical
Quality Control

16.1   THE IMPORTANCE OF QUALITY CONTROL

In this chapter, we introduce an application of statistical methods which is both quite straightforward and far from new. The aim is to exploit statistical techniques in monitoring the quality of the output of a production process. The procedures developed to this end are generally called **statistical quality control methods,** and more recently **statistical process control methods.** In practice, these two terms are often used interchangeably. However, some authors place emphasis on the latter to make it clear that the goal is not simply to inspect a finished product to check that specifications are met. At that stage, it may be that little can be done other than to discard or rework rejects, leading to considerable wastage. On the other hand, the modern literature on statistical process control stresses the importance of monitoring a production process *at each stage* where intermediate output required to meet verifiable standards is produced. The aim is to ensure adequate quality at each stage of the production process, so that time and money are not wasted in continuing work on substandard products. In modern statistical process control then, each stage of a production process is viewed as generating output whose quality should be assessed.

In the U.S. manufacturing industry, statistical quality control methods did not really come into widespread use until the 1980s—a decade which witnessed an explosion of interest in these techniques. Yet as we have indicated, statistical quality control methods are certainly not new. Neither are they at all difficult to understand or implement. Indeed, the basic methods—the ones most commonly used today—are nothing more than fairly routine applications of the statistical techniques discussed in some of the early chapters of this book. Although they were neglected in the United States for many years, the early development of statistical control methods is due to an American, Walter A. Shewhart, who in the 1920s advocated the approaches that underlie the methodology that has so recently achieved wide acceptance. In fact, broad application of Shewhart's ideas in the private manufacturing sector was first achieved in postwar Japan. This development owed much to the influence of another American statistician, W. Edwards Deming, a former colleague of Shewhart. Subsequently, much attention was paid to quality improvement in Japanese manufacturing, and a number of refinements and modifications of the original methods were developed and implemented. Much of this recent work is due to Genichi Taguchi, and his colleagues.

By the end of the 1970s, U.S. industry was facing, as never before, intense foreign competition for domestic markets. Imports of manufactured goods grew dramatically, while many American industries failed to achieve comparable success in foreign markets. The consequences of this development are profound. At the macroeconomic level, the United States has suffered trade deficits for some time. At the microeconomic level, whole industries have gone into decline, while others have been forced to make rapid, and sometimes painful, adjustments to meet the competition. In these circumstances, it is not surprising that American eyes turned toward their most successful competitor—the Japanese. There are, of course, many differences between Japanese and American social and economic organizations. A full discussion of these differences, in an attempt to explain the relative success of Japanese industry, would take us far beyond the scope of this book. For our purposes, it is sufficient to note that many Japanese products available in the American market came to acquire an enviable reputation for quality. It is the recognition by much of America's industry of the need to meet this challenge that explains the rapid growth in the implementation of statistical quality control methods in the United States in the last fifteen years.

Statistical quality control has become the great growth industry of business statistics. In spite of their relative novelty in application, the benefits of these methods should be obvious:

1. *Increased productivity*. If substandard parts are detected early enough and if difficulties with a production process can be anticipated, much wastage of time and material can be avoided. Without increased cost or worker effort, the implementation of a successful statistical process control method should therefore lead to the production of a greater volume of product of satisfactory quality than previously.

2. *Increased sales*. It is now generally agreed that a deserved reputation for product quality is a huge asset in the competitive marketplace. Such a reputation is generally hard-won, but in many industries its absence can prove fatal.

3. *Increased profits*. The net effect of reduced unit costs of production and increased sales is, of course, felt in the corporate bottom line. Quality control methods are now in widespread use because they are profitable.

Although we have said as much as needs to be said about the importance of product quality, we have not yet made clear where statistical methods enter the picture. They do so because the typical quality control procedure, once implemented, must necessarily involve *sampling*. The aim in a quality control exercise is to monitor a production process *on-line*, that is, while it is in operation. Almost inevitably, it will not be feasible to measure the characteristics of every item produced. Instead, relatively small samples of items are drawn from time to time and measurements taken, so that progress over time can be charted and any changes can be noted, and possibly investigated. From our view, the important point is that inference about the process's behavior will be based on sample evidence—a principle with which we are familiar from earlier chapters of this book. In addition, since product measurements are made on-line on the shop floor—and ideally, judgments should be made fairly quickly—it is desirable that relatively simple methods be employed. Typically, these involve some graphical analysis through **control charts,** whose principles can be easily understood, and which can be readily constructed, by production workers.

At a more fundamental level, the importance of statistical ideas in quality control lies in the understanding of *variability* and *chance.* The production process that manufactures *identical* items has not been invented—and never will be. It is inevitable, in practice, that there will be some variability in item characteristics. Therefore, in looking for changes in production characteristics over time, it is important not to be misled by mere chance variability. This discussion should bring to mind our study of hypothesis testing in Chapter 9; and indeed, statistical process control involves elements of hypothesis testing, since sample statistics plotted on control charts are compared with **control limits.** These limits, which are set in accordance with significance levels for hypothesis tests, ensure that the process will very infrequently be interrupted for investigation when apparent deviations from norms are due to chance variability.

In the remainder of this chapter, we will try to provide some flavor of modern statistical control methods.[1] The particular techniques to be discussed are quite straightforward and can be deduced from statistical principles already covered in this book. They are, however, among those in most common use in production management today.

16.2 CONTROL CHARTS FOR MEANS AND STANDARD DEVIATIONS

We consider now the position where a production process yields an output whose characteristic of interest can be measured on a continuum. It is desired to set up a quality control scheme for that process. This can be achieved by taking, over time, a sequence of small samples of output. Typically, in most practical applications, samples of four or five observations are taken, and, to establish a reasonable record of performance, it is desirable to have twenty or more samples. The frequency of sample observations over time depends on the characteristics of the production process. To illustrate, Table 16.1 shows a sequence of twenty samples of five observations on the duration, in milliseconds, of the timing signal emitted by an electronic component. We will explore some of the relevant characteristics of these data.

In the typical application, management will be interested in both the average performance of the process and the variability in performance. Too much variability would indicate that many substandard items are being produced, even if the average performance is adequate. Accordingly, in Table 16.1 we have calculated the sample means and sample standard deviations for each observation period. In establishing the

---

[1] The interested reader can find considerably more details in: R. W. Berger and T. H. Hart, *Statistical Process Control: A Guide for Implementation* (New York: Marcel Dekker, Inc., 1986); G. K. Griffith, *Statistical Process Control Methods for Long and Short Runs* (Milwaukee, WI: ASQC Quality Press, 1989); E. L. Grant and R. S. Leavenworth, *Statistical Quality Control, 6th ed.* (New York: McGraw-Hill, Inc., 1988).

TABLE 16.1 Duration, in milliseconds, of timing signal emitted by an electronic component

SAMPLE NUMBER	SAMPLE OBSERVATIONS					$\bar{x}$	s
1	297	296	297	303	298	298.2	2.77
2	301	301	300	304	297	300.6	2.51
3	297	306	296	302	304	301.0	4.36
4	296	302	299	298	309	300.8	5.07
5	305	304	293	309	293	300.8	7.36
6	298	294	303	306	305	301.2	5.07
7	297	304	299	298	306	300.8	3.96
8	292	292	307	295	300	297.2	6.38
9	295	297	307	304	306	301.8	5.45
10	296	297	309	297	305	300.8	5.85
11	299	301	290	298	297	297.0	4.18
12	303	307	296	298	294	299.6	5.32
13	301	292	313	302	307	303.0	7.78
14	299	298	300	301	295	298.6	2.30
15	299	299	306	303	298	301.0	3.39
16	301	303	297	298	304	300.6	3.05
17	300	296	301	300	304	300.2	2.86
18	295	293	300	299	289	295.2	4.49
19	298	298	306	297	295	298.8	4.21
20	296	303	300	304	299	300.4	3.21

standards to be met by the process, it is also useful to compute the averages of these sample statistics. The overall sample mean, which is simply the average of all 100 sample observations in our example, is

$$\bar{\bar{x}} = (298.2 + 300.6 + \cdots + 300.4)/20 = 299.9$$

The average of the sample standard deviations is

$$\bar{s} = (2.77 + 2.51 + \cdots + 3.21)/20 = 4.48$$

As we will see, this quantity can be used as the basis for an estimate of the unknown process standard deviation, σ, that is, the standard deviation of the entire output of the process.

In this section, we will use the sample means and standard deviations to track process performance. These quantities are plotted on control charts, and we will see how to set control limits to help in understanding the fluctuations over time of the sample mean and standard deviation. Before proceeding, however, it should be noted that while use of the mean is quite standard, in many applications the range rather than the standard deviation is used to assess variability. Presumably, the attraction of this option is that the range—that is, the difference between the largest and smallest sample observation—is more easily calculated on the shop floor where control exercises are implemented on-line. However, this may no longer be the case, given the wide availability of electronic calculators which routinely compute sample means and standard deviations, requiring only the input of the sample observations. We will not discuss here the details of control chart construction when the range is used instead of the standard deviation. The principles of control chart construction and interpretation are essentially the same whichever measure of variability is used, though the details differ somewhat. Details of the analysis when the range is used as the measure of variability are given in Appendix A16.1.

The following box summarizes some of the notation and terminology we are employing.

Notation and Terminology

A sequence of K samples, each of n observations, is taken over time on a measurable characteristic of the output of a production process.

The **sample means** are denoted $\bar{x}_i$ ($i = 1, 2, \ldots, K$). They can be graphed on an $\overline{X}$**-chart.** The average of these sample means is the **overall mean** of all the sample observations

$$\bar{\bar{x}} = \sum_{i=1}^{K} \bar{x}_i / K$$

The **sample standard deviations** are denoted s_i; $i = 1, 2, \ldots, K$. They can be graphed on an s**-chart.** The **average sample standard deviation** is

$$\bar{s} = \sum_{i=1}^{K} s_i / K$$

The **process standard deviation,** σ, is the standard deviation of the population from which the samples were drawn, and it must be estimated from sample data.

AN ESTIMATE OF THE PROCESS STANDARD DEVIATION

As a step toward setting control limits in both the $\overline{X}$-chart and s-chart, it is necessary to estimate the process standard deviation, σ. One possibility would be to base this estimate on the overall sample standard deviation of all the observations—that is, in our example, on the sample standard deviation of all 100 observations. However, in applied quality control work, it is more usual to base an estimate of σ on $\bar{s}$, the average sample standard deviation. Whichever estimate is used, recall from our discussion in Chapter 7 that the sample standard deviation is a biased estimator of the population standard deviation. It is desirable to attempt to correct for this bias. In fact, when it is known that the population distribution is normal, it is possible to find an expression for the expected value of the sample standard deviation. If the sample standard deviation s_i is based on n observations, it can be shown that

$$E(s_i) = c_4 \sigma$$

where c_4 is a number that can be computed as a function of the sample size n. It follows immediately that

$$E(\bar{s}) = c_4 \sigma$$

and hence that an unbiased estimate of the process standard deviation is given by

$$\hat{\sigma} = \bar{s}/c_4 \qquad\qquad (16.2.1)$$

Of course, the population distribution may well not be exactly normal. Nevertheless, it is felt that this correction is worth making and that it will usually reduce the bias inherent in the sample standard deviation as an estimator of the corresponding population quantity.

In Table 16.2, we have set out values of c_4 corresponding to sample sizes ranging from two to ten. Also shown in that table are values for three other **control chart constants.** The notation used may appear strange. In fact, these are just four of a very large number of control chart constants used for various purposes in quality control, and the notation used here for these quantities is standard in the quality control literature. In practical quality control work, tables of control chart constants are routinely available and routinely used. We provide in Appendix A16.2 some details on the derivation of the entries in Table 16.2.

Returning to our example, we found

$$\bar{s} = 4.48$$

From Table 16.2, we see that, for $n = 5$ observations

$$c_4 = .940$$

Therefore, an estimate of the process standard deviation is provided by

$$\hat{\sigma} = \bar{s}/c_4 = 4.48/.940 = 4.77$$

An Estimate of σ

The process standard deviation can be estimated by

$$\hat{\sigma} = \bar{s}/c_4$$

where $\bar{s}$ is the average sample standard deviation, and the control chart constant, c_4, which depends on the sample size n, is tabulated in Table 16.2. If the population distribution is normal, the estimator is unbiased.

CONTROL CHARTS FOR MEANS

In Table 16.1, we listed mean durations for timing signals for a sequence of twenty samples of five observations taken over time. In quality control work, for ease of in-

TABLE 16.2 Some control chart constants

n	c_4	A_3	B_3	B_4
2	.798	2.66	0	3.27
3	.886	1.95	0	2.57
4	.921	1.63	0	2.27
5	.940	1.43	0	2.09
6	.952	1.29	.03	1.97
7	.959	1.18	.12	1.88
8	.965	1.10	.18	1.82
9	.969	1.03	.24	1.76
10	.973	0.98	.28	1.72

terpretation, such information is invariably graphed on a time plot. In this context, that plot is called an $\bar{X}$-chart. Of course, as we saw in Chapter 2, time plots are easily constructed and permit a visual interpretation of any trends.

For production management, it is important to look for signals of deterioration in quality. One possible indication of such a problem would be a sample mean that deviates substantially from the "usual" performance. For example, we see from Table 16.1 that the mean for the eighteenth sample, 295.2, is somewhat lower than the previous ones. To interpret this value, we need in effect to ask whether it is the kind of result one might reasonably expect through sampling variability. In quality control, this judgment is made through comparison with control limits drawn on the control charts. We now see how these limits are derived for $\bar{X}$-charts.

To begin, assume that the process has been operating at a constant level of performance over the whole observation period and that all sample observations can be viewed as having been drawn from the same normal distribution. The mean of that distribution is estimated by the overall mean, $\bar{\bar{x}}$, of all the sample observations, and the standard deviation is estimated by $\hat{\sigma}$ of (16.2.1).

Consider now a single sample of five observations, viewing them as having been drawn from a normal distribution with mean $\bar{\bar{x}}$ and standard deviation $\hat{\sigma}$. Then we know that the sampling distribution of this sample mean is normal, with mean $\bar{\bar{x}}$ and standard error $\hat{\sigma}/\sqrt{n} = \hat{\sigma}/\sqrt{5}$. This result is used as the basis for setting control limits.

When a problem is indicated in practical quality control exercises, some investigative action needs to be taken. This may involve the interruption and thorough investigation of the production process, which can be quite costly. Naturally, it is undesirable that this occur frequently when, in fact, the process is functioning satisfactorily. To guard against the occurrence of too many "false signals" of this sort, it is usual in quality control work to set control limits three standard errors on either side of the mean of the sampling distribution. (These are sometimes called 3-σ limits.) Then, if the distribution of the sample statistic—here the sample mean—is normal, the probability of a value outside the 3-σ limits is

$$P(Z > 3) + P(Z < -3) = 2(.0014) = .0028$$

where Z is a standard normal random variable. (We have used Table 3 of the Appendix here.) Thus, if limits are set in this way, under the assumptions we have made, the probability of a false signal for any particular sample is less than three in one thousand. Of course, typically these assumptions will not be absolutely true, so that this figure is only approximate. Nevertheless, it should provide a reasonable guide, and the use of 3-σ limits is very common.

Returning now to our problem of constructing control charts for sample means, the sampling distribution is centered on the overall mean $\bar{\bar{x}}$, and this **central line** is drawn on the chart. Then, if three-standard error limits are to be used, these are

$$\bar{\bar{x}} \pm 3\hat{\sigma}/\sqrt{n}$$

or, from Eq. (16.2.1)

$$\bar{\bar{x}} \pm 3\bar{s}/(c_4\sqrt{n})$$

We write this as

$$\bar{\bar{x}} \pm A_3\bar{s}$$

where

$$A_3 = 3/(c_4\sqrt{n}) \qquad\qquad (16.2.2)$$

For convenience, values of this control chart constant are given in Table 16.2. The reader is invited to verify that these values could be computed directly from Eq. (16.2.2).

$\bar{X}$-Chart

The $\bar{X}$-chart is a time plot of the sequence of sample means. For convenience in interpretation, three lines are drawn on this chart. The **central line** is

$$CL_{\bar{x}} = \bar{\bar{x}}$$

In addition, there are three-standard error control limits. The **lower control limit** is

$$LCL_{\bar{x}} = \bar{\bar{x}} - A_3\bar{s}$$

and the **upper control limit** is

$$UCL_{\bar{x}} = \bar{\bar{x}} + A_3\bar{s}$$

where the values A_3 are given in Table 16.2.

We are now in a position to draw the $\bar{X}$-chart for the timing signal data of Table 16.1. Referring to Table 16.2 and to our previous calculations, since the sample size is five

$$\bar{\bar{x}} = 299.9 \qquad \bar{s} = 4.48 \qquad A_3 = 1.43$$

The $\bar{X}$-chart is shown in Figure 16.1. The central line is

$$CL_{\bar{x}} = \bar{\bar{x}} = 299.9$$

The lower control limit is

$$LCL_{\bar{x}} = \bar{\bar{x}} - A_3\bar{s} = 299.9 - (1.43)(4.48) = 293.5$$

and the upper control limit is

$$UCL_{\bar{x}} = \bar{\bar{x}} + A_3\bar{s} = 299.9 + (1.43)(4.48) = 306.3$$

Looking at the control chart of Figure 16.1, there seems to be no great cause for concern. None of the sample means is outside the control limits, and indeed the great majority are well within those limits.

CONTROL CHARTS FOR STANDARD DEVIATIONS

To assess the progress of process variability over time, the standard deviations can also be plotted on a control chart. The central line on this chart is the average sample standard deviation, $\bar{s}$, and it is usual to set three-standard error limits. The details are set out in the following box.

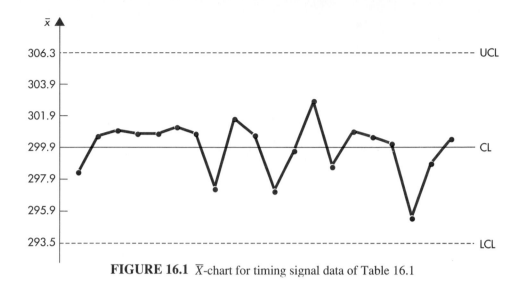

FIGURE 16.1 $\bar{X}$-chart for timing signal data of Table 16.1

---

s-**Chart**

The *s*-chart is a time plot of the sequence of sample standard deviations. The central line on the chart is

$$CL_s = \bar{s}$$

For three-standard error limits, the lower control limit is

$$LCL_s = B_3 \bar{s}$$

and the upper control limit is

$$UCL_s = B_4 \bar{s}$$

where values for the control chart constants[2] B_3 and B_4 are shown in Table 16.2.

The *s*-chart for the timing signal data of Table 16.1 can now be drawn. It is shown in Figure 16.2. We have

$$\bar{s} = 4.48 \qquad B_3 = 0 \qquad B_4 = 2.09$$

Therefore, the three lines on our chart are

$$CL_s = 4.48 \qquad LCL_s = 0 \qquad UCL_s = (2.09)(4.48) = 9.36$$

There does not seem to be cause for undue concern from looking at Figure 16.2. The observed sample standard deviations are generally well below the upper control limit. There is some suggestion of increased variability in the central portion of the observa-

---

[2] In fact, for sample sizes $n \leq 5$, subtracting three standard errors from $\bar{s}$ gives a negative number. Obviously, standard deviations cannot be negative, so the lower limit is taken to be 0. In practice, there will rarely be concern about too *little* variability, so the lower limit is usually not of much interest. More details on the derivation of the constants B_3 and B_4 are provided in Appendix A16.2.

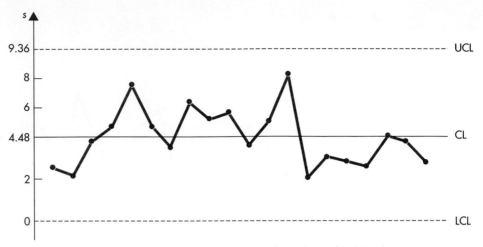

FIGURE 16.2 *s*-Chart for timing signal data of Table 16.1

tion period, for which it might perhaps be worthwhile seeking an explanation in order to learn more about the production process.

FURTHER ANALYSIS OF THE CHARTS

Having developed initial control charts to monitor average performance and variability in performance, some further analysis and interpretation is necessary. Typically, much of this is informal, calling for judgment, aided by experience, rather than formal technical analysis. We will briefly discuss some of the issues that might be involved, noting that the central issue is an assessment of whether or not the performance of the process has been stable over the observation period. If it has not, we are working either with unreliable data, or with data generated by a process subject to serious operating problems. Such data will not provide us with a very reliable indication of what can be expected when the process is operating normally. Essentially, at this stage, the analyst is looking for a pattern of data points distributed more or less randomly around the central line and generally well within the control limits. From this perspective, Figures 16.1 and 16.2 look quite reasonable. In those circumstances, the process under study is said to be **in control,** meaning that its performance characteristics appear to be quite stable. Statistical quality control can be viewed as a means of determining whether a process is in control, as an aid to keeping the process in control and as a mechanism for inducing reduced variability in product quality.

There are a number of ways in which a process might be out of control, since obviously there are many ways in which a sequence of data points can appear nonrandom. Here we will briefly discuss and illustrate three possibilities. Examples of these are graphed in Figure 16.3.

(i) *A value outside the control limits*. The position illustrated in Figure 16.3(a) is clear-cut. Most of the sample statistics (in this particular illustration, the means) are well within the control limits. However, for one sample, the statistic is outside these limits. As we have noted, with three-standard error limits this would be an extremely unusual occurrence for a process that is in control. What we have then is a phenomenon that requires investigation. The analyst

(a) A value outside the control limits

(b) Excessive variability

(c) Trend in sample standard deviations

FIGURE 16.3 Examples of processes out of control

needs to do some detective work, seeking the cause of this extreme value. It will likely emerge that this is not a result of mere chance variability, but arose from peculiar circumstances—often referred to in the literature as **assignable causes.** Perhaps the most common explanation of such phenomena is that an observation value has been incorrectly recorded. It may then be possible to correct this error. Another possibility is that at this particular time, the process was operated by inexperienced personnel. When there are assignable causes for an extreme sample result and some assurance that these will rarely be repeated, this sample should be discarded, and new control limits should be computed from the remaining samples.

(ii) *Excessive variability*. It can happen that although none of the sample values falls outside the control limits, many of those values are far from the central line and relatively close to the limits. Such a situation is illustrated in Figure 16.3(b). Excessive variability in the characteristics of the output of a production process is undesirable, and findings of this sort suggest the desirability of a thorough inspection and overhaul of the process. At this point, the statistician turns the problem over to the engineer.

(iii) *Trends in sample statistics*. The picture presented in Figure 16.3(c) is clearly one of nonrandomness. The sample statistics (here, the standard deviations) do not appear to be randomly dispersed around the central line. Rather, there is a tendency for them to increase over time. Obviously, the impression in Figure 16.3(c) of increasing variability in quality suggests cause for concern, even though no sample value has yet fallen outside the control limits. Perhaps the cause is deteriorating machinery. In any case, the situation clearly calls for further investigation by the engineers.

Only when there is some assurance that a production process is in control is it reasonable to proceed on the basis of calculations such as those made in Table 16.1 and illustrated in Figures 16.1 and 16.2. The control limits computed there can then be used to assess further samples taken on-line—and in this way to look for the development of problems. However, even when the process remains in control, it is desirable that the control limits be recomputed periodically. This is because the characteristics of the production process are likely to evolve over time. For example, the institution and maintenance of a quality control program is likely to heighten awareness in shop floor workers of the importance of quality and of those factors which lead to greater quality. This should lead to reduced variability in product characteristics, and hence to the development of more stringent quality standards. Before proceeding, however, it is necessary to ask whether the product is currently meeting design specifications. We discuss this issue in the next section.

EXERCISES

1. The production process for an electronic component has been monitored, and the strength of electrical emission of the components has been measured. Results are available for a sequence of thirty samples, each of seven observations. The overall mean of the sample observations was 192.6, and the average sample standard deviation was 5.42.

   (a) Use an unbiased estimator to find an estimate of the process standard deviation.

   (b) Find the central line and lower and upper control limits for an $\overline{X}$-chart.

   (c) Find the central line and lower and upper control limits for an s-chart.

2. Measures are taken on the resistance, in ohms, of an electrical component. A sequence of twenty-five samples, each of six observations, was drawn. The overall mean of the sample observations was 93.2 and the average sample standard deviation was 3.67.

   (a) Use an unbiased estimator to find an estimate of the process standard deviation.

   (b) Find the central line and lower and upper control limits for an $\overline{X}$-chart.

   (c) Find the central line and lower and upper control limits for an s-chart.

3. Weights of samples of canned fruit were measured. A sequence of sixteen samples, each of eight observations, was taken. The overall mean of the sample observations was 19.86 ounces, and the average sample standard deviation was 1.23 ounces.

   (a) Use an unbiased estimator to find an estimate of the process standard deviation.
   (b) Find the central line and lower and upper control limits for an $\bar{X}$-chart.
   (c) Find the central line and lower and upper control limits for an s-chart.

4. Traditionally, in British quality control applications, control limits are set at 3.09 standard errors around the mean rather than three standard errors. Referring to Table 3 of the Appendix at the back of this book, explore the consequences and infer the rationale of this specification.

5. The accompanying table shows sample means and standard deviations for a sequence of thirty samples of eight observations each on a quality characteristic of a product.

SAMPLE	$\bar{x}$	s	SAMPLE	$\bar{x}$	s	SAMPLE	$\bar{x}$	s
1	148.2	2.26	11	156.0	4.79	21	148.7	6.28
2	146.4	4.37	12	150.4	3.92	22	149.7	8.92
3	149.9	7.93	13	148.7	8.31	23	151.3	6.20
4	152.8	6.79	14	151.1	7.29	24	150.8	7.39
5	148.7	5.31	15	147.2	3.80	25	147.2	6.97
6	150.6	3.17	16	152.9	4.87	26	141.9	9.68
7	151.5	6.15	17	150.7	3.88	27	152.7	4.28
8	149.2	4.71	18	147.2	8.93	28	148.6	6.51
9	153.9	5.82	19	149.4	6.85	29	150.2	7.29
10	150.6	4.98	20	154.3	7.29	30	148.6	4.73

   (a) Find the overall mean of the sample observations.
   (b) Find the average sample standard deviation.
   (c) Use an unbiased estimator to find an estimate of the process standard deviation.
   (d) Find the central line and lower and upper control limits for an $\bar{X}$-chart.
   (e) Draw the $\bar{X}$-chart and discuss its features.
   (f) Find the central line and lower and upper control limits for an s-chart.
   (g) Draw the s-chart and discuss its features.

6. The accompanying table shows sample means and standard deviations for a sequence of twenty samples of six observations each on contents weights of cans of vegetables, in ounces.

SAMPLE	$\bar{x}$	s	SAMPLE	$\bar{x}$	s	SAMPLE	$\bar{x}$	s
1	20.2	1.9	8	21.0	2.3	15	20.7	1.9
2	18.9	2.7	9	20.6	1.4	16	19.3	2.2
3	19.6	1.7	10	19.1	2.7	17	19.9	3.1
4	20.8	2.3	11	18.8	2.9	18	18.8	2.9
5	19.4	1.2	12	19.3	1.1	19	19.6	2.2
6	19.8	2.1	13	19.8	1.3	20	20.1	1.1
7	20.9	1.6	14	20.2	1.2			

(a) Find the overall mean of the sample observations
(b) Find the average sample standard deviation.
(c) Use an unbiased estimator to find an estimate of the process standard deviation.
(d) Find the central line and lower and upper control limits for an $\overline{X}$-chart.
(e) Draw the $\overline{X}$-chart and discuss its features.
(f) Find the central line and lower and upper control limits for an s-chart.
(g) Draw the s-chart and discuss its features.

16.3 PROCESS CAPABILITY

In Section 16.2, we saw how to use control charts, aided by control limits, to judge whether a process was in control—that is, whether its performance was stable. This is certainly important information, but it is insufficient to assess whether the process is performing adequately to the standards for which it was designed. After all, a consistent performance could be consistently mediocre. Before proceeding further with a quality control or quality improvement program, it is important to determine whether the production process is operating to required specifications. If the process is currently in control, we are in effect asking if it is **capable** of meeting these specifications. This judgment is formed on the basis of data generated by a process that appears to be in control. Therefore, if the sample record includes extreme observations due to assignable causes, these should be discarded before assessing **process capability.** More seriously, when it appears that things have been going wrong over the sample observation period, as for example in cases such as those illustrated in Figures 16.3(b) and (c), corrective action may need to be taken by the engineers. Only when an in-control mode has been established is it possible to go on to assess process capability.

In this section we discuss a common problem, approached through the analysis of sample means and standard deviations. Typically, management will set a range for the values of some characteristic of process output, bounded by **lower and upper specification limits.** For example, in the case of the duration of a timing signal emitted by an electronic component, management may have set a range of tolerable values running from 280 to 320 milliseconds. A process capable of meeting these specifications is one that is very unlikely to produce output not in this range.

For a process that is in control, it is natural to base an assessment of capability on all the sample observations, and, in particular, on estimates of the process mean and standard deviation based on these observations. For the timing signal data, we have already found the estimates[3]

$$\overline{\overline{x}} = 299.9 \qquad \hat{\sigma} = 4.77$$

Then, if the process distribution is assumed to be normal, we have seen that 99.72% of all output should fall within three standard deviations of the mean. It is common, then, in quality control work to calculate the interval $\overline{\overline{x}} \pm 3\hat{\sigma}$. In our example, we have

$$(\overline{\overline{x}} - 3\hat{\sigma}, \overline{\overline{x}} + 3\hat{\sigma}) = (285.6, 314.2)$$

---

[3] In some applications, the sample standard deviation of all the sample observations is used as an estimate of the process standard deviation in place of the estimate used here.

We can regard this as having established the limits within which the process will normally perform. The width of this interval

$$6\hat{\sigma} = (6)(4.77) = 28.6$$

is sometimes called the **natural tolerance** of the process. It provides a measure of the variability in product specifications that can be expected.

Having used the sample data to assess what a production process actually can do, it is only necessary to compare this finding with management specifications of what the process ought to do. What is required is that the interval $\overline{\overline{x}} \pm 3\hat{\sigma}$ lies between, and preferably comfortably between, the lower and upper specification limits. The timing signal data appear quite satisfactory from this point of view. The interval from 285.6 to 314.2 is comfortably between 280 and 320 milliseconds. We might therefore say that the process is capable of meeting these specifications. Notice here that the overall sample mean, $\overline{\overline{x}} = 299.9$, is very near the center, 300 milliseconds, of the tolerance range. In such circumstances, the performance interval is said to be **centered** in the tolerance range. Such centering will often occur and will frequently be desirable. It is not, however, necessary for a process to be capable of meeting standards. As we show in the box below, more formal measures of process capability can be computed.

Two Measures of Process Capability

Assume that management sets **lower and upper tolerance limits,** L and U, for process performance. Process capability is judged by the extent to which $\overline{\overline{x}} \pm 3\hat{\sigma}$ lies between these limits. Two formal measures of capability are:

(i) **Capability Index.** This measure is appropriate when the sample data are **centered** between the tolerance limits, i.e., $\overline{\overline{x}} \simeq (L + U)/2$. The index is

$$Cp = \frac{U - L}{6\hat{\sigma}}$$

A satisfactory value of this index is usually taken to be one that is at least 1.33. [This implies that the **natural tolerance,** $6\hat{\sigma}$, of the process should be no more than 75% of $(U - L)$, the width of the range of acceptable values.]

(ii) **Cpk Index.** When the sample data are not centered, it is necessary to allow for the fact that the process is operating closer to one tolerance limit than the other. This can be done by computing

$$Cpk = \text{Min}\left[\frac{U - \overline{\overline{x}}}{3\hat{\sigma}}, \frac{\overline{\overline{x}} - L}{3\hat{\sigma}}\right]$$

Again, this is taken to be satisfactory if its value is at least 1.33.

For the timing signal data, we have

$$\overline{\overline{x}} = 299.9 \qquad \hat{\sigma} = 4.77 \qquad L = 280 \qquad U = 320$$

Hence, the capability index is

$$Cp = \frac{U - L}{6\hat{\sigma}} = \frac{320 - 280}{(6)(4.77)} = 1.398$$

The *Cpk* index is

$$Cpk = \text{Min} \left[\frac{U - \bar{\bar{x}}}{3\hat{\sigma}}, \frac{\bar{\bar{x}} - L}{3\hat{\sigma}} \right] = \text{Min}(1.405, 1.391) = 1.391$$

In this particular case, since the sample data are, for all practical purposes, centered, the two indices are virtually identical. Both comfortably exceed 1.33, so that we can conclude that the production process is capable of meeting the specifications.

Once process capability has been assessed, there are two possibilities. The process may be found to be incapable of meeting the specifications. This is not a problem for shop-floor production workers. Neither is it a problem for the statistician, who may be able to point to the problem but is unlikely to be equipped to solve it. Rather, the problem must be turned over to management for further analysis and correction. Perhaps the capital equipment is inadequate for the job, possibly through deterioration. Perhaps production workers have been inadequately trained in the operation of that equipment. Perhaps the performance standards that have been set are overly and unnecessarily optimistic. Whatever the case, continued operation and analysis of the process in its current state is of little value.

The happier outcome is that the production process will be found to be capable of meeting the set performance standards. In that case, the quality control process can be continued. The production process should be regularly monitored, and control charts constructed. From time to time, as the process evolves, it is desirable to recompute control limits for these charts. Periodic checks of process capability should also be made. Quality control is not merely a passive activity. Neither is it only a mechanism for detecting problems, though it is certainly valuable for this purpose. The goal of a quality control exercise is improvement in quality, which can be viewed as a reduction in the natural tolerance of the process. These gains can arise from the greater awareness and understanding of good quality and its sources when production workers are involved in the collection and interpretation of data for quality control studies.

EXERCISES

7. Refer to Exercise 1. Management has specified that the strength of electrical emission of components produced by this process should be between 170 and 215.
   (a) Compute the interval $\bar{\bar{x}} \pm 3\hat{\sigma}$ and comment on your finding.
   (b) Find the capability index, *Cp*, and discuss the result.
   (c) Find the *Cpk* index and discuss the result.
8. Refer to Exercise 2. Management has specified that the resistance of components produced by this process should be between 85 and 100 ohms.
   (a) Compute the interval $\bar{\bar{x}} \pm 3\hat{\sigma}$ and comment on your finding.
   (b) Find the capability index, *Cp*, and discuss the result.
   (c) Find the *Cpk* index and discuss the result.
9. Refer to Exercise 3. Management has specified that the weights of canned fruit should be between 18 and 22 ounces.
   (a) Compute the interval $\bar{\bar{x}} \pm 3\hat{\sigma}$ and comment on the result.
   (b) Find and discuss the capability index *Cp*.
   (c) Find and discuss the *Cpk* index.
10. Refer to Exercise 5. Management has specified that the values of the quality characteristic for this process should lie between 130 and 170.

(a) Compute the interval $\bar{\bar{x}} \pm 3\hat{\sigma}$ and comment on your finding.

(b) Find the capability index, Cp, and discuss the result.

(c) Find the Cpk index and discuss the result.

11. Refer to Exercise 6. Management has determined that contents weights should be between 16 and 24 ounces.

(a) Compute the interval $\bar{\bar{x}} \pm 3\hat{\sigma}$ and comment on your finding.

(b) Find the capability index, Cp, and discuss the result.

(c) Find the Cpk index and discuss the result.

16.4 CONTROL CHARTS FOR PROPORTIONS

Now, rather than analyzing numerical data which measures some characteristic of a product, we consider the position where individual product items will be judged to have conformed or not to have conformed to specifications. Again, a sequence of samples is taken over time to assess the evolution of product quality, and the results are plotted on a control chart. Now, the quantity of interest is the proportion of **nonconforming** items in each sample. Obviously, we would like this proportion to be as small as possible, and any increasing trend over time should cause concern.

One important difference in the development of control charts for proportions, compared with the charts of Section 16.2, is that here much larger sample sizes are necessary. This is so because any competently engineered production process is not going to generate a large proportion of nonconforming items. Therefore, to get a reasonable assessment of this measure of quality, a relatively large sample is essential. For many applications, samples of between fifty and two hundred items are recommended, though often larger samples are needed. A rule of thumb often employed in practice is that the average number of nonconforming items per sample should be at least five or six. So, for example, if it is expected that around 1% of all items will fail to conform to standards, samples of at least 500–600 are required. One consequence of the need for large samples is that it may be desirable to take samples of unequal sizes. For example, it may be necessary to inspect the entire output of a day, or of a work shift, to generate sufficient observations. Typically, these numbers will not remain constant over time. In this section, for convenience, we will restrict attention to the case of equal sample sizes, though extension to the case of unequal sample sizes is quite straightforward.

A further important issue in the development of control charts for proportions of nonconforming items concerns the element of subjective judgment inherent in the generation of the data. Nonconformity to standards will be judged by inspectors, and, given the element of subjectivity involved, it is likely that different inspectors will not generate consistent results. In consequence, extra variability, or the appearance of lack of control, in the charts could result from inspector differences. It is important to be aware of this possibility in interpreting control charts for proportions. At the outset, when data are to be generated by more than one inspector, it is necessary to be as specific as possible in setting out the standards for nonconformity.

We will illustrate control charts for proportions through an example. Table 16.3 shows the results from twenty samples, each of 200 observations taken over time, of

TABLE 16.3 Nonconforming items in samples of 200 electronic components

SAMPLE NUMBER	NUMBER NONCONFORMING	$\hat{p}$	SAMPLE NUMBER	NUMBER NONCONFORMING	$\hat{p}$
1	18	.090	11	19	.095
2	15	.075	12	26	.130
3	23	.115	13	11	.055
4	9	.045	14	28	.140
5	17	.085	15	22	.110
6	29	.145	16	14	.070
7	11	.055	17	25	.125
8	21	.105	18	17	.085
9	25	.125	19	23	.115
10	14	.070	20	18	.090

an electronic component. The table shows the numbers, and proportions, of sampled components not conforming to standards. The average of these sample proportions is

$$\overline{p} = (.090 + .075 + \cdots + .090)/20 = .096$$

The following box summarizes the notation used in developing control charts for proportions.

Notation

A sequence of K samples, each of n observations, is taken over time, and the proportions of sample members **not conforming** to standards are determined. These **sample proportions** are denoted $\hat{p}_i$ ($i = 1, 2, \ldots, K$). They can be graphed on a p-chart. If the samples are of the same size, the **average of the sample proportions** is the overall proportion of **nonconforming** items: This is

$$\overline{p} = \sum_{i=1}^{K} \hat{p}_i / K$$

If the process has been operating consistently over the whole observation period, each of the samples can be viewed as having been drawn from a common population. The proportion of nonconforming items in that population is estimated by the average of the sample proportions, $\overline{p}$. Thus, recalling our discussion in Chapter 6 on the sampling distribution of sample proportions, the individual sample proportions $\hat{p}_i$ have sampling distribution with mean estimated by $\overline{p}$, and standard error given by

$$\hat{\sigma}_p = \sqrt{\frac{\overline{p}(1 - \overline{p})}{n}}$$

As with other applications in quality control that we have discussed, standard practice here is to set three-standard error limits on the control charts. Details are given in the following box.

_p_-Chart

The **_p_-chart** is a time plot of the sequence of sample proportions of nonconforming items. The central line is

$$CL_p = \bar{p}$$

For three-standard error limits, the lower control limit[4] is

$$LCL_p = \bar{p} - 3\sqrt{\frac{\bar{p}(1-\bar{p})}{n}}$$

and the upper control limit is

$$UCL_p = \bar{p} + 3\sqrt{\frac{\bar{p}(1-\bar{p})}{n}}$$

We can now draw the _p_-chart for the data of Table 16.3. This is shown in Figure 16.4. The central line on the chart is

$$CL_p = \bar{p} = .096$$

The lower control limit is

$$LCL_p = \bar{p} - 3\sqrt{\frac{\bar{p}(1-\bar{p})}{n}} = .096 - 3\sqrt{\frac{(.096)(.904)}{200}}$$

$$= .096 - .062 = .034$$

FIGURE 16.4 _p_-Chart for electronic components data of Table 16.3

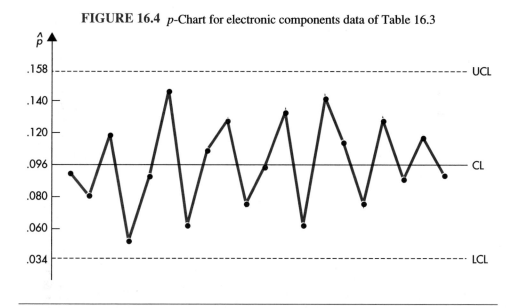

---

[4] The formula for the lower control limit can give a negative value, which is of course an impossible value for a proportion. In that case, the lower control limit is set at 0. In any case, breach of the lower limit will typically not cause concern. It may imply that the process is becoming more reliable. However, another possibility might be poor performance by inspectors in detecting nonconforming items.

and the upper control limit is

$$UCL_p = .096 + .062 = .158$$

Looking at Figure 16.4, it can be seen that all the sample proportions lie between the control limits and that the great majority are well within these limits. There is perhaps a suggestion of moderately high variability in quality, which might warrant further investigation. However, it would not be unreasonable to conclude from the chart that the process is in control. In that case, we might conclude that under current operating conditions, about 9.6% of all items produced will fail to conform to standards.

Interpretation of p-charts is similar to that of the charts of Section 16.2. Sample values that lie outside the control limits are further investigated, and if assignable causes for extreme values are found, these are eliminated and the control limits recalculated. A particular concern would be the appearance of an upward trend over time in a p-chart. This would suggest the possibility of an increasing proportion of nonconforming items—that is, a deterioration in quality. Once it has been established that a process is in control, the limits can be used to evaluate further data. However, as for other control charts, it is good practice to recompute the control limits periodically to account for improved performance as the quality exercise proceeds.

Of course, the analysis of nonconformities in this way may reveal that uncomfortably many substandard items are being produced. In that case, further analysis may be desirable and possible through **Pareto diagrams.** These are essentially bar charts, isolating the individual causes of nonconformity. The various individual problems with the substandard items are listed, and the number of items in each category is calculated. The bar charts may be organized to display either the raw numbers of products with different types of defects or the total costs of correcting these defects. In this way, management should be able to form a quick visual impression of where effort needs to be concentrated to achieve the greatest reduction in the nonconformities rate or in the cost of reworking nonconforming items. In this manner, the quality control exercise will have made a valuable contribution to trouble-shooting.

16.5 CONTROL CHARTS FOR NUMBER OF OCCURRENCES

In Section 4.7 we saw that the Poisson distribution can often be useful in representing the *number of occurrences* of an event. A common application in quality control is where a finished item is inspected, and the number of defects, or imperfections, of a particular type is counted. If items are inspected over time, and *counts* of number of imperfections per item are recorded, this information can be presented in a control chart. This is called a *c-chart*.

A manufacturer of textiles produces bolts of cloth. Periodically, a bolt is carefully inspected, and the number of imperfections is recorded. Table 16.4 shows a sequence of twenty such results, recorded over time. In exercises such as this, it is convenient to have the same inspector examine each item. Then, any apparent trends that appear will not be due to differences in standards applied by, or experience of, different inspectors. In our example, the average number of imperfections per bolt of cloth is

$$\bar{c} = (8 + 8 + \cdots + 6)/20 = 6.6$$

TABLE 16.4 Numbers of imperfections in bolts of cloth

CLOTH BOLT	NUMBER OF IMPERFECTIONS	CLOTH BOLT	NUMBER OF IMPERFECTIONS	CLOTH BOLT	NUMBER OF IMPERFECTIONS
1	8	8	2	15	1
2	8	9	3	16	7
3	6	10	10	17	9
4	8	11	7	18	11
5	9	12	6	19	9
6	5	13	8	20	6
7	7	14	2		

This provides a natural estimate of the population mean number of imperfections per bolt.

The general notation used in constructing control charts for number of occurrences is set out in the following box.

Notation

A sequence of K items is inspected over time. For each item, the number of occurrences of some event, such as an imperfection, is recorded. These *numbers of occurrences* are denoted c_i ($i = 1, 2, \ldots, K$). The *sample mean number of occurrences* is then

$$\bar{c} = \sum_{i=1}^{K} c_i / K$$

The sample mean number of occurrences, $\bar{c}$, provides an estimate of the population mean. Moreover, if the distribution of the number of occurrences is Poisson, the standard deviation of the distribution is the square root of the mean. In our example, then, the standard deviation of the number of occurrences is estimated by

$$\sqrt{\bar{c}} = \sqrt{6.6} = 2.569$$

A control chart for the number of occurrences can be constructed in the usual way. As always, interpretation is facilitated by drawing three-standard error limits on the chart. The following box provides the details.

---

c-Chart

The *c-chart* is a time plot of the number of occurrences of an event. The central line is

$$CL_c = \bar{c}$$

For three-standard error limits, the lower control limit is

$$LCL_c = 0 \qquad \text{if } \bar{c} \leq 9$$
$$= \bar{c} - 3\sqrt{\bar{c}} \qquad \text{if } \bar{c} > 9$$

and the upper control limit is

$$UCL_c = \bar{c} + 3\sqrt{\bar{c}}$$

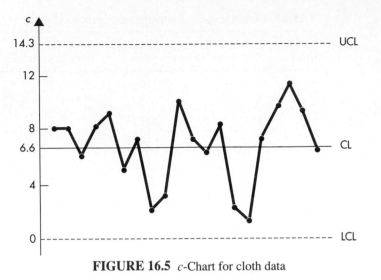

FIGURE 16.5 c-Chart for cloth data

In our example, since $\bar{c}$ is less than nine, the lower control limit is

$$LCL_c = 0$$

The upper control limit is

$$UCL_c = \bar{c} + 3\sqrt{\bar{c}} = 6.6 + 3\sqrt{6.6} = 14.3$$

Figure 16.5 shows the control chart for the data of Table 16.4. Inspection of this c-chart suggests no cause for concern. The observations are all well below the upper control limit and there is no evidence of an increasing number of imperfections over time. It appears, then, that the production process is in control, so that Figure 16.5 presents a fair picture of process capability.

16.6 SUMMARY

The most valuable ingredient of any quality control program is the decision to initiate it. Certainly, the details of the various statistical techniques employed are important and require some study, but the greatest gains are likely to come from the increased awareness of management and workers of the worth of quality improvement. One mechanism for the incorporation of employees into the effort is through the formation of **quality circles**—small groups of people in which quality standards, and possibilities for their improvement, are discussed. Such discussions can lead to valuable suggestions for improvement. They are most likely to do so when the discussions are structured, and when group members are provided with relevant information.

The statistical methods that we have discussed here, and others that are often used, can provide the information necessary for an informed discussion of current quality performance. These methods are not at all difficult to understand, and the emphasis on charts renders interpretation of the data relatively straightforward. This is important, as it allows access to information to a wide range of employees without their needing to understand high-powered technical statistical concepts. Indeed, an understanding of **variability** and its causes should get one far along the road to a capacity for intelligent interpretation of the data. No process will yield perfectly identical pieces of output. There will inevitably be some **natural variability,** which can be put down to chance. An important element of quality control is the recognition of patterns of measurements that are unlikely to reflect natural variability, but rather signal some structural cause that requires investigation.

There are many other quality control techniques beyond those discussed in this chapter, as well as a number of ways in which relevant data might be collected and tabulated. To some extent, the choice of an appropriate approach will depend on individual circumstances. Naturally, the process could be computerized, and statistical quality control computer programs are widely available. As we have seen, for many quality control methods, the calculations and chart construction involved do not constitute a heavy burden. Whether or not to use computers for this purpose may as much as anything depend on an estimate of the costs incurred as well as a judgment of whether this would be preferable for the personnel involved in recording the data.

EXERCISES

12. In the study of an automotive component, thirty samples, each of 250 observations, were taken. The average of the sample proportions of nonconforming items was .056. Find the central line and lower and upper control limits for a p-chart.

13. In the study of a part for aircraft manufacture, twenty-five samples, each of 500 observations, were taken. The average of the sample proportions of nonconforming items was .016. Find the central line and lower and upper control limits for a p-chart.

14. The accompanying table shows proportions of nonconforming items in a sequence of thirty samples, each of 200 observations.

SAMPLE NUMBER	$\hat{p}$	SAMPLE NUMBER	$\hat{p}$	SAMPLE NUMBER	$\hat{p}$
1	.125	11	.135	21	.105
2	.140	12	.170	22	.135
3	.090	13	.105	23	.140
4	.085	14	.095	24	.085
5	.175	15	.130	25	.145
6	.160	16	.145	26	.175
7	.130	17	.155	27	.105
8	.135	18	.090	28	.130
9	.095	19	.125	29	.085
10	.115	20	.145	30	.090

(a) Find the average of the sample proportions.

(b) Find the central line and lower and upper control limits for a p-chart.

(c) Draw the p-chart and discuss its features.

15. The accompanying table shows proportions of nonconforming items in a sequence of twenty samples, each of 500 observations.

SAMPLE NUMBER	$\hat{p}$	SAMPLE NUMBER	$\hat{p}$	SAMPLE NUMBER	$\hat{p}$
1	.048	8	.052	15	.068
2	.062	9	.032	16	.036
3	.056	10	.038	17	.030
4	.060	11	.048	18	.064
5	.038	12	.042	19	.056
6	.042	13	.076	20	.048
7	.066	14	.058		

    (a) Find the average of the sample proportions.
    (b) Find the central line and lower and upper control limits for a p-chart.
    (c) Draw the p-chart and discuss its features.

16. The accompanying table shows numbers of nonconforming items in a sequence of twenty-five samples, each of 250 observations.

SAMPLE NUMBER	NUMBER NONCONFORMING	SAMPLE NUMBER	NUMBER NONCONFORMING	SAMPLE NUMBER	NUMBER NONCONFORMING
1	23	10	15	18	26
2	15	11	25	19	12
3	18	12	17	20	16
4	12	13	11	21	23
5	28	14	25	22	20
6	22	15	19	23	16
7	21	16	23	24	15
8	19	17	21	25	22
9	36				

    (a) Find the sample proportions.
    (b) Find the average of the sample proportions.
    (c) Find the central line and lower and upper control limits for a p-chart.
    (d) Draw the p-chart and discuss its features.

17. A process produces rolls of coated paper. A sequence of twenty rolls was inspected over time and the numbers of imperfections were recorded. The results are shown in the accompanying table.

ROLL	NUMBER OF IMPERFECTIONS	ROLL	NUMBER OF IMPERFECTIONS	ROLL	NUMBER OF IMPERFECTIONS
1	1	8	6	15	2
2	7	9	4	16	6
3	5	10	8	17	8
4	6	11	6	18	12
5	9	12	5	19	5
6	4	13	6	20	4
7	1	14	7		

(a) Find the sample mean number of imperfections per roll.

(b) Find the central line and lower and upper control limits for a *c*-chart.

(c) Draw the *c*-chart and discuss its features.

18. A newspaper reader has very carefully read her local paper for twenty weeks. For each Wednesday's edition she has counted the number of typographical and/or spelling errors. The results are shown in the accompanying table.

WEEK	ERRORS	WEEK	ERRORS	WEEK	ERRORS
1	12	8	21	15	7
2	19	9	14	16	18
3	8	10	7	17	12
4	11	11	13	18	13
5	15	12	19	19	13
6	17	13	11	20	20
7	11	14	10		

(a) Find the sample mean number of errors for these twenty Wednesdays.

(b) Find the central line and lower and upper limits for a *c*-chart.

(c) Draw the *c*-chart and discuss its features.

19. A process manufactures raisin scones. Periodically, a scone is inspected and the number of raisins it contains is counted. The accompanying table shows results for fifteen scones.

SCONE	RAISINS	SCONE	RAISINS	SCONE	RAISINS
1	18	6	16	11	15
2	15	7	13	12	9
3	22	8	18	13	10
4	14	9	14	14	7
5	17	10	12	15	8

(a) Find the sample mean number of raisins per scone.

(b) Find the central line and lower and upper limits for a *c*-chart.

(c) Draw the *c*-chart and discuss its features.

REVIEW EXERCISES

20. Distinguish between each of the following pairs of terms.
   - (a) A process is *in control*, and a process is *capable* of performing to specifications.
   - (b) *Natural variability* and *assignable causes*.
21. In quality control work it is usual to employ three-standard error limits in constructing the charts. Explain the rationale behind, and the implications of, this choice.
22. The accompanying table shows sample means and standard deviations for a sequence of twenty samples of five observations on a quality characteristic of a product.

SAMPLE	$\bar{x}$	s	SAMPLE	$\bar{x}$	s	SAMPLE	$\bar{x}$	s
1	120.3	2.6	8	120.7	1.4	15	120.9	1.9
2	119.5	1.8	9	120.9	2.2	16	119.2	3.1
3	118.4	2.2	10	118.7	2.8	17	119.9	2.2
4	120.9	1.7	11	119.2	2.4	18	118.7	2.6
5	119.3	1.2	12	118.9	1.4	19	120.6	1.4
6	119.7	2.3	13	119.9	1.2	20	119.4	1.9
7	121.1	1.9	14	120.3	1.5			

   - (a) Find the overall mean of the sample observations.
   - (b) Find the average sample standard deviation.
   - (c) Use an unbiased estimator to find an estimate of the process standard deviation.
   - (d) Find the central line and lower and upper control limits for an $\bar{X}$-chart.
   - (e) Draw the $\bar{X}$-chart and discuss its features.
   - (f) Find the central line and lower and upper control limits for an s-chart.
   - (g) Draw the s-chart and discuss its features.
   - (h) Management has specified that the values of the quality characteristic for this process should be between 115 and 125.
       - (i) Compute the interval $\bar{\bar{x}} \pm 3\hat{\sigma}$ and comment on your finding.
       - (ii) Find the capability index, Cp, and discuss the result.
       - (iii) Find the Cpk index and discuss the result.
23. The accompanying table shows sample means and standard deviations for a sequence of twenty-five samples of eight observations on a quality characteristic of a product.

SAMPLE	$\bar{x}$	s	SAMPLE	$\bar{x}$	s	SAMPLE	$\bar{x}$	s
1	347.9	2.37	10	356.1	4.82	18	349.8	6.27
2	349.8	4.26	11	348.7	3.90	19	350.7	5.92
3	346.5	7.81	12	352.1	8.61	20	352.3	9.64
4	352.7	5.62	13	353.6	7.59	21	347.1	3.68
5	350.4	3.17	14	349.1	6.28	22	342.8	6.52
6	348.6	6.09	15	347.4	3.87	23	348.7	7.13
7	351.7	5.27	16	354.3	8.21	24	354.1	4.36
8	353.8	4.31	17	350.5	4.19	25	352.3	5.19
9	349.4	4.97						

(a) Find the overall mean of the sample observations.

(b) Find the average sample standard deviation.

(c) Use an unbiased estimator to find an estimate of the process standard deviation.

(d) Find the central line and lower and upper control limits for an $\overline{X}$-chart.

(e) Draw the $\overline{X}$-chart and discuss its features.

(f) Find the central line and lower and upper control limits for an s-chart.

(g) Draw the s-chart and discuss its features.

(h) Management has specified that the values of the quality characteristic for this process should be between 325 and 375.

    (i) Compute the interval $\overline{\overline{x}} \pm 3\hat{\sigma}$ and comment on your findings.

   (ii) Find the capability index, Cp, and discuss the result.

 (iii) Find the Cpk index and discuss the result.

24. The accompanying table shows proportions of nonconforming items in a sequence of twenty samples, each of 500 observations.

SAMPLE NUMBER	$\hat{p}$	SAMPLE NUMBER	$\hat{p}$	SAMPLE NUMBER	$\hat{p}$
1	.078	8	.080	15	.094
2	.062	9	.068	16	.066
3	.048	10	.076	17	.070
4	.086	11	.064	18	.088
5	.092	12	.068	19	.062
6	.074	13	.058	20	.054
7	.076	14	.082		

(a) Find the average of the sample proportions.

(b) Find the central line and lower and upper control limits for a p-chart.

(c) Draw the p-chart and discuss its features.

25. A department store customer complaints department has recorded the number of complaints received over a period of eighteen weeks. The results are shown in the accompanying table.

WEEK	COMPLAINTS	WEEK	COMPLAINTS	WEEK	COMPLAINTS
1	15	7	20	13	22
2	10	8	11	14	15
3	17	9	15	15	9
4	19	10	15	16	16
5	14	11	19	17	17
6	12	12	10	18	14

(a) Find the sample mean number of complaints per week.

(b) Find the central line and lower and upper limits for a c-chart.

(c) Draw the c-chart and discuss its features.

26. The accompanying table shows sample observations for a sequence of sixteen samples, each of four observations, on a quality characteristic of a product.

SAMPLE NUMBER	SAMPLE OBSERVATIONS			
1	340	346	351	338
2	332	348	330	344
3	339	343	339	347
4	342	338	346	338
5	350	340	345	347
6	344	332	347	351
7	336	348	362	331
8	345	342	349	330
9	356	342	348	329
10	337	361	332	344
11	353	329	323	360
12	348	367	323	320
13	370	354	358	340
14	368	328	339	347
15	366	328	343	351
16	330	323	364	339

(a) Find the sixteen sample means and sample standard deviations.
(b) Find the overall mean of the sample observations.
(c) Find the average sample standard deviation.
(d) Use an unbiased estimator to find an estimate of the process standard deviation.
(e) Find the central line and lower and upper control limits for an $\bar{X}$-chart.
(f) Draw the $\bar{X}$-chart and discuss its features.
(g) Find the central line and lower and upper control limits for an s-chart.
(h) Draw the s-chart and discuss its features.
(i) Refer to the material in Appendix A16.1.
  (i) Find the sixteen sample ranges, and the average sample range.
  (ii) Based on the sample ranges, use an unbiased estimator to estimate the process standard deviation.
  (iii) Based on the sample ranges, find lower and upper control limits for an $\bar{X}$-chart.
  (iv) Find the central line and lower and upper control limits for an R-chart.
  (v) Draw the R-chart and discuss its features.

APPENDIX A16.1

In many practical applications of quality control methods, the sample ranges, rather than the standard deviations, are used to measure variability. In this appendix, we show how the methods of Sections 16.2 and 16.3 are modified in that case.

The range of a set of numbers is just the difference between the largest and the smallest. In Table A16.1 we presented twenty samples, each of five observations, on the duration of a timing signal emitted by an electronic component. The twenty sample ranges are given in Table A16.1. The average sample range is then

$$\overline{R} = (7 + 7 + \cdots + 8)/20 = 10.9$$

Although the individual sample standard deviations are not computed in this approach, it is still useful to estimate the process standard deviation. An estimate is provided by

$$\hat{\sigma} = \overline{R}/d_2 \qquad (A16.1.1)$$

where d_2 and some other useful control chart constants are given in Table A16.2. In our example, samples are of five observations. The estimated process standard deviation is therefore

$$\hat{\sigma} = \overline{R}/d_2 = 10.9/2.326 = 4.69$$

We are assuming here that sample ranges have been calculated, but that sample standard deviations have not. Therefore, it is still possible to plot the $\overline{X}$-chart, exactly as in Section 16.2, with central line provided by the overall mean of the sample observations

$$CL_{\bar{x}} = \overline{\overline{x}}$$

However, now the control limits must be based on the sample ranges instead of the sample standard deviations. These limits are[5]

$$LCL_{\bar{x}} = \overline{\overline{x}} - A_2\overline{R} \qquad UCL_{\bar{x}} = \overline{\overline{x}} + A_2\overline{R}$$

TABLE A16.1 Sample ranges for timing signal data

SAMPLE NUMBER	R	SAMPLE NUMBER	R	SAMPLE NUMBER	R
1	7	8	15	15	8
2	7	9	12	16	7
3	10	10	13	17	8
4	13	11	11	18	11
5	16	12	13	19	11
6	12	13	21	20	8
7	9	14	6		

[5] These are three-standard error limits. In fact, $A_2 = 3/(d_2\sqrt{n})$, corresponding to the expression given in Eq. (16.2.2).

TABLE A16.2 Some control chart constants used in conjunction with the range

n	d_2	A_2	D_3	D_4
2	1.128	1.88	0	3.27
3	1.693	1.02	0	2.57
4	2.059	0.73	0	2.28
5	2.326	0.58	0	2.11
6	2.534	0.48	0	2.00
7	2.704	0.42	.08	1.92
8	2.847	0.37	.14	1.86
9	2.970	0.34	.18	1.82
10	3.078	0.31	.22	1.78

Some values of the control chart constant A_2 are given in Table A16.2. In our example, when $n = 5$, we have

$$LCL_{\bar{x}} = \bar{\bar{x}} - A_2\bar{R} = 299.9 - (.58)(10.9) = 293.6$$

and

$$UCL_{\bar{x}} = \bar{\bar{x}} + A_2\bar{R} = 299.9 + (.58)(10.9) = 306.2$$

The $\bar{X}$-chart is then identical to Figure 16.1, except that the control limits are set at 293.6 and 306.2.

The progress of process variability over time can be assessed through a time plot of the sample ranges. This is known as an R-chart. The R-chart for our timing signal data is shown in Figure A16.1. The central line on the chart is the average sample range; that is

$$CL_R = \bar{R} = 10.9$$

Three-standard error control limits are provided by

$$LCL_R = D_3\bar{R} \qquad UCL_R = D_4\bar{R}$$

FIGURE A16.1 R-Chart for timing signal data

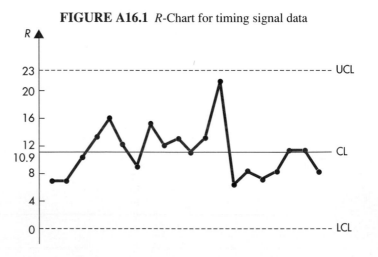

where values of the control chart constants, D_3 and D_4, are given in Table A16.2. For our example

$$LCL_R = 0 \qquad UCL_R = (2.11)(10.9) = 23$$

Inspection of Figure A16.1 suggests no great cause for concern. Only one of the sample ranges is at all close to the upper control limit.

Finally, notice that the process capability calculations of Section 16.3 can still be carried out. Those calculations require an estimate of the process standard deviation. When the analysis is based on sample ranges, that estimate is provided by Eq. (A16.1.1).

APPENDIX A16.2

In this appendix we provide some details of the derivations of the control chart constants used in Section 16.2 and tabulated in Table 16.2.

Suppose that a sample of n observations is drawn from a normal population with standard deviation σ. Let s denote the sample standard deviation. In general, it is known that the sample standard deviation is not an unbiased estimator of the population standard deviation. For a normal population it is possible to show that the expected value of the sample standard deviation is

$$E(s) = c_4\sigma$$

where

$$c_4 = \sqrt{\frac{2}{(n-2)}} \frac{[(n-2)/2]!}{[(n-3)/2]!}; \quad (1/2)! = \sqrt{\pi}/2$$

To illustrate, let $n = 5$. Then

$$c_4 = \sqrt{\frac{2}{4}} \frac{(3/2)!}{(2/2)!} = \sqrt{\frac{1}{2}} (3/2)(1/2)! = \sqrt{\frac{1}{2}} (3/2)(\sqrt{\pi}/2) = .940$$

as given in Table 16.2. Similarly, for $n = 8$

$$c_4 = \sqrt{\frac{2}{7}} \frac{(3!)}{(5/2)!} = \sqrt{\frac{2}{7}} \cdot \frac{6}{(5/2)(3/2)(1/2)!} = \sqrt{\frac{2}{7}} \cdot \frac{6}{(5/2)(3/2)(\sqrt{\pi}/2)} = .965$$

which is the entry shown in Table 16.2. Thus, if sampling is from a normal distribution, s/c_4 provides an unbiased estimator of the population standard deviation.

In Section 16.2, in the discussion leading to Eq. (16.2.2), we provided a derivation of the control chart constant A_3, used in setting control limits for $\bar{X}$-charts. Specifically

$$A_3 = 3/(c_4\sqrt{n})$$

when three-standard error limits are used. For example, for $n = 5$

$$A_3 = 3/(.940\sqrt{5}) = 1.43$$

as given in Table 16.2.

Finally, we consider the sampling distribution of the sample standard deviation when sampling from a normal distribution. The variance of that distribution is

$$\sigma_s^2 = E(s^2) - [E(s)]^2 = \sigma^2 - c_4^2\sigma^2 = \sigma^2(1 - c_4^2)$$

so that the standard error is

$$\sigma_s = \sigma\sqrt{1 - c_4^2}$$

Substituting an unbiased estimator for the unknown population standard deviation then yields the estimate

$$\hat{\sigma}_s = \frac{\bar{s}}{c_4} \sqrt{1 - c_4^2}$$

Three-standard error limits of the sample standard deviation are then

$$\bar{s} \pm 3\hat{\sigma}_s = \bar{s} \pm \frac{3\bar{s}}{c_4} \sqrt{1 - c_4^2}$$

Hence, the lower limit is

$$\bar{s} - \frac{3\bar{s}}{c_4} \sqrt{1 - c_4^2} = B_3\bar{s}$$

where

$$B_3 = 1 - (3/c_4) \sqrt{1 - c_4^2}$$

Similarly, the upper limit is

$$\bar{s} + \frac{3\bar{s}}{c_4} \sqrt{1 - c_4^2} = B_4\bar{s}$$

where

$$B_4 = 1 + (3/c_4) \sqrt{1 - c_4^2}$$

To illustrate, for sample size $n = 5$

$$B_4 = 1 + (3/.940) \sqrt{1 - (.940)^2} = 2.09$$

as given in Table 16.2. Strict application of the formula for B_3 would yield $-.09$ in this case, but since a standard deviation cannot be negative, zero is used as the lower limit here.

In fact, control chart limits could also be based on the chi-square distribution followed by $(n - 1)s^2/\sigma^2$. However, this approach is used less often in practical applications, so we will not discuss its details.

Time Series Analysis and Forecasting

17.1 TIME SERIES DATA: PROBLEMS AND OPPORTUNITIES

In this chapter, we will deal with some of the issues involved in analyzing a special type of data set. Specifically, we will be interested in measurements *over time* on a particular variable. Examples include monthly product sales, quarterly corporate earnings, and daily closing prices for shares of common stock.

Definition

A **time series** is a set of measurements, ordered over time, on a particular quantity of interest.

Time series data typically possess special characteristics that necessitate the development of new statistical methods for their analysis. Virtually all the techniques of data analysis that we have developed so far are based on an assumption of *random sampling*—that is, on the assumption that the available data consist of *independent* observations on the phenomenon of interest. Only very rarely will this assumption of independence be tenable for time series data. For example, consider a series of monthly sales of a manufactured product. Lack of independence might be suspected for at least two reasons. First, if sales were relatively buoyant last month, it is reasonable to suspect that they are more likely than not to remain so in the current month. The general economic conditions that led to high sales volume last month are not likely to undergo an abrupt change in 1 month, so the market features faced by the manufacturer in the current month will, in all probability, be broadly similar to those of the previous month. Thus, we can expect some similarity between sales in adjacent months. Another feature of sales data for many products is *seasonality*. Sales tend to peak at about the same time every year. Hence, if June has historically been a good month for sales of this product in past years, it is more likely than not that June sales in the current year will be relatively high. This too implies a lack of independence in the monthly sales figures.

We have seen that time series are likely to be characterized by certain types of dependence. Thus, an important assumption underlying the great majority of the statistical procedures discussed so far in this text will very probably not hold for time series data. Furthermore, this assumption is usually rather crucial, and the analysis of a time series as if it consisted of independent measurements can produce seriously misleading conclusions. This is the fundamental problem of time series analysis and the reason we must devote a separate chapter to it. We have, in fact, already met the problem in the context of regression analysis in Section 14.8. There we dealt with the problem of estimating regression models when the error terms were autocorrelated—that is, correlated over time. In this chapter, we will restrict ourselves to the analysis of single time series.

We have just discussed a negative aspect of the kinds of dependency patterns likely to be present in time series data. These patterns do create problems, necessitating the development of special techniques of data analysis. However, inherent in this same phenomenon lies an opportunity. It is often possible to exploit any dependencies revealed in the past to produce *forecasts* of future values of a time series. For example, if sales in the current month are rather similar to sales in the immediately preceding months and to sales in the same month in previous years, this information can be used to predict sales in future months.

17.2 INDEX NUMBERS

Before proceeding to a description of statistical methods used in the analysis of time series data, we discuss in this section the construction of a particular type of time series. To motivate our discussion, we begin by posing a question which at first sight may appear deceptively simple. What changes have occurred in the price of automobiles built in the United States in the past 10 years? It almost goes without saying that their prices have risen, but how can this price rise be described *quantitatively?* On the surface, this question may not seem very difficult to answer. One could collect price information about these automobiles in each of the past 10 years and tabulate the data or graph them in a time plot.

However, when one thinks a little more deeply about the problem, a number of difficulties emerge. The first, and perhaps most crucial, is that automobiles are not homogeneous. It is meaningless to ask, "What is the price of an automobile?" It is necessary to be more specific. The price of a large luxury car is very much higher than that of a subcompact. Perhaps, then, one could proceed by comparing the *average* prices of all automobiles built in the United States in each of the past 10 years. Unfortunately, such a comparison might prove misleading. Imagine a year in which relatively many luxury cars and very few subcompacts were sold compared with a year in which there was a preponderance of small-car sales and very few luxury cars were sold. In the latter year, the average price of cars sold would be low compared with that of the previous year, simply because of a change in the market mix. Table 17.1 gives a hypothetical example of a market in which there are just two types of automobile. We see from the table that the price of each type is *higher* in year 2 than in year 1. However, because of the difference in the product mixes sold in the two years, we see from the final column of the table that the average price of all cars sold in year 2 is *lower* than the average price of all cars sold in year 1. Obviously, we would not want to conclude from these data that automobile prices were lower in year 2 than in year 1! Hence, this kind of average is of no value for our purposes.

Another possible solution is to compute the average price of a *single* car of each type. That this procedure is not free from difficulty of interpretation is clear from a second hypothetical example, shown in Table 17.2. Here, we have a market in which subcompact cars are considerably more popular than luxury cars. The price of subcompacts is the same in the two years, while that of luxury cars doubles from year 1 to year 2. Hence, as we see in the final column of the table, the average price of a single subcompact car and a single luxury car is considerably higher in the second year than in the first. But this procedure does not present an accurate picture of the trend in the automobile market, since it gives equal weights to the prices of the two types of car, even though relatively few luxury cars were sold.

These examples demonstrate that to form a reliable picture of the overall price pattern over time, it is necessary to take carefully into account the quantities purchased in each time period. We will see how appropriate weighted averages can be formed.

A similar problem arises because cars are sold with optional "extras," which naturally affect the price. Thus, the average price of subcompacts sold in a year in which consumers opt for many of these extras will be higher than in a year in which they do not, even if the base price is the same in each year. One way out of this difficulty would be to look only at the price of the "stripped-down" version in each year in order to obtain a valid comparison.

Another difficulty arises because of technological improvements. Because of technological advance, a subcompact car of the current model year is a superior product to that sold 10 years ago. It can be argued that some of the increase in price over these 10 years can be attributed to an increase in quality. If this factor is ignored, a simple comparison of prices over this period would overstate the extent of inflation. We will not discuss further the problem of accounting for quality changes when comparing prices over time; it is nevertheless a factor that should not be ignored in assessing such comparisons.

TABLE 17.1 Hypothetical data on automobile prices and sales

YEAR	SUBCOMPACT CARS		LUXURY CARS		ALL CARS
	PRICE (thousand dollars)	NUMBER SOLD (thousands)	PRICE (thousand dollars)	NUMBER SOLD (thousands)	AVERAGE PRICE (thousand dollars)
1	10	5	30	15	25.0
2	11	15	33	5	16.5

TABLE 17.2 Hypothetical data on automobile prices and sales

| YEAR | SUBCOMPACT CARS | | LUXURY CARS | | |
	PRICE (thousand dollars)	NUMBER SOLD (thousands)	PRICE (thousand dollars)	NUMBER SOLD (thousands)	AVERAGE PRICE OF A SINGLE CAR OF EACH TYPE (thousand dollars)
1	10	100	24	1	17
2	10	100	48	1	29

As a final point, we note that the trend in dollar prices of automobiles may not be the most interesting or useful thing to examine. After all, the dollar price of virtually everything has risen steeply in the past 10 years. Perhaps it would be more relevant to compare the price increases of automobiles with those of other products.

The *index number problem* illustrated here arises through our desire to say something about the movement of prices for a *group* of commodities. For example, the price of common stock in each company whose shares are traded on the New York Stock Exchange will change over a 1-month period. We would like to produce a measure of the *aggregate* change in prices. **Index numbers** are designed to attack such problems.

PRICE INDEX FOR A SINGLE ITEM

We begin our discussion of index numbers with a simple case in which we trace the price movements of a single item. The second column of Table 17.3 gives the price of Ford Motor Company stock for each of 12 weeks. As they stand, the actual price figures themselves are not easy to interpret without a little mental arithmetic. This task can be made simpler by expressing each price as a percentage of a single price.

This is done in the third column of Table 17.3. We have chosen the first week as a **base** and have expressed each price as a percentage of the price ($20\frac{5}{8}$) in the base week. For example, the price in the second week is $19\frac{7}{8}$, which is a percentage

$$100\left(\frac{19\frac{7}{8}}{20\frac{5}{8}}\right) = 98.1$$

of the base week price. The percentages calculated in this fashion are called **index numbers** of price. The choice of base period is arbitrary. We could have chosen any other week as our base and expressed all prices as a percentage of the price for that week.

TABLE 17.3 Prices and price index numbers for Ford Motor Company stock over 12 weeks

WEEK	PRICE	PRICE INDEX	WEEK	PRICE	PRICE INDEX
1	$20\frac{5}{8}$	100.0	7	$19\frac{3}{4}$	95.7
2	$19\frac{7}{8}$	98.1	8	$19\frac{7}{8}$	96.9
3	19	93.8	9	$21\frac{1}{2}$	104.3
4	$19\frac{5}{8}$	97.5	10	$22\frac{5}{8}$	110.5
5	$20\frac{5}{8}$	100.0	11	25	123.5
6	$19\frac{7}{8}$	98.1	12	23	113.6

TABLE 17.4 Prices per bushel of three crops in 10 years, and unweighted aggregate index of prices

YEAR	WHEAT	CORN	SOYBEANS	AVERAGE	INDEX OF AVERAGE
1	1.33	1.33	2.85	1.837	100.0
2	1.34	1.08	3.03	1.817	98.9
3	1.76	1.57	4.37	2.567	139.7
4	3.95	2.55	5.68	4.060	221.0
5	4.09	3.03	6.64	4.587	249.7
6	3.56	2.54	4.92	3.673	199.9
7	2.73	2.15	6.81	3.897	212.1
8	2.33	2.02	6.42	3.590	195.4
9	2.97	2.25	6.12	3.780	205.8
10	3.78	2.52	6.28	4.193	228.3

The advantage of using index numbers here lies in the greater ease of interpretation of the numbers. We see immediately from Table 17.3, for instance, that the price of Ford Motor Company stock was 13.6% higher in week 12 than in week 1.

Calculating Price Indices for a Single Item

Suppose that we have a series of observations over time on the price of a single item. To form a **price index,** one time period is chosen as a **base,** and the price in every period is expressed as a percentage of the base period price. Thus, if p_0 denotes the price in the base period and p_1 the price in a second period, the price index for this second period is

$$100\left(\frac{p_1}{p_0}\right)$$

AN UNWEIGHTED AGGREGATE PRICE INDEX

We now consider the problem of how to represent, in the aggregate, price movements for a group of items. Table 17.4 shows the prices paid to U.S. farmers, in dollars per bushel, for wheat, corn, and soybeans over 10 crop years. The table also shows one way of achieving an aggregate price index for these crops. The final two columns of the table give the average price of a bushel of these three crops for each year and an index of these averages, taking the first year as the base.

The resulting *unweighted aggregate index of prices* is easy to calculate. It simply expresses the average price for each year as a percentage of the average price in the base year. However, it suffers from the disadvantage illustrated by the example of Table 17.2. No account is taken of differences in the quantities produced of these crops.

An Unweighted Price Index

Suppose that we have a series of observations over time on the prices of a group of K items. As before, one time period is chosen as a base.

The **unweighted aggregate index of prices** is obtained by calculating the average price of these items in each time period and calculating an index for these average prices. That is, the average price in every period is expressed as a percentage of the average price in the base period. Let p_{0i} denote the price of the ith item in the base period and p_{1i} the price of this item in a second period. The unweighted aggregate index of prices for this second period is

$$100 \left(\frac{\sum_{i=1}^{K} p_{1i}}{\sum_{i=1}^{K} p_{0i}} \right)$$

A WEIGHTED AGGREGATE PRICE INDEX

In forming a price index, it is natural to weight the individual prices by some measure of quantities sold. One possibility is to use average quantities over some or all of the time periods in question. Often quantity information is difficult or expensive to obtain on a regular basis, and indices are based on quantities in a single time period. When these quantities are from the base period, the resulting index is called the *Laspeyres price index*.

The Laspeyres price index, in effect, compares the total cost of purchasing the base period quantities in the base period with what would have been the total cost of purchasing these same quantities in other periods. To illustrate, consider the crop price data of Table 17.4, again with year 1 as base. In that year, production was 1,352 million bushels of wheat, 4,152 million bushels of corn, and 1,127 million bushels of soybeans. Hence, the cost, in million dollars, of the year 1 total output was

$$(1,352)(1.33) + (4,152)(1.33) + (1,127)(2.85) = 10,532$$

In year 2, at the prices then prevailing, the total cost of purchasing the base year quantities would have been

$$(1,352)(1.34) + (4,152)(1.08) + (1,127)(3.03) = 9,711$$

The Laspeyres price index for year 2 is therefore

$$100 \left(\frac{9,711}{10,532} \right) = 92.2$$

Table 17.5 shows the complete index, calculated in this way, for these data.

TABLE 17.5 Laspeyres price index for three crops

YEAR	LASPEYRES INDEX	YEAR	LASPEYRES INDEX	YEAR	LASPEYRES INDEX
1	100.0	5	243.0	9	192.3
2	92.2	6	198.5	10	215.1
3	131.2	7	192.7		
4	212.0	8	178.2		

Comparison of the formula for the Laspeyres price index with that for the unweighted aggregate index of prices is instructive. The difference is that in forming the Laspeyres index, the price of each item is *weighted* by the quantity traded in the base period.

A feature of the construction of Laspeyres price index numbers is that quantity information from only the base period is employed. This is particularly valuable when the collection of quantity information in every time period is either impossible or prohibitively expensive. This could, however, be a disadvantage if for some reason the quantities traded in the period chosen as a base happened to be unrepresentative. This could occur, for example, if the Laspeyres index is computed over a long period of time. The allocation of quantities among the various items may undergo substantial changes over time, so that the original base quantities become outdated. One way around this problem is to construct a **moving Laspeyres price index,** in which the base period is changed from time to time, through the acquisition of quantity information for new base periods. Many published national price indices, such as the Consumer Price Index, are constructed in essentially this way.

A WEIGHTED AGGREGATE QUANTITY INDEX

Price indices are designed to provide a representation of the changes over time in aggregate prices of a group of commodities. We might also want a picture of the evolution of overall quantities traded. Again, any reasonable approach to this problem is likely to result in a *weighted* quantity index, since we would presumably want to give more weight to a change in the quantity purchased of a very expensive item than to a change by the same amount in purchases of an inexpensive item. One procedure for achieving this is through the *Laspeyres quantity index*, which we will illustrate for the quantities produced of wheat, corn, and soybeans, given in Table 17.6.

The Laspeyres quantity index weights the individual quantities by the base period prices. For wheat, corn, and soybeans these are, respectively, 1.33, 1.33, and 2.85. As we have seen, the total value of the year 1 output is 10,532 million dollars. To obtain a quantity index for year 2, we compare with the total value of year 2 production, had year 1 prices prevailed—that is

TABLE 17.6 Production, in millions of bushels, of three crops in ten years

YEAR	WHEAT	CORN	SOYBEANS	YEAR	WHEAT	CORN	SOYBEANS
1	1,352	4,152	1,127	6	2,142	6,266	1,288
2	1,618	5,641	1,176	7	2,026	6,357	1,716
3	1,545	5,573	1,271	8	1,799	7,082	1,843
4	1,705	5,647	1,547	9	2,134	7,939	2,268
5	2,122	5,829	1,547	10	2,370	6,648	1,817

$$(1,618)(1.33) + (5,641)(1.33) + (1,176)(2.85) = 13,006$$

The Laspeyres quantity index for year 2 is therefore

$$100\left(\frac{13,006}{10,532}\right) = 123.5$$

Table 17.7 shows the complete index, calculated in this way.

The Laspeyres Quantity Index

Suppose that we have a group of K items for which information on quantity (produced or traded) is available over a period of time. One period is selected as a base for the index. The **Laspeyres quantity index** in any period is then the total cost of the quantities traded in that period, had the base period prices prevailed, expressed as a percentage of the total cost of the base period quantities.

Let q_{0i} and p_{0i} denote the quantity and price of the ith item in the base period and q_{1i} the quantity of that item in the period of interest. The Laspeyres quantity index for that period is then

$$100\left(\frac{\sum_{i=1}^{K} q_{1i}p_{0i}}{\sum_{i=1}^{K} q_{0i}p_{0i}}\right)$$

CHANGE IN BASE PERIOD

From time to time, officially published series of index numbers are updated by bringing forward the base period. In these circumstances, the value of the original index at the new base point is typically given. As an illustration, columns 2 and 3 of Table 17.8

TABLE 17.7 Laspeyres quantity index for three crops

YEAR	LASPEYRES INDEX	YEAR	LASPEYRES INDEX	YEAR	LASPEYRES INDEX
1	100.0	5	142.3	9	188.6
2	123.5	6	141.0	10	163.0
3	124.3	7	152.3		
4	134.7	8	162.0		

TABLE 17.8 Aggregate Laspeyres price indices for wheat, corn, and soybeans (with base periods year 1 and year 6) and a spliced index (based on year 6)

	BASE YEAR		SPLICED INDEX
YEAR	1	6	(BASE YEAR 6)
1	100.0		50.4
2	92.2		46.4
3	131.2		66.1
4	212.0		106.8
5	243.0		122.4
6	198.5	100.0	100.0
7		94.0	94.0
8		86.7	86.7
9		94.9	94.9
10		107.0	107.0

give Laspeyres price indices for wheat, corn, and soybeans. The second column shows the price index for crop years 1 through 6, using year 1 as the base. The third column gives the Laspeyres price index for crop years 6 through 10, using year 6 as the base. These indices are plotted in Figure 17.1, where the discontinuity in year 6 is obvious.

FIGURE 17.1 Time plots of Laspeyres aggregate price indices for wheat, corn, and soybeans for year 1 through year 6 (year 1 = 100) and year 6 through year 10 (year 6 = 100)

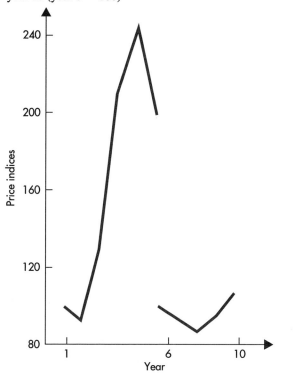

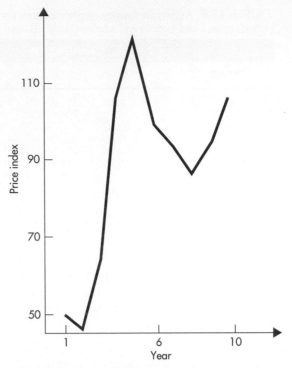

FIGURE 17.2 Spliced aggregate Laspeyres price index for wheat, corn, and soybeans (year 6 = 100)

Given only the information in columns 2 and 3 of Table 17.8, it is difficult to obtain a clear picture of the overall progression of price over this entire period. To do so, we would like to put these two indices on the same footing, obtaining a **spliced index.** In our new index, crop year 6 will be fixed as the base, the index for that year being set at 100. In the original index, based on year 1, the value for year 6 was 198.5. To transform this to 100, we divide by 198.5 and multiply by 100. Similarly, the other index numbers based on year 1 can be converted to base year 6 by dividing each by 198.5 and multiplying the result by 100. For example, the new figure for year 5 is

$$243.0 \left(\frac{100}{198.5} \right) = 122.4$$

The spliced index obtained in this manner is set out in the last column of Table 17.8 and graphed in Figure 17.2, which now presents a continuous picture of price evolution for these commodities over the entire period.

EXERCISES

1. Universities incur many costs in their operation, including the costs of energy, books, laboratory and other equipment, stationery, and labor. Suppose that you are asked to show how price levels faced by your university have changed over the past 10 years. What difficulties would you expect to encounter, and how would you attempt to proceed?

2. The accompanying table shows the price per share of stock in Bank of New York, Inc. for 12 weeks.

WEEK	PRICE	WEEK	PRICE	WEEK	PRICE
1	35	5	35	9	34⅞
2	35⅛	6	34⅞	10	35⅝
3	34⅝	7	35	11	38⅝
4	34⅜	8	34⅝	12	37⅛

(a) Form a price index with week 1 as the base.

(b) Form a price index with week 4 as the base.

3. A restaurant offers three "specials"—steak, seafood, and chicken. Their average prices (in dollars) for the 12 months of last year are shown in the table.

MONTH	STEAK	SEAFOOD	CHICKEN
January	7.12	6.45	5.39
February	7.41	6.40	5.21
March	7.45	6.25	5.25
April	7.70	6.60	5.40
May	7.72	6.70	5.45
June	7.75	6.85	5.60
July	8.10	6.90	5.54
August	8.15	6.84	5.70
September	8.20	6.96	5.72
October	8.30	7.10	5.69
November	8.45	7.10	5.85
December	8.65	7.14	6.21

The following table shows numbers of orders of these specials in each month. Take January as the base.

MONTH	STEAK	SEAFOOD	CHICKEN
January	123	169	243
February	110	160	251
March	115	181	265
April	101	152	231
May	118	140	263
June	100	128	237
July	92	129	221
August	87	130	204
September	123	164	293
October	131	169	301
November	136	176	327
December	149	193	351

(a) Find the unweighted aggregate price index.

(b) Find the Laspeyres price index.

(c) Find the Laspeyres quantity index.

4. The accompanying table shows hourly wage rates over 6 years for three types of employees in a small company.

YEAR	MANUAL	CLERICAL	SUPERVISORY
1	10.60	8.40	16.40
2	11.10	8.70	17.50
3	11.80	9.10	17.90
4	11.90	9.20	18.80
5	12.30	9.60	19.00
6	12.50	9.70	19.30

Take year 1 as base. In that year there were seventy-two manual employees, twenty-three clerical employees, and ten supervisory employees.

(a) Find the unweighted index of hourly wage rates.

(b) Find the Laspeyres index for hourly wage rates.

5. The accompanying table shows a price index for a group of commodities over 6 years. Obtain a spliced index with year 4 as base.

YEAR	1	2	3	4	5	6
BASE YEAR 1	100	108.4	114.3	120.2		
BASE YEAR 4				100	103.5	107.8

6. Explain why it is useful to develop a price index for a group of products—for example, an index of energy prices. What are the advantages of a *weighted* index of prices?

17.3 A NONPARAMETRIC TEST FOR RANDOMNESS

Before discussing techniques for dealing with time series data exhibiting typical patterns of nonrandomness, we will consider a test for randomness in a time series. Among several such tests, the **runs test** is particularly easy to perform. It is nonparametric—that is to say, no assumption is made about the distribution from which the observations were drawn.

To illustrate the test, we will look at a series of sixteen daily observations on an index of the volume of shares traded on the New York Stock Exchange. The data are given in Table 17.9, and graphed in Figure 17.3. A line has been drawn on this figure at the median. For an even number of observations, the median is the average of the middle pair, when the observations are arranged in ascending order. Here, that is

$$\text{Median} = \frac{107 + 108}{2} = 107.5$$

TABLE 17.9 Index of volume of shares traded

DAY	VOLUME	DAY	VOLUME	DAY	VOLUME	DAY	VOLUME
1	98	5	113	9	114	13	109
2	93	6	111	10	107	14	108
3	82	7	104	11	111	15	128
4	103	8	103	12	109	16	92

If this series of observations was random, the volume of shares traded on one day would be independent of that on any other. Then, a high volume would be no more likely to be followed by another high volume than by a low volume. One way to assess evidence of lack of randomness is to look at whether observations are above or below the median. Letting $+$ denote a value above the median, and $-$ a value below the median, we find for the volume of shares traded data

$$- \; - \; - \; - \; + \; + \; - \; - \; + \; - \; + \; + \; + \; + \; + \; -$$

This sequence consists of a *run* of four $-$, followed by a run of two $+$, a run of two $-$, a run of one $+$, a run of one $-$, a run of five $+$, and finally a run of one $-$. In total, there are therefore $R = 7$ runs.

If, as might be suspected here, there was a positive association between adjacent observations in time, we would expect to find relatively few runs. In our example, we ask how likely it is to observe seven or fewer runs if the series is truly random. This requires knowledge of the distribution of the number of runs when the null hypothesis

FIGURE 17.3 Volume of shares traded

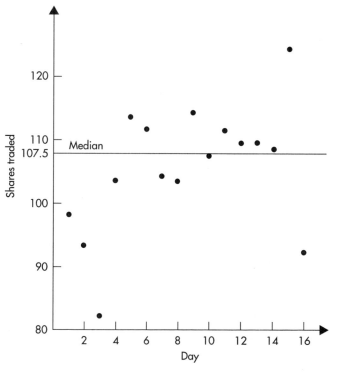

of randomness is true. The cumulative distribution function is tabulated in Table 11 of the Appendix. From that table we see that for a series of $n = 16$ observations, the probability under the null hypothesis of finding 7 or fewer runs is .214. Therefore, the null hypothesis of randomness can only be rejected against the alternative of positive association between adjacent observations at the 21.4% significance level. The evidence in these data against the null hypothesis is not very strong. It should be emphasized that we have not found strong evidence *in favor* of the hypothesis of randomness, but merely failed to find strong evidence against it. Tests of randomness based on small samples such as this have quite low power.

The Runs Tests

Suppose that we have a time series of n observations. (For simplicity, it will be assumed that n is even.) A sequence of signs, with $+$ denoting a value above the median and $-$ a value below, is formed from these data. Let R denote the number of runs in the sequence. The null hypothesis to be tested is of randomness in the time series. Table 11 of the Appendix gives the smallest significance level against which this null hypothesis can be rejected against the alternative of a positive association between observations that are adjacent in time.

If the alternative is the two-sided hypothesis of nonrandomness, the significance level must be doubled if it is less than .5. Alternatively, if the significance level, α, read from the table is bigger than .5, the appropriate significance level for the test against the two-sided alternative is $2(1 - \alpha)$.

For time series of more than twenty observations, the distribution of the number of runs under the null hypothesis can be well approximated by the normal distribution. In fact, it can be shown that under the null hypothesis, the random variable corresponding to

$$Z = \frac{R - \dfrac{n}{2} - 1}{\sqrt{\dfrac{n^2 - 2n}{4(n - 1)}}}$$

has a standard normal distribution. This result can then be used as the basis of a test for randomness when a large number of observations is available. The procedure is described in the box.

The Runs Test: Large Samples

Suppose that we have a time series of n observations, where n is even and moderately large (greater than 20). Define the number of runs, R, as previously. We want to test the null hypothesis

$$H_0: \text{The series is random}$$

The following tests have significance level α:

(i) If the alternative hypothesis is of positive association between adjacent observations, the decision rule is

$$\text{Reject } H_0 \text{ if } \frac{R - \frac{n}{2} - 1}{\sqrt{\dfrac{n^2 - 2n}{4(n - 1)}}} < -z_\alpha$$

(ii) If the alternative is two-sided, of nonrandomness, the decision rule is

$$\text{Reject } H_0 \text{ if } \frac{R - \frac{n}{2} - 1}{\sqrt{\dfrac{n^2 - 2n}{4(n - 1)}}} < -z_{\alpha/2} \qquad \text{or} \qquad \frac{R - \frac{n}{2} - 1}{\sqrt{\dfrac{n^2 - 2n}{4(n - 1)}}} > z_{\alpha/2}$$

EXAMPLE 17.1

Let us consider a classic, frequently analyzed set of data consisting of thirty annual observations on sales (in thousands of dollars) of Lydia E. Pinkham.[1]

The data, together with the corresponding sequence of $+$ and $-$, are shown in the table. Their median is

$$\frac{1,767 + 1,770}{2} = 1,768.5$$

YEAR	SALES	RELATION TO MEDIAN	YEAR	SALES	RELATION TO MEDIAN
1931	1,806	+	1946	2,177	+
1932	1,644	−	1947	1,920	+
1933	1,814	+	1948	1,910	+
1934	1,770	+	1949	1,984	+
1935	1,518	−	1950	1,787	+
1936	1,103	−	1951	1,689	−
1937	1,266	−	1952	1,866	+
1938	1,473	−	1953	1,896	+
1939	1,423	−	1954	1,684	−
1940	1,767	−	1955	1,633	−
1941	2,161	+	1956	1,657	−
1942	2,336	+	1957	1,569	−
1943	2,602	+	1958	1,390	−
1944	2,518	+	1959	1,387	−
1945	2,637	+	1960	1,289	−

We see from the table that the number of runs is $R = 8$. Since we have $n = 30$ observations, the value of the test statistic is

---

[1] G. M. Erickson, "Using ridge regression to estimate directly lagged effects in marketing," *Journal of the American Statistical Association*, 76 (1981), 766–73; K. S. Palda, *The Measurement of Cumulative Advertising Effects* (Englewood Cliffs, N.J.: Prentice Hall, 1964).

$$\frac{R - \frac{n}{2} - 1}{\sqrt{\frac{n^2 - 2n}{4(n-1)}}} = \frac{8 - 15 - 1}{\sqrt{\frac{900 - 60}{116}}} = -2.97$$

From Table 3 of the Appendix, we see that the α value corresponding to $z_\alpha = 2.97$ is .0015. Hence, the null hypothesis of randomness can be rejected against the alternative of positive association between adjacent observations at any significance level above .15%. The evidence in favor of this alternative is quite overwhelming. It is highly improbable that this time series is random.

17.4 COMPONENTS OF A TIME SERIES

In Sections 17.4 through 17.6, we will consider some descriptive ways of measuring the progression through time of a quantity of interest. We will let the series of interest be denoted $X_1, X_2, \ldots, X_n$, so at time t, the observed value of a series is represented by X_t.

One way of thinking about the behavior of an actual observed series is to regard it as being made up of various **components.** Traditionally, four possible components have been considered, with the notion that any or all might be present in any particular series. These components are as follows:

1. Trend component
2. Seasonality component
3. Cyclical component
4. Irregular component

Many time series exhibit a tendency to grow or to decrease fairly steadily over quite long periods of time, and this pattern is identified as **trend.** For example, despite short-run deviations from the trend, measures of national wealth, such as gross domestic product, have moved steadily upward over the years. Such trends will generally not remain constant over time and, indeed, may reverse direction; however, the pattern of evolution is usually rather gradual.

An example of a series exhibiting steady, though by no means constant, upward trend is provided by the data of Table 17.10 and the corresponding graph of Figure 17.4. This series is an index of the amount of consumer credit outstanding.

It is clear from the table, and even more so from the graph that the series is characterized by upward trend, which is much stronger in some years than in others.

TABLE 17.10 Index of consumer credit outstanding

YEAR	CREDIT	YEAR	CREDIT	YEAR	CREDIT	YEAR	CREDIT
1	133	4	171	7	274	10	333
2	155	5	194	8	312	11	343
3	165	6	231	9	313		

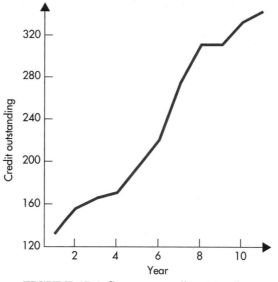

FIGURE 17.4 Consumer credit outstanding

Such a simple graphical display is extremely useful in revealing the major characteristics of a time series. Although more sophisticated techniques are necessary for a fuller analysis, a time plot is invariably a sensible first step in any analysis of a time series.

Many business and economic time series consist of quarterly or monthly observations. Such series often exhibit the phenomenon of **seasonality**—patterns repeated from year to year. As a rather obvious example, retail sales of many products tend to be relatively high in December, because of Christmas shopping. Construction activity in the Midwest is typically low in the winter quarter, due to inclement weather. This seasonal behavior is generally easily spotted when a time series is graphed.

Table 17.11 and Figure 17.5 show earnings per share of a corporation over a period of 8 years. These earnings figures are available quarterly, and from the table one can see evidence of seasonal behavior. The fourth-quarter figures tend to be relatively high, while those in the first quarter are quite low.

This seasonal behavior is quite clear from Figure 17.5, where an obvious pattern repeats each year. The earnings in the second quarter are somewhat higher than those

TABLE 17.11 Earnings per share of a corporation

YEAR	QUARTER			
	1	2	3	4
1	.300	.460	.345	.910
2	.330	.545	.440	1.040
3	.495	.680	.545	1.285
4	.550	.870	.660	1.580
5	.590	.990	.830	1.730
6	.610	1.050	.920	2.040
7	.700	1.230	1.060	2.320
8	.820	1.410	1.250	2.730

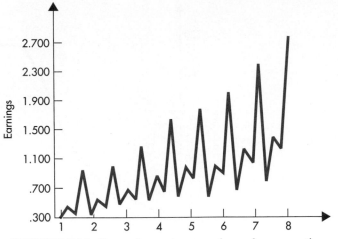

FIGURE 17.5 Quarterly earnings per share of a corporation

of the immediately preceding or succeeding quarter, while those of the fourth quarter are much higher yet. This figure also makes clear that there is another component of the time series. Apart from the obvious seasonality, there is a noticeable upward trend in earnings per share over the period covered by our data. How one approaches the phenomenon of seasonality depends on the objectives. In some applications, such as routine sales forecasting for purposes of inventory control, it is important to obtain as good an assessment as possible of the likely outcome in each future month. In that case, it is clear that any pronounced seasonal pattern, which might reasonably be expected to recur in the future, will provide an important constituent in forecast derivation.

For some other purposes, seasonality can be a nuisance. In many applications, the analyst requires an assessment of overall movements in a time series, uncontaminated by the influence of seasonal factors. For instance, suppose that we have just received the most recent fourth-quarter earnings figures of the corporation of Table 17.11. We already know that these will very likely be a good deal higher than those of the previous quarter. What we would like to do is assess how much of this increase in earnings is due to purely seasonal factors and how much represents real underlying growth. In other words, we would like to produce a time series free from seasonal influence. Such a series is said to be **seasonally adjusted.** We will say a little more about seasonal adjustment in Section 17.6.

Seasonal patterns in a time series constitute one form of regular, oscillatory behavior. In addition, many business and economic time series appear to exhibit oscillatory, or **cyclical,** patterns unconnected with seasonal behavior. These patterns might, for example, mirror business cycles in the economy at large. They are not necessarily regular, but they do follow rather smooth patterns of upswings and downswings. To illustrate, in Figure 17.6, we graph the Lydia E. Pinkham sales data, tabulated in Example 17.1. We see from the figure a decrease in sales to a trough in 1936, followed by an upswing to a peak in the mid-1940s, and thereafter a fairly steady decline. This kind of cyclical pattern is fairly common in business time series, and it is certainly convenient to describe historical behavior in terms of such cyclic movements. However, we are not suggesting that there is sufficient regularity in such historical

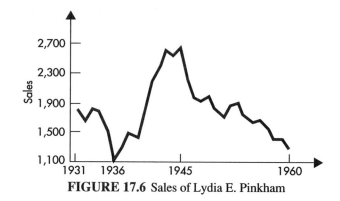

FIGURE 17.6 Sales of Lydia E. Pinkham

patterns to allow the reliable prediction of future peaks and troughs. Indeed, the available evidence suggests that this is not the case.

So far, we have discussed three sources of variability in a time series. If the only components of a series were trend, seasonality, and cycle, we would expect the time plot of that series to be very smooth and rather easily projected forward to produce forecasts. However, as the examples in this section indicate, actual data do not behave in this way. In addition to the components already considered, there will be an **irregular** element, induced by the multitude of factors influencing the behavior of any actual series and whose pattern looks rather unpredictable on the basis of past experience. We might think of this component in much the same way as the error term in a regression model. Its presence is clear in the sales data of Figure 17.6. We might easily draw a smooth curve, with a minimum in 1936 and a maximum in the mid-1940s, quite close to these data points. However, the actual values will deviate to some extent from this curve in no apparently regular fashion.

The conceptual breakdown of a time series into trend, seasonal, cyclical, and irregular components provides us with a very useful vocabulary for describing its behavior. It is often convenient to go beyond verbal description and think in terms of a more formal model. Let X_t denote the value of a series at time t. Then we might think of this series as the sum of its components, through the **additive model**

$$X_t = T_t + S_t + C_t + I_t \qquad (17.4.1)$$

where

T_t = Trend component
S_t = Seasonal component
C_t = Cyclical component
I_t = Irregular component

Alternatively, in some circumstances it might be more appropriate to view a series as the *product* of its constituent components, through the **multiplicative model**

$$X_t = T_t S_t C_t I_t \qquad (17.4.2)$$

In fact, it is not necessary to restrict attention to just these two models. In some circumstances, it may be convenient to treat some factors as additive and others as multiplicative.

Much of the early work in time series analysis concentrated on the isolation of the individual components from a series so that at any point in time, an observation was expressed as a compound of trend, seasonality, cycle, and a residual irregular element. Often this breakdown was achieved through the use of *moving averages*, which will be discussed in the following two sections. This approach has recently been superseded by more modern approaches. An exception, however, is the problem of seasonal adjustment, which requires the extraction from a series of its seasonal component. In Section 17.8, we will discuss one procedure for estimating the components of a time series and show how it can be used in forecasting.

The more modern approach to time series analysis involves the construction of a formal model, in which the various components are either explicitly or implicitly present, to describe the behavior of a data series. In model building, there are two possible treatments of series components. One possibility is to regard them as being *fixed* over time, so that, for example, trend might be represented by a straight line or some other convenient algebraic function. This approach is often valuable in the analysis of physical data but is far less often appropriate in business and economic applications, where experience suggests that any apparently fixed regularities are all too often illusory on closer examination. To illustrate this point, suppose that we considered the Lydia E. Pinkham data for the years 1936 through 1943 only. We see from Figure 17.6 that over this period, there appears to be a steady, fixed upward trend. However, had this "trend" been projected forward a few years from 1943, the resulting forecasts of future sales would have been highly inaccurate. It is only when we look at the picture in future years that we see just how inappropriate a fixed-trend model would have been.

For business and economic data, another treatment of the regular components of a time series is preferable. Rather than regarding them as being fixed for all time, it is generally more sensible to think of them as steadily *evolving* over time. Thus, we need not be committed to fixed trend or seasonal patterns but can allow the possibility that these components change with time. Models of this sort will be considered after we have looked at moving averages.

17.5 MOVING AVERAGES

The irregular component in some time series may be so large that it obscures any underlying regularities, thus rendering difficult any visual interpretation of the time plot. In these circumstances, the actual plot will appear rather jagged, and we may want to *smooth* it to achieve a clearer picture.

This smoothing can be achieved through the method of **moving averages,** which is based on the idea that any large irregular component at any point in time will exert a smaller effect if the observation at that point is averaged with its immediate neighbors. The simplest technique of this kind is called a **simple centered $(2m + 1)$-point moving average.** The idea here is to replace each actual observation X_t by the average of itself and its m neighbors on either side, that is, replace X_t by

$$
\begin{aligned}
X_t^* &= \frac{1}{2m + 1} \sum_{j = -m}^{m} X_{t+j} \\
&= \frac{X_{t-m} + X_{t-m+1} + \cdots + X_t + \cdots + X_{t+m-1} + X_{t+m}}{2m + 1}
\end{aligned}
\tag{17.5.1}
$$

The moving average, X_t^*, is said to be *centered* because X_t is the central value of the sum in the numerator of Eq. (17.5.1).

For example, suppose we set m at 2, so that a 5-point moving average is formed. We then have

$$
X_t^* = \frac{X_{t-2} + X_{t-1} + X_t + X_{t+1} + X_{t+2}}{5}
\tag{17.5.2}
$$

Since the first available observation is X_1, the first moving average of this sort that can be found is

$$
X_3^* = \frac{X_1 + X_2 + X_3 + X_4 + X_5}{5}
$$

This is, of course, just the average of the first five observations. Hence, for the Lydia E. Pinkham data of Example 17.1, we have for the year 1933

$$
X_3^* = \frac{1{,}806 + 1{,}644 + 1{,}814 + 1{,}770 + 1{,}518}{5} = 1{,}710.4
$$

Similarly, X_4^* is the average of the second through sixth observations, and so on. Table 17.12 gives the original and the smoothed series. Notice that when centered moving averages are computed in this way, we necessarily "lose" m observations at each end of the series. Thus, whereas the original series runs from 1931 through 1960, the smoothed series is obtained for 1933 through 1958.

Simple Centered $(2m + 1)$-Point Moving Averages

Let $X_1, X_2, \ldots, X_n$ be n observations on a time series of interest. A smoothed series can be obtained through the use of a simple centered $(2m + 1)$-point moving average, yielding

$$
X_t^* = \frac{1}{2m + 1} \sum_{j = -m}^{m} X_{t+j} \qquad (t = m + 1, m + 2, \ldots, n - m)
$$

TABLE 17.12 Annual sales (X_t) of Lydia E. Pinkham and simple centered 5-point moving average (X_t^*)

t	X_t	X_t^*	t	X_t	X_t^*
1	1,806		16	2,177	2,232.4
2	1,644		17	1,920	2,125.6
3	1,814	1,710.4	18	1,910	1,955.6
4	1,770	1,569.8	19	1,984	1,858.0
5	1,518	1,494.2	20	1,787	1,847.2
6	1,103	1,426.0	21	1,689	1,844.4
7	1,266	1,356.0	22	1,866	1,784.4
8	1,473	1,406.4	23	1,896	1,753.6
9	1,423	1,618.0	24	1,684	1,747.2
10	1,767	1,832.0	25	1,633	1,687.8
11	2,161	2,057.8	26	1,657	1,586.6
12	2,336	2,276.8	27	1,569	1,527.2
13	2,602	2,450.8	28	1,390	1,458.4
14	2,518	2,454.0	29	1,387	
15	2,637	2,370.8	30	1,289	

The smoothed series is graphed in Figure 17.7. It can be seen, by comparison with Figure 17.6, that the series of moving averages is indeed rather smoother than the original data series. This allows us to see even more clearly the underlying oscillatory behavior in these sales figures.

The kind of moving average discussed in this section is just one of many that might have been used. It is often deemed desirable to use a **weighted average,** in which most weight is given to the central observation, with weights for other values decreasing as their distance from the central observation increases. For example, if 5 points are to be used, we might employ, instead of the simple average (17.5.2), the weighted average

$$X_t^* = \frac{X_{t-2} + 2X_{t-1} + 4X_t + 2X_{t+1} + X_{t+2}}{10}$$

In any event, the objective in using moving averages remains the smoothing out of the irregular component in order to allow us to form a clearer picture of the underlying regularities in a time series. The technique is perhaps of most value for descriptive purposes, in the production of graphs such as Figure 17.7.

FIGURE 17.7 Simple centered 5-point moving average of sales of Lydia E. Pinkham

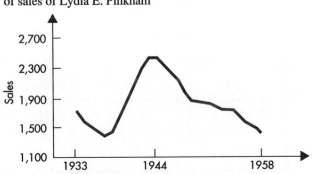

17.6 EXTRACTION OF THE SEASONAL COMPONENT THROUGH MOVING AVERAGES

We now turn to an important application of moving averages. In Section 17.4, we noted that many business and economic time series contain a strong seasonal component. This component can be a nuisance, and the analyst may want to remove it from the series to obtain a keener appreciation of the behavior of other components.

Suppose that we have a quarterly time series with a seasonal component. We produce a series of moving averages whose first term is the average of the first four values of the original series, whose second term is the average of the second through fifth values of the original series, and so on. Each member of the series of moving averages will be constituted from a single observation from each of the four quarters. The series formed in this way should therefore be free from strong seasonal patterns.

For the earnings-per-share data of Table 17.11, the first member of the series of 4-point moving averages is

$$\frac{.300 + .460 + .345 + .910}{4} = .50375$$

The second member is

$$\frac{.460 + .345 + .910 + .330}{4} = .51125$$

The complete series is set out in the third column of Table 17.13.

Although this series of moving averages is free from seasonality, there remains one difficulty. The location in time of the members of the series of moving averages does not correspond precisely with that of the members of the original series. For instance, the first term is the average of the first four observations in the original series. We might therefore regard it as being centered between the second and third observations and write it as

$$X_{2.5}^* = \frac{X_1 + X_2 + X_3 + X_4}{4}$$

Similarly, the second term could be written

$$X_{3.5}^* = \frac{X_2 + X_3 + X_4 + X_5}{4}$$

This difficulty is easily overcome. We can center our series of 4-point moving averages by calculating the averages of adjacent pairs. This yields a series whose first value

$$X_3^* = \frac{X_{2.5}^* + X_{3.5}^*}{2} = \frac{.50375 + .51125}{2} = .5075$$

constitutes the centered moving average corresponding to the third observation of the original series. The remainder of the series of centered moving averages is set out in the final column of Table 17.13. Notice that when moving averages are calculated in this way, we "lose" two observations from each end of the series.

TABLE 17.13 Actual (X_t) earnings per share of a corporation and centered 4-point moving average (X_t*)

t	EARNINGS (X_t)	4-POINT MOVING AVERAGES	CENTERED 4-POINT MOVING AVERAGES (X_t*)
1	.300		
2	.460		
3	.345	.50375	
4	.910	.51125	.5075
5	.330	.53250	.5219
6	.545	.55625	.5444
7	.440	.58875	.5725
8	1.040	.63000	.6094
9	.495	.66375	.6469
10	.680	.69000	.6769
11	.545	.75125	.7206
12	1.285	.76500	.7581
13	.550	.81250	.7888
14	.870	.84125	.8269
15	.660	.91500	.8781
16	1.580	.92500	.9200
17	.590	.95500	.9400
18	.990	.99750	.9763
19	.830	1.03500	1.0163
20	1.730	1.04000	1.0375
21	.610	1.05500	1.0475
22	1.050	1.07750	1.0663
23	.920	1.15500	1.1163
24	2.040	1.17750	1.1663
25	.700	1.22250	1.2000
26	1.230	1.25750	1.2400
27	1.060	1.32750	1.2925
28	2.320	1.35750	1.3425
29	.820	1.40250	1.3800
30	1.410	1.45000	1.4263
31	1.250	1.55250	1.5013
32	2.730		

The series of centered moving averages is plotted in Figure 17.8. For purposes of comparison with the original data series, the scale here is the same as in Figure 17.5. Obviously, most of the seasonality has been removed. Moreover, a byproduct of using moving averages to eliminate seasonality is that the irregular component is also smoothed. The resulting picture thus allows us to judge the nonseasonal regularities in the data. Figure 17.8 is, of course, dominated by upward trend. Closer examination reveals steady earnings growth in the early part of the series, a central portion of rather slower growth, and resumption in the last part of the period of a pattern similar to the early one.

Moving averages can be used as an aid to the seasonal adjustment of series of any period, as described in the box.

A Simple Moving Average Procedure for Seasonal Adjustment

Let X_t ($t = 1, 2, \ldots, n$) be a seasonal time series of period s (so that $s = 4$ for quarterly data and $s = 12$ for monthly data). A centered s-point moving average series, X_t*, is obtained through the following steps, where it is assumed (as is usually the case) that s is even:

(i) Form the s-point moving averages

$$X^*_{t+.5} = \frac{\sum_{j=-(s/2)+1}^{s/2} X_{t+j}}{s} \qquad \left(t = \frac{s}{2}, \frac{s}{2} + 1, \ldots, n - \frac{s}{2}\right)$$

(ii) Form the centered s-point moving averages

$$X^*_t = \frac{X^*_{t-.5} + X^*_{t+.5}}{2} \qquad \left(t = \frac{s}{2} + 1, \frac{s}{2} + 2, \ldots, n - \frac{s}{2}\right)$$

We have seen that the series of centered s-point moving averages can be a useful tool for gaining descriptive insight into the structure of a time series. Since it is largely free from seasonality and embodies a smoothing of the irregular component, it is well suited for the identification of trend and cycle. This series of moving averages has an additional value. It forms the basis for many practical seasonal adjustment procedures. How the adjustment is carried out depends on a number of factors, including the amount of stability one assumes in the seasonal pattern and whether seasonality is viewed as additive or multiplicative. One approach to a multiplicative model is to take logarithms of the data.

We will discuss here a seasonal adjustment approach that is based on an implicit assumption of a very stable seasonal pattern over time. This is known as the **seasonal index method.** Essentially, the assumption is that for any given month or quarter, in each year, the effect of seasonality is to raise or lower the observation by a constant proportionate amount, compared with what it would have been in the absence of seasonal influences.

To illustrate the seasonal index method, we return to our analysis of the corporate earnings data. The seasonally adjusted series is computed in Table 17.14. First, we show the original series X_t, and the series, X_t^*, of centered 4-point moving averages. These are taken from Table 17.13. As a means of assessing the influence of seasonality, the next step is to express X_t as a percentage of X_t^*. Thus, for example, for the third quarter of year 1, we have

FIGURE 17.8 Centered 4-point moving averages for earnings per share of a corporation

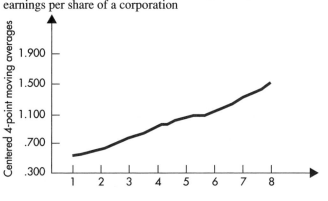

TABLE 17.14 Seasonal adjustment of earnings-per-share of a corporation by the seasonal index method

YEAR	QUARTER	X_t	X_t*	$100\left(\dfrac{X_t}{X_t*}\right)$	SEASONAL INDEX	ADJUSTED SERIES
1	1	.300			61.06	.4913
	2	.460			96.15	.4784
	3	.345	.5075	67.98	72.95	.4729
	4	.910	.5219	174.36	169.84	.5358
2	1	.330	.5444	60.62	61.06	.5405
	2	.545	.5725	95.20	96.15	.5668
	3	.440	.6094	72.20	72.95	.6032
	4	1.040	.6469	160.77	169.84	.6123
3	1	.495	.6769	73.13	61.06	.8107
	2	.680	.7206	94.37	96.15	.7072
	3	.545	.7581	71.89	72.95	.7471
	4	1.285	.7888	162.91	169.84	.7566
4	1	.550	.8269	66.51	61.06	.9008
	2	.870	.8781	99.08	96.15	.9048
	3	.660	.9200	71.74	72.95	.9047
	4	1.580	.9400	168.09	169.84	.9303
5	1	.590	.9763	60.43	61.06	.9663
	2	.990	1.0163	97.41	96.15	1.0296
	3	.830	1.0375	80.00	72.95	1.1378
	4	1.730	1.0475	165.16	169.84	1.0186
6	1	.610	1.0663	57.21	61.06	.9990
	2	1.050	1.1163	94.06	96.15	1.0920
	3	.920	1.1663	78.88	72.95	1.2611
	4	2.040	1.2000	170.00	169.84	1.2011
7	1	.700	1.2400	56.45	61.06	1.1464
	2	1.230	1.2925	95.16	96.15	1.2793
	3	1.060	1.3425	78.96	72.95	1.4531
	4	2.320	1.3800	168.12	169.84	1.3660
8	1	.820	1.4263	57.49	61.06	1.3429
	2	1.410	1.5013	93.92	96.15	1.4665
	3	1.250			72.95	1.7135
	4	2.730			169.84	1.6074

$$100\left(\frac{X_3}{X_3*}\right) = 100\left(\frac{.345}{.5075}\right) = 67.98$$

These percentages are also entered in Table 17.15, where the calculation of the seasonal indices is shown. To assess the effect of seasonality in the first quarter, we find the median of the seven percentages for that quarter. This is the fourth value when they are arranged in ascending order—that is, 60.43. In a similar way, we find the median of X_t as a percentage of X_t* for each of the other quarters.

To obtain seasonal indices, one further minor adjustment is needed. We would like the average of the four seasonal indices to be 100%. However, we see in Table 17.15 that the four medians sum to 395.88. The desired result can be achieved by multiplying each median by (400/395.88). Thus, for the first quarter, we have

$$\text{Seasonal index} = 60.43\left(\frac{400}{395.88}\right) = 61.06$$

TABLE 17.15 Calculation of seasonal indices for earnings-per-share data of a corporation

YEAR	QUARTER				
	1	2	3	4	SUMS
1			67.98	174.36	
2	60.62	95.20	72.20	160.77	
3	73.13	94.37	71.89	162.91	
4	66.51	99.08	71.74	168.09	
5	60.43	97.41	80.00	165.16	
6	57.21	94.06	78.88	170.00	
7	56.45	95.16	78.96	168.12	
8	57.49	93.92			
Median	60.43	95.16	72.20	168.09	395.88
Seasonal index	61.06	96.15	72.95	169.84	400

We interpret this figure as estimating that the effect of seasonality is to lower first-quarter earnings to 61.06% of what they would have been in the absence of seasonal factors.

The seasonal indices, taken from the last row of Table 17.15, are entered in the fifth column of Table 17.14. Notice that the same index is used for any particular quarter in every year. Finally, we obtain our seasonally adjusted series as

$$\text{Adjusted value} = \text{Original value}\left(\frac{100}{\text{Seasonal index}}\right)$$

For example, for the third quarter of year 1, the seasonally adjusted value is

$$.345\left(\frac{100}{72.95}\right) = .4729$$

The complete seasonally adjusted series obtained in this way is given in the final column of Table 17.14, and graphed in Figure 17.9. Notice that there is the suggestion of a little remaining seasonality in the latter part of the period. This suggests that a more elaborate approach, allowing for changing seasonal patterns, may be desirable.

FIGURE 17.9 Seasonally adjusted earnings per share of a corporation

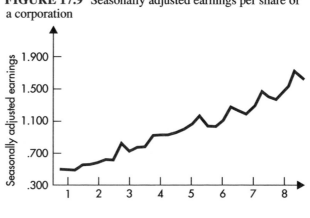

The seasonal index method of seasonal adjustment presented here gives one possible simple attack on the problem. Many important economic time series, such as gross domestic product and its components, employment and unemployment, prices, and wages, have strong seasonal components. Generally, data on such quantities are published by government agencies in both unadjusted and adjusted form. Although they are more complex than the method described here, official adjustment procedures are typically based on moving averages. The seasonal adjustment procedure most commonly employed in official U.S. government publications is the Census X-11 method. It differs from the seasonal index method in allowing for a steadily evolving seasonal pattern over time. It can be shown that in its additive version, X-11 estimates the seasonal component of a monthly time series, to a close approximation, by

$$S_t = \frac{Z_{t-36} + 2Z_{t-24} + 3Z_{t-12} + 3Z_t + 3Z_{t+12} + 2Z_{t+24} + Z_{t+36}}{15}$$

where

$$Z_t = X_t - X_t^*$$

with X_t the original value of the series at time t and X_t^* the corresponding centered 12-point moving average. Of course, if such a procedure is used, some special treatment is needed for values toward the end of the time series, as the expression for the seasonal factor will involve values of the time series that have not yet occurred. A possible way of accomplishing this is to replace unknown future values of a series in the moving average by *forecasts* based on the available data.

EXERCISES

7. The accompanying table shows an index of the value of the U.S. dollar against trading partners' currencies over 12 consecutive months. Use the runs test to test this series for randomness.

MONTH	VALUE	MONTH	VALUE	MONTH	VALUE
1	97.5	5	103.5	9	98.4
2	98.5	6	103.0	10	99.9
3	101.4	7	99.3	11	99.8
4	102.2	8	96.8	12	101.5

8. The table given here shows the inventory-sales ratio for manufacturing and trade in the United States over a period of 12 years. Test this series for randomness using the runs test.

YEAR	RATIO	YEAR	RATIO	YEAR	RATIO
1	1.41	5	1.46	9	1.43
2	1.45	6	1.44	10	1.52
3	1.57	7	1.43	11	1.37
4	1.48	8	1.45	12	1.33

9. The table shows annual returns on a stock market index over 14 years. Test for randomness using the runs test.

YEAR	RETURN (%)	YEAR	RETURN (%)	YEAR	RETURN(%)
1	−7.2	6	21.4	11	5.3
2	6.6	7	22.5	12	16.6
3	18.4	8	6.3	13	31.8
4	32.4	9	32.2	14	−3.1
5	−4.9	10	18.8		

10. The table shows the year-end price of gold (in dollars) over 14 consecutive years. Use the runs test to test this series for randomness.

YEAR	PRICE ($)	YEAR	PRICE ($)	YEAR	PRICE ($)
1	135	6	399	11	405
2	166	7	450	12	486
3	227	8	385	13	410
4	533	9	308	14	369
5	591	10	329		

11. The accompanying table shows private housing units started per thousand of population in the United States over a period of 24 years.

YEAR	STARTS	YEAR	STARTS	YEAR	STARTS
1	8.5	9	6.5	17	5.4
2	6.9	10	7.5	18	7.1
3	7.1	11	7.2	19	9.1
4	7.8	12	7.0	20	9.1
5	8.5	13	9.9	21	7.8
6	8.0	14	11.3	22	5.7
7	7.6	15	9.7	23	4.7
8	5.9	16	6.3	24	4.6

(a) Use the large-sample variant of the runs test to test this series for randomness.
(b) Draw a time plot of this series and comment on the components of the series revealed by this plot.

12. The table shows earnings per share of a corporation over a period of 28 years.

YEAR	EARNINGS	YEAR	EARNINGS	YEAR	EARNINGS
1	50.2	11	20.6	20	22.4
2	33.9	12	21.6	21	12.3
3	20.6	13	27.6	22	20.9
4	25.4	14	36.5	23	42.8
5	32.9	15	49.3	24	86.3
6	31.3	16	45.4	25	73.6
7	18.8	17	35.6	26	47.7
8	14.5	18	30.1	27	56.6
9	17.5	19	25.5	28	53.1
10	23.6				

(a) Use the large-sample variant of the runs test to test this series for randomness.

(b) Draw a time plot of this series and comment on the components of the series revealed by this plot.

13. The accompanying table shows quarterly sales of a corporation over a period of 6 years.

YEAR	QUARTER			
	1	2	3	4
1	272	239	158	219
2	228	198	169	238
3	270	246	203	284
4	299	267	218	293
5	307	258	323	296
6	307	271	197	266

(a) Draw a time plot of this series, and discuss its features.

(b) Use the seasonal index method to seasonally adjust this series. Graph the seasonally adjusted series and discuss its features.

14. The accompanying table shows quarterly sales of a corporation over a period of 6 years.

YEAR	QUARTER			
	1	2	3	4
1	271	199	240	255
2	341	246	245	275
3	351	283	353	292
4	401	282	306	291
5	370	242	281	274
6	356	245	304	279

(a) Draw a time plot of this series, and discuss its features.

(b) Use the seasonal index method to seasonally adjust this series. Graph the seasonally adjusted series and discuss its features.

15. Compute a simple centered 3-point moving average series for the gold price data of Exercise 10. Plot the smoothed series and discuss the resulting graph.

16. Compute simple centered 5-point moving averages for the housing starts data of Exercise 11. Draw a time plot of the smoothed series and comment on your results.

17. Compute a simple centered 7-point moving average series for the corporate earnings data of Exercise 12. Based on a time plot of the smoothed series, what can be said about its regular components?

18. Let

$$X_t^* = \frac{1}{2m+1} \sum_{j=-m}^{m} X_{t+j}$$

be a simple centered $(2m+1)$-point moving average. Show that

$$X_{t+1}^* = X_t^* + \frac{X_{t+m+1} - X_{t-m}}{2m+1}$$

How might this result be used in the efficient computation of series of centered moving averages?

19. The accompanying table shows earnings per share of a corporation over a period of 7 years.

YEAR	QUARTER			
	1	2	3	4
1	.362	.370	.621	.384
2	.389	.389	.639	.431
3	.411	.448	.712	.584
4	.620	.620	.891	.570
5	.540	.690	.870	.680
6	.780	.440	.800	.780
7	.690	.400	1.030	.940

(a) Draw a time plot of these data. Does your graph suggest the presence of a strong seasonal component in this earnings series?

(b) Using the seasonal index method, obtain a seasonally adjusted earnings series. Graph this series, and comment on its behavior.

20. (a) Show that the centered s-point moving average series of Section 17.6 can be written

$$X_t^* = \frac{X_{t-(s/2)} + 2(X_{t-(s/2)+1} + \cdots + X_{t+(s/2)-1}) + X_{t+(s/2)}}{2s}$$

(b) Show that

$$X_{t+1}^* = X_t^* + \frac{X_{t+(s/2)+1} + X_{t+(s/2)} - X_{t-(s/2)+1} - X_{t-(s/2)}}{.}$$

Discuss the computational advantages of this formula in the seasonal adjustment of monthly time series.

21. The accompanying table shows monthly product sales over a period of 3 years. Use the seasonal index method to obtain a seasonally adjusted series.

MONTH	YEAR		
	1	2	3
January	538	636	588
February	620	666	592
March	869	853	670
April	849	753	541
May	947	787	499
June	931	691	511
July	746	680	542
August	740	698	487
September	654	593	486
October	874	721	664
November	759	600	530
December	637	554	472

17.7 SIMPLE EXPONENTIAL SMOOTHING

In the remainder of this chapter, we turn to the possibility of using current and past observations on a time series to obtain forecasts of future values. This problem, though easily stated, can be tricky to resolve satisfactorily. A vast array of forecasting methods are in common use, and to a great extent, the eventual choice will be problem-specific, depending on the resources and objectives of the analyst and the nature of the available data.

In any event, our aim is to use the available observations, $X_1, X_2, \ldots, X_n$, on a series to predict the unknown future values $X_{n+1}, X_{n+2}, \ldots$. Forecasting is of crucial importance in the business environment as a rational basis for decision making. For example, monthly product sales are predicted as a basis for inventory control policy. Forecasts of future corporate earnings are used when making investment decisions.

In this section, we introduce a simple forecasting procedure that is in itself often valuable and forms the basis of some more elaborate methods, one of which we will consider in Section 17.8. This method, known as **simple exponential smoothing,** is appropriate when the series to be predicted is nonseasonal and has no consistent upward or downward trend.

In the absence of trend and seasonality, the objective is to estimate the current *level* of the time series. This estimate is then used as the forecast of all future values. Our position, then, is that we are standing at time n, looking back on the series of observations $X_n, X_{n-1}, X_{n-2}, \ldots$, and we want to form an assessment of the current level of the series. As a prelude, we will consider two extreme possibilities. First, we might simply use the most recent observation, X_n, so that the forecast of all future values would be the latest observation. For some important business series, particularly prices in speculative markets, this is about the best that can be done if forecasts are to be based exclusively on the history of the time series. However, in many applications where the series contains a substantial irregular component, it would be rash to restrict ourselves to only a single value of the series, which could be subject to severe random fluctuations. Rather, we would want to take into account earlier observations also.

At the opposite extreme, we might use as our estimate of current level the simple average of *all* the observations. A moment's reflection will suggest that often this would be absurd, for in forming the average, each value is treated equally. Thus, for example, if future product sales were to be predicted in this way, the same weight would be given to sales many years earlier as to those in the current period. Distant experience is surely far less likely to be relevant to future patterns than are the most recent figures.

Simple exponential smoothing allows a compromise between these extremes, providing a forecast based on a *weighted average* of current and past values. In forming this average, most weight is given to the most recent observation, rather less weight to the immediately preceding value, less to the one before that, and so on. One way to accomplish this is to estimate the level at the current time n by $\overline{X}_n$:

$$\overline{X}_n = (1 - \alpha)X_n + \alpha(1 - \alpha)X_{n-1} + \alpha^2(1 - \alpha)X_{n-2} + \cdots \quad (17.7.1)$$

where α is any number between 0 and 1. For example, if α is fixed at .5, the forecast of future observations of the series is

$$\overline{X}_n = .5X_n + .25X_{n-1} + .125X_{n-2} + \cdots$$

so that a weighted average, with declining weights, is applied to current and past observations in computing the forecasts.

By analogy with (17.7.1), the level of the series at any time t is estimated by

$$\overline{X}_t = (1 - \alpha)X_t + \alpha(1 - \alpha)X_{t-1} + \alpha^2(1 - \alpha)X_{t-2} + \cdots \quad (17.7.2)$$

and, similarly, the level at the previous time period, $(t - 1)$, would be estimated by

$$\overline{X}_{t-1} = (1 - \alpha)X_{t-1} + \alpha(1 - \alpha)X_{t-2} \\ + \alpha^2(1 - \alpha)X_{t-3} + \cdots \quad (17.7.3)$$

Multiplying through Eq. (17.7.3) by α gives

$$\alpha\overline{X}_{t-1} = \alpha(1 - \alpha)X_{t-1} + \alpha^2(1 - \alpha)X_{t-2} + \cdots \quad (17.7.4)$$

Hence, on subtracting (17.7.4) from (17.7.2), we have

$$\overline{X}_t - \alpha\overline{X}_{t-1} = (1 - \alpha)X_t$$

or

$$\overline{X}_t = \alpha\overline{X}_{t-1} + (1 - \alpha)X_t \qquad (0 < \alpha < 1) \qquad (17.7.5)$$

Equation (17.7.5) provides a convenient recursive algorithm for calculating the level estimates. It expresses the level, $\overline{X}_t$, at time t as a weighted average of the previous estimate of level, $\overline{X}_{t-1}$, and the new observation X_t. The weights given to each depend on the choice of α, which is sometimes referred to as the **smoothing constant.**

To begin the calculations, we set

$$\overline{X}_1 = X_1$$

and then apply the formula (17.7.5) in turn for $t = 2, 3, \ldots, n$. To illustrate, we will apply this approach to the Lydia E. Pinkham sales data of Example 17.1. For convenience, the data are shown again in the X_t column of Table 17.16. We begin by setting

$$\overline{X}_1 = X_1 = 1,806$$

Our estimates of levels will be based on choosing the smoothing constant

$$\alpha = .4$$

so that Eq. (17.7.5) becomes

$$\overline{X}_t = .4\overline{X}_{t-1} + .6X_t$$

Hence, we have

$$\overline{X}_2 = .4\overline{X}_1 + .6X_2$$

$$= (.4)(1,806) + (.6)(1,644) = 1,708.8$$

Similarly

$$\overline{X}_3 = .4\overline{X}_2 + .6X_3$$

$$= (.4)(1,708.8) + (.6)(1,814) = 1,771.9$$

TABLE 17.16 Simple exponential smoothing ($\alpha = .4$) of Lydia E. Pinkham sales data

t	X_t	$\overline{X}_t$	t	X_t	$\overline{X}_t$
1	1,806	1,806.0	16	2,177	2,336.5
2	1,644	1,708.8	17	1,920	2,086.6
3	1,814	1,771.9	18	1,910	1,980.6
4	1,770	1,770.8	19	1,984	1,982.6
5	1,518	1,619.1	20	1,787	1,865.2
6	1,103	1,309.4	21	1,689	1,759.5
7	1,266	1,283.4	22	1,866	1,823.4
8	1,473	1,397.2	23	1,896	1,867.0
9	1,423	1,412.7	24	1,684	1,757.2
10	1,767	1,625.3	25	1,633	1,682.7
11	2,161	1,946.7	26	1,657	1,667.3
12	2,336	2,180.3	27	1,569	1,608.3
13	2,602	2,433.3	28	1,390	1,477.3
14	2,518	2,484.1	29	1,387	1,423.1
15	2,637	2,575.8	30	1,289	1,342.6

Continuing in this way, we complete the $\overline{X}_t$ column of Table 17.16.

We see from the table that the most recent estimate of level is provided by

$$\overline{X}_n = \overline{X}_{30} = 1,342.6$$

This value is then used as the forecast of sales in all future years. The observed series and these forecasts are graphed in Figure 17.10.

Forecasting Through Simple Exponential Smoothing

Let $X_1, X_2, \ldots, X_n$ be a set of observations on a nonseasonal time series with no consistent upward or downward trend. The **simple exponential smoothing** method of forecasting then proceeds as follows:

(i) Obtain the *smoothed* series, $\overline{X}_t$, as

$$\overline{X}_1 = X_1$$
$$\overline{X}_t = \alpha\overline{X}_{t-1} + (1 - \alpha)X_t \qquad (0 < \alpha < 1; t = 2, 3, \ldots, n)$$

where α is a **smoothing constant** whose value is fixed between 0 and 1.

(ii) Standing at time n, we obtain forecasts of future values, X_{n+h}, of the series by

$$\hat{X}_{n+h} = \overline{X}_n \qquad (h = 1, 2, 3, \ldots)$$

So far, we have said little about the choice of the smoothing constant, α, in practical applications of simple exponential smoothing. In practice, this choice may be based on either subjective or objective grounds. One possibility is to rely on experience and judgment. For instance, an analyst who wants to predict product demand may have had considerable experience in working with data on similar product lines and thus may know which values of the smoothing constant produce accurate forecasts in this area. Visual inspection of a graph of the available data can also be useful in suggesting an appropriate value for the smoothing constant. If the series appears to contain a substantial irregular element, we would not want to give too much weight to the most recent observation alone, as it may not be strongly indicative of what to

FIGURE 17.10 Sales of Lydia E. Pinkham and forecasts based on simple exponential smoothing

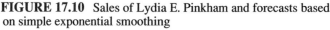
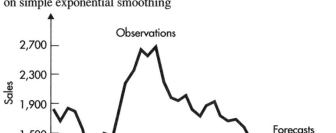

expect in the future. In line with Eq. (17.7.5), this would suggest a relatively high value for the smoothing constant. If, by contrast, the series is rather smooth, we would use a lower value for α.

A more objective approach is to try several different values and see which would have been most successful in predicting historical movements in the time series. We might, for example, compute the smoothed series for values of α of .2, .4, .6, and .8. If $\overline{X}_{t-1}$ is the forecast of X_t made at time $(t-1)$, the error in this forecast will be

$$e_t = X_t - \overline{X}_{t-1}$$

One possibility is to compute, for each trial value of α, the sum of squared forecast errors

$$SS = \sum_{t=2}^{n} e_t^2 = \sum_{t=2}^{n} (X_t - \overline{X}_{t-1})^2$$

The value of α for which this sum of squared forecast errors is smallest will then be used in the prediction of future observations.

Whatever value of the smoothing constant is used, the basic equation (17.7.5) of simple exponential smoothing can be regarded as an **updating mechanism.** At time $(t-1)$, the level of the series is estimated by $\overline{X}_{t-1}$. Then, in the next period, the new observation X_t is used to update this estimate, so that the new estimate of level is a weighted average of the previous estimate and the new observation.

17.8 THE HOLT-WINTERS EXPONENTIAL SMOOTHING FORECASTING MODEL

Many business forecasting procedures in common use are elaborations of the simple exponential smoothing approach. In this section, we will describe one such method, known as the **Holt-Winters model.** Our objective is to allow for trend, and possibly also seasonality, in a time series.

We will begin with the problem of prediction for nonseasonal time series. Here, the objective is to estimate not only the current level of the series but also the trend, where, for this purpose, trend is regarded as the difference between the current level and the preceding level.

The observed value of the series at time t will be denoted X_t, while $\overline{X}_t$ will again be used to represent the estimate of level. The trend estimate is represented as T_t. The principle behind the estimation of these two quantities is much the same as in the simple exponential smoothing algorithm. The two estimating equations are

$$\overline{X}_t = A(\overline{X}_{t-1} + T_{t-1}) + (1-A)X_t \qquad (0 < A < 1) \qquad (17.8.1)$$

$$T_t = BT_{t-1} + (1-B)(\overline{X}_t - \overline{X}_{t-1}) \qquad (0 < B < 1) \qquad (17.8.2)$$

where A and B are smoothing constants whose values are set between 0 and 1.

As in the case of simple exponential smoothing, Eqs. (17.8.1) and (17.8.2) can be viewed as updating formulas by which previous estimates are modified in light of a new observation. The estimate of level, $\overline{X}_{t-1}$, made at time $(t-1)$, taken in conjunction with the trend estimate, T_{t-1}, suggests for time t a level $(\overline{X}_{t-1} + T_{t-1})$. This estimate is modified, in light of the new observation, X_t, to obtain an updated estimate of level, $\overline{X}_t$, in Eq. (17.8.1).

In the same way, trend at time $(t-1)$ is estimated as T_{t-1}. However, once the new observation X_t is available, an estimate of trend is suggested as the difference between the two most recent estimates of level. The trend estimate at time t is then the weighted average given by Eq. (17.8.2).

To begin the computations, we set

$$T_2 = X_2 - X_1 \qquad \text{and} \qquad \overline{X}_2 = X_2$$

Formulas (17.8.1) and (17.8.2) are then applied in turn for $t = 3, 4, \ldots, n$.

The calculations will be illustrated using the data of Table 17.10 on consumer credit outstanding. The observed values of this series are given again in the X_t column of Table 17.17. The initial estimates of level and trend, in year 2, are

$$\overline{X}_2 = X_2 = 155$$

and

$$T_2 = X_2 - X_1 = 155 - 133 = 22$$

We will use Eqs. (17.8.1) and (17.8.2) with $A = .3$ and $B = .4$. These equations are then

$$\overline{X}_t = .3(\overline{X}_{t-1} + T_{t-1}) + .7X_t \qquad (17.8.3)$$

$$T_t = .4T_{t-1} + .6(\overline{X}_t - \overline{X}_{t-1}) \qquad (17.8.4)$$

Setting $t = 3$ in Eq. (17.8.3), we find

$$\overline{X}_3 = .3(\overline{X}_2 + T_2) + .7X_3 = (.3)(155 + 22) + (.7)(165)$$

$$= 168.6$$

Then, using Eq. (17.8.4)

$$T_3 = .4T_2 + .6(\overline{X}_3 - \overline{X}_2) = (.4)(22) + (.6)(168.6 - 155)$$

$$= 16.96$$

TABLE 17.17 Holt-Winters calculations for consumer credit outstanding ($A = .3, B = .4$)

t	X_t	$\overline{X}_t$	T_t	t	X_t	$\overline{X}_t$	T_t
1	133			7	274	266	36
2	155	155	22	8	312	309	40
3	165	169	17	9	313	324	25
4	171	175	11	10	333	338	18
5	194	192	14	11	343	347	13
6	231	223	25				

The calculations continue, now setting $t = 4$ in Eqs. (17.8.3) and (17.8.4). We then find

$$\overline{X}_4 = .3(\overline{X}_3 + T_3) + .7X_4 = (.3)(168.6 + 16.96) + (.7)(171)$$

$$= 175.368$$

and

$$T_4 = .4T_3 + .6(\overline{X}_4 - \overline{X}_3) = (.4)(16.96) + (.6)(175.368 - 168.6)$$

$$= 10.8448$$

The remaining calculations continue in the same way, setting in turn $t = 5, 6, \ldots, 11$.

The results of these calculations are shown in Table 17.17, rounded to the nearest integer.

We now consider the use of these level and trend estimates in forecasting future observations. Given a series $X_1, X_2, \ldots, X_n$, the most recent level and trend estimates are $\overline{X}_n$ and T_n, respectively. In the production of forecasts, it is assumed that this latest trend will continue from the most recent level. Thus, the next value of the series is predicted as

$$\hat{X}_{n+1} = \overline{X}_n + T_n$$

and the following one as

$$\hat{X}_{n+2} = \overline{X}_n + 2T_n$$

In general, standing at time n and looking h time periods into the future, we predict the value of X_{n+h} to be

$$\hat{X}_{n+h} = \overline{X}_n + hT_n$$

From Table 17.17, the most recent level and trend estimates are

$$\overline{X}_{11} = 347 \qquad T_{11} = 13$$

Then, the forecast for consumer credit outstanding in the next year is

$$\hat{X}_{12} = 347 + 13 = 360$$

Similarly, predictions for 2 and 3 years ahead are

$$\hat{X}_{13} = 347 + (2)(13) = 373$$

and

$$\hat{X}_{14} = 347 + (3)(13) = 386$$

Figure 17.11 shows the time series and the first few forecasts. It is a property of this approach that forecasts of future values lie on a straight line.

Forecasting with the Holt-Winters Method: Nonseasonal Series

Let $X_1, X_2, \ldots, X_n$ be a set of observations on a nonseasonal time series. The **Holt-Winters method** of forecasting proceeds as follows:

(i) Obtain estimates of level $\overline{X}_t$ and trend T_t as

$$\overline{X}_2 = X_2 \qquad T_2 = X_2 - X_1$$

$$\overline{X}_t = A(\overline{X}_{t-1} + T_{t-1}) + (1 - A)X_t \qquad (0 < A < 1; t = 3, 4, \ldots, n)$$

$$T_t = BT_{t-1} + (1 - B)(\overline{X}_t - \overline{X}_{t-1}) \qquad (0 < B < 1; t = 3, 4, \ldots, n)$$

where A and B are smoothing constants whose values are fixed between 0 and 1.

(ii) Standing at time n, we obtain forecasts of future values, X_{n+h}, of the series by

$$\hat{X}_{n+h} = \overline{X}_n + hT_n \qquad (h = 1, 2, 3, \ldots)$$

FORECASTING SEASONAL TIME SERIES

We now turn to an extension of the Holt-Winters method, allowing for seasonality. In most practical applications, the seasonal factor is taken to be multiplicative, so that, for example, in dealing with monthly sales figures, we might think of January in terms of a proportion of average monthly sales. As before, the trend component is assumed to be additive.

As for the nonseasonal case, we will use X_t, $\overline{X}_t$, and T_t to denote, respectively, the observed value and level and trend estimates at time t. The seasonal factor will be denoted F_t, so if the time series contains s periods per year, the seasonal factor for the corresponding period in the previous year will be F_{t-s}.

In the Holt-Winters model, the estimates of level, trend, and the seasonal factor are updated by the following three equations:

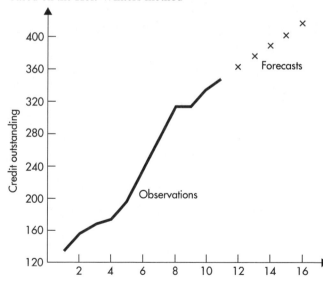

FIGURE 17.11 Consumer credit outstanding, with forecasts based on the Holt-Winters method

$$\overline{X}_t = A(\overline{X}_{t-1} + T_{t-1}) + (1 - A)\frac{X_t}{F_{t-s}} \qquad (0 < A < 1) \qquad (17.8.5)$$

$$T_t = BT_{t-1} + (1 - B)(\overline{X}_t - \overline{X}_{t-1}) \qquad (0 < B < 1) \qquad (17.8.6)$$

$$F_t = CF_{t-s} + (1 - C)\frac{X_t}{\overline{X}_t} \qquad (0 < C < 1) \qquad (17.8.7)$$

where A, B, and C are smoothing constants whose values are set between 0 and 1.

In Eq. (17.8.5), the term $(\overline{X}_{t-1} + T_{t-1})$ represents an estimate of the level at time t, formed one time period earlier. This estimate is then updated when the new observation X_t becomes available. However, here it is necessary to remove the influence of seasonality from that observation by deflating it by the latest available estimate, F_{t-s}, of the seasonal factor for that period. The updating equation for trend, (17.8.6), is identical to that used previously, (17.8.2).

Finally, the seasonal factor is estimated by Eq. (17.8.7). The most recent estimate of the factor, available from the previous year, is F_{t-s}. However, dividing the new observation X_t by the level estimate $\overline{X}_t$ suggests a seasonal factor $X_t/\overline{X}_t$. The new estimate of the seasonal factor is then a weighted average of these two quantities.

Again, we require some preliminary values to begin the computations. As a starting point, we use the first 3 years of data to obtain centered s-point moving averages, as described in Section 17.6.

To illustrate the computations, we will employ the series on earnings per share given in Table 17.13. These data are partially reproduced in the second column of Table 17.18. The final column of that table shows the centered 4-point moving averages, taken from Table 17.13. These are our preliminary estimates of level.

In particular, we will require from this table the level estimate for period 10:

$$\overline{X}_{10} = .7206$$

TABLE 17.18 Initial values for Holt-Winters forecasts of earnings per share of a corporation

t	X_t	$\overline{X}_t$
1	.300	
2	.460	
3	.345	.5075
4	.910	.5219
5	.330	.5444
6	.545	.5725
7	.440	.6094
8	1.040	.6469
9	.495	.6769
10	.680	.7206
11	.545	
12	1.285	

The trend in period 10 can be estimated as the difference in levels between periods 10 and 9; that is

$$T_{10} = \overline{X}_{10} - \overline{X}_9 = .7206 - .6769 = .0437$$

Now, Table 17.18 also provides us with two estimates of the seasonal factor in each of the four quarters. For example, for the third quarter of the year, we have from period 3 the factor .345/.5075 and from period 7 the factor .440/.6094. As our initial estimate of the seasonal factor in the third quarter, we take the average of these two estimates; that is

$$F_7 = \frac{1}{2}\left(\frac{.345}{.5075} + \frac{.440}{.6094}\right) = .701$$

Similarly, for the other three quarters, we have

$$F_8 = \frac{1}{2}\left(\frac{.910}{.5219} + \frac{1.040}{.6469}\right) = 1.676$$

$$F_9 = \frac{1}{2}\left(\frac{.330}{.5444} + \frac{.495}{.6769}\right) = .669$$

$$F_{10} = \frac{1}{2}\left(\frac{.545}{.5725} + \frac{.680}{.7206}\right) = .948$$

Given these initial estimates, the remaining values can be computed. We will use the smoothing constants

$$A = .5 \qquad B = .5 \qquad C = .3$$

Given these values, Eqs. (17.8.5) to (17.8.7) become, for our quarterly model,

$$\overline{X}_t = .5(\overline{X}_{t-1} + T_{t-1}) + .5\left(\frac{X_t}{F_{t-4}}\right) \qquad (17.8.8)$$

$$T_t = .5T_{t-1} + .5(\overline{X}_t - \overline{X}_{t-1}) \qquad (17.8.9)$$

$$F_t = .3F_{t-4} + .7\left(\frac{X_t}{\overline{X}_t}\right) \qquad (17.8.10)$$

The earnings series, X_t, is set out in the second column of Table 17.19.

Formulas (17.8.8) to (17.8.10) are now applied, in turn, for $t = 11, 12, \ldots$. Thus, for period 11, we have from (17.8.8)

$$\overline{X}_{11} = .5(\overline{X}_{10} + T_{10}) + .5\left(\frac{X_{11}}{F_7}\right)$$

$$= .5(.7206 + .0437) + .5\left(\frac{.545}{.701}\right) = .7709$$

TABLE 17.19 Holt-Winters computations for earnings of a corporation ($A = .5, B = .5, C = .3$)

t	X_t	$\overline{X}_t$	T_t	F_t
1	.300			
2	.460			
3	.345			
4	.910			
5	.330			
6	.545			
7	.440			.701
8	1.040			1.676
9	.495			.669
10	.680	.7206	.0437	.948
11	.545	.7709	.0470	.705
12	1.285	.7923	.0342	1.638
13	.550	.8243	.0331	.668
14	.870	.8876	.0482	.971
15	.660	.9359	.0483	.705
16	1.580	.9743	.0433	1.627
17	.590	.9506	.0098	.635
18	.990	.9902	.0247	.991
19	.830	1.0960	.0652	.742
20	1.730	1.1124	.0408	1.577
21	.610	1.0571	−.0072	.594
22	1.050	1.0547	−.0048	.994
23	.920	1.1451	.0428	.785
24	2.040	1.2409	.0693	1.624
25	.700	1.2440	.0362	.572
26	1.230	1.2587	.0254	.982
27	1.060	1.3173	.0420	.799
28	2.320	1.3941	.0594	1.652
29	.820	1.4433	.0543	.569
30	1.410	1.4665	.0388	.968
31	1.250	1.5351	.0537	.810
32	2.730	1.6206	.0696	1.675

Next, using (17.8.9), we have for the trend factor

$$T_{11} = .5T_{10} + .5(\overline{X}_{11} - \overline{X}_{10})$$

$$= (.5)(.0437) + .5\,(.7709 - .7206) = .0470$$

Finally, from Eq. (17.8.10), the seasonal factor is estimated as

$$F_{11} = .3F_7 + .7\left(\frac{X_{11}}{\overline{X}_{11}}\right)$$

$$= (.3)(.701) + .7\left(\frac{.545}{.7709}\right) = .705$$

Continuing in this way, we can obtain the corresponding estimates for period 12. Thus, from (17.8.8), we have the level estimate

$$\overline{X}_{12} = .5\,(\overline{X}_{11} + T_{11}) + .5\left(\frac{X_{12}}{F_8}\right)$$

$$= .5(.7709 + .0470) + .5\left(\frac{1.285}{1.676}\right) = .7923$$

From (17.8.9), the trend estimate is

$$T_{12} = .5T_{11} + .5(\overline{X}_{12} - \overline{X}_{11})$$

$$= (.5)(.0470) + .5(.7923 - .7709) = .0342$$

and from (17.8.10), the seasonal factor is estimated by

$$F_{12} = .3F_8 + .7\left(\frac{X_{12}}{\overline{X}_{12}}\right)$$

$$= (.3)(1.676) + .7\left(\frac{1.285}{.7923}\right) = 1.638$$

The remaining estimates of level, trend, and the seasonal factors are obtained in precisely the same fashion, the results being set out in the final three columns of Table 17.19.

The reader will have formed the impression that the arithmetic burden of carrying out these computations is rather tedious. However, the recursive nature of updating Eqs. (17.8.5) to (17.8.7), in which the same three simple algebraic manipulations are undertaken at each time period, renders them particularly efficient as the basis of an algorithm to be programmed for an electronic computer. With this aid, the arithmetic can be performed very speedily. Moreover, a further advantage for this purpose is that very little information needs to be stored. Once the calculations have begun, it is not necessary to retain all past observations of the time series. All that is necessary is to retain the most recent estimates of level and trend and of the seasonal factors for each period of the last year. Thus, for quarterly data, standing at time t, we need retain only the level and trend estimates $\overline{X}_t$ and T_t and the estimated seasonal factors F_t, F_{t-1}, F_{t-2}, and F_{t-3}. These are then updated when the next observation, X_{t+1}, becomes available. The computational efficiency of this and other exponential smoothing forecasting methods makes them particularly useful in routine sales forecasting for inventory control, where predicted sales for a large number of product lines are required on a regular basis.

Having computed estimates of level, trend, and the seasonal factors, we can exploit these in the production of forecasts of future values of the series. For our earnings example, we need for this purpose the latest estimates of level and trend

$$\overline{X}_{32} = 1.6206 \qquad \text{and} \qquad T_{32} = .0696$$

and the four most recent estimates of the seasonal factors

$$F_{29} = .569 \qquad F_{30} = .968 \qquad F_{31} = .810 \qquad F_{32} = 1.675$$

We now consider the prediction of the next member of the series, X_{33}. To begin, we take our level estimate and add to it the estimate of the trend. Next, we must take into account that observation 33 occurs in the first quarter of the year, so that our result must be multiplied by a seasonal factor for the first quarter, the latest available estimate of which is F_{29}. Hence, X_{33} is predicted by

$$\hat{X}_{33} = (\overline{X}_{32} + T_{32})F_{29} = (1.6206 + .0696)(.569) = .9617$$

Now we consider the prediction of the next value, X_{34}. Since this is two periods ahead of the base from which forecasts are calculated, we add twice the trend estimate to the level estimate. Finally, this must be multiplied by F_{30}, the latest estimate of the seasonal factor in the second quarter of the year. Our forecast then is

$$\hat{X}_{34} = (\overline{X}_{32} + 2T_{32})F_{30} = [1.6206 + (2)(.0696)](.968) = 1.7035$$

We can calculate forecasts as far ahead as needed by continuing in this fashion. Figure 17.12 shows the actual data, together with predicted earnings for the next 2 years. These forecasts seem to reproduce rather well the recent trend and seasonal patterns in the series.

Forecasting with the Holt-Winters Method: Seasonal Series

Let $X_1, X_2, \ldots, X_n$ be a set of observations on a seasonal time series of period s (so that $s = 4$ for quarterly data and $s = 12$ for monthly data). The **Holt-Winters method** of forecasting for such series proceeds as follows:

(i) First we require initial estimates of level, trend, and seasonality. These can be obtained through the method of moving averages. Set

$$\overline{X}_t = \frac{X_{t-(s/2)} + 2(X_{t-(s/2)+1} + \cdots + X_{t+(s/2)-1}) + X_{t+(s/2)}}{2s}$$

for $t = (s/2)+1, (s/2)+2, \ldots, (5s/2)$. The estimate $\overline{X}_{5s/2}$ provides the first needed estimate of level. Trend in this period is estimated by

$$T_{5s/2} = \overline{X}_{5s/2} - \overline{X}_{(5s/2)-1}$$

Initial estimates of the s seasonal factors are then provided by

$$F_{(5s/2)-j} = \frac{1}{2}\left(\frac{X_{(5s/2)-j}}{\overline{X}_{(5s/2)-j}} + \frac{X_{(3s/2)-j}}{\overline{X}_{(3s/2)-j}} \right) \qquad (j = 0, 1, \ldots, s-1)$$

(ii) Beginning at period $[(5s/2)+1]$, we then apply in turn the updating equations

$$\overline{X}_t = A(\overline{X}_{t-1} + T_{t-1}) + (1 - A)\frac{X_t}{F_{t-s}} \qquad (0 < A < 1)$$

$$T_t = BT_{t-1} + (1 - B)(\overline{X}_t - \overline{X}_{t-1}) \qquad (0 < B < 1)$$

$$F_t = CF_{t-s} + (1 - C)\frac{X_t}{\overline{X}_t} \qquad (0 < C < 1)$$

where A, B, and C are smoothing constants, for $t = (5s/2) + 1, \ldots, n$.

(iii) Standing at time n, we compute forecasts of future values, X_{n+h}, of the series by

$$\hat{X}_{n+h} = (\overline{X}_n + hT_n)F_{n+h-s} \qquad (h = 1, 2, \ldots, s)$$

$$= (\overline{X}_n + hT_n)F_{n+h-2s} \qquad (h = s+1, s+2, \ldots, 2s)$$

and so on.

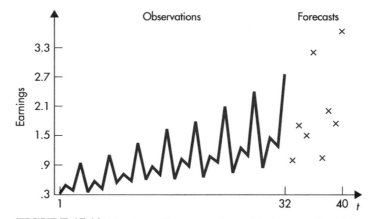

FIGURE 17.12 Earnings of a corporation, with forecasts based on the Holt-Winters method for seasonal series

The actual forecasts obtained through the Holt-Winters approach will depend on the specific values chosen for the smoothing constants. As in our discussion of exponential smoothing in Section 17.7, this choice could be based on either subjective or objective criteria. The analyst's experience with similar data sets might suggest suitable values of the smoothing constants. Alternatively, several sets of possible values can be tried on the available data, and the set that would have yielded the best forecasts can then be retained for future use. The latter approach involves a heavier computational burden but provides the safest course of action when attacking an unfamiliar problem. Given access to a computer program, this is not at all expensive.

EXERCISES

22. Based on the data of Exercise 8, use the method of simple exponential smoothing to obtain forecasts of inventory–sales ratio over the next 4 years. Use a smoothing constant of $\alpha = .4$. Graph the observed time series and the forecasts.

23. Use the method of simple exponential smoothing, with a smoothing constant of $\alpha = .3$, to obtain forecasts of the price of gold in the next 5 years, based on the data of Exercise 10.

24. Using the data of Exercise 11, employ the method of simple exponential smoothing, with smoothing constant $\alpha = .5$, to predict housing starts in the next 3 years.

25. The accompanying table shows earnings per share of a corporation over a period of 18 years.

YEAR	EARNINGS	YEAR	EARNINGS	YEAR	EARNINGS
1	3.63	7	7.01	13	3.54
2	3.62	8	6.37	14	1.65
3	3.66	9	5.82	15	2.15
4	5.31	10	4.98	16	6.09
5	6.14	11	3.43	17	5.95
6	6.42	12	3.40	18	6.26

(a) Using smoothing constants $\alpha = .2, .4, .6,$ and $.8$, find forecasts based on simple exponential smoothing.

(b) Which of the forecasts would you choose to use?

26. (a) If forecasts are based on simple exponential smoothing, with $\overline{X}_t$ denoting the smoothed value of the series at time t, show that the error made in forecasting X_t, standing at time $(t - 1)$, can be written

$$e_t = X_t - \overline{X}_{t-1}$$

(b) Hence, show that we can write

$$\overline{X}_t = X_t - \alpha e_t$$

from which we see that the most recent observation and the most recent forecast error are used to compute the next forecast.

27. Suppose that in the simple exponential smoothing method, the smoothing constant α is set equal to 1. What forecasts will result?

28. Comment on the following statement: "We know that all business and economic time series exhibit variability through time. Yet if simple exponential smoothing is used, the same forecast results for all future values of the time series. Since we know that all future values will not be the same, this is absurd."

29. The table shows an index of industrial production for Canada over a period of 15 years. Use the Holt-Winters procedure, with smoothing constants $A = .3$ and $B = .5$, to obtain forecasts over the next 5 years.

YEAR	INDEX	YEAR	INDEX	YEAR	INDEX
1	79	6	88	11	91
2	74	7	85	12	100
3	78	8	87	13	100
4	80	9	79	14	106
5	83	10	84	15	112

30. The table shows manufacturing hourly earnings in the United States over 24 months. Use the Holt-Winters procedure, with smoothing constants $A = .3$ and $B = .4$, to obtain forecasts for the next 3 months.

MONTH	EARNINGS	MONTH	EARNINGS	MONTH	EARNINGS
1	10.58	9	10.84	17	11.05
2	10.67	10	10.87	18	11.02
3	10.48	11	10.81	19	11.06
4	10.59	12	10.93	20	11.11
5	10.67	13	10.94	21	11.15
6	10.74	14	10.96	22	11.19
7	10.74	15	11.05	23	11.22
8	10.80	16	10.83	24	11.17

31. The accompanying table shows an index of food prices, seasonally adjusted, over a period of 14 months in the United States. Use the Holt-Winters method with smoothing constants $A = .5$ and $B = .5$ to obtain forecasts for the next 3 months.

MONTH	PRICE	MONTH	PRICE	MONTH	PRICE
1	116.6	6	120.3	11	122.6
2	117.1	7	120.6	12	123.6
3	117.8	8	120.8	13	124.2
4	118.9	9	121.2	14	125.0
5	119.5	10	122.1		

32. The table shows percentage profit margins of a corporation over a period of 11 years. Obtain forecasts for the next 2 years, using the Holt-Winters method with smoothing constants $A = .6$ and $B = .6$.

YEAR	PROFIT MARGIN	YEAR	PROFIT MARGIN	YEAR	PROFIT MARGIN
1	8.4	5	6.3	9	8.5
2	7.4	6	7.9	10	7.0
3	7.4	7	7.7	11	5.7
4	7.2	8	7.1		

33. Use the Holt-Winters seasonal method to obtain forecasts of sales up to eight quarters ahead, based on the data of Exercise 13. Employ smoothing constants $A = .6$, $B = .5$, and $C = .4$. Graph the data and the forecasts.

34. Use the Holt-Winters seasonal method to obtain forecasts of sales up to eight quarters ahead, based on the data of Exercise 14. Employ smoothing constants $A = .5$, $B = .4$, and $C = .3$. Graph the data and the forecasts.

17.9 AUTOREGRESSIVE MODELS

A rather different approach to time series forecasting involves using the available data to construct a **model** that might have generated the series of interest. In this section, we will consider a very useful class of such models, while an important broader class will be briefly discussed in the following section.

We have already introduced, in the context of regression models in Section 14.8, the simplest of the models that will be the focus of our attention in this section. Essentially, the idea is to regard a time series as a series of random variables. For practical purposes, we might often be prepared to assume that these random variables all have the same means and variances. However, it would be rash, to say the least, to assume that they were independent of one another. Consider, for example, a series of annual values of product sales. We might suspect that the level of sales in the current period would be related to the levels in the immediately preceding years. Thus, we might expect to find a pattern of correlation through time in our series. Correlation patterns of this kind are sometimes referred to as **autocorrelation.**

In principle, any number of autocorrelation patterns are possible. However, some are considerably more likely to arise than others. A particularly attractive possibility arises when we think of the case of a fairly strong correlation between adjacent observations in time, a less strong correlation between observations two time periods apart, a weaker correlation yet between values three time periods apart, and so on. A very simple autocorrelation pattern of this sort arises when the correlation between adjacent values is some number, say ϕ_1, that between values two time periods apart is ϕ_1^2, that between values three time periods apart is ϕ_1^3, and so on. Thus, if we let X_t denote the value of the series at time t, we have under this model of autocorrelation

$$\text{Corr}(X_t, X_{t-j}) = \phi_1^{j} \qquad (j = 1, 2, 3, \ldots) \qquad (17.9.1)$$

It can be shown that a model of the time series giving rise to the autocorrelation structure (17.9.1) is

$$X_t = \gamma + \phi_1 X_{t-1} + a_t \qquad (17.9.2)$$

where γ and ϕ_1 are fixed parameters and the random variables a_t have means 0 and fixed variances for all t and are not correlated with one another. In (17.9.2), the purpose of the parameter γ is to allow for the possibility that the series X_t has some mean other than 0. Otherwise, this model is the one we used in Section 14.8 to represent autocorrelation in the error terms of a regression equation. It is called a **first-order autoregressive model.**

The first-order autoregressive model (17.9.2) expresses the current value, X_t, of a series in terms of the previous value, X_{t-1}, and a nonautocorrelated random variable a_t. Since the random variable a_t is not autocorrelated, it is unpredictable. It therefore follows that for series generated by the first-order autoregressive model, forecasts of future values depend only on the most recent value of the series. However, in many applications, we would want to use more than this one observation as a basis for forecasting. An obvious extension of the model (17.9.2) would be to make the current value of the series dependent on the *two* most recent observations. Thus, we could use a model

$$X_t = \gamma + \phi_1 X_{t-1} + \phi_2 X_{t-2} + a_t$$

where γ, ϕ_1, and ϕ_2 are fixed parameters. This is called a **second-order autoregressive model.**

More generally, for any positive integer p, the current value of the series can be made (linearly) dependent on the p previous values, through the **autoregressive model of order p:**

$$X_t = \gamma + \phi_1 X_{t-1} + \phi_2 X_{t-2} + \cdots + \phi_p X_{t-p} + a_t \qquad (17.9.3)$$

where $\gamma, \phi_1, \phi_2, \ldots, \phi_p$ are fixed parameters. Equation (17.9.3) depicts the general autoregressive model. In the remainder of this section, we will consider the fitting of such models and their exploitation in forecasting future values.

Suppose that we have a series of observations, $X_1, X_2, \ldots, X_n$. We want to use these to estimate the unknown parameters $\gamma, \phi_1, \phi_2, \ldots, \phi_p$ of the autoregressive model (17.9.3). This can be done through the method of *least squares*. The parameter estimates are taken as the values of $\gamma, \phi_1, \phi_2, \ldots, \phi_p$ for which the sum of squared discrepancies

$$SS = \sum_{t=p+1}^{n} (X_t - \gamma - \phi_1 X_{t-1} - \cdots - \phi_p X_{t-p})^2$$

is smallest. Hence, estimation can be carried out using a multiple regression program, employing the techniques discussed in Chapter 13.

For the data on sales of Lydia E. Pinkham, given in Example 17.1, autoregressive models of orders up to four were estimated by least squares. The fitted first-order model was

$$X_t = 193.27 + .883X_{t-1} + a_t$$
$$(188.92) \quad (.097)$$

(17.9.4)

For the second-order model, we obtained

$$X_t = 313.68 + 1.180X_{t-1} - .358X_{t-2} + a_t$$
$$(192.56) \quad (.187) \qquad (.191)$$

(17.9.5)

The estimated third- and fourth-order models were, respectively

$$X_t = 322.29 + 1.188X_{t-1} - .317X_{t-2} - .057X_{t-3} + a_t$$
$$(215.72) \quad (.206) \qquad (.308) \qquad (.209)$$

(17.9.6)

and

$$X_t = 446.22 + 1.194X_{t-1} - .439X_{t-2} + .286X_{t-3} - .291X_{t-4}$$
$$(232.77) \quad (.211) \qquad (.324) \qquad (.317) \qquad (.210)$$

(17.9.7)

In Eqs. (17.9.4) to (17.9.7), the figures in parentheses beneath the coefficient estimates are the corresponding estimated standard errors.

Given access to a multiple regression computer program, these autoregressive models can be fitted quickly and inexpensively. Table 17.20 shows part of the output for the second-order autoregressive model (17.9.5).

If an autoregressive model is to be used to generate forecasts of future values of a time series, it is necessary to fix a value for p, the order of the autoregression. In making this choice, two considerations must be balanced. We want to choose the order sufficiently large to account for all the important autocorrelation behavior of the series. But too large a value of p will lead to a model with irrelevant parameters and, consequently, inefficient estimation of the parameters that are important.

One possibility is to fix the value of p arbitrarily, perhaps on the basis of past experience with similar data sets. An alternative approach is to set some maximal order, K, of the autoregression and fit, in turn, models of order $p = K, (K - 1), (K - 2), \ldots$. For each value of p, the null hypothesis that the final autoregressive parameter, ϕ_p, of the model is 0 is tested against a two-sided alternative. The procedure terminates when we find a value p for which this null hypothesis is not rejected. Our aim, then, is to test the null hypothesis

$$H_0: \phi_p = 0$$

against the alternative

$$H_1: \phi_p \neq 0$$

The test is based on the fact that, to a good approximation, the parameter estimator divided by its estimated standard error follows a standard normal distribution when the null hypothesis is true. The decision rule, then, is

TABLE 17.20 Part of SAS program output for second-order autoregressive model fitted to Lydia E. Pinkham data

PARAMETER	ESTIMATE	T FOR H0: PARAMETER = 0	STD. ERROR OF ESTIMATE
INTERCEPT	313.68		
XT − 1	1.180	6.31	.187
XT − 2	−.358	−1.87	.191

$$\text{Reject } H_0 \text{ if } \frac{\hat{\phi}_p}{s_p} < -z_{\alpha/2} \qquad \text{or} \qquad \frac{\hat{\phi}_p}{s_p} > z_{\alpha/2}$$

where α is the significance level of the test, $\hat{\phi}_p$ and s_p are the parameter estimate and its standard error, and $z_{\alpha/2}$ is the number for which

$$P(Z > z_{\alpha/2}) = \frac{\alpha}{2}$$

where Z is a standard normal random variable.

We will apply this approach to the Lydia E. Pinkham data, using a 10% significance level for our tests, so from Table 3 of the Appendix

$$z_{\alpha/2} = z_{.05} = 1.645$$

We will fix at 4 the maximum order of autoregression contemplated. Beginning with the fourth-order fitted model (17.9.7), we find

$$\frac{\hat{\phi}_4}{s_4} = \frac{-.291}{.210} = -1.386$$

so the null hypothesis that $\phi_4 = 0$ is not rejected. Turning to the estimated third-order model (17.9.6), we have

$$\frac{\hat{\phi}_3}{s_3} = \frac{-.057}{.209} = -.273$$

Hence, the null hypothesis that $\phi_3 = 0$ is not rejected in this model. Next, consider the estimated second-order autoregressive model (17.9.5). There we find

$$\frac{\hat{\phi}_2}{s_2} = \frac{-.358}{.191} = -1.874$$

For this model, then, the null hypothesis that $\phi_2 = 0$ is rejected by a test of significance level 10%. Accordingly, we will proceed with the second-order model.

Having obtained an appropriate estimated autoregressive model, it is a relatively straightforward matter to compute forecasts of future values of a time series. We will illustrate the procedure by forecasting future sales from the Lydia E. Pinkham data, using the estimated second-order autoregressive model (17.9.5). The last two values in this series were

$$X_{29} = 1,387 \qquad \text{and} \qquad X_{30} = 1,289$$

We now want to predict the next value, X_{31}. Setting $t = 31$ in (17.9.5) gives

$$X_{31} = 313.68 + 1.180X_{30} - .358X_{29} + a_{31}$$

Now, a_{31} is simply a random variable with mean 0, uncorrelated with anything that is known at the time the forecast is made. Our best prediction of this term is therefore 0. Thus, our forecast of X_{31} is

$$\hat{X}_{31} = 313.68 + 1.180X_{30} - .358X_{29}$$

$$= 313.68 + (1.180)(1,289) - (.358)(1,387) = 1,338.15$$

Setting $t = 32$ in (17.9.5), we have

$$X_{32} = 313.68 + 1.180X_{31} - .358X_{30} + a_{32}$$

Once again, our best prediction of a_{32} is simply 0. Moreover, we do not know X_{31}, but we do have its forecast, $\hat{X}_{31}$, so that a natural prediction for sales 2 years ahead is

$$\hat{X}_{32} = 313.68 + 1.180\hat{X}_{31} - .358X_{30}$$
$$= 313.68 + (1.180)(1,338.15) - (.358)(1,289) = 1,431.24$$

Continuing in exactly the same way, we obtain

$$X_{33} = 313.68 + 1.180X_{32} - .358X_{31} + a_{33}$$

Replacing X_{32}, X_{31}, and a_{33} by their forecasts, $\hat{X}_{32}, \hat{X}_{31}$, and 0, then yields the forecast for X_{33} of

$$\hat{X}_{33} = 313.68 + 1.180\hat{X}_{32} - .358\hat{X}_{31}$$
$$= 313.68 + (1.180)(1,431.24) - (.358)(1,338.15) = 1,523.49$$

Proceeding in this fashion, we can compute forecasts as far ahead as required. The data series and the first six forecasts are graphed in Figure 17.13.

The general procedure for computing forecasts based on an estimated autoregressive model is outlined in the box.

Forecasting from Estimated Autoregressive Models

Suppose that we have observations $X_1, X_2, \ldots, X_n$ from a time series and that an autoregressive model of order p has been fitted to these data. Write the estimated model as

$$X_t = \hat{\gamma} + \hat{\phi}_1 X_{t-1} + \hat{\phi}_2 X_{t-2} + \cdots + \hat{\phi}_p X_{t-p} + a_t$$

Standing at time n, we obtain forecasts of future values of the series from

$$\hat{X}_{n+h} = \hat{\gamma} + \hat{\phi}_1 \hat{X}_{n+h-1} + \hat{\phi}_2 \hat{X}_{n+h-2} + \cdots + \hat{\phi}_p \hat{X}_{n+h-p} \qquad (h = 1, 2, 3, \ldots)$$

where for $j > 0$, $\hat{X}_{n+j}$ is the forecast of X_{n+j} standing at time n and for $j \leq 0$, $\hat{X}_{n+j}$ is simply the observed value X_{n+j}.

FIGURE 17.13 Sales of Lydia E. Pinkham and forecasts based on a fitted second-order autoregressive model

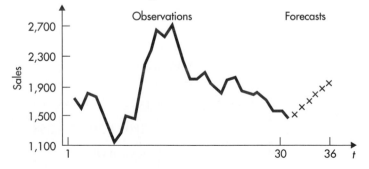

17.10 AUTOREGRESSIVE INTEGRATED MOVING AVERAGE MODELS

In this section, we will briefly introduce an approach to time series forecasting that has become widely used in business applications over the past few years. The models to be discussed include as special cases the autoregressive models discussed in Section 17.9.

In a classic book, George Box and Gwilym Jenkins introduced a methodology sufficiently versatile to provide a moderately skillful user with good results for a wide range of forecasting problems that occur in practice.[2] The essence of the Box-Jenkins approach is the contemplation of a very broad class of models from which forecasts can be derived, together with a methodology for picking, on the basis of the characteristics of the available data, a suitable model for any specific forecasting problem.

The general class of models is the class of **autoregressive integrated moving average models.** These are rather natural extensions of the autoregressive models of Section 17.9. Moreover, the simple exponential smoothing and Holt-Winters predictors of Sections 17.7 and 17.8 can be derived from specific members of this general class, as can many other widely used forecasting algorithms. The models and the Box-Jenkins time series analysis techniques can be generalized to allow for seasonality and also to deal with related time series so that future values of one series can be predicted from information not only on its own past but also on the past of other relevant series. This last possibility allows an approach to forecasting that generalizes the regression procedures discussed in Chapters 12 through 14.

It is not possible in the space available to provide a full discussion of the Box-Jenkins methodology.[3] In essence, it involves three stages:

1. Based on summary statistics that are readily calculated from the available data, the analyst selects a specific model that might be appropriate from the general class. This is not simply a matter of automatically following a set of rules but rather requires a certain amount of judgment and experience. However, one is not forever committed to the model chosen at this stage but can abandon it in favor of some alternative at a later stage of the analysis if that appears desirable.

2. The specific model chosen will almost invariably have some unknown coefficients. These must be estimated from the available data using efficient statistical techniques, such as least squares.

3. Finally, checks are applied to determine whether the estimated model provides an adequate representation of the available time series data. Any inadequacies revealed at this stage may suggest some alternative specification, and the process of model selection, coefficient estimation, and model checking is iterated until a satisfactory model is found.

---

[2] G.E.P. Box and G. M. Jenkins, *Time Series Analysis, Forecasting, and Control* (San Francisco: Holden-Day, 1970).

[3] For an introduction to this methodology, see P. Newbold and T. Bos, *Introductory Business Forecasting* (Cincinnati, OH: South-Western, 2nd ed., 1994).

The Box-Jenkins approach to forecasting has the great advantage of flexibility—a wide range of predictors is available, and choice among them is based on data evidence. Moreover, when this approach to forecasting has been compared with other methods, using actual economic and business time series, it has usually been found to perform very well.[4] Thus, the procedure can be said to have survived the acid test: In practice, it works!

In concluding this brief discussion, note that computer programs for performing a time series analysis through the fitting to data of autoregressive integrated moving average models are widely available. However, the method does have a drawback compared with some of the simpler procedures discussed in earlier sections of this chapter. Because flexibility is allowed in choosing an appropriate model from the general class, the Box-Jenkins approach is more costly in terms of skilled worker time than methods that force a single model structure onto every time series.

EXERCISES

35. Using the data of Table 17.9, estimate a first-order autoregressive model for the index of volume of shares traded. Use the fitted model to obtain forecasts for the next 4 days.

36. The accompanying table shows the volume of transactions (in hundreds of thousands) in shares of a corporation over a period of 12 weeks. Using these data, estimate a first-order autoregressive model, and use the fitted model to obtain forecasts of volume for the next 3 weeks.

WEEK	VOLUME	WEEK	VOLUME	WEEK	VOLUME
1	27.1	5	21.9	9	17.0
2	12.9	6	17.3	10	21.4
3	12.1	7	11.7	11	25.0
4	13.6	8	23.8	12	20.5

37. [*This exercise requires a computer program to carry out the multiple regression calculations.*] Using the data of Exercise 11 on housing starts, estimate autoregressive models of orders 1 through 4. Use the method of Section 17.9 for testing that the order of the autoregression is $(p - 1)$ against the alternative that the order is p, with a significance level of 10%. Select one of these models, and calculate forecasts of housing starts for the next 5 years. Draw a time plot showing the original observations together with the forecasts. Would different forecasts result if a significance level of 5% were used for the tests of autoregressive order?

38. [*This exercise requires a computer program to carry out the multiple regression calculations.*] From the data of Exercise 12 on corporate earnings per share, fit autoregressive models of orders 1 through 4. Use the procedure of Section 17.9 for testing that the order of the autoregression is $(p - 1)$ against the alternative that the true order is p, with 10% significance level. Choose one of these models, and compute forecasts of earnings per share for the next 5 years. Draw a graph showing the original data along with these forecasts. Would the results differ if 5% significance levels were used for the tests?

---

[4] See, for example, P. Newbold and C.W.J. Granger, "Experience with forecasting univariate time series and the combination of forecasts," *Journal of the Royal Statistical Society A, 137* (1974), 131–46.

39. [*This exercise requires a computer program to carry out the multiple regression calculations.*] Refer to the data of Exercise 25 on corporate earnings per share. Fit autoregressive models of orders 1, 2, and 3. Use the procedure of Section 17.9 to test the hypothesis that the order of the autoregression is $(p - 1)$ against the alternative that it is p, at 10% significance level, and thereby select a value for autoregressive order. Use the selected model to generate earnings-per-share forecasts up to 4 years ahead. Draw a time plot of the observations and forecasts. Would different results be obtained with 5%-level significance tests?

40. In Section 17.9, Eqs. (17.9.4)–(17.9.7), fitted autoregressive models of orders 1 through 4 are given for annual sales data. We then selected a model by testing the null hypothesis of autoregression of order $(p - 1)$ against the alternative of autoregression of order p, at the 10% significance level. Repeat this procedure, but testing at the 5% significance level.

(**a**) What autoregressive model is now selected?

(**b**) Obtain forecasts of sales for the next 3 years, based on this selected model.

41. For a certain product, it was found that annual sales volume could be well described by a third-order autoregressive model. The estimated model obtained was

$$X_t = 202 + 1.10X_{t-1} - .48X_{t-2} + .17X_{t-3} + a_t$$

For 1993, 1994, and 1995, sales were 867, 923, and 951, respectively. Calculate sales forecasts for the years 1996 through 1998.

42. For many time series, particularly prices in speculative markets, the *random walk* model has been found to give a good representation of actual data. This model is written

$$X_t = X_{t-1} + a_t$$

Show that if this model is appropriate, forecasts of X_{n+h}, standing at time n, are given by

$$\hat{X}_{n+h} = X_n \qquad (h = 1, 2, 3, \ldots)$$

43. Sometimes it is desirable to extend the model of Exercise 42 to allow for the possibility that the expected change from period to period is not 0. This augmented model, known as the *random walk with drift*, is written

$$X_t = \gamma + X_{t-1} + a_t$$

Show that if this model is appropriate, forecasts of X_{n+h}, standing at time n, are given by

$$\hat{X}_{n+h} = X_n + h\gamma \qquad (h = 1, 2, 3, \ldots)$$

44. [*This exercise requires a computer program to carry out the multiple regression calculations.*] Refer to the data of Exercise 30, showing earnings over 24 months. Denote the observations X_t ($t = 1, 2, \ldots, 24$). Now, form the series of first differences

$$Z_t = X_t - X_{t-1} \qquad (t = 2, 3, \ldots, 24)$$

Fit autoregressive models of orders 1 through 4 to the series Z_t. Using the approach of Section 17.9 for testing that the autoregressive order is $(p - 1)$ against the alternative of order p, with a 10% significance level, select one of these models. Using the selected model, find forecasts for Z_t, $t = 25, 26, 27$. Hence, obtain forecasts of earnings for the next 3 months.

REVIEW EXERCISES ════════════════════════════

45. Refer to Exercise 30, which shows monthly hourly earnings in manufacturing.

(**a**) Obtain an index with month 1 as base.

(**b**) Obtain an index with month 15 as base.

46. A library purchases both books and journals. The accompanying table shows the average prices (in dollars) paid for each and the quantities purchased over a period of 6 years. Use year 1 as base.

YEAR	BOOKS		JOURNALS	
	PRICE	QUANTITY	PRICE	QUANTITY
1	20.4	694	30.1	155
2	22.3	723	33.4	159
3	23.3	687	36.0	160
4	24.6	731	39.8	163
5	27.0	742	45.7	160
6	29.2	748	50.7	155

(a) Find the unweighted aggregate index of prices.
(b) Find the Laspeyres price index.
(c) Find the Laspeyres quantity index.

47. Explain the statement that a time series can be viewed as being made up of a number of components. Provide examples of business and economic time series for which you would expect particular components to be important.

48. In many business applications, forecasts for future values of time series, such as sales and earnings, are made exclusively on the basis of past information on the time series in question. What features of time series behavior are exploited in the production of such forecasts?

49. A manager in charge of inventory control requires sales forecasts for several products, on a monthly basis, over the next 6 months. This manager has available monthly sales records over the past 4 years for each of these products. He decides to use, as forecasts for each of the next 6 months, the average monthly sales over the previous 4 years. Do you think this is a good strategy? Provide reasons.

50. What is meant by the seasonal adjustment of a time series? Explain why government agencies expend a large amount of effort on the seasonal adjustment of economic time series.

51. The accompanying table shows an index of U.S. industrial production over 14 years.

YEAR	INDEX	YEAR	INDEX	YEAR	INDEX
1	68	6	87	11	100
2	74	7	89	12	99
3	80	8	83	13	104
4	86	9	88	14	110
5	89	10	98		

(a) Test this series for randomness using the runs test.
(b) Draw a time plot of these data, and discuss the features revealed by the graph.
(c) Compute the series of simple centered 3-point moving averages. Graph this smoothed series, and discuss its behavior.

52. The following table shows 24 annual observations on sales of a product.

YEAR	SALES	YEAR	SALES	YEAR	SALES
1	853	9	650	17	538
2	693	10	751	18	708
3	715	11	723	19	907
4	785	12	702	20	912
5	851	13	991	21	777
6	797	14	1,129	22	569
7	758	15	972	23	473
8	593	16	631	24	459

(a) Use the large-sample variant of the runs test to test this series for randomness.

(b) Draw a time plot of the data and discuss the characteristics of the series shown by this graph.

(c) Compute the series of simple centered 5-point moving averages. Graph this smoothed series, and discuss its behavior.

53. The table shows quarterly earnings per share of a corporation over 7 years.

YEAR	QUARTER			
	1	2	3	4
1	.786	.668	.863	.807
2	.802	.670	.885	.805
3	.579	.423	.904	.851
4	.430	.409	1.120	.958
5	.680	.460	1.190	.830
6	.766	.440	1.020	.630
7	.690	.600	1.130	.680

(a) Draw a time plot of these data. Does this graph suggest the presence of a strong seasonal component?

(b) Use the seasonal index method to obtain a seasonally adjusted series.

54. The accompanying table shows fifteen monthly values on the price index of a commodity.

MONTH	PRICE	MONTH	PRICE	MONTH	PRICE
1	79	6	89	11	117
2	87	7	94	12	116
3	89	8	92	13	114
4	90	9	88	14	113
5	88	10	96	15	109

(a) Calculate the series of simple centered 3-point moving averages.

(b) Draw a time plot of the smoothed series and comment on its characteristics.

55. Refer to Exercise 52. Use simple exponential smoothing, with smoothing constant $\alpha = .5$, to obtain forecasts of sales for the next 3 years.

56. Refer to Exercise 54. Use the Holt-Winters method, with smoothing constants $A = .3$ and $B = .4$, to obtain forecasts of the price index for the next 4 months.

57. Refer to Exercise 53. Use the Holt-Winters seasonal method, with smoothing constants $A = .4$, $B = .4$, and $C = .2$, to obtain forecasts of this earnings-per-share series for the next 4 quarters.

58. [*This exercise requires a computer program to carry out the multiple regression calculations.*] Using the data of Exercise 52, estimate autoregressive models of orders 1 through 4 for product sales. Using the procedure of Section 17.9 for testing that the autoregressive order is $(p - 1)$ against the alternative that the order is p, with a significance level of 10%, choose one of these models. Compute forecasts for the next 3 years from the chosen model.

59. A second-order autoregressive model was fitted to quarterly data on the ratio of consumer installment debt to personal income in the United States.[5] The estimated model was

$$X_t = 0.021 + 1.74X_{t-1} - .74X_{t-2} + a_t$$

The last two observations of this time series were

$$X_{n-1} = 13.217 \qquad X_n = 13.147$$

Obtain forecasts of X_{n+1}, X_{n+2}, X_{n+3}, and X_{n+4}.

---

[5] Reported in C.W.J. Granger and P. Newbold, *Forecasting Economic Time Series*, 2nd ed. (Orlando, FL: Academic Press, 1986).

CHAPTER 18

Survey Sampling Methods

18.1 INTRODUCTION

Much of statistical inference is concerned with problems of making statements about a population on the basis of information from a sample. In our discussions to this point, two important topics have been treated rather cursorily. First, very little has been said about how one would actually go about selecting the sample members. Second, it has generally been assumed that the number of population members is very large compared with the number of sample members. In this chapter, we concentrate on the problem of a researcher who wants to discover something about a population that is not necessarily large. The investigator intends to collect information on only a subset of the population members and requires guidance as to how to proceed.

The general problem just discussed occurs frequently in business applications. Market researchers often survey human populations to elicit information about product preferences. Auditors typically select a sample of a corporation's accounts receivable, on the basis of which inferences are made about the corresponding population. Personnel directors often require information on employees' attitudes toward proposed new production methods and find it convenient to sample the labor force. Of course, the use of sampling methods is extremely widespread, extending well beyond the field of business. Perhaps the best-known example is the regular survey of voter preferences prior to a presidential election. The information gathered is of interest not only to the general public but also to advisers of candidates who are trying to determine where their efforts should be most heavily concentrated. Such surveys of voters have escalated to the point where voter opinions are sought on all aspects of public policy, and the professional pollster has become an important figure in the politician's entourage.

Before asking how a sample should be taken from a population, we pause to ask, "Why sample at all?" The alternative is to attempt to obtain information from every population member. This would be referred to as a **census** rather than a sample. There are three good reasons why a sample is often preferred to a census. First, in many applications, taking a complete census would be enormously expensive, frequently prohibitively so. Second, information is often required fairly quickly; a full census, even when financially feasible, may take so long to complete that the value of the results is seriously diminished. Finally, with modern statistical methods, it is generally possible to obtain results of the desired level of precision through sampling. Any time and money expended on producing numbers whose apparent precision exceeds the investigator's needs could be better spent elsewhere. Moreover, if a relatively small sample is taken, the gains derived through extra effort in securing accurate information from the sample members could well outweigh the benefits of having information from a larger group which, because of time and cost constraints, may be less reliable. Taken together, these three factors—cost, time, and precision—dictate a preference for a sample rather than a census, on many occasions.

Suppose now that information about a population is required and that the decision has been made to take a sample. It is convenient to think of a sampling study as involving six steps, each aimed at producing the answer to a single question, as set out schematically in Figure 18.1.

We will discuss each of these steps in turn, with reference to a market research problem. Suppose that a publisher intends to bring out a new business statistics text and wants information on the current state of the market. Valuable information might include the number of students enrolled in business statistics courses, the market penetration of existing texts, and instructors' views as to which topics are the most important for their courses. We will assume that the publisher decides to gather data from a sample of college campuses.

FIGURE 18.1   Steps in a sampling study

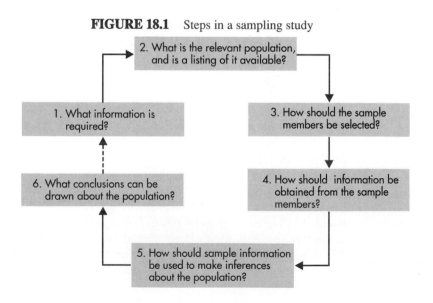

1. WHAT INFORMATION IS REQUIRED?

The answer to this question provides both the motivation and the starting point for the study. If the necessary information is either already available or impossible to obtain, there is no point in carrying out the survey. However, straightforward though the question seems, a rather delicate balance is often needed at this stage. The investigator may have in mind just a single requirement, or there may be several topics of interest. But given that a survey is to be carried out, with all the attendant costs, it is usually worthwhile asking whether further potentially useful information can be gleaned from the study at minimal additional expense. For the publisher of the business statistics text, we have already noted that the most useful questions concern the size of the market, the standing of competitors, and the topics that instructors view as most important. Given that sample members are to be contacted to elicit this information, it may well be worthwhile to ask some additional questions. These may include whether the course is one or two semesters long, whether it is optional or compulsory, the department of the instructor, the procedure for textbook adoption, and the length of time the current text has been in use. Once having started along this road, we may be tempted to allow the list of questions to grow dramatically, because this would not generally increase greatly the cost of carrying out the study. However, there *is* a potential penalty. Respondents are more likely to cooperate in a study that asks relatively few questions and consequently takes up little of their time. Thus, it is important for the investigator to strike a balance whereby questions on central issues are asked (for if an important omission is discovered, it may prove too costly to repeat the whole exercise) and the number of questions asked remains tolerable to potential respondents.

2. WHAT IS THE RELEVANT POPULATION, AND IS A LISTING OF IT AVAILABLE?

It seems rather trite to point out that if inferences are to be made about a particular population, that is the population that must be sampled. Nevertheless, dubious conclusions have often been reached following an otherwise perfectly respectable analysis of survey data precisely because this elementary point has been ignored. Many publications invite the opinions of their readers on particular questions. It would, however, be dangerous to generalize their responses to a wider population. The population studied here is simply the readership of the publication, and this readership is likely to be unrepresentative of the public at large. In many practical studies, the *real* population of interest may be impossible to define. For example, an organization attempting to predict the result of a presidential election is really interested in only people who will, in fact, vote. However, although this is the relevant population, its members are not easy to distinguish. One possibility, of course, is to ask a sample member if he or she intends to vote. However, it is well known that the proportion answering such a question in the affirmative is higher than the proportion who do eventually vote. Another possibility is to ask whether the respondent voted in the previous election, but this too is far from completely satisfactory.

The textbook publisher is likely to regard the relevant population as all instructors (or, perhaps, all colleges) teaching business statistics courses. This population is quite easy to identify, and, as a result of earlier marketing activities, the publisher will almost certainly have a fairly accurate listing of its members.

3. *HOW SHOULD THE SAMPLE MEMBERS BE SELECTED?*

Much of the remainder of this chapter will be devoted to answering this question. Put succinctly, there is no unique way to go about providing the "best" sampling scheme. The appropriate choice will generally depend on the problem at hand and on the resources of the investigator. In Chapter 6, we introduced the notion of **simple random sampling,** in which each potential sample of n members has an equal chance of being chosen. Indeed, all of the data-analytic tools introduced to this point have been based on an assumption that the sample was chosen in such a fashion. There are, however, many circumstances in which alternative sampling schemes might be preferred. Suppose that our publisher is concerned about differences in the treatment of business statistics courses between 2-year and 4-year colleges. It would be important that the sample contain enough colleges of each type to allow reliable conclusions about both to be drawn. However, simple random sampling by no means guarantees attainment of this objective. It is entirely possible, for example, that the sample chosen will contain a preponderance of 4-year colleges. To guard against this possibility, one can draw separate simple random samples of 2-year and 4-year colleges from their respective populations. This is an example of **stratified sampling,** which will be discussed in more detail in Section 18.4. Another matter to be decided at this stage is the number of sample members. Essentially, the choice here depends on the degree of accuracy required and also on the costs involved. We will return to this question in Section 18.5.

4. *HOW SHOULD INFORMATION BE OBTAINED FROM THE SAMPLE MEMBERS?*

This is an extremely important question, the subject of much research. Broadly speaking, two important issues are involved. First, the investigator will want to obtain answers from as high a proportion as possible of the sample members. If the number not responding is high, it will be difficult to be sure that those who do respond are representative of the population at large. For instance, professors failing to supply information to the textbook publisher may be those most heavily involved in research, consulting, or other activities, and their preferences about texts could well differ from those of their colleagues. We have already noted that the number of questions asked in a survey could affect the response rate. The manner in which sample members are contacted is also influential. Frequently, questionnaires are mailed to those selected for the sample, and it often happens that the proportion responding is disappointingly low. Many researchers attempt to improve the response rate by including a covering letter, explaining the purposes of the study and politely soliciting help. An assurance of anonymity may also be valuable. The inclusion of a postpaid envelope for returning the questionnaire is generally worthwhile, and some modest monetary inducement or gift might be promised. Nevertheless, there will almost inevitably be a proportion of nonrespondents, and it is good practice to institute a follow-up inquiry to try to learn something about them. More expensive contact methods, such as telephone calls or home visits by interviewers, are likely to achieve a higher level of response. However, such methods can be costly in terms of time as well as money, and the decision on how to collect information must depend on the investigator's resources and the extent to which nonresponse is thought to be a serious potential problem.

The textbook publisher may decide to mail questionnaires to sample members. This would be inexpensive, so a relatively large initial sample could be drawn. The hope must be that the proportion of nonrespondents is not too high and that the responses obtained are reasonably representative. If it is feared that nonresponse will induce substantial bias should a mail questionnaire be used, a smaller initial sample might be drawn and a greater effort made to contact individual sample members. A feasible strategy might be to ask the company's representatives, who regularly visit campuses, to carry out interviews with the sample members on their next visits. Such a procedure should ensure quite a high response rate. Its major difficulty would be the time taken before all the interviews were completed rather than the additional costs, which would be quite low.

The second point is the obvious desideratum of obtaining answers that are as accurate and as honest as possible. Nothing is to be gained from a highly sophisticated statistical analysis of basically unreliable information. There is an art in designing questions, whether asked through mail survey or by interviewer, in such a way as to extract honest and accurate replies. It is important that the questions be phrased as clearly and unambiguously as possible, so that subjects understand what is being asked. Also, it is well known that respondents can be biased toward providing particular answers by the wording of the question or the tone of an interviewer. Interviewers should in no way convey the impression of having strong views on the subject at hand or of wanting a particular answer. It is also important not to "lead the witness"—questions should be phrased as neutrally as possible. As an extreme example, consider the following two methods of asking essentially the same question:

> **Q.** Which three topics do you regard as most important in your business statistics course?

> or

> **Q.** Do you agree that modern methods of quality management, because of their overwhelming importance in the business world, must now be considered one of the most important topics in any business statistics course?

Of course, no one interested in an accurate picture of instructors' opinions would ask the second question. However, much less clearly biased wording than this has been found to make an appreciable difference to subjects' replies.

As an illustration of this point, Opinion Research Corporation of Princeton, New Jersey, annually surveys public attitudes toward government. Concerned about the influence of question wording, the organization asked the same question in two ways in the 1981 survey. Respondents were asked what programs might best be sacrificed in the event of a severe budget squeeze. Among the list of candidates was "Aid to the needy." This item was selected for cutbacks by only 7% of all respondents. Two months later, when the same question was asked, the description "Aid to the needy" was replaced by "Public welfare." This time the item was chosen for cuts by 39% of respondents!

That interviewers can have an impact on the aggregate response was demonstrated by attempts to assess the approval rating by African-Americans of Ronald Reagan's presidency. In December 1985, a New York Times/CBS poll found an approval rating of 56%. The following month, using African-American interviewers, a Washington Post/ABC poll produced a rating of only 23% approval.

5. HOW SHOULD SAMPLE INFORMATION BE USED TO MAKE INFERENCES ABOUT THE POPULATION?

The greater part of this book has been devoted to providing answers to just this question. In subsequent sections of this chapter, we will discuss methods of inference for particular sampling designs. The chief purpose of the present section is to note the importance of other aspects of a statistical sampling study.

6. WHAT CONCLUSIONS CAN BE DRAWN ABOUT THE POPULATION?

Finally, we come full circle and ask what can be said about the population under study as a result of a statistical investigation. Has the study produced clear answers to the questions that motivated it? Have additional important questions emerged in the course of the study? The investigator at this stage has the task of summarizing and presenting the information gathered. This may involve point or interval estimates, tabular summaries, or graphical presentation of results. What is our best estimate of the number of students enrolled in business statistics courses, and can confidence bands be put around this estimate? Which are the most popular texts at present? What topics do instructors consider most important? Are there significant differences between the 2-year and 4-year college markets? At this stage, the task is to report the findings of the study and to decide how to proceed. It may be that the analysis will suggest the desirability of gathering further information.

It often happens that important unanticipated issues arise during the course of a survey, and the investigator is stimulated to further study of the population. It is for this reason that we have joined step 6 to step 1 with a dashed arrow in Figure 18.1. Suppose that our publisher asks an open-ended question, such as

Q. Our company is planning to bring to market a new business statistics text. Are there any features that you would particularly welcome in such a book?

Assume further that when the questionnaires are returned, an appreciable number mention the possibility of simultaneously marketing a large database containing data on real business problems. Students could get "hands-on" experience in course topics by analyzing these data. Before going to the expense of producing this software, the publisher might find it worthwhile to take another sample in order to assess the chances for success of this venture.

18.2 SAMPLING AND NONSAMPLING ERRORS

When a sample is taken from a population, we will not be able to know *precisely* the value of any population parameter, such as the mean or proportion. Any point estimate will inevitably be in error. We have already discussed one source of error, that resulting from the fact that information is available on only a subset of all the population members. We call this **sampling error.** Given certain assumptions, statistical theory allows us to characterize the nature of the sampling error and to make well-defined probabilistic statements about population parameters. Confidence intervals are examples of such statements. In subsequent sections of this chapter, we will discuss methods of statistical inference for various important sampling schemes. However, it is important to recognize first the potential for another source of error, which cannot be analyzed in such an elegant or clear-cut fashion.

In practical analyses, there is the possibility of an error unconnected with the kind of sampling procedure used. Indeed, such errors could just as well arise if a complete census of the population were taken. These are referred to as **nonsampling errors.** In any particular survey, the potential for nonsampling error exists at a number of places. Examples include the following:

1. *The population actually sampled is not the relevant one.* A celebrated instance of this sort occurred in 1936, when *Literary Digest* magazine confidently predicted that Alfred Landon would win the presidential election over Franklin Roosevelt. In the event, Roosevelt won by a very comfortable margin. This erroneous forecast resulted from the fact that the members of the *Digest's* sample had been taken from telephone directories and other listings, such as magazine subscription lists and automobile registrations. These sources considerably underrepresented the poor, who were predominantly Democrats. The moral of the story is that if one wants to make inference about a population (in this case, the U.S. electorate), it is important to sample that population and not some subgroup of it, however convenient the latter course might appear.

2. *Survey subjects may give inaccurate or dishonest answers.* This could happen because questions are phrased in a manner that is difficult to understand or in a way that appears to make a particular answer seem more palatable or more desirable. Also many questions that one might want to ask are so sensitive that it would be foolhardy to expect uniformly honest responses. Suppose, for example, that a plant manager wants to assess the annual losses to the company caused by employee thefts. In principle, a random sample of employees could be selected and sample members asked, "What have you stolen from this plant in the past 12 months?" This is clearly not the most reliable means of obtaining the required information! In fact, we have already seen one promising possibility for getting around this kind of problem. For a description and illustration of this procedure—*the randomized response approach*—refer to Examples 3.7 and 3.19.

3. *Another possibility arises through nonresponse.* If this is substantial, it can induce additional sampling and nonsampling errors. The sampling error arises because the achieved sample size will be smaller than that intended. Nonsampling error possibly occurs because, in effect, the population being sampled is not the population of interest. The results obtained can be regarded as a random sample *from the population that is willing to respond.* These people may differ in important ways from the larger population. If this is so, a bias will be induced in the resulting estimates.

If it is suspected that nonresponse bias is likely to be troublesome, three possibilities are open. First, the investigator can solicit information through a mechanism known to achieve a relatively high response rate. Second, as far as possible, characteristics of respondents and nonrespondents can be compared, in such matters as age, sex, and race, to see if there are obvious differences between the two groups. Finally, an attempt can be made to contact nonrespondents, some of whom may well be prepared to provide answers to a few key questions. If these differ significantly from the answers of the original respondents, a correction for nonresponse bias can then be made.

There is no general procedure for identifying and analyzing nonsampling errors. But they could be important. The main prescription is that the investigator take care in such matters as identifying the relevant population, designing the questionnaire, and dealing with nonresponse in order to minimize their significance. In the remainder of this chapter, it will be assumed that such care has been taken, and our discussion will center on the treatment of sampling errors.

1. Suppose that you want to conduct a study to determine the views of business majors on your campus as to whether statistics should be a required course. Discuss the steps that you would take in setting up this study, the problems you might expect to encounter, and techniques you might employ to overcome the problems.

2. A campus administrator is interested in the views of students living in dormitories on campus on various aspects of the services provided. You have been approached to carry out a survey. Suggest how you might proceed, following the six steps outlined in Section 18.1.

3. The manager of a campus clothing store is considering introducing some additional brand name items, and wants to assess possible student demand for them. You have been asked to design a survey to elicit this information. Discuss, in detail, how you would proceed.

4. A financial services corporation is considering the possibility of introducing three new types of mutual funds. It is believed that at least initially, most support for these is likely to come from its current customers. The corporation would like to assess the degree of interest these customers have in the proposed new products, preferably learning also relevant characteristics of those people likely to be most interested. You are commissioned to design a study, with a limited budget. How would you proceed?

5. Insurance company executives, aware of substantial increases in certain types of insurance premiums in the last few years, have become concerned about the public image of their industry and the possibility of political repercussions. It has been decided to mount a public relations campaign to educate the public about the reasons for the cost increases. However, there is considerable uncertainty both about the areas in which people have the strongest concerns and the extent to which the factors underlying the price increases for insurance policies are understood. Describe how you could set up a study to obtain relevant information. Follow the steps outlined in Section 18.1.

6. Refer to the study of Exercise 2.
   (a) Within the sampling framework you have designed, do you see the potential for nonsampling errors? If so, what steps would you take to minimize their magnitude?
   (b) Is nonresponse likely to be a serious issue in this study? If so, what might be done about it?

7. Refer to the study of Exercise 3.
   (a) Discuss likely sources of nonsampling errors, and indicate how these could be minimized.
   (b) Would you expect nonresponse to be a serious problem in carrying out this study? If so, how might the problem be alleviated?

8. For the study of Exercise 5, discuss the potential for nonsampling errors and nonresponse. Indicate how you would go about minimizing these problems.

9. One approach to nonresponse of a particular kind is the *recall method*. A survey of households is conducted by having interviewers call on a Thursday evening. Households where no one was home are called again the following Thursday evening. This process can be continued so that households that could not be reached at the first two attempts are recontacted on the next Thursday evening. What might be the value of information obtained in this fashion?

18.3   SIMPLE RANDOM SAMPLING

In the rest of this chapter, we will be interested in problems where a sample of n individuals or objects is to be drawn from a population containing a total of N members. In practical applications, many schemes have been employed for the selection of such samples. The bulk of our discussions will be concentrated on **probability sampling** methods—procedures where some mechanism involving *chance* is used to determine the sample members and the probability of any particular sample being drawn is known.

Definition

Suppose that it is required to select a sample of n objects from a population of N objects. A **simple random sampling** procedure is one in which every possible sample of n objects is equally likely to be chosen.

If a listing of the population members is available, the taking of a simple random sample is straightforward. Suppose that we number the population members from 1 through N. A simple random sample could be achieved by placing N numbered balls in a box, mixing thoroughly, and drawing out n of them. As we noted in Section 6.1, a table of **random numbers** can be used to attain the same objective more efficiently. Essentially, such tables reproduce the properties of drawing balls from boxes, with the proviso that a ball, once drawn, is replaced and could be redrawn. Some random numbers are listed in Table 4 of the Appendix.

Suppose that our population contains 1,000 individuals, numbered 1 through 1,000, and that a random sample of 100 population members is required. The procedure is to start at some arbitrary point in the table, say the top of the fifth column, and read off the last three digits of the random numbers. Thus, the first five are

$$319 \qquad 499 \qquad 166 \qquad 082 \qquad 420$$

The population members with these numbers are then the first five sample members. Continuing in this way, we obtain the rest of our sample, with 000 corresponding to population member 1,000. Any number drawn that has already been obtained is ignored, and the process continues until 100 different numbers have been obtained. This is known as **sampling without replacement.** (An alternative, **sampling with replacement,** which allows the possibility of an individual being included in the sample more than once, will not be discussed here.)

The reader may have guessed that the choice of a population of exactly 1,000 individuals helped make the exposition in the previous paragraph relatively straightforward. Unfortunately, in the real world, populations rarely come in powers of 10! For instance, suppose that we want to sample 100 schools from a list of 1,395 colleges in the United States. Obviously, now, it is necessary to go to four-digit random numbers. Beginning again at the top of the fifth column in the table, we obtain the first five entries:

$$1319 \qquad 4499 \qquad 3166 \qquad 3082 \qquad 5420$$

Notice that only one of these numbers lies between 1 and 1,395. In principle, we could continue drawing until 100 different numbers in this range had been found, discarding all the others. However, this would be a rather time-consuming chore. It can be speeded up by noticing that only numbers up to 13 in the first two digits are of any use to us. Suppose, then, that we adopt the following strategy for the first two digits:

Replace 00, 14, 28, . . . , 84 by 00

Replace 01, 15, 29, . . . , 85 by 01

.   .
.   .
.   .

Replace 13, 27, 41, . . . , 97 by 13

Numbers beginning 98 or 99 will still be ignored. Thus, the five entries given previously become

$$1319 \qquad 0299 \qquad 0366 \qquad 0882 \qquad 1220$$

Continuing in this way, we can complete our sample.

An even quicker procedure is possible if the population list is arranged in some fashion unconnected with the subject of interest. Then, if we want our sample to include, say, one-tenth of the population members, we simply take every tenth name on the list. This is known as **systematic sampling** and is quite commonly used. A systematic sample is analyzed in the same fashion as a simple random sample on the grounds that, relative to the subject of inquiry, the population listing is already in random order. The danger is that there could be some subtle, unsuspected link between the ordering of the population and the subject under study. If this were so, bias would be induced if systematic sampling were employed.

ANALYSIS OF RESULTS FROM SIMPLE RANDOM SAMPLING

We turn now to the analysis of the sample results. We will concentrate on estimating the population mean, total, and proportion. It will be assumed that the sample is sufficiently large that recourse to the central limit theorem is appropriate.

Suppose that the population contains N members and that a simple random sample of size n is taken. We denote by μ the unknown population mean and by x_1, x_2, . . . , x_n the actual observed sample values. Results for the estimation of the population mean are given in the box.

Estimation of the Population Mean

Let $x_1, x_2, \ldots, x_n$ denote the values observed from a simple random sample of size n, taken from a population of N members with mean μ.

(i) The sample mean is an unbiased estimator of the population mean, μ. The point estimate is

$$\bar{x} = \frac{1}{n} \sum_{i=1}^{n} x_i$$

(ii) An unbiased estimation procedure for the variance of the sample mean yields the point estimate

$$\hat{\sigma}_{\bar{x}}^2 = \frac{s^2}{n} \cdot \frac{N-n}{N}$$

---

where

$$s^2 = \frac{1}{n-1} \sum_{i=1}^{n} (x_i - \bar{x})^2$$

is the sample variance.

(iii) Provided the sample size is large, $100(1-\alpha)\%$ confidence intervals for the population mean are given by

$$\bar{x} - z_{\alpha/2}\hat{\sigma}_{\bar{x}} < \mu < \bar{x} + z_{\alpha/2}\hat{\sigma}_{\bar{x}}$$

where $z_{\alpha/2}$ is the number for which

$$P(Z > z_{\alpha/2}) = \frac{\alpha}{2}$$

and the random variable Z follows a standard normal distribution.

Notice that we use the **finite population correction factor** $(N-n)/N$. This factor is similar to one introduced in Section 6.2 and allows us to deal with cases where the number of sample members is not a negligible proportion of the number of population members.[1]

EXAMPLE 18.1

In a particular city, 1,118 mortgages were taken out last year. A random sample of sixty of these had mean amount \$87,300 and standard deviation \$19,200. Estimate the mean amount of all mortgages taken out in this city last year, and find a 95% confidence interval.

Denote the population mean by μ. We have

$$N = 1{,}118 \qquad n = 60 \qquad \bar{x} = 87{,}300 \qquad s = 19{,}200$$

The usual point estimate for the population mean is

$$\bar{x} = 87{,}300$$

To obtain interval estimates, we first find

$$\hat{\sigma}_{\bar{x}}^2 = \frac{s^2}{n} \cdot \frac{N-n}{N} = \frac{(19{,}200)^2}{60} \cdot \frac{1{,}058}{1{,}118} = 5{,}814{,}268$$

By taking the square root, we obtain the estimated standard error

$$\hat{\sigma}_{\bar{x}} = 2{,}411$$

For a 95% confidence interval, from Table 3 of the Appendix, we find

$$z_{\alpha/2} = z_{.025} = 1.96$$

Hence, the 95% confidence interval for the mean amount of all mortgages taken out in this city last year is

---

[1] We saw in Section 6.2 that when sampling from a finite population, the variance of the sample mean is $(\sigma^2/n)[(N-n)/(N-1)]$, where σ^2 is the population variance. It can further be shown, for a finite population that the expected value of the sample variance is $N\sigma^2/(N-1)$. Hence, when the sample variance is used to estimate the population variance, the appropriate finite population correction factor is $(N-n)/N$.

$$87{,}300 - (1.96)(2{,}411) < \mu < 87{,}300 + (1.96)(2{,}411)$$

or

$$82{,}574 < \mu < 92{,}026$$

That is, the interval runs from \$82,574 to \$92,026.

Frequently, interest centers on the population total rather than the mean. For example, the publisher of a business statistics text will want an estimate of the total number of students taking business statistics courses in all U.S. colleges. Inference about the population total is straightforward, the relevant results following from the fact that, in our notation

$$\text{Population total} = N\mu$$

Estimation of the Population Total

Suppose that we have a simple random sample of size n from a population of size N and that the quantity to be estimated is the population total, $N\mu$.

(i) An unbiased estimation procedure for the population total, $N\mu$, yields the point estimate $N\bar{x}$.

(ii) An unbiased estimation procedure for the variance of our estimator of the population total yields the point estimate

$$N^2\hat{\sigma}_{\bar{x}}^2 = \frac{s^2}{n} N(N - n)$$

(iii) Provided the sample size is large, $100(1 - a)\%$ confidence intervals for the population total are obtained from

$$N\bar{x} - z_{\alpha/2}N\hat{\sigma}_{\bar{x}} < N\mu < N\bar{x} + z_{\alpha/2}N\hat{\sigma}_{\bar{x}}$$

EXAMPLE 18.2

From a simple random sample of 400 of the 1,395 colleges in the United States, it was found that the sample mean enrollment during the past year in business statistics courses was 320.8 students, and the sample standard deviation was found to be 149.7 students. Estimate the total number of students enrolled in business statistics courses in the year, and find a 99% confidence interval.

If the population mean is μ, we must estimate $N\mu$, given

$$N = 1{,}395 \qquad n = 400 \qquad \bar{x} = 320.8 \qquad s = 149.7$$

Our point estimate for the total is

$$N\bar{x} = (1{,}395)(320.8) = 447{,}516$$

That is, we estimate a total of 447,516 students in business statistics courses. To obtain interval estimates, we need

$$N^2 \hat{\sigma}_{\bar{x}}^2 = \frac{s^2}{n} N(N-n) = \frac{(149.7)^2}{400} (1{,}395)(995) = 77{,}764{,}413$$

Taking the square root yields

$$N\hat{\sigma}_{\bar{x}} = 8{,}818.4$$

For a 99% confidence interval, from Table 3 of the Appendix, we find

$$z_{\alpha/2} = z_{.005} = 2.575$$

Hence, the 99% confidence interval for the population total is

$$447{,}516 - (2.575)(8{,}818.4) < N\mu < 447{,}516 + (2.575)(8{,}818.4)$$

or

$$424{,}809 < N\mu < 470{,}223$$

Thus, our interval runs from 424,809 to 470,223 students.

Finally, we consider the case where it is required to estimate the proportion, p, of individuals in the population possessing some specific characteristic. Inference about this proportion should be based on the hypergeometric distribution of Section 4.6 when the number of sample members is not very small compared to the number of population members. However, we will again assume that the sample size is large enough to allow the central limit theorem to be invoked. The main results are given in the box.

Estimation of the Population Proportion

Let $\hat{p}$ be the proportion possessing a particular characteristic in a random sample of n observations from a population, a proportion p of whose members possess that characteristic.

(i) The sample proportion is an unbiased estimator of the population proportion, p.

(ii) An unbiased estimation procedure for the variance of our estimator of the population proportion yields the point estimate

$$\hat{\sigma}_{\hat{p}}^2 = \frac{\hat{p}(1-\hat{p})}{n-1} \cdot \frac{N-n}{N}$$

(iii) Provided the sample size is large, $100(1-\alpha)\%$ confidence intervals for the population proportion are given by

$$\hat{p} - z_{\alpha/2}\hat{\sigma}_{\hat{p}} < p < \hat{p} + z_{\alpha/2}\hat{\sigma}_{\hat{p}}$$

EXAMPLE 18.3

From a simple random sample of 400 of the 1,395 colleges in the United States, it was found that business statistics was a two-semester course in 141 of the sampled colleges. Estimate the proportion of all colleges for which the course is two semesters long, and find a 90% confidence interval.

We want to estimate the population proportion, p, given

$$N = 1{,}395 \qquad n = 400 \qquad \hat{p} = \frac{141}{400} = .3525$$

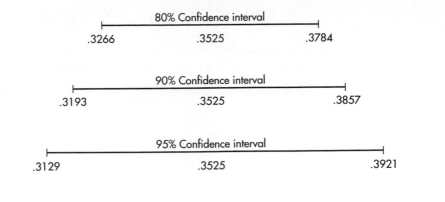

FIGURE 18.2   80%, 90%, 95%, and 99% confidence intervals for population proportion of all colleges in which business statistics is a two-semester course, based on the data of Example 18.3

Our point estimate of p is simply $\hat{p} = .3525$. That is, we estimate that the course is two semesters long in 35.25% of all colleges. To calculate interval estimates, we need

$$\hat{\sigma}_{\hat{p}}^2 = \frac{\hat{p}(1 - \hat{p})}{n - 1} \cdot \frac{N - n}{N} = \frac{(.3525)(.6475)}{399} \cdot \frac{995}{1,395} = .0004079$$

so

$$\hat{\sigma}_{\hat{p}} = .0202$$

For a 90% confidence interval, from Table 3 of the Appendix, we find

$$z_{\alpha/2} = z_{.05} = 1.645$$

The 90% interval is therefore

$$.3525 - (1.645)(.0202) < p < .3525 + (1.645)(.0202)$$

or

$$.3193 < p < .3857$$

Thus, the 90% confidence interval for the percentage of all colleges in which business statistics is a two-semester course runs from 31.93% to 38.57%. Figure 18.2 shows also the 80%, 95%, and 99% confidence intervals for the population proportion, based on these data. Notice that, as always, the greater the probability content, the wider is the confidence interval.

EXERCISES

10. Consult today's *Wall Street Journal* to obtain a list of all stocks traded on the New York Stock Exchange. Using the random numbers of Table 4 of the Appendix, draw a simple random sample of twenty of these stocks. For your sample, find the mean percentage increase in price over the past week.

11. Obtain from your local newspaper a list of all houses advertised for sale in your city. Using the random numbers in Table 4 of the Appendix, draw a simple random sample of fifteen advertisements, and find the sample mean of the advertised prices.

12. A campus has 12,723 students. From a complete list of these students you want to draw a random sample of 100. Explain how you would use a table of random numbers to do this.

13. Take a random sample of fifty pages from this book and estimate the proportion of all pages that contain Figures.

14. A firm employs 189 junior accountants. In a random sample of fifty of these, the mean number of hours overtime billed in a particular week was 9.7, and the sample standard deviation was 6.2 hours. Find a 95% confidence interval for the mean number of hours overtime billed per junior accountant in this firm that week.

15. An auditor, examining a total of 820 accounts receivable of a corporation, took a random sample of sixty of them. The sample mean was $127.43, and the sample standard deviation was $43.27.

   (a) Using an unbiased estimation procedure, find an estimate of the population mean.

   (b) Using an unbiased estimation procedure, find an estimate of the variance of the sample mean.

   (c) Find a 90% confidence interval for the population mean.

   (d) A statistician found, for the population mean, a confidence interval running from $117.43 to $137.43. What is the probability content of this interval?

16. On a particular day, a consumer advice bureau received 125 calls. For a random sample of forty of these calls, it was found that mean time taken in providing the requested advice was 7.28 minutes, and the sample standard deviation was 5.32 minutes. Find a 99% confidence interval for the mean time taken per call.

17. State whether each of the following statements is true or false:

   (a) For a given number of population members and a given sample variance, the larger the number of sample members, the wider is a 95% confidence interval for the population mean.

   (b) For a given number of population members and a given number of sample members, the larger the sample variance, the wider is a 95% confidence interval for the population mean.

   (c) For a given number of sample members and a given sample variance, the larger the number of population members, the wider is a 95% confidence interval for the population mean. Justify your answer.

   (d) For a given number of population members, a given number of sample members, and a given sample variance, a 95% confidence interval for the population mean is wider than a 90% confidence interval for the population mean.

18. Show that our estimate of the variance of the sample mean can be written

$$\hat{\sigma}_{\bar{x}}^2 = s^2 \left(\frac{1}{n} - \frac{1}{N} \right)$$

When $n = N$, it follows that $\hat{\sigma}_{\bar{x}}^2 = 0$. Explain why such a conclusion is to be expected.

19. Using the data of Exercise 14, find a 99% confidence interval for the total number of hours overtime billed by junior accountants in the firm during the week of interest.

20. Using the data of Exercise 15, find a 95% confidence interval for the total amount of these 820 accounts receivable.

21. Using the data of Exercise 16, find a 90% confidence interval for the total amount of time taken in answering these 125 calls.

22. A senior manager, responsible for a group of 120 junior executives, is interested in the total amount of time per week spent by these people in internal meetings. A random sample

of thirty-five of these executives was asked to keep diary records during the next week. When the results were analyzed, it was found that these sample members spent a total of 143 hours in internal meetings. The sample standard deviation was 3.1 hours. Find a 90% confidence interval for the total number of hours spent in internal meetings by all 120 junior executives in the week.

23. A simple random sample of 400 from a total 1,395 colleges in the United States contained 39 colleges that use the text *Statistics Made Difficult and Boring* by J. T. Ripper. Find a 95% confidence interval for the proportion of all colleges using Ripper's text.

24. A business school dean is contemplating a change in the requirements for graduation. At present, business majors are required to take one science course, chosen from a list of possible courses. The proposal is that this be replaced by the requirement that a course in ecology be taken. The business school has 420 students. Of a random sample of 100 of them, fifty-six expressed opposition to this proposal. Find a 90% confidence interval for the proportion of all the school's students opposed to the proposed change in requirements.

25. In a college dormitory, 257 of the residents are freshmen. Of a random sample of 120 of them, thirty-seven indicated strong interest in living in the dormitory next year. Find a 95% confidence interval for the proportion of freshmen in this dormitory with a strong interest in living there next year.

26. A class has 420 students. The final examination is optional—taking it can raise, but not lower, a student's grade. Of a random sample of eighty students, thirty-one indicated that they would take the final examination. Find a 90% confidence interval for the total number of students in this class intending to take the final examination.

18.4   STRATIFIED SAMPLING

Suppose that you decide to investigate the views of students on your campus on the issue of a university's holding shares in corporations that operate in South Africa. This is a sensitive topic, and the framing of appropriately worded questions could be difficult. It is likely that you would want to ask several questions of every sample member and so, given limited resources, would be able to take only a fairly small sample. You would presumably select a simple random sample of, say, 100 students from a list of all students on campus. Suppose, however, that on closer inspection of the records of the sample members, you find that only two of them are business majors, though the population proportion of business majors is far higher than this. Your problem at this stage is twofold. First, you may well be interested in comparing the views of business majors with those of the rest of the student population. This is hardly feasible given their minimal representation in your sample. Second, you may suspect that the views of business majors on this question will differ from those of their fellow students. If that is the case, you would worry about the reliability of inference based on a sample in which this group is seriously underrepresented.

This second point is one on which, up to this stage, we have provided no guidance. You could perhaps console yourself with the thought that since you have taken a random sample, any estimators derived in the usual way will be unbiased, and the resulting inference, in the statistical sense, will be strictly valid. However, a little reflection should convince you that this is scant consolation indeed! All that unbiasedness promises is that if the sampling procedure is repeated a very large number of times and the estimator calculated, its average will be equal to the corresponding population value. But, in fact, you are *not* going to repeat the sampling procedure a large number of times. You have to base your conclusions on *just a single sample*, and the fact that business majors could have been overrepresented in other samples you might have drawn, so that things "average out" in the long run, is not terribly useful.

There is a second tempting possibility, one that is in many ways preferable to proceeding with the original sample. You could simply curse your luck, discard the original sample, and take another. If the constitution of the sample achieved at the second attempt looks more representative of the population at large, you may well be better off to proceed with it. The difficulty now is that the sampling procedure you have adopted—the population is to be sampled until you achieve a sample you like the looks of—is very difficult to formalize, and consequently, the sample results are very hard to analyze with any statistical validity. This is no longer simple random sampling, and the procedures of Section 18.3 are therefore not strictly valid.

Fortunately, a third alternative sampling scheme exists to afford protection against just this type of problem. If it is suspected at the outset that particular identifiable characteristics of population members are germane to the subject of inquiry, or if particular subgroups of the population are of special interest to the investigator, it is not necessary (and probably not desirable) to be content with simple random sampling as a means of selecting the sample members. Instead the population can be broken down into subgroups, or **strata,** and a simple random sample taken from each stratum. The only requirement is that each individual member of the population be identifiable as belonging to one, and only one, of the strata.

Stratified Random Sampling

Suppose that a population of N individuals can be subdivided into K mutually exclusive and collectively exhaustive groups, or **strata. Stratified random sampling** is the selection of independent simple random samples from each stratum of the population.

If the K strata in the population contain $N_1, N_2, \ldots, N_K$ members, then

$$N_1 + N_2 + \cdots + N_K = N$$

There is no need to take the same number of sample members from every stratum. Denote the numbers in the sample by $n_1, n_2, \ldots, n_K$. Then the total number of sample members is

$$n = n_1 + n_2 + \cdots + n_K$$

The population of students whose views are to be canvassed on the subject of investment in South Africa could be divided into two strata—business majors and nonbusiness majors. Less straightforward stratification is also possible. Suppose that on some other topic, you believe that a student's gender and class year (senior, junior, sophomore, or freshman) are both potentially relevant. In that case, to satisfy the requirement that the strata be mutually exclusive and collectively exhaustive, eight strata—senior women, senior men, and so on—are needed.

We will discuss later in this section the question of how to allocate the sampling effort among the strata. Here we note that an attractive possibility, often employed in practice, is *proportional allocation:* The proportion of sample members from any stratum is the same as the proportion of population members in that stratum.

The analysis of the results of a stratified random sample is relatively straightforward. We will denote by $\mu_1, \mu_2, \ldots, \mu_K$ the population means in the K strata and by $\bar{x}_1, \bar{x}_2, \ldots, \bar{x}_K$ the corresponding sample means. Consider a particular stratum, say the jth. Then, since a simple random sample has been taken in this stratum, the stratum sample mean is an unbiased estimator of the population mean μ_j. Also, from an unbiased estimation procedure for the variance of the stratum sample mean, we have the point estimate

$$\hat{\sigma}_{\bar{x}j}^{2} = \frac{s_j^{2}}{n_j} \cdot \frac{N_j - n_j}{N_j}$$

where s_j^{2} is the sample variance in the jth stratum. Inference about individual strata can therefore be made in the same way as in Section 18.3.

Generally, we also want to make inferences about the overall population mean, μ, which is

$$\mu = \frac{N_1\mu_1 + N_2\mu_2 + \cdots + N_K\mu_K}{N} = \frac{1}{N} \sum_{j=1}^{K} N_j\mu_j$$

A natural point estimate is provided by

$$\bar{x}_{\text{st}} = \frac{1}{N} \sum_{j=1}^{K} N_j\bar{x}_j$$

An unbiased estimator of the variance of the estimator of μ follows from the fact that the samples in each stratum are independent of one another, and the point estimate is given by

$$\hat{\sigma}_{\bar{x}_{\text{st}}}^{2} = \frac{1}{N^2} \sum_{j=1}^{K} N_j^{2}\hat{\sigma}_{\bar{x}j}^{2}$$

Inferences about the overall population mean can be based on these results, as summarized in the box.

Estimation of the Population Mean from a Stratified Random Sample

Suppose that random samples of n_j individuals are taken from strata containing N_j individuals ($j = 1, 2, \ldots, K$). Let

$$\sum_{j=1}^{K} N_j = N \qquad \text{and} \qquad \sum_{j=1}^{K} n_j = n$$

Denote the sample means and variances in the strata by $\bar{x}_j$ and $s_j^{2}(j = 1, 2, \ldots, K)$, and the overall population mean by μ.

(i) An unbiased estimation procedure for the overall population mean μ yields the point estimate

$$\bar{x}_{\text{st}} = \frac{1}{N} \sum_{j=1}^{K} N_j\bar{x}_j$$

(ii) An unbiased estimation procedure for the variance of our estimator of the overall population mean yields the point estimate

---

$$\hat{\sigma}_{\bar{x}_{st}}^2 = \frac{1}{N^2} \sum_{j=1}^{K} N_j^2 \hat{\sigma}_{\bar{x}_j}^2$$

where

$$\hat{\sigma}_{\bar{x}_j}^2 = \frac{s_j^2}{n_j} \cdot \frac{N_j - n_j}{N_j}$$

(iii) Provided the sample size is large, $100(1 - \alpha)\%$ confidence intervals for the population mean are obtained from

$$\bar{x}_{st} - z_{\alpha/2}\hat{\sigma}_{\bar{x}_{st}} < \mu < \bar{x}_{st} + z_{\alpha/2}\hat{\sigma}_{\bar{x}_{st}}$$

EXAMPLE 18.4

A restaurant chain has sixty restaurants in Illinois, fifty in Indiana, and forty-five in Ohio. Management is considering adding a new item to the menus. To test the likely demand for this item, it was introduced on the menus of random samples of twelve restaurants in Illinois, ten in Indiana, and nine in Ohio. (This is an example of proportional allocation—20% of population members are included in the sample for each stratum.) Using the subscripts 1, 2, and 3 to denote Illinois, Indiana, and Ohio, respectively, the sample means and standard deviations for numbers of orders received for this item per restaurant in the three states in a week were

$$\bar{x}_1 = 21.2 \qquad s_1 = 12.8$$
$$\bar{x}_2 = 13.3 \qquad s_2 = 11.4$$
$$\bar{x}_3 = 26.1 \qquad s_3 = 9.2$$

Estimate the mean number of weekly orders per restaurant, μ, for all restaurants in this chain.

In our notation, we have

$$N_1 = 60 \qquad N_2 = 50 \qquad N_3 = 45 \qquad N = 155$$
$$n_1 = 12 \qquad n_2 = 10 \qquad n_3 = 9 \qquad n = 31$$

Our estimate of the population mean is

$$\bar{x}_{st} = \frac{1}{N} \sum_{j=1}^{K} N_j \bar{x}_j = \frac{(60)(21.2) + (50)(13.3) + (45)(26.1)}{155} = 20.1$$

Thus, the estimated mean number of weekly orders per restaurant is 20.1.

The next step is to calculate the quantities

$$\hat{\sigma}_{\bar{x}_1}^2 = \frac{s_1^2}{n_1} \cdot \frac{N_1 - n_1}{N_1} = \frac{(12.8)^2}{12} \cdot \frac{48}{60} = 10.923$$

$$\hat{\sigma}_{\bar{x}_2}^2 = \frac{s_2^2}{n_2} \cdot \frac{N_2 - n_2}{N_2} = \frac{(11.4)^2}{10} \cdot \frac{40}{50} = 10.397$$

$$\hat{\sigma}_{\bar{x}_3}^2 = \frac{s_3^2}{n_3} \cdot \frac{N_3 - n_3}{N_3} = \frac{(9.2)^2}{9} \cdot \frac{36}{45} = 7.524$$

Together with the individual stratum sample means, these quantities can be used to compute confidence intervals for the population means of the three strata, exactly as in Example 18.1 (although in this case the sample sizes are too small for comfort). Here, however, we concentrate on the overall population mean. To obtain confidence intervals for this quantity, we need

$$\hat{\sigma}_{\bar{x}_{st}}^2 = \frac{1}{N^2} \sum_{j=1}^{K} N_j^2 \hat{\sigma}_{\bar{x}j}$$

$$= \frac{(60)^2(10.923) + (50)^2(10.397) + (45)^2(7.524)}{(155)^2} = 3.353$$

and, on taking the square root

$$\hat{\sigma}_{\bar{x}_{st}} = 1.83$$

For a 95% confidence interval for the population mean, from Table 3 of the Appendix, we get

$$z_{\alpha/2} = z_{.025} = 1.96$$

Thus, the 95% confidence interval for the mean number of orders per restaurant received in a week is

$$20.1 - (1.96)(1.83) < \mu < 20.1 + (1.96)(1.83)$$

or

$$16.5 < \mu < 23.7$$

The 95% confidence interval runs from 16.5 to 23.7 orders per restaurant. Figure 18.3 shows also 90% and 99% confidence intervals for the mean number of weekly orders per restaurant.

Since the population total is the product of the population mean and the number of population members, these procedures can readily be modified to allow its estimation, as described in the box.

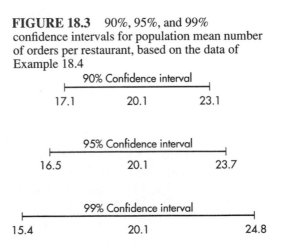

FIGURE 18.3 90%, 95%, and 99% confidence intervals for population mean number of orders per restaurant, based on the data of Example 18.4

Estimation of the Population Total from a Stratified Random Sample

Suppose that we have random samples of n_j individuals from strata containing N_j individuals ($j = 1, 2, \ldots, K$) and that the quantity to be estimated is the population total, $N\mu$.

(i) An unbiased estimation procedure for $N\mu$ leads to the point estimate

$$N\bar{x}_{st} = \sum_{j=1}^{K} N_j \bar{x}_j$$

(ii) An unbiased estimation procedure for the variance of our estimator of the population total yields the estimate

$$N^2 \hat{\sigma}_{\bar{x}_{st}}^2 = \sum_{j=1}^{K} N_j^2 \hat{\sigma}_{\bar{x}_j}^2$$

(iii) Provided the sample size is large, $100(1 - \alpha)\%$ confidence intervals for the population total are obtained from

$$N\bar{x}_{st} - z_{\alpha/2} N\hat{\sigma}_{\bar{x}_{st}} < N\mu < N\bar{x}_{st} + z_{\alpha/2} N\hat{\sigma}_{\bar{x}_{st}}$$

EXAMPLE 18.5

Of the 1,395 colleges in the United States, 364 have 2-year programs and 1,031 are 4-year schools. A simple random sample of forty 2-year schools and an independent simple random sample of sixty 4-year schools were taken. The sample means and standard deviations of numbers of students enrolled in the past year in business statistics courses are given in the table. Estimate the total annual enrollment in business statistics courses.

	2-YEAR SCHOOLS	4-YEAR SCHOOLS
Mean	154.3	411.8
Standard deviation	87.3	219.9

In our notation, we have

$$N_1 = 364 \qquad n_1 = 40 \qquad \bar{x}_1 = 154.3 \qquad s_1 = 87.3$$
$$N_2 = 1{,}031 \qquad n_2 = 60 \qquad \bar{x}_2 = 411.8 \qquad s_2 = 219.9$$

Our estimate of the population total is

$$N\bar{x}_{st} = \sum_{j=1}^{K} N_j \bar{x}_j = (364)(154.3) + (1{,}031)(411.8) = 480{,}731$$

Thus, the estimated total number of students in business statistics courses is 480,731.
Next, we require the quantities

$$\hat{\sigma}_{\bar{x}1}^2 = \frac{s_1^2}{n_1} \cdot \frac{N_1 - n_1}{N_1} = \frac{(87.3)^2}{40} \cdot \frac{324}{364} = 169.59$$

$$\hat{\sigma}_{\bar{x}2}^2 = \frac{s_2^2}{n_2} \cdot \frac{N_2 - n_2}{N_2} = \frac{(219.9)^2}{60} \cdot \frac{971}{1,031} = 759.03$$

Finally

$$N^2\hat{\sigma}_{\bar{x}_{st}}^2 = \sum_{j=1}^{K} N_j^2 \hat{\sigma}_{\bar{x}j}^2 = (364)^2(169.59) + (1,031)^2(759.03) = 829,289,284$$

and, on taking the square root, we obtain

$$N\hat{\sigma}_{\bar{x}_{st}} = 28,797$$

For a 99% confidence interval, from Table 3 of the Appendix, we get

$$z_{\alpha/2} = z_{.005} = 2.575$$

The required 99% interval is therefore

$$480,731 - (2.575)(28,797) < N\mu < 480,731 + (2.575)(28,797)$$

or

$$406,579 < N\mu < 554,883$$

Thus, our 99% confidence interval runs from 406,579 to 554,883 students enrolled.

Next, we consider the problem of estimating a population proportion based on a stratified random sample. Let $p_1, p_2, \ldots, p_K$ be the population proportions in the K strata and $\hat{p}_1, \hat{p}_2, \ldots, \hat{p}_K$ the corresponding sample proportions. If p denotes the overall population proportion, its estimation is based on the fact that

$$p = \frac{N_1 p_1 + N_2 p_2 + \cdots + N_K p_K}{N} = \frac{1}{N} \sum_{j=1}^{K} N_j p_j$$

The procedures are described in the box.

Estimation of the Population Proportion from a Stratified Random Sample

Suppose that we have random samples of n_j individuals from strata containing N_j individuals ($j = 1, 2, \ldots, K$). Let p_j be the population proportion and $\hat{p}_j$ the sample proportion, in the jth stratum, of those possessing a particular characteristic. If p is the overall population proportion:

(i) An unbiased estimation procedure for p yields

$$\hat{p}_{st} = \frac{1}{N} \sum_{j=1}^{K} N_j \hat{p}_j$$

(ii) An unbiased estimation procedure for the variance of our estimator of the overall population proportion yields

$$\hat{\sigma}_{\hat{p}_{st}}^2 = \frac{1}{N^2} \sum_{j=1}^{K} N_j^2 \hat{\sigma}_{\hat{p}j}^2$$

where

$$\hat{\sigma}_{\hat{p}j}^2 = \frac{\hat{p}_j(1 - \hat{p}_j)}{n_j - 1} \cdot \frac{N_j - n_j}{N_j}$$

---

is the estimate of the variance of the sample proportion in the jth stratum.

(iii) Provided the sample size is large, $100(1 - \alpha)\%$ confidence intervals for the population proportion are obtained from

$$\hat{p}_{st} - z_{\alpha/2}\hat{\sigma}_{\hat{p}_{st}} < p < \hat{p}_{st} + z_{\alpha/2}\hat{\sigma}_{\hat{p}_{st}}$$

EXAMPLE 18.6

In the study of Example 18.5, it was found that business statistics was taught by members of the economics department in seven of the 2-year colleges and thirteen of the 4-year colleges in the sample. Estimate the proportion of all colleges in which this course is taught in the economics department.

We have

$$N_1 = 364 \qquad n_1 = 40 \qquad \hat{p}_1 = \frac{7}{40} = .175$$

$$N_2 = 1,031 \qquad n_2 = 60 \qquad \hat{p}_2 = \frac{13}{60} = .217$$

Our estimate of the population proportion is

$$\hat{p}_{st} = \frac{1}{N} \sum_{j=1}^{K} N_j \hat{p}_j = \frac{(364)(.175) + (1,031)(.217)}{1,395} = .206$$

Thus, it is estimated that in 20.6% of all colleges, the course is taught by the economics department.

Next we need the quantities

$$\hat{\sigma}_{\hat{p}_1}^2 = \frac{\hat{p}_1(1 - \hat{p}_1)}{n_1 - 1} \cdot \frac{N_1 - n_1}{N_1} = \frac{(.175)(.825)}{39} \cdot \frac{324}{364} = .003295$$

$$\hat{\sigma}_{\hat{p}_2}^2 = \frac{\hat{p}_2(1 - \hat{p}_2)}{n_2 - 1} \cdot \frac{N_2 - n_2}{N_2} = \frac{(.217)(.783)}{59} \cdot \frac{971}{1,031} = .002712$$

Together with the individual stratum sample proportions, these values can be used to calculate confidence intervals for the two stratum population proportions, exactly as in Example 18.3. Here, we will focus on interval estimation for the overall population proportion, for which we require

$$\hat{\sigma}_{\hat{p}_{st}}^2 = \frac{1}{N^2} \sum_{j=1}^{K} N_j^2 \hat{\sigma}_{\hat{p}_j}^2 = \frac{(364)^2(.003295) + (1,031)^2(.002712)}{(1,395)^2} = .001706$$

so taking the square root yields

$$\hat{\sigma}_{\hat{p}_{st}} = .0413$$

For a 90% confidence interval, from Table 3 of the Appendix, we find

$$z_{\alpha/2} = z_{.05} = 1.645$$

The 90% confidence interval for the population proportion is then

$$.206 - (1.645)(.0413) < p < .206 + (1.645)(.0413)$$

or

$$.138 < p < .274$$

Thus, our interval runs from 13.8% to 27.4% of all colleges.

ALLOCATION OF SAMPLE EFFORT AMONG STRATA

The question of the allocation of the sample effort among the various strata remains to be discussed. Assuming that a total of n sample members is to be selected, how many of these sample observations should be allocated to each stratum? In fact, the survey in question may have multiple objectives, meaning that no clear-cut answer is available. Nevertheless, it is possible to specify criteria for choice that the investigator might keep in mind:

1. If little or nothing is known beforehand about the population and if there are no strong requirements for the production of information about sparsely populated individual strata, a natural choice is **proportional allocation.** Here, the proportion of sample members in any stratum is the same as the proportion of population members in that stratum. Thus, for the jth stratum, we have

$$\frac{n_j}{n} = \frac{N_j}{N}$$

so that

$$n_j = \frac{N_j}{N} \cdot n$$

This intuitively reasonable allocation mechanism is frequently employed and generally provides a satisfactory analysis.

2. Sometimes strict adherence to proportional allocation will produce relatively few observations in strata in which the investigator is particularly interested. In that case, inference about the population parameters of these particular strata could be quite imprecise. In these circumstances, one might prefer to allocate more observations to such strata than is dictated by proportional allocation. In Examples 18.5 and 18.6, 364 of the 1,395 colleges are 2-year schools, and a sample of 100 observations is to be taken. If proportional allocation had been used, the number of 2-year schools in the sample would have been

$$n_1 = \frac{N_1}{N} \cdot n = \frac{364}{1,395} \cdot 100 = 26$$

Since the publisher was particularly interested in acquiring information about this market, it was thought that a sample of only twenty-six observations would be inadequate. For this reason, forty of the 100 sample observations were allocated to this stratum.

3. If the sole objective of a survey is to estimate as precisely as possible an overall population parameter, such as the mean, total, or proportion, and if enough is known about the population, it is possible to derive an **optimal allocation.** If it is required to estimate an overall population mean or total and if the population variances in the individual strata are denoted σ_j^2 it can be shown that the most precise estimators are obtained when

$$n_j = \frac{N_j\sigma_j}{\sum\limits_{i=1}^{K}N_i\sigma_i} \cdot n \qquad (18.4.1)$$

This formula is intuitively plausible. Compared with proportional allocation, it allocates relatively more sample effort to strata in which the population variance is highest. That is to say, a larger sample size is required where the greater population variability exists. Thus, in Example 18.4, where in fact proportional allocation was used, if the differences observed in the sample standard deviations correctly reflect differences in the population quantities, it would have been preferable to have taken fewer observations in the third stratum and more in the first.

An immediate objection arises to the use of formula (18.4.1). It requires knowledge of the population standard deviations, σ_j, whereas very often one will not even have worthwhile estimates of these values before the sample is taken. We will return to this point in the final section of the chapter.

For estimating the overall population proportion, estimators with the smallest possible variance are obtained by choosing sample sizes.

$$n_j = \frac{N_j\sqrt{p_j(1 - p_j)}}{\sum\limits_{i=1}^{K} N_i\sqrt{p_i(1 - p_i)}} \cdot n \qquad (18.4.2)$$

Compared with the proportional allocation, this formula allocates more sample observations to strata in which the true population proportions are closest to .5, for if a proportion is close to 0 or 1, this can be learned with a fair amount of assurance from a relatively small sample. The difficulty in using formula (18.4.2) is that it involves the unknown proportions p_j—the very quantities that the survey is designed to estimate. Nevertheless, sometimes prior knowledge about the population can provide at least a rough ideas as to which strata have proportions closest to .5. In Example 18.6, the sample proportions suggest that the number of 2-year colleges in the sample should have been less than the number resulting from proportional allocation. The same conclusion also holds for this study when one compares the sample standard deviations of Example 18.5 with formula (18.4.1). In spite of this, it was decided that *more*, rather than fewer, 2-year colleges should be included in the sample. The reason for this decision was that in this particular study, the publisher was eager to obtain reliable information about both the 2-year and 4-year college markets.

This illustration serves as an example of an important point. Although the division of sample effort suggested by formulas (18.4.1) and (18.4.2) is often referred to as the *optimum allocation*, it is optimal only with regard to the narrow criterion of efficient estimation of overall population parameters. Frequently, surveys have broader objectives than this, in which case it may well be reasonable to depart from the optimum allocation.

EXERCISES

27. A small town contains a total of 1,800 households. The town is divided into three districts, containing 820, 540, and 440 households, respectively. A stratified random sample of 300 households contains 120, ninety, and ninety households, respectively, from these districts. Sample members were asked to estimate their total energy bills for the winter months. The respective sample means were $290, $352, and $427, and the respective sample standard deviations were $47, $61, and $93.

    (a) Use an unbiased estimation procedure to estimate the mean winter energy bill for all households in this town.

    (b) Use an unbiased estimation procedure to find an estimate of the variance of the estimator of part (a).

    (c) Find a 95% confidence interval for the population mean winter energy bill for households in this town.

28. A college has 152 assistant professors, 127 associate professors, and 208 full professors. The college administration is investigating the amount of time these faculty members spend in meetings in a semester. Random samples of forty assistant professors, forty associate professors, and fifty full professors were asked to keep records of time spent in meetings during a semester. The sample means were 27.6 hours for assistant professors, 39.2

hours for associate professors, and 43.3 hours for full professors. The sample standard deviations were 7.1 hours for assistant professors, 9.9 hours for associate professors, and 12.3 hours for full professors.

(a) Find a 90% confidence interval for the mean time spent in meetings by full professors in this college in the semester.

(b) Using an unbiased estimation procedure, estimate the mean time spent in meetings by all faculty members in this college in the semester.

(c) Find 90% and 95% confidence intervals for the mean time spent in meetings by all faculty members in this college in the semester.

29. A local bus company is planning a new route to serve four housing subdivisions. Random samples of households are taken from each subdivision and sample members are asked to rate on a scale from 1 (strongly opposed) to 5 (strongly in favor) their reaction to the proposed service. The results are summarized in the accompany table.

	SUBDIVISION			
	1	2	3	4
N_i	240	190	350	280
n_i	40	40	40	40
$\bar{x}_i$	2.5	3.6	3.9	2.8
s_i	.8	.9	1.2	.7

(a) Find a 90% confidence interval for the mean reaction of households in subdivision 1.

(b) Using an unbiased estimation procedure, estimate the mean reaction of all households to be served by the new route.

(c) Find 90% and 95% confidence intervals for the mean reaction of all households to be served by the new route.

30. In a stratified random sample of students on a small campus, sample members were asked to rate, on a scale from 1 (poor) to 5 (excellent), opportunities for extracurricular activities. The results are shown in the accompanying table.

	FRESHMEN AND SOPHOMORES	JUNIORS AND SENIORS
N_i	632	529
n_i	50	50
$\bar{x}_i$	3.12	3.37
s_i	1.04	.86

(a) Find a 95% confidence interval for the mean rating that would be given by all freshmen and sophomores on this campus.

(b) Find a 95% confidence interval for the mean rating that would be given by all juniors and seniors on this campus.

(c) Find a 95% confidence interval for the mean rating that would be given by all undergraduate students on this campus.

31. Refer to Exercise 28.

(a) Find a 90% confidence interval for the total amount of time spent in meetings by all full professors in this college in the semester.

(b) Find a 90% confidence interval for the total amount of time spent in meetings by all faculty members in this college in the semester.

32. A company has three divisions, and auditors are attempting to estimate the total amounts of the company's accounts receivable. Random samples of these accounts were taken for each of the three divisions, yielding the results shown in the table.

	DIVISION		
	1	2	3
N_i	120	150	180
n_i	40	45	50
$\bar{x}_i$	$237	$198	$131
s_i	$93	$64	$47

(**a**) Using an unbiased estimation procedure, find a point estimate of the total value of all accounts receivable for this company.

(**b**) Find a 95% confidence interval for the total value of all accounts receivable for this company.

33. Of the 1,395 colleges in the United States, 364 have 2-year programs and 1,031 are 4-year schools. In a random sample of forty 2-year schools, it was found that the text *Statistics Can Be Fun*, by A. N. Optimist was used in ten of the schools. In an independent random sample of sixty 4-year schools, this text was used by eight of the sample members.

(**a**) Find an estimate of the proportion of all colleges using Optimist's text, using an unbiased estimation procedure.

(**b**) Find a 95% confidence interval for the proportion of all colleges using this text.

34. A consulting company has developed a short course on modern business forecasting methods for corporate executives. The first course was attended by 150 executives. From the information they supplied, it was concluded that the technical skills of 100 course members were more than adequate to follow the course material, while those of the remaining fifty were judged barely adequate. After the completion of the course, questionnaires were sent to independent random samples of twenty-five people from each of these two groups in order to obtain feedback that could lead to improved presentation in subsequent courses. Six of the more skilled and fourteen of the less skilled group indicated that they believed the course had been too theoretical.

(**a**) Find an estimate of the proportion of all course members with this opinion, using an unbiased estimation procedure.

(**b**) Find 90% and 95% confidence intervals for this population proportion.

35. A college has 152 assistant professors, 127 associate professors, and 208 full professors. A journalist with the student newspaper was interested in whether faculty members were actually in their offices during posted office hours. She decided to investigate samples of forty assistant professors, forty associate professors, and fifty full professors. Student volunteers were sent to knock on the doors of these sample members during their posted office hours. It was found that thirty-one of the assistant professors, twenty-nine of the associate professors, and thirty-four of the full professors were actually in their offices at these times.

(**a**) Using an unbiased estimation procedure, find a point estimate of the proportion of all faculty members who are in their offices during posted office hours.

(**b**) Find 90% and 95% confidence intervals for the proportion of all faculty members who are in their offices during posted office hours.

36. Refer to Exercise 28. If a total sample of 130 faculty members is to be taken, determine how many of these should be full professors under each of the following schemes:

(**a**) Proportional allocation.

(**b**) Optimum allocation, assuming the stratum population standard deviations are the same as the corresponding sample values.

37. Refer to the data of Exercise 29. If a total sample of 160 households is to be taken, determine how many of these should be from subdivision 1 under each of the following schemes:

   (a) Proportional allocation.
   (b) Optimum allocation, assuming the stratum population standard deviations are the same as the corresponding sample values.

38. Refer to the data of Exercise 30. If a total sample of 100 students is to be taken, determine how many of these should be freshmen and sophomores under each of the following schemes:

   (a) Proportional allocation.
   (b) Optimum allocation, assuming the stratum population standard deviations are the same as the corresponding sample values.

39. Refer to the data of Exercise 32. If a total sample of 135 accounts receivable is to be taken, determine how many of these should be from division 1 under each of the following schemes:

   (a) Proportional allocation.
   (b) Optimum allocation, assuming the stratum population standard deviations are the same as the corresponding sample values.

40. Refer to the data of Example 18.5. If a total sample of 100 colleges is to be taken, determine how many of these should be 4-year schools under each of the following schemes:

   (a) Proportional allocation.
   (b) Optimum allocation, assuming the stratum population standard deviations are the same as the corresponding sample values.

18.5   DETERMINING THE SAMPLE SIZE

An important aspect of the planning of any survey involves the determination of an appropriate number of sample members. Several factors may be relevant. If the procedure for contacting sample members is thought likely to lead to a high rate of nonresponse, this eventuality should be taken into account. In many instances, the resources available to the investigator, in terms of time and money, will place constraints on what can be achieved. In this section, however, we abstract from such considerations and relate sample size to the variances of the estimators of population parameters and consequently to the widths of resulting confidence intervals.

SAMPLE SIZES FOR SIMPLE RANDOM SAMPLING

We begin with the problem of estimating the population mean from a simple random sample of n observations. If the random variable $\overline{X}$ denotes the sample mean, we saw in Section 6.2 that the variance of this random variable is

$$\text{Var}(\overline{X}) = \sigma_{\overline{X}}^2 = \frac{\sigma^2}{n} \cdot \frac{N - n}{N - 1} \qquad (18.5.1)$$

where σ^2 is the population variance. We must now solve Eq. (18.5.1) for the sample size, n. Multiplying through by $(N-1)n$ gives

$$(N-1)\sigma_{\overline{X}}^2 n = N\sigma^2 - \sigma^2 n$$

so

$$[(N-1)\sigma_{\overline{X}}^2 + \sigma^2]n = N\sigma^2$$

and, finally

$$n = \frac{N\sigma^2}{(N-1)\sigma_{\overline{X}}^2 + \sigma^2} \qquad (18.5.2)$$

If the population variance σ^2 is known, Eq. (18.5.2) allows the determination of the sample size n needed to achieve any specified value $\sigma_{\overline{X}}^2$ for the variance of the sample mean. Similar procedures are available if the quantity of interest is the population total.

> **Determination of Sample Size for Estimating Population Mean or Total Through Simple Random Sampling**
>
> Suppose that we want to estimate the mean of a population of N members, which has variance σ^2. If the desired variance, $\sigma_{\overline{X}}^2$, of the sample mean is specified, the required sample size is
>
> $$n = \frac{N\sigma^2}{(N-1)\sigma_{\overline{X}}^2 + \sigma^2}$$
>
> Often it is more convenient to specify directly the width of confidence intervals for the population mean rather than $\sigma_{\overline{X}}^2$. This is easily accomplished since, for example, a 95% confidence interval for the population mean will extend an approximate amount $1.96\sigma_{\overline{X}}$ on each side of the sample mean.
>
> If the object of interest is the population total, we need only note that the variance of the sample estimator of this quantity is $N^2\sigma_{\overline{X}}^2$ and that confidence intervals for it extend an approximate amount $1.96N\sigma_{\overline{X}}$ on each side of $N\overline{x}$.

An obvious difficulty with the practical use of formula (18.5.2) is that it involves the population variance s2, which will typically be unknown. However, an investigator will often have a rough idea of the value of this quantity. In the next section, we will see how it can sometimes be estimated from a preliminary sample of the population.

EXAMPLE 18.7

As in Example 18.1, suppose that in a city last year 1,118 mortgages were taken out and that a simple random sample is to be taken in order to estimate the mean amount of these mortgages. From previous experience of such populations, it is estimated that the population standard deviation is approximately $20,000. A 95% confidence interval for the population mean must extend an amount $4,000 on each side of the sample mean. How many sample observations are needed to achieve this objective?

We have

$$N = 1{,}118 \qquad \sigma = 20{,}000 \qquad 1.96\sigma_{\bar{x}} = 4{,}000 \text{ (so } \sigma_{\bar{x}} = 2{,}041)$$

The required sample size is then

$$n = \frac{N\sigma^2}{(N-1)\sigma_{\bar{x}}^2 + \sigma^2} = \frac{(1{,}118)(20{,}000)^2}{(1{,}117)(2{,}041)^2 + (20{,}000)^2} = 88.5$$

Thus, a simple random sample of eighty-nine observations should suffice to meet our objective.

Next, we consider simple random sampling for the estimation of a population proportion, p. Let $\hat{p}_X$ be the random variable representing the sample proportion. Then, from the properties of the hypergeometric distribution discussed in Section 4.6, it follows that

$$\text{Var}(\hat{p}_X) = \sigma_{\hat{p}X}^2 = \frac{p(1-p)}{n} \cdot \frac{N-n}{N-1}$$

where p is the population proportion. Solving this equation for the sample size gives

$$n = \frac{Np(1-p)}{(N-1)\sigma_{\hat{p}X}^2 + p(1-p)} \tag{18.5.3}$$

Unfortunately, this expression involves the unknown population proportion p, whose estimation is the objective of the study. Two possibilities are open. We could either guess at the value of p or follow the conservative option of replacing $p(1-p)$ in (18.5.3) by its highest possible value, .25.

Determination of Sample Size for Estimating the Population Proportion Through Simple Random Sampling

Suppose that we want to estimate the proportion p of individuals in a population of size N who possess a certain attribute. If the desired variance, $\sigma_{\hat{p}X}^2$, of the sample proportion is specified, the required sample size is

$$n = \frac{Np(1-p)}{(N-1)\sigma_{\hat{p}X}^2 + p(1-p)}$$

The largest possible value for this expression, whatever the value of p, is

$$n_{\max} = \frac{.25N}{(N-1)\sigma_{\hat{p}X}^2 + .25}$$

A 95% confidence interval for the population proportion will extend an approximate amount $1.96\sigma_{\hat{p}X}$ on each side of the sample proportion.

EXAMPLE
18.8

As in Example 18.3, suppose that we want to take a simple random sample of the 1,395 U.S. colleges to estimate the proportion in which the business statistics course is two semesters long. We want to ensure that whatever the true proportion, a 95% confidence interval extends no further than .04 on each side of the sample proportion. How many sample observations should be taken?

We have

$$1.96\sigma_{\hat{p}X} = .04$$

so

$$\sigma_{\hat{p}X} = .0204$$

The sample size needed is then

$$n_{\max} = \frac{.25N}{(N-1)\sigma_{\hat{p}X}^2 + .25} = \frac{(.25)(1,395)}{(1,394)(.0204)^2 + .25} = 420.1$$

Hence, a simple random sample of 421 observations will suffice.

SAMPLE SIZES FOR STRATIFIED RANDOM SAMPLING

It is also possible to derive formulas for the sample size needed to yield a specified degree of precision when stratified random sampling is employed. Let the random variable $\overline{X}_{st}$ denote the estimator of the population mean from stratified sampling and $\overline{X}_j (j = 1, 2, \ldots, K)$ the sample means for the individual strata. It then follows, since

$$\overline{X}_{st} = \frac{1}{N} \sum_{j=1}^{K} N_j \overline{X}_j$$

that the variance of $\overline{X}_{st}$ is

$$\mathrm{Var}(\overline{X}_{st}) = \sigma_{\overline{X}_{st}}^2 = \frac{1}{N^2} \sum_{j=1}^{K} N_j^2 \, \mathrm{Var}(\overline{X}_j)$$

$$= \frac{1}{N^2} \sum_{j=1}^{K} N_j^2 \, \frac{\sigma_j^2}{n_j} \cdot \frac{N_j - n_j}{N_j - 1} \qquad (18.5.4)$$

where the $\sigma_j^2 (j = 1, 2, \ldots, K)$ are the population variances for the K strata. Now, for any choice of $n_1, n_2, \ldots, n_K$, formula (18.5.4) can be used to derive the corresponding variance of the estimator of the population mean. However, the actual total sample size, n, required to achieve a particular value for this variance will depend on the manner in which the sample observations are allocated among the strata. In Section 18.4, we discussed two frequently used procedures, proportional allocation and optimum allocation. In either case, we can substitute for n_j in (18.5.4), solve the resulting equation, and obtain the sample size n. The results are given in the box.[2]

---

[2] In fact, in deriving these formulas, we used the approximation

$$\frac{N_j}{N_j - 1} \approx 1$$

which will cause no difficulty unless the population numbers in individual strata are very small.

Determination of the Sample Size for Stratified Random Sampling

Suppose that a population of N members is subdivided in K strata containing $N_1, N_2, \ldots,$ N_K members. Let σ_j^2 denote the population variance in the jth stratum, and suppose that we want to estimate the overall population mean. If the desired variance, $\sigma_{\bar{X}_{st}}^2$, of the sample estimator is specified, the required total sample size, n, is as follows:

(i) **Proportional allocation:**

$$ n = \frac{\displaystyle\sum_{j=1}^{K} N_j \sigma_j^2}{N\sigma_{\bar{X}_{st}}^2 + \dfrac{1}{N}\displaystyle\sum_{j=1}^{K} N_j \sigma_j^2} $$

(ii) **Optimal allocation:**

$$ n = \frac{\dfrac{1}{N}\left(\displaystyle\sum_{j=1}^{K} N_j \sigma_j\right)^2}{N\sigma_{\bar{X}_{st}}^2 + \dfrac{1}{N}\displaystyle\sum_{j=1}^{K} N_j \sigma_j^2} $$

If stratified random sampling is used to estimate a population proportion, the earlier formulas are modified, $\sigma_{\bar{X}}^2$ being replaced by $\sigma_{\hat{p}_{st}}^2$, the variance of the relevant estimator, and σ_j^2 by $p_j(1 - p_j)$, where p_j is the population proportion in the jth stratum.

EXAMPLE
18.9

As in Example 18.4, suppose that we want to take a stratified random sample to estimate the mean number of orders per restaurant of a new food item when the numbers of restaurants in the three states are

$$ N_1 = 60 \qquad N_2 = 50 \qquad N_3 = 45 $$

Suppose also that the experience of the restaurant chain suggests that the population standard deviations for the three states are likely to be approximately

$$ \sigma_1 = 13 \qquad \sigma_2 = 11 \qquad \sigma_3 = 9 $$

If we require a 95% confidence interval for the population mean extending an amount three orders per restaurant on each side of the sample point estimate, how many sample observations, in total, are needed?

We have

$$ 1.96\, \sigma_{\bar{X}_{st}} = 3 $$

so

$$ \sigma_{\bar{X}_{st}} = 1.53 $$

We also require

$$ \sum_{j=1}^{K} N_j \sigma_j^2 = (60)(13)^2 + (50)(11)^2 + (45)(9)^2 = 19{,}835 $$

and

$$\frac{1}{N} \left(\sum_{j=1}^{K} N_j \sigma_j \right)^2 = \frac{[(60)(13) + (50)(11) + (45)(9)]^2}{155} = 19{,}421$$

For proportional allocation, the sample size needed is

$$n = \frac{\sum N_j \sigma_j^2}{N \sigma_{\bar{X}_{st}}^2 + \dfrac{1}{N} \sum N_j \sigma_j^2}$$

$$= \frac{19{,}835}{(155)(1.53)^2 + 19{,}835/155} = 40.4$$

Thus, a sample of forty-one observations will suffice to produce the required level of precision.

If optimal allocation is to be used, we have

$$n = \frac{\dfrac{1}{N} (\sum N_j \sigma_j)^2}{N \sigma_{\bar{X}_{st}}^2 + \dfrac{1}{N} \sum N_j \sigma_j^2}$$

$$= \frac{19{,}421}{(155)(1.53)^2 + 19{,}835/155} = 39.6$$

so the same degree of reliability can be obtained with forty observations if this method of allocation is used. In this particular case, since the population standard deviations are quite close, this represents only a very small savings compared with proportional allocation.

18.6 OTHER SAMPLING METHODS

So far, we have discussed in some detail simple and stratified random sampling. These are not the only procedures used for choosing a sample. In this section, we consider some alternative methods.

CLUSTER SAMPLING

Suppose that an investigator wants to survey a population spread over a wide geographical area, such as a large city or a state. If either a simple random sample or a stratified random sample is to be used, two immediate problems will arise. First, in order to draw the sample, the investigator will need a reasonably accurate listing of the population members. Such a list may not be available or could perhaps be obtained only at prohibitively high cost. Second, even if the investigator does possess a list of the population, the resulting sample members will almost inevitably be thinly spread over a large area. In that case, contacting each individual sample member by interviewers will be quite costly. Of course, if a mail questionnaire is to be used, this latter problem does not arise. However, this means of contact may lead to an unacceptably high rate of nonresponse, leading the investigator to prefer personal interviews.

Faced with the dilemma of either not having a reliable population listing or wanting to set up personal interviews with sample members when budget resources are tight, the investigator may use an alternative sampling procedure known as **cluster sampling.** This approach is attractive when a population can conveniently be subdivided into relatively small, geographically compact units called **clusters.** For example, a city might be subdivided into political wards or residential blocks. This can generally be achieved even when a complete listing of residents or households is unavailable.

In cluster sampling, a simple random sample of *clusters* is selected from the population, and every individual in each of the sampled clusters is contacted; that is, a complete census is carried out in each of the chosen clusters. In the accompanying box, we list procedures for deriving valid inferences about the population mean and proportion from the results of a cluster sample.

Inferences from Cluster Sampling

Suppose that a population is subdivided into M clusters, that a simple random sample of m of these clusters is selected, and that information is obtained from every member of the sampled clusters. Let $n_1, n_2, \ldots, n_m$ denote the numbers of population members in the m sampled clusters. We denote by $\bar{x}_1, \bar{x}_2, \ldots, \bar{x}_m$ the means for these clusters and by $p_1, p_2, \ldots, p_m$ the proportions of cluster members possessing an attribute of interest. Our objective is to estimate the overall population mean μ and proportion p.

(i) Unbiased estimation procedures give

$$\bar{x}_c = \frac{\sum_{i=1}^{m} n_i \bar{x}_i}{\sum_{i=1}^{m} n_i}$$

and

$$\hat{p}_c = \frac{\sum_{i=1}^{m} n_i p_i}{\sum_{i=1}^{m} n_i}$$

(ii) Estimates of the variances of these estimators, following from unbiased estimation procedures, are

$$\hat{\sigma}_{\bar{x}_c}^2 = \frac{M - m}{Mm\bar{n}^2} \cdot \frac{\sum_{i=1}^{m} n_i^2 (\bar{x}_i - \bar{x}_c)^2}{m - 1}$$

and

$$\hat{\sigma}_{\hat{p}_c}^2 = \frac{M - m}{Mm\bar{n}^2} \cdot \frac{\sum_{i=1}^{m} n_i^2 (p_i - \hat{p}_c)^2}{m - 1}$$

where

$$\bar{n} = \frac{\sum_{i=1}^{m} n_i}{m}$$

is the average number of individuals in the sampled clusters.

(iii) Provided the sample size is large, $100(1 - \alpha)\%$ confidence intervals are obtained from

$$\bar{x}_c - z_{\alpha/2}\hat{\sigma}_{\bar{x}_c} < \mu < \bar{x}_c + z_{\alpha/2}\hat{\sigma}_{\bar{x}_c}$$

and

$$\hat{p}_c - z_{\alpha/2}\hat{\sigma}_{\hat{p}_c} < p < \hat{p}_c + z_{\alpha/2}\hat{\sigma}_{\hat{p}_c}$$

Notice that inferences can be made with relatively little prior information about the population. All that is required is a breakdown into identifiable clusters. We do not even need to know the total number of population members. It is sufficient to know the numbers in each of the *sampled* clusters, and these can be determined during the course of the survey, since a full census is taken in each cluster in the sample. In addition, since sample members will be geographically close to one another within clusters, their contact by interviewers is relatively inexpensive.

EXAMPLE 18.10

A simple random sample of twenty blocks is taken from a residential area containing a total of 1,000 blocks. Each household in the sampled blocks is then contacted, and information is obtained about family incomes. The accompanying table lists mean annual incomes and the proportion of families with incomes below $15,000 per year in the sampled blocks. For this residential area, estimate the mean family income and the proportion of families with incomes below $15,000 per year.

In our notation, we have

$$m = 20 \qquad \text{and} \qquad M = 1,000$$

SMPLED BLOCK	MEAN INCOME (IN DOLLARS)	PROPORTION BELOW $15,000	NUMBER OF HOUSEHOLDS
i	$\bar{x}_i$	p_i	n_i
1	26,283	.1304	23
2	19,197	.4516	31
3	37,911	.1250	24
4	14,527	.6585	41
5	16,753	.5143	35
6	28,312	.2692	26
7	21,646	.3548	31
8	29,312	.1563	32
9	31,829	.1333	30
10	18,412	.3846	39
11	33,893	.0769	26
12	38,409	.0476	21
13	43,911	.0000	20
14	14,699	.4375	32
15	24,921	.1111	36
16	31,827	.0909	33
17	34,436	.0833	24
18	37,647	.0400	25
19	30,026	.1081	37
20	16,493	.3659	41

The total number of households in the sample is

$$\sum_{i=1}^{m} n_i = (23 + 31 + \cdots + 41) = 607$$

To obtain point estimates, we need

$$\sum_{i=1}^{m} n_i \bar{x}_i = (23)(26,283) + (31)(19,197) + \cdots + (41)(16,493) = 15,848,158$$

and

$$\sum_{i=1}^{m} n_i p_i = (23)(.1304) + (31)(.4516) + \cdots + (41)(.3659) = 153$$

Our point estimates are therefore

$$\bar{x}_c = \frac{\sum n_i \bar{x}_i}{\sum n_i} = \frac{15,848,158}{607} = 26,109$$

and

$$\hat{p}_c = \frac{\sum n_i p_i}{\sum n_i} = \frac{153}{607} = .2521$$

Thus, on the basis of this sample evidence, we estimate that for this residential area, mean annual household income is \$26,109 and 25.21% of households have income below \$15,000 per year.

In order to obtain interval estimates, we need the average cluster size

$$\bar{n} = \frac{\sum n_i}{20} = \frac{607}{20} = 30.35$$

Also

$$\frac{\sum_{i=1}^{m} n_i^2 (\bar{x}_i - \bar{x}_c)^2}{m - 1} = \frac{(23)^2 (26,283 - 26,109)^2 + \cdots + (41)^2 (16,493 - 26,109)^2}{19}$$

$$= 69,270,551,000$$

so

$$\hat{\sigma}_{\bar{x}_c}^2 = \frac{M - m}{Mm\bar{n}^2} \cdot \frac{\sum n_i^2 (\bar{x}_i - \bar{x}_c)^2}{m - 1}$$

$$= \frac{(980)(69,270,551,000)}{(1,000)(20)(30.35)^2} = 3,684,914$$

and hence, taking the square root we obtain

$$\hat{\sigma}_{\bar{x}_c} = 1,920$$

For a 95% confidence interval

$$z_{\alpha/2} = z_{.025} = 1.96$$

Hence, a 95% confidence interval for the population mean is

$$26,109 - (1.96)(1,920) < \mu < 26,109 + (1.96)(1,920)$$

or

$$22,346 < \mu < 29,872$$

Our 95% confidence interval for the mean income of all families in this area therefore runs from \$22,346 to \$29,872.

To obtain interval estimates for the population proportion, we first require

$$\frac{\sum_{i=1}^{m} n_i^2(p_i - \hat{p}_c)^2}{m - 1} = \frac{(23)^2(.1304 - .2521)^2 + \cdots + (41)^2(.3659 - .2521)^2}{19}$$

$$= 38.1547$$

Then

$$\hat{\sigma}_{\hat{p}_c}^2 = \frac{M - m}{Mm\bar{n}^2} \cdot \frac{\sum n_i^2(p_i - \hat{p}_c)^2}{m - 1}$$

$$= \frac{(980)(38.1547)}{(1,000)(20)(30.35)^2} = .0020297$$

and so, taking the square root, we obtain

$$\hat{\sigma}_{\hat{p}_c} = .0451$$

Thus, the 95% confidence interval for the population proportion is

$$.2521 - (1.96)(.0451) < p < .2521 + (1.96)(.0451)$$

or

$$.164 < p < .340$$

Our 95% confidence interval for the percentage of households with annual incomes below \$15,000 therefore runs from 16.4% to 34.0%. Figure 18.4 shows also 80%, 90%, and 99% confidence intervals for the proportion of all households in this residential area with annual incomes below \$15,000.

FIGURE 18.4 80%, 90%, 95%, and 99% confidence intervals for population proportion of households in a residential area with annual incomes below \$15,000, based on the data of Example 18.10

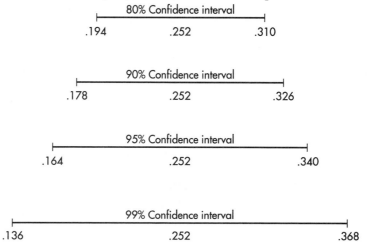

Cluster sampling has a superficial resemblance to stratified sampling. In both, the population is first divided into subgroups. However, the similarity is rather illusory. In stratified random sampling, a sample is taken from *every stratum* of the population, in an attempt to ensure that important segments of the population are given due weight. By contrast, in cluster sampling, a random sample of *clusters* is taken, so that some clusters will have no members in the sample. Since, within clusters, population members will probably be fairly homogeneous, the danger is that important subgroups of the population may be either not represented at all or grossly underrepresented in the final sample. In consequence, while the great advantage of cluster sampling lies in its convenience, this convenience may well be at the cost of additional imprecision in the sample estimates. A further distinction between cluster sampling and stratified sampling is that in the former, a *complete census* of cluster members is taken, while in the latter, a *random sample* of stratum members is drawn. This difference, however, is not essential. Indeed, on occasions, an investigator may draw a random sample of cluster members rather than take a full census.

TWO-PHASE SAMPLING

In many investigations, the population is not surveyed at a single step. Rather, it is often convenient to carry out an initial pilot study in which a relatively small proportion of the sample members are contacted. The results obtained are then analyzed prior to conducting the bulk of the survey. The chief disadvantage of such a procedure is that it can be quite time-consuming. However, this factor may be outweighed by several advantages. One important benefit is that the investigator is able, at modest cost, to try out the proposed questionnaire in order to ensure that the various questions can be thoroughly understood. The pilot study may also suggest additional questions whose potential importance had previously been overlooked. Moreover, this study should also provide an estimate of the likely rate of nonresponse. Should this prove unacceptably high, some modification in the method of soliciting responses might appear desirable.

Conducting a survey in two stages, beginning with a pilot study, is known as **two-phase sampling.** This approach has two further advantages. First, if stratified random sampling is employed, the pilot study can be used to provide estimates of the individual stratum variances. These, in turn, can be employed to estimate the optimum allocation of the sample among the various strata. Second, the results of the pilot study can be used to estimate the number of observations needed to obtain estimators of population parameters with a specified level of precision. The following examples serve to illustrate these points.

**EXAMPLE
18.11**

We begin with a straightforward situation in which a simple random sample is to be used to estimate a population mean. At the outset, relatively little is known about this population, so an initial pilot survey is to be carried out to get some idea of the sample size required.

An auditor wishes to estimate the mean value of accounts receivable in a total population of 1,120 accounts. He wants to produce a 95% confidence interval for the population mean extending approximately $4 on each side of the sample mean. To begin, he takes a simple random sample of 100 accounts, finding a sample standard deviation of $30.27. How many more accounts should be sampled?

Recall from Section 18.5 that the sample size needed can be expressed as

$$n = \frac{N\sigma^2}{(N-1)\sigma_{\bar{x}}^2 + \sigma^2}$$

where $N = 1,120$ is the number of population members in this particular case. In order for the 95% confidence interval to be of the required width, we need

$$1.96\sigma_{\bar{x}} = 4$$

so $\sigma_{\bar{x}}$, the standard deviation of the sample mean, must be

$$\sigma_{\bar{x}} = \frac{4}{1.96} = 2.04$$

The population standard deviation, σ, is unknown. However, as a result of the initial study of 100 accounts receivable, we estimate it to be 30.27. The total number of sample observations needed is therefore

$$n = \frac{(1,120)(30.27)^2}{(1,119)(2.04)^2 + (30.27)^2} = 184.1$$

Since 100 observations have already been taken, an additional eighty-five will suffice to satisfy the auditor's objective.

An investigator intends to take a stratified random sample to estimate mean family income in a town where the numbers in the three stratum districts are

$$N_1 = 1,150 \qquad N_2 = 2,120 \qquad N_3 = 930$$

To begin, she conducts a pilot study, sampling thirty households from each district, obtaining the sample standard deviations $3,657, $6,481, and $8,403, respectively. Suppose that her objective is to obtain, with as small a sample size as possible, a 95% confidence interval for the population mean extending $500 on each side of the sample estimate. How many additional observations should be taken in each district?

The requirement that a specified degree of precision be obtained with as few sample observations as possible implies that optimal allocation must be used. Recall from Eq. (18.4.1) that the numbers n_1, n_2, n_3 to be sampled in the three strata are as follows:

$$n_j = \frac{N_j\sigma_j}{\sum\limits_{i=1}^{3} N_i\sigma_i} \cdot n \qquad (j = 1, 2, 3)$$

where the σ_i are the stratum population standard deviations. Using our sample estimates in place of these quantities, we find

$$n_1 = \frac{(1,150)(3,657)}{(1,150)(3,657) + (2,120)(6,481) + (930)(8,403)} \cdot n = .163n$$

$$n_2 = \frac{(2,120)(6,481)}{(1,150)(3,657) + (2,120)(6,481) + (930)(8,403)} \cdot n = .533n$$

$$n_3 = \frac{(930)(8,403)}{(1,150)(3.657) + (2,120)(6,481) + (930)(8,403)} \cdot n = .303n$$

We have now specified the proportions of the total sample to be allocated to each stratum under the optimal scheme. It remains to determine the total number, n, of sample observations. From Section 18.5, we find

$$n = \frac{\dfrac{1}{N}\left(\displaystyle\sum_{j=1}^{3} N_j \sigma_j\right)^2}{N\sigma_{\bar{X}_{\text{st}}}^2 + \dfrac{1}{N}\displaystyle\sum_{j=1}^{3} N_j \sigma_j^2}$$

where $N = 4{,}200$ is the total number of population members and $\sigma_{\bar{X}_{\text{st}}}^2$ is the variance of the estimator of the population mean. For the 95% confidence interval for the population mean to extend \$500 on each side of the sample estimate, we need

$$1.96\sigma_{\bar{X}_{\text{st}}} = 500$$

so

$$\sigma_{\bar{X}_{\text{st}}} = 255.1$$

As before, we use the estimated standard deviations from the pilot study in place of the unknown population quantities. Hence, we have

$$n = \frac{\dfrac{1}{4{,}200}\,[(1{,}150)(3{,}657)+(2{,}120)(6{,}481)+(930)(8{,}403)]^2}{(4{,}200)(255.1)^2+\dfrac{1}{4{,}200}\,[(1{,}150)(3{,}657)^2+(2{,}120)(6{,}481)^2+(930)(8{,}403)^2]}$$

$$= 503.5$$

Rounding up, we conclude that the total number of sample observations should be 504. These are then allocated among the three strata as

$$n_1 = (.163)(504) = 82$$
$$n_2 = (.533)(504) = 269$$
$$n_3 = (.303)(504) = 153$$

Since thirty households have already been sampled in each stratum, the numbers sampled in the second phase should be 52, 239, and 123.

NONPROBABILISTIC SAMPLING METHODS

We have considered various sampling schemes for which it is possible to specify the probability that any particular sample will be drawn from the population. It is because of this feature of the sampling methods that we are able to make valid statistical inferences based on the sample results. Otherwise, the derivation of unbiased point estimates and confidence intervals with specified probability content could not be achieved with strict statistical validity.

Nevertheless, in many practical applications, **nonprobabilistic methods** are used for selecting sample members, primarily as a matter of convenience. For example, suppose that you want to assess the reactions of students on your campus to some issue of topical interest. One possibility would be to ask all your friends how they feel about it. This group would not constitute a random sample from the population of all students. Accordingly, if you proceed to analyze the data as if they were obtained from a random sample, the resulting inference would lack proper statistical validity.

A more sophisticated version of the approach just described, called **quota sampling,** is commonly used by polling organizations. Interviewers are assigned to a particular locale and instructed to contact specified numbers of people of certain age, race, and sex characteristics. These assigned quotas represent what are thought to be appropriate proportions for the population at large. However, once the quotas are determined, interviewers are granted flexibility in the choice of sample members. Their choice is typically not random. Quota sampling can, and often does, produce quite accurate estimates of population parameters. The drawback is that since the sample is not chosen using probabilistic methods, there is no valid way of determining the reliability of the resulting estimates.

EXERCISES

41. The mean amount of the 812 mortgages taken out in a city in the past year must be estimated. Based on previous experience, a real estate broker knows that the population standard deviation is likely to be about $20,000. If a 95% confidence interval for the population mean is to extend $2,000 on each side of the sample mean, how many sample observations are needed if a simple random sample is taken?

42. A department store has an inventory of 1,420 different products. To estimate the total dollar value of this inventory, an auditor intends to take a simple random sample of products. Based on last year's records, the population standard deviation is estimated to be $160. It is required that a 90% confidence interval for the population total extend $20,000 on each side of its sample estimate. How large a sample size is necessary to satisfy this requirement?

43. A country club wants to poll a random sample of its 320 members to estimate the proportion likely to attend an early-season function. The number of sample observations should be sufficiently large to ensure that a 99% confidence interval for the population proportion extends at most .05 on each side of the sample proportion. How large a sample is necessary?

44. An instructor of a class of 417 students is considering the possibility of a take-home final examination. She wants to take a random sample of class members to estimate the proportion who prefer this form of examination. If it is required that a 90% confidence interval for the population proportion extends at most .04 on each side of the sample proportion, how large a sample is needed?

45. An auditor wants to estimate the mean value of a corporation's accounts receivable. The population is divided into four strata, containing 500, 400, 300, and 200 accounts, respectively. On the basis of past experience, it is estimated that the standard deviations of values in these strata will be $150, $200, $300, and $400, respectively. If a 90% confidence interval for the overall population mean is to extend $25 on each side of the sample estimate, determine the total sample size needed under each of the following schemes:

(**a**) Proportional allocation.

(**b**) Optimal allocation.

46. Mean household income must be estimated for a town that can be divided into three districts. The relevant information is shown in the table.

DISTRICT	POPULATION SIZE	ESTIMATED STANDARD DEVIATION ($)
1	1,150	4,000
2	2,120	6,000
3	930	8,000

If a 95% confidence interval for the population mean, extending $500 on each side of the sample estimate, is required, determine how many sample observations in total are needed under each of the following schemes:

(a) Proportional allocation.

(b) Optimal allocation.

47. A market research organization wants to estimate the mean amounts of time in a week that television sets are in use in households in a city that contains sixty-five precincts. A simple random sample of ten precincts was selected, and every household in each sampled precinct was questioned. The following results were obtained.

SAMPLED PRECINCT	NUMBER OF HOUSEHOLDS	MEAN TIME TELEVISION IN USE (HOURS)
1	28	29.6
2	35	18.4
3	18	32.7
4	52	26.3
5	41	22.4
6	38	31.6
7	36	19.7
8	30	23.8
9	23	25.4
10	42	24.1

(a) Find a point estimate of the population mean amount of time that televisions are in use in this city.

(b) Find a 90% confidence interval for the population mean.

48. A union executive wants to estimate the mean value of bonus payments made to a corporation's clerical employees in the first month of a new plan. This corporation has fifty-two subdivisions, and a simple random sample of eight of these is taken. Information is then obtained from the payroll records of every clerical worker in each of the sampled subdivisions. The results obtained are shown in the table.

SAMPLED SUBDIVISION	NUMBER OF CLERICAL EMPLOYEES	MEAN BONUS ($)
1	69	83
2	75	64
3	41	42
4	36	108
5	59	136
6	82	102
7	64	95
8	71	98

(a) Find a point estimate of the population mean bonus per clerical employee for this month.

(b) Find a 99% confidence interval for the population mean.

49. In the survey of Exercise 47, the households were asked if they had cable television. The numbers having cable are given in the accompanying table.

PRECINCT	1	2	3	4	5	6	7	8	9	10
NUMBER	12	11	10	29	15	13	20	14	9	26

(a) Find a point estimate of the proportion of all households in the city having cable television.

(b) Find a 90% confidence interval for this population proportion.

50. In the survey of Exercise 48, the clerical employees in the eight sampled subdivisions were asked if they were satisfied with the operation of the bonus plan. The results obtained are listed in the table.

SUBDIVISION	1	2	3	4	5	6	7	8
NUMBER SATISFIED	24	25	11	21	35	44	30	34

(a) Find a point estimate of the proportion of all clerical employees satisfied with the bonus plan.

(b) Find a 95% confidence interval for this population proportion.

51. A city is divided into fifty geographical subdivisions. It was required to estimate the proportion of households in the city interested in a new lawn care service. A random sample of three subdivisions contained 611, 521, and 734 households, respectively. The numbers expressing interest in the service were 128, 131, and 172, respectively. Find a 90% confidence interval for the proportion of all households in this city interested in the lawn care service.

52. A bank holds 720 delinquent mortgages on residential properties. It is required to estimate the mean current appraised value of these properties. Initially, a random sample of twenty were appraised, and a sample standard deviation of $37,600 was found. If the bank requires a 90% confidence interval for the population mean extending $5,000 on each side of the sample mean, how many more properties must be appraised?

53. A college has 3,200 undergraduate students and 800 graduate students. Interest is in the amount of money spent in a year on textbooks by these students. Initially, simple random samples of thirty undergraduate students and thirty graduate students were taken. The sample standard deviations for amounts spent were $40 and $58, respectively. It is required that a 90% confidence interval for the overall population mean extends $5 on each side of the sample point estimate. Estimate the smallest total number of additional sample observations needed to achieve this goal.

54. A corporation has a fleet of 480 company cars—100 compact, 180 midsize, and 200 full-size. To estimate the overall mean annual repair costs for these cars, a preliminary random sample of ten cars of each type is selected. The sample standard deviations for repair costs were $105 for compacts, $162 for midsize, and $183 for full-size cars. It is required that a 95% confidence interval for the overall population mean annual repair cost per car extend $20 on each side of the sample point estimate. Estimate the smallest total number of additional sample observations that must be taken.

REVIEW EXERCISES

55. You have been asked to design and carry out a survey in your city on the effectiveness of a radio advertising campaign aimed at promoting a new movie.
    (a) Outline how you would proceed.
    (b) Discuss the possibilities for nonsampling errors and means for minimizing their importance.
    (c) To what extent would you expect nonresponse to be a problem in this survey?

56. Based on a random sample of ten members of your class, estimate the average amount of money per semester spent by class members on textbooks.

57. Carefully explain the distinction between stratified random sampling and cluster sampling. Provide illustrations of sampling problems where each of these techniques might be useful.

58. A test was taken by 90 students. A random sample of ten scores found the following results:

    | 93 | 71 | 62 | 75 | 81 | 63 | 87 | 59 | 84 | 72 |

    (a) Find a 90% confidence interval for the population mean score.
    (b) Without doing the calculations, state whether a 95% confidence interval for the population mean would be wider than or narrower than the interval found in part (a).

59. A corporation has 272 accounts receivable in a particular category. A random sample of fifty of them was taken. The sample mean was $492.36 and the sample standard deviation was $149.92.
    (a) Find a 99% confidence interval for the population mean value of these accounts receivable.
    (b) Find a 95% confidence interval for the total value of these accounts receivable.
    (c) Without doing the calculations, state whether a 90% confidence interval for the population total would be wider than or narrower than the interval found in part (b).

60. The U.S. Senate has 100 members. Information was obtained from the individuals responsible for managing correspondence in sixty-one senators' offices.[3] Of these, thirty-eight specified a minimum number of letters that must be received on an issue before a form letter in response is created.
    (a) Assume these observations constitute a random sample from the population, and find a 90% confidence interval for the proportion of all senators' offices with this policy.
    (b) In fact, information was *not* obtained from a random sample of senate offices. Questionnaires were sent to *all* one hundred offices, but only 61 responded. How does this information influence your view of the answer to part (a)?

61. A corporation employs 148 sales representatives. A random sample of sixty of them was taken, and it was found that for thirty-six of the sample members, volume of orders taken this month was higher than for the same month last year. Find a 95% confidence interval for the population proportion of sales representatives with a higher volume of orders.

62. A company has three subdivisions, employing a total of 970 managers. Independent random samples of managers were taken from each subdivision, and the number of years with the company was determined for each sample member. The results are summarized in the accompanying table.

---

[3] M. J. Culnan, "Processing unstructured organizational transactions: mail handling in the U.S. senate," *Organization Science*, 3 (1992), 117–37.

	SUBDIVISION		
	1	2	3
N_i	352	287	331
n_i	30	20	30
$\bar{x}_i$	9.2	12.3	13.5
s_i	4.9	6.4	7.6

(a) Find a 99% confidence interval for the mean number of years with the company for managers in subdivision 1.

(b) Find a 99% confidence interval for the mean number of years with the company for all managers.

63. Of the 300 pages in a particular book, 180 are primarily nontechnical, while the remainder are technical. Independent random samples of technical and nontechnical pages were taken, and the numbers of errors per page were recorded. The results are summarized in the table.

	TECHNICAL	NONTECHNICAL
N_i	120	180
n_i	20	20
$\bar{x}_i$	1.60	.74
s_i	.98	.56

(a) Find a 95% confidence interval for the mean number of errors per page in this book.

(b) Find a 99% confidence interval for the total number of errors in the book.

64. In the analysis of Exercise 63, it was found that nine of the sampled technical pages and fifteen of the sampled nontechnical pages, contained no errors. Find a 90% confidence interval for the proportion of all pages in this book that have no errors.

65. Refer to the data of Exercise 62. If a total of eighty managers were sampled, determine how many sample members would be from subdivision 1 under each of the following schemes:

(a) Proportional allocation.

(b) Optimum allocation, assuming that the stratum population standard deviations are the same as the corresponding sample quantities.

66. Refer to the data of Exercise 63. If a total of forty pages are to be sampled, determine how many sampled pages would be technical under each of the following schemes:

(a) Proportional allocation.

(b) Optimum allocation, assuming that the stratum population standard deviations are the same as the corresponding sample quantities.

67. You intend to sample the students in your university to assess their views on the adequacy of space in the library. You decide to use a stratified sample by year—freshman, sophomore, and so forth. Discuss the factors you would take into account in deciding how many sample observations to take in each stratum.

68. An automobile dealer has an inventory of 328 used cars. The mean mileage of these vehicles is to be estimated. Previous experience suggests that the population standard deviation is likely to be about 12,000 miles. If a 90% confidence interval for the population mean is to extend 2,000 miles on each side of the sample mean, how large a sample is required if simple random sampling is employed?

69. A simple random sample is to be taken of 527 business majors in a college to estimate the proportion favoring greater emphasis on business ethics in the curriculum. How many observations are necessary to ensure that a 95% confidence interval for the population proportion extends at most .06 on each side of the sample proportion?

70. A population can be divided into K strata, with numbers $N_1, N_2, \ldots, N_K$. Let $\sigma_1, \sigma_2, \ldots, \sigma_K$ denote the stratum population standard deviations, and define

$$\overline{\sigma} = \sum_{j=1}^{K} \frac{N_j \sigma_j}{N}$$

where

$$N = \sum_{j=1}^{K} N_j$$

(a) Show that

$$\sum_{j=1}^{K} N_j (\sigma_j - \overline{\sigma})^2 = \sum_{j=1}^{K} N_j \sigma_j^2 - \frac{1}{N} \left(\sum_{j=1}^{K} N_j \sigma_j \right)^2$$

(b) From the result in (a), deduce that unless the σ_j are all the same

$$\sum_{j=1}^{K} N_j \sigma_j^2 > \frac{1}{N} \left(\sum_{j=1}^{K} N_j \sigma_j \right)^2$$

(c) From the result in (b), deduce that unless the σ_j are all the same, more observations will be required in proportional allocation than under optimal allocation in order to obtain for the population mean a 95% confidence interval of specific width.

(d) Discuss the position when the σ_j are all the same.

71. A market research group takes a random sample of eight of a city's fifty precincts. Every household in each sampled precinct is questioned as to whether it has a central air-conditioning system and also on its summer monthly electricity costs. The results are shown in the table.

SAMPLED PRECINCT	NUMBER OF HOUSEHOLDS	MEAN MONTHLY ELECTRICITY COSTS ($)	NUMBER WITH CENTRAL AIR CONDITIONING
1	38	84	29
2	43	64	22
3	24	49	9
4	37	68	25
5	30	59	13
6	25	77	21
7	47	42	14
8	36	63	21

(a) Find a 95% confidence interval for the population mean summer monthly electricity costs.

(b) Find a 95% confidence interval for the population proportion of households with central air conditioning.

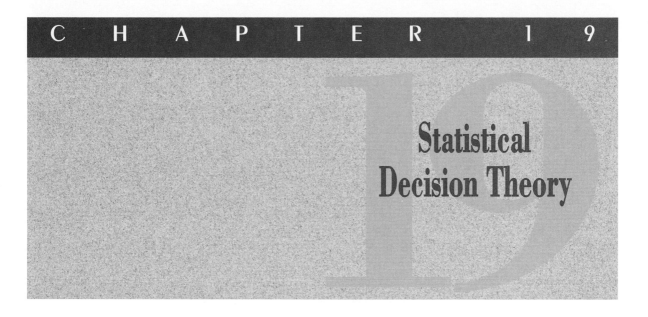

CHAPTER 19

Statistical Decision Theory

19.1 DECISION MAKING UNDER UNCERTAINTY

The topic of this chapter could be characterized as capturing the essence of management problems in any commercial organization. Indeed, the applicability of the subject matter extends further, touching many aspects of our everyday lives. We will be concerned here with the situation in which an individual, a group, or a corporation has available several alternative feasible courses of action. The decision as to which course to follow must be made in a world in which there is uncertainty about the future behavior of the factors that will determine the consequences stemming from the action taken.

We are all constrained to operate in an environment about whose future direction we are uncertain. For example, you may consider attending a baseball game but are doubtful because of the possibility of rain. If you *knew* that it was not going to rain, you would go to the game; if you were *certain* that heavy rain was going to fall for several hours, you would not go. But you are unable to predict the weather with complete assurance, and your decision must be made while contemplating an uncertain future. As another example, at some stage during your final year in college, you will have to decide what to do upon graduation. It is probable that you will have offers of employment from several sources. Graduate school, too, may be a possibility. The decision as to initial career direction is clearly an important one. Certainly you will have acquired information about the alternatives. You will know what starting salaries are on offer, and you will have learned something about the business operations of your future potential employers and how you might fit into these operations.

However, one really does not have a very clear picture of where one will be in a year or two if a particular offer is accepted. This important decision, then, is made in the face of uncertainty about the future.

In the business world, circumstances of this type often arise, as the following examples illustrate:

1. In a recession, a company must decide whether to lay off employees. If the down-turn in business activity is to be short-lived, it may be preferable to retain these workers, who might be difficult to replace when demand improves. If the recession is to be prolonged, however, their retention would be costly. Unfortunately, the art of economic forecasting has not reached the stage where it is possible to predict with great certainty the length or severity of a recession.

2. An investor may believe that interest rates are currently at a peak. In that case, long-term bonds would appear to be very attractive. However, it is impossible to be sure about the future direction of interest rates, and if they were to continue to rise, the decision to tie up funds in long-term bonds would have been suboptimal.

3. Contractors are often required to submit bids for a program of work. The decision to be made is the level at which the bid should be pitched. Two areas of uncertainty may be relevant here. First, the contractor will not know how low a bid will be necessary in order to secure the work. Second, he is not likely to be sure precisely how much it will cost to fulfill the contract. Again, in spite of this uncertainty, some decision must be made.

4. The cost of drilling exploratory offshore oil wells is enormous, and in spite of excellent geological advice, oil companies will not know, before a well is drilled, whether commercially viable quantities of oil will be discovered. The decision as to whether and where to drill in a particular field is one that must be made in an uncertain environment.

In this chapter, our objective is to study methods for attacking decision-making problems of the type just discussed. To make our analysis more concrete, consider the problem of a manufacturer planning to introduce a new candy bar. The manufacturer has available four alternative production processes, denoted A, B, C, and D, ranging in scope from a relatively minor modification of existing facilities to a quite major extension of the plant. The decision as to which course of action to follow must be made at a time when the eventual demand for the product will be unknown. For convenience, we will characterize this potential demand as either "low," "moderate," or "high." It will also be assumed that the manufacturer is able to calculate, for each production process, the profit over the lifetime of the investment for each of the three levels of demand. Table 19.1 shows these profit levels (in dollars) for each production process–level of demand combination.

This particular problem serves to illustrate the general framework for our analysis. A decision maker is faced with a finite number, K, of possible **actions,** which will

TABLE 19.1 Estimated profits of candy bar manufacturer for different production process–level of demand combinations

PRODUCTION PROCESS	LEVEL OF DEMAND		
	LOW	MODERATE	HIGH
A	70,000	120,000	200,000
B	80,000	120,000	180,000
C	100,000	125,000	160,000
D	100,000	120,000	150,000

be labeled $a_1, a_2, \ldots, a_K$. In our example, these actions correspond to the four possible production process adoptions. At the time a particular action must be selected, the decision maker is uncertain about the future of some factor that will determine the consequences of the chosen action. It is assumed that the possibilities for this factor can be characterized by a finite number, H, of **states of nature.** These will be denoted $s_1, s_2, \ldots, s_H$. In the candy bar example, there are three states of nature, corresponding to the three possible levels of demand for the product. Finally, it is assumed that the decision maker is able to specify the monetary rewards, or **payoffs,** for each action–state of nature combination. We will let M_{ij} represent the payoff for action a_i in the event of the occurrence of state of nature s_j. Corresponding to Table 19.1, these payoffs can be displayed in a **payoff table,** whose general form is shown in Table 19.2.

Framework for a Decision Problem

(i) Decision maker has available K courses of **action:**

$$a_1, a_2, \ldots, a_K$$

(ii) There are H possible uncertain **states of nature:**

$$s_1, s_2, \ldots, s_H$$

(iii) For each possible action–state of nature combination, there is an associated monetary **payoff,** M_{ij}, corresponding to action a_i and state of nature s_j.

The decision-making problem, as we have outlined it, is essentially **discrete** in character. That is to say, we have postulated a finite number of available alternative actions and a finite number of possible states of nature. However, many practical problems are **continuous.** The state of nature, for instance, may be more appropriately measured on a continuum than depicted by a number of discrete possibilities. In our example of the candy bar manufacturer, it may be possible to anticipate a range of potential demand levels, rather than simply to specify three levels. Also, in some prob-

TABLE 19.2 General form of payoff table for a decision problem with K possible actions and H states of nature: M_{ij} is the payoff corresponding to action a_i and state of nature s_j.

ACTIONS	STATES OF NATURE			
	s_1	s_2	$\cdots$	s_H
a_1	M_{11}	M_{12}	$\cdots$	M_{1H}
a_2	M_{21}	M_{22}	$\cdots$	M_{2H}
.	.	.		.
.	.	.		.
a_K	M_{K1}	M_{K2}	$\cdots$	M_{KH}

lems, the available actions are most appropriately represented by a continuum. This would be the case, for example, when a contractor must decide on the level at which to bid for a contract. In the remainder of this chapter, we will concentrate on the discrete case. The *principles* involved in the analysis of the continuous case are no different. However, the details of that analysis are based on calculus and will not be considered further here.

When a decision maker is faced with alternative courses of action, the appropriate choice will depend to a considerable extent on the objectives. It is possible to describe various lines of attack that have been employed in the solution of business decision-making problems. However, it must be kept in mind that each individual problem has its own special features and that the objectives of decision makers may vary considerably and indeed be rather complex. A situation of this sort arises when one contemplates the position of a middle manager in a large corporation. In practice, this manager's objectives may differ somewhat from those of the corporation. In making decisions, the manager is very likely to be conscious of his or her own position as well as the overall good of the corporation.

In spite of the individual nature of decision-making problems, we can very easily specify one general rule. It may be possible to eliminate some actions from further consideration under any circumstances. Referring to Table 19.1, consider production process D. The payoff from this process will be precisely the same as that from process C if there is a low level of demand and lower than that from process C if the level of demand were to be either moderate or high. It therefore makes no sense to choose option D, since there is another available choice through which the payoffs can be no lower and could be higher. Since action C is necessarily at least as rewarding as, and possibly more rewarding than, action D, we say that the action C **dominates** action D. If an action is dominated by another available alternative, it is said to be **inadmissible.** Such actions can then be removed from further consideration, as it would be suboptimal to adopt them.

Definitions

If the payoff for action a_j is at least as high as that for a_i, whatever the state of nature, and if the payoff for a_j is higher than that for a_i for at least one state of nature, then action a_j is said to **dominate** action a_i.

Any action that is dominated in this way is said to be **inadmissible.** Inadmissible actions are removed from the list of possibilities prior to further analysis of a decision-making problem.

Any action that is not dominated by some other action and is therefore not inadmissible is said to be **admissible.**

In our analysis of the decision problem of the candy bar manufacturer, we have seen that the action of choosing production process D is inadmissible. Accordingly, this possibility will be dropped from further consideration, and in our subsequent analysis of this problem, we will entertain the possibility of adoption of processes A, B, and C only.

19.2 SOLUTIONS NOT INVOLVING SPECIFICATION OF PROBABILITIES

Before deciding which production process to employ, our manufacturer of candy bars is likely to ask, "What are the chances of each of these levels of demand actually materializing?" In the bulk of this chapter, we will discuss solutions to the decision-making problem that require the specification of outcome probabilities for the various states of nature. However, in this section, we will briefly consider two choice criteria that are not based on such probabilities and in fact have no probabilistic content. Rather, these approaches (and others of the same type) depend only on the structure of the payoff table.

The two procedures considered in this section are called the **maximin criterion** and the **minimax regret criterion.** We will discuss each in relation to the payoff table for the candy bar manufacturer, with the inadmissible strategy of choosing production process D ignored. The manufacturer must therefore select from among three available actions, faced with three possible states of nature.

(i) MAXIMIN CRITERION

Here, we consider the worst possible outcome for each action, whatever state of nature materializes. This *worst outcome* is simply the smallest payoff that could conceivably result. For the candy bar manufacturer's problem, the smallest payoff, whatever production process is used, in fact occurs at the low level of demand. The **maximin criterion** selects the action for which the minimum payoff is highest—that is, we *maximize* the *minimum* payoff. Clearly, as set out in Table 19.3, the maximum value of these minimum payoffs is $100,000, which will occur if production process C is used. The maximin criterion therefore selects this action.

EXAMPLE 19.1

An investor wishes to choose between investing $10,000 for 1 year at an assured interest rate of 12% and investing the same amount over that period in a portfolio of common stocks. If the fixed-interest choice is made, she will be assured of a payoff of $1,200. If the portfolio of stocks is chosen, the return will depend on the performance of the market over the year. If the market is buoyant, a profit of $2,500 is expected; if the market is steady, the expected profit is $500, while for a depressed market, a loss of $1,000 is expected. Set up the payoff table for this investor, and find the maximin choice of action.

TABLE 19.3 Choice of production process C by the maximin criterion

PRODUCTION PROCESS	LEVEL OF DEMAND			MINIMUM PAYOFF	
	LOW	MODERATE	HIGH		
A	70,000	120,000	200,000	70,000	
B	80,000	120,000	180,000	80,000	
C	100,000	125,000	160,000	100,000	← Maximin

The accompanying table shows the payoffs (in dollars), with a negative payoff indicating a loss. The minimum payoff for the fixed-interest investment is $1,200, as this will occur whatever happens in the stock market. The minimum payoff from the stock portfolio is −$1,000 and occurs when the market is depressed. Hence, the largest minimum payoff arises from the fixed-interest investment, which is therefore the action chosen by the maximin criterion.

INVESTMENT	STATE OF THE MARKET			MINIMUM PAYOFF	
	BUOYANT	STEADY	DEPRESSED		
Fixed interest	1,200	1,200	1,200	1,200	← Maximin
Stock portfolio	2,500	500	−1,000	−1,000	

From these illustrations, the general form of the decision rule based on the maximin criterion is clear. This rule is set out in the box.

Decision Rule Based on Maximin Criterion

Suppose that a decision maker has to choose from K admissible actions, $a_1, a_2, \ldots, a_K$, given H possible states of nature. Let M_{ij} denote the payoff corresponding to the ith action and jth state.

For each action, we seek the smallest possible payoff. For the action a_1, for example, this is the smallest of $M_{11}, M_{12}, \ldots, M_{1H}$. Let us denote this minimum M_1^*, where

$$M_1^* = \text{Min}\,(M_{11}, M_{12}, \ldots, M_{1H})$$

More generally, the smallest possible payoff for action a_i is given by

$$M_i^* = \text{Min}\,(M_{i1}, M_{i2}, \ldots, M_{iH})$$

The **maximin criterion** then selects the action a_i for which the corresponding M_i^* is largest.

The positive feature of the maximin criterion for decision making is that it produces the largest possible payoff that can be *guaranteed*. If production process C is used, the candy bar manufacturer is *assured* a payoff of at least $100,000, whatever the level of demand turns out to be. Similarly, for the investor of Example 19.1, the choice of fixed interest makes a *certain* profit of $1,200. In neither example can any available alternative action *guarantee* as much.

However, it is precisely within this guarantee that reservations about the maximin criterion arise, because one must often pay a price for such a guarantee. The price here lies in the forgoing of opportunities to receive a very much larger payoff, through the choice of some other action, *however unlikely* the worst-case situation seems to be. Thus, for example, the candy bar manufacturer may be virtually certain that a high level of demand will result, in which case production process C would be a poor choice, since it yields the lowest payoff at this demand level.

The maximin criterion, then, can be thought of as providing a very cautious strategy for choosing among alternative actions. Such a strategy may, in certain circumstances, be appropriate, but only an extreme pessimist would use it invariably. For this reason, it is sometimes called the *criterion of pessimism*.

(ii) MINIMAX REGRET CRITERION

The decision maker wanting to use the minimax regret criterion must imagine being in the position where a choice of action has been made, one of the states of nature has occurred, and he or she can look back on the choice made either with satisfaction or with disappointment because, as things turned out, some alternative action would have been preferable. Consider once again our candy bar manufacturer. Suppose that the level of demand for the new product turns out to be low. In that case, the best choice of action would have been production process C, yielding a payoff of $100,000. Had this choice been made, the manufacturer would have had 0 **regret.** Had process A been chosen, the resulting profit would have been only $70,000. The extent of the manufacturer's regret, in this eventuality, is the difference between the best payoff that could have been obtained ($100,000) and that resulting from what turned out to be an inferior choice of action. Thus, the regret would be $30,000. Similarly, given low demand, if process B had been chosen, the regret would be

$$\$100,000 - \$80,000 = \$20,000$$

Continuing in this way, we can calculate the regrets involved for moderate and high levels of demand. In each case, the regret is 0 for what would have turned out to be the best choice of action (process C for moderate demand and process A for high demand).

In this way, we can construct a **regret table,** with an entry for each action–state of nature combination. Table 19.4 gives regrets (in dollars) for the candy bar manufacturer's decision problem.

Next, we ask, for each possible course of action, the largest amount of regret that can result. From Table 19.4, these maxima are $30,000, $20,000, and $40,000 for processes A, B, and C, respectively. The **minimax regret criterion** then selects the action for which the maximum regret is smallest. As set out in Table 19.5, the use of this criterion would dictate the choice of production process B.

TABLE 19.4 Regret table for candy bar manufacturer

PRODUCTION PROCESS	LEVEL OF DEMAND		
	LOW	MODERATE	HIGH
A	30,000	5,000	0
B	20,000	5,000	20,000
C	0	0	40,000

TABLE 19.5 Choice of production process B by the minimax regret criterion

PRODUCTION PROCESS	LEVEL OF DEMAND			MAXIMUM REGRET	
	LOW	MODERATE	HIGH		
A	30,000	5,000	0	30,000	
B	20,000	5,000	20,000	20,000	← Minimax regret
C	0	0	40,000	40,000	

EXAMPLE
19.2

Consider again the decision problem of the investor of Example 19.1. What action would be chosen if the minimax regret criterion were followed?

The calculations are set out in the accompanying table. Once again, 0 regret follows from the action that would, in the event, have proved the better alternative. We see, then, that the fixed-interest investment is selected by the minimax regret criterion.

INVESTMENT	STATE OF THE MARKET			MAXIMUM REGRET	
	BUOYANT	STEADY	DEPRESSED		
Fixed interest	1,300	0	0	1,300	← Minimax regret
Stock portfolio	0	700	2,200	2,200	

The general decision rule based on the minimax regret criterion is stated in the box.

Decision Rule Based on Minimax Regret Criterion

Suppose that a payoff table is arranged as a rectangular array, with rows corresponding to actions and columns to states of nature. If each payoff in the table is subtracted from the largest payoff *in its column*, the resulting array is called a **regret table.**

Given the regret table, the action dictated by the **minimax regret criterion** is found as follows:

(i) For each row (action), find the maximum regret.

(ii) Choose the action corresponding to the *minimum* of these *maximum* regrets.

The minimax regret criterion for decision making produces the smallest possible regret that can be *guaranteed*. It does, however, have two serious drawbacks:

1. The logic behind the criterion does not provide a compelling framework for analysis for a wide range of business decision-making problems. Certainly, there is something to be said for not having to shed too many tears over missed opportunities. Nevertheless, in a rational world, decisions ought to be made on rather more substantial grounds.

2. Like the maximin criterion, the minimax regret criterion does not allow the decision-maker to inject personal views as to the likelihood of occurrence of the states of nature into the decision-making process. Since most practical business problems occur in an environment with which the decision maker is at least moderately familiar, this represents a waste of expertise.

EXERCISES

1. An investor is considering three alternatives—a certificate of deposit, a low-risk stock fund, and a high-risk stock fund—for a $20,000 investment. She considers three possible states of nature:

   s_1: Strong stock market
   s_2: Moderate stock market
   s_3: Weak stock market

The payoff table (in dollars) is as follows:

ACTIONS	STATES OF NATURE		
	s	s_2	s_3
Certificate of deposit	1,200	1,200	1,200
Low-risk stock fund	4,300	1,200	−600
High-risk stock fund	6,600	800	−1,500

(a) Are any of these actions inadmissible?

(b) Which action is selected by the maximin criterion?

(c) Which action is selected by the minimax regret criterion?

2. A manufacturer of deodorant is about to expand production capacity to make a new product. Four alternative production processes are available. The accompanying table shows estimated profits, in dollars, for these processes for each of three possible demand levels for the product.

PRODUCTION PROCESS	LEVEL OF DEMAND		
	LOW	MODERATE	HIGH
A	100,000	350,000	900,000
B	150,000	400,000	700,000
C	250,000	400,000	600,000
D	250,000	400,000	550,000

(a) Are any of these actions inadmissible?

(b) Which action is chosen by the maximin criterion?

(c) Which action is chosen by the minimax regret criterion?

3. Another criterion for selecting a decision is the *maximax criterion*, sometimes known as the *criterion of optimism*. This criterion chooses the action with the largest possible payoff.

(a) What action would be chosen by the candy bar manufacturer, with the payoffs of Table 19.1, according to this criterion?

(b) What action would be chosen by the investor of Example 19.1 according to this criterion?

4. The candy bar manufacturer has three admissible actions—processes A, B, and C. When these are considered together, process B is chosen by the minimax regret criterion. Suppose now that a fourth admissible alternative, production process E, is available. Estimated payoffs for this action are $60,000 under low demand, $115,000 for moderate demand, and $220,000 for high demand. Show that when production processes A, B, C, and E are considered together, process A is chosen by the minimax regret criterion. Thus, while adding process E to the available actions does not result in the selection of that process, it does lead to the choice of a different action than would otherwise have been the case. Comment on the intuitive appeal of the minimax regret criterion in light of this example.

5. Consider a decision problem with two possible actions and two states of nature.
   (a) Provide an example of a payoff table according to which both actions are admissible and the same action is chosen by both the maximin criterion and the minimax regret criterion.
   (b) Provide an example of a payoff table according to which different actions are chosen by the maximin criterion and the minimax regret criterion.

6. Consider a decision problem with two admissible actions and two possible states of nature. Formulate a description of the form that the payoff table must take in order that the same action be chosen by the maximin criterion and by the minimax regret criterion.

7. The prospective operator of a shoe store has the opportunity to locate in an established and successful shopping center. Alternatively, at lower cost, he can locate in a new center, whose development has recently been completed. If the new center turns out to be very successful, it is expected that annual store profits from location in it would be $130,000. If the center is only moderately successful, annual profits would be $60,000. If the new center is unsuccessful, an annual loss of $10,000 would be expected. The profits to be expected from location in the established center will also depend to some extent on the degree of success of the new center, as potential customers may be drawn to it. If the new center were to be unsuccessful, annual profit for the shoe store located in the established center would be expected to be $90,000. However, if the new center were moderately successful, this expected profit would be $70,000, while it would be $30,000 if the new center turned out to be very successful.
   (a) Set up the payoff table for the decision-making problem of this shoe store operator.
   (b) Which action is chosen by the maximin criterion?
   (c) Which action is chosen by the minimax regret criterion?

19.3 EXPECTED MONETARY VALUE

We have already suggested quite strongly that an important ingredient in the analysis of a great many business decision-making problems is likely to be the decision maker's assessment of the chances of occurrence of the various states of nature relevant in the determination of the eventual payoff. The criteria discussed in Section 19.2 do not allow the incorporation of this kind of assessment into the decision-making process. However, a manager will almost invariably have a good feeling for the environment in which the decision is to be made and will want this expertise to be taken into account before deciding on a course of action. The candy bar manufacturer will presumably have some experience of the market for his product and, on the basis of that experience, will be able to form a view as to the likelihood of occurrence of low, moderate, or high demand. In this section, we assume that a *probability* of occurrence can be attached to each state of nature, and we will see how these probabilities are employed in arriving at an eventual decision.

Suppose that the candy bar manufacturer knows that of all previous new introductions of this type of product, 10% have met low demand, 50% moderate demand, and 40% high demand. In the absence of any further information, it is then reasonable to postulate, for this particular market introduction, the following probabilities for the states of nature:

$$\text{Probability of low demand} = .1$$

$$\text{Probability of moderate demand} = .5$$

$$\text{Probability of high demand} = .4$$

Notice that since one, and only one, of the states of nature must occur, these probabilities necessarily sum to 1—that is, the states of nature are mutually exclusive and collectively exhaustive.

In solving the decision-making problem, the probabilities for the occurrences of the states of nature are to be employed, together with the payoffs corresponding to each action–state of nature combination. It is therefore convenient to add these probabilities to the payoff table, as in Table 19.6.

In general, when there are H possible states of nature, a probability must be attached to each. We will denote these probabilities by $p_1, p_2, \ldots, p_H$, so probability p_j corresponds to state of nature s_j. Again, these probabilities must sum to 1, so

$$\sum_{j=1}^{H} p_j = 1$$

The general setup of our decision-making problem is shown in Table 19.7.

When choosing an action, the decision maker will see each particular choice as having a specific probability of receiving the associated payoff and will therefore be able to calculate the **expected payoff** arising from each action. If the candy bar manufacturer adopts production process A, he will receive a payoff of $70,000 with probability .1, $120,000 with probability .5, and $200,000 with probability .4. The expected payoff for this action is then the sum of the individual payoffs, weighted by their associated probabilities. These expected payoffs are often called the **expected monetary values** of the actions. For the candy bar manufacturer, the expected monetary values for the three admissible actions are as follows:

Process A: $(.1)(\ 70{,}000) + (.5)(120{,}000) + (.4)(200{,}000) = \$147{,}000$
Process B: $(.1)(\ 80{,}000) + (.5)(120{,}000) + (.4)(180{,}000) = \$140{,}000$
Process C: $(.1)(100{,}000) + (.5)(125{,}000) + (.4)(160{,}000) = \$136{,}500$

TABLE 19.6 Payoffs and state-of-nature probabilities for candy bar manufacturer

PRODUCTION PROCESS	LEVEL OF DEMAND		
	LOW ($p = .1$)	MODERATE ($p = .5$)	HIGH ($p = .4$)
A	70,000	120,000	200,000
B	80,000	120,000	180,000
C	100,000	125,000	160,000

TABLE 19.7 Payoffs, M_{ij}, and state-of-nature probabilities, p_j, for a decision problem with K admissible actions and H possible states of nature

ACTIONS	STATES OF NATURE			
	s_1 (p_1)	s_2 (p_2)	$\cdots$	s_H (p_H)
a_1	M_{11}	M_{12}	$\cdots$	M_{1H}
a_2	M_{21}	M_{22}	$\cdots$	M_{2H}
.	.	.		.
.	.	.		.
.	.	.		.
a_K	M_{K1}	M_{K2}	$\cdots$	M_{KH}

The general form of the definition of expected monetary value is stated in the box.

Expected Monetary Values

Suppose that a decision maker has K possible actions, $a_1, a_2, \ldots, a_K$, and is faced with H states of nature. Let M_{ij} denote the payoff corresponding to the ith action and jth state and p_j the probability of occurrence of the jth state of nature, with

$$\sum_{j=1}^{H} p_j = 1$$

The **expected monetary value**, EMV(a_i), of the action a_i is

$$\text{EMV}(a_i) = p_1 M_{i1} + p_2 M_{i2} + \cdots + p_H M_{iH} = \sum_{j=1}^{H} p_j M_{ij}$$

The expected monetary values associated with the alternative courses of action provide the decision maker with a choice criterion that will be extremely attractive for a great many practical problems. By this criterion, the action with highest expected monetary value is adopted. Hence, following this rule, the candy bar manufacturer would choose production process A. It is interesting to note that neither the maximin criterion nor the minimax regret criterion led to this particular choice. However, we have now added the information that a high level of demand appears much more likely than a low level. This renders process A a relatively attractive option.

Expected Monetary Value Criterion

Given a choice among alternative actions, the **expected monetary value criterion** dictates the choice of the action for which expected monetary value is highest.

The analysis of a decision problem by means of the expected monetary value criterion can be conveniently set out diagrammatically through a mechanism called a **decision tree.** Such a diagram is shown, for the candy bar manufacturer, in Figure 19.1. Beginning at the left-hand side of the figure, branches emerge from the square junction there to represent the three possible actions. Junctions marked by squares are those at which decisions must be made. Next, we reach circular junctions, from which emerge branches, each representing a possible state of nature, to which we attach the associated probability. Finally, at the end of these last branches, the payoffs corresponding to each action–state of nature combination are inserted. The computations proceed from right to left, beginning with these payoffs. For each circular junction, we find the sum of probability times payoff for the emerging branches. This provides the EMV for each action. Finally, the highest of the EMVs is indicated at the square junction. We see that this results from process A, which is therefore chosen by the expected monetary value criterion. This choice of action results in an expected monetary value, or expected profit, of $147,000 for the candy bar manufacturer.

EXAMPLE 19.3

Consider again the investor of Examples 19.1 and 19.2 who must decide between a fixed-interest-rate investment and a portfolio of stocks. Let us assume that this investor is in fact very optimistic about the future course of the stock market, believing the probability that it will be buoyant is .6, while the probability is .2 for each of the other two states. The payoffs and state-of-nature probabilities are therefore those given in the accompanying table. Which investment should be chosen according to the expected monetary value criterion?

FIGURE 19.1 Decision tree for candy bar manufacturer

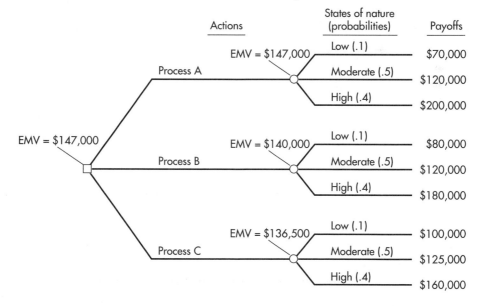

INVESTMENT	STATE OF THE MARKET		
	BUOYANT ($p = .6$)	STEADY ($p = .2$)	DEPRESSED ($p = .2$)
Fixed interest	1,200	1,200	1,200
Stock portfolio	2,500	500	−1,000

Since a payoff of $1,200 will result from the fixed-interest investment, whatever happens in the stock market, the expected monetary value of this investment is $1,200. For the stock portfolio, we have

$$\text{EMV} = (.6)(2,500) + (.2)(500) + (.2)(-1,000) = \$1,400$$

Since this is the higher expected monetary value, the investor would choose the portfolio of common stocks, according to this criterion.

The decision tree for this problem is shown in Figure 19.2. Notice that for the fixed-interest action, there are no sub-branches corresponding to states of nature, since the same payoff ($1,200) materializes whatever the state. This payoff, then, is the expected monetary value for that action.

EXAMPLE 19.4

This example illustrates a problem in which a *sequence* of decisions may be required. The use of decision trees is particularly helpful in solving such problems.

A drug manufacturer holds the patient rights to a new formula for arithritic pain relief. The manufacturer is able to sell the patent for $50,000 or to proceed with intensive tests of the drug's efficacy. The cost of carrying out these tests is $10,000. If the drug is found to be ineffective, it will not be marketed, and the cost of the tests is written off as a loss. In the past, tests of drugs of this type have shown 60% to be effective and 40% ineffective.

If the tests should now reveal the drug to be effective, the manufacturer again has two options available. He can sell the patent rights and test results for $120,000,

FIGURE 19.2 Decision tree for the investor of Example 19.3

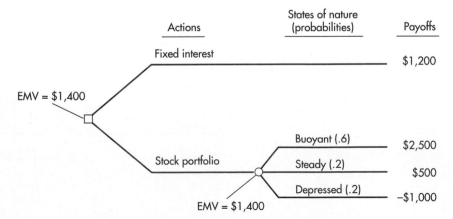

or he can market the drug himself. If the drug is marketed, it is estimated that profits on sales (exclusive of the cost of the tests) will amount to $180,000 if the sales campaign is highly successful but only $90,000 if it is just moderately successful. It is estimated that these two levels of market penetration are equally likely. According to the expected monetary value criterion, how should the drug manufacturer proceed?

It is best to attack this problem through the construction of a decision tree. The completed tree is shown in Figure 19.3. The branches are constructed, beginning on the left-hand side at the first decision point. The manufacturer may decide either to sell the patent, in which case there is nothing further to be done, or to retain it and carry out tests on the drug's efficacy. There are two possible states of nature—the drug is either effective (with probability .6) or ineffective (with probability .4). In the latter case, the story ends. However, if the drug proves to be effective, a second decision must be made—whether to market it or to sell the patent rights and test results. If the former option is adopted, the eventual outcome is determined by the level of marketing success, which could be either moderate or high (each with probability .5).

Next, the payoffs resulting from all action–state of nature combinations are entered on the right-hand side of the diagram. We will begin at the bottom. If the manufacturer's original decision is to sell the patent, he receives $50,000. If the patent is kept but the drug turns out to be ineffective, the manufacturer sustains a loss of $10,000, the cost of carrying out the tests. This is shown as a negative payoff in that amount. If the drug is found to be effective and the patent and test results are then sold, the manufacturer receives $120,000, from which must be subtracted the cost of the tests, leaving a payoff of $110,000. Finally, if the drug is marketed, the payoffs for moderate and high success are, respectively, $90,000 and $180,000, less the cost of the tests, leaving $80,000 and $170,000, respectively.

Having reached this point, we can solve the decision problem by working backward from right to left along the tree. This is necessary because the appropriate action

FIGURE 19.3 Decision tree for the drug manufacturer of Example 19.4

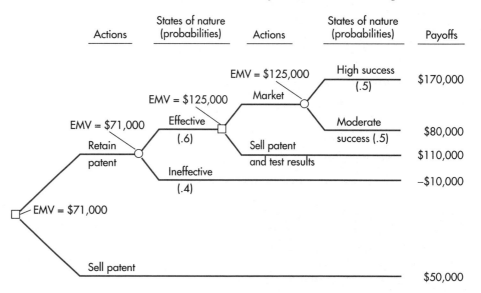

at the first decision point cannot be determined until we have found the expected monetary value of the best available option at the second decision point.

We therefore begin by supposing that initially the patent was retained and the tests proved the drug to be effective. If the patent and test results are sold, a profit of $110,000 will result. The expected monetary value from marketing the drug is

$$(.5)(170,000) + (.5)(80,000) = \$125,000$$

Since this exceeds $110,000, the better option at this stage, by the expected monetary value criterion, is to market the drug. This amount is therefore entered at the square junction of the second decision point and is treated as the payoff that results if the manufacturer's initial decision is to retain the patent and the tests indicate that the drug is effective.

Hence, for the initial decision, the payoff table with state-of-nature probabilities is as shown here. The expected monetary value of selling the patent is the assured $50,000, while the expected monetary value of retaining it is

$$(.6)(125,000) + (.4)(-10,000) = \$71,000$$

Then, by the expected monetary value criterion, the patent should be retained.

ACTIONS	STATES OF NATURE	
	EFFECTIVE ($p = .6$)	INEFFECTIVE ($p = .4$)
Retain patent	125,000	−10,000
Sell patent	50,000	50,000

Thus, we have finally reached the conclusion that if the objective is the maximization of expected monetary value (that is, expected profit), the manufacturer should retain the patent and, if the tests prove the drug to be effective, market it himself. This strategy yields an expected profit of $71,000.

SENSITIVITY ANALYSIS

In our example of the candy bar manufacturer, we found that according to the expected monetary value criterion, production process A should be employed. This decision was based on estimated payoffs for each action–state of nature combination and on estimated probabilities of occurrence for the states of nature. However, often a decision maker will be uncertain about such estimates, so it is useful to ask under what range of specifications of a decision problem a particular action will be optimal under the expected monetary value criterion. **Sensitivity analysis** seeks to answer such questions, the most straightforward case being where a single problem specification is allowed to vary while all other specifications are held fixed.

To illustrate, suppose that the candy bar manufacturer is happy with the assessment that the probability of high demand is .4 but is less sure of the assessments for the other two states of nature. Let p denote the probability of low demand, so that the probability of moderate demand must be $(.6 - p)$. We now ask under what range of values of p adoption of process A would be optimal according to the expected monetary value criterion. Using the payoffs of Table 19.6, the expected monetary values are

$$\text{EMV(A)} = (p)(70,000) + (.6 - p)(120,000) + (.4)(200,000) = 152,000 - 50,000p$$

$$\text{EMV(B)} = (p)(80,000) + (.6 - p)(120,000) + (.4)(180,000) = 144,000 - 40,000p$$

$$\text{EMV(C)} = (p)(100,000) + (.6 - p)(125,000) + (.4)(160,000)$$

$$= 139,000 - 25,000p$$

Choice of process A will remain optimal provided the associated EMV is higher than that of each of the other two processes. Thus, for process A to be preferred to process B, we must have

$$152,000 - 50,000p \geq 144,000 - 40,000p$$

or

$$8,000 \geq 10,000p$$

so

$$p \leq .8$$

This must be so, since, by our assumptions, the probability of low demand cannot exceed .6. Similarly, for process A to be preferred to process C, we require

$$152,000 - 50,000p \geq 139,000 - 25,000p$$

or

$$13,000 \geq 25,000p$$

so

$$p \leq .52$$

We have therefore established that if the payoffs are as postulated in Table 19.6 and the probability of high demand is .4, production process A is the best choice under the expected monetary value criterion provided that the probability of low demand does not exceed .52.

Now suppose that the candy bar manufacturer is uncertain about the estimated payoff of $200,000 for process A under high demand. We shall explore under what range of payoffs process A will be the optimal choice, when all other problem specifications are kept at their initial levels, given in Table 19.6. If we denote by M the payoff for process A under high demand, the expected monetary value for this process is

$$\text{EMV(A)} = (.1)(70,000) + (.5)(120,000) + .4M = 67,000 + .4M$$

The expected monetary values for processes B and C are, as before, $140,000 and $136,500. Therefore, process A will be the best choice according to the expected monetary value criterion, provided that

$$67{,}000 + .4M \geq 140{,}000$$

or

$$.4M \geq 73{,}000$$

so

$$M \geq 182{,}500$$

We have thus shown that if all other specifications are as originally given in Table 19.6, production process A will be selected by the expected monetary value criterion, provided that the payoff for process A under high demand is at least $182,500.

19.4 USE OF SAMPLE INFORMATION: BAYESIAN ANALYSIS

Decisions made in the business world can often involve considerable amounts of money, and the cost of making a suboptimal choice may turn out to be substantial. This being the case, it could well pay the decision maker to make an effort to obtain as much relevant information as possible before the decision is made. In particular, he or she will want to become as thoroughly informed as possible about the chances of occurrence of the various states of nature that determine the eventual payoff.

This feature of any careful analysis of a decision problem has not been apparent in our discussion so far. The candy bar manufacturer, in Section 19.3, assessed the probabilities of low, moderate, and high levels of demand for a new candy bar as .1, .5, and .4, respectively. However, this assessment reflected no more than the historical proportions achieved by previous products. In practice, he might well want to carry out some market research on the prospects for the new product. Given such research, these initial or **prior probabilities** may be modified, yielding new probabilities, called **posterior probabilities,** for the three demand levels. The information (in this case, the market research results) leading to the modification of probabilities for the states of nature will be referred to as **sample information.**

In fact, we saw in Section 3.8 the mechanism for modifying prior probabilities to produce posterior probabilities. This is accomplished through **Bayes' theorem,** which, for convenience, we restate in the box,[1] in the framework of our decision-making problem.

---

[1] Before proceeding further, the reader may wish to review Section 3.8.

Now, suppose that the candy bar manufacturer hires a market research organization to predict the level of demand for his new product.[2] The organization provides a rating of "poor," "fair," or "good," on the basis of its research. A review of the market research company's records reveals the quality of its past predictions in this field. Table 19.8 shows, for each level of demand outcome, the proportion of poor, fair, and good assessments. Thus, for example, on 10% of occasions that demand was high, the assessment was "poor." Thus, in the notation of conditional probability, denoting low, moderate, and high demand levels by s_1, s_2, and s_3, respectively, we have

$$P(\text{Poor} \mid s_1) = .6 \qquad P(\text{Poor} \mid s_2) = .3 \qquad P(\text{Poor} \mid s_3) = .1$$

and so on.

Suppose now that the market research firm is consulted and produces an assessment of "poor" for the prospects of the candy bar. Given this new information, the prior probabilities

TABLE 19.8 Proportion of assessments of each type provided by market research organization for candy bars achieving given levels of demand

ASSESSMENT	LEVEL OF DEMAND		
	LOW (s_1)	MODERATE (s_2)	HIGH (s_3)
Poor	.6	.3	.1
Fair	.2	.4	.2
Good	.2	.3	.7

---

[2] He will, of course, have to pay for this service. In Section 19.5, we discuss the question of whether the returns merit the cost involved.

$$P(s_1) = .1 \qquad P(s_2) = .5 \qquad P(s_3) = .4$$

for the three demand levels can be modified using Bayes' theorem. For a low level of demand, the posterior probability is

$$P(s_1 \mid \text{Poor}) = \frac{P(\text{Poor} \mid s_1)P(s_1)}{P(\text{Poor} \mid s_1)P(s_1) + P(\text{Poor} \mid s_2)P(s_2) + P(\text{Poor} \mid s_3)P(s_3)}$$

$$= \frac{(.6)(.1)}{(.6)(.1) + (.3)(.5) + (.1)(.4)} = \frac{.06}{.25} = .24$$

Similarly, for the other two demand levels, the posterior probabilities are

$$P(s_2 \mid \text{Poor}) = \frac{(.3)(.5)}{.25} = .60$$

$$P(s_3 \mid \text{Poor}) = \frac{(.1)(.4)}{.25} = .16$$

The posterior probabilities can then be employed to calculate the expected monetary values. Table 19.9 shows the payoffs, together with the posterior probabilities for the three demand levels. This is simply a modification of Table 19.6, with the posterior probabilities replacing the prior probabilities of that table.

The expected monetary values for the three production processes can be found in precisely the same manner as before. These are as follows:

PROCESS A: $(.24)(\ 70{,}000) + (.60)(120{,}000) + (.16)(200{,}000) = \$120{,}800$
PROCESS B: $(.24)(\ 80{,}000) + (.60)(120{,}000) + (.16)(180{,}000) = \$120{,}000$
PROCESS C: $(.24)(100{,}000) + (.60)(125{,}000) + (.16)(160{,}000) = \$124{,}600$

We see that if the assessment of market prospects is "poor," according to the expected monetary value criterion production process C should be used. The market research group's assessment has rendered low demand much more likely and high demand considerably less likely than was previously the case. This shift in the view of market prospects is sufficient to induce the candy bar manufacturer to switch his preference from process A (based on the prior probabilities) to process C.

TABLE 19.9 Payoffs for candy bar manufacturer and posterior probabilities for states of nature, given an assessment of "poor" by market research organization

PRODUCTION PROCESS	LEVEL OF DEMAND		
	LOW $(p = .24)*$	MODERATE $(p = .60)*$	HIGH $(p = .16)*$
A	70,000	120,000	200,000
B	80,000	120,000	180,000
C	100,000	125,000	160,000
*Posterior probability.			

Following the same line of argument, we can determine the decisions that would be made if the prospects for the candy bar's market success were rated either "fair" or "good." Again, the posterior probabilities for the three levels of demand can be obtained through Bayes' theorem. For a "fair" assessment, these are

$$P(s_1 \mid \text{Fair}) = \frac{1}{15} \qquad P(s_2 \mid \text{Fair}) = \frac{2}{3} \qquad P(s_3 \mid \text{Fair}) = \frac{4}{15}$$

and, for a "good" assessment

$$P(s_1 \mid \text{Good}) = \frac{2}{45} \qquad P(s_2 \mid \text{Good}) = \frac{1}{3} \qquad P(s_3 \mid \text{Good}) = \frac{28}{45}$$

Using these posterior probabilities, we can now determine the expected monetary values of each of the production processes for each given assessment. Table 19.10 contains these quantities.

As we have already seen, if the assessment is "poor," process C is preferred by the expected monetary value criterion. If any other assessment is made, we would choose to use production process A, according to this criterion.

We recall that for the candy bar manufacturer's problem, when the prior probabilities for levels of demand were used, the optimal decision according to the expected monetary value criterion was to use process A. It can be the case (if an assessment of "poor" is obtained) that a different decision will be made when these prior probabilities are modified by sample information. Hence, it turns out that consulting the market research organization could be valuable for the manufacturer. Of course, if the choice of process A had proved optimal, whatever the assessment, the sample information could not possibly be of value.

EXAMPLE 19.5

In Example 19.4, a drug manufacturer had to decide whether to sell the patent for a pain relief formula before subjecting the drug to thorough testing. (Subsequently, if the patent was retained and the drug found to be effective, a second decision—to market the drug or to sell the patent and test results—also had to be made.) For the initial decision, the two states of nature were

s_1: Drug is effective
s_2: Drug is ineffective

The associated prior probabilities, formed on the basis of previous experience, are

$$P(s_1) = .6 \qquad P(s_2) = .4$$

TABLE 19.10 Expected monetary values for candy bar manufacturer for each of three possible assessments by market research firm

PRODUCTION PROCESS	ASSESSMENT		
	POOR	FAIR	GOOD
A	120,800	138,000	167,556
B	120,000	133,333	155,556
C	124,600	132,667	145,667

The drug manufacturer has the option of carrying out, at modest cost, an initial test before the first decision is made. The test is not infallible. For drugs that have subsequently proved effective, the preliminary test result was positive on 60% of occasions and negative on the remainder. For ineffective drugs, a positive preliminary test result was obtained 30% of the time, the other results being negative. Given the results of the preliminary test, how should the drug manufacturer proceed? Assume that it is still possible to sell the patent for $50,000 if the preliminary test result is negative.

First, we note that if the patent is retained and the exhaustive tests prove the drug to be effective, then in the absence of any sample information on market conditions, the optimal decision at this stage, as in Example 19.4, is to market the drug. The information provided by the preliminary test is irrelevant in that particular decision. However, it could conceivably influence the initial decision as to whether to sell the patent. Accordingly, it is only on this decision that we need to concentrate.

The conditional probabilities of the sample outcomes, given the states of nature, are

$$P(\text{Positive} \mid s_1) = .6 \qquad P(\text{Negative} \mid s_1) = .4$$

$$P(\text{Positive} \mid s_2) = .3 \qquad P(\text{Negative} \mid s_2) = .7$$

If the result of the preliminary test is positive, the posterior probability for the state s_1 (Effective), given this information, is

$$P(s_1 \mid \text{Positive}) = \frac{P(\text{Positive} \mid s_1)P(s_1)}{P(\text{Positive} \mid s_1)P(s_1) + P(\text{Positive} \mid s_2)P(s_2)}$$

$$= \frac{(.6)(.6)}{(.6)(.6) + (.3)(.4)} = .75$$

Further, since the two posterior probabilities must sum to 1, we have

$$P(s_2 \mid \text{Positive}) = .25$$

The accompanying payoff table is the same as in Example 19.4, with these posterior probabilities added.

ACTIONS	STATES OF NATURE	
	EFFECTIVE $(p = .75)*$	INEFFECTIVE $(p = .25)*$
Retain patent	125,000	−10,000
Sell patent	50,000	50,000
*Posterior probability.		

The expected monetary value, if the patent is sold, is $50,000, while if the patent is retained, the expected monetary value is

$$(.75)(125,000) + (.25)(-10,000) = \$91,250$$

Therefore, if the initial test result is positive, the patent should be retained, according to this criterion.

Next, we consider the case where the preliminary test result is negative. The posterior probability for the state s_1 is, by Bayes' theorem

$$P(s_1 \mid \text{Negative}) = \frac{P(\text{Negative} \mid s_1)P(s_1)}{P(\text{Negative} \mid s_1)P(s_1) + P(\text{Negative} \mid s_2)P(s_2)}$$

$$= \frac{(.4)(.6)}{(.4)(.6) + (.7)(.4)} = .4615$$

Hence, the posterior probability for the state s_2 is

$$P(s_2 \mid \text{Negative}) = .5385$$

Once more, if the patent is sold, the expected monetary value is the $50,000 that will be received. If the patent is retained, the expected monetary value of this decision is

$$(.4615)(125,000) + (.5385)(-10,000) = \$52,302.50$$

Thus, even if the preliminary test result is negative, the optimal decision, by the expected monetary value criterion, is to retain the patent.

In this particular example, then, whatever the sample information, the chosen action is the same. The manufacturer should retain the patent in the event of either result emerging from the preliminary test. Since the sample information cannot possibly affect the decision, there is, of course, no point in gathering it. In fact, since performing the preliminary test will not be costless, it will be suboptimal to do so. Thus, we conclude that according to the expected monetary value criterion, the drug manufacturer should retain the patent, and if the thorough tests prove the drug to be effective, he should market it himself. The preliminary test should not be carried out.

19.5 THE VALUE OF SAMPLE INFORMATION

We have seen how sample information can be incorporated into the decision-making process. The potential value of such information lies, of course, in its provision of a better feel for the chances of occurrence of the relevant states of nature. This, in turn, can provide firmer ground on which to base a decision. In this section, we will see how a *monetary* value can be attached to the sample information. This is important, since there will typically be some cost involved in obtaining the sample information, and the decision maker will want to know whether the expected benefits exceed this cost.

In Example 19.5, we considered a situation where the same action was optimal, whatever the sample result. In such a case, the sample information clearly has no value, since the same action would have been taken without it. This is a general rule: If the sample information cannot affect the choice of action, it has value 0.

Accordingly, for the remainder of this section, we will concern ourselves only with circumstances in which the sample result can affect the choice of action. Our example of the candy bar manufacturer planning to introduce a new product is such a case. This manufacturer has to choose from three production processes and is faced with three states of nature, representing different levels of demand for the product. In Section 19.3, we saw that in the absence of sample information and using only the prior probabilities, we choose process A, with an expected monetary value of $147,000.

Now, in practice, having obtained sample information, the decision maker will typically not know which state of nature will occur but will have more firmly grounded probabilistic assessments for these states. However, before discussing the value of sample information in this general framework, it is useful to consider the extreme case where **perfect information** is obtainable—that is, the case where the decision maker is able to gain information that will tell *with certainty* which state will occur. What is the value to the decision maker of having such perfect information?

In the context of our candy bar manufacturer, perfect information corresponds to knowledge of which of the three possible demand levels will actually result. In the absence of any sample information and on the basis of the prior probabilities only, process A will be chosen. However, referring to Table 19.6, we see that if it were known that the level of demand would be low, the best choice would be process C. Since this has a payoff that exceeds by $30,000 that of process A, the value of knowing that demand would be low is $30,000. Similarly, if it were known that moderate demand would result, process C would again be chosen. Here, the payoff from the best available choice exceeds that of process A by $5,000, which is, accordingly, the value of knowing that demand will be moderate. If it were known that high demand would occur, however, process A would be chosen. Thus, this particular knowledge is of no value, since the same decision would have been made without it. We see, therefore, that the value of perfect information depends on the information. Using the prior probabilities of the various states of nature, we can find the **expected value of perfect information.**

For the candy bar manufacturer, the prior probabilities are .1 for low, .5 for moderate, and .4 for high demand. It therefore follows that to this manufacturer, the value of perfect information is $30,000 with probability .1, $5,000 with probability .5, and $0 with probability .4. The expected value of perfect information is, accordingly

$$(.1)(30,000) + (.5)(5,000) + (.4)(0) = \$5,500$$

This dollar amount, then, represents the expected value to the candy bar manufacturer of knowing what level of demand will result.

We now show in the box the general procedure for computing the expected value of perfect information.

Expected Value of Perfect Information

Suppose that a decision maker has to choose from among K possible actions, in the face of H states of nature, $s_1, s_2, \ldots, s_H$. **Perfect information** corresponds to knowledge of which state of nature will arise. The expected value of perfect information is obtained as follows:

(i) Determine which action will be chosen if only the prior probabilities $P(s_1)$, $P(s_2)$, $\ldots, P(s_H)$ are used.

(ii) For each possible state of nature, s_i, find the difference, W_i, between the payoff for the best choice of action, if it were known that state would arise, and the payoff for the action chosen if only the prior probabilities are used. This is the value of perfect information, when it is known that si will occur.

(iii) The expected value of perfect information is then

$$P(s_1)W_1 + P(s_2)W_2 + \cdots + P(s_H)W_H$$

Now, although perfect information will typically not be available, the calculation of the expected value of perfect information can be useful. Since, of course, no sample information can be better than perfect, its expected value cannot be higher than that of the expected value of perfect information. Thus, the expected value of perfect information provides an *upper limit* for the expected value of any sample information. For example, if the candy bar manufacturer is offered information at a cost of $6,000, it is not necessary to inquire further about the quality of this information. It should not be purchased, however reliable, according to the expected monetary value criterion, since its expected value cannot be more than $5,500.

We now turn to the more general problem of assessing the value of sample information that is not necessarily perfect. Again, we will consider the decision-making problem of the candy bar manufacturer, who has the option of obtaining an assessment from a market research organization of the prospects for the new candy bar. These prospects will be rated either "poor," "fair," or "good." We saw in Section 19.4 that in the last two of the three eventualities, process A will still be chosen. Thus, if a "fair" or "good" rating is obtained, the initial choice of action will remain unchanged, and nothing will have been gained from consulting the market research company.

If the prospects are rated "poor," however, we see from Table 19.10 that the optimal choice is process C. This optimal choice would yield an expected monetary value of $124,600, whereas process A, which otherwise would have been used, gives an expected monetary value of $120,800. The difference in these amounts, $3,800, represents the gain from the sample information *if the assessment is "poor."*

Thus, the gains from the sample information are $0 for ratings of "good" or "fair" and $3,800 for a rating of "poor."

We now need to know how likely these gains are to materialize, so in our example, we must find the probability of a "poor" assessment. In general, if A denotes a piece of sample information, and $s_1, s_2, \ldots, s_H$ the H possible states of nature, then

$$P(A) = P(A \mid s_1)P(s_1) + P(A \mid s_2)P(s_2) + \cdots + P(A \mid s_H)P(s_H)$$

For the candy bar example, with s_1, s_2, s_3 denoting low, moderate, and high levels of demand, we have seen that

$$P(s_1) = .1 \qquad P(s_2) = .5 \qquad P(s_3) = .4$$

and

$$P(\text{Poor} \mid s_1) = .6 \qquad P(\text{Poor} \mid s_2) = .3 \qquad P(\text{Poor} \mid s_3) = .1$$

Therefore, the probability of a "poor" assessment is

$$P(\text{Poor}) = P(\text{Poor} \mid s_1)P(s_1) + P(\text{Poor} \mid s_2)P(s_2) + P(\text{Poor} \mid s_3)P(s_3)$$

$$= (.6)(.1) + (.3)(.5) + (.1)(.4) = .25$$

In the same way, using the conditional probabilities of Table 19.8, we obtain the following probabilities for the other two assessments:

$$P(\text{Fair}) = .30 \qquad P(\text{Good}) = .45$$

We see then that the value of the sample information is $3,800 with probability .25, $0 with probability .30, and $0 with probability .45. It therefore follows that the **expected value of the sample information** is

$$(.25)(3,800) + (.30)(0) + (.45)(0) = \$950$$

This dollar amount, then, represents the expected value of the sample information to the decision maker. In terms of the expected monetary value criterion, this sample information will be worth acquiring if its cost is less than its expected value. We define the **expected net value of sample information** as the difference between its expected value and its cost.

Suppose that the market research group charges a fee of $750 for its assessment. The expected net value of this assessment to the candy bar manufacturer is then $950 - 750 = \$200$. Thus, the manufacturer's expected payoff will be $200 higher if the sample information is purchased than if it is not. This amount represents the expected worth of having that information, taking into account its cost. In this case, the manufacturer's optimal strategy is to purchase the market research report and then use production process A if the assessment is either "good" or "fair" and process C if the assessment is "poor." The expected monetary value of this strategy is $147,200—the $147,000 that would result from no sample information plus the expected net value of the sample information.

The general framework for computing the value of sample information is set out in the box.

Expected Value of Sample Information

Suppose that a decision maker has to choose from K possible actions in the face of H states of nature $s_1, s_2, \ldots, s_H$. The decision maker may obtain sample information. Let there be M possible sample results, $A_1, A_2, \ldots, A_M$.

The expected value of sample information is obtained as follows:

(i) Determine which action would be chosen if only the prior probabilities were used.

(ii) Determine the probabilities of obtaining each sample result:

$$P(A_i) = P(A_i \mid s_1)P(s_1) + P(A_i \mid s_2)P(s_2) + \cdots + P(A_i \mid s_H)P(s_H)$$

(iii) For each possible sample result, A_i, find the difference, V_i, between the expected monetary value for the optimal action and that for the action chosen if only prior probabilities are used. This is the value of the sample information, given that A_i was observed.

(iv) The expected value of sample information is then

$$P(A_1)V_1 + P(A_2)V_2 + \cdots + P(A_M)V_M$$

The **expected net value of sample information** is the difference between its expected value and its cost.

According to the expected monetary value criterion, the decision maker should purchase the sample information if its expected net value is positive. Otherwise, the sample information should not be purchased.

The expected value of sample information can be computed in an alternative (but equivalent) manner, which is arithmetically slightly more cumbersome but does provide a convenient way of representing the problem in terms of a sequence of decisions through the construction of a decision tree. The first decision to be made is whether to obtain the sample information. Next, it is necessary to decide which of the alternative actions should be followed.

To illustrate, consider again the problem of the candy bar manufacturer. Figure 19.4 shows the decision trees following from the three possible market research appraisals. These trees have the same general structure as Figure 19.1. The essential difference is that the probabilities associated with the three states of nature are the appropriate *posterior probabilities*, given the specific sample information. These posterior probabilities were found in Section 19.4. The payoffs are now weighted by the posterior probabilities, yielding the expected monetary value of each action, given each possible sample result. These are the expected monetary values shown in Table 19.10. Finally, at the left of each part of Figure 19.4, we show the highest possible expected monetary value for each sample outcome.

This information is transferred to the right of Figure 19.5, in which the decision whether to purchase the market research study is analyzed. If this information is not

FIGURE 19.4 Decision trees for the candy bar manufacturer, given the market research organization assessments of (a) "poor," (b) "fair," (c) "good"

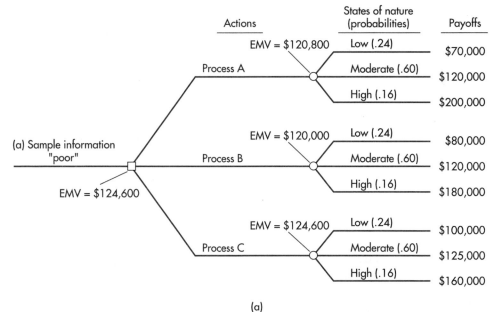

(a)

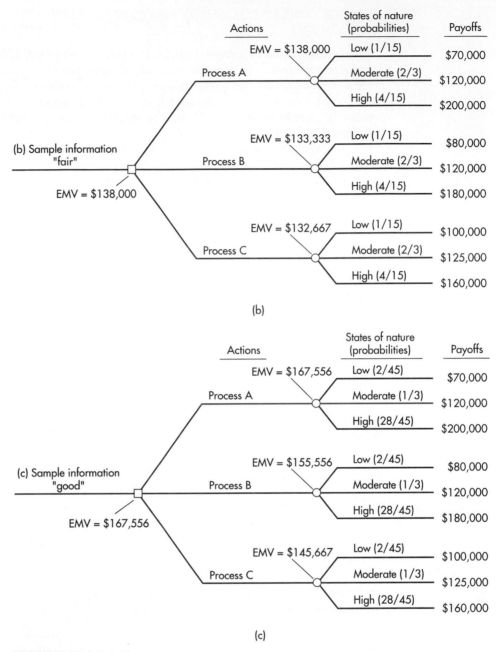

(b)

(c)

FIGURE 19.4 (cont.)

bought, we see, in the bottom part of the figure, an expected monetary value of $147,000. This results from using the prior probabilities and is taken from Figure 19.1.

Turning now to the upper part of Figure 19.5, the expected monetary value that results will depend on the sample outcome. The probabilities are .25 for "poor," .30

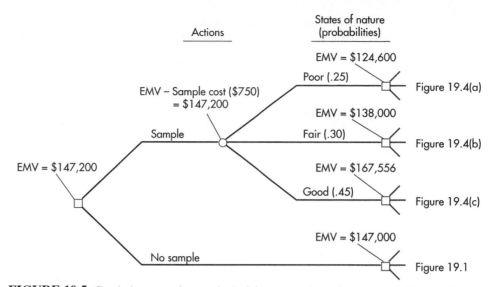

FIGURE 19.5 Candy bar manufacturer's decision to purchase the services of the market research organization

for "fair," and .45 for "good," as we have already seen. Thus, since $124,600 can be expected with probability .25, $138,000 with probability .30, and $167,556 with probability .45, the expected payoff if the sample information is purchased is

$$(.25)(124,600) + (.30)(138,000) + (.45)(167,556) = \$147,950$$

However, it is necessary to subtract from this amount the $750 cost of the sample information, leaving $147,200. Since this is more than the expected payoff when no sample information is obtained, the best strategy, according to the expected monetary value criterion, is to purchase the services of the market research group. The optimal decision has, as indicated at the left of Figure 19.5, an expected monetary value of $147,200.

EXERCISES

8. A student already has offers of employment. She must now decide whether to visit another potential employer for further interviews. She views the time and effort of doing so as a cost of $500, which will be incurred whether or not she takes a job with this employer. If the employer offers a position preferable to her other alternatives, this would be viewed as a benefit worth $5,000 (from which the $500 cost must be subtracted). Otherwise her time and effort would have been wasted.

   (a) Set up the payoff table for the student's decision-making problem.
   (b) Suppose the student believes that the probability is .05 that she would be offered by this employer a position preferable to her other alternatives. According to the expected monetary value criterion, should she visit this potential employer?

9. A manager has to choose between two actions, a_1 and a_2. There are two possible states of nature, s_1 and s_2. The payoffs are shown in the accompanying table. If the manager believes that each state of nature is equally likely to occur, which action should be chosen according to the expected monetary value criterion?

ACTIONS	STATES OF NATURE	
	s_1	s_2
a_1	72,000	51,000
a_2	78,000	47,000

10. The investor of Exercise 1 believes that the probability of a strong stock market is .2, the probability of a moderate stock market is .5, and the probability of a weak stock market is .3.

   (a) Which action should be chosen according to the expected monetary value criterion?

   (b) Draw the decision tree for the investor's problem.

11. Refer to Exercise 2. The deodorant manufacturer knows that historically 30% of new products of this type have met high demand, 40% moderate demand, and 30% low demand.

   (a) According to the expected monetary value criterion, which production process should be used?

   (b) Draw the decision tree for this manufacturer's problem.

12. Consider a decision problem with two admissible actions and two possible states of nature, each of which is equally likely to occur.

   (a) Determine whether each of the following statements is true or false for such problems:

      (i) The action chosen by the expected monetary value criterion will always be the same as the action chosen by the maximin criterion.

      (ii) The action chosen by the expected monetary value criterion will always be the same as the action chosen by the minimax regret criterion.

      (iii) The action chosen by the expected monetary value criterion will always be that for which the average possible payoff is higher.

   (b) Would your answer to statement (iii) in part (a) be the same if the two states of nature were not equally likely to occur?

13. A decision problem has K possible actions and H possible states of nature. If one of these actions is inadmissible, show that it cannot be chosen by the expected monetary value criterion.

14. The shoe store operator of Exercise 7 believes that the probability is .4 that the new shopping center will be very successful, .4 that it will be moderately successful, and .2 that it will be unsuccessful.

   (a) According to the expected monetary value criterion, where should the shoe store be located?

   (b) Draw the decision tree.

15. Refer to the decision-making problem of the investor of Exercises 1 and 10. This investor is comfortable with the assessment of a probability of .2 for a strong market. However, she is less sure of the probability assessments for the other two states of nature. Under what range of probabilities for a weak stock market does the expected monetary value criterion give the choice of action found in Exercise 10?

16. Refer to the problem of the deodorant manufacturer of Exercises 2 and 11.

(a) The manufacturer is comfortable with an assessment that the probability of low demand is .3, but is less secure about the probabilities for the other two demand levels. Under what range of probabilities for moderate demand will the expected monetary value criterion yield the choice of action found in Exercise 11?

(b) Take the remaining problem specifications to be as given in Exercises 2 and 11. Under what range of profits for high demand when process A is used will the expected monetary value criterion give the choice of action found in Exercise 11?

17. Refer to the problem of the shoe store operator of Exercises 7 and 14.

(a) The shoe store operator is happy with the assessment that the probability is .2 that the new shopping center will be unsuccessful but is less sure about the probability assessments for the other two states of nature. Under what range of probabilities that the new shopping center will be very successful will the expected monetary value criterion lead to the choice of action found in Exercise 14?

(b) Assuming that the other problem specifications are as in Exercises 7 and 14, under what range of profit levels for location in the new center if it turns out to be very successful will the expected monetary value criterion lead to the choice of action found in Exercise 14?

18. A manufacturer receives regular contracts for large consignments of parts for the automobile industry. This manufacturer's production process is such that when it is operating correctly, 10% of all parts produced do not meet industry specifications. However, the production process is prone to a particular malfunction, whose presence can be checked at the beginning of a production run. When the process is operated with this malfunction, 30% of the parts produced fail to meet industry specifications. The manufacturer supplies parts under a contract that will yield a profit of $20,000 if only 10% of the parts are defective and a profit of $12,000 if 30% of the parts are defective. The cost of checking for the malfunction is $1,000, and if it turns out that repair is needed, this costs a further $2,000. If incurred, these costs must be subtracted from the profit of the contract. Historically, it has been found that the production process functions correctly 80% of the time. The manufacturer must decide whether to check the process at the beginning of a production run.

(a) According to the expected monetary value criterion, what is the optimal decision?

(b) Draw the decision tree.

(c) Suppose that the proportion of occasions on which the production process operates correctly is unknown. Under what range of values for this proportion would the decision selected in part (a) be optimal, according to the expected monetary value criterion?

19. A contractor has to decide whether to submit a bid for a construction project. It will cost $16,000 to prepare the bid. This cost would be incurred whether or not the bid was accepted. The contractor intends to bid at a level that will produce a $110,000 profit (less the cost of preparing the bid). The contractor knows that 20% of bids prepared in this way have been successful.

(a) Set up the payoff table.

(b) Should a bid be prepared and submitted, according to the expected monetary value criterion?

(c) Under what range of probabilities that the bid will be successful should a bid be prepared and submitted, according to the expected monetary value criterion?

20. On Thursday evening, the manager of a small branch of a car rental agency finds that he has available six cars for rental on the following day. However, he is able to request delivery of additional cars, at a cost of $20 each, from the regional depot. Each car that is rented produces an expected profit of $40. (The cost of delivery of the car must be subtracted from this profit.) Each potential customer requesting a car when none is available is counted a $10 loss in goodwill. On reviewing his records for previous Fridays, the manager finds that the number of cars requested have ranged from six to ten; the percentages are shown in the accompanying table. The manager must decide how many cars, if any, to order from the regional depot.

NUMBER OF REQUESTS	6	7	8	9	10
PERCENT	10	30	30	20	10

(a) Set up the payoff table.

(b) If the expected monetary value criterion is used, how many cars should be ordered?

21. A contractor has decided to place a bid for a project. Bids are to be set in multiples of $20,000. It is estimated that the probability that a bid of $240,000 will secure the contract is .2, the probability that a bid of $220,000 will be successful is .6, and the probability that a bid of $200,000 will be accepted is .8. It is thought that any bid under $200,000 is certain to succeed and any bid over $240,000 is certain to fail. If the manufacturer wins the contract, he must solve a design problem with two possible choices at this stage. He can hire outside consultants, who will guarantee a satisfactory solution, for a price of $80,000. Alternatively, he can invest $30,000 of his own resources in an attempt to solve the problem internally; if this effort fails, he must then engage the consultants. It is estimated that the probability of successfully solving the problem internally is .6. Once this problem has been solved, the additional cost of fulfilling the contract is $140,000.

(a) Potentially, this contractor has two decisions to make. What are they?

(b) Draw the decision tree.

(c) What is the optimal course of action, according to the expected monetary value criterion?

22. A publisher intends to sign a contract for an accounting text with one of three authors, Smith, Brown, or Jones. If the text turns out to be very successful, profits (excluding any extraordinary advertising costs) will be $250,000; if the book is only moderately successful, these profits will be $80,000. In the event that the text fails, a loss of $80,000 will result. The probabilities given in the first table have been conjectured for these states of nature for the three books.

	VERY SUCCESSFUL	MODERATELY SUCCESSFUL	FAILURE
Smith	.2	.6	.2
Brown	.1	.8	.1
Jones	.3	.2	.5

The publisher also has the option of mounting, at a cost of $30,000, an extraordinary advertising campaign for the book once it is published. It is estimated that if this were to be done, the probabilities for the three states of nature would be as shown in the following table:

	VERY SUCCESSFUL	MODERATELY SUCCESSFUL	FAILURE
Smith	.4	.4	.2
Brown	.3	.6	.1
Jones	.5	.2	.3

(a) Draw the publisher's decision tree.

(**b**) According to the expected monetary value criterion, which author should be signed, and should the extraordinary advertising campaign be mounted?

(**c**) Following the calculations in part (b), the publisher has signed a contract with the chosen author. At this point, it is discovered that a clerical error has been made in the marketing department and that in fact the actual cost of the advertising campaign is $40,000. According to the EMV criterion, should the publisher offer to pay the chosen author to withdraw from the contract, and if so, what is the highest sum he should offer?

23. Consider a decision problem with two actions, a_1 and a_2, and two states of nature, s_1 and s_2. Let M_{ij} denote the payoff corresponding to action a_i and state of nature s_j. Assume that the probability of occurrence of state of nature s_1 is p, so the probability of state s_2 is $(1 - p)$.

(**a**) Show that action a_1 is selected by the EMV criterion if

$$p(M_{11} - M_{21}) > (1 - p)(M_{22} - M_{12})$$

(**b**) Hence, show that if a_1 is an admissible action, there is some probability, p, for which it will be chosen. However, if a_1 is not admissible, it cannot be chosen, whatever the value of p.

24. A consultant is considering preparing proposals for one of two contracts. He has the alternative of preparing proposals for neither, but time constraints prevent his preparing proposals for both. The costs of preparation of initial outline proposals are $500 for contract A and $750 for contract B. When the initial proposals have been submitted, responses are obtained from the potential clients. These responses can be categorized as either "positive," "noncommittal," or "negative." The probabilities for the two contracts are shown in the accompanying table. If the response to the initial outline proposal is negative, no contract will be obtained. If the response is not negative, the consultant may provide a more detailed final proposal, at a cost of $1,000 for contract A and $1,500 for contract B. For contract A, the probabilities that this final proposal will be accepted are .9 if the initial response was positive and .4 if it was noncommittal. For contract B, these probabilities are .8 and .2, respectively. If contract A is finally secured, the consultant's profit (from which costs of proposal preparations must be subtracted) is $5,000. For contract B, the corresponding figure is $6,000. The consultant intends to follow the course of action dictated by the EMV criterion.

	POSITIVE	NONCOMMITTAL	NEGATIVE
Contract A	.6	.2	.2
Contract B	.8	.1	.1

(**a**) Draw the decision tree for this consultant.

(**b**) Should the consultant submit an initial outline proposal, and if so, for which project?

(**c**) If the answer to part (b) is "yes," how should the consultant proceed if the response from the selected potential client to the initial proposal is "noncommittal"?

(**d**) This consultant has recently hired a statistician who suggests that it would be better simply to submit the final proposals without going through the stage of preparing initial outline proposals. The costs of proposals prepared in this way would be $1,250 for contract A and $1,875 for contract B. Assuming that the probabilities of final acceptance remain unchanged, is the statistician correct?

25. A manufacturer must decide whether to mount, at a cost of $100,000, an advertising campaign for a product whose sales have been rather flat. It is estimated that a highly successful campaign would add $400,000 (from which the campaign's costs must be subtracted) to profits, a moderately successful campaign would add $100,000, but an unsuccessful campaign would add nothing. Historically, 40% of all similar campaigns have been very successful, 30% moderately successful, and the remainder unsuccessful. This manufacturer consults a media consultant for a judgment on the potential effectiveness of the campaign. This consultant's record is such that she has reported favorably on 80% of campaigns that turned out to be highly successful, 40% of those that were moderately successful, and 10% of unsuccessful campaigns.

(a) Find the prior probabilities for the three states of nature.

(b) In the absence of any report from the media consultant, should this advertising campaign be mounted, according to the EMV criterion?

(c) Find the posterior probabilities for the three states of nature, given that the media consultant reports favorably.

(d) Given a favorable report from the consultant, should the advertising campaign be mounted, according to the EMV criterion?

(e) Find the posterior probabilities for the three states of nature, given that the media consultant does not report favorably.

(f) If the consultant's report is not favorable, should the advertising campaign be mounted, according to the EMV criterion?

26. Refer to Exercise 2. The deodorant manufacturer has four possible production processes from which to choose, depending on the view that is taken of future demand levels. On the basis of past experience, the prior probabilities are .3 for high demand, .4 for moderate demand, and .3 for low demand. The accompanying table shows proportions of "poor," "fair," and "good" assessments for prospects provided by a market research group for similar products that have achieved these demand levels.

ASSESSMENT	LEVEL OF DEMAND		
	LOW	MODERATE	HIGH
Poor	.5	.3	.1
Fair	.3	.4	.2
Good	.2	.3	.7

(a) If the market research group is not consulted, which action should be chosen according to the EMV criterion?

(b) Find the posterior probabilities of the three demand levels, given an assessment of "poor."

(c) Which action should be chosen according to the EMV criterion, given an assessment of "poor"?

(d) Find the posterior probabilities of the three demand levels, given an assessment of "fair."

(e) Which action should be chosen according to the EMV criterion, given an assessment of "fair"?

(f) Find the posterior probabilities of the three demand levels, given an assessment of "good."

(g) Which action should be chosen according to the EMV criterion, given an assessment of "good"?

27. The shoe store operator of Exercise 7 has available two courses of action. His decision is based on his view of the likely level of success of the new shopping center. Historically, 40% of new centers of this type have been very successful, 40% moderately successful, and 20% unsuccessful. A consulting group sells assessments of the prospects of this type of shopping center. The table given here shows the proportion of "good," "fair," and "poor" assessments, given the particular outcome actually resulting.

ASSESSMENT	LEVEL OF SUCCESS		
	VERY SUCCESSFUL	MODERATELY SUCCESSFUL	UNSUCCESSFUL
Good	.6	.3	.2
Fair	.3	.4	.3
Poor	.1	.3	.5

(a) What are the prior probabilities for the three states of nature?

(b) If the shoe store operator does not seek advice from the consulting group, what action should he take, according to the EMV criterion?

(c) What are the posterior probabilities of the three states of nature, given an assessment of "good"?

(d) According to the EMV criterion, given an assessment of "good," what course of action should the shoe store operator adopt?

(e) What are the posterior probabilities of the three states of nature, given an assessment of "fair"? According to the EMV criterion, given an assessment of "fair," which action should be chosen?

(g) What are the posterior probabilities of the three states of nature, given an assessment of "poor"?

(h) If the EMV criterion is followed, which action should be chosen, given a forecast of "poor"?

28. Consider the drug manufacturer of Example 19.5, who had to decide whether to sell the patent for a pain relief formula before subjecting the drug to thorough testing. In the example, we saw that whatever the result of a certain preliminary test of the drug's efficacy, the optimal decision was to retain the patent. Subsequently, this manufacturer developed a superior preliminary test, which again could be carried out at modest cost. For drugs that subsequently proved effective, this new test gave a positive result 80% of the time, while a positive result was obtained for only 10% of the drugs that proved to be ineffective.

(a) Find the posterior probabilities of the two states of nature, given a positive result from this new preliminary test.

(b) According to the EMV criterion, should the patent be sold if the new test result is positive?

(c) Find the posterior probabilities of the two states of nature, given a negative result from the new preliminary test.

(d) According to the EMV criterion, should the patent be sold if the new test result is negative?

(e) Is the optimal choice of action affected by the result of the new preliminary test?

(f) Explain what feature of the preliminary test determines whether its outcome influences the optimal choice of action.

29. In Exercise 18, a supplier of parts to the automobile industry had to decide whether to check the production process for a certain malfunction before starting a production run. The two states of nature were

s_1: Repair not needed (10% of all parts produced fail to meet specifications)

s_2: Repair needed (30% of all parts produced fail to meet specifications)

The prior probabilities, derived from the historical record for this production process, are

$$P(s_1) = .8 \qquad \text{and} \qquad P(s_2) = .2$$

The manufacturer can, before beginning a full production run, produce a single part and check whether it meets specifications, basing a decision on whether to check the production process on the resulting sample information.

(a) If the single part checked meets specifications, what are the posterior probabilities of the states of nature?

(b) If the single part checked meets specifications, should the production process be checked according to the EMV criterion?

(c) If the single part checked does not meet specifications, what are the posterior probabilities of the states of nature?

(d) If the single part checked does not meet specifications, should the production process be checked according to the EMV criterion?

30. Continuing Exercise 29, suppose now that before making a decision on whether to check the production process, *two* parts are made and examined.

(a) If, in fact, repair is not needed, what are the probabilities that both parts, just one part, and neither part will fail to meet specifications?

(b) Compute the same probabilities as in part (a), given that repair of the production process is in fact needed.

(c) Compute the posterior probabilities of the states of nature and determine the optimal action under the expected monetary value criterion, given each of the following circumstances:

(i) Both parts fail to meet specifications.

(ii) Just one part fails to meet specifications.

(iii) Neither part fails to meet specifications.

31. The Watts New Lightbulb Corporation ships large consignments of lightbulbs to big industrial users. When the production process is functioning correctly (which is 90% of the time), 10% of all bulbs produced are defective. However, the process is susceptible to an occasional malfunction, leading to a defective rate of 20%. The Watts New Lightbulb Corporation counts the cost, in terms of goodwill, of a shipment with the higher defective rate to an industrial user as $5,000. If a consignment is suspected to contain this larger proportion of defectives, it can instead be sold to a chain of discount stores, though this involves a reduction of $600 in profits, whether or not the consignment does indeed contain a large proportion of defective bulbs. Decisions by this company are made through the EMV criterion.

(a) A consignment is produced. In the absence of any further information, should it be shipped to an industrial user or to the discount chain?

(b) Suppose that a single bulb from the consignment is checked. Determine where the consignment should be shipped under each of the following circumstances:

(i) This bulb is defective.

(ii) This bulb is not defective.

(c) Suppose that two bulbs from the consignment are checked. Determine where the consignment should be shipped for each of the following situations:

(i) Both bulbs are defective.

(ii) Just one bulb is defective.

(iii) Neither bulb is defective.

(d) Without doing the calculations, indicate how the decision problem could be attacked if 100 bulbs were checked prior to shipping the consignment.

32. Refer to the problem of the investor of Exercise 1.

    (a) Explain what is meant by "perfect information" in the context of this investor's problem.

    (b) The prior probabilities are .2 for a strong stock market, .5 for a moderate stock market, and .3 for a weak stock market. What is the expected value of perfect information to this investor?

33. For the deodorant manufacturer of Exercise 2, the prior probabilities are .3 for high demand, .4 for moderate demand, and .3 for low demand. Find the expected value of perfect information to this manufacturer.

34. For the shoe store operator of Exercise 7, the prior probabilities are .4 that the new shopping center will be very successful, .4 that it will be moderately successful, and .2 that it will be unsuccessful. What is the expected value of perfect information to this shoe store operator?

35. The manufacturer of automobile parts of Exercise 18 must decide whether to check the production process before beginning a full production run. Give that the production process functions correctly 80% of the time, what is the value of perfect information to this manufacturer?

36. In Section 19.5, before showing how to find the expected value of sample information, we discussed separately the determination of the expected value of perfect information. In fact, this was not necessary because perfect information is just a special kind of sample information. Given the general procedure for finding the expected value of sample information, show how to specialize this to the case of perfect information.

37. Refer to Exercise 25. The manufacturer is considering an advertising campaign and first seeks the advice of a media consultant.

    (a) What is the expected value to the manufacturer of the media consultant's advice?

    (b) The media consultant charges a fee of $5,000. What is the expected net value of the consultant's advice?

    (c) This manufacturer faces a two-stage decision problem. First, he must decide whether to purchase advice from the media consultant. Next, he must decide whether to mount the advertising campaign. Draw the complete decision tree, and indicate how the manufacturer should proceed.

38. Refer to Exercise 26. Find the largest fee the deodorant manufacturer should pay to the market research group, according to the expected monetary value criterion.

39. Refer to Exercise 27. Find the expected value to the shoe store operator of an assessment of the shopping center's prospects provided by the consulting group.

40. Refer to Exercise 28. Before deciding whether to sell the patent of a new pain relief formula, the drug manufacturer carries out the new preliminary test. Find the expected value to the manufacturer of the test result.

41. Refer to Exercise 29. The supplier of automobile parts is able to produce and examine a single part before deciding whether to check the production process. What is the expected value of this sample information?

42. Consider the Watts New Lightbulb Corporation of Exercise 31. The corporation can check one or more lightbulbs before deciding whether to ship a consignment to an industrial user or to a discount chain.

    (a) What is the expected value to the corporation of checking a single lightbulb?

    (b) What is the expected value to the corporation of checking two lightbulbs?

    (c) What is the difference between expected values of checking two bulbs and one bulb?

    (d) If the first bulb checked turns out to be defective, what is the expected value of checking the second?

    (e) If the first bulb checked turns out not to be defective, what is the expected value of checking the second?

    (f) Reconcile your answer to part (c) with your answers to parts (d) and (e).

19.6 ALLOWING FOR RISK: UTILITY ANALYSIS

The expected monetary value criterion provides a framework for decision making that has wide practical applicability. That is to say, in many instances, an individual or corporation will believe that the action offering the highest expected monetary value is the preferred course. However, this is not invariably the case, as the following examples illustrate.

1. Many individuals purchase term life insurance through which, for a relatively modest outlay, the insured person's estate is generously compensated in the event of death during the term of the policy. Now, insurance companies are able to calculate the probability of the death of an individual of any given age during a specified period of time. Accordingly, their rates are set in such a way that the price of a policy exceeds the amount of money that is expected to be paid out. The amount of this excess covers the insurance company's costs and provides, on the average, a margin of profit. It then follows that for the person insured, the expected payoff from the life insurance policy is less than its cost. Therefore, if everyone based decisions on the expected monetary value criterion, term life insurance would not be purchased. Nevertheless, many people do buy this form of insurance, demonstrating a willingness to sacrifice something in expected returns for the assurance that the heirs will be provided a financial cushion in the event of death.

2. Suppose that an investor is considering purchasing shares in one or more of a group of corporations, whose prospects he regards as bright. In principle, it is possible to postulate the various states of nature that will influence the returns from investment in each of these corporations. In this way, the expected monetary value of an investment of a fixed amount in each corporation could be determined. According to the expected monetary value criterion, the investor should then put all of his available capital into the corporation for which the expected monetary value is highest. In fact, a great many investors in the stock market do not follow such a strategy. Rather, they spread their cash over a portfolio of stocks. The abandonment of the option of "putting all one's eggs in a single basket," while leading to a lower expected return, provides a hedge against the possibility of losing a good deal of money if the single stock with the highest expected return happens to perform badly. In opting for a portfolio of stocks, the investor is asserting a willingness to sacrifice something in expected monetary value for a smaller chance of a large financial loss.

In each of these examples, the decision maker has exhibited a preference for a criterion of choice other than expected monetary value, and in each circumstance this preference seems to be extremely reasonable. The two examples involve a common ingredient, in addition to expected returns. In both cases, the decision maker wants to take **risk** into account. The purchaser of term life insurance is prepared to accept a negative expected return as the price to be paid for the chance of a large positive return in the event of death. In doing so, he is expressing a *preference for risk*.[3] By contrast, the investor who, in spreading his investment over a portfolio of stocks, accepts a lower expected return in order to reduce the chances of a large loss is expressing an *aversion to risk*.

We have seen that the expected monetary value criterion is inappropriate for decision makers who either prefer or are averse to risk. Fortunately, it is not too difficult to modify this criterion to handle situations in which risk is a relevant factor. Essentially, the idea is to replace the monetary payoffs by quantities that reflect not only the dollar amounts to be received but also the decision maker's attitude to risk.

---

[3] He is, of course, guarding *against* the risk that his family will be financially ill-prepared for his death.

THE CONCEPT OF UTILITY

In Example 19.3, we considered the problem of an investor choosing between a guaranteed fixed-interest investment and a portfolio of stocks. The former yielded a payoff of $1,200, while gains of $2,500 and $500 resulted for the latter if the stock market were to be buoyant or steady, but a loss of $1,000 resulted if it were to be depressed. This investor believed that the respective probabilities for these three states of nature were .6, .2, and .2. In that event, we saw that the expected monetary value from choosing the stock portfolio was $1,400, exceeding by $200 that of the fixed-interest investment. At this juncture, we need to inquire whether this higher expected return merits the risk of losing $1,000, as would occur if the market were depressed. A very wealthy investor, who could quite comfortably sustain such a loss, would almost certainly decide that it did. However, the position of a relatively poor person, to whom a loss of $1,000 would be quite disastrous, may well be different. For such an investor, the payoffs must be replaced by some other quantities that more adequately reflect the calamitous nature of a loss of $1,000. These quantities must measure the value, or **utility,** to the investor of a loss of $1,000 as compared with, for example, gains of $500 or $2,500.

The concept of utility, which plays a central role in microeconomics, provides the basis for the solution of decision-making problems in the presence of risk preference or aversion. To employ it, we need only fairly mild and usually quite reasonable assumptions. Suppose that an individual is faced with several possible payoffs, which may or may not be monetary. It is assumed that the individual can rank in order (possibly with ties) the utility, or satisfaction, that would be derived from each. Thus, if payoff A is preferred to B and B is preferred to C, A must be preferred to C.

We need also to assume that if payoff A is preferred to B and B is preferred to C, there exists a gamble, which offers A with probability p and C with probability $(1 - p)$, such that the decision maker will be indifferent between taking this gamble and receiving B with certainty. Given these and certain other, generally innocuous assumptions whose details need not detain us, it is possible to show that the rational decision maker will choose the action for which expected utility is highest. Consequently, we can analyze the decision problem precisely as in Sections 19.3–19.5, *but with utilities instead of payoffs.* That is to say, we construct a utility table rather than a payoff table and then employ state-of-nature probabilities to compare expected utilities.

We must now discuss how the utilities corresponding to the various payoffs are determined. The possible payoffs for our investor are −$1,000, $500, $1,200, and $2,500. The steps involved in finding the corresponding utilities are stated in the box.

Obtaining a Utility Function

Suppose that a decision maker may receive several alternative payoffs. The transformation from payoffs to **utilities** is obtained as follows:

(i) The units in which utility is measured are arbitrary. Accordingly, we can fix a scale in any convenient fashion. Let L be the lowest and H the highest of all the payoffs. We will assign utility 0 to payoff L and utility 100 to payoff H.

(ii) Let I be any payoff between L and H. We need to determine the probability p such that the decision maker is indifferent between the following alternatives:

    (a) Receive payoff I with certainty

    (b) Receive payoff H with probability p and payoff L with probability $(1 - p)$.

(iii) The utility to the decision maker of payoff I is then $100p$. The curve relating utility to payoff is called a **utility function.**

The first step is straightforward and simply provides us with a convenient metric for measuring utility. The choice of the numbers 0 and 100 to represent the utilities of the lowest and highest payoffs is entirely arbitrary. Any other pair of numbers could equally well be used, as long as the utility of the highest payoff is greater than that of the lowest, without affecting the remaining analysis.

As a practical matter, the second step is the most difficult, partly because it presupposes that the decision maker can manipulate probabilities in a coherent way. In practice, the probability p must be determined by trial and error, through the asking of questions such as the following:

Q. Would you prefer to receive I with certainty or a gamble in which you could obtain H with probability .9 and L with probability .1?

Q. Would you prefer to receive I with certainty or a gamble in which you could obtain H with probability .8 and L with probability .2?

This process is continued until the point of indifference is reached.

The logic of the final step is quite straightforward. Since H has utility 100 and L has utility 0, the **expected utility** if H is obtained with probability p and L with probability $(1 - p)$ is

$$100p + 0(1 - p) = 100p$$

Since the decision maker is indifferent between this gamble and receiving I with certainty, the utility $100p$ is associated with the payoff I.

We now return to our investor. At the first step, we attach utility 0 to the lowest payoff, $-\$1,000$, and utility 100 to the highest, $\$2,500$.

It remains to determine the utilities for the intermediate payoffs, $\$500$ and $\$1,200$. This is achieved by posing to the decision maker a series of questions such as

Q. Would you prefer to receive $\$500$ with certainty or a gamble in which you could obtain a gain of $\$2,500$ with probability p and a loss of $\$1,000$ with probability $(1 - p)$?

Different values of the probability p are tried until the value at which the decision maker is indifferent between the two alternatives is found. This process is repeated for the payoff of $\$1,200$.

Suppose that the investor is indifferent between a payoff of $500 and this gamble with $p = .6$ and between a payoff of $1,200 and the gamble with $p = .8$. The utilities for the intermediate payoffs are then

Payoff $500   Utility = $(100)(.6) = 60$

Payoff $1,200   Utility = $(100)(.8) = 80$

The four utilities for this investor are plotted against the corresponding payoffs as points in Figure 19.6. To indicate the general shape of this investor's utility function, we have drawn a curve through these points. The shape of this curve is interesting, since it characterizes the investor's attitude to risk. As must be the case, utility increases as the payoff increases. However, notice that the *rate of increase* of utility is highest at the lowest payoffs and decreases as payoff increases. This implies a distaste for the lowest payoffs that is more than commensurate with their monetary amounts, indicating *aversion* to risk. This aversion can be seen from the investor's attitude to the gambles offered. For example, the investor is indifferent between a sure payoff of $500 and a gamble in which $2,500 might be won with probability .6 and $1,000 lost with probability .4. The expected monetary value of this gamble is

$$(.6)(2,500) + (.4)(-1,000) = \$1,100$$

which considerably exceeds the equally preferred sure payoff of $500. The amount of this difference provides a measure of the extent of the aversion to risk.

The shape of Figure 19.6 is typical of risk aversion. In Figure 19.7, we show three types of utility functions. The function in part (a) of the figure, where utility increases at a *decreasing* rate as payoff increases, has the same shape as Figure 19.6, once again reflecting an *aversion* to risk. In part (b) of the figure, utility increases at an *increasing* rate as the payoffs become higher. This implies a taste for the highest payoffs that is more than commensurate with the monetary amounts involved, thus showing *preference* for risk. Finally, part (c) of Figure 19.7 shows the intermediate case,

FIGURE 19.6 Utility function for an investor

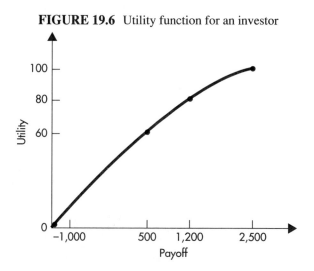

with utility increasing at a *constant* rate for all payoffs. In this case, the monetary values of the payoffs provide a true measure of their utility to the decision maker, who thus demonstrates *indifference* to risk.

The three curves of Figure 19.7 characterize aversion for, preference for, and indifference to risk. However, it is not necessarily the case that a decision-maker will exhibit just one of these attitudes over the whole range of possible payoffs. Figure 19.8 illustrates a more complex situation. Here, for payoffs in the range between M_1 and M_2, the utility function has the shape of Figure 19.7(a), indicating aversion to risk in this payoff range. However, for payoffs of monetary amounts between M_2 and M_3, this utility function has the shape of Figure 19.7(b). Hence, for this range of payoffs, the decision maker exhibits a preference for risk. Finally, in the range of highest

FIGURE 19.7 Utility functions

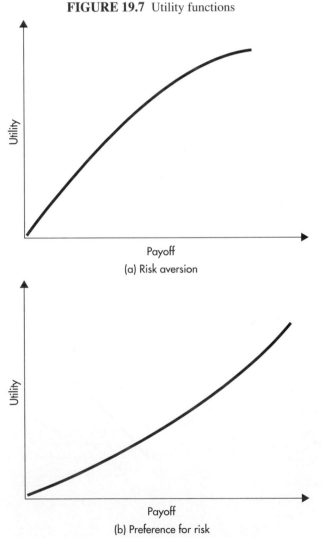

(a) Risk aversion

(b) Preference for risk

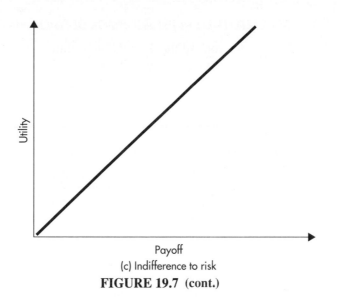

Payoff

(c) Indifference to risk

FIGURE 19.7 (cont.)

payoffs, between M_3 and M_4, the position is once again reversed, the decision maker being averse to risk in this region. Such a utility function can arise in practical problems. For example, an investor may well be averse to sustaining a substantial loss, while being prepared to accept some risk to obtain a fairly high positive return rather than a modest one. However, if a satisfactorily high return can be achieved at modest risk, the investor may be reluctant to risk much more for the possibility of an even higher return.

FIGURE 19.8 Utility function showing aversion to risk for payoffs between M_1 and M_2 and between M_3 and M_4 and preference for risk between payoffs M_2 and M_3

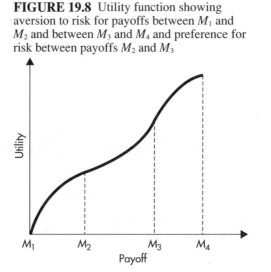

Having determined the appropriate utilities, it remains only to solve the decision-making problem by finding that course of action with the highest expected utility. These expected utilities are obtained in the usual manner, employing the probabilities of the states of nature, as described in the box.

The Expected Utility Criterion

Suppose that a decision maker has K possible actions, $a_1, a_2, \ldots, a_K$, and is faced with H states of nature. Let U_{ij} denote the utility corresponding to the ith action and jth state and p_j the probability of occurrence of the jth state of nature. Then the **expected utility,** $EU(a_i)$, of the action a_i is

$$EU(a_i) = p_1 U_{i1} + p_2 U_{i2} + \cdots + p_H U_{iH} = \sum_{j=1}^{H} p_j U_{ij}$$

Given a choice between alternative actions, the **expected utility criterion** dictates the choice of the action for which expected utility is highest. Under generally reasonable assumptions, it can be shown that this criterion should be adopted by the rational decision maker.

If the decision maker is indifferent to risk, the expected utility criterion and the expected monetary value criterion are equivalent.

Table 19.11 shows the utilities and state-of-nature probabilities for our investor. If the fixed-interest investment is chosen, a utility of 80 is assured, whichever state of nature prevails. For the portfolio of stocks, the expected utility is

$$(.6)(100) + (.2)(60) + (.2)(0) = 72$$

Since this is less than 80, this investor should elect to make the fixed-interest investment, according to the expected utility criterion.

In Example 19.3, we found that investment in the portfolio of stocks was selected by the expected monetary value criterion. However, the incorporation into the analysis of another factor—the extent of this investor's aversion to risk—leads to the conclusion that the fixed-interest option is the better choice. This example serves to illustrate that on occasion, when risk is an important factor, the expected monetary value criterion is inadequate for solving decision-making problems.

The expected utility criterion is the most generally applicable and intellectually defensible of the criteria we have introduced for attacking decision-making problems.

TABLE 19.11 Utilities and state-of-nature probabilities for an investor

INVESTMENT	STATE OF THE MARKET		
	BUOYANT ($p = .6$)	STEADY ($p = .2$)	DEPRESSED ($p = .2$)
Fixed interest	80	80	80
Stock portfolio	100	60	0

Its chief drawback arises from the difficulty of eliciting information about which gambles are regarded as equally attractive as particular assured payoffs. As we have seen, this type of information is essential in the determination of utilities. For a wide range of problems where indifference to risk can safely be assumed, the expected monetary value criterion remains applicable. This would typically be the case, for example, in decision-making in a mature corporation, when the payoffs involved represented only a small proportion of the corporation's total turnover. If, however (as may be the case in the development of a new commercial airliner, for example), possible losses from a project could threaten a corporation with insolvency, the utilities should appropriately reflect an aversion to risk. A company may attempt to spread this risk by forming partnerships with other firms in the industry or with possible customers. Perhaps, also, government may be invited to share or take on the bulk of the risk.

EXERCISES

43. The investor of Exercise 1 has the following six possible payoffs (in dollars):

$$-1,500 \qquad -600 \qquad 800 \qquad 1,200 \qquad 4,300 \qquad 6,600$$

We assign utility 0 to the payoff $-\$1,500$ and utility 100 to the payoff $\$6,600$. For each of the other four payoffs, the investor was asked the question:

Q: Would you prefer to receive payoff I with certainty or a wager in which you gained $\$6,600$ with probability p and lost $\$1,500$ with probability (1 2 p)? The probability p at which the investor was indifferent between these alternatives was recorded. The results obtained are shown in the accompanying table.

PAYOFF	-600	800	1,200	4,300
p	.20	.30	.40	.80

(a) Find the utilities for these four intermediate payoffs.

(b) Assume that the probabilities for the three states of nature are

$$P(s_1) = .2 \qquad P(s_2) = .5 \qquad P(s_3) = .3$$

Which investment should be chosen to maximize expected utility?

44. A decision maker faces a problem in which the possible payoffs (in dollars) are:

$$1,000 \qquad 3,000 \qquad 6,000 \qquad 9,000 \qquad 10,000 \qquad 12,000$$

Utility 0 is assigned to a payoff of $\$1,000$ and utility 100 to a payoff of $\$12,000$. This decision maker is indifferent to risk for payoffs in this range.

(a) Find the utilities for the four intermediate payoffs.

(b) For each intermediate payoff, I, find the probability p such that the decision maker is indifferent between receiving I with certainty and a wager in which $\$12,000$ is received with probability p and $\$1,000$ with probability $(1 - p)$.

45. The shoe store operator of Exercise 7 has six possible payoffs (in dollars):

$$-10,000 \qquad 30,000 \qquad 60,000 \qquad 70,000 \qquad 90,000 \qquad 130,000$$

Assign utility 0 to a loss of $10,000 and utility 100 to a profit of $130,000. For each intermediate payoff I, the probabilities p such that the shoe store operator is indifferent between receiving I with certainty and a gamble in which $130,000 would be gained with probability p and $10,000 lost with probability $(1 - p)$ are shown in the accompanying table.

PAYOFF	30,000	60,000	70,000	90,000
p	.35	.60	.70	.85

(a) What are the utilities for the intermediate payoffs?

(b) Suppose that the probabilities that the new shopping center will be very successful, moderately successful, and unsuccessful are .4, .4, and .2, respectively. Which action should be taken if expected utility is to be maximized?

46. The shoe store operator of Exercise 45 is unsure what value p to attach to indifference between receiving $30,000 with certainty and a gamble in which $130,000 would be gained with probability p and $10,000 lost with probability $(1 - p)$. Assuming that the remaining problem specifications are as in Exercise 45, under what range of values for this probability will the expected utility criterion yield the same choice of action?

47. Consider the contractor of Exercise 19. In fact, this contractor is indifferent between submitting and not submitting a bid. What does this imply about the contractor's utility function?

48. The publisher of Exercise 22 faces a two-stage decision problem, for which the possible eventual payoffs (in dollars) are as follows:

$$-110,000 \qquad -80,000 \qquad 50,000 \qquad 80,000 \qquad 220,000 \qquad 250,000$$

A utility of 0 is assigned to a loss of $110,000 and a utility of 100 to a profit of $250,000. For each intermediate payoff I, the probabilities p such that the publisher is indifferent between payoff I with certainty and a gamble in which $250,000 is gained with probability p and $110,000 lost with probability $(1 - p)$ are given in the accompanying table. If this publisher wants to maximize expected utility, what strategy should he follow?

PAYOFF	−80,000	50,000	80,000	220,00
p	.20	.45	.55	.95

49. Consider the problem of the consultant of Exercise 24, and ignore the option in part (d). The possible payoffs (in dollars) are

$$-2,250 \qquad -1,500 \qquad -750 \qquad -500 \qquad 3,500 \qquad 3,750$$

For each intermediate payoff I, the probabilities p such that the consultant is indifferent between receiving I with certainty and a gamble in which $3,750 is gained with probability p and $2,250 lost with probability $(1 - p)$ are given in the accompanying table. If the consultant wants to maximize expected utility, how should he proceed?

PAYOFF	−1,500	−750	−500	3,500
p	.15	.20	.25	.98

REVIEW EXERCISES

50. We have discussed the following four criteria for decision making:
   - **(i)** Maximin criterion
   - **(ii)** Minimax regret criterion
   - **(iii)** Expected monetary value criterion
   - **(iv)** Expected utility criterion

Briefly outline the philosophies behind these criteria, and discuss their advantages and disadvantages.

51. Of what potential value is sample information in the context of business decision-making? Provide examples of decision-making problems where it would be realistic to expect sample information to be useful.

52. Distinguish among aversion to risk, preference for risk, and indifference to risk. What is the relevance of these concepts to the analysis of business decision-making problems?

53. A consultant is considering submitting detailed bids for two possible contracts. The bid for the first contract costs $100 to prepare, while that for the second contract costs $150 to prepare. If the bid for the first contract is accepted and the work is carried out, a profit of $800 will result. If the bid for the second contract is accepted and the work is carried out, a profit of $1,200 will result. Any costs of bid preparation must be subtracted from these profits. The consultant can, if he wishes, submit bids for both contracts. He does not, however, have the resources to carry out both pieces of work simultaneously. If a bid is submitted and accepted and the consultant is then unable to carry out the work, he counts this as a cost of $200 in lost goodwill. For the decision-making process, there are four possible states of nature:

s_1: Both bids rejected
s_2: Bid for the first contract accepted, bid for the second contract rejected
s_3: Bid for the second contract accepted, bid for the first contract rejected
s_4: Both bids accepted

   (a) The consultant has four possible courses of action. What are they?
   (b) Set out the payoff table for this consultant's decision-making problem.
   (c) Which action is chosen by the maximin criterion?
   (d) Which action is chosen by the minimax regret criterion?

54. Refer to Exercise 53. The consultant believes that the probability is .7 that a bid for the first contract would be accepted and .4 that a bid for the second contract would be accepted. He also believes that the acceptance of one bid is independent of acceptance of the other.

   (a) What are the probabilities for the four states of nature?
   (b) According to the expected monetary value criterion, which action should the consultant adopt, and what is the expected monetary value of this action?
   (c) Draw the decision tree for the consultant's problem.
   (d) What is the expected value of perfect information to this consultant?
   (e) The consultant is offered "inside information" on the prospects of the bid for the first contract. This information is entirely reliable, in the sense that it would allow him to know for sure whether the bid would be accepted. However, no further information is available on the prospects of the bid for the second contract. What is the expected value of this "inside information"?

55. Refer to Exercises 53 and 54. There are nine possible payoffs for this consultant, as follows (in dollars):

| -250 | -150 | -100 | 0 | 550 | 700 | 750 | 950 | 1,050 |

A utility of 0 is assigned to a loss of $250 and a utility of 100 to a profit of $1,050. For each intermediate payoff I, the probabilities p such that the consultant is indifferent between payoff I with certainty and a gamble in which $1,050 is gained with probability p and $250 lost with probability $(1 - p)$ are shown in the accompanying table. According to the expected utility criterion, which action should the consultant choose, and what is the expected utility of this action?

PAYOFF		−150	−100	0	550	700	750	950
p		.05	.10	.20	.65	.70	.75	.85

A P P E N D I X T A B L E S

TABLE 1 Probability function of the binomial distribution

The table shows the probability of x successes in n independent trials, each with probability of success p. For example, the probability of four successes in eight independent trials, each with probability of success .35, is .1875.

n	x					p					
		.05	.10	.15	.20	.25	.30	.35	.40	.45	.50
1	0	.9500	.9000	.8500	.8000	.7500	.7000	.6500	.6000	.5500	.5000
	1	.0500	.1000	.1500	.2000	.2500	.3000	.3500	.4000	.4500	.5000
2	0	.9025	.8100	.7225	.6400	.5625	.4900	.4225	.3600	.3025	.2500
	1	.0950	.1800	.2550	.3200	.3750	.4200	.4550	.4800	.4950	.5000
	2	.0025	.0100	.0225	.0400	.0625	.0900	.1225	.1600	.2025	.2500
3	0	.8574	.7290	.6141	.5120	.4219	.3430	.2746	.2160	.1664	.1250
	1	.1354	.2430	.3251	.3840	.4219	.4410	.4436	.4320	.4084	.3750
	2	.0071	.0270	.0574	.0960	.1406	.1890	.2389	.2880	.3341	.3750
	3	.0001	.0010	.0034	.0080	.0156	.0270	.0429	.0640	.0911	.1250
4	0	.8145	.6561	.5220	.4096	.3164	.2401	.1785	.1296	.0915	.0625
	1	.1715	.2916	.3685	.4096	.4219	.4116	.3845	.3456	.2995	.2500
	2	.0135	.0486	.0975	.1536	.2109	.2646	.3105	.3456	.3675	.3750
	3	.0005	.0036	.0115	.0256	.0469	.0756	.1115	.1536	.2005	.2500
	4	.0000	.0001	.0005	.0016	.0039	.0081	.0150	.0256	.0410	.0625
5	0	.7738	.5905	.4437	.3277	.2373	.1681	.1160	.0778	.0503	.0312
	1	.2036	.3280	.3915	.4096	.3955	.3602	.3124	.2592	.2059	.1562
	2	.0214	.0729	.1382	.2048	.2637	.3087	.3364	.3456	.3369	.3125
	3	.0011	.0081	.0244	.0512	.0879	.1323	.1811	.2304	.2757	.3125
	4	.0000	.0004	.0022	.0064	.0146	.0284	.0488	.0768	.1128	.1562
	5	.0000	.0000	.0001	.0003	.0010	.0024	.0053	.0102	.0185	.0312
6	0	.7351	.5314	.3771	.2621	.1780	.1176	.0754	.0467	.0277	.0156
	1	.2321	.3543	.3993	.3932	.3560	.3025	.2437	.1866	.1359	.0938
	2	.0305	.0984	.1762	.2458	.2966	.3241	.3280	.3110	.2780	.2344
	3	.0021	.0146	.0415	.0819	.1318	.1852	.2355	.2765	.3032	.3125
	4	.0001	.0012	.0055	.0154	.0330	.0595	.0951	.1382	.1861	.2344
	5	.0000	.0001	.0004	.0015	.0044	.0102	.0205	.0369	.0609	.0938
	6	.0000	.0000	.0000	.0001	.0002	.0007	.0018	.0041	.0083	.0156
7	0	.6983	.4783	.3206	.2097	.1335	.0824	.0490	.0280	.0152	.0078
	1	.2573	.3720	.3960	.3670	.3115	.2471	.1848	.1306	.0872	.0547
	2	.0406	.1240	.2097	.2753	.3115	.3177	.2985	.2613	.2140	.1641
	3	.0036	.0230	.0617	.1147	.1730	.2269	.2679	.2903	.2918	.2734
	4	.0002	.0026	.0109	.0287	.0577	.0972	.1442	.1935	.2388	.2734
	5	.0000	.0002	.0012	.0043	.0115	.0250	.0466	.0774	.1172	.1641
	6	.0000	.0000	.0001	.0004	.0013	.0036	.0084	.0172	.0320	.0547
	7	.0000	.0000	.0000	.0000	.0001	.0002	.0006	.0016	.0037	.0078
8	0	.6634	.4305	.2725	.1678	.1001	.0576	.0319	.0168	.0084	.0039
	1	.2793	.3826	.3847	.3355	.2670	.1977	.1373	.0896	.0548	.0312
	2	.0515	.1488	.2376	.2936	.3115	.2965	.2587	.2090	.1569	.1094
	3	.0054	.0331	.0839	.1468	.2076	.2541	.2786	.2787	.2568	.2188
	4	.0004	.0046	.0185	.0459	.0865	.1361	.1875	.2322	.2627	.2734

TABLE 1 Probability function of the binomial distribution (cont.)

n	x	.05	.10	.15	.20	.25	.30	.35	.40	.45	.50
	5	.0000	.0004	.0026	.0092	.0231	.0467	.0808	.1239	.1719	.2188
	6	.0000	.0000	.0002	.0011	.0038	.0100	.0217	.0413	.0703	.1094
	7	.0000	.0000	.0000	.0001	.0004	.0012	.0033	.0079	.0164	.0312
	8	.0000	.0000	.0000	.0000	.0000	.0001	.0002	.0007	.0017	.0039
9	0	.6302	.3874	.2316	.1342	.0751	.0404	.0207	.0101	.0046	.0020
	1	.2985	.3874	.3679	.3020	.2253	.1556	.1004	.0605	.0339	.0176
	2	.0629	.1722	.2597	.3020	.3003	.2668	.2162	.1612	.1110	.0703
	3	.0077	.0446	.1069	.1762	.2336	.2668	.2716	.2508	.2119	.1641
	4	.0006	.0074	.0283	.0661	.1168	.1715	.2194	.2508	.2600	.2461
	5	.0000	.0008	.0050	.0165	.0389	.0735	.1181	.1672	.2128	.2461
	6	.0000	.0001	.0006	.0028	.0087	.0210	.0424	.0743	.1160	.1641
	7	.0000	.0000	.0000	.0003	.0012	.0039	.0098	.0212	.0407	.0703
	8	.0000	.0000	.0000	.0000	.0001	.0004	.0013	.0035	.0083	.0176
	9	.0000	.0000	.0000	.0000	.0000	.0000	.0001	.0003	.0008	.0020
10	0	.5987	.3487	.1969	.1074	.0563	.0282	.0135	.0060	.0025	.0010
	1	.3151	.3874	.3474	.2684	.1877	.1211	.0725	.0403	.0207	.0098
	2	.0746	.1937	.2759	.3020	.2816	.2335	.1757	.1209	.0763	.0439
	3	.0105	.0574	.1298	.2013	.2503	.2668	.2522	.2150	.1665	.1172
	4	.0010	.0112	.0401	.0881	.1460	.2001	.2377	.2508	.2384	.2051
	5	.0001	.0015	.0085	.0264	.0584	.1029	.1536	.2007	.2340	.2461
	6	.0000	.0001	.0012	.0055	.0162	.0368	.0689	.1115	.1596	.2051
	7	.0000	.0000	.0001	.0008	.0031	.0090	.0212	.0425	.0746	.1172
	8	.0000	.0000	.0000	.0001	.0004	.0014	.0043	.0106	.0226	.0439
	9	.0000	.0000	.0000	.0000	.0000	.0001	.0005	.0016	.0042	.0098
	10	.0000	.0000	.0000	.0000	.0000	.0000	.0000	.0001	.0003	.0010
11	0	.5688	.3138	.1673	.0859	.0422	.0198	.0088	.0036	.0014	.0005
	1	.3293	.3835	.3248	.2362	.1549	.0932	.0518	.0266	.0125	.0054
	2	.0867	.2131	.2866	.2953	.2581	.1998	.1395	.0887	.0513	.0269
	3	.0137	.0710	.1517	.2215	.2581	.2568	.2254	.1774	.1259	.0806
	4	.0014	.0158	.0536	.1107	.1721	.2201	.2428	.2365	.2060	.1611
	5	.0001	.0025	.0132	.0388	.0803	.1321	.1830	.2207	.2360	.2256
	6	.0000	.0003	.0023	.0097	.0268	.0566	.0985	.1471	.1931	.2256
	7	.0000	.0000	.0003	.0017	.0064	.0173	.0379	.0701	.1128	.1611
	8	.0000	.0000	.0000	.0002	.0011	.0037	.0102	.0234	.0462	.0806
	9	.0000	.0000	.0000	.0000	.0001	.0005	.0018	.0052	.0126	.0269
	10	.0000	.0000	.0000	.0000	.0000	.0000	.0002	.0007	.0021	.0054
	11	.0000	.0000	.0000	.0000	.0000	.0000	.0000	.0000	.0002	.0005
12	0	.5404	.2824	.1422	.0687	.0317	.0138	.0057	.0022	.0008	.0002
	1	.3413	.3766	.3012	.2062	.1267	.0712	.0368	.0174	.0075	.0029
	2	.0988	.2301	.2924	.2835	.2323	.1678	.1088	.0639	.0339	.0161
	3	.0173	.0852	.1720	.2362	.2581	.2397	.1954	.1419	.0923	.0537
	4	.0021	.0213	.0683	.1329	.1936	.2311	.2367	.2128	.1700	.1208
	5	.0002	.0038	.0193	.0532	.1032	.1585	.2039	.2270	.2225	.1934
	6	.0000	.0005	.0040	.0155	.0401	.0792	.1281	.1766	.2124	.2256
	7	.0000	.0000	.0006	.0033	.0115	.0291	.0591	.1009	.1489	.1934
	8	.0000	.0000	.0001	.0005	.0024	.0078	.0199	.0420	.0762	.1208
	9	.0000	.0000	.0000	.0001	.0004	.0015	.0048	.0125	.0277	.0537
	10	.0000	.0000	.0000	.0000	.0000	.0002	.0008	.0025	.0068	.0161
	11	.0000	.0000	.0000	.0000	.0000	.0000	.0001	.0003	.0010	.0029
	12	.0000	.0000	.0000	.0000	.0000	.0000	.0000	.0000	.0001	.0002
13	0	.5133	.2542	.1209	.0550	.0238	.0097	.0037	.0013	.0004	.0001
	1	.3512	.3672	.2774	.1787	.1029	.0540	.0259	.0113	.0045	.0016
	2	.1109	.2448	.2937	.2680	.2059	.1388	.0836	.0453	.0220	.0095
	3	.0214	.0997	.1900	.2457	.2517	.2181	.1651	.1107	.0660	.0349
	4	.0028	.0277	.0838	.1535	.2097	.2337	.2222	.1845	.1350	.0873

TABLE 1 Probability function of the binomial distribution (cont.)

n	x	.05	.10	.15	.20	.25	.30	.35	.40	.45	.50
	5	.0003	.0055	.0266	.0691	.1258	.1803	.2154	.2214	.1989	.1571
	6	.0000	.0008	.0063	.0230	.0559	.1030	.1546	.1968	.2169	.2095
	7	.0000	.0001	.0011	.0058	.0186	.0442	.0833	.1312	.1775	.2095
	8	.0000	.0000	.0001	.0011	.0047	.0142	.0336	.0656	.1089	.1571
	9	.0000	.0000	.0000	.0001	.0009	.0034	.0101	.0243	.0495	.0873
	10	.0000	.0000	.0000	.0000	.0001	.0006	.0022	.0065	.0162	.0349
	11	.0000	.0000	.0000	.0000	.0000	.0001	.0003	.0012	.0036	.0095
	12	.0000	.0000	.0000	.0000	.0000	.0000	.0000	.0001	.0005	.0016
	13	.0000	.0000	.0000	.0000	.0000	.0000	.0000	.0000	.0000	.0001
14	0	.4877	.2288	.1028	.0440	.0178	.0068	.0024	.0008	.0002	.0001
	1	.3593	.3559	.2539	.1539	.0832	.0407	.0181	.0073	.0027	.0009
	2	.1229	.2570	.2912	.2501	.1802	.1134	.0634	.0317	.0141	.0056
	3	.0259	.1142	.2056	.2501	.2402	.1943	.1366	.0845	.0462	.0222
	4	.0037	.0348	.0998	.1720	.2202	.2290	.2022	.1549	.1040	.0611
	5	.0004	.0078	.0352	.0860	.1468	.1963	.2178	.2066	.1701	.1222
	6	.0000	.0013	.0093	.0322	.0734	.1262	.1759	.2066	.2088	.1833
	7	.0000	.0002	.0019	.0092	.0280	.0618	.1082	.1574	.1952	.2095
	8	.0000	.0000	.0003	.0020	.0082	.0232	.0510	.0918	.1398	.1833
	9	.0000	.0000	.0000	.0003	.0018	.0066	.0183	.0408	.0762	.1222
	10	.0000	.0000	.0000	.0000	.0003	.0014	.0049	.0136	.0312	.0611
	11	.0000	.0000	.0000	.0000	.0000	.0002	.0010	.0033	.0093	.0222
	12	.0000	.0000	.0000	.0000	.0000	.0000	.0001	.0005	.0019	.0056
	13	.0000	.0000	.0000	.0000	.0000	.0000	.0000	.0001	.0002	.0009
	14	.0000	.0000	.0000	.0000	.0000	.0000	.0000	.0000	.0000	.0001
15	0	.4633	.2059	.0874	.0352	.0134	.0047	.0016	.0005	.0001	.0000
	1	.3658	.3432	.2312	.1319	.0668	.0305	.0126	.0047	.0016	.0005
	2	.1348	.2669	.2856	.2309	.1559	.0916	.0476	.0219	.0090	.0032
	3	.0307	.1285	.2184	.2501	.2252	.1700	.1110	.0634	.0318	.0139
	4	.0049	.0428	.1156	.1876	.2252	.2186	.1792	.1268	.0780	.0417
	5	.0006	.0105	.0449	.1032	.1651	.2061	.2123	.1859	.1404	.0916
	6	.0000	.0019	.0132	.0430	.0917	.1472	.1906	.2066	.1914	.1527
	7	.0000	.0003	.0030	.0138	.0393	.0811	.1319	.1771	.2013	.1964
	8	.0000	.0000	.0005	.0035	.0131	.0348	.0710	.1181	.1647	.1964
	9	.0000	.0000	.0001	.0007	.0034	.0116	.0298	.0612	.1048	.1527
	10	.0000	.0000	.0000	.0001	.0007	.0030	.0096	.0245	.0515	.0916
	11	.0000	.0000	.0000	.0000	.0001	.0006	.0024	.0074	.0191	.0417
	12	.0000	.0000	.0000	.0000	.0000	.0001	.0004	.0016	.0052	.0139
	13	.0000	.0000	.0000	.0000	.0000	.0000	.0001	.0003	.0010	.0032
	14	.0000	.0000	.0000	.0000	.0000	.0000	.0000	.0000	.0001	.0005
	15	.0000	.0000	.0000	.0000	.0000	.0000	.0000	.0000	.0000	.0000
16	0	.4401	.1853	.0743	.0281	.0100	.0033	.0010	.0003	.0001	.0000
	1	.3706	.3294	.2097	.1126	.0535	.0228	.0087	.0030	.0009	.0002
	2	.1463	.2745	.2775	.2111	.1336	.0732	.0353	.0150	.0056	.0018
	3	.0359	.1423	.2285	.2463	.2079	.1465	.0888	.0468	.0215	.0085
	4	.0061	.0514	.1311	.2001	.2552	.2040	.1553	.1014	.0572	.0278
	5	.0008	.0137	.0555	.1201	.1802	.2099	.2008	.1623	.1123	.0667
	6	.0001	.0028	.0180	.0550	.1101	.1649	.1982	.1983	.1684	.1222
	7	.0000	.0004	.0045	.0197	.0524	.1010	.1524	.1889	.1969	.1746
	8	.0000	.0001	.0009	.0055	.0197	.0487	.0923	.1417	.1812	.1964
	9	.0000	.0000	.0001	.0012	.0058	.0185	.0442	.0840	.1318	.1746
	10	.0000	.0000	.0000	.0002	.0014	.0056	.0167	.0392	.0755	.1222
	11	.0000	.0000	.0000	.0000	.0002	.0013	.0049	.0142	.0337	.0667
	12	.0000	.0000	.0000	.0000	.0000	.0002	.0011	.0040	.0115	.0278
	13	.0000	.0000	.0000	.0000	.0000	.0000	.0002	.0008	.0029	.0085
	14	.0000	.0000	.0000	.0000	.0000	.0000	.0000	.0001	.0005	.0018
	15	.0000	.0000	.0000	.0000	.0000	.0000	.0000	.0000	.0001	.0002

TABLE 1 Probability function of the binomial distribution (cont.)

n	x	.05	.10	.15	.20	.25	.30	.35	.40	.45	.50
	16	.0000	.0000	.0000	.0000	.0000	.0000	.0000	.0000	.0000	.0000
17	0	.4181	.1668	.0631	.0225	.0075	.0023	.0007	.0002	.0000	.0000
	1	.3741	.3150	.1893	.0957	.0426	.0169	.0060	.0019	.0005	.0001
	2	.1575	.2800	.2673	.1914	.1136	.0581	.0260	.0102	.0035	.0010
	3	.0415	.1556	.2359	.2393	.1893	.1245	.0701	.0341	.0144	.0052
	4	.0076	.0605	.1457	.2093	.2209	.1868	.1320	.0796	.0411	.0182
	5	.0010	.0175	.0668	.1361	.1914	.2081	.1849	.1379	.0875	.0472
	6	.0001	.0039	.0236	.0680	.1276	.1784	.1991	.1839	.1432	.0944
	7	.0000	.0007	.0065	.0267	.0668	.1201	.1685	.1927	.1841	.1484
	8	.0000	.0001	.0014	.0084	.0279	.0644	.1134	.1606	.1883	.1855
	9	.0000	.0000	.0003	.0021	.0093	.0276	.0611	.1070	.1540	.1855
	10	.0000	.0000	.0000	.0004	.0025	.0095	.0263	.0571	.1008	.1484
	11	.0000	.0000	.0000	.0001	.0005	.0026	.0090	.0242	.0525	.0944
	12	.0000	.0000	.0000	.0000	.0001	.0006	.0024	.0081	.0215	.0472
	13	.0000	.0000	.0000	.0000	.0000	.0001	.0005	.0021	.0068	.0182
	14	.0000	.0000	.0000	.0000	.0000	.0000	.0001	.0004	.0016	.0052
	15	.0000	.0000	.0000	.0000	.0000	.0000	.0000	.0001	.0003	.0010
	16	.0000	.0000	.0000	.0000	.0000	.0000	.0000	.0000	.0000	.0001
	17	.0000	.0000	.0000	.0000	.0000	.0000	.0000	.0000	.0000	.0000
18	0	.3972	.1501	.0536	.0180	.0056	.0016	.0004	.0001	.0000	.0000
	1	.3763	.3002	.1704	.0811	.0338	.0126	.0042	.0012	.0003	.0001
	2	.1683	.2835	.2556	.1723	.0958	.0458	.0190	.0069	.0022	.0006
	3	.0473	.1680	.2406	.2297	.1704	.1046	.0547	.0246	.0095	.0031
	4	.0093	.0700	.1592	.2153	.2130	.1681	.1104	.0614	.0291	.0117
	5	.0014	.0218	.0787	.1507	.1988	.2017	.1664	.1146	.0666	.0327
	6	.0002	.0052	.0301	.0816	.1436	.1873	.1941	.1655	.1181	.0708
	7	.0000	.0010	.0091	.0350	.0820	.1376	.1792	.1892	.1657	.1214
	8	.0000	.0002	.0022	.0120	.0376	.0811	.1327	.1734	.1864	.1669
	9	.0000	.0000	.0004	.0033	.0139	.0386	.0794	.1284	.1694	.1855
	10	.0000	.0000	.0001	.0008	.0042	.0149	.0385	.0771	.1248	.1669
	11	.0000	.0000	.0000	.0001	.0010	.0046	.0151	.0374	.0742	.1214
	12	.0000	.0000	.0000	.0000	.0002	.0012	.0047	.0145	.0354	.0708
	13	.0000	.0000	.0000	.0000	.0000	.0002	.0012	.0044	.0134	.0327
	14	.0000	.0000	.0000	.0000	.0000	.0000	.0002	.0011	.0039	.0117
	15	.0000	.0000	.0000	.0000	.0000	.0000	.0000	.0002	.0009	.0031
	16	.0000	.0000	.0000	.0000	.0000	.0000	.0000	.0000	.0001	.0006
	17	.0000	.0000	.0000	.0000	.0000	.0000	.0000	.0000	.0000	.0001
	18	.0000	.0000	.0000	.0000	.0000	.0000	.0000	.0000	.0000	.0000
19	0	.3774	.1351	.0456	.0144	.0042	.0011	.0003	.0001	.0000	.0000
	1	.3774	.2852	.1529	.0685	.0268	.0093	.0029	.0008	.0002	.0000
	2	.1787	.2852	.2428	.1540	.0803	.0358	.0138	.0046	.0013	.0003
	3	.0533	.1796	.2428	.2182	.1517	.0869	.0422	.0175	.0062	.0018
	4	.0112	.0798	.1714	.2182	.2023	.1419	.0909	.0467	.0203	.0074
	5	.0018	.0266	.0907	.1636	.2023	.1916	.1468	.0933	.0497	.0222
	6	.0002	.0069	.0374	.0955	.1574	.1916	.1844	.1451	.0949	.0518
	7	.0000	.0014	.0122	.0443	.0974	.1525	.1844	.1797	.1443	.0961
	8	.0000	.0002	.0032	.0166	.0487	.0981	.1489	.1797	.1771	.1442
	9	.0000	.0000	.0007	.0051	.0198	.0514	.0980	.1464	.1771	.1762
	10	.0000	.0000	.0001	.0013	.0066	.0220	.0528	.0976	.1449	.1762
	11	.0000	.0000	.0000	.0003	.0018	.0077	.0233	.0532	.0970	.1442
	12	.0000	.0000	.0000	.0000	.0004	.0022	.0083	.0237	.0529	.0961
	13	.0000	.0000	.0000	.0000	.0001	.0005	.0024	.0085	.0233	.0518
	14	.0000	.0000	.0000	.0000	.0000	.0001	.0006	.0024	.0082	.0222
	15	.0000	.0000	.0000	.0000	.0000	.0000	.0001	.0005	.0022	.0074
	16	.0000	.0000	.0000	.0000	.0000	.0000	.0000	.0001	.0005	.0018
	17	.0000	.0000	.0000	.0000	.0000	.0000	.0000	.0000	.0001	.0003

TABLE 1 Probability function of the binomial distribution (cont.)

n	x	.05	.10	.15	.20	.25	.30	.35	.40	.45	.50
	18	.0000	.0000	.0000	.0000	.0000	.0000	.0000	.0000	.0000	.0000
	19	.0000	.0000	.0000	.0000	.0000	.0000	.0000	.0000	.0000	.0000
20	0	.3585	.1216	.0388	.0115	.0032	.0008	.0002	.0000	.0000	.0000
	1	.3774	.2702	.1368	.0576	.0211	.0068	.0020	.0005	.0001	.0000
	2	.1887	.2852	.2293	.1369	.0669	.0278	.0100	.0031	.0008	.0002
	3	.0596	.1901	.2428	.2054	.1339	.0716	.0323	.0123	.0040	.0011
	4	.0133	.0898	.1821	.2182	.1897	.1304	.0738	.0350	.0139	.0046
	5	.0022	.0319	.1028	.1746	.2023	.1789	.1272	.0746	.0365	.0148
	6	.0003	.0089	.0454	.1091	.1686	.1916	.1712	.1244	.0746	.0370
	7	.0000	.0020	.0160	.0545	.1124	.1643	.1844	.1659	.1221	.0739
	8	.0000	.0004	.0046	.0222	.0609	.1144	.1614	.1797	.1623	.1201
	9	.0000	.0001	.0011	.0074	.0271	.0654	.1158	.1597	.1771	.1602
	10	.0000	.0000	.0002	.0020	.0099	.0308	.0686	.1171	.1593	.1762
	11	.0000	.0000	.0000	.0005	.0030	.0120	.0336	.0710	.1185	.1602
	12	.0000	.0000	.0000	.0001	.0008	.0039	.0136	.0355	.0727	.1201
	13	.0000	.0000	.0000	.0000	.0002	.0010	.0045	.0146	.0366	.0739
	14	.0000	.0000	.0000	.0000	.0000	.0002	.0012	.0049	.0150	.0370
	15	.0000	.0000	.0000	.0000	.0000	.0000	.0003	.0013	.0049	.0148
	16	.0000	.0000	.0000	.0000	.0000	.0000	.0000	.0003	.0013	.0046
	17	.0000	.0000	.0000	.0000	.0000	.0000	.0000	.0000	.0002	.0011
	18	.0000	.0000	.0000	.0000	.0000	.0000	.0000	.0000	.0000	.0002
	19	.0000	.0000	.0000	.0000	.0000	.0000	.0000	.0000	.0000	.0000
	20	.0000	.0000	.0000	.0000	.0000	.0000	.0000	.0000	.0000	.0000

Reproduced with permission from National Bureau of Standards, *Tables of the Binomial Probability Distribution*, United States Department of Commerce (1950).

TABLE 2 Values of $e^{-\lambda}$

λ	$e^{-\lambda}$	λ	$e^{-\lambda}$	λ	$e^{-\lambda}$	λ	$e^{-\lambda}$
0.00	1.000000	2.60	.074274	5.10	.006097	7.60	.000501
0.10	.904837	2.70	.067206	5.20	.005517	7.70	.000453
0.20	.818731	2.80	.060810	5.30	.004992	7.80	.000410
0.30	.740818	2.90	.055023	5.40	.004517	7.90	.000371
0.40	.670320	3.00	.049787	5.50	.004087	8.00	.000336
0.50	.606531	3.10	.045049	5.60	.003698	8.10	.000304
0.60	.548812	3.20	.040762	5.70	.003346	8.20	.000275
0.70	.496585	3.30	.036883	5.80	.003028	8.30	.000249
0.80	.449329	3.40	.033373	5.90	.002739	8.40	.000225
0.90	.406570	3.50	.030197	6.00	.002479	8.50	.000204
1.00	.367879	3.60	.027324	6.10	.002243	8.60	.000184
1.10	.332871	3.70	.024724	6.20	.002029	8.70	.000167
1.20	.301194	3.80	.022371	6.30	.001836	8.80	.000151
1.30	.272532	3.90	.020242	6.40	.001661	8.90	.000136
1.40	.246597	4.00	.018316	6.50	.001503	9.00	.000123
1.50	.223130	4.10	.016573	6.60	.001360	9.10	.000112
1.60	.201897	4.20	.014996	6.70	.001231	9.20	.000101
1.70	.182684	4.30	.013569	6.80	.001114	9.30	.000091
1.80	.165299	4.40	.012277	6.90	.001008	9.40	.000083
1.90	.149569	4.50	.011109	7.00	.000912	9.50	.000075
2.00	.135335	4.60	.010052	7.10	.000825	9.60	.000068
2.10	.122456	4.70	.009095	7.20	.000747	9.70	.000061
2.20	.110803	4.80	.008230	7.30	.000676	9.80	.000056
2.30	.100259	4.90	.007447	7.40	.000611	9.90	.000050
2.40	.090718	5.00	.006738	7.50	.000553	10.00	.000045
2.50	.082085						

TABLE 3 Cumulative distribution function of the standard normal distribution

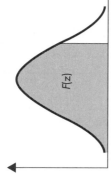

The table shows the probability, $F(z)$, that a standard normal random variable is less than the number z. For example, the probability is .9750 that a standard normal random variable is less than 1.96.

z	F(z)	z	F(z)	z	F(z)	z	F(z)	z	F(z)	z	F(z)
.00	.5000	.31	.6217	.61	.7291	.91	.8186	1.21	.8869	1.51	.9345
.01	.5040	.32	.6255	.62	.7324	.92	.8212	1.22	.8888	1.52	.9357
.02	.5080	.33	.6293	.63	.7357	.93	.8238	1.23	.8907	1.53	.9370
.03	.5120	.34	.6331	.64	.7389	.94	.8264	1.24	.8925	1.54	.9382
.04	.5160	.35	.6368	.65	.7422	.95	.8289	1.25	.8944	1.55	.9394
.05	.5199	.36	.6406	.66	.7454	.96	.8315	1.26	.8962	1.56	.9406
.06	.5239	.37	.6443	.67	.7486	.97	.8340	1.27	.8980	1.57	.9418
.07	.5279	.38	.6480	.68	.7517	.98	.8365	1.28	.8997	1.58	.9429
.08	.5319	.39	.6517	.69	.7549	.99	.8389	1.29	.9015	1.59	.9441
.09	.5359	.40	.6554	.70	.7580	1.00	.8413	1.30	.9032	1.60	.9452
.10	.5398	.41	.6591	.71	.7611	1.01	.8438	1.31	.9049	1.61	.9463
.11	.5438	.42	.6628	.72	.7642	1.02	.8461	1.32	.9066	1.62	.9474
.12	.5478	.43	.6664	.73	.7673	1.03	.8485	1.33	.9082	1.63	.9484
.13	.5517	.44	.6700	.74	.7704	1.04	.8508	1.34	.9099	1.64	.9495
.14	.5557	.45	.6736	.75	.7734	1.05	.8531	1.35	.9115	1.65	.9505
.15	.5596	.46	.6772	.76	.7764	1.06	.8554	1.36	.9131	1.66	.9515
.16	.5636	.47	.6803	.77	.7794	1.07	.8577	1.37	.9147	1.67	.9525
.17	.5675	.48	.6844	.78	.7823	1.08	.8599	1.38	.9162	1.68	.9535
.18	.5714	.49	.6879	.79	.7852	1.09	.8621	1.39	.9177	1.69	.9545
.19	.5753	.50	.6915	.80	.7881	1.10	.8643	1.40	.9192	1.70	.9554
.20	.5793	.51	.6950	.81	.7910	1.11	.8665	1.41	.9207	1.71	.9564
.21	.5832	.52	.6985	.82	.7939	1.12	.8686	1.42	.9222	1.72	.9573
.22	.5871	.53	.7019	.83	.7967	1.13	.8708	1.43	.9236	1.73	.9582
.23	.5910	.54	.7054	.84	.7995	1.14	.8729	1.44	.9251	1.74	.9591
.24	.5948	.55	.7088	.85	.8023	1.15	.8749	1.45	.9265	1.75	.9599
.25	.5987	.56	.7123	.86	.8051	1.16	.8770	1.46	.9279	1.76	.9608
.26	.6026	.57	.7157	.87	.8078	1.17	.8790	1.47	.9292	1.77	.9616
.27	.6064	.58	.7190	.88	.8106	1.18	.8810	1.48	.9306	1.78	.9625
.28	.6103	.59	.7224	.89	.8133	1.19	.8830	1.49	.9319	1.79	.9633
.29	.6141	.60	.7257	.90	.8159	1.20	.8849	1.50	.9332	1.80	.9641
.30	.6179										

TABLE 3 Cumulative distribution function of the standard normal distribution (cont.)

z	F(z)	z	F(z)	z	F(z)	z	F(z)	z	F(z)	z	F(z)
1.81	.9649	2.21	.9864	2.61	.9955	3.01	.9987	3.41	.9997	3.81	.9999
1.82	.9656	2.22	.9868	2.62	.9956	3.02	.9987	3.42	.9997	3.82	.9999
1.83	.9664	2.23	.9871	2.63	.9957	3.03	.9988	3.43	.9997	3.83	.9999
1.84	.9671	2.24	.9875	2.64	.9959	3.04	.9988	3.44	.9997	3.84	.9999
1.85	.9678	2.25	.9878	2.65	.9960	3.05	.9989	3.45	.9997	3.85	.9999
1.86	.9686	2.26	.9881	2.66	.9961	3.06	.9989	3.46	.9997	3.86	.9999
1.87	.9693	2.27	.9884	2.67	.9962	3.07	.9989	3.47	.9997	3.87	.9999
1.88	.9699	2.28	.9887	2.68	.9963	3.08	.9990	3.48	.9997	3.88	.9999
1.89	.9706	2.29	.9890	2.69	.9964	3.09	.9990	3.49	.9998	3.89	1.0000
1.90	.9713	2.30	.9893	2.70	.9965	3.10	.9990	3.50	.9998	3.90	1.0000
1.91	.9719	2.31	.9896	2.71	.9966	3.11	.9991	3.51	.9998	3.91	1.0000
1.92	.9726	2.32	.9898	2.72	.9967	3.12	.9991	3.52	.9998	3.92	1.0000
1.93	.9732	2.33	.9901	2.73	.9968	3.13	.9991	3.53	.9998	3.93	1.0000
1.94	.9738	2.34	.9904	2.74	.9969	3.14	.9992	3.54	.9998	3.94	1.0000
1.95	.9744	2.35	.9906	2.75	.9970	3.15	.9992	3.55	.9998	3.95	1.0000
1.96	.9750	2.36	.9909	2.76	.9971	3.16	.9992	3.56	.9998	3.96	1.0000
1.97	.9756	2.37	.9911	2.77	.9972	3.17	.9992	3.57	.9998	3.97	1.0000
1.98	.9761	2.38	.9913	2.78	.9973	3.18	.9993	3.58	.9998	3.98	1.0000
1.99	.9767	2.39	.9916	2.79	.9974	3.19	.9993	3.59	.9998	3.99	1.0000
2.00	.9772	2.40	.9918	2.80	.9974	3.20	.9993	3.60	.9998		
2.01	.9778	2.41	.9920	2.81	.9975	3.21	.9993	3.61	.9998		
2.02	.9783	2.42	.9922	2.82	.9976	3.22	.9994	3.62	.9999		
2.03	.9788	2.43	.9925	2.83	.9977	3.23	.9994	3.63	.9999		
2.04	.9793	2.44	.9927	2.84	.9977	3.24	.9994	3.64	.9999		
2.05	.9798	2.45	.9929	2.85	.9978	3.25	.9994	3.65	.9999		
2.06	.9803	2.46	.9931	2.86	.9979	3.26	.9994	3.66	.9999		
2.07	.9808	2.47	.9932	2.87	.9979	3.27	.9995	3.67	.9999		
2.08	.9812	2.48	.9934	2.88	.9980	3.28	.9995	3.68	.9999		
2.09	.9817	2.49	.9936	2.89	.9981	3.29	.9995	3.69	.9999		
2.10	.9821	2.50	.9938	2.90	.9981	3.30	.9995	3.70	.9999		
2.11	.9826	2.51	.9940	2.91	.9982	3.31	.9995	3.71	.9999		
2.12	.9830	2.52	.9941	2.92	.9982	3.32	.9996	3.72	.9999		
2.13	.9834	2.53	.9943	2.93	.9983	3.33	.9996	3.73	.9999		
2.14	.9838	2.54	.9945	2.94	.9984	3.34	.9996	3.74	.9999		
2.15	.9842	2.55	.9946	2.95	.9984	3.35	.9996	3.75	.9999		
2.16	.9846	2.56	.9948	2.96	.9985	3.36	.9996	3.76	.9999		
2.17	.9850	2.57	.9949	2.97	.9985	3.37	.9996	3.77	.9999		
2.18	.9854	2.58	.9951	2.98	.9986	3.38	.9996	3.78	.9999		
2.19	.9857	2.59	.9952	2.99	.9986	3.39	.9997	3.79	.9999		
2.20	.9861	2.60	.9953	3.00	.9986	3.40	.9997	3.80	.9999		

TABLE 4 Some uniformly distributed random numbers

85387	51571	57714	00512	61319	69143	08881	01400	55061	82977
84176	03311	16955	59504	54499	32096	79485	98031	99485	16788
27258	51746	67223	98182	43166	54297	26830	29842	78016	73127
99398	46950	19399	65167	35082	30482	86323	41061	21717	48126
72752	89364	02150	85418	05420	84341	02395	27655	59457	55438
69090	93551	11649	54688	57061	77711	24201	16895	64936	62347
39620	54988	67846	71845	54000	26134	84526	16619	82573	01737
81725	49831	35595	29891	46812	57770	03326	31316	75412	80732
87968	85157	84752	93777	62772	78961	30750	76089	23340	64637
07730	01861	40610	73445	70321	26467	53533	20787	46971	29134
32825	82100	67406	44156	21531	67186	39945	04189	79798	41087
34453	05330	40224	04116	24597	93823	28171	47701	76201	68257
00830	34235	40671	66042	06341	54437	81649	70494	01883	18350
24580	05258	37329	59173	62660	72513	82232	49794	36913	05877
59578	08535	77107	19838	40651	01749	58893	99115	05212	92309
75387	24990	12748	71766	17471	15794	68622	59161	14476	75074
02465	34977	48319	53026	53691	80594	58805	76961	62665	82855
49689	08342	81912	92735	30042	47623	60061	69427	21163	68543
60958	20236	79424	04055	54955	73342	14040	72431	99469	41044
79956	98409	79548	39569	83974	43707	77080	08645	20949	56932
04316	01206	08715	77713	20572	13912	94324	14656	11979	53258
78684	28546	06881	66097	53530	42509	54130	30878	77166	98075
69235	18535	61904	99246	84050	15270	07751	90410	96675	62870
81201	04314	92708	44984	83121	33767	56607	46371	20389	08809
80336	59638	44368	33433	97794	10343	19235	82633	17186	63902
65076	87960	92013	60169	49176	50140	39081	04638	96114	63463
90879	70970	50789	59973	47771	94567	35590	23462	33993	99899
50555	84355	97066	82748	98298	14385	82493	40182	20523	69182
48658	41921	86514	46786	74097	62825	46457	24428	09245	86069
26373	19166	88223	32371	11570	62078	92317	13378	05734	71778
20878	80883	26027	29101	58382	17109	53511	95536	21759	10630
20069	60582	55749	88068	48589	01874	42930	40310	34613	97359
46819	38577	20520	94145	99405	47064	25248	27289	41289	54972
83644	04459	73253	58414	94180	09321	59747	07379	56255	45615
08636	31363	56033	49076	88908	51318	39104	56556	23112	63317
92058	38678	12507	90343	17213	24545	66053	76412	29545	89932
05038	18443	87138	05076	25660	23414	84837	87132	84405	15346
41838	68590	93646	82113	25498	33110	15356	81070	84900	42660
15564	81618	99186	73113	99344	13213	07235	90064	89150	86359
74600	40206	15237	37378	96862	78638	14376	46607	55909	46398
78275	77017	60310	13499	35268	47790	77475	44345	14615	25231
30145	71205	10355	18404	85354	22199	90822	35204	47891	69860
46944	00097	39161	50139	60458	44649	85537	90017	18157	13856
85883	21272	89266	94887	00291	70963	28169	95130	27223	35387
83606	98192	82194	26719	24499	28102	97769	98769	30757	81593
66888	81818	52490	54272	70549	69235	74684	96412	65186	87974
63673	73966	34036	44298	60652	05947	05833	27914	57021	58566
37944	16094	39797	63253	64103	32222	65925	64693	34048	75394
93240	66855	29336	28345	71398	45118	01454	72128	09715	29454
40189	76776	70842	32675	81647	75868	21288	12849	94990	21513

Reprinted from *A Million Random Digits with 100,000 Normal Deviates,* by the Rand Corporation (New York: Free Press, 1955), p. 259. Copyright 1955 by the Rand Corporation. Used by permission.

TABLE 5 Cutoff points of the chi-square distribution function

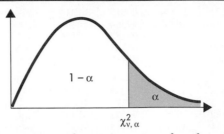

$$\chi^2_{\nu, \alpha}$$

For selected probabilities α, the table shows the values $\chi^2_{\nu,\alpha}$ such that $\alpha = P(\chi^2_\nu > \chi^2_{\nu,\alpha})$, where χ^2_ν is a chi-square random variable with ν degrees of freedom. For example, the probability is .100 that a chi-square random variable with 10 degrees of freedom is greater than 15.99.

ν	.995	.990	.975	.950	.900	.100	.050	.025	.010	.005
1	0.0^4393	0.0^3157	0.0^3982	0.0^2393	0.0158	2.71	3.84	5.02	6.63	7.88
2	0.0100	0.0201	0.0506	0.103	0.211	4.61	5.99	7.38	9.21	10.60
3	0.072	0.115	0.216	0.352	0.584	6.25	7.81	9.35	11.34	12.84
4	0.207	0.297	0.484	0.711	1.064	7.78	9.49	11.14	13.28	14.86
5	0.412	0.554	0.831	1.145	1.61	9.24	11.07	12.83	15.09	16.75
6	0.676	0.872	1.24	1.64	2.20	10.64	12.59	14.45	16.81	18.55
7	0.989	1.24	1.69	2.17	2.83	12.02	14.07	16.01	18.48	20.28
8	1.34	1.65	2.18	2.73	3.49	13.36	15.51	17.53	20.09	21.96
9	1.73	2.09	2.70	3.33	4.17	14.68	16.92	19.02	21.67	23.59
10	2.16	2.56	3.25	3.94	4.87	15.99	18.31	20.48	23.21	25.19
11	2.60	3.05	3.82	4.57	5.58	17.28	19.68	21.92	24.73	26.76
12	3.07	3.57	4.40	5.23	6.30	18.55	21.03	23.34	26.22	28.30
13	3.57	4.11	5.01	5.89	7.04	19.81	22.36	24.74	27.69	29.82
14	4.07	4.66	5.63	6.57	7.79	21.06	23.68	26.12	29.14	31.32
15	4.60	5.23	6.26	7.26	8.55	22.31	25.00	27.49	30.58	32.80
16	5.14	5.81	6.91	7.96	9.31	23.54	26.30	28.85	32.00	34.27
17	5.70	6.41	7.56	8.67	10.09	24.77	27.59	30.19	33.41	35.72
18	6.26	7.01	8.23	9.39	10.86	25.99	28.87	31.53	34.81	37.16
19	6.84	7.63	8.91	10.12	11.65	27.20	30.14	32.85	36.19	38.58
20	7.43	8.26	9.59	10.85	12.44	28.41	31.41	34.17	37.57	40.00
21	8.03	8.90	10.28	11.59	13.24	29.62	32.67	35.48	38.93	41.40
22	8.64	9.54	10.98	12.34	14.04	30.81	33.92	36.78	40.29	42.80
23	9.26	10.20	11.69	13.09	14.85	32.01	35.17	38.08	41.64	44.18
24	9.89	10.86	12.40	13.85	15.66	33.20	36.42	39.36	42.98	45.56
25	10.52	11.52	13.12	14.61	16.47	34.38	37.65	40.65	44.31	46.93
26	11.16	12.20	13.84	15.38	17.29	35.56	38.89	41.92	45.64	48.29
27	11.81	12.88	14.57	16.15	18.11	36.74	40.11	43.19	46.96	49.64
28	12.46	13.56	15.31	16.93	18.94	37.92	41.34	44.46	48.28	50.99
29	13.12	14.26	16.05	17.71	19.77	39.09	42.56	45.72	49.59	52.34
30	13.79	14.95	16.79	18.49	20.60	40.26	43.77	46.98	50.89	53.67
40	20.71	22.16	24.43	26.51	29.05	51.81	55.76	59.34	63.69	66.77
50	27.99	29.71	32.36	34.76	37.69	63.17	67.50	71.42	76.15	79.49
60	35.53	37.48	40.48	43.19	46.46	74.40	79.08	83.30	88.38	91.95
70	43.28	45.44	48.76	51.74	55.33	85.53	90.53	95.02	100.4	104.2
80	51.17	53.54	57.15	60.39	64.28	96.58	101.9	106.6	112.3	116.3
90	59.20	61.75	65.65	69.13	73.29	107.6	113.1	118.1	124.1	128.3
100	67.33	70.06	74.22	77.93	82.36	118.5	124.3	129.6	135.8	140.2

Reproduced with permission from C. M. Thompson, "Tables of percentage points of the chi-square distribution," *Biometrika*, *32* (1941).

TABLE 6 Cutoff points for the Student's *t* distribution

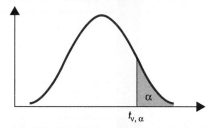

For selected probabilities, α, the table shows the values $t_{\nu,\alpha}$ such that $P(t_\nu > t_{\nu,\alpha}) = \alpha$, where t_ν is a Student's *t* random variable with ν degrees of freedom. For example, the probability is .10 that a Student's *t* random variable with 10 degrees of freedom exceeds 1.372.

ν	α				
	.100	.050	.025	.010	.005
1	3.078	6.314	12.706	31.821	63.657
2	1.886	2.920	4.303	6.965	9.925
3	1.638	2.353	3.182	4.541	5.841
4	1.533	2.132	2.776	3.747	4.604
5	1.476	2.015	2.571	3.365	4.032
6	1.440	1.943	2.447	3.143	3.707
7	1.415	1.895	2.365	2.998	3.499
8	1.397	1.860	2.306	2.896	3.355
9	1.383	1.833	2.262	2.821	3.250
10	1.372	1.812	2.228	2.764	3.169
11	1.363	1.796	2.201	2.718	3.106
12	1.356	1.782	2.179	2.681	3.055
13	1.350	1.771	2.160	2.650	3.012
14	1.345	1.761	2.145	2.624	2.977
15	1.341	1.753	2.131	2.602	2.947
16	1.337	1.746	2.120	2.583	2.921
17	1.333	1.740	2.110	2.567	2.898
18	1.330	1.734	2.101	2.552	2.878
19	1.328	1.729	2.093	2.539	2.861
20	1.325	1.725	2.086	2.528	2.845
21	1.323	1.721	2.080	2.518	2.831
22	1.321	1.717	2.074	2.508	2.819
23	1.319	1.714	2.069	2.500	2.807
24	1.318	1.711	2.064	2.492	2.797
25	1.316	1.708	2.060	2.485	2.787
26	1.315	1.706	2.056	2.479	2.779
27	1.314	1.703	2.052	2.473	2.771
28	1.313	1.701	2.048	2.467	2.763
29	1.311	1.699	2.045	2.462	2.756
30	1.310	1.697	2.042	2.457	2.750
40	1.303	1.684	2.021	2.423	2.704
60	1.296	1.671	2.000	2.390	2.660
∞	1.282	1.645	1.960	2.326	2.576

TABLE 7 Cutoff points for the F distribution

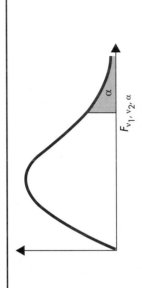

For probabilities $\alpha = .05$ and $\alpha = .01$, the tables show the values $F_{\nu 1, \nu 2, \alpha}$ such that $P(F_{\nu 1, \nu 2} > F_{\nu 1, \nu 2, \alpha}) = \alpha$, where $F_{\nu 1, \nu 2}$ is an F random variable, with numerator degrees of freedom ν_1 and denominator degrees of freedom ν_2. For example, the probability is .05 that an $F_{3, 7}$ random variable exceeds 4.35.

$\alpha = .05$

DENOMINATOR ν_2	1	2	3	4	5	6	7	8	9	10	12	15	20	24	30	40	60	120	∞
1	161.4	199.5	215.7	224.6	230.2	234.0	236.8	238.9	240.5	241.9	243.9	245.9	248.0	249.1	250.1	251.1	252.2	253.3	254.3
2	18.51	19.00	19.16	19.25	19.30	19.33	19.35	19.37	19.38	19.40	19.41	19.43	19.45	19.45	19.46	19.47	19.48	19.49	19.50
3	10.13	9.55	9.28	9.12	9.01	8.94	8.89	8.85	8.81	8.79	8.74	8.70	8.66	8.64	8.62	8.59	8.57	8.55	8.53
4	7.71	6.94	6.59	6.39	6.26	6.16	6.09	6.04	6.00	5.96	5.91	5.86	5.80	5.77	5.75	5.72	5.69	5.66	5.63
5	6.61	5.79	5.41	5.19	5.05	4.95	4.88	4.82	4.77	4.74	4.68	4.62	4.56	4.53	4.50	4.46	4.43	4.40	4.36
6	5.99	5.14	4.76	4.53	4.39	4.28	4.21	4.15	4.10	4.06	4.00	3.94	3.87	3.84	3.81	3.77	3.74	3.70	3.67
7	5.59	4.74	4.35	4.12	3.97	3.87	3.79	3.73	3.68	3.64	3.57	3.51	3.44	3.41	3.38	3.34	3.30	3.27	3.23
8	5.32	4.46	4.07	3.84	3.69	3.58	3.50	3.44	3.39	3.35	3.28	3.22	3.15	3.12	3.08	3.04	3.01	2.97	2.93
9	5.12	4.26	3.86	3.63	3.48	3.37	3.29	3.23	3.18	3.14	3.07	3.01	2.94	2.90	2.86	2.83	2.79	2.75	2.71
10	4.96	4.10	3.71	3.48	3.33	3.22	3.14	3.07	3.02	2.98	2.91	2.85	2.77	2.74	2.70	2.66	2.62	2.58	2.54
11	4.84	3.98	3.59	3.36	3.20	3.09	3.01	2.95	2.90	2.85	2.79	2.72	2.65	2.61	2.57	2.53	2.49	2.45	2.40
12	4.75	3.89	3.49	3.26	3.11	3.00	2.91	2.85	2.80	2.75	2.69	2.62	2.54	2.51	2.47	2.43	2.38	2.34	2.30
13	4.67	3.81	3.41	3.18	3.03	2.92	2.83	2.77	2.71	2.67	2.60	2.53	2.46	2.42	2.38	2.34	2.30	2.25	2.21
14	4.60	3.74	3.34	3.11	2.96	2.85	2.76	2.70	2.65	2.60	2.53	2.46	2.39	2.35	2.31	2.27	2.22	2.18	2.13
15	4.54	3.68	3.29	3.06	2.90	2.79	2.71	2.64	2.59	2.54	2.48	2.40	2.33	2.29	2.25	2.20	2.16	2.11	2.07
16	4.49	3.63	3.24	3.01	2.85	2.74	2.66	2.59	2.54	2.49	2.42	2.35	2.28	2.24	2.19	2.15	2.11	2.06	2.01
17	4.45	3.59	3.20	2.96	2.81	2.70	2.61	2.55	2.49	2.45	2.38	2.31	2.23	2.19	2.15	2.10	2.06	2.01	1.96
18	4.41	3.55	3.16	2.93	2.77	2.66	2.58	2.51	2.46	2.41	2.34	2.27	2.19	2.15	2.11	2.06	2.02	1.97	1.92
19	4.38	3.52	3.13	2.90	2.74	2.63	2.54	2.48	2.42	2.38	2.31	2.23	2.16	2.11	2.07	2.03	1.98	1.93	1.88
20	4.35	3.49	3.10	2.87	2.71	2.60	2.51	2.45	2.39	2.35	2.28	2.20	2.12	2.08	2.04	1.99	1.95	1.90	1.84
21	4.32	3.47	3.07	2.84	2.68	2.57	2.49	2.42	2.37	2.32	2.25	2.18	2.10	2.05	2.01	1.96	1.92	1.87	1.81
22	4.30	3.44	3.05	2.82	2.66	2.55	2.46	2.40	2.34	2.30	2.23	2.15	2.07	2.03	1.98	1.94	1.89	1.84	1.78
23	4.28	3.42	3.03	2.80	2.64	2.53	2.44	2.37	2.32	2.27	2.20	2.13	2.05	2.01	1.96	1.91	1.86	1.81	1.76
24	4.26	3.40	3.01	2.78	2.62	2.51	2.42	2.36	2.30	2.25	2.18	2.11	2.03	1.98	1.94	1.89	1.84	1.79	1.73
25	4.24	3.39	2.99	2.76	2.60	2.49	2.40	2.34	2.28	2.24	2.16	2.09	2.01	1.96	1.92	1.87	1.82	1.77	1.71
26	4.23	3.37	2.98	2.74	2.59	2.47	2.39	2.32	2.27	2.22	2.15	2.07	1.99	1.95	1.90	1.85	1.80	1.75	1.69
27	4.21	3.35	2.96	2.73	2.57	2.46	2.37	2.31	2.25	2.20	2.13	2.06	1.97	1.93	1.88	1.84	1.79	1.73	1.67
28	4.20	3.34	2.95	2.71	2.56	2.45	2.36	2.29	2.24	2.19	2.12	2.04	1.96	1.91	1.87	1.82	1.77	1.71	1.65
29	4.18	3.33	2.93	2.70	2.55	2.43	2.35	2.28	2.22	2.18	2.10	2.03	1.94	1.90	1.85	1.81	1.75	1.70	1.64
30	4.17	3.32	2.92	2.69	2.53	2.42	2.33	2.27	2.21	2.16	2.09	2.01	1.93	1.89	1.84	1.79	1.74	1.68	1.62
40	4.08	3.23	2.84	2.61	2.45	2.34	2.25	2.18	2.12	2.08	2.00	1.92	1.84	1.79	1.74	1.69	1.64	1.58	1.51

TABLE 7 Cutoff points for the F distribution (cont.)

DENOMINATOR v_2	NUMERATOR v_1																		
	1	2	3	4	5	6	7	8	9	10	12	15	20	24	30	40	60	120	∞
60	4.00	3.15	2.76	2.53	2.37	2.25	2.17	2.10	2.04	1.99	1.92	1.84	1.75	1.70	1.65	1.59	1.53	1.47	1.39
120	3.92	3.07	2.68	2.45	2.29	2.17	2.09	2.02	1.96	1.91	1.83	1.75	1.66	1.61	1.55	1.50	1.43	1.35	1.25
∞	3.84	3.00	2.60	2.37	2.21	2.10	2.01	1.94	1.88	1.83	1.75	1.67	1.57	1.52	1.46	1.39	1.32	1.22	1.00

$$\alpha = .01$$

DENOMINATOR v_2	NUMERATOR v_1																		
	1	2	3	4	5	6	7	8	9	10	12	15	20	24	30	40	60	120	∞
1	4052	4999.5	5403	5625	5764	5859	5928	5982	6022	6056	6106	6157	6209	6235	6261	6287	6313	6339	6366
2	98.50	99.00	99.17	99.25	99.30	99.33	99.36	99.37	99.39	99.40	99.42	99.43	99.45	99.46	99.47	99.47	99.47	99.48	99.50
3	34.12	30.82	29.46	28.71	28.24	27.91	27.67	27.49	27.35	27.23	27.05	26.87	26.69	26.60	26.50	26.41	26.32	26.22	26.13
4	21.20	18.00	16.69	15.98	15.52	15.21	14.98	14.80	14.66	14.55	14.37	14.20	14.02	13.93	13.84	13.75	13.65	13.56	13.46
5	16.26	13.27	12.06	11.39	10.97	10.67	10.46	10.29	10.16	10.05	9.89	9.72	9.55	9.47	9.38	9.29	9.20	9.11	9.02
6	13.75	10.92	9.78	9.15	8.75	8.47	8.26	8.10	7.98	7.87	7.72	7.56	7.40	7.31	7.23	7.14	7.06	6.97	6.88
7	12.25	9.55	8.45	7.85	7.46	7.19	6.99	6.84	6.72	6.62	6.47	6.31	6.16	6.07	5.99	5.91	5.82	5.74	5.65
8	11.26	8.65	7.59	7.01	6.63	6.37	6.18	6.03	5.91	5.81	5.67	5.52	5.36	5.28	5.20	5.12	5.03	4.95	4.86
9	10.56	8.02	6.99	6.42	6.06	5.80	5.61	5.47	5.35	5.26	5.11	4.96	4.81	4.73	4.65	4.57	4.48	4.40	4.31
10	10.04	7.56	6.55	5.99	5.64	5.39	5.20	5.06	4.94	4.85	4.71	4.56	4.41	4.33	4.25	4.17	4.08	4.00	3.91
11	9.65	7.21	6.22	5.67	5.32	5.07	4.89	4.74	4.63	4.54	4.40	4.25	4.10	4.02	3.94	3.86	3.78	3.69	3.60
12	9.33	6.93	5.95	5.41	5.06	4.82	4.64	4.50	4.39	4.30	4.16	4.01	3.86	3.78	3.70	3.62	3.54	3.45	3.36
13	9.07	6.70	5.74	5.21	4.86	4.62	4.44	4.30	4.19	4.10	3.96	3.82	3.66	3.59	3.51	3.43	3.34	3.25	3.17
14	8.86	6.51	5.56	5.04	4.69	4.46	4.28	4.14	4.03	3.94	3.80	3.66	3.51	3.43	3.35	3.27	3.18	3.09	3.00
15	8.68	6.36	5.42	4.89	4.56	4.32	4.14	4.00	3.89	3.80	3.67	3.52	3.37	3.29	3.21	3.13	3.05	2.96	2.87
16	8.53	6.23	5.29	4.77	4.44	4.20	4.03	3.89	3.78	3.69	3.55	3.41	3.26	3.18	3.10	3.02	2.93	2.84	2.75
17	8.40	6.11	5.18	4.67	4.34	4.10	3.93	3.79	3.68	3.59	3.46	3.31	3.16	3.08	3.00	2.92	2.83	2.75	2.65
18	8.29	6.01	5.09	4.58	4.25	4.01	3.84	3.71	3.60	3.51	3.37	3.23	3.08	3.00	2.92	2.84	2.75	2.66	2.57
19	8.18	5.93	5.01	4.50	4.17	3.94	3.77	3.63	3.52	3.43	3.30	3.15	3.00	2.92	2.84	2.76	2.67	2.58	2.49
20	8.10	5.85	4.94	4.43	4.10	3.87	3.70	3.56	3.46	3.37	3.23	3.09	2.94	2.86	2.78	2.69	2.61	2.52	2.42
21	8.02	5.78	4.87	4.37	4.04	3.81	3.64	3.51	3.40	3.31	3.17	3.03	2.88	2.80	2.72	2.64	2.55	2.46	2.36
22	7.95	5.72	4.82	4.31	3.99	3.76	3.59	3.45	3.35	3.26	3.12	2.98	2.83	2.75	2.67	2.58	2.50	2.40	2.31
23	7.88	5.66	4.76	4.26	3.94	3.71	3.54	3.41	3.30	3.21	3.07	2.93	2.78	2.70	2.62	2.54	2.45	2.35	2.26
24	7.82	5.61	4.72	4.22	3.90	3.67	3.50	3.36	3.26	3.17	3.03	2.89	2.74	2.66	2.58	2.49	2.40	2.31	2.21
25	7.77	5.57	4.68	4.18	3.85	3.63	3.46	3.32	3.22	3.13	2.99	2.85	2.70	2.62	2.54	2.45	2.36	2.27	2.17
26	7.72	5.53	4.64	4.14	3.82	3.59	3.42	3.29	3.18	3.09	2.96	2.81	2.66	2.58	2.50	2.42	2.33	2.23	2.13
27	7.68	5.49	4.60	4.11	3.78	3.56	3.39	3.26	3.15	3.06	2.93	2.78	2.63	2.55	2.47	2.38	2.29	2.20	2.10
28	7.64	5.45	4.57	4.07	3.75	3.53	3.36	3.23	3.12	3.03	2.90	2.75	2.60	2.52	2.44	2.35	2.26	2.17	2.06
29	7.60	5.42	4.54	4.04	3.73	3.50	3.33	3.20	3.09	3.00	2.87	2.73	2.57	2.49	2.41	2.33	2.23	2.14	2.03
30	7.56	5.39	4.51	4.02	3.70	3.47	3.30	3.17	3.07	2.98	2.84	2.70	2.55	2.47	2.39	2.30	2.21	2.11	2.01
40	7.31	5.18	4.31	3.83	3.51	3.29	3.12	2.99	2.89	2.80	2.66	2.52	2.37	2.29	2.20	2.11	2.02	1.92	1.80
60	7.08	4.98	4.13	3.65	3.34	3.12	2.95	2.82	2.72	2.63	2.50	2.35	2.20	2.12	2.03	1.94	1.84	1.73	1.60
120	6.85	4.79	3.95	3.48	3.17	2.96	2.79	2.66	2.56	2.47	2.34	2.19	2.03	1.95	1.86	1.76	1.66	1.53	1.38
∞	6.63	4.61	3.78	3.32	3.02	2.80	2.64	2.51	2.41	2.32	2.18	2.04	1.88	1.79	1.70	1.59	1.47	1.32	1.00

TABLE 8 Cutoff points for the distribution of the Wilcoxon test statistic

For sample size n, the table shows, for selected probabilities α, the numbers T_α such that $P(T \leq T_\alpha) = \alpha$, where the distribution of the random variable T is that of the Wilcoxon test statistic under the null hypothesis.

n	α				
	.005	.010	.025	.050	.100
4	0	0	0	0	1
5	0	0	0	1	3
6	0	0	1	3	4
7	0	1	3	4	6
8	1	2	4	6	9
9	2	4	6	9	11
10	4	6	9	11	15
11	6	8	11	14	18
12	8	10	14	18	22
13	10	13	18	22	27
14	13	16	22	26	32
15	16	20	26	31	37
16	20	24	30	36	43
17	24	28	35	42	49
18	28	33	41	48	56
19	33	38	47	54	63
20	38	44	53	61	70

Reproduced with permission from R. L. McCormack, "Extended tables of the Wilcoxon matched pairs signed rank statistics," *Journal of the American Statistical Association, 60* (1965).

TABLE 9 Cutoff points for the distribution of Spearman's rank correlation coefficient

For sample size n, the table shows, for selected probabilities α, the numbers $r_{s,\alpha}$ such that $P(r_s > r_{s,\alpha}) = \alpha$, where the distribution of the random variable r_s is that of Spearman's rank correlation coefficient under the null hypothesis of no association.

n	α			
	.050	.025	.010	.005
5	.900	—	—	—
6	.829	.886	.943	—
7	.714	.786	.893	—
8	.643	.738	.833	.881
9	.600	.683	.783	.833
10	.564	.648	.745	.794
11	.523	.623	.736	.818
12	.497	.591	.703	.780
13	.475	.566	.673	.745
14	.457	.545	.646	.716
15	.441	.525	.623	.689
16	.425	.507	.601	.666
17	.412	.490	.582	.645
18	.399	.476	.564	.625
19	.388	.462	.549	.608
20	.377	.450	.534	.591
21	.368	.438	.521	.576
22	.359	.428	.508	.562
23	.351	.418	.496	.549
24	.343	.409	.485	.537
25	.336	.400	.475	.526
26	.329	.392	.465	.515
27	.323	.385	.456	.505
28	.317	.377	.448	.496
29	.311	.370	.440	.487
30	.305	.364	.432	.478

Reproduced with permission from E. G. Olds, "Distribution of sums of squares of rank differences for small samples," *Annals of Mathematical Statistics*, 9 (1938).

TABLE 10 Cutoff points for the distribution of the Durbin-Watson test statistic

Let d_α be the number such that $P(d < d_\alpha) = \alpha$, where the random variable d has the distribution of the Durbin-Watson statistic under the null hypothesis of no autocorrelation in the regression errors. For probabilities $\alpha = .05$ and $\alpha = .01$, the tables show, for numbers of independent variables, K, values d_L and d_U such that $d_L \leq d_\alpha \leq d_U$, for numbers n of observations.

$$\alpha = .05$$

n	K									
	1		2		3		4		5	
	d_L	d_U	d_L	d_U	d_L	d_U	d_L	d_U	d_L	d_U
15	1.08	1.36	0.95	1.54	0.82	1.75	0.69	1.97	0.56	2.21
16	1.10	1.37	0.98	1.54	0.86	1.73	0.74	1.93	0.62	2.15
17	1.13	1.38	1.02	1.54	0.90	1.71	0.78	1.90	0.67	2.10
18	1.16	1.39	1.05	1.53	0.93	1.69	0.82	1.87	0.71	2.06
19	1.18	1.40	1.08	1.53	0.97	1.68	0.86	1.85	0.75	2.02
20	1.20	1.41	1.10	1.54	1.00	1.68	0.90	1.83	0.79	1.99
21	1.22	1.42	1.13	1.54	1.03	1.67	0.93	1.81	0.83	1.96
22	1.24	1.43	1.15	1.54	1.05	1.66	0.96	1.80	0.86	1.94
23	1.26	1.44	1.17	1.54	1.08	1.66	0.99	1.79	0.90	1.92
24	1.27	1.45	1.19	1.55	1.10	1.66	1.01	1.78	0.93	1.90
25	1.29	1.45	1.21	1.55	1.12	1.66	1.04	1.77	0.95	1.89
26	1.30	1.46	1.22	1.55	1.14	1.65	1.06	1.76	0.98	1.88
27	1.32	1.47	1.24	1.56	1.16	1.65	1.08	1.76	1.01	1.86
28	1.33	1.48	1.26	1.56	1.18	1.65	1.10	1.75	1.03	1.85
29	1.34	1.48	1.27	1.56	1.20	1.65	1.12	1.74	1.05	1.84
30	1.35	1.49	1.28	1.57	1.21	1.65	1.14	1.74	1.07	1.83
31	1.36	1.50	1.30	1.57	1.23	1.65	1.16	1.74	1.09	1.83
32	1.37	1.50	1.31	1.57	1.24	1.65	1.18	1.73	1.11	1.82
33	1.38	1.51	1.32	1.58	1.26	1.65	1.19	1.73	1.13	1.81
34	1.39	1.51	1.33	1.58	1.27	1.65	1.21	1.73	1.15	1.81
35	1.40	1.52	1.34	1.58	1.28	1.65	1.22	1.73	1.16	1.80
36	1.41	1.52	1.35	1.59	1.29	1.65	1.24	1.73	1.18	1.80
37	1.42	1.53	1.36	1.59	1.31	1.66	1.25	1.72	1.19	1.80
38	1.43	1.54	1.37	1.59	1.32	1.66	1.26	1.72	1.21	1.79
39	1.43	1.54	1.38	1.60	1.33	1.66	1.27	1.72	1.22	1.79
40	1.44	1.54	1.39	1.60	1.34	1.66	1.29	1.72	1.23	1.79
45	1.48	1.57	1.43	1.62	1.38	1.67	1.34	1.72	1.29	1.78
50	1.50	1.59	1.46	1.63	1.42	1.67	1.38	1.72	1.34	1.77
55	1.53	1.60	1.49	1.64	1.45	1.68	1.41	1.72	1.38	1.77
60	1.55	1.62	1.51	1.65	1.48	1.69	1.44	1.73	1.41	1.77
65	1.57	1.63	1.54	1.66	1.50	1.70	1.47	1.73	1.44	1.77
70	1.58	1.64	1.55	1.67	1.52	1.70	1.49	1.74	1.46	1.77
75	1.60	1.65	1.57	1.68	1.54	1.71	1.51	1.74	1.49	1.77
80	1.61	1.66	1.59	1.69	1.56	1.72	1.53	1.74	1.51	1.77
85	1.62	1.67	1.60	1.70	1.57	1.72	1.55	1.75	1.52	1.77
90	1.63	1.68	1.61	1.70	1.59	1.73	1.57	1.75	1.54	1.78
95	1.64	1.69	1.62	1.71	1.60	1.73	1.58	1.75	1.56	1.78
100	1.65	1.69	1.63	1.72	1.61	1.74	1.59	1.76	1.57	1.78

TABLE 10 Cutoff points for the distribution of the Durbin-Watson test statistic (cont.)

$$\alpha = .01$$

n	K									
	1		2		3		4		5	
	d_L	d_U	d_L	d_U	d_L	d_U	d_L	d_U	d_L	d_U
15	0.81	1.07	0.70	1.25	0.59	1.46	0.49	1.70	0.39	1.96
16	0.84	1.09	0.74	1.25	0.63	1.44	0.53	1.66	0.44	1.90
17	0.87	1.10	0.77	1.25	0.67	1.43	0.57	1.63	0.48	1.85
18	0.90	1.12	0.80	1.26	0.71	1.42	0.61	1.60	0.52	1.80
19	0.93	1.13	0.83	1.26	0.74	1.41	0.65	1.58	0.56	1.77
20	0.95	1.15	0.86	1.27	0.77	1.41	0.68	1.57	0.60	1.74
21	0.97	1.16	0.89	1.27	0.80	1.41	0.72	1.55	0.63	1.71
22	1.00	1.17	0.91	1.28	0.83	1.40	0.75	1.54	0.66	1.69
23	1.02	1.19	0.94	1.29	0.86	1.40	0.77	1.53	0.70	1.67
24	1.04	1.20	0.96	1.30	0.88	1.41	0.80	1.53	0.72	1.66
25	1.05	1.21	0.98	1.30	0.90	1.41	0.83	1.52	0.75	1.65
26	1.07	1.22	1.00	1.31	0.93	1.41	0.85	1.52	0.78	1.64
27	1.09	1.23	1.02	1.32	0.95	1.41	0.88	1.51	0.81	1.63
28	1.10	1.24	1.04	1.32	0.97	1.41	0.90	1.51	0.83	1.62
29	1.12	1.25	1.05	1.33	0.99	1.42	0.92	1.51	0.85	1.61
30	1.13	1.26	1.07	1.34	1.01	1.42	0.94	1.51	0.88	1.61
31	1.15	1.27	1.08	1.34	1.02	1.42	0.96	1.51	0.90	1.60
32	1.16	1.28	1.10	1.35	1.04	1.43	0.98	1.51	0.92	1.60
33	1.17	1.29	1.11	1.36	1.05	1.43	1.00	1.51	0.94	1.59
34	1.18	1.30	1.13	1.36	1.07	1.43	1.01	1.51	0.95	1.59
35	1.19	1.31	1.14	1.37	1.08	1.44	1.03	1.51	0.97	1.59
36	1.21	1.32	1.15	1.38	1.10	1.44	1.04	1.51	0.99	1.59
37	1.22	1.32	1.16	1.38	1.11	1.45	1.06	1.51	1.00	1.59
38	1.23	1.33	1.18	1.39	1.12	1.45	1.07	1.52	1.02	1.58
39	1.24	1.34	1.19	1.39	1.14	1.45	1.09	1.52	1.03	1.58
40	1.25	1.34	1.20	1.40	1.15	1.46	1.10	1.52	1.05	1.58
45	1.29	1.38	1.24	1.42	1.20	1.48	1.16	1.53	1.11	1.58
50	1.32	1.40	1.28	1.45	1.24	1.49	1.20	1.54	1.16	1.59
55	1.36	1.43	1.32	1.47	1.28	1.51	1.25	1.55	1.21	1.59
60	1.38	1.45	1.35	1.48	1.32	1.52	1.28	1.56	1.25	1.60
65	1.41	1.47	1.38	1.50	1.35	1.53	1.31	1.57	1.28	1.61
70	1.43	1.49	1.40	1.52	1.37	1.55	1.34	1.58	1.31	1.61
75	1.45	1.50	1.42	1.53	1.39	1.56	1.37	1.59	1.34	1.62
80	1.47	1.52	1.44	1.54	1.42	1.57	1.39	1.60	1.36	1.62
85	1.48	1.53	1.46	1.55	1.43	1.58	1.41	1.60	1.39	1.63
90	1.50	1.54	1.47	1.56	1.45	1.59	1.43	1.61	1.41	1.64
95	1.51	1.55	1.49	1.57	1.47	1.60	1.45	1.62	1.42	1.64
100	1.52	1.56	1.50	1.58	1.48	1.60	1.46	1.63	1.44	1.65

Reproduced with permission from J. Durbin and G. S. Watson, "Testing for serial correlation in least squares regression, II," *Biometrika, 38* (1951).

TABLE 11 Cumulative distribution function of the runs test statistic

For a given number n of observations, the table shows the probability, for a random time series, that the number of runs will not exceed K.

n	\multicolumn{19}{c}{K}																		
	2	3	4	5	6	7	8	9	10	11	12	13	14	15	16	17	18	19	20
6	.100	.300	.700	.900	1.000														
8	.029	.114	.371	.629	.886	.971	1.000												
10	.008	.040	.167	.357	.643	.833	.960	.992	1.000										
12	.002	.013	.067	.175	.392	.608	.825	.933	.987	.998	1.000								
14	.001	.004	.025	.078	.209	.383	.617	.791	.922	.975	.996	.999	1.000						
16	.000	.001	.009	.032	.100	.214	.405	.595	.786	.900	.968	.991	.999	1.000	1.000				
18	.000	.000	.003	.012	.044	.109	.238	.399	.601	.762	.891	.956	.988	.997	1.000	1.000	1.000		
20	.000	.000	.001	.004	.019	.051	.128	.242	.414	.586	.758	.872	.949	.981	.996	.999	1.000	1.000	1.000

Reproduced with permission from F. Swed and C. Eisenhart, "Tables for testing randomness of grouping in a sequence of alternatives," *Annals of Mathematical Statistics, 14* (1943).

CHAPTER 2

2. **(a)** 26.75 **(b)** 25 **(c)** 22
4. **(a)** 3.125 **(b)** 3
6. **(a)** 5.94 **(b)** 6.35
10. **(a)** 29.52, 5.43 **(b)** 4.75 **(c)** 15 **(d)** 10
12. **(a)** 1.27, 1.13 **(b)** 2
14. **(a)** 5.20, 2.28 **(b)** 7.3 **(c)** 3.975
16. **(a)** 9.83 **(b)** 9.5 **(c)** 28.52, 5.34 **(d)** 8.25
18. **(a)** $195 to $395 **(b)** $154 to $436
20. **(a)** 23,000 to 35,000 **(b)** 23,000 to 35,000
26. **(a)** 3.375 **(b)** 3 **(c)** 3 **(d)** 1.08, 1.04
32. **(b)** .12, .28, .32, .20, .08 **(c)** .12, .40, .72, .92, 1 **(d)** 9.36 **(e)** 4.57 **(f)** 8–12 **(g)** 8–12
34. **(b)** .10, .40, .30, .15, .05 **(c)** 2, 10, 16, 19, 20 **(d)** .10, .50, .80, .95, 1 **(e)** 11.025 **(f)** .27, .52 **(g)** 10.95 **(h)** .77 **(i)** 10.45 to 10.95
36. **(b)** .30, .45, .20, .05 **(c)** .30, .75, .95, 1 **(d)** 1.5 **(e)** .74, .86 **(f)** 1.44 **(g)** 1.29 **(h)** 1 to 2
38. **(b)** $27,700 **(c)** 13,331 **(d)** 24,286
64. **(a)** Yes **(b)** No
66. **(a)** 20.05 **(b)** 20.45 **(c)** 30.1 **(d)** 5.5 **(e)** 16.3 **(f)** 10.6
68. **(b)** 4.92 **(c)** 10.23 **(d)** 3.20 **(e)** 3.80 **(f)** 3.46

CHAPTER 3

2. **(a)** .54 **(b)** .18 **(d)** .46 **(f)** 0 **(h)** .72 **(i)** Yes **(i)** No
6. **(a)** .87 **(b)** .35

8. **(a)** 5,040 **(b)** 1/5,040
10. 1/120
12. 60, 1/60
14. 28
16. **(a)** 150 **(b)** 40/150 = .27 **(c)** 30/150 = .2
18. .35
20. **(a)** No **(b)** No **(c)** No
22. .069
24. **(a)** .56 **(b)** .83
26. .129
28. **(a)** .90 **(b)** .88 **(c)** .925
30. **(a)** .87 **(b)** No
32. .2
34. **(a)** .12 **(b)** .704 **(c)** No **(d)** .333 **(e)** No **(f)** .79 **(g)** .27 **(h)** .87
36. **(a)** .25 **(b)** .32 **(c)** .16 **(d)** .125 **(e)** .212
38. **(a)** .32 **(b)** .25 **(c)** .375 **(d)** .48 **(e)** .44 **(f)** No
40. **(a)** .76 **(b)** .77 **(c)** .43
42. **(a)** .025 **(b)** .445 **(c)** .270
44. **(a)** .475 **(b)** .368 **(c)** .857
46. .375
52. **(a)** True **(b)** True **(c)** True **(d)** True **(e)** False **(f)** False **(g)** False
54. **(a)** False **(b)** False **(c)** True **(d)** False **(e)** False
56. **(a)** .08 **(b)** No **(c)** .27 **(d)** .58
58. **(a)** .105 **(b)** .2625 **(c)** .645 **(d)** .5917 **(e)** No **(f)** No **(g)** No
60. **(a)** .11 **(b)** .69 **(c)** .183 **(d)** No
62. **(a)** .12 **(b)** .70 **(c)** No **(d)** .333 **(e)** .355
64. **(a)** 66 **(b)** 1/6
66. **(a)** .5192 **(b)** .6482 **(c)** Negative
68. .483
70. **(a)** .514 **(b)** .463
72. **(a)** .50 **(b)** .84 **(c)** No **(d)** .98976
74. **(a)** .52 **(b)** .115 **(c)** .885

CHAPTER 4

2. **(c)** .50
4. **(c)** .32 **(d)** .1369
6. **(a)** $P(x) = .4(.6)^{x-1}$ for $x = 1, 2, 3, \ldots$ **(b)** $F(x) = 1 - (.6)^x$ for $x = 1, 2, 3, \ldots$ **(c)** .36
8. 1.25, 1.1675
10. **(a)** 49.9, 1.396 **(b)** 34.2 cents, 2.79 cents
12. **(a)** .2, .18 **(b)** .2, .17
14. 2.62, 1.47
16. 1
18. Strategy 1 has highest expected profit ($650). It should not necessarily be advised, as it is the most risky.
20. **(a)** .53 **(b)** $P(3|0) = 9/19$, $P(4|0) = 7/19$, $P(5|0) = 3/19$ **(c)** $P(0|5) = 1/8$, $P(1|5) = 5/12, P(2|5) = 11/24$ **(d)** .109 **(e)** No

22. **(a)** $P(0, 0) = .54, P(0, 1) = .30, P(1, 0) = .01, P(1, 1) = .15$ **(b)** $P(0|1) = 1/16, P(1|1) = 15/16$ **(c)** .078

24. Because of independence, the joint probabilities are the products of the marginal probabilities, so $P(0, 0) = .0216$, and so on.

26. 28.4, 4.54

28. **(a)** .7351 **(b)** .2321 **(c)** .0328

30. **(a)** .9891 **(b)** .5798

32. **(a)** .000011 **(b)** .3771 **(c)** .2235

34. .032

36. **(a)** 7.5, 2.525 **(b)** $1,875, $631

40. **(a)** .81 **(b)** .28 **(c)** .06

42. .916

44. .38

46. .262

48. **(a)** .267 **(b)** .264

50. **(a)** .171 **(b)** .219

52. .758

54. .83

60. **(a)** 2.21 **(b)** 1.35 **(c)** $913 **(d)** $405.38 **(e)** .35

64. **(a)** .17 **(b)** 2.59, 1.1 **(c)** .191

66. **(a)** .337 **(b)** .593 **(c)** .55, .056

68. The probability of doing at least as well as the analyst by random selection is .167.

70. **(a)** .0907 **(b)** .2213

72. .9918

CHAPTER 5

2. **(b)** $F(x) = .25x$, for $0 \le x \le 4$ **(c)** .25 **(d)** .25

4. **(a)** .2 **(b)** Between .4 and .6

6. $26.4 million, $1 million

8. $54,000, $14,400

10. $1,000, $134.16 (assuming year-to-year independence)

12. Negative values

14. 600, 35.8

16. **(a)** .8849 **(b)** .0918 **(c)** .0446 **(d)** .8413 **(e)** .0233 **(f)** .8403 **(g)** .1141

18. **(a)** .6554 **(b)** .6554 **(d)** .6006 **(e)** $316 to $444

20. **(a)** .2266 **(b)** .2266 **(c)** .5468

22. **(a)** .2148 **(b)** .1587 **(c)** .3692

24. .0668

26. 15.2, 14.8

28. Investment A

30. **(a)** 98.8 **(b)** 183.6 **(c)** .949

32. **(a)** .3721 **(b)** 522.4 **(c)** 400–440 **(d)** 520–560 **(e)** .2922

34. .4990

36. **(a)** .7967 **(b)** .4525 **(c)** .7495 **(d)** 39–41

38. **(a)** .9222 **(b)** .5704

40. .2877

42. (a) .0217 (b) .2514 (c) .7269
44. .2981, .2611
46. .3012
54. (a) 1/6 (b) 2/3 (c) $1,333.33 (d) Let B denote the bid (in thousands of dollars). Then the expected profit is $(B - 10)(20 - B)/12$ thousand dollars. Choose B to maximize this, giving $B = \$15,000$.
56. (c) .75
58. (a) $768.50 (b) $100.05 (c) $165, $34.50
62. (a) .3085 (b) .6826 (c) 79.6 (d) 53.3 to 66.7 minutes (e) .2731
64. (a) .7888 (b) .0062 (c) .0306 (d) 17.9 to 22.1 minutes (e) 19–21 (f) 21–23
66. 23.58%
68. Almost 1.0
70. (a) .16 (b) .135 (c) .393 (d) .050
72. (a) .7745 (b) 137.28 (c) .1587 (d) .0062

CHAPTER 6

2. (a) 1,200 (b) 17,778 (c) 133.33 (d) .1303
4. (a) .9772 (b) .5762 (c) .3108 (d) $114,000–$116,000
6. (a) 5.5 (b) .9909 (c) .8980 (d) .4329 (e) higher, higher, lower
8. (a) 4 (b) .1056 (c) .1587 (d) .4532
10. (a) .26 (b) .20 (c) .23
12. (a) 68 (b) smaller (c) larger
16. (a) .2546 (b) .0951 (c) .0086
18. (a) .424 (b) .00244 (c) .04942 (d) .0618
20. (a) .2 (b) .000889 (c) .0298 (d) .0465
22. .7372
24. (a) .0351 (b) .9236 (c) .4314 (d) higher, higher
26. .05
28. (a) .051 (b) .065 (c) .041
30. .0057
32. (a) .039 (b) .0384 (c) .4906
34. Practically zero.
36. (a) Between .975 and .99 (b) About .975
38. (a) About .01 (b) About .005
40. (a) Yes (b) Yes
42. (a) 221.4 (b) 32.2
44. (a) 2.60 (b) 1.14 (c) 1.23 and 2.34
46. More than .10
52. (a) .0668 (b) .7745 (c) 445.6 (d) 394.4 (e) 123 (f) 76 (g) Smaller
54. (a) .0228 (b) .9544 (c) 13.4 (d) 8.1 (e) Smaller
58. (a) .0262 (b) .3446 (c) .2709 (d) .321
60. .005
62. .6826
64. (a) .374 (b) .440 (c) .032
66. (a) More than .995 (b) Between .9 and .95

CHAPTER 7

2. **(a)** 101.375, 201.696, 14.2   **(b)** mean and variance   **(c)** 25.21   **(d)** .375
4. **(b)** $\bar{X}$ **(c)** 1.25, 1.11
6. **(b)** $\hat{\mu}^{(1)}$ **(c)** 1.29   **(d)** $(X_1 + X_2 + X_3)/3$
10. 45.8%
12. **(a)** $-.15$ **(b)** $p_1(1 - p_1)/20 + p_2(1 - p_2)/12$
14. $\hat{p}(1 - \hat{p})/(n - 1)$, where $\hat{p} = X/n$
18. **(a)** 24.42   **(b)** 85.72   **(c)** 7.14   **(d)** .25   **(e)** .017
22. **(a)** 2.55   **(b)** .025

CHAPTER 8

2. **(a)** $3.99 < \mu < 4.15$ **(b)** Narrower   **(c)** Narrower   **(d)** Wider
4. **(a)** $174.1 < \mu < 201.7$ **(b)** .9596
6. **(a)** $3.72 < \mu < 3.90$ **(b)** Narrower
8. $59.42 < \mu < 61.40$
10. $127.93 < \mu < 187.71$
12. **(a)** $10.8 < \mu < 21.9$ **(b)** Narrower
16. **(a)** $101.5 < \mu < 122.5$ **(b)** Wider
18. $.455 < p < .559$
20. .5528
22. **(a)** $.183 < p < .427$ **(b)** Narrower
24. .8414
26. $23.1 < \sigma^2 < 111.6$
28. $10.9 < \sigma < 19.4$
32. **(a)** $2.99 < \sigma^2 < 13.85$ **(b)** Wider
34. $27.1 < \mu_1 - \mu_2 < 47.5$
36. $-5.57 < \mu_1 - \mu_2 < 40.59$
38. $-3,270 < \mu_1 - \mu_2 < 1,388$
40. $-9.12 < \mu_1 - \mu_2 < -1.52$
42. $-6.3 < \mu_1 - \mu_2 < 2.9$
44. $.031 < p_1 - p_2 < .109$
46. .3328
48. 312
50. 383
52. 664
54. No
56. **(a)** $3.26 < \mu < 3.50$ **(b)** Wider
58. **(a)** $29.2 < \mu < 34.8$ **(b)** $5.0 < \sigma < 9.2$
62. **(a)** $.441 < p < .517$ **(b)** .8472
64. **(a)** $.41 < p < .60$ **(b)** Narrower
66. .7498
68. $-.068 < \mu_1 - \mu_2 < 6.902$
70. $8.43 < \mu_1 - \mu_2 < 34.39$
72. $-.45 < \mu_1 - \mu_2 < -.31$
74. $.02 < p_1 - p_2 < .35$
76. 385

CHAPTER 9

2. Test statistic is -1.8; reject H_0 at 10% level.
4. Test statistic is -3.33; reject H_0 at levels above .04%.
6. .0008
8. .0004
10. **(a)** No **(b)** Yes
12. Test statistic is 1.741; accept H_0 at 5% level.
14. Test statistic is -3.189; reject H_0 at 5% level.
16. Test statistic is 13.08; reject H_0 at 10% level.
18. Test statistic is 46.4; can reject H_0 at 5% level, but not at 2% level.
20. Test statistic is 16.96; cannot reject H_0 at 10% level.
22. Test statistic is -5.62; reject H_0 at 5% level.
24. Test statistic is .64; accept H_0 at 10% level; p-value is .5222.
26. Test statistic is -1.94; can reject H_0 at levels above 2.62%.
28. Test statistic is 2.239; can reject H_0 at 5% level, but not at 2.5% level.
30. Test statistic is 2.04; can reject H_0 at levels above 4.14%.
32. Test statistic is 13.0; can reject H_0 at virtually any level.
34. Test statistic is -1.850; can reject H_0 at 10% level, but not at 5% level.
36. Test statistic is 1.275; cannot reject H_0 at 10% level.
38. Test statistic is -1.465; accept H_0 at 5% level.
40. Test statistic is -8.22; can reject H_0 at virtually any level.
42. Test statistic is -18.4; reject H_0 at 1% level.
44. Test statistic is 7.10; can reject H_0 at 5% level, but not at 1% level.
46. Test statistic is 1.57; cannot reject H_0 at 10% level.
48. .3897
50. .8599
52. .985
54. **(a)** .0082 **(b)** .1151 **(c)** .6554
60. **(a)** False **(b)** True **(c)** True **(d)** False **(e)** False **(f)** True **(g)** False
62. **(a)** Test statistic is $-.56$; accept H_0 at 5% level **(b)** Test statistic is 17.12; accept H_0 at 5% level.
64. **(a)** .0228 **(b)** .0014 **(c)(i)** smaller **(ii)** smaller **(d)(i)** smaller **(ii)** larger
66. 69.66%
68. Test statistic is 2.36; reject H_0 at 5% level.p   834   837
70. Test statistic is 2.217; reject H_0 at 10% level.
72. 7.84%
74. Test statistic is $-.37$; accept H_0 at 10% level.
76. Test statistic is 3.33; reject H_0 at 5% level.
78. Test statistic is -2.30; can reject H_0 at levels above 1.07%.
80. **(a)** Test statistic is -1.20; accept H_0 at 5% level. **(b)** Test statistic is .93; accept H_0 at 5% level.
82. Test statistic is -1.19; accept H_0 at 1% level.
84. .0495
86. No

CHAPTER 10

2. Can reject H_0 against one-sided alternative at 1.96% level but not at .20% level.
4. Test statistic is 2.78; can reject H_0 at levels above .27%.
6. Test statistic is 1.29; can reject H_0 against two-sided alternative at levels above 19.7%.
8. Test statistic is 7; can reject H_0 at 5% level, but not at 2.5% level.
10. Test statistic is -1.73; can reject H_0 at levels above 4.18%.
12. Test statistic is $-.57$; can only reject H_0 against two-sided alternative at levels above 56.86%.
14. Test statistic is $-.39$; can only reject H_0 at levels above 69.66%.
16. Test statistic is 3.45; can reject H_0 at levels above .03%.
18. Test statistic is -4.85; can reject H_0 at very low levels.
22. Can reject H_0 against two-sided alternative at 58.10% level, but not at 26.68% level.
24. Test statistic is 1.43; can reject H_0 at levels above 7.64%.
26. Test statistic is 8; cannot reject H_0 against two-sided alternative at 20% level.
28. Test statistic is -2.42; can reject H_0 against one-sided alternative at levels above .78%.

CHAPTER 11

2. Test statistic is 2.38; cannot reject H_0 at 10% level.
4. Test statistic is 1.51; accept H_0 at 5% level.
6. Test statistic is 3.07; cannot reject H_0 at 10% level.
8. Test statistic is 11.53; can reject H_0 at 1% level, but not at .5% level.
10. Test statistic is 9.63; reject H_0 at 5% level.
12. Test statistic is .44; accept H_0 at 10% level.
14. Test statistic is 11.65; can reject H_0 at .5% level.
16. Test statistic is 6.95; accept H_0 at 1% level.
18. Test statistic is 15.75; reject H_0 at 1% level.
20. Test statistic is 1.70; cannot reject H_0 at 10% level.
22. Test statistic is 1.4; cannot reject H_0 at 10% level.
24. Test statistic is 2.83; cannot reject H_0 at 10% level.
26. Test statistic is 20.3; reject H_0 at 5% level.
28. Test statistic is 1.81; cannot reject H_0 at 10% level.
30. Test statistic is .35; cannot reject H_0 at 10% level.
32. Test statistic is 1.54; cannot reject H_0 at 10% level.
34. Test statistic is 5.80; can reject H_0 at 2.5% level, but not at 1% level.
36. Test statistic is 3.21; can reject H_0 at 10% level, but not at 5% level.

CHAPTER 12

2. **(a)** $-.4066$ **(b)** Test statistic is -1.476; accept H_0 at 10% level.
4. Sample correlation is .057; test statistic is .22; accept H_0 at usual levels.
6. Test statistic is 2.073; can reject H_0 at 2.5% level, but not at 1% level.
8. Test statistic is $-.41$; cannot reject H_0 at 20% level.
10. Rank correlation is .129; cannot reject H_0 at 10% level.
12. **(a)** .681 **(b)** Reject H_0 at .5% level.

14. **(a)** $y = 12.94 - 2.03x$ **(b)** When $x = 0$, expected y is 12.94; each one unit increase in x leads to expected 2.03 unit decrease in y.

16. **(a)** $y = .045 - .224x$ **(b)** Each one unit increase in x leads to expected .224 unit decrease in y.

18. **(a)** $y = -11.5 + .402x$ **(b)** Each one unit increase in x leads to expected .402 unit increase in y.

22. $R^2 = .878$; in the sample 87.8% of variability in sales explained by their linear dependence on price.

24. $R^2 = .538$

26. .766

28. $R^2 = .0121$; in the sample 1.21% of variability in raises explained by their linear dependence on evaluations of teaching.

30. **(a)** 144.47 **(b)** 1.899 **(c)** $-5.07 < \beta < 1.00$ **(d)** Test statistic is -1.476; accept H_0 at 10% level. **(e)** Same

32. **(a)** $y = 3.296 + .539x$ **(b)** $.241 < \beta < .838$

34. Test statistic is -4.073; reject H_0 at 1% level.

36. **(a)** $y = 97.2 - 58.4x$ **(b)** $-67.3 < \beta < -49.5$ **(c)** No

38. Test statistic is 3.002; can reject H_0 at 2.5% level, but not at 1% level.

42. Test statistic is .48; accept H_0 at 10% level.

44. **(a)** 440 **(b)** $404 < Y_{n+1} < 476$, $423 < Y_{n+1} < 457$

46. $-.35 < Y_{n+1} < .44$, $-.07 < Y_{n+1} < .16$

48. $10.1 < Y_{n+1} < 23.2$, $7.8 < Y_{n+1} < 25.4$

52. Test statistic is 2.844; reject H_0 at .05% level.

54. Test statistic is 2.452; reject H_0 at 1% level, but not at .05% level.

56. **(a)** .183 **(b)** Cannot reject H_0 at 10% level.

58. **(a)** .488 **(b)** Cannot reject H_0 at 10% level.

62. **(a)** An increase of one unit in predicted change is associated with an expected increase of .7916 unit in actual change. **(b)** 9.7% of variability in actual change explained by linear relation with predicted change. **(c)** Test statistic is 2.876; reject H_0 at .5% level. **(d)** Test statistic is $-.757$; cannot reject H_0 at 20% level.

64. **(a)** An extra point on skills test leads to an expected extra .2875 point on final score. **(b)** In the sample 11.58% of variability in final score explained by its linear association with skills test score. **(c)** Test statistic is 6.3; reject H_0 at .5% level.

66. **(a)** .2388 **(b)** Test statistic is 2.686; reject H_0 at 5% level. **(c)** $.3 < \beta < 2.3$

CHAPTER 13

2. All else being equal, an increase of one unit in change in equity purchases leads to expected increase of .057 unit in change in stock price. All else being equal, an increase of one unit in change in equity sales leads to expected decrease of .065 unit in change in stock price.

4. **(a)** All else equal, one extra meal per week leads to extra expected weight gain of .653 pound; one extra hour exercise per week leads to extra expected weight loss of 1.345 pounds; one extra beer per week leads to extra expected weight gain of .613 pound. **(b)** No

6. **(a)** .456; 45.6% of variability in milk consumption in the sample is explained by its linear relation with the independent variables **(b)** .416 **(c)** .675 = sample correlation between observed and predicted values of milk consumption

10. **(a)** Test statistic is 2.261; can reject H_0 at 2.5% level, but not at 1% level. **(b)** $.54 < \beta_2 < 1.74$, $.42 < \beta_2 < 1.86$, $.17 < \beta_2 < 2.11$

12. **(a)** Test statistic is $-.410$; cannot reject H_0 at 20% level. **(b)** Test statistic is 13.06; reject H_0 at 1% level.

14. **(a)** All else being equal, an extra \$1 in mean per capita personal income leads to an expected extra \$.04 of net revenue per capita from the lottery **(b)** $.2359 < \beta_2 < 1.5185$ **(c)** Test statistic is -1.383; can reject H_0 at 10% level, but not at 5% level.

16. **(a)** $.18 < \beta_1 < .22$ **(b)** Test statistic is 1.19; cannot reject H_0 at 10% level.

18. **(a)** $.0173 < \beta_5 < .0817$ **(b)** Test statistic is .617; cannot reject H_0 at 20% level. **(c)** Test statistic is 2.108; can reject H_0 at 5% level, but not at 2% level.

20. **(a)** Test statistic is 82.0; can reject H_0 at 1% level.

22. **(a)** Test statistic is 11.31; can reject H_0 at 1% level.

24. Test statistic is 6.24; can reject H_0 at 1% level.

26. Test statistic is 217; can reject H_0 at 1% level.

30. 10.6 pounds

32. 794,000 worker hours

48. **(a)** All else equal, each extra question leads to expected decrease of 1.8345 in percentage response. All else equal, each extra word leads to expected decrease of .0162 in percentage response. **(b)** In the sample, 63.7% of variability in percentage responses explained by their linear dependence on the two independent variables. **(c)** Test statistic is 23.7; reject H_0 at 1% level **(d)** $-3.59 < \beta_1 < -.08$ **(e)** Test statistic is -1.78; can reject H_0 at 5% level, but not at 2.5% level.

52. **(a)** All else equal, each extra point in student's expected score leads on average to extra .469 in actual score. **(b)** $2.475 < \beta_2 < 4.263$ **(c)** Test statistic is 2.096; can reject H_0 at 5% level, but not at 2% level. **(d)** In sample, 68.6% of variability in scores explained by their linear relation with the three independent variables. **(e)** Test statistic is 75; can reject H_0 at 1% level. **(f)** $.828 =$ sample correlation between actual and predicted scores. **(g)** 76

54. **(a)** $110.08 < \beta_6 < 850.00$ **(b)** $803.4 < \beta_7 < 1{,}897.2$ **(c)** Test statistic is -4.93; can reject H_0 at .5% level. **(d)** Test statistic is 6.51; can reject H_0 at .5% level. **(e)** In the sample, 52.39% of variability in minutes played explained by its linear relation with the nine independent variables **(f)** $.724 =$ sample correlation between actual and predicted minutes played.

CHAPTER 14

2. **(a)** All else being equal, expected selling price is higher by \$3,219 if house has a fireplace. **(b)** All else being equal, expected selling price is higher by \$2,005 if house has brick siding. **(c)** $1{,}363 < \beta_4 < 5{,}075$ **(d)** Test statistic is 2.611; can reject H_0 at .5% level.

16. **(a)** A 1% increase in median income leads to an expected .68% increase in store size. **(b)** Test statistic is 8.83; can reject H_0 at .5% level.

24. **(a)** For any observation, the values of the dummy variables sum to one. Since the equation has an intercept term, there is perfect multicollinearity **(b)** β_3 measures the expected difference between demand in the first and fourth quarters, all else equal.

26. Likely to lead to serious specification bias

34. Accept H_0 at 5% level.

36. Accept H_0 at 1% level; test is inconclusive at 5% level.

38. Nothing beyond the appearance of a serious problem of autocorrelated errors.

40. $d = .85$. Can reject hypothesis of no autocorrelation in the errors at 1% level. Serious specification error can lead to the appearance of autocorrelated errors.

46. **(a)** Test statistic is 1.179; accept H_0 at 10% level. **(b)** Test statistic is .495; accept H_0 at 10% level **(c)** Multicollinearity.

50. **(a)** All else being equal, a 1% increase in value of new orders leads to expected decrease of .82% in number of failures.   **(b)** No autocorrelation in errors; reject this hypothesis at 1% level.   **(c)** No   **(d)** .755
52. **(a)** $.035 < \beta < .471$ **(b)** $.253 increase in current period, further $.138 increase next period, $.075 increase two periods ahead, and so on. Total expected increase of $.557.
    (c) Test statistic is .56; cannot reject H_0 at usual levels.

CHAPTER 15

2. **(a)** SSW = 1,342.0; SSG = 836.6; SST = 2,178.6
   (b)

SOURCE	SS	DF	MS	F RATIO
Between groups	836.6	3	278.867	3.95
Within groups	1,342.0	19	70.632	
Total	2,178.6	22		

H_0 is rejected at 5% level but not at 1% level.

4. **(a)**

SOURCE	SS	DF	MS	F RATIO
Between groups	2.433	2	1.2165	0.40
Within groups	36.100	12	3.0083	
Total	38.533	14		

(b) H_0 is not rejected at 5% level.

6. **(a)**

SOURCE	SS	DF	MS	F RATIO
Between groups	23.24	3	7.747	11.80
Within groups	7.88	12	.657	
Total	31.12	15		

(b) H_0 is rejected at 1% level.

8. **(a)**

SOURCE	SS	DF	MS	F RATIO
Between groups	240.93	2	120.465	1.50
Within groups	966.40	12	80.533	
Total	1,207.33	14		

    (b) H_0 is not rejected at 5% level.

10. **(a)** 9.666   **(b)** 1.302; 1.014; -2.316 **(c)** .930
12. Test statistic is 1.18; H_0 is not rejected at 10% level.
14. Test statistic is 9.38; reject H_0 at 1% level, but not at .5% level.
16. Test statistic is .74; cannot reject H_0 at 10% level.
18. Test statistic is 5.245; reject H_0 at 10% level, but not at 5% level.
20. **(a)** Equality of the centers of the population distributions   **(b)** H_0 is not rejected at 10% level.
22. **(a)**

SOURCE	SS	DF	MS	F RATIO
Fertilizers	200.67	2	100.335	4.56
Varieties	62.25	3	20.750	.94
Error	132.00	6	22.000	
Total	394.92	11		

    (b) H_0 is not rejected at 5% level. H_0 is not rejected at 5% level.

24. **(a)**

SOURCE	SS	DF	MS	F RATIO
Regions	230.92	3	76.97	3.22
Colors	74.00	2	37.00	1.55
Error	143.33	6	23.89	
Total	448.25	11		

    (b) H_0 is not rejected at 5% level.

26. $G_1 = -3.5, B_1 = 1.25, \epsilon_{11} = -2.5$.

28. (a)

SOURCE	SS	DF	MS	F RATIO
Agents	268	3	89.333	1.03
Houses	1,152	9	128.000	1.47
Error	2,352	27	87.111	
Total	3,772	39		

(b) H_0 is not rejected at 5% level.

30. (a)

SOURCE	SS	DF	MS	F RATIO
Shows	95.2	2	47.600	3.60
Regions	69.5	3	23.167	1.75
Error	79.3	6	13.217	
Total	244.0	11		

(b) H_0 is not rejected at 5% level.

32. (a)

SOURCE	SS	DF	MS	F RATIO
Contestants	364.50	21	17.3571	19.27
Judges	.81	8	.1013	.11
Interaction	4.94	1,188	.0294	.03
Error	1,069.94	1,385	.9006	
Total	1,440.19			

(b) Null hypothesis of no difference between contestants is rejected at 1% level; the other two null hypotheses are not rejected at 5% level.

34. (a)

SOURCE	SS	DF	MS	F RATIO
Subject types	389.00	3	129.667	5.31
Test types	57.56	2	28.786	1.18
Interaction	146.67	6	24.445	1.00
Error	586.00	24	24.417	
Total	1,179.23	35		

(b) H_0 is not rejected at 5% level.

42.

SOURCE	SS	DF	MS	F RATIO
Between groups	5,165	2	2,582.5	21.48
Within groups	120,802	1,005	120.2	
Total	125,967	1,007		

H_0 is rejected at 1% level.

44. (a)

SOURCE	SS	DF	MS	F RATIO
Between groups	221.34	3	73.780	25.60
Within groups	374.68	130	2.882	
Total	596.00	133		

(b) H_0 is rejected at 1% level.

46.

SOURCE	SS	DF	MS	F RATIO
Between groups	11,438.3028	2	5,719.1514	.79
Within groups	109,200.0000	15	7,280.0000	
Total	120,638.3028	17		

H_0 is not rejected at 5% level.

48. Test statistic is 5.05; H_0 is not rejected at 10% level.

52.

SOURCE	SS	DF	MS	F RATIO
Consumers	37,571.5	124	363.00	1.35
Brands	32,987.3	2	16,493.65	73.42
Error	55,710.7	248	224.64	
Total	126,269.5	374		

H_0 is rejected at 1% level.

54. (a)

SOURCE	SS	DF	MS	F RATIO
SAT scores	.82667	2	.41333	24.79
Incomes	.00667	2	.00333	.20
Error	.06667	4	.01667	
Total	.90000	8		

(b) H_0 is not rejected at 5% level.   **(c)** H_0 is rejected at 1% level.

56. (a) 3.3   **(b)** 0   **(c)** .0667 **(d)** .4333

58.

SOURCE	SS	DF	MS	*F* RATIO
Prices	.178	2	.0890	.09
Countries	4.365	2	2.1825	2.32
Interaction	1.262	4	.3155	.33
Error	93.330	99	.9427	
Total	99.135	107		

None of the three null hypotheses is rejected at 5% level.

60. (a)

SOURCE	SS	DF	MS	*F* RATIO
SAT scores	2.20111	2	1.10056	66.02
Incomes	.01778	2	.00889	.53
Interaction	.10223	4	.02556	1.53
Error	.15000	9	.01667	
Total	2.47112	17		

(b) H_0 is not rejected at 5% level.   (c) H_0 is rejected at 1% level.   (d) H_0 is not rejected at 5% level.

CHAPTER 16

2. (a) 3.855   (b) 93.2, 88.5, 97.9   (c) 3.67, .11, 7.23
4. Under normality, probability is .002 of a value outside the limits.
6. (a) 19.84,   (b) 1.99   (c) 2.09   (d) 19.84, 17.27, 22.41   (f) 1.99, .06, 3.92
8. (a) (81.6, 104.8)   (b) .65   (c) .59 [Process not capable]
10. (a) (131.36, 168.60)   (b) 1.07   (c) 1.07 [Process not capable]
12. .056, .012, .100
14. (a) .125   (b) .125, .055, .195
16. (b) .080   (c) .080, .029, .131
18. (a) 13.55 (b) 13.55, 2.51, 24.59
22. (a) 119.825   (b) 1.985   (c) 2.112   (d) 119.825, 116,986, 122.664   (f) 1.985, 0, 4.149
(h)(i) (113.5, 126.2) (ii) .79 (iii) .76 [Process not capable]
24. (a) .0723   (b) .0723, .0376, .1070
26. (b) 343.44   (c) 11.51   (d) 12.49   (e) 343.44, 324.68, 362.20   (g) 11.51, 0, 26.12
(h)(i) Average range = 25.94 (ii) 12.60 (iii) 324.51, 362.37 (iv) 25.94, 0, 59.14

CHAPTER 17

2. (a) 100, 102.5, 99.3, 98.2, 100.0, 99.6, 100.0, 99.3, 99.3, 100.7, 110.7, 106.1   (b) 101.8, 104.4, 101.1, 100, 101.8, 101.5, 101.8, 101.1, 101.1, 102.5, 112.7, 108.0
4. (a) 100, 105.4, 109.6, 112.7, 115.5, 117.2   (b) 100, 104.8, 110.5, 112.1, 115.7, 117.5
8. $R = 7$; H_0 is rejected only at high significance levels
10. $R = 5$; H_0 is rejected against one-sided alternative at 7.8% level, but not at 2.5% level

12. **(a)** $R = 7$; test statistic is -3.08; H_0 is rejected against one-sided alternative at .1% level
16. Values for years 3 and 4 are 7.8 and 7.7
22. All forecasts are 1.36.
24. All forecasts are 5.2.
32. 6.7, 6.5
36. $X_t = 18.515 - .032X_{t-1} + a_t$; 17.9, 17.9, 17.9
40. **(a)** Order 1 **(b)** 1,331, 1,369, 1,402
46. **(a)** 100, 110.7, 117.9, 128.0, 144.5, 159.8 **(b)** 100, 110.5, 116.4, 124.4, 138.2, 150.9
    (c) 100, 104.1, 100.4, 105.6, 106.3, 105.2
52. **(a)** $R = 10$; test statistic is -1.25; can reject H_0 against one-sided alternative at levels above 10.56%. **(c)** Values for years 3 and 4 are 779 and 768.
54. **(a)** Values for months 2 and 3 are 85 and 88.7.

CHAPTER 18

14. $8.2 < \mu < 11.2$
16. $5.49 < \mu < 9.07$
20. $95,489 < N\mu < 113,136$
22. $403 < N\mu < 577$
24. $.49 < p < .63$
26. $129 < Np < 197$
28. **(a)** $40.8 < \mu_3 < 45.8$ **(b)** 37.33 **(c)** $36.03 < \mu < 38.63$, $35.78 < \mu < 38.88$
30. **(a)** $2.84 < \mu_1 < 3.40$ **(b)** $3.14 < \mu_2 < 3.60$ **(c)** $3.05 < \mu < 3.41$
32. **(a)** 81,720 **(b)** $77,542 < N\mu < 85,898$
34. **(a)** .347 **(b)** $.255 < p < .439$, $.238 < p < .456$
36. **(a)** 56 **(b)** 65
38. **(a)** 54 **(b)** 59
40. **(a)** 74 **(b)** 88
42. 281
44. 211
46. **(a)** 498 **(b)** 471
48. **(a)** 91.7 **(b)** $70.7 < \mu < 112.7$
50. **(a)** .451 **(b)** $.380 < p < .522$
52. 107
54. 130
58. **(a)** $69.1 < \mu < 80.3$ **(b)** Wider
60. **(a)** $.56 < p < .69$
62. **(a)** $7.0 < \mu_1 < 11.4$ **(b)** $9.8 < \mu < 13.4$
64. $.48 < \mu < .72$
66. **(a)** 16 **(b)** 22
68. 76

CHAPTER 19

2. **(a)** Choice of process D is inadmissible **(b)** Process C **(c)** Process A
8. **(b)** No
10. **(a)** Low-risk stock fund

12. **(a)(i)** False **(ii)** True **(iii)** True   **(b)** No
14. New center with EMV $74,000 per annum
16. **(a)** Less than 33/70   **(b)** More than $816,667
18. **(a)** Check the process, with EMV = $18,600   **(b)** At most 5/6
20. **(b)** 2 cars, with EMV $16
22. **(b)** Jones, with the campaign; EMV $87,000   **(c)** Yes, up to $5,000.
24. **(b)** An outline proposal for contract B should be submitted; EMV $1,890.   **(c)** Detailed final proposal should not be submitted, since expected return would be −$300. **(d)** Yes; the best strategy now is to submit a final proposal for contract B; EMV $2,085.
26. **(a)** Process A; EMV $440,000   **(b)** .5, .4, .1   **(c)** Process C; EMV $345,000   **(d)** 9/31, 16/31, 6/31   **(e)** Process C; EMV $395,161   **(f)** 2/13, 4/13, 7/13   **(g)** Process A; EMV $607,692
28. **(a)** 12/13 for effective, 1/13 for ineffective   **(b)** Retain; EMV $114,615   **(c)** .25 for effective; .75 for ineffective   **(d)** Sell; EMV $50,000   **(e)** Yes
30. **(a)** .01, .18, .81   **(b)** .09, .42, .49   **(c)(i)** 4/13, 9/13. Check, EMV $17,615 **(ii)** 12/19, 7/19. Check, EMV $18,263 **(iii)** .8687, .1313. Check, EMV $18,737
32. **(a)** Knowledge of future course of market   **(b)** $1,000
34. $24,000 per annum
38. $23,000
42. **(a)** $34   **(b)** $55.80   **(c)** $21.80   **(d)** None   **(e)** $24.29   **(f)** Multiplying $24.29 by the probability (.89) that the first bulb is not defective gives $21.80
44. **(a)** 200/11, 500/11, 800/11, 900/11   **(b)** 2/11, 5/11, 8/11, 9/11
46. At most .475
48. Should sign Smith and not mount advertising campaign, EU 57
54. **(a)** .18, .42, .12, .28   **(b)** Bid for both contracts; EMV $510   **(d)** $204   **(e)** $79

Acceptance of hypothesis, 325
Acceptance sampling, 162
Actions, 782
Addition rule of probabilities, 97
Additive model, 695
Adjusted coefficient of determination, 492
Admissible action, 784
Allocation among strata, 758
Alternative hypothesis, 324
Analysis of variance:
    one-way, 598
    population model for, 605
    for regression, 507
    two-way:
        more than one observation per cell, 624
        one observation per cell, 613
Arrival process, 169
Assignable causes, 654
Attributes, 113
Autocorrelated errors, 572
Autocorrelation in time series, 723
Autoregressive integrated moving average models, 728
Autoregressive models:
    for regression errors, 573
    for time series, 723
Average sample standard deviation, 647
Aversion to risk, 818, 821

Bar charts, 53
Base for index numbers, 680
Base period change, 684
Basic outcomes, 75
Bayes' theorem, 113
    alternative statement, 116
    and decision making, 798
Bell-shaped curve, 194
Bernoulli distribution, 157
Best asymptotic normal estimator, 266
Best linear unbiased estimator, 451, 488
Between-groups variability, 599
Bias, 261
Binomial distribution:
    and control charts, 660
    introduced, 157

mean and variance of, 160
normal approximation to, 211
Poisson approximation to, 170
probability function of, 158
and sample proportion, 234
and sign test, 387
tabulated, 829
using tabulated probabilities for, 161
Birthday problem, 103
Bivariate probabilities, 108
Blocking variable, 613
Blocks, 613
Bowman-Shelton test, 413
Box-and-whisker plots, 59

Capability, 656
Capability index, 657
Categorical data, 405
Census, 736
Census X-11, 704
Centered moving average, 697
Centered performance interval, 657
Central limit theorem, 207
    and confidence intervals, 281
    and distribution of sample mean, 230
    and distribution of sample proportion, 235
    and hypothesis tests, 337
    and normal approximation to binomial and Poisson distributions, 210
Central line, 650
Central tendency, 8
Chi-square distribution:
    and central limit theorem, 208
    and contingency tables, 416
    and goodness of fit tests, 407
    introduced, 245
    and sampling distribution of sample variance, 245
    tabulated, 838
    using tabulated probabilities of, 247
Class marks, 40
Classes for grouped data, 30
Cluster sampling, 767
Coefficient of determination, 454, 491
Coefficient estimation, 536

Coincidences, 66
Collectively exhaustive events, 78
Combinations, 95
Complement of event:
    defined, 78
    probability of, 96
Component bar chart, 54
Components of time series, 692
Composite hypothesis, 324
Computer packages:
    for analysis of variance, 630
    for regression, 517
Conditional probability, 98
Conditional probability function, 146
Confidence interval:
    from cluster sampling, 769
    defined, 272
    for difference between means, 300
    for difference between proportions, 309
    for population mean, 273, 285
    for population proportion, 292
    for population variance, 294
    for predictions from regression, 464
    for regression coefficients, 461, 498
    and sample size, 314
    from simple random sampling, 745
    from stratified sampling, 753
Consistent estimator, 266
Contingency tables, 415
Continuity correction, 211
Continuous random variable:
    defined, 130
    expectation of, 186
    introduced, 179
    linear function of, 188
    mean of, 187
    probability distribution for, 180
    standard deviation of, 187
    variance of, 187
Control chart constants, 648
Control charts:
    introduced, 645
    for means, 650, 671
    for numbers of occurrences, 662
    for proportions, 659
    for ranges, 672
    for standard deviations, 650
Control limits, 645, 650

Corrected coefficient of determination, 492
Correlation:
    and coefficient of determination, 454
    and covariance, 428
    for population, 428
    of ranks, 436
    sample, 432
    testing for, 433
Covariance:
    and correlation, 428
    defined:
        for continuous random variables, 190
        for discrete random variables, 149
    and statistical independence, 151, 190
Criterion of optimism, 789
Criterion of pessimism, 786
Cumulative distribution function:
    defined, 180
    relation to probability density function, 184
Cumulative frequency, 30
Cumulative mass function, 133
Cumulative probability function, 143
Cumulative relative frequency, 30
Cyclical component, 692

Decision making, 5, 781
    and sample information, 798
Decision rule for hypothesis test, 325
Decision tree 792
    and value of sample information, 807
Degrees of freedom, 246
Dependence in regression, 442
Dependent variable, 444
Design of experiments, 559
Differences of random variables, 152, 191
Discrete random variable:
    defined, 130
    expectation of, 135
    linear function of, 139
    mean of, 136
    probability distributions for, 131
    standard deviation of, 138
    variance of, 138
Dispersion, 14
Distribution-free tests, 385
Dominating action, 784
Dummy variables, 538
Durbin-Watson test, 575
    tables for, 843
Durbin's h-test, 584

Efficiency, 261
    and regression, 451, 488

Emotive statements, 61
Empty set, 77
Error sum of squares, 454, 491
Error term in regression, 445
Error variance estimation, 459, 492
Estimate, 257
Estimator, 257
Event, 76
Evolving trend, 696
Excessive variability, 654
Expectation, 155
Expected monetary value, 790
Expected monetary value criterion, 792
Expected net value of sample information, 806
Expected payoff, 791
Expected utility, 820
Expected utility criterion, 824
Expected value, 135
    for continuous random variable, 186
    for discrete random variable, 136
Expected value of perfect information, 804
Expected value of sample information, 806
Explanatory power of regression, 452, 489
Exponential distribution, 216
    and Poisson distribution, 217
Exponential smoothing:
    Holt-Winters method, 712
    simple, 708
Extreme observations, 13

F distribution, 366
    tabulated, 840
Factorials, 92
Fair bets, 85
Finite population correction factor, 230, 235, 745
First order autoregressive model:
    for regression errors, 573
    for time series, 724
First quartile, 25
Forecasting:
    from autoregressive integrated moving average models, 728
    from autoregressive models, 723
    through Holt-Winters method, 712
    introduced, 4, 678
    from regression models, 463, 511
    through simple exponential smoothing, 708
Frequency, 30

Gauss-Markov theorem, 451, 488
Goodness of fit tests, 405
    with unknown parameters, 410

Graphical size comparisons, 64
Grouped data, 29
    numerical summary of, 37

Heteroscedasticity, 566
Histogram, 29
Holt-Winters method, 712
    for seasonal series, 715
Hypergeometric distribution:
    introduced, 163
    mean and variance, 165
    probability function of, 165
Hypothesis, 323
Hypothesis tests:
    for autocorrelated errors, 575, 584
    concepts, 323
    for contingency tables, 417
    for correlation, 433
    decision rules for, 325
    for difference between means, 352
    for difference between proportions, 360
    for equality of variances, 366, 435
    for goodness of fit, 407
    for heteroscedasticity, 570
    measuring power of, 369
    nonparametric, 385
    for normality, 412
    in one-way analysis of variance, 602
    for population mean, 329, 339
    for population proportion, 348
    for population variance, 344
    for randomness, 688
    in regression, 462, 499, 505
    in two-way analysis of variance, 619, 627

In control, 652
Inadmissible action, 784
Inadmissible estimator, 266
Independent attributes, 113
Independent events, 101
Independent random variables, 148, 190
Independent samples, 301, 355, 395, 595
Independent variables, 444
Index number problem, 680
Index numbers, 678
    base for, 680
Indifference to risk, 822
Interaction, 624
Interquartile range:
    for grouped data, 42
    for set of numbers, 25
Intersection of events:
    defined, 77
    probability of, 99

Interval estimate, 272
Interval estimator, 272
Irregular component, 692

Joint cumulative distribution function, 190
Joint cumulative probability function, 149
Joint probability, 110
Joint probability function, 145
Jointly distributed random variables, 144, 190

Kruskal-Wallis test, 606
Kurtosis, 413

Lagged dependent variables, 541
    and autocorrelated errors, 584
Laspeyres price index, 682
Laspeyres quantity index, 683
Least squares estimation, 446, 485
Level of confidence, 272
Level of test, 328
Linear association:
    and correlation, 427
    and regression, 442
Linear function of random variables, 139, 188
Linear regression model, 441
Loaded statements, 61
Log linear model, 554
Lower control limit, 650
Lower specification limit, 656
Lying with statistics, 61

Maintained hypothesis, 324
Mann-Whitney test, 394
Marginal distribution function, 190
Marginal probability, 110
Marginal probability function, 145
Matched pairs, 301, 352, 391, 435, 595
Maximax criterion, 789
Maximin criterion, 785
Maximum likelihood method, 266
Mean:
    and central limit theorem, 207
    of continuous random variable, 187
    of discrete random variable, 136
    for grouped data, 40
    of set of numbers, 8
Mean absolute deviation, 23
Mean squared error, 265
Mean squares, 601
Media reports, 317
Median:
    for grouped data, 42
    relative efficiency of, 262
    of set of numbers, 12

Minimax regret criterion, 787
Minimum variance unbiased estimator, 263
MINITAB program, 517
Modal class, 45
Mode, 14
Model building, 535
Model specification, 536
Model verification, 537
Models for time series, 723
Most efficient estimator, 263
Moving averages, 696
    and seasonal adjustment, 699
Moving Laspeyres price index, 683
Multicollinearity, 558
Multiple correlation, 494
Multiple observation values, 37
Multiple regression model, 477
Multiplication rule of probabilities, 99
Multiplicative model, 695
Mutually exclusive events, 77

Natural tolerance, 657
Natural variability, 665
Nonconforming items, 659
Nonlinear models, 553
Nonparametric tests, 385, 436, 606, 688
Nonprobabilistic sampling methods, 774
Nonresponse, 741
Nonsampling error, 741
Normal distribution:
    as approximation to binomial distribution, 211
    as approximation to Poisson distribution, 213
    and central limit theorem, 207
    cumulative distribution function of, 197
    and distribution of sample mean, 230
    introduced, 194
    mean and variance of, 195
    probability density function of, 195
    range probabilities for, 197, 200
    and rule of thumb, 20
    standard, 198
    tables for, 834
    test for, 412
Normal equations, 531
Null hypothesis, 324
Numerical information, 1,6
Numerical summary:
    central tendency, 8
    dispersion, 14
    for grouped data, 37

Occurrence of event, 76
One-sided alternatives, 324

One-way analysis of variance, 598
Opinion surveys, 317
Optimal allocation, 758
Ordering, 91
Outcomes of experiment, 75
Overall mean, 647

p-value, 333
Parameter, 257
Parameter estimation, 536
Pareto diagram, 662
Partial correlation, 493
Partial regression coefficients, 479
Payoff table, 783
Payoffs, 783
Perfect information, 804
Perfect multicollinearity, 560
Permutations, 93
Pie charts, 57
Point estimate, 258
Point estimator:
    choice of, 265
    defined, 258
    efficiency of, 261
    unbiasedness of, 260
Poisson distribution:
    as approximation to binomial distribution, 170
    and control charts, 663
    and exponential distribution, 217
    goodness of fit test for, 411
    introduced, 166
    mean and variance of, 167
    normal approximation to, 213
    probability function of, 167
Population, 3, 7, 223
Population mean, 10
Population multiple regression, 483
Population proportion, 234
Population regression line, 445
Population standard deviation, 18
Population total, 746
Population variance, 18
Posterior probability, 114
    and decision making, 798
Postulates of probability, 86
Power:
    introduced, 326
    measurement of, 369
Prediction:
    from linear regression, 463
    from multiple regression, 511
Preference for risk, 818, 821
Price index:
    single item, 680
    unweighted aggregate, 681
    weighted aggregate, 683
Principle of randomness, 224

Prior probability, 114
  and decision making, 798
Probability:
  addition rule of, 97
  bivariate, 108
  conditional, 98
  introduced, 3, 74
  joint, 110
  marginal, 110
  meaning of, 83
  multiplication rule of, 99
  posterior, 114, 798
  postulates of, 86
  prior, 114, 798
  relative frequency concept of, 83
  subjective, 85
Probability content of interval, 272
Probability density function, 182
Probability distributions:
  for continuous random variables, 180
  for discrete random variables, 131
Probability function, 131
Probability mass function, 131
Probability sampling, 742
Probability value, 333
Process capability, 656
Process standard deviation, 647
Proportional allocation, 751, 758

Quadratic dependence, 553
Quality circles, 664
Quality control, 643
Quantitative information, 2
Quantity index, 683
Quartiles:
  for grouped data, 42
  for set of numbers, 25
Queuing, 169, 216
Quota sampling, 775

Random experiment, 75
Random numbers:
  introduced, 224
  tabulated, 837
  use of tables, 743
Random sample, 224
Random variables:
  continuous, 179
  differences of, 152, 191
  discrete, 130
  independent, 148, 190
  jointly distributed, 144, 190
  linear function of, 139, 188
  sums of, 152, 191

Randomized blocks, 614
Randomized response, 82, 99
Randomness:
  principle of, 224
  test for, 688
Range, 24
  and control charts, 671
Range probabilities, 181
Rank correlation, 436
Ranks, 391
Regression:
  assumptions, 450, 487
  and autocorrelated errors, 572
  computer packages for, 517
  confidence intervals for, 461, 498
  dummy variables in, 538
  estimation, 446, 485
  explanatory power of, 452, 489
  and heteroscedasticity, 566
  hypothesis tests for, 462, 499, 505
  and lagged dependent variables, 541, 584
  linear model, 441
  multicollinearity in, 558
  multiple model, 477
  nonlinear models in, 553
  prediction from, 463, 511
  specification bias in, 556
Regression sum of squares, 454, 491
Regret table, 787
Rejection of hypothesis, 325
Relationships, 4
Relative efficiency, 261
Relative frequency, 30
Relative frequency concept of probability, 83
Replication, 624
Residuals, 452, 489
Risk, 19, 819
Robustness, 250, 377
Rule of thumb, 21
Runs test, 688
  table for, 846

Sample:
  defined, 3, 7
  introduced, 223
  random, 224
Sample correlation coefficient, 432
Sample information in decision making, 798
  value of, 803
Sample mean:
  defined, 11, 227
  as efficient estimator, 263

  sampling distribution of, 227
  as unbiased estimator, 261
Sample multiple regression, 486
Sample proportion:
  defined, 234
  as efficient estimator, 263
  sampling distribution of, 234
  as unbiased estimator, 261
Sample regression line, 448
Sample size estimation, 314, 762
Sample space, 75
Sample standard deviation, 21, 244
Sample variance:
  defined, 21, 244
  as efficient estimator, 263
  sampling distribution of, 244
  as unbiased estimator, 261
Sampling, 3, 223
  acceptance, 162
  cluster, 767
  probability, 742
  quota, 775
  simple random, 224, 742
  stratified, 750
  systematic, 744
  two-phase, 772
  with replacement, 743
  without replacement, 743
Sampling distribution:
  introduced, 225
  of sample mean, 227
  of sample proportion, 234
  of sample variance, 244
Sampling error, 740
Scale, 63
Scatter plots, 58
Seasonal adjustment, 694, 699
Seasonal index method, 701
Seasonality, 693
Seasonality component, 692
  extraction of, 699
Second order autoregressive model, 724
Sensitivity analysis, 796
Sequence of decisions, 794
Service times, 216
Set of outcomes, 76
Sets of regression parameters, 505
Sign test, 386
Significance level, 326
Simple centered moving average, 697
Simple exponential smoothing, 708
Simple hypothesis, 324
Simple random sample, 224, 742
Skewness, 46, 413
Slope of regression line, 444
Smoothing constant, 710

Spearman's rank correlation coefficient, 436
   table for, 842
Specification bias, 556
Specification limits, 656
Standard assumptions for regression, 450, 487
Standard deviation:
   of continuous random variable, 187
   of discrete random variable, 138
   for grouped data, 41
   interpretation of, 19
   population, 18
   sample, 21
Standard error, 229
Standard normal distribution, 198
   tabulated, 834
States of nature, 783
Statistic, 225, 257
Statistical Analysis System (SAS) program, 517
Statistical decision theory, 781
Statistical Package for the Social Sciences (SPSS), 518
Statistical process control, 643
Statistical quality control, 643
Statistically independent events, 101
Statistically independent random variables, 148, 190
   and covariance, 151, 190
Stem-and-leaf diagrams, 35
Strata, 751
   allocation among, 758

Stratified sampling, 750
   and sample size, 765
Student's t distribution, 282
   tabulated, 839
Subjective probability, 85
Summation notation, 9
Sums of random variables, 152, 191
Sums of squares decomposition, 454, 491, 601, 618, 628
Survey sampling methods, 735
Symmetric distribution, 49
Systematic sampling, 744

Tchebychev's rule, 20
Third quartile, 25
Time plots, 56
   scale for, 63
Time series:
   components of, 692
   introduced, 677
   seasonal adjustment of, 694, 699
Total sum of squares, 454, 491
Tree diagram, 92
Trend component, 692
Trends in control charts, 654
Two-phase sampling, 772
Two-sided alternative, 324
Two-way analysis of variance:
   more than one observation per cell, 624
   one observation per cell, 613
Types I and II errors, 326

Unbiased estimation, 260
Uncertainty, 2
   decision making under introduced, 5, 781
Uniform distribution, 180
   and central limit theorem, 208
Union of events:
   defined, 78
   probability of, 97
Unweighted aggregate price index, 681
Updating mechanism, 712
Upper control limit, 650
Upper specification limit, 656
Utility, 819
Utility function, 820

Value of sample information, 803
Variance:
   of continuous random variable, 187
   of discrete random variable, 138
   for grouped data, 40
   population, 16
   sample, 21
Venn diagram, 77

Waiting-lines, 19, 216
Weighted aggregate price index, 682
Weighted aggregate quantity index, 683
Weighted average, 698
Wilcoxon test, 391
   table for, 842
Within-groups variability, 599